T0189459

Handbook of
Dynamic Data Driven Applications Systems

Erik P. Blasch • Frederica Darema
Sai Ravela • Alex J. Aved

Editors

Handbook of Dynamic Data Driven Applications Systems

Volume 1

Second Edition

 Springer

Editors
Erik P. Blasch
Air Force Office of Scientific Research
Arlington, VA, USA

Frederica Darema (iD)
InfoSymbiotics Systems Society
Boston, MA, USA

Sai Ravela (iD)
Earth, Atmospheric and Planetary Sciences
Massachusetts Institute of Technology
Cambridge, MA, USA

Alex J. Aved
Air Force Research Lab
Rome, NY, USA

ISBN 978-3-030-74570-7   ISBN 978-3-030-74568-4   (eBook)
https://doi.org/10.1007/978-3-030-74568-4

1st edition: © Springer Nature Switzerland AG 2018
2nd edition: © This is a U.S. government work and not under copyright protection in the U.S.; foreign copyright protection may apply 2022

This Springer imprint is published by the registered company Springer Nature Switzerland AG
The registered company address is: Gewerbestrasse 11, 6330 Cham, Switzerland

Contents

Contents

Part IX   Cyber-Aware: Security and Computing

Part X   Systems-Aware: Design Methods

About the Editors

Erik P. Blasch is a program officer with the Air Force Office of Scientific Research. His focus areas are in multi-domain (space, air, ground) data fusion, target tracking, pattern recognition, and robotics. He has authored 750+ scientific papers, 22 patents, 30 tutorials, and 5 books. Recognitions include the Military Sensing Society Mignogna leadership in data fusion award, IEEE Aerospace and Electronics Systems Society Mimno best magazine paper award, IEEE Russ bioengineering award, and founding member of the International Society of Information Fusion (ISIF). Previous appointments include adjunct associate professor at Wright State University, exchange scientist at Defense Research and Development Canada, and officer in the Air Force Research Laboratory. Dr. Blasch is an associate fellow of AIAA, fellow of SPIE, and fellow of IEEE.

Frederica Darema retired as Senior Executive Service (SES) member and director of the Air Force Office of Scientific Research, Arlington, Virginia, where she led the entire basic research investment for the AF and served as research director in the Air Force's Chief Data Office, and as associate deputy assistant secretary at the Air Force Office for Science, Technology and Engineering. Prior career history includes: research staff positions at the University of Pittsburgh, Brookhaven National Laboratory, and Schlumberger-Doll; management and executive-level positions at the T. J. Watson IBM Research Center and the IBM Corporate Strategy Group, the National Science Foundation, and the Defense Advanced Research Projects Agency; and director of the AFOSR Directorate for Information, Math, and Life Sciences. Dr. Darema, PhD in nuclear physics, is a fellow of the Institute of Electrical and Electronics Engineers (IEEE), among other professional recognitions. She pioneered the DDDAS paradigm, and since 2000, she has organized and led research initiatives, programs, workshops, conferences, and other forums to foster and promote DDDAS-based science and technology advances.

Sai Ravela, PhD, directs the Earth Signals and Systems Group (ESSG) in the Earth Atmospheric and Planetary Sciences (EAPS) Department at the Massachusetts Institute of Technology. His primary interests are in statistical pattern recognition, stochastic nonlinear systems, and computational intelligence with application to earth, planets, climate, and life. Dr. Ravela has pioneered dynamic data driven observing systems for wildlife and fluids, the latter with application from the laboratory to localized atmospheric phenomena. He has advanced several DDDAS topics with new methods for application to coherent fluid dynamical regimes. Dr. Ravela proposed and co-organized the Dynamic Data Driven Environmental Systems Science Conference (DyDESS 2014, Cambridge), and then co-organized the first, second, and third general DDDAS conferences (2016 Hartford, 2017 Cambridge, 2020 MIT/Online). Dr. Ravela also teaches machine learning with system dynamics and optimization, which introduces the informative approach, a key DDDAS concept, to design learning and hybrid stochastic systems and solve inverse problems and inference.

Alex J. Aved is a senior researcher with the Air Force Research Laboratory, Information Directorate, Rome, NY, USA. His research interests include multimedia databases, stream processing (via CPU, GPU, or coprocessor), and dynamically executing models with feedback loops incorporating measurement and error data to improve the accuracy of the model. He has published over 50 papers and given numerous invited lectures. Previously, he was a programmer at the University of Central Florida and database administrator and programmer at Anderson University.

Chapter 1
Introduction to the Dynamic Data Driven Applications Systems (DDDAS) Paradigm

Erik P. Blasch, Frederica Darema ⓘ, and Dennis Bernstein

Abstract Dynamic Data Driven Applications Systems (DDDAS) is a paradigm for systems analysis and design, and a framework that dynamically couples high-dimensional physical and other analysis models and methods, run-time measurements, and computational architectures. Some of the foremost early applications of DDDAS successes range from environmental assessment of adverse weather and natural disasters such as tornadic activity, hurricane formation and trajectory, wildfire monitoring and volcanic plume detection and tracking, to real-time structural health monitoring in aerospace systems and electrical power grids operation, and to medical and societal applications. Monitoring, understanding and predicting behaviors of complex and dynamic systems with DDDAS principles has expanded over the years to demonstrate new and advanced capabilities in other applications that span space situational awareness, unmanned aerial vehicle (UAV) design and operation, and complex systems adaptive management and security applications. Recent efforts reflect the digital age of information management such as multimedia analysis, electrical power grid control, other civilian infrastructures, and biohealth concerns. Underlying DDDAS developments are advances in sensor design, signal processing and filtering, as well as computational architectures and communications. The book highlights for the reader DDDAS-based advances, with more information available in the DDDAS society's website: www.1dddas.org.

Keywords Dynamic Data Driven Application Systems · Hurricane · Data Assimilation loop · Sensor reconfiguration loop · Feedback control · High-dimensional modeling · Weather forecasting · Volcanic ash detection ·

E. P. Blasch (✉)
Air Force Office of Scientific Research, Arlington, VA, USA
e-mail: erik.blasch.1@us.af.mil

F. Darema
InfoSymbiotics Systems Society, Boston, MA, USA

D. Bernstein
Department of Aerospace Engineering, University of Michigan, Ann Arbor, MI, USA
e-mail: dsbaero@umich.edu

E. P. Blasch et al. (eds.), *Handbook of Dynamic Data Driven Applications Systems*,
https://doi.org/10.1007/978-3-030-74568-4_1

Wildfire monitoring · Orbital awareness · Structural health monitoring ·
Self-aware · Estimation · Context · Cyber networks ·
Sensing-learning-adaptation · Autonomy · Smart sensing · Autonomy in use
(AIU) · Machine learning

1.1 Introduction

The methods presented in the book capture the DDDAS paradigm and the essence
of DDDAS-based systems' analysis and design. Invariably, the DDDAS paradigm
and ensuing frameworks proposed by one of the authors (Dr. Frederica Darema)
inspires many researchers for engineering and science advances.

As articulated by Dr. Darema who pioneered the DDDAS paradigm[1] [1–5]:

*"in DDDAS, instrumentation data and executing application models of these systems
become a dynamic feedback control loop, whereby measurement data are dynamically
incorporated into an executing model of the system in order to improve the accuracy of the
model (or simulation), or to speed-up the simulation, and in reverse the executing application model controls the instrumentation process to guide the measurement process. DDDAS
presents opportunities to create new capabilities through more accurate understanding,
analysis, and prediction of the behavior of complex systems, be they natural, engineered,
or societal, and to create decision support methods which can have the accuracy of full-
scale simulations, as well as to create more efficient and effective instrumentation methods,
such as intelligent management of Big Data, and dynamic and adaptive management of
networked collections of heterogeneous sensors and controllers. DDDAS is a unifying
paradigm, bringing together computational and instrumentation aspects of an application
system, which extends the notion of Big Computing to span from the high-end to the real-
time data acquisition and control, and it's a key methodology in managing and intelligently
exploiting Big Data."*

DDDAS (Dynamic Data Driven Applications Systems), beginning in 1998–
1999, is a paradigm in which computation and instrumentation aspects of an
application system are dynamically integrated in a feedback control loop, in the
sense that instrumentation data can be dynamically incorporated into the executing
model of the application, and in reverse the executing model can control the
instrumentation [6]. Such approaches have shown to enable more accurate and
faster modeling and analysis of the characteristics and behaviors of a system.
Methods based on the DDDAS paradigm can exploit data in intelligent ways to
provide new capabilities, including: (1) analysis and understanding of the behaviors
of complex systems and dynamic conditions; (2) decision support systems with
the accuracy of full-scale modeling; (3) efficient data collection and data mining
(including heterogeneous and distributed data); and (4) complex systems resource
management, such as heterogeneous collections of sensors and controllers, and
optimized operations of systems-of-systems.

---

[1]Darema coined the term DDDAS in 1999, but she conceived the key concepts of the paradigm
itself in 1980, when she was working in large nuclear radiation transport modeling for oil
exploration through nuclear accelerator neutron and gamma-ray measurements; between 1980 and
through the 80's, in organizational private communications Darema discussed about "DDDAS"
ideas under the title "Gedanken Laboratory" and presented it in [3].

The DDDAS paradigm, and opportunities and challenges in exploiting the DDDAS paradigm have been discussed in a series of workshops, starting with the National Science Foundation (NSF) workshop in March of 2000 [7], and subsequent ones. Notably, shortly after the March 2000 workshop, Kelvin Droegemeier and his team applied the DDDAS paradigm for analysis of a March 2000 tornadic event in Dallas, Texas; the event had been missed by the then forecasting models, and Droegemeier showed that using DDDAS they would have correctly predicted the onset and path of the tornado [8]. The reports from this and subsequent forums, identified new science and technology capabilities, inspired by and enabled through the DDDAS paradigm. New capabilities include modeling approaches, algorithm developments, systems software, and instrumentation methods, as well as the need for synergistic multidisciplinary research among these areas [9]. DDDAS brings together practitioners of application domains, researchers in mathematics, statistics, electrical engineering, and computer sciences, and designers involved in the development of instrumentation systems and methods. Through a series of forums and sponsored funding programs, research efforts commenced to address the challenges and create new frontiers in complex and dynamic systems' capabilities. As shown through the increasing body of work, DDDAS is applicable to many areas, such as: (1) engineering: aerospace-, civil-, electrical- and mechanical-engineering, and nanotechnologies; (2) systems: manufacturing, transportation, and energy systems; (3) science: materials, environmental-, weather-, climate-sciences, and biomedical sciences; as well as (4) decision support for: operations in civilian and industrial infrastructures, medical diagnosis and treatment, multimedia analysis, and cyber security evaluation. This book presents examples of advances through DDDAS to inform and motivate scientists, engineers and developers who may use the DDDAS paradigm and exploit it in these in such and many other science and technology areas.

The remainder of this chapter seeks to provide the reader a better understanding of the DDDAS paradigm and its applicability. Section 1.2 discusses the features of the DDDAS paradigm. Section 1.3 highlights, as examples, the methods of estimation and assimilation for processing data. Section 1.4 presents key components in enabling DDDAS methods. Section 1.5 provides a review of major areas where DDDAS has been applied in the last 20 years. Section 1.6 provides an overview of the book contents. Section 1.7 discusses DDDAS future directions, and Sect. 1.8 presents a summary on the book scope.

1.2   What Is DDDAS?

Consider an approaching hurricane (e.g., the 2005 "Katrina" event [10, 11]). A meteorological model of the storm can be constructed, constituted from the atmospheric aspects of the storm system, and its interface with ground, littoral, or aqueous (especially oceanic) aspects. However, the model has limited predictive value without knowledge of initial and varying conditions, boundary conditions, inputs, parameters and states, especially dynamic ones, such as velocities and accelerations - all these data collected with various sensor measurements, spanning many spatial positions, time-scales, and modalities. In order to make predictions, data are needed to estimate unknown quantities. Although the storm can be imaged at low resolution by satellite, measurements by aircraft with high resolution are expensive and limited in range, and therefore the size of the storm makes it impossible to obtain detailed measurements over a large area.

In a scenario such as the dynamic environmental example above, in the DDDAS-based approach, the (physical) model of the system can be used to select adaptively (by the executing model) measurements (needed for example to improve the predictive accuracy of the model), and in return the executing model guiding and reconfiguring the sensors and their modalities, so that data useful in improving the model accuracy are collected. Thus, through the selected measurements, the information content of the data is enhanced, for the ultimate objective of accurately predicting the path and intensity of the storm. At the same time, the data collected by the sensors enhances the accuracy of the model by providing estimates of initial and varying conditions, boundary conditions, and dynamic inputs, parameters, and states. The integration of on-line and off-line (archival) data with the executing model creates a positive feedback loop, where the model judiciously guides the sensor selection and data collection, from which ("in return") the sensor data improves the accuracy of the model; the other aspect of the DDDAS paradigm is to use the on-line (or archival) data to replace parts of the computation to speedup the modeling, and in return the executing model can request additional data to be collected or from archival storage, and use these data to further speedup the modeling; these approaches can be combined to speed-up and make the modeling more accurate.

The hurricane example illustrates the essence of Dynamic Data Driven Applications Systems (DDDAS). DDDAS is a paradigm and conceptual framework that synergistically and dynamically integrates models and data in order to facilitate and improve the analysis and prediction of the characteristics and behaviors of physical phenomena, engineered systems, societal systems. The term "physical" is used here in the broader sense of any model that represents the reality of a system (natural, engineered, or other system). In a broader context, DDDAS encompasses adaptive state estimation that uses an *instrumentation reconfiguration loop* (IRL) as shown in Fig. 1.1, in [12]. The IRL loop seeks to reconfigure the sensors in order to enhance the information content of the measurements. The sensor reconfiguration is guided adaptively by the simulation of the physical process. Consequently, the sensor reconfiguration is *dynamic*, and the overall process is (dynamic) *data driven*.

The core of DDDAS is the *data augmentation loop* (DAL), which integrates instrumentation data to drive the physical system simulation modeling (of an actual system) so that the trajectory of the simulation more closely follows the trajectory of the physical system. The dynamic data assimilation (which combines theory with observations) in DAL, uses input data if input sensors are available. An innovative feature of DDDAS, which goes beyond the traditional "data assimilation" methods, is the additional *instrumentation reconfiguration loop* (IRL), shown in Fig. 1.1, which controls the instrumentation system (such as the set of sensors, actuators, sensor executing models and sensors signal analysis), to collect additional data in

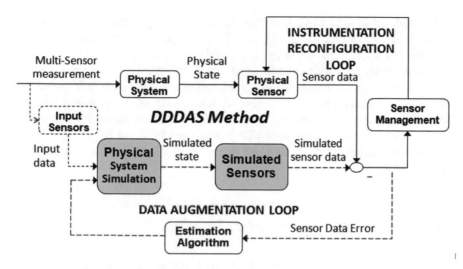

Fig. 1.1   A Depiction of Dynamic Data Driven Applications Systems (DDDAS) feedback loop

targeted ways, where data are needed to improve or speedup the model, or apply coordinated control of sensors or actuators. For example if the instrumentation consists of a set of physical sensors, in DDDAS the executing model (or simulation) adaptively guides the physical sensors, in a coordinated way, in order to enhance the information content of the collected data. The *dynamic data augmentation* and the *instrumentation* reconfiguration feedback loops are **computational** and physical feedback loops. The simulation guides the instrumentation reconfiguration and what data to be collected, and in turn, uses this additional, selected data, to improve the accuracy of the physical system simulation. This "meta" (positive) feedback loop is the essence of DDDAS.

Key aspects of DDDAS include the algorithmic and statistical methods that can incorporate dynamically the measurement data with that of the high-fidelity modeling and simulation, and as needed invoke models of higher or lower levels of fidelity (or resolution) depending on the dynamic data inputs.

1.3   State Estimation and Data Assimilation

The goal of **state estimation** is to combine models with data in order to estimate model states that are not directly measured. State estimation is a foundational area of research in systems and control. Relevant techniques date from the 1960's in the form of the Kalman filter and the Luenberger observer. An observer is a model that emulates the dynamics of a physical system and is driven by instrumentation data in order to approximate unmeasured states. The Kalman filter is a stochastically optimal observer that estimates unmeasured states. In large-scale physics applications, such as applications involving structures or fluids, state estimation is called *data assimilation*.

The Kalman filter was developed for linear systems. However, most real applications involve nonlinear dynamics, and the development of observers and filters for nonlinear systems is a challenging problem that remains largely unsolved. Numerous techniques, which can be described as suboptimal, ad hoc, application-based, or approximate, have been developed, and many of these methods are widely used. These techniques include the extended Kalman filter (KF), ensemble Kalman filter (EKF), ensemble adjustment Kalman filter (EnAKF), unscented Kalman filter (UKF), stochastic integration filter (SIF), and particle filters (PF) [13, 14]. As discussed in the next Section, DDDAS is an advanced adaptive state estimation methodology.

1.3.1 DDDAS and Adaptive State Estimation

State estimation algorithms are based on prior information about the (physical) system [15]. The information typically includes a model of the (physical) system as well as knowledge of the initial state, inputs (e.g., disturbances), and instrumentation (e.g., sensor data) noise. Likewise, stochastic representation, for example, as a statistical description of the disturbances and instrumentation-data noise, is one method to process the information. An adaptive state estimation algorithm may attempt to learn and update online the information, states, and parameters.

DDDAS uses adaptation in a different sense. In particular, DDDAS seeks to reconfigure the instrumentation during operation, in real-time. Instrumentation reconfiguration, driven by the model of the system, enhances the information content of the measurements. The information reconfiguration loop is shown in Fig. 1.1. Together, the integration of the data into the executing model (dynamic data augmentation) loop and the sensor reconfiguration loop are central to methods using the DDDAS paradigm.

1.3.2 Does DDDAS Use Feedback Control?

DDDAS uses computational feedback, in addition to physical feedback. As Fig. 1.1 shows, state estimation is a *feedback process*, where the instrumentation data corrects the simulation of the physical system. The data augmentation feedback loop is implemented in computation, and thus has no effect on the physical system.

DDDAS employs an additional feedback loop by reconfiguring the instrumentation based on the sensor data, much like the KF method. The instrumentation reconfiguration feedback loop is also computational, and thus does not affect the response of the physical system. In contrast, feedback control uses physical inputs (such as forces and moments) in order to affect the behavior of a physical system, such as an aircraft autopilot that drives the control surfaces and modifies the aircraft trajectory. Consequently, DDDAS employs two computational feedback loops, *in addition to the physical feedback control.* The power of DDDAS is to also use simulated data from a high-dimensional model to augment measurement systems, for systems analysis and design, and to leverage statistical methods, simulation, and computation architectures.

1.4 DDDAS Methods

The DDDAS paradigm and ensuing framework, as the term "Applications Systems" in the name implies, has been applied to many applications where modeling and data collection are utilized in engineering and scientific analysis, but also for other application areas such as financial and societal systems. To enable such capabilities through DDDAS, synergistic and multidisciplinary advances are needed along four science and technology axes: (1) modeling and simulation methods of real-world applications, (2) their associated mathematical (numeric and non-numeric) and statistical algorithms, (3) instrumentation and measurement methods, and (4) computer systems software, as shown in Fig. 1.2.

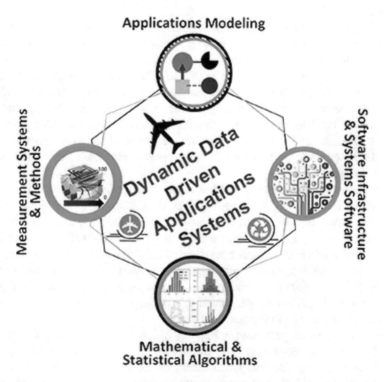

Fig. 1.2 Characteristic attributes, or characteristic or inherent elements of DDDAS

Instrumentation methods include multidomain components in real-world situations such as for example, terrestrial and space sensors monitoring the atmosphere; avionics sensors detecting air movements, computer vision detecting vehicles on a terrain road network, or sonar sensing of water currents and turbulence in the ocean. Representing the application are comprehensive, high-fidelity simulation models as well as model abstractions and models of lower fidelities, such as for example those in the case-study areas referenced above, the space Global ionosphere–thermosphere model (GITM) model, the National Climate Atmospheric Reference (NCAR) model, ground-based vehicle traffic models, and oceanic radar scatter models. The dynamic integration of modeling and the instrumentation data requires software systems to process the dynamically changing computational and communication requirements of the application models and algorithms, which change depending on the dynamic data inputs and model parameters; such include: models with good convergence properties under perturbation from dynamic data inputs, and invocation of other models (representing other modalities of the system and/or different levels of abstraction) depending on the dynamic data inputs. The seamlessly integrated coordination of high-end with real-time computing requires new hardware and software approaches in the fields of optimization, data flow, and architectures, together with modeling and instrumentation methods for real world applications.

The key developments of the DDDAS-based dynamic integration of executing application models with the application instrumentation, and the support runtime software (computer "systems-software") include: **theory, algorithms, and computation,** which the book seeks to highlight. The theory includes mathematical advances including numeric and non-numeric (e.g., retrospective cost modeling, graph-, agent-based, etc); while the algorithms support new methods (e.g., ensemble Kalman filter, Particle filter, optimization techniques). The computational considerations align with developments in the computer networking and communications areas for cases such as non-convex optimization, data flow architectures, and systems design.

The **challenges** to enable DDDAS include data modeling, context processing, and content application. To bring together data, context and content requires addressing issues in model fidelity, dimensions, and usability such as how many parameters are needed for system control. When data are collected, they need to be preprocessed to determine whether the inherent information matches the context. An example is: clutter reduction, sensor registration, and confuser analysis in vehicle tracking. Finally, another key challenge is that of sampling, as shown in Fig. 1.3. Sampling is the multi-resolution needed to monitor the situation, environment and network context to explain the content desired.

Three examples are presented in Fig. 1.4 which demonstrate DDDAS methods applied to enhance awareness. The examples are from the areas of air, space, and cyberspace, where modeling, instrumentation, and systems software have been designed for realistic platforms and actual environments. On the left is weather modeling with nonlinear tracking methods for unmanned aerial vehicle (UAV) flight routing. The middle includes multi-domain robotics of space and ground vehicles

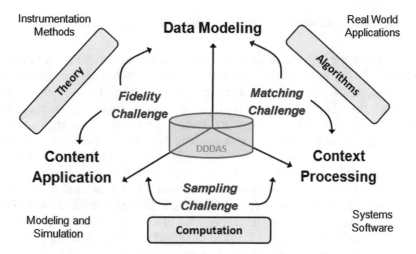

Fig. 1.3 DDDAS challenges and processes

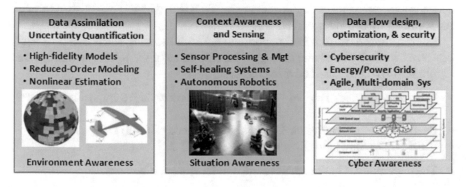

Fig. 1.4 DDDAS Awareness Examples

with filtering methods for distributed autonomous coordinated control. Finally, the cyber example comes from power grids performance that integrates cyber physical systems (CPS) [16] with the internet of things (IoT). It should be noted that DDDAS is a more powerful paradigm than CPS (which was coined by the embedded systems community), as DDDAS involves comprehensive models of the system under study, and where said models interact with the instrumentation aspects of the system and cognizantly control the instrumentation, as for example demonstrated for power grids in [17] for optimized power grids operation.

1.5   DDDAS Research Areas of Historical Development

The impact of the DDDAS concept has been manifested for almost two decades, starting with the initial NSF workshop in March 2000 that brought together researchers, engineers, scientists, and developers [7]. The March 2000 workshop introduced the DDDAS paradigm to the research community, and articulated the need for multidisciplinary research harnessing the power of theory, modeling, instrumentation, and (computer) software and hardware advances to instantiate applications-systems-level opportunities. As articulated in that workshop and in the subsequent ones in 2006 and 2010, and in the 2005 NSF Program Solicitation, the DDDAS environments spanned and integrated the high-end and the real-time computing, and computing at the sensors and controllers side – what was called later the IoT and Edge Computing. The proliferation of DDDAS impact is demonstrated in the literature, as shown in Fig. 1.5. The statistics from Fig. 1.5 only capture those papers that explicitly call-out DDDAS as the underlying paradigm; while many other papers that have briefly acknowledged DDDAS are not included in Fig. 1.5. There is a growing trend in approaches using DDDAS, which is established through the website (www.1dddas.org).

Many forums have provided opportunities for showcasing science and technology advances in DDDAS and through DDDAS. Some of the primary meetings that highlighted DDDAS-based advances include:

- IEEE International Parallel and Distributed Processing Symposium (IPDPS) [18];
- International Conference on Computational Science (ICCS) [19]; and
- IEEE Winter Simulation Conference (WSC) [20, 21].

The opportunities have expanded into engineering conferences:

- IEEE American Controls Conference (ACC) [22];
- ISIF International Conference on Information Fusion (Fusion) [23];

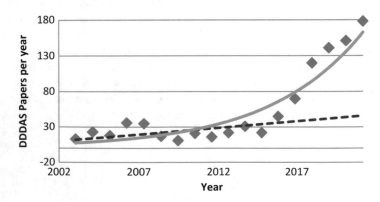

Fig. 1.5 DDDAS Trends of papers per year (dashed line 2002–2016; solid line 2002–2020)

- AIAA Aviation [24]; and
- ASME Embedded Systems and Applications [25, 26].

These and other science forums have hosted DDDAS workshops, panels, and presentations; such include: Data Stream (STREAM), American Geophysical Union (AGU), American Society of Mechanical Engineers (ASME), International Conference in Computational Sciences (ICCS), and Society for Industrial and Applied Mathematics (SIAM).

Along the way, numerous meetings and workshops were convened, including the **D**ynamic **D**ata-driven **E**nvironmental **S**ystems **S**cience Conference (DyDESS) (2014). DyDESS focused on scientific methods in environmental sciences, such as: (1) Perspectives from Ocean State Estimation; (2) Imaging Earth's interior with active and passive source seismic data; (3) Objective Detection of Lagrangian Vortices in Unsteady Velocity Data; and (4) Data Assimilation and Controls for atmospheric mutiscale dimensional processing. The DDDAS/InfoSymbiotics conference (2016) spurred the genesis of this book, which includes research work presented at that conference, as well as other work done over the years, starting in 2000.

Over the years, many researchers have embraced the DDDAS concept with a variety of applications, as shown in Fig. 1.6, which is an illustration from the AFOSR-NSF 2010 Workshop Report [7]. Areas of interest shown in the illustration include adverse weather events (e.g., tornadoes, hurricanes, etc), environmental (e.g., atmospheric contaminant transport, wildfires, etc), aerospace (e.g., UAV swarms, decision support modeling, etc), and medical imaging, among many others. The DDDAS community is dedicated to showcasing scientific and technological advances in complex systems modeling and instrumentation methods. The next section cites a set of publications over the last 20 years, organizing them into the areas of theory, methods, and systems analysis and design.

The history of DDDAS extends over four decades, from the inception of the concept in 1980 to the last two decades of developments by the broader scientific communities, academic, industry, and federal labs in the US and internationally. To organize the diverse set of applications, three areas are highlighted here: (1) **theory**, (2) **methods**, and (3) **designs**. Key areas for theory are based in the scientific areas with large data collections and complex models. Methods include various engineering designs for a broad set of domains – space, air, and ground, where DDDAS supports dynamic response and control. Finally, examples are presented that include elements needed to support applications that require systems design and computational architectures. Given the large size of the DDDAS literature, various taxonomies could be highlighted; however, the organization here is an effort to provide the reader with perspectives of the wide-ranging influence the DDDAS paradigm has had on the scientific, development, and design communities.

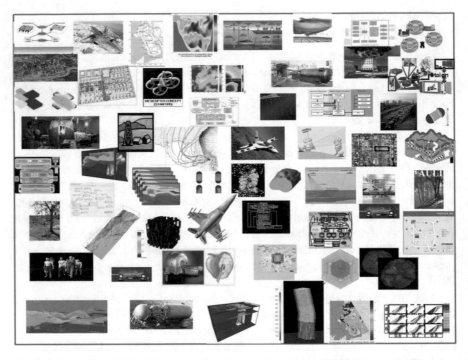

Fig. 1.6 Examples of DDDAS impact (From: Report of the August 2010 Multi-Agency Workshop on Info/Symbiotics/DDDAS: The power of Dynamic Data Driven Applications Systems, AFOSR-NSF (Air Force Office of Scientific Research-National Science Foundation), 2010 [7])

1.5.1   Theory: Modeling and Analysis

The DDDAS paradigm began with enhancing the phenomenology of *science and engineering models* such that, measurement information would (dynamically and adaptively) improve the resulting model. In 2003, several projects were launched that demonstrated key attributes in DDDAS, including faster and more accurate modeling, measurement information, dynamic data assimilation and adaptive sampling (going beyond the traditional data assimilation), incorporated into multiphysics [27], atmospheric modeling [28], and ocean forecasting [29]; as well as pandemics [30] and enterprise resource planning [17], discussed later (Sect. 5.3) in the context of application systems design. An application that benefited from the DDDAS principles using science models was oil well placement [31].

As the DDDAS methods showed promise in science applications, a key area was in *weather forecasting* [8]. Researchers assessed tornado prediction [32], weather and climate analysis [33], and chemical transport models [34]. Simultaneously, DDDAS began addressing theoretical uncertainty and quantifying error minimization (Uncertainty Quantification - UQ) [35]. Some years later, Ravela et al. [36] and others began to use the information from weather forecasting (e.g., coherent fluid analysis) for advances in applications controls for UAVs and aircraft routing.

Along with weather forecasting, another set of environmental systems-related applications on *wildfire monitoring* were developed, such as agent-based simulations for fire propagation modeling [37], which remains of interest to the present. A set of researchers, led by Mandel and Coen with their initial work [38], continued to use the DDDAS paradigm for inclusion of advanced physical models of wildfire prediction with that of real-time sensing. Such work includes the CAWFE® (Coupled Atmosphere-Wildland Fire Environment) modeling system, which together with various sensors such as the Visible Infrared Imaging Radiometer Suite (VIIRS), provided analysis of smoke plume detection [39] in the United States. The wildfire assessment method was extended to other geographic locations such as in Europe [40]. Furthermore, fire detection and mitigation sought to understand the management of water distribution [41].

Another example in the environmental systems area, is that of *volcanic ash detection* by Bursik and Singla, et al. [42]. Atmospheric analysis can have impacts on commercial air transport, such as the 2010 eruption of the Eyjafjallajökull volcano in Iceland. The particulates in the air from an eruption could have disastrous effects, for example on combustion engines of an aircraft flying through the sky region affected by volcanic ash spread. Likewise, with the detection of changes in the weather content, environmental wind context, and navigational data could be used to alter the air traffic management of the networked skies. Advances in uncertainty quantification were incorporated into the ash movement modeling so as to prepare aviation for future events and provide passenger safety [43]. Uncertainty quantification helps in estimating error reduction in complex modeling and estimation methods [44].

Additional science and engineering applications benefitting from DDDAS based methods include areas for bio-sensing and analysis for *medical applications*. One example is using image recognition for tracking human responses to stress and expressions. Metaxas et al. [45] developed DDDAS-based methods using image recognition and face tracking [46]. Other examples include using the sensing to update models of humans in support of neurosurgery [47]. As a third set of examples, Oden et al. [48, 49] utilized DDDAS principles for laser treatment of cancer. In each of these cases, DDDAS methods have supported enhancements in medical treatment through advanced modeling. Other DDDAS-based developments presented in this book include diagnostics, chemical treatment, and pandemics.

1.5.2 Methods: Domain Applications

Building upon the DDDAS principles for science and engineering applications, another area of influence are developments which applied the DDDAS-based dynamic data assimilation analysis to that of control and filtering. As highlighted earlier, an extension of the scientific modeling of the air environment was extended to the atmospheric environment for *orbital awareness*. Bernstein et al. [50] utilized the DDDAS principle for dynamic data assimilation, to use actual data to impart information into a model in aspects (of the system under study) not captured as well by the analytical (physical) model, and applied it in the case of the global ionosphere-thermosphere model (GITM). While it was applied as a scientific analysis, it showed how DDDAS can be applied for *system-level model-based* adaptive control and sensing. Simulations were conducted to determine the effects on planetary motion [51] and movement of atmospheric elements [52]. A third example extends these developments for the Retrospective Cost Model Refinement (RCMR) that includes modeling, sensing and control [53]. The capabilities achieved through this work provide for advances in satellite protection, orbital sensing, and understanding the far-earth environment.

Protection of aerial and space-based platforms, such as satellites, is also a key area for DDDAS-based advanced capabilities, including *structural health monitoring* (SHM), as exemplified by several research efforts. Farhat, Michopoulos, Chang et al. [54] utilized the DDDAS principles towards SHM of structural and materials assessments, while Korobenko and Bazilevs et al. followed with aircraft composite structures work which is featured in this book. Creating an accurate model, with DDDAS-based embedded sensing, supports real-time response to a dynamically changing environment. Additionally, developments include reduced-order modeling (ROM) such that the ensemble of models can be refined over model parameters, uncertainty estimation, and sensing bias [55]. Oden et al. [56] provided additional benefits of SHM for damage assessment and others highlighted modeling updates that account for materials damage [57]. The book highlights recent advancements in SHM using the DDDAS paradigm such as for aerospace systems.

Expanding DDDAS-based SHM methods to create real-time decision support systems, Willcox and Allaire et al. [58] have utilized online/offline modeling in support of *self-aware vehicles* which paves the way for autonomous systems. Included in their research is a focus on the model dimensionality for operational performance [59]. As a second example, Mohseni et al. have utilized a wide variety of air and water autonomous systems and applied DDDAS for control and atmospheric sensing [60]. The monitoring of the environment was combined to support the health monitoring of the vehicles in a changing environment. These developments have been incorporated into the control of soaring vehicles [61]. The third example includes on-board avionics to sense fault detection [62]. Varela et al. has led a group to bring together the computational modeling with that of instrumentation (e.g., pitot tubes, electronics) health assessment for safe flight [63]. Typically, estimation theory is employed for self-aware vehicles.

To achieve the capabilities for analysis over multiple domains requires the coordination and *estimation* across the techniques employed. Using the ensemble Kalman filter, Sandu et al. [64] addressed the computational aspects of dynamic data assimilation for aerosol in the atmosphere while Ravela et al. [65] devised methods for aerial platforms and underwater sensors positioning. Other work examined methods to improve forecasting prediction [66]. If the DDDAS methods are able to forecast the movements, they can use field alignment to estimate vehicle locations such as with quadrature information [67, 68]. Likewise, the fidelity of the parameters affects the estimation of model accuracy [69], which enables a mixture of ensembles [70].

Estimation methods are elements of *data fusion* techniques. The integration of measurements includes data, sensor, and information fusion. Information fusion aligns well with the DDDAS principles [71], however in DDDAS the data fusion is inherently dynamic. Such an example is an array of sensors whose operation is guided by dynamic data-driven model for target detection and classification [72]. DDDAS hence can improve pattern recognition [73] or classification especially if data analysis is performed over features [74]. Recent methods have combined heterogeneous data in support of nonlinear classification of moving objects using signal and pixel data [75].

Moving entity analysis includes *object estimation*. Hoffman et al. [76] used DDDAS-based modeling for adaptive sensor control in analysis of hyperspectral data to gather relevant features of the moving object. Fujimoto et al. [77] used similar DDDAS-based methods for ground vehicle-movement analysis, while others advanced the methods for multidimensional assignment in support of aerial vehicle monitoring [78].

In adaptive context-aware applications, the DDDAS concept leverages models such as scene, roads, or other terrain information. *Context aware* approaches were investigated [79], along with methods for measurement models which learn through state-augmenting contexts [80]. These methods were furthered by the information fusion community for context-enhanced information fusion which shows how DDDAS techniques can improve tracking over many operating conditions for robust performance [81].

Building on theory and methods, a number of efforts have demonstrated new capabilities for complex systems design and operation.

1.5.3   Analysis and Design: Systems and Architectures

The third section of this overview discusses systems architecture and systems analysis and design, for example for energy networks and cyber network analysis, and other systems design, with recent efforts also exploiting cloud computing. In the early methods of DDDAS, there was a need for scalable applications-systems' *architectures,* and agent-based systems where evaluated [82]. DDDAS showed promise for supply chain analysis to improve the logistics and movement of parts [83]. In addition, the advent of web-based methods have provided a use case for distributed simulations for computer data streaming [84]. Web-based methods afford query languages for DDDAS designs [85] and analysis [86].

The distributed aspects of network analysis were adapted to be DDDAS-based and applied for power systems and *energy* analysis [87, 88]. Power analysis as a function of microgrids is aimed to support not only traditional uses such as residential buildings and other regional environments, but also the power and energy available for Internet of Things (IoT), and such also include "IoT" within a given system such as for example in an aircraft which requires an adequate model of the energy distribution [89]. As for ground vehicles, the energy consumption can be improved both locally for a car and globally for traffic [90].

In networks, whether power grids, or complex equipment or infrastructure, the comprehensive (system-model) and real-time analysis which can take into account global effects (such as multiple components or systems-of-systems) can improve situation awareness, for example for disaster management [91]. A DDDAS-based *systems approach* applied to smart cities and urban infrastructures, supported assessment of emissions effects on the climate [92]. Likewise, with systems-analysis, DDDAS-based methods can support the design of embedded electronics for signal processing [93]. Such methods were further analyzed for adaptive video stream processing [94, 95].

Recent trends have changed the network application to include communication and *cyber networks*. Early work, DDDAS-based, utilized web services to monitor the network health [96]. Subsequently, DDDAS-based methods for societal applications involved monitoring and trust in a (societal) network [97]; other DDDAS-based methods for trust and privacy, relied on trust analysis for sensing control and assignment [98]. Recent efforts include extending these, and a comprehensive analysis of DDDAS and the coordination of trust was explored by Blasch and Hariri et al. [99, 100].

Finally, the application of the DDDAS concept in heterogeneous and distributed *computing* has shown promise for advancements in systems-software for dynamic and adaptive runtime support and with Quality of Service (QoS) optimization. An example of QoS optimization improvement using DDDAS is provided in [101]. The use of a cloud-based system was successful for real-time tracking of targets from Wide Area Motion Imagery (WAMI) streaming data [102]. DDDAS-based methods for cloud computing were used in [103], for example using edge sensors to manage the data streams between internet of things (IoT) networked devices and those of sensors at the edge. A review by Darema et al. [104] discusses how DDDAS-based methods support of wide range of applications and their environments, such as distributed behavior model orchestration in cognitive IoT environments and their capabilities.

1.6 Book Overview

This book was inspired as an extension of the Proceedings of the 2016 DDDAS workshop in Hartford Connecticut. The book chapters reflect both research work conducted over the years starting in the 1990's as well as presentations in the 2016 forum. Additional material on chapters in this book are available at the DDDAS website (www.1dddas.org). This website also hosts an archival record of DDDAS-based work conducted over the years, including software methods and data to support the DDDAS analysis. To overview some of the contributions, the Table 1.1 below lists the book chapters highlighting their theory, simulation, data, and application content. The reader can use this table to for example focus on those chapters where the theoretical content and application context is of interest to their research and analysis.

1.7   DDDAS Future

Three emerging areas where DDDAS can have profound impact, include: (1) data science learning; (2) autonomy through adaptation; and (3) systems design with smart sensing – as shown in Fig. 1.7.

Data movement and ***data science*** are future efforts aligned with the growth of artificial intelligence (AI), machine learning, and deep networks methods. These growing areas of interest follow from the recent trend in big data. The original DDDAS paradigm calls out modeling and *big data* (and in particular models and "dynamic" big-data) as an overarching theme that utilizes algorithms, models, and computation, to harness data availability and control the data collection (and more broadly the instrumentation of a system). Algorithms still need to be adapted to the dynamic environment. For example, neural networks do interpolation through modeling, but are not good at extrapolation to changing environments nor do they provide explanation of resolved decisions. If, on the other hand, instrumentation methods capturing data are integrated with high-dimensional modeling of the situation context, then such constructs within AI can be realizable for analysis, design, and adaptive management efforts.

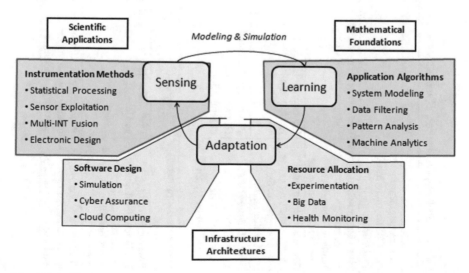

Fig. 1.7 DDDAS future areas

Table 1.1 Book chapters summary of approaches

	Theory	Simulation	Data	Application
Measurement aware: assimilation, uncertainty quantification				
Tractable non-Gaussian representations in dynamic data driven coherent fluid mapping	Reduced order modeling with ensemble filtering	Atmospheric plumes	UAV tracking plume detection	Unmanned aerial systems
Dynamic data-driven adaptive observations in data assimilation for multi-scale systems	Information-theoretic particle filtering	Lorenz 1963 Weather data	Weather augmented nonlinear flight	Sensor selection in dynamic flight
Dynamic data-driven uncertainty quantification via generalized polynomial Chaos	Polynomial Chaos and GMM uncertainty quantification	Satellite tracking	Ionosphere-thermosphere models	Orbital awareness
Signals aware: processes monitoring				
Towards learning Spatio-temporal data stream relationships for failure detection in avionics	Declarative data estimation and learning	Airplane sensor data	Aircraft weight, airflow measurements	Avionics sensor failure
Markov modeling via spectral analysis for combustion instabilities	Reduced-order Markov modeling w maximum entropy partitioning	Time-series combustion modeling	Gas, pressure, temperature	Combustion engine diagnostics

Dynamic space-time model for syndromic surveillance with particle filters and Dirichlet process	Particle filters with Dirichlet processes	Biohealth outbreak	Indiana public health emergency surveillance sys.	Health protection
Structures aware: health modeling				
A computational steering framework for large-scale composite structures. Part I: parametric-based design and analysis	Variational multiscale fluid structure interaction (FSI)	Isogeometirc analysis (IGA) approach lie finite-element modeling	Structures composite element relation network with ultrasonic sensor	Composite wing control for aerodynamic flight
Development of intelligent and predictive self-healing composite structures using dynamic data driven applications systems	Modified beam theory	Structures crack and delanation healing	Double-cantilever beam fracture and healing test	Structural self-healing
Dynamic data-driven approach for unmanned aircraft systems and aeroelastic response analysis	Bayesian copula model	Aeroelastic unsteady, vortex lattice method with finite element model (UVLM-FEM)	Sensor strain measurements	UAV wing analysis

(continued)

Table 1.1 (continued)

	Theory	Simulation	Data	Application
Environment aware: earth, biological and space systems				
Transforming wildfire detection and prediction using new and underused sensor and data sources integrated with modeling	Ensemble Kalman filter with adaptive simulation invocation of data	Coupled atmosphere-wildland fire environment modeling tools	Visible infrared imaging radiometer suite (VIIRS) satellite data	Wildfire detection and prediction
DDDAS for identification of biomarkers in DNA methylation	Hierarchical clustering for dimension reduction	DNA sequencing through locus score information	GEO DataSets of lung Cancer	Biomarkers in DNA methylation
Photometric method for 3D reconstruction of space object	Photometric stereo imaging using structure from motion methods	Synthetic images generated from ray-tracer engine	Light detection and ranging (LIDAR)	Resident space object detection
Situation aware: tracking methods				
Aided optimal search: data-driven target pursuit from on-demand delayed binary observations	Sparse Gaussian mixture model w/ mixed-integer programming	Partially observably Markov decision processes for optimal search	Unattended ground sensors for object estimation	UAV/AGV coordination for surveillance

Optimization of multi-target tracking within a sensor network via information guided clustering	Information-driven sensor querying with entropy likelihood	Particle filter prediction	Unattended ground sensors for object estimation	Sensor network management
Data-driven prediction of confidence and EVAR in time-varying datasets	Entropic value at risk w/ real-time adaptive prediction of time-varying and obscure rewards	Predicted information gain w multiplayer bandit	European research area data: Temperature, windfall, rain, ozone	Environmental awareness
Context aware: coordinated control				
DDDAS for attack detection and isolation of control systems	DDDAS-inspired anomaly isolation and response	Nonlinear three tank Luenberger observer	Cyber attacks modeling	Cyber attacks of industrial control systems
Approximate local utility design for potential game approach to cooperative sensor network planning	Information theoretic methods	Game theoretic neighbor utility	Lorenz-95 model	Sensor grid weather forecasting

(continued)

Table 1.1 (continued)

	Theory	Simulation	Data	Application
Dynamic sensor-actor interactions for path planning in an uncertain threat field	Fisher information theoretic methods	Actor–driven sensor reconfiguration in threat field	Grid-based sensor field	Wildfires, atmospheric contaminants
Energy aware: power systems				
Energy-aware dynamic data-driven distributed traffic simulation for energy and emissions reduction	Kinematic modeling of vehicles with cellular automata	EPA MOtor Vehicle Emissions Simulator (MOVES) model	Federal Highway Administrations Next Generation Simulation (NGSIM) data	Vehicle emissions monitoring
A dynamic data-driven optimization framework for demand side management microgrids	Load demand from wind turbines, diesel, and solar energy optimization	Interruption load management (ILM) analysis	Florida Automated Weather Network (FAWN) data	Microgrid CO_2 emissions
Dynamic data driven partitioning of smart grid for improving power efficiency by combining K-means and fuzzy methods	Fuzzy logic market-based optimization	GridLAB-D simulation	IEEE-13, IEEE-37 and IEEE-123 bus test feeders	Renewable energy sources energy
Process aware: image and video computing methods				
Design of a dynamic data-driven system for multispectral video processing	Gaussian mixture model pixel-level fusion	Lightweight dataflow spectral run-time system model	Hyperspectral band subset processing	Multi-spectral image processing

Light field and plenoptic point cloud compression	Self-similarity based light field video encoding	Bi-direction motion estimation and compensation	Dense camera array images	Lenslet-based and camera array image processing
On compression of machine-derived context sets for fusion of multi-modal sensor data	Graph-theoretic problem of maximal clique enumeration	D-Markov context set compression	Time-series symbolic dynamic filtered data	Context-based sensor data for surveillance
Cyber aware: security and computing systems				
Simulation-based optimization as a service for dynamic data-driven applications systems	K-greedy coordinate decent (CD) method	Simulation-based optimization as a service	Dynamic traffic light control	Cloud-based large scale discrete variable decision decision
Privacy and security issues in DDDAS systems	Laplace perturbation analysis a-differential privacy	PREDICT (privacy and secuRity enhancing dynamic information collection and moniToring)	Data stream collection of multimedia data	Intelligent data collection

(continued)

Table 1.1 (continued)

	Theory	Simulation	Data	Application
Multimedia content analysis with dynamic data driven applications systems (DDDAS)	Qurey-based dataflow target detection and tracking	Live-video computing (LVC) database management system (LVC-DBMS) system	Parking lot image and text data	Multimodal surveillance
Systems aware: combined design methods				
Parzen Windows: simplest regularization algorithm	Non parametric least-squares learning	Gaussian sensor simulation	Sonar sensing, Stuctures ID, Financial transactions, Medical Iris detection, Ionosphere,	General analysis for broad engineering systems
Multiscale DDDAS framework for damage prediction in aerospace composite structures: From wind turbines to UAV	Isogeometric analysis (IGA) and finite element modeling	Surrogate management framework of beam displacement	Structural health monitoring data	Wing composite structures
A dynamic data-driven stochastic state-awareness framework for the next generation of bio-inspired fly-by-feel aerospace vehicles	AutoRegressive pooling of sensor data	Vector-dependent functionally pooled models	Piezoelectric lead-zirconate titanate (PZT), strain gauges, and temp sensors	Fly-by-feel aerospace vehicle

The second area, **Autonomy through adaptation**, includes many aspects, from autonomy in traditional vehicles [105] to recent data science methods such as data at rest, data in motion, and data in use concepts [106, 107]. While the data concepts (i.e., at rest, in motion, and in use) were promoted by the software community, these labels were mostly for the movement of data and not the processing of the data. The processing of the data, augmented with modeling can be a hallmark of future autonomous systems. Autonomy at rest (AAR) leverages data science to combine or fuse the data, while autonomy in motion (AIM) supports the interaction among platforms such as UAVs. DDDAS is focused on autonomy in use (AIU). Autonomous systems dynamically interact with their environments, so there is a need for not only complex modeling (which needs to consider not only the model of one isolated system but also the other systems with which a given system interacts with), as well as methods in which real-time distributed sensing updates the models. Together, modeling, sensing, and data movement, as has been articulated by the DDDAS paradigm, are future trends to achieve autonomous solutions.

The third growth area, is in **smart sensing** through networked systems and software, or architectures [108], to move and process data with high performance computing over a wide variety of (heterogeneous collections of) sensors, such as visual [109] and radar [110, 111] sensors. The coordination of social modeling, internet of things (IoT), and power grids require systems and software developments to coordinate the dynamic data. The DDDAS efforts will expand from DDDAS-based principles, while leveraging other developments in autonomy and learning. Additionally, smart sensing includes not only the data exploitation, but also information collection, processing, fusion, and analysis [112, 113].

Fundamental basic research in DDDAS will be gathered from, and contribute to, scientific applications, mathematical foundations, and infrastructure architectures [114]. Specifically, advances in theory, methods, and systems analysis and design will continue to expand the science and engineering capabilities stemming from the DDDAS principles [115]. The book highlights recent accomplishments while future research projects and presentations in professional forums will showcase emerging developments.

1.8 Summary

The book organizes DDDAS-based developments in three parts of the different areas that are prominent in DDDAS methods: theory, methods, and complex and dynamic systems' analysis and design as shown in Fig. 1.8. The first part, *theory*, discusses some of the key fundamental approaches researchers have used including dynamic data assimilation, process modeling and filtering, and estimation. The second part, *methods*, includes key interactions between the theory and the use cases such as structural analysis for structural health monitoring, systems control for component processing, and image rendering for situation evaluation. Finally, the third part, (systems) *analysis* and *design*, includes recent advanced capabili-

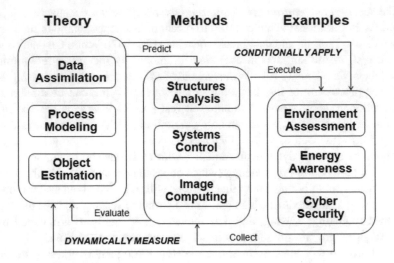

Fig. 1.8 DDDAS methods presented in the book

ties for domain applications including situation awareness through environmental assessment, energy awareness such as power grids, and cyber awareness concerning privacy and security protections.

The readers of this book will benefit from DDDAS theory developments such as object estimation, information fusion, and sensor management. The recent interest in UAVs provides a case example for new and advanced methods, including command and control, swarm analysis, and structural health monitoring. Finally, the set of applications presented are examples which leverage and extend science models, where big data dynamically integrated with modeling as per the DDDAS paradigm, to create more powerful models and thus extend the modeling foundations for important applications, as shown in the example of weather forecasting, volcanic ash assessment, and wildfire monitoring, among many other applications areas. In the last two decades, DDDAS has resulted in many systems currently studied by academics, researchers, practitioners, and industrialists. This book helps to capture and organize these results for the reader. The DDDAS community encourages discussion, comments, and contributions through the website: www.1dddas.org.

Acknowledgements Work presented in this book was supported in part by the DDDAS Program of the Air Force Office of Scientific Research (AFOSR) as well as other funding agencies. The views and conclusions contained herein are those of the authors and should not be interpreted as necessarily representing the official policies or endorsements, either expressed or implied, of the Air Force Research Laboratory or the U.S. Government, or any other funding entities.

References

1. A. Aved, E. Blasch, Dynamic Data Driven Applications Systems (DDDAS), (2104) Website, www.1dddas.org.
2. F. Darema, Grid Computing and Beyond: The Context of Dynamic Data Driven Applications Systems. Proceedings of the IEEE, 93 (3):692–697, (2005)
3. F. Darema, Parallel Applications and the Gedanken Laboratory, *Conference of the Society of Engineering Sciences*, (1990)
4. F. Darema et al., DDDAS: Dynamic Data Driven Applications Systems, US National Science Foundation (2005). https://www.nsf.gov/pubs/2005/nsf05570/nsf05570.htm
5. F. Darema, The Next Generation Program, (1998). http://www.nsf.gov/pubs/1999/nsf998/nsf998.htm
6. F. Darema, New software architecture for complex applications development and runtime support, *Int. J. High-Performance Computation, Special Issue on Programming Environments, Clusters, and Comp. Grids for Sci. Comp.*, 14(3), (2000)
7. *Report of the August 2010 Multi-Agency Workshop on Info/Symbiotics/DDDAS: The power of Dynamic Data Driven Applications Systems*, AFOSR-NSF (2010), available at https://s3.amazonaws.com/static.1dddas.org/docs/2010_DDDAS-InfoSymbioticsReport.pdf
8. B. Plale, D. Gannon, D. Reed, S. Graves, K. Droegemeier, B. Wilhelmson, M. Ramamurthy, Towards dynamically adaptive weather analysis and forecasting in LEAD, *International Conference Computational Science* (2005).
9. F. Darema, The Next Generation Software Program, *International Journal of Parallel Programming* 33 (2–3): 73–79, (2005). https://doi.org/10.1007/s10766-005-4785-6.
10. G. Allen, Building a Dynamic Data Driven Application System for Hurricane Forecasting, *International Conf. on Computational Science*, 1034–1041 (2007)
11. G. Allen, P. Bogden, R.A. Luettich, Jr, E. Seidel, R. Twilley, Designing a Dynamic Data Driven Application System for Coastal and Environmental Modeling, *Grid-Based Problem Solving Environments*, 275–293 (2007)
12. D.S. Bernstein, A. Ridley, J. Cutler, A. Cohn, Transformative Advances in DDDAS with Application to Space Weather Monitoring, Project Report, Univ. Michigan (2015)
13. C. Yang, M. Bakich, et al., Pose Angular-Aiding for Maneuvering Target Tracking, *Int. Conf. on Info Fusion* (2005)
14. J. Dunık, O. Straka, et al., Random-Point-Based Filters: Analysis and Comparison in Target Tracking, *IEEE Tr. on Aerospace and Elec. Sys.*, 51(2): 1403–1421, (2015)
15. E.P. Blasch, E. Bosse, D.A. Lambert, *High-Level Information Fusion Management and Systems Design*, Artech House, Norwood, MA (2012)
16. US National Science Foundation, Cyber-Physical Systems (CPS) Program Solicitation, https://www.nsf.gov/pubs/2010/nsf10515/nsf10515.htm
17. N. Celik, S. Lee, K. Vasudevan, Y.-J. Son, DDDAS-based multi-fidelity simulation framework for supply chain systems, *IIE Transactions*, 42(5):325–341 (2010). https://doi.org/10.1080/07408170903394306
18. F. Darema, The Next Generation Software Workshop – IPDPS'07, *IEEE Int'l Parallel and Distributed Processing Symposium (IPDPS)*, (2007)
19. F. Darema, Cyberinfrastructures of Cyber-applications-systems, *Procedia Computer Science*, 1 (1): 1287–1296 (2010). https://doi.org/10.1016/j.procs.2010.04.143.
20. A.R. Chaturvedi, Society of simulation approach to dynamic integration of simulations, *IEEE Winter Simulation Conference*, 2125–2131 (2006)
21. R. Fujimoto, J. Barjis, et al., Dynamic Data Driven Application Systems: Research Challenges and Opportunities, *Winter Simulation Conference*, 664–678 (2018)
22. S. Sarkar, P. Chattopdhyay, A. Ray, S. Phoha, M. Levi, Alphabet size selection for symbolization of dynamic data-driven systems: An information-theoretic approach, *American Control Conference (ACC)*, 5194–5199 (2015)

23. V. Maroulas, K. Kang, I.D. Schizas, M.W. Berry, A learning drift homotopy particle filter, *International Conference on Information Fusion*, 1930–1937 (2015)
24. E. Blasch, Enhanced air operations using JView for an air-ground fused situation awareness UDOP, *IEEE/AIAA Digital Avionics Systems Conference* (DASC) (2013). https://doi.org/10.1109/DASC.2013.6712597
25. F. Darema, et al., Panel on *Unifying Directions for Systems Engineering, ASME*/IEEEInternational Conf. on Mechatronic and Embedded Sys. and App. (2011)
26. F. Darema, Y.-J. Son, A. Patra, AFOSR Panel: Dynamic Data Driven Application Systems (DDDAS) in the Age of Big Compute and Big Data, *ASME/IDETC International Design Engineering Technical Conferences* (2014)
27. J. Michopoulos, Ddema: A data driven environment for multiphysics applications, *International Conference Computational Science* (2003)
28. G. Carmichael, D.N. Daescu, A. Sandu, T. Chai, Computational aspects of chemical data assimilation into atmosphere models, *International Conference Computational Science* (2003)
29. C. Evangelinos, R. Chang, P.F.J. Lermusiaux, N.M. Patrikalakis, Rapid real-time interdisciplinary ocean forecasting using adaptive sampling and adaptive modeling and legacy codes: Component ecapsulation using xml, *International Conference Computational Science* (2003)
30. J. Mandel, J. D. Beezley, L. Cobb, A. Krishnamurthy, Data Driven Computing by the Morphing Fast Fourier Transform Ensemble Kalman Filter in Epidemic Spread Simulations, DDDAS/ICCS Workshop, *Procedia Computer Sci.*, 1, 1221–1229 (2010)
31. M. Parashar, V. Matossian, W. Bangerth, H. Klie, B. Rutt, T. Kurc, U. Catalyurek, J. Saltz, M.F. Wheeler, Towards dynamic data-driven optimization of oil well placement, *International Conference Computational Science*, (2005)
32. T.B. Trafalis, I. Adrianto, M.B. Richman, Active learning with support vector machines for tornado prediction, *International Conference Computational Science* (2007)
33. L. Ramakrishnan, Y. Simmhan, B. Plale, Realization of dynamically adaptive weather analysis and forecasting in LEAD: Four years down the road, *International Conference Computational Science* (2007)
34. L. Zhang, A. Sandu, Data assimilation in multiscale chemical transport models, *International Conference Computational Science* (2007)
35. N. Roy, H.-L. Choi, D. Gombos, J. Hansen, J. How, S. Park, Adaptive observation strategies for forecast error minimization, *International Conference Computational Science* (2007)
36. S. Ravela, Quantifying uncertainty for coherent structures, *Procedia Computer Science*, 9, 1187–1196 (2012)
37. J. Michopoulos, P. Tsompanopoulou, E. Houstis, A. Joshi, Agent-based simulation of data-driven fire propagation dynamics, *International Conference Computational Science* (2004)
38. J. Mandel, J.D. Beezley, L.S. Bennethum, S. Chakraborty, J.L. Coen, C.C. Douglas, J. Hatcher, M. Kim, A. Vodacek, A dynamic data driven wildland fire model, *International Conference Computational Science* (2007)
39. J.D. Beezley, S. Chakraborty, J.L. Coen, C.C. Douglas, J. Mandel, A. Vodacek, Z. Wang, Real-time data driven wildland fire modeling, *International Conference Computational Science* (2008)
40. R. Rodriguez-Aseretto, M.D. Leo, A. Cortés, J.S. Miguel-Ayanz, A data-driven model for big forest fires behavior prediction in Europe, *Procedia Computer Science*, 18, 186–1870 (2013)
41. L. Wang, D. Chen, W. Liu, Y. Ma, Y. Wu, Z. Deng, DDDAS-Based Parallel Simulation of Threat Management for Urban Water Distribution Systems, *Computing in Science & Engineering* 16(1): 8–17 (2014). https://doi.org/10.1109/MCSE.2012.89
42. A.K. Patra, M.I. Bursik, J. Dehn, M. Jones, M. Pavolonis, E.B. Pitman, T. Singh, P. Singla, E.R. Stefanescu, S. Pouget, P. Webley, Challenges in developing DDDAS based methodology for volcanic ash hazard analysis - effect of numerical weather prediction variability and parameter estimation, *Procedia Computer Science* 18, 1871–1880 (2013)
43. A.K. Patra, E.R. Stefanescu, R.M. Madankan, M.I. Bursik, E.B. Pitman, P. Singla, T. Singh, P. Webley, Fast construction of surrogates for UQ central to DDDAS application to volcanic ash transport, *Procedia Computer Science* 29: 1227–1235 (2014)

44. V.H.V.S. Rao, A. Sandu, A posteriori error estimates for DDDAS inference problems, *Procedia Computer Science* 29, 1256–1265 (2014)
45. D. Metaxas, S. Venkataraman, C. Vogler, Image-based stress recognition using a model-based dynamic face tracking system, *International Conference Computational Science* (2004)
46. D. Metaxas, G. Tsechpenakis, Z. Li, Y. Huang, A. Kanaujia, Dynamically adaptive tracking of gestures and facial expressions, *International Conference Computational Science* (2006)
47. A. Majumdar, A. Birnbaum, D. Choi, A. Trivedi, S.K. Warfield, K. Baldridge, P. Krysl, A dynamic data driven grid system for intra-operative image guided neurosurgery, *International Conference Computational Science* (2005)
48. J.T. Oden, K.R. Diller, C. Bajaj, J.C. Browne, J. Hazle, I. Babuska, J. Bass, L. Demkowicz, Y. Feng, D. Fuentes, S. Prudhomme, M.N. Rylander, R.J. Stafford, Y. Zhang, Development of a computational paradigm for laser treatment of cancer, *International Conference Computational Science* (2006)
49. C. Bajaj, J.T. Oden, K.R. Diller, J.C. Browne, J. Hazle, I. Babuska, J. Bass, L. Bidaut, L. Demkowicz, A. Elliott, Y. Feng, D. Fuentes, B. Kwon, S. Prudhomme, R.J. Staord, Y. Zhang, Using cyber-infrastructure for dynamic data driven laser treatment of cancer, *International Conference Computational Science* (2007)
50. I.S. Kim, J. Chandrasekar, A. Ridley, D.S. Bernstein, Data assimilation using the global ionosphere-thermosphere model, *International Conference Computational Science*, (2006)
51. S. Ravela, J. Marshall, C. Hill, A. Wong, S. Stransky, Real-time observatory for laboratory simulation of planetary circulation, *International Conference Computational Science* (2007)
52. A.V. Morozov, A.J. Ridley, D.S. Bernstein, N. Collins, T.J. Hoar, J.L. Anderson, Data assimilation and driver estimation for the Global Ionosphere–Thermosphere Model using the Ensemble Adjustment Kalman Filter, *Journal of Atmospheric and Solar-Terrestrial Physics* 104, 126–136 (2013)
53. A.G. Burrell, A. Goel, A.J. Ridley, D.S. Bernstein, Correction of the Photoelectron Heating Efficiency Within the Global Ionosphere-Thermosphere Model Using Retrospective Cost Model Refinement, *Journal of Atmospheric and Solar-Terrestrial Physics*, 124, 30–38 (2015).
54. C. Farhat, J.G. Michopoulos, F.K. Chang, L.J. Guibas, A.J. Lew, Towards a dynamic data driven system for structural and material health monitoring, *International Conference Computational Science* (2006)
55. J. Cortial, C. Farhat, L.J. Guibas, M. Rajashekhar, Time-parallel exploitation of reduced-order modeling and sensor data reduction for structural and material health monitoring DDDAS, *International Conference Computational Science* (2007)
56. E.E. Prudencio, P.T. Bauman, D. Faghihi, J.T. Oden, K. Ravi-Chandar, S.V. Williams, A dynamic data driven application system for real-time monitoring of stochastic damage, *Procedia Computer Science* 18, 2056–2065 (2013)
57. E.E. Prudencio, P.T. Bauman, D. Faghihi, K. Ravi-Chandar, J.T. Oden, A Computational Framework for Dynamic Data Driven Material Damage Control, Based on Bayesian Inference and Model Selection, *International Journal for Numerical Methods in Engineering* 102 (3-4): 379–403 (April 2015). https://doi.org/10.1002/nme.4669
58. D. Allaire, J. Chambers, R. Cowlagi, D. Kordonowy, M. Lecerf, L. Mainini, F. Ulker, K. Willcox, A baseline offine/online DDDAS capability for self-aware aerospace vehicles, *Procedia Computer Science*, 18, 1959–1968 (2013)
59. D. Allaire, D. Kordonowy, M. Lecerf, L. Mainini, K. Willcox, Multi-fidelity DDDAS methods with application to a self-aware aerospace vehicle, *Procedia Computer Science* 29, 1182–1192 (2014)
60. L. Peng, K. Mohseni, Sensor driven feedback for puff estimation using unmanned aerial vehicles, *International Conference on Unmanned Aircraft Systems (ICUAS)*, 562–569, (2014). https://doi.org/10.1109/ICUAS.2014.6842298.
61. E. Blasch, P. Paces, P. Kostek, K. Kramer, Summary of Avionics Technologies, *IEEE Aerospace and Electronics Systems Magazine* 30(9): 6–11, (Sept. 2015)

62. W. Silva, E. W. Frew, W. Shaw-Cortez, Implementing path planning and guidance layers for dynamic soaring and persistence missions, *International Conference on Unmanned Aircraft Systems* (ICUAS), 92–101, (2015). https://doi.org/10.1109/ICUAS.2015.7152279

63. S. Imai, E. Blasch, A. Galli, F. Lee, C.A. Varela, Airplane Flight Safety Using Error-Tolerant Data Stream Processing, *IEEE Aerospace and Electronics Systems Magazine*, 32(4): 4–17 (April 2017)

64. A. Sandu, W. Liao, G.R. Carmichael, D. Henze, J.H. Seinfeld, T. Chai, D. Daescu, Computational aspects of data assimilation for aerosol dynamics, *International Conference Computational Science* (2004)

65. S. Ravela, Amplitude-position formulation of data assimilation, *International Conference Computational Science* (2006)

66. B. Jia, K.D. Pham, E. Blasch, D. Shen, Z. Wang, G. Chen, Cooperative Space Object Tracking using Space-based Optical Sensors via Consensus-based Filters, *IEEE Tr. on Aerospace and Electronics Systems*, 52(3): 1908–1936 (2016)

67. S. Ravela, Two extensions of data assimilation by field alignment, *International Conference Computational Science* (2007)

68. P. Tagade, S. Ravela, On a quadratic information measure for data assimilation, *American Control Conf.*, 598–603 (2014)

69. T.C. Henderson, N. Boonsirisumpun, The impact of parameter estimation on model accuracy assessment, *Procedia Computer Science* 18, 1969–1978 (2013)

70. P. Tagade, H. Seybold, S. Ravela, Mixture ensembles for data assimilation in dynamic data-driven environmental systems, *Procedia Computer Science* 29: 1266–1276 (2014)

71. E.P. Blasch, Dynamic data driven applications system concept for information fusion," *Procedia Computer Science* 18, 1999–2007 (2013)

72. N. Virani, S. Marcks, S. Sarkar, K. Mukherjee, A. Ray, S. Phoha, Dynamic data driven sensor array fusion for target detection and classification, *Procedia Computer Science*, 18, 2046–2055 (2013)

73. E. Blasch, G. Seetharaman, F. Darema, Dynamic Data Driven Applications Systems (DDDAS) modeling for Automatic Target Recognition, *Proc. SPIE* 8744 (2013)

74. B. Smith, P. Chattopadhyay, A. Ray, T.R. Damarla, Performance robustness of feature extraction for target detection & classification, *IEEE American Control Conference*, (2014)

75. T. Chin, Jr., K. Xiong, E. Blasch, CRAMStrack: Enhanced Nonlinear RSSI Tracking Using Circular Multi-Sectors for Threat Detection, *Journal of Signal Processing Systems*, June (2020)

76. B. Uzkent, M.J. Hoffman, A. Vodacek, J.P. Kerekes, B. Chen, Feature matching and adaptive prediction models in an object tracking DDDAS, *Procedia Computer Science* 18, 1939–1948 (2013)

77. R. Fujimoto, A. Guin, M. Hunter, H. Park, R. Kannan, G. Kanitkar, M. Milholen, S. Neal, P. Pecher, A dynamic data driven application system for vehicle tracking, *Procedia Computer Science* 29, 1203–1215 (2014)

78. B. Uzkent, M.J. Hoffman, A. Vodacek, Integrating Hyperspectral Likelihoods in a Multi-dimensional Assignment Algorithm for Aerial Vehicle Tracking, *IEEE Journal of Selected Topics in Applied Earth Observations and Remote Sensing* 9(9): 4325–4333, (2016). https://doi.org/10.1109/JSTARS.2016.2560220

79. N. Nguyen, M.H.H. Khan, Context Aware Data Acquisition Framework for Dynamic Data Driven Applications Systems (DDDAS), *IEEE Military Communications Conf.*, 334–341 (2013). https://doi.org/10.1109/MILCOM.2013.65

80. N. Virani, J-W. Lee, S. Phoha, A. Ray, Learning context-aware measurement models," *American Control Conference* (ACC), 4491–4496 (2015). https://doi.org/10.1109/ACC.2015.7172036

81. L. Snidaro, J. Garcia Herrero, J. Llinas, E. Blasch, *Context-Enhanced Information Fusion: Boosting Real-World Performance with Domain Knowledge*, Springer (2016)

82. A. Chaturvedi, J. Chi, S. Mehta, D. Dolk, SAMAS: Scalable architecture for multi-resolution agent-based simulation, *International Conference Computational Science*, (2004)

83. N. Koyuncu, S. Lee, K.K. Vasudevan, Y-J. Son, P. Sarfare, DDDAS-basedmulti-fidelitysimulation for onlinepreventivemaintenancescheduling in semiconductorsupply chain, *Winter Simulation Conference*, 1915–1923, (2007) https://doi.org/10.1109/WSC.2007.4419819

84. A. Boukerche, F.M. Iwasaki, R.B. Araujo, E.B. Pizzolato, Web-Based Distributed Simulations Visualization and Control with HLA and Web Services, *IEEE/ACM International Symposium on Distributed Simulation and Real-Time Applications*, 17–23, (2008). https://doi.org/10.1109/DS-RT.2008.30

85. A.J. Aved, E. Blasch, Multi-INT Query Language for DDDAS Designs, *Procedia Computer Science* 51, 2518–2523 (2015)

86. E. Blasch, S. Phoha, Special Issue: Dynamic Data-Driven Applications Systems (DDDAS) concepts in Signal Processing, *J. Signal Processing Systems* (2017) https://doi.org/10.1007/s11265-017-1253-7

87. E.H. Abed, N.S. Namachchivaya, T.J. Overbye, M.A. Pai, P.W. Sauer, A. Sussman, Data driven power system operations, *International Conference Computational Science*, (2006)

88. N. Celik, A.E. Thanos, J.P. Saenz, DDDAMS-based dispatch control in power networks, *Procedia Computer Science* 18, 1899–1908 (2013)

89. E. Frew, B. Argrow, A. Houston, C. Weiss, J. Elston, An energy-aware airborne dynamic data-driven application system for persistent sampling and surveillance, *Procedia Computer Science* 18, 2008–2017 (2013)

90. S. Neal, R. Fujimoto, M. Hunter, Energy consumption of Data Driven traffic simulations, *Winter Simulation Conference (WSC)*, 1119–1130 (2016). https://doi.org/10.1109/WSC.2016.7822170

91. G. R. Madey, A.-L. Barabsi, N.V. Chawla, M. Gonzalez, D. Hachen, B. Lantz, A. Pawling, T. Schoenharl, G. Szabo, P. Wang, P. Yan, Enhanced situational awareness: Application of DDDAS concepts to emergency and disaster management, *International Conference Computational Science* (2007)

92. R.M. Fujimoto, N. Celik, H. Damgacioglu, M. Hunter, D. Jin, Y-J. Son, J. Xu, Dynamic data driven application systems for smart cities and urban infrastructures, *Winter Simulation Conference*, 1143–1157, (2016). https://doi.org/10.1109/WSC.2016.7822172

93. K. Sudusinghe, I. Cho, M. Van der Schaar, S.S. Bhattacharyya, Model based design environment for data-driven embedded signal processing systems, *Procedia Computer Science* 29, 1193–1202 (2014).

94. S. Chakravarthy, A. Aved, S. Shirvani, M. Annappa, E. Blasch, Adapting Stream Processing Framework for Video Analysis, *Procedia Computer Science*, 51, 2648–2657, (2015)

95. H. Li, K. Sudusinghe, Y. Liu, J. Yoon, M. Van Der Schaar, E. Blasch, S.S. Bhattacharyya, Dynamic, Data-Driven Processing of Multispectral Video Streams, *IEEE Aerospace and Electronics Systems Magazine*, 32 (4): 50–57 (June 2017)

96. P. Chew, N. Chrisochoides, S. Gopalsamy, G. Heber, T. Ingraffea, E. Luke, J. Neto, K. Pingali, A. Shih, B. Soni, P. Stodghill, D. Thompson, S. Vavasis, P. Wawrzynek, Computational science simulations based on web services, *International Conference Computational Science* (2003)

97. O. Onolaja, R. Bahsoon, G. Theodoropoulos, Conceptual framework for dynamic trust monitoring and prediction, *Procedia Computer Science*, 1, 1241–1250 (2010)

98. L. Pournajaf, L. Xiong, V. Sunderam, Dynamic data driven crowd sensing task assignment, *Procedia Computer Science*, 29: 1314–1323 (2014)

99. E. Blasch, Y. Al-Nashif, S. Hariri, Static versus dynamic data information fusion analysis using DDDAS for cyber trust, *Procedia Computer Science*, 29, 1299–1313, 2014.

100. Y. Badr, S. Hariri, Y. Al-Nashif, E. Blasch, "Resilient and Trustworthy Dynamic Data-Driven Application Systems (DDDAS) Services for Crisis Management Environments," *Procedia Computer Science*, 51, 2623–2637 (2015)

101. T. Chen, R. Bahsoon, G. Theodoropoulos, Dynamic qos optimization architecture for cloud-based DDDAS, *Procedia Computer Science*, 18, 1881–1890 (2013)

102. R. Wu, B. Liu, Y. Chen, E. Blasch, H. Ling, G. Chen, A Container-based Elastic Cloud Architecture for Pseudo Real-time Exploitation of Wide Area Motion Imagery (WAMI) Stream, *The Journal of Signal Processing Systems*, 1–13 (Nov. 2016). https://doi.org/10.1007/s11265-016-1206-6.

103. S. Shekar, Dynamic Data Driven Cloud Systems for Cloud-Hosted CPS, *IEEE International Conference on Cloud Engineering Workshop (IC2EW),*195–197(2016). https://doi.org/10.1109/IC2EW.2016.38

104. C.-S. Li, F. Darema, V. Chang, Distributed behavior model orchestration in cognitive internet of things solution, *Enterprise Information Systems*, 12, 414–434 (2017). https://doi.org/10.1080/17517575.2017.1355984

105. G. Seetharaman, A. Lakhotia, et al., Unmanned Vehicles Come of Age: The DARPA Grand Challenge, *IEEE Computer Society Magazine*, 39(12): 26–29 (2006)

106. E. Blasch, D. Shen, B. Jia, Z. Wang, G. Chen, Y. Chen, K. Pham, Autonomy in use for space situation awareness, *Proc. SPIE, 11017* (2019)

107. E. Blasch, B. Pokines, Analytical Science for Autonomy Evaluation, *IEEE National Aerospace and Electronics Systems Conference* (2019)

108. T. El-Ghazawi, V. Solker, V, Narayana, et al., Dynamically Adaptive Hybrid Nanoplasmonic Networks on Chips (NoCs), AD1096804, Technical Report (2019)

109. Y. Zheng. E. Blasch, Z. Liu, *Multispectral Image Fusion and Colorization*, SPIE, Bellingham, Washington (2018)

110. T. Mukherjee, P. Kumar, D. Pati, et al., LoSI: Large Scale Location Inference through FM Signal Integration and Estimation, *IEEE Big Data Mining and Analytics*, 2(4): 319–348 (Dec 2019). https://doi.org/10.26599/BDMA.2019.9020013.

111. U. Majumder, E. Blasch, D. Garren, *Deep Learning for Radar and Communications Automatic Target Recognition*, Artech House (2020).

112. R. Xu, Yu Chen, et al., An Exploration of Blockchain-Enabled Decentralized Capability-based Access Control Strategy for Space Situation Awareness, *Optical Engineering*, 58(4), 041609 (2019). https://doi.org/10.1117/1.OE.58.4.014609

113. E. Blasch, J. S. Tiley, D. Sparkman, S. Donegan, M. Cherry, Data fusion methods for materials awareness, *Proc SPIE 11423*, (2020)

114. F. Darema, E. Blasch, DDDAS Solutions for Border Patrol and Emergency Response Environments, *IEEE Future Networks: Enabling 5G and Beyond* (Oct. 2020)

115. E. Blasch, R. Bohn, J. Gato, et al., Future Direction of DDDAS/InfoSymbiotics and Collaborations with Related Initiatives, *Int'l., Conf. on DDDAS,* (2020)

Part I
Measurement-Aware: Data Assimilation, Uncertainty Quantification

Chapter 2
Tractable Non-Gaussian Representations in Dynamic Data Driven Coherent Fluid Mapping

Sai Ravela ⓘ

Abstract This chapter discusses the elements of a Dynamic Data Driven Applications System in the context of mapping coherent environmental fluids using autonomous small unmanned aircraft. The application and and its underlying system dynamics and optimization are presented along with three key ideas. The first is that of a dynamically deformable reduced model, which enables efficacious prediction by solving non-Gaussian problems associated with coherent fluids. The second is the use of ensemble learning in nonlinear estimation, which mitigates model errors in the form of bias, reduces sampling burdens in estimation whilst offering direct state space adjustments for filtering and smoothing and producing compact posterior ensembles. The third idea is the use of tractable variational information theoretic inference in estimation that also requires minimal resampling and allows for gradient-based inferences for non-Gaussian high-dimensional problems with few samples.

Keywords Data assimilation · Information theoretic learning · Ensemble learning · Cooperative Autonomous Observing Systems · Mixture Ensemble filter · Boosted Mixture Ensemble filters · Fast ensemble smoothers · Mixture smoothers · Variational non-Gaussian inference · Minimally sampled estimation · Unmanned aircraft systems · Coherent fluids · Coherent structures · Fluid SLAM · Plume monitoring · Adaptive observation · Quadratic mutual information · Renyi entropy

S. Ravela (✉)
Earth, Atmospheric and Planetary Sciences, Massachusetts Institute of Technology, Cambridge, MA, USA
e-mail: ravela@mit.edu

© The Author(s), under exclusive license to Springer Nature Switzerland AG 2022
E. P. Blasch et al. (eds.), *Handbook of Dynamic Data Driven Applications Systems*,
https://doi.org/10.1007/978-3-030-74568-4_2

35

2.1 Introduction

The existence of feedbacks between simulating and observing processes is a key characteristic of the Dynamic Data Driven Applications Systems (DDDAS) wherein predictions and their uncertainties control the observations/instrumentation and, in reverse, measurements constrain models. The interaction is multifaceted; data can entrain empirical models to augment physics-based counterparts, data may empirically parameterize numerical model inadequacies, or state and parameter estimation may assimilate data. In turn, physical laws and numerical model simulations provide constraints and prior beliefs for adaptive information gathering, active learning and empirical model identification. In the DDDAS paradigm, the symbiosis between simulations and observations extends across model (and sensor) fidelities; such as reduced models derived from higher-fidelity models for efficacious realtime operation and, in reverse, detailed models learned from local simple models to handle dynamical regimes and variable conditions.

This chapter is concerned with the reconstruction of localized atmospheric phenomena such as plumes, jets, vortices, using remote and in-situ sensors on autonomous small Unmanned Aerial/Aircraft Systems (sUAS) to produce detailed one-, two- and three-dimensional maps of the physical, chemical or biological variables. The applications range from the study of benign but poorly understood phenomena such as sea breeze fronts to hazardous ones such as volcanic plumes and cyclones. Our DDDAS investigations produced the first autonomous plume hopper [26] for convective and volcanic regimes, snapshots of this research at the Popocatepetl volcano in Mexico as shown in Fig. 2.1.

Fig. 2.1 MIT Cooperative Autonomous Observing System at the Popocatepetl Volcano in an experiment to gather and produce SO_2 maps using sUAS for in-situ and remote sensing. Shown here is an aircraft in flight, flight path and inversion for concentration, typical sensors, the aircraft and press coverage

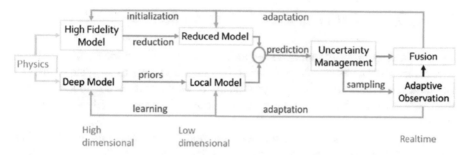

Fig. 2.2 The symbiosis of information transfer between a hierarchy of models reduced from higher fidelity models to afford efficacious realtime prediction with uncertainty quantification and, in reverse, from adaptively sampled data to models learned from larger data contexts using the Dynamic Data Driven Applications Systems framework

2.1.1 Systems Dynamics and Optimization

DDDAS enables new "autonomous field instruments" for investigating poorly understood phenomena in the atmosphere from the boundary layer to the stratosphere. A closer look at these applications reveals a common Systems Dynamics Optimization (SDO) cycle, shown in Fig. 2.2. Detailed high-fidelity models, often run offline, are reduced to predict and quantify uncertainty up to a short time horizon in realtime, targeting supplementary data to assimilate with primary data and, increasingly, by augmenting models with model parameterizations learned from data.

This chapter highlights work that encompasses all elements of the DDDAS' SDO cycle. This includes our Itzamna I9 aircraft series (see Fig. 2.1) that advances the popular SkyWalker X8 that we first introduced for autonomous environmental mapping. It includes instrumentation for imaging plumes using Infrared/Ultraviolet (IR/UV) cameras, SkyCandy, an embedded platform design for running MES-PAC (Model Estimation Sampling Planning and Control) stack. Additionally, new algorithms were also developed for inference [27] reduced modeling [28], assimilation [30], uncertainty quantification for coherent fluids [25] and smooth flows [37], cooperative observation [5], non-linear high-dimensional inference approaches using ensemble learning [32], tractable information theoretic learning [38] and, more recently, manifold learning. These approaches extend easily to other problems including two-point boundary value problems, receding horizon problems, and most recently deep learning. These approaches have enabled broader applications such as in animal biometrics and storm tracking [9, 42].

It is beyond the scope of this chapter to describe these algorithms in detail, however, we focus here on the DDDAS study of volcanic plumes in Fig. 2.1 and then describe two procedures for inference that can influence every element of the DDDAS cycle. The inference approaches are reproduced from [32, 38] for this handbook.

2.1.2 Dynamically Deformable Reduced Models

The DDDAS cycle in this application system (see Fig. 2.3) includes a novel reduced model that assimilates remote and in-situ SO_2 measurements to estimate plumes. A key contribution is to develop fast dynamically deformable reduced models wherein the mean state and bases describing the reduced model are treated as deformable fields.

The pairwise mutual deformation between model snapshots is marginalized in a correspondence-free manner to estimate the reduced model [25, 28]. The mean and bases also deform dynamically in the presence of remote observations. Using the dynamic measurements, the reduced model continually adapts to changing shape and structure of the observed coherent plume field.

A new formulation replaces the classical Karhunen-Loeve (KL) expansion $x_t = \bar{x} + u\Sigma\eta_t$, for a time mean $\bar{x}$ (ensemble mean) and eigenvectors u, eigenvalues Σ and reduced variable η_t (stochastic variable), with a deformable expansion $\hat{x}_t = \bar{x} \circ q + (u \circ q)\Sigma\eta_t$, where the deformation field q is estimated by from model predictions and data [28]. Data assimilation also adjusts the reduced variable η_t online; this is a novel formulation of the position-amplitude assimilation problem [30] for reduced models. In the plume application, remote sensing of tracers is used to estimate the deformation field q. The predictions from the reduced model with uncertainty quantified serves as the basis for planning sampling paths to take supplementary in-situ measurements to further estimate the reduced stochastic variable η_t (or $\Sigma\eta_t$).

In Fig. 2.3, the high fidelity simulation initially produces a poor reduced model (only the mean field is shown) and differs in amplitude and phase from the SO_2 remote observations used. The sUAS plan for in-situ sensing using two independent sampling paths is thus also initially poor. As the bases adapt in deformation space, so do sampling plans because they are transported by the deformation field e.g. through levelsets. These plans in turn enable more accurate in-situ information to be gathered for assimilation into the reduced variable. The benefit of this process

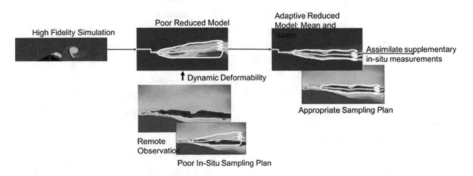

Fig. 2.3 A dynamically deformable approach is used to adapt reduced models and plans from high-fidelity simulations for sampling supplementary in-situ observations and assimilating them. Here remote ultraviolet (UV) observation of SO_2 are used to illustrate deformability [17]

is that it incorporates physics and data. Nevertheless, nonlinear approaches using reduced model ensembles are also feasible using the methods discussed in the next two sections.

2.1.3 Nonlinear High Dimensional Inference

Optimizing the performance of the closed DDDAS cycle and its loop elements in such coherent fluid mapping systems can in general be viewed in terms of probabilistic inference for non-linear, high-dimensional systems with non-Gaussian uncertainties. To see this, consider a dynamical system $x_{t+\Delta t} = f(x_t, u_t; \alpha)$, where $x_t, x_{t+\Delta t} \in \mathcal{R}^n$ is an n-dimensional discrete state vector and $f(\cdot, \cdot)$ is a possibly non-linear model with u_t as inputs. For simplicity, the model is illustrated without "process noise", utilizing instead the epistemic uncertainties of the initial conditions as the primary source of uncertainty. Measurements $y_{t'} \in \mathcal{R}^m$ are assumed to be related by a linear or linearized observation equation $y_{t'} = H\hat{x}_{t'} + v_{t'}$ where $\hat{x}_{t'}$ is the *true* but unknown state vector, H is a measurement process, and $v_{t'} \sim \mathcal{N}(0, R)$ the (additive) Gaussian measurement uncertainty.

Inference problems pertaining to state estimation are commonly solved for distributions $p(x_t|y_{0:t})$, $p(x_0|y_{0:t})$, or $p(x_{0:t}|y_{0:t})$ and parameter estimation using $p(\alpha|y_{0:t})$ [29], but unknown environmental inputs and observing system controls are also of interest. Similarly, the adaptive sampling problem for supplementary observations $p(z_{t:t+k\Delta t}|y_{0:t})$ can be studied as an inference problem, just as model reduction discussed in the previous section. Here, we use sequential Bayesian state estimation as an exemplar to illustrate the central issues.

Sequential Bayesian state estimation includes: (a) *prediction*, which uses a model to propagate the state forward in time; (b) *filtering*, where the current model state is updated recursively using experimental observations up to the current time; and (c) *smoothing*, which uses the current observations to update the model state at previous times. Approaches include classical schemes such as Kalman [14] filters and smoothers, the Ensemble Kalman filter (EnKF) and smoother [11, 29], Particle filter and smoother [2], and variants [6, 8].

However, the tractability of inference such as in high-dimensional numerical model state spaces is challenging, as is the emergence of non-Gaussian uncertainties in nonlinear processes, for example, as multimodal or heavy tailed distributions [23]. To compound matters, grossly inadequate environmental observations complicate inference from data and models. Current practice offers two primary alternatives. On the one hand are rank-reduced, localized or multiscale ensemble Kalman filters and variants. These methods ease linearization issues and produce direct state update equations. Recognizing the operational use of ensemble forecasts and the methods by which they are generated, the *direct adjustment of individual ensemble members*, often incorporating balance constraints and other dynamical sampling procedures is beneficial. Nevertheless, the Gaussian assumption can be problematic, for example, for localized phenomena [28, 30]. On the other hand, non-parametric

Bayesian inference, notably the Particle Filter [2], can be attractive for non-Gaussian estimation but tractability in higher dimensions is challenging.

The DDDAS community recognizes that efficient high-dimensional non-Gaussian estimation is essential in many applications. It would benefit high-dimensional DDDAS applications if non-Gaussian variational inference was possible, thus mitigating the need for extensive resampling whilst retaining the advantage of direct state adjustment. Emerging approaches include kernel [15, 38] and mixture density representations [1, 12, 34–36] in information-theoretic [38] and classical formulations.

In the remaining discussion of this chapter, using Bayesian sequential state estimation as the exemplar of inference problems characteristic in the DDDAS cycle, we describe two techniques that advance the state of the art. One key observation from the approaches presented is that non-Gaussian inference that is characteristic of non-linear problems can be tractably approached in a variational information theoretic manner. A second key conclusion is that in the presence of sparse samples, high dimensions and model error, minimum variance estimation cannot be ignored. These conclusions are obtained by developing two types of sequential solutions; the first using a mixture ensemble (particle mixture) filtering framework with ensemble learning, and the second is a filtering solution using information theoretic learning.

2.2   Ensemble Learning in Mixture Ensembles

The simplicity with which Gaussian Mixture Models (GMM) [20] apply to non-Gaussian estimation makes them attractive for state estimation [1]. We are interested in both the filtering and smoothing problems. For a Markov process, the recursive nature of the estimation process allows us to consider the Bayesian "update" at a single time instance, i.e. $p(x \mid y) \propto p(y \mid x)p(x)$. Non-Gaussian priors are modeled as mixtures of Gaussians as defined by [20]

$$p(x; \theta) = \sum_{m=1}^{M} \alpha_m \ \mathcal{N}(x; \boldsymbol{\mu}_m, \boldsymbol{P}_m). \tag{2.1}$$

Here, the parameter θ includes M, the number of mixture components, $\alpha_m = p(z_m)$ are the mixture weights representing the probability of a mixture element z_m, and $\mathcal{N}(x; \boldsymbol{\mu}_m, \boldsymbol{P}_m)$ are multivariate normal distributions with means $\boldsymbol{\mu}_m$ and covariances $\boldsymbol{P}_m$. The mixture weights are constrained by $\sum_{m=1}^{M} \alpha_m = 1$.

When high-dimensional coherent fluid models are simulated using an ensemble, then any ensemble member x_e has a finite probability of belonging to every other mixture element in a GMM. This fact is modeled through a weight vector,

$$\omega_{em} = \frac{\mathcal{N}(x_e; \boldsymbol{\mu}_m, \boldsymbol{P}_m)\alpha_m}{\sum_{j=1}^{M} \mathcal{N}(x_e; \boldsymbol{\mu}_j, \boldsymbol{P}_j)\alpha_j} \tag{2.2}$$

The GMM parameters are typically estimated using Maximum Likelihood Estimation (MLE)[1] via the Expectation Maximization (EM) [20] together with model selection criteria. To calculate the mixture parameters, we first define $N_m = \sum_{e=1}^{N} \omega_{em}$ for an ensemble of size N, then determine

$$
\alpha_m = \frac{N_m}{N}; \quad \mu_m = \frac{\sum_{e=1}^{N} \omega_{em} x_e}{N_m}; \quad P_m = \frac{\sum_{e=1}^{N} \omega_{em} \left(x_e - \mu_m\right)\left(x_e - \mu_m\right)^T}{N_m}
$$

$$(2.3)$$

In time-dependent GMM-filtering, an ensemble is propagated, mixture parameters are estimated and then a measurement update is applied to solve two inference problems. The first for "state" $p(x|y)$ that assesses the posterior means μ_m^a and covariances P_m^a. Using $\mathcal{K}(P_m^f)$ as a Kalman gain, then:

$$
\mu_m^a = \mu_m^f + \mathcal{K}(P_m^f)\left(y - H\mu_m^f\right); \qquad (P_m^a)^{-1} = \left((P_m^f)^{-1} + H^T R^{-1} H\right)
$$

$$(2.4)$$

The second step is "parameter estimation" $\alpha_m^a = p(z_m|y) \propto \sum_e p(y|x_e)p(x_e|z_m)$ α_m^f which yields the mixture weight update as a *convolution of two Gaussians*:

$$
\alpha_m^a = \frac{\mathcal{N}\left(y; H\mu_m^f, HP_j^f H^T + R\right)\alpha_m^f}{\sum_{j=1}^{M} \mathcal{N}\left(y; H\mu_j^f, HP_j^f H^T + R\right)\alpha_j^f}
$$

$$(2.5)$$

The parametric posterior distribution is sampled to produce a new ensemble and the filtering process repeats.

2.2.1   Mixture Ensemble Filter and Smoother

Seybold et al. show [32] that the GMM filter is inefficient because it requires explicit synthesis of moments and it would be advantageous to perform the updates directly in ensemble space. Several attempts have been made at ensemble formulations. Bengtsson et al. [3] propose clustering and individual Kalman updates based on cluster membership. Smith [34] uses EM with Bayes Information Criterion (BIC) but projects the GMM onto an approximate posterior Gaussian distribution. Dovera and Rossa [7] sample an index according to the posterior mixture weight and update the corresponding ensemble member using EnKF. Frei and Kunsch [12] extend this scheme by using balanced sampling to determine the ensemble member for update. Although dimensionality issues could be reduced by these methods, managing ensemble members' associations with mixture elements is difficult. But, this is also

---

[1] Maximum a posteriori (MAP) problem can also be solved.

unnecessary. The mixture filter can be expressed as a compact ensemble transform that needs no ad hoc association rules, and the posterior ensemble can be resampled using effective sample size measures [2] akin to the particle filter.

For the measurement update, there are two equations [32]. The first is a solution to $p(\mathbf{x}|\mathbf{y})$ using the ensemble mean as a constraint, so that:

$$\mathbf{x}_e^a \equiv \mathbf{x}_e + \sum_{m=1}^{M} \{\mathcal{K}(\mathbf{P}_m)\,(\mathbf{d}_{em} - \mathbf{H}\omega_{em}\mathbf{x}_e)\} \tag{2.6}$$

where, $\mathbf{d}_{em} = \omega_{em}\mathbf{y}$ is without perturbed observations and $\mathbf{d}_{em} = \alpha_m\mathbf{y}_e$ is with perturbed observations. This is different from Tagade's earlier proposal [36].

The second equation is for the posterior weights, obtained by solving for $w_{em}^a = p(z_m|\mathbf{x}_e, \mathbf{y}) \propto p(\mathbf{y}|\mathbf{x}_e)p(\mathbf{x}_e|z_m)p(z_m)$ analogously to Eq. 2.2. Note that this implies a recursive weight update; $w_{em}^a \propto p(\mathbf{y}|\mathbf{x}_e)w_{em}^f$. This is in essence a Gaussian mixture particle filter. It can also be evaluated without explicitly constituting covariances. The posterior ensemble and weights can be evaluated for effective sample size [2] and resampled to avoid sample degeneracy.

Even more interestingly, the ensemble update is a compact transform [32]:

$$A^a = A^f \sum_{m=1}^{M} \Xi_m \circ (W_m^N)^T = A^f \Xi \tag{2.7}$$

A^f is the forecast ensemble, A^a is the estimated ensemble and $W_m^N(1 : N, e) = w_{em}$. The compact matrix Ξ in ensemble size $N \times N$ in the sense of Evensen [11] is a weakly nonlinear transformation of the prediction. This is the compact *Mixture Ensemble Filter (MEnF)* that was not shown hitherto Seybold et al. [32] As a compact ensemble transform, MEnF immediately enables the derivation of a fast mixture ensemble smoother (MEnS) akin to EnKS [11]. Ravela and McLaughlin [29] showed, the smoothing equation is a recursion so that fixed interval estimation is of order $O(L)$ for interval L via a forward-backward pass, and fixed-lag estimation is of order $O(1)$ via a first-in-first out queue. The MEnF/S shares the advantages of a particle filter but enables direct ensemble adjustment without running into dimensionality issues. This was a breakthrough in tractable inference by Seybold et al. [32] and improved upon Tagade et al. solution [36].

2.3 Nonlinear Filtering Must Reduce Total Variance

Seybold et al. [32] also show that GMM-based filtering either explicitly or in ensemble space becomes problematic in the presence of model error. Mixture modes are statistically estimated and the total variance includes the variance of the means which becomes significant as the number of mixture members increases. Current GMM-based filters have no representation for this component. So, when

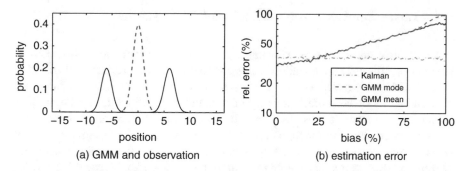

Fig. 2.4 Bi-modal example depicts worsening GMM estimation error with bias because it does not account for the variance of the means; for details see [32]

model error manifests as a bias relative to the GMM modes, convergence can be extremely slow. A simple experiment shows that beyond a very small bias, GMM performance is worse than the ensemble Kalman filter. In such a case, minimizing overall variance cannot be ignored, especially if estimating estimation uncertainty is also important. In general, non-Gaussian estimation cannot lose sight of minimizing variance, particularly when the confidence in real-world models is low.

Seybold et al. [32] considered a bimodal prior with mean at zero. The modes are positioned at $\mu_m = \pm 6\sigma$ with a variance of $\sigma_m^2 = 1$ each of weight $\alpha_m = 0.5$, as shown in Fig. 2.4a. Imagine now a measurement in between, dotted line. When the measurement lies in between the two mixture modes, the system defines the bias as 100% [32]. Consider the truth to be stationary and a measurement with noise variance $\sigma_r^2 = 1$. For comparison, a Kalman filter is compared with a prior variance equal to the total variance of the GMM. Because truth is stationary, we expect some convergence in the estimated mean and covariance for each filter. The estimation error is tracked over five filtering iterations per trial repeatedly over a large number of trials. The GMM on average performs far worse than the EnKF. Figure 2.4b shows the average normalized RMS estimation error comparing the Kalman estimate's posterior mean, the GMM's dominant mode, and its mean, respectively, with truth. As shown by Seybold et al. [32], the convergence is also much slower.

The slow convergence is because the total variance in GMM, which includes the variance of the means, is not accounted. As a result, the filter converges slower under bias and with a larger estimation error. The EnKF has a larger initial Kalman gain and rapidly reduces overall variance. Clearly, as the modes fragment, GMM filter will lose track of the total variance. This is particularly the case when model errors are present, which is almost always in the real world. The question remains, how can non-Gaussian Bayesian estimation also minimize total variance?

2.4   Ensemble Learning with a Stacked Cascade

A hierarchical approach can accomplish global variance reduction where GMMs targeted at different regularization scales are combined. In a variation of this idea, an ensemble propagated to the filtering step is assumed to have an imprecise distribution, modeled through a group of probability functions to handle multiple objectives such as in this case for jointly tracking the local mode and reducing total variance. Each objective function produces a *weak* estimator. For example, EnKF is weak for non-Gaussianity while GMM cannot account for the variance of means. The ensemble of estimators is used to learn in the framework of *Ensemble Learning* to produce a better estimator than anyone alone.

A machine learning view of Bayesian estimators is as (nonlinear) regression machines. Multiple regression machines form an ensemble of regression machines and, here, we consider two ensemble transforms; $\mathcal{M}_g$, the GMM, and $\mathcal{M}_e$, the EnKF. In principle, a variety of methods are feasible. Seybold et al. [32] used stacking [41] or stacked generalization, and cascaded generalization [13]. The resulting estimator is called the *Boosted Mixture Ensemble Filter (B-MEnF)*, combines the two using the "stacked cascade" and outperforms either one.

Figure 2.5 depicts an iterative process for combining the two machines. At each iteration, Stacking [41] combines the outputs. A Cascade Generalization [13] then follows and continues to the next iteration. During stacking, the "meta-learner" selects the outputs of the regression machine with the lower error to perturbed measurements (the truth is unknown) [10]; a higher posterior probability criterion is also applicable. Ideally, cascading continues till the model complexity of estimated posterior ensemble GMMs no longer improves.

Stacking arguably reduces bias and cascading reduces variance. Using bootstrap sampling of the ensemble with perturbed measurements prevents overfitting, which is a conventional approach in many randomized learning problems.

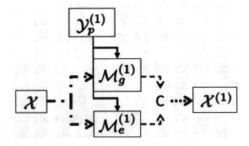

Fig. 2.5 The Stacked-Cascade shown for a single iteration. Stacked generalization of $\mathcal{M}_e$ and $\mathcal{M}_g$ picks the ensemble member with lower posterior error. A cascade of stacked machines uses perturbed observations for training and testing, and a bootstrap ensemble for training

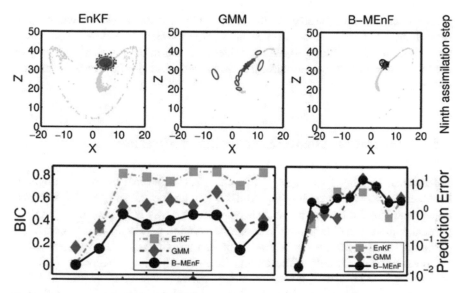

Fig. 2.6 An example of B-MEnF applied to the Lorenz-63 problem [32]. The results show superior performance over GMM due to boosting, producing approximately the same error but at a lower uncertainty

2.4.1 Application Example

We describe an identical twin experiment on a Lorenz-63 system [19] reproduced from [32]. This system exhibits two characteristic attractors at very long timescales. Even at the integration time scale used here, the distribution of ensemble members is nongaussian [32].

Figure 2.6 presents the filter results in a 2D X-Z projection for EnKF (left column), GMM (middle column) at the first assimilation (top) step and after nine assimilation cycles (bottom). The right column shows the result of B-MEnF. The predicted point cloud is in light gray and dark points depict the posterior point cloud. Solid lines indicate probability contours. A red star marks truth.

A Gaussian model works well initially but, as the attractor structure becomes nongaussian EnKF ensemble members disperse farther, suggesting that the GMM better constrains the uncertainty over time. A convex combination of the two smallest eigenvalues of the forecast error covariance regularizes EM to produce reasonable GMM clusters, but there is sensitivity to the regularization parameter. As the posterior ensemble point cluster depicts, filtering with Gaussian measurement noise leaves (see Eq. 2.3) one dominant posterior mode and the remaining are degenerate.

Although all three estimators are comparable in error, however, without any resampling whatsoever, B-MEnF produces posterior GMMs of lower complexity than EnKF or GMM alone. B-MEnF tightens the ensemble better by drawing on the local mode and overall variance. It allows non-Gaussian inference with minimal re-sampling.

2.5 Information Theoretic Learning in Filtering

We continue seeking approaches to non-Gaussian variational inference mitigating the need for extensive resampling whilst retaining the advantage of direct state adjustment that the EnKF and variants provide. One way is by considering a more general summary measure than variance or correlation. For example, kurtosis is commonly used in Independent Component Analysis (ICA) to identify linear modes for non-Gaussian variables. The mutual information, using Shannon's definition of entropy, is also a well known summary measure that is characterized by its "distribution free" property. For non-Gaussian random variables it generalizes as divergence from independence.

Thus, one might devise a mutual information measure using the joint and marginal probabilities of measurements and states to synthesize filters and smoothers. For example, Tomita et al. [39] have used a measure of mutual information based on the Shannon entropy [33] to derive a linear and a non-linear filter. Unfortunately, because it is difficult to calculate gradient terms directly from the usual definition of mutual information, one must resort to sampling methods making this approach intractable for many high dimensional applications.

Kapur [16] provides an inspiring generalization of entropy that unifies several alternatives. He derives a cross-entropy quadratic measure alternative to Kullback-Leibler divergence directly corresponding to the Bhattacharya measure. When applied to calculating mutual information, one thus arrives at a quadratic measure of mutual information, from which gradients can be calculated relatively easily thus admitting an optimization framework for non-Gaussian inference. This was noted early as an exciting development for Data Assimilation [24] and has been used in feature extraction with other emerging applications in machine learning [18, 22, 40].

Tagade and Ravela [38] use Kapur's quadratic mutual information on the Lorenz-95 problem. The quadratic mutual information is interpreted in terms of an *information potential* expressed by ensembles of model state or experimental observations in a kernel density representation [21], following Torkkola [22, 40], but can be approached using reproducing kernel Hilbert space (RKHS) also (which we have not done here). The filtering problem is posed as maximization of the approximated information potentials. The gradients of the information potentials are obtained analytically to derive a filter. The proposed approach allows, similar to MEnF/B-MEnF, for direct state adjustment for non-Gaussian inference. This is discussed here with a double well example [35].

2.5.1 Tractable Information Theoretic Approach

Consider the *filtering* problem and let x, y and $\hat{x}$ denote the model state, experimental observations and the estimate at the current time T respectively. Dropping the time subscript, define an arbitrary (possibly non-linear) filter as:

$$\hat{x} = F(x, y). \tag{2.8}$$

Our objective is to determine the mapping $F(x, y)$ by maximizing *Conditional Mutual Information* $\hat{F}(x, y) = F(x, y)\mathcal{J}(y; \hat{x}|x)$. We call this a "Mutual Information Filter" (MuIF).

To derive a tractable approach, we note that entropy is often used as a measure of uncertainty [33], with the mutual information quantified using the Kullback-Leibler measure for the cross entropy [4]. Though the Shannon entropy is the most widely used measure of entropy, it is possible to use a wide array of different definitions of entropy as pointed out by Kapur [16]. Renyi entropy [31] is obtained by relaxing Shannon's third axiom. For a random variable X, Renyi entropy of order α is defined as:

$$\mathcal{R}_\alpha(X) = \frac{1}{1 - \alpha} \log \int (f_X(\mathbf{x}))^\alpha \, d\mathbf{x} = \mathcal{V}_\alpha(X), \tag{2.9}$$

where $\alpha > 0$ and $\alpha \neq 1$. In particular, Renyi entropy of order 2 and the associated *Quadratic Mutual Information* is attractive. When $\alpha = 2$, $\mathcal{R}_2(X)$ is a quadratic Renyi entropy, given by:

$$\mathcal{R}_2(X) = -\log(\mathcal{V}_2(\mathbf{x})), \tag{2.10}$$

where $\mathcal{V}_2(\mathbf{x})$ is *quadratic information potential*, which represents expected value of the Probability Distribution Function (PDF) of $\mathbf{x}$. Since the logarithm is a monotonic function, entropy optimization can be achieved by optimizing $\mathcal{V}_2(\mathbf{x})$. Further, as $\mathcal{R}_2(X)$ is a lower bound of the Shannon Entropy [22], quadratic Renyi entropy is expected to be more efficient than the Shannon entropy for entropy maximization.

Following the definition of Renyi entropy, different measures of divergence and associated mutual information are proposed in the literature [16]. In particular, the Euclidean distance between the PDFs, given by

$$D_e(f_X, g_X) = \int (f_X(\mathbf{x}) - g_X(\mathbf{x}))^2 \, d\mathbf{x}. \tag{2.11}$$

Kapur's *quadratic mutual information* is given by

$$\mathcal{J}(X; Y) = D_e(f_{XY}(\mathbf{x}, \mathbf{y}), f_X(\mathbf{x}) f_Y(\mathbf{y}))$$
$$= \mathcal{V}_J - 2\mathcal{V}_C + \mathcal{V}_M, \tag{2.12}$$

where, $\mathcal{V}_J$ and $\mathcal{V}_M$ are the quadratic information potential of the joint and the marginal PDFs, while $\mathcal{V}_C$ is the cross information potential [22].

Using a Parzen window estimation with the Gaussian kernel [21, 22, 24, 40], $G(\mathbf{x}, \Sigma)$ with $\Sigma = \sigma^2 I$ typically, we may approximate any PDF to an arbitrary accuracy [21]; inference is non-Gaussian. Using the convolution property of Gaussian kernels and the Parzen window estimates of the PDFs, estimates of the information potentials $\hat{\mathcal{V}}_J$, and $\hat{\mathcal{V}}_C$, and $\hat{\mathcal{V}}_M$ and their gradients may be readily evaluated [38]. This is further sped up using hashing and indexing techniques to retrieve close neighbors to evaluate these terms.

Tagade and Ravela [38] define an ensemble matrix of model predictions $\mathbf{A} = [\mathbf{x}_i; i = 1, \ldots, N_s] \in \mathcal{R}^{n \times N_s}$, another for perturbed observations $\mathcal{Z} = [\mathbf{z}_i; i = 1, \ldots, N_s] \in \mathcal{R}^{m \times N_s}$, with perturbed observation defined as $\mathbf{z}_i = \mathbf{y} + \mathbf{v}_i$, where $\mathbf{v}_i$ denotes a sample from the PDF of the measurement error. Using the filter (2.8), an ensemble matrix of the estimated states, $\hat{\mathbf{x}} \in \mathcal{R}^n$, can similarly be defined as: $\mathcal{F} = [F(\mathbf{x}_i, \mathbf{z}_i); i = 1, \ldots, N_s] \in \mathcal{R}^{n \times N_s}$. The ensemble matrix $\mathcal{F}$ can be populated to reinitialize the system dynamics. Tagade and Ravela [38] propose a *steepest-gradient-ascent*, letting the solution at the current iteration be denoted by $F(\mathbf{x}, \mathbf{z})_k$. Then,

$$F(\mathbf{x}, \mathbf{z})_{k+1} = F(\mathbf{x}, \mathbf{z})_k + \eta \nabla \mathcal{J}(\mathbf{z}; \hat{\mathbf{x}}|\mathbf{x}), \qquad (2.13)$$

where ∇ denotes the gradient, while η is a user defined step size. This evaluation produces gradients of information potentials or information forces and can be directly calculated. When F is suitably parameterized, for example $\hat{\mathbf{x}} = \mathbf{x} + \mathcal{K}(\mathbf{z} - \mathbf{x})$, then gradients with respect to the parameter can be estimated and updated instead by evaluating $\mathcal{J}(\mathbf{z}; \mathcal{K}|\mathbf{x})$. In this linear example, $\mathcal{K}$ is akin to a Kalman gain, which they call the information gain.

The application of MuIF to the filtering problem on Lorenz-95 by Tagade and Ravela [38] is shown in Fig. 2.7. A comparison on the double well system [35] is

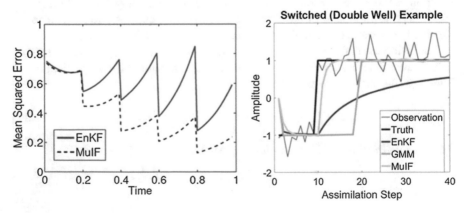

Fig. 2.7 A comparison of EnKF and MuIF on a Lorenz-95 problem [38] and a double well problem [35]

also shown. Its performance is comparable to mixtures, and can track the switching well. We note that although the evaluation of mutual information can be expensive considering all pairs of interactions between the model and observation samples, the use of hashing techniques and indexing techniques have shown considerable scalability. Such approximate inference is, we posit, promising for coherent fluid mapping, especially when the ensemble sizes are relatively small. Further, Parzen windowing is problematic in high dimensions, approaches based on RKHS can be developed.

2.6 Application Example

The estimation methodology previously developed is applied to a key aspect of the coherent fluid mapping problem, extending Sect. 2.1. The example illustrated is of dynamically adapting sampling paths using tracer hot spots. This is posed as a Bayesian estimation problem and illustrated using the B-MEnF approach.

The approach uses a DDDAS model hierarchy; the high fidelity model simulation is reduced using the approach in Sect. 2.1, reduced model ensemble realizations produce an ensemble of wind-efficient sampling plans. These plans are adapted using extrapolated remote tracer (e.g., SO_2) measurements to sample tracer hot-spots, which is important in hazardous plumes. Features are detected and extrapolated from the current remotely sensed image, and assembled into a sampling time window using a previously described [25, 26] approach. The targeted features and prior ensemble of plans are fused, producing a posterior distribution of sampling paths for an sUAS to execute that is both energy efficient and targets the tracer features. This framework allows for further adaption during flight.

In Fig. 2.8, an initial ensemble of plans produced by only considering winds depicts a downwind trajectories from the plume start to the right. The low, neutral and high shear model regimes produce a non-Gaussian distribution, shown in trajectories and shading. A mixture is an appropriate model in this case. The measurements are specified as time extrapolated hotspots [25, 26]. Initial plans are based on winds, but rather than replan, the model-driven sample plans are dynamically adapted to incorporate tracer sampling preferences. The posterior flight plan distribution is compact and convergence is rapid using B-MEnF. Similar results are obtained with the mutual information filter.

2.7 Conclusions

We discussed the overall structure of DDDAS applications for mapping coherent fluids and its loop elements. We described one application instance and focused on a novel deformable reduced model that adapts with and is robust to non-Gaussian errors. We then focused on nonlinear and non-Gaussian inference using

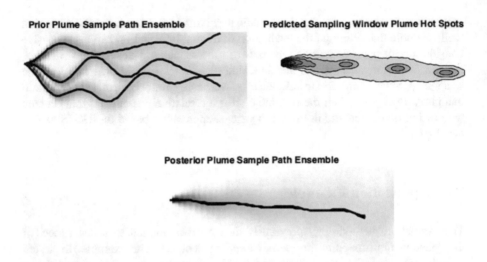

Fig. 2.8 A prior ensemble of sample plans using only winds (top) is adapted with tracer measurements to include hotspots (middle) to produce a posterior set of sampling plans (bottom). The shading indicates sampling uncertainty

two approaches; a Boosted Mixture Ensemble filter (B-MEnF) and a Mutual Information Filter (MuIF). We further discussed their application adapting sampling plans.

Whilst mixture approaches seem promising for non-Gaussian estimation, they actually perform worse than EnKF in the presence of bias. The absence of a total variance objective is the culprit. The compact MEnF reduces dimensionality issues, mitigates sampling problems and directly enables smoothing. B-MenF, a stacked-cascade ensemble learner, reduces uncertainty better than either GMM or EnKF alone and, in experiments here, it needed no resampling. We posit that Ensemble Learning (analogous to multi-model ensembles) can be an efficient way to deal with model error and bias in high-dimensional non-Gaussian systems.

Kapur's quadratic mutual information is approximated using an ensemble-based kernel-density estimate of model state and experimental observations. The approximated quadratic mutual information is integrated with the steepest-gradient-ascent algorithm to maximize the mutual information. The proposed algorithm is depicted for Lorenz-95 model and the double well, outperforming EnKF and with similar performance as a mixture approach.

Acknowledgements This work was in part supported by AFOSR(FA9550-12-1-0313) and NSF DBI-1146747, the MISTI seed fund, a Seaver award and an ESI seed grant. Any opinions, findings, and conclusions or recommendations expressed in this material are those of the author(s) and do not necessarily reflect the views of NSF or AFOSR or MISTI. Special thanks to K. Emanuel, J. How, H.-L. Choi, J. Salas, P. Tagade, C. Denamiel, H. Seybold, R. Westlund, O. Gonzalez, B. Rosas and many undergraduate students and collaborators of ESSG.

References

1. D.L. Alspach, H.W. Sorenson, Nonlinear bayesian estimation using gaussian sum approxima-tions. IEEE Trans. Autom. Control **17**, 439–448 (1972)
2. M.S. Arulampalam, S. Maskell, N. Gordon, T. Clapp, A tutorial on particle filters for online nonlinear/non-gaussian bayesian tracking. IEEE Trans. Signal Proc. **50**(2), 174–188 (2002)
3. T. Bengtsson, C. Snyder, D. Nychka, Toward a nonlinear ensemble filter for high-dimensional systems. J. Geophys. Res. **108**, 8775 (2003)
4. H.L. Choi, Adaptive sampling and forecasting with mobile sensor networks. Ph.D. thesis, Massachusetts Institute of Technology, 2009
5. H.-L. Choi, S.-J. Lee, A potential game approach for information-maximizing cooperative planning of sensor networks. IEEE Trans. Control Syst. Technol. **23**(6), 2326–2335 (2015)
6. S.C. Choi, R. Wette, Maximum likelihood estimation of the parameters of the Gamma distribution and their bias. Technometrics **11**, 683–690 (1969)
7. L. Dovera, E.D. Rossa, Multimodal ensemble Kalman filtering using gaussian mixture models. Comput. Geosci. **15**, 307–323 (2011)
8. J. Dunik, O. Straka, M. Simandl, E. Blasch, Sigma-point set rotation for derivative-free filters in target tracking applications. J. Adv. Inf. Fusion **11**(1), 91–109 (2016)
9. J. Duyck, C. Finn, A. Hutcheon, P. Vera, J. Salas, S. Ravela, Sloop: a pattern retrieval engine for individual animal identification. Pattern Recognit. **48**(4), 1059–1073 (2015)
10. S. Dzeroski, B. Zenko, Is combining classifiers better than selecting the best one? in *Proceedings of the Nineteenth International Conference on Machine Learning (ICML '02)* (Morgan Kaufmann, San Francisco, 2004) pp. 255–273
11. G. Evensen, The ensemble Kalman filter: theoretical formulation and practical implementation. Ocean Dyn. **53**, 343–367 (2003)
12. M. Frei, H.R. Kunsch, Mixture ensemble Kalman filters. Comput. Stat. Data Anal. **58**, 127–138 (2013)
13. J. Gama, P. Brazdil, Cascade generalization. Mach. Learn. **41**(3), 315–343 (2000)
14. A. Gelb, *Applied Optimal Estimation* (The MIT Press, Cambridge, 1974)
15. I. Hoteit, D.T. Pham, G. Triantafyllou, G. Korres, A new approximate solution of the optimal nonlinear filter for data assimilation in meteorology and oceanography. Mon. Weather Rev. **136**, 317–334 (2008)
16. J.N. Kapur, *Measures of Information and Their Applications* (Wiley, New Delhi, 1994)
17. C. Kern, C. Werner, T. Elias, A.J. Sutton, P. Lubcke, Applying UV cameras for SO2 detection to distant or optically thick volcanic plumes. J. Volcanol. Geotherm. Res. **262**, 80–89 (2013)
18. R. Liu, D.F. Gillies, An estimate of mutual information that permits closed-form optimization. Entropy **15**, 1690–1704 (2013)
19. E.N. Lorenz, Deterministic nonperiodic flow. J. Atmos. Sci. **20**, 130–141 (1963)
20. G.J. McLachlan, T. Krishnan, *The EM Algorithm and Extensions* (Wiley-Interscience, Hoboken, 2008)
21. E. Parzen, On the estimation of probability density function and the mode. Ann. Math. Stat. **33**, 1065 (1962)
22. J.W. Principe, J.W. Fisher, D. Xu, *Information Theoretic Learning* (Wiley, New York, 2000)
23. J. Prüher, F. Tronarp, T. Karvonen, S. Särkkä, O. Straka, Student-t process quadratures for filtering of non-linear systems with heavy-tailed noise, in *International Conference on Information Fusion*, Piscataway, 2017
24. S. Ravela, Data assimilation by maximizing mutual information. Geophys. Res. Abstr. **10**, EGU2008–A–11090 (2008)
25. S. Ravela, Quantifying uncertainty for coherent structures. Proc. Comput. Sci. **9**, 1187–1196 (2012)
26. S. Ravela, Mapping coherent atmospheric structures with small unmanned aircraft systems, in *AIAA InfotechAerospace (IA) Conference, Guidance, Navigation, and Control and Co-located Conferences, (AIAA 2013-4667)*, 2013

27. S. Ravela, Spatial inference for coherent geophysical fluids by appearance and geometry, in *Winter Conference on Applications of Computer Vision*, 2014
28. S. Ravela, Dynamic data-driven deformable reduced models for coherent fluids. Proc. Comput. Sci. **51**, 2464–2473 (2015)
29. S. Ravela, D. McLaughlin, Fast ensemble smoothing. Ocean Dyn. **57**, 123–134 (2007)
30. S. Ravela, K. Emanuel, M. McLaughlin, Data assimilation by field alignment. Physica D **230**, 127–145 (2007)
31. A Renyi, On measure of entropy and information, in *Fourth Symposium on Mathematical Statistics and Probability*, Berkeley, 1961
32. H. Seybold, S. Ravela, P. Tagade, Ensemble learning in non-gaussian data assimilation. Lect. Notes Comput. Sci. **8964**, 227–238 (2015)
33. C.E. Shannon, A mathematical theory of communication. Bell Syst. Tech. J. **27**, 379–423 (1948)
34. K.W. Smith, Cluster ensemble Kalman filter. Tellus **59**, 749–757 (2007)
35. T. Sondergaard, P.F.J. Lermusiaux, Data assimilation with gaussian mixture models using dynamically orthogonal field equations. Part 1: theory and scheme. Mon. Weather Rev. **141**, 1737–1760 (2013)
36. P. Tagade, H. Seybold, S. Ravela, Mixture ensembles for data assimilation in dynamic data-driven environmental systems, in *Proceedings of the International Conference on Computational Science, ICCS 2014*, Cairns, 10–12 June 2014, pp. 1266–1276
37. P.M. Tagade, H.-L. Choi, A dynamic bi-orthogonality based approach for uncertainty quantification of stochastic systems with discontinuities. ASME J. Verification, Validation Uncertain. Quantif. **2**(1), 011003–011012 (2017)
38. P.M. Tagade, S. Ravela, A quadratic information measure for data assimilation, in *American Control Conference*, Portland, 2014
39. Y. Tomita, S. Omatu, T. Soeda, An application of the information theory to filtering problems. Inf. Sci. **11**, 13–27 (1976)
40. K. Torkkola, Feature extraction by non-parametric mutual information maximization. J. Mach. Learn. Res. **3**, 1415–1438 (2003)
41. D.H. Wolpert, Stacked generalization. Neural Netw. **5**, 241–259 (1992)
42. C.M. Yang, S. Ravela, Deformation invariant image matching by spectrally controlled diffeomorphic alignment, in *2009 IEEE 12th International Conference on Computer Vision*, Piscataway, 2009, pp. 1303–1310

Chapter 3
Dynamic Data-Driven Adaptive Observations in Data Assimilation for Multi-scale Systems

Hoong C. Yeong, Ryne Beeson, N. Sri Namachchivaya, Nicolas Perkowski, and Peter W. Sauer

Abstract This chapter considers several research topics that encompass the area of *Dynamic Data Driven Applications Systems* (DDDAS), and describes the multidisciplinary methods required for the analysis and prediction of complex systems. It focuses on developing new algorithms and tools for the collection, assimilation and harnessing of data by threading together ideas from random dynamical systems to information theory. A general overview of the multi-scale signal and observation processes, the multidisciplinary methods required for their analysis, and a new particle filtering algorithm that combines homogenization with filtering theory are presented. Importance sampling and control methods are then used as a basic and flexible tool for the construction of the proposal density inherent in particle filtering for approximating the real time filtering of chaotic signals. Finally the chapter describes an *information theoretic* method, which follows naturally from the expected uncertainty minimization criterion, for dynamic sensor selection in filtering problems. It is compared with a strategy based on finite-time Lyapunov exponents of the dynamical system, which provide insight into error growth due to signal dynamics.

H. C. Yeong (✉) · R. Beeson · N. S. Namachchivaya
Department of Aerospace Engineering, University of Illinois at Urbana-Champaign, Urbana, IL, USA
e-mail: hyeong2@illinois.edu; rbeeson2@illinois.edu; navam@illinois.edu

N. Perkowski
Institut für Mathematik, Humboldt-Universität zu Berlin, Berlin, Germany
e-mail: perkowsk@math.hu-berlin.de

P. W. Sauer
Department of Electrical and Computer Engineering, University of Illinois at Urbana-Champaign, Urbana, IL, USA
e-mail: psauer@illinois.edu

Keywords Nonlinear filtering · Homogenization · Dimensional reduction · Stochastic partial differential equation (SPDE) · Particle filtering · Information flow · Sensor selection · Kullback-Leibler · Lyapunov exponents · Singular vectors · Homogenized Hybrid Particle Filter (HHPF)

3.1 Introduction

The focus of this chapter is based on the DDDAS paradigm that includes the confluence of three areas, namely random dynamical systems, control and estimation (data assimilation), and information theory. Mathematical models are valuable tools for understanding complex systems. However, these models are considerably uncertain. The uncertainty can be attributed to: the inability of models to capture important physical processes; inadequate use of observations to constrain and initialize the models; and uncertainties in determining model updates. An emerging challenge for inference and prediction of large-scale complex systems is to efficiently *analyze and assimilate* the ever-increasing high dimensional data produced by the vast number of engineered and natural systems. On the stochastic side, the crucial field of modeling sub-grid scale phenomena has been increasingly moving towards stochastic "parameterizations" [7]. The enormous complexity of the problems continues to pose challenges for predicting interactions among the physical and environmental systems. These unique challenges due to the interactions among uncertainties, nonlinearities, and observations will be detailed in this chapter.

This chapter integrates ideas from *random dynamical systems*, *homogenization methods*, *nonlinear filtering* and *Markov Chain Monte Carlo* methods to develop a general collection of new mathematical techniques that dynamically assimilate new data from observations for prediction. As we shall show, the concept of integrating random dynamical systems, homogenization methods and nonlinear filtering always sounds clear enough at a distance, but the closer one gets to the proofs, the vaguer the subtleties of these interactions become. Key tools to explore these issues in a canonical way are explained in [2, 4, 14, 16, 31]. Novel results, contributions and their significance in *three* important areas of research within DDDAS are presented below.

The content of this chapter is organized as follows. A general overview of the multi-scale signal and observation processes, the multidisciplinary methods required for their analysis, and relevant new results achieved in data assimilation for coarse grained dynamics, are given in Sects. 3.2 and 3.3. The reduction technique, examined in Sect. 3.2, entails an averaging result for the fast motion associated with perturbed dynamics. The section overviews the well known results associated with the martingle problem. Section 3.3 addresses the effects of the multiscale signal and observation processes via the study of the Zakai equation. Section 3.3 describes a lower dimensional stochastic partial differential equation (PDE) (Zakai type equation) that was constructed in a canonical way to addresses the effects of the multiscale signal and observation processes and provide an example of implementation on a toy problem. Finally Sect. 3.4 utilizes the Kullback-Leibler divergence as a measure of information flow in adaptive sensing. The strategy is suitable for quantifying the information by a future measurement with the goal of reducing analysis uncertainty of the coarse grained signal. A methodology using singular vectors of the linear tangent map is also employed as a tool for improving analysis for model update.

3.2   Dimensional Reduction and Homogenization

A general overview of the multiscale signal and observation processes and relevant results achieved in DDDAS, the multidisciplinary methods required for their analysis, and relevant new results achieved in data assimilation for the coarse grained dynamics are presented in this section. The analytical core of this part of the work is *dimensional reduction*. In large complex systems, non-linearities of the governing physical processes allow energy transfer between different scales, and many aspects of this complex behavior can be represented by stochastic models. In such problems with scale separation, one of the most studied models of random perturbations is represented by a diffusive Markov process $\{(X_t^\varepsilon, Z_t^\varepsilon); t \geq 0\}$ whose semigroup of transition operators T^ε is generated by $\mathscr{L}^\varepsilon$, a second order elliptic (partial) differential operator as explained in [14]. X^ε and Z^ε are the slow and fast components of the system, respectively, and $\varepsilon > 0$ is the timescales separation parameter – the ratio of the timescale of the fast dynamics to that of the slow. Small ε indicates wide timescales separation between the slow and fast components. On the slow timescale, high dimensional multi-scale stochastic systems often behave like a smaller, reduced-order model (ROM); however, the reduced-order model is not known a priori. In these problems, extracting coarse-grained dynamics is at heart a problem of weak convergence of stochastic processes, or more exactly weak convergence of the laws of Markov processes. One of the preeminent modern frameworks for considering convergence of the laws of Markov processes is that of the *martingale problem* [12, 41], which was used in [31, 32] to develop the reduced models. These stochastically averaged, lower-dimensional models are strictly valid only in the limit of infinitesimally small noise. Nonetheless, they provide qualitatively useful results and are helpful in developing inexpensive lower-dimensional computational models as shown in [34].

The starting point for the work presented here is the stochastic version of a $(m + n)$-dimensional multi-scale dynamical system:

$$dX_t^\varepsilon = b(X_t^\varepsilon, Z_t^\varepsilon)dt + \sigma(X_t^\varepsilon, Z_t^\varepsilon)dW_t, \tag{3.1a}$$

$$dZ_t^\varepsilon = \frac{1}{\varepsilon} f(X_t^\varepsilon, Z_t^\varepsilon)dt + \frac{1}{\sqrt{\varepsilon}} g(X_t^\varepsilon, Z_t^\varepsilon)dV_t, \tag{3.1b}$$

where $X^\varepsilon \in \mathbb{R}^m$ and $Z_t^\varepsilon \in \mathbb{R}^n$ are the slow and fast components, respectively, and $W_t \in \mathbb{R}^k$ and $V_t \in \mathbb{R}^l$ are independent k- and l-dimensional standard Brownian motions, respectively. The vector field and diffusion coefficients are $b : \mathbb{R}^{m+n} \to \mathbb{R}^m, \sigma : \mathbb{R}^{m+n} \to \mathbb{R}^{m \times k}, f : \mathbb{R}^{m+n} \to \mathbb{R}^n, g : \mathbb{R}^{m+n} \to \mathbb{R}^{n \times l}$. All the functions above are assumed to be Borel-measurable. For fixed $x \in \mathbb{R}^m$ at the fast timescale, define

$$dZ_t^x = f(x, Z_t^x)dt + g(x, Z_t^x)dV_t.$$

In other words, Z^x is a version of Z^ε, the solution of (3.1b), with $X^\varepsilon = x$ fixed. Assume that for all $x \in \mathbb{R}^m$, Z^x is ergodic and converges rapidly to its unique stationary distribution $p_\infty(x; \cdot)$.

The primary result of stochastic dimensional reduction is a self-contained description of the coarse-grained dynamics without fully resolving the dynamics described in the fast scale. It has been shown [36] that, as scaling parameter ε tends to zero, the limiting process of X^ε is a Markov process $\overline{X}$ with the generator $\mathscr{L}$:

$$\mathscr{L} = \sum_{i=1}^m \overline{b}_i(x)\frac{\partial}{\partial x_i} + \frac{1}{2}\sum_{i,j=1}^m \overline{a}_{ij}(x)\frac{\partial^2}{\partial x_i \partial x_j}, \tag{3.2}$$

where

$$\overline{b}(x) = \int_{\mathbb{R}^n} b(x, z)p_\infty(x; dz), \quad \overline{a}(x) = \int_{\mathbb{R}^n} (\sigma\sigma^T)(x, z)p_\infty(x; dz)$$

are the homogenized drift and diffusion coefficients of the slow components. In general, the limiting description of the coarse-grained dynamics will take values in a reduced space (which in the setting of (3.1) is $\mathbb{R}^m \subset \mathbb{R}^{m \times n}$). The geometry of the reduced space can be found from the coarse-grained dynamics as shown in a series of papers [32, 34] on stochastic dimensional reduction. In other words, when ε is small, $\overline{X}$ behaves stochastically like X^ε with the effects of the fast component Z^ε averaged out. The results of [23] and chapter 5 of [6] provides dimensional reduction in slow-fast systems driven by real and white noise, respectively, using a geometric singular perturbation approach.

Consider the following simple signal model [37, 42] to illustrate the effect of homogenization:

$$\dot{X}_t^\varepsilon = -(Z_t^\varepsilon)^3 + \sin(\pi t) + \cos(\sqrt{2}\pi t), \qquad X_0^\varepsilon = x_0 \in \mathbb{R}, \tag{3.3a}$$

$$dZ_t^\varepsilon = -\frac{1}{\varepsilon}(Z_t^\varepsilon - X_t^\varepsilon)dt + \frac{1}{\sqrt{\varepsilon}}dV_t, \qquad Z_0^\varepsilon = z_0 \in \mathbb{R}. \tag{3.3b}$$

For a fixed $X_t^\varepsilon = x$, the solution of (3.3b) is the Ornstein-Uhlenbeck process with stationary density

$$\mu(z|x) = \frac{1}{\sqrt{\pi}}\exp\{-(z - x)^2\}, \qquad z \in \mathbb{R}. \tag{3.4}$$

As $\varepsilon \to 0$, one can show that [42] $X_t^\varepsilon \to \overline{X}_t$ strongly, where $\overline{X}_t$ satisfies

$$\dot{\overline{X}}_t = -(\overline{X}_t)^3 - \frac{3}{2}\overline{X}_t + \sin(\pi t) + \cos(\sqrt{2}\pi t), \qquad \overline{X}_0 = x_0, \tag{3.5}$$

i.e. the dynamics of $\overline{X}$ is that of (3.3a) with Z^ε effects averaged w.r.t. the stationary density (3.4).

If we are only interested in studying the system behavior at the slow timescale, i.e. in X^ε, then, when timescales separation is large, $\overline{X}$ provides a good representation of the distribution without having to explicitly resolve the fast dynamics. In the next Section, we describe the data assimilation procedure based on the reduced-order dynamics of $\overline{X}$.

3.3 Data Assimilation in Multi-scale Systems

Data assimilation involves blending information from observations of the actual system states with information from dynamical models to estimate the system states. Common features of observations data are: (i) complex structures – complexity in relations between different parts of the data and the nature of the data itself; (ii) noisy – measurements are inherently subject to random fluctuations; (iii) indirect observations – the desired state is not directly observed. This section deals with assimilation of such data in complex, multiscale systems using filtering theory.

Continuous time state estimation for linear stochastic systems is based on a single unifying theme, namely that state estimation is equivalent to projection onto a closed linear subspace generated by an observation process in a Hilbert space of random variables. This formulation leads to optimal linear estimation and prediction procedures, such as the Kalman-Bucy filter (see, for example, [5, 17]), which is widely used in stochastic optimal control problems. In the nonlinear setting, state estimation is equivalent to restricting the probability measure of the signal to the space of information generated by the observation process. The resulting conditional measure is governed by a stochastic partial differential equation (see, for example, [5]), which in practice can be solved using numerical techniques. The results presented here combines stochastic dimensional reduction and nonlinear filtering theory to provide a rigorous theoretical framework for the development of lower dimensional nonlinear filters for estimating coarse-grained dynamics in multi-scale signals. In practice, stochastic integration approximation methods for the solution of the nonlinear filtering problem have been developed, and can be categorized into global and local methods. Global methods appproximate a probability density function on the entire state space while local methods approximate filtered nonlinear functions in local regions. In the numerical examples of this chapter, we use global methods, a particle filter and the ensemble Kalman filter. For descriptions and analyses of stochastic local methods and comparison with the ensemble Kalman filter, see, for example [10].

The nonlinear filtering problem is framed by augmenting the dynamics of the state (3.1) by an observation process Y^ε. Information about the signal/state is available only indirectly through sensors, modeled as $h(x, z)$, corrupted by sensor noise B:

$$Y_t^\varepsilon = \int_0^t h(X_s^\varepsilon, Z_s^\varepsilon)ds + B_t \tag{3.6}$$

with Borel-measurable $h : \mathbb{R}^{m+n} \to \mathbb{R}^d$ and B is assumed to be a d-dimensional standard Brownian motion that is independent of W and V. The only available information about the signal/state of the system up to time t is contained in the observation σ-field $\mathscr{Y}_t^\varepsilon \overset{\text{def}}{=} \sigma\{Y_s^\varepsilon : 0 \leq s \leq t\}$ of the observations at times s up to t. This section describes some results for the best estimate of statistics of the slow state X_t^ε based on the information contained in $\mathscr{Y}_t^\varepsilon$ generated by the observation process Y^ε, which depends also on the fast process Z^ε. Since the fast process Z^ε rapidly attains its invariant measure, standard averaging techniques suggest that as $\varepsilon \searrow 0$, we should replace the dynamics of the slow process by $\overline{X}$. In other words, we can average out the effects of the fast process Z^ε and regard $\{\overline{X}_t, t \geq 0\}$ as the reduced dynamical model, to be utilized for filtering on a lower-dimensional space compared to the original space of the multiscale signal. When filtering on the reduced space for the signal, the corresponding averaged sensor function $\overline{h}$ should be utilized. However, the true observation Y^ε should still be used, because it may not be possible to obtain "averaged" measurements in practice, and "averaged" measurements may result in some loss of information.

Stochastic dimensional reduction and nonlinear filtering techniques were used in [16, 35] to construct the reduced-order filter and show that it is close to the true filter in the limit of wide timescale separation (small ε). Below, we briefly describe the results, in terms of the density function as in [35]. The results of [16] are in terms of filters (conditional expectation of continuous, bounded functions of the signal).

For $A \in \mathscr{B}(\mathbb{R}^m)$, let $\overline{\pi}_t^{\varepsilon, x}(A, \mathbf{Y}_{[0, t]}^\varepsilon) \overset{\text{def}}{=} \mathbb{P}\{\overline{X}_t \in A | \mathscr{Y}_t^\varepsilon\}$ denote the conditional probability of the homogenized process at time t, given observations up to time t. The homogenized process generated by $\mathscr{L}^{\lambda}$ is combined with the actual observation Y^ε in defining the recursive stochastic PDE for the conditional density $\overline{p}_t(\cdot, \mathscr{Y}_t^\varepsilon)$ for $\overline{\pi}_.^{\varepsilon, x}$. Define $\overline{h}(x) = \int h(x, z) p_\infty(x, dz)$, where $p_\infty(x, \cdot)$ is the invariant density for the fast process with x fixed. Let

$$\overline{\pi}_t^\varepsilon(A, \mathbf{Y}_{[0, t]}^\varepsilon) = \int_{x \in A} \overline{p}_t^\varepsilon(x) dx = \frac{\int_{x \in A} \overline{u}_t^\varepsilon(x) dx}{\int_{x \in \mathbb{R}^n} \overline{u}_t^\varepsilon(x) dx}, \tag{3.7}$$

where $\overline{u}_t^\varepsilon(x)$ is governed by the stochastic PDE

$$d\overline{u}_t^\varepsilon(x) = \mathscr{L}^* \overline{u}_t^\varepsilon(x) dt + \overline{h}(x) \overline{u}_t^\varepsilon(x) dY_t^\varepsilon, \tag{3.8}$$

with $\overline{u}_0^\varepsilon(x) = p_0(x)$. We emphasize that $\overline{\pi}_t^\varepsilon$ is not the standard nonlinear filter introduced earlier, but is a "hybrid" entity derived by using the statistics of the limiting process $\{\overline{X}_t\}$ together with the "non-limiting"/true observation process $\{Y_t^\varepsilon\}$. Using (3.8) and (3.7), it is shown in [35] that the x-marginal of the original conditional density, $\int_{\mathscr{Z}} p_t^\varepsilon(\cdot, z, \mathscr{Y}_t^\varepsilon) dz$, is close to the homogenized conditional density $\overline{p}_t(\cdot, \mathscr{Y}_t^\varepsilon)$. Similar results for the filter $\mathbb{E}[\varphi(\overline{X}_t)|\mathscr{Y}_t^\varepsilon]$, for bounded, continuous functions φ on $\mathbb{R}^m$, are obtained in [16], by invoking a dual representation of the filtering equation and using existing probabilistic estimates to bound the error between the true and homogenized filters.

Remark 1 In most real applications, for example weather prediction models, the observation and signal processes are within the same environment; hence signal and sensor noises are correlated. Our work on the hybrid coarse grained filter $\overline{\pi}_t^{\varepsilon}$ in [16, 35] is in the uncorrelated signal and sensor noises setting, but is currently being extended to the correlated noise setting.

This theory is enabled using an efficient class of filtering methods called particle methods, which invoke sequential Monte Carlo and importance sampling techniques (see, for example, [24, 37]) to recursively approximate the solution to the stochastic PDE (3.8). Particle methods involve the simulation of a sample of independent particles of the signal according to the signal's stochastic law, and reweighting and resampling particles to incorporate information from the observations. The resulting sample represents the posterior conditional distribution of the signal given observations. Based on the results for the homogenized filter, particle methods and averaging techniques have been combined to approximate the hybrid filtering equation solution in a multiscale setting, called the *Homogenized Hybrid Particle Filter* (HHPF), developed in [37].

We apply the HHPF to the example given by (3.3a) and (3.3b) to illustrate its potential for high-dimensional complex problems. To do so, we augment the signal process with an following observation process $Y_t^{\varepsilon} = \frac{1}{2}(X_t^{\varepsilon})^2 + B_t$, which can be written in differential form

$$dY_t^{\varepsilon} = X_t^{\varepsilon} \left\{ -(Z_t^{\varepsilon})^3 + \sin(\pi t) + \cos(\sqrt{2}\pi t) \right\} dt + dB_t.$$

The averaged sensor function is

$$h(X_t) = -(\overline{X}_t)^4 - \frac{3}{2}(\overline{X}_t)^2 + \{\sin(\pi t) + \cos(\sqrt{2}\pi t)\}\overline{X}_t.$$

The results from a particle filter and the HHPF are given in Fig. 3.1a, b, respectively. Both results are also compared with the analytical solution (3.5). The sample

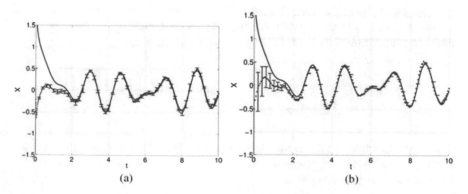

(a)   (b)

Fig. 3.1 Filter estimates for a particle filter (448 s) versus the HHPF (15 s). (**a**) PF estimate (red), True signal (blue). (**b**) HHPF estimate (red), True signal (blue)

standard deviation are represented by the error bars. The time taken for these simulations are 448 and 15 s respectively. The filter estimate in Fig. 3.1b is sparse in time compared to that of Fig. 3.1a, because numerical integration in the HHPF can be performed at a coarser timestep (slow timescale) than is required when homogenization is not utilized (fast timescale). Hence, the dramatic decrease in computation time.

In [25], particle methods are adapted for dynamical systems which are inherently chaotic and for observations that are sparse in time. A control is superimposed on the particle dynamics to drive particles to locations most representative of the next available observations, while still trying to remain faithful to the original signal dynamics. This control is obtained by minimizing a utility functional that is quadratic in the relative distance of particle locations from the next observed locations, and the control effort. An importance sampling step, in addition to that for the observation likelihood, is required to realize the measure change needed to compensate for the addition of control in the signal dynamics. The control can be interpreted as steering particles gradually toward locations indicated by the next observation. The optimization also results in minimal weight variance for each particle.

Evaluation of the optimal control is based on the Feynman-Kac representation and Malliavin derivative, which can become computationally overwhelming for nonlinear signals. However, the solution can be obtained explicitly for linear systems. The linear control strategy is implemented as a suboptimal solution for filtering a noisy version of the 3-dimensional Lorenz '63 model [26] for nonperiodic flow in atmospheric convection. The signal and observation processes are given as:

$$d \begin{bmatrix} X_t^1 \\ X_t^2 \\ X_t^3 \end{bmatrix} = \begin{bmatrix} -\sigma & \sigma & 0 \\ \rho & -1 & 0 \\ 0 & 0 & -\beta \end{bmatrix} \begin{bmatrix} X_t^1 \\ X_t^2 \\ X_t^3 \end{bmatrix} dt + \begin{bmatrix} 0 \\ -X_t^1 X_t^3 \\ X_t^1 X_t^2 \end{bmatrix} dt + \alpha \, dW_t \tag{3.9a}$$

$$dY_k = h X_k dt + g \, dB_k \tag{3.9b}$$

We use the standard parameters $\sigma = 10$, $\rho = 8/3$, and $\beta = 28$ in the signal equations. The signal and sensor noise is simulated as a vector of Gaussian random numbers premultiplied by the following correlation matrices,

$$Q \stackrel{\text{def}}{=} \alpha\alpha^T = \begin{bmatrix} 1 & 0.5 & 0.25 \\ 0.5 & 1 & 0.5 \\ 0.25 & 0.5 & 1 \end{bmatrix} \quad \text{and} \quad R \stackrel{\text{def}}{=} gg^T = \begin{bmatrix} 2 & 0 & 0 \\ 0 & 2 & 0 \\ 0 & 0 & 2 \end{bmatrix}$$

The sensor function is a 3×3 identity matrix, $h \stackrel{\text{def}}{=} I_{3\times3}$. Observations are recorded every $\Delta t = 0.2$, which corresponds to roughly 1/4 of the error doubling time for the deterministic Lorenz '63 system.

The filtering results are shown in Fig. 3.2a, b. Implementation of the suboptimal control was sufficient to ensure consistent tracking of the signal, even when the inter-observations interval is large. The difference between the estimated state $\hat{\mathbf{x}}_t = (\hat{X}_t^1, \hat{X}_t^2, \hat{X}_t^3)$ and the true state $\mathbf{x}_t = (X_t^1, X_t^2, X_t^3)$ of the system constitutes the root-mean-square error (RMSE), $\|\mathbf{x}_t - \hat{\mathbf{x}}_t\|^2$, which is amplified in between observations in chaotic systems that have positive Lyapunov exponents. The particle filter without any control can miss the transitions from one wing of the Lorenz butterfly to the other, as can be seen in Fig. 3.2a. For the same initial sample, Fig. 3.2b shows that the particle filter with the approximate linear control is able to track transitions in the true signal.

The filtering algorithm described so far can be supplemented by a sensor design scheme that extracts better observations (that contain the maximum amount of information), which has the potential to further reduce the error in the analysis of the initial state for the forecast. Using information-theoretic formulations and information flow, adaptive sensing can be designed to extract more information content at a given observation time. Section 3.4 considers sensor selection with the goal of improving the analysis at observation times, by looking at mutual information between the signal and observation. Additionally, in chaotic systems, error growth and uncertainty can be characterized by Lyapunov exponents. Specifically, for a chaotic system, solutions settle near a subset of the state space, called an attractor. However, state trajectories are sensitive to initial conditions, i.e. trajectories starting from initial conditions that are close can deviate far apart in the future. This sensitivity to initial conditions is characterized by (finite time) Lyapunov exponents. Observations can potentially be improved by constructing a sensor function that is more sensitive in unstable directions (directions corresponding to positive Lyapunov exponents).

3.4 Information-Theoretic Sensor Selection Strategy

This section proposes a method for selecting sensor models to collect data that contain useful information for making predictions. With the emergence of sensing concepts that capitalize upon the rapidly increasing availability of controllable sensor degrees of freedom, ranging from sensor operating mode to physical control of the platforms carrying the sensors, there is a need for new strategies for information collection. Effort will be focused on sensor selection and placement for environmental problems through construction of information theoretic utility functions that contain essential information for the estimation problem – specifically state uncertainty as quantified by conditional entropy. In this context, the sensor selection task can be seen as choosing a sensor whose observations provide the most information about the quantity that is being estimated.

The work on optimal sensor path/placement based on information theoretic concepts that is presented here was initiated in [27]. Information-based sensor optimization is not unfamiliar in dynamic estimation problems and has been studied, see for example [1, 11, 15, 19, 29, 40, 43]. In [27], a sensor control scheme is implemented in the update step of the nonlinear filtering algorithm for a single,

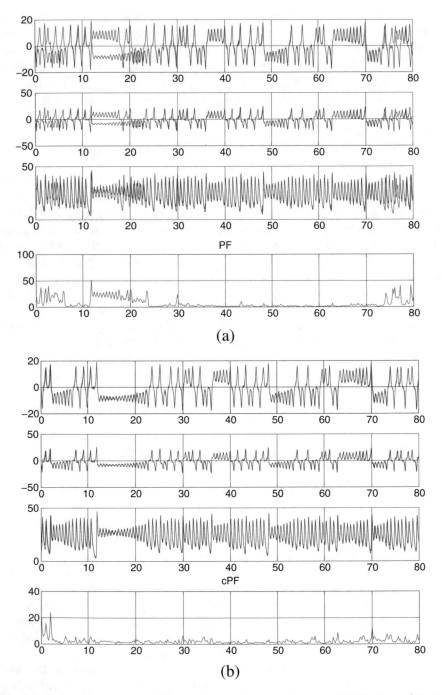

Fig. 3.2 Particle filter estimates of 3 components of Lorenz '63 system. RMSE, $||\mathbf{x}_t - \hat{\mathbf{x}}_t||_2$, is shown in the bottom-most plots. (**a**) Particle filter without control. (**b**) Particle filter with control

dynamic-sensor system. The control is determined by maximizing an information utility function that quantifies the amount of information that observations contribute to the filtering posterior. Here, we first consider information maximization in the discrete-time filtering setting, as in [27], for the sensor selection problem. The continuous-time setting is considered in Sect. 3.4.2 via an information flow equation. For a general introduction to information theory, see for example [8].

We describe the information maximization problem in this section by representing the signal as a single component X, without distinguishing different timescales. Consider the discrete-time signal with observation

$$X_{k+1} = b(X_k) + W_k, \qquad X_0 = x_0 \in \mathbb{R}^m$$

$$Y_k = h_{\theta_k}(X_k) + B_k, \qquad Y_0 = 0_{d \times 1},$$

where $b : \mathbb{R}^m \to \mathbb{R}^m$, $h : \mathbb{R}^m \to \mathbb{R}^d$, $W_k \sim \mathcal{N}(0, Q)$, $Q \in \mathbb{R}^{m \times m}$, $B_k \sim \mathcal{N}(0, R)$, $R \in \mathbb{R}^{d \times d}$, and θ_k is a "control" that allows us to modify the sensor function to maximize the information utility at observation times.

Let $p(x_k | y_{0:k-1})$ and $p(x_k | y_{0:k}; \theta_k)$ denote the prior and posterior densities respectively. The kth observation is modified via θ_k, such that we maximize the information gained from the observation. Hence θ_k comes in as a parameter in the posterior. θ_k can represent a modification on the sensor dynamics for moving sensors or a sensor selection decision from an array of stationary sensors. [27] studies the dynamic sensor problem while here we consider the sensor selection setting. The control history $\theta_{0:k-1}$ is implicitly included in the density notation by considering that they are already incorporated in $y_{0:k-1}$.

The information gain can be quantified by the Kullback-Leibler (KL) divergence of the posterior and prior densities, $D_{KL}(p(x_k | y_{0:k}; \theta_k) || p(x_k | y_{0:k-1}))$, a "metric" of the difference between the two densities. This KL divergence is dependent on Y_k, which is only available after θ_k has been determined. In order to use this KL divergence to determine the optimal θ_k, this KL divergence is averaged over all possible Y_k based on the prior, which is the best knowledge of the distribution of X_k before the posterior is obtained. Hence the posterior in the KL divergence is a "virtual posterior". The utility function that we propose is the following:

$$I(x_k, y_{0:k}; \theta_k) \stackrel{\text{def}}{=} \int_{\mathcal{Y}} D_{KL}(p(x_k | y_{0:k}; \theta_k) || p(x_k | y_{0:k-1})) \, p(y_k | y_{0:k-1}; \theta_k) dy_k,$$

$$(3.10)$$

where

$$p(y_k | y_{0:k-1}; \theta_k) = \int_{\mathcal{X}} p(y_k | x_k; \theta_k) p(x_k | y_{0:k-1}) dx_k \qquad (3.11)$$

is the density of the expected observation, given the prior. The optimal θ_k is determined as

$$\theta_k^* = \arg\max_{\theta \in \Theta} I(x_k, y_{0:k}; \theta_k),$$

where Θ is the set of admissible controls or the set of sensor arrays. The resulting observation constructs a posterior that is far from the prior in the KL divergence sense, but still obeys the signal dynamics specified by the prior.

A simple application of Bayes' Theorem relates the KL divergence to conditional entropy of the signal given observation:

$$\int_{\mathscr{Y}} D_{KL}(p(x_k|y_{0:k}; \theta_k)||p(x_k|y_{0:k-1})) \, p(y_k|y_{0:k-1}; \theta_k) dy_k$$

$$= \int_{\mathscr{Y}} \left(\int_{\mathscr{X}} p(x_k|y_{0:k}; \theta_k) \log \frac{p(x_k|y_{0:k}; \theta_k)}{p(x_k|y_{0:k-1})} \, dx_k \right) p(y_k|y_{0:k-1}; \theta_k) dy_k$$

$$= -\int_{\mathscr{X}} p(x_k|y_{0:k-1}) \log p(x_k|y_{0:k-1}) dx_k$$

$$+ \int_{\mathscr{Y}} \int_{\mathscr{X}} p(x_k|y_{0:k}; \theta_k) \log p(x_k|y_{0:k}; \theta_k) dx_k \, p(y_k|y_{0:k-1}; \theta_k) dy_k$$

$$= H(X_k) - H(X_k|Y_k; \theta_k). \tag{3.12}$$

Equation (3.12) is the difference between the entropy of X_k and the conditional entropy of X_k given Y_k. Hence, maximizing the KL divergence between the posterior and prior is equivalent to minimizing the conditional entropy of signal given observation. Note that the entropy of quantities at time k in (3.12) are averaged over densities conditioned with respect to $Y_{0:k-1}$, which are assumed known at time k. This is the definition of entropy that we use in discrete time from here on.

The mutual information between X_k and $Y_{0:k}$,

$$-\int_{\mathscr{X} \times \mathscr{Y}} p(x_k, y_{0:k}; \theta_k) \log \frac{p(x_k)p(y_{0:k}; \theta_k)}{p(x_k, y_{0:k}; \theta_k)} \, dx_k dy_{0:k},$$

measures the error in assuming independence of signal and observations when they are not. Equivalently, it is the amount of information that the observation contains about the signal. Based on its definition, mutual information between signal and observation should be equivalent to the difference in entropy of the signal and conditional entropy of the signal given observation. It can be seen, via an application of Bayes' Theorem, that

$$-\int_{\mathscr{X} \times \mathscr{Y}} p(x_k, y_{0:k}; \theta_k) \log \frac{p(x_k)p(y_{0:k}; \theta_k)}{p(x_k, y_{0:k}; \theta_k)} \, dx_k dy_{0:k} = H(X_k) - H(X_k|Y_k; \theta_k)$$

$$\tag{3.13a}$$

$$= H(Y_k; \theta_k) - H(Y_k|X_k; \theta_k)$$

$$\tag{3.13b}$$

This gives another interpretation of the utility function (3.10): Relating (3.13) to (3.12), maximizing KL divergence between the posterior and prior (3.10) is equivalent to maximizing the mutual information between the signal and observation.

By (3.12) or (3.13a), maximizing the information utility with respect to θ can be achieved by minimizing the conditional entropy

$$H(X_k|Y_k;\theta_k) = -\int_{\mathcal{Y}}\int_{\mathcal{X}} p(x_k|y_{0:k};\theta_k)\log p(x_k|y_{0:k};\theta_k)dx_k\, p(y_k|y_{0:k-1};\theta_k)dy_k.$$
(3.14)

Unless the densities involved are explicitly known, $H(X_k|Y_k;\theta_k)$ has to be approximated computationally. An example of numerical approximation of such information theoretic quantities is demonstrated in [9], where importance sampling is utilized. This can be computationally intensive, considering samples of the signal and observations have to be generated and their importance sampling weight calculated appropriately according to (3.14). In addition, sampling of observations has to be performed for different parametrizations of θ. However, in the linear case, evaluation of (3.14) is simplified using Kalman filter statistics, as described in Sect. 3.4.1.

Since KL divergence is a measure of the difference between two densities, maximizing the KL divergence between the prior and posterior does not directly lead to a better posterior density for signal estimation. For example, [43] shows empirically for the linear Gaussian case that increasing or decreasing the posterior error covariance relative to the prior's both increase KL divergence, the latter which is desired for signal estimation. Averaging the KL divergence over future observations in (3.10) is based on a different motivation, but it addresses this question. From the interpretation (3.12), maximizing (3.10) is equivalent to minimizing uncertainty of signal given observation, which gives a better posterior for signal estimation compared to the prior. In the linear Gaussian case, this leads to minimizing the determinant of the posterior error covariance explicitly.

3.4.1 The Linear Case

Consider the linear case, where the required densities are known Gaussians: The posterior is given by the Kalman filter, while the density of expected observations, based on (3.11), is determined from the observation likelihood and Kalman filter prior.

Using (3.13a), the conditional entropy of X_k given Y_k can be maximized by

$$\theta_k^* = \arg\min_{\theta\in\Theta}\left|P_{k|0:k}^\theta\right|,$$

$$P_{k|0:k}^\theta = P_{k|0:k-1} - P_{k|0:k-1}(h_k^\theta)^*(R + h_k^\theta P_{k|0:k-1}(h_k^\theta)^*)^{-1}h_k^\theta P_{k|0:k-1},$$
(3.15)

where $P^{\theta_k}_{k|0:k}$ and $P_{k|0:k-1}$ are the Kalman filter posterior and prior error covariances, respectively, and h^θ_k is the sensor matrix at time k. Alternatively, using (3.13b), the mutual information between X_k and Y_k can be maximized by

$$\theta^*_k = \arg \max_{\theta \in \Theta} \left| R + h^\theta_k P_{k|0:k-1} (h^\theta_k)^* \right|. \tag{3.16}$$

This is the same as the criteria in [11].

In order to illustrate the relation between KL divergence/mutual information maximization with the filtering procedure, we consider the linear Gaussian setting with a specific family of sensor matrices. Specifically, for all k, let $h^\theta_k \in \mathbb{R}^{m \times m}$ be a matrix chosen according to our control θ_k, which takes values from an admissible set Θ, defined as follows

$$\Theta \overset{\text{def}}{=} \left\{ \begin{bmatrix} 1 \\ 0 \\ \vdots \\ 0 \\ 0 \end{bmatrix}, \begin{bmatrix} 0 \\ 1 \\ \vdots \\ 0 \\ 0 \end{bmatrix}, \ldots, \begin{bmatrix} 0 \\ 0 \\ \vdots \\ 1 \\ 0 \end{bmatrix}, \begin{bmatrix} 0 \\ 0 \\ \vdots \\ 0 \\ 1 \end{bmatrix} \right\} = \{e_1, e_2, \ldots, e_{m-1}, e_m\} \tag{3.17}$$

The rule for constructing the sensor function is given as $h^\theta_k \overset{\text{def}}{=} \theta_k \otimes \theta_k$, which implies that h^θ_k will always be a zero matrix with one entry on the diagonal equal to 1. The goal is to choose $\theta_k = e_{i*}$ such that $h^\theta_k = e_{i*} \otimes e_{i*}$ maximizes information gain based on (3.10). This is representative of an array of m sensors, of which each sensor observes one component of the signal, and only one of the m sensors is to be switched on at each observation time.

Using either (3.15) or (3.16), and the Leibniz formula for matrix determinants, the sensor selection strategy can be determined as: Choose $\theta_k = e_{i*}$ if

$$P_{i*i*} \sum_{\mathfrak{p} \in \Gamma^m} \text{sgn}(\mathfrak{p}) \prod_{j=1, j \neq i*}^{m} R_{j\mathfrak{p}_j}$$

$$> P_{ii} \sum_{\mathfrak{p} \in \Gamma^m} \text{sgn}(\mathfrak{p}) \prod_{j=1, j \neq i}^{m} R_{j\mathfrak{p}_j} \quad \text{for all} \quad i = 1, 2, \ldots, m, \ i \neq i^*,$$

$$\tag{3.18}$$

where P_{ii} is the iith diagonal element of the prior error covariance matrix, R_{ij} is the ijth element of the observation noise covariance matrix, and Γ^m is the set of $m!$ permutations of the indices $1, \ldots, m$. $\sum_{\mathfrak{p} \in \Gamma^m} \text{sgn}(\mathfrak{p}) \prod_{j=1, j \neq i}^{m} R_{j\mathfrak{p}_j}$ is the ii cofactor of R; that is, the determinant of R with row and column i removed. If the observation noise is independent across components, i.e. R is diagonal, then (3.18) becomes

$$P_{i^*i^*} \prod_{j \neq i^*}^{m} R_{jj} > P_{ii} \prod_{j \neq i}^{m} R_{jj} \iff \frac{P_{i^*i^*}}{P_{ii}}$$

$$> \frac{\prod_{j \neq i}^{m} R_{jj}}{\prod_{j \neq i^*}^{m} R_{jj}} \quad \text{for all} \quad i = 1, 2, \ldots, m, \ i \neq i^*, \tag{3.19}$$

i.e. component i^* is selected for observation if the ratio of prior error of i^* to the prior error in other components is greater than the ratio of observation noise in other components to observation noise in the ith component. This implies that even if a component has large prior error, it will not be selected for observation if its observation noise component is large relative to other components. The same interpretation applies when the observation noise components are not independent, as the ii cofactor of R in (3.18) is a measure of the magnitude of the observation noise with the ith component removed.

3.4.2 Information Flow for the Coarse Grained Dynamics

In this section, we quantify the time evolution of uncertainty about the signal and mutual information between signal and observation. The same information theoretic concepts as in the discrete-time sensor selection problem are used, but now we will revert to the continuous-time setting.

Consider the multiscale system (3.1), and (3.6). By the results presented in Sect. 3.3, estimation of the coarse-grained dynamics of (3.1) can be performed using the limiting $\mathbb{R}^m$-process generated by $\mathscr{L}$. Hence, we utilize the reduced-order filter that is given by the density $\overline{p}^\varepsilon(x) = \frac{\overline{u}^\varepsilon(x)}{\int_{\mathscr{X}} \overline{u}^\varepsilon(\zeta) \, d\zeta}$ for multiscale estimation in this subsection. We also denote the unconditioned density of limiting homogenized process by $\overline{p}$, i.e. the solution to the Fokker-Planck/forward Kolmogorov equation with generator $\mathscr{L}^\dagger$.

As discussed in the discrete-time segment of this section, the mutual information $\overline{I}_t^\varepsilon(\overline{X}_t, \mathbf{Y}_{[0,t]}^\varepsilon)$ is equal to the Kullback-Leibler divergence between the joint distribution of $(\overline{X}_t, \mathbf{Y}_{[0,t]}^\varepsilon)$ and the product distribution of $\overline{X}_t$ and $\mathbf{Y}_{[0,t]}^\varepsilon$. It quantifies the reduction in the uncertainty of $\overline{X}_t$ due the knowledge of $\mathbf{Y}_{[0,t]}^\varepsilon$. It can be thought of as the observation-derived information on coarse grained dynamics in the reduced-order filter at time t. $\overline{I}_t^\varepsilon \equiv 0$ would imply that the observations up to time t are completely useless for estimating $\overline{X}_t$.

The mutual information flow equation for a diffusion process with no timescale separation has been obtained in [30]. We determine the equivalent equation for the multiscale setting, using the reduced-order filter of Sect. 3.3. Denote the entropy and conditional entropy of the coarse-grained dynamics by

$$\overline{H}_t^{\overline{\rho}}(\overline{X}_t)\overset{\text{def}}{=}-\mathbb{E}\left[\log\overline{\rho}_t(\overline{X}_t)\right]\quad\text{and}\quad\overline{H}_t^{\overline{u}^\varepsilon}(\overline{X}_t|\mathbf{Y}_{[0,t]}^\varepsilon)\overset{\text{def}}{=}-\mathbb{E}\left[\log\overline{u}_t^\varepsilon(\overline{X}_t)\right],$$

where $\overline{\rho}$ is the solution of the Fokker-Planck equation with generator $\mathscr{L}^{\dagger}$ and $\overline{u}^\varepsilon$ satisfies the stochastic PDE with generator $\mathscr{L}^{\dagger}$, driven by Y^ε, (3.8). We first determine the time rates of change of the entropies. Define

$$\overline{l}_t^{\overline{\rho}}(x)\overset{\text{def}}{=}-\log\overline{\rho}_t(x)\quad\text{and}\quad\overline{l}_t^{\overline{u}^\varepsilon}(x)\overset{\text{def}}{=}-\log\overline{u}_t^\varepsilon(x).$$

For fixed x, we have

$$\frac{d\overline{l}_t^{\overline{\rho}}(x)}{dt}=-\frac{\mathscr{L}^*\overline{\rho}_t(x)}{\overline{\rho}_t(x)}\quad\text{and}\quad d\overline{l}_t^{\overline{u}^\varepsilon}(x)=-\frac{\mathscr{L}^*\overline{u}_t^\varepsilon(x)}{\overline{u}_t^\varepsilon(x)}dt-\overline{h}^*(x)dY_t^\varepsilon.$$

The results of [20] provide an extension of Itô's lemma for when $\overline{l}^{\overline{\rho}}$ and $\overline{l}^{\overline{u}^\varepsilon}$ are functions of the stochastic process $\overline{X}$. We obtain

$$d\overline{l}_t^{\overline{\rho}}(\overline{X}_t)=\left\{tr\left(\nabla\overline{b}(\overline{X}_t)\right)-\frac{1}{2}tr\left((\sigma\sigma^*)(\overline{X}_t)\left[\nabla^2\log\overline{\rho}_t(\overline{X}_t)\right]\right)\right\}dt$$
$$-\left[\nabla^T\log\overline{\rho}_t(\overline{X}_t)\right]\left[(\sigma\sigma^*)^{\frac{1}{2}}(\overline{X}_t)dW_t\right]$$

and

$$d\overline{l}_t^{\overline{u}^\varepsilon}(\overline{X}_t)=\left\{tr\left(\nabla\overline{b}(\overline{X}_t)\right)-\frac{1}{2}tr\left((\sigma\sigma^*)(\overline{X}_t)\left[\nabla^2\log\overline{u}_t^\varepsilon(\overline{X}_t)\right]\right)\right\}dt$$
$$-\left[\nabla^T\log\overline{u}_t^\varepsilon(\overline{X}_t)\right]\left[(\sigma\sigma^*)^{\frac{1}{2}}(\overline{X}_t)dW_t\right]$$
$$+\frac{1}{2}\left\{\|h(X_t^\varepsilon,Z_t^\varepsilon)-\overline{h}(\overline{X}_t)\|^2-\|h(X_t^\varepsilon,Z_t^\varepsilon)\|^2\right\}dt-\overline{h}^*(\overline{X}_t)dB_t.$$

Taking the expected values, we obtain the respective rates of change of entropies:

$$\frac{d\overline{H}_t^{\overline{\rho}}(\overline{X}_t)}{dt}=\mathbb{E}\left[tr\left(\nabla\overline{b}(\overline{X}_t)\right)\right]+\frac{1}{2}\mathbb{E}\left[\left\|(\sigma\sigma^*)^{\frac{1}{2}}(\overline{X}_t)\nabla\log\overline{\rho}_t(\overline{X}_t)\right\|^2\right]\quad(3.20)$$

and

$$\frac{d\overline{H}_t^{\overline{u}^\varepsilon}(\overline{X}_t|\mathbf{Y}_{[0,t]}^\varepsilon)}{dt} = \mathbb{E}\left[tr\left(\nabla\overline{b}(\overline{X}_t)\right)\right]dt + \frac{1}{2}\mathbb{E}\left[\left\|(\sigma\sigma^*)^{\frac{1}{2}}(\overline{X}_t)\nabla\log\overline{u}_t^\varepsilon(\overline{X}_t)\right\|^2\right]dt$$

$$+ \frac{1}{2}\mathbb{E}\left[\left\|h(X_t^\varepsilon, Z_t^\varepsilon) - \overline{h}(\overline{X}_t)\right\|^2 - \left\|h(X_t^\varepsilon, Z_t^\varepsilon)\right\|^2\right]dt.$$

$$(3.21)$$

Let

$$\overline{H}_t^{\overline{p}^\varepsilon}(\overline{X}_t|\mathbf{Y}_{[0,t]}^\varepsilon) \overset{\text{def}}{=} -\mathbb{E}\left[\log\overline{p}_t^\varepsilon(\overline{X}_t)\right] = \overline{H}_t^{\overline{u}^\varepsilon}(\overline{X}_t|\mathbf{Y}_{[0,t]}^\varepsilon) + \mathbb{E}\left[\log\int_{\mathcal{X}}\overline{u}_t^\varepsilon(\zeta)\,d\zeta\right].$$

$$(3.22)$$

The normalizer of the conditional density is (see, for example, Lemma 3.29 of [5])

$$\int_{\mathcal{X}}\overline{u}_t^\varepsilon(\zeta)\,d\zeta = \exp\left\{\int_0^t\widehat{\overline{h}}_s^\varepsilon\,dY_s^\varepsilon - \frac{1}{2}\int_0^t\|\widehat{\overline{h}}_s^\varepsilon\|^2\,ds\right\},$$

where $\widehat{\overline{h}}_s^\varepsilon \overset{\text{def}}{=} \mathbb{E}\left[\overline{h}(\overline{X}_t)\,\big|\,\mathcal{Y}_t^\varepsilon\right]$. Then, (3.22) along with (3.21) gives us the rate of change of conditional entropy for the coarse grained dynamics:

Lemma 1 *Under conditions for existence of the limiting process generated by $\mathscr{L}^\dagger$, the rate of change of entropy of that limiting process is given by (3.20). Under conditions for the filter convergence results of [16], the rate of change of the conditional entropy of the limiting process given observations history is*

$$\frac{d\overline{H}_t^{\overline{p}^\varepsilon}(\overline{X}_t|\mathbf{Y}_{[0,t]}^\varepsilon)}{dt} = \mathbb{E}\left[tr\left(\nabla\overline{b}(\overline{X}_t)\right)\right] + \frac{1}{2}\mathbb{E}\left[\left\|(\sigma\sigma^*)^{\frac{1}{2}}(\overline{X}_t)\nabla\log\overline{p}_t^\varepsilon(\overline{X}_t)\right\|^2\right]$$

$$- \frac{1}{2}\left\{\mathbb{E}\left[\left\|h(X_t^\varepsilon, Z_t^\varepsilon) - \widehat{\overline{h}}_t^\varepsilon\right\|^2\right] - \mathbb{E}\left[\left\|h(X_t^\varepsilon, Z_t^\varepsilon) - \overline{h}(\overline{X}_t)\right\|^2\right]\right\}.$$

$$(3.23)$$

Remark 2 $\overline{H}_t^{\overline{p}}(\overline{X}_t)$ is the uncertainty in our knowledge about $\overline{X}_t$ on $\mathbb{R}^m$. Equation (3.20) describes the time rate of change of this uncertainty. If the signal is deterministic, then $\overline{\sigma\sigma^*} \equiv 0$ and the rate of change is equal to the expected value of the trace of the gradient of the nonlinear vector field that governs $\overline{X}$. The uncertainty in this case is due to the error in the initial condition, so the expectation is taken with respect to the density that has been propagated forward from the initial density by the generator $\mathscr{L}^\dagger$ given by (3.2) (with $\overline{\sigma\sigma^*} \equiv 0$). For a small deviation $\delta\overline{X}_0$ from an initial $\overline{X}_0$, the rate of change is given by

$$\dot{\delta\overline{X}}_t = \nabla\overline{b}(\overline{X}_t)\delta\overline{X}_t,$$

therefore, $\nabla \overline{b}$ represents the growth rate of an initial error. At a fixed time t, $tr\left(\nabla \overline{b}(\overline{X}_t)\right)$ is equal to the sum of eigenvalues of $\nabla \overline{b}(\overline{X}_t)$, which indicates the growth or shrinkage of $\delta \overline{X}_t$ from time t to a small δt ahead, a "volumetric change".

In the conventional interpretation of the Fisher information, the second moment of $\nabla \log \overline{\rho}$ represents the sensitivity of $\overline{\rho}(\overline{X})$ to changes in $\overline{X}$. In (3.20), $\nabla \log \overline{\rho}$ is stretched by the diffusion coefficient. The corresponding second moment can be interpreted as the sensitivity of $\overline{\rho}$ to $\overline{X}$, amplified by the diffusion effect, i.e. the sensitivity of $\overline{\rho}$ to the stochastic effects of the signal dynamics. This contributes to the growth in uncertainty about $\overline{X}$ due to diffusion in (3.20). In fact, [30] defines this as the Fisher information.

Remark 3 $\overline{H}_t^{\overline{\rho}^\varepsilon}(\overline{X}_t | \mathbf{Y}_{[0,t]}^\varepsilon)$ is the uncertainty in our knowledge about $\overline{X}_t$ on $\mathbb{R}^m$ given information from $\mathbf{Y}_{[0,t]}^\varepsilon$. Equation (3.23) contains the same terms as (3.20) that capture uncertainty growth due to the signal dynamics. In addition, it contains a dissipative term, $\mathbb{E}\left[\left\|h(X_t^\varepsilon, Z_t^\varepsilon) - \widehat{\overline{h}}_t^\varepsilon\right\|^2\right]$, due to information from the sensor function. This contributes to a reduction in uncertainty growth. However, this reduction is penalized by the fact that the homogenized sensor function $\overline{h}$ is used in the reduced-order filter, in the form of the error $\mathbb{E}\left[\left\|h(X_t^\varepsilon, Z_t^\varepsilon) - \overline{h}(\overline{X}_t)\right\|^2\right]$.

Recall that mutual information between the signal and observation is equivalent to the reduction in uncertainty about the signal given observations, i.e. the difference between the entropy and conditional entropy given observations. Hence, Lemma 1 leads to the following rate of change of mutual information:

Theorem 1 *Under conditions for the filter convergence results of* [16], *the rate of change of the mutual information between the limiting process (the coarse grained dynamics) of the signal that is generated by $\overline{\mathscr{L}}^*$ and observations history is*

$$\frac{d\overline{I}_t^\varepsilon(\overline{X}_t, \mathbf{Y}_{[0,t]}^\varepsilon)}{dt} = \frac{1}{2}\left\{\mathbb{E}\left[\left\|h(X_t^\varepsilon, Z_t^\varepsilon) - \widehat{\overline{h}}_t^\varepsilon\right\|^2\right] - \mathbb{E}\left[\left\|h(X_t^\varepsilon, Z_t^\varepsilon) - \overline{h}(\overline{X}_t)\right\|^2\right]\right\}$$

$$- \frac{1}{2}\left\{\mathbb{E}\left[\left\|(\sigma\sigma^*)^{\frac{1}{2}}(\overline{X}_t)\nabla \log \overline{p}_t^\varepsilon(\overline{X}_t)\right\|^2\right] - \mathbb{E}\left[\left\|(\sigma\sigma^*)^{\frac{1}{2}}(\overline{X}_t)\nabla \log \overline{\rho}_t(\overline{X}_t)\right\|^2\right]\right\}$$

(3.24)

Remark 4 Based on interpretations in Remarks 2 and 3, the right side of (3.24) consists of an information growth rate from the sensor function and a dissipation rate due to sensitivity of the conditional density to stochasticity of signal dynamics. The information growth is penalized by the fact that the homogenized sensor function is used in place of the true sensor function. As the filter estimate improves with more observations, the difference between $\widehat{\overline{h}}^\varepsilon$ and $h(X^\varepsilon, Z^\varepsilon)$ should decrease, bar the error due to homogenization, and information growth will decrease. A statistical mechanics interpretation of information flow for the Kalman-Bucy filter is presented in [28], providing a thermodynamic entropy analog to information flow within a partially-observed linear system.

3.4.3   Finite-Time Lyapunov Exponents and Singular Vectors

In this section we make some preliminary connections between finite-time Lyapunov exponents (FTLE) and singular vectors (SV), and the rate of entropy growth given in Sect. 3.4.2. Lyapunov exponents describe the average asymptotic rate of separation for initial conditions that start close to each other in a dynamical system. Corresponding to each unique Lyapunov exponent is a linear subspace of the tangent space, which is spanned by Lyapunov vectors [33] and [39]. The finite-time equivalent definition provides the same geometric intuition, but is defined for a finite interval of time; for example, in the data assimilation case, this would be the time between observations. To define the FTLE and SV, we first recall that the fundamental matrix of a system, denoted as $\Phi_t \stackrel{\text{def}}{=} D\varphi(t, \omega, x)$, satisfies the variational equation

$$d\delta X_t = Df(\varphi(t, \omega)x)\delta X_t dt + Dg(\varphi(t, \omega)x)\delta X_t \circ dW_t,$$

$X_t = \varphi(t, \omega)x$ is an integral curve of the flow φ for a specified initial condition $X_0 = x$ and sample ω [2, 21]. For smooth and bounded f and g, the existence and uniqueness of Φ_t in the setting of random dynamical systems has been rigorously justified by Arnold and Scheutzow [3]. The main point is that Φ_t maps small perturbations of the process X_t at time 0 to perturbations at time t. Formally,

$$\delta X_t = \Phi_t \delta X_o$$

Note that in the additive noise case (i.e. g a constant matrix), the Jacobian is

$$\Phi_t \stackrel{\text{def}}{=} D\varphi(t, \omega, x) = X_0 + \int_0^t Df(\varphi(s, \omega)x)D\varphi(s, \omega)ds,$$

and therefore this relation provides us with a direct procedure for computing Φ_t given initial condition X_0 and the integrated solution X_t.

For a process $X_t \in \mathbb{R}^n$, Φ_t is an $\mathbb{R}^{n \times n}$ matrix. Any matrix can be written in a singular value decomposition (SVD). The SVD of Φ_t is given as

$$\Phi_t = U\Sigma V^*,$$

where U is a unitary matrix of *left-singular vectors* of Φ_t and V a unitary matrix of *right-singular vectors*. Σ is a diagonal matrix with non-negative elements along the diagonal called *singular values*. The singular values are ordered: $\sigma_1 \geq \sigma_2 \geq \ldots \geq \sigma_n \geq 0$. A key relationship between U, V and Σ is that they satisfy the normal equations for Φ_t; that is $\Phi_t^* \Phi_t V = V\Sigma^2$ and $\Phi_t \Phi_t^* U = U\Sigma^2$. Consider now a relation for the maximal finite-time Lyapunov exponent λ_{max}^t and associated vector ξ_{max},

$$\lambda_{max}^t \overset{\text{def}}{=} \frac{1}{|t|} \log ||\Phi_t \xi_{max}||_2 = \ldots = \frac{1}{|t|} \log \sqrt{< \xi_{max}, V \Sigma^2 V^* \xi_{max} >} \qquad (3.25)$$

For simplicity, assume σ_1 is unique. Then this relation implies that the top finite-time Lyapunov exponent is $\frac{1}{|t|} \log \sigma_1$ and a perturbation in the direction of v_1 (i.e. the first column vector of V) will be stretched more (if $\sigma_1 > 1$) or contracted less (if $\sigma_1 < 1$), than any other unit vector, during the interval $[0, t]$. Importantly, the form of the SVD also implies that perturbations in the v_1 subspace of the domain will be mapped to the subspace spanned by u_1 in the codomain. This provides the motivation to rewrite the SVD decomposition of Φ_t as the following: $\Phi_t = \sum_i^n \sigma_i \cdot u_i \otimes v_i$.

The singular values and vectors provide rather sharp information regarding the dynamical stretching that occurs during a time interval $[0, t]$ along a solution X_t. This is in contrast to the entropy forms given in Sect. 3.4. For example, in (3.20) the term, $\mathbb{E}\left[tr\left(\nabla \overline{b}(\overline{X}_t)\right)\right]$, accounts for the expected volumetric rate-of-change due to the dynamical stretching, but does not explicitly provide the subspaces with fast-growth. These specific subspaces are of interest in the adaptive observation process and being able to explicitly identify them are of value, hence our motivation to explore the use singular values and vectors.

3.4.4 Sensor Selection and the Lorenz 1963 Model

In this final section, we use the noisy version of the Lorenz 1963 model given in (3.9a) as a testbed for exploring the effectiveness of sensor selection using methods based on relative entropy and singular vectors. For the standard model parameters given in Sect. 3.3, the deterministic version of the Lorenz 1963 model has Lyapunov exponents with values 0.906, 0.0, and -14.572. The Lorenz model is in fact chaotic, implied by the existence of the positive Lyapunov exponent and bounded motion on an attractor.

We augment the observation process of (3.9b) so that the sensor function is constructed according to $h_k^\theta \overset{\text{def}}{=} \theta_k \otimes \theta_k$ and θ_k is selected from the admissible control set Θ defined in (3.17) (see the end of Sect. 3.4.1 for details). We will first describe the criteria for sensor selection using relative entropy and singular vectors, then provide some relations between the two criteria, and lastly present the numerical setup and results. We end with some concluding remarks.

3.4.4.1 Sensor Selection with Kullback-Leibler Divergence

In the numerical results to follow, we will use the Ensemble Kalman Filter (EnKF) [13]. The EnKF is a Monte Carlo based filter that uses ensemble integrations under the full nonlinear dynamics, but assumes Gaussian statistics in the analysis scheme. An analysis of the ensemble Kalman filter scheme can be found in [10]. Using this filtering scheme, we apply the results given in Sect. 3.4.1 on choosing θ_k in the linear Gaussian setting. For example, when our sensor noise is uniform, then (3.19) says that we would choose $\theta_k = e_1 = [1, 0, 0]^T$ if

$$P_{1,1} > P_{2,2} \quad \text{and} \quad P_{1,1} > P_{3,3}$$

Where $P_{i,i}$ is the i-th diagonal entry of the prior error covariance, $P_{k|0:k-1}$. The logic for choosing θ_k as a different element of Θ is similar.

3.4.4.2 Sensor Selection with Singular Vectors

A criteria for choosing θ_k based on singular vectors can be framed using (3.25), which says that the largest dynamical stretching during a finite time interval will occur in the subspaced spanned by v_1. These perturbations will be stretched by σ_1 and mapped to the u_1 subspace at time t. Hence, if one assumes that error is uniform after observation $k - 1$ or if entropy growth due to the deterministic dynamics dominates, then the best approach to reducing uncertainty due to dynamical stretching is to choose $\theta_k = u_1$ at observation k. Therefore, in the numerical results that follow, we use the following criteria in the singular vector case,

$$\theta_k \overset{\text{def}}{=} e_i \quad \text{where} \quad i = \arg \max |u_{1,i}|, \quad i \in \{1, 2, 3\},$$

where $u_{1,i}$ is the i-th entry of the u_1 left-singular vector. Essentially, this choice of θ_k is equivalent to an orthogonal projection first onto the subspace spanned by u_1 and then a truncation by performing a second orthogonal projection onto the subspace of the canonical frame $\{e_i\}$ that corresponds to the largest entry of u_1.

3.4.4.3 Influence of Singular Values in Discrete-Time, Linear Gaussian Case

Before presenting the numerical results, we inspect the influence of the dynamical stretching, given by the singular values and vectors in the linear Gaussian case. Recall Eq. (3.13b), which provides the utility function to be maximized in terms of difference in entropy and conditional entropy. In the linear Gaussian case, it can be determined to be

$$I(X_k, Y_{0:k}; \theta_k) = \log |R + h_k^\theta P_{k|0:k-1} (h_k^\theta)^*| - \log |R| \tag{3.26}$$

We have used the strictly monotonic property of log to remove unnecessary scalings. Assuming R to be invertible, we have

$$\theta_k^* = \arg\max_{\theta_k \in \Theta} |I + h_k^\theta P_{k|0:k-1}(h_k^\theta)^* R^{-1}| \tag{3.27}$$

The prior error covariance, $P_{k|0:k-1}$, is updated according to the following relation,

$$P_{k|0:k-1} = \Phi_{k,k-1} P_{k-1|0:k-1} \Phi_{k,k-1}^* + Q, \tag{3.28}$$

where $\Phi_{k,k-1} = U \Sigma V^*$ is our tangent linear propagator from $k-1$ to k and Q is the signal error covariance. Since the determinant of a matrix is equivalent to the product of it's eigenvalues, we can substitute (3.28) into (3.27), yielding

$$\theta_k^* = \arg\max_{\theta_k \in \Theta} \prod (1 + \lambda_i)$$

$$\text{where} \quad \lambda_i \in \rho(h_k^\theta \left[\Phi_{k,k-1} P_{k-1|0:k-1} \Phi_{k,k-1}^* + Q \right] (h_k^\theta)^* R^{-1}),$$

where $\rho(\cdot)$ is the spectrum. Let $R = cI$, where $c \in \mathbb{R} \setminus \{0\}$ and I the identity matrix, which is a reasonable assumption for most problems. We let $||Q|| <<$ $||\Phi_{k,k-1} P_{k-1|0:k-1} \Phi_{k,k-1}^*||$; that is the stretching due to noise is small compared to the influence of the deterministic dynamics. Next let the $k-1$ posterior error covariance be expressed in an eigendecomposition (also an SVD form) as

$$P_{k-1|0:k-1} = \sum_i \tilde{\lambda}_i \cdot \tilde{E}_i \quad \text{where} \quad \tilde{E}_i \stackrel{\text{def}}{=} \tilde{e}_i \otimes \tilde{e}_i$$

We similarly write the SVD decomposition of $\Phi_{k,k-1}$ in a more compact notation as

$$\Phi_{k,k-1} = \sum_i \sigma_i \cdot S_i \quad \text{where} \quad S_i \stackrel{\text{def}}{=} u_i \otimes v_i$$

Using these statements and the SVD decomposition of $\Phi_{k,k-1}$ yields,

$$\theta_k^* \approx \arg\max_{\theta_k \in \Theta} \prod (1 + \lambda_i) \quad \text{where} \quad \lambda_i \in \rho \left(h_k^\theta \left[\sum_{i,j,k} \sigma_i \tilde{\lambda}_j \sigma_k \cdot S_i \tilde{E}_j S_k^* \right] (h_k^\theta)^* \right)$$

To see how singular values and KL divergence interact, we constrain the admissible set of controls to be the left singular vectors; that is $\Theta \stackrel{\text{def}}{=} \{u_1, u_2, u_3\}$. Then we have

$$\theta_k^* = u_i \quad \text{where} \quad i = \arg\max_{i \in \{1,2,3\}} \lambda_i \quad \text{and} \quad \lambda_i \in \rho \left(\sigma_i^2 \sum_j \tilde{\lambda}_j \{< v_i, \tilde{e}_j >\}^2 \cdot u_i \otimes u_i \right)$$

What is now clear, is that our KL divergence criteria should yield similar results to orthogonal projection onto the subspace spanned by the leading left singular vector when either: the posterior error at $k - 1$ is nearly uniform and/or the largest error components at $k - 1$ are nearly aligned with v_1 (the right singular vector associated with σ_1) and/or the dynamical stretching into the u_1 subspace dominates any other subspace complementary to u_1 as well as signal and sensor noise.

3.4.4.4   Numerical Results

We now present the numerical results of our study. As mentioned, these results are produced using the EnKF. The simulation parameters are: integration step size of $\delta t = 0.01$ with a split RK4 method, an observation step size of $\Delta t = 40\delta t = 0.4$, a total simulation time of $t_f = 80.0$, and the number of particles was $\mathcal{N}_p = 4$. The observation time update $\Delta t = 0.4$ is roughly $1/2$ of the error doubling time, which is ~ 0.77 time units. Because the Lorenz model has a positive Lyapunov exponent of 0.906, one can expect a significant amount of the entropy growth between observations due to dynamical stretching.

In Fig. 3.3, we will compare the statistical results from 500 trials of each of the following four sensor cases and sensor covariances (to be given in (3.29)), for a total of 4000 simulations.

Identity: $h_k \overset{\text{def}}{=} I_{3\times3}$; the sensor function is the identity matrix and hence all states are always observed. This provides us with a generous lower bound on performance for normalized sensor functions.

KL: h_k^θ; is chosen according to the KL divergence criteria given in Sect. 3.4.4.1.

SV: h_k^θ; is chosen according to the singular vector criteria presented in Sect. 3.4.4.2.

Random: h_k; is a zero matrix with one diagonal entry chosen randomly to be 1 at each observation k. This criteria provides some idea of how sensitive the particular filtering problem is to well chosen sensor functions.

Lastly, we will compare the effectiveness of these four sensor selections with two different sensor covariances. Namely a *Uniform* and a *Non-Uniform* sensor covariance given in (3.29). The numerical results are shown in Fig. 3.3, which shows the distribution of RMSE from 500 experiments for each sensor selection criteria. In each column, the vertical axis is RMSE, while the *Uniform* (blue) (left) and *Non-Uniform* (green) (right) curves are the normalized distributions of RMSE for uniform and non-uniform sensor noises, respectively. The dashed lines indicate the respective quartiles.

$$R = \underbrace{\begin{bmatrix} 2 & 0 & 0 \\ 0 & 2 & 0 \\ 0 & 0 & 2 \end{bmatrix}}_{\text{Uniform}} \qquad R = \underbrace{\begin{bmatrix} 0.5 & 0 & 0 \\ 0 & 4 & 0 \\ 0 & 0 & 0.5 \end{bmatrix}}_{\text{Non-Uniform}} \qquad (3.29)$$

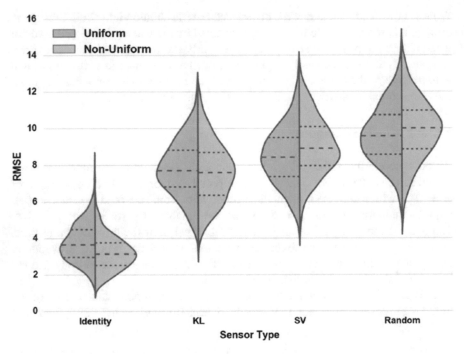

Fig. 3.3 A comparison of sensor functions for a noisy Lorenz 1963 model with *Uniform* (blue) and *Non-Uniform* (green) sensor noise. 500 trials of each case are simulated. The average root mean square error (RMSE) distribution of runs is plotted for each and dashed lines represent the quartiles of the distribution (the mean being the darker center dashed line)

The **Identity** case shown in Fig. 3.3 provides us with a best case scenario for the simulation trials. It is a full rank sensor matrix (i.e. rank $H_{\text{Id}} = 3$), whereas the other three cases are rank 1. The average root mean square error (RMSE) for the four sensor selection criteria under Uniform noise is:

$$\textbf{Identity} = 3.77, \quad \textbf{KL} = 7.78, \quad \textbf{SV} = 8.48, \quad \textbf{Random} = 9.66$$

In the case of our Non-Uniform noise, the average RMSE is:

$$\textbf{Identity} = 3.21, \quad \textbf{KL} = 7.62, \quad \textbf{SV} = 9.02, \quad \textbf{Random} = 9.91$$

In the Uniform noise case, both the sensor selections using KL divergence and singular vectors outperform a random selection. On average, the KL divergence does slightly better than the singular vectors criteria, which is a positive indication of how our information centric formulation is able to account for uncertainty in error at a time step $k - 1$ into the k observation selection. In the Non-Uniform noise case, Fig. 3.3 and the RMSE values given above show that the performance of the KL divergence criteria is not effected, but the singular vector criteria, which does not account for corruption in the observation process, is strongly hindered.

3.5   Conclusions

In summary, engineered and natural systems of interest are of high dimension and contains several scales. The current data are great in number, complex, often of extremely high dimension, and frequently noisy. The bottleneck has been the lack of availability of good statistical techniques that quickly and effectively extract useful information and assimilate them in real time. This chapter presented new information theory-based methods for the distributed collection and assimilation of data in a multiscale environment, in particular, results that deal with the measures of the quality and variability of the data involved as well as collecting and assimilating them. The second section described results on dimensional reduction driven by either additive or multiplicative white noise. The third section dealt with the vital issue of the curse of high dimension in data assimilation. Understanding how the *scaling* interacts with *filtering* opened the bottleneck to overcome some of the computational issues of large scale systems.

In the context of filtering applications, the reduced-order nonlinear filtering equations [16, 24, 37] provided estimation of coarse-grained dynamics (slow dynamics) without requiring explicit knowledge of the fast dynamics, hence reducing computational complexities and information storage requirements. The final section presented a sensor selection strategy intended to improve predictability through mutual information between the signal and observation. In addition, a rate of change of mutual information between the homogenized version of the signal and real observations history is obtained. A strategy based on finite-time Lyapunov exponents of the dynamical system was shown to provide clearer insight into error growth due to signal dynamics and is computationally more efficient compared to the mutual information method. Known connections between Lyapunov exponents and dynamical entropy can be used to further the understanding of error growth [22] and [38]. A numerical experiment using a noisy Lorenz '63 model shows the overall superiority of the mutual information approach while the finite-time Lyapunov exponents approach performs well when sensor noise is uniform. The information theoretic studies of [43] and [18] found different sensitivities of varying orders of Renyi divergence (from 0 to 1, KL divergence corresponds to order 1) to differences between densities. The effects of different orders of Renyi divergence in the cost function of Sect. 3.4 on the sensor selection problem here remains to be explored.

Acknowledgments The authors acknowledge the support of the AFOSR under grant numbers FA9550-12-1-0390 and FA9550-16-1-0390.

References

1. E.H. Aoki, A. Bagchi, P. Mandal, Y. Boers, A theoretical look at information-driven sensor management criteria, in *Proceedings of the 14th International Conference on Information Fusion (FUSION)* (IEEE, Chicago, 2011), pp. 1180–1187
2. L. Arnold, *Random Dynamical Systems*, Springer Monographs in Mathematics (Springer, Berlin, 1998)
3. L. Arnold, M. Scheutzow, Perfect cocycles through stochastic differential equations. Probab. Theory Relat. Fields **101**, 65–88 (1995)
4. L. Arnold, N.S. Namachchivaya, K.L. Schenk, Toward an understanding of stochastic hopf bifurcations: a case study. J. Bifurcation Chaos **6**, 1947–1975 (1996)
5. A. Bain, D. Crisan, Fundamentals of stochastic filtering (Springer, Berlin, 2009).
6. N. Berglund, B. Gentz, Noise-induced phenomena in slow-fast dynamical systems: a sample paths approach, (Springer, London, 2006)
7. R. Buizza, M. Miller, T.N. Palmer, Stochastic simulation of model uncertainties. Q. J. R. Meteorol. Soc. **125**, 2887–2908 (1999)
8. T.M. Cover, J.A. Thomas, *Elements of Information Theory*, 2nd edn. (Wiley-Interscience J.A., Hoboken, 2006)
9. A. Doucet, B.-N. Vo, C. Andrieu, M. Davy, Particle filtering for multi-target tracking and sensor management, in *Proceedings of the 5th International Conference on Information Fusion (FUSION)* (IEEE, Annapolis, MD, 2002), pp. 474–481
10. J. Dunik, O. Straka, M. Simandl, E. Blasch, Random-point-based filters: analysis and comparison in target tracking. IEEE Trans. Aerosp. Electron. Syst. **51**(2), 1403–1421 (2015)
11. E. Ertin, J.W. Fisher, L.C. Potter, Maximum mutual information principle for dynamic sensor query problems in *Information Processing in Sensor Networks*. Lecture Notes in Computer Science, vol. 2634 (Springer, Berlin, 2003), pp. 405–416
12. S.N. Ethier, T.G. Kurtz, *Markov Processes: Characterization and Convergence* (Wiley, New York, 1986)
13. G. Evensen, The ensemble Kalman Filter: theoretical formulation and practical implementation. Ocean Dyn. **53**(4), 343–367 (2003)
14. M.I. Freidlin, A.D. Wentzell, *Random Perturbations of Dynamical Systems*. Grundlehren der Mathematischen Wissenschaften, 260 (Springer, Berlin, 1998)
15. C. Kreucher, J. Wegrzyn, M. Beauvais, R. Conti, Multiplatform information-based sensor management: an inverted UAV demonstration, in *Defense and Security Symposium, International Society for Optics and Photonics: 65780Y-65780Y, 2007*
16. P. Imkeller, N.S. Namachchivaya, N. Perkowski, H.C. Yeong, Dimensional reduction in nonlinear filtering: a homogenization approach. Ann. Appl. Probab. **23**(6), 2161–2603 (2013)
17. A.H. Jazwinski, *Stochastic Processes and Filtering Theory* (Academic, New York, 1970)
18. C. Kreucher, K. Kastella, A.O. Hero III, Information based sensor management for multitarget tracking, in *Proceedings of SPIE 5204, Signal and Data Processing of Small Targets*, vol. 480 (San Diego, CA, 2003)
19. C.M. Kreucher, A.O. Hero, K.D. Kastella, M.R. Morelande, An information-based approach to sensor management in large dynamic networks. Proc. IEEE **95**(5), 978–999 (2007)
20. H. Kunita, Some extensions of Itô's formula. Séminaire de probabilités (Strasbourg), vol. 15 (Springer, Berlin/Heidelberg, 1981), pp. 118–141
21. H. Kunita, *Stochastic Flows and Stochastic Differential Equations* (Cambridge University Press, Cambridge, 1990)
22. F. Ledrappier, L.-S. Young, The metric entropy of diffeomorphisms: part I: characterization of measures satisfying Pesin's Entropy formula. Ann. Math. **122**(3), 509–539 (1985)
23. J. Li, K. Lu, P.W. Bates, Geometric singular perturbation theory with real noise. J. Differ. Equ. **259**(10), 5137–5167 (2015)
24. N. Lingala, N.S. Namachchivaya, N. Perkowski, H.C. Yeong, Particle filtering in high-dimensional chaotic systems. Chaos **22**, 047509 (2012)

25. N. Lingala, N.S. Namachchivaya, N. Perkowski, H.C. Yeong, Optimal nudging in particle filters. Probab. Eng. Mech. **32**, 21–30 (2014)
26. E.N. Lorenz, Deterministic nonperiodic flow. J. Atmos. Sci. **20**, 130–141 (1963)
27. M. Mamlouk, Information based sensor control in a two-vortex flowfield. M.S. Thesis, University of Illinois-Urbana Champaign, Department of Aerospace Engineering, Urbana, Illinois (2013)
28. S. Mitter, N. Newton, Information and Entropy Flow in the Kalma-Bucy Filter. J. Stat. Phys. **118**(1), 145–176 (2005)
29. S. Martinez, F. Bullo, Optimal sensor placement and motion coordination for target tracking. Automatica **42**, 661–668 (2006)
30. E. Mayer-Wolf, M. Zakai, On a formula relating the Shannon information to the Fisher information for the filtering problem, in *Filtering and Control of Random Processes: Proceedings of the E.N.S.T.-C.N.E.T. Colloquium*, Paris, 23–24 Feb 1983, vol. 61 (Springer, Berlin/Heidelberg, 1984), pp. 164–171
31. N.S. Namachchivaya, R.B. Sowers, Rigorous stochastic averaging at a center with additive noise. Meccanica **37**(2), 85–114 (2002)
32. N.S. Namachchivaya, R.B. Sowers, L. Vedula, Nonstandard reduction of Noisy Duffing-van der Pol equation. J. Dyn. Syst. **16**(3), 223–245 (2001)
33. V.I. Oseledec, A Multiplicative Ergodic Theorem. Lyapunov characteristic numbers for dynamical systems. Trans. Moscow Math. Soc. **19**, 197–231 (1968)
34. K. Onu, N.S. Namachchivaya, stochastic averaging of surface waves. Proc R Soc A **466**(3), 2363–2381 (2010)
35. J.H. Park, N.S. Namachchivaya, R.B. Sowers, Dimensional reduction in nonlinear filtering. Nonlinearity **23**(2), 305–325 (2010)
36. G.C. Papanicolaou, D. Stroock, S.R.S. Varadhan, Martingale approach to some limit theorems, in *Papers from the Duke Turbulence Conference, Duke University*, Durham, 1976, paper no. 6 (Duke University, Durham, 1977)
37. J.H. Park, N.S. Namachchivaya, H.C. Yeong, Particle filters in a multiscale environment: homogenized hybrid particle filter. J. Appl. Mech. **78**(6), 1–10 (2011)
38. Y. Pesin, Characteristic Lyapunov exponents and smooth ergodic theory. Rus. Math. Surv. **32**(4), 55–114 (1977)
39. D. Ruelle, Ergodic theory of differentiable dynamical systems. Publ. IHES **50**, 27–58 (1979)
40. A. Ryan, J.K. Hedrick, Particle filter based information-theoretic active sensing. Robot. Auton. Syst. **58**(5), 574–584 (2010)
41. D.W. Stroock, S.R.S. Varadhan, Multidimensional diffusion processes Grundlehren der Mathematischen Wissenschaften 233 (Springer, Berlin, 1979)
42. E. Weinan, D. Liu, E. Vanden-Eijnden, Analysis of multiscale methods for stochastic differential equations. Commun. Pure Appl. Math. **58**, 1544–1585 (2005)
43. C. Yang, I. Kadar, E. Blasch, M. Bakich, Comparison of information theoretic divergences for sensor management, in *Proceedings of SPIE 8050, Signal Processing, Sensor Fusion, and Target Recognition XX*, 80500C, Bellingham, 2011

Chapter 4
Dynamic Data-Driven Uncertainty Quantification via Polynomial Chaos for Space Situational Awareness

Richard Linares, Vivek Vittaldev, and Humberto C. Godinez

Abstract Knowledge of all space objects in orbit and the space environment is collected and maintained by the Space Surveillance Network (SSN). This task is becoming more difficult as the number of objects currently tracked increases due to breakup events and improvements in sensor detection capabilities. The SSN is tasked with maintaining information on over 22,000 objects, 1,100 of which are active. In particular, low-Earth orbiting satellites are heavily influenced by atmospheric drag which is difficult to model due to fluctuations in the upper atmospheric density. These fluctuations are caused by variations in the Solar energy flux which heats Earth's atmosphere causing it to expand. This research uses probabilistic models to characterize and account for the fluctuations in the Earth's atmosphere. By correctly estimating the fluctuations, our work contributes to improving the ability to determine the likelihood of satellite collisions in space.

The main focus of this chapter is the application of a new Polynomial Chaos based Uncertainty Quantification (UQ) approach for Space Situational Awareness (SSA). The challenge of applying UQ to SSA is the long term integration problem, where simulations are used to forecast physics over long temporal and/or spatial extrapolation intervals. This chapter applies a Polynomial Chaos (PC) expansion and Gaussian Mixture Models (GMMs) in a hybrid fashion for UQ applied to satellite tracking. This chapter uses the GMM-PC approach for orbital UQ and the PC approach for atmospheric density UQ. Two different application examples are

R. Linares (✉)
Department of Aeronautics and Astronautics, Massachusetts Institute of Technology, Cambridge, MA, USA
e-mail: linaresr@mit.edu

V. Vittaldev
Department of Aerospace Engineering and Engineering Mechanics, The University of Texas at Austin, Austin, TX, USA
e-mail: v.vittaldev@utexas.edu

H. C. Godinez
Applied Mathematics Group, Los Alamos National Laboratory, Los Alamos, NM, USA
e-mail: hgodinez@lanl.gov

© The Author(s), under exclusive license to Springer Nature Switzerland AG 2022
E. P. Blasch et al. (eds.), *Handbook of Dynamic Data Driven Applications Systems*,
https://doi.org/10.1007/978-3-030-74568-4_4

shown. The first example demonstrates the GMM-PC approach for orbital UQ for a low Earth orbit satellite under the influence of atmospheric perturbations. The second example demonstrates the PC approach for atmospheric density UQ, where a physics-based model is used to capture the uncertainty of the atmospheric density under uncertain Solar conditions. These two examples are not combined under this work but the tools developed provide a framework for an unified understanding of UQ for low Earth orbiting satellites.

Keywords Satellite drag · Uncertainty quantification · Satellite orbits · Polynomial chaos

4.1 Introduction

Recent events in space, including the collision of Russia's Cosmos 2251 satellite with Iridium 33 and China's Feng Yun 1C anti-satellite demonstration, have stressed the capabilities of the space community and its ability to provide accurate and actionable impact probability estimates because of the additional debris objects that were generated. For example, the Space Surveillance Network (SSN) has the unique challenge of tracking more than 22,000 Space Objects (SOs) and providing critical collision avoidance warnings to military, NASA, and commercial operators. However, due to the large number of SOs and the limited number of sensors available to track them, it is impossible to maintain persistent surveillance resulting in large observation gaps [1]. This inherent latency in the catalog information results in sparse observations and large propagation intervals between measurements and close approaches. The large propagation intervals coupled with nonlinear SO dynamics results in highly non-Gaussian probability distribution functions (pdfs). In particular, satellites in Low-Earth Orbit (LEO) are heavily influenced by atmospheric drag which is difficult to model [2]. Uncertainties in atmospheric drag must be folded into estimation models to accurately represent the position uncertainties for calculating impact probabilities or conjunction assessments (CA). This process then separates naturally into a prediction and correction cycle, where estimates are used to predict the orbital position at a future time and observations are used to improve or correct these predictions while decreasing uncertainty. The difficulty in this process lies in representing the non-Gaussian uncertainty and accurately propagating it [3]. Accurate assessment of confidence in position knowledge will be a significant improvement, particularly for the space situational awareness (SSA) community. The contribution of this chapter is the application of PC [4] and GMM-PC [5] to satellite tracking with upper atmospheric UQ.

A number of upper atmospheric models exist which can be classified as either empirical or physics-based models [6, 7]. The current Air Force standard is the High Accuracy Satellite Drag Model (HASDM) [8], which is an empirical model based on observations of calibration satellites. These satellite observations are used to determine atmospheric model parameters based on their orbit determination solutions. Although the HASDM model is accurate for determining the current state of the upper atmospheric environment, it has no forecasting capability which limits its effectiveness for CA calculations. A number of physics-based models exist, two of which are the Global Ionosphere-Thermosphere Model (GITM) [9] and the Thermosphere-Ionosphere-Electrodynamics General Circulation Model (TIE-GCM) [6, 7]. These are physics-based models that solve the full Navier-Stokes equations for density, velocity, and temperature for a number of neutral and charged chemical species components. The improved modeling and prediction capabilities of these models come at a high computational cost. The models are very high-dimensional, solving Navier-Stokes equations over a discretized spatial grid involving 2000–10,000 state variables and 12–20 inputs and internal parameters. Satellite CA calculations usually involves long propagation intervals (3–8 days) resulting in nonlinear transformation and non-Gaussian errors.

This nonlinearity and high-dimensionality results in the so-called *curse of dimensionality* [10], where the combination of increasing problem dimension and order of nonlinearity, causes the number of required evaluations to grow in a super-linear manner. The *curse of dimensionality* as related to atmospheric models is a difficulty that this chapter addresses. Additionally, CA requires full knowledge of the probability density function (pdf) to calculate the impact probability as opposed to traditional state estimation and data assimilation approaches which only require the first two moments (mean and covariance). This chapter presents a new approach that solves for the full pdf.

A common but computationally intensive method of propagating uncertainty is the use of Monte Carlo (MC) simulations [11, 12]. Randomly generated samples from the initial uncertainty distribution are propagated through the function of interest. MC approaches require on the order of millions of propagations[1] to generate statistically valid UQ solutions. Parallelizing the computations on multiprocessor central (CPUs) or on Graphics Processing Units (GPUs) reduces the runtime of the simulations significantly [13–15] at the cost of increasing the difficulty of implementation [16]. Reducing the number of sample points required for a result with satisfactory confidence bounds is possible through importance sampling. Although the computational cost can be prohibitive for most applications due to the slow convergence, the generality of MC techniques makes them an ideal benchmark to compare other methods.

A spectrum of techniques exists that propagate the state and uncertainty of an initially Gaussian distribution through a nonlinear function, such as orbit propagation [17]. Computational cost is traded for accuracy of the pdf. Using the first order Taylor series expansion of the dynamics to linearly propagate the covariance matrix lies on one extreme; while the MC simulation lies on the other extreme of computational cost. Two techniques that occupy a range within this spectrum of computational cost are Gaussian Mixture Models (GMMs) [18] and Polynomial Chaos (PC) expansion [4].

GMMs can approximate any pdf using a weighted sum of Gaussian distributions with the approximation improving in an L_1-norm sense with increasing number of elements [18]. When the initial distribution is Gaussian, the approximate GMM

---

[1]This number is problem dependent.

for this case has spatially distributed means and each element has smaller variance than that of the initial Gaussian distribution (i.e., differential entropy). Using the GMM approximation, each Gaussian component is propagated through the nonlinear function using State Transition Tensors (STTs) [19], sigma-point based methods [20, 21], quadrature, or cubature[2] [22–24]. Each element has a smaller uncertainty than the initial Gaussian distribution at epoch and therefore, the Gaussian assumption for each element should hold for propagation times that are at least as long, or longer than the original distribution. The weighted sum of the Gaussian elements after propagation approximates the resulting forecast pdf while having the ability to approximate non-Gaussian distributions. GMMs have been successfully used in many uncertainty propagation applications such as orbit estimation [25, 26], orbit determination [27, 28], and conjunction assessment [29, 30].

The PC [4] approach uses orthogonal polynomial (OP) expansions as a surrogate model for quantifying uncertainty. The most suited polynomial is chosen using the Wiener-Askey scheme and depends on the initial uncertainty distribution [31]. It is also possible to compute optimal orthogonal polynomials for arbitrary pdfs that are not part of the Wiener-Askey scheme using arbitrary PC (aPC) [32]. For Gaussian distributions, Hermite polynomials are the corresponding OPs [4, 31]. For the multidimensional case, the coefficients of the multivariate polynomials are computed such that a mapping of the random variable from the initial time to the final time is approximated. Once the polynomial coefficients are computed, sampling from the PC polynomial approximation generally has a lower computational cost than a full-blown MC run. The PC approach has been used in many fields for uncertainty quantification of computationally intensive models [33–36]. In orbital mechanics, PC has been previously used for uncertainty propagation [37, 38] and conjunction assessment [39, 40].

Reference [5] used PC and GMM in a hybrid fashion to quantify state uncertainty for spacecraft. Including a GMM with the PC (GMM-PC) was shown to reduce the overall order required to achieve a desired accuracy. Reference [5] converted the initial distribution into a GMM, and PC was used to propagate each of the elements. Splitting the initial distribution into a GMM reduces the size of the covariance associated with each element and therefore, lower order polynomials can be used. The GMM-PC effectively reduces the function evaluations required for accurately describing a non-Gaussian distribution that results from the propagation of a state with an initial Gaussian distribution through a nonlinear function. The current chapter uses the GMM-PC method, developed by Ref. [5], for the satellite orbital UQ with atmospheric drag. Additionally, the PC method is used for UQ applied to upper atmospheric models without splitting the initial uncertainty into a GMM.

The organization of this chapter is as follows. First, the GMMs are discussed. Next, the PC approach is outlined and discussed. Following this the GMM-PC approach is discussed. Additionally, results are shown for simulated examples for both orbital and atmospheric UQ. Finally, discussions and conclusions are provided.

---

[2]Multidimensional quadratures.

4.2 Gaussian Mixture Models

A GMM approximates any PDF in an L_1-distance sense by using a weighted sum of Gaussian probability distribution functions [18].

$$p(\mathbf{x}) = \sum_{i=1}^{N} \alpha_i \, p_g\left(\mathbf{x}; \boldsymbol{\mu}_i, \mathbf{P}_i\right) \tag{4.1}$$

where $p_g\left(\mathbf{x}; \boldsymbol{\mu}_i, \mathbf{P}_i\right)$ is a multivariate Gaussian pdf with mean $\boldsymbol{\mu}_i$ and covariance $\mathbf{P}_i$, N is the number of Gaussian probability distribution functions, and α_i is a positive non-zero weight, which satisfies the following constraint:

$$\sum_{i=1}^{N} \alpha_i = 1 \tag{4.2}$$

where $\forall \alpha_i > 0$. For uncertainty propagation, the initial Gaussian distribution is split into a GMM and each element is propagated through the nonlinear function. Standard Gaussian propagation techniques such as State Transition Matrices (STTs) [19] or sigma-point methods [20, 21] are commonly used to approximate the Gaussian elements post propagation. Although each element remains Gaussian, the weighted sum forms a non-Gaussian approximation of the true distribution. Modifications of this procedure exist, where the weights can be updated post-propagation [41] or the elements can be further split into more elements or merged mid-propagation [25]. However, these modifications are not considered for this work.

Instead of forming a GMM approximation of the initial multivariate Gaussian distribution, a univariate GMM library of the standard normal distribution is formed [25, 27, 30, 42]. The univariate library is applied along a column of the square-root factor of the covariance matrix in order to form a GMM approximation of a multivariate Gaussian. The univariate splitting library has to be computed only once and is stored in the form of a lookup table. Finding the univariate library is converted to an optimization problem where the distance between the GMM and the standard normal distribution is minimized. The L_2 distance is used instead of L_1 because a closed-form solution exists for the L_2 distance between a GMM and a Gaussian distribution. A library where all the standard deviations in the split are the same (homoscedastic), $\sigma = \sqrt{1/N}$, and odd N up to 39 elements is used in this work [43, 44]. With increasing N, σ decreases and therefore, the differential entropy of each element decreases as seen in Fig. 4.1.

To apply the univariate splitting library to a multivariate Gaussian distribution $\mathbf{p}_G \sim \mathcal{N}(\boldsymbol{\mu}, \mathbf{P})$, the univariate splitting library is applied along a column of the square-root $\mathbf{S}$ of the covariance matrix:

$$\mathbf{P} = \mathbf{S}\mathbf{S}^T \tag{4.3}$$

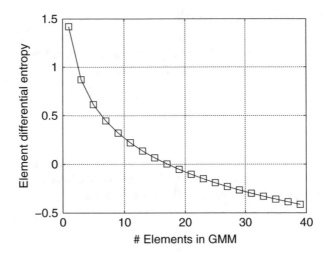

Fig. 4.1 Differential entropy per element

For an n-dimensional state, the covariance matrix of each element after the split is:

$$\mathbf{P}_i = [\mathbf{s}_1 \ldots \sigma \mathbf{s}_k \ldots \mathbf{s}_n][\mathbf{s}_1 \ldots \sigma \mathbf{s}_k \ldots \mathbf{s}_n]^T \qquad (4.4)$$

where $\mathbf{s}_k$ is the desired column of $\mathbf{S}$ that the split is along. The means of the multivariate GMM are:

$$\boldsymbol{\mu}_i = \boldsymbol{\mu} + \mu_i \mathbf{s}_k \qquad (4.5)$$

where μ_i are the univariate library mixture split locations [43, 44]. If Cholesky or spectral decomposition is used to generate $\mathbf{S}$, the possible splitting options are limited to $2n$ directions. However, it is possible to apply the univariate splitting direction along any desired direction by generating a square-root matrix with one column parallel to the input direction [45]. For extremely non-linear problems, splitting along a single direction may not account for the entire non-linearity of the problem. Therefore, splitting the initial multivariate distribution in multiple directions is required in order to better approximate the non-Gaussian behavior post-propagation [44, 46]. In such cases the splitting library can be applied recursively as a tensor product to split along multiple directions.

4.3 Polynomial Chaos

The idea of PC originates from a chapter from Norbert Wiener [4], where the term *chaos* is used to refer to uncertainty. This theory has been used frequently

Table 4.1 The Wiener-Askey scheme where α and β are pdf specific parameters [50]

Distribution type	Density	Polynomial	Weight	Range of x
Normal	$\frac{1}{\sqrt{2\pi}}e^{\frac{-x^2}{2}}$	Hermite	$e^{\frac{-x^2}{2}}$	$[-\infty, \infty]$
Uniform	$\frac{1}{2}$	Legendre	1	$[-1, 1]$
Beta	$\frac{(1-x)^\alpha(1+x)^\beta}{2^{\alpha+\beta+1}B(\alpha+1,\beta+1)}$	Jacobi	$(1-x)^\alpha(1+x)^\beta$	$[-1, 1]$
Exponential	e^{-x}	Laguerre	e^{-x}	$[0, \infty]$
Gamma	$\frac{x^\alpha e^{-x}}{\Gamma(\alpha+1)}$	Generalized laguerre	$x^\alpha e^{-x}$	$[0, \infty]$

for UQ and is now also being used in the Aerospace field [37, 39, 47–49]. In PC, the uncertainty in variables through a transformation is represented by a series of orthogonal polynomials

$$u(\xi, t) = \sum_{i=0}^{\infty} c_i(t)\Psi_i(\xi) \tag{4.6}$$

where $u(\xi, t)$ is the output of interest. In Eq. (4.6) ξ is a random variable. The orthogonal polynomials Ψ_i are defined by the following inner product in a Hilbert space:

$$\int_{-\infty}^{\infty} \Psi_m(\xi)\Psi_n(\xi)w(\xi) = 0 \tag{4.7}$$

Based on the distribution of the random variable, the orthogonal polynomial type and weighing function, $w(\xi)$ from Eq. (4.7), are chosen from the Weiner-Askey [31] scheme found in Table 4.1.

Since most applications assume the initial distribution to be Gaussian, Hermite polynomials are chosen according to the Wiener-Askey scheme. This chapter applies the normalized probabilists Hermite polynomials where the weight function is changed to:

$$w(\xi) = \frac{1}{\sqrt{2\pi}}e^{\frac{-\xi^2}{2}} \tag{4.8}$$

The new weight function assumes that the distribution has a mean of 0 and a standard deviation of 1, which effectively normalizes and improves the numerical properties. The normalized Hermite polynomials can be found by using the following recursive relation:

$$(n+1)! \times \Psi_{n+1}(\xi) = \xi\Psi_n(\xi) - n\Psi_{n-1}(\xi) \tag{4.9}$$

where

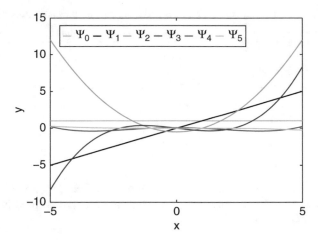

Fig. 4.2 Normalized probabilists Hermite polynomials

Table 4.2 Two-dimensional multivariate polynomials up to order 2

Order	Multi-index	Multivariate polynomial
0	$\alpha_0 = [0, 0]$	$\Psi_{\alpha 0}(\xi) = 1$
1	$\alpha_1 = [1, 0]$	$\Psi_{\alpha 1}(\xi) = \Psi_1(\xi_1)$
1	$\alpha_2 = [0, 1]$	$\Psi_{\alpha 2}(\xi) = \Psi_1(\xi_2)$
2	$\alpha_3 = [2, 0]$	$\Psi_{\alpha 3}(\xi) = \Psi_2(\xi_1)$
2	$\alpha_4 = [0, 2]$	$\Psi_{\alpha 4}(\xi) = \Psi_2(\xi_2)$
2	$\alpha_5 = [1, 1]$	$\Psi_{\alpha 5}(\xi) = \Psi_1(\xi_1)\Psi_2(\xi_1)$

$$\Psi_0 = 1 \qquad \Psi_1 = \xi \tag{4.10}$$

In reality, the infinite series from Eq. (4.6) is truncated at some order. The orthogonal univariate Hermite polynomials up to order 5 can be seen in Fig. 4.2. The conjunction problem depends on the full position and velocity of the satellite and is therefore a multivariate problem that requires orthogonal multivariate polynomials. Multivariate polynomials can be created using the multi-index notation. Two-dimensional multivariate polynomials up to order 2 can be seen in Table 4.2. The multivariate polynomial can then be written as:

$$u(\xi, t) = \sum_{i=0}^{L} c_i(t)\Psi_{\alpha i}(\xi) \tag{4.11}$$

where L is given by

$$L = \frac{(n + l)!}{n! l!} \tag{4.12}$$

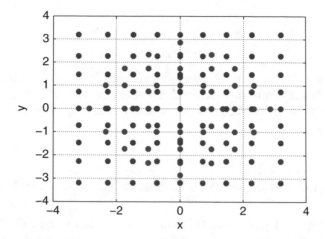

Fig. 4.3 Difference between a full (red) and sparse (blue) two-dimensional quadrature grid

where n is the dimension of ξ and l is the maximum order of the truncated univariate polynomial. A given order $\bar{L}$ of the multivariate polynomial equals the sum of the elements of the multi-index vector. If the output is also a vector function of dimension n, $u(\xi, t)$, $n \times L$ coefficients $c_i(t)$ have to be computed.

The final challenge is to determine the coefficients $c_i(t)$. The two major methods used to determine these coefficients are the Intrusive method and the Non-intrusive method. The intrusive method requires knowledge of the propagation function that determines the evolution of the random vector of inputs. This then results in a system of equations that need to be solved for $c_i(t)$. The intrusive method cannot be used with black-box dynamics, and therefore is not considered in this work. The non-intrusive method does not require any knowledge of the propagation function. Given that we can solve the system for a specified initial condition, we use the projection property (Galerkin Projection) for approximating Eq. (4.11):

$$c_i(t) = \int u(\xi, t) \Psi_i(\xi) p(\xi) d\xi \qquad (4.13)$$

where $p(\xi)$ is the pdf of ξ.

The coefficients in the non-intrusive method can be solved using either Least Squares (LS), or a quadrature method. When LS is implemented, the initial states are randomly sampled. If the quadrature method is used, the initial states are chosen based on the node locations of the quadrature rule. The number of initial states to be used can be vastly reduced by using Compressive Sampling (CS) when using LS, and by using Sparse Grids (SG) when using the quadrature method. In this work, the quadrature method is used with a Smolyak SG (SSG) [51]. The SSG uses fewer grid points than a full tensor product quadrature as can be seen in Fig. 4.3. In the quadrature method, a grid is generated with N_q node points, where each node has a location ξ_n and weight q_n associated with them. The coefficients $c_i(t)$ are then found using the following summation:

$$c_i(t) = \sum_{n=1}^{N_q} q_n u(\boldsymbol{\xi}_n, t) \Psi_{\alpha i}(\boldsymbol{\xi}_n) \tag{4.14}$$

It should be noted that the node points are generated from a zero mean and identity covariance matrix multivariate distribution for numerical accuracy. The initial points are simply scaled to the actual mean and covariance inside the transformation function $u(\xi, t)$.

4.4 Polynomial Chaos with Gaussian Mixture Models

Reference [5] developed the GMM-PC method and this section provides a brief introduction to the method. Both PC and GMMs can represent non-Gaussian distributions with lower computational cost than that of a full blown MC simulation. However, they both have their limitations. The biggest problem with PC is the *curse of dimensionality*. The number of coefficients required with increasing order and increasing dimension for multivariate polynomials can be computed from Eq. (4.12) and seen in Fig. 4.4a. The number of nodes where computation has to be carried out also increases rapidly with increasing order and dimension as seen in Fig. 4.4b. When GMMs are used for multivariate applications, the univariate library is applied along one specified direction. Thus, the spectral direction along which the splitting is carried out can play a very important role in the quality of the resulting non-Gaussian distribution after a nonlinear transformation [30].

A combination of GMMs with PC results in a theory that can outperform each of the separate theories due to them complementing each other [5]. This chapter

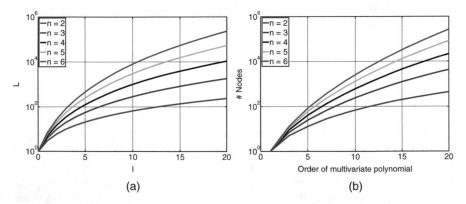

(a)   (b)

Fig. 4.4 *Curse of Dimensionality* with Polynomial Chaos. (**a**) Terms required for multivariate polynomials. (**b**) Number nodes for a Smolyak grid

uses the GMM-PC approach for orbital UQ, while the PC approach is applied to atmospheric density UQ providing the interaction between this two forms of UQ. In the GMM-PC method, each of the mixture elements is represented by a PC expansion. The GMMs splitting reduces the size of the distribution that each PC expansion has to account for. This is analogous to reducing the range for Taylor series expansion (TSE), or the Finite Element Method (FEM). Therefore, we use more simple elements (lower order PC expansions) over smaller subdomains (a GMM) to approximate the final non-Gaussian distribution over a larger domain. The benefit can be seen in a very simple test case where an initial Gaussian distribution of a state in polar coordinates is converted to Cartesian coordinates. Since this transformation is non-linear, the resulting distribution becomes non-Gaussian. The true (MC) and approximated distributions can be seen in Fig. 4.5. The PC approximation is much better than the strictly Gaussian approximation as can be seen in Fig. 4.5a, b. Combining PC and GMM, however, results in a much lower discrepancy between the MC and approximated distributions.

4.5 Global Ionosphere-Thermosphere Model

The novel GMM-PC methods implemented for the problem of SSA (orbit estimation and propagation). The major source of uncertainty in orbital propagation is the ionosphere-thermosphere environment. Therefore, this work accurately characterize the uncertainty in the ionosphere-thermosphere through the PC approach. For this purpose, this work uses a physics-based model, the Global Ionosphere-Thermosphere Model (GITM).

The Global Ionosphere-Thermosphere Model (GITM) [9] is a physics based model that solves the full Navier-Stokes equations for density, velocity, and temperature for a number of neutral and charged components. The model explicitly solves for the neutral densities of O, O_2, $N(^2D)$, $N(^2T)$, $N(^4S)$, N_2, NO, H, and He; and the ion species $O^+(^4S)$, $O^+(^2D)$, $O^+(^2P)$, O_2^+, N^+, N_2^+, NO^+, H^+, and He^+. It also contains chemistry between species of ions and neutrals, ions and electrons, and neutral and neutrals. In addition, GITM self-consistently solves for the neutral, ion, and electron temperature; the bulk horizontal neutral winds; the vertical velocity of the individual species; and the ion and electron velocities. To account for solar activity GITM can use $F_{10.7}$ as a proxy EUV spectrum measurements.

Some of the more important features of GITM are: adjustable resolution; non-uniform grid in the altitude and latitude coordinates; the dynamics equations are solved without the assumption of hydrostatic equilibrium; the advection is solved for explicitly, so the time-step in GITM is approximately 2–4 s; the chemistry is solved for explicitly, so there are no approximations of local chemical equilibrium; the ability to choose different models of electric fields and particle precipitation patterns; the ability to start from NRLMSISE-00 empirical model [6, 7] or the international reference ionosphere (IRI) model [52] solutions; and the ability to use

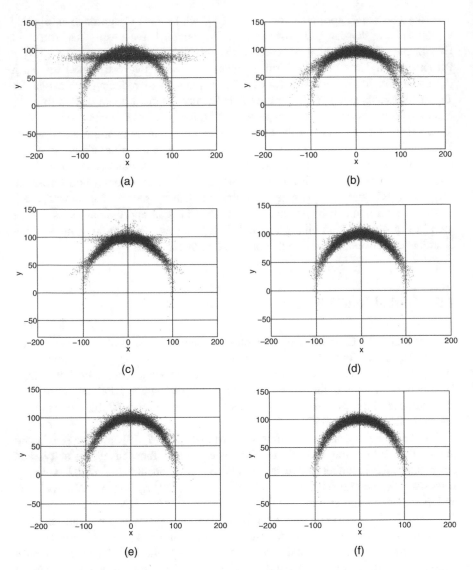

Fig. 4.5 True distribution (blue) and approximated distribution (red) after conversion from Polar coordinates to Cartesian coordinates. (**a**) Gaussian approximation using the Unscented Transform. (**b**) Polynomial Chaos approximation. (**c**) GMM approximation with 3 elements. (**d**) PC GMM approximation with 3 elements. (**e**) GMM approximation with 5 elements. (**f**) PC GMM approximation with 5 elements

a realistic (or ideal) magnetic field determined at the time of the model run. The main parameter of interest is $F_{10.7}$, which is a measure of the solar radio flux at 10.7 cm wavelength and is used as a proxy in GITM for solar activity. Figure 4.6

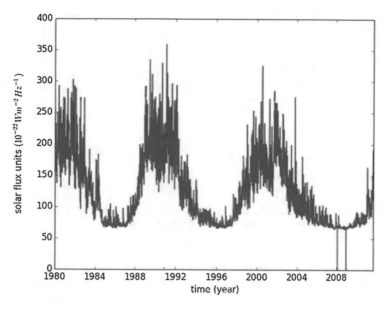

Fig. 4.6 $F_{10.7}$

shows the $F_{10.7}$ solar radio flux index from 1980 up to approximately 2011, where the 11-year solar cycle is clearly visible in the high and low activity peaks.

4.6   Results

Two simulation studies are conducted, where the first case investigates the orbital position UQ problem, while the second case investigates the atmospheric density UQ problem. The first case uses the GMM-PC approach for the orbital position UQ problem and the second case uses the PC approach (without GMM splitting) to study the atmospheric density UQ problem. The results for these two cases are discussed in this section.

4.6.1   Orbital Uncertainty Quantification

In this section, a test simulation is carried out to investigate the validity of the GMM-PC method develop by Ref. [5] for an orbital application. The non-linearity of the orbital equations combined with the presence of perturbation such as the atmosphere, make the orbital pdf non-Gaussian with increasing flight time. Thus, this test case propagates a satellite in an almost circular LEO orbit at an altitude of

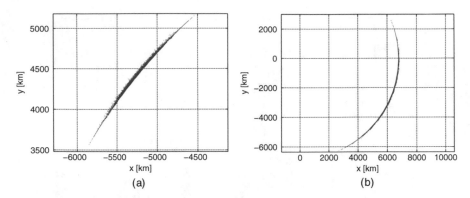

Fig. 4.7 MC reults (blue) and PC GMM results (red) for the test orbit. (**a**) Distribution after a time of flight of 1 day. (**b**) Distribution after a time of flight of 5 days

approximately 450 km, under the influence of atmospheric drag simulated using the Jacchia-Bowman 2008 (JB2008) Empirical Thermospheric Density Model [53].

A Gaussian distribution was generated about an initial condition of the orbit. A MC and a GMM-PC simulation was then carried out for 1 day (Fig. 4.7a) and for 5 days (Fig. 4.7b). The simulation was only carried out as a planar 2-dimensional trajectory for simplicity, but can easily be extended to a full 3-dimensional simulation in the future. As can be seen in the results found in Fig. 4.7, the final distribution is highly non-Gaussian. However, the GMM-PC simulation with orders of magnitude fewer runs is able to represent the final distribution well.

4.6.2   Initial Results for Atmospheric Density Forecasting

Low-Earth orbiting (LEO) satellites are heavily influenced by atmospheric drag, which is very difficult to model accurately. One of the main sources of uncertainty is input parameter uncertainty. These input parameters include F10.7, AP, and solar wind parameters. These parameters are measured constantly and these measurements are used to predict what these parameters will be in the future. The predicted values are then used in the physics-based models to predict future atmospheric conditions. Therefore, for the forward prediction of orbital uncertainty, the uncertainty of the atmospheric density due to these parameters must be characterized.

These simulation examples focus on using the PC technique for UQ of physics-based atmospheric models. Unlike the last case this case just studies the use of PC for UQ of the atmospheric density. The PC approach is used to quantify the forecast uncertainty due to uncertainty in F10.7, Ap-index (a measure of the general level of geomagnetic activity over the globe for a given day), and solar wind parameters. The PC approach is used to preform UQ on future atmospheric conditions. As part of this CA process, accurate and consistent UQ is required for the atmospheric models used.

In this section, initial results for the PC UQ applied to the GITM model is discussed. The goal here is to use a physics based atmospheric density model for obtaining accurate density forecast to be used in conjunction assessments. The GITM model has a number of input parameters that can be derived from observations but the model also needs forecasts of its inputs and these forecasted values may be highly uncertain. Therefore, we look at the uncertainty in the forecasted density based on the uncertainty of these inputs. The main input parameter that drives the main dynamics in the GITM model is F10.7 (see Fig. 4.6). Two simulation cases are considered here, the first case uses quiet solar condition model input parameters and the second case uses active solar condition model input parameters. The first case only considers F10.7 as an input parameter. While the second case considers uncertainty in $F10.7$, Interplanetary Magnetic Field (IMF) in GSM coordinates (nT) (B_x, B_y, B_z), Solar Wind (km/s) V_x, and Hemispheric power HPI. The result for this simulation are shown in Fig. 4.8. The time period for the simulations shown is Oct 21–26, 2002.

For these simulations, parameters are modeled as constant during forecast but random. In the first case, F10.7 is assumed to have a normal distribution $\mathcal{N}(165.98, 8.34^2)$. For the first case, one dimensional quadrature points are used as simulation ensembles and the PC model is fit using one dimensional Hermite polynomials. The parameters for the second case are modeled as constant during forecast but random. The random variables have the following distribution $\mathcal{N}(\mu, P)$, with $\mu = [165.98, -1.45, 0.06, -0.5, -551.79, 38.07]^T$ and the covariance given by

$$\mathbf{P} = \mathrm{diag}\left([8.33^2, 4.84^2, 4.10^2, 2.15^2, 105.1^2, 38.87^2]\right) \tag{4.15}$$

For the second case, the Smolyak Sparse Cubature are used as simulation ensembles and fit to multi-dimensional Hermite polynomials. From the figure it is clear that the uncertainty has a complex behavior across geographic locations. Moreover, the difference in the test cases highlight the fact the Solar conditions can drastically effect the model's accuracy. From the figures it is seen that during storm conditions (Fig. 4.8d) the uncertainty can be as large as 30% but only 5% during quiet times (Fig. 4.8b).

4.7 Conclusion

The combination of Polynomial Chaos (PC) expansion with Gaussian Mixture Models (GMMs) results in a framework than can efficiently capture the evolution of an initially Gaussian distribution into a highly non-Gaussian distribution through a non-linear transformation. This worked shows a Dynamic Data-Driven Applications

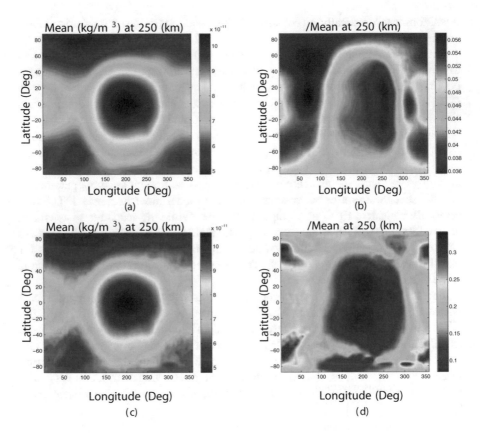

Fig. 4.8 Uncertainty quantification for atmospheric density for Oct 21–26, 2002. (**a**) Case I: Mean density. (**b**) Case I: Mean density uncertainty. (**c**) Case II: Mean density. (**d**) Case II: Mean density uncertainty

Systems (DDDAS) approach that can update UQ estimates based on observed data of changing Solar conditions. In particular, F10.7, Ap-index (geomagnetic activity), and Solar wind parameters from observational data can be used to develop a pdf of expected atmospheric drag. Using an initial GMM reduces the domain covered by the PC and thus, lower order polynomials can be used to get accurate results. Increasing the order of the polynomials increases the computational load in an exponential manner, while increasing the number of elements may result in a near linear increase in the computational load. Increasing the polynomial order only marginally increases the accuracy after a certain order.

This work applies the GMM-PC approach to the orbital Uncertainty Quantification (UQ) problem. It was shown that the GMM-PC approach outperformed the PC approach for the cases considered of Solar conditions. Additionally, the PC approach was applied to physics-based atmospheric models. It was shown that the uncertainty in atmospheric density models have a complex behavior across geographic locations. The test cases shown in this work highlight the fact the Solar conditions can drastically effect the model accuracy. The test cases showed that during Solar storm conditions the uncertainty can be as large as 30% but only 5% during quiet times. This work provides initial results of the GMM-PC applied to orbital propagation of uncertainty and the PC approach applied to atmospheric density.

Acknowledgments The first author wish to acknowledge support of this work by the Air Force's Office of Scientic Research under Contract Number FA9550-18-1-0149 issued by Erik P. Blasch.

References

1. R. Oliva, E. Blasch, R. Ogan, Applying aerospace technologies to current issues using systems engineering: 3rd AESS chapter summit. IEEE Aerosp. Electron. Syst. Mag. **28**(2), 34–41 (2013)
2. D.S. Bernstein, A. Ridley, J. Cutler, A. Cohn, Transformative advances in DDDAS with application to space weather monitoring. Technical report, Department of Aerospace Engineering, University of Michigan, Ann Arbor, 2015
3. H. Chen, G. Chen, E. Blasch, K. Pham, Comparison of several space target tracking filters. Proc. SPIE **7330**, 73300I (2009)
4. N. Weiner, The homogeneous chaos. Am. J. Math. **60**(4), 897–936 (1938)
5. V. Vittaldev, R.P. Russell, R. Linares, Spacecraft uncertainty propagation using gaussian mixture models and polynomial chaos expansions. J. Guid. Control. Dyn. **39**, 2615–2626 (2016)
6. A. Hedin, A revised thermospheric model based on mass spectrometer and incoherent scatter data: Msis-83. J. Geophys. Res. **88**, 10170–10188 (1983)
7. J. Picone, A. Hedin, D. Drob, A. Aikin, NRLMSISE-00 empirical model of the atmosphere: statistical comparisons and scientific issues. J. Geophys. Res. **107**(A12), 1468 (2002)
8. M.F. Storz, B.R. Bowman, M.J.I. Branson, S.J. Casali, W.K. Tobiska, High accuracy satellite drag model (HASDM). Adv. Space Res. **36**(12), 2497–2505 (2005)
9. A. Ridley, Y. Deng, G. Toth, The global ionosphere–thermosphere model. J. Atmos. Sol.-Terr. Phys. **68**, 839–864 (2006)
10. R. Bellmam, *Dynamic Programming* (Princeton University Press, Princeton, 1957)
11. C. Sabol, C. Binz, A. Segerman, K. Roe, P.W. Schumacher, Probability of collision with special perturbations dynamics using the monte carlo method, paper AAS 11-435, in *AAS/AIAA Astrodynamics Specialist Conference*, Girdwood, 31 Jul–4 Aug 2011
12. R.W. Ghrist, D. Plakalovic, Impact of non-gaussian error volumes on conjunction assessment risk analysis, paper AIAA 2012-4965, in *AIAA/AAS Astrodynamics Specialist Conference*, Minneapolis, 13–16 Aug, 2012
13. N. Arora, V. Vittaldev, R.P. Russell, Parallel computation of trajectories using graphics processing units and interpolated gravity models. J. Guid. Control. Dyn. **38**, 1345–1355 (2015). Accepted for Publication
14. H. Shen, V. Vittaldev, C.D. Karlgaard, R.P. Russell, E. Pellegrini, Parallelized sigma point and particle filters for navigation problems, paper AAS 13-034, in *36th Annual AAS Guidance and Control Conference*, 1–6 Feb, Breckenridge, 2013
15. N. Nakhjiri, B.F. Villac, An algorithm for trajectory propagation and uncertainty mapping on GPU, paper AAS 13-376, in *23rd AAS/AIAA Space Flight Mechanics Meeting*, Kauai, 2013
16. S.-Z. Ueng, M. Lathara, S.S. Baghsorkhi, W.-M. W. Hwu, *Languages and Compilers for Parallel Computing, ch. CUDA-Lite: Reducing GPU Programming Complexity* (Springer, Berlin/Heidelberg, 2008), pp. 1–15

17. A.B. Poore, Propagation of uncertainty in support of SSA missions, in *25th AAS/AIAA Space Flight Mechanics Meeting*, Williamsburg, 2015
18. D.L. Alspach, H.W. Sorenson, Nonlinear Bayesian estimation using gaussian sum approximations. IEEE Trans. Autom. Control **17**(4), 439–448 (1972)
19. R.S. Park, D.J. Scheeres, Nonlinear mapping of gaussian statistics: theory and applications to spacecraft trajectory design. J. Guid. Control. Dyn. **29**(6), 1367–1375 (2006)
20. S. Julier, J.K. Uhlmann, Unscented filtering and nonlinear estimation. Proc. IEEE **92**, 401–402 (2004)
21. M. Norgaard, N.K. Poulsen, O. Ravn, New developments in state estimation for nonlinear systems. Automatica **36**(11), 1627–1638 (2000)
22. I. Arasaratnam, S. Haykin, Cubature Kalman filters. IEEE Trans. Autom. Control **54**(6), 1254–1269 (2009)
23. D.F. Crouse, On measurement-based light-time corrections for bistatic orbital debris tracking. IEEE Trans. Aerosp. Electron. Syst. **51**(3), 2502–2518 (2015)
24. B. Jia, K.D. Pham, E. Blasch, D. Shen, Z. Wang, G. Chen, Cooperative space object tracking using space-based optical sensors via consensus-based filters. IEEE Trans. Aerosp. Electron. Syst. **52**(4), 1908–1936 (2016)
25. K.J. DeMars, R.H. Bishop, M.K. Jah, Entropy-based approach for uncertainty propagation of nonlinear dynamical systems. J. Guid. Control. Dyn. **36**(4), 1047–1057 (2013)
26. K. Vishwajeet, P. Singla, M. Jah, Nonlinear uncertainty propagation for perturbed two-body orbits. J. Guid. Control. Dyn. **37**(5), 1415–1425 (2014)
27. J.T. Horwood, N.D. Aragon, A.B. Poore, Gaussian sum filters for space surveillance: theory and simulations. J. Guid. Control. Dyn. **34**(6), 1839–1851 (2011)
28. K.J. DeMars, M.K. Jah, A probabilistic approach to initial orbit determination via gaussian mixture models. J. Guid. Control. Dyn. **36**(5), 1324–1335 (2013)
29. K.J. DeMars, Y. Cheng, M.K. Jah, Collision probability with Gaussian mixture orbit uncertainty. J. Guid. Control. Dyn. **37**(3), 979–985 (2014)
30. V. Vittaldev, R.P. Russell, Collision probability for resident space objects using Gaussian mixture models, paper AAS 13-351, in *23rd AAS/AIAA Spaceflight Mechanics Meeting*, Kauai, 2013
31. D. Xiu, G.E. Karniadakis, The wiener-askey polynomial chaos for stochastic differential equations. SIAM J. Sci. Comput. **24**, 619–644 (2002)
32. S. Oladyshkin, W. Nowak, Data-driven uncertainty quantification using the arbitrary polynomial chaos expansion. Reliab. Eng. Syst. Saf. **106**, 179–190 (2012)
33. D.M. Luchtenburga, S.L. Bruntonc, C.W. Rowleyb, Long-time uncertainty propagation using generalized polynomial chaos and flow map composition. J. Comput. Phys. **274**, 783–802 (2014)
34. X. Li, P.B. Nair, Z. Zhang, L. Gao, C. Gao, Aircraft robust trajectory optimization using nonintrusive polynomial chaos. J. Aircr. **51**(5), 1592–1603 (2014)
35. L. Mathelin, M.Y. Hussaini, T.A. Zang, Stochastic approaches to uncertainty quantification in CFD simulations. Numer. Algorithms **38**(1–3), 209–236 (2005)
36. M. Dodson, G.T. Parks, Robust aerodynamic design optimization using polynomial chaos. J. Aircr. **46**(2), 635–646 (2009)
37. B.A. Jones, A. Doostan, G.H. Born, Nonlinear propagation of orbit uncertainty using nonintrusive polynomial chaos. J. Guid. Control. Dyn. **36**(2), 415–425 (2013)
38. V. Vittaldev, R. Russell, R. Linares, Spacecraft uncertainty propagation using gaussian mixture models and polynomial chaos expansions. J. Guid. Control Dyn. **39**(12), 2615–2626 (2016)
39. B.A. Jones, A. Doostan, Satellite collision probability estimation using polynomial chaos. Adv. Space Res. **52**(11), 1860–1875 (2013)
40. B.A. Jones, N. Parrish, A. Doostan, Postmaneuver collision probability estimation using sparse polynomial chaos expansions. J. Guid. Control. Dyn. **38**(8), 1425–1437 (2015)
41. G. Terejanu, P. Singla, T. Singh, P.D. Scott, Uncertainty propagation for nonlinear dynamic systems using gaussian mixture models. J. Guid. Control. Dyn. **31**(6), 1623–1633 (2008)

42. M.F. Huber, T. Bailey, H. Durrant-Whyte, U.D. Hanebeck, On entropy approximation for gaussian mixture random vectors, in *IEEE International Conference on Multisensor Fusion and Integration for Intelligent Systems (MFI 2008)*, 2008, pp. 181–188

43. V. Vittaldev, R.P. Russell, Multidirectional Gaussian mixtrure models for nonlinear uncertainty propagation. CMES **111**(1), 83–117 (2016)

44. V. Vittaldev, R.P. Russell, Uncertainty propagation using gaussian mixture models. In *SIAM Conference on Uncertainty Quatification*, (Savannah, GA 2014)

45. J.M. Aristoff, J.T. Horwood, T. Singh, A.B. Poore, Nonlinear uncertainty propagation in orbital elements and transformation to cartesian space without loss of realism, in *AIAA/AAS Astrodynamics Specialist Conference*, San Diego, Aug 4–Aug 7, 2014

46. V. Vittaldev, R.P. Russell, Collision probability using multidirectional gaussian mixture models, in *25th AAS/AIAA Space Flight Mechanics Meeting*, Williamsburg, 2015

47. R. Madankan, P. Singla, T. Singh, P.D. Scott, Polynomial-chaos-based Bayesian approach for state and parameter estimations. J. Guid. Control. Dyn. **36**(4), 1058–1074 (2013)

48. S. Hosder, R.W. Walter, R. Perez, A non-intrusive polynomial chaos method for uncertainty propagation in CFD simulations, in *44th AIAA Aerospace Sciences Meeting and Exhibit*, Reno, 2006

49. S. Hosder, R.W. Walter, Non-intrusive polynomial chaos methods for uncertainty quantification in fluid dynamics, in *48th AIAA Aerospace Sciences Meeting Including the New Horizons Forum and Aerospace Exposition*, Orlando, 2010

50. D. Xiu, G.E. Karniadakis, The wiener–askey polynomial chaos for stochastic differential equations. SIAM J. Sci. Comput. **24**(2), 619–644 (2002)

51. S.A. Smolyak, Quadrature and interpolation formulas for tensor products of certain classes of functions. Doklady Akademii nauk SSSR, **1**(4), 240–243 (1963)

52. K. Rawer, D. Bilitza, S. Ramakrishnan, Goals and status of the international reference ionosphere. Rev. Geophys. **16**, 177 (1978)

53. B.R. Bowman, W.K. Tobiska, F.A. Marcos, C.Y. Huang, C.S. Lin, W.J. Burke, A new empirical thermospheric density model jb2008 using new solar and geomagnetic indices, AIAA 2008–6483, in *AIAA/AAS Astrodynamics Specialist Conference*, Honolulu, 2008

Part II
Signals-Aware: Process Monitoring

Chapter 5
Towards Learning Spatio-Temporal Data Stream Relationships for Failure Detection in Avionics

Sida Chen, Shigeru Imai, Wennan Zhu, and Carlos A. Varela

Abstract Spatio-temporal data streams are often related in complex ways, for example, while the airspeed that an aircraft attains in cruise phase depends on the weight it carries, it also depends on many other factors. Some of these factors are controllable such as engine inputs or the airframe's angle of attack, while others contextual, such as air density, or turbulence. It is therefore critical to develop failure models that can help recognize errors in the data, such as an incorrect fuel quantity, a malfunctioning pitot-static system, or other abnormal flight conditions. In this paper, we extend our PILOTS programming language [1] to support machine learning techniques that will help data scientists: (1) create parameterized failure models from data and (2) continuously train a statistical model as new evidence (data) arrives. The linear regression approach learns parameters of a linear model to minimize least squares error for given training data. The Bayesian approach classifies operating modes according to supervised offline training and can discover new statistically significant modes online. As shown in Tuninter 1153 simulation result, dynamic Bayes classifier finds discrete error states on the fly while the error signatures approach requires every error state predefined. Using synthetic data, we compare the accuracy, response time, and adaptability of these machine learning techniques. Future dynamic data driven applications systems (DDDAS) using machine learning can identify complex dynamic data-driven failure models, which will in turn enable more accurate flight planning and control for emergency conditions.

Keywords Data streaming · Spatio-temporal data · Declarative programming · Linear regression · Bayesian classification and learning

S. Chen (✉) · S. Imai · W. Zhu · C. A. Varela
Rensselaer Polytechnic Institute, Troy, NY, USA
e-mail: chens15@rpi.edu; imais@rpi.edu; zhuw5@rpi.edu; cvarela@cs.rpi.edu

© The Author(s), under exclusive license to Springer Nature Switzerland AG 2022
E. P. Blasch et al. (eds.), *Handbook of Dynamic Data Driven Applications Systems*,
https://doi.org/10.1007/978-3-030-74568-4_5

5.1   Introduction

Detecting and recognizing patterns from streaming data generated by multiple aircraft sensors has become an important research area for flight safety. In the Air France flight 447 accident in 2009, iced pitot tubes caused an error in air speed data, and the pilots failed to react correctly, leading to crash [2]. While there have been advances in information fusion [3] and virtual modeling [4] for avionics control and user warnings, there is still a need for further research in methods that allow for fault detection and recovery techniques to be easily realized and implemented with minimal risk of software errors. Using redundant information provided by different sensors, this tragedy might have been avoided by using a Dynamic Data-Driven Applications Systems (DDDAS) [5] approach based information from the avionics models and sensor measurements. DDDAS can expand the flight safety envelope of automation and support pilots with real-time decision making.

In some situations, detecting and recovering from sensor data errors is non-trivial, even for human experts and flight assistant systems. In the Tuninter 1153 flight accident in 2005, the fuel quantity indicator of a different aircraft model was installed, causing the instrument to display an incorrect amount of fuel, which led to fuel exhaustion of the aircraft [6]. This accident might have been avoided if the weight error could be detected by checking the relationship between lift and weight during the flight cruise phase. Lift depends on airspeed, air density, wing surface area, and coefficient of lift. The coefficient of lift itself depends on the angle of attack and this relationship will change with different aircraft types. Understanding such complex relationships from multiple sensor data streams is critical to accurately detecting sensor faults. In this chapter, we propose using machine learning techniques to estimate parameterized models of aircraft sensor data relationships, and statistically determine aircraft operating modes.

Using offline training parameters and known relationships and models among redundant streaming data from prior research, we have been able to detect and correct for sensor data errors using actual flight accident data [7, 8]. However, aircraft models might change due to significant aircraft emergencies, e.g. damage to a wing or loss of engines. To get more accurate results, an online system should be able to incrementally update model parameters, and detect new modes that may not be in the offline training data set. The naïve Bayes classifier is a suitable method for offline training and incremental learning, but needs to be extended to detect previously unknown modes.

The Programming Language for spatiO-Temporal data Streaming applications (PILOTS) was developed for run-time system fault detection and correction in data streams, which is especially important for flight safety. PILOTS has evolved gradually to date. The PILOTS programming language was first designed in 2012 and proposed the concept of error signatures [9]. Next, PILOTS included a compiler and a runtime system [1] and then added error detection and correction support to the compiler and the runtime [10]. Finally, PILOTS was applied to data streams obtained from actual accidents, Air France 447 [2] and Tuninter

1153 [6], and confirmed the effectiveness of its error detection and correction capabilities [7, 8, 11].

In this chapter, we extend PILOTS to support machine learning techniques including linear regression for linear models, and Bayesian classification and learning for dynamic models. Synthetic data streams are used to verify and compare these approaches. Using the X-Plane flight simulator [12], flight sensor data is generated to train the relationship between angle of attack and coefficient of lift during cruise phase. With the training results and the relationship between lift and weight during cruise phase, PILOTS is able to detect and correct for weight data errors using error functions and error signatures. The model is constructed using a dynamic Bayes classifier for offline training and incremental online learning of different modes, which also detects new modes as the streaming data switches to an unknown pattern.

The rest of the chapter is organized as follows. Section 5.2 describes error signature-based error detection and correction methods within the PILOTS programming language and the architecture of its runtime system. Section 5.3 discusses the design and implementation of the machine learning component in PILOTS. Section 5.4 describes an instance of the machine learning component to estimate parameters for a linear model using regression. Section 5.5 introduces the dynamic Bayesian classification and online learning. Section 5.6 presents the methods and results of the machine learning techniques using a case study of airplane weight error detection and correction. Section 5.7 identifies related work. Finally we briefly describe future research directions and conclude the paper in Sect. 5.8.

5.2 Background

PILOTS[1] is a highly-declarative programming language that has been applied to both the Air France 447 [2] and the Tuninter 1153 [6] accidents data, showing that PILOTS was able to successfully detect the data errors in both cases [11], and provide a potential method to warn of the error in the case of Air France 447 [8].

5.2.1 Error Detection and Correction Methods

Error functions are used to detect possible faults among redundant input stream data. An error function should have the zero value if there is no error in the input data, such as when the whole system is working in the normal mode.

---

[1]All sample programs in this paper use v.0.3.2. PILOTS v.0.3.2 is available at http://wcl.cs.rpi.edu/pilots.

For example, in the cruise phases of a flight, the lift equals the weight of the airplane. The lift can also be calculated using other input data, including airframe's angle of attack, air density, temperature, pressure and air speed. In this case, an error function could simply be defined as:

$$e(lift, weight) = lift - weight \qquad (5.1)$$

The lift in Eq. 5.1 is calculated using sensor input data. In the normal cruise phase mode, the value of Eq. 5.1 should be zero. If there is an error in the weight indicator, and the input weight data is lower than the real weight, Eq. 5.1 should be greater than zero. Similarly, if the input weight data is higher than the real weight, Eq. 5.1 should be smaller than zero. Thus, the validity of the input data could be determined from the value of the error function.

The values of input data are assumed to be sampled periodically from corresponding spatio-temporal data streams. Thus, an error function e changes its value as time proceeds and can be represented as $e(t)$.

Error signatures An *error signature* is a constrained mathematical function pattern that is used to capture the characteristics of an error function $e(t)$. Using a vector of constants $\bar{K} = \langle k_1, \ldots, k_m \rangle$, a function $f(t, \bar{K})$, and a set of constraint predicates $\bar{P} = \{p_1(\bar{K}), \ldots, p_l(\bar{K})\}$, where the error signature $S(\bar{K}, f(t, \bar{K}), \bar{P}(\bar{K}))$ is defined as follows:

$$S(f(t, \bar{K}), \bar{P}(\bar{K})) \triangleq \{ f \mid p_1(\bar{K}) \wedge \cdots \wedge p_l(\bar{K}) \}. \qquad (5.2)$$

Mode likelihood vectors Given a vector of error signatures $\langle S_0, \ldots, S_n \rangle$, we calculate $\delta_i(S_i, t)$, the distance between the measured error function $e(t)$ and each error signature S_i by:

$$\delta_i(S_i, t) = \min_{g(t) \in S_i} \int_{t-\omega}^{t} |e(t) - g(t)| dt. \qquad (5.3)$$

where ω is the window size. Note that our convention is to capture "normal" conditions as signature S_0. The smaller the distance δ_i, the closer the raw data is to the theoretical signature S_i. *Mode likelihood vector* is defined as $L(t) = \langle l_0(t), l_1(t), \ldots, l_n(t) \rangle$ where each $l_i(t)$ is designed as:

$$l_i(t) = \begin{cases} 1, & \text{if } \delta_i(t) = 0 \\ \frac{\min\{\delta_0(t), \ldots, \delta_n(t)\}}{\delta_i(t)}, & \text{otherwise.} \end{cases} \qquad (5.4)$$

Mode estimation Using the mode likelihood vector, the final mode output is estimated as follows. Observe that for each $l_i \in L, 0 < l_i \leq 1$ where l_i represents the ratio of the likelihood of signature S_i being matched with respect to the likelihood of the best signature.

Because of the formulation of $L(t)$, the largest element l_j will always be equal to 1. Given a threshold $\tau \in (0, 1)$, the system checks for one likely candidate l_j that is sufficiently more likely than its successor l_k by ensuring that $l_k \leq \tau$. Thus, element j is the most likely mode by choosing the error signature S_j. If $j = 0$ then the system is in *normal mode*. If $l_k > \tau$, then regardless of the value of k, *unknown error* mode (-1) is assumed.

Error correction Whether or not a known error mode i is recoverable is application and problem dependent. If there is a mathematical relationship between an erroneous value and other independently measured values, the erroneous value can be replaced by a new value estimated from the other independently measured values.

5.2.2   Spatio-Temporal Data Stream Processing System

Figure 5.1 shows the architecture of the PILOTS runtime system, which implements the error detection and correction methods as described in Sect. 5.2.1. It consists of three parts: the *Data Selection*, the *Error Analyzer*, and the *Application Model* modules. The Application Model obtains homogeneous data streams $(d'_1, d'_2, \ldots, d'_N)$ from the Data Selection module, and then it generates outputs $(o_1, o_2, \ldots, o_M)$ and data errors $(e_1, e_2, \ldots, e_L)$. The Data Selection module takes heterogeneous incoming data streams $(d_1, d_2, \ldots, d_N)$ as inputs. Since this runtime is assumed to be working on moving objects, the Data Selection module is aware of the current

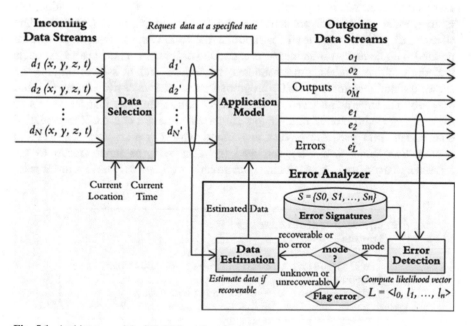

Fig. 5.1 Architecture of the PILOTS runtime system

location and time. Thus, it returns appropriate values to the Application Model by
selecting or interpolating data in time and location, depending on the data selection
method specified in the PILOTS program. The Error Analyzer collects the latest
ω error values from the Application Model and keeps analyzing errors based on
the error signatures. If it detects a recoverable error, then it replaces an erroneous
input with the estimated one by applying a corresponding estimation equation. The
Application Model computes the outputs based on the estimated inputs produced by
the Error Analyzer.

5.3 Design of Machine Learning Component

The PILOTS system can detect and correct for errors in data streams using models
that define the relations between data streams, for example the relationship between
wind speed, air speed, and ground speed. For non-trivial relations or relations with
unknown parameters, we introduce prediction functionality using machine learning
for PILOTS.

5.3.1 Prediction in PILOTS Programming Language

To support prediction in the PILOTS declarative language, a new data selection method `predict` is defined in addition to `closest`, `euclidean`, and
`interpolate`. Method predict $(model, d'_{i_1}, d'_{i_2}, \cdots, d'_{i_n})$ takes the identifier
of the model as used for prediction as the first argument, $model$, and the data
streams, $d'_{i_1}, d'_{i_2}, \cdots, d'_{i_n}$, used for input as the following arguments. `predict`
method is implemented as an interface, accepting different machine learning models
including online models, offline models, regressors, and classifiers. Figure 5.2
shows a simple example PILOTS program `PredictionTest`, where $a(t)$ and
$b(t)$ are data streams retrieved by `closest` method meaning that the values of
$a(t)$ and $b(t)$ with closest timestamp t to current time are chosen. The predicted
data stream $c(t)$ uses the prediction method with `linear_regression` as
a predictive model with $a(t)$, retrieved by `closest`, as input stream to the
`linear_regression`. Assuming data streams $a(t)$ and $b(t)$ have a linear rela-

```
program PredictionTest;
  inputs
    a,b (t) using closest (t);
    c (t) using predict(linear_regression, a);
  outputs
    difference: b - c at every 1 sec;
end
```

Fig. 5.2 A simple PILOTS program example outputting error

tionship, which is captured by the linear_regression, $c(t)$ is the prediction result of the linear_regression from $a(t)$. The outputs section compares $c(t)$ with $b(t)$ to produce pairwise difference between actual data (stream b) and output of the linear_regression (stream c).

5.3.2   Prediction in PILOTS Runtime

Figure 5.3 shows the updated PILOTS runtime system with the addition of machine learning of models from data. To support the new prediction feature in PILOTS language syntax, Data Selection is altered to support communication to outside components through a socket. When Application Model requests p from Data Selection module, it first computes the input vector $\mathbf{x} = [d'_{i_1} d'_{i_2} \cdots d'_{i_n}]^T$ using data selection method defined for each d_i, and then sends *model* along with input vector $\mathbf{x}$ to the Learning Engine where the prediction is made by requested *model* using input vector $\mathbf{x}$. The online Learning Engine updates the dynamic online learning model for every prediction made and gives prediction result p back to the Data Selection component, which sends the prediction result to the Application Model as requested. The offline Learning Engine trains learning models using three major parts: (1) *training definition* including learning hypothesis, learning algorithm configuration, preprocessing methods and data file configuration; (2) *learning algorithms* such as least squares, Bayesian classifier or others; (3) *training data*, which refers to data stored in files. The other parts of the PILOTS runtime system remain the same (see Fig. 5.1) to maintain backward compatibility.

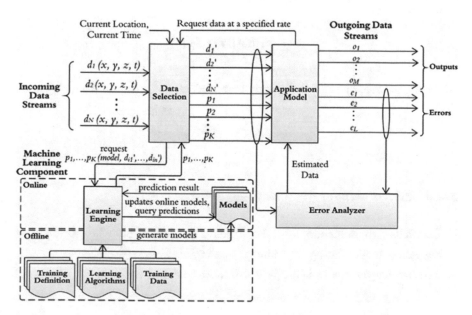

Fig. 5.3 The updated PILOTS runtime architecture with machine learning components

5.4 Data-Driven Learning of Linear Models

Linear regression is a well-studied and powerful tool for estimating inter-variable relations in linear models. The equation for a linear regression model is

$$y = X\beta + \epsilon$$

where

$$y = \begin{pmatrix} y_1 \\ y_2 \\ \vdots \\ y_n \end{pmatrix}, X = \begin{pmatrix} x_{11} & \cdots & x_{1m} \\ x_{21} & \cdots & x_{2m} \\ \vdots & \ddots & \vdots \\ x_{n1} & \cdots & x_{nm} \end{pmatrix}, \beta = \begin{pmatrix} \beta_1 \\ \beta_2 \\ \vdots \\ \beta_m \end{pmatrix}, \epsilon = \begin{pmatrix} \epsilon_1 \\ \epsilon_2 \\ \vdots \\ \epsilon_n \end{pmatrix}$$

where y_i is a dependent variable; x_{ij} is an independent variable; β_i is the regression coefficient; and ϵ_i is an error term.

5.4.1 Learning Algorithm

There are multiple methods to solve linear models. One of the learning algorithms implemented in the PILOTS system is ordinary least squares, of which the target is minimizing the square of the Euclidean norm $||y - X\beta||^2$ by finding the best coefficient vector $\hat{\beta}$

$$\hat{\beta} = \arg\min_{\beta} ||y - X\beta||^2$$

Assuming the columns in X are linearly independent, $\hat{\beta}$ is retrieved from the closed form

$$\hat{\beta} = (X^T X)^{-1} X^T y$$

5.4.2 Linear Model Accuracy

- **Coefficient of determination**: This metric is used to evaluate goodness of regression model fitting on training set $R^2 = 1 - \frac{\sum_i (y_i - \hat{y}_i)^2}{\sum_i (y_i - \bar{y})^2}$ where y_i is measured/dependent variable, $\hat{y}_i$ is estimated variable, and $\bar{y}$ is the average of all y_i.

- **Root Mean Squared Error**: This metric is used to evaluate the amount of error produced by prediction on average $RMSE = \sqrt{\frac{1}{n} \sum_{i=1}^{n} (y_i - \hat{f}(x_i))^2}$ where $\hat{f}$ is an estimator, x_i is an independent variable vector $[x_{i1} \; x_{i2} \; \cdots \; x_{im}]^T$.

5.5 Statistical Learning of Dynamic Models

Naïve Bayes classifiers [13, 14] are commonly used in supervised training and classification. For continuous data, if the values of samples in each class are assumed to be normally distributed, the classifiers are called Gaussian naïve Bayes classifiers [15]. In the training phase, tagged samples of different classes are processed to train the parameters of the classifier. The parameters include the mean value, standard variance, and prior probability of each class. In the testing phase, the trained Naive Bayes classifier decides the class of untagged input samples.

One limitation of the traditional naïve Bayes classifier is that the input samples in the testing phase will only be classified into classes that appeared in the training phase. If a sample of a previously unknown class appears, it will be classified into one of the known classes, even if the probability that it belongs to that class is very low. However, with dynamic stream data, new modes not in the training set could occur in some complex situations. For example, if a Bayes classifier is trained to recognize the "normal weight" and "underweight" modes of the weight indicator on an airplane during flights, and a previously unknown mode "overweight" appears in testing phase, the classifier will not be able to detect this new mode, but will classify the samples to "normal weight" or "underweight" based on the value and prior probability of the modes.

To tackle this limitation of the naïve Bayes classifier, we extend it into a dynamic Bayes classifier that has two phases: (1) *Offline*: Supervised learning, which is the same as Gaussian naïve Bayes classifiers. (2) *Online*: Unsupervised dynamic incremental learning, that classifies samples in known modes, updates parameters of the model, and create new modes for samples in previously unknown modes. Because PILOTS focuses on processing stream data during flights and deciding the normal or error operational modes of an airplane, the words "mode" and "class" are used interchangeably and have the same meaning in this paper.

5.5.1 Offline Supervised Learning

5.5.1.1 Gaussian Naïve Bayes Classifiers

In a Gaussian naïve Bayes classifier [15], each input sample X is described by a feature vector $(x_1, \ldots, x_n)$, and each sample is classified into a target class $y \in \{y_1, \ldots, y_m\}$. In this chapter, we consider samples of only one feature x, but the results can be generalized to n features. By Bayes' theorem, the conditional probability $P(y|x)$ is:

$$P(y|x) = \frac{P(y)P(x|y)}{P(x)} \tag{5.5}$$

As the samples in each feature are assumed to be normally distributed, $P(x|y)$ is calculated by:

$$P(x|y) = \frac{1}{\sqrt{2\pi\sigma_y^2}} e^{-\frac{(x-\mu_y)^2}{2\sigma_y^2}} \tag{5.6}$$

where μ_y is the mean of the values in x associated with class y, and σ_y is the standard deviation of the values in x associated with class y.

The corresponding classifier $\hat{y}$ is:

$$\hat{y} = \arg\max P(y|x) \tag{5.7}$$

Because $P(x)$ is the same for each class, $\hat{y}$ is:

$$\hat{y} = \arg\max P(y|x) = \arg\max P(y)P(x|y) \tag{5.8}$$

5.5.1.2 Offline Learning Phase

In the offline supervised learning phase, input data tagged with mode labels are processed by a Gaussian naïve Bayes classifier. The mean value μ_y, standard deviation σ_y, and the prior probability $P(y)$ of each mode y, are calculated by the classifier, as in Fig. 5.4.

5.5.2 Dynamic Online Unsupervised Learning

5.5.2.1 Major and Minor Modes

To support dynamically changing modes during the online learning phase, the concepts of *major* and *minor* modes are introduced. Major modes represent statistically significant patterns and are generated during offline supervised learning phase or converted from Minor modes during online learning phase. Minor modes represent noise in data stream, and are created with unique mode identity (ID) during online learning phase when a new sample isn't in $\mu \pm 2\sigma$ of any existing modes. A minor mode can be converted into major mode, if the number of samples in a minor mode exceeds certain threshold, which is used to diminish impact of noise and distinguish actual patterns.

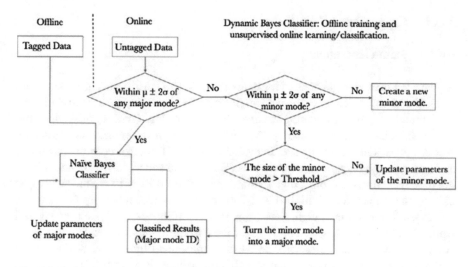

Fig. 5.4 Online classification and incremental learning using dynamic Bayes classifier

5.5.2.2 Online Learning Phase

The process of dynamic online unsupervised learning is shown in Fig. 5.4. The parameters of initial major modes are from the training results of the offline training phase. As untagged samples are processed, if the value is within $\mu \pm 2\sigma$ of any major mode, the sample will be classified by naive Bayes classifier, and the parameters are incrementally updated. If the value is not within $\mu + 2\sigma$ of any major mode, but is within $\mu \pm 2\sigma$ of a minor mode, it will be classified into the closest minor mode, and the parameters of minor modes are updated accordingly. Finally, if the value of the sample is not within $\mu \pm 2\sigma$ of any major or minor mode, a new minor mode will be created for this sample. σ of the new minor mode is initially set as the average σ of the existing major modes. When the size of the minor mode is greater than a threshold, we start to calculate and use the real σ of the minor mode. The reason is that the σ might be biased if the number of samples is too small. Each time when the parameters of a minor mode are updated, if the number of samples exceeds a certain threshold, it will be upgraded into a major mode.

5.6 Case Study: Airplane Weight Estimation

To help prevent accidents caused by fuel quantity indicator errors such as the Tuninter 1153 flight accident, we use the X-Plane flight simulator to generate flight sensor data and simulate airplane weight error scenarios. With the synthetic data, machine learning techniques are applied to infer airplane model parameters from data, airplane weight error detection and actual weight estimation.

5.6.1   Experimental Settings

5.6.1.1   Data Generation

X-Plane 9.7 is used to generate flying data of ATR72-500 in different altitudes, gross weights and power settings. The data is split by selecting 3 flights' 25 cruise phases, 1251 minutes in total, as training set, and a 20-minutes flight with 4 cruise phases as testing set. The model is trained by 25 cruise phases in the training set and tested by 4 cruise phases in the testing set. To evaluate the PILOTS error detection accuracy and effectiveness on various error ranges of overweight and underweight conditions, the data is modified as following: To simulate stable overweight condition, weight data in the range from 1 to 100 and 750 to 800 s is multiplied by 0.9; for the underweight condition, weight data from 1025 to 1099 s is multiplied by 1.1 and from 390 to 490 s is multiplied by 1.05; for the unstable overweight and underweight conditions, weight data from 570 to 648 s is multiplied by normal deviates with mean at 1 and standard deviation at 0.1, and weight data from 291 to 377 s is multiplied with uniformly distributed random variables from uniform with range from 0.9 to 1.1. The cruise phases of testing set lie between 5 to 164, 230 to 395, 470 to 688 and 780 to 1108 s. The weight data is visualized as "measured" in Fig. 5.10.

5.6.1.2   Implementation and Evaluation of Learning Algorithms

For learning algorithms, the Sci-Kit package is used for the implementation of least squares algorithm and evaluation of the trained models.

5.6.2   Aerodynamic Model Parameter Estimation by Linear Regression

Synthetic data with simple relationships is used to verify the integration of machine learning approaches into PILOTS. In this example, simulated ATR-72 500 airplane data is used for PILOTS to detect weight error and generate estimations of actual weight in the data streams. The relation between coefficient of lift and angle of attack is investigated and under certain assumptions about known variables, the estimation of weight from angle of attack, ambient temperature, ambient pressure and true air speed is made possible using linear regression by the PILOTS learning component.

5.6.2.1 Assumption

To simulate and test linear regression implemented in PILOTS machine learning component, we assume certain known variables. The following variables are assumed to be correctly measured and known: gross weight W, ambient pressure p, true airspeed v, wing surface area S, special gas constant for dry air R', and ambient temperature T.

5.6.2.2 Linear Regression Model

In cruise phase, when yaw, roll angles are close to zero and pitch is small, we assume $L = W$, in which L is total lift and W is gross weight. Based on the assumption, PILOTS estimates W by the lift equation:

$$W = L = \frac{1}{2}v^2 S\rho C_l, \tag{5.9}$$

where ρ is air density and C_l is coefficient of lift. From the ideal gas law, $\rho = \frac{p}{R'T}$ so replace ρ with $\frac{p}{R'T}$ in Eq. 5.9 to get:

$$W = \frac{pv^2 S C_l}{2R'T} \tag{5.10}$$

and by transforming Eq. 5.10, C_l, coefficient of lift could be represented by:

$$C_l = \frac{2W R'T}{pv^2 S}. \tag{5.11}$$

Generally C_l depends on the shape of airfoil and the shape of an aircraft. To roughly estimate C_l, the complex physical model is simplified using Thin-Airfoil theory, which predicts a linear relationship [16] between coefficient of lift, C_l, and the angle of attack, α, for low values of α, as shown in Fig. 5.5 between dashed vertical lines. This relationship can be expressed as:

$$C_l = \beta_1 \alpha + \beta_2 + \epsilon \tag{5.12}$$

where ϵ is noise and α is known while β_1 and β_2 are distinct values for different aircrafts. A linear model could be formulated as the following:

$$y = X\beta + \epsilon \tag{5.13}$$

$$y = \begin{pmatrix} C_{l_1} \\ C_{l_2} \\ \vdots \\ C_{l_n} \end{pmatrix}, \quad C_{l_i} = \frac{2W_i R'T_i}{p_i v_i^2 S}, \quad X = \begin{pmatrix} \alpha_1 & 1 \\ \alpha_2 & 1 \\ \vdots & \\ \alpha_n & 1 \end{pmatrix}, \quad \beta = \begin{pmatrix} \beta_1 \\ \beta_2 \end{pmatrix}$$

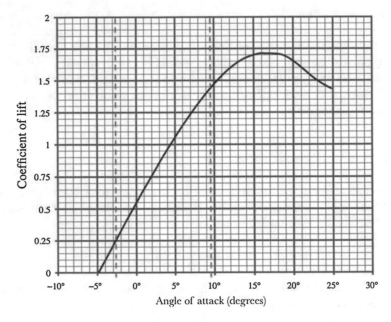

Fig. 5.5 Coefficient of lift as a function of angle of attack for a cambered airfoil. (Adapted from https://en.wikipedia.org/wiki/Lift_coefficient)

Because each column in X is independent, the least squares method defined in Sect. 5.4.1 is used to retrieve $\hat{\beta}$, and predict $\hat{W}$ using the following equation:

$$\hat{W} = \frac{pv^2 S(\hat{\beta}_1 \alpha + \hat{\beta}_2)}{2R'T} \tag{5.14}$$

which is substituted in the linear estimation of C_l, in Eq. 5.10.

5.6.3 Error Detection and Correction Using Error Signatures

5.6.3.1 PILOTS Program

The linear regression model is trained with synthetic data using training parameters as shown in Fig. 5.6. `data` defines the training file including file type and schema similar to Fig. 5.7 as an example, and constants used in features and labels; `preprocessing` defines the preprocessing methods used on the training set; and `model` contains functions for features, labels and training algorithms. The error function e is given by Eq. 5.15 as the percentage of discrepancy between predicted weight $\hat{W}$ and measured weight W. The vector of error signatures uses a threshold of 3.5% because this number is more rigorous than the percentage of discrepancy

```
{
  "data":{
    "file": ["training.csv"],
    "type": "csv",
    "header_type": "csvheader",
    "schema": "schema.json",
    "constants": {"S": 61.0, "R": 286.9}
  },
  "preprocessing":{
    "unit_transformation": {"v":"m/s", "p":"pascal","t":"kelvin","w":"newton","a
        ":"radian"}
  },
  "model":{
    "features": ["{a}"],
    "labels": ["2*{w}/({v}**2*({p}/{R}/{t})*{S})"],
    "algorithm":{
    "id": "linear_regression",
    "param": {},
    "save_file": "regression.estimator"
    }
  }
}
```

Fig. 5.6 Offline training parameters for the linear regression model

```
{
  "names": ["v","p","t","w","a"],
  "units": ["knot","in_Hg","celsius","force_pound","degree"]
}
```

Fig. 5.7 Example data schema file

Table 5.1 Vector of error signatures for weight correction

| | Error signature | |
Mode	Function	Constraints
Normal	$e = k$	$-0.035 < k < 0.035$
Underweight	$e = k$	$k > 0.035$
Overweight	$e = k$	$k < -0.035$

between error weight and actual weight in Tuninter 1153 accident, which is about 10%. A PILOTS program named WeightCorrection implementing the vector of error signatures in Table 5.1 is shown in Fig. 5.8. If the error signature s_1 or s_2 is detected, the program estimates weight using Eq. 5.14. The data selection module computes v', a', p', te', w' using data points with the closest time stamp, and uses a' as an input matrix to predict cl' using model the with id linear_regression.

$$e = \frac{W - \hat{W}}{W} \qquad (5.15)$$

```
program WeightCorrection;
    /* v = true air speed (m/s), a = angle of attack (Radian) */
    /* p = pressure (Pa), te = temperature (K), w = gross weight (N) */
    /* cl = coefficient of lift, R = 286.9 J/(kg K), S = 61(m^2)*/
    inputs
        v, a, p, te, w (t) using closest(t);
        cl (t) using predict(linear_regression, a);
    outputs
        corrected_weight: w at every 1 sec;
    errors
        e: (w - p*(v*v)*61*cl/(2*286.9*te))/w;
    signatures
        s0(K): e = K, -0.035 < K < 0.035          ''Normal'';
        s1(K): e = K, K > 0.035                    ''Underweight''
            estimate w = p*(v*v)*61*cl/(2*286.9*te);
        s2(K): e = K, K < - 0.035                  ''Overweight''
            estimate w = p*(v*v)*61*cl/(2*286.9*te);
end
```

Fig. 5.8 A declarative specification of `WeightCorrection` PILOTS program using error signature

5.6.3.2 Error Detection

Evaluation Criteria: We evaluate the performance of error detection based on *accuracy* and *response time*, which are defined as follows:

- **Accuracy** evelutes how accurately the algorithm determines the true mode. Assuming the true mode transition $m(t)$ is known for $t = 0, 1, 2, \ldots, T$, let $m'(t)$ for $t = 0, 1, 2, \ldots, T$ be the mode determined by the error detection algorithm. We define $accuracy(m, m') = \frac{1}{T} \sum_{t=0}^{T} p(t)$, where $p(t) = 1$ if $m(t) = m'(t)$ and $p(t) = 0$ otherwise.
- **Maximum/Minimum/Average Response Time** assesses how quickly the algorithm reacts to mode changes. Let a tuple (t_i, m_i) represent a mode change point, where the mode changes to m_i at time t_i. Let

$$M = \{(t_1, m_1), (t_2, m_2), \ldots, (t_N, m_N)\},$$

and

$$M' = \{(t_1', m_1'), (t_2', m_2'), \ldots, (t_{N'}', m_{N'}')\},$$

where M and M' are the sets of true mode changes and detected mode changes respectively. For each $i = 1 \ldots N$, PILOTS finds the smallest t_j' such that $(t_i \leq t_j') \wedge (m_i = m_j')$; if not found, let t_j' be t_{i+1}. The response time r_i for the true mode m_i is given by $t_j' - t_i$. The maximum, minimum, and average response time are defined by $\max_{1 \leq i \leq N} r_i$, $\min_{1 \leq i \leq N} r_i$, and $\frac{1}{N} \sum_{i=1}^{N} r_i$ respectively.

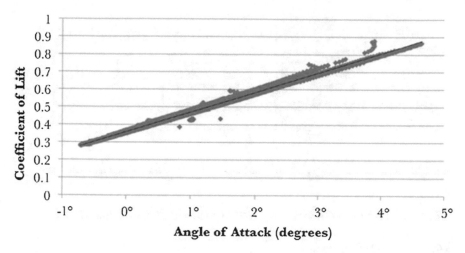

Fig. 5.9 The linear relation between angle of attack and coefficient of lift in cruise phase of training set

5.6.3.3 Software Parameter Settings

See Sect. 5.6.1.1 for data generation. PILOTS program `WeightCorrection` in Fig. 5.8 is executed with different combinations of window sizes $\omega \in \{1, 2, 4, 8, 16\}$ and thresholds $\tau \in \{0.2, 0.4, 0.6, 0.8, 0.99\}$ to investigate the accuracy and average response time.

5.6.3.4 Results

Figure 5.9 shows the training result of linear relationship between angle of attack and coefficient of lift, where the learned parameters are $\beta_1 = 6.3888$ and $\beta_2 = 0.3589$. The evaluation of the trained model gives $R^2 = 0.9949$, $RMSE = 0.00794$, showing a strong linear relationship with low in-sample error. Using Eq. 5.9, we compute the training error between measured weight and estimated weight, resulting in $RMSE = 2687N$.

Figure 5.10 shows the estimated weight and measured weight during the 18 min flight where $\omega = 1$ and $\tau = 0.99$, the best among all combinations in accuracy and response time. The PILOTS program can successfully detect and give estimated weight under overweight and underweight conditions in cruise phases, with root mean squared error close to 1617N on average. The program performs the best in system failure simulation regions where the weight drifts by 10% or 5%, and performs well in random error simulation regions. The overall accuracy is 97.6% and the minimum response time is 0 s; maximum response time is 84 s and the average response time is 1.45 s. Outside cruise phase, the program does not estimate weight properly as the assumption $L = W$ does not hold.

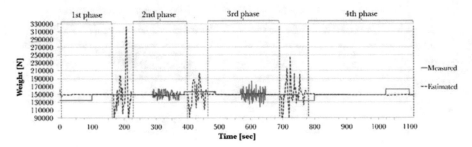

Fig. 5.10 Error detection and correction using $\omega = 1, \tau = 0.99$ for X-Plane simulated data

5.6.4 *Error Detection Using the Dynamic Bayes Classifier*

5.6.4.1 PILOTS Program

We use $\hat{W} - W$ as the feature for the dynamic Bayes classifier. Estimated weight is calculated by Eq. 5.9 using the method described in Sect. 5.6.2. The dynamic Bayes classifier is trained with both "normal" (mode 0) and "underweight" (mode 1) tagged data in the offline learning phase as described in Experimental Settings. Figure 5.11 shows the parameters setting for the offline training phase. `data.file` is the input file for training. `data.constants` are parameters we used for features. `model.features` are features for Bayes classifier. In this example, the feature is the discrepancy between estimated weight $\hat{W}$ by Eq. 5.14 and measured weight W. `model.algorithm.param` is the software parameters setting. A PILOTS program shown in Fig. 5.12 named `WeightErrorMode` is used for the online learning and classification to detect different weight error modes.

5.6.4.2 Mode Prediction Evaluation

We use the same evaluation criteria for major mode prediction: accuracy and response time as in Sect. 5.6.3.2.

5.6.4.3 Experimental Settings

See Sect. 5.6.1.1 for data generation. We use the same testing data, and 8000 s training data in cruise phase modified as follows: weight data in the range from 1526 to 3129 second are multiplied by 1.1 to simulate overweight mode. There are two major modes in the tagged training data: mode 0 for normal status and mode 1 for overweight status. For online learning, we set the threshold of the sample number to turn a minor mode into a major mode to 100. The sample number threshold for calculating σ of a new mode instead of using average σ is also set as 100. Figure 5.13 shows the feature and tagged mode of training data.

```
{
  "data":{
    "file": ["bayes_error_train.csv"],
    "type": "csv",
    "header_type": "csvheader",
    "schema":"bayes_schema.json",
    "constants": {"Beta_1": 6.38883559, "Beta_2": 0.35885757, "S": 61.0}
  },
  "preprocessing":{
    "unit_transformation": {"v":"m/s", "p":"pascal","t":"kelvin","w":"newton","a
        ":"radian"}
  },
  "model":{
    "features": ["({w}-0.5*({v}**2*({p}/286.9/{t})*{S})*({Beta_1}*{a}+{Beta_2}))
        "],
    "labels": ["{mode}"],
    "algorithm": {
      "id": "bayesonline",
      "param": {"sigma_scale": 2, "threshold": 100},
      "save_file": "bayes_online.estimator",
      "serialize_function": "to_json",
      "deserialize_function": "load_json"
    }
  }
}
```

Fig. 5.11 Offline training parameters for the dynamic Bayes classifier

```
program WeightErrorMode;
  /* v = true air speed (m/s), a = angle of attack (Radian) */
  /* p = pressure (Pa), te = temperature (K), w = gross weight (N) */
  inputs
    v, a, p, te, w (t) using closest(t);
    mode (t) using predict(bayes, v, a, p, te, w);
  outputs
    estimated_mode: mode at every 1 sec;
end
```

Fig. 5.12 A declarative specification of the `WeightErrorMode` PILOTS program using the dynamic Bayes classifier

5.6.4.4 Results

Figure 5.14 shows the results of weight error mode detection by dynamic Bayes classifier. Using the same testing data as in Fig. 5.10, the dynamic Bayes classifier successfully detects three major modes in the cruise phases: mode 0 for normal status, mode 1 for underweight status, and mode 3 for overweight status. Mode 0 and mode 1 are major modes that appeared in the tagged training data, mode 3 is a new major mode detected by the classifier during the online incremental learning and prediction phase. Mode 2 and mode 4 to 24 are minor modes generated by the noise and non-cruise phase data in the testing set. The accuracy of major mode detection is 86.3% and the average response time is 3.43 s.

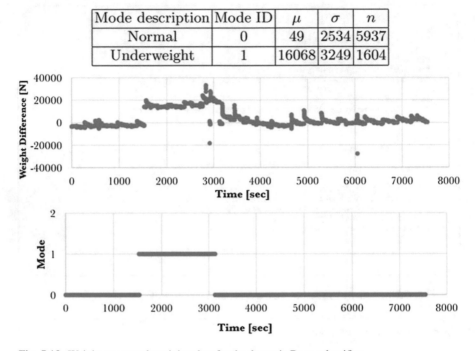

Mode description	Mode ID	μ	σ	n
Normal	0	49	2534	5937
Underweight	1	16068	3249	1604

Fig. 5.13 Weight error mode training data for the dynamic Bayes classifier

5.6.5 Comparison Between Error Signatures and Dynamic Bayes Classifier

The average response time of the error signatures approach with 0.035 as threshold, $\omega = 1$, and $\tau = 0.99$, is 58% shorter than that of the dynamic Bayes classifier, and the error signatures approach is 11.3% more accurate than the dynamic Bayes classifier. However, the dynamic Bayes classifier discovers discrete error states dynamically and automatically while the error signatures approach is static, that is, every signature must be predefined manually.

5.7 Related Work

Stream data processing has been an important technique in flight safety systems. Fault detection, isolation, and reconfiguration (FDIR) has also been actively studied in the control community [17]. The FDIR systems evaluate a set of residuals (what we call error functions) to detect if a fault has occurred, then isolate the type of the fault, and reconfigure the system to recover from the fault. To alleviate the effect of noise on residuals, robust residual generation techniques,

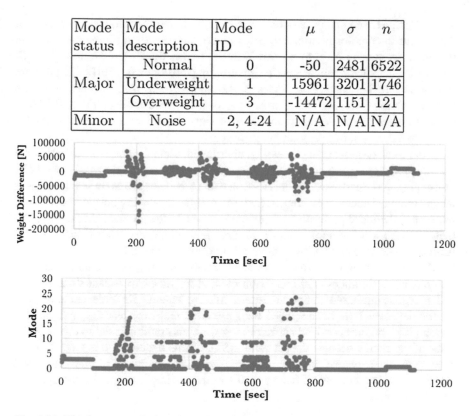

Mode status	Mode description	Mode ID	μ	σ	n
	Normal	0	-50	2481	6522
Major	Underweight	1	15961	3201	1746
	Overweight	3	-14472	1151	121
Minor	Noise	2, 4-24	N/A	N/A	N/A

Fig. 5.14 Weight error mode detection using dynamic Bayes classifier

such as a Kalman Filter based approach [18], have been used. Error residuals from different sources including ground speed, estimated wind speed, and propeller speed, are used to successfully detect and isolate airspeed sensor faults [19]. In some study, the residuals are not considered as binary value, but are assumed to have different distributions according to different modes [20]. The false positive and false negative detection rate of a FDIR method can be evaluated by several statistical models [21, 22]. The PILOTS language was designed for spatio-temporal data stream filtering, error detection and correction. PILOTS has been shown to detect and recover from sensor errors using actual flight data from commercial accidents [8]. The PILOTS framework enables users to implement fault detection and correction with tens of lines of code to describe error conditions.

There have been many systems that combine data stream processing and data base management, i.e., Data Stream Management Systems (DSMS). PLACE [23] and Microsoft StreamInsight [24] are DSMS-based systems supporting spatio-temporal streams. Also, the concept of the moving object data base (MODB) which adds support for spatio-temporal data streaming to DSMS is discussed in [25]. Also, a DSMS-based traffic congestion estimation system has been proposed [26].

These DSMS-based spatio-temporal stream management systems support general continuous queries for multiple moving objects such as "Find all the cars running within a diameter of X from a point Y in the past Z time". Unlike these DSMS-based systems which handle multiple spatio-temporal objects, a PILOTS program is assumed to be moving and tries to extrapolate data that is relevant to the current location and time. This approach narrows down the applicability of PILOTS; however, users can more easily design error signatures to estimate data on the fly thanks to the declarative programming approach.

In the context of big data processing, distributed, scalable, and fault-tolerant data streaming systems have been widely used. Such systems include MillWheel [27], Storm [28], and Spark Streaming [29]. Since these systems are expected to run over many computer nodes, they are designed to continue producing correct results with reasonably degraded performance even in the case of node failures. Unlike PILOTS, they are not aware of application-level data failures. On the other hand, PILOTS itself does not have any fault-tolerance mechanism to node failures.

Machine learning techniques have been widely used in stream data processing. There is a multi-dimensional regression method for time-series data streams [30], and a regression-based temporal pattern mining scheme for data streams [31]. Neural networks have been applied for supervised real-time learning and classification [32], and unsupervised active mining methods could be used to estimate the error of the model on new data streams [33]. In this chapter, we extend PILOTS to support linear regression of stream data, and also combined offline supervised learning and dynamic online incremental learning as implemented by the dynamic Bayes classifier.

5.8 Discussion and Future Work

In this chapter, we extend the PILOTS programming language to support machine learning techniques. A linear regression approach is applied to learn the relationship between coefficient of lift and the angle of attack during flights. With the training results, and models to calculate airplane weight during cruise phase, the PILOTS program successfully detects and give estimated weight under underweight and overweight conditions in simulated flight data by using error signatures. In this case, we only consider possible weight errors, while other sensor data like airspeed needs additional signatures to ensure its correctness. Using dynamic Bayes classifier, when the system is trained by normal and underweight data, the PILOTS program is able to detect a new mode when an overweight situation occurs in the online learning phase. Error signatures and dynamic Bayes classifier both have their advantages and limitations. Error signatures detect and correct for data errors, while dynamic Bayes classifier only detects for data errors, but is not able to fix them. Dynamic Bayes classifier detects statistically significant new modes during the online learning phase, while error signatures can only detect pre-defined modes.

When using the dynamic Bayes classifier to detect weight error, we noticed that the system not only detects "normal", "underweight", "overweight" modes, but also classifies "5% overweight" and "15% overweight" as two different modes, see Fig. 5.15. This information is useful if different strategies need to be taken for different extent of weight errors, otherwise it would be unnecessarily misleading to classify them into different modes. Thus, the dynamic Bayes classifier should be adjusted to the requirements of various use cases. This would result in a semi-supervised online learning approach.

Future work includes exploring distributed computing for large scale data processing to get higher efficiency. For the dynamic Bayes classifier, it would be helpful to involve human feedback in the online learning phase, especially when a new mode is detected, to get more accurate classification parameters and decision making. Techniques are needed to add error correction to the dynamic Bayes classifier and learning. Take the weight error case for example, for any mode except the normal mode, simply using the estimated weight instead of detected weight as error correction. Machine learning techniques could also be used to learn parameters in error signatures from data. Another possible direction is to combine

Mode status	Mode description	Mode ID	μ	σ	n
Major	Normal	0	-33	2462	6544
	Underweight	1	15898	3312	1708
Minor	5% Overweight	2	-6922	239	54
	15% Overweight	3	-17450	277	91

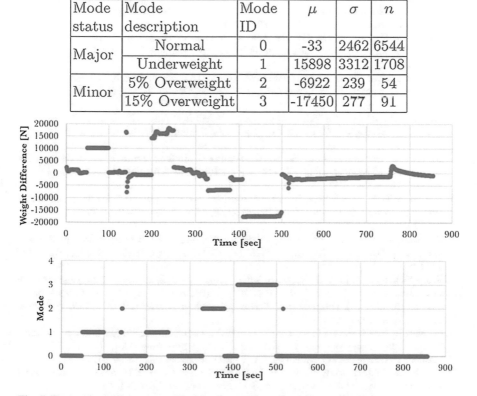

Fig. 5.15 Another weight error mode detection using dynamic Bayes classifier

logic programming and probabilistic programming, as in ProbLog [34], to help analyze spatio-temporal stream data. Finally, uncertainty quantification [35] is an important future direction to associate confidence to data and error estimations in support of decision making.

Acknowledgments This research is partially supported by the DDDAS program of the Air Force Office of Scientific Research, Grant No. FA9550-15-1-0214, NSF Grant No. 1462342, and a Yamada Corporation Fellowship.

References

1. S. Imai, C.A. Varela, Programming spatio-temporal data streaming applications with high-level specifications, in *3rd ACM SIGSPATIAL International Workshop on Querying and Mining Uncertain Spatio-Temporal Data (QUeST) 2012*, Redondo Beach, Nov 2012
2. Bureau d'Enquêtes et d'Analyses pour la Sécurité de l'Aviation Civile, Final Report: On the accident on 1st June 2009 to the Airbus A330-203 registered F-GZCP operated by Air France flight AF 447 Rio de Janeiro – Paris. https://www.bea.aero/fileadmin/documents/docspa/2009/f-cp090601.en/pdf/f-cp090601.en.pdf. Accessed 15 Sept 2016
3. E.P. Blasch, D.A. Lambert, P. Valin, M.M. Kokar, J. Llinas, S. Das, C. Chong, E. Shahbazian, High level information fusion (HLIF): survey of models, issues, and grand challenges. IEEE Aerosp. Electron. Syst. Mag. **27**(9), 4–20 (2012)
4. J.T. Oden, E.E. Prudencio, P.T. Bauman, Virtual model validation of complex multiscale systems: applications to nonlinear elastostatics. Comput. Methods Appl. Mech. Eng. **266**, 162–184 (2013)
5. F. Darema, Dynamic data driven applications systems: a new paradigm for application simulations and measurements, in *Computational Science-ICCS 2004* (Springer, Berlin/Heidelberg, 2004), pp. 662–669
6. A.N. per la Sicurezza del Volo, Final report: accident involving ATR 72 aircraft registration marks TS-LBB ditching off the coast of Capo Gallo (Palermo – Sicily), 6 Aug 2005. Accessed 31 Mar 2015
7. S. Imai, R. Klockowski, C.A. Varela, Self-healing spatio-temporal data streams using error signatures, in *2nd International Conference on Big Data Science and Engineering (BDSE 2013)*, Sydney, Dec 2013
8. S. Imai, A. Galli, C.A. Varela, Dynamic data-driven avionics systems: inferring failure modes from data streams, in *Dynamic Data-Driven Application Systems (DDDAS 2015)*, Reykjavik, June 2015
9. S. Imai, C.A. Varela, A programming model for spatio-temporal data streaming applications, in *Dynamic Data-Driven Application Systems (DDDAS 2012)*, Omaha, June 2012, pp. 1139–1148
10. R.S. Klockowski, S. Imai, C. Rice, C.A. Varela, Autonomous data error detection and recovery in streaming applications, in *Proceedings of the International Conference on Computational Science (ICCS 2013). Dynamic Data-Driven Application Systems (DDDAS 2013) Workshop*, May 2013, pp. 2036–2045
11. S. Imai, E. Blasch, A. Galli, W. Zhu, F. Lee, C.A. Varela, Airplane flight safety using error-tolerant data stream processing. IEEE Aerosp. Electron. Syst. Mag. **32**(4), 4–17 (2017)
12. Laminar Research, X-Plane. http://www.x-plane.com/. Accessed 15 Sept 2016
13. I. Rish, An empirical study of the naive Bayes classifier, in *IJCAI 2001 workshop on empirical methods in artificial intelligence*, vol. 3 (IBM, New York, 2001), pp. 41–46
14. E.T. Jaynes, *Probability Theory: The Logic of Science* (Cambridge University Press, Cambridge, 2003)

15. G.H. John, P. Langley, Estimating continuous distributions in Bayesian classifiers, in *Proceedings of the Eleventh conference on Uncertainty in artificial intelligence* (Morgan Kaufmann Publishers Inc., 1995), pp. 338–345
16. J.D. Anderson Jr, *Fundamentals of Aerodynamics* (Tata McGraw-Hill Education, New York, 2010)
17. I. Hwang, S. Kim, Y. Kim, C.E. Seah, A survey of fault detection, isolation, and reconfiguration methods. IEEE Trans. Control Syst. Technol. **18**(3), 636–653 (2010)
18. T. Menke, P. Maybeck, Sensor/actuator failure detection in the Vista F-16 by multiple model adaptive estimation. IEEE Trans. Aerosp. Electron. Syst. **31**, 1218–1229 (1995)
19. S. Hansen, M. Blanke, Diagnosis of airspeed measurement faults for unmanned aerial vehicles. IEEE Trans. Aerosp. Electron. Syst. **50**, 224–239 (2014)
20. C. Svärd, M. Nyberg, E. Frisk, M. Krysander, Data-driven and adaptive statistical residual evaluation for fault detection with an automotive application. Mech. Syst. Signal Process. **45**(1), 170–192 (2014)
21. A. Zolghadri, Advanced model-based FDIR techniques for aerospace systems: today challenges and opportunities. Prog. Aerosp. Sci. **53**, 18–29 (2012)
22. J. Marzat, H. Piet-Lahanier, F. Damongeot, E. Walter, Model-based fault diagnosis for aerospace systems: a survey, in *Proceedings of the Institution of Mechanical Engineers, Part G: Journal of Aerospace Engineering*, vol. 226, Jan 2012, pp. 1329–1360,
23. M.F. Mokbel, X. Xiong, W.G. Aref, M.A. Hammad, Continuous query processing of spatio-temporal data streams in PLACE. GeoInformatica **9**, 343–365 (2005)
24. M.H. Ali, B. Chandramouli, B.S. Raman, E. Katibah, Spatio-temporal stream processing in Microsoft StreamInsight. IEEE Data Eng. Bull. **33**(2), 69–74 (2010)
25. K. An, J. Kim, Moving objects management system supporting location data stream, in *Proceedings of the 4th WSEAS International Conference on Computational Intelligence, Man-Machine Systems and Cybernetics*, CIMMACS'05, Stevens Point, Wisconsin (World Scientific and Engineering Academy and Society (WSEAS), 2005), pp. 99–104
26. S. Geisler, C. Quix, S. Schiffer, M. Jarke, An evaluation framework for traffic information systems based on data streams, Trans. Res. Part C Emerging Technol. **23**, 29–55 (2012)
27. T. Akidau, A. Balikov, K. Bekiroğlu, S. Chernyak, J. Haberman, R. Lax, S. McVeety, D. Mills, P. Nordstrom, S. Whittle, Millwheel: fault-tolerant stream processing at internet scale. Proc. VLDB Endow. **6**(11), 1033–1044 (2013)
28. The Apache Software Foundation, Apache Storm. http://storm.apache.org/, 2015. Accessed 15 Sept 2016
29. M. Zaharia, T. Das, H. Li, S. Shenker, I. Stoica, Discretized streams: an efficient and fault-tolerant model for stream processing on large clusters, in *Proceedings of the 4th USENIX conference on Hot Topics in Cloud Computing* (USENIX Association, 2012), pp. 10–10
30. Y. Chen, G. Dong, J. Han, B. W. Wah, J. Wang, Multi-dimensional regression analysis of time-series data streams, in *Proceedings of the 28th International Conference on Very Large Data Bases* (VLDB Endowment, 2002), pp. 323–334
31. W.-G. Teng, M.-S. Chen, P.S. Yu, A regression-based temporal pattern mining scheme for data streams, in *Proceedings of the 29th International Conference on Very large data bases-Volume 29* (VLDB Endowment, 2003), pp. 93–104
32. G.A. Carpenter, S. Grossberg, J.H. Reynolds, Artmap: supervised real-time learning and classification of nonstationary data by a self-organizing neural network. Neural Netw. **4**(5), 565–588 (1991)
33. W. Fan, Y.-A. Huang, H. Wang, S.Y. Philip, Active mining of data streams, in *Proceedings of the 2004 SIAM International Conference on Data Mining* (SIAM, 2004), pp. 457–461
34. L. De Raedt, A. Kimmig, H. Toivonen, Problog: a probabilistic prolog and its application in link discovery, in *International Joint Conference on Artificial Intelligence*, vol. 7, 2007, pp. 2462–2467
35. D. Allaire, D. Kordonowy, M. Lecerf, L. Mainini, K. Willcox, Multifidelity DDDAS methods with application to a self-aware aerospace vehicle, in *DDDAS 2014 Workshop at ICCS'14*, June 2014, pp. 1182–1192

Chapter 6
Markov Modeling via Spectral Analysis: Application to Detecting Combustion Instabilities

Devesh K. Jha, Nurali Virani, and Asok Ray

Abstract Effective representation of temporal patterns to infer generative models from measurement data is critical for dynamic data-driven application systems (DDDAS). Markov models are often used to capture temporal patterns in sequential data for statistical learning applications. This chapter presents a methodology for reduced-order Markov modeling of time-series data based on spectral properties of stochastic matrix and clustering of directed graphs. Instead of the common Hidden Markov model (HMM)-inspired techniques, a symbolic dynamics-based approach is used to infer an approximate generative Markov model for the data. The time-series data is first symbolized by partitioning the continuous domain to obtain a discrete-valued signal. The size of temporal memory of the discretized symbol sequence is then estimated using spectral properties of the stochastic matrix created from the symbol sequence for a first-order Markov model of the symbol sequence. Then, a graphical method is used to cluster the states of the corresponding high-order Markov model to infer a reduced-size Markov model with a non-deterministic algebraic structure. A Bayesian inference rule captures the parameters of the reduced-size Markov model from the original model. The proposed idea is illustrated by creating Markov models for pressure time-series data from a swirl stabilized combustor where some controlled protocols are used to induce instability. Results demonstrate complexity modeling of the underlying

This work has been supported in part by the U.S. Air Force Office of Scientific Research under Grant No. FA9550-15-1-0400. This work was conducted when all authors were at The Pennsylvania State University.

D. K. Jha
Mitsubishi Electric Research Laboratories, Cambridge, MA, USA

N. Virani
GE Research, Niskayuna, NY, USA

A. Ray (✉)
Department of Mechanical and Nuclear Engineering, The Pennsylvania State University, University Park, PA, USA
e-mail: axr2@psu.edu

Markov model as the system operating condition changes from stable to unstable which is useful in combustion applications such as detection and control of thermo-acoustic instabilities.

Keywords Bayesian inferencing · Combustion processes · Detection and estimation · Dynamic data-driven modeling · Hidden Markov modeling · Markov processes · Model order reduction · Novelty detection · Thermo-acoustic instabilities · Time series analysis

6.1 Motivation and Introduction

The underlying theory of symbolic time-series analysis (STSA) [1, 2] has led to the development of signal representation tools in the paradigm of dynamic data-driven application systems (DDDAS) [3, 4], where time series of sensor signals are partitioned to obtain respective symbol strings. In general, STSA is a nonlinear technique for representation of temporal patterns in sequential data, where the underlying continuous attributes are projected onto a symbolic space. This step is followed by identification of concise probabilistic patterns for compression of the discretized information. Within this framework, *finite-memory* Markov models have been shown to be a reasonable *finite-memory* approximation (or representation) of systems with fading memory (e.g., engineering systems that exhibit stable orbits or mixing) [5, 6].

Once the continuous data are discretized, the memory estimate for the discretized sequence is used for compression as a finite-memory Markov process, which is represented by a state transition matrix. The transition matrix is estimated by a maximum likelihood estimator (MLE) under the assumption of infinite data and uniform priors for all elements of the transition matrix. In contrast to the probabilistic finite state automaton (PFSA)-based approach to infer a Markov model for time-series data presented in [5–7], an alternative method has been proposed in this chapter, where the constraints of the deterministic algebraic structure of finite-state automata are relaxed to allow non-deterministic transitions for the PFSA inferred from the time-series data. This task has been performed by making a trade-off for lower complexity of the generated model (possibly) at the expense of resolution loss. The proposed concept is validated for model inferencing using time-series data from a swirl-stabilized combustor and identify the different stages of the complex instability phenomenon from a completely data-driven perspective. We also illustrate the changes in the model structure and discuss their physical interpretations based on the data from the process.

Hidden Markov Modeling (HMM) is the most-widely used statistical learning tool for modeling time-series data [8] where the data is modeled as a Markov process with unobserved states. The learning task is to infer the states and the corresponding parameters of the Markov chain. In contrast to HMM, some other non-linear techniques have also been proposed for Markov modeling of time-series data where the states of the Markov chain are some collection of words of different lengths which can be obtained from the time-series data up on projecting the data to a discrete space with finite cardinality [5–7, 9, 10]. The common concept in all these techniques, based on Markov modeling of discrete sequences, is that the Markov chain is induced by probabilistic version of a deterministic FSA [5]. While the PFSA-based inference provides a consistent, deterministic graph structure for learning, the deterministic algebraic structure is generally redundant and can often lead to large number of states in the induced Markov model. Merging the states of the PFSA for dimensionality reduction is often inconsistent due to the algebraic constraints [6]. Some other approaches for state aggregation in Markov chains could be found in [11–14]. However, these papers present aggregation of states in a Markov chains; construction of the Markov chain from data is never considered. It is important that these two problems (i.e., state merging and Markov chain construction) be studied together for analysis of dynamic data-driven application systems (DDDAS) [3, 4]. Moreover, the optimal model selection is inspired by *wrapper*-based techniques where the system searches for the best one in all the above techniques as the similarity is measured between the Markov chains of different dimensions obtained by merging certain parts of the state-space.

This chapter presents a Markov modeling technique for time-series data where the size of temporal memory of the symbolic data is estimated by using the spectral properties of a PFSA whose states are words of length one [15, 16]. Next the states are merged and the deterministic algebraic properties associated with PFSA are removed, where the states of the Markov chain is now some collection of words from its alphabet of length estimated in the last step. The parameters of the reduced-order Markov model are estimated using a Bayesian inference technique from the parameters associated with the higher-order Markov model. The final model obtained is a generative model for the data; however, some information is lost as parts of the deterministic structure of a finite state automaton (FSA) are removed. This approach is used to construct Markov models for pressure data obtained from a combustion instability [17–19] phenomenon, which is a highly non-linear thermo-acoustic process and very hard to model completely using first principles of physics. This chapter addresses data-driven modeling for real-time detection of changes in the underlying process. Specifically these data-driven models can assist prediction and control of combustion instabilities and thus, allow for more reliable and efficient operation of modern-day combustors such as those used in aircraft gas turbine engines or in gas-fired power plants.

6.2   Background and Mathematical Preliminaries

Symbolic analysis of time-series data is a recent approach where continuous sensor data are converted to symbol sequences via partitioning of the continuous domain [5, 20]. The dynamics of the symbols sequences are then modeled as a Probabilistic Finite State Automata (PFSA), which is defined as follows:

Definition 1 (PFSA) A Probabilistic Finite State Automata (PFSA) is a tuple $G = (\mathcal{Q}, \mathcal{A}, \delta, M)$ where

- $\mathcal{Q}$ is a finite set of states of the automata;
- $\mathcal{A}$ is a finite alphabet set of symbols $a \in \mathcal{A}$;
- $\delta : \mathcal{Q} \times \mathcal{A} \rightarrow \mathcal{Q}$ is the state transition function;
- $M : \mathcal{Q} \times \mathcal{A} \rightarrow [0, 1]$ is the $|\mathcal{Q}| \times |\mathcal{A}|$ emission matrix. The matrix $M = [m_{ij}]$ is row stochastic such that m_{ij} is the probability of generating symbol a_j from state q_i.

For symbolic analysis of time-series data, a class of PFSAs called the D-Markov machine have been proposed [5] as a sub-optimal but computationally efficient approach to encode the dynamics of symbol sequences as a finite state machine. For most stable and controlled engineering systems that tend to forget their initial conditions, a finite length memory assumption is reasonable. The states of this PFSA are words over $\mathcal{A}$ of length D (or less); and state transitions are described by a sliding block code of memory D and anticipation length of one [21]. The dynamics of this PFSA can both be described by the $|\mathcal{Q}| \times |\mathcal{Q}|$ state transition matrix Π or the $|\mathcal{Q}| \times 1$ state visit probability vector p. The alphabet size or the level of coarse-graining of the continuous domain is driven by the resolution level required to capture the dynamics of the system—domain knowledge or data-driven partitioning techniques [22] can be used for this purpose. Estimating the depth of historical influences, on the other hand, requires estimation of the decay-rate of the memory of a dynamical system.

For systems with fading memory it is expected that the predictive influence of a symbol progressively diminishes further into the future. Formally depth is defined as follows:

Definition 2 (Depth) Let $\vec{s} = s_1 \ldots s_k s_{k+1} s_{k+2} \ldots$ be the observed symbol sequence where each $s_j \in \mathcal{A} \ \forall j \in \mathbb{N}$. Then, the depth of the process generating $\vec{s}$ is defined as the length D such that:

$$\Pr(s_k|s_{k-1}, \ldots, s_1) = \Pr(s_k|s_{k-1}, \ldots, s_{k-D}) \tag{6.1}$$

An accurate estimation of depth for the symbolic dynamical process is required for the precise modeling of the underlying dynamics of the discrete sequence. Next an information-theoretic metric is introduced, which is used for merging the states of the Markov model later in next section.

Definition 3 (Kullback-Leibler Divergence) The Kullback-Leibler (K-L) divergence of a discrete probability distribution P from another distribution $\tilde{P}$ is defined as follows.

$$D_{\text{KL}}(P \| \tilde{P}) = \sum_{x \in X} p(x) \log \left(\frac{p(x)}{\tilde{p}(x)} \right)$$

It is noted that K-L divergence is not symmetric; however, it can be converted to a symmetric distance as follows: $d(P, \tilde{P}) = D_{KL}(P\|\tilde{P}) + D_{KL}(\tilde{P}\|P)$. This is defined as the K-L distance between the distributions P and $\tilde{P}$.

This distance is used to determine the structure in the set of the states of the PFSA-based Markov model whose states are words, over the alphabet of the PFSA, of length equal to the depth estimated for the discretized sequence.

6.3   Proposed Approach

This section presents the details of the proposed approach for inferring a Markov model from the time-series data. As discussed earlier, the first step is the discretization of the time-series data to generate a discrete symbol sequence. It is possible to optimize the symbolization of time-series using an optimization criterion and the details are available in literature (e.g., see [17]). The data are discretized using the unbiased principle of entropy maximization of the discrete sequence using Maximum Entropy Partitioning (MEP) [23]. The proposed approach consists of three critical steps and is also shown in Fig. 6.1 for pedagogical purposes. A psuedo-code for the proposed method is also provided in the appendix for clarity.

- Estimate the approximate size of temporal memory (or order) of the symbol sequence.
- Cluster the states of the high-order Markov model.

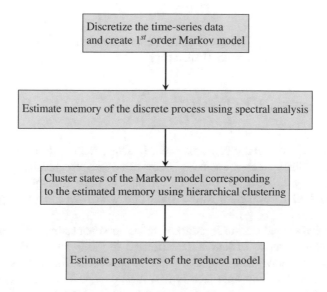

Fig. 6.1 Flowchart for the proposed reduced-order modeling

- Estimate the parameters of the reduced-order Markov model (i.e., the Transition matrix).

Memory of the discrete sequence is estimated using a recently introduced method based on the spectral analysis of the 1st order Markov model induced by a PFSA [15, 16]. The key ideas behind the three steps are explained next.

6.3.1 Estimation of Reduced-Order Markov Model

Depth D of a symbol sequence has been redefined in [15] as the number of time steps after which probability of current symbol is independent of any past symbol i.e.:

$$\Pr(s_k|s_{k-n}) = \Pr(s_k) \ \forall n > D \tag{6.2}$$

Note that dependence in the proposed definition (Eq. 6.2) is evaluated on individual past symbols using $\Pr(s_k|s_{k-n})$ as opposed to the assessing dependence on words of length D using $\Pr(s_k|s_{k-1}, \ldots, s_{k-D})$. It is shown that if the observed process is *forward causal* then observing any additional intermediate symbols $s_{k-1}, \ldots, s_{k-n+1}$ cannot induce a dependence between s_k and s_{k-n} if it did not exist on individual level.

Let $\boldsymbol{\Pi} = [\pi_{ij}^{(1)}]$ be the one-step transition probability matrix of the PFSA G constructed from this symbol sequence i.e.

$$\boldsymbol{\Pi} = \Pr(s_k|s_{k-1}) \tag{6.3}$$

Then using the distance of the transition matrix after steps from the stationary point, depth can be defined as a length D such that

$$\left|\text{trace}\left(\boldsymbol{\Pi}^n\right) - \text{trace}\left(\boldsymbol{\Pi}^\infty\right)\right| \leq \sum_{j=2}^{J} \left|\lambda_j\right|^n < \epsilon \ \forall n > D \tag{6.4}$$

J is number of non-zero eigenvalues of $\boldsymbol{\Pi}$. Thus, the depth D of the symbol sequence is estimated for a choice of ϵ by estimating the stochastic matrix for the one-step PFSA. Next, another pass of data is done through the module to estimate the PFSA parameters whose states are words over $\mathscr{A}$ of length D, i.e., $\boldsymbol{\Pi} = \Pr(s_k|s_{k-1}, \ldots, s_{k-D})$.

The states of the reduced-order Markov model are then estimated by partitioning the set of words over $\mathscr{A}$ of length D estimated in the last step. This is done by using an agglomerative hierarchical clustering approach. The advantage of using the hierarchical clustering approach is that it helps visualize the structure of the set of the original states using an appropriate metric. Agglomerative hierarchical clustering is a bottom-up clustering approach [24] that generates a sparse network (e.g., a binary tree) of the state set $\mathscr{Q}$ (where $|Q| = |\mathscr{A}^D|$) by successive addition of edges between the elements of $\mathcal{Q}$. Initially, each of the states $q_1, q_2, \ldots, q_n$ is in its own cluster $C_1, C_2, \ldots, C_n$ where $C_i \in \mathcal{C}$, which is the set of all clusters for the hierarchical cluster tree. The distance between any two states, q_i and q_j, in $\mathcal{Q}$ is measured by using the K-L distance between the symbol emission probabilities conditioned on these states, i.e.,

$$d(q_i, q_j) = D_{\mathrm{KL}}(\mathrm{Pr}(\mathcal{A}|q_i) \| \mathrm{Pr}(\mathcal{A}|q_j)) + D_{\mathrm{KL}}(\mathrm{Pr}(\mathcal{A}|q_j) \| \mathrm{Pr}(\mathcal{A}|q_i)) \qquad (6.5)$$

In terms of the distance measured by Eq. (6.5), the pair of clusters that are nearest to each other are merged and this step is repeated till only one cluster is left. The tree structure displays the order of splits in the state set of the higher-order Markov model and is used to aggregate the states close to each other. The set of states clustered together could be obtained based on the number of final states required in the final Markov model.

Remark 1 (**Stopping Criterion for Merging**) The stopping criterion for the algorithm could be reached based on the modeling objective. In the absence of any defined end objective, the criterion for stopping the algorithm could be found using approaches like Minimum description length (MDL) for signal representation. If stopping criterion corresponds to another end objective (e.g., class separability), then a Bayesian inference rule could be used to arrive at a consistent cardinality of clusters in $\mathcal{Q}$. However, in this chapter, the algorithm is terminated by fixing the desired number of states (N_{max}) a priori. For a detailed discussion, interested readers are referred to [17, 25, 26].

Remark 2 The final Markov model is a finite depth approximation of the original time-series data. However, compared to the PFSA-based D-Markov machines in [5, 6], the current aggregated model has a non-deterministic algebraic structure, i.e., the same symbol emissions from a state can lead to different states. While this leads to some information loss as compared to the models in [5, 6], this facilitates compression of the size of the model as per the application requirements. For example, even though the optimal model might require a higher finite memory adding all words corresponding to that length might not be necessary to preserve the statistical behavior or class separability. Furthermore, the aggregated model would allow faster convergence rates for the symbol emission probabilities which can be calculated using Glivenko-Cantelli theorem [27]. For a detailed discussion interested readers are referred to [17].

6.3.2   Estimation of Parameters for the Reduced-Order Markov Model

The parameters of the Markov model obtained after clustering the states of the original PFSA with $|\mathcal{A}|^D$ states is obtained using a Bayesian inference technique using the parameters estimated for the PFSA. In this proposed approach, the state

State
Cluster

Original
State

Emitted
Symbol

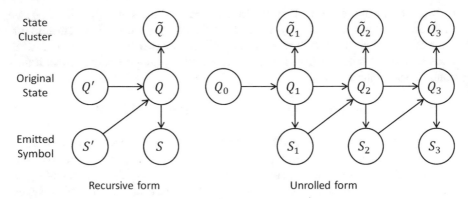

Recursive form   Unrolled form

Fig. 6.2 Graphical models representing dependencies between the random variables

transition matrix $\boldsymbol{\Pi}$, the emission matrix $\boldsymbol{M}$, and the state probability vector $\boldsymbol{p}$ of the original PFSA model G are available, along with the deterministic assignment map $f : \mathscr{Q} \to \widetilde{\mathscr{Q}}$ of the state in $\mathscr{Q}$ (i.e., state set of original model) to one of the state in $\widetilde{\mathscr{Q}}$ (i.e., state set of the reduced order model). Since the reduced order model can represented by the tuple $\widetilde{G} = (\widetilde{\mathscr{Q}}, \widetilde{\boldsymbol{\Pi}})$, where $\widetilde{\boldsymbol{\Pi}} = [\tilde{\pi}_{ij}]$ is the state transition matrix, a Bayesian inference technique is employed to infer the individual values of transition probabilities $\tilde{\pi}_{ij} = \Pr(\tilde{q}_{k+1} = j \mid \tilde{q}_k = i)$ for all $i, j \in \widetilde{\mathscr{Q}}$.

Let Q_k be the random variable denoting the state of PFSA model at some time step $k \in \mathbb{N}$ and S_k denotes the symbol emitted from that state, this probabilistic emission process is governed by the emission matrix $\boldsymbol{M}$. The state of the reduced order model is obtained from a deterministic mapping of the state of the PFSA model, thus the state of this model is also a random variable, which is denoted by $\widetilde{Q}_k = f(Q_k)$. The Bayesian network representing the dependencies between these variables is shown in the recursive as well as unrolled form in the Fig. 6.2. The conditional density $\Pr(\widetilde{Q}_k = \tilde{q} \mid Q_k = q)$ can be evaluated by checking if state q belongs to the state cluster $\tilde{q}$ and assigning the value of 1 if true, else assign it the value of 0. Since it is known that $\widetilde{\mathscr{Q}}$ partitions the set $\mathscr{Q}$, the conditional density is well-defined. Thus, it can be written as

$$\Pr(\widetilde{Q}_k = \tilde{q} \mid Q_k = q) = \mathrm{I}_{\tilde{q}}(q), \tag{6.6}$$

where I is the indicator function with $\mathrm{I}_{\tilde{q}}(q) = 1$, if element q belongs to the set $\tilde{q}$, else it is 0. The derivation of the Markov model $\Pr(\widetilde{Q}_{k+1} \mid \widetilde{Q}_k)$ using $\Pr(Q_{k+1} \mid Q_k)$, stationary probability vector $\boldsymbol{p}$, and assignment map f is shown ahead.

$$\Pr(\widetilde{Q}_{k+1} \mid \widetilde{Q}_k) = \sum_{q \in \mathscr{Q}} \Pr(\widetilde{Q}_{k+1}, Q_{k+1} = q \mid \widetilde{Q}_k) \tag{6.7}$$

(Marginalization)

$$= \sum_{q \in \mathcal{Q}} \Pr(Q_{k+1} = q \mid \widetilde{Q}_k) \Pr(\widetilde{Q}_{k+1} \mid Q_{k+1} = q) \qquad (6.8)$$

(Factorization using Fig. 6.2)

$$= \sum_{q \in \mathcal{Q}} \Pr(Q_{k+1} = q \mid \widetilde{Q}_k) \, \mathrm{I}_{\widetilde{Q}_{k+1}}(q) \qquad (6.9)$$

(using (6.6))

$$= \sum_{q \in \widetilde{Q}_{k+1}} \Pr(Q_{k+1} = q \mid \widetilde{Q}_k). \qquad (6.10)$$

where $\Pr(Q_{k+1} \mid \widetilde{Q}_k)$ is obtained from Bayes' rule as

$$\Pr(Q_{k+1} \mid \widetilde{Q}_k) = \frac{\Pr(\widetilde{Q}_k \mid Q_{k+1}) \Pr(Q_{k+1})}{\sum_{q \in \mathcal{Q}} \Pr(\widetilde{Q}_k \mid Q_{k+1} = q) \Pr(Q_{k+1} = q)}. \qquad (6.11)$$

By following the steps to obtain (6.10),

$$\Pr(\widetilde{Q}_k \mid Q_{k+1}) = \sum_{q \in \widetilde{Q}_k} \Pr(Q_k = q \mid Q_{k+1}). \qquad (6.12)$$

where $\Pr(Q_k \mid Q_{k+1})$ results from Bayes' rule as

$$\mathrm{P}_1(Q_k \mid Q_{k+1}) = \frac{\Pr(Q_{k \mid 1} \mid Q_k) \Pr(Q_k)}{\sum_{q \in \mathcal{Q}} \Pr(Q_{k+1} \mid Q_k = q) \Pr(Q_k = q)}. \qquad (6.13)$$

It is noted that, for the distribution $\Pr(Q_k)$ and $\Pr(Q_{k+1})$, a stationary probability $\boldsymbol{p}$ is available. Using Eqs. (6.10), (6.11), (6.12), and (6.13) together, one can easily obtain the state transition matrix $\widetilde{\boldsymbol{\Pi}}$ of the reduced order model. Once the state cluster set $\widetilde{\mathcal{Q}}$ and state transition matrix $\widetilde{\boldsymbol{\Pi}}$ are available, the reduced order model is completely defined. The pseudocode for the proposed approach is given next.

6.3.3   Pseudocode of the Main Algorithm

This section summarizes proposed approach as a pseudo-code (see Algorithm 1), which will be used to find the model parameters in the training phase. The parameters in the testing phase are estimated using the clustering map $f = f_{N_{\max}}$. The rest of the chapter will demonstrate the utility of these models in a practical problem of modeling combustion instabilities from time-series data.

Algorithm 1 Reduced order Markov modeling

Input: The observed symbol sequence $\vec{s} = \{s_1 \ldots s_k s_{k+1} s_{k+2} \ldots | s_i \in \mathscr{A} \forall i \in \{1, 2, \ldots\}\}$
Output: The final D-Markov model, $\mathscr{M} = (\tilde{\mathscr{Q}}, \tilde{M}, \tilde{\Pi})$
1   Estimate the Π matrix for 1-step Markov model using frequency counting with an uniform prior
2   Estimate the size of temporal memory, $D(\epsilon)$ for $\vec{s}$ using Eq. (6.4)
3   Estimate M and Π for the $D(\epsilon)$-Markov model using frequency counting with an uniform prior
4   Initialize hierarchical clustering with $\mathscr{C}_{|\mathscr{Q}|} = \{q_i \mid q_i \in \mathscr{Q}\}$
5   **for** $i = |\mathscr{Q}| - 1, \ldots, 1$ **do**
6   find distinct clusters $A, B \in \mathscr{C}_{i+1}$ minimizing $d(A, B)$, where $d(A, B) = \max d(q_i, q_j)$ with
        $q_i \in A$ and $q_j \in B$
7       $\mathscr{C}_i := (\mathscr{C}_{i+1} \setminus \{A, B\}) \cup \{A \cup B\}$
8   **return** *Hierarchy of state clusters* $\mathscr{C}_1, \ldots, \mathscr{C}_{|\mathscr{Q}|}$ *and state-to-cluster mappings* $f_i : \mathscr{Q} \to \mathscr{C}_i$
    $\forall i \in \{1, \ldots, |\mathscr{Q}|\}$
9   Calculate the parameters of reduced model using $\tilde{\mathscr{Q}} = \mathscr{C}_{N_{max}}$, $f = f_{N_{max}}$ and Eqs. (6.10)
    through (6.13), where N_{max} is the maximum number of states

---

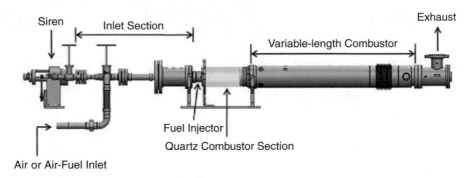

Fig. 6.3 Schematic drawing of the test apparatus

6.4 Combustion Experiment Details

This section presents the experimental details for collecting data to analyze the complex non-linear phenomena that occurs during the instability phenomena, in a laboratory-scale combustor. A swirl-stabilized, lean-premixed, laboratory-scale combustor was used to perform the experimental study. Figure 6.3 shows a schematic drawing of the variable-length combustor. The combustor consists of an inlet section, an injector, a combustion chamber, and an exhaust section. The combustor chamber consists of an optically-accessible quartz section followed by a variable length steel section.

High pressure air is delivered to the experiment from a compressor system after passing through filters to remove any liquid or particles that might be present. The air supply pressure is set to 180 psig using a dome pressure regulator. The air is pre-heated to a maximum temperature of 250°C by an 88kW electric heater. The fuel for this study is natural gas (approximately 95% methane). It is supplied to the system at a pressure of 200 psig. The flow rates of the air and natural gas are measured by

Table 6.1 Operating conditions

Parameters	Value
Equivalence ratio	0.525, 0.55, 0.60, 0.65
Inlet velocity	25–50 m/s in 5 m/s increments
Combustor length	25–59 inch in 1 inch increments

thermal mass flow meters. The desired equivalence ratio and mean inlet velocity is set by adjusting these flow rates with needle valves. For fully pre-mixed experiments (FPM), the fuel is injected far upstream of a choke plate to prevent equivalence ratio fluctuations. For technically pre-mixed experiments (TPM), fuel is injected in the injector section near the swirler. It mixes with air over a short distance between the swirler and the injector exit. Tests were conducted at a nominal combustor pressure of 1 atm over a range of operating conditions, as listed in Table 6.1. Other details, which are reported in [4], are skipped for brevity (Fig. 6.4).

6.5 Results and Discussion

This section presents details of the analyses completed by using the pressure time-series data to infer the underlying reduced-order Markov model. Time-series data is first normalized by subtracting the mean and dividing by the standard deviation of its elements; this step corresponds to bias removal and variance normalization. Data from engineering systems is typically oversampled to ensure that the underlying dynamics can be captured. Due to coarse-graining from the symbolization process, an over-sampled time-series may mask the true nature of the system dynamics in the symbolic domain (e.g., occurrence of self loops and irrelevant spurious transitions in the Markov chain). Time-series is first down-sampled to find the next crucial observation (see Fig. 6.5 for the autocorrelation plot). The first minimum of auto-correlation function generated from the observed time-series is obtained to find the uncorrelated samples in time. The data sets are then down-sampled by this lag. To avoid discarding significant amount of data due to downsampling, down-sampled data using different initial conditions is concatenated. Further details of this preprocessing can be found in [15].

The continuous time-series data set is then partitioned using maximum entropy partitioning (MEP), where the information rich regions of the data set are partitioned finer and those with sparse information are partitioned coarser. In essence, each cell in the partitioned data set contains approximately an equal number of data points under MEP. A ternary alphabet with $\mathscr{A} = \{0, 1, 2\}$ has been used to symbolize the continuous combustion instability data. As discussed in Sect. 6.4, sets of time-series data from different phases have been analyzed, as the combustion process emerges from stable through the transient to the unstable region.

Figure 6.4 demonstrates the observed changes in the behavior of the data as the combustion operating condition changes from stable to unstable. As seen, there is a change in the empirical distribution which changes from a unimodal-Gaussian to

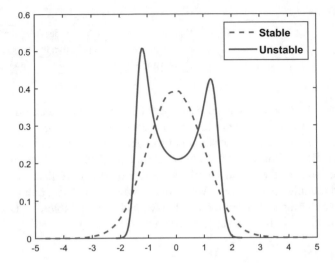

(a) Probability density function for the pressure time-series data

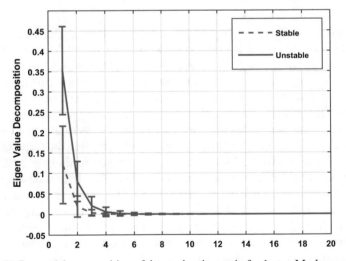

(b) Spectral decomposition of the stochastic matrix for 1-step Markov model

Fig. 6.4 (**a**) shows the change in the empirical density calculated for the pressure time-series data as the process deviates from the stable operating condition to unstable operating condition; (**b**) shows the spectral decomposition of the 1-step stochastic matrix for the data under stable and unstable operating conditions

a multi-modal Gaussian (bi-modal in Fig. 6.4) as the operating condition changes from stable to unstable. Selected 150 samples of pressure data from the stable and unstable phases each are analyzed and compared.

First, the expected size of temporal memory is compared during the two phases. There are changes in the Eigen value decomposition rate for the 1-step stochastic

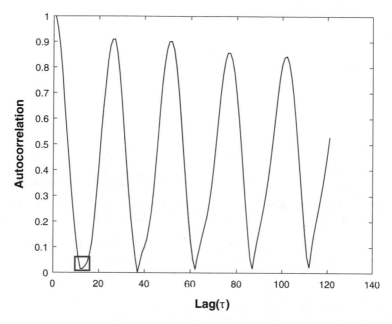

Fig. 6.5 Autocorrelation function of time-series data in the unstable phase of combustion. The time-series data is down-sampled by the lag marked in the red square. It is noted that the individual time-series have their own down-sampling lags

matrix calculated from the data during the stable and unstable behavior, irrespective of the combustor length and inlet velocity. During stable conditions, the Eigen values very quickly go to zero as compared to the unstable operating condition. This suggests that the size of temporal memory of the discretized data increases as the system move to the unstable operating condition. This indicates that under the stable operating condition, the discretized data behaves as symbolic noise as the predictive power of Markov models remain unaffected even if the order of the Markov model is increased. On the other hand, the predictive power of the Markov models can be increased by increasing the order of the Markov model during unstable operating condition, indicating more deterministic behavior. An $\epsilon = 0.05$ is chosen to estimate the depth of the Markov models for both the stable and unstable phases. Correspondingly, the depth was calculated as 2 and 3 for the stable and unstable conditions (see Fig. 6.4).

The corresponding $D(\epsilon)$ is used to construct the Markov models next. First a PFSA whose states are words over $\mathscr{A}$ of length $D(\epsilon)$ is created and the corresponding maximum-likely parameters (M and Π) are estimated. Then, the hierarchical clustering algorithm using K-L distance is used to cluster and aggregate the states. It is noted that individual models are created for every sample of data, i.e., every sample is partitioned individually so that the symbols will have different meaning for every sample. Consequently, each sample will have a different state-space when viewed in the continuous domain. Thus, the mean behavior of the

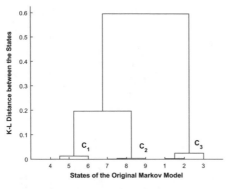

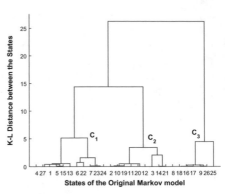

(a) Hierarchical cluster tree of the states
during stable behavior

(b) Hierarchical cluster tree of the states
during unstable behavior

Fig. 6.6 (**a**) shows hierarchical cluster tree for the states of the original Markov model obtained
during stable combustion process; (**b**) shows the same during unstable behavior

samples is not shown during any operating regime as the state-space would be
inconsistent (even though the cardinality could be the same).

Figure 6.6 shows the hierarchical cluster tree that details the structure of the
state-space for the PFSA with depth $D(\epsilon)$ for a typical sample during stable and
unstable behavior. The cluster tree also suggests the symbolic noise behavior of the
data during the stable regime (the states are very close to each other based on the
K-L distance). However, clearly a coarse clustering of states in the model during
the unstable behavior would lead to significant information loss (as the states are
statistically different). However, to compare the two Markov models, the cardinality
of the final models are kept the same. The algorithm is terminated with 3 states in the
final Markov model during the stable as well as the unstable regime. The parameters
of the final Markov model are then estimated using the PFSA models of depth $D(\epsilon)$
using the dynamic Bayesian network approach explained in Sect. 6.3.2.

Figure 6.7 presents some results to show the class separability and changes
in the Markov models as the states are aggregated. As the model is computed
individually for every sample, comparing the stochastic matrices directly is not
consistent. Instead a measure is introduced to model the complexity of the Markov
model for every sample as follows: $\eth = \max_{q_i, q_j \in \mathcal{Q}} d(q_i, q_j)$ (where d is defined in
Eq. (6.5)). Essentially, the measure $\eth$ represents the maximum divergence between
the symbol emission probabilities from the states of the Markov model created.
Then, the statistics of $\eth$ obtained for the Markov models are compared during stable
and unstable conditions. In Fig. 6.7a, it could be seen that the measure $\eth$ is clearly
able to separate the stable and unstable conditions with the original model.

Figure 6.7b shows the results with the final aggregated model with just 3 states.
As seen in Fig. 6.7b, there is some information loss upon model reduction; however,
there is still good class separability. Another point to note is that while there is

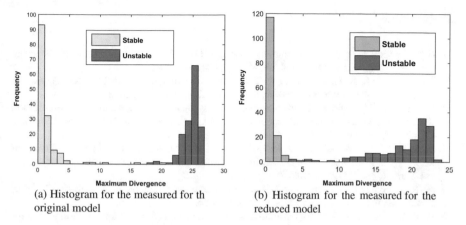

(a) Histogram for the measured for th original model

(b) Histogram for the measured for the reduced model

Fig. 6.7 (**a**) shows the class separability with the original bigger model; (**b**) shows changes after state aggregation

significant change in the set with unstable operating condition, there isn't much change in the behavior of the measure during stable operating condition.

6.6 Conclusions and Future Work

This chapter has presented a methodology for Markov modeling of time-series data for dynamic data-driven application systems (DDDAS) [3, 4]. The technical approach is based on the concepts of symbolic dynamics, where the memory size of the discretized time-series data is estimated to infer the equivalence class of states based on KL distance. The proposed concepts have been tested on experimental data from a swirl-stabilized combustor apparatus used to study unstable thermo-acoustic phenomena during the combustion process. The proposed approach affords the complexity of inferring the time-series data based on a Markov model. Use of Bayesian methods to infer models with various end objectives (e.g., class separability and clustering) is a topic of future research. Another important topic of future work is consistency analysis of the spectral method for memory estimation of the considered class of Markov models. Using multi-dimensional partitioning techniques from [28], this work can be readily extended to multi-variate time-series data.

Acknowledgments The authors would like to thank Professor Domenic Santavicca and Mr. Jihang Li of Center for Propulsion, Penn State for kindly providing the experimental data for combustion used in this work. Benefits of technical discussion with Dr. Shashi Phoha at Penn State are also thankfully acknowledged.

References

1. P. B. Graben, "Estimating and improving the signal-to-noise ratio of time series by symbolic dynamics," *Physical Review E*, vol. 64, no. 5, p. 051104, 2001.
2. C. S. Daw, C. E. A. Finney, and E. R. Tracy, "A review of symbolic analysis of experimental data," *Review of Scientific Instruments*, vol. 74, no. 2, pp. 915–930, 2003.
3. F. Darema, "Dynamic data driven applications systems: New capabilities for application simulations and measurements," in *5th International Conference on Computational Science - ICCS 2005*, Atlanta, GA; United States, 2005.
4. S. Sarkar, S. Chakravarthy, V. Ramanan, and A. Ray, "Dynamic data-driven prediction of instability in a swirl-stabilized combustor," *International Journal of Spray and Combustion*, vol. 8, no. 4, pp. 235–253, 2016.
5. A. Ray, "Symbolic dynamic analysis of complex systems for anomaly detection," *Signal Processing*, vol. 84, no. 7, pp. 1115–1130, July 2004.
6. K. Mukherjee and A. Ray, "State splitting and merging in probabilistic finite state automata for signal representation and analysis," *Signal Processing*, vol. 104, pp. 105–119, 2014.
7. I. Chattopadhyay and H. Lipson, "Abductive learning of quantized stochastic processes with probabilistic finite automata," *Philosophical Transactions of the Royal Society of London A: Mathematical, Physical and Engineering Sciences*, vol. 371, no. 1984, p. 20110543, 2013.
8. C. M. Bishop, *Pattern recognition and machine learning*. Springer, 2006.
9. C. R. Shalizi and K. L. Shalizi, "Blind construction of optimal nonlinear recursive predictors for discrete sequences," in *Proceedings of the 20th Conference on Uncertainty in Artificial Intelligence*, ser. UAI '04, 2004, pp. 504–511.
10. Y. Seto, N. Takahashi, D. K. Jha, N. Virani, and A. Ray, "Data-driven robot gait modeling via symbolic time series analysis," in *American Control Conference (ACC), 2016*. IEEE, 2016, pp. 3904–3909.
11. K. Deng, Y. Sun, P. G. Mehta, and S. P. Meyn, "An information-theoretic framework to aggregate a markov chain," in *American Control Conference, 2009. ACC'09*. IEEE, 2009, pp. 731–736.
12. B. C. Geiger, T. Petrov, G. Kubin, and H. Koeppl, "Optimal kullback–leibler aggregation via information bottleneck," *Automatic Control, IEEE Transactions on*, vol. 60, no. 4, pp. 1010–1022, 2015.
13. M. Vidyasagar, "A metric between probability distributions on finite sets of different cardinalities and applications to order reduction," *Automatic Control, IEEE Transactions on*, vol. 57, no. 10, pp. 2464–2477, 2012.
14. Y. Xu, S. M. Salapaka, and C. L. Beck, "Aggregation of graph models and markov chains by deterministic annealing," *Automatic Control, IEEE Transactions on*, vol. 59, no. 10, pp. 2807–2812, 2014.
15. A. Srivastav, "Estimating the size of temporal memory for symbolic analysis of time-series data," *American Control Conference, Portland, OR, USA*, pp. 1126–1131, June 2014.
16. D. K. Jha, A. Srivastav, K. Mukherjee, and A. Ray, "Depth estimation in Markov models of time-series data via spectral analysis," in *American Control Conference (ACC), 2015*. IEEE, 2015, pp. 5812–5817.
17. D. K. Jha, "Learning and decision optimization in data-driven autonomous systems," Ph.D. dissertation, The Pennsylvania State University, 2016.
18. D. K. Jha, A. Srivastav, and A. Ray, "Temporal learning in video data using deep learning and Gaussian processes," *International Journal of Prognostics and Health Monitoring*, vol. 7, no. 22, p. 11, 2016.
19. S. Sarkar, D. K. Jha, A. Ray, and Y. Li, "Dynamic data-driven symbolic causal modeling for battery performance & health monitoring," in *Information Fusion (Fusion), 2015 18th International Conference on*. IEEE, 2015, pp. 1395–1402.

20. J. Lin, E. Keogh, L. Wei, and S. Lonardi, "Experiencing SAX: a novel symbolic representation of time series," *Data Mining and Knowledge Discovery*, vol. 15, no. 2, pp. 107–144, October 2007.
21. D. Lind and B. Marcus, *An introduction to symbolic dynamics and coding.*   Cambridge University Press, 1995.
22. S. Garcia, J. Luengo, J. A. Saez, V. Lopez, and F. Herrera, "A survey of discretization techniques: Taxonomy and empirical analysis in supervised learning," *IEEE Transactions on Knowledge and Data Engineering*, vol. 99, no. PrePrints, 2012.
23. V. Rajagopalan and A. Ray, "Symbolic time series analysis via wavelet-based partitioning," *Signal Processing*, vol. 86, no. 11, pp. 3309–3320, November 2006.
24. R. Xu and D. Wunsch, "Survey of clustering algorithms," *Neural Networks, IEEE Transactions on*, vol. 16, no. 3, pp. 645–678, 2005.
25. D. K. Jha, N. Virani, J. Reimann, A. Srivastav, and A. Ray, "Symbolic analysis-based reduced order markov modeling of time series data," *Signal Processing*, vol. 149, pp. 68–81, 2018.
26. N. Virani, D. K. Jha, A. Ray, and S. Phoha, "Sequential hypothesis tests for streaming data via symbolic time-series analysis," *Engineering Applications of Artificial Intelligence*, vol. 81, pp. 234–246, 2019.
27. V. N. Vapnik, *Statistical learning theory.*   Wiley New York, 1998, vol. 1.
28. N. Virani, J.-W. Lee, S. Phoha, and A. Ray, "Information-space partitioning and symbolization of multi-dimensional time-series data using density estimation," in *2016 American Control Conference (ACC).*   IEEE, 2016, pp. 3328–3333.

Chapter 7
Dynamic Space-Time Model for Syndromic Surveillance with Particle Filters and Dirichlet Process

Hong Yan, Zhongqiang Zhang, and Jian Zou

Abstract Massive spatio-temporal data are challenging for statistical analysis due to their low signal-to-noise ratios and high-dimensional spatio-temporal structure. To resolve these issues, we propose a novel Dirichlet process particle filter (DPPF) model. The Dirichlet process models a set of stochastic functions as probability distributions for dimension reduction, and the particle filter is used to solve the nonlinear filtering problem with sequential Monte Carlo steps where the data has a low signal-to-noise ratio. Our data set is derived from surveillance data on emergency visits for influenza-like and respiratory illness (from 2008 to 2010) from the Indiana Public Health Emergency Surveillance System. The DPPF develops a dynamic data-driven applications system (DDDAS) methodology for disease outbreak detection. Numerical results show that our model significantly improves the outbreak detection performance in real data analysis.

Keywords Syndromic surveillance · Space-time model · Dirichlet process · Particle filters · Outbreak detection

7.1 Background

Significant morbidity and mortality are potentially caused by communicable diseases if not detected in time. The recent Ebola outbreak in West Africa has infected more than 30,000 people and killed over 11,000 [6]. Enhancement of the ability to model and predict disease outbreaks and hotspots could help to improve our decision-making strategies, such as when to close schools and how to allocate vaccines. With the development of modern technologies, it is imperative to collect and analyze data from surveillance so that such communicable diseases can be predicted and infection can be contained days or weeks before outbreaks.

H. Yan · Z. Zhang · J. Zou (✉)
Department of Mathematical Sciences, Worcester Polytechnic Institute, Worcester, MA, USA
e-mail: jzou@wpi.edu

© The Author(s), under exclusive license to Springer Nature Switzerland AG 2022   147
E. P. Blasch et al. (eds.), *Handbook of Dynamic Data Driven Applications Systems*,
https://doi.org/10.1007/978-3-030-74568-4_7

Several syndromic surveillance systems have been put in use nationally in recent years, such as the Center for Disease Control (CDC)'s BioSense program, Early Aberration Response System (EARS) and Electronic Surveillance System for the Early Notification of Community-Based Epidemics (ESSENCE), as reviewed by [4]. The data set used in this chapter is derived from emergency department (ED) visits for influenza-like illness and respiratory illness in the Indiana Public Health Emergency Surveillance System (PHESS). Indiana has the largest Health Information Exchange, including a comprehensive coverage of individual information. The data are collected in nearly real time, which means data can be obtained within seconds with almost no delay in reporting.

In our analysis, we choose three-year visits data from 2008 to 2010. There are several difficulties in analyzing the real surveillance data. First, the daily data in three years contain both time and spatial covariates, with a dimension of 1096×92 (1096 days and 92 counties). Second, the existing algorithms do not perform well enough to accurately detect the outbreaks. For example, a huge number of false alarms have been generated in outbreak detections using the existing CDC algorithm. Thus, there is a need to develop a novel framework to achieve dimension reduction and computational efficiency through dynamic data-driven applications systems (DDDAS).

There are two important challenging issues that should be addressed: high-dimension and low signal-to-noise ratio in a spatio-temporal dynamic structure. Both of them have influences on the performance of outbreak detection. Many existing spatio-temporal methods, e.g., [16, 22, 36], articulate variations associated with covariate information and uncertainty quantification. Zou et al. [38] propose a Bayesian framework incorporates Gaussian Markov random field and spatio-temporal conditional autoregressive models. The framework allows timely outbreak detections for syndromic surveillance systems, while providing a systematic means for quantifying spatial and temporal uncertainty.

Application system DDDAS is a paradigm that dynamically inputs data to improve outcome accuracy and algorithm efficiency. It is a popular topic and has been employed to many applications [27–31, 35]. In this chapter, we propose a novel hierarchal Bayesian framework to accommodate these two issues: by first applying the method of Dirichlet process to cluster our data and then use a hidden Markov model which is solved with a particle filter technique. The DDDAS-related DPPF framework will be detailed in Sect. 7.2. The benefits of combining Dirichlet process with particle filters are three-fold. First, the employment of Dirichlet process achieves dimension reduction and automatic selection of number of spatial clusters without the need of a pre-specified cluster number. Second, our model is semi-parametric and incorporates spatial dependency through a DDDAS approach. Third, as compared to traditional methods such as the Kalman filter, particle filters obtain hidden variables effectively especially in our nonlinear model.

A Dirichlet process is a non-parametric Bayesian method which allows relaxation of the parametric assumption and significantly enhances model versatility. In a clustering problem, the most salient advantage of Dirichlet process is the automatic selection of the number of clusters, in contrast of being specified by the experimenter than most existing machine learning methods, see [1, 3, 13, 15] and more recent developments in [12] (stick-breaking processes), [10] (local Dirichlet process), [32] (nested Dirichlet process), and [34] (hierarchical Dirichlet processes). Bayesian nonparametric spatial modeling with Dirichlet process has been applied to many applications of spatio-temporal data analysis [7, 11, 17, 18, 24].

The main purpose of a Hidden Markov model (HMM) is to identify the hidden states from observed dynamical data. HMM based methods have been widely used for surveillance data, see [19, 23, 25, 26, 37]. To solve for the hidden states, one can use stochastic filters, Kalman filter [21], particle filter or ensemble Kalman filter [2, 5, 14, 33] develops MEnF filter by combining Gaussian mixture models and ensemble filter. It achieves dimension and uncertainty reductions. Compared to a traditional HMM, the employment of Dirichlet process achieves dimension reduction and reduces the between-group dependency for filtering.

The rest of the chapter is organized as follows. In Sect. 7.2, we present our proposed DPPF model and all methods. We apply the DPPF model to the real data from the Indiana Public Health Emergency Surveillance System (PHESS) and discuss the outbreak detection results in Sect. 7.3. Concluding remarks are discussed in Sect. 7.4.

7.2 Methodology

This section presents our semi-parametric DPPF model which consists of two parts: Dirichlet process and particle filters. An adjacency matrix is employed to further accommodate the spatial information after clustering with the Dirichlet process. Outbreak detection performance is measured by statistical process control charts.

Counts of discrete cases are usually assumed to be from a Poisson distribution. In the influenza-like illness surveillance data, the number of syndrome counts within each day in a certain spatial region is collected and the counts are assumed to follow a Poisson distribution. Counts of the ith region on time t is denoted by y_{it}, x_{i1t} is time stamp and x_{i2t} represents day of the week. The spatial effect θ_i follows a Dirichlet process and θ_i is for the region (county) i. The semi-parametric model is as follows.

$$y_{it}|\theta_i \sim \text{Poisson}(\exp(\beta_1 x_{i1t} + \beta_2 x_{i2t} + \theta_i)), \quad i=1,\ldots,n, \ t=1,\ldots,T, \quad (7.1)$$

$$\theta_i|G \sim G, \quad i=1,\ldots,n, \quad (7.2)$$

$$G|\alpha, G_0 \sim \text{DP}(\alpha G_0), \quad G_0 = \mathcal{N}(\mu, \Sigma), \ \alpha > 0, \quad (7.3)$$

$$\mathbb{E}[y_{\lambda_{jl},t}] = \xi_{jt}, \quad \lambda_{jl} \in C_j, \ l=1,\ldots,n_j, \ j=1,\ldots,m, \quad (7.4)$$

$$\xi_t = A\zeta_t + \mathbf{v}_t, \quad \xi_t, \mathbf{v}_t \in \mathbb{R}^m, \ A \in \mathbb{R}^{m\times m}, \quad (7.5)$$

$$\zeta_t = D\zeta_{t-1} + \zeta_{t-1}(1 - \frac{\zeta_{t-1}}{k}) + \mathbf{w}_t, \quad \zeta_t, \mathbf{w}_t \in \mathbb{R}^m, \ D \in \mathbb{R}^{m\times m}. \quad (7.6)$$

The set $C_j = \{\lambda_{j1}, \lambda_{j2}, \ldots, \lambda_{jn_j}\}$ consists of all the indices of counties clustered into the jth group from Dirichlet process (7.1), (7.2), and (7.3). After the clustering using Dirichlet process (7.5), (7.2), and (7.3), data are aggregated by clusters to obtain $\boldsymbol{\xi}_t$ which serves as observations in the nonlinear filter (7.5) and (7.6). The nonlinear filter finally estimates the hidden variable $\boldsymbol{\zeta}_t \in \mathbb{R}^m$ on clusters.

Now we describe the computation of hyper-parameters, $\boldsymbol{\beta}$, A, D, k and the Gaussian noise $\mathbf{v}_t$, $\mathbf{w}_t$ from (7.5) and (7.6). The covariance matrix Q of $\mathbf{w}_t$ is diagonal and the covariance matrix R of $\mathbf{v}_t$ is a compound symmetry covariance matrix. Capacity is mimicked by parameter k with a large initial value. The basline spatial effect of θ_i is a normal distribution $G_0 = \mathcal{N}(\boldsymbol{\mu}, \Sigma)$. Both $\boldsymbol{\mu}$ and Σ are the mean and variance from a normal distribution which are assumed to have informative priors $\boldsymbol{\mu} \sim \mathcal{N}(\boldsymbol{\mu}_0, \Sigma_0)$ and $\Sigma \sim \mathrm{IW}(a, b)$ respectively. $\mathrm{IW}(a, b)$ is the inverse Wishart distribution with scale matrix a and degrees of freedom b. We assume that the $\boldsymbol{\beta}$'s are from a multivariate normal distribution $\boldsymbol{\beta} \sim \mathcal{N}(\boldsymbol{\beta}_0, \Sigma_\beta)$. The concentration parameter $\alpha > 0$ is assumed to have a Gamma prior $\alpha \sim \Gamma(a_0, b_0)$. Both of the noises $\mathbf{w}_t$ and $\mathbf{v}_t$ are from normal distributions with $\mathbf{w}_t \sim \mathcal{N}(0, Q)$ and $\mathbf{v}_t \sim \mathcal{N}(0, R)$ respectively. A maximum likelihood estimation (MLE) is used to obtain initial estimations of A, D, k, Q and R.

7.2.1 Dirichlet Process

Compared to many traditional clustering algorithms, a Dirichlet process could automatically obtain the number of clusters without a pre-specified number of clusters. In the DPPF model, the spatial effect is assumed to be from a Dirichlet process.

In (7.1), (7.2), and (7.3) the normal distribution $G_0 = \mathcal{N}(\boldsymbol{\mu}, \Sigma)$ has mean $\boldsymbol{\mu}$ and a covariance Σ, both of which have informative priors $\boldsymbol{\mu} \sim \mathcal{N}(\boldsymbol{\mu}_0, \Sigma_0)$ and $\Sigma \sim \mathrm{IW}(a, b)$ respectively. The distribution $\mathrm{IW}(a, b)$ is the inverse Wishart distribution with scale matrix a and degrees of freedom b. We also assume that the $\boldsymbol{\beta}$'s obey a normal distribution $\boldsymbol{\beta} \sim \mathcal{N}(\boldsymbol{\beta}_0, \Sigma_\beta)$. The concentration parameter $\alpha > 0$ is assumed to have a Gamma prior $\alpha \sim \Gamma(a_0, b_0)$. Posterior distribution of θ_i is given by

$$\pi(\theta_i | \theta_1, \ldots, \theta_{i-1}, \alpha, \boldsymbol{\mu}, \Sigma) = \frac{\alpha}{\alpha + i - 1} G_0(\boldsymbol{\mu}, \Sigma)$$

$$+ \frac{1}{\alpha + i - 1} \sum_{j=1}^{i-1} \delta_{\theta_j}(\theta_i), \ i = 2, \cdots, m. \quad (7.7)$$

A small α implies small probability that θ_i is a new value drawn randomly from G_0, which leads to a small number (m) of distinct values of $\boldsymbol{\theta}$; and a large α indicates there will be more clusters, i.e., larger m.

In practice, it often requires to choose "the best" from many clustering results obtained from a Dirichlet processes. Thus, a rule is needed to select a optimal clustering results from Dirichlet process since the clustering from Dirichlet process is not unique due to the use of a sequential Markov Chain Monte Carlo. To this end, we propose a preference-based selection principle, which fully utilizes all the clustering information from the Dirichlet processes. Since the adjacency matrix is not a well-known construct associated with a Dirichlet process, we define a quantitative index, called the *influential index* and use it to find optimal clustering results.

The influential index is calculated as follows. Denote the column summation of the adjacency matrix M by $S = \{s_1, s_2, \ldots, s_n\}$, where n is the number of regions and $s_i = \sum_{j=1}^{n} M_{ij}$. Here M_{ij} is set to be $1/n_i$ when regions i and j are adjacent and otherwise 0, where n_i is the number of neighbors of region i. After the Dirichlet process, data are aggregated from the same cluster by adding all the elements from M column-wise and row-wise, so that the same cluster has a unique label. In some sense, s_k is what the region k contributes to all its neighbors. Assume that there are L clustering results from the Dirichlet process and in the lth clustering result, there are c_l clusters/groups, $1 \leq l \leq L$. Denote the lth clustering result by $D_l = \{\tau_{l1}, \tau_{l2}, \ldots, \tau_{lc_l}\}$, $1 \leq l \leq L$, where τ_{lk} contains all labels of regions in the kth cluster of the lth clustering result. Then the selection is determined by the largest value(s) of the influential index defined as:

$$\text{Ind}_l = \sum_{k=1}^{c_l} |\tau_{lk}| \sum_{i \in \tau_{lk}} s_i, \quad 1 \leq l \leq L. \tag{7.8}$$

where $|\tau_{lk}|$ is the number of elements in set τ_{lk}. If Ind_l for some $1 \leq l \leq L$ has the largest value, then the lth clustering is used for later data processing.

7.2.2   Particle Filter

To model incidence rates after clustering through Dirichlet process, we employ a particle filter, i.e., a number of independent random variables called particles are used to estimate the hidden variables. The particles are sampled directly from the state space, representing the posterior distribution. New observations are involved to update the posterior probabilities and the system is propagated recursively according to Bayesian rule.

Note the (7.5) and (7.6) have Markov linear observations. With a further assumption on $\mathbf{w}_t$ and $\mathbf{v}_t$ as Gaussian random variables, the goals of the nonlinear filter $\mathbb{E}[\boldsymbol{\zeta}_t | \boldsymbol{\xi}_t]$'s for $t = 1, 2, \ldots, T$ are Gaussian which can be solved explicitly. Even though this problem can be solved by the classical Kalman filter [20], our model is nonlinear and the evaluation of nonlinear functional is a challenge even with Gaussian parameters. We then use instead a particle filter technique to solve the problem, which is achieved by sequential Monte Carlo methods. In a sequential Monte Carlo simulation, the prior and the posterior distributions are approximated by discrete distributions. With a resampling technique, this particle filter is an efficient implementation [9]. The recursive nature and relative low cost are the advantages of a particle filter approach.

We assume that there are J particles. Then ζ_t could be drawn from the posterior distribution,

$$\zeta_{t+1}|\zeta_t, \xi_{t+1} \sim \mathcal{N}(\mu, \Sigma), \tag{7.9}$$

$$\mu = \Sigma(Q^{-1}g(\zeta_t) + A'R^{-1}\xi_{t+1}), \tag{7.10}$$

$$\Sigma = (Q^{-1} + A'R^{-1}A)^{-1}. \tag{7.11}$$

In practice, the nonlinear functional of $\zeta_{i,t+1}$ is evaluated by

$$\mathbb{E}[f(\zeta_{t+1})|\zeta_t, \xi_{t+1}] \approx \sum_{j=1}^{J} f(\zeta_{t+1}^{(j)}|\zeta_t, \xi_{t+1})p_{t+1}^{(j)},$$

where $\zeta_{t+1}^{(j)}$ are Monte Carlo samples (often called particles) and the weights $p_{t+1}^{(j)}$ can be obtained recursively:

$$p_{t+1}^{(j)} \propto p_t^{(j)}\exp(-\eta^{(j)}), \quad j = 1, \ldots, J.$$

$$\eta^{(j)} = \frac{1}{2}(\xi_{t+1} - Ag(\zeta_t^{(j)}))^{\mathsf{T}}K^{-1}(\xi_{t+1} - Ag(\zeta_t^{(j)})),$$

$$K = R + AQA^{\mathsf{T}},$$

where $g(\zeta_{t-1}) = D\zeta_{t-1} + \zeta_{t-1}(1 - \frac{\zeta_{t-1}}{k})$ as demonstrated in Eq. (7.6).

7.2.3 Evaluation of the Method

A popular statistical quality control chart – exponentially weighted moving average (EWMA) control chart is employed to evaluate the proposed DPPF method. Control charts are usually used to detect violations that depart from a specified center or the sample center. Since the focus is on the detection of an outbreak of a certain disease, the violations below the center line are not of interest for our surveillance data analysis.

In practice, we would like an early signal for out-of-control process to indicate an abnormality, and hence a dynamic indicator of a possible disease outbreak. Since large control limits will result in an increase of out-of-control average run length (ARL) for any shift and reduce the power of the chart, the results are reported in

the EWMA chart with control limit up to 4σ. The 4σ threshold is selected for two reasons. First, it may be difficult to detect the true positives if large control limits is used, especially for true positive rate (TPR) and negative predictive value (NPV) as the detection effectiveness decreases as control limit increases. Second, if control limits are too large in the EWMA chart, it will result in large type II errors.

Outbreak detection performances are evaluated by comparing the detected results with the true outbreaks. The benchmark set consists of the label of points that identify the points as outbreaks or not. Points are defined as true positives if they are outbreaks in both benchmark and EWMA detection results. True negatives are regular periods that are not detected as outbreaks in EWMA. False positive and false negative points are defined similarly. Five indices are reported, accuracy (ACC), sensitivity (TPR), specificity (SPC), positive predictive value (PPV) and negative predictive value (NPV).

7.3 Applications with Indiana Surveillance Data

The surveillance data of this study come from the Indiana Public Health Emergency Surveillance System (PHESS). The dataset contains emergency department visits for influenza-like illness and respiratory illness. There are about seven million observations in the data set, ranging from 2008 to 2010. The DPPF model is applied to the real data by first clustering through Dirichlet process and then obtaining hidden variables by particle filters as described in Sect. 7.2. After the Dirichlet process steps, the 92 counties in Indiana are clustered into 25 spatial groups. As a comparison, we also consider another method involving the regional labor market information as discussed in [39], which clusters the counties into 11 regions. Detection performance by our DPPF model is compared to the results by the following three methods: (1) using the raw data with 92 counties; (2) using regional labor market data with 11 regions; and (3) dimension reduced data by Dirichlet process without filtering.

Time series plot of the 25 groups after Dirichlet process is in Fig. 7.1. The highest value is around 670 days with the largest outbreak, which is in October, 2009. The CDC 2009–2010 influenza season report [8] confirms that the peak of weekly percentage of visits for influenza like illness is indeed at the end of October, 2009. This peak is higher than all three previous flu seasons, as shown in Fig. 7.1. Such a high peak will dominate the process and make it difficult to discover other moderate and small outbreaks. The time series plot of filtered states is shown in Fig. 7.2. The magnitudes of the filtered states are smaller than those of observations and the overall shape of the latent states is similar to the raw data.

Figure 7.3 shows the clustering results for real data after the Dirichlet process. Average incidence rate for each of the clusters is provided in a heat map, which is an Indiana state map with 92 counties. Colors in the map present the average incidence rate of each cluster for the corresponding season. The average value increases with the darkness of the color, from white to dark red. The last season of 2009 has a

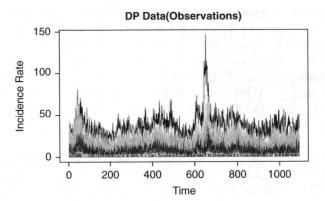

Fig. 7.1 Time series plot for DP data

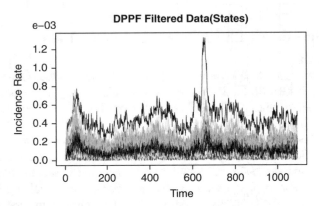

Fig. 7.2 Time series plot for DPPF data

relatively dark color, which implies the high level of incidence rate during this time. This period is the outbreak of the 2009 H1N1 activity.

To evaluate different methods in outbreak detection, we refer to the CDC's influenza season summary [8]: *"the proportion of specimens testing positive for influenza first exceeded 10% during the week ending January 12, 2008 (week 2), peaked at 32% during the week ending February 9, 2008 (week 6), and declined to <10% during the week ending April 19, 2008 (week 16). The proportion was above 10% positive for 14 consecutive weeks"*. Thus we obtain the first outbreak from 01/12/2008 to 04/19/2008 (99 days).

According to the CDC report for the past decade, the flu peak month is usually during December to March. However, the H1N1 pandemic during this period complicated the situation and there were both common flu season and the H1N1 outbreak. The second outbreak period, which is also the H1N1 period, occurred from 08/30/2009 to 12/12/2009 (104 days). We use the averaged value within each cluster and each season for our analysis. By comparing the results spatially, we can

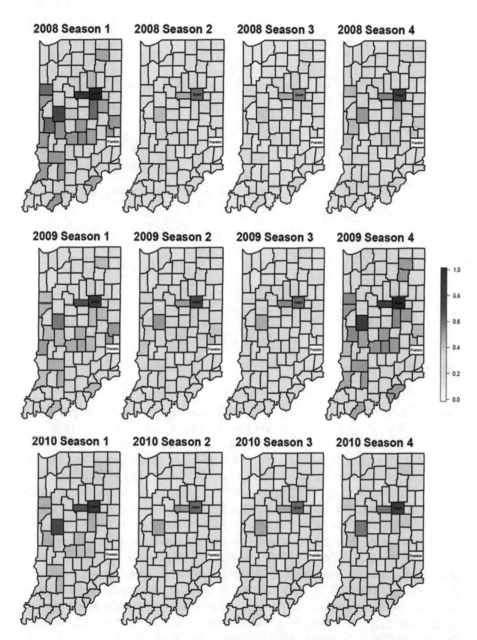

Fig. 7.3 Indiana Surveillance Data Clustered by Dirichlet Process. Incidence rate of each cluster is a standardized value and scaled to 0–1. Counties with darker color has higher relative incidence rate. Grant county has the highest incidence rate and Franklin has the lowest incidence rate

see that Grant county has the highest incidence rate and Franklin has the lowest incidence rate. However, in seasons without severe outbreaks, such as the second

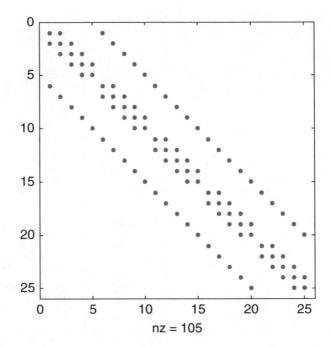

Fig. 7.4 Diffusion Matrix

and third season in 2010, the differences of incidence rate are not significant. We could narrow the time window to one month or even one week to discover more detailed information. In this section, we show the clustering results in seasons for an overall dynamics of the influenza-like illness. We also observe that the first season of 2008 has relatively high incidences except for the highest peak. This is again confirmed by the CDC 2007–2008 influenza-like illness seasonal report, which implies there was an outbreak during the first flu season of 2008.

The filtered data from DPPF model is related with the values of model parameters initially estimated from minimizing the negative log likelihood. For the matrix A in (7.5), we define it as a simple tri-diagonal matrix with the same diagonal value and same off diagonal non-zero value. The matrix D has a block tri-diagonal structure as demonstrated in Fig. 7.4. This is motivated by mimicking the structure of a diffusion matrix discretized from finite difference for Laplacian in a popular type of logistic model. In our model, we have 25 groups and thus D is a 25 by 25 symmetric sparse matrix with diagonal values at 4 and off-diagonals (dotted) at -1.

Figure 7.5 displays outbreak detection results using the real data. Five popular performance measures in classification evaluation have been presented, and our DPPF model shows advantages in almost all of them. Different type of indices show different behaviors as the control limits increase. Generally speaking, for all the four methods in this comparison, ACC, SPC and PPV increase as control limit increase from 1σ to 4σ. For the other two indices, TPR and NPV show the decreasing trends.

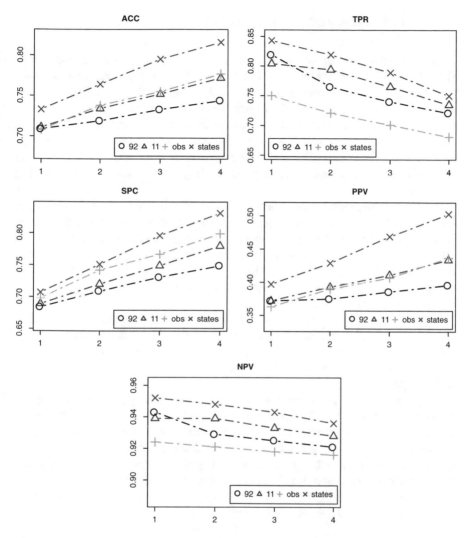

Fig. 7.5 Indiana surveillance data outbreak detection with diagonal Q matrix. (X-axis: control limits. Y-axis: index value. Black ○: raw data (92 counties) results. Red △: regional labor market (11 regions) results. Green +: Dirichlet process results. Blue ×: DPPF results when A is a tri-diagonal matrix)

Except for PPV, the detection precisions of our DPPF model are greater than 70%, and could reach as high as more than 90%. The DPPF still performs the best even for PPV, while all four methods have relatively low detection accuracy. Here we limit the control limits up to 4σ. If the control limit is too large, most of the points will stay within the limits, thus the EWMA chart fails to detect all the outbreaks. This explains why there is a decreasing trend in TPR and NPV when control limits increase.

7.4   Conclusions and Future Work

To accommodate low signal-to-noise ratios and high-dimensional spatio-temporal structure in health surveillance data, we propose a novel hierarchical Bayesian framework that incorporates both spatial and temporal effects via Dirichlet processes and particle filters. Our model (DPPF) is a data driven approach for spatio-temporal dynamics with efficient dimension reduction which provides effective and early detections of outbreaks. The DPPF achieves high accuracy with low signal-to-noise ratio and detects small shifts in the data. Moreover, the computational cost of the DPPF method is significantly lower than a Bayesian approach for the full data dimension.

Since the independence and normality assumptions in statistical control charts are often violated, the use of raw data to do outbreak detection with control charts could be problematic. Our DPPF model is strategically strengthened using the Dirichlet processes for dimension reduction without pre-specifing the number of clusters and reducing the between-cluster spatial dependencies for filtering. The non-parametric property of Dirichlet process enhances model flexibility and affords dynamic data driven detections.

The particle filter provides hidden variable estimation. Compared to the traditional hidden Markov models for surveillance, our DPPF model makes it possible for dynamic states estimation. The numerical results demonstrate that the proposed methodology is effective in modeling and predicting the dynamic patterns of the outbreak process.

The methodology presented here is naturally appealing for a wide range of modeling problems. The DPPF framework will enable public health practitioners in cases of the infeasibility and potential undesirability of likelihood-based inference for massive spatio-temporal outbreak detection. Our parameter estimates are chosen to achieve as close a match as possible, according to an optimal filtering framework, between the observed and fitted values of selected statistical properties. Ongoing research includes investigation of different setup of the filter models in our DPPF framework, such as various A and D matrices.

References

1. C.E. Antoniak, Mixtures of Dirichlet processes with applications to Bayesian nonparametric problems. Ann. Stat. **2**, 1152–1174 (1974)
2. C.H. Bishop, B.J. Etherton, S.J. Majumdar, Adaptive sampling with the ensemble transform Kalman filter. Part I: theoretical aspects. Mon. Weather Rev. **129**(3), 420–436 (2001)
3. D. Blackwell, J.B. MacQueen, Ferguson distributions via pólya urn schemes. Ann. Stat. **1**, 353–355 (1973)
4. R. Brookmeyer, D.F. Stroup, *Monitoring the Health of Populations: Statistical Principles and Methods for Public Health Surveillance* (Oxford University Press, New York, 2003)
5. G. Burgers, P. Jan van Leeuwen, G. Evensen, Analysis scheme in the ensemble Kalman filter. Mon. Weather Rev. **126**(6), 1719–1724 (1998)

6. K. Burghardt et al., Testing modeling assumptions in the West Africa Ebola outbreak. Sci. Rep. **6**, 34598 (2016). https://doi.org/10.1038/srep34598
7. B. Cai, A.B. Lawson, M. Hossain, J. Choi, R.S. Kirby, J. Liu et al., Bayesian semiparametric model with spatially–temporally varying coefficients selection. Stat. Med. **32**(21), 3670–3685 (2013)
8. CDC, *Weekly u.s. influenza surveillance report*, 2007–2008, 2008–2009, 2009–2010 (2016)
9. A.J. Chorin, M. Morzfeld, X. Tu, A survey of implicit particle filters for data assimilation, in *State-Space Models*, ed. by Y. Zeng, S. Wu (Springer, New York, 2013), pp. 63–88
10. Y. Chung, D.B. Dunson, The local Dirichlet process. Ann. Inst. Stat. Math. **63**(1), 59–80 (2011)
11. J.A. Duan, M. Guindani, A.E. Gelfand, Generalized spatial Dirichlet process models. Biometrika **94**(4), 809–825 (2007)
12. D.B. Dunson, J.-H. Park, Kernel stick-breaking processes. Biometrika **95**(2), 307–323 (2008)
13. M.D. Escobar, M. West, Bayesian density estimation and inference using mixtures. J. Am. Stat. Assoc. **90**(430), 577–588 (1995)
14. G. Evensen, Sequential data assimilation with a nonlinear quasi-geostrophic model using monte carlo methods to forecast error statistics. J. Geophys. Res. Oceans **99**(C5), 10143–10162 (1994)
15. T.S. Ferguson, A Bayesian analysis of some nonparametric problems. Ann. Stat. **1**, 209–230 (1973)
16. R.D. Fricker, B.L. Hegler, D.A. Dunfee, Comparing syndromic surveillance detection methods: ears versus a cusum-based methology. Stat. Med. **27**, 3407–3429 (2008)
17. M. Fuentes, B. Reich, Multivariate spatial nonparametric modelling via kernel processes mixing. Stat. Sin. **23**(1), 75–97 (2013)
18. A.E. Gelfand, A. Kottas, S.N. MacEachern, Bayesian nonparametric spatial modeling with Dirichlet process mixing. J. Am. Stat. Assoc. **100**(471), 1021–1035 (2005)
19. P.J. Green, S. Richardson, Hidden Markov models and disease mapping. J. Am. Stat. Assoc. **97**(460), 1055–1070 (2002)
20. M.S. Grewal, A.P. Andrews, A.K. Filtering, *Theory and practice using matlab*, 3rd edn. (Wiley, Hoboken, 2001)
21. R.E. Kalman, A new approach to linear filtering and prediction problems. J. Basic Eng. **82**(1), 35–45 (1960)
22. K. Kleinman, Generalized linear models and generalized linear mixed models for small-area surveillance, in *Spatial and Syndromic Surveillance for Public Health*, ed. by A.B. Lawson, K. Kleinman (Wiley, West Sussex, 2005), pp. 77–94
23. L. Knorr-Held, S. Richardson, A hierarchical model for space–time surveillance data on meningococcal disease incidence. J. R. Stat. Soc. Ser. C Appl. Stat. **52**(2), 169–183 (2003)
24. A. Kottas, J.A. Duan, A.E. Gelfand, Modeling disease incidence data with spatial and spatio temporal Dirichlet process mixtures. Biom. J. **50**(1), 29–42 (2008)
25. A.B. Lawson, K. Kleinman et al., *Spatial and Syndromic Surveillance for Public Health* (Wiley, New York, 2005)
26. Y. Le Strat, F. Carrat, Monitoring epidemiologic surveillance data using hidden Markov models. Stat. Med. **18**(24), 3463–3478 (1999)
27. J. Mandel, J.D. Beezley, *An Ensemble Kalman-Particle Predictor-Corrector Filter for Non-Gaussian Data Assimilation* (Springer, Berlin/Heidelberg, 2009), pp. 470–478
28. J. Mandel, J.D. Beezley, A.K. Kochanski, V.Y. Kondratenko, M. Kim, Assimilation of perimeter data and coupling with fuel moisture in a wildland fire–atmosphere DDDAS. Proc. Comput. Sci. **9**, 1100–1109 (2012)
29. J. Mandel, L.S. Bennethum, M. Chen, J.L. Coen, C.C. Douglas, L.P. Franca, C.J. Johns, M. Kim, A.V. Knyazev, R. Kremens, V. Kulkarni, G. Qin, A. Vodacek, J. Wu, W. Zhao, A. Zornes, *Towards a Dynamic Data Driven Application System for Wildfire Simulation* (Springer, Berlin/Heidelberg, 2005), pp. 632–639

30. A. Patra, M. Bursik, J. Dehn, M. Jones, M. Pavolonis, E.B. Pitman, T. Singh, P. Singla, P. Webley, A DDDAS framework for volcanic ash propagation and hazard analysis. Proc. Comput. Sci. **9**, 1090–1099 (2012)

31. A.K. Patra, M. Bursik, J. Dehn, M. Jones, R. Madankan, D. Morton, M. Pavolonis, E.B. Pitman, S. Pouget, T. Singh et al., Challenges in developing DDDAS based methodology for volcanic ash hazard analysis–effect of numerical weather prediction variability and parameter estimation. Proc. Comput. Sci. **18**, 1871–1880 (2013)

32. A. Rodriguez, D.B. Dunson, A.E. Gelfand, The nested Dirichlet process. J. Am. Stat. Assoc. **103**(483), 1131–1154 (2008)

33. H. Seybold, S. Ravela, P. Tagade, *Ensemble Learning in Non-Gaussian Data Assimilation* (Springer, Cham, 2015), pp. 227–238

34. Y.W. Teh, M.I. Jordan, M.J. Beal, D.M. Blei, Hierarchical Dirichlet processes. J. Am. Stat. Assoc. **101**, 1566–1581 (2006)

35. A. Vodacek, J.P. Kerekes, M.J. Hoffman, Adaptive optical sensing in an object tracking DDDAS. Proc. Comput. Sci. **9**, 1159–1166 (2012)

36. L.A. Waller, B.P. Carlin, H. Xia, A. Gelfand, Hierarchical spatio-temporal mapping of disease rates. J. Am. Stat. Assoc. **92**, 607–617 (1997)

37. R.E. Watkins, S. Eagleson, B. Veenendaal, G. Wright, A.J. Plant, Disease surveillance using a hidden Markov model. BMC Med. Inform. Decis. Mak. **9**(1), 1 (2009)

38. J. Zou, A.F. Karr, D. Banks, M.J. Heaton, G. Datta, J. Lynch, F. Vera, Bayesian methodology for the analysis of spatial–temporal surveillance data. Stat. Anal. Data Min. **5**(3), 194–204 (2012)

39. J. Zou, A.F. Karr, G. Datta, J. Lynch, S.J. Grannis, A Bayesian spatio-temporal approach for real-time detection of disease outbreaks: a case study. BMC Med. Inform. Decis. Mak. **14**(108), 1–18 (2014)

Part III
Structures-Aware: Health Modeling

Chapter 8
A Computational Steering Framework for Large-Scale Composite Structures: Part I—Parametric-Based Design and Analysis

A. Korobenko, M.-C. Hsu, and Y. Bazilevs

Abstract Recent advances in simulation, optimization, structural health monitoring, and high-performance computing create a unique opportunity to combine the developments in these fields to formulate a Dynamic Data-Driven Applications Systems (DDDAS) Interactive Structure Composite Element Relation Network (DISCERN) framework. DISCERN consists of the following items and features: a structural health monitoring (SHM) system, an advanced structural modeling and fluid-structure interaction (FSI) simulation, sensitivity analysis, optimization and control modules. High-performance computing (HPC) is employed to enhance the efficiency and effectiveness of the system. The intended application of the DISCERN framework is the analysis of medium-to-large-scale composite structures. These include aerospace structures, such as military aircraft fuselage and wings, helicopter blades, and unmanned aerial vehicles, and civil structures, such as wind turbine blades and towers. The proposed DISCERN framework continuously and dynamically integrates the SHM data into the analysis of these structures. This capability allows one to: (1) Shelter the structures from excessive stress levels during operation; (2) Make informed decisions to perform structural maintenance and repair; and (3) Predict the remaining fatigue life of the structure. In Part I we present the computational framework for parametric-based design and analysis of these structures, and in Part II we discuss the optimization and control modules within the proposed DISCERN framework, including the integration of the FSI simulations.

A. Korobenko (✉)
Department of Mechanical and Manufacturing Engineering, University of Calgary, Calgary, AB, Canada
e-mail: artem.korobenko@ucalgary.ca

M.-C. Hsu
Department of Mechanical Engineering, Iowa State University, Ames, IA, USA

Y. Bazilevs
School of Engineering, Brown University, Providence, RI, USA

© The Author(s), under exclusive license to Springer Nature Switzerland AG 2022
E. P. Blasch et al. (eds.), *Handbook of Dynamic Data Driven Applications Systems*,
https://doi.org/10.1007/978-3-030-74568-4_8

Keywords Adjoint-based control · Continuum damage model · Isogeometric analysis · Kirchhoff–Love shells · Progressive damage · Fatigue damage

8.1 Introduction

Dynamic Data-Driven Applications Systems (DDDAS) [15] is a framework in which measurement data collected for a given physical system are used to dynamically update a computational model of that system. Using measurement data, the computational model geometry, boundary conditions, forcing, and material parameters may be updated to better represent physical reality. At the same time, the properly updated computational model is able to produce higher-fidelity outputs for the quantities of interest for which measurements are not readily available. As such, DDDAS is a framework in which measurement and simulation co-exist in a symbiotic environment.

Recent developments in computational mechanics, optimization, structural health monitoring (SHM), and high-performance computing (HPC) create a unique opportunity to formulate a DDDAS framework wherein computational steering can be used for the class of medium to large-scale structural applications [8] (see Fig. 8.1 for an illustration). These include aerospace structures such as aircraft fuselage and wings, helicopter blades, unmanned aerial vehicles, and civil structures

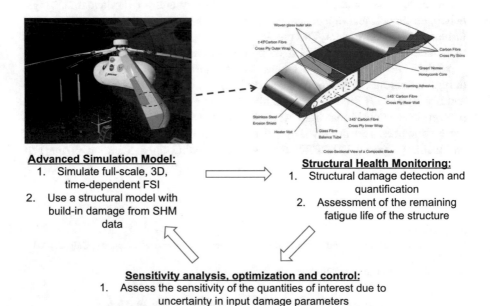

Fig. 8.1 Illustration of the proposed DISCERN framework

such as wind turbine blades and towers. Computational steering enables real-time monitoring and control of structures to minimize fatigue loads, and thereby lengthen structural life, prevent premature failure, and predict the onset of failure. There are several well-known damage scenarios that occur in composite structures primarily resulting from manufacturing. The ability to shelter these structures from excessive fatigue loading, in real time and under fully operational status, results in fewer hours spent on structural maintenance and repair, and could ultimately lead to significant cost savings. The computationally intensive components of this DDDAS framework necessitate utilization of HPC.

Many applications of DDDAS involve not only updating of the computational model on the basis of sensor data, but also adjustment of the model and physical system input parameters to optimize a desired outcome. For example, in [29], the authors developed and deployed a DDDAS framework for computational steering of the laser-guided surgery for prostate cancer treatment. The temperature and location of the laser were dynamically controlled to achieve maximum damage to the cancerous tissue. In our case, we are interested in a DDDAS framework for large-scale structures exposed to aerodynamic loading, such as aircraft fuselage and wings, for which we call our methodology DDDAS Interactive Structure Composite Element Relation Network (DISCERN).

As part of the DISCERN framework, we are interested in dynamically controlling structures to ensure their operation in safe conditions, and to minimize the onset and progression of structural damage. In most cases, the fluid–structure interaction (FSI) [9] effect is important and needs to be included in the underlying computational model. Furthermore, because the FSI effect is significant for damage modeling, a successful dynamic control strategy for our application system must be able to take FSI coupling into account. Such a dynamic control strategy for time-dependent FSI, first proposed in [4], is described in this chapter. The proposed control strategy is based on the simultaneous solution of the primal and adjoint (or sometimes called dual) FSI problems. The solutions of both primal and adjoint FSI problems are used to adjust the control parameters of the application system. Because both primal and adjoint FSI problems involve coupling between the primal and dual fluid and structural mechanics degrees of freedom, the control strategy automatically takes FSI coupling into account.

In this book chapter we present the first two modules of the DISCERN framework focusing on interactive parametric design-through-analysis platform. We present a design-through-analysis platform based on isogeometric analysis (IGA) that offers a user-friendly interface for the entire design process, including geometry modeling, assignment of model material parameters, loads, and boundary conditions, computational analysis, and post-processing. The platform also offers the flexibility to dynamically incorporate data during the different stages of the process. Although we target users that have elementary knowledge of geometry modeling, mechanical and structural design, mechanics of solids, structures, and fluids, and numerical methods, the platform can also be used by experts in these areas.

8.2 Elements of the DISCERN Framework

The proposed platform provides a closed-loop design method for engineering applications as depicted in Fig. 8.2. Once a basic model has been designed through CAD software, simulation may be performed directly using this model after distributing material parameters and specifying boundary and load conditions on model surfaces. After inspecting the solution, the designer can then make a judgment where to improve the current design. Because the original geometry is modeled parametrically, changing the design according to the analysis results would consist of simply adjusting input parameters. As a result, within this closed-loop design process, the user could conceivably create and optimize designs within a shorter timeframe using a single platform. Subsequent sections will detail the contents of the design and analysis components shown in Fig. 8.2. In Part II we will focus on the optimization and control components.

8.2.1 Parametric-Based Design and Interactive Visual Programming

The concept of *parametric modeling* is central to design in many fields of engineering and beyond (e.g., architecture [42]). Currently parametric modeling is used in conjunction with solid geometry modeling that employs geometric primitives and Boolean operations (e.g., SOLIDWORKS [40]). The use of parametric modeling with modern Spline technology like NURBS or T-splines is not common, and presents a novel research direction in IGA. The proposed work builds on the concept of parametric modeling and provides a fairly general and convenient approach for creating parametric designs, which make use of NURBS and T-spline geometry

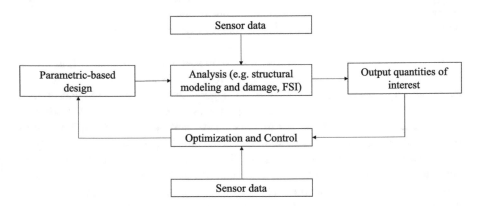

Fig. 8.2 Elements of the DISCERN platform

description, using the visual programming concept. The proposed approach is applicable to a large class of geometries, including surface and volumetric descriptions.

We base our developments on Rhino [33] CAD software. Rhino gives designers a variety of functions that are required to build complex, multi-patch NURBS surfaces [31]. Recently, additional functionality was added in Rhino to create and manipulate T-spline surfaces [1, 39], which is an important enhancement allowing one to move away from a fairly restrictive NURBS-patch-based geometry design to a completely unstructured, watertight surface definition while respecting all the constraints imposed by analysis [37]. Rhino also features an enhanced *graphic programming design tool* for parametric design called Grasshopper [17], and utilizes free and open-source software development kits (SDK) [34] for plug-in development. Furthermore, Rhino is relatively transparent as compared to other CAD software in that it provides the user with the ability to interact with the system through the so-called "plug-in" commands. All of these features are well aligned with our goals, and we exploit them in the design of our IGA-based design-through-analysis platform.

As the visual programming interface, Grasshopper moves away from the traditional paradigm of writing a text file with program instructions, which is then fed to an off-the-shelf compiler to produce an executable file. This approach is bug-prone and often requires significant programming education and expertise. In contrast, using Grasshopper, the program is written in terms of "components" with pre-defined functionality, and "wire connections" between the components that serve as conduits of input and output data. As a result, using an intuitive arrangement of components and connections, one can rapidly generate an analysis model, establish parametric control, and link the model to the desired solver and visualization modalities. In the case when new functionality is needed, a traditional programming approach may be employed to create new components, which are then added to the library of the existing ones, and may be flexibly used by the designer. An example of Grasshopper parametric geometry design of an wind turbine blade is shown in Fig. 8.3.

8.2.2 Analysis

In this work we present the modeling of the thin-shell composite structures based on IGA, however, depending on the targeted application the analysis part can be easily augmented with additional modules. The interested reader can refer to Part II to read about the fluid-structure interaction (FSI) analysis module. Moreover, the integral part of the analysis within the DDDAS paradigm is the data coming from sensors, observations, and other sources (depending on the application). The data can be used to set material properties, loads, and boundary conditions The platform we present in this work naturally enables dynamic integration of the data into analysis for accurate prediction of the structural response. In Part II we also discuss how data can be integrated into the Optimization module.

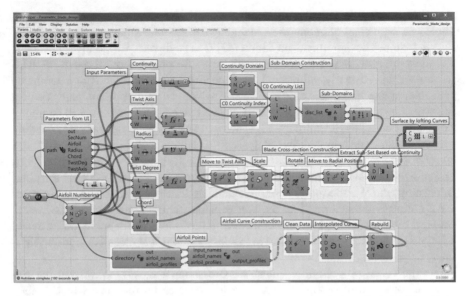

Fig. 8.3 Grasshopper generative algorithm for parametric geometry design of wind turbine blade

8.2.2.1 Modeling of Thin-Shell Composites Using Isogeometric Analysis

We start with a description of Isogeometric Analysis (IGA), which presents a core structural modeling platform in this work. IGA is a recently introduced FEM-like simulation methodology that relies on the geometry representation of Computer-Aided Design (CAD), Computer Graphics (CG), and animation [3, 13, 21]. In IGA the geometry and computational solution fields are represented using the same functional description. The most widely used discretization in IGA makes use of non-Uniform Rational B-Splines (NURBS) [31], but other alternatives, such as T-splines [2, 38], are currently being developed and routinely used. As a result of this choice, integration of structural design and computational analysis is greatly simplified. This single representation of the geometry and solution fields allows a direct interaction with as-build geometry, which is needed at different stages of modeling and simulation. IGA is an inherently higher-order accurate technique, and, in addition, the basis functions in IGA are of higher-order continuity than standard FEM. This additional smoothness property is a distinguishing feature of IGA, and is beneficial in many applications of computational mechanics (see, e.g., [13]).

Aerospace and civil composite structures of interest in this work, such as aircraft fuselage, wings, and wind turbine blades, are geometrically complex, curved thin shells. As a result, to simulate such structures at full scale and with sufficient geometric detail, discretization of thin shell theories are employed for computational efficiency, and are key to structural modeling of laminated composites. Isogeometric shell analysis was recently proposed in [10] to address the shortcomings of standard finite element technology for thin shells. It was found that higher-order continuity

(C^1 and above) of the IGA basis functions significantly improved the per-degree-of-freedom accuracy and robustness of thin shell discretizations as compared to the FEM. Furthermore, the increased continuity of IGA discretizations enabled the use of shell kinematics without rotational degrees of freedom and the development of a new class of Kirchhoff–Love shell formulations [11, 22, 23], leading to further computational cost savings associated with the analysis of thin structures. The isogeometric rotation-free Kirchhoff–Love shell formulation was successfully applied in the context of fluid-structure interaction modeling of wind turbines in [5–7, 24]. In what follows, we present the basics of the thin shell formulation employed in this work.

The rotation-free Kirchhoff–Love shell variational formulation may be stated as follows: Find the shell midsurface displacement $\mathbf{y}^h$, such that $\forall \mathbf{w}^h$,

$$
\int_{\Gamma_0^s} \mathbf{w}^h \cdot \rho_0 h_{th} \left(\frac{\mathrm{d}^2 \mathbf{y}^h}{\mathrm{d}t^2} - \mathbf{f}^h \right) \mathrm{d}\Gamma
$$

$$
+ \int_{\Gamma_0^s} \delta \bar{\boldsymbol{\epsilon}}^h \cdot \left(\mathbf{A}\bar{\boldsymbol{\epsilon}}^h + \mathbf{B}\bar{\boldsymbol{\kappa}}^h \right) \mathrm{d}\Gamma
$$

$$
+ \int_{\Gamma_0^s} \delta \bar{\boldsymbol{\kappa}}^h \cdot \left(\mathbf{B}\bar{\boldsymbol{\epsilon}}^h + \mathbf{D}\bar{\boldsymbol{\kappa}}^h \right) \mathrm{d}\Gamma
$$

$$
+ \int_{\Gamma_0^b} \delta \bar{\boldsymbol{\kappa}}^h \cdot \mathbf{D}^b \bar{\boldsymbol{\kappa}}^h \, \mathrm{d}\Gamma - \int_{(\Gamma_t^s)_h} \mathbf{w}^h \cdot \mathbf{h}^h \, \mathrm{d}\Gamma = 0. \tag{8.1}
$$

In the above formulation, Γ_0^s and Γ_t^s is the shell midsurface in the reference and deformed configuration, respectively, $\bar{\boldsymbol{\epsilon}}$ and $\bar{\boldsymbol{\kappa}}$ are the vectors of membrane-strain and curvature-change coefficients, respectively, in the local coordinate system, ρ is the through-thickness-averaged density, $\delta\bar{\boldsymbol{\epsilon}}^h$ and $\delta\bar{\boldsymbol{\kappa}}^h$ are the variations of the membrane-strain and curvatures-change vectors, respectively, $(\Gamma_t^s)^h$ is the shell subdomain with a prescribed traction boundary condition, and $\mathbf{h}^h$ is the prescribed traction vector. Furthermore, Γ_0^b denotes the so-called bending strip domain, which is a key construct of the bending-strip method developed in [22]. The latter technique allows direct application of rotation-free Kirchhoff–Love shell formulation to geometrically complex structures comprised of multiple surface patches, including non-manifold situations. To model a composite shell, the classical laminated plate theory [32] is employed. We denote the thickness of the kth ply by t_k, and its centroid by $\bar{z}_k$. With these definitions, in Eq. (8.1), the extensional, coupling, and bending stiffnesses, given by $\mathbf{A}$, $\mathbf{B}$, and $\mathbf{D}$ matrices, respectively, may be computed for any layup as

$$
\mathbf{A} = \int_{h_{th}} \overline{\mathbf{C}} \, d\xi_3 = \sum_{k=1}^{n} \overline{\mathbf{C}}_k t_k, \tag{8.2}
$$

$$\mathbf{B} = \int_{h_{th}} \xi_3 \overline{\mathbf{C}} \, d\xi_3 = \sum_{k=1}^{n} \overline{\mathbf{C}}_k t_k \overline{z}_k, \tag{8.3}$$

$$\mathbf{D} = \int_{h_{th}} \xi_3{}^2 \overline{\mathbf{C}} \, d\xi_3 = \sum_{k=1}^{n} \overline{\mathbf{C}}_k \left(t_k \overline{z}_k^2 + \frac{t_k^3}{12} \right). \tag{8.4}$$

Here, $\overline{\mathbf{C}}_k$ is a constitutive material matrix for the kth ply in the local coordinate system given by

$$\overline{\mathbf{C}}_k = \mathbf{T}^T (\phi_k) \, \tilde{\mathbf{C}}_k \, \mathbf{T}(\phi_k), \tag{8.5}$$

$$\mathbf{T}(\phi) = \begin{bmatrix} \cos^2 \phi & \sin^2 \phi & \sin \phi \cos \phi \\ \sin^2 \phi & \cos^2 \phi & -\sin \phi \cos \phi \\ -2 \sin \phi \cos \phi & 2 \sin \phi \cos \phi & \cos^2 \phi - \sin^2 \phi \end{bmatrix}, \tag{8.6}$$

where ϕ denotes the fiber orientation angle in the ply, and $\tilde{\mathbf{C}}$ is the constitutive matrix for the orthotropic material written with respect to the principal material axes (or lamina axes) of the ply (see [22] for more details).

The present thin shell formulation is suitable in the regime of large displacements because the strain measures $\overline{\varepsilon}$ and $\overline{\kappa}$ are derived from the Green–Lagrange strain and, as a result, are insensitive to rigid-body translation and rotation. The St. Venant–Kirchhoff material constitutive law is assumed in the above developments. The details of the constitutive matrix $\tilde{\mathbf{C}}$ for the case of fatigue damage are shown in the next section. The Kirchhoff–Love shell equations are discretized in the Galerkin framework using smooth spline functions (NURBS or T-Splines), and are integrated in time using the Generalized-α method [12].

8.2.2.2   The Structural Health Monitoring (SHM) System

The biggest modeling challenge is to use an output of a structural monitoring system and "convert" it into a quantifiable structural response (e.g. damage) that is used to update the IGA simulation model. Another challenge is to enable the prediction of structural response of the updated model and to estimate the future response of the structure (e.g. the remaining fatigue life of the structure). This is known as the *prognosis step* of SHM.

The damage prediction is the most critical aspect of the structural response. The types of damage often encountered in composite structures, and which are of interest here, are local buckling of composite fibers (in-plane and/or out-of-plane fiber waviness), disbonding at the spar-panel adhesive, resin-starved areas, and delamination of the sandwich panel. These specific defects are being considered today as typical of aerospace and civil composite structures, and are the subject of current research by several groups. Experimental investigations of such phenomena are necessary to establish a reliable correspondence between the recorded sensor/measurement data, the type, extent, and location of damage that occurred, and how to build this information into an advanced computational model of the structure.

The defect detection effort involves both ultrasonic sensor arrays and infrared thermographic imaging. The ultrasonic sensor arrays consist of either bulk piezo-electric transducers or the flexible Macro-Fiber Composite (MFC) transducers. Both devices have been used extensively in a variety of projects involving damage detection in composite structures in [16, 27, 30]. For damage detection and location, the sensors are used in an Acoustic Emission (AE) (passive) mode, as well as in an active mode of ultrasonic guided wave testing. In a *passive mode*, location of active damage may be performed using the traditional triangulation of time-of-flight information. In an *active mode*, several guided wave schemes may be employed, including traditional pitch-catch schemes and more elaborated diffraction-based schemes. In addition to the ultrasonic sensor array, large-field inspections may be conducted by Infrared Thermographic methods aided by a statistical image processing approach, recently developed in [26]. The statistical approach, which is based on a Multivariate Outlier Analysis of the infrared thermographic images, was recently proven to enhance the defect contrast in aerospace-type composite panels.

While in this work we present the analysis module for the pristine structures, in [25] the authors discussed the DISCERN framework for damage prediction in multilayer composite structures typically used in energy and aerospace application.

8.3 NREL Phase VI Wind Turbine Blade

The proposed framework is applied to the parametric geometry design of an NREL Phase VI wind turbine blade [18, 19] that requires a considerable number of parametric inputs, including the geometric continuity of each cross section, airfoil type, radial airfoil location, and chord length. This NREL wind turbine blade has 25 airfoil cross sections. It gradually changes from a cylindrical cross section at the hub center to an S809 airfoil [41] cross section along the blade to the blade tip. The main input parameters are shown in Fig. 8.5a. The S809 airfoil data points shown in Fig. 8.4 can be stored in a text file and imported via the interface.

We first show the standard workflow for creating parametric model of the NREL Phase VI wind turbine blade and how this model can be used for the analysis.The workflow for parametric design and geometry modeling of the NREL Phase VI wind turbine blade is shown on Fig. 8.5b. In Fig. 8.3 the leftmost group of components named "Input Parameters" represents operations on input data such as surface continuity, airfoil type, radial position, twist angle and axis, and chord length. The group includes the in-house developed VBScript (Visual Basic Scripting Edition) component for reading these input parameters from a user interface. The user interface is shown in Fig. 8.5a and is developed using C# RhinoCommon Plug-in SDK [35]. The group of components named "Airfoil Curve Construction" imports unit-chord-length airfoil data given by the users and constructs smooth NURBS curves interpolating through each set of airfoil data points. The "rebuild" function

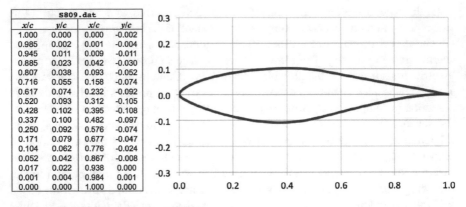

s809.dat			
x/c	y/c	x/c	y/c
1.000	0.000	0.000	-0.002
0.985	0.002	0.001	-0.004
0.945	0.011	0.009	-0.011
0.885	0.023	0.042	-0.030
0.807	0.038	0.093	-0.052
0.716	0.055	0.158	-0.074
0.617	0.074	0.232	-0.092
0.520	0.093	0.312	-0.105
0.428	0.102	0.395	-0.108
0.337	0.100	0.482	-0.097
0.250	0.092	0.576	-0.074
0.171	0.079	0.677	-0.047
0.104	0.062	0.776	-0.024
0.052	0.042	0.867	-0.008
0.017	0.022	0.938	0.000
0.001	0.004	0.984	0.001
0.000	0.000	1.000	0.000

Fig. 8.4 S809 airfoil data and profile [41]

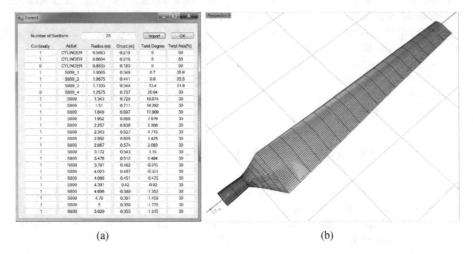

(a)   (b)

Fig. 8.5 NREL Phase VI wind turbine blade parametric design and geometry modeling. (**a**) User interface for parametric design. (**b**) NREL Phase VI wind turbine blade

is then used on these curves to make sure that all the NURBS airfoil profiles have the same number of control points and knot vectors. This operation ensures that the NURBS surface generated by skinning (or lofting) along this series of profile curves will have the desired parameterization.

Based on the input parameters corresponding to blade cross sections, each airfoil profile is relocated such that the twist axis is aligned to the origin, scaled by the chord length, and rotated according to the twist degree. The modified airfoil profiles are then moved to their corresponding radial positions along the twist axis, which is also the blade-pitched axis. This procedure is performed by the group of components named "Blade Cross-section Construction" in Fig. 8.3. Due to the inherent discontinuity of sharp transition between different blade design zones, the input data are separated into different subdomains using the group of components

Fig. 8.6 T-spline surface of
the NREL Phase VI wind
turbine blade

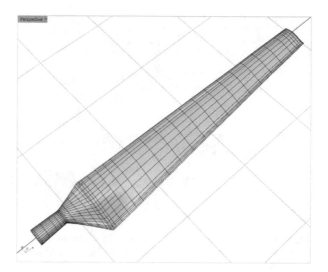

named "Sub-Domain Construction". After all subsets of blade cross-section curves
are prepared, individual NURBS surfaces are generated by skinning (or lofting)
along the curves within each subset. This is done by the rightmost component shown
in Fig. 8.3. The multi-patch NURBS surface generated through this procedure is
conforming between different patches.

Next, a multi-patch NURBS surface is converted to a single T-spline surface
using the Autodesk T-Splines Plug-in for Rhino [1, 36] to have better modeling
features, such as local refinement and coarsening. Figure 8.6 shows the T-spline
surface of the wind turbine blade to which local refinement has already been added,
and from which unwanted knots have been removed.

Remark 1 We note that a geometric model may be constructed using different
procedures and algorithms depending on the designer's preferences and the level
of familiarity with the tool. The example shown in Fig. 8.3 is one of the many ways
of achieving the same goal.

Remark 2 Quite often a volumetric representation of the geometry is needed for
analysis. The reader is referred to [20] for discussion on possible extensions of the
current geometry modeling platform to handle volumes.

8.3.1   Setting Material Properties, Loads, and Boundary Conditions

The next logical step towards analysis is to define the material properties, loads, and
boundary conditions. The user interface for setting these properties and conditions
depends on the selection and assignment of T-spline surface elements. The user

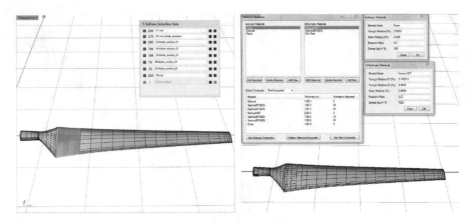

Fig. 8.7 Left: Select and assign elements to different sets using "TsSelSet" command. Right: Composite layups can be defined and assigned to T-spline sets using the in-house developed user interface

interface shown in Fig. 8.7 allows the user to define composite layups consisting of any number of layers of user-defined isotropic or orthotropic materials. Each layer is assigned a material, thickness, and fiber orientation. This approach to composite definition is similar to that employed by Sandia National Laboratories' Numerical Manufacturing And Design Tool (NuMAD) [28]. The resulting composite layup designs can then be assigned to specific T-spline surface elements. We use the classical laminated plate theory [6, 14] to homogenize the material through-thickness constitutive behavior for a given composite layup. For the sake of simplicity, the material we use in the following analysis is aluminum, which is isotropic and has Young's modulus of 70 GPa and Poisson's ratio of 0.35. The blade is assumed to have eight regions of constant thickness, which decreases from root to tip. Finally, we apply the clamped boundary condition at the root by selecting two rows of control points, and select four different pressure load areas on the pressure side of the blade surface, as shown in Fig. 8.8.

8.3.2 Simulation Results

The pressure load of 45 kPa is applied on the selected zones of the blade surface as shown in Fig. 8.8. The resultant force due to the pressure load is 2.315 kN. The blade is clamped at the root and, in addition, loaded by gravity. Dynamic simulation is employed with a time-step size of 0.001 s. The analysis results are shown in Fig. 8.9. The deformed T-spline surface is visualized by adding the displacement field to the control point coordinates.

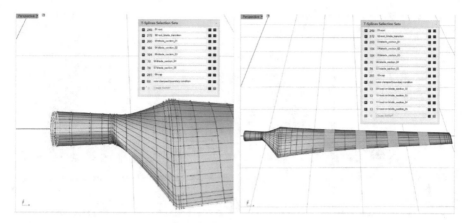

Fig. 8.8 Left: Select control points to set clamped boundary condition. Right: Select elements to assign pressure loads on several upper-surface areas

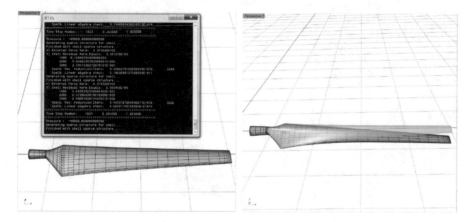

Fig. 8.9 Left: Isogeometric shell analysis. Right: Deformed T-spline surface

8.3.3 Visualization of IGA Results

To have a deeper understanding of the analysis results, one may perform post-processing of quantities of interest such as the maximum in-plane principal Green–Lagrange strain (MIPE) from shell displacement. The steady-state results are shown in Fig. 8.10. The higher MIPE area is concentrated around the sharp transition from the cylindrical root to the airfoil cross sections. This analysis result could provide guidance for potential design improvement.

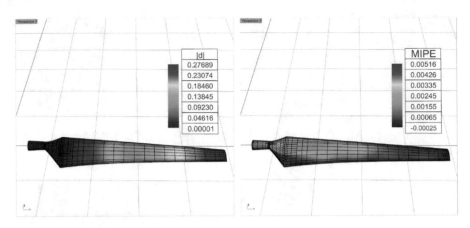

Fig. 8.10 Displacement (left) and MIPE (right) contours of the isogeometric shell analysis result

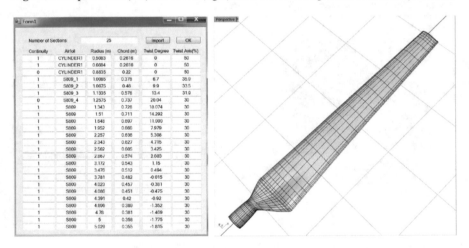

Fig. 8.11 New design parameters and the corresponding modified wind turbine blade geometry

8.3.4 Parametric Design Modification

The design of the NREL Phase VI wind turbine blade can be easily modified to have a larger root by using the parametric design user interface as shown in Fig. 8.11. Figure 8.12 shows an overlapping of the original and modified designs, where the red wireframe represents the new geometry, and the black wireframe represents the original geometry. After following the same platform steps, the new deformation and MIPE results are shown in Fig. 8.13. Figure 8.14 shows the comparison of MIPE between the redesigned and original cases. The maximum value of MIPE of the whole blade drops by 18.4% compared to the original design, and the maximum displacement decreases by 11.7%. This illustrates how

Fig. 8.12 The comparison between the original (black wireframe) and modified (red wireframe) geometry

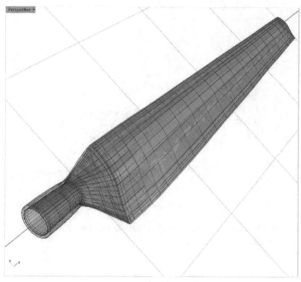

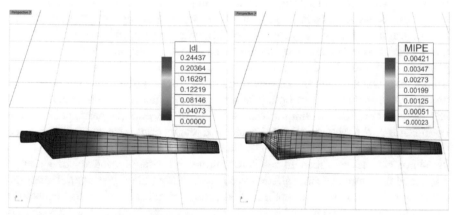

Fig. 8.13 Displacement (left) and MIPE (right) contours of the isogeometric shell analysis results of the modified wind turbine blade

the structural design improvements may be achieved within the same IGA design-through-analysis platform.

8.4   Conclusions

A DDDAS framework for large-scale composite structures based on continually and dynamically injected sensor data is proposed. The DDDAS Interactive Structure Composite Element Relation Network (DISCERN) framework consists of several parts. In this chapter we presented first two modules focusing on a computational

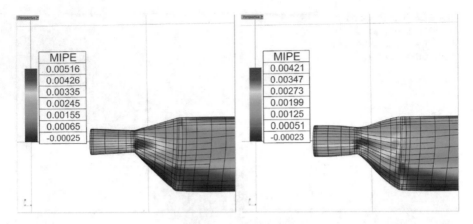

Fig. 8.14 The comparison of the MIPE contour distributions of the original (left) and modified (right) designs

framework for parametric design and modeling using isogeometric analysis. The framework is based on Grasshopper, an algorithmic modeling interface that abides by and uniquely integrates a number of important design philosophies and that also contains powerful geometry manipulation functions that enable the parametric generation of models suitable for IGA. In the context of this unified design framework, which features consistent geometry descriptions throughout design and analysis, analysis-driven optimization even of complex designs is natural and relatively simple. It is a unique framework in that it enables parametric design optimization of a variety of CAD-generated engineering structures using IGA. Overall, this framework demonstrates how the benefits of IGA within DDDAS paradigm can be leveraged in realistic engineering design contexts to generate optimized designs and design alternatives based on high-fidelity structural analysis, reducing designer labor. The optimization procedure presented here is necessarily limited in scope. The more sophisticated optimization modules are discussed in Part II of the paper.

Acknowledgments This work was supported by the AFOSR Grant FA9550-12-1-0005, AFOSR Grant FA9550-16-1-0131, ARO grant No. W911NF-14-1-0296. The authors greatly acknowledge this support.

References

1. Autodesk T-Splines Plug-in for Rhino. http://www.tsplines.com/products/tsplines-for-rhino.html. 2014.
2. Y. Bazilevs, V. M. Calo, J. A. Cottrell, J. A. Evans, T. J. R. Hughes, S. Lipton, M. A. Scott, and T. W. Sederberg. Isogeometric analysis using T-splines. *Computer Methods in Applied Mechanics and Engineering*, 199:229–263, 2010.

3. Y. Bazilevs, L. Beirao da Veiga, J. A. Cottrell, T. J. R. Hughes, and G. Sangalli. Isogeometric analysis: Approximation, stability and error estimates for *h*-refined meshes. *Mathematical Models and Methods in Applied Sciences*, 16:1031–1090, 2006.
4. Y. Bazilevs, M.-C. Hsu, and M.T Bement. Adjoint-based control of fluid–structure interaction for computational steering applications. *Procedia Computer Science*, 18:1989–1998, 2013.
5. Y. Bazilevs, M.-C. Hsu, J. Kiendl, and D. J. Benson. A computational procedure for prebending of wind turbine blades. *International Journal for Numerical Methods in Engineering*, 89:323–336, 2012.
6. Y. Bazilevs, M.-C. Hsu, J. Kiendl, R. Wüchner, and K.-U. Bletzinger. 3D simulation of wind turbine rotors at full scale. Part II: Fluid–structure interaction modeling with composite blades. *International Journal for Numerical Methods in Fluids*, 65:236–253, 2011.
7. Y. Bazilevs, M.-C. Hsu, and M. A. Scott. Isogeometric fluid–structure interaction analysis with emphasis on non-matching discretizations, and with application to wind turbines. *Computer Methods in Applied Mechanics and Engineering*, 249-252:28–41, 2012.
8. Y. Bazilevs, A.L. Marsden, F. Lanza di Scalea, A. Majumdar, and M. Tatineni. Toward a computational steering framework for large-scale composite structures based on continually and dynamically injected sensor data. *Procedia Computer Science*, 9:1149–1158, 2012.
9. Y. Bazilevs, K. Takizawa, and T. E. Tezduyar. *Computational Fluid–Structure Interaction: Methods and Applications*. John Wiley & Sons, Chichester, 2013.
10. D. J. Benson, Y. Bazilevs, M.-C. Hsu, and T. J. R. Hughes. Isogeometric shell analysis: The Reissner–Mindlin shell. *Computer Methods in Applied Mechanics and Engineering*, 199:276–289, 2010.
11. D. J. Benson, Y. Bazilevs, M.-C. Hsu, and T. J. R. Hughes. A large deformation, rotation-free, isogeometric shell. *Computer Methods in Applied Mechanics and Engineering*, 200:1367–1378, 2011.
12. J. Chung and G. M. Hulbert. A time integration algorithm for structural dynamics with improved numerical dissipation: The generalized-α method. *Journal of Applied Mechanics*, 60:371–75, 1993.
13. J. A. Cottrell, T. J. R. Hughes, and Y. Bazilevs. *Isogeometric Analysis: Toward Integration of CAD and FEA*. Wiley, Chichester, 2009.
14. I. M. Daniel and O. Ishai. *Engineering Mechanics of Composite Materials*. Oxford University Press, New York, NY, 1994.
15. F. Darema. Dynamic data driven applications systems: A new paradigm for application simulations and measurements. *in proceedings of ICCS 2004 4th International Conference on Computational Science*, pages 662–669, 2004.
16. F. Lanza di Scalea, H. Matt, I. Bartoli, S. Coccia, G. Park, and C. Farrar. Health monitoring of uav wing skin-to-spar joints using guided waves and macro fiber composite transducers. *Journal of Intelligent Material Systems and Structures*, 18:373–388, 2007.
17. Grasshopper. http://www.grasshopper3d.com/. Accessed 27 May 2016.
18. M. M. Hand, D. A. Simms, L. J. Fingersh, D. W. Jager, J. R. Cotrell, S. Schreck, and S. M. Larwood. Unsteady aerodynamics experiment phase VI: Wind tunnel test configurations and available data campaigns. Technical Report NREL/TP-500-29955, National Renewable Energy Laboratory, Golden, CO, 2001.
19. M.-C. Hsu, I. Akkerman, and Y. Bazilevs. Finite element simulation of wind turbine aerodynamics: Validation study using NREL Phase VI experiment. *Wind Energy*, 2012. In review.
20. M.-C. Hsu, C. Wang, A. J. Herrema, D. Schillinger, A. Ghoshal, and Y. Bazilevs. An interactive geometry modeling and parametric design platform for isogeometric analysis. *Computers and Mathematics with Applications*, 70(7):1481–1500, 2015.
21. T. J. R. Hughes, J. A. Cottrell, and Y. Bazilevs. Isogeometric analysis: CAD, finite elements, NURBS, exact geometry, and mesh refinement. *Computer Methods in Applied Mechanics and Engineering*, 194:4135–4195, 2005.

22. J. Kiendl, Y. Bazilevs, M.-C. Hsu, R. Wüchner, and K.-U. Bletzinger. The bending strip method for isogeometric analysis of Kirchhoff–Love shell structures comprised of multiple patches. *Computer Methods in Applied Mechanics and Engineering*, 199:2403–2416, 2010.
23. J. Kiendl, K.-U. Bletzinger, J. Linhard, and R. Wüchner. Isogeometric shell analysis with Kirchhoff–Love elements. *Computer Methods in Applied Mechanics and Engineering*, 198:3902–3914, 2009.
24. A. Korobenko, M.-C Hsu, I. Akkerman, J. Tippmann, and Y. Bazilevs. Structural mechanics modeling and FSI simulation of wind turbines. *Mathematical Models and Methods in Applied Science*, 23:249–272, 2013.
25. A. Korobenko, M. Pigazzini, X. Deng, and Y. Bazilevs. Multiscale dddas framework for damage prediction in aerospace composite structures. In E. Blasch, S. Ravela, and A. Aved, editors, *Handbook of Dynamic Data Driven Applications Systems*, pages 677–696. Springer, 2018.
26. A. Manohar and F. Lanza di Scalea. Wavelet aided multivariate outlier analysis to enhance defect contrast in thermal images. *Experimental Techniques, Society for Experimental Mechanics*, 2011. in press.
27. H. Matt, I. Bartoli, and F. Lanza di Scalea. Ultrasonic guided wave monitoring of composite wing skin-to-spar bonded joints in aerospace structures. *Journal of the Acoustical Society of America*, 118:2240–2252, 2005.
28. Numerical Manufacturing And Design Tool (NuMAD). http://energy.sandia.gov/energy/renewable-energy/wind-power/rotor-innovation/numerical-manufacturing-and-design-tool-numad/. 2015.
29. J. T. Oden, K. R. Diller, C. Bajaj, J. C. Browne, J. Hazle, I. Babuska, J. Bass, L. Demkowicz, Y. Feng, D. Fuentes, S. Prudhomme, M. N. Rylander, R. J. Stafford, and Y. Zhang. Dynamic data-driven finite element models for laser treatment of prostate cancer. *Num. Meth. PDE*, 23:904–922, 2007.
30. G. Park, C. Farrar, F. Lanza di Scalea, and S. Coccia. Performance assessment and validation of piezoelectric active-sensors in structural health monitoring. *Smart Materials and Structures*, 15:1673–1683, 2006.
31. L. Piegl and W. Tiller. *The NURBS Book (Monographs in Visual Communication), 2nd ed.* Springer-Verlag, New York, 1997.
32. J. N. Reddy. *Mechanics of Laminated Composite Plates and Shells: Theory and Analysis, 2nd ed.* CRC Press, Boca Raton, FL, 2004.
33. Rhino. http://www.rhino3d.com/. Accessed 27 May 2016.
34. Rhino Developer Docs. http://developer.rhino3d.com/. Accessed 27 May 2016.
35. RhinoCommon. http://developer.rhino3d.com/guides/rhinocommon. Accessed 27 May 2016.
36. M. A. Scott, T. J. R. Hughes, T. W. Sederberg, and M. T. Sederberg. An integrated approach to engineering design and analysis using the Autodesk T-spline plugin for Rhino3d. ICES REPORT 14-33, The Institute for Computational Engineering and Sciences, The University of Texas at Austin, September 2014, 2014.
37. M. A. Scott, X. Li, T. W. Sederberg, and T. J. R. Hughes. Local refinement of analysis-suitable T-splines. *Computer Methods in Applied Mechanics and Engineering*, 2012. Accepted for publication.
38. T. W. Sederberg, D.L. Cardon, G.T. Finnigan, N.S. North, J. Zheng, and T. Lyche. T-spline simplification and local refinement. *ACM Transactions on Graphics*, 23(3):276–283, 2004.
39. T.W. Sederberg, J. Zheng, A. Bakenov, and A. Nasri. T-splines and T-NURCCS. *ACM Transactions on Graphics*, 22(3):477–484, 2003.
40. SolidWorks. http://www.solidworks.com/. Accessed 27 May 2016.
41. D. M. Somers. Design and experimental results for the S809 airfoil. Technical Report NREL/SR-440-6918, National Renewable Energy Laboratory, Golden, CO, 1997.
42. M. Stavric and O. Marina. Parametric modeling for advanced architecture. *International Journal of Applied Mathematics and Informatics*, 5(1):9–16, 2011.

Chapter 9
Development of Intelligent and Predictive Self-Healing Composite Structures Using Dynamic Data-Driven Applications Systems

Mishal Thapa, Bodiuzzaman Jony, Sameer B. Mulani, and Samit Roy

Abstract This chapter presents an intelligent self-healing design of fiber-reinforced polymer (FRP) composites for predictive self-healing using the Dynamic Data-Driven Application Systems (DDDAS) paradigm through damage prognosis and a non-autonomous self-healing protocol. The proposed intelligent self-healing structural concept is composed of three inter-connected modules: (1) a damage sensing module, (2) a damage-prognosis module, and (3) a self-healing module. The current study focuses on developing the self-healing module of the proposed intelligent self-healing structural system - repeatable self-healing of FRP using thermoplastic healing agents and shape memory polymers (SMP) in FRP composites structures. This self-healing mechanism is motivated by the bio-mimetic process of '*close then heal*' mechanism where the SMP complements the cracks' closing, and the thermoplastic healing agent performs the healing process. For this purpose, double-cantilever beam (DCB) tests were carried out to quantify the healing efficiency in terms of Mode-I interlaminar fracture toughness (G_{Ic}) following the ASTM D5528-13 testing protocol, and the healing efficiencies of seven different healing cycles were assessed to test the repeatability of the healing mechanism. The tests showed promising healing efficiencies ranging from *58%* to *73%* in terms of regaining the fracture toughness of virgin specimens. Furthermore, fractography analysis using Scanning Electron Microscopy (SEM) and the optical microscope of the fractured FRP composite specimens were also carried out qualitatively to understand the mechanisms responsible for enhancing healing efficiency.

Keywords Repeatable self-healing · Thermoplastic healing agent · Delamination · Mode-I Interlaminar fracture toughness

M. Thapa · B. Jony · S. B. Mulani · S. Roy (✉)
The Department of Aerospace Engineering and Mechanics, The University of Alabama, Tuscaloosa, AL, USA
e-mail: mthapa@crimson.ua.edu; jbodiuzzaman@crimson.ua.edu; sbmulani@eng.ua.edu; sroy@eng.ua.edu

© The Author(s), under exclusive license to Springer Nature Switzerland AG 2022
E. P. Blasch et al. (eds.), *Handbook of Dynamic Data Driven Applications Systems*,
https://doi.org/10.1007/978-3-030-74568-4_9

9.1 Introduction

The concept of Dynamic-Data Driven Application Systems (DDDAS) refers to the recursive process of evolving the mathematical model of a system by continuously incorporating additional data from the measurement process of the system's response into the model [1]. One of the most common examples of the DDDAS paradigm is a series of Kalman Filters (KF) in which the KF is a convergence observer in which the gain of the observer is continuously updated based on the integrated difference between the actual measurements and those predicted from a possibly uncertain model [2]. One of the areas that exhibit great potential for applying the DDDAS paradigm is of composites. structural health monitoring (SHM) and self-healing. The DDDAS paradigm for structures includes a damage prognosis model, damage-sensing analysis, and recursive self-healing, followed by the updates to the damage model.

Fiber-reinforced polymer (FRP) composites are commonplace in the aerospace, automotive, wind energy, marine, and sporting goods industries because of their superior specific mechanical properties (high specific strength and stiffness) when compared to traditional engineering materials. However, these benefits are susceptible to various manufacturing defects, such as fiber misalignment, voids, and thermal stresses due to the curing. Furthermore, the in-plane laminated construction of the FRP system results in inherent vulnerability to out-of-plane loadings such as those experienced under dynamic impact events. Along with these manufacturing issues, there exist various thermal, hygrothermal, and aging effects which could eventually lead to the formation of considerable internal damage (macro and micro-cracks) [3], and compromise the structural integrity and service life [4] of laminated FRP structures. To minimize these drawbacks, composite structures go through regular manual labor-intensive inspection using non-destructive testing (NDT) and evaluation (NDE). Based on the NDE results, less extensively damaged parts may be repaired or replaced for the case of extensive damage. However, detection, repair, and replacement processes result in lengthy downtime and high maintenance costs. Researchers have explored biologically inspired self-healing concepts as an alternative to traditionally expensive repair techniques to combat the drawbacks of damage detection and repair in FRP composites.

Since the inception of the self-healing concept about three decades ago [5], various self-healing methods have been developed and implemented in composites, which can be broadly classified as *autonomous* and *non-autonomous* self-healing [6]. The pre-embedded liquid resin delivery system is based on the *autonomous* approach where healing is performed automatically in response to the rupture or damage in the composite. The *autonomous* approach employs either capillary tubes or spherical capsules as storage vessels for the healing resin [7–20], followed by the rupturing of the healing agent contained in a capillary tube or spherical capsules by the progression of structural damage. The rupture of the healant-container results in the bleeding of the uncured resin, which then reacts with the solid catalysts dispersed in the matrix material or mix with the liquid curing agent contained within the matrix. Eventually, polymerization of liquid healing agent re-bonds the fracture surfaces and "heals" the cracks, thereby restoring the mechanical performance of the FRP composite structure to an acceptable level. However, some of the major disadvantages of the autonomous approach are: (1) the reliance on liquid resin delivery system, (2) ensuring the survival of the healant container vessels during the manufacturing process, (3) the need for simultaneous crack propagation and rupture of the healant containers [21], (4) difficulty in closing large cracks, (5) the reduction in composite strength due to leftover empty vessels after healing that act as voids and/or inclusions, and (6) repeatability of healing, once all the healing agents have been consumed [22].

On the other hand, most of these drawbacks are absent in the proposed *non-autonomous* self-healing process. There are two approaches to of achieving *non-autonomous* healing. The first approach is intrinsic healing, where the matrix of the composite has the inherent healing capability through thermal reaction [23, 24], hydrogen bonding [25, 26], or molecular diffusion [27]. The second approach is the addition of mendable thermoplastic additives to the matrix during the manufacturing stage. Upon damage detection, healing is realized through thermoplastic melting and bonding of the fracture surfaces by melted healant upon heat application. This method has advantages over other methods mentioned earlier in this chapter because of its simplicity and repeatability, and it can be applied to a wide range of thermoset/thermoplastic combinations as long as the polymers are compatible with each other [5].

Since their inception, both the *autonomous* and *non-autonomous* self-healing have gained considerable success in regaining their original "pristine" property. Yet, most of these healing methods are challenging to control. Moreover, the studies related to coordination between self-healing, damage assessment, control, and feedback are minimal.

All these factors highlight a need for the next-generation intelligent composite structure [28], which can detect and assess the severity of the damage and can initiate the required healing based on that assessment. One of the primary challenges for such a system is the capability of detecting the damage and starting the healing process in time before the damage becomes irreparable. Therefore, the combination of damage-sensing and self-healing subsystems demands a recursive algorithm capable of incorporating the information of the micro-scale changes identified by the sensing mechanism into a damage model to prognosticate the threat of any probable macro-scale damage caused due to those changes. Using the damage-sensing and self-healing approach, early initiation of damage can be assessed, and '*predictive self-healing*' can be performed by triggering the healing process at the right time and location before irreparable damage occurs. Such a recursive algorithm based intelligent FRP composite system has been proposed by the authors that incorporates the DDDAS paradigm with damage-sensing and self-healing modules. The proposed system has predictive self-healing capability through monitoring micro-scale changes and dynamically integrating them into a recursively updated damage prognosis model.

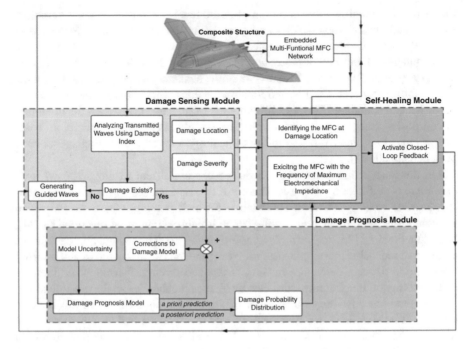

Fig. 9.1 DDDAS damage-tolerant intelligent self-healing concept flowchart

9.1.1 Overview of the Proposed Intelligent Structure

The proposed intelligent self-healing structural concept is composed of a damage sensing module, a damage-prognosis module, and a self-healing module, as depicted in the flowchart in Fig. 9.1. The damage-sensing module is based on a novel guided-wave SHM technique, which is implemented through an embedded active multifunctional network of Macro-Fiber Composite (MFC, supplied by Smart Material Corp.). The embedded damage-sensing system will use guided waves coupled with a novel damage index called 'Normalized Correlation Moment' [29]. The system can detect damage, find the location of the damage, and evaluate the severity of the damage. In this chapter, the methods to develop the optimum self-healing module for an intelligent damage tolerant structure is presented. The 'close-then-heal' methodology [30] has been considered in this study, where thermoplastic shape memory polymer (SMP) and caprolactone polymer (CAPA) were used respectively for closing and then healing the macro-cracks and delamination in FRP coupons by heating it above the glass transition temperature of the SMP. The details of the double-cantilever beam test specimen fabrication, fracture analysis using a scanning electron microscope (SEM), and the results obtained are presented in the subsequent sections. Some of the authors' studies related to self-healing composites can also be found in [31–34].

9.2 Experimental Section

9.2.1 Double-Cantilever Beam (DCB) Test Specimen Fabrication

9.2.1.1 Materials

For our experiments, liquid two-part epoxy resin system SC-780 (di-glycidyl ether of Bisphenol-F epoxy (DGEBA) and hardener agent) obtained from Applied Poleramic, Inc. were used as received. The toughened epoxy resin system (SC-780) was selected because of its low curing temperature (37 °C). Also, 16 plies of unidirectional Uni-Web IM7 carbon fiber (12K) (with an average carbon fiber diameter of 5.2 μm) procured from Soller Composites, LLC was used as the reinforcing material. On the other hand, CAPA 6506 [35] supplied by Perstorp UK Limited in powder form was used as the healant. CAPA is a high molecular weight 50,000 linear polyester derived from a caprolactone monomer, which has a particle density of 1.1 g/cm^3 and a melting temperature of 58–60 °C. The CAPA was selected as the healant because of its healing repeatability [36]. Polyurethane-based SMP [37] fibers were used to bring the macroscopic crack surfaces closer to assist the molecular scale healing with CAPA. The SMP was procured from SMP Technologies Inc. as a 1.75 mm diameter filament and then programmed and thinned (0.05 mm diameter) using additive manufacturing before applying it in the FRP composite laminate. SMP was selected because of its excellent capability of crack closing [36]. A flowchart of the composite laminate manufacturing process incorporating healing agents is shown in Fig. 9.2.

9.2.2 Manufacturing of DCB Test Specimens

The FRP composite laminate was prepared by a hand layup procedure following the ASTM D5528-13 standard [38], as shown in Fig. 9.2. Sixteen carbon fiber plies (0.254 m × 0.254 m) were cut from the supplied unidirectional weaved carbon fiber rolls and used for preparing the unidirectional laminate (0_{16}^0). The 15 wt. % CAPA (36.5 gm) was mixed with liquid SC-780 part A (200 gm) resin by a shear mixer at 500 rpm for 15 minutes. SC-780 part B hardener (44 gm) was then added to the mixture and mixed for another 15 minutes at the same rpm. The mixed resin was used for hand layup of the plies. And a pre-crack was created on one end of the laminate by inserting a 12.5 μm thick and 0.0635 m wide Polytetrafluoroethylene (PTFE film/DuPont Teflon, Chemours Company) film at the mid-plane of the laminate. The thinned SMP filaments (with a total amount of three gm) were also sprinkled in the mid-layer while laying up the laminate. The final consolidation was performed using a programmable compression molding machine by utilizing the curing cycle at 37 °C for two hours with 4.5 kN force. From each laminate, six DCB

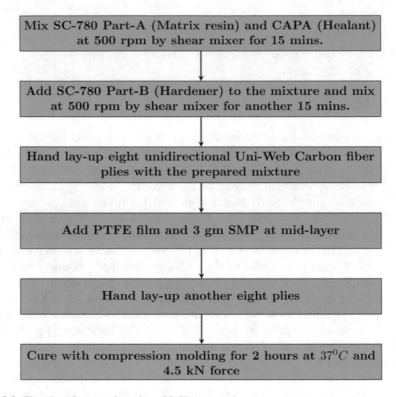

Fig. 9.2 Flowchart for manufacturing of DCB test specimen

specimens (*0.21 m × 0.04 m × 0.005 m*) with *0.04 m* pre-crack were obtained by using a diamond saw, and then a pair of piano hinges were bonded to the pre-crack end of the specimens with the epoxy adhesive (Fig. 9.3) for proper load alignment during testing.

9.2.3 Fracture and Healing Protocols

The DCB specimens were used to evaluate *Mode-I* interlaminar fracture toughness and healing performance by following the *ASTM D5528-13* standard [38]. The DCB specimens were loaded through the bonded hinges in quasi-static tension on an MTS test machine load frame using displacement control method (*2.5 mm/min*) to induce *Mode-I* fracture along the midply interlaminar region. The initial pre-crack region (a_0) from the hinge-loading line to the interior PTFE film termination interface was approximately *0.038 m*. The loading was carried out until the crack propagated to the *0.0254 m* from the initial pre-crack end. Specimens were then unloaded (*25 mm/min*) and removed from the MTS load-frame for healing. The data

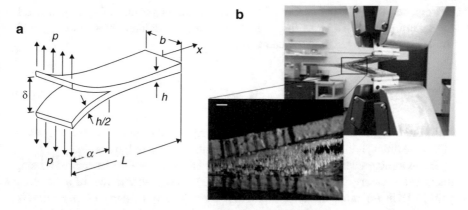

Fig. 9.3 (**a**) DCB test specimen geometry, (**b**) DCB test specimen in quasi-static tension with an enlarged view of crack propagation (scale bar = *1.5 mm*)

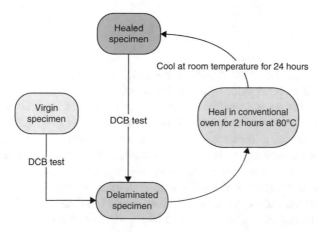

Fig. 9.4 Healing protocol flowchart for mendable epoxy specimens

for time, load, and crosshead displacement during the testing were collected using Q-test software. Afterward, healing was accomplished by keeping the delaminated specimen in an oven at *80 °C* for 2 hours and then cooling at room temperature for the next 24 hours, as shown in the flowchart in Fig. 9.4.

9.2.4   Fracture Analysis

DDDAS includes the use of a system's model to understand the underlying physics. One of the methods of characterizing the physics of self-healing is fracture toughness (crack resisting strength) in the DCB test, which is based on linear elastic fracture and beam mechanics. The strain energy release rate, $G[M / T^2]$, can be expressed in terms of the release of strain energy (dU) per unit of specimen width for an infinitesimal increase in crack length (da) for delamination growing self-similarly under a constant displacement [39].

$$G = -\frac{1}{b}\frac{dU}{da} \tag{9.1}$$

In Eq. (9.1), U represents the total strain energy of the specimen, b is the width of the specimen, and a is the delamination length, as depicted in Fig. 9.3a.

By assuming each arm of the DCB specimen as a cantilever beam and using linear beam theory, the expression for the strain energy release rate of a perfectly built-in DCB (clamped at the delamination front) is given by Eq. (9.2). Here, G_{Ic} represents the Mode-I interlaminar fracture toughness, P is the load, and δ is the load-point displacement as illustrated in Fig. 9.3a.

$$G_{Ic} = \frac{3P\delta}{2ba} \tag{9.2}$$

However, Eq. (9.2) overestimates the G_{Ic} as it assumes the beam is perfectly built (no rotation occurs at the delamination front) [38] and neglects the contribution of shear deformation and rotation at the delamination front [40]. To accommodate the effect of this rotation and shear deformation in the DCB specimen, a slightly longer effective delamination $a + |\Delta|$ is assumed, where Δ is the crack length correction factor to account for the contributions from shear and rotation. The correction term Δ is determined from the intercept of a least-squares plot of the cube root of compliance of the DCB specimen as a function of the delamination length. Therefore, the *modified beam theory* (MBT) that accounts for the rotation and shear deformation is given, as shown by Eq. (9.3), and was used in this study.

$$G_{Ic} = \frac{3P\delta}{2b\,(a + |\Delta|)} \tag{9.3}$$

For the healing efficiency calculations, Eq. (9.4) was considered, which defines the ability of a healed sample to recover crack growth resistance [41]. Here, G_{Ic}^{Virgin} is the average virgin (i.e., uncracked) critical strain energy release rate over a given delamination length and G_{Ic}^{Healed} is the average critical strain energy release rate over the same delamination length of a healed specimen.

$$\eta_{G_{Ic}} = \frac{G_{Ic}^{Healed}}{G_{Ic}^{Virgin}} \times 100\% \tag{9.4}$$

9.3   Results and Discussions

To demonstrate the DDDAS-based self-healing capability and repeatability, the DCB fracture and healing test cycle, as depicted in Fig. 9.4 were carried out seven times on four replicate specimens. This section presents the results obtained from these DCB tests as well as fractography analysis of the damaged specimens to understand the fracture characteristics of the healed specimens.

9.3.1   Fracture Test Results

The load vs. crosshead displacement plot for four different DCB specimens containing SMP and CAPA are shown in Fig. 9.5. As seen in Fig. 9.5a for virgin specimens before healing, the load-displacement curves demonstrated a linear increment of the load until it reached a peak load. On further increasing the load, an unstable growth of the crack was observed, followed by a decrease in load beyond peak load. Interestingly, different trends were observed after the peak load even for specimens (Table 9.1) obtained from the same unidirectional laminate as demonstrated by the sudden dip in load for Specimen-1 and Specimen-2 (Fig. 9.5a), which indicates a large sudden crack jump in the midplane of the DCB specimen.

On the other hand, a complex oscillatory load-displacement pattern for Specimen-3 and Specimen-4 was observed during the DCB tests. This pattern is similar to stick-slip crack growth and refers to the transition between ductile (stable) and brittle (unstable) crack growth [40]. The different trends of the specimens after the peak load also suggest the different amount of energy required for the crack propagation as well as the fracture toughness.

Once delamination was created in the virgin specimen, as depicted in Fig. 9.3, the healing operation was carried out by placing the DCB specimens in an oven at $80\,^{\circ}C$ for two hours. During the healing process, the SMP became thermally activated and helped to narrow the gap between crack surfaces. In addition, the diffusion of melted CAPA took place, which was followed by polymerization and bonding of the healants to the delamination crack surfaces upon cooling. Seven successive healing and DCB fracture tests were then carried out on the healed specimens to demonstrate the healing capability and repeatability. As shown in Fig. 9.5b–h, the load-displacement curve for all the specimens demonstrates linear behavior initially, as observed for the virgin specimen. However, there was no decrease in the load after the deviation from the linear trend, as seen for the virgin case until the crack propagated $25.4\,mm$ (1 in.) from the pre-crack end. This is attributed to the ductile characteristic of the thermoplastic rich zones, which was activated after heating at $80\,^{\circ}C$. Here, it is to be noted that the melting temperature of CAPA is $58–60\,^{\circ}C$ [35]. Hence the thermoplastic healants did not demonstrate this ductile characteristic for the virgin specimens, which was cured at $37\,^{\circ}C$ whereas it demonstrated this behavior upon heating at $80\,^{\circ}C$. The different trends of load-displacement behavior

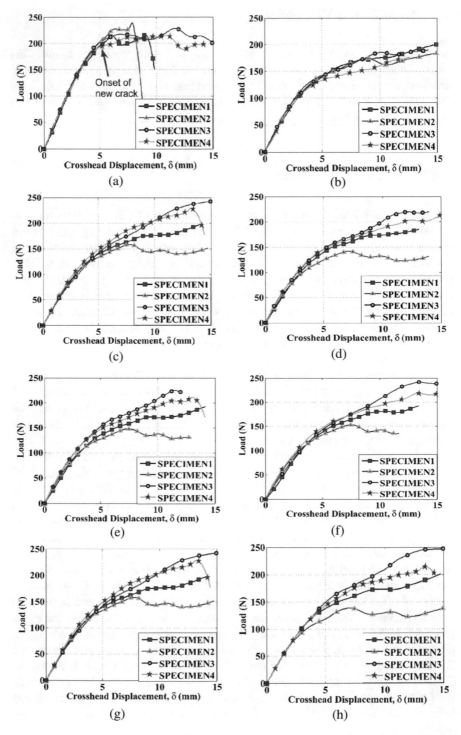

Fig. 9.5 Load versus crosshead displacement behavior of DCB specimens for different healing cycles. (**a**) Virgin. (**b**) First heal. (**c**) Second heal. (**d**) Third heal. (**e**) Fourth heal. (**f**) Fifth heal. (**g**) Sixth heal. (**h**) Seventh heal

Table 9.1 Virgin specimen peak load characteristics

Specimen	Delamination length, a (mm)	Peak load, P_{max} (N)	Crosshead displacement, δ (mm)
1	52.39	216.46	9.04
2	46.03	239.13	7.90
3	49.00	228.24	11.64
4	47.29	214.53	10.95

Fig. 9.6 Load vs. crosshead displacement for seven healing cycles, including virgin fracture for DCB Specimen-2

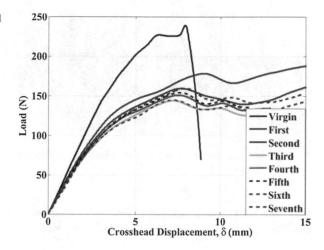

for the healed specimens also suggest that the crack may have propagated along a different path in a stable manner compared with the virgin fracture specimen.

After completing the first healing cycle, the healing and fracture of the specimens were performed six more times under similar conditions. However, Fig. 9.5c–h showed a considerable variation of crack propagation and trends of load with crosshead displacement for each healing cycle. In these plots, the peak load was clearly observed for Specimen-2, and also the decreasing pattern after the peak load was observed. This suggests a smaller fracture toughness and low resistance to crack propagation in the mid-layer for Specimen-2 compared to the other specimens, which can be attributed to the lack of enough healants or improper melting of healants in the cracked plane. Nonetheless, the similar trends in the linear region and nearby location of the separation of the linear trend for different specimens suggest similar values of G_{Ic}.

Furthermore, a summary of the load-displacement plot of Specimen-2 is provided for seven healing cycles in Fig. 9.6 to demonstrate the healing repeatability as described earlier. From this plot, it is evident that the stiffness of the healed specimens is slightly lower than that of the virgin specimen. Similar trends in the non-linear region from the second healing to seventh healing also indicate the propagation of the crack along the same path in the mid-layer. Therefore, this similarity among the load-displacement curves of the specimen for different healing cycles provides good evidence of the healing repeatability of thermoplastic healants.

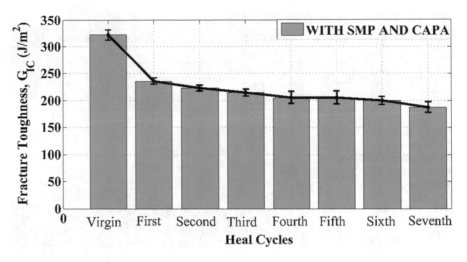

Fig. 9.7 Bar chart showing average Mode-I interlaminar fracture toughness plotted as a function of healing cycles

It is to be noted that thermoplastic healants underwent only physical changes during the subsequent healing cycles. No chemical reactions like the thermoset healants were involved, one of the main reasons for healing repeatability [36].

9.3.2 Quantification of Healing Efficiency

The self-healing ability and repeatability over multiple cycles are further demonstrated quantitatively by calculating the averaged critical fracture toughness of four replicate specimens that marks the onset of delamination initiation. The average toughness was also used to compute the average healing efficiency given by Eq. (9.4) for four replicate specimens as a function of healing cycles. Here, only the fracture toughness has been used for the healing efficiency analysis since the delamination is a complex phenomenon. A quantitative evaluation of the effects of interlaminar fracture on the strength properties is difficult. As can be seen from the bar chart in Fig. 9.7, the average G_{Ic} value for the virgin specimen is 271.64 (J/m^2), and the healing efficiency shows a steady decline with the number of healing cycle, which is as expected. The healing efficiency plot in Fig. 9.8 showed that a fracture healing efficiency of 73.33% was obtained after the first healing cycle compared with 58.20% after the seventh healing cycle. This decrease in G_{Ic} and η_{GIc} with subsequent healing cycles might be due to the breakage of SMP and CAPA fibrils with subsequent healing as evident during the DCB test (Fig. 9.10c), as well as due to potential thermal degradation of the thermoplastic healants with subsequent healing cycles at $80\ ^{\circ}C$ which is well above the melting temperature (i.e., 58–$60\ ^{\circ}C$) of the CAPA particles. Nonetheless, the healed specimens demonstrated

Fig. 9.8 The average healing efficiency (η_{GIc}) of the healed specimens as a function of the healing cycle

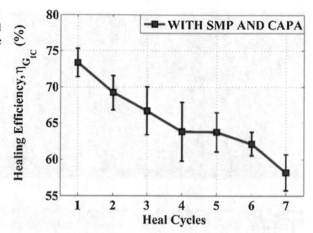

good healing repeatability because of the mendable nature of the thermoplastic healants and yielded more than 50% healing efficiency even after the seventh fracture and healing cycle.

Furthermore, the coefficient of variation (COV), which is the ratio of the standard deviation value to the mean value, was found to be less than 6% for G_{Ic} and less than 7% for η_{GIc} among all healing cycles. This suggested an excellent agreement in the G_{IC} and η_{Gc} values obtained from different specimens.

9.3.3 Fractography Using Scanning Electron Microscopy (SEM)

The SEM imaging analysis of the fracture surfaces of the healed specimens was carried out to understand the mechanisms responsible for the healing as well as degradation of the healing efficiency with subsequent healing cycles.

One of the most important criteria for partially or fully regaining the virgin fracture toughness is the presence of sufficient amount of healants in the fractured region [42, 43]. The complex region with elastomeric behavior and fibrillations (as shown in Fig. 9.9a) at the pre-crack end suggests the existence of the thermoplastic healant in the crack plane, and thus it supported the healing repeatability obtained in our study. Also, the highly irregular surface indicates the ductile fracture of the healant that is responsible for the resistance to crack growth. In addition, the uneven surface in Fig. 9.9b suggests crack tortuosity and crack deflection along the thermoplastic rich zone, which results in high fracture toughness for crack propagation. Similarly, the plane surface near the far end of the crack in Fig. 9.9c suggests crack growth along the matrix region with less resistance. It indicates interfacial debonding as one of the dominant modes for failure. However, less evidence of broken carbon fibers suggests the absence of the fiber bridging from

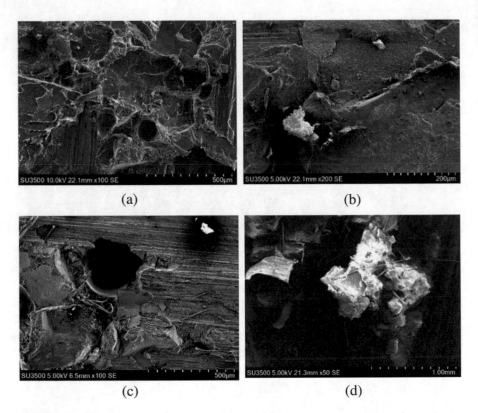

Fig. 9.9 The SEM images of the fracture surfaces of the healed specimens containing SMP and CAPA. (a) Near pre-crack end. (b) In the middle-zone of crack region. (c) Near crack end. (d) Cluster of CAPA+SMP

the SEM imaging. In fact, the damage propagates preferentially along the mixture of thermoset and thermoplastic than propagating through the fiber because of the lower requirement of fracture energy for crack growth along the matrix rich mid-layer. Therefore, one way to obtain higher healing efficiency is by choosing a tougher thermoplastic healant than currently used in this research.

One of the reasons for the unstable crack growth and reduced healing efficiency is the agglomeration of the thermoplastic healant, as seen in Fig. 9.9d [40]. Therefore, the healing efficiency of the specimens can be increased if the thermoplastic healant with low melting temperature, low viscosity, and high diffusivity is used. Also, uniform dispersion of the healant is another way of preventing the agglomeration of the thermoplastic healant and increasing the healing efficiency. Furthermore, the ability of the healants to form a strong bond with the epoxy will lead to higher healing performance.

The micrographic edge view of the crack region is provided in Fig. 9.10. For this purpose, the edges of the virgin specimens were polished before the DCB tests were carried out as shown in Fig. 9.10a at *1.27 cm (0.5 in)* from the pre-crack end. The

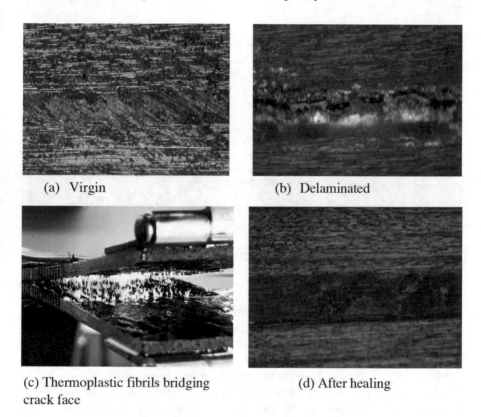

(a) Virgin   (b) Delaminated

(c) Thermoplastic fibrils bridging   (d) After healing
crack face

Fig. 9.10 Optical images for (**a**) Virgin specimen. (**b**) Delaminated specimen. (**c**) White healant fibrils during DCB fracture. (**d**) Healed specimen with no visible crack

interfacial debonding and kinking of the cracks during propagation along the matrix at the same location as in Fig. 9.10a is clearly visible from the delaminated figure in Fig. 9.10b. In addition, the thin thermoplastic fibrils that bridge the delamination surfaces and offer resistance for crack growth can be clearly seen in Fig. 9.10c. These bridging ligaments suggest the plastic deformation of the healants that allow the transfer of interlaminar stress across the delamination crack. This, in turn, provides the extrinsic toughening due to the lowering of the stress at the crack tip [44]. Finally, the edge view of the healed specimen in Fig. 9.10d shows the repair of the crack leaving behind very little sign of a visible crack.

9.3.4 Parametric Sensitivity Analysis

The results provided and discussed in this chapter provided evidence of the excellent healing ability and repeatability of thermoplastic SMP and CAPA as healing agents. Work is currently underway to improve the healing efficiency, to reduce the healing

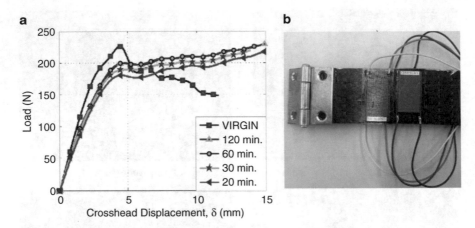

Fig. 9.11 (a) Load vs. crosshead displacement plot for different healing time for a DCB specimen, (b) DCB specimen with the MFC for healing

time for specimens in the oven, and also the use of Macro-Fiber Composite (MFC) piezo actuated heating system to replace the heating of the specimens in the oven.

Recently, a parametric sensitivity study at different time durations for heating the specimens with SMP and CAPA in an oven was assessed. To this end, the manufacturing cycle was changed to get a finer and homogenous mixture of the healants and also to prevent the formation of a cluster of CAPA particles during manufacture. Preliminary results from the sensitivity study as presented in Fig. 9.11a revealed that reducing healing time from 120 minutes to *20* minutes does not have any significant effect on the fracture behavior. Therefore, thermoplastic healants with much shorter heating time will ultimately offer substantially lower power requirements for healing and enhanced safety of the structure.

Furthermore, the possibility of achieving self-healing with the MFC actuated heating system rather than heating in an oven is currently being explored. To test MFC actuated healing ability, two MFCs (M2814-P1: *28 mm × 14 mm*) are attached on both the top and bottom surfaces of the specimen to provide sufficient heat for the crack-region in the mid-layer as shown in Fig. 9.11b. This set up will allow the MFCs to carry out healing with activation of SMP and melting of the CAPA by enough heat generation through ultrasonic excitation. Although the preliminary results are promising with this system, it will require additional parametric sensitivity study to determine the effect of excitation voltage and frequency on healing efficiency.

The development of dynamic data-driven damage modeling using finite element analysis (FEA) of the DCB specimens is also being carried out to model damage initiation and progression accurately. This FEA model will be a key part of the damage prognosis model inherent in the DDDAS paradigm.

9.4 Concluding Remarks

To achieve an intelligent self-healing system for composite structures, a novel SHM DDDAS paradigm is presented that combines a damage sensing network, a damage prognosis module, and self-healing mechanisms. The SHM DDDAS can sense damage using sensors, which then updates the prognosis module and activates the self-healing mechanism using an embedded MFC network. One of the main advantages of the SHM DDDAS approach is that it offers predictive self-healing to prevent the damage from becoming irreparable.

In this chapter, the self-healing capability of carbon fiber composites using mendable thermoplastic healants was presented for repeated fracture/healing cycles. The self-healing is performed by a two-step, '*close then heal*' technique where the SMP fibers help in bringing fracture surfaces of the macro-cracks close together, followed by molecular scale healing with CAPA through melting, diffusion, polymerization, and adhesion to the fracture surfaces. The DCB test data for specimens containing thermoplastic healants demonstrated that the fracture specimens were able to regain their virgin critical fracture toughness by as much as *73%* after the first healing cycle. The results also showed that the self-healing was repeatable, and a healing efficiency of *58%* was obtained after the seventh healing cycle. The healing mechanism of the thermoplastic healants was also evident from the SEM and optical micrograph images where the ductile fracture of the thermoplastic healants, fibril formation, tortuosity of the crack path, and the ligaments bridging the crack surfaces were observed that are responsible for offering resistance to crack propagation. These observations suggest that the healing efficiency can be increased by selecting thermoplastic healants with low melting temperature, low viscosity, high diffusivity, and the ability to form strong adhesion to the fracture surfaces.

Furthermore, to reduce the time and energy consumed during self-healing of the Mode-I interlaminar fracture, a parametric study based on varying time duration for heating the specimens was conducted. The results show that it is feasible to achieve similar healing efficiency even with only *20–30* minutes of heating. In addition, the healing of the fracture specimens with the MFC actuated heating system instead of oven heating has shown great promise. Work is currently underway to combine a damage sensing network and a dynamic data-driven damage prognosis module with the intelligent self-healing system, where initial developments have shown promising results.

Acknowledgments Funding for this work has been provided by the AFOSR Dynamic Data-Driven Application System Directorate (FA9550-17-1-0033). Scanning electron microscopy was carried out in the **Optical Analysis Facility,** which is supported by the Department of Biological Sciences. The authors would like to thank Professor Mark E. Barkey and Dr. Paul G. Allison for allowing to use of their lab facilities for various testing. The support of the Department of Aerospace Engineering and Mechanics at The University of Alabama, Tuscaloosa, is also acknowledged.

References

1. C. Farhat et al., Towards a Dynamic Data Driven System for Structural and Material Health Monitoring (Springer, Berlin/Heidelberg, 2006)
2. C.R. Farrar, N.A.J. Lieven, Damage prognosis: the future of structural health monitoring. Philos. Trans. R. Soc. A Math. Phys. Eng. Sci. 365(1851), 623–632 (2007)
3. R.S. Trask, C.J. Norris, I.P. Bond, Stimuli-triggered self-healing functionality in advanced fibre-reinforced composites. J. Intell. Mater. Syst. Struct. 25(1), 87–97 (2014)
4. G. Li, V.D. Muthyala, Impact characterization of sandwich structures with an integrated orthogrid stiffened syntactic foam core. Compos. Sci. Technol. 68(9), 2078–2084 (2008)
5. J. Nji, G. Li, Damage healing ability of a shape-memory-polymer-based particulate composite with small thermoplastic contents. Smart Mater. Struct. 21(2), 025011 (2012)
6. K.A. Williams, D.R. Dreyer, C.W. Bielawski, The underlying chemistry of self-healing materials. MRS Bull. 33(8), 759–765 (2011)
7. J. Lee et al., Fracture behaviour of a self-healing microcapsule-loaded epoxy system. Ex-press Polym Lett 5(3), 246–253 (2011)
8. B.J. Blaiszik et al., Self-healing polymers and composites. Annu. Rev. Mater. Res. 40(1), 179–211 (2010)
9. E.B. Murphy, F. Wudl, The world of smart healable materials. Prog. Polym. Sci. 35(1), 223–251 (2010)
10. S.R. White et al., Autonomic healing of polymer composites. Nature 409, 794 (2001)
11. R.S. Trask, G.J.Williams, I.P. Bond, Bioinspired self-healing of advanced composite structures using hollow glass fibres. J. R. Soc. Interface 4(13), 363–371 (2007)
12. R.S. Trask, I.P. Bond, Biomimetic self-healing of advanced composite structures using hollow glass fibres. Smart Mater. Struct. 15(3), 704 (2006)
13. J.W.C. Pang, I.P. Bond, 'Bleeding composites'—damage detection and self-repair using a biomimetic approach. Compos. A. Appl. Sci. Manuf. 36(2), 183–188 (2005)
14. J.W.C. Pang, I.P. Bond, A hollow fibre reinforced polymer composite encompassing self-healing and enhanced damage visibility. Compos. Sci. Technol. 65(11), 1791–1799 (2005)
15. E.N. Brown, S.R. White, N.R. Sottos, Microcapsule induced toughening in a self-healing polymer composite. J. Mater. Sci. 39(5), 1703–1710 (2004)
16. J. Yang et al., Microencapsulation of isocyanates for self-healing polymers. Macromolecules 41(24), 9650–9655 (2008)
17. S.H. Cho et al., Polydimethylsiloxane-based self-healing materials. Adv. Mater. 18(8), 997–1000 (2006)
18. C. Dry, Procedures developed for self-repair of polymer matrix composite materials. Compos. Struct. 35(3), 263–269 (1996)
19. M.R. Kessler, N.R. Sottos, S.R. White, Self-healing structural composite materials. Com-pos. A. Appl. Sci. Manuf. 34(8), 743–753 (2003)
20. S.M. Bleay et al., A smart repair system for polymer matrix composites. Compos. A. Appl. Sci. Manuf. 32(12), 1767–1776 (2001)
21. S.A. Hayes et al., A self-healing thermosetting composite material. Compos. A. Appl. Sci. Manuf. 38(4), 1116–1120 (2007)
22. G. Li, H. Meng, J. Hu, Healable thermoset polymer composite embedded with stimuli-responsive fibres. J. R. Soc. Interface 9(77), 3279–3287 (2012)
23. X. Chen et al., A thermally re-mendable cross-linked polymeric material. Science 295(5560), 1698–1702 (2002)
24. T.A. Plaisted, S. Nemat-Nasser, Quantitative evaluation of fracture, healing and re-healing of a reversibly cross-linked polymer. Acta Mater. 55(17), 5684–5696 (2007)
25. P. Cordier et al., Self-healing and thermoreversible rubber from supramolecular assembly. Nature. 451, 977–980 (2008)
26. D. Montarnal et al., Versatile one-pot synthesis of supramolecular plastics and self-healing rubbers. J. Am. Chem. Soc. 131(23), 7966–7967 (2009)

27. R.P. Wool, K.M. O'Connor, A theory crack healing in polymers. J. Appl. Phys. 52(10), 5953–5963 (1981)
28. D.A. Hurley, D.R. Huston, Coordinated sensing and active repair for self-healing. Smart Mater. Struct. 20(2), 025010 (2011)
29. S. Torkamani et al., A novel damage index for damage identification using guided waves with application in laminated composites. Smart Mater. Struct. 23(9), 095015 (2014)
30. G. Li, N. Uppu, Shape memory polymer based self-healing syntactic foam: 3-D confined thermomechanical characterization. Compos. Sci. Technol. 70(9), 1419–1427 (2010)
31. M. Thapa et al., Development of intelligent and predictive self-healing composite structures using dynamic data-driven applications systems. Handbook of Dynamic Data Driven Applications Systems, Editors:, Blasch, E., Ravela, S. and Aved, A., Springer Nature. 173–191 (2018)
32. B. Jony et al., Repeatable self-healing of thermosetting fiber reinforced polymer composites with thermoplastic healant. Smart Mater. Struct. 28 (2), 025037 (2019)
33. M. Thapa et al., Experimental characterization of shape memory polymer enhanced thermoplastic self-healing carbon/epoxy composites. AIAA Scitech 2019 Forum. 1112 (2019)
34. N.J. Vishe et al., Healing of Mode-I Fatigue Crack in Fiber Reinforced Composites using Thermoplastic Healants. AIAA Scitech 2020 Forum, 2104 (2019)
35. Product data sheet CAPA 6506, 16 Oct 2014, PERSTORP (2014), https://www.perstorp.com/products/capa_6506
36. G. Li, O. Ajisafe, H. Meng, Effect of strain hardening of shape memory polymer fibers on healing efficiency of thermosetting polymer composites. Polymer 54(2), 920–928 (2013)
37. Shape memory polymer presentation e-catalogue, SMP Technologies Inc., http://www.smptechno.com/pdf/smpvsspresentation100218.pdf
38. Standard test method for Mode-I interlaminar fracture toughness of unidirectional fiber-reinforced polymer matrix composites, ASTM D5528, 10/01/2013
39. C. Larco, R. Pahonie, M. Mihaila-Andres, Experimental study on mode I fracture of fibredux unidirectional prepreg. AIP Conf. Proc. 1836(1), 020037 (2017)
40. M.R. Kessler, S.R.White, Self-activated healing of delamination damage in woven composites. Compos. A. Appl. Sci. Manuf. 32(5), 683–699 (2001)
41. J.F. Patrick et al., Continuous self-healing life cycle in vascularized structural composites. Adv. Mater. 26(25), 4302–4308 (2014)
42. H. Ghazali, L. Ye, M.Q. Zhang, Interlaminar fracture of CF/EP composite containing a dual-component microencapsulated self-healant. Compos. A. Appl. Sci.Manuf. 82, 226–234 (2016)
43. C.H. Wang et al., Interlayer self-healing and toughening of carbon fibre/epoxy composites using copolymer films. Compos. A. Appl. Sci. Manuf. 43(3), 512–518 (2012)
44. K. Pingkarawat et al., Healing of carbon fibre-epoxy composites using thermoplastic additives. Polym. Chem. 4(18), 5007–5015 (2013)

Chapter 10
Dynamic Data-Driven Approach for Unmanned Aircraft Systems Aero-elastic Response Analysis

R. Kania, A. Kebbie-Anthony, X. Zhao, S. Azarm, and B. Balachandran

Abstract In this chapter, we will discuss how DDDAS ideas can be used to enhance the autonomy of an unmanned system, while accounting for nonlinear behavior of the system. Our approach is illustrated in the context of the unmanned aerial vehicle, such as the SensorCraft. It will be shown as to how DDDAS can be used to enhance the performance envelope as well as avoid aero-elastic instabilities, while reducing the need for user input. The DDDAS methodology and its application to this field are described in a framework that consists of an offline component and an online component.

During the offline phase, user supplied mission objectives such as required payload along with initial data such as weather forecasts and operation history of the aircraft are used to simulate and optimize for creating a robust optimal mission configuration, all prior to take-off of the SensorCraft. In this phase, with the aero-elastic simulator, preliminary stability envelopes are constructed to determine the flutter boundary of the aircraft with damage and without damage to the aircraft. By using available simulation results, an initial meta-model is trained offline. During the online phase, sensor data is to be acquired for the decision support process. This data is to be filtered and then fused with the meta-model to achieve a fast and reasonable estimate of the system response compared to those obtained from the computationally expensive aero-elastic simulator. As the responses are estimated and updated, they are evaluated based on the objectives so that optimal maneuvers can be determined with assistance of a decision support system. The DDDAS framework is composed of these three components, namely, the aero-elastic simulator, data-driven prediction scheme, and decision support system. The aero-elastic simulation is used to obtain information on the unmanned vehicle's dynamic response and this information is combined with sensor data for use in the online application of a decision support system.

R. Kania · A. Kebbie-Anthony · X. Zhao · S. Azarm · B. Balachandran (✉)
Department of Mechanical Engineering, University of Maryland, College Park, MD, USA
e-mail: balab@umd.edu

© The Author(s), under exclusive license to Springer Nature Switzerland AG 2022
E. P. Blasch et al. (eds.), *Handbook of Dynamic Data Driven Applications Systems*,
https://doi.org/10.1007/978-3-030-74568-4_10

Keywords Aero-elasticity · Active robust optimization · Co-simulation · Decision support system · Sensor data · Data fusion

10.1 Introduction

Uncertainty in physical responses and changes in environmental conditions will always be limiting factors to reckon with for determining the performance of an unmanned aircraft vehicle (UAV) system. Additionally, several recent UAVs (e.g., SensorCraft) are being designed with long, thin wings, which make the aircraft system more susceptible to aero-elastic instabilities. In order to increase flight effectiveness, nonlinear aero-elasticity needs to be addressed in the design and operation of such systems. In addition, instabilities and post-instability behavior need to be taken into account as well. To utilize aero-elastic models effectively, decisions need to be made optimally, given uncertainty in the environment.

A standard approach for addressing aero-elastic effects takes place in the design phase. Linearized aero-elastic models, calibrated with experimental data, are used to predict speeds at which the considered aircraft can experience flutter (oscillatory) behavior. The aircraft design is considered safe to fly only when the maximum operating speed of the aircraft is well below the minimum aero-elastic onset speed [20]. Over the decades, studies of linearization methods have matured, and these methods have been successfully utilized. More recently, machine learning techniques have been applied to the problem of estimating the stability envelope by having as inputs data from multiple models of various fidelity levels and constructing a Support Vector Machine (SVM). Once trained, the SVM can be used to predict which aero-elastic flight regime a given configuration will fall into. The boundary between these classifications can be used to describe a flight envelope, with aero-elastically stable operation on one side, and unstable operation on the other [19]. Both linearized models and machine learning classifiers have the same drawback in that they do not consider post-instability behavior. That is, they cannot be used to predict the nature of the behavior following an aero-elastic instability and cannot be used to make useful predictions after the onset of an instability.

The SensorCraft was conceived as a novel surveillance platform and a set of design goals were put forth in 2002. These goals include flight durations upwards of 40 hours with different flight regimes, and an aircraft with a number of integrated sensors [24].

To meet the long flight duration objective, designers had to adopt atypical wing structures which offer high efficiency. These structures fall into three categories, namely, the Diamond Wing, Box Wing, and Strut- (Truss-) Braced Wing configurations (Fig. 10.1) [5]. As shown in Fig. 10.1, in each one of the designs, the aircraft has long and flexible wings that are reinforced with a strut or secondary wing. Although increased length and flexibility are shown to improve efficiency, they open the door to aero-elastic instabilities such as flutter that are typically avoided in modern aircraft designs. Systems with flexible wings can exhibit complex, nonlinear motions (e.g., [10]). Nonlinear aero-elasticity and the complex dependence of the

Fig. 10.1 Various wing
designs for SensorCraft.
(Adapted from Cavallaro and
Demasi [5])

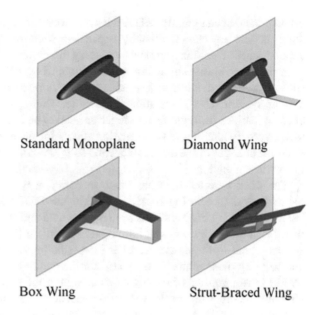

Standard Monoplane   Diamond Wing

Box Wing   Strut-Braced Wing

system behavior on the many determining factors make it difficult to predict and
almost impossible for a pilot (onboard or remote) to successfully navigate the
aircraft. So, these designs require a decision support system to help the pilot tailor
flight configuration options with considerations of nonlinear aero-elasticity.

With an observation platform, such as the SensorCraft, there are a number of
objectives that are sought with each mission. An operator would want to maximize
the amount and the quality of data collected. Taking the vehicle itself into account,
minimizing damage or maximizing the useful life of the aircraft may also be desired
goals to account for in a mission. The first priority of an observation platform will
likely be the maximization of data quality. Consider then a scenario where turbulent
conditions are detected in the flight path during a mission. Passing through such an
obstacle will certainly muddle any images or sensor readings and may even force
an object tracker to relocate its target. The alternative, however, is to maneuver
under, over, or around, if possible. Making a maneuver could have all of the same
negative effects. What then, is the operator to do in order to minimize disruptions
to the observations? This is where a decision support system can be invaluable. A
decision support system can be used to calculate the effect each maneuver, or non-
maneuver, will have on the objective and determine an optimal path forward, even
taking into consideration uncertainty in the environmental factors. Decision support
systems will be discussed in more detail later in this chapter, including an outline
for how to handle multiple competing mission goals.

Often decisions are made while ignoring aero-elasticity because of the difficulty
in considering nonlinearity. However, as better performance and efficiency of
aircraft are sought, nonlinear physics becomes critical for making predictions
and dealing with system behavior. Therefore, nonlinear aero-elastic models are
required to capture dynamic instabilities such as flutter and associated limit-cycle

oscillations that can greatly reduce the operational lifetime of the aircraft. However, these models are computationally expensive. Meta-models can be considered to approximate the nonlinear models, reducing the number of execution calls required of the full aero-elastic simulations. In addition, worst-case scenarios for uncertainty can be predicted in advance to produce an envelope inside which a safe unmanned aircraft system (UAS) operation is possible. Then, as disturbances and changes become realized in-flight, fewer scenarios need to be analyzed to determine optimal maneuvers. Evaluating fewer scenarios allows for faster updating of the models to real-time changes of the environment and suggested maneuvers to be better matched to a current situation.

The work reported here has much in common with adaptive structural health planning and monitoring research. Within the DDDAS [6] literature, structural health monitoring of aircraft has been investigated and shown to benefit greatly from it; for example, the studies of Farhat and Amsallem [7] and Allaire et al. [3]. The common goal of these researchers is the prediction of failure in aircraft structures and tailoring planned missions to best suit the remaining capabilities of the aircraft. Online sensor readings can only be used to infer the current status of the aircraft's structural health. Conversely, simulations can accurately predict such failures before they ever occur. However, the exact operating conditions of the aircraft cannot be known beforehand. Once the conditions are known, a simulation will take time to run. Generally, the accuracy of the simulated prediction will be related to the computational time. With all of these tradeoffs, very accurate and timely failure predictions become nearly impossible to achieve; so, safety margins must be added to prevent system failure. The DDDAS paradigm provides one solution; that is, to combine the above tools and get a faster and more accurate prediction.

The decision support system is shown in Fig. 10.2 as an input-output block. From the viewpoint of a pilot or operator, the decision support system inputs are the current system response and sensor readings from the aircraft and the outputs are possible optimal solutions that will help maintain or lead to aero-elastically stable flight. Internally, based on the available information, new simulations can be performed to fill any gaps. Simulations of differing fidelity levels can be used depending on the needs of the situation; for example, what accuracy is required and how much time is available. The results are fused together with the data to

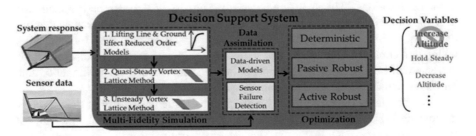

Fig. 10.2 Schematic of decision support system

validate that the model can be used to accurately represent the UAS at the current time and detect any sensors that may have failed and readings are being obtained with insufficient accuracy. The fused response prediction is then used to optimize future maneuvers. Again, multiple levels of fidelity, or robustness here, are available to select for different situations. The final outputs are values of decision variables, which provide optimized solutions. In the presence of multiple objectives, multiple optimal decision will be suggested and the pilot's preference will be used to select from among them.

The quintessential DDDAS framework has three components: theory, modeling and simulation, and dynamic data. The theory is integral to the development of the entire framework and one can use it to shape how simulations are carried out and data modeling are constructed. Once the framework is established, there are dynamic interactions between the simulations and the data driven modeling, and the information that is generated from this interactive combination is used to make system predictions. The fourth, as of yet unnamed, component is the application system which contains and benefits from the DDDAS construct.

The implementation of DDDAS schemes, which combine the above components, has been shown effective in a number of fields with the same general structure. Problems that require timely solutions to intensive simulations in order to perform an application in real time can be found in such areas in environmental analysis, robotics, image processing, and embedded computing. Modeling of atmospheric conditions, such as air currents is a well-known computationally intensive task that is often delegated to super computers. During unfolding catastrophes such as wild fires and the release of airborne contaminants, there is not sufficient time to run a simulation and to act on its predictions. Benefits to weather forecasting have been shown in the studies of Fisher et al. [8], prediction of the spread of wildfires in Mandel et al. [18] and Rodriguez, Cortés, and Margalef [23], and the identification of airborne contaminants [1, 2, 16]. Enhanced performance has been noted with vehicle system applications, especially, for unmanned aerial vehicles [17, 21] and ground vehicles [15]. Finally, in the field of image processing, target tracking, which requires fast and accurate computations, has been aided through DDDAS [25]. This is by no means a complete listing of the systems to which DDDAS has been successfully applied, but it should serve to inform the reader of the breadth of this powerful methodology. It should also be seen how the problem under consideration in this chapter fits neatly into the range of other DDDAS applications.

The rest of the chapter is organized as follows. First, the structure of the DDDAS framework is described, highlighting the interactions among the major components. Then, the formalism behind the aero-elastic co-simulation is presented. After that, the authors provide a section on the data-driven prediction framework. In it, the use of online sensor data to supplement the co-simulation is detailed. Finally, the authors explain the decision support system and how it can be used for data-driven predictions.

10.2 Framework

The framework for the DDDAS methodology discussed in this chapter is illustrated
in Fig. 10.3. Beginning in the offline phase, initial data that is provided by the
user, based on known or estimated operating conditions and mission parameters
is used to determine a number of aero-elastic simulations to perform. The results
are used to both determine a data-driven model for predicting system responses, and
to tailor an initial flight envelope for which an optimal mission plan can be found.
After the beginning of the mission or take-off, the operation shifts to the online
phase. Starting at the top of Fig. 10.3, in the online phase, sensor data is obtained
from sensors located on the SensorCraft and fused with current model predictions.
Further detail on how data fusion is performed is given in a later section. As with
the offline initial data, the now fused data is used to design a set of simulation
experiments. The data-driven model is updated to incorporate the new results. The
model is validated against holdout data, and analysis is performed to detect faulty
sensor measurements. The new predicted responses are then fused with incoming
data, and the cycle is repeated. Based on the data-driven model, optimization studies
are carried out to determine optimal maneuvers that are feasible with the predicted
aero-elastic response. The results are then provided to a pilot so that he/she may
make well informed decisions on how to proceed further with a maneuver.

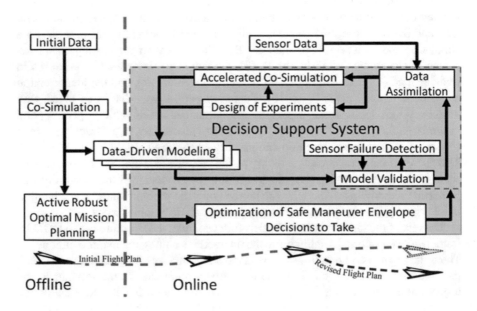

Fig. 10.3 DDDAS framework for decision support system

10.3   Aero-Elastic Simulation

A central component of the proposed DDDAS framework that was mentioned before is the aero-elastic simulation and the underlying basis for this simulation. Generally speaking, aero-elasticity of a system such as the UAS includes structural dynamics and aerodynamics and some form of coupling between them. The structural dynamics depends on inertial effects, elastic effects, and the aerodynamic loads acting on the structure. Reduced-order models developed by using methods such as the finite element method can be used to study the structural dynamics of a system. The aerodynamic forces can be obtained through computational fluid dynamics and methods such as the unsteady, vortex lattice method. Once one has constructed models to describe the structural dynamics and aerodynamics, it is possible to recreate aero-elastic effects wherein the fluid flow exerts a force on the considered UAS system, the UAS system responds to the loads, and the system response in turn alters the fluid flow around it. Because of this naturally occurring feedback, an aero-elastic simulation can be difficult and time consuming.

As shown in Fig. 10.2, in the envisioned decision support system, three fidelity-level models are incorporated to capture static, dynamic, and aero-elastic responses of the system. Given the modular nature of the approach, this approach is not limited to these three models and other models could be used as well in the DDDAS framework. When modeling fluid flows, one option is to use commercial solvers meant for Computational Fluid Dynamics (CFD). In these solvers, it is common to use a grid method, wherein one discretizes the flow field and numerically solves the governing equations, such as the Navier-Stokes equations. In some of the commercial packages, one can couple CFD with a structural solver allowing for fluid-structure interactions to be studied. Although such methods are ubiquitous, it has been shown that using instead, a grid-free vortex method provides sufficient accuracy to predict forces on the scale that is sought here. One advantage of vortex methods in the current study is the levels of fidelity available. As shown in Fig. 10.2, lifting line theory in combination with a simple ground effect model can be used to generate quite a fast, low accuracy estimate of the aerodynamic forces by assuming the lifting surfaces form a one-dimensional line of vortices at a given instant in time. Improvements can be made to the quasi-steady model by considering a two-dimensional lattice of vortices in the method called the vortex lattice method (VLM). As aero-elasticity responses are dynamic in nature, a model in which one accounts for unsteady behavior as well would be appropriate. This unsteady behavior can be captured by using the so-called unsteady, vortex lattice method (UVLM). This scheme can be strongly coupled with a structural model to create a co-simulation of aero-elastic dynamics, as done in the current work as well as prior work of the group members (e.g., [22]). Co-simulation (e.g., [12]) here refers to the partitioning of a coupled system into subsystems that are separately simulated (but numerically integrated) with a suitable exchange of states at predefined time instances to account for the coupling.

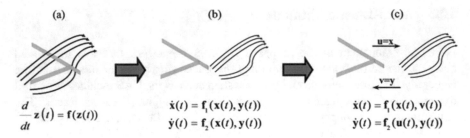

(a)   (b)   (c)

$$\frac{d}{dt}z(t) = f(z(t))$$

$$\dot{x}(t) = f_1(x(t), y(t))$$
$$\dot{y}(t) = f_2(x(t), y(t))$$

$$\dot{x}(t) = f_1(x(t), v(t))$$
$$\dot{y}(t) = f_2(u(t), y(t))$$

Fig. 10.4 Co-simulation process for a system in airflow: (**a**) wing in airflow, (**b**) partitioning, and (**c**) co-simulation

In Fig. 10.4, the representative steps involved in the co-simulation process for a SensorCraft wing in airflow are depicted. At the initial stage, the coupled system (structure in airflow) is represented by the continuous system, wherein the state vector is given by $z(t) = \begin{pmatrix} x(t) \\ y(t) \end{pmatrix}$. Here $x(t)$ and $y(t)$ are the state vectors associated with the structure and the velocity/pressure fields of airflow, respectively. In the next stage of the co-simulation process, one partitions the dynamic system into two subsystems as follows:

$$\frac{d}{dt}z(t) = \frac{d}{dt}\begin{pmatrix} x(t) \\ y(t) \end{pmatrix} = \begin{pmatrix} f_1(x(t), y(t)) \\ f_2(x(t), y(t)) \end{pmatrix} \Rightarrow \begin{array}{c} \dot{x}(t) \\ \dot{y}(t) \end{array} = \begin{array}{c} f_1(x(t), y(t)) \\ f_2(x(t), y(t)) \end{array}$$

(10.1)

The final stage of the co-simulation process involves exchanging information bi-directionally between the two subsystems. This is accomplished by using a prediction to represent the unknown state vector in the different subsystems. Therefore, to simulate the $\dot{x}(t)$ subsystem, a prediction $v(t)$ is needed for its $y(t)$ input. Similarly, to simulate the $\dot{y}(t)$ system, a prediction $u(t)$ is needed for its $x(t)$ input. After substituting the predictions into (10.1), the system can be written as

$$\begin{pmatrix} \dot{x}(t) \\ \dot{y}(t) \end{pmatrix} = \begin{pmatrix} f_1(x(t), v(t)) \\ f_2(u(t), y(t)) \end{pmatrix}$$

(10.2)

in which the structure's state is simulated by using the predicted airflow states and the airflow state is simulated by using the predicted structure states. Further information on co-simulation of complex systems can be found in Kalmar-Nagy and Stanciulescu [12].

The two subsystems are computational implementations of models intended for the UAS structural dynamics and the aerodynamics. The first subsystem, Simulator 1, is the UAS structural model. In Simulator 1, one utilizes the finite element method (FEM) to simulate the motions of the representative SensorCraft wings by using beam elements. The structural dynamics of the SensorCraft is studied by using the mass and stiffness matrix along with the load vector. Here,

Fig. 10.5 Beam representation of joined-wing aircraft wing

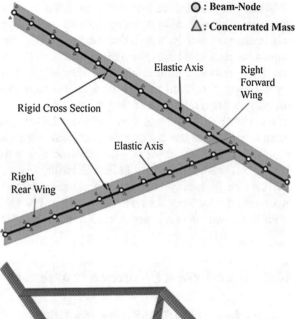

Fig. 10.6 Representative aerodynamic mesh of full joined-wing aircraft

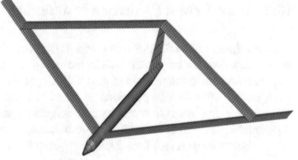

geometric stiffness effects are also taken into account to study buckling. In Fig. 10.5, the beam representation of the right wing of a representative SensorCraft is shown. The beam nodal points are represented by circles distributed along the center lines of both wings. The mass of the wings is concentrated into point masses collocated with the nodal points. The second subsystem, Simulator 2, is used to simulate the aerodynamics. For Simulator 2, one utilizes the UVLM to determine the aerodynamic loads acting on the representative SensorCraft. The wake, considered to be vorticity-containing regions where viscous effects cannot be ignored, is convected behind the aircraft. Through the convection of the wake, the aerodynamic loads (lift and drag) for the system are estimated. The mesh used for the aerodynamic model of the full joined-wing aircraft is shown in Fig. 10.6. To capture the aerodynamic effects with the highest fidelity level, a very refined mesh is used. A representative treatment of UVLM-FEM based co-simulation can be found in the work Roccia et al. [22]. It is envisaged that in future efforts such co-simulations will be coupled with experimental data obtained for flight systems (e.g., [10]).

When one obtains aero-elastic simulation results with this level of fidelity, this does come at a high computational cost. Even with modern computing enhancements such as parallelization and GPU computing, these computations cannot be performed fast enough to enable real-time decision support. If they could be performed sufficiently fast, simulations alone still lack information on current flight conditions needed to relate their results to the physical system. Both issues, speed and relevance of the provided information, can be addressed by using online sensor data. A main thrust of the DDDAS paradigm is the integration of simulation and sensor data to produce data with the accuracy of high fidelity simulations and instantaneous information available from sensor data. The method used in this work is described in the following section. Additionally, computations can be algorithmically accelerated through approximation methods such as the fast multipole method. An application of the fast multipole method to the above described co-simulation is demonstrated in Kebbie-Anthony et al. [14].

10.4   Data-Driven Prediction Framework

A central feature of a DDDAS framework is dynamic data usage. In the last section, the authors detailed the co-simulation method used to simulate UAS aero-elastic responses. An important feature of the DDDAS paradigm is the use of dynamic data modeling to offset the computational costs of complex physics simulators to allow for real-time deployment. In this section, a dynamic data-driven prediction system is presented. The authors combine the aero-elastic simulation results with dynamic sensor data to support real-time decision making for a SensorCraft.

For the decision support system, it is crucial to have a fast and accurate system prediction environment based on the current flight conditions. As mentioned in the preceding section, simulations are used to estimate global system responses of the entire system. The UVLM based simulations can be used to obtain an accurate prediction of the system's behavior. However, due to the computational expense, it is impractical to use UVLM for online predictions. On the other hand, a low-fidelity simulation, such as a VLM based simulation, can be executed to estimate global system behavior in a timely manner, but with a decreased accuracy. Also available during online performance are the numerous sensors embedded in every aircraft (and more for a developing prototype) which can be used to obtain a continuous stream of environmental and structural response data from the aircraft. Given that most sensors can be used primarily to obtain measurements in regions spatially local to them, there is an inherent information mismatch when using this sensor data with spatially, global simulation results. There is a need to develop a data-driven prediction framework based on available simulation data and local sensor data, with high computational efficiency and reasonable accuracy comparable to the high-fidelity simulation.

Certain assumptions are made in this prediction framework. First, measurements from sensors used in the framework refer to measurements of endogenous system

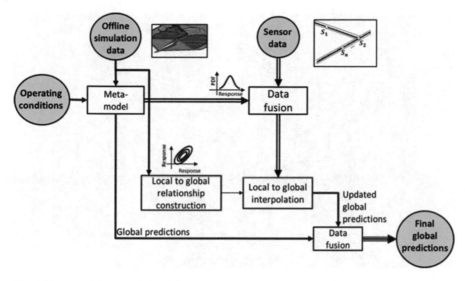

Fig. 10.7 Data driven prediction framework

properties, and the sensors are assumed to be used for measurements of local, discretely located response data. It is assumed that each sensor is free of systematic error but subject to independent random noise. The uncertainty level produced by noise is assumed to be known as it can usually be found in a specification sheet for any given sensor. Together, the sensor data and the available simulation data are considered as training inputs for the model. Finally, the spatially, global system behavior is assumed to be dependent on each other, or correlated, since they are sharing the exact same operating variables.

In Fig. 10.7, the authors illustrate the overall process of the data-driven prediction framework. The training inputs, the sensor data, and the simulation data, are shown at the top of the framework and these are used to construct the model. Through this model, data are fused to make global predictions, for the considered operating conditions. As with the DDDAS framework, the data-driven prediction system is composed of an offline phase and online phase. Following Fig. 10.7 (see also Fig. 10.3), during the offline stage, a meta-model can be constructed based on available simulation results. The next step is to capture pairwise statistical relationships between each local response (associated with sensor location) and each global response. During the online stage, the meta-model is used to make global estimates of the aircraft performance for the current operating conditions. For local responses, sensor measurements and the meta-model estimations are fused together based on their levels of uncertainty. The next is to update the global prediction by utilizing local and global statistical relationships constructed by utilizing a Bayesian Copula model [11] during the offline stage. Finally, these updated global predictions are fused with meta-model for global predictions.

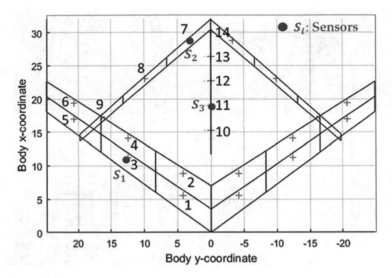

Fig. 10.8 VLM aerodynamic mesh of joined-wing aircraft lifting surface with representative sensor locations

10.5 Case Study

An aerodynamic case study of a joined-wing aircraft is used to demonstrate the proposed prediction framework. In Fig. 10.8, the considered aircraft layout is shown. The quantities of interest are the strains simulated at 14 different locations on the aircraft. Out of the 14 locations, three locations have sensors that are used to measure strain as is shown in Fig. 10.8. All three sensors are assumed to be susceptible to noise with assumed distributions at varying levels. The operating conditions considered are air density, freestream speed, and flight altitude. The VLM based formulation is employed as the aerodynamic model for purposes of illustration. In ongoing work, the UVLM based formulation is being used. This extension and more details on a dynamic prediction framework can be found in Zhao et al. [26].

The aerodynamic case study is started with an offline stage. Gaussian regression has been used to construct a meta-model, with training based on results obtained through VLM simulations for 10 operating conditions (see Table 10.1). Sensor locations are chosen to be at the root of the fore wing, near the wing joints, and the vertical tail at points coincident with panel numbers 3, 7, and 11, respectively. The spatial coincidence of the sensor locations and simulation model control points; that is, the centers of the aerodynamic mesh panels, allows for the development of pairwise statistical relationships between the model values at the sensor locations and every other point. Correlation is established between every point where there is a sensor and every other point in turn. With 14 locations being considered, and 3 sensors, 13 correlations need to be computed for each sensor for a total of 39 pairwise statistical relationships. Once the relationships have been characterized,

Table 10.1 Ten operating conditions evaluated for training process

Training point number	Flight speed (m/s)	Air density (kg/m³)	Altitude (m)
1	89.23	1.29	66.69
2	99.07	1.31	94.39
3	70.24	1.21	58.65
4	46.44	1.08	96.96
5	78.94	1.14	64.27
6	87.25	1.26	79.17
7	69.49	1.08	71.51
8	61.89	1.13	80.44
9	45.57	1.18	88.21
10	57.46	1.03	52.15

Table 10.2 Ten operating conditions evaluated for testing process

Test point number	Flight speed (m/s)	Air density (kg/m³)	Altitude (m)
1	80.71	1.12	98.69
2	89.37	1.17	51.72
3	64.04	1.19	87.25
4	54.64	1.25	70.12
5	46.98	1.11	81.35
6	99.22	1.28	65.33
7	83.83	1.06	75.46
8	73.05	1.04	56.61
9	63.34	1.23	60.19
10	42.29	1.29	94.62

responses at any of the 14 locations can be inferred from sensor data at the 3 sensor points.

Ten operating conditions were randomly generated to represent online operations and validate the prediction accuracy as, shown in Table 10.2. A prediction based solely on the meta-model is compared with the proposed approach, in the meta-model prediction and the simulated sensor data are fused. Both results are compared with the VLM results at the ten operating conditions.

In Fig. 10.9, the authors show the prediction errors at the 14 locations. They present the root mean squared error (RMSE) for meta-model without sensor fusion and meta-model with proposed sensor fusion in Fig. 10.9(a). Note that with the addition of more sensors, the RMSE is reduced at a majority of the 14 locations. At locations 12 and 14, the unadjusted meta-model has slightly lower RMSE, but the difference is insignificant especially since there is improvement in the STD. In Fig. 10.9(b), the authors show that a more consistent reduction in the standard deviations is achieved with additional sensors. The average RMSE and STD prediction errors at the 14 locations are presented in Table 10.3.

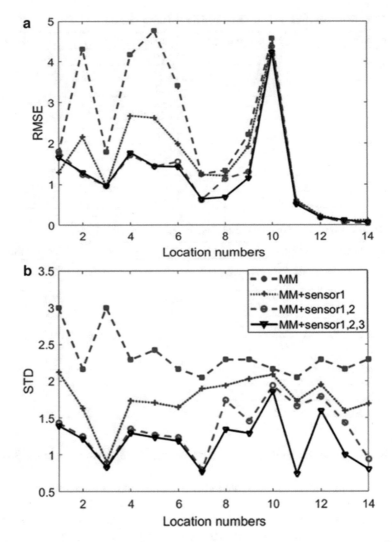

Fig. 10.9 Normalized predictions for 14 location responses: (**a**) root mean square error (RMSE) and (**b**) standard deviation (STD) comparisons

Table 10.3 Statistical prediction results comparison

	Meta-model (MM)	MM and Sensor 1	MM and Sensors 1, 2	MM and Sensors 1, 2, 3
RMSE	2.56	1.79	1.32	1.37
STD	2.44	1.66	1.29	1.14

10.6   Decision Support

Now that the DDDAS framework for data driven predictions has been used to determine a probability distribution for the current state estimate and future state predictions, the next question is how can that information be used to make a flight decision? This area of active research is addressed in this section.

By using the state predictor, maneuvers can be evaluated for their potential impact on mission objectives and optimal maneuvers can be determined. Computational assistance for pilots is especially important due to the aero-elastic susceptibility of SensorCraft designs. Aero-elastic effects are highly nonlinear making them particularly difficult to predict and all but nullifying the efficacy of employing intuition for avoidance. For some applications, that may be acceptable, but here, the price of failure is very steep. So even unlikely events that may only occur in the tails of their probability distributions need to be in the forefront of design considerations. The matter is further complicated when we consider that a given mission may have multiple objectives. As stated at the introduction of this chapter, maximizing data collection, maximizing quality of data, minimizing aircraft damage, and maximizing aircraft operational lifetime are some of the objectives that may figure into how decisions are made. Some of these clearly align with each other. Minimizing damage and maximizing data quality, for example, will most likely lead to many of the same choices since any damage to the aircraft may damage the sensors or introduce noise into the measurements. Other objectives could often be at odds with each other. Maximizing the operational lifetime of the SensorCraft may interfere with the amount of data collected if the operator is unwilling to take certain risks that could lead to the release of valuable data, and/or situations wherein there is excessive stress on the wings. Determining which objectives take priority, when, and by how much is an important task that can greatly affect the maneuvering behavior. Balancing optimality for multiple competing objectives while maintaining a measure of feasibility for all of them is a central function of the decision support system.

When uncertainty is introduced, due to measurement error, modeling error, and so on, extra precautions need to be included in the decision making process. There are two standard approaches for incorporating this uncertainty. The simplest and most widespread, is to treat the problem as if it were deterministic, assuming that any uncertain event will take on its most likely value and then optimize. When some guarantee of feasibility is sought, the possible outcomes of the uncertain events are enumerated and a robust solution, one that is insensitive to uncertainties, is found that satisfies all of the constraints for all eventualities. In the case of an aircraft, or really any system with controls, the optimization can benefit from separating the decision variables into current decisions and future decisions. In a technique developed for chemical plant design called flexible optimization [9], one considers design variables that need to be determined before an uncertain event occurs and operational variables as operations that can be determined after the occurrence. After the event takes place, only one of its possible outcome scenarios can be realized. The plant can be designed so that for each distinct scenario, a distinct operation is optimized. The topic of operationally flexible robust optimization with multiple objectives is elaborated upon in greater detail by Azarm and Lee [4]. A method for searching for the worst case scenarios instead of doing an exhaustive sweep has been investigated by Kania, Azarm, and Balachandran [13].

$$
\begin{aligned}
&\underset{x_d, x_{op1}, \dots, x_{opi}, \dots, x_{opI} \forall p}{\text{minimize}} \quad E\left[f_{m,i}\left(x_d, x_{opi}, p_i\right)\right] \quad m = 1, \dots, M \\
&s.t. : g_{j,i}\left(x_d, x_{opi}, p_i\right) \leq 0 \quad j = 1, \dots, J, \quad i = 1, \dots, I \\
&\quad \underset{\forall p \quad x_{op} \quad j \in J}{\text{maxminmax}} g_{j,i}\left(x_d, x_{op}, p\right) \leq 0 \\
&\forall p : \quad p_l \leq p \leq p_u; \quad \forall p_i : \quad p_l \leq p_i \leq p_u
\end{aligned}
\tag{10.3}
$$

where x_d contains the design variables; x_{op} contains the operational variables; p contains the uncertain parameters; p_l and p_u contain the lower and upper bounds of the uncertain parameters respectively; x_{opi} contains the operational variables corresponding to the ith discrete value of p; $f_{m,i}$ contains the mth objective function evaluated at the ith discrete value of p; and $g_{j,i}$ contains the jth constraint evaluated at the ith discrete value of p.

In Eq. (10.3), the authors show the general form of an optimization of M objectives that is robust with operational flexibility to I possible scenarios of the uncertain events p_i. For each of these, there is a separate operational variable x_{opi} that is optimized, with only a single value of the design variables x_d.

For the SensorCraft considered in this chapter, this means that the system can be designed for its operation during different types of missions, or preflight parameters can be designed for uncertain events that might require distinct maneuvers. In order to get the most performance out of the system while considering aero-elastic instabilities, it is desired that each maneuver be optimized and guaranteed, within some limits, to be feasible/stable. For updating the optimal solution, one frequently requires a model that can be evaluated in a short time, but the cost of inaccuracy (possible destruction of an aircraft) makes a high fidelity model desirable. Most often, these two criteria are mutually exclusive. The DDDAS framework discussed in the previous section allows for a method by using the accuracy of the nonlinear aero-elastic simulation with the real-time sensor data to achieve a prediction that is both fast and accurate. These properties mean that not only can the DDDAS based decision support system be used to aid in the design, but it can also be employed as a form of finite horizon controller. The data-driven prediction framework shows how predictions can be made for aero-elastic stability in future time steps. Instead of considering the design variables of flexible optimization to be of a different nature than the operational variables, maneuvers can be treated as both. There is a maneuver that must be taken at the current time, while the uncertain conditions are unknown, and also a maneuver that should be taken later, after some of the unknowns become known. These can have the same variables, but divided into now and later.

Fig. 10.10 One-step
look-ahead decision support
based on state estimator and
predictor

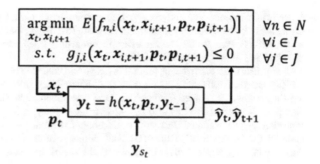

$$\arg\min_{x_t, x_{i,t+1}} E\left[f_{n,i}\left(x_t, x_{i,t+1}, p_t, p_{i,t+1}\right)\right] \quad \forall n \in N$$
$$s.t. \quad g_{j,i}\left(x_t, x_{i,t+1}, p_t, p_{i,t+1}\right) \le 0 \quad \forall i \in I$$
$$\forall j \in J$$

$$y_t = h(x_t, p_t, y_{t-1})$$

$$y_{s_t}$$

Referring to Fig. 10.10, the lower block with outputs $\hat{y}_t$ and $\hat{y}_{t+1}$, current
and future aero-elastic state elements is the data-driven prediction system. These
estimates are used in the decision support system to determine the feasibility of
tentative maneuvers. Maneuvers consist of decision variables x, with the subscripts
t and $t + 1$ denoting the current time step and the future time step, respectively. The
future maneuver x_{t+1} is divided into I possible maneuvers wherein the ith maneuver
corresponds to the ith possible scenario for the uncertain event. By optimizing for
time t and possible values for time $t + 1$ a one-step look ahead method of decision
support has been created. Each maneuver that is selected to execute by the operator
is optimal and feasible, and also chosen to enhance the optimality and feasibility of
the future maneuver.

Where x's are state vectors, p's are uncertain parameters, y's are system
responses, and $\hat{y}$'s are system response predictions. The subscript t corresponds
to the current time during online operation, with $t + 1$ representing estimates of a
future time, and $t - 1$ being the previous time step. The subscript i indicates which
of the I possible outcome scenarios for the next time step is being considered.

10.7 Concluding Remarks

In this chapter, a DDDAS framework for a decision support system has been
developed to make use of aero-elastic simulation capabilities, system response
predictions, and optimization under uncertainty. By accelerating high-fidelity simulations with an approximation method, such as the fast multipole method and using
the proposed data-driven prediction system, it is expected that accuracy can be
achieved for the needed decision making. With computationally cheaper function
evaluations, online optimization would be feasible. Additionally, incorporating
measures of robustness that take operational variables into account would mean that
the resulting decision support system can help pilots realize efficient performance
with thin, flexible wing aircraft such as the SensorCraft.

Acknowledgements The authors gratefully acknowledge partial support received for this work through AFOSR DDDAS Program Grant FA9550-15-1-0134. They also express their appreciation to Dr. Erik P. Blasch and Dr. Frederica Darema of AFOSR, for the constructive suggestions provided during the course of this work.

For SensorCraft related data, the authors have had extended interactions with researchers in the AFRL supported Collaborative Center for Multidisciplinary Sciences at Virginia Tech, Blacksburg, VA (in particular, Dr. Robert Canfield) and Dr. Robert Scott of the NASA Langley Research Center, Hampton, VA. The team has also benefited from ongoing collaborations with Professor Sergio Preidikman of the National University of Córdoba, Argentina on UVLM studies and fluid-structure simulations. Thanks are also due to Dr. Nail Gumerov of the University Of Maryland Institute Of Advanced Computer Studies for his help with the use of the fast multipole method.

References

1. Akcelik, V., Biros, G., Draganescu, A., Ghattas, O., Hill, J., and van Bloeman Waanders, B. (2005). "Dynamic data-driven inversion for terascale simulations: real-time identification of airborne contaminants." *Proceedings of SC2005*, pp. 43–58. Seattle, WA.
2. Akcelik, V., Biros, G., Draganescu, A., Ghattas, O., and Hill, J. (2006). "Inversion of airborne contaminants in a regional model." In: *Int. Conf. Comput. Sci.* (ICCS), vol. 3993, pp. 481–488. Reading, UK
3. Allaire, D., Kordonowy, D., Lecerf, M., Mainini, L., and Willcox, K. (2014). "Multifidelity DDDAS methods with application to a self-aware aerospace vehicle." *Procedia Computer Science* 29: 1182–1192.
4. Azarm, S. and Lee, Y.-T. (2016) "Multi-objective robust optimization formulations with operational flexibility and discretized uncertainty." *Proceedings of the International Design Engineering Technical Conferences*, Charlotte, NC, August 21–24.
5. Cavallaro, R., and Demasi, L. (2016). "Challenges, ideas, and innovations of joined-wing configurations: A concept from the past, an opportunity for the future." *Progress in Aerospace Sciences*, 87, 1–93.
6. Darema, F. (2004). "Dynamic data driven applications systems: A new paradigm for application simulations and measurements." *Computational Science-ICCS* 2004: 662–669.
7. Farhat, C., and Amsallem, D. (2008) "Recent advances in reduced-order modeling and application to nonlinear computational aeroelasticity." 46th AIAA Aerospace Sciences Meeting and Exhibit, Reno, NV.
8. Fisher, M., Nocedal, J., Trémolet, Y., and Wright, S. J. (2009). "Data assimilation in weather forecasting: a case study in PDE-constrained optimization." *Optimization and Engineering* 10.3: 409–426.
9. Halemane, K. P. and Grossman, I. E. (1983) "Optimal process design under uncertainty," *AIChE Journal*, 29(3), 425–433.
10. Hsu, S. T.-S., Fitzgerald, T., Nguyen, V., Patel, T., and Balachandran, B. (2017). "Motion visualization and estimation for flapping wing systems." *Acta Meccanica Sinica*, 33(2), 1806–1822.
11. Huard, D., Evin, G., and Favre, A.C. (2006) "Bayesian copula selection." *Computational Statistics & Data Analysis,* 51(2), 809–822.
12. Kalmar-Nagy, T. and Stanciulescu, I. (2014) "Can complex systems really be simulated?" *Applied Mathematics and Computation*, 227, 199–211.
13. Kania, R., Azarm, S., and Balachandran, B., (2016) "Use of operationally flexible robust optimization in dynamic data driven application systems." *InfoSymbiotics/Dynamic Data Driven Application Systems Conference*, Hartford, CT, August 9.

14. Kebbie-Anthony, A., Gumerov, N., Predikman, S., Balachandran, B., and Azarm, S. (2017). "Fast multipole method for nonlinear, unsteady aerodynamic simulations." *SciTech* [accepted 2017].
15. Khaleghi, A. M., Xu, D., Lobos, A., Minaejan, S., Son, Y.-J., and Liu, J. (2013). "Agent-based hardware-in-the-loop simulation for UAV/UGV surveillance and crowd control system." *Proceedings of the 2013 Winter Simulation Conference: Simulation: Making Decisions in a Complex World*. IEEE Press.
16. Lieberman, C., Fidkowski, K.W., and van Bloemen Waanders, B. (2013). "Hessian-based model reduction: largescale inversion and prediction." *Int. J. Numer. Methods Fluids* 71, 135–150.
17. Madey, G. R., Blake, R. M., Poellabauer, C., Lu, H., McCune, R. R., and Wei, Y. (2012). "Applying DDDAS principles to command, control and mission planning for UAV swarms." *Procedia Computer Science* 9: 1177–1186.
18. Mandel, J., Bennethum, L., Beezley, J., Coen, J., Douglas, C., Kim, M., and Vodacek, A. (2008). "A wildland fire model with data assimilation." *Math. Comput. Simul.* 79, 584–606.
19. Missoum, S., Dribusch, C., and Beran, P. (2010). "Reliability-based design optimization of nonlinear aeroelasticity problems." *Journal of Aircraft*, 47(3), 992.
20. Njuguna, J. (2007). "Flutter prediction, suppression and control in aircraft composite wings as a design prerequisite: A survey." *Structural Control and Health Monitoring*, 14(5), 715–758.
21. Peng, L., Lipinski, D., and Mohseni, K. (2014). "Dynamic data driven application system for plume estimation using UAVs." *Journal of Intelligent & Robotic Systems* 74.1-2: 421–436.
22. Roccia, B., Preidikman, S., and Balachandran, B. (2017) "Computational dynamics of flapping wings in hover flight: a co-simulation strategy." *AIAA Journal* 55(6): 1806–1822.
23. Rodriguez, R., Cortés, A., and Margalef, T. (2009). "Injecting dynamic real-time data into a DDDAS for forest fire behavior prediction." *In: Int. Conf. Comput. Sci. (ICCS)*, vol. 5454, pp. 489–499. Baton Rouge, LA.
24. Tilmann, C. P. (2002). "Emerging aerodynamic technologies for high-altitude long-endurance SensorCraft UAVs." Air Force Research Lab Wright-Patterson AFB OH Air Vehicles Directorate. Retrieved from http://www.dtic.mil/get-tr-doc/pdf?AD=ADA428754
25. Uzkent, B., Hoffman, M. J., Vodacek, A., Kerekes, J. P., and Chen, B. (2013). "Feature matching and adaptive prediction models in an object tracking DDDAS." *Procedia Computer Science* 18: 1939–1948.
26. Zhao, X., Kania, R., Kebbie-Anthony, A., Azarm, S., and Balachandran, B. (2017). "Dynamic data-driven aero-elastic response prediction." *SciTech* [accepted 2017].

Part IV
Environment-Aware: Earth, Biological, and Space Systems

Chapter 11
Transforming Wildfire Detection and Prediction Using New and Underused Sensor and Data Sources Integrated with Modeling

Janice L. Coen, Wilfrid Schroeder, and Scott D. Rudlosky

Abstract Wildfire management relies upon prompt detection of new ignitions and timely anticipation of a fire's growth as influenced by local terrain, fuel characteristics and condition, and weather, notably wind. Recent advances include the CAWFE modeling system, which couples a *numerical weather prediction model* optimized for modeling fine-scale airflows in complex terrain with fire behavior algorithms, capturing how the fire "creates its own weather", and ingests spatially refined (375-m pixels) *satellite active fire detection* products from Visible Infrared Imaging Radiometer Suite (VIIRS), igniting simulated fires 'in progress'. Assuming regular fire mapping data, this allows an accurate forecast of fire growth for the next 12–24 h; sequences of these simulations may maintain a reasonable forecast of fire growth from detection it until it is extinguished. However, accurately anticipating a fire's growth is a difficult forecasting challenge because of accumulating model error, stochastic processes, and intervention (i.e. firefighting), data may be missing, and some conditions are inherently less predictable. Here, we develop and apply algorithms (steered by other data) to distill new and existing (but underutilized) sources of data on wildfire detection and mapping, develop and apply algorithms to integrate asynchronous data on wildfire detection and monitoring with coupled weather–wildland fire models, and assess the improvement in wildfire detection time and forecasted fire growth. We investigate the use of additional datasets from satellites with fire detection algorithms and adjacent non-utilized passes of VIIRS to enhance simulations of the 2015 Canyon Creek Complex. These additional asynchronous data allowed 1–3 h earlier fire detection by remote sensing, allowed forecasts to begin and be delivered that much earlier, and introduced

J. L. Coen (✉)
National Center for Atmospheric Research, Boulder, CO, USA
e-mail: janicec@ucar.edu

W. Schroeder
University of Maryland, College Park, MD, USA

S. D. Rudlosky
NOAA NEDIS/STAR/SCSB, College Park, MD, USA

© The Author(s), under exclusive license to Springer Nature Switzerland AG 2022
E. P. Blasch et al. (eds.), *Handbook of Dynamic Data Driven Applications Systems*,
https://doi.org/10.1007/978-3-030-74568-4_11

several additional simulations into the cycling forecast of a three-day fire growth period. By updating the anticipated fire growth forecast more frequently, these supplemental simulations improved fire growth forecast and compensated where standard, scheduled observations were missing or obscured by clouds.

Keywords Numerical weather prediction · Fire behavior · CAWFE · Satellite active fire detection · Dynamic data driven application system · Wildfire forecast

11.1   Introduction

Wildfires are a costly natural hazard that presents a detection, monitoring, and forecasting challenge. Lightning outbreaks may produce thousands of cloud-to-ground strikes, leading to numerous ignitions. Historically, fires are indicated by the appearance of smoke plumes and mapping data collected once nightly by aircraft such as the National Infrared Operations (NIROPs), directed toward the highest priority fires. Since 1999, satellite borne instruments such as the Moderate Resolution Imagine Spectroradiometer (MODIS) [1, 2] have shown promise in fire detection and indicating overall extent of large fires multiple times per day during daytime and nighttime. More recent spaceborne instruments with finer resolution such as the Visible and Infrared Imaging Radiometer Suite (VIIRS) [3] have shown utility both in delineating fire extent at scales relevant for fire behavior and detecting lower intensity and smaller fires. While available in near real time through operational sites, integration with fire management and growth forecasting operations continues.

Ignitions may lie stagnant until conditions become drier and windier, and then grow rapidly in size and complexity in episodic runs that occur on a small proportion of days. Operational forecasting of a fire's growth still largely relies on kinematic models (i.e., [4]) based on semi-empirical relationships between the rate of spread of the leading edge of a fire (the flaming front) and environmental factors that influence it including the terrain slope, fuel characteristics and moisture condition, and wind, either from a nearby measurement or coarse atmospheric model diagnosis or prediction. More recent research advances include improved modeling tools, such as the CAWFE® (Coupled Atmosphere-Wildland Fire Environment) modeling system, which two-way couples a numerical weather prediction (NWP) model optimized for modeling fine-scale airflows in complex terrain with fire behavior algorithms, to more realistically model how wildfires unfold. CAWFE models the weather in the fire environment at hundreds of meters (resolution finer than current operational forecast models), the fire behavior, and its feedback to the weather – notably producing fire-winds that further impact fire behavior.

However, accurately anticipating a fire's growth is intrinsically a difficult forecasting challenge because of nonlinearity, accumulating model error, stochastic processes, and intervention (i.e. firefighting). Events can extend for weeks or even months - much longer than a weather model forecast is valid, are impacted by external factors such as firefighting, and contain processes such as the ignition of new fires by ember spotting that cannot be treated in a deterministic manner. By integrating these tools, prior work suggested accurate forecasting of the unfolding of a wildfire was within reach. It demonstrated that integrating CAWFE and the 12-hourly VIIRS active fire detection product, igniting fires 'in progress' using the VIIRS fire mapping data, allowed accurate simulation of fire growth for at least the next 12–24 h [5]. By applying sequences of these simulations, a practice referred to in the weather prediction community as 'cycling', they suggested that this technique could be used to maintain a good forecast of upcoming fire behavior from first detection until the fire was extinguished.

Despite these scientific advances, challenges remain. As in many other complex systems, weather forecasts are often performed in traditional ways with scheduled forecasts and data collection, limited ingestion of data that are expected to be available at initialization, and no steering between data and model. Data may be missing, obscured, or incomplete while nonlinear models are prone to rapid error accumulation. In fire applications, these are challenges: (i) remote and/or undetected fire ignition sources and (ii) fast-moving and/or complex-behavior wildfires. The first challenge is typically associated with lightning strikes in the western U.S. creating smoldering fires that go undetected for days until a smoke plume is seen and reported. In that case, early detection and early triggering of prediction systems is key. The second challenge describes fires occurring during weather regimes where predictability is very short, approximately a few hours. While VIIRS active fire detection data is available in near real time at least every 12 h, observational gaps may still exist, as substantial fire growth may occur between consecutive satellite passes or data may be obscured by clouds, sun glint, or topography, negatively impacting intelligence used for fire suppression and growth prediction. To address the two challenges above, data from existing and new sensors must be used to maximum benefit.

This work investigates how dynamic data driven application techniques that employ new and existing underutilized wildfire detection and mapping data sources tightly integrated with coupled weather-fire behavior modeling could transform wildfire detection and prediction. Initially, the data supplementing the primary VIIRS active fire detection product include additional data distilled from adjacent underutilized VIIRS passes and remote sensing data from polar-orbiting satellites with different resolution and revisit frequencies. We discuss these data, develop and apply algorithms to integrate asynchronous data on wildfire detection and monitoring with the CAWFE coupled weather–wildland fire model, and assess the improvement in wildfire detection time and forecasted fire growth. These methods and data have been used to enhance simulations of Oregon's 2015 Canyon Creek Complex, demonstrating the improvement due to incorporation of Dynamic Data Driven Application System (DDDAS) techniques. Outcomes included faster detection time, earlier forecasts enabling earlier response using the information, and improved forecast skill throughout simulated periods.

11.2 Background

11.2.1 Forecasting Approaches

As a forecasting problem, wildfires present numerous challenges. First, during a long-lasting fire, a simulation initialized at ignition could lose most of its fidelity before the time of active fire spread or period of interest due to error growth arising from imperfect initialization data and model physics. Second, wildfires may grow for weeks to months whereas weather forecast skill decreases rapidly with time, with state-of-the-art synoptic-scale models essentially losing all skill after 12 days [6]. Thus, no single weather forecast can cover a long-lived event accurately. Moreover, processes such as spotting, in which embers lofted by the fire may ignite new fires, cannot be modeled deterministically and fire suppression can impact the fire growth, requiring routine diagnostics and re-initialization.

To address this, a new method [5] introduced a fire perimeter defined by VIIRS pixel-based fire detection data into CAWFE at a time corresponding to the observation, allowed the fire to evolve, and compared the simulated and observed fire extent at the time of the next VIIRS data (~12 h later). They found that simulations represented fire growth well for 12–24 h after each initialization in comparison to later satellite passes but strayed from mapped area with time, as expected. They proposed forecasts be done using a *cycling approach*, in which a series of CAWFE simulations would be started at regular 12-hourly intervals, initialized with cycled large-scale weather forecasts and the fire location 'in progress' using successive VIIRS perimeters. They suggested that this system could largely overcome the decrease in skill with time that a single forecast would experience and could be used to predict even a long-lived fire's extent from first detection until extinction. Despite that major advancement, additional work is required in order to determine the optimum cycling frequency and the net gain in predictive skills resulting from additional observations and model invocation.

Alternative data assimilation approaches (e.g., [7]) to wildfire modeling propose to use the Ensemble Kalman Filter technique, in which a suite of simulations with slightly varying initial conditions is run, compared with mapped fire location, and adjusted toward the observation. However, when applied to wildfires by varying the fire location, the method fails to meet the criteria that the ensemble members be independent. In addition, the computational cost of running dozens of simulations is unnecessary. The method was developed to adjust intertwined atmospheric state variables, but, as applied in coupled weather-fire models, the fire extent is essentially an external forcing and no special handling to avoid unbalancing the model state is needed. Instead, [5] showed that the extent of the observed fire, already in progress, could simply be introduced into a weather simulation without making the simulation become unstable. Other approaches have attempted to steer coupled weather-fire model simulations by assimilating fuel moisture data from surface weather stations [8]. The argument against such an approach is that compared to other environmental factors such as wind, the fuel moisture impact is very weak [9] and, because the fuel moisture data are extremely sparse, the actual spatial variability of fuel moisture is unknown and not represented in the data. Moreover, when the event is strongly forced – either by ambient winds or fire winds generated by ample fuels and complex terrain – details of fuel composition, amount, and moisture are not essential to capturing the event's character [9]. Hence, *our approach emphasizes methodologies that keep the simulated weather and fire system up-to-date using high frequency cycling triggered by the arrival of new data distilled with iterative adaptive algorithms.*

In practice, the idealized modeling scenario proposed by [5] could experience both challenges and opportunities. For example, the weather regime could be more unpredictable and 12-hourly updates on fire mapping data may not be frequent enough to maintain skill. In addition, the routine fire mapping data might be missing for the fire of interest because of cloud obscuration or other observation conditions affecting data fidelity and/or availability (e.g., variable pixel resolution as a function of observation angles, terrain or canopy obscuration, partial block-out zones due to sun glint, sensor downtime). However, as noted, prior and subsequent VIIRS overpasses may provide additional fire detection data, and additional sensors and data products are coming online, such as the Landsat-8 active fire detection product [10]. These factors form the basis of a dynamic-data-driven approach.

11.2.2   The 2015 Canyon Creek Wildfire Complex

Between 0500 UTC (12:00 AM) and 1100 UTC (4:00 AM) on August 12, 2015 a lightning storm passing over the Malheur National Forest (NF) in eastern Oregon ignited at least 12 new fires. These fires received initial attack but two - the Berry Creek Fire in the Strawberry Mountain Wilderness and the Mason Springs Fire in the Malheur NF – escaped. On August 14, prefrontal winds of 18 m s^{-1} (40 mph) drove the fires to the northeast, causing the two fires to merge forming the Canyon Creek Complex and increasing the fire size from 242 ha (600 acres) to 13,759 ha (34,000 acres). With the passage of a dry cold front, winds shifted and drove the fire to the southeast into the Strawberry Wilderness (Fig. 11.1). The complex was contained November 5, 2015, at 44,621 ha (110,261 acres).

Space borne observations providing either detection or mapping of the Canyon Creek Complex include both VIIRS and Landsat-8 data and begin during the lightning storm itself. These observations, which cluster around mid-night and early afternoon, cover the first growth period, examined here, and extend throughout the incident.

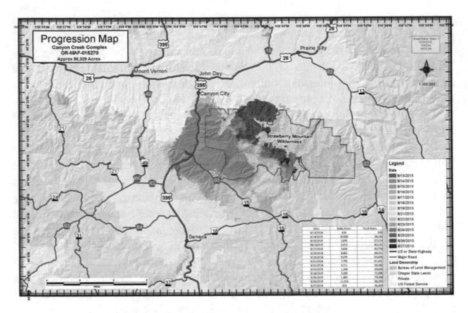

Fig. 11.1 Canyon Creek Complex progression map. (Image courtesy of U.S.D.A. Forest Service (Available at https://inciweb.nwcg.gov/incident/map/4495/24/48177/))

11.3 Methods

11.3.1 Wildland Fire Detection, Mapping, and Monitoring

Many wildfires continue to be reported by the detection of a smoke plume. Mapping of fire extent is conducted by the National Infrared Operations (NIROPs) on high-priority fires. This airborne mapping is limited to nighttime to maximize the thermal contrast of the fire from its background and provides a single mosaic of the entire fire perimeter per visit. Satellite-borne remote sensing instruments measure radiances in the short wave and thermal infrared bands, which guide the delineation of near real-time fire extent maps from individual satellite imagery. In contrast with visual detection and airborne mapping, satellite borne instruments have the potential to routinely detect and monitor wildfires worldwide.

11.3.1.1 The Visible and Infrared Imaging Radiometer Suite (VIIRS)

The VIIRS multispectral instrument lies aboard the Suomi National Polar-orbiting Partnership (S-NPP), a preparatory mission to the upcoming Joint Polar Satellite System (JPSS) [11]. The VIIRS land product suite includes two active fire detection global data sets available at least every 12 h, namely: a baseline 750 m product and a 375 m product using the higher resolution imager bands. Both detection

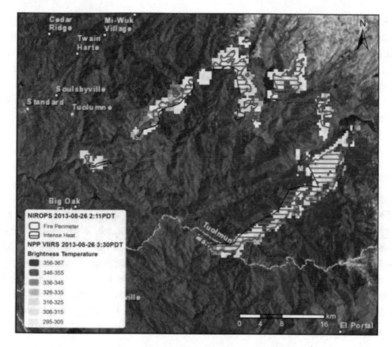

Fig. 11.2 Near-coincident VIIRS 375 m and National InfraRed Operations (NIROPS) active fire mapping of the Rim Fire, CA, on 26 August 2013. NIROPS data include fire perimeter (solid blue contour) and areas of intense heat (dashed blue polygons). VIIRS data describe actively burning pixels with associated radiometric temperature color-coding

algorithms are built on the heritage MODIS fire product, using primarily the middle- and thermal-infrared spectral data to detect sub-pixel fire activity associated with biomass burning [3, 12]. Compared to other global data sets, the higher resolution 375 m VIIRS fire product enables early detection of fires as small as 5 m^2 at night, as well as improved mapping of large fires. The algorithm's performance is largely driven by the scene's condition, to which detection tests are automatically adjusted to avoid false alarms associated with other radiometrically bright features (e.g., clouds, sun-glint zones, highly reflective rooftops). Tuning is performed to balance false alarm and omission error rates at global scales. Both VIIRS 750 m and 375 m fire algorithms are currently running in near real-time for the U.S. at the USDA Remote Sensing Applications Center. The VIIRS 375 m product has been validated against airborne infrared data over western U.S. fires achieving comparable results (Fig. 11.2).

The S-NPP/VIIRS sampling frequency is a function of latitude. Global wall-to-wall coverage is achieved every 12 h, with nominal equator crossing times of 1:30 P.M. (ascending node) and 1:30 A.M. (descending node). Mid-latitudes are sampled least twice a day, with some alternating days experiencing up to four observations (two in the afternoon and two in the morning).

Additional observations may sometimes be obtained from prior or subsequent overpasses, which are each separated from the primary pass most optimal for detection (i.e., closer to nadir) by the orbital period 102 minutes (corresponding to ~14.11 orbits per day). Detection performance and thus whether useful data can be obtained from these passes depends on the viewing conditions - observation angle and thus pixel size, orientation of a fire on topography, and the presence of clouds or solar illumination.

11.3.1.2 Landsat

Landsat-8 (launched in February 2013) carries the Operational Land Imager (OLI) and Thermal Infrared Sensor (TIRS) [13]. Flying in a polar orbit, Landsat-8 has a 16-day revisit time and provides primarily daytime data, although data acquisition may vary according to geographical orientation and science objectives or special applications (e.g., on-demand nighttime acquisition in support of wildfire mapping). Landsat-class data have been successfully demonstrated to detect actively burning fires [14, 15]. The Landsat-8 active fire detection algorithm [10] builds upon algorithms in those works using near infrared ($\approx$0.8 μm) and shortwave infrared ($\approx$2.2 μm) to classify pixels containing an active fire.

11.3.2   Coupled Weather-Wildland Fire Modeling

The CAWFE® (Coupled Atmosphere-Wildland Fire Environment) modeling system combines a NWP model with a fire behavior module, allowing it to capture atmospheric motions in complex terrain, the impact of spatially and temporally varying weather on fire behavior, interactions of fire with the atmosphere, and the impact of these feedbacks on fire behavior. It can simulate overall rate and direction of spread and distinguishing characteristics of landscape-scale wildfires and, in contrast to simpler models, provide deeper understanding of and capture distinctive dynamic events and transitions in fire behavior.

The 3D meteorological *Clark-Hall* model (described in [16, 17]) in CAWFE is non-hydrostatic and based on the Navier-Stokes equations of motion, a thermodynamic equation, and a conservation of mass equation using the anelastic approximation. Vertically stretched terrain-following coordinates allow detailed simulation of airflow at horizontal resolutions of hundreds of kilometers while telescoping in to focus at approximately a hundred meters in complex terrain. The outer of several interactive, nested modeling domains are initialized and boundary conditions are updated with gridded atmospheric states from model forecasts or analyses. Its solution methods and options were designed to allow it to excel at fine scales (100 s of m) in extremely complex terrain.

CAWFE's fire module, detailed in [18–20], is based on semi-empirical relationships. A rate of spread formula [4] is used to estimate surface fire spread as a function of terrain, fuel properties, and wind at the fire line, the latter of which may be affected by the fire. It estimates post-frontal fuel consumption as per [21], to track sensible and latent heat release from different fuel classes, and smoke particulate release via an emission factor. A simple radiation treatment distributes sensible and latent heat fluxes and particulates from the fire into the lowest atmospheric grid levels, based on fire observations [22, 23]. A surface fire heat flux exceeding an empirically defined threshold may ignite a crown fire, which is simulated to spread through canopies at a rate given by other empirical relationships [24]. Weather and fire are coupled so that the fire's heat and water vapor fluxes alter the atmosphere's state, notably producing fire winds, and the evolving atmospheric state affects fire behavior.

The weather model component has been used to simulate many meteorological phenomena including precipitation formation, terrain-induced turbulence, and windstorms. CAWFE simulations have been tested against *in situ* measurements and incident team maps (2002 Big Elk Fire in Pinewood Springs, CO [18]), fires mapped by airborne infrared instruments (the 2002 Troy Fire and the Santa Ana-driven 2006 Esperanza Wildfire, [9] (Fig. 11.3a) and VIIRS data (the 2012 High Park Fire [25] (Fig. 11.3b) and the 2012 Little Bear Fire [5])). In contrast to simpler models, case studies using CAWFE showed that, provided the atmospheric model can capture the atmospheric flow, the distinguishing features of events – the overall spread rate, direction, and fire behavior phenomena – can be modeled and distinctive dynamic events and transitions in behavior, such as the splitting of fires into multiple heading regions, the confluence of terrain, wind and fuel effects into blow-ups, fires drawn up canyons orthogonal to the wind, fire whirls and inclined roll vortices, and the transition to a running crown fire, can be captured.

(a)   (b)

Fig. 11.3 CAWFE simulations of the (**a**) 2006 Esperanza Fire near Cabazon, CA, reproduced from Coen and Riggan (2014) and (**b**) 2012 High Park Fire near Fort Collins, CO, reproduced from Coen and Schroeder (2015). The heat flux produced by the fire is shown in the color bar in each figure, along with smoke (misty white field), and near surface wind speed and direction (vectors)

11.4   Experiment Design and Results

Traditional approaches operate routinely at regular intervals at the simulation level – input data is gathered, model simulation is launched, output is examined. Even using the cycling approach of [5], new simulations are triggered on a regular schedule, nominally each 12 h (or 24 h, if clouds obscure the scene), as new VIIRS data become available.

Using a dynamic data-driven approach, we create an adaptive simulation invocation system based on the arrival of new fire detection data. By using asynchronous data such as extra VIIRS passes, simulations can be initialized more frequently, so that the most recent simulation is more current than a traditional approach would provide and, unlike an older forecast that has accumulated error, should maintain higher skill.

The National Centers for Environmental Prediction (NCEP) Final Operational Global Analyses, prepared operationally every 6-hours on a $1° \times 1°$ grid were used to provide initial conditions and later boundary conditions for the outermost domain of a 72-hour Weather Research and Forecasting (WRF) model simulation with two nested domains with 30-km and 10-km horizontal spatial resolution, encompassing the period 12 UTC August 13–12 UTC August 16. The WRF simulation dynamically downscaled the atmospheric analyses to initialize and provide boundary conditions for a sequence of CAWFE simulations.

11.4.1   Dynamic Data Driven Model Invocation

The CAWFE model was used to simulate a sequence of periods during the Canyon Creek Complex over a domain centered on the Malheur NF of central Oregon using four nested domains with horizontal resolutions of 10 km, 3.33 km, 1.11 km, and 370 m. CAWFE provided an updated simulation initiated twice daily at 0600 UTC (11 PM) and 1800 UTC (11 AM). The spatial map of fuel models is given by LANDFIRE (https://wwww.landfire.gov).

In each simulation, the fire was initialized in progress using the most recent active fire detection data, either from Landsat-8, the standard VIIRS observation, or prior or subsequent passes, where observations were successfully obtained. Simulations of the weather, fire growth, and interactions between weather and fire were then carried out until 12 UTC August 16, by which time this period of growth had ended. In a standard approach, this experimental design supports the introduction of standard 1:30 AM and 1:30 PM VIIRS observations. In this demonstration of Dynamic Data Driven Model invocation, additional simulations are performed introducing asynchronous observations from Landfire-8 and VIIRS observations from prior or subsequent overpasses. Evaluations of the simulations were made against later observations.

11.4.2   Results: Impact on Fire Detection

The August 12 3:07 A.M. VIIRS observation (Fig. 11.4a) had the potential to provide an early indicator of ignition but lightning strikes either had not yet occurred or had not yet become established, were impacted by rain, or under cloud cover, and no active fire was detected. The first detection from remote sensing occurred during the 11:43 AM Landsat-8 overpass (Fig. 11.4b), one of three observations that occurred late morning to early afternoon on August 12. Landsat-8 detected two ignitions. Soon after, at 12:53 PM, a VIIRS observation (Fig. 11.4c) detected three fire starts – the additional fire start became the Mason Springs fire. A VIIRS observation on the subsequent VIIRS pass at 2:30 PM (Fig. 11.4d) detected these same three starts, amidst scattered clouds that could be obscuring other ignitions. If approximately 2:30 PM is considered the time of the standard VIIRS observation, by considering additional data sources (the Landsat-8 and 12:53 PM VIIRS supplemental observations), *detections were observed 1 h 10 min – 2 h 53 min earlier than the standard detection time alone.*

Approximately 12 h later, the Aug. 13 2:50 AM VIIRS nighttime observation (Fig. 11.4e) detected four ignitions, the new start being the Berry Creek fire. (It cannot be determined whether this was present at 2:30 PM, as clouds covered this location.) Data from the subsequent VIIRS pass at 4:26 AM did not intersect the modeling domain (Fig. 11.4f). Later that day, two close VIIRS observations (centered at 12:36 PM (Fig. 11.5a) – a supplemental observation – and 2:12 PM (Fig. 11.5b)) confirmed the four ignitions remained and showed slight growth only on the Mason Springs Fire. Nearly 12 h later, the Aug. 14 nighttime observations produced the standard observation at 2:32 AM (Fig. 11.5c), showing some growth on the Mason Springs fire, and a pass at 4:09 AM (Fig. 11.5d) that produced no data. Later that morning, a Landsat image covering some other part of Oregon could have provided an update but did not intersect the modeling domain (Fig. 11.5e), leaving an update to wait until the 1:55 PM standard VIIRS observation (Fig. 11.5f), which showed the Mason Springs Fire had overrun the Berry Creek Fire during significant growth to the northeast.

The next sequences of images contain two close in time VIIRS observations – at Aug. 15 2:09 AM (Fig. 11.6a) and 3:51 AM (Fig. 11.6b). The prior indicates the fire shifted directions and ran to the southeast. The second, a supplementary pass, the indicated the fire's run had ceased.

11.4.3   Results: Impact on Fire Prediction

Figure 11.7 shows a sequence of simulations that were performed with the 11 A.M. August 13 CAWFE simulation, in which the wildfire was initialized with VIIRS active fire detections at 12:36 P.M. (Fig. 11.7a) and 2:12 P.M. (Fig. 11.7b) on August 13 and 2:32 A.M. on August 14 (Fig. 11.6c). The first simulation, Expt. A, hints

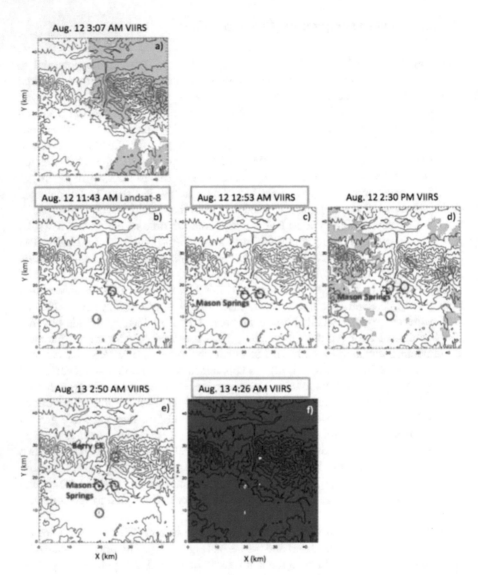

Fig. 11.4 Satellite active fire detection data over the innermost modeling domain. Each row includes successful observations within the 3 h period encompassing the afternoon or nighttime VIIRS observation. Light gray shading indicates cloud cover. Red-filled polygons indicate pixels in which active fire has been detected. Charcoal indicates no data could be obtained. Dark red indicates areas where in prior observations, active fire was detected. Titles indicate the observation time; an orange box indicates an additional observations outside the standard twice-daily VIIRS observation

at the first rapid growth of the fire to the northeast by 26.9 h and the run to the southeast by 39.2 h –features apparent in the last row, which shows the observations at these times for comparison. As a supplemental simulation enabled by successfully

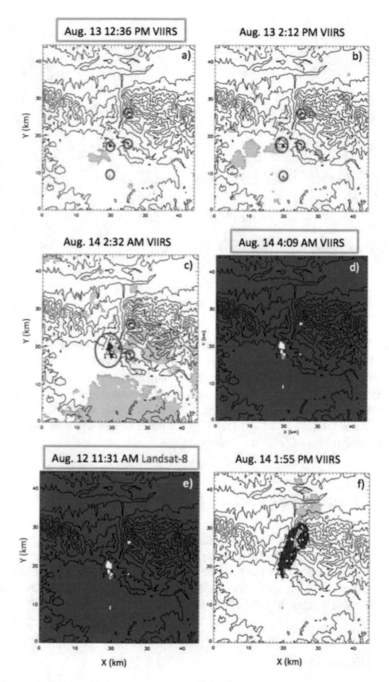

Fig. 11.5 Similar to Fig. 11.4, at later times

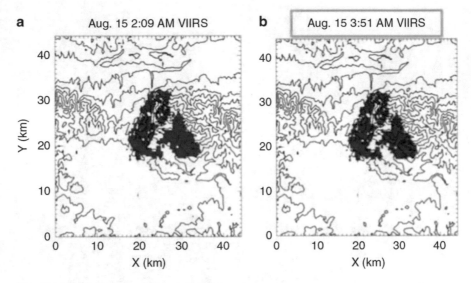

Fig. 11.6 Similar to Figs. 11.4 and 11.5, at later times

extracting a fire detection from the VIIRS pass preceding the standard detection, this simulation would provide a heads up that active fire growth was imminent 1 h 36 min earlier. The next simulation (Expt. B) supports and refines this prediction. The third simulation (Expt. C), begun with the supplemental observation nearly 12 h later, further refines the simulation, restricting the overprediction of growth that Expts. A and B showed through 17.2 h, and refining the prediction of growth episodes to the northeast and southeast seen in the observations.

11.4.4 Integrated Results

We found that (1) incorporating other sensors (fire detection products from Landsat 8 and prior and subsequent VIIRS passes) enabled earlier fire detection and initiation of simulations, making a forecast available 1.5–3 h earlier, and (2) considering prior and subsequent VIIRS passes often could be used to launch additional simulations – an additional 4, making 10 simulations possible.

11.5 Discussion

The detection and prediction of subsequent growth of wildland fires is time-sensitive work of critical importance, upon which important management decisions are made and resources based. Like many other applications, this is currently done in a

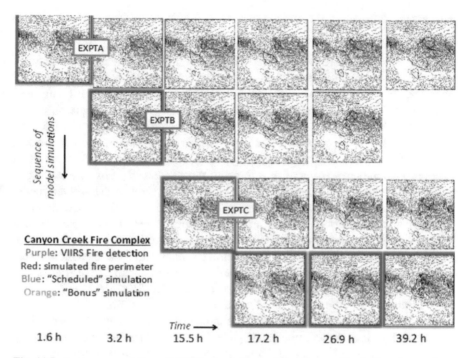

Fig. 11.7 A sequence of three CAWFE simulations of the Canyon Creek Complex at times (indicated on the x-axis) after 11 AM August 13. Fire extent in images highlighted by magenta are the observed active fire detections

traditional manner with rigorous scheduling of routine, repeated modeling relying on fixed detection algorithms and regular, periodic input data arrival. This work, employing modeling, new sensors, and underutilized active fire detection data, begins to explore the improvement DDDAS techniques make on wildland fire detection and forecasting, highlighting the benefits toward mitigating the societal impacts of a widespread natural hazard.

Prior work presented forecasting scenarios through which the new generation of coupled weather fire models could provide a forecast throughout the life of a fire using cycling techniques and regularly ingested active fire detection data, however this was only the beginning.

In practice, it is more complex, as data may also be obscured by clouds, not available, or have errors or gaps. In addition, errors exist in the weather forecast and there are some situations with high uncertainty in which phenomena are predictable over only short time periods. There are also opportunities – as "extra" data may be available by prior or subsequent satellite passes or other sensors (and may help us sustain a regular forecast).

11.6   Conclusions

In this work, DDDAS techniques were applied to improve how wildland fires are detected, mapped, and predicted in a specific case, the Canyon Creek wildfire complex. As one of several improvements, DDDAS techniques were being used to create an adaptive control system for seeking new data and invoking model simulations based on their availability. By looking at a specific example, we demonstrated how supplemental fire data outside the standard, routine forecast schedule (e.g. Landsat 8/OLI or asynchronous S-NPP/VIIRS active fire detection data) enabled remote sensing of fires to occur more frequently, possibly leading to earlier detection, triggered earlier (and more frequent) dynamic data-driven model invocation that led to simulation output that can be acted upon sooner and indicated significant growth periods earlier, maintained better forecast accuracy, and can compensate for the negative impacts of missing scheduled data. Specifically, it could lead to earlier detection of fires, allowing more to be extinguished before they become difficult to manage (a national security concern, as arsonists can create multiple ignitions during conditions favorable for fire growth and all must be detected early), and better forecasting throughout the fires' lifetimes.

The work has broader implications as integrating data from new or underutilized sensors and from an algorithmic perspective, the "go find the fire in the data" step is equivalent to launching an additional measuring device or platform such as a UAS or directing a sensor when to collect data. The results could affect NWP and fire remote sensing and have broad application across other fields, as simulations of natural systems. It also has broad application across other forecasting systems, which are often nonlinear and suffer error buildup, and are currently done in a traditional manner with rigorous scheduling of routine, repeated modeling relying on fixed detection algorithms and regular, periodic input data arrival.

Acknowledgements The National Science Foundation (NSF) under grant 1462247 and the National Aeronautics and Space Administration under awards NNH11AS03 and NNX12AQ87G supported this work. NSF sponsors the National Center for Atmospheric Research. Any opinions, findings, and conclusions or recommendations expressed in this material are the authors' and do not reflect the views of NSF.

References

1. Giglio, L., Descloitres, J., Justice, C.O., and Kaufman, Y. J. (2003). An enhanced contextual fire detection algorithm for MODIS. *Remote Sensing of Environment,* 87, 273–282.
2. Justice, C.O., Giglio, L., Korontzi, S., et al. (2002). The MODIS fire products. *Remote Sensing of Environment,* 83, 244–262.
3. Schroeder, W., Oliva, P., Giglio, L., and Csiszar, I. (2014). The new VIIRS 375 m active fire detection data product: Algorithm description and initial assessment. *Remote Sensing of Environment,* 143, 85–96.

4. Rothermel, R. C. (1972) A Mathematical Model For Predicting Fire Spread. USDA Forest Service Research Paper INT-115.
5. Coen, J. L., and Schroeder W. (2013) Use of spatially refined remote sensing fire detection data to initialize and evaluate coupled weather-wildfire growth model simulations. *Geophys. Res. Lett.* 40,5536–5541.
6. Stern, H., and Davidson, N.E. (2015) Trends in the skill of weather prediction at lead times of 1-14 days. *Quart. J. Royal Meteor. Soc.,* 141, 2726–2736.
7. Rochoux, M. (2014) Towards a more comprehensive monitoring of wildfire spread - Contributions of model evaluation and data assimilation strategies, Ph.D. thesis, Ecole Centrale Paris.
8. Mandel, J., Amram, S., Beezley, J. D., Kelman, G., Kochanski, A. K., Kondratenko, V. Y., Lynn, B. H., Regev, B., and Vejmelka, M. (2014) Recent advances and applications of WRF-SFIRE, *Nat. Hazards Earth Syst. Sci.* Discuss., 14, 2829–2845.
9. Coen, J. L. and Riggan P. J. (2014) Simulation and thermal imaging of the 2006 Esperanza wildfire in southern California: Application of a coupled weather-wildland fire model. *Intl. J. Wildland Fire,* 23,755–770.
10. Schroeder, W., P. Oliva, L. Giglio, B. Quayle, E. Lorenze, F. Morelli, (2015) Active fire detection using Landsat-8/OLI data. Remote Sensing of Environment. (In press.)
11. Justice, C.O., Róman, M.O., Csiszar, I., et al. (2013). Land and cryosphere products from Suomi NPP VIIRS: Overview and status. *Journal of Geophysical Research Atmospheres.*
12. Csiszar, I., Schroeder, W., Giglio, L., *et al.,* (2014). Active fires from the Suomi NPP Visible Infrared Imaging Radiometer Suite: Product status and first evaluation results. *Journal of Geophysical Research Atmospheres,* doi: https://doi.org/10.1002/2013JD020453.
13. Roy, D., Wulder, M.A., Loveland, T.R., et al. (2014). Landsat-8: Science and product vision for terrestrial global change research. *Remote Sensing of Environment,* 145, 154–172.
14. Giglio, L., Csiszar, I., Restás, Á., Morisette, J. T., Schroeder, W., Morton, D., & Justice, C. O. (2008). Active fire detection and characterization with the Advanced Spaceborne Thermal Emission and Reflection Radiometer (ASTER). *Remote Sensing of Environment,* 112, 3055–3063.
15. Schroeder, W., Prins, E., Giglio, L., Csiszar, I., Schmidt, C., Morisette, J., & Morton, D. (2008). Validation of GOES and MODIS active fire detection products using ASTER and ETM+ data. *Remote Sensing of Environment,* 112, 2711–2726.
16. Clark, T. L., Hall W. D., and Coen J. L. (1996) Source Code Documentation for the Clark-Hall Cloud-scale Model Code Version G3CH01. NCAR Technical Note NCAR/TN-426+STR, DOI: https://doi.org/10.5065/D67W694V.
17. Clark, T. L., Keller T., Coen J., Neilley P., Hsu H. and Hall W.D. (1997) Terrain-induced Turbulence over Lantau Island: 7 June 1994 Tropical Storm Russ Case Study. *J. Atmos. Sci.,* 54,1795–1814.
18. Coen, J. L. (2005) Simulation of the Big Elk Fire using coupled atmosphere – fire modeling. *Intl. J. Wildland Fire,*14,49–59.
19. Coen, J.L. (2013) Modeling Wildland Fires: A Description of the Coupled Atmosphere-Wildland Fire Environment Model (CAWFE). NCAR Technical Note NCAR/TN–500+STR, 38 pp.
20. Clark, T, Coen J. L., Latham D. (2004) Description of a coupled atmosphere–fire model. *Intl. J. Wildland Fire* ,13,49–63.
21. Albini, F. A. (1994) PROGRAM BURNUP: A simulation model of the burning of large woody natural fuels. Final Report on Research Grant INT-92754-GR by U.S.F.S. to Montana State Univ., Mechanical Engineering Dept.
22. Clements, C.B., Zhong S., Goodrick S., *et al.* (2007) Observing the Dynamics of Wildland Grass Fires: FireFlux—A Field Validation Experiment. *Bull. American Meteor. Soc.,*88:1369–1382.
23. Coen, J. L., Mahalingam S., Daily J. (2004) Infrared imagery of crown-fire dynamics during FROSTFIRE. *J. Appl. Meteor.,* 43,1241–1259.

24. Rothermel, R. C. (1991), Predicting behavior and size of crown fires in the northern Rocky Mountains, Res. Paper INT-438. Ogden, UT: U.S. Dep. of Agriculture, Forest Service, Intermountain Forest and Range Experiment Station, 46 p.
25. Coen, J. L. and Schroeder W. (2015) The High Park Fire: Coupled weather-wildland fire model simulation of a windstorm-driven wildfire in Colorado's Front Range. *J. Geophys. Res. Atmos.* 120,131–146.

Chapter 12
Dynamic Data Driven Application Systems for Identification of Biomarkers in DNA Methylation

Haluk Damgacioglu, Emrah Celik, Chongli Yuan, and Nurcin Celik

Abstract The term 'epigenetic' refers to all heritable alterations that occur in a given gene function without having any change on the DeoxyriboNucleic Acid (DNA) sequence. Epigenetic modifications play a crucial role in development and differentiation of various diseases including cancer. The specific epigenetic alteration that has garnered a great deal of attention is DNA methylation, i.e., the addition of a methyl-group to cytosine. Recent studies have shown that different tumor types have distinct methylation profiles. Identifying idiosyncratic DNA methylation profiles of different tumor types and subtypes can provide invaluable insights for accurate diagnosis, early detection, and tailoring of the related treatment for cancer. In this study, our goal is to identify the informative genes (biomarkers) whose methylation level change correlates with a specific cancer type or subtype. To achieve this goal, we propose a novel high dimensional learning framework inspired by the dynamic data driven application systems paradigm to identify the biomarkers, determine the outlier(s) and improve the quality of the resultant disease detection. The proposed framework starts with a principal component analysis (PCA) followed by hierarchical clustering (HCL) of observations and determination of informative genes based on the HCL predictions. The capabilities and performance of the proposed framework are demonstrated using a DNA methylation dataset stored in GEO DataSets on lung cancer. The preliminary results demonstrate that our

H. Damgacioglu · N. Celik (✉)
Department of Industrial Engineering, University of Miami, Coral Gables, FL, USA
e-mail: haluk.damgacioglu@uth.tmc.edu; celik@miami.edu

E. Celik
Department of Mechanical and Aerospace Engineering, University of Miami, Coral Gables, FL, USA
e-mail: e.celik@miami.edu

C. Yuan
Purdue University, Department of Chemical Engineering, West Lafayette, IN, USA
e-mail: cyuan@purdue.edu

© The Author(s), under exclusive license to Springer Nature Switzerland AG 2022
E. P. Blasch et al. (eds.), *Handbook of Dynamic Data Driven Applications Systems*,
https://doi.org/10.1007/978-3-030-74568-4_12

241

framework outperforms the conventional clustering algorithms with embedded dimension reduction methods, in its efficiency to identify informative genes and outliers, and removal of their contaminating effects at the expense of reasonable computational cost.

Keywords Dynamic data driven application systems · DNA methylation · Hierarchical clustering · Principal component analysis · Outlier detection

12.1 Introduction

The term 'epigenetic' refers to all heritable alterations that occur in a given gene function without having any change on the DNA sequence. Epigenetic modifications, i.e., DNA methylation and histone post-translational modifications, regulate the transcription state of a gene, and play crucial roles in cell differentiation and proliferation [18, 33]. Accumulating evidence suggests that aberrant epigenetic changes are affiliated with various diseases such as diabetes, schizophrenia, and cancers [19, 20, 31]. Compared with genetic alterations, aberrant epigenetic modifications typically occur at an early-stage of disease. They can thus be reversed given proper interventions. The study of epigenetics is emerging but fast-growing field of science as epigenetic biomarker and therapies promise for the detection and treatment of a broad array of diseases [17, 20]. One of the most important epigenetic alteration is DNA methylation, i.e., the addition of a methyl-group to DNA. The most prevalent DNA methylation is the covalent addition of a methyl group to the 5-carbon position of the cytosine to form a 5-methylcytosine (5mC) occurring within a CpG dinucleotide, a DNA sequence in which a cytosine and guanine appear consecutively. CpG methylation is commonly affiliated with gene silencing and most abundant in heterochromatin regions.

Recent research has shown a significant interest in understanding of the correlation between aberrant DNA methylation and cancer [20, 21, 31]. These studies revealed that cancer cells have different methylation profiles from normal cells. DNA methylation can not only be used to differentiate different tumor types, but also to distinguish tumor subtypes [25, 35, 39]. Medical understanding of DNA methylation and its implications in the biology of cancer has significantly advanced in the past years, due to the high-throughput DNA-sequencing-based methylation analysis. Herein, data mining techniques for the collected high-throughput data play an increasingly important role in extracting useful information for a wide range of applications such as identifying cancer diagnosis and prognostic biomarkers.

Clustering algorithms are powerful tools for identifying idiosyncratic DNA methylation profile of different tumor types and subtypes. Basically, cluster analysis groups similar data points into same groups. Amongst the clustering algorithms presented in the literature, hierarchical clustering (HCL) is widely used for DNA methylation analysis. Variants of HCL has also been applied to the analysis of different DNA methylation patterns in different cancer types or subtypes. For instance, [39] and [8] used agglomerative hierarchical clustering algorithm for identification of aberrant DNA methylation profiles in lung cancer subtypes and lung adenocarcinoma, pleural mesothelioma, and nonmalignant pulmonary tissues, respectively, while [38] performed a two-way hierarchical clustering analysis to characterize the DNA methylation profiles for clear cell sarcoma of the kidney and other pediatric renal tumors. While HCL is relatively easy to implement and comes at the expense of low computational cost when compared to other clustering algorithms such as k-means, it is still a greedy algorithm and sensitive to outliers (or influential data points). Like most clustering algorithms, HCL assumes all information to be equally important for clustering. This assumption, however, is unlikely to be valid in most real systems and causes HCL to mark a significant number of points as outliers, which further necessitates an implementation of a dimension reduction algorithm.

In DNA methylation analysis, the data is very complex with thousands of genes being collected from a single patient making the determination of an informative set of genes (biomarkers) crucial for accurate identification of cancer-related DNA Methylation profiles. To this end, several dimension reduction algorithms have been proposed in the literature for the characterization of informative biomarkers. For instance, the study [39] determined seven informative genes among 24 genes using Mann-Whitney U-test, while [8] chose 500 genes with the highest variance from thousands of genes. Another study implemented a two-way hierarchical clustering to find out an informative loci [38].

In this study, we propose a dynamic data driven hierarchical clustering (3D-HCL) framework motivated by the dynamic data driven application systems (DDDAS) paradigm founded by Darema [11–15]. The proposed 3D-HCL framework embodies an HCL algorithm with a threefold capability to detect the outliers, identify the set of informative biomarkers, and define the clusters in an efficient manner using the newly measured data from the real system. 3D-HCL initializes with a principal component analysis (PCA). Then the HCL is run as an application system and based on the results of the HCL, the outlier detection score, the cluster membership score and the informative locus score are calculated. Here, these scores steer the measurement process (in our case, informative biomarkers) based on the results of the developed clustering algorithm (HCL) for the next iteration. The bidirectional information flow between HCL and the proposed scores continues until a termination condition is satisfied. These scores are also used for real-time classification of new samples. Based on the classification results, the orchestration module can call the biomarker identification module to retrieve information from the new samples or add the samples to the cluster structure.

In this study, our proposed DDDAS based framework addresses two major issues in HCL for performing data analysis in large and complex datasets such as DNA methylation. First, the performance of all clustering algorithms is highly dependent on the performance of their embedded dimension reduction (feature selection) algorithm. To the best of our knowledge, there does not exist a single universal algorithm that promises reasonable results for all datasets. The literature presents many dimension reduction algorithms for DNA methylation analysis whose performance is dependent on the data utilized for analysis. Hence, a successful implementation of a traditional HCL would require testing with several different dimension reduction algorithms. However, our proposed 3D-HCL framework is generically designed such that multiple dimension reduction algorithms are not required in succession. While 3D-HCL is initialized with a dimension reduction algorithm, the results are minimally affected by the selected initial set of informative biomarkers. The proposed framework identifies the most informative loci at each iteration, and these loci are updated based on the informative score calculated at each iteration. Second, HCL is sensitive to outliers and noise. In the literature, outliers are also called as *influential data points* as they can affect the results obtained from a clustering algorithm to a significant extent. In order to mitigate this impact of outliers and make our 3D-HCL less sensitive to influential data points (i.e., outliers), we further equipped our proposed framework with an outlier detection algorithm based on a fast distance-based measure.

The proposed work is also novel in the eminent DDDAS literature. DDDAS has its power in its ability to create a symbiotic feedback loop between the real system and its application. Dynamic data obtained from the real system is incorporated into an executing application where the application in turn steers the measurement process of the real system. As such, DDDAS has been applied to a variety of areas such as supply chain systems [4, 6, 7], distributed electric microgrids [16, 26, 34, 36, 37, 43], smart energy management [23, 28, 44, 45], data fusion analysis [1, 3, 41, 42], transportation systems [22, 32], and surveillance and crowd control [5, 29] amongst many others. This study introduces a new dynamic data driven learning framework for identification of informative biomarkers based on the DDDAS paradigm that not only provides measures for detecting outliers but also presents an orchestration procedure for the symbiotic feedback loop between the learning mechanism and the real system application. Here, the performance of the proposed 3D-HCL framework on learning mechanism is tested on the lung cancer methylation data. Our results show that the symbiotic feedback loop increases the accuracy of the learning mechanism by updating informative biomarkers based on the information obtained from clustering algorithm in the unsupervised training dataset and the real time classification results of new samples.

The proposed framework has been designed in a generic manner for wide applicability in data system with various dimensionalities. The performance of the proposed framework is demonstrated using real lung cancer DNA methylation data obtained from GEO DataSets [8] where the results reveal that our proposed framework outperforms the conventional HCL algorithm in differentiating lung cancer tissues with 3% versus 33% error margins. Last but not least, this study provides a validation for dynamic updating of massive databases for *in vivo* DNA methylation analysis. In such an analysis, dynamically obtained data can be processed fast in a computationally efficient way. To this end, our proposed DDDAS 3D-HCL can be considered as an online learning mechanism fed by dynamic and big data as well as archival information.

12.2   DNA Methylation Data

Bisulfite treatment, also known as bisulfate conversion, is used to determine a DNA methylation pattern. Bisulfite treatment converts unmethylated cytosines to uracil while methylated residues remain unaffected [40]. Samples are then subject to DNA sequencing to identify specific changes in the DNA sequence that can directly inform the methylation level of a specific CpG site.

Bisulfite conversion provides methylated and unmethylated intensities at the each CpG sites to measure DNA methylation level. Beta value as defined in Eq. 12.1 is commonly used to measure DNA methylation status.

$$\beta_i = \frac{max\,(m_i, 0)}{max\,(m_i, 0) + max\,(u_i, 0) + \alpha} \tag{12.1}$$

In Eq. 12.1, m_i and u_i represent measured ith methylated and unmethylated probe intensities, respectively. In order to avoid having negative values in probe intensities, any negative values are reset to 0. To prevent probes with very low expression levels from dominating results, an adjustment factor (α) is used. In this study, α is set to 100 as recommended by [2]. The beta value ranges between 0 and 1. A value of zero means that every copy of the CpG island in the probe is unmethylated, whereas a value of one indicates that all copies of the CpG site are completely methylated.

12.3   Proposed DDDAS-Based Learning Framework (3D-HCL)

The proposed DDDAS-based learning framework first identifies: (1) candidate clusters of samples based on their DNA methylation levels and (2) informative CpG regions (biomarkers) whose methylation level change correlates with specific clusters (i.e., cancer type or subtype). The components of the proposed DDDAS-based learning framework are explained in detail in this section (see Fig. 12.1 for overview).

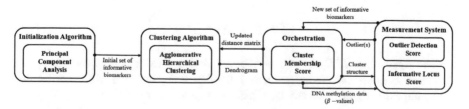

Fig. 12.1 Overview of the proposed DDDAS 3D-HCL framework

12.3.1 Initialization Algorithm: Principal Component Analysis

Principal component analysis (PCA) is a widely known dimension reduction algorithm in the literature [9]. PCA performs dimensionality reduction by identifying correlations in the data while preserving as much of the variance in the high dimension data as possible. PCA converts a set of correlated variables into a set of linearly uncorrelated variables called principal components using orthogonal transformation. The steps of the principal component analysis are explained below.

Let X is an $n \times m$ matrix consisting of m dimensional observation (in our case loci) of n samples.

Step 1 Centralize the data by subtracting the mean of each variable (observation) as shown below.

$$\tilde{X} = \begin{bmatrix} x_{11} - \bar{X}_1 & \cdots & x_{1m} - \bar{X}_m \\ \vdots & \ddots & \vdots \\ x_{n1} - \bar{X}_1 & \cdots & x_{nm} - \bar{X}_m \end{bmatrix} \tag{12.2}$$

Here, x_{ij} is the data for sample i and observation j, $\bar{X}_j$ is the mean of variable j and $\tilde{X}$ is the centralized data matrix.

Step 2 Compute the covariance matrix C from $\tilde{X}$ by using:

$$C = \frac{1}{m} \tilde{X}^T \tilde{X} \tag{12.3}$$

Step 3 Calculate the eigenvectors and the eigenvalues by solving the following equation for each variable

$$C \times \vec{u}_i = \lambda_i \times \vec{u}_i \tag{12.4}$$

In the equation above $\vec{u}_i$ represents the ith eigenvector and λ_i corresponds to the ith eigenvalue. Also, each pair of eigenvector must satisfy the following conditions. These conditions ensure that the eigenvectors are orthogonal to each other.

$$\vec{u}_i^T \times \vec{u}_j = 1 \; if \; i = j \tag{12.5}$$

$$\vec{u}_i^T \times \vec{u}_j = 0 \; if \; i \neq j \tag{12.6}$$

The eigenvalues of C shows how much variance is explained by corresponding eigenvector. In dimensionality reduction, the first p eigenvectors which correspond to the largest p eigenvalues are used instead of an $n \times m$ matrix.

12.3.2 Clustering Algorithm: Hierarchical Clustering

Hierarchical clustering (HCL) is a widely used clustering algorithm in DNA methylation analysis to identify the DNA methylation profiles affiliated with certain cancer subtypes [8, 38, 39]. The "bottom-up" approach (agglomerative) and the "top down" (divisive) approach are the main strategies in HCL. In *agglomerative*, each data point starts in its own cluster, and pairs of clusters are merged until only one cluster remains, while in *divisive*, all data points belong to one cluster at the beginning, and they are split until each of them is in its own cluster. The agglomerative approach is more commonly applied in the literature as it is generally faster than the divisive approach in terms of computational complexity. However, it should be noted that the HCL may still perform worse in terms of solution quality as the merges in agglomerative and the splits in divisive are both determined using a greedy algorithm. Additionally, HCL provides good and understandable visualization for users, and unlike other commonly used algorithms such as k-means, HCL does not require a prior knowledge of number of clusters. Due to these reasons, hierarchical agglomerative clustering is adopted as a learning mechanism in this study. For brevity, HCL abbreviation is also used for hierarchical agglomerative clustering in the rest of the paper.

As discussed above, HCL starts with having each observation in a separate cluster, then repeatedly merges the closest pair of clusters until only one cluster is left. In this work, we base the merging operation on an average linkage where the closest pair of clusters are identified as in the following equation.

$$D_{avg}\left(C_i, C_j\right) = \frac{1}{|C_i||C_j|} \sum_{x \in C_i} \sum_{y \in C_j} d_{xy} \tag{12.7}$$

In Eq. 12.7, $D_{avg}\left(C_i, C_j\right)$ shows the average link (distance) between cluster i and cluster j, $|C_i|$ represents the cardinality of cluster i and d_{xy} shows the distance between data point x and point y. Since the DNA methylation levels for all probes are properly scaled using the β_i values, Euclidean distance (as shown in Eq. 12.8) is used without any standardization method as a distance metric.

$$d_{ij} = \sqrt{\sum_{g \in \theta} \left(\beta_i^g - \beta_j^g\right)^2} \tag{12.8}$$

In Eq. 12.8, β_i^g is the beta value of probe g of point i and θ is the set of informative probes. HCL builds a tree-based hierarchical representation (dendrogram) using the Eqs. 12.7 and 12.8 and clusters are obtained by cutting the dendrogram at a desired level.

12.3.3 Orchestration Procedure: Cluster Membership Score Based Algorithm

In clustering problems, cluster assignments are made on the basis of a similarity measure, Euclidean distance in our case. Even if the clusters are formed based on the measure, the similarity measure may not answer such detailed questions related with the results of clustering algorithm, such as labeling, determining right number of clusters, detecting outliers or border points, etc. To this end, in this study, we propose a cluster membership score that shows the membership degree of a point to a cluster. The cluster membership score is developed based on the definition of an uncertainty classification measure proposed by [10, 27] for a probabilistic distance clustering algorithm. Here, we adapt the definition of uncertainty classification measure to HCL for better understanding of the clusters. The cluster membership score is explained in detail below.

Let $d\left(i, C_j\right)$ is the average of distances between observation i and observations assigned to cluster j.

Definition 1 Let m_i is the cluster membership measure of observation i. It is the harmonic mean of the distances $\left\{d\left(x, C_j\right) : j \in \{1, \ldots, k\}\right\}$ divided by their geometric mean.

$$
m_i = k \left(\prod_{j=1}^{k} \rho_j(i)\right)^{\frac{1}{k}} \text{ where } \rho_j(i) = \frac{\prod_{u \neq j} d\left(i, C_j\right)}{\sum_{v=1}^{k} \prod_{t \neq v} d\left(i, C_t\right)} \tag{12.9}
$$

The proposed score is ranging from 0 to 1. A value of zero indicates that the point is certainly a member of a cluster whereas a value of one shows the current information do not explain the membership of a point.

Definition 2 Let M_j denotes the cluster validation score for given cluster structure. The cluster validation score is the mean of the cluster membership scores of data points assigned to the corresponding cluster.

$$
M_j = \frac{\sum_{i \in C_j} m_i}{|C_j|} \tag{12.10}
$$

Based on the definition of cluster membership score, the low values of M_j indicate that cluster j is explained and separated well from the other clusters with the given information (in our case, identified set of informative CpG regions). This score is designed to help orchestration of the information flow between hierarchical clustering, and outlier detection algorithm and dimension reduction algorithm. Also, it determines when the framework will be terminated.

12.3.4   Outlier Detection Algorithm

Outliers can arise from DNA methylation data due to measurement errors and/or the dynamic nature in epigenetic mechanisms. Identification of outliers can eliminate their contaminating effect on the methylation data and tremendously increase the performance of clustering algorithm. Because of greedy mechanism used in merging clusters, HCL is sensitive to outliers and it can result in 'trivial' clusters. To this end, outlier detection and removal are important tasks to improve the performance of clustering algorithm in DNA methylation analysis.

Outliers (or influential points) can be defined as data points, distant from the remainder of the data points. HCL can result in meaningless clusters due to outliers (an example is shown in Results Section). In this study, we propose fast distance measure for detecting outliers. This measure is designed by assuming that while normal data points have a dense neighborhood whereas outliers are far apart from their neighbors and thus have a less dense neighborhood.

Let o_i represents the outlier score of data point i. It is number of points that are closer than distance p.

$$o_i = \sum_{j=1}^{N} \delta \left(d_{ij}, p \right) \tag{12.11}$$

In Eq. 12.11, $\delta \left(d_{ij}, p \right)$ is a function such that it is 1 if $d_{ij} \leq p$ and it is 0, if otherwise. The data points with small o_i values are considered as outliers. Here, o_i values are highly dependent on the parameter p. Small p values can find that all points are normal while large p can mark normal points as outliers. Therefore, selection of p is very important. In this study, p is determined as average of distance between data points. Other outlier detection algorithms, similar with the proposed one in this study, can be found in the literature [30].

12.3.5   Dimension Reduction Algorithm: Locus Information Score Based Algorithm

In conventional application of HCL on a high-dimensional space, dimension reduction algorithm (or feature selection algorithm) finds a set of informative attributes and then HCL forms clusters based on this set. However, since the results of any clustering algorithm are highly dependent on selected attributes, this approach can failure in most of the real systems especially dynamic, complex systems such as a DNA sequence. Also, PCA has two important drawbacks. First, since PCA performs dimensionality reduction using orthogonal transformation, it complicates the identification biomarkers associated with diseases in DNA methylation analysis. Second, PCA does not take into account the contaminating effect of outliers in determining the principal components. To address these issues, we developed a *locus informative score* inspired by [24].

Let Inf_l^j denotes the information score of locus l for the cluster j. Based on the cluster structure found by HCL, it is calculated as follows.

$$Inf_l^j = \frac{\left| \mu_{i \in C_j}\left(\beta_i^l\right) - \mu_{t \notin C_j}\left(\beta_t^l\right) \right|}{\sigma_{i \in C_j}\left(\beta_i^l\right) + \sigma_{t \notin C_j}\left(\beta_t^l\right)} \tag{12.12}$$

In Eq. 12.12, β_i^l is the beta value of locus l for sample (point) i, and μ and σ are the mean and standard deviation for the given set of beta values, respectively. The higher Inf_l^j scores mean that the locus l is informative to differentiate the cluster j from the other clusters. In this study, if Inf_l^j is greater than 1 for any cluster, the locus l is considered as an informative biomarker.

12.4 Results and Discussion

In this work, the capabilities and performance of the proposed DDDAS-based framework are demonstrated using lung cancer DNA methylation data obtained from the Gene Expression Omnibus (GEO) repository at the National Center for Biotechnology Information archives with accession number GSE16559 [8]. In this section, we first demonstrate each step of our framework to build groups of samples with related methylation profiles on the training dataset. Then, we show how to incorporate test data into the 3D-HCL and correlate test results with 3D-HCL predictions.

12.4.1 Learning from Training Data

The training dataset used in our experiments is a part of larger data and consists of 33 samples and two clusters, namely Non-malignant pulmonary and lung adenocarcinoma. At the initialization step of the proposed learning framework, PCA is applied to all 1505 probes with DNA different methylation levels for all samples. When the number of variables (in our case, number of probes) is larger than the number of samples, PCA reduces the dimensionality to, the number of samples (at best). In this specific example, PCA results in 32 components without loss of information. To select the initial set of informative biomarkers, we start by looking at the cumulate variance explained by a set of principal components (Fig. 12.2).

As shown in Fig. 12.2, the first few components have the largest variance among all components. In fact, while the first three components retain 60% of the original variance, the last 19 components are only able to explain 10% of the variation of the original data. Because some variance is expected in the original DNA methylation

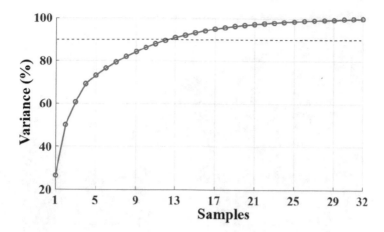

Fig. 12.2 Cumulative variance explained by a set of principal components

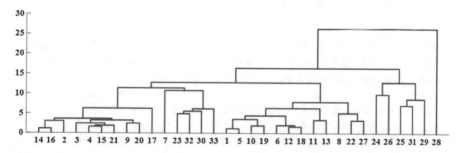

Fig. 12.3 Dendrogram obtained from HCL (Solution 1)

dataset due to the contained outliers; in this work, the components that explains 90% of the variance (13 of them) are chosen to initialize the framework.

Next, hierarchical clustering was run with the distance matrix calculated based on the components found by PCA using the Eq. 12.8. Figure 12.3 illustrates the dendrogram obtained from HCL. As shown in the figure, HCL could not find any meaningful clusters. Similar results were recorded when using conventional approach that incorporated PCA as a dimension reduction algorithm and HCL as a clustering algorithm. Error rate of this conventional approach was also recorded as 33%.

In the solution, cluster 2 has only one member which is sample 28. In this example, since cluster validation score for cluster 2 was zero and the cardinality of cluster was one, an outlier score of each data point was calculated based on the current distance matrix and shown in Fig. 12.4.

The outlier score of point 28 is zero, meaning that there is no point closer to the point 28 than p, mean of the distance matrix. The point was marked as outlier and removed from distance matrix. Then, HCL was applied to the 32 samples. It should be noted here that after outlier removal, the points were re-indexed based

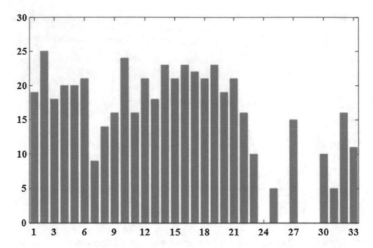

Fig. 12.4 Outlier score of each data point

on their position with respect to outlier point index. In Solution 2, HCL resulted in more meaningful clusters with error rate of 18% as shown in Fig. 12.5a. Since the cluster validation scores of both clusters were less than 0.8, the outlier removing algorithm was not executed. Next, the informative probes were determined based on the cluster formation obtained Solution 2 using the Eq. 12.12. The distance matrix was re-calculated with respect to the new set of informative probes and HCL was applied to the new distance matrix. The result of the algorithm was shown in Fig. 12.5b. Here, the error rate was down to 3.03% and the cluster validation scores of cluster 1 and cluster 2 were down to 0.36 and 0.65, respectively. The same procedure is repeated to obtain Solution 3 where the results are shown in Fig. 12.5c. While Solution 4 presents the same clustering formation as was in Solution 3, cluster validation scores are better for both clusters in Solution 4 due to an updated set of informative biomarkers. Since the same solutions were obtained in consecutive runs, the algorithm is terminated.

The cluster validation scores of both clusters in each run were illustrated in Fig. 12.6. It is expected that cluster validation score decreases after each run with updating the set of informative probes based on the obtained clusters. However, the validation scores of clusters in Solution 1 were smaller than the those in Solution 2. Here, in Solution 1, cluster 2 consists of only point 28 which is far from the other data points and obviously, the cluster validation score is 0 for cluster 2. Also, since the point 28 is far from the points, in Solution 1, the cluster validation score of cluster 1 was smaller than other solutions. This issue can be explained as the effect of influential points on the cluster validation score that the users should bear in mind.

After the recursive procedure is terminated, there is one more step to finalize the solution. In this step, the outlier(s) was re-assigned to the closest cluster based on the results of HCL. The closest cluster is the one that has the minimum average

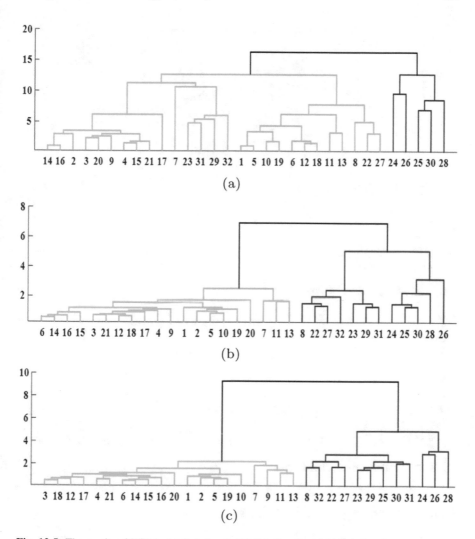

Fig. 12.5 The results of HCL in (**a**) Solution 2, (**b**) Solution 3, and (**c**) Solution 4

distance between outlier and the points assigned to corresponding cluster. The result after the finalization step was represented in Fig. 12.7. The error rate is 3.03%, the proposed procedure mis-assigned only point 8 (non-malignant pulmonary) to the lung adenocarcinoma cluster.

The proposed dynamic data driven high dimensional learning framework clusters the samples and identifies the biomarkers associated with these clusters. The proposed framework results in 72 probes that help classify the new samples without having to conduct a complete analysis. The original data and identified informative probes were represented in Fig. 12.8a and b, respectively.

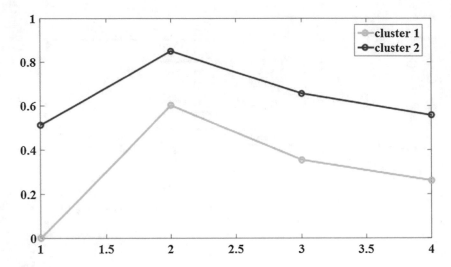

Fig. 12.6 Cluster validation scores

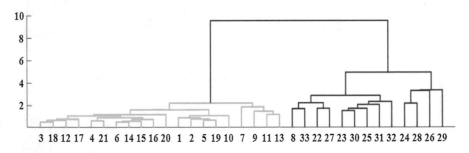

Fig. 12.7 Solution after finalization step

12.4.2 Learning from Test Data

The discriminative model obtained from learning algorithm based on the training dataset eases the classification of the test data without running the learning algorithm. This is the main motivation of the most of the learning algorithms proposed in the literature. However, especially in high dimensional data, training dataset may not reflect all of the different groups that are possible within the system (in our case, cancer types and subtypes) causing the discriminative model outputting incorrect predictions when used with the test data. For example, in unsupervised DNA methylation analysis, the biomarkers identified using a dimension reduction algorithm and a discriminative model (cluster structure in our case) are heavily dependent on each other and thus training dataset can mislead the results of a discriminative model. Here, we conduct two sets of experiments where in the first set of experiments, we demonstrate the capabilities of 3D-HCL in real-time

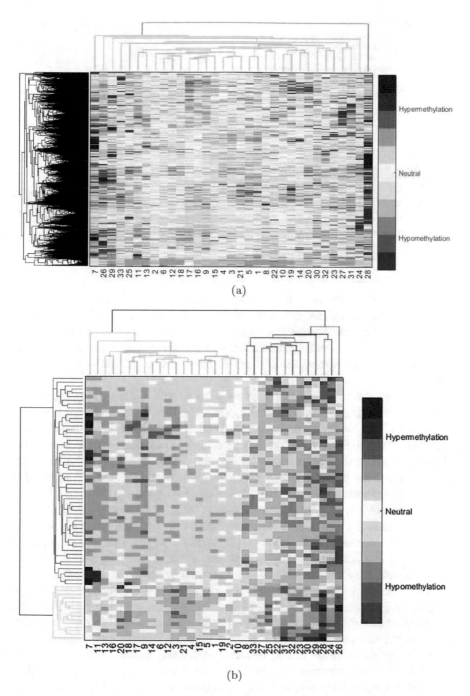

Fig. 12.8 Original data and identified informative probes. (**a**) Original data. (**b**) Identified biomarkers

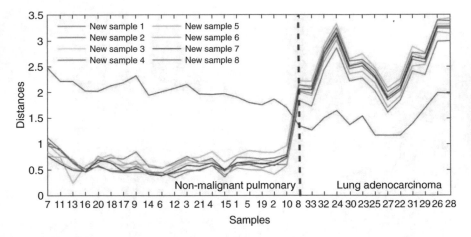

Fig. 12.9 Classification of 8 non-malignant pulmonary samples

classification of the test data, then in the second set of experiments, we show the performance of our framework in the updating of the discriminative model with respect to test data predictions in the case that training data do not reflect the true representation of the new samples. In the first set of experiments, we classify the 8 non-malignant pulmonary samples where the results of 3D-HCL are shown in Fig. 12.9.

Figure 12.9 shows the distance between each sample in the training set and the newly obtained sample. As seen in the figure, the new samples except sample 4 have similar DNA methylation profiles based on the biomarkers identified using the discriminative model. Here, the orchestration module calculates m_i and decides the class of each new sample i without running the clustering algorithm. The cluster membership of the samples except sample 4 is smaller than 0.2 which means that the identified biomarkers explain the class of these samples. However, membership score of sample 4 is quite high (approximately 0.85). This shows that this sample can be considered as an outlier or can come from a different cluster that has not been considered in training dataset. Since this data point is far from all of the samples in both the training and test datasets, it is marked as an outlier. Our outlier detection algorithm also classifies the point as an outlier with respect to its o_i score.

In the second experiment, the test dataset includes 12 pleural mesothelioma samples which have not been considered in the training dataset. Similar to Fig. 12.9, Fig. 12.10 shows the dissimilarity value between the pleural mesothelioma samples, and the non-malignant pulmonary and lung adenocarcinoma samples. Here, m_i values of the samples in this test dataset are approximately 0.90. Here the orchestration module decides that all these samples belong to a different cluster since these samples have similar DNA methylation profiles based on the identified biomarkers. Then, to identify the new set of biomarkers that separates these samples from the samples in the training dataset, the locus informative score (see Eq. 12.12)

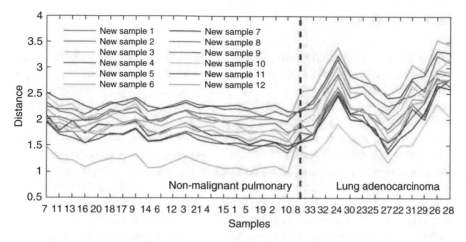

Fig. 12.10 Classification of 12 pleural mesothelioma samples

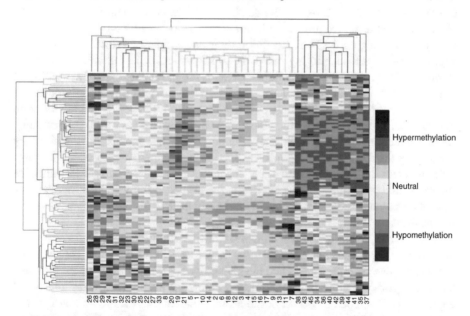

Fig. 12.11 Identified informative biomarkers after new test data

is calculated for each locus assuming that the samples in the new dataset belong to a new cluster. Based on inf_l^j values, 42 additional loci are labeled as informative biomarkers. The results of updated learning model are represented in Fig. 12.11. The results show that the symbiotic feedback loop increases the accuracy of the learning mechanism by updating informative biomarkers based on the information obtained from the test data. As such, the accuracy of the updated learning model is 97.78%.

12.5 Conclusion

In this work, a dynamic data driven applications systems (DDDAS) high dimensional learning framework, namely 3D-HCL, is introduced for identifying idiosyncratic DNA methylation profile of different tumor types and/or subtypes. The proposed framework is composed of five algorithms, (1) principal component analysis that initializes the framework by determining initial set of informative biomarkers, (2) hierarchical clustering algorithm that clusters the points (samples) into groups which represent cancer types or subtypes, (3) outlier detection algorithm that finds outliers and removes their contaminating effect on the input of HCL, (4) informative probe selection procedure which identifies the biomarkers associated with clusters obtained by learning mechanism, and (5) orchestration procedure that coordinates the information flow between HCL and outlier detection algorithm and informative probe selection procedure based on the designed cluster membership score. The performance of the proposed framework was demonstrated using real lung cancer data obtained from GEO database [8]. The performance of the proposed DDDAS-based recursive procedure is noted as very promising on the case study in terms of detecting outliers and removing their contaminating effect, finding meaningful clusters, and identifying biomarkers. In particular, in the selected dataset, traditional HCL results in approximately 33% error and fails to identify meaningful clusters. Our improved iterative procedure, however successfully differentiates the non-malignant pulmonary and lung adenocarcinoma with 3% error and identifies an aberrant DNA methylation profile associated with these cancer types. Interestingly, we observed that outliers have a significant effect on dimension reduction by misleading the determination of informative genes. Our proposed procedure is also able to detect and remove the outliers from the methylation dataset to minimize their potential contamination. Collectively, the proposed framework paves the way towards analyzing complex DNA methylation data using data driven learning mechanisms.

The future venues of this work involves itself with the testing of the proposed algorithm using datasets collected from a larger number of patients. The outcome of these studies will further validate the capability and performance of the DDDAS learning algorithm while improving its accuracy. In this study, a threshold based algorithm is developed based on designed informative locus score so that the predefined threshold value can affect the identification of informative biomarkers. Here, an optimal mechanism or automatic fine-tuning mechanisms for the threshold parameter can be investigated. Lastly, in its current form, the hierarchical clustering algorithm expects the number of clusters as a pre-determined parameter. The future work will focus on the exploration of a cluster membership score that will help optimize the number of clusters used in run-time.

The proposed 3D-HCL framework is tested on a real lung cancer DNA methylation dataset. As demonstrated in Sect. 12.4 the feedback loop between the clustering and identification of biomarkers provides more accurate results of aberrant DNA methylation profiles associated with cancer. The results of this study show that

DDDAS based methodologies can provide invaluable insight into accurate cancer diagnosis, early detection, and treatment tailoring especially the research in the analysis of time-course data, and complex and comprehensive studies involving very large number of genes and samples such as Human Genome Project. In time-course methylation analysis, the proposed 3D-HCL framework can be further investigated to identify groups of biomarkers whose expressions are not stable over time, and then classify the new samples based on these identified biomarkers by steering the timing of data collection. In conclusion, this study highlights that DDDAS based learning methodologies offer not only more accurate results but also more efficient experimental designs for analyzing and understanding of genetic and epigenetic blueprint in the complex and comprehensive projects.

Acknowledgments This project is supported by the AFOSR DDDAS.

References

1. Aved A (2013) Scene understanding for real time processing of queries over big data streaming video. University of Central Florida
2. Bibikova M, Lin Z, Zhou L, Chudin E, Garcia EW, Wu B, Doucet D, Thomas NJ, Wang Y, Vollmer E, et al (2006) High-throughput dna methylation profiling using universal bead arrays. Genome research 16(3):383–393
3. Blasch E, Al-Nashif Y, Hariri S (2014) Static versus dynamic data information fusion analysis using dddas for cyber security trust. Procedia Computer Science 29:1299–1313
4. Blasch E (2018) Dddas advantages from high-dimensional simulation. In: Winter Simulation Conference (WSC) 2019, pp 1418–1429
5. Blasch E, Aved A (2015) Dynamic data-driven application system (dddas) for video surveillance user support. In: Procedia Computer Science, vol 51, pp 2503–2517
6. Blasch E, Xu R, Nikouei S, Chen Y (2018) A study of lightweight dddas architecture for real-time public safety applications through hybrid simulation. In: Winter Simulation Conference (WSC) 2019, pp 762–773
7. Celik N, Lee S, Vasudevan K, Son YJ (2010) Dddas-based multi-fidelity simulation framework for supply chain systems. IIE Transactions 42(5):325–341
8. Christensen BC, Marsit CJ, Houseman EA, Godleski JJ, Longacker JL, Zheng S, Yeh RF, Wrensch MR, Wiemels JL, Karagas MR, et al (2009) Differentiation of lung adenocarcinoma, pleural mesothelioma, and nonmalignant pulmonary tissues using dna methylation profiles. Cancer research 69(15):6315–6321
9. Cunningham JP, Ghahramani Z (2015) Linear dimensionality reduction: Survey, insights, and generalizations. Journal of Machine Learning Research 16:2859–2900
10. Damgacioglu H, Iyigun C (2012) Uncertainity and a new measure for classification uncertainity. In: Uncertainty Modeling in Knowledge Engineering and Decision Making, World Scientific, pp 925–930
11. Darema F (1996) On the parallel characteristics of engineering/scientific and commercial applications: differences, similarities and future outlook. In: Keane J (ed) Parallel Commercial Processing
12. Darema F (2002) Dynamic data driven application systems. Internet Process Coordination p 149

13. Darema F (2004) Dynamic data driven applications systems: A new paradigm for application simulations and measurements. In: International Conference on Computational Science, Springer, pp 662–669
14. Darema F (2011) Computational model and environments. Journal of Algorithms and Computational Technology 5(4):545–600
15. Darema F (2012, June) New frontiers through computer and information science. Presented at the 2012 International Conference on Computational Science (ICCS), Omaha, NE.
16. Darville J, Celik N (2020) Simulation optimization for unit commitment using a region-based sampling (rbs) algorithm. In: Proceedings of the 2020 Institute of Industrial and Systems Engineers
17. Devaskar SU, Raychaudhuri S (2007) Epigenetics–a science of heritable biological adaptation. Pediatric research 61:1R–4R
18. Eccleston A, DeWitt N, Gunter C, Marte B, Nath D (2007) Epigenetics. Nature 447(7143):395–395
19. Egger G, Liang G, Aparicio A, Jones PA (2004) Epigenetics in human disease and prospects for epigenetic therapy. Nature 429(6990):457–463
20. Esteller M (2008) Epigenetics in cancer. New England Journal of Medicine 358(11):1148–1159
21. Esteller M, Corn PG, Baylin SB, Herman JG (2001) A gene hypermethylation profile of human cancer. Cancer research 61(8):3225–3229
22. Fujimoto R, Guensler R, Hunter M, Kim HK, Lee J, Leonard II J, Palekar M, Schwan K, Seshasayee B (2006) Dynamic data driven application simulation of surface transportation systems. In: International Conference on Computational Science, Springer, pp 425–432
23. Fujimoto RM, Celik N, Damgacioglu H, Hunter M, Jin D, Son YJ, Xu J (2016) Dynamic data driven application systems for smart cities and urban infrastructures. In: Winter Simulation Conference (WSC), 2016, IEEE, pp 1143–1157
24. Golub TR, Slonim DK, Tamayo P, Huard C, Gaasenbeek M, Mesirov JP, Coller H, Loh ML, Downing JR, Caligiuri MA, et al (1999) Molecular classification of cancer: class discovery and class prediction by gene expression monitoring. science 286(5439):531–537
25. Holm K, Hegardt C, Staaf J, Vallon-Christersson J, Jönsson G, Olsson H, Borg Å, Ringnér M (2010) Molecular subtypes of breast cancer are associated with characteristic dna methylation patterns. Breast Cancer Research 12(3):1
26. Hunter M, Biswas A, Fujimoto R (2018) Energy efficient middleware for dynamic data driven application systems. In: Proceedings of the 2018 Winter Simulation Conference, pp 628–639
27. Iyigun C, Ben-Israel A (2009) Semi-supervised probabilistic distance clustering and the uncertainty of classification. In: Advances in data analysis, data handling and business intelligence, Springer, pp 3–20
28. Jin D, Nicole D (2015) Parallel simulation and virtual-machine-based emulation of software-defined networks. In: ACM Transactions on Modeling and Computer Simulation (TOMACS), vol 1, pp 1–27
29. Khaleghi AM, Xu D, Wang Z, Li M, Lobos A, Liu J, Son YJ (2013) A dddams-based planning and control framework for surveillance and crowd control via uavs and ugvs. Expert Systems with Applications 40(18):7168–7183
30. Knox EM, Ng RT (1998) Algorithms for mining distancebased outliers in large datasets. In: Proceedings of the International Conference on Very Large Data Bases, Citeseer, pp 392–403
31. Laird PW, Jaenisch R (1996) The role of dna methylation in cancer genetics and epigenetics. Annual review of genetics 30(1):441–464
32. Lecerf M, Allaire D, Willcox K (2015) Methodology for dynamic data-driven online flight capability estimation. AIAA Journal 53(10):3073–3087
33. Li E, Beard C, Jaenisch R (1993) Role for dna methylation in genomic imprinting. Nature 366(6453):362–365
34. Shi X, Damgacioglu H, Celik N (2015) A dynamic data-driven approach for operation planning of microgrids. Procedia Computer Science 51:2543–2552

35. Siegmund KD, Laird PW, Laird-Offringa IA (2004) A comparison of cluster analysis methods using dna methylation data. Bioinformatics 20(12):1896–1904
36. Thanos AE, Shi X, Sáenz JP, Celik N (2013) A dddams framework for real-time load dispatching in power networks. In: Proceedings of the 2013 Winter Simulation Conference: Simulation: Making Decisions in a Complex World, IEEE Press, pp 1893–1904
37. Thanos AE, Bastani M, Celik N, Chen CH (2017) Dynamic data driven adaptive simulation framework for automated control in microgrids. IEEE Transactions on Smart Grid 8(1):209–218
38. Ueno H, Okita H, Akimoto S, Kobayashi K, Nakabayashi K, Hata K, Fujimoto J, Hata Ji, Fukuzawa M, Kiyokawa N (2013) Dna methylation profile distinguishes clear cell sarcoma of the kidney from other pediatric renal tumors. PloS one 8(4):e62,233
39. Virmani AK, Tsou JA, Siegmund KD, Shen LY, Long TI, Laird PW, Gazdar AF, Laird-Offringa IA (2002) Hierarchical clustering of lung cancer cell lines using dna methylation markers. Cancer Epidemiology Biomarkers & Prevention 11(3):291–297
40. Wang RYH, Gehrke CW, Ehrlich M (1980) Comparison of bisulfite modification of 5-methyldeoxycytidine and deoxycytidine residues. Nucleic acids research 8(20):4777–4790
41. Xu J, Zhang S, Huang E, Chen C, Lee L, Celik N (2014) Efficient multi-fidelity simulation optimization. Winter Simulation Conference, pp 3940–3951
42. Xu J, Zhang S, Huang E, Chen C, Lee L, Celik N (2016) Multi-fidelity optimization with ordinal transformation and optimal sampling. Asia-Pacific Journal of Operational Research 33(3):165–170
43. Yavuz A, Darville J, Celik N, Xu J, Chen C, Langhals B, Engle R (2020) Advancing self healing capabilities in interconnected microgrids via ddas with relational database management. In: Proceedings of the 2020 Winter Simulation Conference
44. Ye C, Ding Y, Wang P, Lin Z (2019) A data-driven bottom-up approach for spatial and temporal electric load forecasting. In: IEEE Trans Power Syst, vol 34, pp 1966–1979
45. Zhou K, Chen Y, Xu Z, Lu J, Hu Z (2018) A smart-community demand response load scheduling method based on consumer clustering. 2nd IEEE Conference Energy Internet Energy System Integration

Chapter 13
Photometric Stereopsis for 3D Reconstruction of Space Objects

Xue Iuan Wong, Manoranjan Majji and Puneet Singla

Abstract The use of photometric stereopsis approaches to estimate the geometry of a resident space object (RSO) from image data is detailed. The set of algorithms and methods for shape estimation form an integral element of a Dynamic Data Driven Application System (DDDAS) for enhancing space situational awareness, where, sensor tasking and scheduling operations are carried out based upon the RSO orbital and geometric attributes, as estimated from terrestrial and space-based sensor systems. Techniques for estimating the relative motion between successive frames using image features are used for data alignment before surface normal estimation. Mathematical models of photometry and imaging physics are exploited to infer the surface normals from images of the target object under varied illumination conditions. Synthetic images generated from physics based ray-tracing engine are used to demonstrate the utility of the proposed algorithms.The proposed framework results in a estimates of the surface shape of the target object, which can subsequently used in forward models for prediction, data assimilation and subsequent sensor tasking operations. Sensitivity analysis is used to quantify the uncertainty of reconstructed surface.

Keywords Space situation awareness (SSA) · Light detection and ranging (LIDAR) · Photometric stereo · Lambertian surface model · Scale Invariant Feature Transformation (SIFT) · Space Object Light Attribute Rendering (SOLAR) · Itokawa model · Apollo model

Xue Iuan Wong
Research Engineer, Ford Motor Company
e-mail: xuewong@buffalo.edu

Manoranjan Majji
Associate Professor, Aerospace Engineering, Director, Land, Air and Space Robotics Laboratory, Texas A & M University
e-mail: mmajji@tamu.edu

Puneet Singla
Associate Professor, Department of Aerospace Engineering, The Pennsylvania State University
e-mail: psingla@psu.edu

© The Author(s), under exclusive license to Springer Nature Switzerland AG 2022   263
E. P. Blasch et al. (eds.), *Handbook of Dynamic Data Driven Applications Systems*,
https://doi.org/10.1007/978-3-030-74568-4_13

13.1 Introduction

Space situation awareness (SSA), including space surveillance and characterization of all space objects and environments, is critical for national and economic security. SSA is the ability to detect, track and characterize passive and active space objects. In light of the large number of resident space objects, (RSOs, > 20,000) and the generally accepted notion that our knowledge about the number and nature of most of the objects is severely limited to none, an unmet and urgent need exists for accurate tracking and characterization of RSOs. In addition to orbit parameters, RSO shape and size attributes are necessary to characterize long term evolution of the orbital states, especially for objects in the low and mid Earth orbital regimes. Dynamic Data Driven Application Systems (DDDAS) provide an important avenue to monitor resident space objects, by enabling mechanisms to infer their shape, state and number, and simultaneously providing a data driven feedback loop about which future measurements are to be made to maintain the RSO uncertainties in the catalog below acceptable threshold values. Such a framework comprises of an interplay between various algorithms and methods, catering to different SSA products. Fig 13.1 provides a notional overview of such a system called INFOrmation and Resource Management (INFORM) conceived by the authors for SSA applications.

An important aspect of space exploration and situational awareness involves the characterization of surface geometry of space objects. Surface geometry estimates are then utilized by the forward models for uncertainty propagation and subsequent resource allocation operations for catalogue maintenance, conjunction assessment and other SSA product generation. While astronomers are more interested in measuring the geometry of natural space objects such as asteroid and planetoids, the measurement of man-made objects such as spacecraft enable better characterization of resident space objects of interest in space situational awareness applications.

Common methods applied in space object's surface measurement are based on stereo vision [22], laser scanning [6], and photoclinometry [27]. Traditional

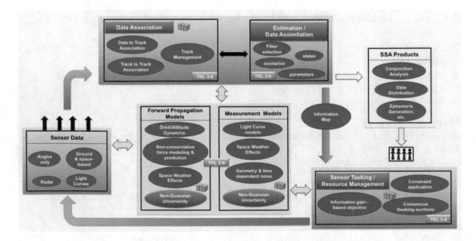

Fig. 13.1 INFORM Framework: A DDDAS for SSA Applications

methods of binocular stereopsis [11, 32] estimate the 3D shape of an object by triangulating image feature correspondences from two or more images obtained from viewpoints. Determination of pixel correspondences across multiple images is accomplished by extracting feature points in images and matching with the aid of descriptors. Binocular stereopsis or its multiview counterparts cannot provide a dense surface reconstruction of bland, textureless surfaces. An example for application of stereopsis in surface measurement is the Chinese Chang-E II lunar probe mission [22]. A series of images taken during the lunar probe landing process are used to recover 3D map of the landing zone. In this process, the measurements at different position but roughly along the same direction are used in conjunction with an adaptive Markov field algorithm [25] to recover pixel correspondences for dense surface reconstruction. In addition to being computationally expensive, multiview stereo techniques require high resolution imagery to establish feature correspondences. In RSO images with ground or space based telescopes, it is difficult to acquire images at high resolution with a finite depth of field. Light Detection and Ranging (LIDAR) is a time of flight measurement system that scans a collimated LASER to obtain range measurements. Being a reliable approach for surface scanning, LIDARs are widely used in space missions. For example, the measurement of Mercury's terrain in MESSENGER mission were obtained through LIDAR [6]. The need for specialized instrumentation obviates the use of LIDARs for shape estimation of RSOs.

Photoclinometry, also known as "shape from shading" is an approach for estimating surface shape of space objects. Unlike the other methods discussed previously, shape from shading does not directly measure surface geometry but estimates surface slope. The central idea behind photoclinometry is to infer shape by exploiting the dependence of surface slope on the intensity gradient of the surface in an image. Light reflection on a surface is governed by the reflectance model, or photometric function, which is a function of the geometry, surface material properties, and illumination (light polarity, wave length, incidence angle, etc.). Surface geometry given by the gradient may be parameterized in terms of the azimuth and polar angles with respect to a body fixed coordinate system. Since photoclinometry has an intensity measurement for each surface point, the estimates of surface slope from single image is an underdetermined problem. In order to solve surface gradient from the given information, photoclinometry defines additional constraints such as brightness and smoothness to provide regularity for the estimation problem. Given the illumination condition and an image that captures the reflected light of a surface, photoclinometry estimates surface gradients based on a reflectance model. Surface gradients are then integrated to estimate local surface geometry. The advantage of photoclinometry is the capability of reconstructing a high resolution surface with a finite set of images of comparable resolution. However, due to the requirement of constraint equations, photoclinometry can only estimate local geometry of a smooth surface up to certain accuracy. Practical applications utilize it as a source of auxiliary information for data assimilation with other measurements of surface geometry.

Photometric stereo [15] uses image observations of an object from various illumination conditions to deduce the shape and reflectance characteristics of the object. Similar to shape from shading, photometric stereo infers surface gradients from reflectance model and light measurements. In comparison to photoclinometry, photometric stereo does not require the definition of extra constraint equations to make this inference. Additional image requirements made with the same relative pose under variant illumination conditions are used in lieu of the photoclinometry constraints. Photometric stereo provides better accuracy in estimating surface gradients. In SSA applications, where the telescope observations of a target are available, it becomes the method of choice for shape estimation and forms the basis for shape estimation in the INFORM DDDAS framework. Photometric stereo has the same disadvantage as photoclinometry in terms of the fact that only surface gradients are estimated. Surface shape has to be estimated through spatial integration, which suffers from quality degradation when surface discontinuities exist. Thus for mapping applications, photometric stereo technique is less practical as compared to traditional texture based stereo technique. Image observations of an object also carry relative pose information. Structure from motion algorithms provides the basis for deriving relative pose estimates from image features. To this end, we ask the following question: *given a sequence of images of a space object, how do we utilize photometric stereo to provide high resolution surface reconstructions along with camera relative pose estimates?*

Application of photometric stereo has been confined to controlled laboratory environment, owing to various limitations. First, photometric stereo requires a controlled illumination environment. In various outdoor environments, lighting is usually uncontrollable [1, 40]. In the space environment however, Sun is the predominant light source, with known reference location.

A key challenge associated with photometric stereo is related to establishing pixel correspondences. Within the controlled environment where there is no relative motion between camera and object, pixel correspondences can be directly established by comparing pixel entries uniformly across different frames. In case of uncontrollable environment, when the object is allowed to move relative to the camera, this assumption is violated and one cannot assign contiguous pixel patches to belong to the same parts of the object across different frames. To solve this problem, multi-view photometric stereo [13] introduces the concepts from the multi-view stereo [34] to first estimate a rough surface and then iteratively optimize a cost function based upon the error between the estimate surface normal and depth gradient. Method proposed by Higo [14] attempts to solve for both object shape and normal vector simultaneously by posing an optimization problem that estimates a best fitting surface to attain to photometric consistency. Another multi-view stereo method developed by Zhou [41] focuses on materials with isotropic reflection (identical diffuse constant). A set of iso-depth contours [2] are first estimated from images and the 3D position of a sparse set of surface points are determined through the application of structure from motion methods. A complete surface reconstruction is then accomplished by propagating depth from determined surface points along the iso-depth contour. Passive photometric stereo [21] also makes use of structure from motion methods to first determine set of sparse surface points. Instead of propagating depth from surface points, they estimate a piecewise planar surface and then iteratively corrects this surface until it converges.

The INFORM based DDDAS approach for shape estimation is similar to Zhou's method [41] and passive photometric stereo [21]. It utilizes structure from motion methods to estimate a sparse set of surface points. Estimation of an iso-contour line is not necessary in our formulation. Further, the assumption of isotropic surface is also relaxed. We also obviate the necessity to construct a piecewise linear surfaces for iterative corrections. The INFORM based DDDAS method to estimate RSO surface geometry starts by applying structure from motion methods to detect a set of surface points in object space. This accomplishes sparse 3D reconstruction of these surface points. Each of these surface points are projected back into images to recover their reflected intensity along different illumination directions. Photometric stereo is then applied to estimate their surface normals. By assuming distance between two adjacent pixels is small, we then utilize the surface normal estimates to broadcast depth value among the adjacent pixels with finite difference approach. The process of propagating surface point and estimating the local normal vector is repeated until all pixels with valid measurements are traversed. To this end, the algorithm consists of three main steps. 1) Estimating the initial surface point with structure from motion and feature correspondences, 2) Estimating surface normal of aligned pixel patches using photometric stereo, and 3) Estimating dense surface using the depth propagation algorithm. Note that the proposed method does not solve large scale optimization problem iteratively. The surface propagation process being a local function is amenable to parallelization. Therefore, the proposed algorithm is more computationally efficient when compared to most of the multi-view photometric stereo algorithms including passive photometric stereo. The proposed algorithm also does not assume isotropic surface. Therefore, it is more general when compared to Zhou's method [41].

The rest of this chapter is organized as follows. Section 2 provides the problem statement. Introduction to photometric stereo is given in section 3 and a brief summary of structure from motion method is provided in section 4. Section 5 develops an algorithm to implement the photometric stereo to estimate 3D surface of RSOs. Section 6 details the experiment results. Section 7 draws the conclusions on the DDDAS approach.

13.2   Problem Statement and Background

Technical details of the problem statement involving photometric stereopsis are discussed in this section. Assume that sun is the only light source and that the reflected light from planets are neglected. Reflected light from the natural or man-made space object is captured by the imaging system. Sensor system includes a digital imager with appropriate optical elements for imaging process. A similar sensor system for SSA applications is considered by Jia et al., [18]. It is of interest to

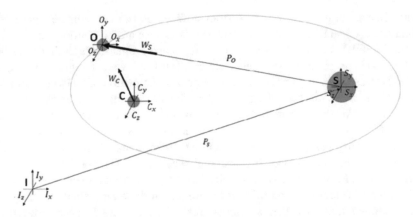

Fig. 13.2 Coordinate systems and geometry of the problem

obtain a 3D reconstruction of the RSO surface from a set of images obtained under different illumination conditions.

Photometric stereopsis process mainly comprises of three major components, namely the light source, the object, and the observer. To develop mathematical model associated with imaging process, an inertial frame denoted by I is defined as shown in Fig. 13.2. It is assumed that a point light source with known position with respect to inertia frame is used as the source for the imaging process. Assume that distance between light source and object is large when compared to the size of object, such that object's surface is illuminated by a source at infinity along the vector $\mathbf{w}_s$. The reflected light ray then arrives at object's surface and is assumed to have identical illumination direction over the entire workspace.

Due to the relative motion, object experiences translation and rotation relative to the light source and the observer. Therefore, the light incidence direction with respect to object's surface varies from frame to frame. Assume the object is rotating about its own center of gravity with a rotational velocity of ω_o. The relative orientation R_{OS} is then computed by integrating the following equation with initial attitude, $R_{OS}(t_0)$:

$$\dot{R}_{OS}(t) = -[\omega_o \times] R_{OS}(t) \tag{13.1}$$

$[\omega_o \times]$ is the cross product matrix [33]. The light incidence direction, $\mathbf{w}_s$, on the object's surface is given in the $\mathbf{O}$ frame by the equation:

$$\mathbf{w}_s(t) = R_{OS}^T(t) \frac{\mathbf{p}_O}{|\mathbf{p}_O|} \tag{13.2}$$

where $\mathbf{p}_O$ is position of the object $\mathbf{O}$ with respect to the source $\mathbf{S}$ expressed in the object coordinate system.

Consider an observer $\mathbf{C}$, orbiting the object O be described by the vector $\mathbf{p}_c$, the vector $\mathbf{w}_c$ represents the line of sight from the observer to the object. Observation

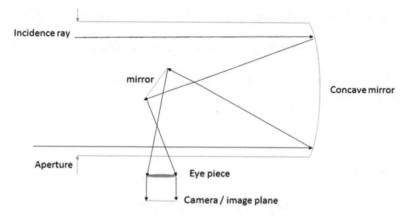

Fig. 13.3 Simplified model of telescopic lens system

of the object is projected on a 3D image frame that is aligned with the coordinate system that is affixed **C**. We assume that the sensor is located at the observer, with its axes aligned with the coordinates of the observer.

Assume that there is a telescopic lens attached to the camera, or a camera with a small field of view. In such optical systems such as telephoto lens, the rays of reflected light from the object to the image are parallel to each other. The light transport physics in the telephoto optics is markedly different from traditional camera systems, where a pin-hole projection model is found to be more appropriate [11]. Telephoto optics are more aptly modeled by utilizing an orthographic projection model.

Telescopic lens model in Fig. 13.3 shows that an orthographic projection simplifies the process of image formation as a close approximation to telescopic lens system. To this end, we assume an orthographic projection model is suitable for SSA applications of interest in this chapter.

13.3   Photometric Stereo

13.3.1   Formulation

Based on the geometry of the image formation process, we now provide a brief introduction to photometric stereopsis. Assuming a Lambertian reflectance model for the surface [30], the relationship between incidence light direction, $\mathbf{w}_s$ and reflected radiance, l_r is given as:

$$l_r = k_d l_s \mathbf{n}_x \cdot \mathbf{w}_s \tag{13.3}$$

where $\mathbf{n}_x = [n_x, n_y, n_z]$ represents the surface normal vector, k_d is the Lambertian reflectance coefficient, and l_s represents the incidence light radiance. Using the

Lambertian reflection model, the magnitude of reflected radiance, l_r, is written as:

$$l_r = k_d l_s (n_x w_{s,x} + n_z w_{s,y} + n_z w_{s,z}), \quad \mathbf{w}_s = [w_{s,x}, w_{s,y}, w_{s,z}] \tag{13.4}$$

Dividing l_r with l_s we define the normalized radiance, $|l|$ (or the gain of the reflection process) as:

$$|l| = \frac{l_r}{l_s} = k_d (n_x w_{s,x} + n_z w_{s,y} + n_z w_{s,z}) \tag{13.5}$$

This can be written as:

$$|l| = k_d [w_{s,x}, w_{s,y}, w_{s,z}][n_x, n_y, n_z]^T \tag{13.6}$$

Given at least three measurements of l_r at different incidence illumination directions, one can solve for components of $k_d \mathbf{n}$ in Eq. 13.6 using a system of linear equations. Assuming we have k number of measurements; the linear system of equations is given as:

$$
\begin{bmatrix} |l|_1 \\ |l|_2 \\ . \\ . \\ . \\ |l|_k \end{bmatrix} = \begin{bmatrix} w_{s,x,1} & w_{s,y,1} & w_{s,z,1} \\ w_{s,x,2} & w_{s,y,2} & w_{s,z,2} \\ & . & \\ & . & \\ & . & \\ w_{s,x,k} & w_{s,y,k} & w_{s,z,k} \end{bmatrix} \begin{bmatrix} k_d n_x \\ k_d n_y \\ k_d n_z \end{bmatrix} \tag{13.7}
$$

Eq. 13.7 can be written in the matrix form as:

$$\mathbf{l} = W_s [k_d \mathbf{n}_x] \tag{13.8}$$

where $\mathbf{l} \in \mathbb{R}^{k \times 1}$, $W_s \in \mathbb{R}^{k \times 3}$. The vector $[k_d \mathbf{n}_x]$ is given by the following least squares solution:

$$[k_d \mathbf{n}_x] = (W_s^T M W_s)^{-1} W_s^T M \mathbf{l} \tag{13.9}$$

where M is a weight matrix. Note that the Lambertian model follows a cosine distribution when incidence angle is less than $\pi/2$ rad. It will truncated at zero for any incidence angle larger than $\pi/2$ rad. However, 0 intensity does not necessarily a product of incidence angle larger or equal to $\pi/2$. It could be a result of shadowing or masking. Therefore, we exclude measurements of zero intensity from applying to photometric stereo.

Knowing that the normal vector is a unit vector, $\mathbf{n}$ is therefore normalized direction vector of $[k_d \mathbf{n}]$, and k_d is its length. The reflectance coefficient k_d can therefore be simultaneously estimated.

$$\mathbf{n} = \frac{[k_d\mathbf{n}]}{|[k_d\mathbf{n}]|} \tag{13.10}$$

$$k_d = |[k_d\mathbf{n}]| \tag{13.11}$$

Photometric stereo estimates the surface normal with the least squares solution. Therefore, more consistent measurements leads to a more accurate solution. However, photometric stereo solution is undefined when the coefficient matrix W_s is of rank less than 3. This frequently implies that all of the $\mathbf{w}_s$ lie on the same plane. When all the measurements are distributed on a plane, we do not have enough information to correctly estimate the normal vector for each surface point. In the present INFORM framework, which is a DDDAS for shape estimation of RSOs, the principal light source is the sun. Variation of intensity of the reflected light is caused by the relative pose of the RSO with respect to the light source. In the event that the relative pose is invariant through the imaging process, the coefficient matrix ceases loses rank. Photometric stereopsis, therefore relies heavily on the observability of the normal vector for each image pixel.

13.3.2   Modified Photometric Stereo

Solving surface normal with linear least square is a simple and elegant approach. However, the solution of the least squares problem involves the use of redundant parameterization of the normal vector components along with the coupling of the reflectance coefficient. Minimal parameterization of the normal vector in terms of azimuth angle and the polar angle is written in Eq. 13.12 as

$$\mathbf{n_x} = \big[\, sin(\xi)sin(\Omega)\ cos(\xi)sin(\Omega)\ cos(\Omega) \,\big] \tag{13.12}$$

ξ is azimuth angle, and Ω is polar angle measured in terms of body frame coordinate. Using the definition of the normal vector of Eq. 13.12 and substituting it into the Lambertian model, we get:

$$|l| = k_d \big(w_{s,x}sin(\xi)sin(\Omega) + w_{s,y}cos(\xi)sin(\Omega) + w_{s,z}cos(\Omega) \big) \tag{13.13}$$

We use the Gaussian Least Square differential Correction (GLSDC) algorithm [7] as the non-linear least square solver in this problem to solve for the unknown diffusivity constant, polar angle and azimuth angle. The state vector containing these three unknown is defined as follows:

$$\mathbf{x} = \big[\, k_d\ \Omega\ \xi \,\big]$$

Iteration process for estimating the elements of the state vector $\mathbf{x}$ in the GLSDC is setup to minimize the error functional

$$\Delta y_k = \mathbf{l} - \hat{\mathbf{l}}(\hat{\mathbf{x}}_k) \tag{13.14}$$

where vector $\mathbf{l}$ is intensity measurement, and $\hat{\mathbf{l}}(\hat{\mathbf{x}})$ is predicted intensity vector solved with estimated parameter vector $\hat{\mathbf{x}}$. If the error vector is larger then a given threshold, a differential correction to estimate parameters is applied as:

$$\hat{\mathbf{x}}_{k+1} = \hat{\mathbf{x}}_k + \Delta \mathbf{x}_k \tag{13.15}$$

$$\Delta \mathbf{x}_k = (H_k^T H_k)^{-1} H_k^T \Delta y \tag{13.16}$$

The Jacobian matrix of the Lambertian model with respect to each unknown term is solved about the previous estimated state $\hat{\mathbf{x}}_k$ as:

$$H_k = \left[\begin{array}{ccc} \frac{\partial |l|}{\partial k_d} & \frac{\partial |l|}{\partial \Omega} & \frac{\partial |l|}{\partial \xi} \end{array} \right]_{\hat{\mathbf{x}}_k} \tag{13.17}$$

$$\frac{\partial |l|}{\partial k_d} = w_{s,x} sin(\xi) sin(\Omega) + w_{s,y} cos(\xi) sin(\Omega) + w_{s,z} cos(\Omega)$$

$$\frac{\partial |l|}{\partial \Omega} = k_d (w_{s,x} sin(\xi) cos(\Omega) + w_{s,y} cos(\xi) cos(\Omega) - w_{s,z} sin(\Omega))$$

$$\frac{\partial |l|}{\partial \xi} = k_d (w_{s,x} cos(\xi) sin(\Omega) - w_{s,y} sin(\xi) sin(\Omega))$$

Differential corrections of Eq. 13.15 are applied until the norm of the error vector Δy_k of Eq. 13.14 drops below a pre-defined threshold value or the error change between two successive iterations gets small. Do note that when the polar angle is equal to zero, term $\frac{\partial |l|}{\partial \xi}$ is equal to zero as well. This indicates that we lose observability on the azimuth angle when polar angle is equal to zero. Losing observability in azimuth angle does not affect the final solution, but causes singularity when solving correction term with Eq. 13.16. A simple solution to avoid such a problem is to drop the terms related to azimuth angle when polar angle equals zero:

$$H = \begin{cases} \left[\begin{array}{ccc} \frac{\partial |l|}{\partial k_d} & \frac{\partial |l|}{\partial \Omega} & \frac{\partial |l|}{\partial \xi} \end{array} \right] & \Omega \neq 0 \\ \left[\begin{array}{cc} \frac{\partial |l|}{\partial k_d} & \frac{\partial |l|}{\partial \Omega} \end{array} \right] & \Omega = 0 \end{cases} \tag{13.18}$$

An appropriate choice for the measurement sensitivity matrix can be when the estimated value is sufficiently small, near convergence. Modified photometric stereo is different from original photometric stereo in terms of usage of the non-linear model and the parametrization of normal vector. Given identical measurement sets and using the Lambertian surface assumption, both algorithms yield the same result. Therefore, if computing predicted uncertainty is not required, it is unnecessary to replace original photometric stereo with modified photometric stereo. The point of using modified photometric stereo is to remedy the fact that normal vector directly estimated from original photometric stereo is subject to unit vector constraint, which makes the uncertainty calculations more complex as compared to the two angle parametrization.

Without explicitly relying on the surface normal's unit vector constraint as in traditional photometric stereo, modified photometric stereo is also compatible with more complex photometric function such as the Lunar-Lambert model traditionally applied in photoclinometric methods. In this chapter, we focuses on developing a framework that has the flexibility in choice of the photometric function, and therefore will restrict our discussions to Lambertian model. However, we note that proposed algorithm is also compatible with other photometric functions, and it is expected to yield better estimation results when applying better choice of photometric functions for various surfaces.

13.3.3 Surface Reconstruction and Depth Estimation

After solving for the normal vector for each pixel on an image, we obtain a normal map that indicates the local normal vector. Rendering of normal map allows to reconstruct appearance of the object at different illumination conditions under fixed view-point direction. For INFORM framework and its utility in the DDDAS for SSA product generation, a 3D surface map is desired. To recover a 3D surface from normal map, a common method is to integrate the surface gradient [9, 20]. Defining two components of the surface gradient as:

$$p = \frac{\partial z}{\partial x}$$

$$q = \frac{\partial z}{\partial y}$$

where p and q indicate surface gradient along x and y direction, respectively. The normal vector is related to surface gradient through:

$$\mathbf{n} = \frac{[p, q, 1]}{\sqrt{p^2 + q^2 + 1}}$$

Therefore, surface gradient may be recovered from the normal vector estimates by making use of the following relationship:

$$p = \frac{n_x}{n_z} \qquad (13.19a)$$

$$q = \frac{n_y}{n_z} \qquad (13.19b)$$

Assume that position x and y of a surface point are available in the object space. The depth of each surface point is then propagated from adjacent surface point the using finite difference operator given as follows:

$$
\begin{aligned}
z_{u,v} = \tfrac{1}{4}((z_{u+1,v} &- \tfrac{(p_{u+1,v}+p_{u,v})\delta x}{2}) \\
+(z_{u-1,v} &+ \tfrac{(p_{u-1,v}+p_{u,v})\delta x}{2}) \\
+(z_{u,v+1} &- \tfrac{(q_{u,v+1}+q_{u,v})\delta y}{2}) \\
+(z_{u,v-1} &+ \tfrac{(q_{u,v-1}+q_{u,v})\delta y}{2}))
\end{aligned}
\qquad (13.20)
$$

where δx and δy are the deflection along x, y directions on the surface.

If the surface is smooth, following the integrability constraint (Eqs. 13.21), propagation of depth from each direction should return identical results.

$$\frac{\partial^2 z}{\partial x \partial y} = \frac{\partial^2 z}{\partial y \partial x} \qquad (13.21)$$

Assumption of integrability will only work on a smooth surface. In most real objects, there are surface discontinuity that leads to violation of this assumption. Propagating the depth value across discontinuous sections leads to erroneous surface reconstruction. Therefore, it is essential to identify surface discontinuities before proceeding to the integration.

Wang [38] proposes to detect discontinuities using three subsequent operations. First, the angles between a pixel and four of its adjacent pixels are computed to establish a threshold to detect a discontinuity. A non-photorealistic (NPR) camera [31] (a method to re-render an image in a non-photorealistic way but to enforce the boundary and occlusion) is then applied to input images for depth edge detection. Finally, feature detection techniques are applied on color coded normal map (Rendering an image by coloring each element in normal vector with RGB color) to detect discontinuity in color gradients. Once the discontinuities are detected, reconstruction process will simply have to avoid them during integration to resolve error caused by discontinuity.

Another solution to this problem is to integrate the normal map by imposing integrability constraints through regularization [16]. A quadratic regularization proposed by Horn [16] is to search for a surface that minimizes the following function:

$$\epsilon(\hat{z}) = \int \int [\nabla \hat{z}(x, y) - [p, q]]^2 dx dy \qquad (13.22)$$

where $\hat{z}$ is the estimated depth. Eq. 13.22 can be approximated by the following discrete form:

$$\epsilon(\hat{z}) = \sum\sum \left[\frac{z_{u+1,v} - z_{u,v}}{\delta x} - \frac{p_{u+1,v} + p_{u,v}}{2} \right]^2 + \left[\frac{z_{u,v+1} - z_{u,v}}{\delta y} - \frac{q_{u,v+1} + q_{u,v}}{2} \right]^2$$

$$(13.23)$$

Minimizing Eq. 13.23 in Euler form by setting $\nabla\epsilon = 0$ leads to the following expression:

$$z_{u,v} = \frac{z_{u+1,v} + z_{u-1,v} + z_{u,v+1} + z_{u,v-1}}{4} - \frac{p_{u+1,v} + p_{u,v} + q_{u,v+1} + q_{u,v}}{8}$$

$$(13.24)$$

Since all depth values are unavailable initially, Eq. 13.24 sets initial depth to zero and updates the estimated surface iteratively. An improved scheme of this method to include boundary conditions, and an extension into other regularization method is proposed by Horn [16].

Integrating surface normals to derive a depth estimate is an open research problem in computer graphics. This is because most of the proposed methods can not effectively deal with discontinuity in surface, due to the limited information about an object's surface with observations from a single view-point direction. In this chapter, we propose to reconstruct surface by sequentially solving the photometric stereo and normal vector integration problems. This requires accurate estimates of both normal vector and surface point location to proceed. Our solution to this problem depends on the fact that we have a sparse set of surface points with known positions distributed on the object's surface. Let each of these surface points serve as reference points and broadcast the depth value toward entire surface. If there is discontinuity detected along path of propagation, we will simply stop going any further and let other broadcast processes estimate the location of surface point from other sides of the discontinuity. This method allow us to bypass some of the discontinuities in the surface. Although there is no guarantee that proposed method uniformly resolves issues associated with surface discontinuities due to the information available to us, this method allows us to minimize the error in surface reconstruction.

Having introduced photometric stereo for estimation of surface normals from a sequence of image captured under different illumination directions, we have looked at a modified photometric stereo that allows more efficient computation of the sensitivity terms. This forms an integral element of shape estimation methods in INFORM SSA framework. However, until this point, we have assumed that the relative motion between camera and object is stationary. Therefore, there is no problem in establishing pixel correspondences. In realistic situations, relative motion always exists and therefore establishing pixel correspondences can be fairly difficult. In order to solve this problem, we will first introduce structure from motion methods that allow the recovery of relative pose estimates in addition to rough shape. Rough shape estimation process form sparse feature correspondences is known as sparse stereo.

13.4   Photometric stereo In Motion

To resolve the issue of relative motion between the camera and the object, we now develop a framework that combines structure from motion algorithms with photometric stereo. There are two stages of the photometric stereo in motion algorithm. An initialization stage for estimating the initial condition for the relative pose. This is followed by a propagation stage for estimating the dense 3D surface. During the initialization stage, Scale Invariant Feature Transformation (SIFT) [23] is first applied to detect a set of feature points in the reference image. Each of this feature is then tracked over subsequent sequence with the Kanade–Lucas–Tomasi (KLT) tracker [24] to form set of feature tracks. Object space coordinates and the orientation of each image frame with respect to reference image frame are estimated by the application of structure from motion methods on corresponding feature tracks. During our study, factorization method [36] is being applied as the structure from motion method that provide relative pose and sparse structure estimation. Normal vector of each surface points is then estimated with photometric stereo by using intensity of feature track as input. Set of estimated surface points with the normal vector now defines the initial conditions for the propagation stage.

Propagation stage defines pixels with known object space coordinates and associated normal vector as base pixels, and defines their adjacent pixels that are without either position or normal vector as forward pixels. During propagation, each surface point are propagated spatially to these forward pixels from the base pixel with finite difference method that will be introduced in subsequent discussion. Projecting propagated surface points onto each image with the orthographic model recovers their measured reflected intensity in the image frame. Knowing the pixel value of the projected surface point, photometric stereo is then applied to estimate normal vector from all forward pixels. With both normal vector and location in object space determined, a forward pixel is now updated to be a base pixel. Propagation process is repeated until there are no valid pixels (pixel value > 0) in the image. A flow chart summarizing this algorithm is given in Fig. 13.4.

Note that for each frame in the image sequence, the proposed algorithm does not require any iteration process at pixel level or surface level. We also do not require expensive pre-computations, therefore we conclude our proposed algorithm yields better computational efficiency in comparison to other algorithms. Since photometric stereo is solved explicitly at each pixel location there no necessity to assume isotropic surface.

Propagation of the surface points for orthographic projected image assuming unit distance between surface points corresponding to two adjacent pixels, required us to

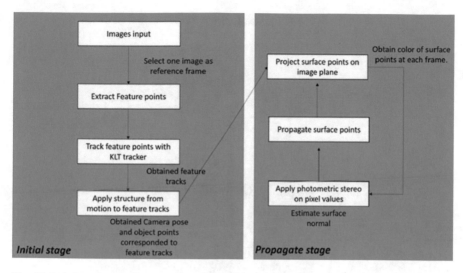

Fig. 13.4 A flow chart for proposed photometric stereo in motion algorithm

assume that surface slope remain constant in between two adjacent surface points:

$$z_{u+1,v} = z_{u,v} + \frac{\partial z_{u,v}}{\partial u} du \qquad (13.25)$$

Surface slope is recovered using sparse Eq. 13.19. During its application, the term n_z in normal vector can be close to zero and may lead to errors in computing the correct surface slope. When this condition occurs, the propagation process is stopped.

We assume unit distance between pixels, therefore $du = dv = 1$. Since this number does not indicate real displacement between surface points, reconstructed surface has scale ambiguity. Proposed method can sequentially update surface point location and surface point normal vector at each pixels from any pixel that has valid surface point and normal vector information. Note that this process is highly parallelizable and depth corresponding to various pixel patches may be inferred simultaneously.

13.5   Covariance Analysis

To predict the precision of reconstruction, a commonly used technique is to evaluate the uncertainty of estimated result by considering error and noise introduced from different sources. The method for computing error covariance in this research is based on sensitivity analysis of each participated algorithm.

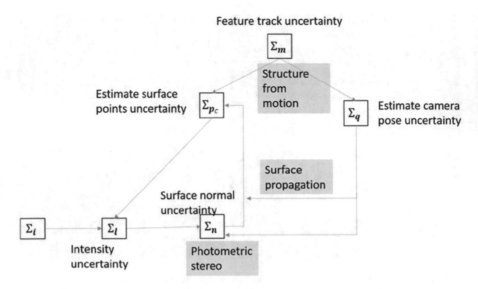

Fig. 13.5 Covariance analysis flowchart. Starting form the error covariance of feature track (Σ_m), it is propagated to the covariance of camera pose (Σ_q) and the covariance of initial surface point (Σ_{p_c}) through structure from motion method. Error covariance of the normal vector (Σ_n) is a function of the covariance of the measurement intensity (Σ_l), and covariance of the camera pose. Uncertainty of measured intensity is related to the image noise covariance (Σ_i), and error caused by projection of surface points on image plane. Uncertainty of surface points and normal vector is propagated toward other surface points through surface propagation process

Fig.13.5 is a roadmap for uncertainty propagation of proposed algorithms, that form a key element of the DDDAS. It illustrates propagation of uncertainty from one module to another. Since outputs of one algorithm form inputs to other algorithms, the uncertainty analysis can be inferred as the sensitivity of the algorithm's output with respect to input uncertainty. The remainder of this section derives the sensitivity analysis of each component, starting from raw sensor noise and ultimately compute the error covariance of reconstructed surface. Note that the error covariance of feature track, and Factorization's shape and motion matrix are derived in a parallel paper by the authors [39].

13.5.1 Raw Sensor Noise and the Intensity Uncertainty

Raw sensor noise includes image noise and the uncertainty associated with the uncertainty of the camera's intrinsic parameters. Orthographic projection model has image noise alone. Perspective projection model has uncertainties associated with both image and camera intrinsic parameters. Intrinsic parameter uncertainty may be obtained from the camera calibration process [4].

Image noise is measured with Immerkaer's method [17], which estimates the image noise variance by taking the difference of two Laplacian of the images. It can be shown that the estimation of noise using this method involves a convolution operation with the following kernel:

$$C = \begin{bmatrix} 1 & -2 & 1 \\ -2 & 4 & -2 \\ 1 & -2 & 1 \end{bmatrix} \tag{13.26}$$

A global image noise standard deviation is then compute by :

$$\sigma_i = \sqrt{\frac{\pi}{2}} \frac{1}{6(w-2)(h-2)} \sum |l(x,y) * C| \tag{13.27}$$

where w and h are the width and height of the image. To obtain local intensity variance, w and h with size of a local window are used. These calculations initialize the covariance analysis of subsequent image operations.

13.5.2   Covariance of the Normal Vector Estimates

Using our definition of modified photometric stereo, uncertainties of the estimated polar angle and azimuth angle are first computed. Covariance of the normal vector is then solved using these parameters. Eq. 13.16 therefore directly serves as the sensitivity of estimated parameters, with respect to the variation of intensity.

Other than intensity, estimation of normal vector and diffuse constant k_d also depend on light source direction. Light source direction corresponding to each frame is estimated from image frame orientation with respect to the reference frame. Since the light source depends on estimated value carrying uncertainty, it is also a random variable. It is necessary to compute the sensitivity of the estimated parameter with respect to the light source direction. Using Eq. 13.16 that solves for the sensitivity of the parameter with respect to the intensity variation, sensitivity with respect to the light source direction is calculated using following expressions:

$$\frac{\partial \mathbf{x}}{\partial \mathbf{w}_i} = \frac{\partial \mathbf{x}}{\partial |l|} \frac{\partial |l|}{\partial \mathbf{w}_i} \tag{13.28}$$

$$\frac{\partial |l|}{\partial \mathbf{w}_i} = k_d \mathbf{n} \tag{13.29}$$

$$\frac{\partial \mathbf{x}}{\partial |l|} = (H^T H)^{-1} H^T \tag{13.30}$$

where matrix H is the Jacobian matrix obtained using Eq. 13.18. Error covariance of the estimated surface's azimuth angle and polar angle, along with diffuse constant are then approximated using the following expression:

$$\Sigma_{\mathbf{x}} = \left[H \, \frac{\partial \mathbf{x}}{\partial \mathbf{w}_i} \right] \left[\begin{array}{cc} \Sigma_l & 0 \\ 0 & \Sigma_{\mathbf{w}_i} \end{array} \right] \left[H^T \, \frac{\partial \mathbf{x}}{\partial \mathbf{w}_i}^T \right]^T \tag{13.31}$$

where $\Sigma_{\mathbf{w}_i}$ is uncertainty covariance of light source direction and Σ_l is uncertainty covariance of measurement intensity. During the propagation phase, Σ_l will has to consider uncertainty caused by error in estimated camera frame orientation and error in the propagated surface depth. This is because we use this information to acquire the intensity by the back projection technique. Sensitivity of the intensity with respect to camera frame orientation and surface depth can be modeled by using local intensity gradient. However, since there is no guarantee that the projection error is small enough for approximating the local sensitivity information, we use an unscented transform [19] to approximate the intensity measurement uncertainty. We assume that there is an error in estimating the camera pose and the surface point location. It result in an error in the projection coordinates on the image plane and then causes subsequent error in intensity measurements. Since there is an intensity measurement corresponding to each image plane coordinate, the variance of measurement intensity can be measured as the intensity variation within a region bounded by an area specified by projected image plane location error. The projected image plane location error is estimated by first selecting a set of sigma points, and solving for their projected coordinates on the image. Bounding areas are computed as a rectangle with length equal to maximum distance between projected sigma points.

Light source direction is transformed by utilizing the rotational matrix $R^{(i)}$ at i^{th} frame. Since orientation of the camera is estimated through factorization, results from out recent research provide the corresponding estimation error covariance $\Sigma_{\mathbf{q}}$. Where, orientation of the camera at each frame is parametrized using the Classical Rodrigoues Parameters (CRP), $q = [q_1, q_2, q_3]^T$ [33]. The rotation matrix in terms of CRP is written as:

$$R = \frac{1}{\sqrt{1 + q^T q}} \begin{bmatrix} 1 + q_1^2 - q_2^2 - q_3^2 & 2(q_1 q_2 + q_3) & 2(q_1 q_3 - q_2) \\ 2(q_1 q_2 - q_3) & 1 - q_1^2 + q_2^2 - q_3^2 & 2(q_2 q_3 + q_1) \\ 2(q_1 q_3 + q_2) & 2(q_2 q_3 - q_1) & 1 - q_1^2 - q_2^2 + q_3^2 \end{bmatrix} \tag{13.32}$$

Each image frame is a measurement of object at different orientation. Collecting all n measurement frames into a vector $\mathbf{q}$:

$$\mathbf{q} = [q^{(1)}, q^{(2)}, ..., q^{(n)}] \tag{13.33}$$

where $q^{(j)}$ indicates the CRP of the jth frame. The light source direction $\mathbf{w}_i^{(n)}$ at each frame expressed in terms of the image space coordinate using the rotational matrix $R^{(n)}$ and light source direction expressend in the reference frame $w_i^{(0)}$ is written as:

$$\mathbf{w}_i^{(n)} = R^{(n)} \mathbf{w}_i^{(0)}$$

Substituting into Eq. 13.32 and taking partial derivatives leads to:

$$\frac{\partial w_{i,x}}{\partial q} = \frac{\partial}{\partial q} R_{11}(q) w_{i,x}^0 + \frac{\partial}{\partial q} R_{12}(q) w_{i,y}^0 + \frac{\partial}{\partial q} R_{13}(q) w_{i,z}^0 \tag{13.34}$$

$$\frac{\partial w_{i,y}}{\partial q} = \frac{\partial}{\partial q} R_{21}(q) w_{i,x}^0 + \frac{\partial}{\partial q} R_{22}(q) w_{i,y}^0 + \frac{\partial}{\partial q} R_{23}(q) w_{i,z}^0 \tag{13.35}$$

$$\frac{\partial w_{i,z}}{\partial q} = \frac{\partial}{\partial q} R_{31}(q) w_{i,x}^0 + \frac{\partial}{\partial q} R_{32}(q) w_{i,y}^0 + \frac{\partial}{\partial q} R_{33}(q) w_{i,z}^0 \tag{13.36}$$

The partial derivative of each rotation matrix elements with respect to CRPs are computed from Eq. 13.32. Error covariance of the light source direction is then propagated from the uncertainty of estimated camera orientation CRP using:

$$\Sigma_{\mathbf{w}_i} = \frac{\partial \mathbf{w}_i}{\partial q} \Sigma_q \frac{\partial \mathbf{w}_i}{\partial q}^T \tag{13.37}$$

where $\frac{\partial \mathbf{w}_i}{\partial q}$ is a matrix with each element computed from Eqs. 13.34 - 13.36, and Σ_q is computed from the uncertainty analysis of the corresponding camera pose estimation algorithm. Since the camera orientation at different frames may be assumed to be uncorrelated with each other, error covariance is computed independently for each frame.

Given the uncertainty in estimated normal vector's azimuth angle and polar angle, the normal vector uncertainty is compute from local sensitivity of Eq. 13.12 as:

$$\Sigma_{\mathbf{n}} = \begin{bmatrix} \frac{\partial \mathbf{n}}{\partial \Omega} & \frac{\partial \mathbf{n}}{\partial \xi} \end{bmatrix} \begin{bmatrix} \sigma_\Omega^2 & \sigma_{\Omega,\xi} \\ \sigma_{\Omega,\xi} & \sigma_\xi^2 \end{bmatrix} \begin{bmatrix} \frac{\partial \mathbf{n}}{\partial \Omega} & \frac{\partial \mathbf{n}}{\partial \xi} \end{bmatrix}^T \tag{13.38}$$

$$\frac{\partial \mathbf{n}}{\partial \Omega} = \begin{bmatrix} sin(\xi)cos(\Omega) & cos(\xi)cos(\Omega) & sin(\Omega) \end{bmatrix}$$

$$\frac{\partial \mathbf{n}}{\partial \xi} = \begin{bmatrix} cos(\xi)sin(\Omega) & -sin(\xi)sin(\Omega) & 0 \end{bmatrix}$$

where σ_Ω and σ_ξ are the standard deviations of the estimated polar angle and azimuth angle. Since they correlated, the correlation term $\sigma_{\Omega,\xi}$ does not equal to zero, these elements are extracted from Σ_X computed by Eq. 13.31. Note that when

$\Omega = 0$, we do not have an estimate of ξ and therefore we assume normal vector in this case is not a function of ξ, such that term $\frac{\partial \mathbf{n_x}}{\partial \xi}$ is equal to zero.

13.5.3 Error Covariance of The Surface Points

As outlined in the introduction, our reconstruction process uses the estimates of the normal vectors to propagate the surface points in order to estimate a densely reconstructed surface. Surface points propagation of orthographic configuration only solve for depth, while coordinate along x and y direction are deterministic. The propagation of surface depth along the x direction leads to the following equation:

$$z_{u+1,v} = z_{u,v} + \frac{n_x}{n_z}$$

Sensitivity of the propagated depth is solved using:

$$\delta z_{u+1,v} = \begin{bmatrix} 1 & \frac{1}{n_z} & -\frac{n_x}{n_z^2} \end{bmatrix} \begin{bmatrix} \delta z_{u,v} & \delta n_x & \delta n_z \end{bmatrix}^T \tag{13.39}$$

Error estimate of the depth can thus be computed using the covariance written as:

$$\sigma_{z,u+1,v}^2 = \begin{bmatrix} 1 & \frac{1}{n_z} & -\frac{n_x}{n_z^2} \end{bmatrix} \begin{bmatrix} \sigma_{z,u,v}^2 & 0 & 0 \\ 0 & \sigma_{n,x}^2 & \sigma_{n,xz} \\ 0 & \sigma_{n,xz} & \sigma_{n,z}^2 \end{bmatrix} \begin{bmatrix} 1 \\ \frac{1}{n_z} \\ -\frac{n_x}{n_z^2} \end{bmatrix} \tag{13.40}$$

where the elements $\sigma_{n,x}^2$, $\sigma_{n,xz}$, and $\sigma_{n,z}^2$ of Eq. 13.40 are computed from estimated normal vector error covariance calculations outlined earlier.

Estimation of the error covariance not only serves as a measure of estimation accuracy, but may also be used as criteria for terminating the surface propagation process. Estimated covariance is computed following the surface point location and normal vector carried out for each pixel. Therefore, uncertainty estimates are available during the propagation process. Since surface propagation is a numerical integration process, error in previous step is accumulated to subsequent steps. In order to avoid propagating error into the future that leads to larger error, propagation process on a surface points may be terminated when the error covariance exceeds certain threshold.

13.6 Simulation and Experiment

Experimental measurement data sets to evaluate the proposed algorithms are generated by using a ray tracer based imaging engine called Space Object Light Attribute Rendering (SOLAR) System. This SOLAR system allows us to implement physically plausible reflectance models of object's surface, along with physical optical systems for realistic camera projection and image formation emulations. The SOLAR system is based on an in-house ray tracing engine. Inter-reflection, light refraction, optical elements modeling, etc are implemented as software blocks in the renderer. Since ray tracer renders a scene by explicitly tracing the path of light incident on each pixel of camera from the scene, it is computationally expensive when compared to commonly used rasterization techniques applied in computer graphics engines such as OpenGL [28] and DirectX [10]. However, ray tracer engine is more suitable for applications, where physically consistent image formation is important over real time rendering. Therefore, we utilize this engine to generate measurement data for demonstration of our algorithms that utilize space application.

Measurement data sets from two object models are synthesized for demonstration purposes. Itokawa asteroid model [3] is rendered to provide measurements of natural space object with diffuse surface. Apollo-Soyuz [5] spacecraft model is implemented to provide measurements of a high specular man-made object with surface discontinuity. Itokawa model has richer surface feature in comparison to the Apollo model. This allows factorization method to has better performance on Itokawa model. In case of the Apollo model, we assume the existence of painted fiducials on the surface, such that it is able to provide some feature points over a large but smooth surface. Each of the object models are rendered under three different conditions to evaluate the performance of the proposed algorithms. First, both objects are rendered with pure Lambertian model and relative motion between camera and object is held stationary. Subsequent emulation scenario renders both Apollo and Itokawa models using pure Lambertian model, while camera-object relative motion is not stationary to evaluate the performance of proposed photometric stereo in motion algorithms. For third set of experiments, we use the Oren-Nayar model [29] to render the Itokawa model and generate its synthetic measurement. The Apollo model is rendering with Torrance-Sparrow model [37]. Both of these models are considered as physically plausible reflectance model. While the Oren-Nayar model is a diffuse reflection model for rough surfaces, Torrance-Sparrow is a specular reflection model. This experiment is to evaluate the performance of proposed algorithms when using Lambertian model to approximate more complex and realistic light reflection.

A focused Newtonian telescope model without lens aberrations is implemented in the SOLAR system as the optics attached to the camera to validate assumption of orthographic projection.

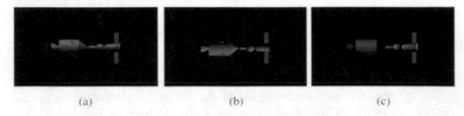

(a)   (b)   (c)

Fig. 13.6 3 out of 10 measurements of Apollo model, (a) $\mathbf{w}_i = [0, 0.707107, 0.707107]$, (b) $\mathbf{w}_i = [0.353553, -0.612372, 0.707107]$, (c) $\mathbf{w}_i = [-0.612372, 0.353553, 0.707107]$

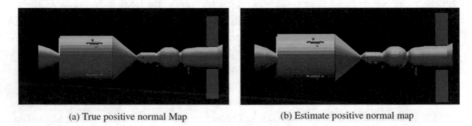

(a) True positive normal Map   (b) Estimate positive normal map

Fig. 13.7 A comparison of true positive normal map and photometric stereo estimate positive normal map

13.6.1 Stationary Observation of Lambertian Surface

We use the case of no relative motion between the observer and the object to provide a base line understanding of photometric stereo performance when ideal conditions are satisfied perfectly (i.e., stationary relative pose during measurement, light source direction at each frame is perfectly known and object is isotropic Lambertian surface). It is assumed that the object is located at inertia frame origin, with the camera frame's negative z axis pointing toward the object centroid. It is assumed that the light source is initially oriented along the direction of $\mathbf{w}_{i,0} = [0, 0.707, 0.707]$ and rotated about z axis for 2π rad over 10 frames.

Three out of ten measurements of Apollo model are shown in Fig. 13.6.

Since camera-object relative pose remains constant throughout measurement sequence, we can directly implement photometric stereo to estimate normal vector at each pixel. A collection of normal vectors for each pixel is stored as a normal map. The normal vectors are colored by following the Blue-Green-Red (BGR) color channel scheme for visualization purposes. Values in x direction are plotted as blue, while the values in y and z directions are plotted in green and red, respectively. The intensity of each color is the magnitude of normal vector component. Since colors do not have negative value, we plot a positive normal map that plots only the positive component in a normal vector (Fig. 13.7), and a negative normal map that plot only the negative components of a normal vector (Fig. 13.8).

For better comparison between estimate and true normal map, we define an error function that governs the error between the two normal vector as 1 minus the

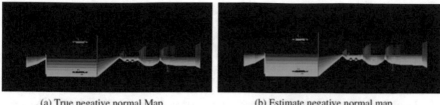

(a) True negative normal Map   (b) Estimate negative normal map

Fig. 13.8 A comparison of true negative normal map and photometric stereo estimate negative normal map

Fig. 13.9 Normal vector estimation error map

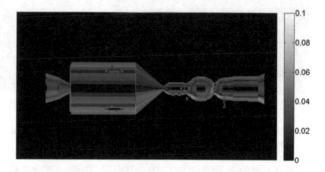

absolute value of dot product of estimate normal vector, $\mathbf{n}_{est}$ and true normal, $\mathbf{n}_t$:

$$e = 1 - |\mathbf{n}_{est} \cdot \mathbf{n}_t| \qquad (13.41)$$

Error of estimated normal vector computed by Eq. 13.41 are visualized as color map in Fig. 13.9. A visual inspection of the error color map shows that the maximum error is about 0.08 located at regions near the edges of the object. It also shows that the surfaces that are oriented along the camera bore-sight have small errors. This experiment result demonstrates that under the ideal conditions, photometric stereo is able to provide good estimates of the surface normal.

Estimation of surface geometry in this experiment is accomplished by integrating surface normal along the surface, starting from an arbitrary initial point with a positive surface depth value.

Fig. 13.10 shows estimated surface for the various view of the Apollo model. From these plots, we can infer that the surface estimated from the normal map integration can provide accurate results in areas with smaller surface discontinuities. Automated means of detecting continuous region in an image remains a research challenge.

Following a similar procedure, we have the estimated normal map for Itokawa model. The normal maps are shown in Figs. 13.11 - 13.12.

Normal vector error map is plotted in Fig. 13.13. It is evident that the error levels are equivalent to those of the Apollo model.

Fig. 13.10 Estimated object surface through normal map integration at different view directions

(a) True positive normal Map   (b) Estimate positive normal map

Fig. 13.11 A comparison of true positive normal map and photometric stereo estimated positive normal map

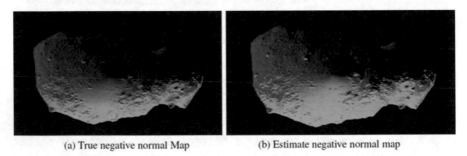

(a) True negative normal Map   (b) Estimate negative normal map

Fig. 13.12 A comparison of true negative normal map and photometric stereo estimated negative normal map

Fig. 13.14 are snapshots of various views of the estimate surface of Itokawa computed by integrating surface normal map. Estimate surface is poorer than that of the Apollo due to the lack of observability of surface normal at different locations along the edge. On the other hand, estimated Itokawa surface does not suffer from errors caused by surface discontinuity.

Experimental results of this section show that traditional photometric stereo is able to provide good estimates of the surface normal. Surface geometry is then estimated by integrating the estimated surface normal to produce an model for surface geometry.

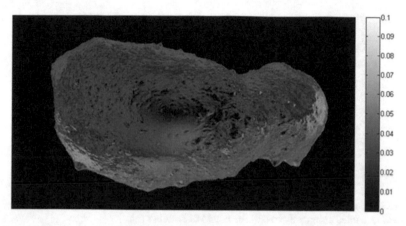

Fig. 13.13 Normal vector estimation error map

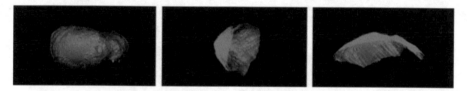

Fig. 13.14 Estimated object surface through normal map integration along different view points

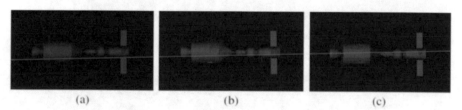

(a)   (b)   (c)

Fig. 13.15 3 out of 50 measurements of Apollo model in motion. (a) $\mathbf{w}_c = [0, 0.0, -1]$, (b) $\mathbf{w}_c = [-0.1508, -0.1431, -0.9781]$, (c)$\mathbf{w}_c = [0.1525, 0.1025, -0.9830]$

13.6.2   Observation of Lambertian Surface From Non-Stationary View Point

When relative motion between camera and object is no longer stationary, traditional photometric stereo is not directly applicable. This experiment is to evaluate performance of our photometric stereo in motion approach under assumption that the surface reflectance is Lambertian in nature.

Figs. 13.15 show 3 out of 50 measurements of Apollo model. Illumination direction is aligned with view direction in this case because light source is assumed to be affixed in the camera frame. Note that this assumption is not necessary and that the light source direction is free to move around. Set of feature points extracted by

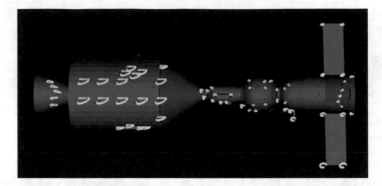

Fig. 13.16 Feature tracks as input to structure from motion method, red ellipse at the end of each track are estiamted uncertainty covariance bound of feature track

Fig. 13.17 A comparison of factorization estimated camera orientation (red dot) and true camera orientation(blue dot) after translated into view direction relative to object

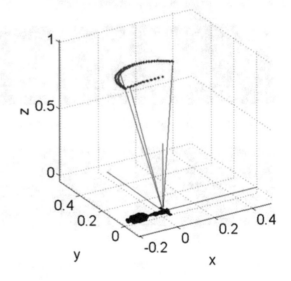

SIFT and tracked by KLT tracker in this case are plotted as yellow dots in Fig. 13.16. The red ellipse located at the end of each feature track in Fig. 13.16 are estimated feature track error covariance bound of last feature point in a track. Theses are computed using methods developed by the authors in a related recent research [39].

Feature tracks are supplied to the Factorization algorithm for computing relative pose of each frame. To demonstrate the performance of Factorization, a comparison of estimated orientation with respect to the true camera orientation is shown in Fig. 13.17. Each red and blue dot plotted in Fig. 13.17 indicate the view direction from camera to the object plotted in object fixed frame. This plot shows that factorization method is able to estimate camera orientation with reasonably accuracy.

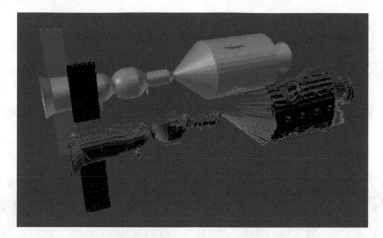

Fig. 13.18 A side to side comparison of estimated space craft surface(front) to true object surface(back). A scaling parameter determined empirically is applied to the estimated surface so that we can compare the estimated surface and true surface in same scale

Using the initial condition provided by the Factorization method, we use the method developed in this work to estimate a surface and normal map for the Apollo model. Estimation results are rendered in Figs. 13.18 - 13.20.

Estimated surface in Fig. 13.18 shows that proposed method can provide a reasonable estimate of the surface geometry. Estimation errors incurred in Fig. 13.18 are relatively large when compared to result in Fig. 13.10. This is attributed to the fact that the proposed method works under the non ideal conditions, where the original photometric stereo are not applicable. The reconstructed surface also shows that the proposed method is able to resolve the surface discontinuity issue by making use of additional information from motion alignment of matching pixel patches.

A comparison of estimated normal vectors in Figs. 13.19 -13.20 demonstrates that estimation of surface normal is generally accurate over a large fraction of the surface. Large errors in surface normal estimation occur near the edge of surface segments. This is caused by the error in object points to image projection as the variation of intensity near such region are large, owing to poor observability of depth in orthographic projection.

In addition to the estimation of surface geometry and surface normals, we also derive methods to compute the covariance associated with both the estimates. For visualization purposes, estimation error variance is first translated to standard deviation, and plotted as a color map. In case of the normal vector uncertainty, a direction map and a magnitude map are plotted separately. The direction map indicates the distribution of error in x, y, and z direction within a normal vector. A magnitude map is used to indicate the magnitude of uncertainty of corresponded pixel. Since surface depth is a scalar variable, the surface depth standard deviation map only plots the estimated standard deviation of surface depth value.

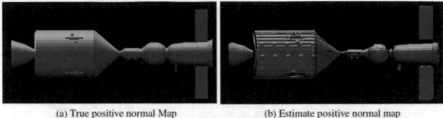

(a) True positive normal Map   (b) Estimate positive normal map

Fig. 13.19 A comparison of true positive normal map and estimated positive normal map

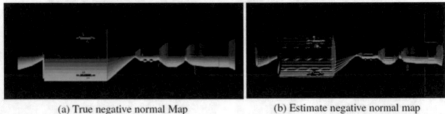

(a) True negative normal Map   (b) Estimate negative normal map

Fig. 13.20 A comparison of true negative normal map and estimated negative normal map

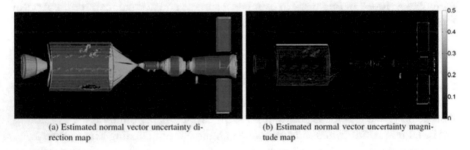

(a) Estimated normal vector uncertainty di-   (b) Estimated normal vector uncertainty magni-
rection map   tude map

Fig. 13.21 Estimated normal vector uncertainty standard deviation (a) direction map (b) magnitude map

Fig. 13.21 shows the estimated standard deviation of the estimated normal vector. The direction map indicates that a large fraction of the uncertainty in estimated normal vector is distributed along the direction with minimum magnitude. While the magnitude map indicates large estimation error are concentrated around region closed to the edge. This is equivalent to loss of observability and similar to Fig. 13.22. Fig. 13.22 is the estimated standard deviation of the surface depth estimates, patch like distribution of surface depth uncertainty correpond to pixel patches used by the depth estimation algorithm. A poor starting solution depth therefore is propagated to the patch that is computed from that solution.

After examining the performance of the proposed algorithm on a man-made object, we now repeat the experiments on Itokawa asteroid that represents natural space object without surface discontinuity. Three out of a total of 50 input images

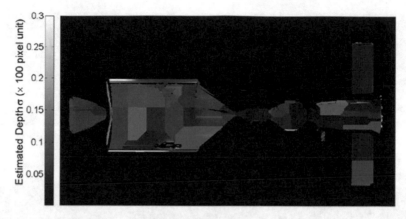

Fig. 13.22 Estimate surface depth standard deviation map

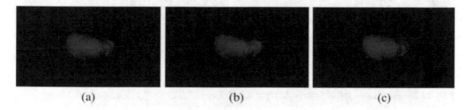

(a)   (b)   (c)

Fig. 13.23 3 out of 50 measurements of Itokawa model in motion. (a) $\mathbf{w}_c = [0, 0.0, -1]$, (b) $\mathbf{w}_c = [-0.1508, -0.1431, -0.9781]$, (c) $\mathbf{w}_c = [0.1525, 0.1025, -0.9830]$

Fig. 13.24 A side to side comparison of empirically scaled Itokawa surface estimates (front) with true object surface (back)

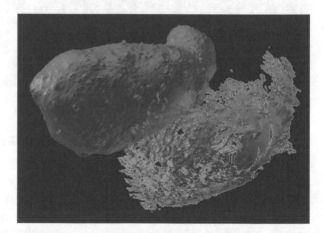

for Itokawa experiment are shown in Fig. 13.23. Estimated Itokawa surface is shown in Fig. 13.24.

Comparing the estimated surface of Itokawa through proposed method in Fig. 13.24 and from original photometric stereo in Fig. 13.10, we see that estimation result in case of the motion stereo algorithm is actually better. This can be attributed

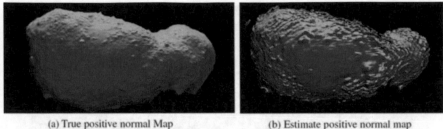

(a) True positive normal Map   (b) Estimate positive normal map

Fig. 13.25 A comparison of true positive normal map and estimated positive normal map

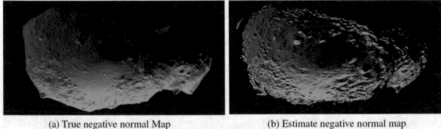

(a) True negative normal Map   (b) Estimate negative normal map

Fig. 13.26 A comparison of true negative normal map and estimated negative normal map

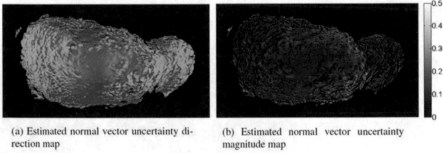

(a) Estimated normal vector uncertainty di-   (b) Estimated normal vector uncertainty
rection map   magnitude map

Fig. 13.27 Standard diviation of the estimated normal vector(a) direction map (b) magnitude map

to the use of large number of observations that yield better observability and improved imaging geometry. This experiment also shows that the concept of using multiple initial surface points estimated from structure from motion method, and then propagated for constructing a dense surface with photometric stereo is indeed feasible.

A comparison of estimation results in Figs. 13.25 - 13.26 shows that the estimation of normal vector with proposed approach fairs better for semi-convex geometries that have contiguous regions. Estimated uncertainties result are graphically rendered in Figs. 13.27 - 13.28.

Fig. 13.28 Estimate surface depth standard deviation map

This set of experiments demonstrate the application of the proposed algorithm in estimating the surface geometry of both man-made and natural objects. Experimental results indicate that performance of proposed approach on a continuous surface is better than performance on a surface with discontinuities. These algorithms demonstrate optimism as elements of the INFORM framework to derive RSO shape estimates as a part of the DDDAS for SSA applications.

13.6.3   Observation of Non-Lambertian Surface From Non-Stationary View Point

After demonstrating the utility of the proposed algorithms in reconstructing the Lambert surface, we now move on to evaluate the performance of proposed algorithm in reconstruction of non-Lambertian surface.

Man-made space objects are usually coated with materials that have high reflectance in order to reflect heat from radiation. Based on this fact, it is natural to assume that most of the man-made space objects have high specular reflection. Therefore, their reflectance should be modeled with specular reflection models. Torrance-Sparrow is considered a physics based specular reflectance model, although it is not as comprehensive as other methods such as HTSG model [12].

Given a set of measurements of Apollo model rendered by Torrance Sparrow model in Fig. 13.29, it is desired to estimate the shape of the object of interest. Direct application of the photometric stereo on measurements with specular component will result large error in the estimated normal vector. Therefore, measurements with specular components will need to be removed before the estimation of the normal vector. Since the specular reflection is concentrated around specular peak direction, when there are sufficient number of measurements, the specular component can

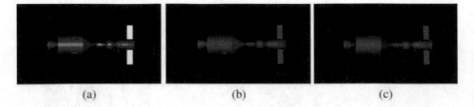

(a)   (b)   (c)

Fig. 13.29 3 out of 100 measurements of Apollo model in motion, (a) specular component is clearly brighter than diffuse component. (b-c) specular component is not captured because camera direction is off from specular peak direction

Fig. 13.30 A side to side comparison of empirically scaled estimate Apollo surface (front) to true object surface (back) with measurement rendered with Torrance Sparrow model

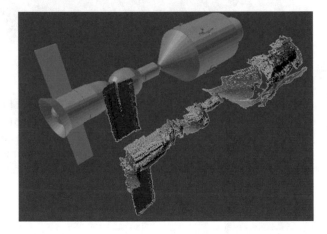

be removed as outliers. In this experiment, we use RANdom SAmple Consensus (RANSAC) algorithm [8] to search for outlier measurements with specular component and reject them. A downside of using RANSAC is that large amount of measurements are required in order to detect specular reflection. Therefore, we increase the number of image measurements to 100 frames in this experiment. Once the measurements with specular reflections are removed, remaining images are assumed to be purely diffuse and photometric stereo in motion algorithm is applied to estimate the surface geometry.

Figs. 13.30 - 13.34 are the depth estimation results of the Apollo model from measurements with specular reflection. Reconstruction shows that the estimation result is relatively poor in comparison to the estimates obtained from the idealized case where the reflectance is a pure Lambertian surface. This is because RANSAC cannot remove all the measurement hypotheses that have specularity. Developing a better method to remove specular reflection has been a active study in the research community. Methods such as SUV color space transform [26] and specular free image [35] are developed for this purpose. However, most of these methods require color information. Man-made spacecraft are typically textureless and theses methods are not directly applicable. Currently, removing specular with RANSAC remains the most popular method that applicable to general surface.

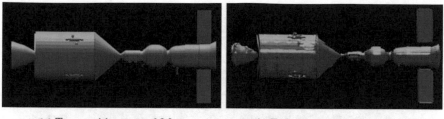

(a) True positive normal Map   (b) Estimate positive normal map

Fig. 13.31 A comparison of true positive normal map and estimated positive normal map

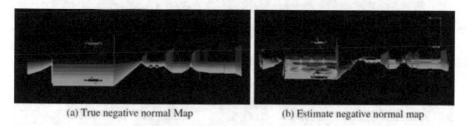

(a) True negative normal Map   (b) Estimate negative normal map

Fig. 13.32 A comparison of true negative normal map and estimated negative normal map

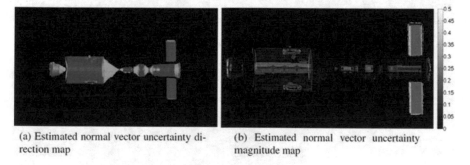

(a) Estimated normal vector uncertainty di-   (b) Estimated normal vector uncertainty
rection map   magnitude map

Fig. 13.33 Standard deviation of the estimated normal vectors uncertainty (a) direction map (b) magnitude map

Natural space objects such as asteroid generally have a relatively diffuse surface, while carrying weak directional reflection properties like specular reflection. Oren-Nayar model [29] is a diffuse model that is developed to model such weak directionally diffuse reflection on a rough surface. Lambertian can serve as an approximation to Oren-Nayar surface when surface roughness is removed. Therefore, we are directly supplying measurement generated from Oren-Nayar model into proposed algorithm for surface estimation.

Figs. 13.35 shows a subset of input images for Itokawa model rendered from Oren-Nayar model. Estimation result obtained by using this data set is shown in Fig. 13.36 - 13.40.

Fig. 13.34 Estimate surface depth standard deviation map

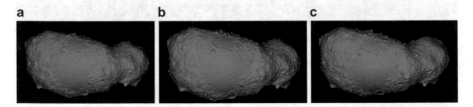

Fig. 13.35 3 out of 50 measurements of Itokawa model rendered by Oren Nayar model

Fig. 13.36 A side to side
comparison of empirically
scaled Itokawa surface
estimates (front) with true
object surface (back) with
measurement rendered with
Oren-Nayar model

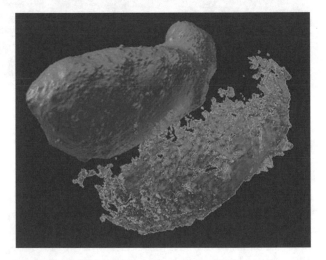

Results of estimation of the surface of the Itokawa model rendered with
Oren-Nayar reflectance model show that its estimation accuracy is as good as measurement rendered with Lambertian model. The fact that the model reconstruction
operations using the algorithms developed here are modestly robust to reflectance

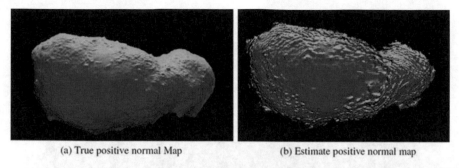

(a) True positive normal Map

(b) Estimate positive normal map

Fig. 13.37 A comparison of true positive normal map and the estimated positive normal map

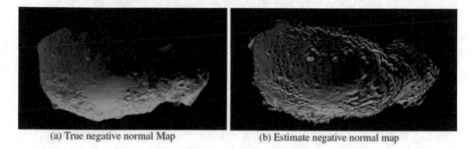

(a) True negative normal Map

(b) Estimate negative normal map

Fig. 13.38 A comparison of true negative normal map and the estimated negative normal map

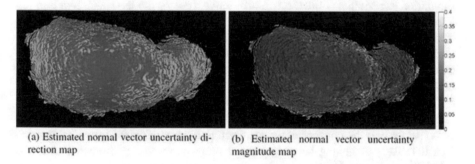

(a) Estimated normal vector uncertainty direction map

(b) Estimated normal vector uncertainty
magnitude map

Fig. 13.39 Estimated normal vector uncertainty standard deviation (**a**) direction map (**b**) magnitude map

model forms a basis of optimism towards the applicability of the proposed approach to reconstruct the surfaces of weekly specular object from image data. Since the true reflectance characteristics are generally unknown, the approaches discussed here-in as a part of the DDDAS for SSA applications seems promising.

Fig. 13.40 Estimate surface depth standard deviation map

13.7 Conclusion

A photometric stereopsis in motion approach for space object dense surface reconstruction based on structure from motion and photometric stereo is discussed in this chapter. It forms an integral component of the RSO shape estimation algorithms in an innovative INFORM framework that is DDDAS for SSA applications. Emulation experiments utilizing two different geometry models, each representing a man-made and natural RSO are used to demonstrate the utility of photometric stereopsis algorithms under non-ideal illumination, surface reflectance and relative motion conditions. Experimental results show that the algorithms discussed are capable of providing valid surface geometry estimates even when the assumption of diffuse surface is not exactly valid. It is shown that the use of photometry for shape estimation provides an alternative to textured based stereopsis solutions that fail to produce any reconstruction in bland surfaces. Experiment results also demonstrate that the concept of using structure from motion for initialization, and then iteratively switching between surface propagation and photometric stereo is a feasible approach for dense surface reconstruction when relative motion exists between the object and the observer.

Acknowledgements This work is based upon work supported by the AFOSR grant FA9550-15-1-0313. Drs. Erik P. Blasch, Sai Ravella and Frederica Darema are acknowledged for the technical discussions. The authors are also grateful to the inputs of the anonymous reviewers. Their inputs enhanced the quality of the chapter extensively.

References

1. Ackermann J, Langguth F, Fuhrmann S, Goesele M (2012) Photometric stereo for outdoor webcams. In: Computer Vision and Pattern Recognition (CVPR), 2012 IEEE Conference on, pp 262–269, doi:10.1109/CVPR.2012.6247684
2. Alldrin N, Kriegman D (2007) Toward reconstructing surfaces with arbitrary isotropic reflectance : A stratified photometric stereo approach. In: Computer Vision, 2007. ICCV 2007. IEEE 11th International Conference on, pp 1–8, doi:10.1109/ICCV.2007.4408881
3. Barnouin O, Kahn H E (2012) Amica images with geometry backplanes v1.0. hay-a-amica-3-amicageom-v1.0. =http://sbn.psi.edu/pds/resource/amicageom.html
4. Bouguet J Y (2004) Camera calibration toolbox for matlab
5. Carbajal M (2009) Apollo soyuz. URL http://http://nasa3d.arc.nasa.gov/detail/apollo-soyuz-c
6. Cavanaugh JF, Smith JC, Sun X, Bartels AE, Ramos-Izquierdo L, Krebs DJ, McGarry JE, Trunzo R, Novo-Gradac AM, Britt JL, et al (2007) The mercury laser altimeter instrument for the messenger mission. In: The Messenger Mission to Mercury, Springer, pp 451–479
7. Crassidis JL, Junkins JL (2011) Optimal estimation of dynamic systems. CRC press
8. Fischler MA, Bolles RC (1981) Random sample consensus: A paradigm for model fitting with applications to image analysis and automated cartography. Commun ACM 24(6):381–395, doi:10.1145/358669.358692, URL http://doi.acm.org/10.1145/358669.358692
9. Frankot RT, Chellappa R (1988) A method for enforcing integrability in shape from shading algorithms. Pattern Analysis and Machine Intelligence, IEEE Transactions on 10(4):439–451
10. Gray K (2003) Microsoft DirectX 9 programmable graphics pipeline. Microsoft Press
11. Hartley R, Zisserman A (2003) Multiple view geometry in computer vision. Cambridge university press
12. He XD, Torrance KE, Sillion FX, Greenberg DP (1991) A comprehensive physical model for light reflection. In: Proceedings of the 18th annual conference on Computer Graphics and interactive techniques
13. Hernandez C, Vogiatzis G, Cipolla R (2008) Multiview potometric stereo. IEEE Transaction on Pattern Analysis and Machine Interlligence 30(3)
14. Higo T, Matsushita Y, Joshi N, Ikeuchi K (2009) A hand-held photometric stereo camera for 3-d modeling. In: Computer Vision, 2009 IEEE 12th International Conference on, pp 1234–1241, doi:10.1109/ICCV.2009.5459331
15. Horn B (1975) Obtaining Shape From Shading Information. McGraw-Hill New York
16. Horn BK, Brooks MJ (1986) The variational approach to shape from shading. Computer Vision, Graphics, and Image Processing 33(2):174–208
17. Immerkaer J (1996) Fast noise variance estimation. Computer vision and image understanding 64(2):300–302
18. Jia B, Pham KD, Blasch E, Shen D, Wang Z, Chen G (2016) Cooperative space object tracking using space-based optical sensors via consensus-based filters,. IEEE Transactions on Aerospace and Electronic Systems 52(3):1908–1936
19. Julier SJ, Uhlmann JK (1997) New extension of the kalman filter to nonlinear systems. In: AeroSense'97, International Society for Optics and Photonics, pp 182–193
20. Klette R, Schluens K (1996) Height data from gradient maps. In: Photonics East'96, International Society for Optics and Photonics, pp 204–215
21. Lim J, Ho J, Yang MH, Kriegman D (2005) Passive photometric stereo from motion. In: Computer Vision, 2005. ICCV 2005. Tenth IEEE International Conference on, vol 2, pp 1635–1642 Vol. 2, doi:10.1109/ICCV.2005.185
22. Liu Z, Wan W, Peng M, Zhao Q, Xu B, Liu B, Liu Y, Di K, Li L, Yu T, Wang B, Zhou J, Chen H (2014) Remote sensing mapping and localization techniques for teleoperation of chang'e-3 rover. Journal of Remote Sensing 18(5)
23. Lowe D (1999) Object recognition from local scale-invariant features. In: Computer Vision, 1999. The Proceedings of the Seventh IEEE International Conference on, vol 2, pp 1150–1157 vol.2, doi:10.1109/ICCV.1999.790410

24. Lucas BD, Kanade T (1981) An iterative image registration technique with an application to stereo vision. IJCAI 81
25. M P, K D, Z L (2014) Adaptive markov random field model for dense matching of deep space stereo images. Journal of Remote Sensing 18(1)
26. Mallick SP, Zickler TE, Kriegman DJ, Belhumeur PN (2005) Beyond lambert : Reconstructing specular surface using color. In: Computer Vision and Pattern Recognition, IEEE
27. McEwen AS (1991) Photometric functions for photoclinometry and other applications. Icarus 92(2):298–311
28. OpenGL A, Woo M, Neider J, Davis T (1999) Opengl programming guide. Addison-Wesley
29. Oren M, Nayar SK (1994) Generalization of lambert's reflectance model. In: Proceedings of 21st annual conference on Computer Graphics and Interactive Technique, ACM
30. Pharr M, Humphreys G (2004) Physically based rendering: From theory to implementation. Morgan Kaufmann
31. Raskar R, Tan KH, Feris R, Yu J, Turk M (2004) Non-photorealistic camera: depth edge detection and stylized rendering using multi-flash imaging. In: ACM Transactions on Graphics (TOG), ACM, pp 679–688
32. Scharstein D, Szeliski R (2002) A taxonomy and evaluation of dense two-frame stereo correspondence algorithms. International journal of computer vision 47(1-3):7–42
33. Schaub H, Junkins JL (2003) Analytical mechanics of space systems. Aiaa
34. Seitz SM, Curless B, Diebel J, Scharstein D, Szeliski R (2006) A comparison and evaluation of multi-view stereo reconstruction algorithms. In: Computer vision and pattern recognition, 2006 IEEE Computer Society Conference on, IEEE
35. Tan RT, Nishino K, Ikeuchi K (2004) Separating reflection component based on chromaticity and noise analysis. IEEE transactions on Pattern Analysis and Machine Intelligence 26(10)
36. Tomasi C, Kanade T (1992) Shape and motion from image streams under orthography: a factorization method. International Journal of Computer Vision 9(2)
37. Torrance KE, Sparrow EM (1967) Theory for off-specular reflection from roughened surface. Journal of the Optical Society of America 57(9)
38. Wang Y, Bu J, Li N, Song M, Tan P (2012) Detecting discontinuities for surface reconstruction. In: Pattern Recognition (ICPR), 2012 21st International Conference on, IEEE, pp 2108–2111
39. XueIuan Wong MM (2016) An efficient method for klt-tracker uncertainty quantification and its application. Image and vision computing (Under Review)
40. Yu LF, Yeung SK, Tai YW, Terzopoulos D, Chan T (2013) Outdoor photometric stereo. In: Computational Photography (ICCP), 2013 IEEE International Conference on, pp 1–8, doi:10.1109/ICCPhot.2013.6528306
41. Zhou Z, Wu Z, Tan P (2013) Multi-view photometric stereo with spatially varying isotropic materials. In: Computer Vision and Pattern Recognition (CVPR), 2013 IEEE Conference on, IEEE, pp 1482–1489

Part V
Situation Aware: Tracking Methods

Chapter 14
Aided Optimal Search: Data-Driven Target Pursuit from On-Demand Delayed Binary Observations

Luca Carlone, Allan Axelrod, Sertac Karaman, and Girish Chowdhary

Abstract We consider the following search problem: an autonomous robot (the *searcher*) needs to locate and reach a *target* moving in a field scattered with *Unattended Ground Sensors* (UGS). The searcher has very limited information about the target: (i) it has an initial distribution (the *prior*) describing the probability of the target being at a given location at the initial time, and (ii) it can interrogate nearby sensors; each sensor records a binary measurement, describing whether or not the target passed in the proximity of the sensor at some point in time. Then the goal for the searcher is to estimate the trajectory of the target, and plan a maneuver that allows reducing the uncertainty about the current target state. We refer to this problem as *aided optimal search*, in that the search process is aided by an external infrastructure (the ground sensors). The paper adopts a *Dynamic Data-Driven Appplications Systems* (DDDAS) paradigm, in which the data collected by the searcher is used to update the belief on the trajectory of the target, and the searcher actively steers the measurement process to improve its knowledge about the location of the target. In particular, we make two main contributions. The first regards the target trajectory estimation. We show how to perform optimal Bayesian inference from binary measurements using a Gaussian Mixture Model (GMM). One of the main insights is that parameterizing the GMM in the information filter (inverse covariance) form allows huge computational savings: the information matrix of each mixture component is a very sparse (block-tridiagonal) matrix, which allows us to deal with a GMM with thousands of components in a fraction of a second. The second contribution regards planning: we propose a Mixed-Integer Programming (MIP) approach to plan the optimal searcher path, which minimizes the uncertainty about the position of the target. The key idea here is the use of sampling to decouple the complexity of the MIP from the length of the trajectory of

L. Carlone (✉) · S. Karaman
Massachusetts Institute of Technology, Cambridge, MA, USA
e-mail: lcarlone@mit.edu; sertac@mit.edu

A. Axelrod · G. Chowdhary
Coordinated Science Lab, University of Illinois at Urbana-Champaign, Urbana, IL, USA
e-mail: allanma@okstate.edu; girishc@illinois.edu

© The Author(s), under exclusive license to Springer Nature Switzerland AG 2022
E. P. Blasch et al. (eds.), *Handbook of Dynamic Data Driven Applications Systems*,
https://doi.org/10.1007/978-3-030-74568-4_14

the target. We demonstrate the proposed strategy in extensive simulations, reporting statistics about success rate and computational time for different scenarios and target motion models. The proposed search strategy largely outperforms greedy strategies (e.g., visiting the most likely target position).

Keywords Optimal search · Dynamic target pursuit · Pursuit evasion · Multimodal estimation · Trajectory estimation · Unattended ground sensors · Sensor networks · Gaussian mixture model · Sparse Gaussian mixture model · Bayesian estimation · Mixed-integer programming · Trajectory smoothing

14.1 Introduction

Unmanned robots are being widely adopted for social and civil applications. Unmanned Aerial Vehicles (UAVs), for instance, are finding applications in monitoring and surveillance, disaster response, inspection, precision agriculture, and entertainment. The motivations behind the use of these vehicles are manifold: they are small, agile, and relatively inexpensive. Moreover, in military applications, UAVs enable the human operator to lead the mission without being exposed to unnecessary risks. In most of the mentioned applications, however, the UAV is teleoperated, i.e., the human operator supplies low level controls to guide the robot, which has very limited autonomy. A higher degree of autonomy would be very desirable, in order to alleviate the workload on the human operator, to reduce the amount of training needed to operate the vehicles, and to unleash applications involving the simultaneous use of multiple robots.

This paper pushes the boundary of autonomous operation in a *search* task: an autonomous robot (the *searcher*) needs to search for and reach a *target* moving in a field scattered with *Unattended Ground Sensors* (UGS). In order to complete this task, the searcher has to collect information about the motion of the target, and has to exercise decision making to decide on the best search strategy. The search task has important applications in a *Urban Search and Rescue* (USAR) setting, where the goal is to locate and provide support to a victim as quickly as possible. Other applications include tracking of ground vehicles in a road network using UAVs [2, 59], and intruder detection and tracking in security scenarios.

Target search is a *data-driven task*: while in principle it is possible to carefully model the dynamics of the target, the uncertainty in the model structure and parameters would lead to a quick error accumulation between the predicted and the actual target location. The only way to reduce this uncertainty is to collect sensor data about the state of the target. In this sense, our search problem must be addressed within the DDDAS paradigm [27, 28], since it requires integrating prior knowledge about the target (i.e., its motion model) with the sensor data dynamically sampled from the ground sensors. Within the DDDAS paradigm we face two challenges: the first is how to optimally fuse the prior information about the target with the newly available sensor data; and the second is how to choose the sensor data which is more

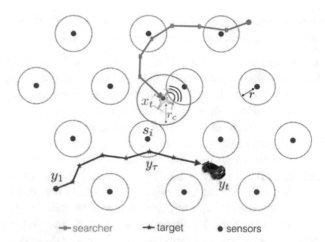

Fig. 14.1 A target moves in a field of unattended ground sensors (UGS). Each UGS records if the target passed within a sensing radius (r, dotted blue circles) from the sensor position at some point in time. For instance, sensor i, at position s_i, records a detection of the target at time $\tau = \{1, \ldots, t\}$, where t is the current time. A searcher is deployed in the same region with the goal of locating the target. The searcher has prior knowledge on the state of the target at the initial time (y_1) and can interrogate sensors within a communication radius (r_c, solid green circle) around its current location (x_t)

informative to localize the target. In the following we provide a detailed description of our problem setup.

We consider a challenging setup in which the searcher has very limited information about a fast-moving target: (i) it has an initial distribution (the *prior*) describing the probability of the target being at a given location at the initial time, and (ii) it can interrogate nearby sensors; each sensor records a binary measurement, describing whether or not the target passed in the proximity of the sensor at some point in time. A graphical representation of the problem is given in Fig. 14.1. This setup is realistic when the robot operates in a field scattered with inexpensive, low-power UGS: these sensors can detect the target via seismic, acoustic, infrared, and optical sensing [11], and can operate continuously for extended periods of time, without any maintenance. On the other hand, our setup makes target search particularly challenging: (i) the searcher has to actively gather data, i.e., data is made available *on-demand*: in this sense the problem is close to *sensor selection* [44], while having the extra complexity of the sensor selection being connected to the location of the searcher (it can only interrogate sensors within a sensing radius); and (ii) the searcher receives *delayed* measurements of the target state: for instance, the searcher may visit a sensor at time t and the sensor returns a detection of the target at time $\tau < t$. Moreover, these measurements are binary in nature ("detection" or "no detection"), making the estimation of the target trajectory a particularly challenging instance of recursive optimal estimation; and (iii) finally, the computation of the optimal search strategy involves complex decision making that has to ponder the advantage in visiting a given sensor and has to respect the dynamics of the searcher.

In this sense, the search problem falls in the class of Partially Observably Markov Decision Processes (POMDPs), which are intractable in general.

Contribution We provide two main contributions. The first addresses optimal target trajectory estimation. While most related work on optimal search considers relatively simple instance of Bayesian inference to estimate the posterior of the target state, our setup (with delayed measurements) requires to estimate the entire trajectory of the target which leads to a high-dimensional estimation problem (also known as *trajectory smoothing*). We show that when the dynamics of the target are described by a linear Gaussian model, and modeling the prior at the initial time as a Gaussian Mixture Model (GMM), we can perform optimal Bayesian estimation from binary measurements in closed form. Similarly to other applications of GMMs to Bayesian estimation [6, 65], the number of mixture components in our model quickly grows over time. However, we show that parametrizing the GMM in information (inverse covariance) form leads to a *sparse* GMM (i.e., a GMM in which the information matrices are very sparse). This insight enables us to perform optimal estimation using thousands of mixture components in a fraction of a second. We also discuss two alternatives to perform *GMM reduction* when the number of components becomes too large.

The second contribution regards the design of a search strategy that minimizes the uncertainty about the state of the target. We first formulate a finite-horizon optimal control problem, which involves the target posterior distribution. Then we take a particle-based approximation of the posterior, which allows us to phrase the problem as a mixed-integer convex program (MIP). While solving a mixed-integer programming is NP-hard, efficient implementations of branch-and-bound techniques exist, allowing us to solve problems with many sensors (≈ 100) and long horizons (≈ 50 steps). A key idea in our approach is to use a different representation of the trajectory posterior in the estimation and in the planning part. For estimation, we use a Gaussian Mixture Model, which allows optimal inference and can easily deal with large uncertainty about the target state (on the other hand, the use of a particle filter for trajectory estimation would lead to particle depletion [66]). For planning, instead, we use a *sampling-based posterior*, which leads to a convex problem and can be more easily attacked using standard solvers.

As a further contribution, we provide a thorough numerical evaluation of the proposed approach, for different performance characteristics of the target (i.e., speed, agility) and increasing uncertainty in the initial target state, comparing it against a greedy planner which always moves towards the most likely target location. Empirical evidence confirms that our approach largely outperforms the greedy baseline.

Paper organization Section 14.2 reviews related literature, while Sect. 14.3 provides preliminaries and notation. Section 14.4 formalizes our problem setup. Section 14.5 describes a sparse Gaussian Mixture Model for optimal trajectory smoothing. Section 14.6 discusses a MIP-based search strategy. Section 14.7 reports numerical results. Section 14.8 concludes the paper.

14.2 Related Work

The first body of related work is the literature on **optimal search** (OS). In OS a searcher needs to plan a path that allows detecting one or more targets in a known environment. OS is also known as "one-sided search" in that the target is static or moves according to some policy which is independent on the state of the searcher. OS played an important role in maritime warfare [48]; we refer the reader to [67] for a general overview. OS is usually formulated over a graph in which vertices are potential positions of the searcher and the target, while edges denote traversability between locations. Therefore, the goal of the search strategy is to minimize the expected time before the target is detected or to maximize the detection probability in presence of false detections [45]. Assaf and Zamir [7] study a box-searching problem (one or more targets are hidden in boxes and the searcher can inspect any of them), in which one disregards searcher's motion, and show that visiting the most probable target location is the optimal search strategy. On the other hand, when the searcher cannot "teleport", the problem, also referred to as the *optimal path search* problem, has been shown to be NP-complete even when the target is stationary [69]. Washburn [72] presents an iterative forward-and-backward algorithm. Eagle [31] proposes a dynamic programming approach, while branch and bound is used in [32]. Bourgault et al. [15, 16] consider single or multiple searchers moving in a continuous obstacle-free environment; they propose a Bayesian approach to predict the target state, and use an optimal control formulation to drive the searcher towards a static or drifting target. Lau et al. [52, 53] consider a search problem in a discretized indoor environment with multiple stationary targets; a dynamic programming approach is given in [52], while branch and bound is adopted in [53]. Sato et al. [62] extend the branch-and-bound approach [53] to consider a resource-constrained searcher moving in a discretized 3D space. Hollinger et al. [38] consider a search problem with multiple searchers, and use submodularity to establish performance guarantees when sequentially computing search policies across the team.

The second body of related work is the literature on **pursuit evasion** (PE). In PE, a pursuer chases an evader, which actively tries to avoid capture (for this reason PE is also known as "adversarial search" or "worst-case search"). PE is usually formulated over a graph and it is assumed that both the pursuer and the evader have exact knowledge of the position of the players at each time step (e.g., the *cops-and-robbers game* [3]). The case in which the players can observe each other position only if they are at the same vertex is known as the *hunter-and-rabbit game* [1]. The case in which the players have local visibility (i.e., can only see the adversary when it is close enough) has been considered in [40, 41]. Related work also investigates PE problems in continuous space, where the position of the players is not confined to the nodes of a graph. A popular PE problem in the continuous domain is the *lion-and-man game* [5], in which the players move in the 2D quadrant. The lion-and-man game has been also studied in a limited-sensing setup, in which the pursuers can only detect the evader within a given distance, and the evader moves only if the pursuer is nearby [14]. PE in polygonal environments with limited visibility is considered in [35]. Shen et al. [63], Blasch et al. [12], and Jia et al. [43] consider extensions to three-dimensional PE games. PE is related to the literature on *differential games*, which also considers the dynamics of pursuer and evader, see e.g., the *homicidal chauffeur game* and the general overview in [9]. An excellent survey on PE and OS is given in [25].

Our search problem can be also formulated as a **partially observable Markov decision process** (POMDP). In that case, the *state* of the POMDP includes both the state of the searcher and the state of the target (a POMDP model of the search problem is given in [38]). The *actions* in the corresponding POMDP would only control the motion of the searcher, while the *observations* correspond to detections of the target. The POMDP would then reward the searcher for visiting the same locations as the target. POMDP are intractable in general [46], although sampling-based approaches [8, 57, 64], and belief compression [60] enabled the solution of relatively large POMDPs. In the context of target search, the computational cost soon becomes impractical when searching over a large environment [38]. A related literature is also the one on **belief space planning** in robotics, where a robot looks for a suitable motion strategy in order to drive its belief (posterior distribution over the state of the robot and possibly the external world) towards a desired state. Recent work considers belief space planning in continuous domain; Bai et al. [8] use sampling to update an initial policy. Platt et al. [58] use linear quadratic regulation (LQR) to compute locally optimal policies. Erez and Smart [33] use an extended Kalman Filter (EKF) and a Gaussian Mixture Model for the belief and applied local optimization techniques for planning. Van den Berg et al. [70] relax assumptions about the measurements collected over the planning horizon, while Indelman et al. [39] investigate belief space planning within a smoothing and mapping framework.

Another set of related works is the one in the area of **unattended ground sensors** (UGS) and **DDDAS**. The literature on sensor networks is very broad and an extensive review is outside the scope of this work; we refer the interested reader to [24] for an historical perspective. We limit our review to few related works, including the work of Duarte and Hu [30] and Blasch et al. [11], discussing how to use a sensor network to classify moving vehicles, and the works on target pursuit in a road network instrumented with UGS [20, 21, 49–51]. Choi and How [23] and Choi et al. [22] investigate the *sensor targeting problem*, in which a set of sensors must be deployed to observe a phenomenon of interest. Casbeer et al. [17] and Ahmed et al. [2] investigate Bayesian estimation to localize a moving target in a road network from UGS detections. Blasch et al. [10] consider different metrics for sensor scheduling, in order to observe a moving target. Niu and Varshney [56] study maximum likelihood estimation of the target position from quantized data. Krishnamoorthy et al. [49] study the problem of capturing an intruder in a road network using an UAV and propose a backward recursive scheme to construct the set of UAV locations from which capture is guaranteed. Krishnamoorthy et al. [50] analyze the optimal worst-case time to capture an intruder on a Manhattan grid. Chen et al. [20, 21] compute intruder pursuit policies on road networks using decision trees. Krishnamoorthy et al. [51] and Casbeer et al. [18] provide conditions and policies under which intruder capture is guaranteed. While the problem setup in these works is very close to the one presented in our paper, a key difference is that our intruder search is performed in a continuous space, rather than in a discrete road network. Fujimoto et al. [34] propose a DDDAS system for vehicles tracking from live images, and discuss an architecture to implement a *sense-predict-adapt* DDDAS cycle. DDDAS approaches have also been considered for tracking different dynamic phenomena, including water contaminants [29], wildfires [55], and hurricanes [4].

Other related problems The problem at hand also intersects other lines of research. We mention them for completeness, and refer the reader to the corresponding papers for details. In *Informative Path Planning* problems, the goal is to plan a path that maximizes some information-collection objective, possibly under additional constraints such as path length or total time limit; recent literature includes polylogarithmic approximations [54], sampling-based methods [47], and branch and bound [37]. In *Prize-collecting* Traveling Salesman problems (TSP) an agent moves on a graph: each node has a price for visiting it and a penalty for not visiting it; then the goal is to find a tour that obtains at least a given profit, while minimizing the length of the tour and the penalty for not visiting some nodes [13]. In the *orienteering* problem an agent has to reach a given node in a graph, while visiting as many nodes as possible along the way, such that the path is shorter than a given bound; recent literature includes guaranteed approximations [19], and MIP-based algorithms [71]. A variant of the orienteering problem is the *optimal tourist problem* [73] in which the reward collected at a node is a function of the time spent at that node.

Novelty and challenges Despite the large amount of related work in OS and PE, few key features make our setup unique. The first feature is the presence of the unattended ground sensors. Rather than using just onboard sensors, the searcher can collect measurements using an infrastructure of sensors scattered in the environment. For this reason we refer to our problem as *aided optimal search*. The sensor measurements are delayed in the sense that they provide information on past states of the target. This requires more sophisticated search policies for two reasons. First, the searcher has to reason over the entire trajectory of the target, rather than on its current state. Computationally, this means that the state of the target (for both estimation and planning) is high-dimensional and grows over time. This rules out dynamic programming and POMDP approaches, which are known to be slow even in standard instances of optimal search [38, 52]. Second, the possibility of measuring past states creates complex interdependence among the reward collected when visiting different locations in the environment. For instance, consider the case in which a searcher inspects an environment consisting of two areas (say A and B) separated by a single narrow passage. If the searcher knows that the target started in the area A, a single measurement at a UGS located at the narrow passage can radically change the interest of the searcher towards visiting the entire area B.

The second feature of our setup is that, contrarily to most literature on optimal search and UGS, our searcher operates in continuous space and we want to enforce motion constraints (e.g., dynamics, speed limits) during the computation of the search strategy. This makes the formulation more realistic and enables extensions which also take into account resource constraints (e.g., time, fuel) for the searcher.

14.3 Notation and Preliminaries

Vector norms and matrices We use the symbol $\mathbf{I}_n$ to denote the $n \times n$ identity matrix; we denote with $\mathbf{0}_{n \times m}$ the $n \times m$ matrix of zeros. The Euclidean norm of a vector x is denoted with $\|x\|_2$; we also use the following norms: $\|x\|_\infty \doteq \max_{i=1,\dots,n} |x_i|$ (ℓ_∞-norm); $\|x\|_1 \doteq \sum_{i=1,\dots,n} |x_i|$ (ℓ_1-norm).

Multivariate Gaussian Distributions We use the notation $\mathcal{N}_\mathcal{P}(x; \mu, \Sigma)$ to denote a d-dimensional multivariate Gaussian with mean $\mu \in \mathbb{R}^d$ and covariance matrix $\Sigma \in \mathbb{R}^{d \times d}$:

$$\mathcal{N}_\mathcal{P}(x; \mu, \Sigma) = \frac{\det(\Sigma)^{-\frac{1}{2}}}{(2\pi)^{\frac{d}{2}}} \exp\left\{ -\frac{1}{2}(x - \mu)^\mathsf{T} \Sigma^{-1}(x - \mu) \right\} \tag{14.1}$$

When convenient, we parametrize the multivariate Gaussian in *information form*:

$$\mathcal{N}(x; \eta, \Omega) = \frac{\det(\Omega)^{\frac{1}{2}}}{(2\pi)^{\frac{d}{2}}} \exp\left\{ -\frac{1}{2}(x - \Omega^{-1}\eta)^\mathsf{T} \Omega(x - \Omega^{-1}\eta) \right\} \tag{14.2}$$

where the matrix Ω is called the *information matrix* and η is the *information vector*. It can be readily seen that whenever Ω, Σ are positive definite, the descriptions (14.1) and (14.2) are equivalent, and are related by:

$$\mathcal{N}_\mathcal{P}(x; \mu, \Sigma) = \mathcal{N}(x; \Sigma^{-1}\mu, \Sigma^{-1}) \tag{14.3}$$

which tells that the information matrix is the inverse of the covariance, $\Omega = \Sigma^{-1}$, and $\mu = \Sigma \ \eta = \Omega^{-1}\eta$. To denote that a random vector x is Normally distributed we write $x \sim \mathcal{N}_\mathcal{P}(\mu, \Sigma)$ or $x \sim \mathcal{N}(\eta, \Omega)$.

Gaussian Mixture Model (GMM) A GMM is a probability density function (pdf) described by the following expression:

$$\mathcal{M}_\mathcal{P}(x; \{\mu_j, P_j, \alpha_j\}_{j=1}^m) = \sum_{j=1}^m \alpha_j \mathcal{N}_\mathcal{P}(x; \mu_j, P_j) \tag{14.4}$$

where m is the number of mixture components, and α_j are the *mixture coefficients*, with $\sum_{j=1}^m \alpha_j = 1$. It is usually assumed that $\alpha_j \geq 0$, which, together with $\sum_{j=1}^m \alpha_j = 1$, guarantees that (14.4) is a valid pdf. However, one can allow for negative α_j as long as the pdf remains positive everywhere [74].

Assuming $P_1, \dots, P_m$ to be positive definite, we can equivalently parametrize the GMM in information form, as follows:

$$\mathcal{M}(x; \{\eta_j, \Omega_j, \alpha_j\}_{j=1}^m) = \sum_{j=1}^m \alpha_j \mathcal{N}(x; \eta_j, \Omega_j) \tag{14.5}$$

which is the same as (14.4) for $\Omega_j = P_j^{-1} > 0$, and $\eta_j = \Omega_j \, \mu_j$, $j = 1, \ldots, m$. To denote that a random vector x is distributed according to a GMM we write $x \sim \mathcal{M}(\{\eta_j, \Omega_j, \alpha_j\}_{j=1}^m)$. A GMM is said to be *sparse*, if Ω_j, $j = 1, \ldots, m$ are sparse matrices.

14.4 Problem Statement

The target A target moves in a planar region $\mathcal{R}$ and we call $p_t^y \in \mathbb{R}^2$ and $v_t^y \in \mathbb{R}^2$ the position and the velocity of the target at time t, respectively. Therefore, $y_t \doteq [p_t^y \; v_t^y] \in \mathbb{R}^4$ is the *state* of the target at time t. We assume that the dynamics of the target are described by the following *process model*:

$$y_{t+1} = A y_t + w_t \tag{14.6}$$

where $A \in \mathbb{R}^{4 \times 4}$ is a known matrix, and $w_t \in \mathbb{R}^4$ is a random vector. This model, for instance, encompasses a velocity random walk in which the target applies unknown (stochastic) accelerations. We assume that w_t is Normally distributed: $w_t \sim \mathcal{N}(0, \Omega_w)$. The process model can be equivalently written in terms of transition probability:

$$\mathbb{P}\,(y_{t+1}|y_t) = \mathcal{N}(y_{t+1} - A y_t; 0, \Omega_w) \tag{14.7}$$

We also assume that we are given a prior distribution of the target state at the initial time:

$$y_1 \sim \mathcal{M}(\{\eta_{1,j}, \Omega_{1,j}, \alpha_{1,j}\}_{j=1}^m) \tag{14.8}$$

for $m \geq 1$ and some known $\eta_{1,j}, \Omega_{1,j}, \alpha_{1,j}$, $j = 1, \ldots, m$. For instance, we can assume that y_1 is distributed according to a single Gaussian ($m = 1$) with large covariance, or we can use multiple components, corresponding to multiple hypotheses on the initial state of the target. Modeling the prior as a GMM is indeed a mild assumption as GMM can approximate generic continuous pdfs with arbitrary accuracy [65].

In this chapter, we are interested in the *trajectory* of the target. Therefore, rather than estimating the most recent state y_t, our goal is to compute a posterior distribution over the following vector:

$$y_{1:t} = \begin{bmatrix} y_1 \\ \vdots \\ y_t \end{bmatrix} \in \mathbb{R}^{4t} \tag{14.9}$$

The sensors The region in which the target is moving is scattered with N *unattended ground sensors* (UGS), see Fig. 14.1. The position of the sensors is denoted as $s_i \in \mathbb{R}^2$, $i = 1, \ldots, N$. We assume that, when interrogated at time t, a sensor $i \in \{1, \ldots, N\}$ provides a time-stamped binary measurement z_t. The measurement is described by the tuple $z_t = (i, \tau, b)$, where i is the unique identifier of the sensor, $b \in \{0, 1\}$ is the binary reading, and $\tau \in \{1, \ldots, t\}$ is a time stamp. A value $z_t^1 \doteq (i, \tau, b = 1)$ indicates that the target was in the proximity of sensor i at time τ; more precisely, we have a *detection* when the target passed within a sensing radius r from the sensor. On the other hand, $z_t^0 \doteq (i, \tau, b = 0)$ indicates that the target never passed near sensor i.

The searcher We assume that the motion of the searcher is governed by the following (deterministic) linear dynamics:

$$x_{t+1} = A_x x_t + B_x u_t \tag{14.10}$$

where $x_t \in \mathbb{R}^4$ is the *pursuer state*, including its 2D position and velocity, $u_t \in \mathbb{R}^2$ is the control action, and A_x and B_x are given matrices of suitable dimensions. In practice, (14.10) represents a double integrator, in which at each time step the pursuer decides its acceleration commands u_t. We consider a realistic scenario in which the controls are bounded, i.e.,

$$\|u_t\| \le \bar{U}, \quad \forall \, t \tag{14.11}$$

where $\bar{U}$ is a given upper bound. We also assume that the maximum velocity of the pursuer is limited, i.e.,

$$\|Sx_t\| \le \bar{S}, \quad \forall \, t \tag{14.12}$$

where $\bar{S}$ is a given speed limit, and the matrix $S \in \mathbb{R}^{2 \times 4}$ extracts the 2D velocity from the state vector x_t.

The searcher knows the position of the sensors $s_i \in \mathbb{R}^2$, $i = 1, \ldots, N$ and can interrogate a sensor within a communication radius r_c from its current position. More precisely, a measurement is received from sensor i at time t, if and only if:

$$\|Px_t - s_i\| \le r_c \tag{14.13}$$

where $P \in \mathbb{R}^{2 \times 4}$ extracts the 2D position from the state x_t.

14.5 Target Trajectory Estimation Via Sparse Gaussian Mixture Model

This section describes our approach to estimate the trajectory of the target from binary measurements. The proposed approach is based on Bayesian smoothing: at each time step the posterior is predicted using the process model (14.7); then,

binary measurements (if available) are included in the posterior in the update
step. More formally, denoting with $Z_{1:t}$ all the measurements collected till time
t, our incremental smoother computes the posterior probability $\mathbb{P}(y_{1:t+1}|Z_{1:t+1})$
by updating the posterior at the previous time step $\mathbb{P}(y_{1:t}|Z_{1:t})$. Section 14.5.1
describes the prediction phase. Section 14.5.2 discusses the measurement update.

14.5.1 Prediction

The prediction phase computes the prior distribution at time $t+1$, i.e.,
$\mathbb{P}(y_{1:t+1}|Z_{1:t})$, from the posterior at time t, i.e., $\mathbb{P}(y_{1:t}|Z_{1:t})$, and the transition
probability $\mathbb{P}(y_{t+1}|y_t)$. The following relations are general and independent on the
choice of the prior and transition probabilities:

$$\mathbb{P}(y_{1:t+1}|Z_{1:t}) = \mathbb{P}(y_{1:t}, y_{t+1}|Z_{1:t}) = \text{(using the chain rule)}$$

$$\mathbb{P}(y_{t+1}|y_{1:t}, Z_{1:t})\,\mathbb{P}(y_{1:t}|Z_{1:t}) = \text{(using the Markov property)}$$

$$\mathbb{P}(y_{t+1}|y_t)\,\mathbb{P}(y_{1:t}|Z_{1:t}) \tag{14.14}$$

The previous equation shows that the prior distribution can be computed as a product
of the posterior at the previous time and the transition probability. Note that we
operate in a smoothing framework, hence we do not marginalize out past states as
in standard Bayesian filtering.

Let us assume that our probability prior at time t is a GMM with m mixture
components:

$$\mathbb{P}(y_{1:t}|Z_{1:t}) = \mathcal{M}(y_{1:t}; \{\eta_{t,j}, \Omega_{t,j}, \alpha_{t,j}\}_{j=1}^m) \tag{14.15}$$

Substituting our choice of priori (14.15) and transition probability (14.7) in (14.14),
we demonstrate that (see Appendix A for a complete derivation):

$$\mathbb{P}(y_{1:t+1}|Z_{1:t}) = \mathcal{M}(y_{1:t+1}; \{\bar{\eta}_{t+1,j}, \bar{\Omega}_{t+1,j}, \bar{\alpha}_{t+1,j}\}_{j=1}^m) \tag{14.16}$$

where $\bar{\eta}_{t+1,j}$, $\bar{\Omega}_{t+1,j}$, and $\bar{\alpha}_{t+1,j}$ are computed as:

$$\boxed{\begin{aligned}
\bar{\eta}_{t+1,j} &= S_{1:t}^\mathsf{T}\eta_{t,j} \\
\bar{\Omega}_{t+1,j} &= S_{1:t}^\mathsf{T}\Omega_{t,j}S_{1:t} + S_{t:t+1}^\mathsf{T}\Omega^w S_{t:t+1} \\
\bar{\alpha}_{t+1,j} &= \alpha_{t,j}
\end{aligned}} \tag{14.17}$$

and the matrices $S_{1:t} \in \mathbb{R}^{4t \times 4(t+1)}$ and $S_{t:t+1} \in \mathbb{R}^{4 \times 4(t+1)}$ are defined such that:

$$S_{1:t}\, y_{1:t+1} = y_{1:t} \qquad S_{t:t+1}\, y_{1:t+1} = y_{t+1} - Ay_t \tag{14.18}$$

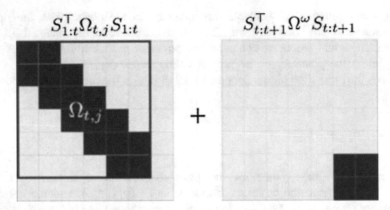

Fig. 14.2 The prediction of the information matrix of each mixture component in (14.17) preserves a block tridiagonal structure of the information matrices. In particular, it is possible to see that the matrix $S_{1:t}$ in (14.18) can be written explicitly as $S_{1:t} = [\mathbf{L}_{4t} \quad \mathbf{0}_{4t \times 4}]$; therefore the product $S_{1:t}^\mathsf{T} \Omega_{t,j} S_{1:t}$ only adds rows and columns of zeros to the matrix $\Omega_{t,j}$ (each white block in the figure denote a 4×4 zero matrix, while the blue blocks may contain nonzero entries). Similarly, we note that $S_{t:t+1}$ in (14.18) can be written as $S_{t:t+1} = [\mathbf{0}_{4 \times 4(t-1)} \quad -A \quad \mathbf{I}_4]$, which implies that the product $S_{t:t+1}^\mathsf{T} \Omega^w S_{t:t+1}$ is zero everywhere except the four bottom-right blocks

Note that the prediction step in (14.16) can be implemented efficiently, even for large number of mixture components, since $S_{1:t}$ and $S_{t:t+1}$ have few nonzero entries and the term $S_{t:t+1}^\mathsf{T} \Omega^w S_{t:t+1}$ can be pre-calculated (it is independent on the mixture component). Therefore, if $\Omega_{t,j}$ is a sparse matrix, also $\bar{\Omega}_{t+1,j}$ is sparse, for $j = 1, \ldots, m$. More precisely, the prediction produces block-tridiagonal matrices, see Fig. 14.2.

14.5.2 Update

The update phase computes the posterior distribution at time $t + 1$, i.e., $\mathbb{P}(y_{1:t+1} | Z_{1:t+1})$, from the prior at time $t + 1$, i.e., $\mathbb{P}(y_{1:t+1} | Z_{1:t})$, and the measurement likelihood $\mathbb{P}(z_{t+1} | y_{1:t+1})$. The following relations are general and independent on the choice of the prior and likelihood function:

$$\mathbb{P}(y_{1:t+1} | Z_{1:t+1}) = \mathbb{P}(y_{1:t+1} | Z_{1:t}, z_{t+1}) = \text{(using the Bayes rule)}$$

$$\frac{\mathbb{P}(z_{t+1} | Z_{1:t}, y_{1:t+1}) \, \mathbb{P}(y_{1:t+1} | Z_{1:t})}{\int \mathbb{P}(z_{t+1} | Z_{1:t}, y_{1:t+1}) \, \mathbb{P}(y_{1:t+1} | Z_{1:t}) \, dy_{1:t+1}} = \text{(using the Markov property)}$$

$$\frac{\mathbb{P}(z_{t+1} | y_{1:t+1}) \, \mathbb{P}(y_{1:t+1} | Z_{1:t})}{\int \mathbb{P}(z_{t+1} | y_{1:t+1}) \, \mathbb{P}(y_{1:t+1} | Z_{1:t}) \, dy_{1:t+1}} \tag{14.19}$$

The first step towards the computation of the posterior distribution is to define the likelihood function for our problem.

Measurement Likelihood We first recall that p_τ^y is the position of the target at time $\tau \in \{1, \ldots, t\}$, and we introduce a sparse matrix $U_\tau \in \mathbb{R}^{2 \times 4t}$ that is such that:

$$U_\tau y_{1:t} = p_\tau^y \qquad (14.20)$$

In Sect. 14.4 we gave a deterministic description of the measurements. We have a detection at sensor i if:

$$\|U_\tau y_{1:t} - s_i\| \leq r \qquad (14.21)$$

at some time $\tau \in \{1, \ldots, t\}$. In this Section, we conveniently give a probabilistic description of the binary measurements: the probability of the target being detected at time τ is a continuous function of its distance from the target. More formally, the likelihood of a detection ($b = 1$), time-stamped with τ, at sensor i, is:

$$\mathbb{P}\left(z_t^1 | y_{1:t}\right) = \mathbb{P}\left(b = 1 | y_\tau, s_i\right) = \exp\left\{-\frac{\|U_\tau y_{1:t} - s_i\|^2}{r^2}\right\} \qquad (14.22)$$

Eq. (14.22) describes the likelihood of a detection, given the target trajectory $y_{1:t}$. The model in (14.22) states that the sensor detects the target with probability 1 when $U_\tau y_{1:t} = p_\tau^y = s_i$ (i.e., when the target position at time τ coincides with the sensor position s_i), while the probability decays exponentially fast when the target moves farther from the sensor position. While this model makes intuitive sense (i.e., the chance of detecting the target quickly decays when the target is far from the sensor), the key advantage of using this model is that it enables a closed-form computation of the Bayesian update, as shown later in this section. A similar observation is reported in [42], which uses binary measurements within a Kalman filter; in hindsight, our approach is an extension of the filter presented in [42] to a full smoothing setup.

Using the detection probability (14.22), we write the probability of having no detections ($b = 0$) from sensor i at time τ as:

$$\mathbb{P}\left(z_t^0 | y_{1:t}\right) = 1 - \mathbb{P}\left(z_t^1 | y_{1:t}\right) \qquad (14.23)$$

We use the symbol "z_t" to denote a generic binary measurement, while we use z_t^1 and z_t^0 when distinguishing the outcome of the measurement is important. While the two outcomes may appear similar, they impact the update phase presented in the rest of this section in a very different manner, since they are described by different likelihood functions. Note that the subscript "t" in z_t denotes the time at which the estimator becomes "aware" of the new measurement (i.e., when the searcher interrogates the sensor), and this is different in general from the detection time τ.

We now show that if the prior is a GMM – as in our case, see (14.16) – and the likelihood functions are the ones described in (14.22) and (14.23), then the posterior probability remains a GMM. The update equations change depending on whether the measurement has $b = 1$ (detection) or $b = 0$ (no detection). We discuss the two cases separately in the following.

Detection ($b = 1$) When the searcher acquires a measurement $z_t^1 = (i, \tau, b = 1)$, the expression of the measurement likelihood is described in Eq. (14.22). Substituting (14.14) and (14.22) into (14.19) we prove that (derivation in Appendix B):

$$\mathbb{P}(y_{1:t+1}|Z_{1:t+1}) = \mathcal{M}(y_{1:t+1}; \{\eta_{t+1,j}, \Omega_{t+1,j}, \alpha_{t+1,j}\}_{j=1}^m) \qquad (14.24)$$

where $\eta_{t+1,j}$, $\Omega_{t+1,j}$, and $\alpha_{t+1,j}$ are computed as:

$$\begin{cases} \eta_{t+1,j} = \bar{\eta}_{t+1,j} + U_\tau^\mathsf{T} \frac{s_i}{r} \\ \Omega_{t+1,j} = \bar{\Omega}_{t+1,j} + \frac{1}{r^2} U_\tau^\mathsf{T} U_\tau \\ \alpha_{t+1,j} = \frac{\bar{\alpha}_{t,j}\beta_{t+1,j}}{\sum_{j=1}^m \bar{\alpha}_{t,j}\beta_{t+1,j}} \end{cases} \qquad (14.25)$$

and the scalars $\beta_{t+1,j}$ are computed by evaluating a Normal distribution at s_i:

$$\beta_{t+1,j} = \mathcal{N}_\mathcal{P}(s_i; U_\tau \bar{\Omega}_{t+1,j}^{-1} \bar{\eta}_{t+1,j}, U_\tau \bar{\Omega}_{t+1,j}^{-1} U_\tau^\mathsf{T} + r^2) \qquad (14.26)$$

Note that an efficient implementation would not perform matrix inversions to compute (14.26), but would rather resort to a sparse linear system solver.

No detection ($b = 0$) The case in which the sensor did not detect the target, i.e., $z_t^0 = (i, \tau, b = 0)$, is different from the detection case in a subtle way. In the derivation, the main different lies in the expression of the measurement likelihood. Substituting (14.14) and (14.23) into (14.19) we can demonstrate that the posterior probability is given by (cf. Appendix B):

$$\begin{aligned} \mathbb{P}(y_{1:t+1}|Z_{1:t+1}) = &\mathcal{M}(y_{1:t+1}; \{\eta_{t+1,j}^+, \Omega_{t+1,j}^+, \alpha_{t+1,j}^+\}_{j=1}^m) + \\ &\mathcal{M}(y_{1:t+1}; \{\eta_{t+1,j}^-, \Omega_{t+1,j}^-, \alpha_{t+1,j}^-\}_{j=1}^m) \end{aligned} \qquad (14.27)$$

where $\eta_{t+1,j}^+, \Omega_{t+1,j}^+, \alpha_{t+1,j}^+, \eta_{t+1,j}^-, \Omega_{t+1,j}^-, \alpha_{t+1,j}^-$ are computed as follows:

$$\begin{cases} \eta_{t+1,j}^+ = \bar{\eta}_{t+1,j} & \eta_{t+1,j}^- = \bar{\eta}_{t+1,j} + U_\tau^\mathsf{T} \frac{s_i}{r} \\ \Omega_{t+1,j}^+ = \bar{\Omega}_{t+1,j} & \Omega_{t+1,j}^- = \bar{\Omega}_{t+1,j} + \frac{1}{r^2} U_\tau^\mathsf{T} U_\tau \\ \alpha_{t+1,j}^+ = \frac{\bar{\alpha}_{t,j}}{1 - \sum_{j=1}^m \bar{\alpha}_{t,j}\gamma_{t+1,j}} & \alpha_{t+1,j}^- = \frac{-\bar{\alpha}_{t,j}\gamma_{t+1,j}}{1 - \sum_{j=1}^m \bar{\alpha}_{t,j}\gamma_{t+1,j}} \end{cases} \qquad (14.28)$$

and the terms $\gamma_{t+1,j}$ can be computed as follows:

$$\gamma_{t+1,j} = 2\pi r^2 \beta_{t+1,j} \qquad (14.29)$$

where $\beta_{t+1,j}$ is defined as in (14.26). Note that each "no detection" event doubles the number of mixture components, as can be seen from (14.27).

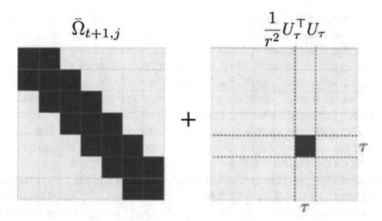

Fig. 14.3 The update step in our smoother preserves the sparsity structure of the information matrix of each mixture component. In particular, the matrix $\frac{1}{r^2} U_\tau^{\mathsf{T}} U_\tau$, appearing in the update Eq. (14.25) is a block diagonal matrix with a single nonzero diagonal block in position τ

We conclude by observing that the update step does not alter the sparsity structure of the information matrices of each Gaussian component. In Eq. (14.28), the components labeled with "+" have the same information matrix of the prediction step, while the sum in the expression of the "−" components (which is the same appearing in (14.25)) only adds nonzero diagonal blocks, as shown in Fig. 14.3.

GMM Reduction So far we showed how to perform efficient trajectory smoothing in information form. Our approach enables fast computation by leveraging sparse matrix manipulation and it is parsimonious in terms of memory consumption as the number of nonzero entries in each information matrix grows linearly in the length of the trajectory (since the matrices are block tridiagonal) rather than quadratically (as it would happen when performing smoothing in covariance form).

Despite these advantages, the number of GMM components keeps increasing whenever we include a "no detection" measurement in our estimator. Therefore, it is of interest to devise strategies to reduce the number of components when their number exceeds a given upper bound (for instance, in our tests, we limit the number of mixture components to $m = 10^4$). The literature on GMM reduction offers three main families of approaches to approximate a given GMM with one having a smaller number of mixture components. We give a high-level overview here, while we refer the reader to [26, 61] for a comprehensive treatment. The first approach is *pruning* and consisting of simply discarding components whose weights $\alpha_{t,j}$ are small (e.g., $\alpha_{t,j} \leq 10^{-5}$). The second approach is based on *merging* and consists in replacing two or more mixture components in the original GMM with a single "merged" component; the parameters describing the "merged" components are usually computed via iterative optimization. The third approach is based on *sampling*: when the original GMM becomes too large, we sample from it and we fit a GMM with less components to the samples (fitting a GMM to a set of samples can be performed via Expectation-Maximization [36, §8.5]). While reduction via merging or sampling are feasible in our context, a naive implementation of these techniques would not preserve the sparsity of the information matrices.

For our experiments we test two alternative approaches to limit the growth of the mixture components. The first approach is very simple yet effective: since the number of mixture components only grows when we incorporate a "no detection" measurement, we avoid including these measurements after we reach the allowed number of mixture components. The second approach is based on sampling; however, rather than sampling the entire target trajectory and fitting a high-dimensional GMM (this would lead to large dense information matrices), we only sample the current target state, say at time t and fit a 4-dimensional GMM. This is the same as "re-initializing" the smoother, which starts with a new GMM (with a small number of components) at time t, and produces a sparse GMM posterior after time t. While this solution is computationally efficient, it implies that we "forget" the trajectory before time t; and hence, we cannot incorporate delayed measurements regarding the state of the target before time t. In both approaches, we also prune mixture components with very small weights.

14.6 Ground-Sensor-Aided Search Via Mixed-Integer Convex Programming

This section describes a search strategy to minimize the uncertainty about the target location over a finite time horizon. We provide a general formulation of the optimal search in Sect. 14.6.1. Then we provide a sampling-based approximation in Sect. 14.6.2: this approximation leads to a mixed-integer convex program, which can be solved reliably (at least for medium-sized problems) using standard solvers.

14.6.1 Ground-Sensor-Aided Optimal Search

We consider a receding-horizon planner in which the searcher has to plan the optimal motion for L look-ahead steps, starting from its current state $\bar{x}_t$. Recalling that $\mathbb{P}(y_{1:t}|Z_{1:t})$ is the posterior over the target trajectory at time t, the receding-horizon planner minimizes the uncertainty associated to the target posterior at the end of the time horizon, namely $\mathbb{P}(y_{1:t+L}|Z_{1:t+L})$ while satisfying the motion dynamics (14.10), the acceleration limit (14.11) and the speed limit (14.12).

We observe that the measurements collected during the future look-ahead steps are unknown: the searcher does not know a priori whether a given sensor detected the target or not. Related work tackles the detection ambiguity issue by taking the optimistic assumption that future measurements will be in agreement with the current belief [58], or by trying to reason probabilistically over the outcome of future measurements [39, 70]. In our formulation, we take the conservative assumption that the searcher always obtains a "no detection" from each sensor interrogated during the L lookahead steps. This choice has the advantage that the plan remains optimal as long as the searcher does not get an actual detection. In practice, this means that the searcher only needs to re-plan its trajectory after getting a new detection (which happens rarely at the beginning of the search), or when the current plan have been executed.

Let us assume that $f(\cdot)$ is a function that takes a probability distribution as input and returns a measure of the uncertainty in the distribution; for instance, $f(\cdot)$ can be the trace of the covariance of the distribution, the determinant of the covariance, or the entropy. Then, our search problem is phrased as an optimization problem (detailed explanation follows):

$$\min_{\substack{x_t,\ldots,x_{t+L},\\ u_t,\ldots,u_{t+L},\\ \mathcal{P}_{1:t},\ldots,\mathcal{P}_{1:t+L}}} f(\mathcal{P}_{1:t+L})$$

subject to

(initial searcher state at time t) $x_t = \bar{x}_t$

(searcher dynamics, Eq. 14.10) $x_{\tau+1} = A_x x_\tau + B_x u_\tau$

(max searcher speed, Eq. 14.12) $\|S x_\tau\| \leq \bar{S}$

(max searcher acc., Eq. 14.11) $\|u_\tau\| \leq \bar{U}$

(initial target posterior at time t) $\mathcal{P}_{1:t} = \mathbb{P}(y_{1:t}|Z_{1:t})$

(target posterior evolution) $\mathcal{P}_{1:\tau+1} = \mathcal{B}(\mathcal{P}_{1:\tau}, z_\tau^0)$

(measurements) $z_\tau^0 = (i, \tau, 0)$ if $\|P x_\tau - s_i\| \leq r_c$

$$\forall \tau = t, \ldots, t+L, \quad \forall i = 1, \ldots, N$$

$$(14.30)$$

The optimization variables are the future controls $u_{t:t+L}$, the future searcher states $x_{t:t+L}$, and the future target posteriors $\mathcal{P}_{1:t}, \ldots, \mathcal{P}_{1:t+L}$. The objective rewards the minimization of the uncertainty of the target posterior at the end of the horizon $\mathcal{P}_{1:t+L}$. The first four constraints regard the searcher. The constraint $x_t = \bar{x}_t$ enforces that the initial state of the searcher matches the actual searcher state at the time of planning, i.e., $\bar{x}_t$. The subsequent constraints enforce dynamics and motion constraints, as per Eqs. (14.10), (14.11), and (14.12). The last set of constraints describes the evolution of the target trajectory posterior over the time horizon. The constraint $\mathcal{P}_{1:t} = \mathbb{P}(y_{1:t}|Z_{1:t})$ fixes the initial condition for the posterior $\mathcal{P}_{1:t}$, i.e., at planning time t the posterior $\mathcal{P}_{1:t}$ has to match the actual target trajectory posterior $\mathbb{P}(y_{1:t}|Z_{1:t})$ (this is the GMM that we estimated in Sect. 14.5). In the constraint $\mathcal{P}_{1:\tau+1} = \mathcal{B}(\mathcal{P}_{1:\tau}, z_\tau^0)$, the function $\mathcal{B}(\mathcal{P}_{1:\tau}, z_\tau^0)$ represents a Bayesian smoother (as the one presented in Sect. 14.5): the smoother takes as input the

---

[1]In practice, the most challenging part of the problem is indeed the initial phase of the search in which the uncertainty about the target is large and most of the interrogated sensors are far from the actual trajectory of the target.

posterior at time τ and the measurements z_τ^0 and returns the posterior at the next time $\tau + 1$. Note that $\mathcal{B}(\cdot, \cdot)$ is a deterministic function, and indeed the evolution of the posterior is deterministic, given the measurements. The last constraint ($z_\tau^0 = (i, \tau, 0)$ if $\|Px_\tau - s_i\| \le r_c$) states that a measurement $z_\tau^0 = (i, \tau, 0)$ becomes available, whenever sensor i (at position s_i) is within the communication radius from the searcher position at time τ (i.e., Px_τ), cf. with Eq. (14.13). The communication constraint is the key interface between the searcher and the target, and indeed it is the only way in which the searcher can modify the evolution of the target posterior. Problem (14.30) is a deterministic optimization problem (the stochasticity about future measurements has been removed by assuming future measurements to be "no detections").

Remark 1 (Challenges in the general formulation (14.30)) Two main aspects in (14.30) make it a particularly complex optimization problem. The first issue is that the posterior $\mathcal{P}_{1:\tau}$ (which is an optimization variable) is an infinite dimensional object in general. This issue is mitigated when a finite-dimensional parametrization of the posterior is adopted, as we did in Sect. 14.5. In that case, the actual optimization variables are the parameters (information matrix, information vector, and weight) of each component in the GMM; moreover, the Bayesian smoother $\mathcal{B}(\cdot, \cdot)$ can be written explicitly using the prediction Eq. (14.17) and the update Eq. (14.25). However, also in this case, the Bayesian smoother leads to nonconvex equality constraints, making the resulting optimization hard to solve globally. In the next section we circumvent this issue by adopting a sampling-based approximation of the posterior. The second issue is connected with the "if" statement that controls the acquisition of future measurements. In the next section we introduce binary variables to model the fact that a measurement from sensor i is acquired only when the searcher is within communication radius from the sensor position s_i.

14.6.2 Sampling-Based Aided Search via Convex Mixed-Integer Programming

In this section we approximate the posterior about the trajectory of the target with a set of K weighted samples, as commonly done in particle filtering. More formally, we approximate the posterior at time t as:

$$\mathbb{P}(y_{1:t} | Z_{1:t}) \approx \sum_{k=1}^{K} \bar{\omega}_t^{(k)} \delta(y_{1:t} - \bar{y}_{1:t}^{(k)}), \qquad (14.31)$$

where $\delta(\cdot)$ denotes the Dirac delta function, $\bar{y}_{1:t}^{(k)} \in \mathbb{R}^{4t}$ is the k-th trajectory hypothesis, and the weights $\bar{\omega}_t^{(k)}$ are such that $\bar{\omega}_t^{(k)} \ge 0, \forall k$, and $\sum_{k=1}^{K} \bar{\omega}_t^{(k)} = 1$. Each sample $\bar{y}_{1:t}^{(k)}$ represents a potential trajectory of the target. In practice, we compute the sample-based posterior (14.31) by sampling our sparse GMM (this can be done via acceptance-rejection sampling as shown in the experimental section).

The sample-based approximation (14.31) allows rewriting problem (14.30) as:

$$\min_{\substack{x_t,\ldots,x_{t+L},u_t,\ldots,u_{t+L}, \\ \omega_t^{(k)},\ldots,\omega_{t+L}^{(k)},y_{1:t}^{(k)},\ldots,y_{1:t+L}^{(k)},\forall k}} f(\omega_{t+L}^{(k)},y_{1:t+L}^{(k)})$$

subject to

(searcher constraints) $x_t = \bar{x}_t$, $x_{\tau+1} = A_x x_\tau + B_x u_\tau$, $\|S x_\tau\| \le \bar{S}$, $\|u_\tau\| \le \bar{U}$

(target posterior at time t) $\{\omega_t^{(k)}, y_{1:t}^{(k)}\}_{k=1}^K = \{\bar{\omega}_t^{(k)}, \bar{y}_{1:t}^{(k)}\}_{k=1}^K$

(target posterior evolution) $\{\omega_{\tau+1}^{(k)}, y_{1:\tau+1}^{(k)}\}_{k=1}^K = \mathcal{B}(\{\omega_\tau^{(k)}, y_{1:\tau}^{(k)}\}_{k=1}^K, z_\tau^0)$

(measurements) $z_\tau^0 = (i, \tau, 0)$ if $\|P x_\tau - s_i\| \le r_c$

$\forall \tau = t, \ldots, t+L$, $\forall i = 1, \ldots, N$

$$(14.32)$$

The only difference between (14.32) and (14.30) is that we substituted the posterior $\mathcal{P}_{1:\tau}$ with its sample-based parametrization $\{\omega_\tau^{(k)}, y_{1:\tau}^{(k)}\}_{k=1}^K$, which is now part of our optimization variables; with slight abuse of notation we kept the same symbols for the objective function $f(\cdot)$ and for the smoother $\mathcal{B}(\cdot, \cdot)$, while these functions will be implemented in a different way when using the sample-based approximation.

Our goal in this section is to reformulate the objective function $f(\cdot)$ as a convex function, and the Bayesian smoother $\mathcal{B}(\cdot, \cdot)$ and the "if" statement as convex constraints. Since all other constraints in (14.32) are already convex, this would make our search problem a convex program, which can be solved globally; the price to pay for convexity is that our reformulation requires the introduction of binary variables.

Bayesian recursion as a convex constraint In our sample-based approximation, the Bayesian smoother $\mathcal{B}(\cdot, \cdot)$ leads to a simple constraint on the evolution of the weights in the particle filter.

We can write explicitly the Bayesian recursion for our particle filter as [68, §4.2] (for all samples $k = 1, \ldots, K$):

$$\begin{cases} y_{1:\tau+1}^{(k)} = A y_{1:\tau}^{(k)} + \bar{w}_\tau & \text{(particle prediction)} \\ \omega_{\tau+1}^{(k)} = \omega_\tau^{(k)} \mathbb{P}\left(z_\tau^0 | y_{1:\tau}^{(k)}\right) & \text{(weight update)} \end{cases} \qquad (14.33)$$

where $\bar{w}_t$ is a realization of the random noise $w_t \sim \mathcal{N}(0, \Omega_w)$, while $\mathbb{P}\left(z_\tau^0 | y_{1:\tau}^{(k)}\right)$ is the likelihood of the measurement z_τ^0 given the k-th particle trajectory $y_{1:\tau}^{(k)}$. Note that if no measurement is acquired (i.e., when the searcher cannot interrogate a sensor), the weights remain unchanged:

$$\omega_{\tau+1}^{(k)} = \omega_\tau^{(k)} \qquad k = 1, \ldots, K \qquad (14.34)$$

Before substituting the Bayesian smoother (14.33), in (14.32), we note that after sampling the realization of the noise $\bar{w}_\tau$, Eq. (14.33) uniquely defines the future evolution of the particles $y_{1:\tau}^{(k)}$ for all $\tau = t+1, \ldots, t+L$. Therefore, we can precompute the trajectories $y_{1:\tau}^{(k)}$ and the measurement likelihood $\mathbb{P}\left(z_\tau^0|y_{1:\tau}^{(k)}\right)$ before-hand; in particular, for each sensor i and for each sample k, we precompute the likelihood of receiving a "no detection" from sensor i, by evaluating the likelihood function (14.23) at $y_{1:\tau}^{(k)}$. Let us use the shorthand $p_i^{(k)}$ for the resulting likelihoods:

$$p_{i\tau}^{(k)} = \mathbb{P}\left(z_\tau^0|y_{1:\tau}^{(k)}\right) \tag{14.35}$$

Therefore, we can now rewrite (14.32) as:

$$\min_{\substack{x_t,\ldots,x_{t+L},u_t,\ldots,u_{t+L}, \\ \omega_t^{(k)},\ldots,\omega_{t+L}^{(k)},y_{1:t}^{(k)},\ldots,y_{1:t+L}^{(k)},\forall k}} f(\omega_{t+L}^{(k)}, y_{1:t+L}^{(k)})$$

subject to

(searcher constraints) $x_t = \bar{x}_t$, $x_{\tau+1} = A_x x_\tau + B_x u_\tau$, $\|S x_\tau\| \leq \bar{S}$, $\|u_\tau\| \leq \bar{U}$

(target posterior at time t) $\{\omega_t^{(k)}, y_{1:t}^{(k)}\}_{k=1}^K = \{\bar{\omega}_t^{(k)}, \bar{y}_{1:t}^{(k)}\}_{k=1}^K$

(target posterior evolution) $y_{1:\tau+1}^{(k)} = A y_{1:\tau}^{(k)} + \bar{w}_t$

$\qquad\qquad \omega_{\tau+1}^{(k)} = \omega_\tau^{(k)} p_{i\tau}^{(k)}$ if $\|P x_\tau - s_i\| \leq r_c$

$\qquad\qquad \omega_{\tau+1}^{(k)} = \omega_\tau^{(k)}$ if $\|P x_\tau - s_i\| \geq r_c$

$\qquad\qquad \forall \tau = t,\ldots,t+L$, $i=1,\ldots,N$, , $k=1,\ldots,K$

$$\tag{14.36}$$

Note that the "if" statements allow applying a different weight update depending on whether or not we got a measurement from sensor i, according to (14.33) and (14.34).

As remarked above, the evolution of $y_{1:\tau}^{(k)}$ for all $\tau = t+1,\ldots,t+L$ is uniquely defined (i.e., we have no way of changing it using our control actions), hence we can safely remove $y_{1:\tau}^{(k)}$ from the optimization, and pre-compute the terminal state $y_{1:t+L}^{(k)}$ which appears in the objective; let us call this terminal state as $\bar{y}_{1:t+L}^{(k)}$ to denote that it is known and let us drop the constraints related to $y_{1:\tau}^{(k)}$ from (14.36):

$$\min_{\substack{x_t,\ldots,x_{t+L},u_t,\ldots,u_{t+L}, \\ \omega_t^{(k)},\ldots,\omega_{t+L}^{(k)}}} f(\omega_{t+L}^{(k)}, \bar{y}_{1:t+L}^{(k)})$$

subject to

(searcher constraints) $x_t = \bar{x}_t$, $x_{\tau+1} = A_x x_\tau + B_x u_\tau$, $\|S x_\tau\| \leq \bar{S}$, $\|u_\tau\| \leq \bar{U}$

(weights at time t) $\omega_t^{(k)} = \bar{\omega}_t^{(k)}$,

(weights evolution) $\omega_{\tau+1}^{(k)} = \omega_\tau^{(k)} p_{i\tau}^{(k)}$ if $\|P x_\tau - s_i\| \leq r_c$

$\qquad\qquad \omega_{\tau+1}^{(k)} = \omega_\tau^{(k)}$ if $\|P x_\tau - s_i\| \geq r_c$

$\qquad\qquad \forall \tau = t,\ldots,t+L$, $i=1,\ldots,N$, , $k=1,\ldots,K$

$$\tag{14.37}$$

So far, by using a sample-based approximation, we rephrased the original problem (14.30), including infinite dimensional pdfs, into one with simpler constraints, in which the action of the searcher on the evolution of the target posterior is captured by the weights associated to each sample.

Uncertainty minimization as a convex objective In this section we provide a more explicit expression for the uncertainty metric $f(\cdot)$ in the objective of (14.37). In particular, we select $f(\cdot)$ to be the trace of the covariance of the posterior of the target position at the end of the horizon. Since we approximated our posterior using a weighted set of samples, the resulting sample covariance (remembering that, for any $\tau \in \{1 \dots, t\}$, U_τ is a matrix that extracts the position at time τ from the target state) is:

$$\mathrm{cov}(U_{t+L} y_{1:t+L}) = U_{t+L}\mathrm{cov}(y_{1:t+L})U_{t+L}^{\mathsf{T}} =$$

$$\sum_{k=1}^{K} \omega_{t+L}^{(k)} (U_{t+L}\bar{y}_{1:t+L}^{(k)} - U_{t+L}\mu_{1:t+L})(U_{t+L}\bar{y}_{1:t+L}^{(k)} - U_{t+L}\mu_{1:t+L})^{\mathsf{T}}$$

where $\mu_{1:t+L} = \sum_{k=1}^{K} \omega_{t+L}^{(k)} \bar{y}_{1:t+L}^{(k)}$ is the sample mean. The trace of the sample covariance is:

$$\mathrm{tr}\left(\sum_{k=1}^{K} \omega_{t+L}^{(k)} (U_{t+L}\bar{y}_{1:t+L}^{(k)} - U_{t+L}\mu_{1:t+L})(U_{t+L}\bar{y}_{1:t+L}^{(k)} - U_{t+L}\mu_{1:t+L})^{\mathsf{T}}\right) =$$

$$\sum_{k=1}^{K} \omega_{t+L}^{(k)} \| U_{t+L}\bar{y}_{1:t+L}^{(k)} - U_{t+L}\mu_{1:t+L} \|^2$$

$$(14.38)$$

The function in (14.38) is not convex in $\omega_{t+L}^{(k)}$ since also $\mu_{1:t+L}$ depends on the weights at the end of the horizon. To avoid this nonconvexity, we compute the sample mean using the initial sample weights $\bar{\omega}_t^{(k)}$, rather then the ones at time $t + L$:

$$\bar{\mu}_{1:t+L} = \sum_{k=1}^{K} \bar{\omega}_t^{(k)} \bar{y}_{1:t+L}^{(k)} \tag{14.39}$$

This approximation is motivated by computational considerations (i.e., it leads to a convex objective), and it is empirically shown to lead to effective search policies. Moreover, it has the advantage that the square in (14.38) can be precomputed before the optimization. To simplify notation, we define the following scalars, which are computed before planning:

$$d_k \doteq \| U_{t+L}\bar{y}_{1:t+L}^{(k)} - U_{t+L}\bar{\mu}_{1:t+L} \|^2 \qquad k = 1, \dots, K. \tag{14.40}$$

Roughly speaking, d_k represents the squared distance between the position of the k-th sample trajectory at time $t + L$ and the sample mean. Using the expression of the trace of the covariance (14.38) and the definition of d_k in (14.40), our objective function becomes:

$$f(\omega_{t+L}^{(k)}, \bar{y}_{1:t+L}^{(k)}) = \sum_{k=1}^{K} \omega_{t+L}^{(k)} d_k \tag{14.41}$$

which is a linear function of the unknown weights.

Substituting the objective (14.41) in (14.37) and applying the change of variables $v_\tau^{(k)} = \log(\omega_\tau^{(k)})$, we get:

$$\min_{\substack{x_t,\dots,x_{t+L},u_t,\dots,u_{t+L}, \\ v_t^{(k)},\dots,v_{t+L}^{(k)}}} \sum_{k=1}^{K} \exp(v_{t+L}^{(k)}) d_k$$

subject to

(searcher constraints) $x_t = \bar{x}_t$, $x_{\tau+1} = A_x x_\tau + B_x u_\tau$, $\|S x_\tau\| \le \bar{S}$, $\|u_\tau\| \le \bar{U}$

(weights at time t) $v_t^{(k)} = \log \bar{\omega}_t^{(k)}$

(weights evolution) $v_{\tau+1}^{(k)} = v_\tau^{(k)} + \log p_{i\tau}^{(k)}$ if $\|P x_\tau - s_i\| \le r_c$

$\qquad\qquad\qquad v_{\tau+1}^{(k)} = v_\tau^{(k)}$ if $\|P x_\tau - s_i\| \ge r_c$

$\qquad\qquad\qquad \forall \tau = t,\dots,t+L$, $i=1,\dots,N$, , $k=1,\dots,K$

$$\tag{14.42}$$

which is now a convex problem, except the "if" conditions which appear in the constraints. Recall that $\bar{x}_t$, d_k, $\bar{\omega}_t^{(k)}$, $p_{i\tau}^{(k)}$, are known quantities, while the optimization variables are now the future searcher control and state, and the logarithm of the weights, i.e., $v_t^{(k)}, \dots, v_{t+L}^{(k)}$.

Writing the "if" statements using binary variables So far, we showed how to compute our search strategy by solving the optimization problem (14.42). Problem (14.42) is convex, although it includes "if" statements which depend on some of the optimization variables (i.e., the searcher position $P x_\tau$). These kind of constraints cannot be directly fed to a standard solver, hence in this section we show how to write them in a more explicit form by using binary variables.

Let us introduce a set of integer variables $b_{i\tau}$, such that, if $b_{i\tau} = 1$, then the searcher is within communication radius from sensor i at time τ, or $b_{i\tau} = 0$ otherwise. Using $b_{i\tau}$, we can rewrite the two constraints which include the "if" statements in (14.42) using a single equality constraint:

$$v_{\tau+1}^{(k)} = v_\tau^{(k)} + b_{i\tau} \log p_{i\tau}^{(k)} \tag{14.43}$$

When $b_{i\tau} = 1$ we have a measurement from sensor i, hence we apply the update $v_{\tau+1}^{(k)} = v_\tau^{(k)} + \log p_{i\tau}^{(k)}$, otherwise Eq. (14.43) reduces to $v_{\tau+1}^{(k)} = v_\tau^{(k)}$.

Now we only remain to enforce that $b_{i\tau} = 1$ if and only if the searcher is within a distance r_c from sensor i. We enforce this condition by adding the following constraint to our optimization problem:

$$\|P x_\tau - s_i\| \le r_c + (1 - b_{i\tau})\mathcal{M} \tag{14.44}$$

where $\mathcal{M} \in \mathbb{R}$ is a large constant. In (14.44), when $b_{i\tau} = 1$ the constraint becomes $\| Px_\tau - s_i \| \le r_c$, while for $b_{i\tau} = 0$ the constraint (14.44) vanishes, since the right-hand side is made arbitrarily large by $\mathcal{M}$. Therefore, whenever $\| Px_\tau - s_i \| \ge r_c$, the only way to satisfy the constraint (14.44) is to set $b_{i\tau} = 0$: this is exactly the desired behavior in which $b_{i\tau}$ must be zero whenever $\| Px_\tau - s_i \| \ge r_c$, i.e., when the searcher position is further than r_c from the sensor. Conversely, whenever $\| Px_\tau - s_i \| \le r_c$ the optimization encourages $b_{i\tau}$ to be one, since this yields a smaller objective.[2]

We are now ready to provide the final statement of our finite-horizon search strategy. By substituting the condition (14.43) in place of the two constraints with the "if" statement in (14.42), and by adding the extra constraint (14.44), we get:

$$
\min_{\substack{x_t,\ldots,x_{t+L},u_t,\ldots,u_{t+L}, \\ v_t^{(k)},\ldots,v_{t+L}^{(k)} \\ b_{i\tau}, i=1,\ldots,N, \tau=1,\ldots,L}} \sum_{k=1}^{K} \exp(v_{t+L}^{(k)}) d_k
$$

subject to

(searcher constraints) $x_t = \bar{x}_t$, $x_{\tau+1} = A_x x_\tau + B_x u_\tau$, $\| S x_\tau \| \le \bar{S}$, $\| u_\tau \| \le \bar{U}$

(weights at time t) $v_t^{(k)} - \log \bar{\omega}_t^{(k)}$

(weights evolution) $v_{\tau+1}^{(k)} = v_\tau^{(k)} + b_{i\tau} \log p_{i\tau}^{(k)}$

$\| Px_\tau - s_i \| \le r_c + (1 - b_{i\tau})\mathcal{M}$

$\forall \tau = t,\ldots,t+L$, $i=1,\ldots,N$, , $k=1,\ldots,K$

(14.45)

Problem (14.45) is a mixed-integer convex problem, with $L \cdot N$ binary variables, where N is the number of sensors and L is the number of look-ahead steps in the horizon. The following remark provides a more intuitive explanation of the search strategy resulting from (14.45).

Remark 2 (Intuitive Explanation of Problem (14.45)) In problem (14.45) the target trajectory posterior is represented as a set of weighted samples. The objective function in (14.45) rewards the minimization of the weights of the samples. In particular, the objective rewards minimizing weights of samples having large d_k. From (14.40), d_k is essentially the (squared) distance of the terminal position of the particle from the mean. Therefore, the objective tries to minimize the weight of samples that fall far from the mean, hence trying to reduce the spread of the target position posterior. In order to reduce the weight of a sample k, the optimization encourages many binary variables $b_{i\tau}$ to be one (this will decrease $v_{\tau+1}^{(k)}$, since $p_{i\tau}^{(k)} \le 1$ and $\log p_{i\tau}^{(k)} \le 0$). However, $b_{i\tau} = 1$ which can only happen if the searcher is close enough to sensor i. Therefore, problem (14.45) rewards the searcher to pass in proximity of the sensors, while respecting the motion constraints of the searcher.

---

[2] When $b_{i\tau} = 1$, the weight update is $v_{\tau+1}^{(k)} = v_\tau^{(k)} + \log p_{i\tau}^{(k)} \le v_\tau^{(k)}$ (recall: $p_{i\tau}^{(k)} \le 1$ hence $\log p_{i\tau}^{(k)}$ is negative), leading to a smaller objective.

Further Computational Remarks So far we have been agnostic about the type of norms used to measure distances. While an intuitive choice if the Euclidean norm, computational reasons suggest otherwise. If we use the ℓ_1 or the ℓ_∞ norm, all the constraints in (14.45) become linear constraints. Moreover, if we use the first-order expansion $\exp(v_{t+L}^{(k)}) \approx \text{const} + v_{t+L}^{(k)}$, then also the objective becomes a linear function. Using these two linear approximations, we rephrase (14.45) as a mixed-integer *linear* program (MILP), for which fast specialized solvers exist.

14.7   Numerical Experiments

The numerical results in this section show that the proposed approach can effectively reduce the uncertainty about the target location and has a higher success rate in finding the target, compared to a greedy strategy. The section is organized as follows. Section 14.7.1 describes the simulation scenario. Section 14.7.2 provides implementation details for the tested algorithms. Section 14.7.3 describes a typical simulation outcome, that highlights the key features of the proposed approach, compared to a greedy strategy. Section 14.7.4 reports the results of a Monte Carlo analysis, providing statistics regarding the performance of the proposed approach for different motion profiles of the target (i.e., changing maximum speed, agility) and increasing uncertainty on the initial target state.

14.7.1   The Scenario

The scenario in which the search takes place is a square region $\mathcal{R}$ of size $500\,\text{m} \times 500\,\text{m}$. Unattended ground sensors are uniformly spaced within $\mathcal{R}$. We consider a scenario with 100 sensors, each one having sensing radius $r = 20\,\text{m}$ (Fig. 14.4).

The searcher successfully accomplishes its task if it is able to localize the target before it escapes the region $\mathcal{R}$ and before a maximum time $\bar{T}$ is elapsed (we set $\bar{T} = 100$). A target is localized when the uncertainty on its current position is below a given threshold. In particular, the current position covariance $\bar{\Sigma}$ can be computed from our Gaussian Mixture model $\mathcal{M}(\{\eta_{t,j}, \Omega_{t,j}, \alpha_{t,j}\}_{j=1}^m)$ as:

$$\bar{\Sigma} = \sum_{j=1}^m \alpha_{t,j} \left(U_t \Omega_{t,j}^{-1} U_t^{-1} + U_t (\mu_{t,j} - \bar{\mu})(\mu_{t,j} - \bar{\mu})^{\mathsf{T}} U_t^{\mathsf{T}} \right) \tag{14.46}$$

where $U_t \in \mathbb{R}^{2 \times 4t}$ is the matrix that extracts the position at time t from the state, as defined in (14.20), $\mu_{t,j} = \Omega_{t,j}^{-1} \eta_{t,j}$ is the mean of each mixture component, and $\bar{\mu} = \sum_{j=1}^m \alpha_{t,j} \mu_{t,j}$ is the mean of the GMM. Note that we never invert $\Omega_{t,j}$: we rather solve sparse (tridiagonal) linear systems, which makes the cost of computing the covariance (14.46) negligible. Therefore the target is said to be localized if the

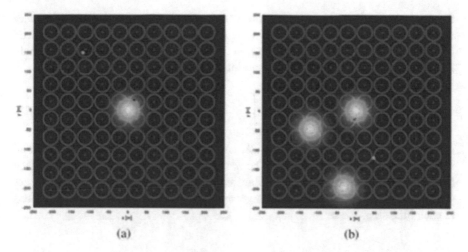

Fig. 14.4 Test scenario: the target (in red) moves in a square region $\mathcal{R}$. The region contains uniformly spaced ground sensors (cyan dots); the sensing radius of each sensor is shown as a circle. The position of the searcher (in green) is randomly drawn within $\mathcal{R}$; the searcher has an initial distribution on the target position, shown as a background color (light yellow denotes high probability, blue is low probability). (**a**) unimodal initial distribution, (**b**) multimodal initial distribution.

marginal position standard deviation (i.e., the square root of the diagonal entries of $\bar{\Sigma}$) falls below a threshold that we set to be equal to half of the sensing radius of the sensors:

$$\bar{\sigma} \doteq \sqrt{\max(\operatorname{diag}(\bar{\Sigma}))} \leq r/2 \qquad (14.47)$$

The searcher dynamics is described by a double integrator, with maximum speed bounded by $\bar{S} = 10\text{m/s}$ and maximum acceleration bounded by $\bar{U} = 5\,\text{m/s}^2$. The searcher starts with zero velocity and its initial position is randomly drawn within $\mathcal{R}$. The searcher is provided with an initial distribution over the target state (Fig. 14.4). The initial target posterior is a Gaussian with zero mean and information matrix Ω_1 (more details below). The communication radius r_c (the distance at which the searcher can interrogate a sensor) is set to $r_c = 20\,\text{m}$.

The target initial state is drawn according to the initial distribution $y_1 \sim \mathcal{N}(0, \Omega_1)$. In particular, we set $\Omega_1 = \operatorname{blkdiag}((\sigma_p^1)^2 \mathbf{I}_2, (\sigma_v^1)^2 \mathbf{I}_2)$, where σ_p^1 and σ_v^1 are the standard deviations of the initial target position and velocity, respectively. The nominal values for these parameters are:

$$\sigma_p^1 = 20\,\text{m} \qquad , \qquad \sigma_v^1 = \kappa_v \frac{\bar{S}}{3} \qquad (14.48)$$

where κ_v is a constant parameter, called the *speed factor*. The condition $\sigma_v^1 = \kappa_v \bar{S}/3$ guarantees that with high probability (within 3σ from the mean), the velocity of the target is smaller than κ_v times the velocity of the pursuer. Since the capture must happen before the target escapes the region $\mathcal{R}$, considering high target speed (comparable to the one of the searcher, i.e., $\kappa_v = 1$) makes the problem extremely challenging.[3] The target follows the motion model (14.6) with:

$$A = \begin{bmatrix} \mathbf{I}_2 & \mathbf{I}_2 \Delta t \\ \mathbf{0} & \mathbf{I}_2 \end{bmatrix} \tag{14.49}$$

where Δt is a time step (conventionally set to 1). In (14.6), $w_t \sim \mathcal{N}(0, \Omega_w)$ and $\Omega_w = \mathrm{blkdiag}((\sigma_p^w)^2 \mathbf{I}_2, (\sigma_v^w)^2 \mathbf{I}_2)$. The matrix Ω_w is related to the "agility" of the target: when the entries of this matrix are small, the target moves at constant speed, while when the entries are large, the target applies aggressive (random) accelerations at each time step. We set

$$\sigma_p^w = 0.1 \, \mathrm{m} \quad , \quad \sigma_v^w = \kappa_a \, \sigma_v^1 \tag{14.50}$$

where κ_v is a constant parameter, called the *agility factor*.

A visual understanding of the impact of the parameters κ_v and κ_a on the target trajectory is provided by Fig. 14.5. Figure 14.5 shows 10 realizations of the (random) target trajectory for different values of these parameters; for the sake of visualization all trajectories start at the origin and are simulated for 100 time steps. Fig. 14.5b shows a scenario in which the speed factor κ_v is large and the agility factor κ_a is small; in this case, the target tends to move quickly (due to the large initial speed) along straight trajectories (a small κ_a implies that the target only makes small adjustments at each time step). On the other hand, Fig. 14.5c shows a scenario in which κ_v is small, and κ_a is large; in this case the trajectory can be very irregular, with sudden changes in direction. We note that in both cases most of the trajectories escape the scenario within the first 100 time steps (we only display the portion of trajectory within the region $\mathcal{R}$), and for this reason we set the maximum time to be $\bar{T} = 100$. In this section we consider $\kappa_v = 0.3$ and $\kappa_a = 0.01$, while we investigate the effect of these parameters on the search results in Sect. 14.7.4.

14.7.2 The Algorithms: Implementation Details

Proposed approach The GMM-based estimation of Sect. 14.5 is implemented in Matlab, which can efficiently solve sparse linear systems. We set $m = 10^4$ as maximum number of mixture components in the GMM. After this quota is reached, the estimator does not accept "no detection" measurements (i.e., the belief is

---

[3]Think about the extreme case in which the target and the searcher have the same speed: then if the target moves in the opposite direction with respect to the searcher position, *no* search strategy can make the searcher reach the target before it escapes the region $\mathcal{R}$.

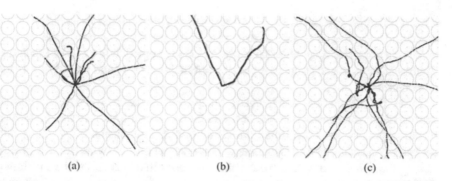

Fig. 14.5 Target motion profiles: examples of target trajectories obtained from the motion model (14.6) for different speed (κ_v) and agility factors (κ_a). Each figure shows 10 realizations of the (random) target trajectory, starting from the center of the scenario. (**a**) Low speed, Low agility $\kappa_v = 0.3$, $\kappa_a = 0.01$. (**b**) High speed, Low agility $\kappa_v = 1$, $\kappa_a = 0.01$. (**c**) Low speed, High agility $\kappa_v = 0.3$, $\kappa_a = 0.2$

predicted but not updated). We also prune mixture components with weight smaller than 10^{-5}. From this distribution, we draw $K = 500$ samples to be used in the MIP (14.45). The linear version of the MIP (14.45) is solved using IBM CPLEX and returns a set of controls for the next L lookahead steps. We use a time horizon of $L = 40$. After the search strategy is computed, the robot follows the planned trajectory until a detection occurs (the plan remains valid until we get a detection, see Sect. 14.6.2). When a detection occurs, the plan is recomputed. We impose an upper bound on the central processor unit (CPU) time required by the MIP: after 300 s, if the MIP has not returned an optimal solution we interrupt the optimization and use the current solution.

Greedy approach We benchmark the proposed approach against a greedy algorithm that tries to reach the most likely position of the target. The estimation part of the greedy approach is still based on the GMM model, with minor changes discussed later in this section. From the GMM, we compute the maximum likelihood target position by discretizing the environment in 10×10 m cells and by evaluating the GMM at the center of each cell. The cell position attaining the maximum probability value is chosen to be the maximum likelihood estimate; we denote the maximum likelihood estimate with $x_{\mathcal{G}}$. In order to plan a path that reaches $x_{\mathcal{G}}$ as quickly as possible, we solve the following convex program:

$$\min_{x_t,\ldots,x_{t+L},u_t,\ldots,u_{t+L}} \sum_{\tau=t}^{t+L} \|x_\tau - x_{\mathcal{G}}\|$$
$$\text{subject to}$$
$$\text{(searcher constraints)}\quad x_t = \bar{x}_t \ , \quad x_{\tau+1} = A_x x_\tau + B_x u_\tau \ , \quad \|S x_\tau\| \leq \bar{S} \ , \quad \|u_\tau\| \leq \bar{U}$$
$$\forall \tau = t,\ldots,t+L$$

$$(14.51)$$

which computes a path over an horizon L that minimizes the distance from the goal location $\|x_\tau - x_{\mathcal{G}}\|$, while satisfying the motion constraints for the searcher.

Also in this case we choose $L = 40$ and we set the searcher dynamics and the speed and acceleration bounds as discussed in the previous section. Since the cost of solving (14.51) is negligible, we apply the greedy approach in a Model Predictive Control fashion: at each step we replan the optimal trajectory and we only apply the first control action.

From the estimation standpoint, a major difference between the proposed approach and the greedy one lies in the reduction scheme we use for the GMM. In our approach, we bound the number of GMM components by rejecting "no detection" measurements; this strategy, however, would not work for the greedy strategy: consider the case in which the searcher already reached the maximum GMM components quota (10^4 components). Then, if the estimator is not allowed to include new measurements, the maximum likelihood estimate x_G tends to remain in the same location, leading the searcher to be stuck at x_G, even when the target was not found at that location. For this reason, in the greedy approach we use a sampling-based GMM reduction, as described in Sect. 14.5. In particular, we apply this reduction scheme after the quota of $m = 10^4$ mixture components is reached. After sampling this large mixture, we fit a smaller one with 10 components. Also in this case, we prune components with weight smaller than 10^{-5}.

14.7.3 A Typical Result

A typical outcome of our search strategy is reported in Fig. 14.6a1–d1. The figures show the initial position of the searcher (green circle, on the top right), the posterior over the current target position (figure background color), and the planned trajectory (in yellow). Figure 14.6a1 shows the trajectory planned by the proposed approach at the start of the search. Figure 14.6b1 shows the execution of the planned trajectory till time $t = 30$ (green), while the trajectory still to be executed if shown in yellow. Figure 14.6c1 shows the change in the target posterior after the first detection (at time $t = 37$) and the newly planned trajectory (yellow line). Figure 14.6d1 trajectory executed till time $t = 51$, right before the searcher intersects the target. A natural behavior emerges from our MIP search: the plan leads the searcher to circle around the peak of the distribution; since the searcher does not know in which direction the target is heading, the smartest strategy is to circle around the initial target location, and interrogate sensors in that area, so to gain intelligence on which direction the target took. Note that the searcher cleverly prefers to follow a wavy path in order to visit as many sensors as possible.

For comparison, we report the initial outcome of the execution of the greedy strategy in Fig. 14.6a2–d2; each figure reports the peak of the position posterior (maximum likelihood estimate) as a black square. The greedy searcher directly points towards the peak of the posterior, and, in doing so, it spreads the probability distribution, increasing the entropy of the resulting posterior (Fig. 14.6b2). After that, the greedy searcher points towards the next peak and again, by visiting the peak, it "splits" the posterior (Fig. 14.6c2); the overall results of the greedy strategy is the creation of multiple distant trajectory hypotheses, which soon become

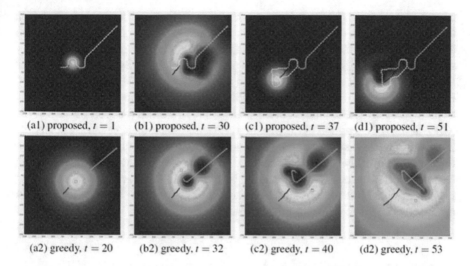

(a1) proposed, $t = 1$ (b1) proposed, $t = 30$ (c1) proposed, $t = 37$ (d1) proposed, $t = 51$

(a2) greedy, $t = 20$ (b2) greedy, $t = 32$ (c2) greedy, $t = 40$ (d2) greedy, $t = 53$

Fig. 14.6 Snapshots taken during different phases of the search. (**a1**) trajectory planned by the proposed approach (yellow line) at the beginning of the search. (**b1**) trajectory executed till time $t = 30$ (green), trajectory still to be executed (yellow), and posterior distribution. (**c1**) first detection at time $t = 37$ and newly planned trajectory by the proposed approach (yellow line). (**d1**) trajectory executed till time $t = 51$, right before the searcher intersects the target. (**a2**)–(**d2**) trajectory executed by the greedy approach (green line) and peak of the posterior (black square)

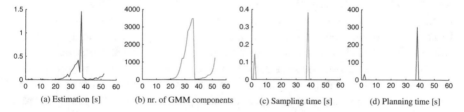

(a) Estimation [s]   (b) nr. of GMM components   (c) Sampling time [s]   (d) Planning time [s]

Fig. 14.7 Timing results. The x-axis reports the time steps of the simulation, the y-axis reports: (**a**) time required to perform recursive estimation (GMM prediction and update) at each time step. (**b**) number of GMM components at each time step. (**c**) time required to sample the GMM to produce the samples used in the MIP formulation (14.45). (**d**) time required to solve the MIP program (14.45) using CPLEX. In all plots, time is expressed in seconds

extremely hard to follow for the searcher. The advantage of the proposed approach is twofold: first, it is aware of the sensors, hence leading the searcher to visit as many sensors as possible along the path; second, it considers the posterior over the *entire trajectory of the target*; on the other hand, the greedy approach only uses the posterior about the latest target position.

We report the timing for each aspect of the proposed approach in Fig. 14.7 for a typical execution (more statistics are reported in the next section). Our estimation model is very efficient as shown in Fig. 14.7a: our non-optimized Matlab implementation can perform estimation over a GMM with thousands mixture components in around a second; the corresponding number of components is given in Fig. 14.7b. Figure 14.7c shows the time required to sample the GMM to produce the trajectory hypotheses used in the MIP (14.45). The sampling time is usually small since sampling can be parallelized (`parfor` loop in Matlab) and only requires sparse matrix-vector operations thanks to the sparsity of our GMM model. Finally, Fig. 14.7d shows the time required to solve the MIP (14.45); this is the dominant cost of our approach. The two peaks correspond to the two times the searcher solves the MIP: during the execution of the plan no further computation is needed. Usually the first peak is smaller, since the target trajectory hypotheses only cross few sensors and the optimizer quickly determines that there is no advantage in visiting the remaining sensors (hence it sets the corresponding binary variables to zero). While planning is computational intensive, it has to be executed only occasionally and usually 2–4 optimizations suffice to localize the target.

14.7.4 Monte Carlo Analysis

In this section, we provide quantitative results to assess the performance of the proposed approach in large-scale simulated experiments. We compute statistics about timing and performance of our approach in scenarios of increasing complexity.

Success rates and timing We consider the simulation setup of Sect. 14.7.1, with nominal values for the speed and agility factors ($\kappa_v = 0.3$, $\kappa_a = 0.01$). We run 30 Monte Carlo simulations and in each simulation we record whether: (i) the target was localized (label: `Loc`), (ii) it escaped the region $\mathcal{R}$ (label: `Esc`), or (iii) the maximum time $\bar{T}$ elapsed (label: `Max`). We also consider the target localized when it is within the sensing radius of the searcher. Figure 14.8a shows the histogram of the simulation outcomes comparing the proposed approach against the greedy search. In nominal conditions, the proposed approach can correctly localize the target in more than 90% of the tests, while the greedy approach only localizes the target

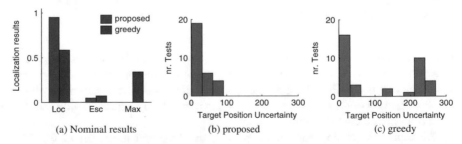

(a) Nominal results   (b) proposed   (c) greedy

Fig. 14.8 (a) Percentage of runs in which the target was localized ("Loc" bar), escaped the region $\mathcal{R}$ ("Esc" bar), or was not found before the time limit ("Max" bar). The bar plot compares the proposed approach (blue) against the greedy approach (red). Histograms of the position uncertainty of the target at the end of the test for (b) the proposed approach and (c) the greedy approach

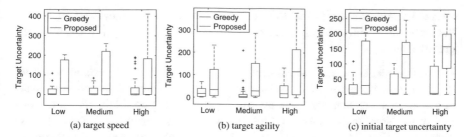

Fig. 14.9 Statistics about the terminal target position uncertainty, comparing the proposed approach against a greedy search strategy. Statistics are computed over 30 Monte Carlo runs. The figures provide statistics for increasing (**a**) target speed, (**b**) target agility, and (**c**) initial uncertainty about the target state

in 60% of the runs. In particular, in all tests the proposed approach was able to localize the target in the allotted time. In few runs the target was able to escape: we are considering challenging scenarios with quickly moving targets and unfortunate extractions of the initial target state can result in large target speeds. Figure 14.8b, c give further insights on the performance of the two approaches, showing the histogram of the target uncertainty $\bar{\sigma}$ at the end of the runs. The histogram Fig. 14.8b confirms that in most tests, the proposed approach is able to correctly reduce the uncertainty on the target location. On the other hand, Fig. 14.8c shows that in many runs the greedy search leads to very poor estimation of the target location. The mean estimation time, averaged over the 30 runs, is around 0.22 s, while the maximum estimation time is 12.40 s (with $1.46 \cdot 10^4$ mixture components); average planning time is 39.51 s while the maximum matches our upper bound (300 s).

Increasing target speed   In this section, we consider more challenging scenarios, with increasing target speed, showing that the performance of the proposed approach degrades gracefully when the complexity of the search instance increases; on the other hand, we will see that the performance of a greedy search quickly becomes unacceptable. As mentioned in Sect. 14.7.1 the target speed is controlled by the speed factor κ_v. Figure 14.9a shows the box plot of the target uncertainty $\bar{\sigma}$ (at the end of the runs) for increasing target speed (Low: $\kappa_v = \frac{1}{3}$, Medium: $\kappa_v = \frac{1}{2}$, High: $\kappa_v = 1$). In the box plot, the central line indicates the median, and the bottom and top edges of the box indicate the 25th and 75th percentiles, respectively. The size of the box produced by the proposed approach remains small, confirming that in most tests our search strategy is able to localize the target. On the other hand, the box of the target uncertainty quickly increases with increasing target speed when using a greedy search.

Increasing target agility   As mentioned in Sect. 14.7.1 the target agility is controlled by the agility factor κ_a. Figure 14.9b shows the box plot of the target uncertainty $\bar{\sigma}$ (at the end of the runs) for increasing target agility (Low: $\kappa_a = 0.03$, Medium: $\kappa_a = 0.1$, High: $\kappa_a = 0.2$). The size of the box produced by the proposed approach increases gracefully for increasing target agility, confirming that in most tests our search strategy is able to localize the target. On the other hand, the box of the target uncertainty quickly increases with increasing target agility when using a greedy search.

Increasing target initial uncertainty We present a final set of tests in which we increase the complexity of the search by making the initial distribution over the target location multimodal, as shown in Fig. 14.4b. Figure 14.9c shows the box plot of the target uncertainty $\bar{\sigma}$ (at the end of the runs) for increasing initial target uncertainty (Low: 1 mode, Medium: 2 modes, High: 3 modes). To generate the initial target distribution we set one mode at the center of the scenario (as done in the previous tests): from this mode we generate the initial state of the target. Then we add further modes having mean position uniformly drawn in the square $\mathcal{R}$. The searcher only has access to the GMM being the sum of all these modes: this corrresponds to the case in which the prior knowledge about the target position is unreliable and includes multiple (possibly inaccurate) hypotheses. The median target uncertainty remains fairly constant for the proposed approach, confirming that in most of the runs the target is localized; the size of the box increases gracefully with the number of modes in the initial target distribution. On the other hand, the median target uncertainty quickly increases when using the greedy approach.

14.8 Conclusion

We considered an *aided optimal search* problem in which a searcher has to find a target moving in a 2D field scattered with unattended ground sensors. The searcher is "blind" in the sense that it cannot directly detect the target, and it has to leverage opportunistic information gathered by the UGS in its communication range. Each UGS records a binary measurement which indicates whether the target passed in its neighborhood or not; moreover, the UGS records a timestamp at which the last detection occurred. This setup is challenging for two reasons. First, the sensors possibly provide information about past states of the target, hence requiring the searcher to reason over the entire trajectory of the target rather than on its current location. Computationally, the estimation of the target trajectory is an inference problem over a large continuous state space. The second challenge is connected to the fact that the searcher can only interrogate sensors within its communication range. Therefore, the searcher has to devise effective motion policies that are opportunistic in visiting sensors which are informative to estimate the current location of the target.

We adopt a *Dynamic Data-Driven Applications Systems* (DDDAS) paradigm, in which the data collected by the searcher is used to update the belief on the trajectory of the target, and the searcher actively steers the measurement process to improve its knowledge about the location of the target. More specifically, we propose two main contributions that address these two challenges. The first contribution is a sparse Gaussian Mixture Model to perform optimal Bayesian estimation over the trajectory of the target. We show that parameterizing the GMM in information (inverse covariance) form leads to a sparse GMM, enabling estimation over GMM with thousands of mixture components in a fraction of a second. The second contribution regards decision making. We propose a finite-horizon planning approach that computes the optimal searcher trajectory that minimizes the uncertainty about the target location. By using a sampling-based approximation, this search strategy leads to a mixed-integer convex program, which can be solved in reasonable time in small and medium instances. We validate the proposed contributions in extensive simulations including Monte Carlo runs testing the performance of our approach against a greedy search for increasing target speed and agility, and increasing uncertainty about the initial target location.

This work opens different avenues for future work. From the theoretical standpoint, it is interesting to devise sufficient conditions (e.g., maximum target speed or agility) to guarantee that the target is localized, or to derive upper bounds on the optimal search time. From the algorithmic standpoint, it is interesting to substitute the MIP-based search with possibly suboptimal but more efficient search techniques. Finally, another interesting avenue for future work includes testing the proposed approach in realistic search problems using a setup similar to the one described in [2].

A   Prediction Equations

In this section we derive the equations for the prediction phase of our incremental smoother. We start with a lemma, which will be useful to simplify the derivation later on.

Lemma 1 (From measurement to state space) *Given a multivariate Gaussian* $\mathcal{N}(Ax; \eta, \Omega)$, *with* $A \in \mathbb{R}^{d \times d}$ *and full rank, then the multivariate Gaussian can be written equivalently as:*

$$\mathcal{N}(Ax; \eta, \Omega) = \mathcal{N}(x; A^T \eta, A^T \Omega A) \tag{14.52}$$

Proof. We prove the claim by inspection. We write explicitly the right-hand side of (14.52) as:

$$\mathcal{N}(x; A^T \eta, A^T \Omega A) = k \exp\left\{ -\tfrac{1}{2}[x - (A^T \Omega A)^{-1} A^T \eta]^T \times \right.$$
$$(A^T \Omega A)[x - (A^T \Omega A)^{-1} A^T \eta]\right\} = \tag{14.53}$$
$$k \exp\left\{ -\tfrac{1}{2}\left[x^T(A^T \Omega A)x - 2\eta^T Ax + \eta^T A(A^T \Omega A)^{-1} A^T \eta \right]\right\}$$

From the fact that A is square and full rank (hence invertible), the previous simplifies to:

$$k \exp\left\{-\tfrac{1}{2}\left[(Ax)^\mathsf{T}\Omega(Ax) - 2\eta^\mathsf{T}Ax + \eta^\mathsf{T}\Omega^{-1}\eta\right]\right\} =$$
$$k \exp\left\{-\tfrac{1}{2}\left[(Ax - \Omega^{-1}\eta)^\mathsf{T}\Omega(Ax - \Omega^{-1}\eta)\right]\right\} = \mathcal{N}(Ax; \eta, \Omega) \tag{14.54}$$

which proves the claim. □

We can now focus on the derivation of the prediction equations. Let us start from the general prediction Eq. (14.14):

$$\mathbb{P}(y_{1:t+1}|Z_{1:t}) = \mathbb{P}(y_{t+1}|y_t)\,\mathbb{P}(y_{1:t}|Z_{1:t}) \tag{14.55}$$

Substituting our choice of prior probability (14.15) and transition probability (14.7), we get:

$$\mathbb{P}(y_{1:t+1}|Z_{1:t}) = \mathcal{N}(y_{t+1} - Ay_t; 0, \Omega_w)\mathcal{M}(y_{1:t}; \{\eta_{t,j}, \Omega_{t,j}, \alpha_{t,j}\}_{j=1}^m) =$$
$$\mathcal{N}(y_{t+1} - Ay_t; 0, \Omega_w)\sum_{j=1}^m \alpha_{t,j}\mathcal{N}(y_{1:t}; \eta_{t,j}, \Omega_{t,j}) =$$
$$\sum_{j=1}^m \alpha_{t,j}\mathcal{N}(y_{t+1} - Ay_t; 0, \Omega_w)\mathcal{N}(y_{1:t}; \eta_{t,j}, \Omega_{t,j}) \tag{14.56}$$

Now we use the definition of $S_{1:t}$ and $S_{t:t+1}$, given in (14.18), which we substitute in (14.56):

$$\mathbb{P}(y_{1:t+1}|Z_{1:t}) = \sum_{j=1}^m \alpha_{t,j}\mathcal{N}(S_{t:t+1}y_{1:t+1}; 0, \Omega_w)\mathcal{N}(S_{1:t}y_{1:t+1}; \eta_{t,j}, \Omega_{t,j}) \tag{14.57}$$

We can develop each summand as follows:

$$\mathcal{N}(S_{t:t+1}y_{1:t+1}; 0, \Omega_w)\mathcal{N}(S_{1:t}y_{1:t+1}; \eta_{t,j}, \Omega_{t,j}) =$$
$$\frac{[\det(\Omega_w)\det(\Omega_{t,j})]^{\frac{1}{2}}}{(2\pi)^{\frac{4(t+1)}{2}}}\exp\left\{-\tfrac{1}{2}\left(\begin{bmatrix} S_{1:t} \\ S_{t:t+1}\end{bmatrix}y_{1:t+1} - \begin{bmatrix}\Omega_{t,j}^{-1}\eta_{t,j} \\ 0\end{bmatrix}\right)^\mathsf{T} I \times \right.$$
$$\left.\begin{bmatrix}\Omega_{t,j} & 0 \\ 0 & \Omega_w\end{bmatrix}\left(\begin{bmatrix} S_{1:t} \\ S_{t:t+1}\end{bmatrix}y_{1:t+1} - \begin{bmatrix}\Omega_{t,j}^{-1}\eta_{t,j} \\ 0\end{bmatrix}\right)\right\} =$$
$$\mathcal{N}\left(\begin{bmatrix} S_{1:t} \\ S_{t:t+1}\end{bmatrix}y_{1:t+1}; \begin{bmatrix}\eta_{t,j} \\ 0\end{bmatrix}, \begin{bmatrix}\Omega_{t,j} & 0 \\ 0 & \Omega_w\end{bmatrix}\right) \tag{14.58}$$

Noting that the matrix $\begin{bmatrix} S_{1:t} \\ S_{t:t+1}\end{bmatrix}$ is square and full rank, we apply Lemma 1 and simplify the previous expression as:

$$\mathcal{N}(S_{t:t+1}y_{1:t+1}; 0, \Omega_w)\mathcal{N}(S_{1:t}y_{1:t+1}; \eta_{t,j}, \Omega_{t,j}) =$$
$$\mathcal{N}(y_{1:t+1}; S_{1:t}^\mathsf{T}\eta_{t,j}, S_{1:t}^\mathsf{T}\Omega_{t,j}S_{1:t} + S_{t:t+1}^\mathsf{T}\Omega_{t,j}S_{t:t+1}) \tag{14.59}$$

Substituting (14.59) back into (14.57), we obtain:

$$\mathbb{P}\left(y_{1:t+1}|Z_{1:t}\right) = \sum_{j=1}^{m} \alpha_{t,j} \mathcal{N}(y_{1:t+1}; S_{1:t}^{\mathsf{T}}\eta_{t,j}, S_{1:t}^{\mathsf{T}}\Omega_{t,j}S_{1:t} + S_{t:t+1}^{\mathsf{T}}\Omega_{t,j}S_{t:t+1})$$
$$(14.60)$$

which coincides with Eqs. (14.16) and (14.17).

B   Update Equations

In this section we derive the equations for the update phase of our incremental smoother. We start with a lemma, which will be useful to simplify the derivation later on.

Lemma 2 (Update in Information Form) *Given two multivariate Gaussians* $\mathcal{N}(x; \bar{\eta}, \bar{\Omega})$ *and* $\mathcal{N}(Ax; \eta_a, \Omega_a)$, *with* $x \in \mathbb{R}^d$ *and* $A \in \mathbb{R}^{d_a \times d}$ *(full row rank,* $d_a \le d$), *then the following equality holds:*

$$\mathcal{N}(Ax; \eta_a, \Omega_a)\mathcal{N}(x; \bar{\eta}, \bar{\Omega}) = \kappa \mathcal{N}(x; \bar{\eta} + A^{\mathsf{T}}\eta_a, \bar{\Omega} + A^{\mathsf{T}}\Omega_a A) \qquad (14.61)$$

where κ *is a constant independent on* x.

Proof. We prove the claim by inspection. We write explicitly the left-hand side of (14.61) as:

$$\mathcal{N}(Ax; \eta_a, \Omega_a)\mathcal{N}(x; \bar{\eta}, \bar{\Omega}) = \frac{\det(\bar{\Omega})^{\frac{1}{2}}}{(2\pi)^{\frac{d}{2}}} \frac{\det(\Omega_a)^{\frac{1}{2}}}{(2\pi)^{\frac{d_a}{2}}} \times$$

$$\exp\left\{ -\frac{1}{2}\left[(Ax - \Omega_a^{-1}\eta_a)^{\mathsf{T}}\Omega_a(Ax - \Omega_a^{-1}\eta_a) + (x - \bar{\Omega}^{-1}\bar{\eta})^{\mathsf{T}}\bar{\Omega}(x - \bar{\Omega}^{-1}\bar{\eta}) \right] \right\} =$$

(developing the squares and introducing κ to denote constant factors)

$$\kappa \times \exp\left\{ -\frac{1}{2}\left[x^{\mathsf{T}}(\bar{\Omega} + A^{\mathsf{T}}\Omega_a A)x - 2x^{\mathsf{T}}(\bar{\eta} + A^{\mathsf{T}}\eta_a) + \eta_a^{\mathsf{T}}\Omega_a^{-1}\eta_a + \bar{\eta}^{\mathsf{T}}\bar{\Omega}^{-1}\bar{\eta} \right] \right\} =$$

(including constants at the exponent in κ)

$$\kappa \times \exp\left\{ -\frac{1}{2}\left[x^{\mathsf{T}}(\bar{\Omega} + A^{\mathsf{T}}\Omega_a A)x - 2x^{\mathsf{T}}(\bar{\eta} + A^{\mathsf{T}}\eta_a) \right] \right\} =$$

(reincluding more convenient constants at the exponent)

$$\kappa \times \exp\left\{ -\frac{1}{2}\left[x^{\mathsf{T}}(\bar{\Omega} + A^{\mathsf{T}}\Omega_a A)x - 2x^{\mathsf{T}}(\bar{\eta} + A^{\mathsf{T}}\eta_a) + \right.\right.$$
$$\left.\left. (\bar{\eta} + A^{\mathsf{T}}\eta_a)^{\mathsf{T}}(\bar{\Omega} + A^{\mathsf{T}}\Omega_a A)^{-1}(\bar{\eta} + A^{\mathsf{T}}\eta_a) \right] \right\} =$$

(isolating the Gaussian term, up to constant)

$$\kappa \times \mathcal{N}(x; \bar{\eta} + A^{\mathsf{T}}\eta_a, \bar{\Omega} + A^{\mathsf{T}}\Omega_a A)$$

$$(14.62)$$

A simple way to explicitly compute the constant κ is to observe that:

$$\int \mathcal{N}(Ax; \eta_a, \Omega_a)\mathcal{N}(x; \bar{\eta}, \bar{\Omega})dx = \qquad (14.63)$$

$$\int \kappa \times \mathcal{N}(x; \bar{\eta} + A^\mathsf{T} \eta_a, \bar{\Omega} + A^\mathsf{T} \Omega_a A) dx = \kappa \tag{14.64}$$

Hence κ is the result of a convolution of two Gaussian distributions, which can be computed as [68, page 209]

$$\kappa = \mathcal{N}_\mathcal{P}(\Omega_a^{-1} \eta_a; A \bar{\Omega}^{-1} \bar{\eta}, A \bar{\Omega}^{-1} A^\mathsf{T} + \Omega_a^{-1}) \tag{14.65}$$

and this concludes the proof.   □

Detection ($b_{it} = 1$) Let us start from the general update Eq. (14.19):

$$\mathbb{P}(y_{1:t+1} | Z_{1:t+1}) = \frac{\mathbb{P}(z_{t+1} | y_{1:t+1}) \, \mathbb{P}(y_{1:t+1} | Z_{1:t})}{\int \mathbb{P}(z_{t+1} | y_{1:t+1}) \, \mathbb{P}(y_{1:t+1} | Z_{1:t}) \, dy_{1:t+1}} \tag{14.66}$$

Let us focus on the term $\mathbb{P}(z_{t+1} | y_{1:t+1}) \, \mathbb{P}(y_{1:t+1} | Z_{1:t})$. First of all, we rewrite the measurement likelihood as:

$$\begin{aligned}
&\mathbb{P}(b_{it} = 1 | y_{1:t}) = \exp\left\{ -\frac{\|p_{\tau_{it}}^y - s_i\|^2}{r^2} \right\} = \\
&\exp\left\{ -\frac{\|U_{1:t+1} y_{1:t+1} - s_i\|^2}{r^2} \right\} = \frac{1}{\gamma} \mathcal{N}(U_{1:t+1} y_{1:t+1} ; \frac{s_i}{r^2}, \frac{1}{r^2})
\end{aligned} \tag{14.67}$$

which stresses the fact that the measurement likelihood can be seen as a "scaled" multivariate Gaussian, with γ being the normalization factor (the expression of this term is irrelevant for the subsequent derivation). Let us now substitute the prior probability (14.16) and the measurement likelihood (14.67) in (14.66):

$$\begin{aligned}
&\frac{\mathbb{P}(z_{t+1} | y_{1:t+1}) \mathbb{P}(y_{1:t+1} | Z_{1:t})}{\int \mathbb{P}(z_{t+1} | y_{1:t+1}) \mathbb{P}(y_{1:t+1} | Z_{1:t}) dy_{1:t+1}} = \\
&\frac{\frac{1}{\gamma} \mathcal{N}(U_{1:t+1} y_{1:t+1} ; \frac{s_i}{r^2}, \frac{1}{r^2}) \sum_{j=1}^m \bar{\alpha}_{t+1,j} \mathcal{N}(y_{1:t+1} ; \bar{\eta}_{t+1,j}, \bar{\Omega}_{t+1,j})}{\int \frac{1}{\gamma} \mathcal{N}(U_{1:t+1} y_{1:t+1} ; \frac{s_i}{r^2}, \frac{1}{r^2}) \sum_{j=1}^m \bar{\alpha}_{t+1,j} \mathcal{N}(y_{1:t+1} ; \bar{\eta}_{t+1,j}, \bar{\Omega}_{t+1,j}) dy_{1:t+1}} = \\
&\frac{\mathcal{N}(U_{1:t+1} y_{1:t+1} ; \frac{s_i}{r^2}, \frac{1}{r^2}) \sum_{j=1}^m \bar{\alpha}_{t+1,j} \mathcal{N}(y_{1:t+1} ; \bar{\eta}_{t+1,j}, \bar{\Omega}_{t+1,j})}{\int \mathcal{N}(U_{1:t+1} y_{1:t+1} ; \frac{s_i}{r^2}, \frac{1}{r^2}) \sum_{j=1}^m \bar{\alpha}_{t+1,j} \mathcal{N}(y_{1:t+1} ; \bar{\eta}_{t+1,j}, \bar{\Omega}_{t+1,j}) dy_{1:t+1}} = \\
&\frac{\sum_{j=1}^m \bar{\alpha}_{t+1,j} \mathcal{N}(U_{1:t+1} y_{1:t+1} ; \frac{s_i}{r^2}, \frac{1}{r^2}) \mathcal{N}(y_{1:t+1} ; \bar{\eta}_{t+1,j}, \bar{\Omega}_{t+1,j})}{\int \sum_{j=1}^m \bar{\alpha}_{t+1,j} \mathcal{N}(U_{1:t+1} y_{1:t+1} ; \frac{s_i}{r^2}, \frac{1}{r^2}) \mathcal{N}(y_{1:t+1} ; \bar{\eta}_{t+1,j}, \bar{\Omega}_{t+1,j}) dy_{1:t+1}}
\end{aligned}$$

which, using Lemma 2, becomes:

$$\frac{\sum_{j=1}^m \bar{\alpha}_{t+1,j} \, \beta_{t+1,j} \, \mathcal{N}(y_{1:t+1} ; \eta_{t+1,j}, \Omega_{t+1,j})}{\int \sum_{j=1}^m \bar{\alpha}_{t+1,j} \, \beta_{t+1,j} \, \mathcal{N}(y_{1:t+1} ; \eta_{t+1,j}, \Omega_{t+1,j}) dy_{1:t+1}} \tag{14.68}$$

where $\eta_{t+1,j}$ and $\Omega_{t+1,j}$ are defined as in (14.25). Observing that the integral of each Gaussian at the denominator of (14.68) is one, the previous simplifies to

$$\left(\frac{\bar{\alpha}_{t+1,j}\,\beta_{t+1,j}}{\sum_{j=1}^{m}\bar{\alpha}_{t+1,j}\,\beta_{t+1,j}}\right)\mathcal{N}(y_{1:t+1}\;;\;\eta_{t+1,j},\Omega_{t+1,j}) \tag{14.69}$$

which matches the expression of (14.25).

No detection ($b_{it}=0$) In this case, the measurement likelihood is:

$$\mathbb{P}(b_{it}=0|y_{1:t}) = 1 - \exp\left\{-\frac{\|p_{\tau_{it}}^{y}-s_i\|^2}{r^2}\right\} = 1 - \frac{1}{\gamma}\mathcal{N}(U_{1:t+1}y_{1:t+1}\;;\;\frac{s_i}{r^2},\frac{1}{r^2}) \tag{14.70}$$

where $\gamma = 2\pi r^2$ (this is the inverse of the normalization factor of the Gaussian).

Let us now substitute the prior probability (14.16) and the measurement likelihood (14.70) in (14.66):

$$\frac{\mathbb{P}(z_{t+1}|y_{1:t+1})\mathbb{P}(y_{1:t+1}|Z_{1:t})}{\int \mathbb{P}(z_{t+1}|y_{1:t+1})\mathbb{P}(y_{1:t+1}|Z_{1:t})dy_{1:t+1}} =$$

$$\frac{(1-\frac{1}{\gamma}\mathcal{N}(U_{1:t+1}y_{1:t+1}\;;\;\frac{s_i}{r^2},\frac{1}{r^2}))\sum_{j=1}^{m}\bar{\alpha}_{t+1,j}\mathcal{N}(y_{1:t+1}\;;\;\bar{\eta}_{t+1,j},\bar{\Omega}_{t+1,j})}{\int(1-\frac{1}{\gamma}\mathcal{N}(U_{1:t+1}y_{1:t+1}\;;\;\frac{s_i}{r^2},\frac{1}{r^2}))\sum_{j=1}^{m}\bar{\alpha}_{t+1,j}\mathcal{N}(y_{1:t+1}\;;\;\bar{\eta}_{t+1,j},\bar{\Omega}_{t+1,j})dy_{1:t+1}} =$$

(integral of the GMM at the denominator is 1)

$$\frac{(1-\frac{1}{\gamma}\mathcal{N}(U_{1:t+1}y_{1:t+1}\;;\;\frac{s_i}{r^2},\frac{1}{r^2}))\sum_{j=1}^{m}\bar{\alpha}_{t+1,j}\mathcal{N}(y_{1:t+1}\;;\;\bar{\eta}_{t+1,j},\bar{\Omega}_{t+1,j})}{1-\sum_{j=1}^{m}\bar{\alpha}_{t+1,j}\frac{1}{\gamma}\int\mathcal{N}(U_{1:t+1}y_{1:t+1}\;;\;\frac{s_i}{r^2},\frac{1}{r^2})\mathcal{N}(y_{1:t+1}\;;\;\bar{\eta}_{t+1,j},\bar{\Omega}_{t+1,j})dy_{1:t+1}} =$$

(from the definition of $\beta_{t+1,j}$)

$$\frac{(1-\frac{1}{\gamma}\mathcal{N}(U_{1:t+1}y_{1:t+1}\;;\;\frac{s_i}{r^2},\frac{1}{r^2})\sum_{j=1}^{m}\bar{\alpha}_{t+1,j}\mathcal{N}(y_{1:t+1}\;;\;\bar{\eta}_{t+1,j},\bar{\Omega}_{t+1,j})}{1-\sum_{j=1}^{m}\bar{\alpha}_{t+1,j}\frac{1}{\gamma}\beta_{t+1,j}} =$$

$$\frac{\sum_{j=1}^{m}\bar{\alpha}_{t+1,j}\mathcal{N}(y_{1:t+1}\;;\;\bar{\eta}_{t+1,j},\bar{\Omega}_{t+1,j})}{1-\sum_{j=1}^{m}\bar{\alpha}_{t+1,j}\frac{1}{\gamma}\beta_{t+1,j}} -$$

$$\frac{\sum_{j=1}^{m}\bar{\alpha}_{t+1,j}\frac{1}{\gamma}\mathcal{N}(U_{1:t+1}y_{1:t+1}\;;\;\frac{s_i}{r^2},\frac{1}{r^2})\mathcal{N}(y_{1:t+1}\;;\;\bar{\eta}_{t+1,j},\bar{\Omega}_{t+1,j})}{1-\sum_{j=1}^{m}\bar{\alpha}_{t+1,j}\frac{1}{\gamma}\beta_{t+1,j}} =$$

(note that gamma does not simplify)

$$\frac{\sum_{j=1}^{m}\bar{\alpha}_{t+1,j}\mathcal{N}(y_{1:t+1}\;;\;\bar{\eta}_{t+1,j},\bar{\Omega}_{t+1,j})}{1-\sum_{j=1}^{m}\bar{\alpha}_{t+1,j}\frac{1}{\gamma}\beta_{t+1,j}} -$$

$$\frac{\sum_{j=1}^{m}\bar{\alpha}_{t+1,j}\frac{1}{\gamma}\mathcal{N}(U_{1:t+1}y_{1:t+1}\;;\;\frac{s_i}{r^2},\frac{1}{r^2})\mathcal{N}(y_{1:t+1}\;;\;\bar{\eta}_{t+1,j},\bar{\Omega}_{t+1,j})}{1-\sum_{j=1}^{m}\bar{\alpha}_{t+1,j}\frac{1}{\gamma}\beta_{t+1,j}} =$$

(using Lemma 2 in each term of the second sum)

$$\frac{\sum_{j=1}^{m} \bar{\alpha}_{t+1,j}}{1-\sum_{j=1}^{m} \bar{\alpha}_{t+1,j} \frac{1}{\gamma} \beta_{t+1,j}} \mathcal{N}(y_{1:t+1} \; ; \; \bar{\eta}_{t+1,j}, \bar{\Omega}_{t+1,j}) +$$

$$\frac{\sum_{j=1}^{m} -\bar{\alpha}_{t+1,j} \frac{1}{\gamma} \beta_{t+1,j}}{1-\sum_{j=1}^{m} \bar{\alpha}_{t+1,j} \frac{1}{\gamma} \beta_{t+1,j}} \mathcal{N}(y_{1:t+1} \; ; \; \bar{\eta}_{t+1,j} + U_{1:t+1}^{\mathsf{T}} \frac{s_i}{r^2}, \bar{\Omega}_{t+1,j} + \frac{1}{r^2} U_{1:t+1}^{\mathsf{T}} U_{1:t+1})$$

which coincides with (14.25).

References

1. M. Adler, H. Räcke, N. Sivadasan, C. Sohler, B. Vöcking, Randomized pursuit-evasion in graphs. Comb. Probab. Comput. **12**(3), 225–244, (2003)
2. N. Ahmed, D. Casbeer, Y. Cao, D. Kingston, Bayesian hidden markov models for UAV-enabled target localization on road networks with soft-hard data. in *SPIE Defense and Security Symposium*, 2015
3. M. Aigner, M. Fromme, A game of cops and robbers. Discret. Appl. Math. **8**(1), 1–12 (1984)
4. G. Allen, Building a dynamic data driven application system for hurricane forecasting, in *Computational Science – ICCS 2007* (Springer, Berlin/Heidelberg, 2007), pp. 1034–1041
5. L. Alonso, A.S. Goldstein, E.M. Reingold, Lion and man: upper and lower bounds. INFORMS J. Comput. **4**(4), 447–452 (1992)
6. D. Alspach, H. Sorenson, Nonlinear bayesian estimation using gaussian sum approximations. IEEE Trans. Autom. Control **17**(4), 439–448 (1972)
7. D. Assaf, S. Zamir, Optimal sequential search: a bayesian approach. Ann. Stat. **13**(3), 1213–1221 (1985)
8. H. Bai, H. David, W.S. Lee, Integrated perception and planning in the continuous space: a POMDP approach, in *Robotics: Science and Systems (RSS)*, 2013
9. T. Basar, G.J. Olsder, *Dynamic Noncooperative Game Theory*. Classics in Applied Mathematics, 2nd edn. (SIAM, Philadelphia, 1999)
10. E. Blasch, P. Maupin, A. Jousselme, Sensor-based allocation for path planning and area coverage using ugss, in *IEEE National Aerospace and Electronics Conference (NAECON)*, 2010, pp. 361–368
11. E. Blasch, J. Dezert, P. Valin, DSmt applied to seismic and acoustic sensor fusion, in *IEEE National Aerospace and Electronics Conference (NAECON)*, 2011, pp. 79–86
12. E.P. Blasch, K. Pham, D. Shen, Chen G, Orbital satellite pursuit-evasion game-theoretical control, in *IEEE International Conference on Information Science, Signal Processing and Application (ISSPA)*, 2012
13. A. Blum, M.L. Furst, Approximation algorithms for orienteering and discounted-reward TSP, in *Symposium on Foundations of Computer Science*, 2003, pp. 46–55
14. S.D. Bopardikar, F. Bullo, J.P. Hespanha, Sensing limitations in the lion and man problem, in *American Control Conference*, 2007, pp. 5958–5963
15. F. Bourgault, T. Furukawa, H.F. Durrant-Whyte, Coordinated decentralized search for a lost target in a Bayesian world, in *IEEE/RSJ International Conference on Intelligent Robots and Systems (IROS)*, 2003, pp. 48–53
16. F. Bourgault, T. Furukawa, H.F. Durrant-Whyte, Optimal search for a lost target in a Bayesian world, in *International Conference on Field and Service Robotics, Springer Tracts in Advanced Robotics (STAR)*, 2006, pp. 209–222

17. D. Casbeer, K Meier, Y Cao, Estimating the state of an intruder with a UAV and unattended ground sensors, in *AIAA Infotech Aerospace Conference*, 2013, pp. 4269–4275
18. D. Casbeer, K. Krishnamoorthy, P. Chandler, M. Pachter, Moving ground target isolation by a UAV using predicted observations, in *IEEE Conference on Decision and Control*, 2014, pp. 4284–4289
19. C. Chekuri, N. Korula, M. Pál, Improved algorithms for orienteering and related problems. ACM Trans. Algorithms **8**(3), 1–27 (2012)
20. H. Chen, K. Krishnamoorthy, W. Zhang, D. Casbeer, Continuous-time intruder isolation using unattended ground sensors on graphs, in *American Control Conference*, 2014, pp. 5270–5275
21. H. Chen, K. Krishnamoorthy, W. Zhang, D. Casbeer, Intruder isolation on a general road network under partial information. IEEE Trans. Control Syst. Technol. **25**(1), 222–234 (2017)
22. H.L. Choi, J.P. How, J.A. Hansen, Ensemble-based adaptive targeting of mobile sensor networks, in *2007 American Control Conference*, 2007, pp. 2393–2398
23. H.L. Choi, J.P. How, Efficient targeting of sensor networks for large-scale systems. IEEE Trans. Control Syst. Technol. **19**(6), 1569–1577 (2011)
24. C.-Y. Chong, S.P. Kumar, Sensor networks: evolution, opportunities, and challenges, in *Proceedings of the IEEE*, 2003, pp. 1247–1256
25. T. Chung, G. Hollinger, V. Isler, Search and pursuit-evasion in mobile robotics: a survey. Auton. Robot. **31**(4), 299–316 (2011)
26. D. Crouse, P. Willett, K. Pattipati, L. Svensson, A look at gaussian mixture reduction algorithms, in *14th International Conference on Information Fusion*, 2011, pp. 1–8
27. F. Darema, Dynamic data driven applications systems: a new paradigm for application simulations and measurements, in *Computational Science – ICCS 2004: 4th International Conference, Krakow, Poland, 6–9 June 2004, Proceedings, Part III*, eds. M. Bubak, G.D. van Albada, P.M.A. Sloot, J.J. Dongarra. Lecture Notes in Computer Science, vol. 3038 (Springer, Heidelberg, 2004), pp. 662–669
28. F. Darema, Grid computing and beyond: the context of dynamic data driven applications systems. Proc. IEEE **93**(3), 692–697 (2005)
29. C.C. Douglas, M.J. Cole, P. Dostert, Y. Efendiev, R.E. Ewing, G. Haase, J. Hatcher, M. Iskandarani, C.R. Johnson, R.A. Lodder, Dynamically identifying and tracking contaminants in water bodies, in *Computational Science – ICCS 2007: 7th International Conference, Beijing, 7th International Conference, 27–30 May 2007, Proceedings, Part I*, eds. Y. Shi, G.D. van Albada, J.J. Dongarra, P.M.A. Sloot. Lecture Notes in Computer Science, vol. 4487 (Springer, Heidelberg, 2007), pp. 1002–1009
30. M.F. Duarte, Y.H. Hu, Vehicle classification in distributed sensor networks. J. Parallel Distrib. Comput. **64**(7), 826–838 (2004)
31. J.N. Eagle, The optimal search for a moving target when the search path is constrained. Oper. Res. **32**, 1105–1115 (1984)
32. J.N. Eagle, J.R. Yee, An optimal branch-and-bound procedure for the constrained path, moving target search problem. Oper. Res. **32**(1), 110–114 (1990)
33. T. Erez, W.D. Smart, A scalable method for solving high-dimensional continuous POMDPs using local approximation, in *Conference in Uncertainty in Artificial Intelligence (UAI)*, 2010
34. R. Fujimoto, A. Guin, M. Hunter, H. Park, R. Kannan, G. Kanitkar, M. Milholen, S. Neal, P. Pecher, A dynamic data driven application system for vehicle tracking. Proc. Comput. Sci. **29**, 1203–1215 (2014)
35. L. Guibas, J. Latombe, S. LaValle, D. Lin, R. Motwani, Visibility-based pursuit-evasion in a polygonal environment. Int. J. Comput. Geom. Appl. **9**(5), 471–494 (1999)
36. T. Hastie, R. Tibshirani, J.H. Friedman, *The Elements of Statistical Learning* (Springer, New York, 2001)
37. G. Hollinger, G. Sukhatme, Stochastic motion planning for robotic information gathering, in *Robotics: Science and Systems (RSS)*, 2013
38. G. Hollinger, S. Singh, J. Djugash, A. Kehagias, Efficient multi-robot search for a moving target. Int. J. Robot. Res. **28**(2), 201–219 (2009)

39. V. Indelman, L. Carlone, F. Dellaert, Planning in the continuous domain: a generalized belief space approach for autonomous navigation in unknown environments. Int. J. Robot. Res. **34**(7), 849–882 (2015)
40. V. Isler, S. Kannan, S. Khanna, Randomized pursuit-evasion with local visibility. SIAM J. Discret. Math. **1**(20), 26–41 (2006)
41. V. Isler, N. Karnad, The role of information in the cop-robber game. Theor. Comput. Sci. Spec. Issue Graph Search. **3**(399), 179–190 (2008)
42. R. Ivanov, N. Atanasov, M. Pajic, G. Pappas, I. Lee, Robust estimation using context-aware filtering, in *Allerton Conference on Communication, Control, and Computing*, 2015
43. B. Jia, K.D. Pham, E. Blasch, D. Shen, Z. Wang, G. Chen, Cooperative space object tracking using space-based optical sensors via consensus-based filters. IEEE Trans. Aerosp. Electron. Syst. **52**(3), 1908–1936 (2016)
44. S. Joshi, S. Boyd, Sensor selection via convex optimization. IEEE Trans. Signal Process. **57**, 451–462 (2009)
45. J. Kadane, Optimal whereabouts search. Oper. Res. **19**(4), 894–904 (1971)
46. L.P. Kaelbling, M.L. Littman, A.R. Cassandra, Planning and acting in partially observable stochastic domains. Artif. Intell. **101**(1), 99–134 (1998)
47. S. Karaman, E. Frazzoli, Sampling-based algorithms for optimal motion planning. Int. J. Robot. Res. **30**(7), 846–894 (2011)
48. B.O. Koopman, The theory of search. Part III: the optimum distribution of searching effort. Oper. Res. **5**(5), 613–626 (1957)
49. K. Krishnamoorthy, D. Casbeer, P. Chandler, M. Pachter, S. Darbha, UAV search & capture of a moving ground target under delayed information, in *IEEE Conference on Decision and Control*, 2012, pp. 3092–3097
50. K. Krishnamoorthy, S. Darbha, P.P. Khargonekar, D. Casbeer, P. Chandler, M. Pachter, Optimal minimax pursuit evasion on a manhattan grid, in *IEEE Conference on Decision and Control*, 2013, pp. 3421–3428
51. K. Krishnamoorthy, D. Casbeer, P. Chandler, M. Pachter, Pursuit on a graph using partial information, in *American Control Conference*, 2015, pp. 4269–4275
52. H. Lau, S. Huang, G. Dissanayake, Optimal search for multiple targets in a built environment, in *IEEE/RSJ International Conference on Intelligent Robots and Systems (IROS)*, 2005, pp. 3740–3745
53. H. Lau, S. Huang, G. Dissanayake, Probabilistic search for a moving target in an indoor environment, in *IEEE/RSJ International Conference on Intelligent Robots and Systems (IROS)*, 2006, pp. 3393–3398
54. J.J. Lim, H. Pirsiavash, A. Torralba, Parsing IKEA objects: fine pose estimation, in *International Conference on Computer Vision (ICCV)*, 2013, pp. 2992–2999
55. J. Mandel, L.S. Bennethum, J.L. Coen M. Chen, C.C. Douglas, L.P. Franca, Towards a dynamic data driven application system for wildfire simulation, in *Computational Science – ICCS 2005* (Springer, Berlin/Heidelberg, 2005)
56. R. Niu, P.K. Varshney, Target location estimation in sensor networks with quantized data. IEEE Trans. Signal Process. **54**(12), 4519–4528 (2006)
57. S.C.W. Ong, S.W. Png, D. Hsu, W.S. Lee, Planning under uncertainty for robotic tasks with mixed observability. Int. J. Robot. Res. **29**(8), 1053–1068 (2010)
58. R. Platt Jr., R. Tedrake, L.P. Kaelbling, T. Lozano-Pérez, Belief space planning assuming maximum likelihood observations, in *Robotics: Science and Systems (RSS)*, 2010, pp. 587–593
59. S. Rasmussen, D. Kingston, Development and flight test of an area monitoring system using unmanned aerial vehicles and unattended ground sensors, in *International Conference on Unmanned Aircraft Systems (ICUAS)*, 2015
60. N. Roy, G. Gordon, S. Thrun, Finding approximate POMDP solutions through belief compression. J. Artif. Intell. Res. **23**, 1–40 (2005)
61. A.R. Runnalls, Kullback-Leibler approach to gaussian mixture reduction. IEEE Trans. Aerosp. Electron. Syst. **43**(3), 989–999 (2007)

62. H. Sato, J.O. Royset, Path optimization for the resource-constrained searcher. Nav. Res. Logist. **57**(5), 422–440 (2010)
63. D. Shen, G. Chen, H. Ling, K.D. Pham, E. Blasch, Methods and devices for demonstrating three-player pursuit-evasion game. U.S. Patent application Publication 2016/0121204 A1, 5 May 2016
64. D. Silver, J. Veness, Monte-Carlo planning in large POMDPs, in *Advances in Neural Information Processing Systems (NIPS)*, 2010, pp. 2164–2172
65. H.W. Sorenson, D.L. Alspach, Recursive bayesian estimation using gaussian sums. Automatica **7**, 465–479 (1971)
66. C. Stachniss, G. Grisetti, W. Burgard, Recovering particle diversity in a Rao-Blackwellized particle filter for SLAM after actively closing loops, in *IEEE International Conference on Robotics and Automation (ICRA)*, 2005, pp. 667–672
67. L.D. Stone. *Theory of Optimal Search*, 2nd edn. (Academic, San Diego, 1989)
68. S. Thrun, W. Burgard, D. Fox, *Probabilistic Robotics* (The MIT Press, Cambridge, 2005)
69. K.E. Trummel, J.R. Weisinger, The complexity of the optimal searcher path problem. Oper. Res. **34**(2), 324–327 (1986)
70. J. Van Den Berg, S. Patil, R. Alterovitz, Motion planning under uncertainty using iterative local optimization in belief space. Int. J. Robot. Res. **31**(11), 1263–1278 (2012)
71. P. Vansteenwegen, W. Souffriau, D.V. Oudheusden, The orienteering problem: a survey. Eur. J. Oper. Res. **209**, 1–10 (2011)
72. A.R. Washburn, Search for a moving target: the FAB algorithm. Oper. Res. **31**(4), 739–751 (1983)
73. J. Yu, J. Aslam, S. Karaman, D. Rus, Optimal tourist problem and anytime planning of trip itineraries. arXiv: 1409.8536 (2015)
74. B. Zhang, C. Zhang, Finite mixture models with negative components, in *International Conference on Machine Learning and Data Mining in Pattern Recognition*, 2005, pp. 31–41

Chapter 15
Optimization of Multi-target Tracking Within a Sensor Network Via Information Guided Clustering

Alexander A. Soderlund and Mrinal Kumar

Abstract This work presents a new algorithm for rapid and efficient clustering of sensing nodes within a heterogeneous wireless sensor network. The objective is to enable optimal sensor allocation for localization uncertainty reduction in multi-target tracking. The proposed algorithm is built on three metrics: (i) sensing feasibility; (ii) measurement quality to maximize information utility; and, (iii) communication cost to minimize data routing time. The derived cluster is employed as the search-space for optimal sensor allocation via maximizing the uncertainty reduction of the expected probability distribution over a target's state-space. Theoretical analysis is used to show advantage of the proposed method in terms of information utility over the widely used Euclidean distance based clustering approach. The analysis is verified via simulated target tracking examples, in terms of metrics of information utility and computational expenditure. Simulations also reveal relationships between sensor field density and the extent of information gain over competing methods.

Keywords State estimation · Target tracking · Autonomous systems · Sensor network · Information-driven sensor querying · Clustering

15.1 Introduction

Autonomous target tracking is a multifaceted problem that involves many phases of computational operations working in succession to generate an accurate target state estimate (e.g., position, velocity, etc.) in real-time. The quantity of interest at any given time is the target's state probability density function, also referred to as its *belief state*. Target-tracking in the Bayesian framework involves the following two-step recursion [1]: (i) propagation of the target's belief state through

A. A. Soderlund (✉) · M. Kumar
Department of Mechanical and Aerospace Engineering, The Ohio State University, Columbus, OH, USA
e-mail: soderlund.3@osu.edu; kumar.672@osu.edu

© The Author(s), under exclusive license to Springer Nature Switzerland AG 2022   345
E. P. Blasch et al. (eds.), *Handbook of Dynamic Data Driven Applications Systems*,
https://doi.org/10.1007/978-3-030-74568-4_15

its assumed dynamics model to a future point where sensor input is anticipated; and (ii) assimilating received sensor data to update the propagated belief state, typically in a step of Bayesian information fusion. Autonomous execution of this recursive cycling through the target's *prior* and *posterior* belief states (output of steps (i) and (ii), respectively) within a wireless sensor network (WSN) has become an emerging topic of research interest in recent years. In particular, there is emphasis on improving the information fusion step by optimizing the incoming measurements of the target via optimal sensor selection [2–8].

The practice of incorporating sensors' data within a distributed sensor network to localize a moving target's position was demonstrated by Dommermuth [9], who implemented the closest point of approach (CPA) method to track a low-flying aircraft with a low number (4–5) of acoustic sensors for a set number of network configurations. This method was improved upon by the work of Yang et al. [10] who enhanced the CPA method to successfully predict a target's location within a randomized sensor configuration, albeit still with a small number of sensors. In expanding the challenge of target tracking to a field comprised of hundreds of sensors, a sensor selection optimization performed on the full network is neither computationally efficient nor effective [11] as valuable target detections are lost while appointing and activating sensing nodes. To maintain tracking feasibility in real-time, it is necessary to create a manageable subset of sensors (a cluster) from which the optimal sensor(s) can then be selected to make target measurements.

"Clustering"[1] is itself a form of sensor selection, where potential clusters in their simplest form are derived from sensor-target proximity [11–13] which activate a subset of the WSN (active sensors can observe a target inside its sensing radius, passive sensors cannot). This activation approach is essentially based on the Euclidean distance between the sensor and the target and is referred to here as the Euclidean Clustering Algorithm[2] (ECA) in the sequel.

In the literature, clustering methods are largely dependent on the nature of the wireless sensor network being used. These methods differ in processing structure (centralized vs. distributed), sensor type (homogeneous vs. heterogeneous) and cluster-head location (static vs dynamic) [14]. Successful target tracking in a WSN was demonstrated by Yang and Sikdar [15] with the use of static clusters, where the leader nodes are established at the outset of the tracking operation. In an architecture like this, the static leader nodes may fail, resulting in the loss of event-monitoring within an entire cluster. Moreover, there are occasions where the target travels along discontinuous cluster boundaries or into areas not covered within clusters' perimeters. This boundary problem was addressed by Wang et al. [16] by introducing a hybrid clustering approach that, while still keeping the fundamental

---

[1]The use of the term differs throughout the literature. In this study, "clustering" only pertains the act of reducing the set of potential nodes for further sensor selection.

[2]"ECA" is used as an umbrella term for clustering procedures that prioritize chosen sensors' proximity to predicted target positions. Obviously, not all proximity-based methods are identical and vary depending on the application.

architecture of static clusters, allowed for on-demand dynamic clusters to form when a target approached a static boundary and accompany the target to the next static cluster. A system architecture composed entirely of dynamic clusters, while more computationally intensive, forms updated sensor clusters as the target belief-state evolves through the environment. In the WSN architecture used in this work, a single optimal sensor selected on expected information gain performance is designated as a dynamic cluster-head, also known as a *leader node*, that performs measurement acquisition and consequent routing of the target data back to a designated processing base station (known as a sensor-to-sink data transfer).

Sensor selection based on predicted information utility has been demonstrated previously. Zhao et al. [17] implemented dynamic clustering under the information driven sensor querying (IDSQ) approach, where the selection of dynamic cluster-heads are constrained on potential information utility contribution (Mahalanobis distance to the target belief distribution) and communication cost from data-routing (measured by Euclidean distance between communicating sensors). The approach was applied to the tracking of a single target in a two-dimensional field of wireless sensors using IDSQ while treating the entire sensor set as a single cluster. This was modified further by performing cluster-head selection based on the information gain provided by optimizing the mutual information between the posterior and prior target beliefs [2]. Tharmarasa et al. [6] clustered bearing-only sensor sets predicated on predicted information gain due to each sensor's probability of detection, and a similar procedure was employed by Hernandez et al. [3] in a Euclidean distance-based sensor redeployment scheme. There is also precedent for clustering sensors with energy consumption considerations in concordance with target localization, as was done by Qian et al. [18], and Zou and Chakrabarty [5].

All clustering and sensor selection methods discussed thus far are essentially procedures rooted in tradeoffs made between tracking performance and computational efficacy. If this latter concern were removed, the *Exhaustive Search* method introduced by Kaplan [19] was designed to serve as a baseline approach upon which practical selection schemes would be compared. This method iterates through all possible subsets of a bearing-only WSN that would yield the global minimum in terms of the Mean Square positional error of the target, and was shown to be computationally NP-hard. Kaplan's nearly-optimal variation of this exhaustive search, the Global Node Selection (GNS) method, was modified by Capponi et al. [20] for areal proximity sensors that minimized the predicted Cramér-Rao Lower Bound (CRLB) of the posterior target belief state. A computationally exhaustive search (CES) method inspired by GNS will be treated as a baseline against which we compare this work's computational and uncertainty reduction performance.

This review of literature suggests that a well-designed sensor clustering algorithm must account for several factors simultaneously, namely, *cost* incurred from data-routing (such as communication bandwidth and transmit time) [21, 22], *information utility* potential [2, 6, 7, 17], and target detection *feasibility* [5, 23, 24]. The contribution of this work is the design and demonstration of a multi-phase sensor clustering method that accounts for the above described clustering factors within a centralized and heterogeneous WSN. Its objective is to achieve provably lower target state uncertainty (or higher information utility) compared to that of the Euclidean distance approach while also maintaining low computational expenditure. Named *Information-Guided Rapid Clustering Algorithm (IGRCA)*, it relies on available sensor location and activation data, predicted target distribution parameters and a directed data routing network that results in *rapidly* computed feasibility, information utility, and routing time metrics. The new clustering approach is compared (analytically as well as through numerical simulations) with the cluster of closest sensors in tracking applications involving a variety of sensor densities and number of targets being tracked. It is shown to be superior in terms of state uncertainty reduction and comparable in computational expenditure.

The work proceeds as follows: Sect. 15.2 describes the target tracking operation within a centralized dynamic prediction-based WSN through the use of Euclidean distance-based clusters. Section 15.3 describes the mathematical basis and implementation of a comprehensive clustering algorithm that improves upon the Euclidean method within a heterogeneous wireless sensor set. This is followed by the optimization of an information theoretic metric, namely, the expected differential entropy to identify the optimal sensor from among the cluster to be tasked with the measurement. Section 15.4 describes the measurement model and target dynamics within an extended Kalman filter (EKF) tracking framework. Section 15.5 presents rigorous theoretical analysis to demonstrate the advantage of IGRCA over the closest-sensor approach in terms of information utility. Numerical simulations are presented in Sect. 15.6 to support the analysis. Performance of IGRCA is evaluated and compared with nearest-neighbor Euclidean approach and the computationally exhaustive search in terms of multiple metrics, including information gain, target state uncertainty reduction, and algorithm running time. Tracking of multiple simultaneous targets with nonlinear dynamics is considered, but it is assumed in these simulations that data association is not required (e.g., representing a scenario involving friendly targets that identify themselves). Conclusions and directions for future research are given in Sect. 15.7.

15.2 Target Tracking and Motivating Problem

The goal of minimizing uncertainty whilst tracking a moving target within a WSN comprised of n sensing nodes presents an assortment of issues, e.g. a majority of the sensors will not be able to make a measurement of the target (either it does not lie in the sensor's field or is out of its sensing range). Of the subset of sensors where a measurement is possible (a subset of k nodes where $k \leq n$), it requires the optimization of an appropriate cost function over the space of the entire feasible set in order to identify the sensor that provides the most information gain. This process involves a computational burden of order $\mathcal{O}(k)$ and underscores the need for clustering: valuable computation time can be saved by running the sensor-selection procedure over a *reduced* sensor set, while also enabling increased frequency of measurements to be made throughout the tracking duration. This study considers both optimization problems, namely: (1) the cluster formation step, followed by, (2) the identification of the optimal sensor within the cluster. The information guided rapid clustering algorithm (IGRCA) follows a three stage selection process in the following order: sensing feasibility, information utility, and communication cost. Results provided in Sect. 15.6 display the benefits of this process in terms of quality of measurements, or, more directly, in terms of reduction in target uncertainty. The focus of this study is to design the IGRCA and demonstrate its benefits, whereby all tracking simulations that require the data fusion operation use the extended Kalman filter due to its overall simplicity, minimal processing requirements and low number of required data fields (target state and covariance). First, we formulate in Sect. 15.2.1 the fundamental problem to be solved in terms of tracking a single target within a WSN environment. In Sect. 15.2.2, this problem is solved with the application of a general Euclidean clustering algorithm (ECA). The shortcomings of this algorithm are exploited to derive the merits of the IGRCA, which attempts to solve the identical hypothetical tracking problem in Sect. 15.3.

15.2.1 Problem Formulation

Consider a target maneuvering through a two-dimensional environment containing a set of wirelessly-connected sensors (see Fig. 15.1a). This sensor set, comprised of n nodes (hundreds to thousands), [25] is represented as

$$\mathcal{W} = \{S_1, \ S_2, \ S_3, \dots \ S_i, \dots, \ S_n\} \tag{15.1}$$

The current time instant is labeled $k - 1$. Motion of each target is assumed to be governed by a discrete time dynamics model:

$$\mathbf{x}_k = \mathbf{f}(\mathbf{x}_{k-1}) + \mathbf{v}_{k-1} \tag{15.2}$$

where the system process noise $\mathbf{v}_{k-1}$ is assumed to possess a zero-mean multivariate Gaussian distribution $\mathbf{v}_{k-1} \sim \mathcal{N}(0, \mathbf{Q}_{k-1})$. A general sensor model (in terms of modality) is represented by the following relationship,

$$\mathbf{z}_k = \mathbf{h}_k(\mathbf{x}_k) + \mathbf{w}_k \tag{15.3}$$

where the sensor noise is also assumed to be Gaussian: $\mathbf{w}_k \sim \mathcal{N}(0, \mathbf{R}_k)$. The probability density function of a target's state, commonly referred to as its *belief state*, is parameterized using a Gaussian density function with the mean-covariance pair $(\mathbf{x}_{k-1}^+, \mathbf{P}_{k-1}^+)$. In this notation, the superscript "+" denotes *posterior* values, i.e., the mean and covariance conditioned on all sensor information available up to time $k - 1$. The prior belief parameters at time k can be obtained via propagation through the dynamics model given above and are denoted as $(\hat{\mathbf{x}}_k, \hat{\mathbf{P}}_k)$. Within the network $\mathcal{W}$ there are $m \leq n$ sensing nodes which can feasibly observe the target at the next

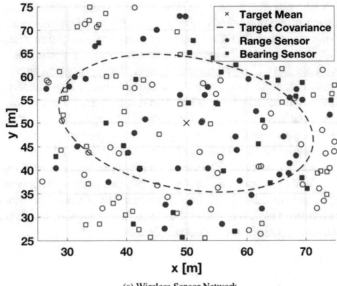

(a) Wireless Sensor Network

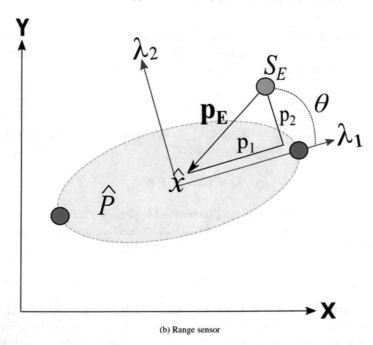

(b) Range sensor

Fig. 15.1 (a) Complete wireless sensor set $\mathcal{W}$ tasked with tracking a target. Filled markers represent sensors where a measurement is feasible. (b) Zoomed-in view illustrating a range sensor S_E (blue circle) with sensing vector $\mathbf{p}_E$ has two optimal locations (orange circles) at a distance d away from the target mean

timestep k. The inclusion of data from any one of these feasible sensors, S_i, will result in a posterior belief state $(\mathbf{x}_{i,k}^+, \mathbf{P}_{i,k}^+)$ and the set of possible posterior matrices corresponding to each feasible sensor is represented as:

$$\mathscr{P}_k = \{\mathbf{P}_{1,k}^+, \mathbf{P}_{2,k}^+, \ldots, \mathbf{P}_{i,k}^+, \ldots \mathbf{P}_{m,k}^+\}$$

The fundamental sensor selection problem is the identification of the sensor node S^* whose measurement corresponds to the maximum information gain of the resulting posterior covariance $\mathbf{P}_{*,k}^+$ (measured via metrics such as differential entropy or Fisher Information). Of course, the construction of such a set with advantageous computational and quality constraints (i.e., routing time and statistical relevance) is the primary focus of this work.

As this one-step lookahead approach needs to dictate a sensing decision based on predicted dynamics before the target arrives at its position at time k, a computationally-rapid state estimation scheme must be run at time $k - 1$. The Extended Kalman Filter (EKF) [1] has been adopted due to its efficiency and ease of implementation. The EKF estimates the state under a Bayesian framework that involves a two-step recursion: (i) propagation of the target's current belief state through a linearized dynamics model to a future point where a measurement is anticipated, resulting in the prior state belief; and (ii) fusion of the received sensor information with this prior belief to update the state to a posterior belief state. These two steps are detailed in Sects. 15.2.1.1 and 15.2.1.2 respectively.

The above problem has been adapted within the EKF paradigm by employing linearized versions of $\mathbf{f}_k$ and $\mathbf{h}_k$, which are obtained from their corresponding first-order Taylor series expansions, involving Jacobian matrices $\mathbf{F}_k = \frac{\partial \mathbf{f}_k}{\partial \mathbf{x}}\Big|_{(\mathbf{x}_{k-1})}$ and $\mathbf{H}_k = \frac{\partial \mathbf{h}_k}{\partial \mathbf{x}}\Big|_{\hat{\mathbf{x}}_k}$, both evaluated at the prior belief mean $\hat{\mathbf{x}}_k$. The use of the EKF relies on the assumption that the propagated state is close to the true state ($\hat{\mathbf{x}}_k \approx \mathbf{x}_k$). The filter proceeds as follows:

15.2.1.1 Prediction

In the EKF framework, given the current belief represented by the posterior state estimate and error covariance, $(\mathbf{x}_{k-1}^+, \mathbf{P}_{k-1}^+)$ the predicted prior belief at time k is given by:

$$\hat{\mathbf{x}}_k = \mathbf{f}_k(\mathbf{x}_{k-1}^+) \tag{15.4}$$

with its associated prior state covariance matrix

$$\hat{\mathbf{P}}_k = \mathbf{F}_k \mathbf{P}_{k-1}^+ \mathbf{F}_k^T + \mathbf{Q}_k, \text{ where } \mathbf{F}_k(\hat{\mathbf{x}}_k) = \frac{\partial \mathbf{f}_k}{\partial \mathbf{x}}\Big|_{(\mathbf{x}_{k-1})} \tag{15.5}$$

15.2.1.2 Update

The measurement model is linearized about the predicted prior mean:

$$\tilde{\mathbf{z}}_k = \mathbf{H}_k \hat{\mathbf{x}}_k + \mathbf{w}_k, \text{ where } \mathbf{H}_k(\hat{\mathbf{x}}_k) = \left.\frac{\partial \mathbf{h}_k}{\partial \mathbf{x}}\right|_{\hat{\mathbf{x}}_k} \qquad (15.6)$$

and used to construct the Kalman gain:

$$\mathbf{K}_k = \hat{\mathbf{P}}_k \mathbf{H}_k(\hat{\mathbf{x}}_k)^T [\mathbf{H}_k(\hat{\mathbf{x}}_k)\hat{\mathbf{P}}_k \mathbf{H}_k(\hat{\mathbf{x}}_k)^T + \mathbf{R}_k]^{-1} \qquad (15.7)$$

The fusion step results in the following update equations, resulting in the final posterior belief state and covariance at time k.

$$\mathbf{x}_k^+ = \hat{\mathbf{x}}_k + \mathbf{K}_k(\mathbf{z}_k - \mathbf{h}_k(\hat{\mathbf{x}}_k)) \qquad (15.8)$$

$$\mathbf{P}_k^+ = (\mathbf{I} - \mathbf{K}_k \mathbf{H}_k(\hat{\mathbf{x}}_k))\hat{\mathbf{P}}_k \qquad (15.9)$$

A processing node within the WSN (the base station) is responsible for computing Eqs.(15.4), (15.5), (15.6), (15.7), (15.8) and (15.9), where the choice of $\mathbf{H}_k(\hat{\mathbf{x}}_k)$ in the measurement model is dependent on the output type $\mathbf{h}_k$ of the optimally chosen sensor (detailed in Sect. 15.3.4).

Within this recursive EKF framework of alternating predictions and updates, we will attempt to estimate the state of the target with reduced uncertainty. This requires a predictive solution to the sensor selection problem by way of optimizing on expected information-theoretic measures. The solution given via application of the ECA will be demonstrated in the next section, following a brief review of sensor network architecture.

15.2.2 Motivation: The Euclidean Cluster

Recall that each member of the wireless heterogeneous sensor network $\mathcal{W}$ is a node capable of sensing, where each sensor S_i is defined by its two-dimensional position $\mathbf{S}_i = [S_{x,i}, S_{y,i}]^T$, measurement output type (relative bearing of target, relative range to target, etc.), and sensing field of view Λ_i. The following assumptions are made regarding the sensors within $\mathcal{W}$:

1. Node locations $\mathbf{S}_i$ are uniformly distributed within a square sensing field of area $\Omega_T = [\omega \times \omega]\, m^2$.
2. Maximum sensing range ρ_i (in meters) and angular range ψ_i (in radians) are identical for each sensor, but sensor orientation is uniformly randomized between $[0, 2\pi]$ for simplicity.

The assumptions above do not limit the scope of the methodology developed in this work and are made primarily for the sake of simplicity. Given assumptions (1) and (2), the probability p_f that an observation of the target is feasible by m sensors at any point in a dense field can be related by the Poisson distribution, shown by Sikdar and Yang [15]:

$$p_f = \sum_{i=0}^{m} \frac{e^{-\lambda\left(\frac{\psi}{2}\pi\rho^2\right)}\left(\lambda\left(\frac{\psi}{2}\pi\rho\right)^2\right)^i}{i!} \tag{15.10}$$

which treats target detection as being affected by field density λ, the number of nodes per unit area, and sensor characteristics. Note that the use of the Poisson distribution is somewhat arbitrary and motivated largely by its historical success in similar contexts. In scenarios where successful detection depends on complex interactions among the target(s), potential sensors and their respective environments, more advancements are needed for accurately capturing the probability of detection.

The general form of the closest-sensor cluster operates by considering the group of one or more sensing nodes S_i^* that lie closest in terms of Euclidean distance to the target's predicted point of approach [3, 9, 11–14, 14, 15, 20]. As it may be computationally prohibitive to iterate over all elements of $\mathscr{W}$, the field is sorted into a subset based on a Euclidean distance metric from the propagated mean $\hat{\mathbf{x}}_k$. Let the relative position vector between the propagated state mean $\hat{\mathbf{x}}_k$ and position S_i be

$$\mathbf{p}_i^k = \hat{\mathbf{x}}_k - S_i \tag{15.11}$$

The Euclidean cluster $\mathscr{E}_k \subseteq \mathscr{W}$ constructed at time step k is composed of $t \leq n$ sensors

$$\mathscr{E}_k = \{S_1, \ S_2, \ S_3, \ldots, \ S_i, \ldots, \ S_t\}, \quad \forall \quad |\mathbf{p}_i^k| \leq \rho_i \tag{15.12}$$

where t is a user-defined value that can vary between 1 and the maximum number of feasible sensors. $\mathscr{E}_k$ is obtained from Steps 1–8 of the Euclidean clustering algorithm (ECA), tabulated in Algorithm 1. A visual example of the ECA output cluster is displayed in Fig. 15.2.

The ECA is non-optimal, as the sensing nodes within $\mathscr{E}_k$ may not be in position to make a measurement (field of view Λ_i is not considered in the cluster selection). In practice, the primary advantage of using $\mathscr{E}_k$ for sensor selection is its computationally efficient assembly, but this quick generation also makes the cluster prone to (i) target-loss [16], a rare instance where $\mathscr{E}_k$ is entirely made up of infeasible sensors and the target proceeds unobserved, and (ii) the loss in higher potential information gain [2, 17] due to superior sensors lying at advantageous orientations to the propagated belief state but not with appropriately-small Euclidean distances to be clustered using Algorithm 1. This effect will be more ostensibly studied in Sect. 15.5. To avoid track loss, sensing feasibility is the first issue addressed in the construction of the IGRCA.

Algorithm 1 Euclidean clustering algorithm

1: Given the current state of the target, $\mathbf{x}_{k-1}$ and $\mathbf{P}_{k-1}$ compute the prior belief values $\hat{\mathbf{x}}_k$ and $\hat{\mathbf{P}}_k$
   at the next time-step k.
2: **while** $t < n$ **do**
3:     Iterate through $\mathscr{W}\backslash\mathscr{E}_k$ and return closest sensor S_E with Eq. (15.12).
4:     $t \leftarrow t + 1$.
5:     $\mathscr{E}_k \leftarrow \mathscr{E}_k \cup S_E$.
6: **end while**
7: **if** The number of elements of $\mathscr{E}_k$ is 0, return prior as posterior **then**
8:     Go to step 1.
9: **else**
10:    Iterate through $\mathscr{E}_k$ and perform simulated measurements at time k to compute expected
       entropy H_i with Eq. (15.19) for each sensor.
11:    Determine the optimal sensor S_i^* by identifying the minimal expected entropy H_i^*.
12:    Route the current belief data to S_i^*.
13:    S_i^* performs a measurement and routes the information back to the base station for data
       aggregation and fusion.
14: **end if**
15: Repeat step 1.

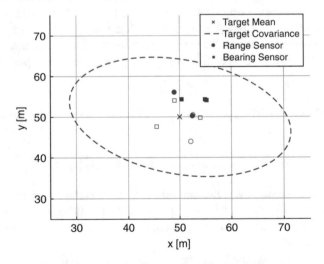

Fig. 15.2 Cluster of sensors $\mathscr{E}_k$ selected based on sensor-target proximity. The faded markers in
the Euclidean set represent infeasible sensors

15.3 Information Guided Rapid Clustering Algorithm

To achieve the dual goal of maintaining low localization error while also avoiding loss of target tracks, a new clustering algorithm is developed here that is
computationally comparable to the Euclidean approach in real-time target tracking
scenarios. This method, called the Information Guided Rapid Clustering Algorithm
(IGRCA), is composed of three sequential clustering steps that include sensing

feasibility (Sect. 15.3.1), information utility (Sect. 15.3.2), and communication cost (Sect. 15.3.3). This clustering procedure culminates in a final optimal sensor selection step (Sect. 15.3.4) that tasks a chosen node with observing the target. While the principles underlying the IGRCA construction in this section mention the single target tracking case for clarity, the IGRCA is easily adaptable to the multiple target scenarios analyzed in Sect. 15.6.

15.3.1 Sensing Feasibility

Recall that the current time label is $(k - 1)$ and optimal sensor selection is required for the next time step, labeled k. The IGRCA initially considers only nodes within the WSN $\mathcal{W}$ that can feasibly sense the target. This requires, at every propagated step, an updated *Region of Feasibility* constructed as

$$\Lambda_k = \Lambda_1 \cup \Lambda_2 \cup \ldots \Lambda_i \cup \cdots \cup \Lambda_m \text{ where } \hat{\mathbf{x}}_k \in \text{int}(\Lambda_i)$$

where $\text{int}(\Lambda_i)$ represents the interior of a circular sector within the Euclidean plane Ω_T, defined by radius ρ_i and central angle ψ_i with sensor location $\mathbf{S}_i$ at its origin. A binary value is attached to all nodes within $\mathcal{W}$ whose field of view Λ_i was included in the creation of Λ_k, akin to the binary proximity sensors demonstrated previously [23]. The resulting cluster satisfying the feasibility condition comprises of $m \leq n$ elements $\mathcal{F}_k \subseteq \mathcal{W}$ at time step k, and is constructed as

$$\mathcal{F}_k = \{S_1, \ S_2, \ S_3, \ldots, \ S_i, \ldots, \ S_m\}, \quad \forall \ \Lambda_i \in \Lambda_k \tag{15.13}$$

Generation of the set $\mathcal{F}_k$ (call it the *feasibility cluster*) requires $\mathcal{O}(n)$ operations. The cluster $\mathcal{F}_k$ guarantees a feasible measurement at time step k, except of-course, when the predicted target location is outside the field of view of every sensor $S_i \in \mathcal{W}$. See Fig. 15.6a for an example of the feasibility cluster in Sect. 15.3.5.

15.3.1.1 A Note on Feasibility

For the sensor types introduced below in Sect. 15.3.2.2 (Radar, Sonar, direction of arrival (DOA), etc.), previous target-tracking studies, e.g. Refs. [6, 26] have adopted a so-called Swerling I model which, while a target lies in the sensor's field of view, performs a measurement with probabilistic target detection as opposed to the binary detection discussed above in Sect. 15.3.1. While implementing a simulated probability of detection for each measurement provides a more realistic target tracking scenario, it does not affect the credibility of a direct algorithm comparison, which is the primary focus of this work. However, it should be noted that the detrimental effect on a sensor's ability to observe a target due to the sensor's operating distance (see Ref. [27]) is retained in the the measurement noise variance model in Sect. 15.4.2.

15.3.2 Information Utility

While the cluster $\mathscr{F}_k$ ensures that a measurement will take place at time step k, it provides no guarantee regarding information utility. The second stage of selection seeks to retain the sensor nodes with the greatest "potential to reduce uncertainty of the target's posterior belief state" at time k. This is loosely referred to as *information utility*. The potential information utility of each node is revealed by incorporating two sensor-specific measures: (i.) the Mahalanobis distance to the propagated (prior) state belief at time k, and (ii.) the mode (range, bearing, etc.) that dictates the appropriate measurement model and output type. These criteria are detailed further in Sects. 15.3.2.1 and 15.3.2.2, respectively. The cluster resulting from application of ranking each sensor within $\mathscr{F}_k$ by information utility (see Fig. 15.6b) is referred to as $\mathscr{Q}_k$ ("the quality cluster").

15.3.2.1 Mahalanobis Distance

Given a probability distribution in $\mathfrak{R}^N$ with known mean and covariance, the unitless Mahalanobis distance is a scalar measure of the "statistical relevance" of a point to the said belief distribution [28]. This metric, defined in Eq. (15.14) below, is computed easily given the sample point $\mathbf{p}$ and the distribution mean $\boldsymbol{\mu}$ and covariance Σ,

$$M = \sqrt{(\mathbf{p} - \boldsymbol{\mu})^T \, \Sigma^{-1} (\mathbf{p} - \boldsymbol{\mu})} \tag{15.14}$$

In an object-sensing application, treating the sensor as the sample point from the target's state distribution will express this "relevance" as the sensor's information utility regarding a target state update, and geometrically represents a closer alignment of the relative position vector between the mean and the sensor with respect to the eigen-directions of the target's uncertainty covariance matrix. In the current application, only static "positional sensors" are used (e.g. those measuring range and bearing). On the other hand, the target's belief state is jointly composed of its four-dimensional state-vector, $\mathbf{x} = [x, \ \dot{x}, \ y, \ \dot{y}]^T$, which of-course, also includes velocity components. Thus the target's full-state prior distribution at time step k is $\mathcal{N}(\hat{\mathbf{x}}_k, \hat{\mathbf{P}}_k)$, parameterized by a four-dimensional mean vector and a four-dimensional covariance ellipsoid. Therefore, in order to reconcile the positional sensors with the target's belief state, we use only the so-called *positional restrictions* of $(\hat{\mathbf{x}}_k, \hat{\mathbf{P}}_k)$, denoted by $\hat{\mathbf{x}}_{k_{\text{pos}}} = [\hat{x}_k, \ \hat{y}_k]^T$ and $\hat{\mathbf{P}}_{k_{\text{pos}}} = \begin{bmatrix} \sigma_{k_x}^2 & \sigma_{k_{xy}} \\ \sigma_{k_{xy}} & \sigma_{k_y}^2 \end{bmatrix}$. For each sensor location $\mathbf{S}_i$ within the feasibility cluster $\mathscr{F}_k$ at time step k, the Mahalanobis distance from Eq. (15.14) is translated to:

$$M_i^k = \sqrt{(\mathbf{S}_i - \hat{\mathbf{x}}_{k_{\text{pos}}})^T \hat{\mathbf{P}}_{k_{\text{pos}}}^{-1} (\mathbf{S}_i - \hat{\mathbf{x}}_{k_{\text{pos}}})} \tag{15.15}$$

Essentially, a given sensor's Mahalanobis distance from the target's propagated positional belief state is equivalent to the number of standard deviations away the sensor's two-dimensional location is from the propagated (prior) mean target position, $\hat{\mathbf{x}}_{pos}$. The positional covariance $\hat{\mathbf{P}}_{pos}$ as defined above can be geometrically represented by an ellipse of eccentricity e and body-fixed principal axes that are aligned along the eigenvectors of $\hat{\mathbf{P}}_{pos}$, namely, λ_1 and λ_2, originating from the target mean position, $\hat{\mathbf{x}}_{pos}$: see Fig. 15.1b. Consider the relative sensing angle, θ, defined as the angle between the major axis of the prior belief covariance ellipse, λ_1, and the sensor-target relative position vector ($\mathbf{p}_i^k$ from Eq. (15.11)):

$$\theta = \arccos\left(\frac{\mathbf{p}_i^k \cdot \lambda_1}{|\mathbf{p}_i^k|\,|\lambda_1|}\right), \quad \theta \in \left[-\frac{\pi}{2}, \frac{\pi}{2}\right] \tag{15.16}$$

Note that the Mahalanobis distance defined in Eq. (15.15) is related to the relative sensing angle: for a range sensor at Euclidean distance d from the mean, the sensing locations with minimum Mahalanobis distance lie along λ_1 (shown as orange circles in Fig. 15.1b), i.e., where the angle θ is minimized.

Mahalanobis distance is simply a measure of a sensor's geometric relation to a belief state, but in the special instance where a sensor's output relays a constraint on that belief state (i.e., a range or bearing of the target) then the Mahalanobis metric is synonymous with information utility [29]. Two points that are equidistant from the mean may have a corresponding Mahalanobis metric that differ by several orders of magnitude, depending on the respective vectors' alignments to the uncertainty distribution's major axis' eigenvector. In the scenario shown in Fig. 15.3, range sensors A and B are physically equidistant from the target mean. However, because sensor A has a more favorable relative sensing angle than sensor B, it is closer to the target in terms of Mahalanobis distance than sensor B. It consequently provides greater uncertainty reduction along the major axis of the prior covariance, and would be chosen over sensor B in a direct Mahalanobis distance comparison.

15.3.2.2 Sensing Mode and Quality Cluster Creation

A sensor's modality (range, bearing etc.) is a primary factor that affects the selection process. Unlike the range sensors shown in Fig. 15.3 which provide a relative distance measurement along its sensing vector $\mathbf{p}$, bearing sensors sense along an axis orthogonal to $\mathbf{p}$ and output the angle of the received signal. As a result of this orthogonality, the Mahalanobis distance for bearing sensors is computed with a belief state covariance $\hat{\mathbf{P}}_{k_{pos}}$ rotated by $90°$ in the body-fixed reference frame. In the inertial frame, this is expressed as $\hat{\mathbf{P}}_{k_{pos}}^{\text{Bearing}} = \begin{bmatrix} \sigma_{k_y}^2 & -\sigma_{k_{xy}} \\ -\sigma_{k_{xy}} & \sigma_{k_x}^2 \end{bmatrix}$.

Due to the difference in measurement models, observations incorporated from range and bearing sensors at the same Mahalanobis distance do not, in general, gain equal amounts of information after the update stage (Eqs. (15.6), (15.7), (15.8) and (15.9)). When evaluated in terms of the differential entropy of the posterior

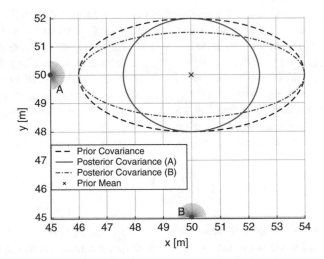

Fig. 15.3 Sensor selection between sensors A and B results in differing updated error ellipses. Rays extending from the sensors represent their respective fields of view

density (an information metric that indicates a distribution's level of randomness, formally defined below in Sect. 15.3.4), it is apparent that there is a belief-state dependent Mahalanobis. The crossover value is actually:

$$M_C = \left(\frac{R_b}{R_r \sqrt{\lambda_1 \lambda_2}} \right)^{\frac{1}{2}}$$

where $\frac{R_r}{R_b}$ is the ratio of range to bearing sensor noise variance. Bearing sensors selected with a lower Mahalanobis metric than M_C tend to offer greater information utility (i.e., a smaller differential entropy) than any range sensor available in the Mahalanobis interval $[0, M_C)$. Figure 15.4 depicts the relation between a given sensor's Mahalanobis distance, modality (red square or blue dot), and the expected differential entropy resulting from that sensor's measurement.

Thus, in order to implement the "information utility clustering" step, each member node of the feasible cluster $\mathscr{F}_k$ is initially ranked by their Mahalanobis distance, M_i^k, relative to the propagated target prior density. This Mahalanobis-ranked set is then sorted via sensing modality, where all bearing sensors with Mahalanobis metric lower than the crossover values $M_i^k < M_C$ take precedence, succeeded by Mahalanobis-sorted range sensors. From this ranked set $\widetilde{\mathscr{F}}_k$, a user-defined number of sensors (ℓ) is retained, producing the *quality cluster* $\mathscr{Q}_k \subseteq \widetilde{\mathscr{F}}_k$ of $\ell \leq m$ elements:

$$\mathscr{Q}_k = \{S_1, \ S_2, \ S_3, \ldots, \ S_i, \ldots, \ S_\ell\}, \quad \text{such that} \quad M_i^k \leq M_L^k \tag{15.17}$$

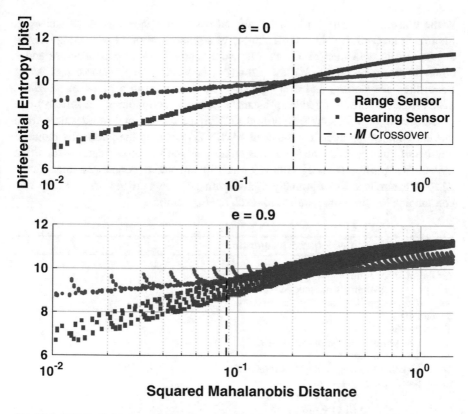

Fig. 15.4 Effect of sensor modality (range and bearing sensors are blue dots and red squares, respectively) and Mahalanobis distance on Expected Differential Entropy. A prior positional uncertainty ellipse with area of 10π m^2 is considered at two eccentricities of $e = 0$ and $e = 0.9$, respectively

where M_L^k is a time-varying Mahalanobis distance upper bound and is an outcome of what nodes are available at the time of clustering, which depends on the size of sensors retained, ℓ. While this limit on retained nodes is open for further on-line optimization, in the interests of computational overhead the implementation of a node density-based limit has been found to provide adequate results.

15.3.3   Communication Cost

The final clustering step, designed to reduce the computational cost of routing information from a sensor to a processing node (and vice versa), is applied to the quality set $\mathcal{Q}_k$. In this context, the computational cost (also known as the *cost of delay* [30] between the sensor and sink) is represented as the routing time, τ_k, required to activate a sensor S_i at the look-ahead timestep k based on the predicted target positional mean $\hat{\mathbf{x}}_k$. The routing time is computed as $\tau_k = 2\nu\varphi_i$, where ν

is the transmission rate (in bps) for all sensors within the network $\mathcal{W}$ and φ_i is the minimum (and time-invariant) number of communication links to complete the sensor-to-sink data transfer. Given a network topology of $\mathcal{W}$ with n nodes and z communication links, the shortest paths [31] between a single-source processing node (the base station) and every possible sensing node in a graph of weighted edges (treated here as Euclidean distances between communicating sensors) can be computed with Dijkstra's algorithm [32]. Since the optimal routing time from one communicating node to another in a WSN is driven by the minimally required number of links between the two nodes rather than the shortest distance, a modified Dijkstra's algorithm (see Algorithm 2) was implemented to construct a final cluster $\mathcal{C}_k$. An example of an optimally-routed path is shown in Fig. 15.5, where five communication links are required to reach the base station.

Algorithm 2 Modified Dijkstra's algorithm

1: Initialize $\mathcal{V} \leftarrow \mathcal{W}$ as the set of sensors.
2: **for all** $S_i \in \mathcal{V}$. **do**
3:     $\varphi_i \leftarrow 1$ {Minimum transmissions possible}.
4:     $d[S_i] \leftarrow \infty$ {Distance from sink to sensor}.
5: **end for**
6: **while** $\mathcal{V}$ **not** $\varnothing$ **do**
7:     Find sensor $S_i \in \mathcal{V}$ with minimum $d[S_i]$.
8:     Remove S_i from $\mathcal{V}$.
9:     Initialize $\mathcal{Y}$ as neighboring sensor set of S_i.
10:     **for all** sensor $y \in \mathcal{Y}$ **do**
11:         **if** $d[S_i] + d[S_i, y] < d[y]$ **then**
12:             $d[y] \leftarrow d[S_i] + d[S_i, y]$
13:             **return** $\varphi_y \leftarrow \varphi_i + 1$
14:             {Increment communication chain}
15:         **end if**
16:     **end for**
17: **end while**

Algorithm 2 has a computational running time of $\mathcal{O}((n + z)\ln(n))$, where z is the number of possible communication links. All optimal routing times are sensor-dependent and computed off-line. Successful operation of Algorithm 2 scales well for practical sensor densities and communication ranges; a useful advantage given the network density may not be known a priori in a realistic tracking scenario. After returning the shortest number of links φ_i for each node within $\mathcal{Q}_k$, the *cost* cluster of $r \leq \ell$ elements $\mathcal{C}_k \subseteq \mathcal{Q}_k$ at time step k is constructed as

$$\mathcal{C}_k = \{S_1, S_2, S_3, \ldots S_i, \ldots, S_r\}, \quad \forall \ \varphi_i \leq \varphi_L \tag{15.18}$$

Analogous to the creation of the quality cluster $\mathcal{Q}_k$, $\mathcal{C}_k$ is generated by the retention of a user-defined number of r sensors within $\mathcal{Q}_k$ that will potentially make the measurement. Hence, the bound φ_L is a time-varying value. An example of the final rapid cluster $\mathcal{C}_k$ is presented in Fig. 15.6c.

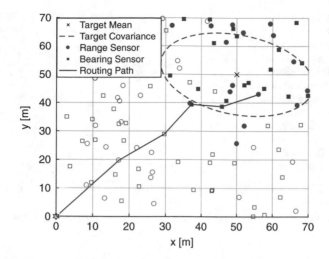

Fig. 15.5 Data transfer from sensor to sink within a $\mathcal{W}$ of 125 sensors. ($\varphi = 5$ message links)

15.3.4   Final Optimal Sensor Selection

Once the IGRCA cluster has been constructed, the optimal sensor from this set must be identified which will ultimately be tasked with making the measurement of the target at time step k. The objective is to select the sensor that will result in the "least" posterior uncertainty. This is obviously "awkward" because posterior densities at time k would require sensor measurements at that time, which has not yet occurred. In implementing the *one-step lookahead* procedure employed with the IDSQ approach (as in Ref. [17]), we compute the expected differential entropy of the simulated posterior target belief state as an information utility measure to predict the optimal sensor S^*. Measured in bits, this scalar metric measures the level of *randomness* within a distribution. In a target tracking application, sensors with measurements that result in a lower differential entropy of a posterior density represent greater reduction in uncertainty. Letting $\mathbf{P}_k^+$ be the *simulated* posterior covariance of dimension n with look-ahead posterior mean $\mathbf{x}_k^+$, the differential entropy of a Gaussian distribution is defined as:

$$H(\mathcal{N}(\mathbf{x}_k^+, \mathbf{P}_k^+)) = \frac{1}{2} \log_2 \left[(2\pi \exp)^n \left| \mathbf{P}_k^+ \right| \right] \tag{15.19}$$

The sensor S^* responsible for the minimum differential entropy within the final cluster $\mathcal{C}_k$ of r nodes is selected as the measurement-taking leader node for the next timestep k.

Fig. 15.6 (**a**) Sensor subset $\mathscr{F}_k$ generated with Eq. (15.13). (**b**) Sensor subset $\mathscr{Q}_k$ generated with Eq. (15.17). The remaining range and combined sensors tend along the major axis of the error ellipse, while bearing sensors lie along the minor axis. (**c**) The final output of the IGRCA $\mathscr{C}_k$ retains the cost-effective nodes

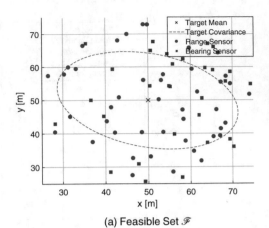

(a) Feasible Set $\mathscr{F}$

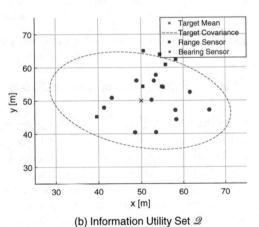

(b) Information Utility Set $\mathscr{Q}$

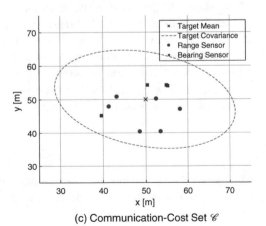

(c) Communication-Cost Set $\mathscr{C}$

15.3.4.1   A Note on the Use of Two Separate Information Gain Metrics

We point out that from above, the Mahalanobis distance was used as the information theoretic metric to construct the sensor cluster $\mathcal{Q}_k$, whereas a different metric, namely differential entropy, was utilized to identify the optimal sensor S_k^* from within the cluster $\mathcal{Q}_k$. A criticism of this approach is that given its direct mapping to target uncertainty reduction, differential entropy and not the Mahalanobis distance, represents a better choice for creating the quality cluster ($\mathcal{Q}_k$) in Sect. 15.3.2. It should be noted that Mahalanobis distance and the expected differential entropy convey two different pieces of information utility: While the Mahalanobis metric simply predicts the geometric advantage of a given sensor (via distance and orientation to the greatest axis of uncertainty), the simulated differential entropy measures the *effect* that a given sensor's measurement would have on the resulting belief state. The predicted Mahalanobis distance only has to evaluate Eq. (15.15) for each sensor, as opposed to the predicted differential entropy that must make use of each sensor's measurement model and algebraically manipulate Eqs. (15.6), (15.7) and (15.9) to achieve an analytical expression for Eq. (15.19) given the prior covariance. For the measurement and variance models we outline further down in Sect. 15.4.2, it was empirically determined that the average additional time expended (when compared to the average Mahalanobis computation time) to assign expected differential entropy values to a group of feasible sensors grows linearly with the cluster size. Thus, the use of the Mahalanobis distance as an information utility metric is beneficial to rapidly clustering large numbers of sensors that favor uncertainty reduction while differential entropy operates as an additional utility metric on a final reduced set.

15.3.5   Procedure of the IGRCA

The step-wise procedure that constructs the final sensor cluster $\mathcal{C}_k$ from the full wireless sensor network $\mathcal{W}$ (presented in Fig. 15.1a) is outlined in Algorithm 3. The algorithm can be summarized in terms of generation of the following sequence of nested sensor sets at time k:

$$\underbrace{\mathcal{W}}_{\text{WSN (Fig. 15.1a)}} \supseteq \underbrace{\mathcal{F}_k}_{\text{Feasible Set (Fig. 15.6a)}} \supset \underbrace{\mathcal{Q}_k}_{\text{Utility Set (Fig. 15.6b)}} \supset \underbrace{\mathcal{C}_k}_{\text{IGRCA Output(Fig. 15.6c)}}$$

An alternative is to rank each feasible sensor S_i according to an objective function value (see Zhao et al. [17]) as follows

$$\Phi^k(S_i) = \alpha_1 M_i^k + \alpha_2 \varphi_i^k, \text{ where } \alpha_1 + \alpha_2 = 1$$

where at every time step k the final cluster is constructed by ranking each node within $\mathscr{F}_k$ by Φ^k and retaining a user-specified r nodes with the lowest objective values Φ^k. While this method allows for simultaneous consideration of both information utility and routing cost at the time of clustering, it was determined that the subset approach is more cost-effective and results in near-identical overall target uncertainty reduction.

Algorithm 3 Information guided rapid clustering algorithm

1: Compute the optimal routing paths via Algorithm 2.
2: Given the current state of the target $\mathbf{x}_{k-1}$ and $\mathbf{P}_{k-1}$ compute the prior belief values $\hat{\mathbf{x}}_k$ and $\hat{\mathbf{P}}_k$ at the next time-step k.
3: Iterate through $\mathscr{W}$ and return $\mathscr{F}_k$ with Eq. (15.13).
4: **if** The number of elements of $\mathscr{F}_k$ is 0, return prior as posterior **then**
5:      Go to step 1.
6: **else**
7:      Iterate through $\mathscr{F}_k$ and return $\mathscr{Q}_k$ with Eq. (15.17).
8:      Reorder $\mathscr{F}_k$ into $\tilde{\mathscr{F}}_k$.
9:      Iterate through $\mathscr{Q}_k$ and return $\mathscr{C}_k$ with Eq. (15.18).
10:     Iterate through $\mathscr{C}_k$ and perform simulated measurements at time k to compute expected entropy H_i with Eq. (15.19) for each sensor.
11:     Determine the optimal sensor S^* by identifying the minimal expected entropy H_k^*.
12:     Route the current belief data to S^*.
13:     S^* performs a measurement and routes the information back to the base station for data aggregation and fusion.
14: **end if**
15: Repeat step 2.

15.4   Target Dynamics and Sensor Measurement Models

In this section, the dynamics and measurement models laid out in Sect. 15.2.1 are specified for the specialized case of multiple maneuvering targets being tracked with the measurements generated by the activated nodes of a wireless sensor network. These models are implemented in the succeeding information utility analysis given in Sect. 15.5 and in the simulation studies discussed in Sect. 15.6.

15.4.1   System Model

For tracking applications, it is advantageous for the sensor-selection algorithm to account for sudden directional shifts in a target's trajectory as it maneuvers within the sensing environment. Consider a state-space χ partitioned into two regions ($\chi = \chi_1 \cup \chi_2$) defined below:

1. The comprehensive sensing boundary of the wireless sensor network $\mathcal{W}$ of n sensors, defined as $\chi_1 = \{\Lambda_1 \cup \Lambda_2 \cup \Lambda_3, \ldots \Lambda_{n-1} \cup \Lambda_n \cup \Omega_T\}$, where Ω_T is the user-defined test area (in m^2) that the set $\mathcal{W}$ is responsible for covering.
2. The portion of χ in which the target cannot be sensed, defined as $\chi_2 = \chi \setminus \chi_1$.

Each member of the partition (here χ_1 and χ_2) admits a unique set of system dynamics equations, defined by their corresponding state transition matrices $\mathbf{A}_1$ and $\mathbf{A}_2$, thereby resulting in a piecewise affine system (a switching state system) [33, 34]. To simulate this behavior, a switching function was introduced by Olfati-Saber and Sandell [35] into the system dynamics that applies an orthogonal force to the target at the time step in which it escapes, redirecting it back into the sensor field. This allows for the tracking of agents with unpredictable path-deviation or obstacle-avoidance behavior within a bounded environment. In the simulations presented in Sect. 15.6, the base station is able to predict when an object will encounter a switch in its trajectory, and will account for an object's new dynamics in the prior state prediction. The target position dictates the state transition dynamics into two models, one for inside and the other for outside the sensor field. A binary switching function with scalar input η that represents a component of the target position vector $\eta \in \{x_t, y_t\}$ enables switching between these modes

$$\Gamma(\eta) = \begin{cases} 1, & \text{if } \eta \geq 0 \\ -1, & \text{otherwise} \end{cases}$$

We extend the above definition to include a user-defined boundary distance a:

$$\mu(\eta) = \frac{\Gamma((a-\omega)+\eta) + \Gamma(a-\eta)}{2},$$

where a target may exit the boundaries of the test area Ω_T for a where "a" represents the distance from the origin (along the x or y directions) within the test area a before encountering an orthogonal direction shift from the switching matrix:

$$\mathbf{M(x)} = \begin{bmatrix} \mu(x) & 0 \\ 0 & \mu(y) \end{bmatrix}.$$

The linearized state transition form of Eq. (15.2) is now defined as

$$\mathbf{F(x)} = \mathbf{M(x)} \otimes \mathbf{A}_1 + (\mathscr{I}_2 - \mathbf{M(x)}) \otimes \mathbf{A}_2,$$

where, $\otimes$ denotes the Kronecker Product, $\mathbf{A}_1 = \begin{bmatrix} 1 & \Delta T \\ 0 & 1 \end{bmatrix}$ (applied when $[x_t, \ y_t]^T \in X_1$) and $\mathbf{A}_2 = \begin{bmatrix} 1 & \Delta T \\ -\Delta T c_1 & 1 - \Delta T c_2 \end{bmatrix}$ (applied when $[x_t, \ y_t]^T \in X_2$) with user-defined constants $a, c_1, c_2 > 0$, and step-size in time ΔT. Equation (15.2) becomes

$$\mathbf{x}_{k+1} = \mathbf{F}(xk)xk + \mathbf{B}\mathbf{v}_k \tag{15.20}$$

where $\mathbf{B} = \mathscr{I}_2 \otimes \begin{bmatrix} \frac{\Delta T^2 \sigma_q}{2} \\ \Delta T \sigma_q \end{bmatrix}$ with process noise variance σ_q^2. Equation (15.20) is used to generate the target trajectories with randomized initial states described in the results section below (Sects. 15.6.3 and 15.6.3.3).

15.4.2 Measurement Model

We consider a heterogeneous wireless sensor network comprised of both bearing-only (i.e., passive sonar [36, 37] and Angle-of-Arrival antenna arrays [38, 39]) and range-only (i.e., radar [40] or acoustic amplitude [2]) sensors. The output of each sensor-type is a function of the relative position between the sensor $S_i = [S_{x,i} \ S_{y,i}]$ and the target's location:

$$\mathbf{h}_k(\mathbf{x}_k) = \begin{cases} \sqrt{\tilde{x}_k^2 + \tilde{y}_k^2} & \text{for range sensor} \\ \arctan \frac{\tilde{y}_k}{\tilde{x}_k} & \text{for bearing sensor} \end{cases} \tag{15.21}$$

where $\tilde{x}_k = x_k - S_{x,i}$ and $\tilde{y}_k = y_k - S_{y,i}$ are the predicted relative positions and angle between the sensing node and the target at time k. The Jacobians of these measurement models (see Refs. [40, 41] for the derivation of range-only and bearing-only models, respectively) are

$$\mathbf{H}_k(\hat{\mathbf{x}}_k) = \begin{cases} \begin{bmatrix} \frac{\tilde{x}_k}{\sqrt{\tilde{x}_k^2 + \tilde{y}_k^2}} & 0 & \frac{\tilde{y}_k}{\sqrt{\tilde{x}_k^2 + \tilde{y}_k^2}} & 0 \end{bmatrix}, & \text{(range sensor)} \\[4mm] \begin{bmatrix} \frac{-\tilde{y}_k}{\tilde{x}_k^2 + \tilde{y}_k^2} & 0 & \frac{\tilde{x}_k}{\tilde{x}_k^2 + \tilde{y}_k^2} & 0 \end{bmatrix}, & \text{(bearing sensor)} \end{cases} \tag{15.22}$$

In addition to the measurement matrices, the noise variance $R_i^k(d_k)$ for each sensor i is related to its relative position to the target, based on the received signal strength model [8, 29, 42, 43] (present in acoustic amplitude and sonar sensors) which is a function of the sensor's distance d away from the target at time k, an amplifying constant κ and an additional randomized error $r_i \sim \text{Gamma}(r_\alpha, r_\beta), r_i << d$ which represents inherent mechanical error made during observation.

$$R_i^k(d_k) = \kappa (d_k + r_i) \tag{15.23}$$

Measurements routed to the base station also carry an attached binary mode value to indicate whether the data carries a relative distance or bearing value.

$$\varrho = \begin{cases} 0 & \text{for range sensor} \\ 1 & \text{for bearing sensor} \end{cases} \tag{15.24}$$

This allows the base station to compute Eqs.(15.7), (15.8) and (15.9) with the correct measurement and noise forms.

15.5 Analysis

As outlined in Sect. 15.3.2, two characteristics are key in sensor selection: (i) relative location to the target and (ii) sensing modality. In this section, we rigorously lay out the relationship between a sensor's relative position to the target and the potential information gain from its measurement. The analysis presented here supports IGRCA's use of Mahalanobis distance as the information metric for sensor clustering. The range sensor is considered first, followed by an extension to bearing sensors. First, we clarify our notation in regards to frame of reference and state an information gain result that is well known.

15.5.1 Frame of Reference

Recall that in this work we are concerned only with "positional sensors" (range/bearing measurements), whereby the developments below use *positional restrictions* of the mean vector and covariance matrix, defined in Sect. 15.3.2.1 as $\hat{\mathbf{x}}_{\text{pos}} = [\hat{x}, \ \hat{y}]^T$ and $\hat{\mathbf{P}}_{\text{pos}} = \begin{bmatrix} \sigma_x^2 & \sigma_{xy} \\ \sigma_{xy} & \sigma_y^2 \end{bmatrix}$. In the sequel, this covariance matrix is described within a "body-fixed frame" with the target position at the origin, i.e. $\hat{\mathbf{x}}_{\text{pos}} = [0, \ 0]^T$ and $\hat{\mathbf{P}}_{\text{pos}} = \begin{bmatrix} \lambda_1 & 0 \\ 0 & \lambda_2 \end{bmatrix}$. This transformation from the inertial reference frame is performed such that the greatest eigenvalue of the positional covariance matrix $\mathbf{e}_1$ correlates to the eigenvector of the major axis of the uncertainty ellipse within the inertial frame, λ_1 (see Fig. 15.1b for both reference frames). Analogously, the relative position vector in the inertial frame (used in Eq. (15.22)), $\mathbf{p} = [\tilde{x}, \ \tilde{y}]^T$ is redefined within this principal axis coordinate system as $\mathbf{p} = [p_1, \ p_2]^T$.

Lemma 1 *Consider a target with positional mean and covariance $\hat{\mathbf{x}}_{\text{pos}}$ and $\hat{\mathbf{P}}_{\text{pos}}$ respectively, and a range sensor S_E with position $\mathbf{S}_E$ and relative sensing vector $\mathbf{p}_E = \mathbf{S}_E - \hat{\mathbf{x}}_{\text{pos}}$ at a distance $\|\mathbf{p}_E\| = d$ from the target. Sensor locations that provide optimal target uncertainty reduction lie along the principal major axis $\mathbf{e}_1$ of $\hat{\mathbf{P}}_{\text{pos}}$.*

Proof The following result is well known and interested readers may refer to Appendix C.5 of Zhao's and Guibas' work in [29].

The amount of uncertainty reduction along a sensing axis $\mathbf{p}_E$ is directly proportional to the predicted information gain, represented geometrically by the reduction in volume of the uncertainty hyperellipsoid

$$\mathscr{I} \propto \det(\hat{\mathbf{P}}) - \det(\mathbf{P}^+) \tag{15.25}$$

A range sensor (blue circle in Fig. 15.1b) provides measurement information $\mathbf{z}$ parallel to the sensing vector $\mathbf{p}_E$. The surface area of the resulting updated covariance $\hat{\mathbf{P}}_{\mathrm{pos}}^+$ is lowest if $\mathbf{p}_E$ originates from the points of optimal information gain (orange circles in Fig. 15.1b) which lie along the uncertainty ellipse's longest axis $(\mathbf{e}_1)$ [44].   □

Before presenting further results, additional notation and definitions are needed. Consider Lemma 1 applied to a uniformly distributed sensor field. A range sensor obtained as the outcome of optimization of Euclidean distance is represented as S_E with relative vector $\mathbf{S}_E$ from the expected target position $\hat{\mathbf{x}}_{\mathrm{pos}}$. It is represented in the **body-fixed** frame as $\mathbf{p}_E = [p_1, p_2]^{\mathrm{T}}$ with a Euclidean distance $d = \sqrt{\mathbf{p}_E \cdot \mathbf{p}_E}$ from the expected target mean. Its squared Mahalanobis distance S_E from the target pdf is then:

$$M_E^2 = \mathbf{p}_E^T \, \hat{\mathbf{P}}_{\mathrm{pos}}^{-1} \, \mathbf{p}_E = \frac{1}{\lambda_1 \lambda_2} [\lambda_2 p_1^2 + \lambda_1 p_2^2] \tag{15.26}$$

Next, consider a circle of radius d circumscribed by the sensing vector $\mathbf{p}_E$ around the mean position $\hat{\mathbf{x}}_{\mathrm{pos}}$. Depending on the quadrant in which S_E lies, its position vector $\mathbf{p}_E$ can be mapped to a new (hypothetical) location $\mathbf{p}_Q$ that has a shorter projection l_Q to the major axis vector $\mathbf{e}_1$ than that of the original projection (l_E) from $\mathbf{p}_E$. A shorter projection coincides with higher information gain (see Lemma 1). Figure 15.7 illustrates four possible locations (red circles) for the sensor S_E, and the respective rotational paths (pink sectors) wherein a resulting rotation of $\mathbf{p}_E$ anywhere within the sector will entail a shorter projection to the major axis. The direction of rotation applied to sensing vector $\mathbf{p}_E$ and the nearest major axis vertex is quadrant-dependent, as specified in (15.27). The angle of S_E with respect to major axis, θ_E, is always measured from the major axis to $\mathbf{p}_E$. Similarly, the angle θ_Q of the resulting vector, $\mathbf{p}_Q$, is also measured from the nearest major axis. For simplicity, let $\gamma = \theta_E - \theta_Q$.

$$R_3 = \begin{cases} \begin{bmatrix} \cos\gamma & \sin\gamma \\ -\sin\gamma & \cos\gamma \end{bmatrix}, & \text{for } \gamma \in \text{Quadrants I or III} \\[2ex] \begin{bmatrix} \cos\gamma & -\sin\gamma \\ \sin\gamma & \cos\gamma \end{bmatrix}, & \text{for } \gamma \in \text{Quadrants II or IV} \end{cases} \tag{15.27}$$

Lemma 2 *Let a range sensor S_E at distance d from the target mean position, $\hat{\mathbf{x}}_{\mathrm{pos}}$, and relative angle γ with respect to the major axis of the target's positional*

Fig. 15.7 Possible S_E
locations in all four quadrants
are depicted each with an
associated circular sector
(pink path) where a lower
Mahalanobis distance resides.
In the first quadrant case,
$E_E = E_Q$ but $M_Q < M_E$

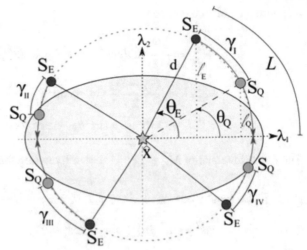

*covariance, $\mathbf{e}_1$, be selected as the optimal sensor via the ECA algorithm. Let the
corresponding Mahalanobis distance w.r.t. the target pdf be M_E. If $\theta_E \neq 0$, S_E
subtends an arc, L, of radius d on to $\mathbf{e}_1$ along which Mahalanobis distance from
the target pdf is less than or equal to M_E and another range sensor S_Q with
corresponding Mahalanobis distance M_Q, if placed on this arc, would be preferred
over S_E by IGRCA.*

Proof $M_Q \leq M_E$ is shown below in the first quadrant case, with the vector $\mathbf{p}_E$
described in polar form as (d, θ_E), where $\theta_E \in [0, \frac{\pi}{2}]$. A clockwise rotation of $\mathbf{p}_E$
through an angle of $\gamma \in [0, \theta_E]$, will yield the following rotated sensing vector

$$\mathbf{p}_Q = R_3 \mathbf{p}_E = \begin{bmatrix} p_1 \cos \gamma + p_2 \sin \gamma \\ -p_1 \sin \gamma + p_2 \cos \gamma \end{bmatrix} \tag{15.28}$$

and the polar conversions of $p_1 = d \cos \theta_E$ and $p_2 = d \sin \theta_E$ restate M_E^2 as:

$$M_E^2 = \frac{d^2}{\lambda_1 \lambda_2} [\lambda_2 \cos^2 \theta_E + \lambda_1 \sin^2 \theta_E] \tag{15.29}$$

The squared Mahalanobis distance $M_Q^2 = \mathbf{p}_Q^T \hat{\mathbf{P}}_{pos}^{-1} \mathbf{p}_Q$ in the body-fixed form of
Eq. (15.26) is done with the substitution of $\mathbf{p}_Q = R_3 \mathbf{p}_E$ in Eq. (15.28):

$$M_Q^2 = \frac{1}{\lambda_1 \lambda_2} [\lambda_2 p_1^2 \cos^2 \gamma + 2\lambda_2 p_1 p_2 \sin \gamma \cos \gamma$$
$$+ \lambda_2 p_1^2 \sin^2 \gamma + \lambda_1 p_2^1 \sin^2 \gamma$$
$$- 2\lambda_1 p_1 p_2 \sin \gamma \cos \gamma + \lambda_1 p_2^2 \cos^2 \gamma]$$

and with the polar conversion

$$M_Q^2 = \frac{d^2}{\lambda_1\lambda_2}[\lambda_2(\cos^2\gamma\cos^2\theta_E + \sin^2\gamma\sin^2\theta_E)$$

$$+ \frac{(\lambda_2 - \lambda_1)}{2}\sin 2\gamma\sin 2\theta_E$$

$$+ \lambda_1(\cos^2\gamma\sin^2\theta_E + \sin^2\gamma\cos^2\theta_E)]$$

The desired inequality $M_Q^2 \le M_E^2$ is shown by noting that

$$[\lambda_2(\cos^2\gamma\cos^2\theta_E + \sin^2\gamma\sin^2\theta_E) + \frac{(\lambda_2 - \lambda_1)}{2}\sin 2\gamma\sin 2\theta_E$$

$$+ \lambda_1(\cos^2\gamma\sin^2(\theta_E) + \sin^2\gamma\cos^2\theta_E)]$$

$$\le [\lambda_2\cos^2\theta_E + \lambda_1\sin^2\theta_E]$$

which reduces to

$$\lambda_2 \le \lambda_2\cos^2\theta_E + \lambda_1\sin^2\theta_E \tag{15.30}$$

We combine the above with an expression of eccentricity in terms of the covariance eigenvalues, $e^2 = 1 - \frac{\lambda_2}{\lambda_1}$ to get

$$1 \le \cos^2\theta_E + \frac{\sin^2\theta_E}{(1 - e^2)} \tag{15.31}$$

By the definition of Lemma 2, the rotated sensing vector $\mathbf{p}_Q$ will have a resulting relative angle $\theta_Q \le \theta_E$. Since $\theta_Q = \theta_E$ *if and only if* $\gamma = 0$, the nontrivial result provides the following relation:

$$\theta_Q < \theta_E \implies M_Q < M_E \tag{15.32}$$

$\square$

As expected, the quantities in Eq. (15.31) are equal when the eccentricity is zero. The proof is similar for γ in quadrant cases $II - IV$, and the conclusions are the same: for $e \neq 0$, $\mathbf{p}_E$ can be rotated to a vector $\mathbf{p}_Q$ that has a shorter projection l_Q to the major axis vector $\mathbf{e}_1$ than that of the sensing vector $\mathbf{p}_E$, with a lower Mahalanobis distance (see Eq. (15.32) and Fig. 15.7). There are two instances where $\mathbf{p}_E$ and $\mathbf{p}_Q$ are the same vector:

1. Eccentricity of uncertainty ellipse is zero.
2. The closest Euclidean point already lies along the major principal axis: polar points $(d,0)$, and (d,π)

The following lemma concerns sensors at points located within the first quadrant of the body-fixed reference frame.

Lemma 3 *Consider two sensors S_E and S_Q on a circular arc of radius d at Mahalanobis distance M_E and M_Q from the target state pdf. Then*

$$M_Q < M_E \implies \theta_Q < \theta_E \qquad (15.33)$$

where, θ_E and θ_Q are the angular positions of S_E and S_Q respectively, measured from the major axis.

Proof We are given two points in the first quadrant described by (d, θ_E) and (d, θ_Q) and assume that condition $M_Q^2 < M_E^2$. Using Eq. (15.29) from Lemma 2, $M_Q^2 < M_E^2$ becomes:

$$\lambda_2 \cos^2 \theta_Q + \lambda_1 \sin^2 \theta_Q < \lambda_2 \cos^2 \theta_E + \lambda_1 \sin^2 \theta_E$$

substituting $\lambda_2 = \lambda_1 z$ where $z = (1 - e^2)$,

$$= z \cos^2 \theta_Q + \sin^2 \theta_Q < z \cos^2 \theta_E + \sin^2 \theta_E$$

$$= z \frac{1 + \cos 2\theta_Q}{2} + \frac{1 + \cos 2\theta_Q}{2} < z \frac{1 + \cos 2\theta_E}{2} + \frac{1 + \cos 2\theta_E}{2}$$

$$= z (\cos u - \cos v) < (\cos u - \cos v), \text{ with } u = 2\theta_Q \text{ and } v = 2\theta_E$$

which holds *if $u < v$*. Thus, $M_Q < M_E \implies \theta_Q < \theta_E$ as $0 \le z < 1$.   □

Theorem 1 *Consider two sensors S_E and S_Q at polar coordinates (d, θ_E) and (d, θ_Q) respectively in the body-fixed reference frame. If their Mahalanobis distance from the target state-pdf is M_E and M_Q respectively, then*

$$\theta_Q < \theta_E \iff M_Q < M_E \qquad (15.34)$$

Proof Combining Lemmas 2 and 3 results in Eq. (15.34) (applicable within the first quadrant).   □

While Lemma 3 may seem redundant to Lemma 2 in its construction, it is crucially different in what knowledge is assumed for their respective proofs. As the Mahalanobis distance metric implicitly contains both Euclidean distance and relative angle information (such as γ for each sensor), the *if and only if* statement provided by Eq.(15.34) allows an algorithm supplied with Mahalanobis distance information to sort sensors in terms of information optimality, as demonstrated by Lemma 4 below.

Lemma 4 *Given two range sensors S_E and S_Q at positions described by (d, θ_E) and (d, θ_Q) in the first quadrant such that $\theta_Q < \theta_E$, the expected Fisher Information of S_Q is greater than that of S_E, i.e.*

$$\theta_Q < \theta_E \implies \mathscr{I}_Q > \mathscr{I}_E$$

Proof The measurement error variances R_E and R_Q of sensors S_E and S_Q respectively are each assumed to be $\kappa_r(d + r_0)^3$ The target's prior covariance with body-fixed principal axes is represented as the diagonal matrix:

$$\hat{\mathbf{P}} = \begin{bmatrix} \lambda_1 & 0 & 0 & 0 \\ 0 & \lambda_3 & 0 & 0 \\ 0 & 0 & \lambda_2 & 0 \\ 0 & 0 & 0 & \lambda_4 \end{bmatrix} \tag{15.35}$$

and the resulting the Kalman gain from Eq. (15.7) becomes:

$$\mathbf{K} = \begin{bmatrix} \dfrac{dp_1\lambda_1}{\lambda_1 p_1^2 + \lambda_2 p_2^2 + d^2\kappa_r(d+r_0)} \\ 0 \\ \dfrac{dp_2\lambda_2}{\lambda_1 p_1^2 + \lambda_2 p_2^2 + d^2\kappa_r(d+r_0)} \\ 0 \end{bmatrix}$$

Thus the posterior covariance can be obtained from Eq. (15.9) as

$$\mathbf{P}^+ = \begin{bmatrix} \dfrac{\lambda_1(\lambda_2 p_2^2 + d^2\kappa_r(d+r_0))}{\lambda_1 p_1^2 + \lambda_2 p_2^2 + d^2\kappa_r(d+r_0)} & 0 & \dfrac{-\lambda_1\lambda_2 p_1 p_2}{\lambda_1 p_1^2 + \lambda_2 p_2^2 + d^2\kappa_r(d+r_0)} & 0 \\ 0 & \lambda_3 & 0 & 0 \\ \dfrac{-\lambda_1\lambda_2 p_1 p_2}{\lambda_1 p_1^2 + \lambda_2 p_2^2 + d^2\kappa_r(d+r_0)} & 0 & \dfrac{\lambda_2(\lambda_1 p_1^2 + d^2\kappa_r(d+r0))}{\lambda_1 p_1^2 + \lambda_2 p_2^2 + d^2\kappa_r(d+r_0)} & 0 \\ 0 & 0 & 0 & \lambda_4 \end{bmatrix}$$

leads to the predicted Fisher Information metric (defined as the determinant of the inverse of the posterior covariance) $\mathscr{I} \equiv det\left((\mathbf{P}_k^+)^{-1}\right)$

$$\mathscr{I} = \frac{\lambda_1 p_1^2 + \lambda_2 p_2^2 + d^2\kappa_r(d+r_0)}{\lambda_1\lambda_2\lambda_3\lambda_4 d^2\kappa_r(d+r_0)} \tag{15.36}$$

where, $p_1 = d\cos\theta$ and $p_2 = d\sin\theta$. Since $\lambda_2 = \lambda_1(1 - e^2)$, Eq. (15.36) can be rephrased as

$$\mathscr{I}(e, \theta) = \frac{\kappa_r(d+r_0) + \lambda_1(\cos^2\theta + (1-e^2)\sin^2\theta)}{\kappa_r(d+r_0)\lambda_1^2\lambda_3\lambda_4(1-e^2)} \tag{15.37}$$

i.e. the Fisher Information can be treated as a bivariate function of the positional covariance eccentricity (e) and the relative sensing angle, θ (Fig. 15.8). In order to

---

[3]For simplicity, the error term r_0 is a positive constant, $r_0 \ll d$.

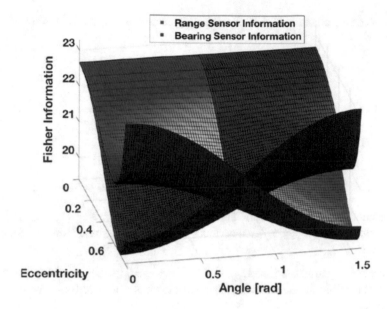

Fig. 15.8 Fisher Information $\mathscr{I}$ surfaces (blue and red), generated by a range and bearing sensor respectively, are assumed to lie 1 m from the target. From this distance, each sensor type observes belief state distributions at varying eccentricities and sensing angles

compare the Fisher Information of any two sensors, hold the eccentricity value of the target distribution as a constant and take the partial derivative of $\mathscr{I}$ with respect to θ:

$$\frac{\partial \mathscr{I}}{\partial \theta} = \frac{\sin 2\theta(-e^2)}{\kappa_r(d + r_0)\lambda_1\lambda_3\lambda_4(1 - e^2)} \leq 0, \quad \forall \theta \in (0, \frac{\pi}{2})$$

Hence, for targets with non-circular distributions ($e \neq 0$) and for nonnegative sensor white-noise r_0:

$$\theta_E > \theta_Q \implies \mathscr{I}_Q > \mathscr{I}_E$$

$\square$

Theorem 2 *Given a common sensor field, a cluster $\mathscr{Q}$ of n sensors derived from the IGRCA will provide greater or equal information gain than any Euclidean cluster $\mathscr{E}$ of equal number.*

$$\sum_i^n \mathscr{I}_Q^i \geq \sum_i^n \mathscr{I}_E^i$$

Where $\mathscr{I}^i$ is the Fisher Information provided by sensor S_i.

Proof Reorder clusters $\mathscr{E}$ and $\mathscr{Q}$ according to ascending Mahalanobis distance, such that

$$\mathscr{E} = \{E_1, \ E_2, \ E_3, \ldots, \ E_i, \ldots, \ E_n\},$$

$$\text{where } M_{E_1} \leq M_{E_2} \ldots M_{E_{n-1}} \leq M_{E_n}$$

and

$$\mathscr{Q} = \{Q_1, \ Q_2, \ Q_3, \ldots, \ Q_i, \ldots, \ Q_n\},$$

$$\text{where } M_{Q_1} \leq M_{Q_2} \ldots M_{Q_{n-1}} \leq M_{Q_n}$$

Consider an arbitrary sensor pair (E_i, Q_i) where $i \in \{1, 2, \ldots, n\}$. The information gain for Q_i is greater than or equal to E_i based on the following arguments:

- Theorem 1 guarantees that $M_{Q_i} < M_{E_i} \iff \theta_{Q_i} < \theta_{E_i}$, and thus the sensor with the minimal Mahalanobis distance also has optimized relative angle and distance.
- Lemma 4 guarantees that $\theta_{Q_i} < \theta_{E_i} \implies \mathscr{I}_{E_i} < \mathscr{I}_{Q_i}$.
- Lemma 1 guarantees that a higher Fisher Information metric is proportional to a higher uncertainty reduction in the target distribution's positional belief state.

Thus, the *optimal* sensor will always lie within the IGRCA cluster $\mathscr{Q}$. As both $\mathscr{E}$ and $\mathscr{Q}$ are constructed on sorting sensors by increasing Euclidean and Mahalanobis distance respectively, then extending this inequality to the entire cluster of n sensors by selecting any pair of sensors without replacement and comparing them directly on information gain, the resulting *sum* of Fisher information for each cluster yields the following inequality:

$$\sum_i^n \mathscr{I}_Q^i \geq \sum_i^n \mathscr{I}_E^i$$

$\square$

15.5.2 *Extension to Bearing Sensors*

Theorem 2 can easily be extended to bearing sensors. The corresponding optimal locations are found along the minor axis ($\mathbf{e}_2$) of the uncertainty ellipse, as bearing sensors provide a measurement orthogonal to a range sensor's sensing axis. Due to the difference in measurement models, Lemma 4 is adapted into Corollary 1 as follows.

Corollary 1 *Given two bearing sensors S_E and S_Q in the first quadrant described by (d, θ_E) and (d, θ_Q) and the condition $\theta_Q > \theta_E$, then the Fisher Information provided by S_Q is greater than that of S_E.*

$$\theta_Q > \theta_E \implies \mathscr{I}_Q > \mathscr{I}_E$$

Proof Implementing the bearing model with variance amplification factor κ_b in Eq. (15.21), the Kalman gain becomes

$$\mathbf{K} = \begin{bmatrix} \dfrac{-p_2 \lambda_1 (p_1^2 + p_2^2)}{\lambda_2 p_1^2 + \lambda_1 p_2^2 + (p_1^2 + p_2^2)^2 \kappa_b (d + r_0)} \\ 0 \\ \dfrac{p_1 \lambda_2 (p_1^2 + p_2^2)}{\lambda_2 p_1^2 + \lambda_1 p_2^2 + (p_1^2 + p_2^2)^2 \kappa_b (d + r_0)} \\ 0 \end{bmatrix}$$

and resulting Fisher information metric $\mathscr{I} \equiv det\big((\mathbf{P}_k^+)^{-1}\big)$, using the same substitutions ($p_1 = d \cos \theta$, $p_2 = d \sin \theta$ and $\lambda_2 = \lambda_1 (1 - e^2)$) outlined above:

$$\mathscr{I} = \frac{\lambda_1 (1 - e^2)(\cos^2 \theta + \sin^2 \theta) + d^2 \kappa_b (d + r_0)}{\lambda_1^2 \lambda_3 \lambda_4 (1 - e^2) d^2 \kappa_b (d + r_0)} > 0 \qquad (15.38)$$

for $\theta \in (0, \frac{\pi}{2})$ and partial derivative with respect to θ:

$$\frac{\partial \mathscr{I}}{\partial \theta} = \frac{\sin 2\theta (e^2)}{\kappa_b (d + r_0) d^2 \lambda_1 \lambda_3 \lambda_4 (1 - e^2)} \geq 0, \quad \forall \theta \in \left(0, \frac{\pi}{2}\right)$$

$\square$

The preceding section has demonstrated that regardless of the sensor-type selected, the use of the Mahalanobis metric will *always* yield an information gain greater than or equal to its Euclidean counterpart. This effect is borne out in the probability surfaces described in Sect. 15.6.2 below.

15.6 Simulation Results

In this section, we evaluate the proposed IGRCA algorithm through three separate numerical simulation tests. The first test (Sect. 15.6.2) compares IGRCA with ECA at a large number of test target locations in the domain of interest. Algorithms are evaluated in terms of the probability of providing greater information gain, and the strict inequality in favor of IGRCA is confirmed. Both point-wise and cumulative estimates over the test area are computed, which demonstrate the superior information gain IGRCA provides over a large number of simulated target positions. The second test (Sect. 15.6.3) compares the performance of IGRCA and ECA with a globally exhaustive algorithm (CES) in terms of cumulative target state uncertainty in multi-target tracking. Three targets, each with dynamics described in Sect. 15.4.1 are considered. The final test (Sect. 15.6.3.3) displays the response of the three algorithms to an increasing number of targets, measured in both cumulative target state uncertainty and average computational time. These tests require the definition of several performance metrics, given below.

15.6.1 Performance Metrics

1. **Fisher Information:** The determinant of the Fisher Information matrix, $\mathscr{I}$, provides a direct measure of information gain from the update step. Recall that the information utility metrics of Sect. 15.3.2, namely sensor modality and Mahalanobis distance are aimed at reducing target state uncertainty, represented by the covariance $\mathbf{P}_k$. It is known that the determinant of the Fisher information matrix, $\mathscr{I} = det(\mathbf{P}_k^{-1})$, which is nothing but the volume form of the inverse of the Gaussian updated belief uncertainty [29], is a scalar measure of *information gain*. Therefore, it is used here to compare the outcome of measurement updates in target tracking via ECA and IGRCA.

2. **Algorithm Win Probability (AWP):** Given a general target location in the sensing field, the IGRCA Algorithm Win Probability is defined as the probability that the IGRCA cluster $\mathscr{C}$ provides information gain ($\mathscr{I}$) *strictly greater than* the ECA cluster $\mathscr{E}$. Let the optimal sensor resulting from IGRCA and ECA be S_R and S_E, respectively with corresponding information gains $\mathscr{I}_R$ and $\mathscr{I}_E$. Of-course, if the target's prior positional covariance is circular ($e = 0$), the Mahalanobis and Euclidean distances are equivalent ($M_i^k = |\mathbf{p}_i^k|$), causing both clustering algorithms to return identical clusters assuming all nodes are feasible ($\mathscr{F} = \mathscr{W}$), such that $\mathscr{I}_R = \mathscr{I}_E$. In the more general case however, i.e. for $e \neq 0$, $\mathscr{I}_R \geq \mathscr{I}_E$. On the basis of these observations, we conduct a Monte Carlo simulation by drawing prior positional covariance ellipse eccentricity samples, $\{e_j\}_{j=1}^N \sim Unif([0, 1])$, to estimate the probability that IGRCA information gain is *strictly* greater than ECA information gain at a given target location in the sensing field:

$$\text{AWP}(x_t, y_t) = P(\mathscr{I}_R > \mathscr{I}_E | x = x_t, y = y_t) = \frac{1}{N} \sum_{i=1}^N \alpha_i \qquad (15.39)$$

where, (x_t, y_t) is a generic target location in the sensing field and α_i is a binary success indicator for when the optimal sensor lies *only* within the IGRCA cluster:

$$\alpha_i = \begin{cases} 1, & \text{if } S^* \in \mathscr{C} \setminus (\mathscr{C} \cap \mathscr{E}) \\ 0, & \text{otherwise} \end{cases}$$

Eq. (15.39) can also be used to determine a scalar cumulative measure (*Cumulative Win Probability*, or, CWP) by sweeping over target locations over the entire sensing domain:

$$\text{CWP} = P\left(\mathscr{I}_R > \mathscr{I}_E\right) = 1 - P\left(\mathscr{I}_R = \mathscr{I}_E\right)$$
$$= 1 - \sum_{i,j} P\left(\mathscr{I}_R = \mathscr{I}_E \mid x = x_i, y = y_j\right) P(x = x_i, y = y_j)$$

(15.40)

where, the theorem of total probability is used to obtain Eq. (15.40). The arguments of the preceding expressions are reversed (i.e., $\mathscr{I}_E > \mathscr{I}_R$) to calculate the AWP and CWP of the ECA.

3. **Trace of the Posterior Cramér-Rao Lower Bound:** A scalar value that indicates the overall amount of uncertainty for multiple target states. Sect. 15.3.2 and Fig. 15.3 both illustrate the reduction in positional uncertainty of a target as an acceptable metric for a sensor's utility. The posterior Cramér-Rao Lower Bound (PCRLB) [45–47] for a Gaussian distribution with a posterior Fisher Information matrix $\mathscr{I}$ is defined as $\mathbf{J} = \mathscr{I}^{-1}$. To extend this measure to the full state vector and for M independently maneuvering targets described by the dynamics in Eq. (15.20), a scalar metric that corresponds to the overall amount of state uncertainty for the target set (from Ref. [6]) is given by

$$trace(\mathbf{J}_k^{-1}) = \sum_{i=1}^{M} trace(\mathbf{P}_k^i)$$

(15.41)

where

$$\mathbf{J}_k^{-1} = \begin{bmatrix} \mathbf{P}_k^1 & & \\ & \ddots & \\ & & \mathbf{P}_k^M \end{bmatrix}$$

(15.42)

is the block-diagonal matrix comprised of posterior covariance matrices for each target at time k: $\mathbf{P}_k^i$, where $i = 1, \ldots, M$. Over the course of a multi-target tracking application, a clustering algorithm that produces lower $trace(\mathbf{J}_k^{-1})$ values indicates superior performance in regards to information utility. In this work, the identities of the targets in Sects. 15.6.3 and 15.6.3.3 below were assumed to be known throughout each simulation run, i.e. perfect data-association is assumed.

4. **Algorithm Run Time:** In tracking scenarios involving maneuvering targets with dynamic behavior, it is beneficial to implement a sensor-selection algorithm that is computationally efficient in (a) target propagation and construction of sensor clusters, (b) determination of the optimal sensor, and (c) sending/receiving target information throughout the network. These parts are represented, respectively, as cluster creation time, ζ_k, sensor selection time, β_k, and routing time, τ_k, in wall-

clock seconds. The algorithm run time (ξ_k) is comprised of all computing and routing time expended to track a target for a single timestep k, $\xi_k = \zeta_k + \beta_k + \tau_k$.

(a) **Cluster creation time** ζ_k is the execution time of steps 1–8 of Algorithm 3 for the IGRCA and Algorithm 1 for the ECA.

(b) **Sensor selection time** β_k is the execution time of steps 9–10 of Algorithm 3 for the IGRCA and steps 9–11 of Algorithm 1 for the ECA.

(c) **Routing time** τ_k is the routing time derived from the number of links, φ, required to transmit information between the base station and a sensor, and was defined above in Sect. 15.3.3. In practice, this routing time is much lower than the required update frequency, $\tau_k \ll f_{\text{Update}}^{-1}$.

Note that expanding the tracking application to account for a total number of targets M yields a higher total algorithm run time per round of measurements, such that $\sum_{t=1}^{M} \xi_k^t = \sum_{t=1}^{M} \zeta_k^t + \sum_{t=1}^{M} \beta_k^t + \sum_{t=1}^{M} \tau_k^t$. As the base station computes and transmits information sequentially, $\xi_k^t > \xi_k^{t-1} > \cdots > \xi_k^1$. In the scenario where $\xi_k^t > f_{\text{Update}}^{-1}$, the base station recognizes that targets $\{t, t + 1, \ldots, M\}$ will not be measured at time k before the next series of updates begin for time $k + 1$. To account for this, targets are ranked into an ordered set $\mathscr{T}_k$ at the end of each round of data fusion (time k) by the trace of their corresponding posterior covariance matrices:

$$\mathscr{T}_k = \{T_1, T_2, T_3, \ldots, T_i, \ldots, T_M\},$$

where $trace(\mathbf{P}_k^1) \geq trace(\mathbf{P}_k^2) \ldots trace(\mathbf{P}_k^{M-1}) \geq trace(\mathbf{P}_k^M)$. Targets with higher uncertainty are prioritized for measurement in the next round (time step $k + 1$) of measurements.

15.6.2 Algorithm Win Probability: Simulation

IGRCA has an advantage in terms of directly accounting for information utility in relatively sparse fields where the target's uncertainty ellipse is elongated, such that the role of Mahalanobis distance to the target distribution becomes important. To verify this, AWP (Eq. (15.39)) was computed over target locations within a discretized sample space $\Omega_T = [100 \times 100]\,\text{m}^2$ with a resolution of 1 m (total of 10^4 test points). Two sensor fields densities of 100 and 1000 range-only sensing nodes were uniformly distributed over Ω_T.

The Algorithm Win Probabilities (Eq. (15.39)) of both clustering methods over each possible target position $[x_t, \ y_t]^T \in \Omega_T$ and at varying sensor densities are depicted as a surface plot over the test domain in Fig. 15.9. Each location on the 2D test plane is mapped according to an "Algorithm Win Indicator" value where positive values represent the IGRCA AWP at the location. Conversely, negative

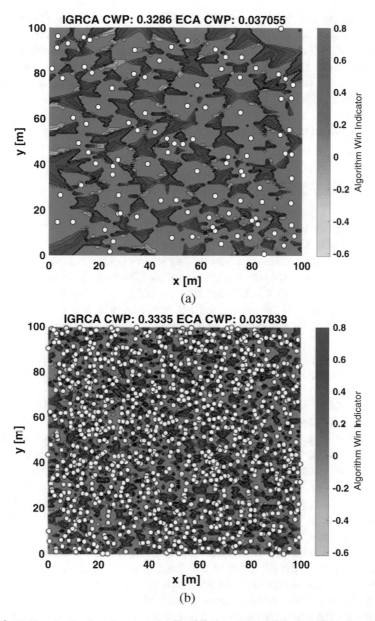

Fig. 15.9 Uniformly distributed sensor sets $\mathscr{W}$ and their corresponding algorithm win probability maps. Dots represent sensor locations. The "Algorithm Win Indicator" shows the AWP value on each location for each clustering method. Positive values correspond to IGRCA superiority and negative values to the ECA. (**a**) Sparse sensor field. (**b**) Dense sensor field

values on the surface plot represent ECA AWP. The surfaces indicate that regardless of sensor density, IGRCA is strictly better than ECA in regions of the test domain where sensors (white dots) are sparse. While AWP describes algorithmic superiority on a micro level, the CWP (Eq. (15.40)) provides a macro picture and is shown for all four cases (accounting for sensor distribution and clustering algorithm) are displayed in the titles of Fig. 15.9a, b. It is interesting to note that for a given type of sensor distribution, the CWP appears to be largely invariant with sensor density. The reason behind this is not clear at this point and is the subject of further research.

15.6.3 Multiple Target Tracking

Target localization uncertainty results were compiled for IGRCA, ECA and the CES (Computationally Exhaustive Search) method. To determine the *globally optimal* sensor in terms of predicted uncertainty reduction via CES,[4] each feasible sensor within $\mathscr{F}_k$ is iterated over with a predictive Fisher information computation and an associated trace of the PCRLB. In the absence of lost target tracks, the uncertainty reduction $(trace(\mathbf{J}_k^{-1}))$ provided by CES operates as a lower baseline for the aforementioned clustering methods to be compared against.

15.6.3.1 Comparative Posterior CRLB: Various Sensor Densities

To test scalability at varying sensor field densities (see Eq. (15.10)), ten separate uniformly distributed WSN's, each with a base station housed at $[-1 \ -1]^T$ m, were generated for each simulation of one hundred multi-target tracking simulations, ranging from a sparse 100 sensor set to a dense field of 1000 nodes that provides the algorithms with increased parity in regards to sensor feasibility. Each simulation was comprised of three targets maneuvering simultaneously over a test area of $\Omega_T = [100 \times 100] \, m^2$. Each sensor was assigned a randomized sensing mode and orientation at the start of simulation. The initial state of target i, where $i = 1, 2, 3$, $\mathbf{x}_{i0} = [x_{i0} \ y_{i0} \ \dot{x}_{i0} \ \dot{y}_{i0}]^T$, was initialized at the start of each simulation with initial position and velocity components randomized according to: $\{x_{i0}, \ y_{i0}\} \sim Unif([0, 100])$ m and $\{\dot{x}_{i0}, \ \dot{y}_{i0}\} \sim Unif([-10, 10])$ m/s. A maximum communication range of 25 m was assumed for each sensor, according to the 802.11b wireless communication standard, along with an angular range of π radians for the field of view and sensing range of $\rho_i = 25$ m. For the dynamics introduced in Sect. 15.4.1, values of $\Delta T = 0.01$ s, $c_1 = 0.75$, $c_2 = 1$, $\sigma_q = 5$ were used. The base station queried the sensor set for updated measurements of all targets at a constant rate $f_{\text{Update}} = 10$ Hz, and each tracking scenario was performed

---

[4]This study utilizes an exhaustive search to locate a *single* optimal sensor, as opposed to a conventional graph neuron set.

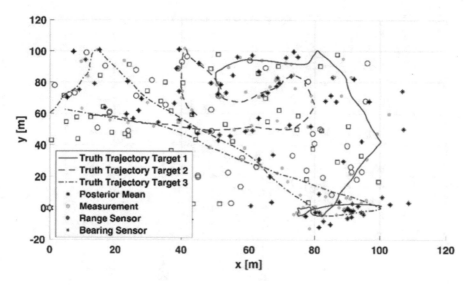

Fig. 15.10 Example run of three simulated targets being tracked with the IGRCA approach over the course of 30 s

over the course of 30 s. An example of a multi-target run is presented in Fig. 15.10. As expected from the construction of subsets $\mathcal{D}_k$ and $\mathcal{C}_k$, the IGRCA tends to favor sensors closer to the base station (housed near the origin of sensing grid) and along the target's major uncertainty axis. Regardless of sensor density, the IGRCA consistently produced significantly lower posterior $trace(\mathbf{J}_k^{-1})$ relative to ECA. In environments with a low number of available sensors, the IGRCA performed comparably with CES, as the optimal sensor is often collected in the quality filter step of Algorithm 3. At a higher sensor density, the CES algorithm significantly outperforms both IGRCA and ECA in maintaining a lower posterior $trace(\mathbf{J}_k^{-1})$ (as expected, at a higher computational cost). The mean (over all targets) $trace(\mathbf{J}_k^{-1})$ among all runs is presented for two sensor fields in Fig. 15.11.

Therefore, as far as minimization of target uncertainty is concerned, IGRCA significantly outperforms ECA and is on par with CES for moderate sensing field densities. Of course, this study does not consider computational expenditure, which is studied next, including a study of how algorithm performance varies with an increasing number of targets.

15.6.3.2 Computational Expenditure

The algorithm run time (ξ_k), including its various components, i.e. clustering (ζ_k), selection (β_k) and routing (τ_k) times defined in Sect. 15.6.1 were compiled and averaged over one hundred randomized tracking scenarios for a varying number of targets ($M = 1, \ldots, 6$): see Fig. 15.12. As expected, CES is unambiguously

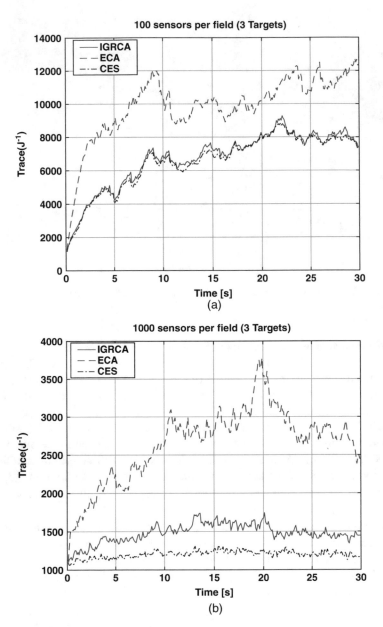

Fig. 15.11 Comparison of clustering methods IGRCA, ECA, and CES over 100 randomized multi-target simulations at different sensor densitie. (**a**) 100 sensors. (**b**) 1000 sensors

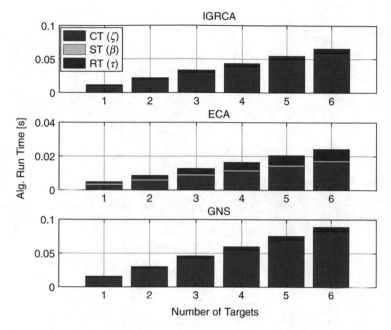

Fig. 15.12 Comparison of algorithm run times per timestep

the most expensive, regardless of target number. The bulk of its algorithm run time lies in its clustering stage (ζ_k), as it must iterate through $\mathrm{card}(\mathscr{F})$ feasible sensors and perform expensive matrix inversions per each node. In contrast, the IGRCA's use of Mahalanobis distance as a utility metric, while not as proficient as Fisher Information in regards to uncertainty reduction, requires much fewer computational steps. Furthermore, the cost "filtering" via $\mathscr{C}$ allows the IGRCA to benefit from consistently lower routing times, further reducing its algorithm run time, even with an initial overhead cost included for running Algorithm 2 at the start of each tracking simulation. Across all tracking scenarios, the ECA is superior to the IGRCA and CES in computational expenses. If this computational cost surpasses the measurement update limit, the ability of a centralized tracking network to maintain low target state uncertainty is negatively impacted as pertinent information regarding the object is not available for data fusion. Section 15.6.3.3 below reveals the resulting overall localization uncertainty when total algorithmic run time induces the loss of measurement updates.

15.6.3.3 Comparative Posterior CRLB: Various Number of Targets

To determine the effect of an increasing number of targets on (a) algorithm run time ξ_k (measured in seconds), and (b) overall level of target uncertainty (measured in $trace(\mathbf{J}_k^{-1})$), six scenarios were considered with an increasing number

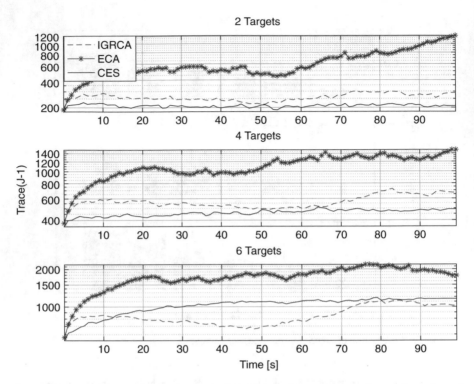

Fig. 15.13 Comparison of clustering methods with overall target uncertainty and number of tracked objects. Simulations were performed on a uniformly distributed field of 400 sensors

of simultaneously maneuvering of targets ($M = 1, \ldots, 6$). One hundred simulations were performed on each case with every target's initial state $\hat{\mathbf{x}}_0$ randomized at the start of each run. A sensor field of 400 uniformly distributed heterogeneous nodes was used and the results are shown in Fig. 15.13.

Note that in all cases, the ECA incurs the highest values of $trace(\mathbf{J}_k^{-1})$, due to its comparably lower information utility subset of sensors. This reduced quality is a direct result of (i) infeasible sensors that were added to the cluster, lowering the chances to select the optimal sensor, and (ii) the sensors were not clustered based on any information theoretic measure comparable to Mahalanobis distance or expected differential entropy. For a small number of targets, CES returns the lowest uncertainty as expected, because it performs a rigorous search for the optimal sensor for each target. However, as the number of targets increases, the computational load underlying the maximization of sensor utility can rise to the point where the search for optimal sensors cannot be completed before the next measurement is due, i.e. $\xi_k^t > f_{\text{Update}}^{-1}$. Consequently, the cumulative uncertainty among all targets can grow as the clustering algorithm starts missing measurement updates due to incomplete computations. This is typically not a problem for ECA (computationally least expensive), but can rapidly become a concern for CES (most expensive) as it

Table 15.1 Computation: average fraction of timesteps where missed measurement occurred

Algorithm	$M = 1$	$M = 2$	$M = 3$	$M = 4$	$M = 5$	$M = 6$
IGRCA (mean tracks lost)	0	0	0	0	0	0.0143
ECA (mean tracks lost)	0	0	0	0	0	0
CES (mean tracks lost)	0	0	0	0.0032	0.0675	0.3685

starts missing an increasing number of measurement updates, causing uncertainty to grow. For the IGRCA and CES, algorithm run time is largely dependent on the number of feasible sensors (clustering time ζ_k) and position of the target, which influences routing time (τ_k). Table 15.1 displays the average frequency of missed measurements over the course of a run, in $\frac{f_{\text{Update}} * (\#\text{Missed Meas.})}{\text{Simulation Time}}$. The update frequency was set at $f_{\text{Update}} = 10\,\text{Hz}$.

When the number of targets is small (≤ 3), the tracking performance of all three algorithms is unaffected and as mentioned above, CES and IGRCA provide comparable $trace(\mathbf{J}_k^{-1})$, both significantly better than ECA. For six targets, CES misses at least one target measurement roughly 36% of the time. The consequences are noted in Fig. 15.13, where the total target uncertainty for CES exceeds that of the IGRCA for a limited time. It was found through additional simulations that when $M = 8$, the IGRCA method outperforms the CES for the entirety of the simulation.

15.7 Conclusion

This work presents a nested sensor clustering algorithm with the aim of minimizing target uncertainty in multiple target tracking applications within a wireless sensor field. The overall approach is to increase "sensor utility" (as characterized by the Mahalanobis distance), while also keeping computational overhead under control. It is rigorously shown that the new information guided algorithm outperforms the Euclidean clustering algorithm in terms of information utility, which is based purely on the distance of the target(s) from available sensors. At the same time, numerical simulations reveal that the new approach is on par with globally exhaustive searches (e.g., CES) in terms of target uncertainty reduction, which can be computationally prohibitive as the number of targets increase. Future work will focus on improving the proposed method by accounting for unpredictable target dynamics, data association complications, and implementing measurement reception error with probabilistic message loss.

Acknowledgments This work was supported by the Air Force Office of Scientific Research Grant No. AFOSR FA9550-15-1-0330.

References

1. J.L. Crassidis, J.L. Junkins, *Optimal Estimation of Dynamic Systems*. Chapman & Hall/CRC Applied Mathematics & Nonlinear Science, 2nd edn. (Chapman & Hall/CRC, Boca Raton, 2011)
2. J. Liu, J. Reich, F. Zhao, Collaborative in-network processing for target tracking. EURASIP J. Appl. Signal Process. **4**, 378–391 (2003). 616720
3. M.L. Hernandez, T. Kirubarajan, Y. Bar-Shalom, Multisensor resource deployment using posterior Cramer-Rao bounds. IEEE Trans. Aerosp. Electron. Syst. **40**, 399–416 (2004)
4. P.V. Pahalawatta, D. Depalov, T.N. Pappas, A.K. Katsaggelos, Detection, classification, and collaborative tracking of multiple targets using video sensors, in *Information Processing in Sensor Networks* (Springer, Berlin, 2003), pp. 529–544
5. K. Chakrabarty, Y. Zou, Sensor deployment and target localization based on virtual forces, in *Twenty-Second Annual Joint Conference of the IEEE Computer and Communications*, San Francisco, 2003, pp. 71–75
6. M. Hernandez R. Tharmarasa, T. Kirubarajan, Large-scale optimal sensor array management for multitarget tracking. IEEE Trans. Syst. Man Cybern. **37**(5), 803–814 (2007)
7. X. Shen, S. Liu, P.K. Varshney, Sensor selection for nonlinear systems in large sensor networks. IEEE Trans. Aeros. Electron. Syst. **50**(4), 2664–2678 (2014)
8. T. Wang, Z. Peng, J. Liang, S. Wen, M.Z.A. Bhuiyan, Y. Cai, J. Cao, Following targets for mobile tracking in wireless sensor networks. ACM Trans. Sensor Netwo. (TOSN) **12**(4), 31 (2016)
9. F.M. Dommermuth, The estimation of target motion parameters from CPA time measurements in a field of acoustic sensors. J. Acoust. Soc. Am. **83**(4), 1476–1480 (1988)
10. Q. Yang, A. Lim, K. Casey, R. Neelisti, Real-time target tracking with CPA algorithm in wireless sensor networks, in *5th Annual IEEE Communications Society Conference on Sensor, Mesh and Ad Hoc Communications and Networks*, San Francisco, 2008, pp. 305–312
11. T. Ahmed O. Demigha, W. Hidouci, On energy efficiency in collaborative target tracking in wireless sensor network: a review. IEEE Commun. Surv. Tutorials **15**(3), 1210–1222 (2013)
12. A. Cerpa, J. Elson, D. Estrin, L. Girod, M. Hamilton, J. Zhao, Habitat monitoring: application driver for wireless communications technology. SIGCOMM Comput. Commun. Rev. **31**(2 supplement), 20–41 (2001)
13. A. Farina, G. Golino, A. Capponi, C. Pilotto, Surveillance by means of a random sensor network: a heterogeneous sensor approach, in *2005 7th International Conference on Information Fusion*, Philadelphia, ed. by E. Blasch, vol. 2, 2005
14. J. Lin, W. Xiao, F. L. Lewis, L. Xie, Energy-efficient distributed adaptive multisensor scheduling for target tracking in wireless sensor networks. IEEE Trans. Instrum. Meas. **58**(6), 1886–1896 (2009)
15. B. Sikdar, H. Yang, A protocol for tracking mobile targets using sensor networks, in *IEEE International Workshop on Sensor Network Protocols and Applications*, Anchorage, 2003, pp. 73–77
16. Z. Wang, W. Lou, Z. Wang, J. Ma, H. Chen, A novel mobility management scheme for target tracking in cluster-based sensor networks, in *International Conference on Distributed Computing in Sensor Systems* (Springer, Santa Barbara, 2010), pp. 172–186
17. J. Reich F. Zhao, J. Shin, Information-driven dynamic sensor collaboration. IEEE Signal Process. Mag. **19**, 61–72 (2002)
18. Y. Zhang J. Qian, X. Jin, Energy-efficient node selection for acoustic source localization in wireless sensor network, in *6th International Conference on Wireless Communications Networking and Mobile Computing*, Shenzhen, 2010, pp. 1–5
19. L.M. Kaplan, Global node selection for localization in a distributed sensor network. IEEE Trans. Aerosp. Electron. Syst. **42**(1), 113–135 (2006)

20. A. Capponi, C. Pilotto, G. Golino, A. Farina, L. Kaplan, Algorithms for the selection of the active sensors in distributed tracking: comparison between frisbee and GNS methods, in *9th International Conference on Information Fusion*, Florence, 2006, pp. 1–8

21. D. Estrin C. Intanagonwiwat, R. Govinda, Directed diffusion: a scalable and robust communication paradigm for sensor networks, in *6th Annual International Conference on Mobile Computing and Networking*, San Diego, 2003, pp. 56–67

22. T. Yum X. Zhu, L. Shen, Hausdorff clustering and minimum energy routing for wireless sensor networks. IEEE Trans. Veh. Technol. **58**(2), 990–997 (2009)

23. U. Madhow, J. Singh, R. Kumar et al., Multiple-target tracking with binary proximity sensors. ACM Trans. Sensor Netw. **8**(1), 3–13 (2011)

24. D. Wang, Y. Wang, Energy-efficient node selection for target tracking in wireless sensor networks. Int. J. Distrib. Sensor Netw. **9**(1), 1–6 (2013)

25. C.S. Raghavendra, K.M. Sivalingam, T. Znati, *Wireless Sensor Networks* (Springer, New York, 2006)

26. S. Blackman, R. Popoli, *Design and Analysis of Modern Tracking Systems (book)*. (Artech House, Norwood, 1999)

27. R. Stolkin, I. Florescu, Probability of detection and optimal sensor placement for threshold based detection systems, IEEE Sensors J. **9**(1), 57–60 (2009)

28. P.C. Mahalanobis, On the generalised distance in statistics., in *Proceedings of the National Institute of Sciences of India*, vol. 2 (Baptist Mission Press, 1936), pp. 49–55

29. L. Guibas F. Zhao, *Wireless Sensor Networks: An Information Processing Approach* (Morgan Kaufmann Publishers, Amsterdam, 2004)

30. S.M.H. Jalilolghadr, M. Sabaei. Proposed a new algorithm for real-time applications in routing of wireless sensor networks, in *Proceedings of the International Conference on Management and Artificial Intelligence,* Bali, 2011, pp. 1–3

31. B. Krishnamachari, D. Estrin, S. Wicker, Modelling data-centric routing in wireless sensor networks. IEEE Infocom **2**, 39–44 (2002)

32. T. Cormen, C. Leiserson, R. Rivest, C. Stein, *Introduction to Algorithms* (The MIT Press, Cambridge, 2010)

33. M. Morari F. Borrelli, A. Bemporad, *Predictive Control for Linear and Hybrid Systems* (Cambridge University Press, Cambridge, 2015)

34. M. Johansson, A. Rantzer, Computation of piecewise quadratic lyapunov functions for hybrid systems, in *1997 European Control Conference (ECC)*, Brussels, July 1997, pp. 2005–2010

35. N. Sandell, R. Oltafi-Saber, Distributed tracking in sensor networks with limited sensing range, in *American Control Conference*, Seattle, 2008, pp. 3158–3163

36. V.J. Aidala, Kalman filter behavior in bearings-only tracking applications. IEEE Trans. Aerosp. Electron. Syst. **15**(1), 29–39 (1979)

37. S. Nardone, A.G. Lindgren, K. Gong, Fundamental properties and performance of conventional bearings-only target motion analysis. IEEE Trans. Autom. Control **29**(9), 775–787 (1984)

38. P. Rong, M. Sichitiu, Angle of arrival localization for wireless sensor networks, in *2006 3rd Annual IEEE Communications Society on Sensor and Ad Hoc Communications and Networks, SECON'06*, vol. 1 (IEEE, Reston, 2006), pp. 374–382

39. P. Kułakowski, J. Vales-Alonso, E. Egea-López, W. Ludwin, J. García-Haro, Angle-of-arrival localization based on antenna arrays for wireless sensor networks. Comput. Electr. Eng. **36**(6), 1181–1186 (2010)

40. B. Ristic, S. Arulampalam, J. McCarthy, Target motion analysis using range-only measurements: algorithms, performance and application to ingara isar data. Technical report, Defence Science and Technology Organisation Electronics and Surveillance Research, Salisbury, 2001

41. N Peach, Bearings-only tracking using a set of range-parameterised extended kalman filters. IEEE Proc. Control Theory Appl. **142**(1), 73–80 (1995)

42. F. Zhao, L. Guibas (eds.), *Information Processing in Sensor Networks* (Springer, Berlin/Heidelberg, 2003) pp. 412–415

43. D.P. Spanos, R. Olfati-Saber, R.M. Murray, *Approximate distributed Kalman filtering in sensor networks with quantifiable performance, in Proceedings of the 4th International Symposium on Information Processing in Sensor Networks*, Los Angeles, 2005
44. J. Thomas T. Cover, *Elements of Information Theory* (Wiley, Hoboken, 2006)
45. P. Tichavsky, C.H. Muravchik, A. Nehorai, Posterior cramer-rao bounds for discrete-time nonlinear filtering. IEEE Trans. Signal Process. **46**(5), 1386–1396 (1998)
46. N. Gordon, B. Ristic, S. Arulampalam, *Beyond the Kalman Filter* (Artech House, Boston, 2004)
47. C. Yang, L. M. Kaplan, E. Blasch, M. Bakich, Optimal placement of heterogeneous sensors for targets with Gaussian priors. IEEE Trans. Aerosp. Electron. Syst. **49**(3), 1637–1653 (2013)

Chapter 16
Data-Driven Prediction of Confidence for EVAR in Time-Varying Datasets

Allan Axelrod, Luca Carlone, Girish Chowdhary, and Sertac Karaman

Abstract The key challenge for Dynamic Data Driven Applications Systems (DDDAS) operating in time-varying environments is to predict when the learned model may lose relevance. If the learned model loses relevance, then the autonomous system is at risk of making wrong decisions. *The Entropic Value at Risk* (EVAR) is a computationally efficient and coherent risk measure that can be utilized to quantify this model relevance. The value of EVAR is calculated with respect to an assumed confidence value; e.g., a 90% confidence may be desired for robust decision-making. Without a model on the confidence value directly, there is no guarantee that EVAR calculations will reflect the uncertainty present in dynamic real-world environments. In this paper, we present a Bayesian model and learning algorithms to predict the state-dependent confidence necessary for calculating the EVAR in time-varying datasets. We discuss applications of the data-driven EVAR to a monitoring problem, in which a DDDAS agent has to chose a set of sensing locations in order to maximize the expected EVAR of the acquired data. In this way, the DDDAS agent can learn a model on an underlying phenomenon of interest by prioritizing the areas where the model is most likely incorrect but highly valued. We empirically demonstrate the efficacy of the presented model and learning algorithms on five real-world datasets. We show that, overall, the EVAR-Real-time Adative Prediction of Time-varying and Obscure Rewards (EVAR-RAPTOR) algorithm outperforms EVAR-Predicted Information Gain* (EVAR-PIG*) as well as naive searches such as random and sequential search across these five real-world datasets.

Keywords Entropic value at risk (EVAR) · EVAR-Real-time Adaptive Prediction of Time-varying and Obscure Rewards (EVAR-RAPTOR) · Information gain · Conditional value at risk (CVAR) · Poisson exposure distribution (Ped) · N-armed restless bandit · Temperature · CASTNet ozone

A. Axelrod (✉) · G. Chowdhary
Coordinated Science Lab, University of Illinois at Urbana-Champaign, Urbana, IL, USA
e-mail: allana2@illinois.edu; girishc@illinois.edu

L. Carlone · S. Karaman
Massachusetts Institute of Technology, Cambridge, MA, USA
e-mail: lcarlone@mit.edu; sertac@mit.edu

389

16.1   Introduction

Dynamic Data Driven Applications Systems (DDDAS) must select actions that are appropriate to the environment in which they operate [1–3]. Yet, without precise knowledge of the environment, DDDAS are at risk of selecting suboptimal actions. Many autonomy and adaptive control architectures utilize online learning to improve system's environmental model. However, in time-varying environments, learned models may lose relevance over time. The key challenge facing DDDAS in time-varying environments is therefore to predict and quantify how quickly environmental models lose relevance, and to take appropriate data-gathering actions that minimizes the risk of making wrong decisions due to inaccurate environmental models. In order to address these challenges, we must first answer what uncertainty measure best captures changes in the environment and design data-driven stochastic models that define how this uncertainty measure evolves over time.

In this Chapter, our goal is to lay the modeling and algorithmic foundations for DDDAS to predict the risk of making the wrong decision in the face of time variations. We use an exploration problem as a motivating example: our DDDAS agent is operating in a field with N sensing locations which are measuring some underlying time-varying phenomenon of interest (e.g., temperature, rainfall). Due to sensing constraints, the agent can only acquire information from $\kappa < N$ of these sensing locations at each time step. Therefore, the goal of the agent is to learn a predictive model that can help identify the subset of sensing locations which are most likely to help the agent maintain an up-to-date model of the environment. If the agent could determine the predictive model, then the risk of the agent overestimating in a time-varying environment can be *proactively* mitigated.

In quantifying predictive uncertainty, it is natural to use variance (VAR) or distribution tail probabilities. While such measures describe an expected distance of a sample from the mean of the current stochastic model, neither address how the stochastic model changes as a result of new observations. By contrast, uncertainty measures such as the information gain [4], the entropic value at risk (EVAR) [5], and the conditional value at risk (CVAR) [6] all describe uncertainty in how the model will change due to new observations.

While both CVAR and EVAR provide an intuitive bound on how the expectation of our model changes due to new observations, EVAR is more computationally efficient than CVAR and is the tightest upper bound on CVAR when both have the same confidence γ [5]. As we will show, EVAR can also incorporate the information gain, and so we examine EVAR as a comprehensive measure of the uncertainty.

Our main contribution is a Bayesian model and learning algorithms for predicting the spatio-temporal evolution of the EVAR (in our running example, this is our risk of over-estimation at each sensing location). We first present a generalization of the Poisson Exposure Distribution (Ped) [7, 8], which we call the *Poisson exposure process* (Pep). Then, we use Pep to model the evolution of the information gain term in the EVAR.

The Pep is a useful form of the Lévy process because it has the same domain as the information gain term in EVAR and because it has an analytical Bayesian update; moreover, we can establish probabilistic accuracy guarantees on the corresponding information gain estimate. which we show affords probabilistic accuracy guarantees. The key advantage of the Pep is that it allows us to overcome the assumption of identically distributed samples utilized in algorithms such as *Predicted Information Gain* (PIG) [9]. We develop an EVAR-variant of our *Real-time Adaptive Prediction of Time-varying and Obscure Rewards (RAPTOR)* algorithm [10] called (EVAR-RAPTOR). We show that the EVAR-RAPTOR algorithm outperforms the EVAR exploration variant of PIG, as well as sequential and random search, in simulations over four real-world datasets.

The rest of this paper is structured as follows. Section 16.2 provides preliminary concepts and formally introduces the information gain and the EVAR. Section 16.3 presents our problem formulation, tailoring it to an exploration problem (analogous to steering for DDDAS). Moreover, it presents our Pep-based model for the evolution of the information gain and, by extension, of the EVAR. Section 16.4 gives practical algorithms to predict the EVAR and established formal performance guarantees for them. Section 16.5 compares the proposed algorithms against related approaches. Section 16.6 concludes the chapter.

16.2 Preliminaries

This section reviews relevant probabilistic inequalities (Sect. 16.2.1), properties of Lévy processes (Sect. 16.2.2), and the definition of information gain (Sect. 16.2.3) which is used in the definition of the entropic value at risk (Sect. 16.2.4).

16.2.1 Probabilistic Inequalities

Here we review the Chebyshev inequality (Lemma 1) and the Bienaymé-Chebyshev inequality (Lemma 2).

Lemma 1 (Chebyshev Inequality [11]) *Let the random variables* $Z(t_1), \ldots,$ $Z(t_n) \in [0, +\infty)$ *be independent trials. Let* $\bar{Z} = \sum_{j=1}^{n} Z(t_j)$ *and* $\mu = \mathbb{E}(\bar{Z})$. *Then for any* $k > 0$,

$$Pr(|\bar{Z} - \mu| \geq k) \leq \frac{\text{VAR}(\bar{Z})}{k^2}. \tag{16.1}$$

The Chebyshev inequality in Lemma 1 is defined in terms of the summation of random variables. Hence, a sampling bound obtained directly from the Chebyshev inequality bounds the cumulative error between all expected and sampled random variable values, rather than the error of an individual sample. In contrast, the Bienaymé-Chebyshev inequality, reviewed in Lemma 2 below, provides a bound on individual samples.

Lemma 2 (Bienaymé-Chebyshev Inequality [11]) *Let the random variables* $Z(t_1), \ldots, Z(t_n) \in [0, +\infty)$ *be independent and identically distributed trials. Let* $\bar{Z} = \frac{1}{n} \sum_{j=1}^{n} Z(t_j)$ *and* $\mu = \mathbb{E}(\bar{Z})$. *Then with* $k > 0$,

$$Pr\left(\left|\bar{Z} - \mu\right| \geq k\right) \leq \frac{\text{VAR}(\bar{Z})}{nk^2}. \tag{16.2}$$

In the rest of this work, we are going to use similar inequalities to quantify how well the system is able to predict the information gain at a given sensing location. The guarantees offered by the Bienaymé-Chebyshev inequality are desirable, namely it provides error bounds on the next sample. One limitation, however, lies in the fact that the samples are required to be identically distributed; this is undesirable in this context, since we want to study time-varying distributions that are sampled over time. In Sect. 16.4 we extend the Bienaymé-Chebyshev inequality to account for non-identically distributed samples.

16.2.2 Lévy Process

Here, we review the properties of Levy processes and how these properties allow the information gain to be modeled as a random variable. A Levy process $\mathscr{L}$ for the random variable Z has the following properties for increments $\Delta Z(\Delta t) > 0$ [12]:

1. $\mathscr{L}$ has independent and stationary increments,
2. $\Delta Z(0) = 0$ with probability one,
3. $\forall k > 0$ and $\forall \Delta t > 0$, $\lim_{\Delta t \to 0} f(\Delta Z(\Delta t) > k) = 0$.

Property 2 is crucial as it shows that a Lévy process can incorporate deterministic realizations of a stochastic process. To briefly illustrate this, let's say that we observe a realization of ΔZ. At the time of the observation, the value Δt becomes 0, while the value of Δt had formerly been positive prior to the observation. Then, by Property 2, $\Delta Z(\Delta t)$ when $\Delta t = 0$ is deterministic, while $\Delta Z(\Delta t)$ when $\Delta t > 0$ is stochastic.

16.2.3 Information Gain and Exploration

Exploration can be viewed as an information-collecting task, hence a means of quantifying the information collected is essential to guide decision-making for exploration. Exploration strategies conventionally use some form of the posterior variance [13–17] or the information-entropy [18–24] to quantify the information gained by a given action. While both strategies make intuitive sense, they are mathematically imprecise descriptors of the information gain which, due to a theorem of uniqueness in information theory [4], is defined as

$$I(P(Y)||P_0(Y)) = \int_{P(Y) \ll P_0(Y)} P(y) \ln \frac{P(y)}{P_0(y)} dy. \tag{16.3}$$

Here, Y is a random variable, $P_0(Y)$ is a given prior distribution, $P(Y)$ is the posterior distribution (after the exploration action is undertaken), and $P(Y) \ll P_0(Y)$ (i.e., $P(Y)$ is absolutely continuous with respect to $P_0(Y)$) which means that $P_0(Y = c) = 0$ implies that $P(Y = c) = 0$.

16.2.4   Entropic Value at Risk (EVAR) Risk Measure

A *risk measure* assigns a real value to a random variable Y that quantifies the uncertainty associated with a variable. Examples of risk measures include value-at-risk (VaR), variance (VAR), and Conditional Value at Risk (CVAR). Ahmadi-Javid [5] introduced the *Entropic Value at Risk* (EVAR) measure that addresses computational and coherency shortcomings of VAR and CVAR.

The EVAR of a real-valued random variable Y, with *confidence level* $1 - \gamma$ (with $\gamma \in (0, 1]$), is defined as

$$\text{EVAR}_{1-\gamma}(Y) \doteq \inf_{\theta > 0} \{\theta^{-1} \ln \left(\mathbb{E}_{P_0} \left[e^{\theta Y} \right] / \gamma \right) \}. \tag{16.4}$$

The importance of the EVAR lies in the fact that, with confidence level $1 - \gamma$, it upper bounds the value of the posterior expectation [5]:

$$\text{EVAR}_{1-\gamma}(Y) = \sup_{\substack{P(Y) \ll P_0(Y) \\ I(P(Y)||P_0(Y)) \leq -\ln(\gamma)}} \{\mathbb{E}_P(Y)\}. \tag{16.5}$$

Therefore, predicting the EVAR would help to upper-bound uncertainty in a time-varying environment. The Donsker-Varadhan variational formula is used to prove the dual form of EVAR and will be useful to defining a data-driven EVAR. Hence, we use the Donsker-Varadhan variational formula.

Lemma 3 (Donsker-Varadhan Variational Formula (In Lemma 3.1 of [5]))

$$\ln \left(\mathbb{E}_{P_0}[e^X] \right) = \sup_{P \ll P_0} \{\mathbb{E}_P[X] - I\left(P(x)||P_0(x) \right)\}. \tag{16.6}$$

In this work, we will be using the following form of Lemma 3,

$$\ln \left(\mathbb{E}_{P_0}[e^X] \right) + I\left(P(x)||P_0(x) \right) = \sup_{P \ll P_0} \{\mathbb{E}_P[X]\}. \tag{16.7}$$

16.3 Formulation: Exploration as Multi-play N-Armed Restless Bandits

In this Chapter, we consider the following exploration problem: there exists a set of N sensing locations in a spatial domain from which we may observe a time-varying phenomenon. We denote the set of all sensing locations as $\Omega \doteq \{1, \ldots, N\}$. In particular, each sensing location $i \in \Omega$ is associated to a stochastic process Y_i that we want to estimate. At each time t, sensor i observes a *sample* $y_i(t)$ of the process Y_i. However, due to resource constraints (e.g., cost), we cannot acquire samples from all the N sensors but only from a subset of them, i.e., we can only observe the outcome of $\kappa \leq N$ sensors, where κ is a given upper bound. Therefore, the problem we address in this Chapter is learning how to select the subset of Ω, having cardinality κ, where the phenomena Y_i exhibit the greatest change, as quantified by EVAR. Note that while for clarity of presentation we tailor our problem formulation to a sensing task, the formulation can be extended to model risk-aware applications in mobile robotics, or asset selection in portfolio optimization.

16.3.1 Multi-play N-Armed Restless Bandit Formulation

In our formulation, we focus on the exploration task, where only κ of $N \geq \kappa$ sensing locations may be sampled at any given time instant t (episode) within the sensor set Ω. Feedback from the selected subset of sensors $\mathscr{S}^*(t) \subset \Omega$ is used to update the models of each time-varying process Y_i. We also associate a second stochastic process to each sensing location, which models the evolution of the information gain at each location. We denote this information gain process with the symbol Z_i, for all $i \in \Omega$. For simplicity, each sensor location $i \in \Omega$ is assumed to be statistically independent.

Similar to previous work [10, 25–28] we model the exploration problem as a multi-play N-armed restless bandit problem. In this formulation, each *arm* of the bandit corresponds to a sensor $i \in \Omega$. Therefore, the overall goal is to select the best set of κ bandit arms such that some measure on exploration reward is optimized. We call $\mathscr{S}^*(t)$ the set of sensing locations (arms) selected at time t.

The key difference with respect to our previous work is that we learn to select the subset of arms with the most entropic value at risk (EVAR), rather than selecting the subset with the largest information gain [10, 25–27]. Intuitively, since the sensing locations observe time-varying phenomena, the EVAR at a given location changes over time. Therefore, our goal is to use a data-driven approach that can dynamically learn which sensing location is best to sample.

More formally, the objective of our exploration policy is to maximize the total EVAR obtained in each episode of the exploration task. This can be achieved by visiting the sensing locations which are expected to have the most EVAR:

$$\mathscr{S}^{\star}(t) \doteq \underset{\mathscr{S} \subset \Omega}{\operatorname{argmax}} \sum_{i \in \mathscr{S}} \mathbb{E}\left[\text{EVAR}_{1-\gamma_i}(Y_i)\right]$$
$$\text{subject to Card}(\mathscr{S}) = \kappa, \tag{16.8}$$

where $\text{Card}(\cdot)$ denotes the cardinality of a set. In Sect. 16.4 we go one step further and we provide probabilistic bounds that assess the quality of our EVAR estimate at each location. This allows discussing when the "informed policy" of Eq. (16.8) is expected to perform better than a naive policy (e.g., random or sequential sensor selection).

16.3.2 Data-Driven EVAR

Conventionally, EVAR is calculated using an assumed confidence level γ. However, for time-varying environments, it is critical that a data-driven confidence level be implemented. To reach a data-driven confidence γ for EVAR, we will first present an equivalent form of EVAR by adding the constraint $(I(P(Y)||P_0(Y) \leq -\ln(\gamma).)$ from (16.5) to the Donsker-Varadhan variational formula in Lemma 3; i.e.,

$$\text{EVAR}_{1-\gamma}(Y) = \ln\left(\mathbb{E}_{P_0}\left[e^Y\right]\right) - \ln(\gamma) = \sup_{\substack{P(Y) \ll P_0(Y) \\ I(P(Y)||P_0(Y)) \leq -\ln(\gamma)}} \mathbb{E}_P[Y]. \tag{16.9}$$

We will next show that (16.7) is the lower-bound case of EVAR across all confidence levels γ. We define the lower-bound confidence $\gamma^\star \leq \gamma$ as

$$\gamma^\star \doteq e^{-I(P(Y)||P_0(Y))} \leq \gamma. \tag{16.10}$$

We insert $\gamma^\star$ into (16.9) to yield

$$\text{EVAR}_{1-\gamma^\star}(Y) = \ln\left(\mathbb{E}_{P_0}\left[e^Y\right]\right) - \ln(\gamma^\star) \leq \text{EVAR}_{1-\gamma}(Y). \tag{16.11}$$

We include explicit definition of $\gamma^\star$ into the previous equation to obtain

$$\text{EVAR}_{1-\gamma^\star}(Y) = \ln\left(\mathbb{E}_{P_0}\left[e^Y\right]\right) + I(P(Y)||P_0(Y)), \tag{16.12}$$

which is equivalent to (16.7).

16.3.2.1 Requirement for Predicting Data-Driven EVAR

It is now clear that, in order to predict the data-driven $\text{EVAR}_{1-\gamma^\star}$, we need to learn a model of the information gain $I(P(Y)||P_0(Y))$. In the following section we show

how to model the information gain as a Lévy process $Z = I(P(Y)||P_0(Y))$; since in our case we have N processes (one for each sensing location), we define $Z_i = I(P(Y_i)||P_0(Y_i))$, and, we rewrite the policy (16.8) as:

$$\mathcal{S}^*(t) \doteq \underset{\mathcal{S} \subset \Omega}{\operatorname{argmax}} \sum_{i \in \mathcal{S}} \left(\mathbb{E}\left[Z_i \right] + \ln\left(\mathbb{E}_{P_0}(e^{Y_i}) \right) \right)$$

$$\text{subject to } \operatorname{Card}(\mathcal{S}) = \kappa, \tag{16.13}$$

16.3.3   Modeling the Information Gain

The data received as $y_i \sim Y_i$ from the selected subset of sensors, $\mathcal{S}^*(t)$, informs our model on the data process Y_i. Similarly, the information gain z_i of the data y_i informs our model on the information process Z_i. Formally, we use the following hierarchical model, with additional discussion on this model in the beginning of Sect. 16.5.3,

$$y_i \sim Y_i$$
$$z_i \sim Z_i|y_i . \tag{16.14}$$

We model Z_i as a stochastic variable to form a predictive model on what the information gain of our next sample will be at location i. In Sect. 16.3.3.2 we describe the stochastic model that we use to describe the evolution of Z_i. Our model is based on the Poisson Exposure Distribution (Ped), which we recall in Sect. 16.3.3.1.

16.3.3.1   Poisson Exposure Distribution (Ped) Likelihood

The Ped was introduced by [7] to model a continuous and monotonically increasing output resulting from a Poisson-distributed input. Since the Ped likelihood has a similar domain to the information gain and its expectation equivalently represents the average information gain used in [9], the Ped likelihood will be integral in forming a comparable baseline algorithm.

Definition 1 The probability density function of the Ped is defined as

$$f(z) = C_\Lambda \frac{\Lambda^z e^{-\Lambda}}{\Gamma(z+1)}, \tag{16.15}$$

where $\Lambda > 0$ is the distribution mean, C_Λ is the normalizing constant, $z \in \mathbb{R}$ is the random variable, and Γ is the gamma function.

Moreover, the Ped has an analytical Bayesian update using the Gamma distribution, which models the parameter Λ.

Fact 1 *The Gamma distribution is a conjugate prior of the Ped such that*

$$G\left(\Lambda|\alpha+z,\beta+1\right) \propto Ped\left(z|\Lambda\right)G\left(\Lambda|\alpha,\beta\right). \tag{16.16}$$

where $G\left(\Lambda|\alpha,\beta\right)$ is the Gamma distribution with shape parameter α and rate parameter β.

Proof *See Proposition 1 in [10] for details.*

16.3.3.2   Poisson Exposure Process (Pep) Model

Since we are interested in modeling a time-varying information gain at each sensing location in our environment, we must generalize the Ped to incorporate time as a dependent argument. The hidden Markov model (HMM) for the Ped as proposed in [7] parallels our problem where we cannot observe so-called informative events arriving at each location. However, we depart from [7] to extend the Ped to model phenomena that are dependent upon non-constant time intervals.

Definition 2 The probability density function of the Pep is defined as

$$f(z|\Lambda(t)) = C_{\Lambda(t)}\frac{(\Lambda(t))^z e^{-\Lambda(t)}}{\Gamma(z+1)}, \tag{16.17}$$

where $\Lambda(t)$ is the time-varying mean, $C_\Lambda(t)$ is the normalizing constant, and $z \in \mathbb{R}$ is the random variable. A Pep is called homogeneous if $\frac{d}{dt}\Lambda(t) = \lambda \ \forall \ t$, otherwise the Pep is called inhomogeneous.

In [7], the maximum likelihood estimate of the Poisson exposure distribution, and therefore the Pep by extension, was found to be highly nonlinear. However, as Definition 2 mathematically is similar in form to the Poisson process in (16.17), we show that the conjugate prior of the Pep is identical to that of the Poisson process as shown in Fact 2.

Fact 2 *The gamma distribution is a conjugate prior of the homogeneous Poisson exposure process (Pep) such that*

$$G\left(\lambda t|\alpha+z,\beta+t\right) \propto Pep\left(z|\lambda t\right)G\left(\lambda t|\alpha,\beta\right). \tag{16.18}$$

Proof *See Corollary 5.1 in [10] for details.*

16.4   Algorithms and Probabilistic Guarantees

While Facts 1 and 2 provide a simple analytical update for the homogeneous Pep, we still need to demonstrate conditions when the homogeneous Pep model will be provably accurate. Until we have a provably accurate regression, we cannot rely on information-driven (informed) exploration using the Pep. Hence, we adopt the strategy of uninformed-to-informed exploration, where we start performing the exploration task with a sequential search strategy (an uninformed policy) and transition to an informed policy once provable accuracy guarantees are available.

To prove probabilistic accuracy guarantees, we leverage the Chebyshev and Bienaymé-Chebyshev inequalities. The guarantees offered by the Bienaymé-Chebyshev inequality are desirable, namely that we now have error bounds on the next sample. Moreover, the independent and identically distributed condition is satisfactory for time-invariant distributions such as the Ped, which we show in Sect. 16.4.1. However, we are also interested in error bounds for our next sample in a time-varying environment. Therefore, we theoretically derive incremental variable changes (which are ideally suited for the homogeneous Pep) for the Chebyshev inequality, hence relaxing the assumption of identically distributed samples.

16.4.1   The Time-Invariant Case: Ped-Based Exploration

The regression in the Predicted Information Gain (PIG) algorithm [9] calculates the information gain for a sensing location i as the expectation of the random variable Z_i which models our belief over the information gain at each location:

$$\mathbb{E}[Z_i] = \frac{1}{n_i} \sum_{j=1}^{n_i} Z_i(t_j) \qquad (16.19)$$

where (16.19) is a time-invariant expectation. As only the expectation in (16.19) is used to drive the PIG algorithm to explore, we may equivalently use the Ped regression from Fact 1 in place of (16.19). As in our prior work in the prediction of the information gain [26, 27], we must modify the PIG algorithm from [9] into PIG* to facilitate a fair comparison to RAPTOR. In this work, we further modify PIG* to become EVAR-PIG* (Algorithm 1) to facilitate a fair comparison with our proposed algorithm, EVAR-RAPTOR (Algorithm 2). To provide a probabilistic bound for the Ped analytical update of PIG* shown in Fact 1, we leverage the Bienaymé-Chebyshev inequality.

Theorem 1 (Chebyshev Inequality for PIG, $k = \Lambda$) *Let $Z(t_1), \ldots, Z(t_n)$ be independent and identically distributed Poisson exposure distribution trials. Let $\bar{Z}(t_n) = \frac{1}{n} \sum_{j=1}^{n} Z(t_j)$ and $\Lambda = \mathbb{E}[\bar{Z}(t_n)]$. Then,*

$$Pr\left(|\bar{Z} - \Lambda| \geq \Lambda\right) \leq \frac{1}{n\Lambda}. \qquad (16.20)$$

Proof This proof proceeds along the line of the proof of Theorem 2, but where $k = \lambda$ and noting that $\beta = n$.

Using the results from Theorem 1, we develop an uninformed-to-informed exploration bound for PIG in Corollary 1.

Corollary 1 (Accuracy Bound for PIG, $k = \Lambda$) *If the environment statistics are time-invariant, then, given an accuracy threshold $0 < c \leq 1$, it holds $Pr\left(|\bar{Z} - \Lambda| \geq \Lambda\right) < c$ if the following condition is satisfied:*

$$n_b > \frac{1}{\Lambda_b c}, \qquad \text{with} \qquad b = \operatorname*{argmax}_i \frac{1}{n_i \Lambda_i}, \tag{16.21}$$

where n_i is the number of samples at location i and Λ_i is the Ped mean.

Proof This proof proceeds along the line of the proof of Corollary 2, but where the left hand side is $Pr(|\bar{Z} - \Lambda| \geq \Lambda)$ and $\beta = n$.

Algorithm 1 EVAR-PIG*

Input: sensor set $\Omega = \{1, \ldots, N\}$, subset size κ
Initialize $(\alpha_i, \beta_i, \Lambda_i, n_i) \leftarrow 0 \; \forall \, i$
for each time t and for each sensor i **do**
    $\mathbb{E}[EVAR_{1-\gamma_i^*}] \leftarrow \Lambda_i + \ln\left(\mathbb{E}_{n_i}\left[e^{cY}\right]\right)$
    if Corollary 1 **then**
        $\mathscr{S}(t) \leftarrow (16.13)$
    else
        $\mathscr{S}(t) \leftarrow$ Sequential sampling
    end if
    if $i \in \mathscr{S}(t)$ and $n_i{=}1$ **then**
        Initialize belief on Y_i
    else
        Update belief on Y_i (16.38) $\forall \, i \in \mathscr{S}(t)$
        if $\min_i n_i \geq 2$ **then**
            Update belief Λ_i (16.16) $\forall \, i \in \mathscr{S}(t)$
        end if
    end if
    $n_i \leftarrow n_i + 1 \; \forall \, i \in \mathscr{S}(t)$
end for

Corollary 1 is the accuracy condition that we implement for the uninformed-to-informed variant of the PIG algorithm, shown in Algorithm 1. Note that the informed exploration variant of PIG is simply Algorithm 1 for this class of bandit problems when the accuracy threshold is assumed to be satisfied upon the initialization of the PIG algorithm [9].

16.4.2 The Time-Varying Case: Pep-Based Exploration

Since Corollary 1 is only valid in an environment with time-invariant statistics, we are compelled to develop an analogous result which is valid in time-varying environments. Before we derive probability bounds for the Pep, we briefly review the properties of a Lévy process [12] for the increment $\Delta Z(\Delta t) > 0$ in the random variable Z:

1. ΔZ has independent and stationary increments,
2. $\Delta Z(0) = 0$ with probability one,
3. $\forall\, a > 0$ and $\forall\, \Delta t > 0$, $\lim_{\Delta t \to 0} P(\Delta Z(\Delta t) > a) = 0$.

The above properties are used in Theorem 2 and Corollary 2 below.

Lemma 4 (Chebyshev Inequality) [11], $k = \lambda$ *Let* $\Delta Z(t_1), \ldots, \Delta Z(t_n) > 0$ *be independent Poisson exposure process increments so that* $Pr(\Delta Z(t_i)) = p_i$. *Let* $\bar{Z}(t_n) = \sum_{j=1}^{n} \Delta Z(t_j)$ *and* $\Lambda(t_n - t_1) = \lambda\beta = \mathbb{E}[Z(t_n)]$. *Then,*

$$Pr\left(|\bar{Z} - \lambda\beta| \geq \lambda\right) \leq \frac{1}{\lambda}. \tag{16.22}$$

Since we are using a homogeneous Pep with stationary increments, we may extend Lemma 4 to provide a sequential-in-time bound as shown in Lemma 5.

Lemma 5 (Time Inequality, $k = \lambda$) *Let* $\Delta Z(t_1), \ldots, \Delta Z(t_n) > 0$ *be independent Poisson exposure process increments so that* $Pr(\Delta Z(t_i)) = p_i$. *Let* $\bar{Z}(t_n) = \frac{1}{t_n} \sum_{j=1}^{n} \Delta Z(t_j)$ *and* $\frac{d}{dt}\Lambda(\Delta t) = \lambda = \mathbb{E}[\bar{Z}(t_n)]$. *Then,*

$$Pr\left(|\bar{Z} - \lambda| \geq \lambda\right) \leq \frac{1}{\lambda\beta}. \tag{16.23}$$

Proof From Lemma 1, we know that

$$Pr(|\bar{Z} - \mu| \geq k) \leq \frac{Var(Z)}{k^2}. \tag{16.24}$$

Inserting the mean and variance of our gamma distribution model on homogeneous Pep into (16.24) yields

$$Pr(|\bar{Z} - \frac{\alpha}{\beta}| \geq k) \leq \frac{\frac{\alpha}{\beta^2}}{k^2}, \tag{16.25}$$

which simplifies to

$$Pr(|\bar{Z} - \lambda\beta| \geq k) \leq \frac{\lambda}{\beta k^2}. \tag{16.26}$$

In assigning, $\lambda = k$, we resolve the proof.

$$Pr(|\bar{Z} - \lambda\beta| \geq \lambda) \leq \frac{1}{\lambda\beta}. \qquad (16.27)$$

We now consider a so-called bi-homogeneous Pep with $\Lambda(\Delta t, \Delta n) = \lambda t n$, where λ is the *information gain per unit-time per sample* (i.e., $\frac{d}{dt}\frac{d}{dn}\Lambda(t, n) = \lambda \ \forall \ t, n > 0$). We further propose a gamma posterior distribution model for the bi-homogeneous Pep under consideration as

$$G\left(\lambda \mid \alpha_i = \frac{\alpha_{(i,1)} + \alpha_{(i,2)}}{2}, \beta_i = \beta_{(i,1)}\beta_{(i,2)}\right), \qquad (16.28)$$

where an analytical update for the parameters is given in Fact 3.

Fact 3 *The parameters for the proposed gamma distribution in* (16.28) *are analytically updated such that*

$$\begin{aligned} G\left(\lambda\Delta t|\alpha_{(i,1)} + z, \beta_{(i,1)} + \Delta t\right) &\propto Pep\left(z|\lambda\Delta t\right) G\left(\lambda\Delta t|\alpha_{(i,1)}, \beta_{(i,1)}\right) \\ G\left(\lambda\Delta n|\alpha_{(i,2)} + z, \beta_{(i,2)} + \Delta n\right) &\propto Pep\left(z|\lambda\Delta n\right) G\left(\lambda\Delta n|\alpha_{(i,2)}, \beta_{(i,2)}\right) \end{aligned} \qquad (16.29)$$

Proof The proof follows directly from Fact 2.

A key benefit of the bi-homogeneous Pep here is that we can derive a tighter inequality which does not require identically distributed samples, as stated in Theorem 2.

Theorem 2 (Chebyshev Inequality for RAPTOR, $k = \lambda^{\frac{3}{4}}$) *Let* $\Delta Z(t_1), \ldots,$ $\Delta Z(t_n) > 0$ *be independent Poisson exposure process increments. Let* $\bar{Z}(t_n) = \frac{1}{n t_n}\sum_{j=1}^{n} \Delta Z(t_j)$ *and* $\frac{d}{dt}\frac{d}{dn}\Lambda(\Delta t, \Delta n) = \lambda = \mathbb{E}[\bar{Z}(t_n)]$. *Then,*

$$Pr\left(|\bar{Z} - \lambda| \geq \lambda^{\frac{3}{4}}\right) \leq \frac{1}{\sqrt{\alpha\beta}} = \frac{1}{\sqrt{\alpha n(t_n - t_1)}}, \qquad (16.30)$$

where α and β are both defined in (16.28).

Proof From Chebyshev's inequality, we know that

$$Pr(|\bar{Z} - \mu| \geq k) \leq \frac{\text{VAR}(\bar{Z})}{k^2}. \qquad (16.31)$$

Inserting the mean ($\lambda = \frac{\alpha}{\beta}$) and variance ($\frac{\alpha}{\beta^2}$) of our gamma distribution model on homogeneous Pep into (16.31) yields

$$Pr(|\bar{Z} - \lambda| \geq k) \leq \frac{\frac{\alpha}{(\beta)^2}}{k^2}, \qquad (16.32)$$

which simplifies to

$$Pr(|\bar{Z} - \lambda| \geq k) \leq \frac{\lambda}{\beta k^2}. \tag{16.33}$$

In assigning, $k = \lambda^{\frac{3}{4}}$ and noting that $\beta = n(t_n - t_1)$ due to (16.28), we resolve the proof:

$$Pr(|\bar{Z} - \lambda\beta| \geq \lambda^{\frac{3}{4}}) \leq \frac{1}{\sqrt{\alpha\beta}} = \frac{1}{\sqrt{\alpha n(t_n - t_1)}}. \tag{16.34}$$

Remark 1 (On the selection of k in Theorem 2) We select k in terms of λ such that: (1) the error bound is constant and (2) the probability bound decreases with the total sampling time, number of samples, and increase in information gain. This limits the selection of k to λ with an exponent between $\frac{1}{2}$ to 1, non-inclusive.

While our sample and time inequality in Theorem 2 provides an error bound for learning a single bi-homogeneous Pep, it does not yet provide a condition for the transition between uninformed and informed exploration across all bandit arms. This is given in the following corollary.

Corollary 2 (Accuracy Bound for RAPTOR)   *If the environment statistics are time-varying, then, given an accuracy threshold $0 < c \leq 1$, it holds $Pr\left(|\bar{Z} - \lambda| \geq \lambda^{\frac{3}{4}}\right) < c$ if the following conditions are satisfied:*

$$t_{n_b} > t_{1_b} + \frac{1}{n_b \alpha_b c^2}, \quad \text{and} \quad \frac{1}{\sqrt{\alpha_b \beta_b}} < c \tag{16.35}$$

where $b = \underset{i}{\arg\max} \ \frac{1}{\sqrt{\alpha_i \beta_i}}$, n_i is the number of samples at location i, α_i is the total increase in the information gain at location i, and β_i is the total duration that location i has been observed.

Proof When the right-hand side of (16.34) is between 1 and 0, we have meaningful guarantees on the error of our regression; i.e., when

$$\frac{1}{\sqrt{\alpha_b \beta_b}} < c, \tag{16.36}$$

where $0 < c \leq 1$ and $\beta = n(t_n - t_1)$. Then meaningful guarantees are available at a sensing location i when

$$t_{n_i} > t_{1_i} + \frac{1}{n_i \alpha_i c^2}. \tag{16.37}$$

Consequently, meaningful guarantees are available across the entire sensing domain once $t_{n_i} > t_{1_i} + \frac{1}{n_b \alpha_b c^2}$, where $b = \underset{i}{\mathrm{argmax}} \ \frac{1}{n_i \alpha_i c^2}$.

The bound in Theorem 2 extends the Chebyshev inequality such that a result analogous to the Bienaymé-Chebyshev inequality is achieved, but where samples need not be identically distributed. Moreover, guarantees on the bi-homogeneous Pep regression by Theorem 2 provide a principled condition for transitioning from uninformed exploration to informed exploration in Corollary 2.

Algorithm 2 EVAR-RAPTOR

Input: sensor set $\Omega = \{1, \ldots, N\}$, subset size κ
Initialize $(\alpha_i, \beta_i, \lambda_i, n_i, \Delta t_i) \leftarrow 0 \ \forall \ i$
for each epoch at time t and for each sensor i **do**
　　$\mathbb{E}[Z_i | \Delta t_i, \Delta n_i] \leftarrow \lambda_i \Delta t_i \Delta n_i + Z_i(t_{n_i}) + \ln \left(\mathbb{E}_{n_i} \left[e^{cY} \right] \right)$
　　if Corollary 2 **then**
　　　　$\mathscr{S}(t) \leftarrow$ (16.13)
　　else
　　　　$\mathscr{S}(t) \leftarrow$ Sequential sampling
　　end if
　　if $i \in \mathscr{S}(t)$ and $n_i{=}1$ **then**
　　　　Initialize belief on Y_i
　　else
　　　　Update belief on Y_i (16.38) $\forall \ i \in \eta_t$
　　　　if $\underset{i}{\min} \ n_i \geq 2$ **then**
　　　　　　Update belief λ_i (16.29) $\forall \ i \in \eta_t$
　　　　end if
　　end if
　　$n_i \leftarrow n_i + 1 \ \forall \ i \in \mathscr{S}(t)$
　　$\Delta t_i \leftarrow \Delta t_i + 1 \ \forall \ i \in \mathscr{S}(t)$
end for

16.5   Experimental Evaluation

The empirical results in this section quantify the advantage of our proposed risk-aware strategy. The risk-aware performance of each algorithm is assessed in terms of the maximum available EVAR at each time step of the simulation; this maximum value is assessed in an omniscient post-processing of the data.

16.5.1   Evaluation Setup

For our experiments, we use the Intel Berkeley temperature dataset [29], the European Research Area (ERA) temperature dataset [30], the Ireland windspeed dataset [31], the Washington rainfall dataset [32], and the Clean Air Status and

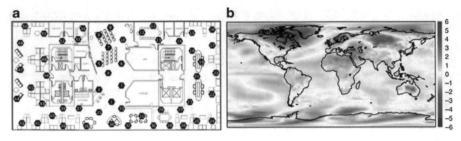

Fig. 16.1 Both the Intel (indoor) and ERA (outdoor) temperature datasets are shown. (**a**) The Intel research lab in Figure 16.1a shows 54 sensors, but the data file from [29] has 58 sensor feeds in their data file. Due to sensor quality constraints, we use 52 of the 58 sensor feeds. The temperature is recorded in Celsius. (**b**) The magnitude, in Celsius, of anomalies in the European Research Area (ERA) interim datset, relative to the means of the ERA-interim dataset for the year 2010 is shown [34]

Trends Network (CASTNet) Ozone concentration dataset [33]. Each dataset reports the evolution of an environmental variable (e.g., temperature) at N geographic locations.

The **Intel Temperature dataset** contains the temperature measured (in Celsius) of the Intel lab at Berkeley between February 29th and April 5th of 2004 [29]. Due to quality of the recorded data, and to the presence of short or corrupted sensor feeds, we use approximately 5 days worth of data across 52 sensor feeds; i.e., $N = 52$.

The **European Research Area (ERA) temperature dataset** contains the measured temperature at an altitude of 2 meters around the world. We use data between January 1st 2011 to January 1st 2014 [30]. We limited our analysis to 50 randomly selected sensor feeds and a subset size of 6; i.e., $N = 50$ and $\kappa = 6$ (Fig. 16.1).

The **Ireland windspeed dataset** contains measured windspeed (in meters per second) at 12 stations across Ireland between 1961–1978 [31]. We use all 12 sensing stations for experimentation and a subset size of 2; i.e., $N = 12$ and $\kappa = 2$.

The **Washington rainfall dataset** (in millimeters) has 272 sensing locations across Washington state from 1949–1994 [32]. We use 25 locations, since not all areas received rain, and a subset size of 2; i.e., $N = 25$ and $\kappa = 2$ (Figs. 16.2 and 16.3).

The **CASTNet ozone dataset** (in parts per billion) has 80 operational sensing locations, of which we use $N = 60$ locations based on the duration of data available at each site. The dataset reports the 8-h daily maximum ozone concentrations which were compressed and missing entries in the monthly dataset were filled using the average concentration for that year [33]. As the dataset is originally based on the 8-h maximum concentrations of ozone, this dataset particularly suits the use of EVAR as an uncertainty measure. The CASTNet data used spans 16.5 years, from halfway through 1995 to the end of 2011.

We create additional simulated datasets, by applying a scaling factor d to each random variable in the five real-world datasets mentioned above. The original data, which would have been paired with a scaling factor of $d = 1$ resulted in

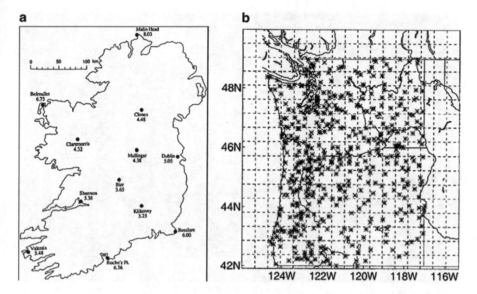

Fig. 16.2 The Ireland windspeed (left) and Washington rainfall (right) datasets are shown. (**a**) The Windspeed in Ireland was measured in knots and on an hourly basis at 12 sensing stations between the years 1961–1978. (**b**) The Washington rainfall dataset records rainfall in centimeters. The data was recorded between 1949 and 1994 on a daily basis. The 272 sensors are denoted by the asterisks on the map

computational memory shortages due to the large values of e^Y, and were therefore excluded. However, scalings ranging from $d = 10^{-5}$ and $d = 10^{-1}$ were usable on a machine with 8GB of RAM.

16.5.2   Assumptions on Prior and Posterior Distributions

The environmental variables Y_i are modeled using a normal distribution at each sensing location i. For each sample received, we calculate the frequentist variance σ_i^2 of the normal distribution. Using the calculated variance, we apply the following Bayesian update for the normal distribution

$$\mu_{(p,i)} = \frac{\frac{n_i}{\sigma_i^2}\mu_{(P_{00},i)} + \frac{y_i}{\sigma_{(P_{00},i)}^2}}{\frac{n_i}{\sigma_i^2} + \sigma_{(P_{00},i)}^{-2}} \text{ and } \sigma_{P_0}^2 = \left(\frac{\sigma^{-2}}{n_i} + \sigma_{P_0}^{-2}\right)^{-1}, \qquad (16.38)$$

where $\mu_{(p,i)}$ is the posterior mean, $\mu_{(p_0,i)}$ is the prior mean, $\sigma_{(p,i)}^2$ is the posterior variance, $\sigma_{(p_0,i)}^2$ is the prior variance, and y_i is the sample mean [35]. The information gain of the posterior normal distribution is then computed as

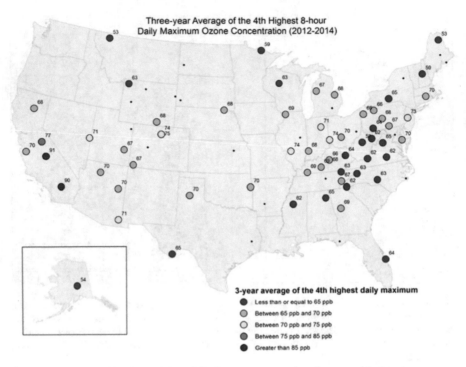

Fig. 16.3 An example of the CASTNET Ozone concentration dataset, with data in parts per billion, is shown above [33]

$$I(P(Y)||P_0(Y)) = 0.5\left[\ln\left(\frac{\sigma^2_{P_0}}{\sigma^2_P}\right) + tr\left[\left(\sigma^2_{P_0}\right)^{-1}\sigma^2_P\right] - 1\right.$$

$$\left. + (\mu_P - \mu_{P_0})^T \left(\sigma^2_{P_0}\right)^{-1}(\mu_P - \mu_{P_0})\right], \qquad (16.39)$$

where 1 is the dimensionality of the data which we use for experiments [36]. We then calculated the EVAR as

$$\text{EVAR}_{1-\gamma^\star} = \ln\left(\mathbb{E}_{P_0}(e^{dY})\right) + I(P(dY)||P_0(dY)), \qquad (16.40)$$

where $\gamma^\star = e^{-I(P(dY)||P_0(dY))}$ is the lower bound of γ and d is the scaling parameter.

16.5.3   EVAR-Seeking Algorithms and Results

This section discusses the performance of the proposed learning algorithm, EVAR-RAPTOR (Algorithm 2). To ensure clarity, we briefly state the impact of scaling our random variable Y on $\text{EVAR}_{1-\gamma^*}(Y)$. From (16.40), we see that $\text{EVAR}_{1-\gamma^*}(Y)$ is calculated using an expectation on e^Y using a prior belief $P_0(Y)$ and the information gain $I(P||P_0)$. We outline the properties of both parts of $\text{EVAR}_{1-\gamma^*}(Y)$ below.

The expectation, itself, on the prior belief $\mathbb{E}_{P_0}[e^Y]$ is not a random variable. By contrast, when only the prior P_0 is known for the information gain $I(P||P_0)$, then the information gain becomes a conditional expectation on a function of a random variable; i.e., $I(P||P_0|P_0) = \mathbb{E}_P[\ln\left(\frac{P}{P_0}\right)|P_0]$, where a conditional expectation is a random variable. Unlike the expected value based on the prior belief, the information gain is also scale-invariant. As a result, the information gain is a scale-invariant random variable. Moreover, each different scaling d applied to our random variable Y serves to transition from $\text{EVAR}_{1-\gamma^*}(Y)$ being dominated by the prior belief $\mathbb{E}_{P_0}[e^Y]$ to being dominated by the information gain $I(P||P_0)$.

While in (16.40) a change in the scaling parameter d affects the value of $\ln\left(\mathbb{E}\left[e^{dY}\right]\right)$, it does not affect the value of the information gain, $I(P(dY)||P_0(dY))$ [37]. As $\ln\left(\mathbb{E}\left[e^{dY}\right]\right)$ is an expectation based on the prior in (16.38), it is deterministic and given. Hence, as the scaling parameter d increases, the proportion of EVAR that is stochastic decreases. Resultantly, if the regression for the information gain is accurate, then we should see a consistent EVAR prediction performance across a range of values for the scaling parameter d across all datasets.

Although sequential and random sampling methods allocate statistically even sensing effort, their performance is highly inconsistent across the five datasets. This motivates the use of information-driven approaches to predict EVAR; i.e., EVAR-PIG* and EVAR-RAPTOR. It is immediately clear from Figs. 16.4, 16.5, 16.6, 16.7 and 16.8 that both EVAR-PIG* and EVAR-RAPTOR outpeform sequential and random sampling across all five datasets and variable scalings. It is important to emphasize that the regressions and derived bounds used for (16.39) distinguish the empirical performance of EVAR-PIG* and EVAR-RAPTOR. Since, overall, EVAR-RAPTOR outperforms all baseline algorithms across the five datasets and all scalings, we conclude that the bi-homogeneous Pep regression is the key reason for the performance increase.

However, a single contradictory result in Fig. 16.7a shows that EVAR-PIG* outperforms EVAR-RAPTOR for a particular set of conditions in the Washington rainfall dataset; i.e., a scaling of $d = 10^{-1}$, subset $\kappa = 2$ and set $N = 25$. It is worth noting that it is known that RAPTOR outperforms PIG* in predicting the information gain; this, in combination with the fact that the information gain is scale-invariant, means that the difference in performance is largely due to the expected values of the prior belief; i.e., that the EVAR of the Washington rainfall dataset is mostly stationary when a scaling of $d = 10^{-1}$ is used. This helps to explain why EVAR-PIG* also has performance closely matching that of

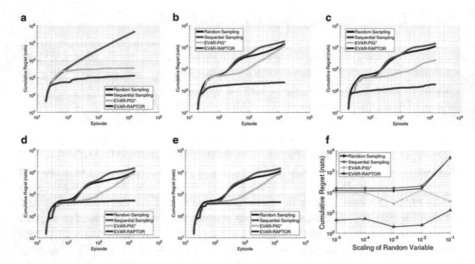

Fig. 16.4 The EVAR-RAPTOR algorithm outperforms all baselines and has the most consistent performance across all scalings of the **Intel temperature dataset.** (**a**) Regret of scaling $d = 10^{-1}$. (**b** Regret of scaling $d = 10^{-2}$. (**c**) Regret of scaling $d = 10^{-3}$. (**d**) Regret of scaling $d = 10^{-4}$. (**e**) Regret of scaling $d = 10^{-5}$. (**f**) Regret of each scaling

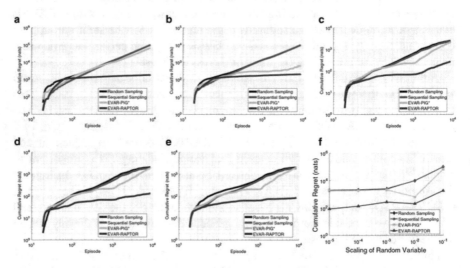

Fig. 16.5 The EVAR-RAPTOR algorithm outperforms all baselines and has the most consistent performance across all scalings of the **ERA daily temperature dataset.** (**a**) Regret of scaling $d = 10^{-1}$. (**b**) Regret of scaling $d = 10^{-2}$. (**c**) Regret of scaling $d = 10^{-3}$. (**d**) Regret of scaling $d = 10^{-4}$. (**e**) Regret of scaling $d = 10^{-5}$. (**f**) Regret of each scaling

EVAR-RAPTOR when the scaling is changed to $d = 10^{-2}$ in Fig. 16.7b, but then EVAR-PIG* becomes steadily less competitive as the scaling decreases further, remembering that the scaling affects the stochasticity of EVAR.

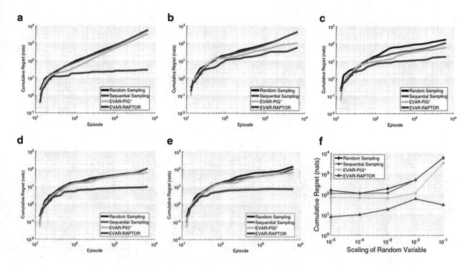

Fig. 16.6 The EVAR-RAPTOR algorithm outperforms all baselines and has the most consistent performance across all scalings of the **Ireland windspeed dataset.** (**a**) Regret of scaling $d = 10^{-1}$. (**b**) Regret of scaling $d = 10^{-2}$. (**c**) Regret of scaling $d = 10^{-3}$. (**d**) Regret of scaling $d = 10^{-4}$. (**e**) Regret of scaling $d = 10^{-5}$. (**f**) Regret of each scaling

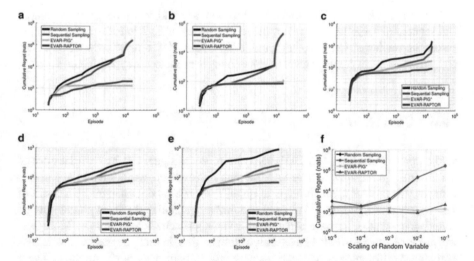

Fig. 16.7 The EVAR-RAPTOR algorithm has the most consistent performance across all scalings of the **Washington rainfall dataset**, but is outperformed by EVAR-PIG* only at the scaling of $d = 10^{-1}$. This result is more thoroughly discussed in Sect. 16.5.3. (**a**) Regret of scaling $d = 10^{-1}$. (**b**) Regret of scaling $d = 10^{-2}$. (**c**) Regret of scaling $d = 10^{-3}$. (**d**) Regret of scaling $d = 10^{-4}$. (**e**) Regret of scaling $d = 10^{-5}$. (**f**) Regret of each scaling

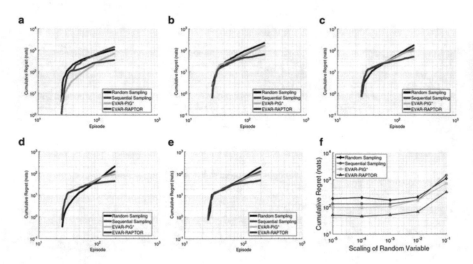

Fig. 16.8 The EVAR-RAPTOR algorithm outperforms all baselines and has the most consistent performance across all scalings of the **CASTNet ozone dataset.** (a) Regret of scaling $d = 10^{-1}$. (b) Regret of scaling $d = 10^{-2}$. (c) Regret of scaling $d = 10^{-3}$. (d) Regret of scaling $d = 10^{-4}$. (e) Regret of scaling $d = 10^{-5}$. (f) Regret of each scaling

In summary, EVAR-PIG* appears to be about as good, if not better, than random and sequential sampling. However, the performance of EVAR-PIG* is inconsistent across the scaling d. On the other hand, EVAR-RAPTOR outperforms all baselines and is consistent in performance, despite changes in the scaling parameter d.

16.6 Conclusion

In the context of steering a DDDAS system, we mitigate the risk of data-driven models losing relevance in time-varying environments as quantified by the entropic value at risk (EVAR), which helps to quantify how a model changes as a result of new observations. While EVAR is conventionally calculated with a predetermined confidence value γ, here we use a data-driven approach to determine γ. Moreover, we propose the EVAR-RAPTOR algorithm which learns to predict the EVAR available at different sensing locations with probabilistic accuracy guarantees. These probabilistic guarantees allow us to accurately learn and predict (EVAR) values in real-world datasets, even when the random environmental variable is scaled by a constant. Empirical results on four real-world datasets demonstrate empirically that EVAR-RAPTOR has consistently superior performance in predicting EVAR values for data generated by time-varying distributions.

Acknowledgments This work is sponsored by the Air Force Office of Scientific Research Award Number FA9550-14-1-0399, and the Air Force Office of Scientific Research Young Investigator Program Number FA9550-15-1-0146.

References

1. F. Darema, Dynamic data driven applications systems: a new paradigm for application simulations and measurements, in *International Conference on Computational Science*, Krakow (Springer, 2004), pp. 662–669 https://link.springer.com/book/10.1007/b97988
2. F. Darema, Grid computing and beyond: the context of dynamic data driven applications systems. Proc. IEEE **93**(3), 692–697 (2005)
3. F. Darema, DDDAS, a key driver for large-scale-big-data and large-scale-big-computing. Proc. Comput. Sci. **51**, 2463 (2015)
4. A. Hobson, A new theorem of information theory. J. Stat. Phys. **1**(3), 383–391 (1969)
5. A. Ahmadi-Javid, Entropic value-at-risk: a new coherent risk measure. J. Optim. Theory Appl. **155**(3), 1105–1123 (2012)
6. R.T. Rockafellar, S. Uryasev, Optimization of conditional value-at-risk. J. Risk **2**, 21–42 (2000)
7. T. Kim, A.V. Nefian, M.J. Broxton, Photometric recovery of ortho-images derived from apollo 15 metric camera imagery, in *Advances in Visual Computing* (Springer, 2009), pp. 700–709
8. T. Kim, A.V. Nefian, M.J. Broxton, Photometric recovery of apollo metric imagery with lunar-lambertian reflectance. Electron. Lett. **46**(9), 631–633 (2010)
9. D.Y. Little, F.T. Sommer, Learning and exploration in action-perception loops. Front. Neural Circuits **7**, 1–19 (2013)
10. A.M. Axelrod, Learning to exploit time-varying heterogeneity in distributed sensing using the information exposure rate. Master's thesis, Oklahoma State University, 2015
11. C.C. Heyde, E. Seneta, Studies in the history of probability and statistics. XXXI. The simple branching process, a turning point test and a fundamental inequality: a historical note on I.J. bienaymé. Biometrika **59**(3), 680–683 (1972)
12. D. Applebaum, Lévy processes: from probability to finance and quantum groups. Not. AMS **51**(11), 1336–1347 (2004)
13. M. Tokic, Adaptive ε-greedy exploration in reinforcement learning based on value differences, in *KI 2010: Advances in Artificial Intelligence* (Springer, 2010), pp. 203–210
14. W. Jouini, D. Ernst, C. Moy, J. Palicot, Upper confidence bound based decision making strategies and dynamic spectrum access, in *2010 IEEE International Conference on Communications (ICC)*, Cape Town (IEEE, 2010), pp. 1–5 http://icc2010.ieee-icc.org/
15. A. Carpentier, A. Lazaric, M. Ghavamzadeh, R. Munos, P. Auer, Upper-confidence-bound algorithms for active learning in multi-armed bandits, in *Algorithmic Learning Theory* (Springer, 2011) pp. 189–203
16. C. Gehring, D. Precup, Smart exploration in reinforcement learning using absolute temporal difference errors, in *Proceedings of the 2013 International Conference on Autonomous Agents and Multi-agent Systems*, Saint Paul. International Foundation for Autonomous Agents and Multiagent Systems, 2013, pp. 1037–1044 https://dl.acm.org/citation.cfm?id=2484920
17. D. Russo, B. Van Roy, An information-theoretic analysis of Thompson sampling. arXiv preprint arXiv:1403.5341 (2014)
18. J.C. Principe, D. Xu, Information-theoretic learning using Renyis quadratic entropy, in *Proceedings of the First International Workshop on Independent Component Analysis and Signal Separation*, Aussois, France, 1999, pp. 407–412 https://scholar.googleusercontent. com/scholar.bib?q=info:IFH_36rOMQgJ:scholar.google.com/&output=citation&scisig= AAGBfm0AAAAAW3GA7DJPrAxvpEvPRhC_z9ovoHvVeTWe&scisf=4&ct=citation&cd=-1&hl=en&scfhb=1

19. P. Reverdy, R.C. Wilson, P. Holmes, N.E. Leonard, Towards optimization of a human-inspired heuristic for solving explore-exploit problems, in *CDC*, Maui, 2012, pp. 2820–2825 http://www.ieeecss.org/CAB/conferences/cdc2012/

20. D. Ryabko, Time-series information and learning, in *2013 IEEE International Symposium on Information Theory Proceedings (ISIT)*, Istanbul (IEEE, 2013), pp. 1392–1395 http://www.proceedings.com/19451.html

21. S.G. Nora Ayanian, Persistent monitoring of stochastic spatio-temporal phenomena with a small team of robots, in *Proceedings of Robotics: Science and Systems*, Berkeley, California, USA, July 2014 http://rll.berkeley.edu/RSS2014/

22. D. Russo, B. Van Roy, Learning to optimize via information-directed sampling, in *Advances in Neural Information Processing Systems*, Montreal, 2014, pp. 1583–1591 https://nips.cc/Conferences/2014/

23. J.M. Hernández-Lobato, M.A. Gelbart, R.P. Adams, M.W. Hoffman, Z. Ghahramani, A general framework for constrained bayesian optimization using information-based search. arXiv preprint arXiv:1511.09422 (2015)

24. H. Ding, D.A. Castañón, Optimal solutions for adaptive search problems with entropy objectives. arXiv preprint arXiv:1508.04127 (2015)

25. A.M. Axelrod, S.A. Karaman, G.V. Chowdhary, Exploitation by informed exploration between isolated operatives for information-theoretic data harvesting, in *Conference on Decision and Control (CDC)*, Osaka, vol. 54, 2015

26. A. Axelrod, G. Chowdhary, Uninformed-to-informed exploration in unstructured real-world environments, in *Self-Confidence In Autonomous Systems*, Washington, DC (AAAI, 2015)

27. A. Axelrod, G. Chowdhary, A hybridized bayesian parametric-nonparametric approach to the pure exploration problem, in *Bayesian Nonparametrics: The Next Generation*, Montreal. Neural Information Processing Systems, 2015

28. A. Axelrod, G. Chowdhary, *The Explore-Exploit Dilemma in Nonstationary Decision Making under Uncertainty*, 1st edn. (Springer, New York, 2015), pp. 2198–4182

29. P. Bodik, W. Hong, C. Guestrin, S. Madden, M. Paskin, R. Thibaux, Intel lab data. Technical report, Intel Berkely Research Lab, Feb 2004

30. P. Berrisford, D.P. Dee, K. Fielding, M. Fuentes, P. Kallberg, S. Kobayashi, S. Uppala, *The era-interim archive* (European Center for Medium Range Weather Forecasts, Reading, 2009)

31. J. Haslett, A.E. Raftery, Ireland wind data set. Technical report, Trinity College and University of Washington, pp. 1961–1978

32. M. Widmann, C.S. Bretherton, Validation of mesoscale precipitation in the NCEP reanalysis using a new gridcell dataset for the northwestern united states. J. Clim. **13**(11), 1936–1950 (2000)

33. Clean Air Status and Trends Network (CASTNET), Accessed Hourly Ozone data at www.epa.gov/castnet on Sept 2015

34. D.P. Dee, S.M. Uppala, A.J. Simmons, P. Berrisford, P. Poli, S. Kobayashi, U. Andrae, M.A. Balmaseda, G. Balsamo, P. Bauer et al., The era-interim reanalysis: configuration and performance of the data assimilation system. Q. J. R. Meteorol. Soc. **137**(656), 553–597 (2011)

35. A. Gelman, J.B. Carlin, H.S. Stern, D.B. Dunson, A. Vehtari, D.B. Rubin, *Bayesian data analysis*, 3rd edn. (CRC Press, Boca Raton, 2013)

36. J. Duchi, *Derivations for Linear Algebra and Optimization* (Berkeley, 2007)

37. M.J Schervish, *Theory of Statistics* (Springer, New York, 2012)

Part VI
Context-Aware: Coordinated Control

Chapter 17
DDDAS for Attack Detection and Isolation of Control Systems

Luis Francisco Combita, Jairo Alonso Giraldo, Alvaro A. Cardenas, and Nicanor Quijano

Abstract In the last decade, the security of control systems has become a research priority. Attack detection, isolation and reconfiguration are necessary to maintain a control system safe, even in the presence of attacks. In this work, we exploit some tools from fault-tolerant control systems and analyze them under a security framework leveraging the insights from Dynamic Data Driven Applications Systems (DDDAS). In particular, we propose DDDAS Anomaly Isolation and Response (DDDAS-AIR), an architecture for secure control systems that relies on simulations of the physical system to help us reconfigure the sensors in order to mitigate the impact of the attack. This chapter demonstrates the proposed mechanisms with a three-tanks system under attack, and shows how the evaluation of traditional fault-detection systems needs to be reconsidered for attacks instead of natural faults.

Keywords Anomaly isolation and response (AIR) · Cyber attack · Fault detection · Isolation and reconfiguration (FDIR)

17.1 Introduction

The widespread adoption of embedded sensors is giving us new opportunities to measure and understand the dynamic behavior of physical systems. To leverage these new opportunities, DDDAS [1] has emerged as a new paradigm to dynamically

L. F. Combita (✉)
Department of Electronical Engineering, Universidad Distrital Francisco Jose de Caldas, Bogotá, Colombia
e-mail: lfcombita@udistrital.edu.co; ca.luis10@uniandes.edu.co

J. A. Giraldo · A. A. Cardenas
Department of Computer Science, University of Texas at Dallas, Richardson, TX, USA
e-mail: jairo.giraldo@utdallas.edu; alvaro.cardenas@utdallas.edu

N. Quijano
Department of Electrical Engineering, Universidad de Los Andes, Bogotá, Colombia
e-mail: nquijano@uniandes.edu.co

© The Author(s), under exclusive license to Springer Nature Switzerland AG 2022
E. P. Blasch et al. (eds.), *Handbook of Dynamic Data Driven Applications Systems*,
https://doi.org/10.1007/978-3-030-74568-4_17

combine data from a variety of sources, augment data with simulations, and obtain more accurate predictions and precise controls. DDDAS has proven to be useful in diverse applications that include industrial control [2], risk management [3], social networks [4], controls of swarms [5], microgrid control [6], and dispatch control in power networks [7].

Recently, the DDDAS paradigm has also been incorporated in cyber-security and privacy studies [8–11]. While computer security research initially focused on security mechanisms to prevent attacks, it is now accepted that preventing attacks is not enough, and systems need to detect and respond to attacks. Detecting and responding automatically to attacks is particularly important in control systems because they are required to send real-time continuous control actions to maintain the safety of the system. If an attacker takes partial control of a system, a failure to respond automatically in real-time can have severe negative consequences such as destruction of equipment or even loss of life. In the literature, researchers have focused their attention mostly on preventive actions that aim to decrease the likelihood of attacks by reducing vulnerabilities. Surprisingly, little attention has been given to isolation and reconfiguration in the presence of adversaries, where the objective is to identify the location of the attack and generate actions that mitigate and neutralize the attacks, thus reducing its impact over the system [12]. The DDDAS paradigm is particularly well-suited to help us model the problem of detecting and responding to attacks against control systems because by definition, the paradigm encourages developers to think in terms of how to use models of the physical system to guide the data acquisition, how data acquisition can change the operation and simulation of the models, and in particular, on how to dynamically reconfigure the control system based on the outputs of computation, model simulations, and sensor inputs.

Leveraging these characteristics, in this chapter we propose a DDDAS-inspired Anomaly Isolation and Response (DDDAS-AIR) architecture and analysis for the security of control systems. DDDAS-AIR can run the simulation of the physical system under control and the output of these computations can then lead us to reclassify sensors, actuators, and controllers as more trustworthy or less trustworthy. Our DDDAS-AIR algorithm can dynamically reconfigure the selection of sensors that are trusted, creating synthetic data to mitigate the lack of missing sensor observations in order to drive the system to a safe place. In particular, in this Chapter, we start by exploring classical notions of fault detection and isolation in control systems, and then show how to study them under adversarial conditions by proposing new attack models and metrics of performance.

17.2   Problem Formulation

Consider the linear, time-invariant, discrete-time system described by

$$x(k + 1) = Ax(k) + Bu(k)$$
$$y(k) = Cx(k), \qquad\qquad (17.1)$$

where $A \in \mathbb{R}^{n \times n}$, $B \in \mathbb{R}^{n \times m}$, $C \in \mathbb{R}^{p \times n}$, $x(k) \in \mathbb{R}^n$ represents the state of the system, $u(k) \in \mathbb{R}^m$ represents the input of the system, and $y(k) \in \mathbb{R}^p$ represents the output of the system. This representation [13] can be used to describe the dynamic behavior of industrial processes, where $u(k)$ is designed to ensure that $y(k)$ converges to a desired reference $r^*(k)$ under certain conditions.

17.2.1   Cyber-Attacks in Control Systems

Integrity attacks denote the types of cyber-attacks where a set of sensors or actuators are compromised, which allow attackers to inject arbitrary values [14]. Equation (17.1) can be extended to include these two types of attacks as follows

$$
\begin{aligned}
x(k+1) &= Ax(k) + Bu(k) + F_a f_a(k) \\
y^a(k) &= Cx(k) + F_s f_s(k),
\end{aligned}
\tag{17.2}
$$

where $F_a \in \mathbb{R}^{n \times m}$, $F_s \in \mathbb{R}^{p \times n}$, $f_a \in \mathbb{R}^m$ represents false data injection on actuators, $y^a(k) \in \mathbb{R}^p$ represents the compromised sensor measurement, and $f_s \in \mathbb{R}^p$ represents false data injection on sensors.

Attacks on sensors consist on replacing $y(k)$ (the real sensor measurement) with $y^a(k) = y(k) + F_s f_s(k)$ (any data value output from the sensor), i.e. a new input the attack $f_s(k)$, is added to the system. Attacks on actuators consist on modifying the input of the plant (the control signal sent to the process by the controller or the Programmable Logic Controller) adding a new input, the attack $f_a(k)$. This modification affects directly the action that the actuators may execute.

Integrity attacks and faults on control systems share some similarities in that the sensor or control signals change from the real values and become less trustworthy; however, while faults are typically random and non-strategic, cyber-attacks are strategic, more deceptive, and potentially more dangerous for the safety of the system. The objective of the attacker can be economical profit, stealing private information, or causing malfunction or safety hazards in a control process. The differences between attacks and faults are significant, and as a consequence we cannot use directly the existing tools from the fault detection literature to detect attacks. In this Chapter, we show a new way to analyze and compare traditional fault-detection systems considering the adversarial nature of attacks.

17.3   DDDAS Anomaly Isolation and Response

In order to design attack-resilient systems, we need to (i) detect that an attack is taking place; (ii) identify (isolate) the attacked device(s); and (iii) reconfigure the system and/or change its operation to mitigate the attack (e.g., replace the sensed measurements by their estimate [15]). In this work we aim to design novel strategies for attack detection, isolation and reconfiguration by extending concepts from fault detection and isolation theory [16].

In particular, motivated by the DDDAs paradigm [1], we propose a new DDDAS Anomaly Isolation and Response (DDDAS-AIR) architecture to increase the resiliency of control systems, as illustrated in Fig. 17.1. The architecture has an anomaly detection module that uses the sensor values from the field and compares them to the simulation of the system. If there are errors between the results from the simulation and the values from the field, then DDDAS-AIR will reconfigure the controller to operate in a more conservative (an potentially expensive) way while at the same time asking for more data (from potentially more expensive sensors) to confirm or reject the anomaly.

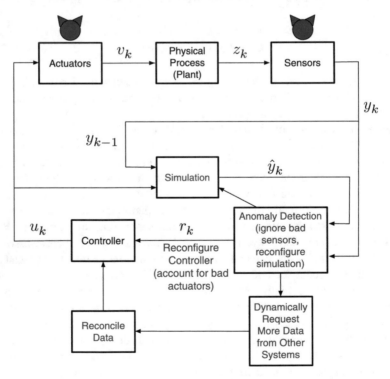

Fig. 17.1 The components of DDDAS-AIR (in blue) have an anomaly detection module that compares the sensor values from the field and compares them to the simulation of the system. If there are errors between them then it will reconfigure the controller to operate in a more conservative (and potentially expensive way) while at the same time asking for more data (from potentially more expensive sensors) to confirm or reject the anomaly

17.3.1 Anomaly Detection

Anomaly detection mechanisms are used to detect unexpected system behavior. There are two important techniques to detect anomalies: Fault Detection, Isolation and Reconfiguration (FDIR) and Data Stream Management Systems (DSMS). FDIR is commonly used in the control community to develop Fault-Tolerant Control Systems. DSMS are predominant on transportation systems [17]. This approach is based on the utilization of the logical redundancy that exists between fault-independent sensor data. However, not all control systems have this kind of redundancy on sensors, and this is the reason why analytical redundancy is developed instead. *Analytical redundancy* uses mathematical models to simulate the physical system and then uses the simulation results to compare them to sensor values received form the process.

Anomaly detection using analytical redundancy is composed by two parts: (i) residual generation and (ii) decision making. One of the most common ways to obtain residuals is by comparing the measurement $y(k)$ with its estimated $\hat{y}(k)$, such that $r(k) = |y(k) - \hat{y}(k)|$, where the absolute value is calculated element-wise. Residuals are close to zero when there is no difference between the actual system measurement and the values obtained from the estimation. These residuals can be different to zero due to faults, noise, attacks, and modeling errors. A *stateless* decision-making module produces an alert when the residuals are greater than a specific threshold τ:

$$D(k) = \begin{cases} 1, & \text{if } r(k) > \tau \\ 0, & \text{if } r(k) \leq \tau. \end{cases}$$

The estimated system can be obtained using an estimator, which requires both the input and the output of the system. In addition, it is required that the system state is fully observable, i.e., the information of all state variables can be derived from the output and the input of the system, in a finite time. The basic idea behind these kind of observers or filter-based approaches is to estimate the outputs of the system from the measurements by using either Luenberger Observers (LO) in deterministic scenarios or Kalman filters in stochastic scenarios.

The Luenberger observer can be described by:

$$z(k + 1) = Az(k) + Bu(k) + L(y(k) - Cz(k))$$
$$\hat{y}(k) = Cz(k), \tag{17.3}$$

where $z(k) \in \mathbb{R}^n$ is the estimated state vector, L is the estimator gain, and A, B, C from (17.1) are the matrices used to describe the dynamical behavior of the plant. The idea behind Luenberger observers is to add a weighting of the error between the output $y(k)$ and the estimated output $Cz(k)$ to the state equation in order to ensure that the estimation error converges to zero. In order to simplify the notation (without loss of generality), the rest of the Chapter will focus on systems where $C = I$, i.e., all the states are measurable; however, results can be easily extended to the case where $C \neq I$.

Let us define the estimation error as $e(k) = x(k) - z(k)$. In the presence of an attack, the estimation error can be described by

$$e(k + 1) = (A - LC)e(k) + F_a f_a(k),$$

where it is clear that, if there is no anomaly and the matrix $\bar{A} = A - LC$ has all eigenvalues inside the unit circle, then $e(k)$ converges to zero as k tends to ∞.

The residual $r(k + 1) = y^a(k + 1) - \hat{y}(k + 1)$ in the presence of the two types of attacks described above, when the matrix C is an identity matrix I, is given by

$$r(k + 1) = (A - L)r(k) + F_a f_a(k) + F_s f_s(k + 1) - (A - L)F_s f_s(k).$$

Let us define $\delta(k) = F_a f_a(k) + F_s f_s(k + 1) - (A - L)F_s f_s(k)$ so that

$$r(k + 1) = (A - L)r(k) + \delta(k).$$

Solving the difference equation we obtain

$$r(k) = (A - L)^k r(0) + \sum_{m=0}^{k-1} (A - L)^{k-m-1}\delta(m).$$

Note that if $(A - L)$ have all eigenvalues inside the unit circle, the estimation error will converge to a linear combination of the cumulative effect of $\delta(m)$ over time.

In this work, we assume that only sensor attacks take place in the system, and no more than one sensor is attacked simultaneously. The residuals under attack are given by

$$r(k + 1) = |y^a(k + 1) - \hat{y}(k + 1)|$$
$$= |x(k + 1) + F_s f_s(k + 1) - z(k + 1)|$$
$$= |e(k + 1) + F_s f_s(k + 1)|.$$

Clearly, the presence of anomalies can cause $r(k)$ to be greater than τ and we can detect attacks, but it depends on the appropriate selection of τ.

17.3.2 Anomaly Isolation

Anomaly detection only indicates that there is an attack, but it does not necessarily identify which particular device is sending the misleading data. To identify the compromised devices, we can use anomaly isolation ideas. There are several isolation proposals in the literature, and in this chapter we focus on the use of structured residuals. *Structured residuals* are obtained via the design of observers that are insensitive to some specific disturbances such as Unknown Input Observers (UIOs). The Unknown Input Observer (UIO) is a generalization of the LO [16]. A full-order observer is defined as:

$$w(k+1) = Fw(k) + TBu(k) + K_{12}y^a(k)$$
$$z(k) = w(k) + Hy^a(k), \qquad (17.4)$$

where $z(k) \in \mathbb{R}^n$ is the estimated state vector, and $w(k) \in \mathbb{R}^n$ is the state vector of this full-order observer, which is computed by the linear transformation $w(k) = Tx(k)$. F, T, and K_{12} are matrices that must be designed such the unknown input f_a or f_s is decoupled from the other inputs, and other design requirements.

In the system described by (17.2) there are anomalies on sensors and actuators. In this Chapter, we focus our attention on anomalies in sensors, i.e., $f_a = 0$. Combining the observer in (17.4) with the system in (17.2), the estimation error $e(k) = x(k) - z(k)$ is governed by the equation:

$$e(k+1) = [A - HCA - K_1C]e(k) + [(A - HCA - K_1C) - F]w(k)$$
$$+ [(I - HC) - T]Bu(k) + [(A - HCA - K_1C)H - K_2]y^a(k)$$
$$- K_1F_sf_s(k) - HF_sf_s(k+1).$$
$$(17.5)$$

If the following equations hold:

$$T = I - HC, \quad F = TA - K_1C, \quad K_2 = FH, \quad K_{12} = K_1 + K_2, \qquad (17.6)$$

then the estimation error dynamic is given by

$$e(k+1) = Fe(k) - K_1F_sf_s(k) - HF_sf_s(k+1), \qquad (17.7)$$

and the magnitude of the residual is given by

$$r(k) = |Ce(k) + F_sf_s(k)|. \qquad (17.8)$$

Notice from (17.7) that if all eigenvalues of F are inside unit circle, the estimation error converges to a linear combination of the attack (similar to the LO).

Now, in order to identify the location of the attack, it is necessary to design p residual calculators, where the jth $r^j(k)$ does not depend on the sensor j. As a consequence, it is possible to combine all the $r^j(k)$ and determine in which one the attack occurred. For instance, let us consider 3 sensors. If sensor 1 is compromised, the residuals in 1 will be 0, but in 2 and 3 will be different from zero, which indicates that the attack was not in 2 and 3. Therefore, the same conditions described above in (17.6) should be satisfied for each residual calculator, where all matrices omit the jth row. Readers are urged to read [16] for more insights on fault isolation.

17.4   Obtaining a Simulation Model

The design of Luenberger and Unknown Input Observers requires a mathematical model to describe the dynamical behavior of the controlled system. Roughly speaking, there are two ways to obtain these models, using first-principles, or learning them from datasets. In a *first-principles approach*, engineers use physical laws to describe the dynamic evolution of a system. This is not always a practical approach because a formal definition of a system takes more resources and in some large and complex processes, this would be practically infeasible. *Learning* the behavior of the system based on inputs and outputs is a more general and practical approach, and also matches the DDDAS philosophy of refining models based on sensor data.

One of the main challenges from learning a state-space system from input-output data of the control system is that the selection of the model order is not obvious. In this work, we assume that the order system parameter is known a priori. This fact is important because, higher order models increase the complexity of the model, and it is known that there is a trade-off between model complexity versus accuracy [18].

The models of the systems can be input-output descriptions or space-state representations. The UIOs are usually designed from a state-space description of the system. The identification based on subspace methods produces directly a state-space representation from input-output data. These methods use concepts and algorithms from numerical linear algebra. In addition to this, subspace algorithms are not iterative and therefore there are not convergence problems, which also reduces the execution time of the algorithms. The main idea of identification-based on subspace methods algorithms is to use the input-output observations to estimate the state of the system, then to define a value for the order of the system, and finally to use linear algebra to determine the space-state matrices that are the parameters of the system in this representation.

17.5   Case Study

17.5.1   Description of the System

In order to illustrate the DDDAS-AIR framework, an example is shown with a nonlinear three-tanks system with two pumps as actuators to drive water into the tanks [19]. The output variables of the system are the water level in each one of the tanks. These variables are measured with one sensor for each tank. The schematic diagram of the system is shown in Fig. 17.2.

The control system objective is to reach a desired water level by adjusting the amount of inlet water in the two tanks. The dynamical behavior of the system (assuming $L_1 > L_3 > L_2$) is given by a set of three first order nonlinear differential equations, as follows

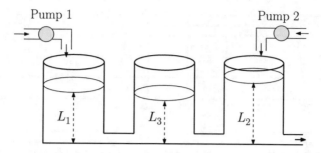

Fig. 17.2 Three tanks system

Table 17.1 Parameter values of the three tank system

Parameter	Symbol	Value
Tank cross sectional area	S	$0.0154\,\text{m}^2$
Cross sectional area inter-tanks	S_n	$5 \times 10^{-5}\,\text{m}^2$
Inter-tanks outflow coefficient	$\mu_{13} = \mu_{32}$	0.5
Emptying outflow coefficient	μ_{20}	0.6
Maximum flow rate	$Q_{i\,max}$ $(i \in [1\ 2])$	$1.5 \times 10^{-4}\,\text{m}^3\,\text{s}^{-1}$
Maximum level	$L_{j\,max}$ $(j \in [1\ 2\ 3])$	$0.62\,\text{m}$

$$S\frac{d}{dt}L_1(t) = Q_1(t) - q_{13}(t),$$

$$S\frac{d}{dt}L_2(t) = Q_2(t) + q_{32}(t) - q_{20}(t),$$

$$S\frac{d}{dt}L_3(t) = q_{13}(t) - q_{32}(t), \qquad (17.9)$$

$$q_{13}(t) = \mu_{13}\, S_n\, \text{sign}\,[L_1(t) - L_3(t)]\, \sqrt{2\,g\,L_1(t) - L_3(t)},$$

$$q_{32}(t) = \mu_{32}\, S_n\, \text{sign}\,[L_3(t) - L_2(t)]\, \sqrt{2\,g\,L_3(t) - L_2(t)},$$

$$q_{20}(t) = \mu_{20}\, S_n\, \sqrt{2\,g\,L_2(t)},$$

where $q_{13}(t)$ represents the water flow-rate from tank 1 to tank 3, $q_{32}(t)$ represents the water flow-rate from tank 3 to tank 2, $q_{20}(t)$ represents the water flow-rate of tank 2 draining the water out of the system, $Q_1(t)$ and $Q_2(t)$ represents the input water flow-rate to tanks 1 and 2 respectively, $L_1(t)$, $L_2(t)$, and $L_3(t)$ are the levels of the tanks 1, 2, and 3 respectively, S represents the cross sectional area of the tanks, S_n represents the cross sectional area of the pipes between tanks, μ_{13} represents the outflow coefficient from tank 1 to tank 3, μ_{32} represents the outflow coefficient from tank 3 to tank 2, and μ_{20} represents the outflow coefficient of tank 2 emptying.

The parameter values of the three tanks system are shown in Table 17.1.

The operation point of the system is given by

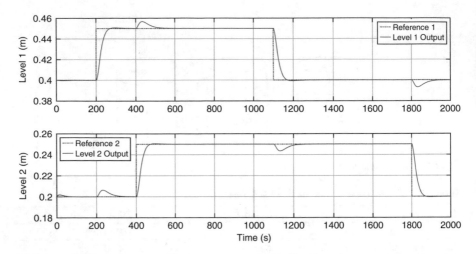

Fig. 17.3 Response of the closed loop control system without attacks, the outputs exhibit overshoots and undershoots as a consequence of a change in the other reference input

$$L_{1_{oper}} = 0.4\,\text{m}\,, \qquad L_{2_{oper}} = 0.2\,\text{m}\,, \qquad L_{3_{oper}} = 0.3\,\text{m}\,,$$

where $L_{j_{oper}}$ $(j \in [1, 2, 3])$ represents the level of tank j, and

$$Q_{1_{oper}} = 3.5018 \times 10^{-5}\,\text{m}^3\,\text{s}^{-1}\,, \qquad Q_{2_{oper}} = 3.1838 \times 10^{-5}\,\text{m}^3\,\text{s}^{-1}\,,$$

where $Q_{i_{oper}}$ $(i \in [1, 2])$ represents the input flow rates needed to reach the required levels, when the system does not have any disturbance.

The system is managed using a PI controller that aims to take the levels L_1 and L_2 to some desired references R_1 and R_2 respectively. This closed-loop controlled system is strongly coupled, i.e., changes on each input have an effect on the three outputs. Figure 17.3 shows the controlled system outputs, without any attack.

17.5.2 Obtaining the Model System from I/O Data

As we showed before, there is an exact mathematical model description of the system as described in (17.9). However, we can linearize that set of equations around the operation point described by $L_{j_{oper}}$ $(j \in [1, 2, 3])$ and $Q_{i_{oper}}$ $(i \in [1, 2])$ to obtain a set of three linear first order differential equations that can be arranged in a continuous-state representation given by

$$\dot{x}_c(t) = A_c x_c(t) + B_c u_c(t)$$
$$y_c(t) = C_c x_c(t), \qquad\qquad (17.10)$$

where the subindex c means that is a continuous-time model of the system.

If we have input/output system data, we can obtain an approximation of the state representation of the system in discrete-time, which would be equivalent to the discretization of (17.10) with sampling time T_s [20]. T_s can be determined from the elapsed time between two consecutive input/output data, and the obtained model have the shape of (17.1), using subspace identification techniques and a similarity transformation, with

$$A = \begin{bmatrix} 0.9899 & 0.0005 & 0.0098 \\ 0.0004 & 0.9804 & 0.0095 \\ 0.0108 & 0.0107 & 0.9784 \end{bmatrix},$$

$$B = \begin{bmatrix} 60.1584 & 0.1660 \\ -0.3848 & 60.1895 \\ 0.4138 & 0.1935 \end{bmatrix}, \tag{17.11}$$

$$C = \begin{bmatrix} 1 & 0 & 0 \\ 0 & 1 & 0 \\ 0 & 0 & 1 \end{bmatrix},$$

and $T_s = 1\ s$.

17.5.3 Detection of Sensor Attacks

Anomaly detection leverages LO or UIO to simulate the evolution of the process to specific inputs, and then uses the expected results to compare them with sensor information. As explained previously, UIOs are designed to be insensible to one anomaly, and for this reason they use less information of the plant to obtain the estimation. As a consequence, the error between the true value of the variable and its estimation through UIOs is larger than through LO.

Figure 17.4 illustrates the effects of sensor attacks. It is important to note that measurements from the three tank levels are available, but only two of them are controllable because there are only two control inputs on the plant. The purpose of the attacker is to modify the level of the tanks, which in the worst case can lead to an overflow of the tanks. The attacks in this Chapter focus on the modification of the true information of the sensors of the plant, i.e., the true values of the water level on the tanks of the plant. Examples of these attacks and their effect on the outputs of the plant are shown in Fig. 17.4.

The attack to sensor 1 *subtracts a constant* value to the sensor during the attack time interval, and the effect on the output of the system is an increment of the water level in tank 1.

The attack on sensor 2 is a *triangular deviation* (in time) from the real value and the false value. The effect of this attack is to produce a triangular-shaped change

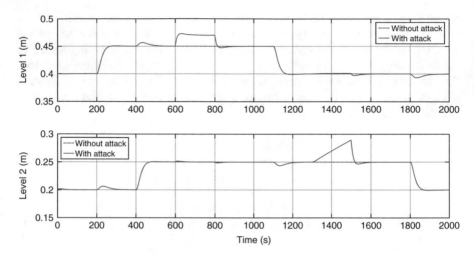

Fig. 17.4 Response of the closed-loop control system with/without attacks, the outputs show how the level of the water change with the attack, and the maximum level could overpass the physical height of the tanks, which in practice will be an overflow of water

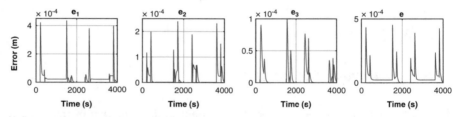

Fig. 17.5 Residuals obtained from Luenberger Observer. $e_1 = |y_1 - \hat{y}_1|$, $e_2 = |y_2 - \hat{y}_2|$, $e_3 = |y_3 - \hat{y}_3|$, and $e = \|y - \hat{y}\|$

rate in the output variable. This type of attack is more difficult to detect than the abrupt square-shaped attack in sensor 1.

The model described in (17.1) with parameters defined in (17.11) is used to design a LO and a set of UIOs. These observers are used to evaluate the residual of the system-states. The residual between the output system variables and their expected values obtained from the LO and the UIOs simulations without attacks is illustrated in Fig. 17.5, which shows the residual for the three water level of the system obtained with LO. Figure 17.6 shows the residual for the three water level of the system obtained with UIOs. In these figure, it is clear that the absolute value of the residual for UIOs is greater than the absolute value of the residual for LO. As a consequence of the residuals from UIOs are larger than from LO, there are larger attacks that remain undetected when UIOs are used to detect attacks than when a LO is used. For this reason, a better detection of attacks can be achieved using LOs.

The result of the detection process is shown in Fig. 17.7. The anomaly detection system generates an alert when one or more attacks are detected, and is "off" when

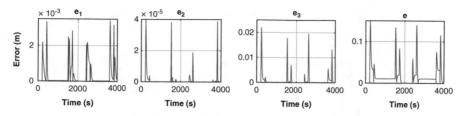

Fig. 17.6 Residuals obtained from Unknown Input Observers. $e_1 = |y_1 - \hat{y}_1|$, $e_2 = |y_2 - \hat{y}_2|$, $e_3 = |y_3 - \hat{y}_3|$, and $e = \|y - \hat{y}\|$

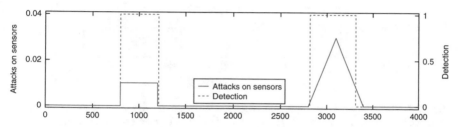

Fig. 17.7 The dotted blue line depicts the detection, 1 on detection signal, means there is an attack on a sensor, and 0 means there is no attack on sensors. The red line shows the attacks applied to sensors of the system

no attacks are detected. The detection is "on" (alert) when the residual between the sensor value and its estimated value are greater than a threshold. Only when attacks are larger than the threshold difference between the output of the system and the estimated output, will they be detected. This fact can be used by an attacker, whom can then design attacks that cannot be detected.

The parametric plots in Fig. 17.7 are calculated by comparing the system outputs under attack $y^a(k)$ with the reference output $y^{ref}(k)$ from the system without attack. Let Δ be the impact metric defined by $\sum_{k=0}^{k_f} \|y^{ref}(k) - y^a(k)\|$ for all the time of the simulation k_f. In the same way, let $E[T_{fa}]$ be the Expected Time Between False Alarms (TMBFA) that can be obtained for different τ. Recall that increasing τ decreases the number of false alarms, but it allows an attacker to inject stronger attacks that will take longer to be detected. Figure 17.8 illustrates the trade-off between false alarms and impact of the attack for LO and UIOs using the metric proposed in [21].

Figure 17.8 is one of the fundamental contributions of the DDDAS-AIR approach, because it clearly shows a comparison of traditional fault-detection algorithms against attacks (not random faults). Figure 17.8 shows why LO models should be used as a first line of defense against attacks instead of relying only on UIOs. While in traditional Fault-Detection theory UIOs are used by themselves to isolate faults (without the need of LOs), when attacks are considered, there is a need to have LOs as a first line of defense, because they limit the impact of undetected attackers in the system far more than UIOs, as illustrated in Fig. 17.8.

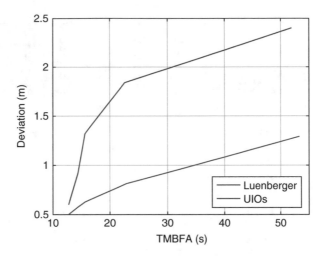

Fig. 17.8 These curves depict the relation between the maximum deviation on the output, before an attack is detected for Unknown Input Observer (UIO) and Luenberger Observer (LO)

Clearly, using LO decreases the adversary effects in the system, but using LOs alone would not enable us to identify the source of the attack. LO could be used for systems with very small number of sensors or systems that shut down in the presence of an attack. On the other hand, UIO allows an attacker to launch stronger attacks, but when detected, it will be able to identify the source of the attack and take specific actions. These results suggest that a good strategy to reduce the impact of sensor attacks on control systems is to use LO and then UIOs.

17.5.4 Isolation of Sensor Attacks

The knowledge about the existence of an attack is not enough to develop adequate actions to mitigate the effect of the attacks. Therefore, it is necessary in addition to the detection of attacks, to know the place where the attack occurs. This mechanism is known as the *isolation of the attack*. This procedure is based in the UIOs [16], and these results are shown in Fig. 17.9. The top part of Fig. 17.9 shows that the attack is detected on sensor 1 (not sensors 2 or 3), while the bottom part shows that the attack is coming from sensor 2 (not sensors 1 or 3). These results also show that for our selected thresholds, the Attack Isolation system for sensor 1 has no false alarms, while the Attack Isolation system for sensor 2 has intermittent false alarms. The reason for this phenomenon is because the model obtained from data for output 1 is more accurate than the model obtained for output 2. Having said that, in both cases the duration of false alarms is short when compared with the alert duration when under attack.

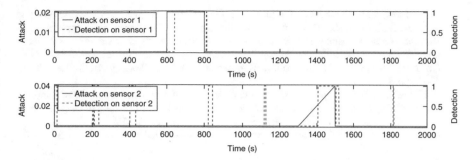

Fig. 17.9 The dotted blue line depicts the isolation of attacks. Top figure shows the attack detection on sensor 1. Bottom figure shows the attack detection on sensor 2. The red line shows the attacks applied to each sensor of the system

17.6 Conclusions and Future Work

In this chapter, we have presented an overall framework for attack detection, isolation, and response, called DDDAS-AIR. The results demonstrate the differences between detection and isolation, and the comparative approaches between fault detection and attack detection. In particular, the primary contribution of this chapter is an illustration of how attack-detection needs LOs as a first line of defense, and relies on UIOs once an attack has been detected. While in traditional Fault-Detection theory UIOs are used by themselves to isolate faults (without the need of LOs), when considering attacks a LO is needed as a first line of defense, because they limit the impact of undetected attacks in the system far more than UIOs, as illustrated in Fig. 17.8.

In future work we will analyze the next major step of our framework: attack response. Our preliminary results suggest that when attacks are detected on sensors, the attacks can be isolated and then used together with the simulation of the system to estimate the missing values. In future work we will also consider attacks to actuators.

Acknowledgments This work was partially supported by Comision de Estudios No. 015 de 2014 by Universidad Distrital Francisco José de Caldas, and is also partially supported by Colciencias 727 de 2015. The work at UT Dallas is based upon work supported by the Air Force Office of Scientific Research under award number FA9550-17-1-0135.

References

1. F. Darema, Dynamic data driven applications systems: a new paradigm for application simulations and measurements, in *Proceedings of the Computational Science – ICCS 2004: 4th International Conference, Kraków, Poland, 6–9 June 2004, Part III*, eds. by M. Bubak, G.D. van Albada, P.M.A. Sloot, J. Dongarra (Springer, Berlin/Heidelberg, 2004), pp. 662–669
2. Q. Zeng, Q. Zhang, Z. Yang, A dynamic data-driven application simulation model for oil spill emergency decision in port water area. Transport **30**(4), 406–410 (2015)

3. G.R. Madey, A.-L. Barabási, N.V. Chawla, M. Gonzalez, D. Hachen, B. Lantz, A. Pawling, T. Schoenharl, G. Szabó, P. Wang, P. Yan, Enhanced situational awareness: application of DDDAS concepts to emergency and disaster management, in *Proceedings of the Computational Science – ICCS 2007: 7th International Conference, Beijing, China, 27–30 May 2007, Part I*, eds. by Y. Shi, G.D. van Albada, J. Dongarra, P.M.A. Sloot (Springer, Berlin/Heidelberg, 2007), pp. 1090–1097

4. C. Kennedy, G. Theodoropoulos, Intelligent management of data driven simulations to support model building in the social sciences, in *Proceedings of the 2006 International Conference on Computational Science* (Springer, Berlin/Heidelberg, 2006), pp. 562–569

5. R.R. McCune, G.R. Madey, Control of artificial swarms with DDDAS. Proc. Comput. Sci. **29**, 1171–1181 (2014)

6. A.E. Thanos, M. Bastani, N. Celik, C.H. Chen, Dynamic data driven adaptive simulation framework for automated control in microgrids. IEEE Trans. Smart Grid **8**, 209–218 (2017)

7. N. Celik, A.E. Thanos, J.P. Saenz, DDDAMS-based dispatch control in power networks. Proc. Comput. Sci. **18**, 1899–1908 (2013)

8. L. Xiong, V. Sunderam, Security and privacy dimensions in next generation DDDAS/infosymbiotic systems: a position paper. Proc. Comput. Sci. **51**, 2483–2492 (2015)

9. G. Dsouza, G. Rodriguez, Y. Al-Nashif, S. Hariri, Building resilient cloud services using DDDAS and moving target defence. Int. J. Cloud Comput. **2**(2–3) 171–190 (2013)

10. G. Dsouza, S. Hariri, Y. Al-Nashif, G. Rodriguez, Resilient dynamic data driven application systems (RDDDAS). Proc. Comput. Sci. **18**, 1929–1938 (2013)

11. E. Blasch, Y. Al-Nashif, S. Hariri, Static versus dynamic data information fusion analysis using dddas for cyber security trust. Proc. Comput. Sci. **29**, 1299–1313 (2014)

12. L.F. Cómbita, J. Giraldo, A.A. Cárdenas, N. Quijano, Response and reconfiguration of cyber-physical control systems: a survey, in *Proceedings of the 2015 IEEE 2nd Colombian Conference on Automatic Control (CCAC)* (IEEE, Manizales, 2015), pp. 1–6

13. C.-T. Chen, *Linear Systems Theory and Design* (Oxford University Press, New York, 1984)

14. A.A. Cardenas, S. Amin, S. Sastry, Secure control: towards survivable cyber-physical systems, in *Proceedings of the 28th International Conference on Distributed Computing Systems Workshops*, June 2008, pp. 495–500

15. A.A. Cárdenas, S. Amin, Z.-S. Lin, Y.-L. Huang, C.-Y. Huang, S. Sastry, Attacks against process control systems: risk assessment, detection, and response, in *Proceedings of the 6th ACM Symposium on Information, Computer and Communications Security, ASIACCS'11*, New York (ACM, 2011), pp. 355–366

16. J. Chen and R.J. Patton, *Robust Model-Based Fault Diagnosis for Dynamic Systems* (Kluwer Academic Publishers, Norwell, 1999)

17. S. Imai, E. Blasch, A. Galli, W. Zhu, F. Lee, C.A. Varela, Airplane flight safety using error-tolerant data stream processing. IEEE Aerosp. Electron. Syst. Mag. **32**(4), 4–17 (2017)

18. P. van Overschee, B. de Moor, *Subspace Identification for Linear Systems: Theory, Implementation, Applications* (Springer, Boston, 1996)

19. Amira, *Laboratory Setup: Three-Tank System DTS200* (Amira GmbH, Duisburg, 2002)

20. C.L. Phillips, H.T. Nagle, *Digital Control System Analysis and Design*, 3rd edn. (Prentice-Hall, Inc., Upper Saddle River, 1995)

21. D.I. Urbina, J.A. Giraldo, A.A. Cardenas, N.O. Tippenhauer, J. Valente, M. Faisal, J. Ruths, R. Candell, H. Sandberg, Limiting the impact of stealthy attacks on industrial control systems, in *Proceedings of the 2016 ACM SIGSAC Conference on Computer and Communications Security, CCS'16*, New York (ACM, 2016), pp. 1092–1105

Chapter 18
Approximate Local Utility Design for Potential Game Approach to Cooperative Sensor Network Planning

Su-Jin Lee and Han-Lim Choi

Abstract This paper addresses information-based sensing point selection from a set of candidate sensing locations, which determines a set of measurement points maximizing the mutual information between the sensor measurements and the variables of interest. A potential game approach has been applied to implementing distributed decision making for cooperative sensor planning. When a sensor network consists of a large number of sensing agents, the local utility function for a sensing agent requires a lot of computation, because the local utility function depends on the other agents decisions while each sensing agent is inherently faced with limitations in both its communication and computational capabilities. Accordingly, a local utility function for each agent should be approximated to accommodate limitations in information gathering and processing. We propose an approximation method of a local utility function using only a part of the decisions of other agents. The part of the decisions that each agent considers is called the *neighboring set* for the agent. The error induced by the approximation is also analyzed, and to keep the error small we propose a neighbor selection algorithm that choose the neighbor set for each agent in a greedy way. The selection algorithm is based on the information structure of measurement variables taken by the agents. We illustrate the approximation method and the neighbor selection algorithm through a numerical simulation on simplified weather forecasting.

Keywords Sensor networks · Informative planning · Mutual information · Potential game · Local utility design

S.-J. Lee · H.-L. Choi (✉)
Department of Aerospace Engineering, Korea Advanced Institute of Science and Technology, Yuseong, Daejeon, Republic of Korea
e-mail: hanlimc@kaist.ac.kr

© The Author(s), under exclusive license to Springer Nature Switzerland AG 2022
E. P. Blasch et al. (eds.), *Handbook of Dynamic Data Driven Applications Systems*,
https://doi.org/10.1007/978-3-030-74568-4_18

18.1   Introduction

A sensor network consists of a large number of sensing agents, which communicate with other agents in a network or a central station. Each sensor node generally has its own processing unit and a power unit. In some cases, an agent can have a mobile unit so that it moves to the specified location to take measurements. The data about the variables of interest through the measurements taken by sensor nodes are delivered into other agents or a central unit to analyze the data and extract information of the sensed environment. A sensor network extends the ability to gather information to a larger area, however each agent also has limitations in resources such as communication bandwidth, computation capability, and available energy. To prolong the operation time of sensing agents, it is important to find out the sensing locations for a sensor network that give the maximum information about the variables of interest. Here, Dynamic Data Driven Applications Systems (DDDAS) concept can be applied to steer the agents of a sensor network and take efficient measurements [1, 9]. DDDAS illustrates a paradigm where a system incorporates data obtained from simulation into the control of the system to improve the ability for sensors to gather information efficiently. This sensor network planning problem can be formulated as an optimization problem maximizing mutual information between the measurement variables and the variables of interest in various contexts [5, 11, 13, 14].

   To make a sensor network scalable, the the distributed/decentralized implementation of the optimization problem is needed. There are two main research directions aimed at designing the procedure finding out the most informative sensing locations. The two directions can be differentiated by the number of solving a local optimization problem for each agent until obtaining a solution. One way can be described as a single run algorithm such as local greedy and sequential greedy decisions [14, 20], which obtain the sub-optimal solution after solving the local optimal problem only once. While these algorithms are simple to implement and especially a sequential greedy algorithm guarantees the worst-case performance when the objective function satisfies submodularity, they are subject to some limitations. Since each agent selects the sensing locations by solving only one problem, these single run algorithms cannot fully take advantage of possible information flows, and thus the decisions can be arbitrary suboptimal. Also, the mutual information in general does not satisfy the submodularity, specifically for a weather forecast. The other direction is an iterative algorithm which generates a sequence of solutions to converge to an approximate optimal solution [5, 12, 13]. An iterative method solves the optimization problem approximately at first, and then more accurately with updated set of information as the iterations progress [3]. A game-theoretic method is one of the iterative algorithms, which finds a solution through a decision making process called a *repeated game*, i.e., the same set of games being played over and over again until converged to a solution. Especially, a potential game approach provides a systematic framework for designing distributed implementation of multiagent systems and many learning algorithms to converges to an optimal solution [16, 18].

In [7], we addressed the distributed implementation of a sensor network planning by applying a potential-game approach. Potential games have been applied to many engineering problems, due to their desirable static (e.g., existence of a pure strategy Nash equilibrium) and dynamic properties (e.g., convergence to a Nash equilibrium with simple learning algorithms) [4, 18]. Since a potential game formulates the centralized optimization into distributed version by considering each decision maker as a player in a game, the multiagent systems can be easily transformed to the game formation and implemented in a distributed way. The formulation of a multiagent problem as a potential game consists of two steps: (1) game design in which the the agents are selfish entities and possible actions are defined and (2) learning design which involves specifying a distributed learning algorithm that lead to a desirable collective behavior of the system [11]. For *game design*, we proposed the conditional mutual information of the measurement variables conditioned on the other agents' decisions as a local utility function for each agent. This conditional mutual information is shown to be aligned with the global objective function for a sensor network. The system-wide objective is maximizing the mutual information between the whole sensor selection and the variables of interest. For a *learning algorithm*, the joint strategy fictitious play (JSFP) is adopted. With two design steps we showed that the potential game approach for distributed cooperative sensing provides better performance than other distributed/decentralized decision making algorithms, such as the local greedy and the sequential greedy algorithms, through the numerical examples of weather forecast and target tracking.

However, the computation of the local utility function for each agent requires a lot of resources. This computational burden results in part from the complexity of the local utility function itself, and in part from the dependency of the function on all of the agents decisions. To reduce the computational burden, an approximate local utility that only depends on the neighboring agents' decisions was suggested and investigated [5]. Since it is not possible for each agent to know the decisions from the other agents actions for a sensor network consisting of a large number of sensors, this approximate local utility function also enables us to improve communication efficiency. As a result, the local utility function for each agent is computed by considering only the actions of its neighboring agents. Here, the neighboring agents for each agent are defined by a set of agents that are located within a prespecified distance from the agent. When selecting neighboring agents for each agent, the correlation between the measurement variables is not considered at all. However, in some cases, such as a weather forecast example the measurements taken at close locations have little correlation with each other. Thus, the optimality gap of the potential game with the neighboring agents is larger than the potential game with the full information about the other agents and even the sequential greedy algorithm because the error incurred by neglecting the correlated variables is not negligible.

This work presents an approximation method for computing local utility function to address this computational problem and provide a good performance comparing to the previous work. We propose a greedy neighbor selection algorithm to consider correlation structure of the information space in which the cooperative sensing decision is made. The greedy selection algorithm for each agent adds a neighboring agent one by one, which has maximum mutual information about the variables of interest conditioned on the measurement variables of the agent and its pre-selected neighbors. With the determined neighbor set for each agent, we also propose a similar approximation method for computing a local utility function to the previous work. A numerical example on idealized weather forecasting is presented, showing that the approximation utility functions depending on the neighbor set selected by the proposed algorithm outperform the approximation method with the neighboring agents which are located close in Euclidean distance.

18.2 Background

The primary task of a sensor network is to gather information from a physical environment in order to estimate the *verification variables*. The verification variables $\mathbf{x}_v$ are the variables of interest that we want to know. They are a part of the state variables representing the physical environment and cannot be observed directly through the measurements.

In a problem of our concern, we assume that the physical environment can be represented with a finite set of measurable states, $\mathbf{x}_S = \{x_{s_1}, \ldots, x_{s_n}\}$ and the verification variables $\mathbf{x}_v$ in spatial-temporal space. The subscript $S = \{s_1, s_2, \ldots, s_n\}$ denotes the set of sensing locations for a sensor network, and is referred to as a *search space* S for a sensor network, and x_s represents the state variable at the sensing location $s \in S$. Sensors make measurements of the states in the search space corrupted with some noise, v_s as shown in the measurement model,

$$z_s = x_s + v_s. \tag{18.1}$$

Since the verification variables $\mathbf{x}_v$ are correlated with the states in the search space by a joint probability distribution, sensor measurements are correlated with the verification variables and have information about them.

A sensor network planning problem can be rephrased as *selecting the state variables to take measurements out of the search space*, so that the amount of information about the verification variables is maximized.

18.2.1 Information Measures

The amount of information about a random variable is equivalent to the uncertainty involved in the random variables of the states. Entropy is a widely used measure for the quantification of the uncertainty, computed in terms of a probability distribution of a random variable. With the entropy, mutual information is derived to measure the reduction in the uncertainty of the state variables, and will be adopted as an objective function for evaluating the expected performance of measurements to be taken by a sensor network.

18.2.1.1   Entropy

The entropy of a continuous random variable x, referred to as differential entropy, is defined as the negative expected value of the logarithm of the probability density function $f_x(x)$ of the random variable x [8].

Definition 1   The entropy $\mathcal{H}(x)$ of a continuous random variable x with probability density function $f_x(x)$ is defined as

$$\mathcal{H}(x) \triangleq -\mathbb{E}_x\left[\log f_x(x)\right] = -\int_S f_x(x) \log f_x(x) dx \tag{18.2}$$

where $\mathbb{E}_x[\cdot]$ denotes expectation over x, and S is the support of the random variable x, which represents the set where $f_x(x) > 0$.

As shown in the above definition of entropy, entropy is not dependent on the value of x itself but rather than depends on the shape of the distribution $f_x(x)$.

The definition of entropy for a single random variable extends to the the entropy of a random vector **x** consisting several random variables $x_1, x_2, \ldots, x_n$ using the multiple integral.

$$\mathcal{H}(\mathbf{x}) = \mathcal{H}(x_1, x_2, \ldots, x_n)$$

$$= \int_S f_{\mathbf{x}}(x_1, \ldots, x_n) \log\left(f_{\mathbf{x}}(x_1, \ldots, x_n)\right) dx_1 \ldots dx_n. \tag{18.3}$$

where $f_{\mathbf{x}}(x_1, \ldots, x_n)$ is the joint probability density function of the random vector $\mathbf{x} = [x_1, \ldots, x_n]^T$. Specifically, if **x** is a Gaussian random vector with mean $\mu_{\mathbf{x}}$ and covariance matrix $P(\mathbf{x}) \triangleq \mathbb{E}[(\mathbf{x} - \mu_{\mathbf{x}})(\mathbf{x} - \mu_{\mathbf{x}})^T]$, then its entropy is expressed as

$$\mathcal{H}(\mathbf{x}) = \frac{n}{2} \log(2\pi e) + \frac{1}{2} \log(|P(\mathbf{x})|). \tag{18.4}$$

As stated above, the entropy depends only on the shape of the distribution, thus results in a function of the determinant of the covariance matrix $|P(\mathbf{x})|$ only.

The conditional entropy for a single random variable is defined as

$$\mathcal{H}(x|z) = \mathbb{E}_z\left[\mathcal{H}(x|z=z)\right]$$

$$= -\int_{S_z} f_x(z) \int_{S_{x|z}} f_{x|z}(x|z) \log(f_{x|z}(x|z)) dx dz$$

$$= -\int_{S_z} \int_{S_{x|z}} f_{x,z}(x, z) \log(f_{x|z}(x|z)) dx dz$$

$\mathcal{H}(x|z)$ is an expected entropy of the conditional distribution taken over all possible values of z. It represents a measure of uncertainty that will remain in x *on the average* before the specific value of z is given. Likewise, the conditional entropy of a Gaussian random vector can be represented by a function of the determinant of the conditional covariance matrix. When two random vectors $\mathbf{x} = [x_1, \ldots, x_n]^T$,

$\mathbf{z} = [z_1, \ldots, z_m]^T$ have a multivariate normal distribution, the conditional random vector $\mathbf{x}$ conditioned on the other random vector $\mathbf{z}$ also have a multivariate normal distribution. Thus

$$\mathcal{H}(\mathbf{x}|\mathbf{z}) = \frac{n}{2} \log(2\pi e) + \frac{1}{2} \log(|P(\mathbf{x}|\mathbf{z})|). \tag{18.5}$$

Here, the conditional covariance matrix for a Gaussian can be computed as

$$P(\mathbf{x}|\mathbf{z}) = P(\mathbf{x}) - P(\mathbf{x}, \mathbf{z}) P^{-1}(\mathbf{x}) P(\mathbf{z}, \mathbf{x}). \tag{18.6}$$

$P(\mathbf{x}, \mathbf{z})$ represents the covariance between $\mathbf{x}$ and $\mathbf{z}$ and is defined by $P(\mathbf{x}, \mathbf{z}) \triangleq \mathbb{E}[(\mathbf{x} - \mu_{\mathbf{x}})(\mathbf{z} - \mu_{\mathbf{z}})^T]$. With the notation of conditional entropy and the product rule of probabilities, the following chain rule is derived.

$$\mathcal{H}(\mathbf{x}, \mathbf{z}) = \mathcal{H}(\mathbf{z}) + \mathcal{H}(\mathbf{x}|\mathbf{z}) = \mathcal{H}(\mathbf{x}) + \mathcal{H}(\mathbf{z}|\mathbf{x}). \tag{18.7}$$

That is, the measure of the uncertainty contained in two random vectors is the sum of the uncertainty of one random vector and the uncertainty of the other random vector conditioned on the first one. The chain rule for entropy can be expressed in terms of individual random variables as

$$\begin{aligned} \mathcal{H}(\mathbf{x}, \mathbf{z}) = {} & \mathcal{H}(x_1) + \mathcal{H}(x_2|x_1) + \cdots + H(x_n|x_1, \ldots, x_{n-1}) \\ & + \mathcal{H}(z_1|\mathbf{x}) + \mathcal{H}(z_2|\mathbf{x}, z_1) + \cdots + \mathcal{H}(z_m|\mathbf{x}, z_1, \ldots, z_{m-1}). \end{aligned} \tag{18.8}$$

18.2.1.2 Mutual Information

Mutual information represents the amount of information contained in one random variable about the other random variable. Specifically, It quantifies the amount of the uncertainty reduction in one random variable x due to the observation of the other random variable z, thus it can be represented by the difference between the entropy of a random variable and its conditional entropy conditioned on the other random variable.

$$\mathcal{I}(x; z) = \mathcal{H}(x) - \mathcal{H}(x|z) \tag{18.9}$$

By the chain rule of the entropy in (18.7), the mutual information can be shown to be commutative.

$$\begin{aligned} \mathcal{I}(x; z) = {} & \mathcal{H}(x) - \mathcal{H}(x|z) = \mathcal{H}(x) - (\mathcal{H}(x, z) - \mathcal{H}(z)) \\ = {} & \mathcal{H}(z) - \mathcal{H}(z|x) = \mathcal{I}(z; x) \end{aligned} \tag{18.10}$$

It means that the mutual information contained in random variable x about random variable z is equal to the information contained in z about x. Thus the mutual information can be thought of a measure of the mutual dependency between two random variables. Another form of mutual information uses the expectation from the second equality in (18.10).

$$
\mathcal{I}(x; z) = \mathcal{H}(x) + \mathcal{H}(z) - \mathcal{H}(x, z) = \mathbb{E}\left[\log\left(\frac{p_{x,z}(x, z)}{p_x(x)p_z(z)}\right)\right] \quad (18.11)
$$

The mutual information between two random vectors $\mathbf{x} \in \mathbb{R}^n$ and $\mathbf{z} \in \mathbb{R}^m$ is defined in the same way, and holds the chain rule as well.

$$
\mathcal{I}(\mathbf{x}; \mathbf{z}) = \mathcal{I}(x_1; \mathbf{z}) + \mathcal{I}(x_2; \mathbf{z}|x_1) + \cdots + \mathcal{I}(x_n; \mathbf{z}|x_1, \ldots, x_{n-1})
$$

$$
= \mathcal{I}(z_1; \mathbf{x}) + \mathcal{I}(z_2; \mathbf{x}|z_1) + \cdots + \mathcal{I}(z_m; \mathbf{x}|z_1, \ldots, z_{m-1}). \quad (18.12)
$$

When the two random vectors are jointly Gaussian, the mutual information can be expressed with covariance matrix using (18.4) and (18.5)

$$
\mathcal{I}(\mathbf{x}; \mathbf{z}) = \frac{1}{2}\log(|P(\mathbf{x})|) - \frac{1}{2}\log(|P(\mathbf{x}|\mathbf{z})|). \quad (18.13)
$$

In case of two Gaussian random variables, the correlation between two random variables is enough to represent the mutual information.

$$
\mathcal{I}(x; z) = \frac{1}{2}\log\left(\frac{|P(x)|}{|P(x|z)|}\right) = \frac{1}{2}\log\left(\frac{P(x)}{P(x) - P(x, z)^2/P(z)}\right)
$$

$$
= -\frac{1}{2}\log\left(1 - \rho_{x,z}^2\right) \quad (18.14)
$$

where $\rho_{x,z}^2 \triangleq \frac{P(x,z)^2}{P(x)P(z)}$ is the correlation of x and z, and has the value between -1 and 1. To derive a theorem for the subsequent Sections, a property of mutual information related to three random variables is given [13]

$$
\mathcal{I}(x; y|z) - \mathcal{I}(x; y) = \mathcal{I}(x; z|y) - \mathcal{I}(x; z)
$$

$$
= \mathcal{I}(z; y|x) - \mathcal{I}(z; y) \quad (18.15)
$$

18.2.2   Game-Theoretic Architecture

Potential games are applied to many engineering optimization problems (such as cooperative control and resource allocation problems) due to their static (existence of Nash equilibrium) and dynamic good property (simple learning algorithm). This section provides the required game-theoretic background to develop the results in the Chapter.

18.2.2.1   Strategic Form Game

A finite game in strategic form consists of three components [10]. First of all there is a finite set of players $\mathcal{N} = \{1, 2, \ldots, N\}$, and each player selects one of actions from the strategy space, $\mathcal{A}_i$, for each player $i \in \mathcal{N}$. Lastly, a player receives the utility after all the players select their own actions, which is represented as a utility function $u_i : \mathcal{A} \to \mathbb{R}$, for each player $i \in \mathcal{N}$. With these elements, a finite strategic form game instance is defined by the tuple $\langle \mathcal{N}, \{A_i\}_{i \in \mathcal{N}}, \{u_i\}_{i \in \mathcal{N}} \rangle$. In this setting, each player has a preference structure over the actions that the player can select, according to its utility function u_i. A joint strategy space of a game is denoted by a N-fold Cartesian product of every action set $\mathcal{A} = \prod_{i \in \mathcal{N}} \mathcal{A}_i$, which represents a set of all possible combinations of actions for all players to choose. $a = (a_1, a_2, \ldots, a_N) \in \mathcal{A}$ is the collection of strategies of all players, called a strategy profile, where $a_i \in \mathcal{A}_i$ denotes the strategy chosen by player $i \in \mathcal{N}$. For notational convenience, the strategy space can be expressed as $a = (a_i, a_{-i})$, where $a_{-i} = (a_1, \ldots, a_{i-1}, a_{i+1}, \ldots, a_N)$ denotes the collection of actions of players other than player i.

A utility function u_i for player i reflects a preference of player i over its possible actions $\mathcal{A}_i$. Given other players' actions, each player would try to maximize the payoff, selecting an action that gives the maximum payoff. If every player selects the action with the maximum payoff assuming that other player's actions do not change and the chosen action is consistent with the belief that other players assumed about the player's action, and it is also true for all the players, then there is no reason for every player to change his action in this strategy profile. It follows a solution concept in a non-cooperative game, a Nash equilibrium. Formally, a strategy profile $a^* \in \mathcal{A}$ is a (pure) Nash equilibrium if

$$u_i(a_i^*, a_{-i}^*) \geq u_i(a_i, a_{-i}^*) \tag{18.16}$$

for every $a_i \in \mathcal{A}_i$ and every player $i \in \mathcal{N}$. A Nash equilibrium is a strategy profile in which no player can improve its utility by deviating unilaterally from its profile.

18.2.2.2   Potential Game

A potential game is a non-cooperative game in which the incentive of the players changing their actions can be expressed by a single function, called the *potential function*, which corresponds the global objective of a system in many engineering problems. That the player tries to maximize its utility is equivalent to maximizing the global objective for a system [19]. Formally, a finite non-cooperative game $\mathcal{G} = \langle \mathcal{N}, \{\mathcal{A}_i\}_{i \in \mathcal{N}}, \{u_i\}_{i \in \mathcal{N}} \rangle$ is a potential game if there exists a scalar function $\phi : \mathcal{A} \to \mathbb{R}$ such that

$$u_i(a_i', a_{-i}) - u_i(a_i'', a_{-i}) = \phi(a_i', a_{-i}) - \phi(a_i'', a_{-i}) \tag{18.17}$$

for every $i \in \mathcal{N}$, $a_i', a_i'' \in \mathcal{A}_i$, $a_{-i} \in \mathcal{A}_{-i}$. The function ϕ is referred to as a potential function of the game $\mathcal{G}$. The property of a potential game in (18.17) is called perfect alignment between the potential function and the player's local utility functions. This means that the amount of the change in the global objective caused by the unilateral change in one of the actions is equal the change in the local utility function of the corresponding agent. This results in two important properties of potential games. First, a potential game guarantees the existence of pure strategy Nash equilibrium. Since the joint strategy space is finite, there always exists at least one maximum value of the potential function. This strategy profile maximizing the potential function locally or globally is a pure Nash equilibrium. Hence, every potential game possesses at least one pure Nash equilibrium. The second important property is about the dynamics of a game. Many learning algorithms for finding out a Nash equilibrium in potential games are established and proven to have guaranteed asymptotic convergence to a Nash equilibrium [17].

18.3 Sensor Network Planning as a Potential Game

The goal of sensor network planning problems is to find out the optimal sensing locations that maximizes the mutual information between the verification variables and the measurements taken at those locations. In [7], we proposed a potential game formulation for distributed sensor network planning problem. Each sensing agent is considered as a player of the game and the action set of an agent is a search space for each sensor. For a local utility we showed that the local objective function defined by the conditional mutual information of an agent conditioned on the other agents' sensing decisions lead to a potential game, with the potential function being the original mutual information.

18.3.1 Cooperative Sensor Planning for Maximum Information

In this Chapter, we consider a sensor targeting problem where a network of N mobile sensing agents deployed in a relatively large domain (see Fig. 18.1). A mobile sensing agent is a vehicle carrying sensors on it, an unmanned aerial vehicle (UAV) is one example. The whole search space for a sensor network is divided up into small sensing regions[1] to which each sensing agent is designated and within

---

[1]The search region for an agent can be overlapped with other agents. In a sensor management problem, sensors are spatially installed at fixed positions and the goal is to determine which sensor node to turn ON/OFF. Then, the search space selecting a sensor node to turn on can be considered as the whole search space, that is, all the positions at which the sensors are installed.

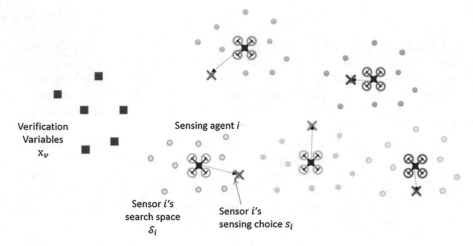

Fig. 18.1 A deployment of a sensor network in a search space. Each sensing agent is designated to a prespecified sensing region which is assumed to be finite dimensional. The sensing agent select the future sensing locations within the designated search space [7]

each region the agent selects sensing points; $S_i \subset S$ denotes the search space for a sensing agent i and we consider the region to be finite dimensional in the spatial and/or temporal space.

In a cooperative sensing problem, a sensor network tries to obtain a meaningful information about the verification variables through the measurements taken by the sensors, so that the verification variables are estimated with sufficient accuracy. Since the sensor network has limited resources, the sensor network should select the set of sensing points that gives the information about the verification variables as much as possible to reduce the number of measurements. Therefore, the cooperative sensing problem can be stated as selecting the most informative set of sensing points over the search space S. The informativeness about the variables of interest x_v through measurements $z_{s_{1:N}}$ can be quantified using mutual information. Here, the subscript $s_{1:N} = \{s_1, \ldots, s_N\}$ denotes the set of the sensing locations for N sensors and i-th sensing location s_i is selected from its designated region S_i, that is $s_i \in S_i$. $z_{s_{1:N}} = [z_{s_1}, \ldots, z_{s_N}]$ is the random vector that represents the measurement variables taken at the locations $s_{1:N} \subset S$. Therefore, the mathematical formulation of the cooperative sensing problem can be given by the optimization that seeks to find out the set of sensing points, $s_{1:N}$ that gives the maximum mutual information about the variables of interest x_v.

$$s_{1:N}^* = \arg \max_{s_{1:N}:s_i \in S_i} \mathcal{I}(x_v; z_{s_{1:N}}) \qquad (18.18)$$

The sensor network planning problem is a combinatorial optimization problem. To find out the optimal solution, we need to search for a combinatorial number of candidate sets of sensing locations. Some distributed decision architecture

---

Algorithm 1 Learning algorithm (u_i, F_i)

1: Choose the strategy using local greedy strategy
2: **while** Convergence Criteria not satisfied **do**
3:     **for** $i \in \{1, \ldots, N\}$ **do**
4:         Perform local optimization at each agent i
5:         Update the strategy according to the update rule, $s_i(t) = F_i(s(0), \ldots, s(t-1); u_i)$
6:     **end for**
7: **end while**

---

have been proposed to solve this computational complexity. Greedy strategies are often adopted due to their simple implementation. Although the greedy algorithms provide a good result, they are still subject to some limitations. Since the greedy strategies obtain a solution with a single run of an optimization problem for each agent, it is not possible to improve their solution performance by communicating agents' decisions. Game theoretic architecture provides a systematic iterative framework for considering other agents' decisions.

18.3.2 Sensor Selection as Potential Game

To formulate a sensor planning problem as a strategic form game, each sensing agent is considered as a player in a game who tries to maximize its local utility function, $\tilde{u}_i(s_i, s_{-i})$, where s_i is the set of sensing locations for sensor i, and s_{-i} represents the set of sensing locations other than sensor i's selections. In [7], we previously showed that the conditional mutual information of sensor i's measurements conditioned on the other agents sensing decisions leads to a potential game with a global objective function

$$\phi(s_i, s_{-i}) = \mathcal{I}(x_v; z_{s_i}, z_{s_{-i}}) = \mathcal{I}(x_v; z_{s_{1:N}}). \tag{18.19}$$

The local utility function can be represented by

$$u_i(s_i, s_{-i}) = \mathcal{I}(x_v; z_{s_i} | z_{s_{-i}}) \tag{18.20}$$

The solution of the designed potential game can be obtained by using a repeated game. At each stage of the game, each agent updates its decision based on the other agents' decisions up to the previous stages. With some randomness and the local optimization process, each agent either keeps its previous decision unchanged or selects the action of maximum payoff. The general structure of learning algorithms is summarized in Algorithm 1.

The selection rule F_i determines the specific learning algorithm. Among many learning rules, we adopted a *joint strategy fictitious play (JSFP)* [18]. In JSFP, each player assumes that other players play randomly according to the joint empirical frequencies, $f_{-i}(s_{-i}; t)$, which represents the frequency with which all players but

i have selected a joint action profile $\mathbf{s}_{-i}$ up to stage $t - 1$. In local optimization step at each stage, a player computes the expected local utility for action $\mathbf{s}_i \in \mathcal{S}_i$ with the joint action model of its opponents given by

$$u_i(\mathbf{s}_i, f_{-i}(t)) = \mathbb{E}_{f_{-i}(t)}[u_i(\mathbf{s}_i, \mathbf{s}_{-i})] \tag{18.21}$$

In [18], the predicted utilities $u_i(\mathbf{s}_i, f_{-i}(t))$ for each $\mathbf{s}_i \in \mathcal{S}_i$ can be expressed with a simple recursion rule

$$u_i(\mathbf{s}_i, f_{-i}(t)) = \frac{1}{t}\sum_{\tau=0}^{t-1} u_i(\mathbf{s}_i, \mathbf{s}_{-i}(\tau))$$

$$= \frac{t}{t+1}u_i(\mathbf{s}_i; t) + \frac{1}{t+1}u_i(\mathbf{s}_i, \mathbf{s}_{-i}(t)),$$

We showed that the JSFP for a sensor network planning problem can be converged to a Nash equilibrium by using [18, Theorem 2.1] and specifying the termination condition of the algorithm and demonstrated the efficiency of Nash equilibrium solutions through the weather forecast example in [7].

The equation for the local utility function shows that it requires the decisions of all of the agents, results in large computation and communication costs, especially the required computation grows exponentially in case of using a particle filter for estimating the target states. Thus we need to approximate the local utility function.

18.4 Approximate Local Utility Design

In the game-theoretic formulation, the conditional mutual information of an agent conditioned on the other agents' decisions defines a local utility function for each agent. Rewriting the local utility function (18.20) in a backward scheme,

$$u_i(\mathbf{s}_i, \mathbf{s}_{-i}) = \mathcal{I}(x_v; z_{\mathbf{s}_i}|z_{\mathbf{s}_{-i}}) = \mathcal{H}(z_{\mathbf{s}_i}|z_{\mathbf{s}_{-i}}) - \mathcal{H}(z_{\mathbf{s}_i}|x_v, z_{\mathbf{s}_{-i}}) \tag{18.22}$$

In this section, we propose an approximation method to lessen the computational burden of obtaining the local utility function. The method is to modify the form of the local utility function itself simply by removing some of conditioning variables, which represent the decisions of other agents.

18.4.1 Neighbors with Correlation

We propose the approximation method for computing the local utility function which limits the number of the conditioning variables, not using all of the decisions from a sensor network. Removing some of the conditioning variables is accomplished by using the correlation structure of the information space, making the local utility function depend on the part of the decisions.

$$\tilde{u}_i(s_i, s_{N_i}) = \mathcal{I}(x_v; z_{s_i} | z_{s_{N_i}}) \tag{18.23}$$

where s_{N_i} is the set of the measurement selections correlated with sensing agent i's decision, referred to as a neighbor set of sensing agent i and $z_{s_{N_i}}$ denotes the corresponding measurement variables. The neighbor set s_{N_i} is a subset of s_{-i}. To reduce the computation, the neighbor set should be a strict subset of s_{-i}. We quantify the error incurred by the approximation and arrange the error bound into the following lemma.

Lemma 18.1 *Let Δ_{u_i} denote the difference between the approximate local utility for sensor i and the true value of (18.20), then*

$$\begin{aligned} \Delta_{u_i} &= c_1(s_{-i}) - \mathcal{I}(x_v; z_{s_{-N_i}} | z_{s_i \cup s_{N_i}}) \\ &= c_2(s_{-i}) + \mathcal{I}(z_{s_i \cup s_{N_i}}; z_{s_{-N_i}}) - \mathcal{I}(z_{s_i \cup s_{N_i}}; z_{s_{-N_i}} | x_v) \end{aligned} \tag{18.24}$$

where $s_{-N_i} \triangleq s_{1:N} \setminus \{s_i \cup s_{N_i}\}$ is the set of the sensing locations that sensor i does not consider in computing its approximate utility, and $c_1(s_{-i})$, $c_2(s_{-i})$ encompass the terms that are constant with respect to the i-th sensing agents selection.

Proof The conditional mutual information of (18.20) and (18.23) can be expanded using chain rule (18.12)

$$\begin{aligned} \Delta_{U_i} &= \mathcal{I}(x_v; z_{s_i} | z_{s_{N_i}}) - \mathcal{I}(x_v; z_{s_i} | z_{s_{-i}}) \\ &= [\mathcal{I}(x_v; z_{s_{1:N}}) - \mathcal{I}(x_v; z_{s_{N_i}}) - \mathcal{I}(x_v; z_{s_{-N_i}} | z_{s_i \cup s_{N_i}})] \\ &\quad - [\mathcal{I}(x_v; z_{s_{1:N}}) - \mathcal{I}(x_v; z_{s_{-i}})]. \end{aligned}$$

Cancelling out common terms results in the first equation in (18.24) and rewriting the third term using (18.15)

$$\begin{aligned} \Delta_{U_i} &= \mathcal{I}(x_v; z_{s_{-i}}) - \mathcal{I}(x_v; z_{s_{N_i}}) - \mathcal{I}(x_v; z_{s_{-N_i}}) + \mathcal{I}(z_{s_i \cup s_{N_i}}; z_{s_{-N_i}}) \\ &\quad - \mathcal{I}(z_{s_i \cup s_{N_i}}; z_{s_{-N_i}} | x_v) \\ &= c(s_{-i}) + \mathcal{I}(z_{s_i}, z_{s_{N_i}}; z_{s_{-N_i}}) - \mathcal{I}(z_{s_i}, z_{s_{N_i}}; z_{s_{-N_i}} | x_v). \end{aligned}$$

Remark 18.2 When it is assumed that the measurement variables are conditionally independent given the verification variable, the error of the approximate local utility can be simplifed as

$$\Delta_{U_i} = c(s_{-i}) + \mathcal{I}(z_{s_i \cup s_{N_i}}; z_{s_{-N_i}}) \tag{18.25}$$

The conditional independence makes the last term in (18.24) be zero, then the error can be represented with a mutual information between the sensing selections related with sensing agent i and the others. In this case, the sensing locations that are correlated with sensing agent i's search space are selected as a neighbor set of sensing agent i regardless of the verification variables. For example, this is the case for a target tracking example.

Remark 18.3 In a non-cooperative game, each agent tries to maximize its own payoff with the other agents' decisions fixed. Thus, adding a constant to the utility function for the fixed other agents' actions has no effect on the decision of the agent. In (18.24), the common term $c_1(\mathbf{s}_{-i})$ and $c_2(\mathbf{s}_{-i})$ for all the strategies of agent i doesn't affect the preference structure of sensing agent i [4]. Note that a Nash equilibrium is defined in terms of payoff differences for varying actions of each agent, suggesting that games with identical preference structure share the same equilibrium sets. Thus, if the term that depends on the selection of agent i is zero, the game with approximate local utility functions will have the same equilibrium sets with the game with the true value of (18.20).

18.4.2 Determination of the Neighbor Set

The error incurred by the approximation of the local utility function can be considered in two ways. In the first equation of (18.24), the error is represented as the mutual information between the verification variables and the measurement variables of which is not in the neighbor set of agent i. If after conditioning on the measurement selections of sensing agent i and its neighbors, the measurement variables at $\mathbf{s}_{-N_i}$ have little information about the target variables, the error becomes small enough to approximate the local utility function with sufficient accuracy. That is, the measurement variables at $\mathbf{s}_{-N_i}$ have no new information about the verification variables other than the measurements at $\mathbf{s}_i$ and $\mathbf{s}_{N_i}$.

In the other way, the error is the difference between the prior mutual information and the posterior mutual information conditioning on the target states as shown in the second equation of (18.24). It amounts to the mutual information of the variables at $\mathbf{s}_i \cup \mathbf{s}_{N_i}$ and $\mathbf{s}_{-N_i}$ projected onto the subspace generated by the target states [21].

To make the error sufficiently small, it is important to decide which measurement variables be included in the neighbor set for each agent. In most of the cases, the measurement variables taken at the close locations are correlated with each other, and in contrast the measurements taken at the distant locations from sensing agent i's search space have little correlation with agent i's selection. Thus, each sensing agent can approximate its utility function by considering the neighbor set consisted of the sensing agent close to each agent. However, in weather forecast example, there is no connection between the closeness in Euclidean distance and correlation among variables. Weather dynamics is highly nonlinear and thus the neighbor set should be chosen in different way to the usual cases. For a weather forecast example,

---

Algorithm 2 Neighbors selection algorithm for weather forecast example(i, $P_0 = P(z_{\mathcal{S}_{-i}})$, $P_v = P(z_{\mathcal{S}_{-i}}|x_v)$)

1: $s_{\mathcal{N}_i} := \emptyset$
2: $s_{-\mathcal{N}_i} := s_{\mathcal{S}_{1:N}} \setminus s_{\mathcal{S}_i}$
3: **for** $j \in \{1, \dots, n\}$ **do**
4: **for** $y \in s_{-\mathcal{N}_i}$ **do**
5:   $\Delta_y = \log(\frac{P_0(z_y)}{P_l(z_y)})$
6: **end for**
7: $y^* = \arg\max_{y \in s_{-\mathcal{N}_i}} \Delta_y$
8: $s_{\mathcal{N}_i} := s_{\mathcal{N}_i} \cup y^*$
9: $s_{-\mathcal{N}_i} := s_{-\mathcal{N}_i} \setminus y^*$
10: $P_0 = P_0(z_{s_{-\mathcal{N}_i}}) - P_0(z_{s_{-\mathcal{N}_i}}, z_{y^*}) P_0(z_{y^*}, z_{s_{-\mathcal{N}_i}}) / P_0(z_{y^*})$
11: $P_v = P_v(z_{s_{-\mathcal{N}_i}}) - P_v(z_{s_{-\mathcal{N}_i}}, z_{y^*}) P_v(z_{y^*}, z_{s_{-\mathcal{N}_i}}) / P_v(z_{y^*})$
12: **end for**

---

the sequential greedy scheme is proposed. Every sensing agent conducts the greedy scheme to determine its neighbor set. The algorithm is simply adding sensing agents in sequence, choosing the next sensor which has maximum mutual information about the target states conditioned on the measurement variables of a sensing agent's search space and its pre-selected neighbors. Using the first error bound in (18.24), the algorithm greedily selects the next sensing agent j that maximizes:

$$\mathcal{I}(z_{s_j}; x_v | z_{s_i \cup s_{N_i}}) = \mathcal{H}(z_{s_j} | z_{s_i \cup s_{N_i}}) - \mathcal{H}(z_{s_j} | z_{s_i \cup s_{N_i}}, x_v). \tag{18.26}$$

In Algorithm 2, we outlines the greedy neighbor selection algorithm.

If we leave out the measurement variables that have little correlation with sensor i s selection, we can approximate the local utility function with a small error. This approximation reduces the burden of computation significantly, however it cannot be showed that the approximate local utility function satisfies the alignment with the global objective, thus we cannot say that the game with the approximate local utility function is a potential game. The performance of the game with the proposed local utility function should be studied in future work.

18.4.3 Computation Time Analysis

The main burden for the computation of utility functions is caused by conditioning variables the decisions from all of the agents. For a multivariate normal distribution, a local utility function (18.20) is rewritten using the backward scheme [6] and the mutual information for a Gaussian variables (18.13) with additive white Gaussian measurement noise,

$$u_i(\mathbf{s}_i, \mathbf{s}_{-i}) = \mathcal{I}(x_v; z_{\mathbf{s}_i} | z_{\mathbf{s}_{-i}}) = \mathcal{H}(z_{\mathbf{s}_i} | z_{\mathbf{s}_{-i}}) - \mathcal{H}(z_{\mathbf{s}_i} | x_v, z_{\mathbf{s}_{-i}})$$

$$= \frac{1}{2} \log |P(z_{\mathbf{s}_i} | z_{\mathbf{s}_{-i}})| - \frac{1}{2} \log |P(z_{\mathbf{s}_i} | x_v, z_{\mathbf{s}_{-i}})|$$

$$= \frac{1}{2} \log \left| P(z_{\mathbf{s}_i}) - P(x_{\mathbf{s}_i}, x_{\mathbf{s}_{-i}}) P(z_{\mathbf{s}_{-i}})^{-1} P(x_{\mathbf{s}_{-i}}, x_{\mathbf{s}_i}) \right|$$

$$- \frac{1}{2} \log \left| P(z_{\mathbf{s}_i} | x_v) - P(x_{\mathbf{s}_i}, x_{\mathbf{s}_{-i}} | x_v) P(z_{\mathbf{s}_{-i}} | x_v)^{-1} P(x_{\mathbf{s}_{-i}}, x_{\mathbf{s}_i} | x_v) \right|$$

where $P(z_{\mathbf{s}}) = P(x_{\mathbf{s}}) + R_{\mathbf{s}}$, $P(z_{\mathbf{s}} | x_v) = P(x_{\mathbf{s}} | x_v) + R_{\mathbf{s}}$ denote the covariance matrices of measurement variables at sensing selections $\mathbf{s}$, and $R_{\mathbf{s}}$ denotes the measurement noise covariance. As shown above, the most time-consuming term is the computation of the inverse of matrices relating to the other agents' decisions in obtaining a local utility function. Inversion of $n \times n$ symmetric positive matrix requires approximately $\frac{2}{3} n^3$ floating-point operations [2], and thus computation time for the conditional mutual information increases proportional to the cubic of the number of sensing agents ($\mathcal{O}(N^3)$). For a large sensor network, the computation of a utility function for an agent becomes intractable. However, the approximate local utility function depending on the neighbor sensing agents' decisions ensures that the computation time of a utility function for each agent stays within fixed limits as there are limited number of neighbors around each agent.

18.5   Numerical Example

A sensor targeting example for weather forecast is presented to demonstrate the validity of the proposed local utility function and the selection algorithm of the neighboring set. In Sect. 18.5.1 we describe a sensor targeting problem for weather forecast. In Sect. 18.5.2 we compare the performance of the approximate local utility function with other algorithms.

18.5.1   Sensor Targeting for Weather Forecast

The proposed game-theoretic method is demonstrated on a sensor targeting example for weather forecast using Lorenz-95 model. The Lorenz-95 model [15] is an idealized chaos model that is implemented for the initial verification of numerical weather prediction. In this example, we adopt a same sensor targeting scenario as [6], in which a 2-D extension of the original 1-D Lorenz-95 model was developed and used. The 2-D model represents the global weather dynamics of the midlatitude region of the northern hemisphere as follows [7]:

$$\dot{y}_{ij} = \left(y_{i+1,j} - y_{i-2,j} \right) y_{i-1,j} + \frac{2}{3} \left(y_{i,j+1} - y_{i,j-2} \right) y_{i,j-1} - y_{ij} + \bar{y},$$

$$(i = 1, \dots, L_{on}, \ j = 1, \dots, L_{at}) \qquad (18.27)$$

where y_{ij} denotes a scalar meteorological quantity, such as vorticity or temperature, at the ith longitudinal and jth latitudinal grid point, and each of which corresponds to the state variable at the point. At the sensing location ij the measurement model is given by

$$z_{ij} = y_{ij} + v_{ij}$$

where v_{ij} is additive sensing noise, with $v_{ij} \sim \mathcal{N}(0, R_{ij})$ for all possible sensing locations. In the weather forecast, the agent takes measurements of meteorological quantities directly corrupted with some noise. The size of the whole region is $L_{on} = 36$ longitudinal and $L_{at} = 9$ latitudinal grid points, which are corresponds to 694×694 km.

The sensor targeting problem for the weather forecast can be rephrased as selecting the most informative sensing locations in the predefined search region at $t_s = 0.05$ (equivalent to 6 h) to reduce the uncertainty in the verification variables. The verification variables correspond to y in the verification region at the verification time $t_v = 0.55$ (equivalently to 66 h). While unattended ground sensors of size 93 is already deployed and takes measurements every 6 h, the decision should be made to choose additional sensing locations for mobile sensing agents, such as UAVs at t_s. Using the Ensemble square root filter [22] with the above weather dynamics, the joint probability distribution of the measurement variables at t_s and the verification variables at t_v can be approximated by a multivariate Gaussian distribution obtained from the samples of the filter (See [6] for more detail setting of the problem). With the covariance matrix of the measurement variables and the verification variables $P(x_{\mathcal{S}_{1:N}} \cup x_v)$, the problem can be treated as a static sensor selection problem in which decides where to make measurements out of a finite set of candidate locations. The backward scheme proposed in [6] is utilized to calculate the mutual information of the global objective function, which is proven to be efficient in computing the impact of each measurement variables combinations on the uncertainty reduction (18.18).

$$\mathcal{I}(x_v; z_s) = \mathcal{I}(z_s; x_v) = H(z_s) - H(z_s | x_v)$$

$$= \frac{1}{2} \log(|P(z_s)|) - \frac{1}{2} \log(|P(z_s | x_v)|)$$

$$= \frac{1}{2} \log(|P(x_s) + R_s|) - \frac{1}{2} \log(|P(x_s | x_v) + R_s|). \quad (18.28)$$

For the given covariance matrix $P(x_{\mathcal{S}_{1:N}} \cup x_v)$ obtained from the ensemble square root filter, the two covariance matrices $P(x_{\mathcal{S}_{1:N}} | x_v)$ and $P(x_{\mathcal{S}_{1:N}})$ are computed prior to the selection process. The unconditioned covariance matrix for the measurement variables $P(x_{\mathcal{S}_{1:N}})$ is formed by simply removing the rows and columns corresponding to the verification variables from $P(x_{\mathcal{S}_{1:N}} \cup x_v)$. The conditional covariance matrix $P(x_{\mathcal{S}_{1:N}} | x_v)$ is computed by conditioning $P(x_{\mathcal{S}_{1:N}})$ on the verification variables x_v. Once these two covariance matrices are obtained, then the selection process for each sensing agent is equivalent to the selection of corresponding principal submatrix and calculation of determinants.

In a potential game each agent computes the local utility function defined by the conditional mutual information between the measurement selection and the verification variables conditioned on the other agents' action. We calculate the local utility using the backward scheme as the mutual information of the global objective.

$$
\begin{aligned}
u_i(\mathbf{s}_i, \mathbf{s}_{-i}) &= \mathcal{I}(x_v; z_{\mathbf{s}_i} | z_{\mathbf{s}_{-i}}) = \mathcal{I}(z_{\mathbf{s}_i}; x_v | z_{\mathbf{s}_{-i}}) \\
&= H(z_{\mathbf{s}_i} | z_{\mathbf{s}_{-i}}) - H(z_{\mathbf{s}_i} | x_v, z_{\mathbf{s}_{-i}}) \\
&= \frac{1}{2} \log \left(\left| P(z_{\mathbf{s}_i} | z_{\mathbf{s}_{-i}}) \right| \right) - \frac{1}{2} \log \left(\left| P(z_{\mathbf{s}_i} | x_v, z_{\mathbf{s}_{-i}}) \right| \right)
\end{aligned}
\tag{18.29}
$$

Here, we should calculate the two matrices $P(z_{\mathcal{S}_i} | z_{\mathbf{s}_{-i}})$ and $P(z_{\mathcal{S}_i} | x_v, z_{\mathbf{s}_{-i}})$ over the search space of agent i before optimizing the agent's selection. For the obtained covariance matrices $P(x_{\mathcal{S}_{1:N}} | x_v)$ and $P(x_{\mathcal{S}_{1:N}})$ from the backward scheme the two conditional covariance matrices $P(z_{\mathcal{S}_i} | z_{\mathbf{s}_{-i}})$ and $P(z_{\mathcal{S}_i} | x_v, z_{\mathbf{s}_{-i}})$ are computed by conditioning on the other agents' sensing selections respectively. If the number of sensing points each agent selects is one, then the covariance matrix for one sensing point become a scalar which is a corresponding diagonal elements in the matrix.

The approximate local utility is computed in the same way of computing the local utility (18.29) with the exception of the conditioning variables. The conditioning variables are reduced to the neighboring measurements instead of all the other agents' decisions.

$$
\begin{aligned}
\tilde{u}_i(\mathbf{s}_i, \mathbf{s}_{N_i}) &= \mathcal{I}(z_{\mathbf{s}_i}; x_v | z_{\mathbf{s}_{N_i}}) \\
&= H(z_{\mathbf{s}_i} | z_{\mathbf{s}_{N_i}}) - H(z_{\mathbf{s}_i} | x_v, z_{\mathbf{s}_{N_i}}) \\
&= \frac{1}{2} \log \left(\left| P(z_{\mathbf{s}_i} | z_{\mathbf{s}_{N_i}}) \right| \right) - \frac{1}{2} \log \left(\left| P(z_{\mathbf{s}_i} | x_v, z_{\mathbf{s}_{N_i}}) \right| \right)
\end{aligned}
\tag{18.30}
$$

18.5.2 Comparative Results

The proposed game-theoretic method using approximation of the local utility has been tested for three different sensing topologies – nine sensors in 3×2 format in two different search spaces, and fifteen sensors in 2×3 format in larger region than the first and second cases, as described in Table 18.1. An oceanic region of size 12×9 (in longitude $\times$ latitude) is considered as a potential search region, among which the whole search space $\mathcal{S}_{1:N}$ is chosen and each agent is assigned its own sensing region $\mathcal{S}_i$ separated from the other agents.

$$
\mathcal{S}_i \cap \mathcal{S}_j = \emptyset, \ \forall i \neq j
$$

Table 18.1 Topology of example cases ($a \times b$: a grids in longitude, b grids in latitude)

Case	N	n_i	$S_{1:N}$	S_i
1	9	1	9×6	3×2
2	9	1	9×6	3×2
3	15	1	10×9	2×3

The number of sensing locations for each agent is set to be one for all the cases as in [7], because the global optimal solution cannot be obtained in tractable time. We compare the proposed method to seven different strategies:

- *Global optimal:* The global optimal solution for the cooperative sensor network planning problem in (18.18) is obtained by exhaustive search.
- *Local greedy:* Local greedy strategy maximizes the mutual information of its own selection as shown in below

$$\max \mathcal{I}(z_{s_i}; x_v).$$

- *Sequential greedy:* Each agent select the sensing location which gives the maximum mutual information conditioned on the preceding agents' decisions.

$$\max \mathcal{I}(z_{s_i}; x_v | z_{s_{1:i-1}})$$

- *Iterative greedy:* Agents make decisions based on the latest outcome with the same local utility function as (18.20). The decisions are made iteratively.
- *JSFP w/ inertia:* Implementation of Algorithm 1 of [7] with inertia, i.e., an agent is reluctant to change its action to a better one with some probability (in this example, with probability $\alpha = 0.3$ an agent chooses a better action)
- *JSFP w/o inertia:* Implementation of Algorithm 1 of [7] without inertia.
- *Approximate JSFP with 2-hop neighborhood w/ inertia:* Iterative process with local utility functions defined as (18.23). In this strategy, the neighbors are determined in terms of multi-hop in inter-agent communication.
- *Approximate JSFP with correlation based neighborhood w/ inertia:* Iterative process with local utility functions defined as (18.23). The neighbors are determined by Algorithm 2 using the correlation structure of the search space.

The resulting objective values for the seven different strategies are given in Table 18.2, and the histories of objective values in the iterative procedure are shown in Fig. 18.2. The results for iterative algorithms with inertia are obtained from Monte-Carlo simulation and represent average objective values. Case 3 is different from the other two cases in that a larger sensor network is considered, and the global optimal solution cannot be obtained in tractable time. However, from the examples of small sensor networks we consider that the optimal solution of the third case may be close to the JSFP with full information. Thus, we can consider the objective value for the JSFP with full information as a lower bound for the optimal solution.

Table 18.2 Objective values
for seven different strategies

Strategy	Case 1	Case 2	Case 3
Global optimal	2.1556	1.7563	N/A
Local greedy	1.9136	1.6668	2.3105
Sequential greedy	1.9739	1.6959	2.6131
JSFP-full w/o inertia	2.1424	1.7427	2.8337
JSFP-full w/ inertia	2.1487	1.7479	2.8886
JSFP-appr 2 hop w/ inertia	2.1401	1.7026	2.7087
JSFP-appr corr w/ inertia	2.1400	1.7519	2.8292

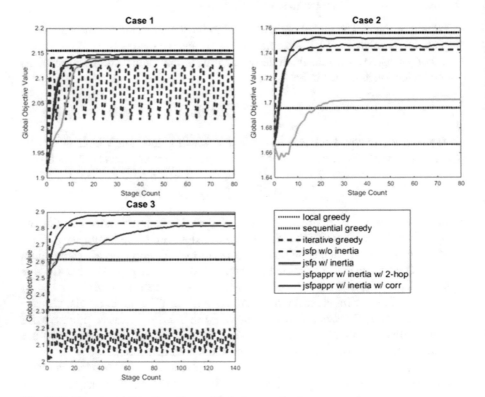

Fig. 18.2 Histories of objective values with stage count for three cases

For case 1 and 3, the results for the iterative greedy method also are added to verify
the previous result and compare the method with the proposed algorithm.

Before addressing the results of the proposed method, we verify some trends
that is already shown in [7]. The JSFP solutions converge to a solution which is
better than ones from the greedy algorithms. The iterative greedy method does not
converge and its unstable solution is lower than the JSFP solutions as shown in Case
1 and Case 3. As our previous work, we consider the sequential greedy solution as
a baseline for comparing the performance of different strategies, since it guarantees
the worst-case performance in polynomial time, even though the guarantee is

applied to the problems in which the objective functions satisfy some conditions. Unfortunately, the mutual information for weather forecasting does not satisfy those conditions, however the sequential greedy algorithm gives better solution than a simple local greedy method. First, note that the proposed method for finding out an approximate solution should give an objective value higher than sequential greedy algorithm's solutions. The JSFP with approximate local utility functions also presents a better performance than the sequential greedy strategy. The approximate local utility function based on the correlation always gives a better solution than the ones depending on the actions of the neighbors selected by physical distance. In all cases, the objective value for the approximate JSFP with correlation based neighborhood is close to the JSFP with full information. The important thing to note here is that the number of conditioning variables used for computing the utility functions is half of the JSFP with full information. As mentioned in Sect. 18.4.3, the computation time for the conditional mutual information increases proportional to the cubic of the conditioning variables. Therefore, the computation time for the approximate local utility function is reduced by a factor of approximately 8. However, the convergence time for the JSFP with approximation takes more time than the JSFP with full information. For the cases with small networks (Case 1 and Case 2) the difference between the convergence time is small, however a larger sensor network needs more time to converge with the approximate utility than with the exact utility function. The analysis of convergence time will be future work.

18.6 Conclusion

We presented an approximation method for computing the local utility function for a sensor network planning problem formulated as a potential game to find out the optimal sensing points selection in tractable time. A local utility function of each agent that depends on the neighboring measurement variables is presented, and a neighbor selection algorithm is proposed to keep the error induced by the approximation small. A sensor targeting example for weather forecast demonstrated that a potential game formulation with the approximation local utility function gives good performance close to a potential game with full information and results in a better solution than previous work [5] in which the approximation local utility function depending on the neighboring agents' actions was proposed but the neighboring agents are specified in terms of physical distance.

Acknowledgments This work was supported by Agency for Defence Development under the research contract "Persistent Information-Gathering with Airborne Surveillance and Communication Networks in Fading Environments".

References

1. http://www.dddas.org/
2. B.S. Andersen, J.A. Gunnels, F. Gustavson, J. Was'niewski, A recursive formulation of the inversin of symmetric positive definite matrices in packed storage data format. Lect. Notes Comput. Sci. **2367**, 287–296 (2002)
3. S. Boyd, N. Parikh, E. Chu, B. Peleato, J. Eckstein, Distributed optimization and statistical learning via the alternating direction method of multipliers. Found. Trends. Mach. Learn. **3**(1), 1–122 (2010)
4. O. Candogan, I. Menache, A. Ozdaglar, P.A. Parrilo, Flows and decompositions of games: harmonic and potential games. Math. Oper. Res. **36**(3), 474–503 (2011)
5. H.-L. Choi, A potential game approach for distributed cooperative sensing for maximum mutual information, in *Proceedings of American Control Conference*, Washington, DC, 2013
6. H.-L. Choi, J.P. How, Efficient targeting of sensor networks for large-scale systems. IEEE Trans. Control Syst. Technol. **19**(6), 1569–1677 (2011)
7. H.-L. Choi, S.-J. Lee, A potential-game approach for information-maximizing cooperative planning of sensor networks. IEEE Trans. Control Syst. Technol. **23**(6), 2326–2335 (2015)
8. T.M. Cover, J.A. Thomas, *Elements of Information Theory* (Wiley-Interscience, Chichester, 1991)
9. F. Darema, Dynamic data driven applications systems: a new paradigm for application simulations and measurements, in *Computational Science-ICCS 2004*, 2004, pp. 662–669
10. D. Fudenberg, J. Tirole, *Game Theory* (MIT Press, Cambridge, 1991)
11. R. Gopalakrishnan, J.R. Marden, A. Wierman, An architectural view of game theoretic control. ACM SIGMETRICS Perform. Eval. Rev. **38**(3), 31–36 (2011)
12. B. Grocholsky, *Information-Theoretic Control of Multiple Sensor Platforms*, PhD thesis, University of Sydney, 2002
13. G.M. Hoffmann, C.J. Tomlin, Mobile sensor network control using mutual information methods and particle filters. IEEE Trans. Autom. Control **55**(1), 32–47 (2010)
14. A. Krause, A. Singh, C. Guestrin, Near-optimal sensor placements in gaussian processes: theory, efficient algorithms and empirical studies. J. Mach. Learn. Res. **9**(2), 235–284 (2008)
15. E.N. Lorenz, K.A. Emanuel, Optimal sites for supplementary weather observations: simulation with a small model. J. Atmosp. Sci. **55**(3), 399–414 (1998)
16. J.R. Marden, G. Arslan, J.S. Shamma, Regret based dynamics: convergence in weakly acyclic games, in *Proceedings of the 6th International Joint Conference on Autonomous Agents and Multiagent Systems* (ACM, Honolulu, Hawaii, 2007), p. 42
17. J.R. Marden, G. Arslan, J.S. Shamma, Cooperative control and potential games. IEEE Trans. Syst. Man Cybern. Part B (Cybern.) **39**(6), 1393–1407 (2009)
18. J.R. Marden, G. Arslan, J.S. Shamma, Joint strategy fictitious play with inertia for potential games. IEEE Trans. Autom. Control **54**(2), 208–220 (2009)
19. D. Monderer, L. Shapley, Potential games. Games Econom. Behav. **14**(1), 124–143 (1996)
20. L.V. Nguyen, S. Kodagoda, R. Ranasinghe, G. Dissanayake, Information-driven adaptive sampling strategy for mobile robotic wireless sensor network. IEEE Trans. Control Syst. Technol. **24**(1), 372–379 (2016)
21. M.S. Pinsker, *Information and Information Stability of Random Variables and Processes* (Holden-Day, Oxford, 1964)
22. J.S. Whitaker, H.M. Hamill, Ensemble data assimilation without perturbed observations. Mon. Weather Rev. **130**(7), 1913–1924 (2002)

Chapter 19
Dynamic Sensor-Actor Interactions for Path-Planning in a Threat Field

Benjamin S. Cooper and Raghvendra V. Cowlagi

Abstract We consider the problem of planning the path of a vehicle, which we refer to as the *actor*, to traverse a threat field with minimum threat exposure. The threat field is an unknown, time-invariant, and strictly positive scalar field defined on a compact 2D spatial domain – the actor's *workspace*. The threat field is estimated by a network of mobile sensors that can measure the threat field pointwise at their locations. All measurements are noisy. The objective is to determine a path for the actor to reach a desired goal with minimum *risk*, which is a measure sensitive not only to the threat exposure itself, but also to the uncertainty therein. A novelty of this problem setup is that the actor can communicate with the sensor network and request that the sensors position themselves such that the actor's risk is minimized. Future applications of this problem setup include, for example, delivery (by an actor) of emergency supplies to a remote location that lies within/beyond a region afflicted by wildfire or atmospheric contaminants (the threat field). We formulate this problem on a grid defined on the actor's workspace, which defines a topological graph $\mathcal{G}$. The threat field is assumed to be finitely parameterized by coefficients of spatial basis functions. Least squares estimates of these parameters are constructed using measurements from the sensors and the actor. Whereas edge transitions in the graph $\mathcal{G}$ are deterministic, the transition *costs* depend on the threat field estimates, and are deterministic but unknown. The actor and the sensors interact iteratively. At each iteration, Dijkstra's algorithm is used to determine a minimum risk path in the graph $\mathcal{G}$ for the actor. Next, a set of grid points "near" this path are identified as points of interest. Finally, the next set of sensor locations is determined to maximize the confidence of threat field estimates on these points of interest, the threat field estimate is accordingly updated, and the iteration repeats. We explore the effect of initial sensor placement on the convergence of the iterative planner-sensor as well as discuss convergence properties with respect to the relative number of parameters and sensors available.

B. S. Cooper · R. V. Cowlagi (✉)
Aerospace Engineering Program, Worcester Polytechnic Institute, Worcester, MA, USA
e-mail: rvcowlagi@wpi.edu

© The Author(s), under exclusive license to Springer Nature Switzerland AG 2022
E. P. Blasch et al. (eds.), *Handbook of Dynamic Data Driven Applications Systems*,
https://doi.org/10.1007/978-3-030-74568-4_19

Keywords Interactive planning · Path-planning · Motion-planning · Parameter
estimation · Sensor placement · Sensor networks

19.1 Introduction

An expanding variety of applications drives the need for autonomy of unmanned
aerial and terrestrial vehicles. There are two major components of vehicular
autonomy: (1) sensing and situational awareness in the vehicle's environment, and
(2) motion-planning and control to achieve autonomous motion in this environment.
These two components can be identified with the observer/estimator and the
controller subsystems, respectively, in a traditional control systems framework.
Mirroring a common practice in control systems design, a "principle of separation"
between these two components is often assumed, as evident from discussions in
textbooks on autonomous mobile vehicles, e.g., [31]. The separation entails that
the collection and processing of sensor data is independent of the specific motion-
planning problem at hand. In this paper, we study a specific motion-planning
problem and a sensor setup where the removal of such separation between the two
components of autonomy can be beneficial.

We address planar path-planning for a mobile vehicle, which we call the *actor*
vehicle, to traverse a compact planar workspace W with minimum exposure to
a spatially varying scalar field, which we call the *threat field*. The values taken
by the threat field over W are estimated by a finite number of sensors that can
take pointwise measurements of the threat field. We study the problem of sensor
placement. However, in a departure from the typical approach of placing sensors
to determine an optimal estimate of the threat field, we study sensor placement
to optimize the actor's performance. By explicitly relating the problem of sensor
placement to the actor's motion-planning problem, we remove the separation
between the sensing and planning components. This problem setup also reflects a
growing research interest in *distributed autonomy,* where a heterogeneous team of
mobile vehicles collaboratively executes a common task.

19.1.1 Literature Review

Different facets of the proposed problem are addressed in different domains of
the literature. The primary domains include path- and motion-planning under
uncertainty, sensor management, and parameter estimation of a distributed process,
while additional insights are provided by the literature in the areas of simultaneous
localization and mapping (SLAM), target tracking and localization, planning for
stochastic systems, optimal design of experiments, and distributed control systems.

The literature on *sensor management* addresses optimal placement of sensors
to estimate distributed processes [17, 33], including the atmospheric dispersal of

gases [11], the spread of volcanic ash [23], and the identification and control of structural vibrations [29]. Guidance and coordination strategies for mobile sensors are also discussed [12, 24, 25] for envisioned implementations using teams of unmanned aerial, terrestrial, or underwater vehicles (UXVs).

A typical performance metric used to characterize optimal sensor placement is maximum information, or equivalently, minimum entropy [9]. Maximization of a characteristic, such as the determinant, the trace, or the largest eigenvalue, of the Fisher information matrix (FIM) is another frequently used performance metric. Other metrics include the classical least squared error in parameter estimates, mutual information, Battacharya coefficients, Hellinger distance, and Kullback-Lieber divergence [9, 17, 27].

Examples of integrated approaches to estimation and control, which disregard the aforementioned separation principle, are found in the literature on guidance and coordination strategies for mobile sensor networks to maximize an information metric. In particular, target tracking and localization are widely addressed applications of mobile sensor networks [1, 13, 25]. A distinction between task- and information-driven performance metrics for parameter estimation is discussed in Ref. [18], which concludes that for a specific task such as target tracking, a task-specific performance metric (e.g., squared tracking error) is beneficial.

The literature on motion-planning and control for mobile vehicles encompasses several major approaches. Applications of optimal control theory are widely discussed for vehicle guidance [3, 7], including numerical methods for trajectory optimization [5, 14]. These methods are difficult to apply in situations involving several state constraints, such as obstacles in the vehicle's environment. The robotics literature addresses this issue by geometric path-planning algorithms based on workspace grids or cell decompositions [6, 28] and visibility roadmaps [22]. Within the last two decades, randomized sampling-based methods including probabilistic roadmaps (PRM) [16], and rapidly exploring random trees (RRT) [15, 20] have addressed efficient motion-planning in large dimensional configuration- or state spaces.

Motion-planning under uncertainty is typically formulated as a Markov Decision Process (MDP) or a partially observable MDP (POMDP), and can be solved using dynamic programming (DP) [4]. Unfortunately, a naïve implementation of DP is, in general, computationally intractable for practical applications. To this end, belief space roadmaps are discussed for motion-planning under uncertainty [2, 30]. Typical sources of uncertainty in motion-planning include motion uncertainty due to vehicle modeling errors, uncertainty in the vehicle's states due to measurement noise, and uncertainty in the environment map [19], the latter of discussed in the proposed work. The literature on simultaneous localization and mapping (SLAM) algorithms addresses [8, 21] the simultaneous reduction in uncertainty in the environment map and in the vehicle's state, by estimating parameters that describe environmental features. SLAM methods may also involve planning, typically formulated as an MDP [8] that reflects the uncertainties in the map and in the vehicle state.

19.1.2 Proposed Work and Contributions

We consider the problem of planning the path of a vehicle, which we refer to as the *actor*, to traverse a threat field with minimum threat exposure. The threat field is an unknown, time-invariant, and strictly positive scalar field defined on a compact 2D spatial domain $\mathcal{W}$. The threat field is estimated by a network of mobile sensors that can measure the threat field pointwise at their locations. All measurements are noisy. The objective is to determine a path for the actor to reach a desired goal with minimum expected threat exposure over the estimated path. A novelty of this problem setup is we seek sensor placements that minimize the actor's expected threat exposure. Future applications of this problem setup include, for example, delivery (by an actor) of emergency supplies to a remote location that lies within/beyond a region afflicted by wildfire or atmospheric contaminants (the threat field).

We formulate this problem on a grid defined on the actor's workspace, which defines a topological graph $\mathcal{G}$. The threat field is assumed to be finitely parameterized by coefficients of spatial basis functions. Least squares estimates of these parameters are constructed using measurements from the sensors and the actor. Whereas edge transitions in the graph $\mathcal{G}$ are deterministic, the transition *costs* depend on the threat field estimates, and are therefore deterministic but unknown. The sensor locations change iteratively. At each iteration, Dijkstra's algorithm is used to determine a path with minimum threat exposure in the graph $\mathcal{G}$ for the actor. Next, a set of grid points "near" this path are identified as points of interest. Finally, the next set of sensor locations is determined to maximize the confidence of threat field estimates on these points of interest, the threat field estimate is accordingly updated, and the iteration repeats.

The contributions of this Chapter are as follows. The Chapter breaks new ground in dynamic data-driven autonomy, in that an explicit bidirectional interaction between a path-planning algorithm and a sensor network are separate from the actor vehicle. Prior works in the literature have focused either on the problem of finding paths with minimum expected threat exposure (e.g. [26]) or on the problem of distributed estimation of a spatio-temporally varying scalar field (e.g. [12, 23]). To the best of the authors' knowledge, this paper is the first to consider an "orchestration" of a sensor network using graphical methods to acquire measurements *most relevant to a concurrent path-planning problem*. A prior work [32] has considered such "orchestration" of an onboard sensor, namely, gimbaled pointing of an electro-optical/infrared camera. We focus on autonomy (namely, path-planning on a grid) and a simple implementation of mobile sensor networks (namely, least-squares estimation of a finitely parameterized field) to emphasize the *interactions* between these entities. The proposed work includes the study of a heuristic method to determine a domain of the actor's interest for guiding sensor placement. We study the iterative process that results from the computation of this domain, the subsequent sensor placement, and replanning by the actor with newly acquired sensor data.

The rest of the Chapter is organized as follows. In Sect. 19.2, we introduce the main elements of the problem. In Sect. 19.3 we describe a dynamic actor-sensor interaction that results in a sensor placement strategy. In Sect. 19.4, we illustrate examples of the proposed reconfiguration strategy, and present numerical simulation results to discuss convergence of the actor-sensor interactions. We conclude the Chapter in Sect. 19.5 with comments about the future work.

19.2 Problem Formulation

Let $\mathcal{W} \subset \mathbb{R}^2$ be a closed square region, called the *workspace*, in which the actor and the sensors move. In this workspace, we formulate a grid consisting of N_G^2 uniformly placed in N_G rows and N_G columns. The coordinates in a prespecified Cartesian coordinate axis system of the ith grid point are denoted by $\mathbf{x}_i$, for each $i = 1, \ldots, N_G^2$. We consider a strictly positive scalar field $c : \mathcal{W} \rightarrow \mathbb{R}^2_{>0}$, called the *threat field*, which represents unfavorable regions with higher intensity. The actor is assumed to traverse grid points according to a "4−connectivity rule," i.e., the actor can traverse from the ith grid point to immediately adjacent grid points in the same row or the same column. In this Chapter, we neglect vehicle kinematic and dynamic constraints that can restrict this motion, while noting that such constraints can in the future be incorporated in the proposed grid-world problem setup [10]. We also assume that the actor vehicle has no uncertainties in localization or in motion on the grid: i.e., the current grid-point location of the actor is known, and the effect of moving to an adjacent grid-point is deterministic.

The actor's motion-planning problem is formulated as a graph search problem. To this end, we define a graph $\mathcal{G} = (V, E)$, where each vertex in V is uniquely associated with a grid point, and labeled with superscripts as $v^1, v^2, \ldots, v^{N_G^2}$. The edge set E is defined as the set of pairs of vertices associated with adjacent grid points. Edge transition costs are assigned by a scalar function $\bar{g} : E \rightarrow \mathbb{R}^2_{>0}$ defined as

$$\bar{g}((v^i, v^j)) = c(\mathbf{x}_j), \tag{19.1}$$

for each pair $i, j \in \{1, \ldots, N_G^2\}$, such that $(v^i, v^j) \in E$.

A *path* in the graph $\mathcal{G}$ between two prespecified vertices v^{i_s} and v^{i_g} is a sequence $\mathbf{v} = (v_0, v_1, \ldots, v_P)$, without repetition, of successively adjacent vertices with $v_0 = v^{i_s}$ and $v_P = v^{i_g}$. Note that indices of vertices in this sequence are denoted using *sub*scripts. The *cost* $\bar{\mathcal{J}}(\mathbf{v}) \in \mathbb{R}^2_{>0}$ of this path is the sum of transition costs of each edge in the path, i.e., $\bar{\mathcal{J}}(\mathbf{v}) = \sum_{k=1}^{P} \bar{g}((v_{k-1}, v_k))$. The actor's motion-planning problem is now formulated as the problem of finding a path with minimum cost between the actor's initial location at grid point $i_s \in \{1, \ldots, N_G^2\}$ and a destination grid point $i_g \in \{1, \ldots, N_G^2\}$.

Uncertainty in the actor's motion-planning problem arises from uncertainty in the knowledge of the threat field. That is to say, edge transitions in the graph $\mathcal{G}$ are deterministic, but the transition *costs*, which depend on the threat field estimates, are unknown but estimated through measurements. We assume that the threat field is finitely parameterized as

$$c(\mathbf{x}) = \sum_{n=1}^{N_P} \theta_n \phi_n(\mathbf{x}) = \Phi(\mathbf{x})\Theta, \qquad (19.2)$$

where $\phi_n : \mathcal{W} \rightarrow \mathbb{R}^2$ are prespecified spatial basis functions, $\Phi(\mathbf{x}) := [\phi_1(\mathbf{x}) \ \phi_2(\mathbf{x}) \ \ldots \ \phi_{N_P}(\mathbf{x})]$, and $\Theta := [\theta_1 \ \theta_2 \ \ldots \ \theta_{N_P}]^{\mathrm{T}}$. We assume that a finite number N_S of sensors take pointwise measurements to estimate the parameter vector Θ. These sensors are assumed to be located at grid points, and the set of these grid points is denoted by $\mathbf{s} = \{s_1, s_2, \ldots, s_{N_S}\} \subset \{1, \ldots, N_G^2\}$. The measurement taken by each sensor is $z_k := c(\mathbf{x}_{s_k}) + \eta_k$, where $\eta_k \sim \mathcal{N}(0, \sigma_k^2)$, for each $k = 1, \ldots, N_S$. Finally, we assume that the number of sensors is "small," i.e., $N_S \ll N_G^2$.

The actor can avail of the estimates of the threat field parameters, and therefore the actor's motion-planning problem is reformulated by considering estimated edge transition costs based on the measured threat field, via Eq. (19.1). Informally, the problem of interest in this Chapter is then defined as follows.

Problem 19.1 Find a set of sensor locations $\mathbf{s} := \{s_1^*, s_2^*, \ldots, s_{N_S}^*\} \subset \{1, \ldots, N_G^2\}$, and a path $\mathbf{v}^*$ in the graph $\mathcal{G}$ with minimum expected cost.

Note that this problem involves an explicit dependence between the sensor locations and the actor's motion-planning problem. It is an open research question to determine whether a set of sensor locations that optimizes a typical performance metric (e.g., trace of the FIM), also minimizes the expected cost of the actor's path. The solution of Problem 19.1 may require the formulation of a new sensor placement strategy. In what follows, we present a preliminary investigation of these issues based on simulation experiments.

19.3 Actor-Driven Sensor Reconfiguration

For a given set $\mathbf{s}_0$ of sensor locations, let $\hat{\Theta}_{\mathbf{s}_0}$ and $P_{\mathbf{s}_0}$ denote the mean and covariance matrix of the least squares estimate of the parameter Θ. Precisely:

$$\hat{\Theta}_{\mathbf{s}_0} := H^{\mathrm{L}}(\mathbf{s}_0)\mathbf{z}, \qquad (19.3)$$

$$P_{\mathbf{s}_0} := (H^{\mathrm{T}}(\mathbf{s}_0)R^{-1}H(\mathbf{s}_0))^{-1}. \qquad (19.4)$$

Here $R = \mathrm{diag}(\sigma_1^2, \ldots, \sigma_{N_S}^2)$ is the measurement error covariance matrix, $\mathbf{z} = [z_1 \ldots z_{N_S}]^{\mathrm{T}}$, and $H(\mathbf{s}_0)$ is defined as

$$H(\mathbf{s}_0) := \left[\Phi^{\mathrm{T}}(\mathbf{x}_{s_{1,0}}) \ \Phi^{\mathrm{T}}(\mathbf{x}_{s_{2,0}}) \ \ldots \ \Phi^{\mathrm{T}}(\mathbf{x}_{s_{N_S,0}}) \right]^{\mathrm{T}}.$$

Heuristic Iterative Algorithm for Path-Domain Threat Estimation

---

procedure **Initialize**
  1: Set initial sensor placement $s_0 \subset \{1, \ldots, N_G^2\}$.
  2: Execute Dijkstra's algorithm to determine $v_{s_0}^*$.
  3: Set iteration counter $\ell = 1$.

procedure **Main**
  1: **Initialize**
  2: **while** $\neg StopCondition$ **do**
  3:    Identify a minimal set $\{n_1, n_2, \ldots, n_{N_Q}\}$, with $N_Q \leqslant N_P$, such that the union
       $\mathcal{W}_Q \subseteq \mathcal{W}$ of significant support regions of the basis functions $\phi_{n_1}, \ldots, \phi_{n_{N_Q}}$
       covers all of the grid points associated with the path $v_{s_{\ell-1}}^*$.
  4:    Place sensors at grid points in the set $s_\ell \subset \{1, \ldots, N_G^2\}$ such that $x_s \in \mathcal{W}_Q$ for
       each $s \in s_\ell$.
  5:    Execute Dijkstra's algorithm to determine $v_{s_\ell}^*$.
  6:    Increment iteration counter $\ell = \ell + 1$, and evaluate $StopCondition$.

Fig. 19.1 Pseudo-code for a heuristic iterative algorithm to solve Problem 19.1

The expected cost $\mathcal{J}(\mathbf{v}) = E[\bar{\mathcal{J}}(\mathbf{v})]$ of a path $\mathbf{v} = (v_0, v_1, \ldots, v_P)$ in $\mathcal{G}$ then follows from Eq. (19.1):

$$\mathcal{J}(\mathbf{v}) := \sum_{k=1}^{P} E[\bar{g}((v_{k-1}, v_k))] = \sum_{k=1}^{P} \Phi(\mathbf{x}_k)\hat{\Theta}_{s_0}.$$

For the given set s_0 of sensor locations, the actor's motion-planning problem of finding a path $v_{s_0}^*$ in $\mathcal{G}$ with minimum expected cost can be solved using a standard path optimization algorithm such as Dijkstra's algorithm [4].

The main innovation in the proposed work is that we seek to solve Problem 19.1 by the following iterative approach. At each iteration, numbered by $\ell = 0, 1, \ldots$, we attempt to find a new set s_ℓ of sensor locations, and an associated path $v_{s_\ell}^*$ in $\mathcal{G}$ with minimum expected cost, such that

$$\lim_{\ell \to \infty} \mathcal{J}(v_{s_\ell}^*) = \bar{\mathcal{J}}(\mathbf{v}^*), \tag{19.5}$$

where $\mathbf{v}^*$ is the true optimal path. The process of finding the set s_ℓ based on the actor's optimal path $v_{s_{\ell-1}}^*$ in the previous iteration is called *sensor reconfiguration*.

A formal proof of the existence of the limit and convergence in Eq. (19.5) is beyond the scope of this Chapter. In what follows, we investigate a heuristic sensor reconfiguration strategy, and study the results of simulation experiments with this strategy.

We assume that the basis functions ϕ_n, $n = 1, \ldots, N_P$, are Gaussian functions of the form $\phi_n(\mathbf{x}) := \frac{1}{\sqrt{(2\pi)^k |\Sigma_n|}} \exp(-\frac{1}{2} \cdot (\mathbf{x} - \bar{\mathbf{x}}_n)^T \Sigma_n^{-1} (\mathbf{x} - \bar{\mathbf{x}}_n))$, where Σ_n is positive semi-definite and $\bar{x}_n \in \mathcal{W}$ are prespecified for each $n = 1, \ldots, N_P$ and in our workspace, $k = 2$. Whereas these basis functions do not have compact support in $\mathbb{R}^2$, we identify the region $\{x : \|x - \bar{x}_n\| \le 3\sqrt{|\Sigma_n|}\} \cap \mathcal{W}$ as the region of *significant support* for the basis function ϕ_n. This region of *significant support* simply reflects the rapidly decaying influence of a single basis function in the global workspace. The proposed sensor reconfiguration strategy is then described in the algorithm in Fig. 19.1.

The conceptual rationale for this algorithm is that the subregion in the workspace $\mathcal{W}$ "of interest" to the actor is relatively small. Therefore, the regions of significant support of a small number of basis functions may suffice to cover this region of the actor's interest. These basis functions are identified in Line 3 of the algorithm in Fig. 19.1. Consequently, sensors may be placed to reduce the estimation errors of the parameters associated with these basis functions, at the expense of tolerating higher estimation errors in other parameters. Specifically, these parameters are θ_{n_i}, where $i \in \{1, 2, \ldots, N_Q\}$, as defined in Line 3.

The method of sensor placement within the smaller subregion $\mathcal{W}_Q$ identified in Line 3 is a topic of ongoing research. For the simulation experiments reported in this Chapter, we choose s_ℓ (Line 4) by arbitrarily selecting N_S unique grid points within the subregion $\mathcal{W}_Q$.

The stopping criteria for this algorithm, denoted by the boolean variable *StopCondition* in Lines 2 and 6 in Fig. 19.1, are user-specified, and depend on the properties of convergence of the limit in Eq. (19.5), if such properties are known. For the simulation experiments reported in this Chapter, we adopt the simple criterion of reaching a prespecified maximum number of iterations.

19.4   Results and Discussion of Numerical Simulation Experiments

The set of simulation experiments reported in this section are all performed assuming a square workspace $\mathcal{W} = [-1, 1] \times [-1, 1]$. As previously stated, the threat field basis functions are set to be Gaussian functions. The locations of "peaks" $\bar{x}_n$ of these Gaussian functions are assigned to ensure uniform separation between peaks, and coverage of the workspace $\mathcal{W}$. The values for v_n are obtained for each experiment by sampling uniform distributions over $\mathcal{W}$ and $[0, (\frac{2}{N_P})^2]$, respectively, for each $n = 1, \ldots, N_P$. The true values of the parameters θ_n are obtained for each experiment by sampling the normal distribution $\mathcal{N}(0, 1)$. The number of grid points is fixed at $N_G^2 = 400$. The number of parameters N_P is varied between 1 and 50 for different experiments. Figure 19.2 illustrates an example of a threat field overlaid with grid points, with $N_P = 25$.

Next, we discuss the observed effects of naïve sensor placement strategies for initializing the algorithm in Fig. 19.1. For this discussion, the true threat field is the same as illustrated in Fig. 19.2. For this field, the true optimal path is shown for reference in Fig. 19.3. To compare the actor's paths resulting from the proposed

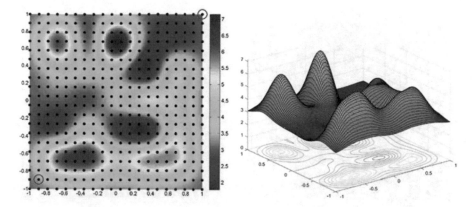

Fig. 19.2 (**Left**) The *Grid-world* overlaid with the true threat field. Sensors can occupy any of the grid point positions. The start and goal locations are marked as red circles (the start location is at the bottom-left). (**Right**) 3D visualization of true threat field where height indicates severity or intensity of threat

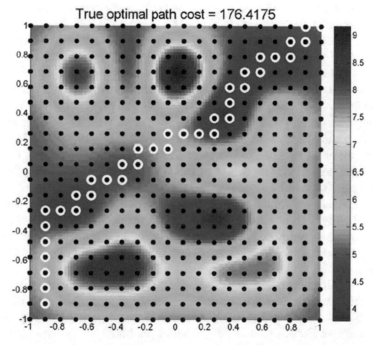

Fig. 19.3 A threat field consisting of a summation of $N_P = 25$ parameters or 25 2D Gaussian peaks. The minimum threat exposure path, shown in connected white circles, is determined as a ground-truth reference, using the true threat field

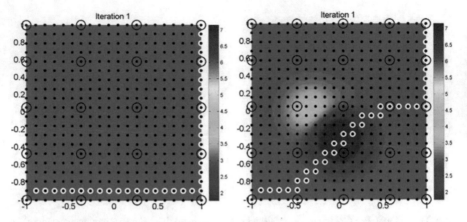

Fig. 19.4 Estimated threat field and resultant actor's path with minimum expected cost in the initialization stage of the proposed algorithm, with uniformly-spaced sensor placement: S(**Left**) $N_S = 20$. and (**Right**) $N_S = 25$

algorithm to the true optimal path, we define the *incurred cost* of the actor's path as the cost computed using the true field values.

We are interested in situations where the number of sensors N_S is comparable to the number of threat field parameters N_P. Figure 19.4 illustrates the estimated threat field when sensors are initially placed at uniformly spaced locations in the workspace. The threat field parameter estimates here are "corrected," such that if the n_{th} term on the diagonal of the covariance matrix P_{s_0} is larger than a prespecified threshold, then the parameter estimate $\hat{\theta}_n$ is set to zero. With $N_S = 20 < N_P$, all of the resulting parameter estimates are zero (left image in Fig. 19.4). With $N_S = 25 = N_P$, only two of the resulting parameter estimates are non-zero (i.e., only two out of $N_P = 25$ elements of the diagonal of matrix P_{s_0} are below the threshold). However, there is a significant difference in the incurred costs of the actor's path.

Similar results of initialization are observed for other placement strategies. Specifically, Fig. 19.5 illustrates the estimated threat field when sensor placements are initially clustered near the actor's start location. Figure 19.6 illustrates the estimated threat field when sensor are placed in a "diagonal strafing" configuration as indicated.

These initialization examples indicate significant differences in the incurred cost of the initial path of the actor for different sensor placements. Next, we discuss the iterative sensor reconfiguration proposed in the algorithm in Fig. 19.1. An objective of this discussion is to study whether the initial sensor placement affects the convergence properties of the proposed algorithm. Figure 19.7 illustrates the application of the proposed algorithm, with sensor locations ($N_S = 25$) and actor paths at several intermediate iterations (the iteration number is denoted ℓ). This example indicates a convergence of the sensor placement locations and of the actor's path. Note also that the sensor placement shown in Fig. 19.7h results in a

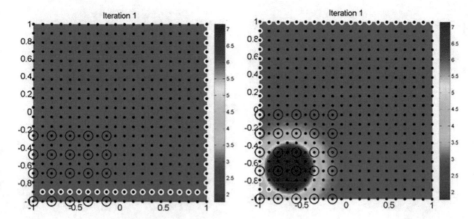

Fig. 19.5 Estimated threat field and resultant actor's path with minimum expected cost in the initialization stage of the proposed algorithm, with sensor placement clustered near the actor's start location: **(Left)** $N_S = 20$. **(Right)** $N_S = 25$

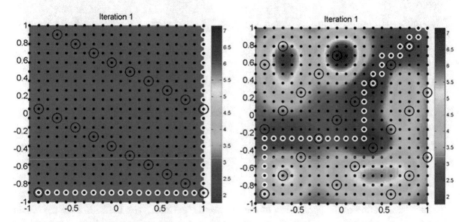

Fig. 19.6 Estimated threat field and resultant actor's path with minimum expected cost in the initialization stage of the proposed algorithm, with sensor placement in a "diagonal strafing" configuration: **(Left)** $N_S = 20$. **(Right)** $N_S = 25$

worse[1] threat field estimate compared to that obtained by the "diagonal strafing" placement shown in Fig. 19.6. However, the incurred cost of the actor's path is lower with the sensor placement in Fig. 19.7h. This observation corroborates the premise of the proposed work that actor-driven sensor placement strategies may result in performance improvements for the actor, as compared to a separated, information-driven sensor placement strategy.

---

[1] As quantified by the trace of the estimation error covariance matrix P.

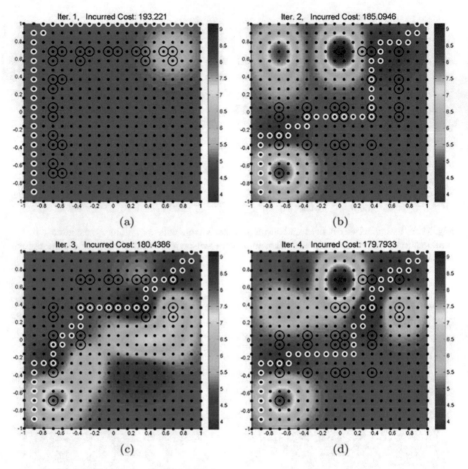

Fig. 19.7 Illustration of the application of the proposed algorithm, with indications of the sensor placement and actor's path with minimum expected cost at several intermediate iterations. (**a**) $\ell = 1$. (**b**) $\ell = 2$. (**c**) $\ell = 3$. (**d**) $\ell = 4$. (**e**) $\ell = 7$. (**f**) $\ell = 8$. (**g**) $\ell = 9$. (**h**) $\ell = 10$

In what follows, we discuss issues related to convergence and optimality (i.e., comparison of the incurred cost with the cost of the true optimal path).

We conducted simulation experiments involving the application of the algorithm in Fig. 19.1 with different combinations of N_P and N_S to observe the convergence behavior of this algorithm. Figure 19.8 shows a summary of results of these experiments for every pair (N_P, N_S) for $N_P \in \{1, 4, 9, 16, 25, 36, 49\}$, and $N_S \in \{1, 2, \ldots, 60\}$. The following three types of behaviors of the proposed algorithm are observed.

1. **Practical convergence to the true optimal path:** The incurred costs of paths found in Line 5 of the algorithm in Fig. 19.1 converge to within a "small" interval of the cost of the true optimal path. This is the desired ideal behavior of the

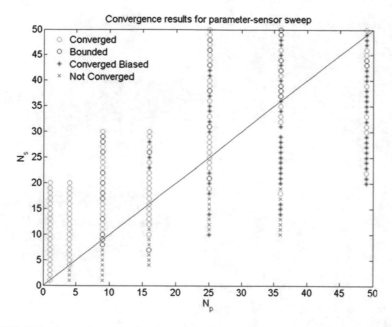

Fig. 19.8 Summary of observed convergence behavior of the proposed algorithm for various pairs (N_P, N_S)

algorithm. This behavior is typically observed in the reported simulations when N_P is relatively small and $N_S \geq N_P$. In Fig. 19.9, the pairs (N_P, N_S) at which this behavior is observed are indicated by green-colored circles. This behavior is observed to be independent of the initial sensor placement strategy. Figure 19.9 illustrates an example of the iterative and convergent changes in expected and incurred costs of the actor's path.

2. **Convergence to a sub-optimal path:** The incurred costs of paths found in Line 5 of the proposed algorithm converge to a value significantly different from the cost of the true optimal path. This behavior is typically observed in the reported simulations when the number of parameters is relatively large. In Fig. 19.9, the pairs (N_P, N_S) at which this behavior is observed are indicated by red-colored asterisk marks. Figures 19.10 and 19.11 illustrate example of the iterative and convergent changes in expected and incurred costs of the actor's path. As indicated in Fig. 19.11, the difference between the true optimal cost and the incurred cost at which the proposed algorithm converges can be large.

3. **Non-convergence or bounded oscillations:** The incurred costs of paths found in Line 5 of the proposed algorithm do not converge, but they may oscillate in a bounded interval containing the cost of the true optimal path. These two behaviors are typically observed in the reported simulations when N_P is relatively small and $N_S < N_P$. In Fig. 19.9, the pairs (N_P, N_S) at which this behavior is observed are indicated by red-colored cross marks and blue-colored circles. Figure 19.12 illustrates an example of the iterative and non-convergent changes

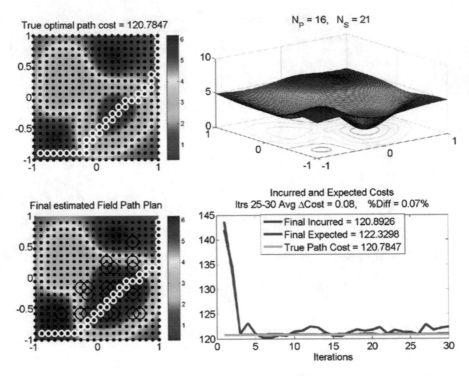

Fig. 19.9 An example illustrating practical convergence of the actor's incurred cost to the true optimal cost. Here, $N_P = 16$ and $N_S = 21$

in expected and incurred costs of the actor's path. Figure 19.13 illustrates an example of the iterative changes in expected and incurred costs with bounded oscillations.

The first two behavior types are acceptable, especially if the sub-optimality of the incurred or expected costs of the actor in the second behavior type can be theoretically bounded. At this time, we do not have such bounds available. Instead, we conducted another set of experiments to observe such sub-optimality as a function of the number of sensors and the number of parameters. Figure 19.14 shows a summary of the results of these experiments for every pair (N_P, N_S) for $N_P \in \{1, 4, 9, 16, 25, 36, 49\}$, and $N_S \in \{1, 2, \ldots, 60\}$. For each pair, five experiments were conducted with different true parameter values. Figure 19.14 indicates the percentage difference between the incurred cost of the actor's path, as determined by the proposed algorithm after 30 iterations, and the true optimal cost. The map indicated in Fig. 19.14 is obtained after interpolating values for (N_P, N_S) pairs where experiments were not conducted.

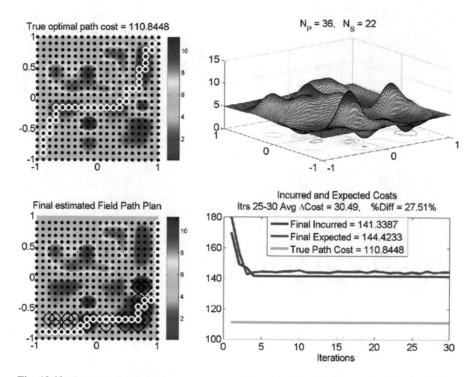

Fig. 19.10 An example illustrating convergence of the actor's incurred cost to a suboptimal value. Here, $N_P = 36$ and $N_S = 22$

The salient observations from Fig. 19.14 are as follows.

1. The observed sub-optimality is typically less than 10% in the region $N_S \geq N_P$.
2. The worst cases of sub-optimality typically occur when N_S is significantly smaller than N_P.
3. The occurrences of the second type of behavior of the proposed algorithm (i.e. convergence to a sub-optimal path) are more frequent when N_P is relatively large (specifically, greater than 25 in these experiments).
4. In the region $N_S < N_P$ close to the line $N_S = N_P$, convergence to sub-optimal paths is frequently observed. Furthermore, the observed sub-optimality is typically less than 20%.

The last observation is of particular interest: when $N_S < N_P$, a poor estimate (as measured by the trace of the estimation error covariance matrix) of the threat field is obtained, but the proposed algorithm can place these sensors such that the actor's motion-planning problem can yet be solved without significant sub-optimality. For example, with $N_P = 36$ and with N_S as low as 20, no more than 10% sub-optimality was observed in the actor's path.

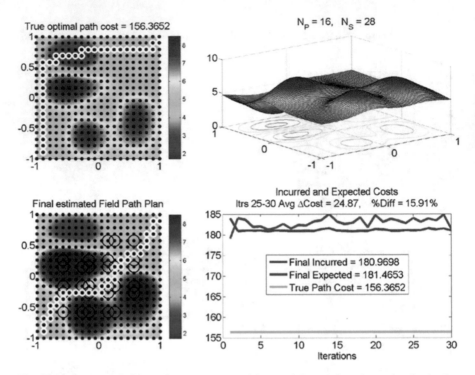

Fig. 19.11 An example illustrating convergence of the actor's incurred cost to a suboptimal value. Here, $N_P = 16$ and $N_S = 28$

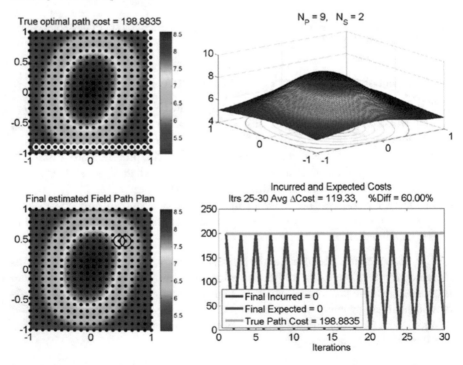

Fig. 19.12 An example illustrating non-convergent behavior of the proposed algorithm. Here, $N_P = 9$ and $N_S = 2$

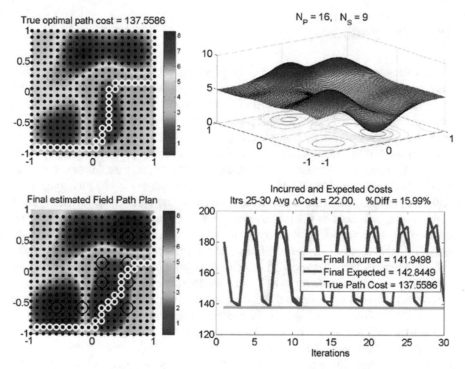

Fig. 19.13 An example illustrating bounded oscillations of the actor's incurred cost near the true optimal cost. Here, $N_P = 16$ and $N_S = 9$

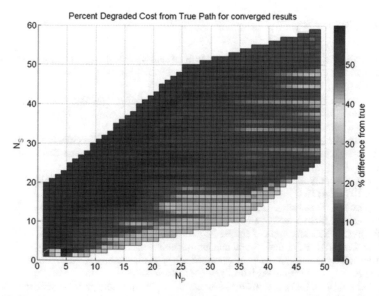

Fig. 19.14 Summary of observed sub-optimality of actor paths resulting from the proposed algorithm for various pairs (N_P, N_S)

19.5 Conclusions

In this Chapter, we discussed a motion-planning problem where the decision-making entity, namely, the actor, is allowed to influence the placement of sensors that provide measurements in the actor's environment. We proposed a specific and heuristic algorithm to change sensor placements iteratively, and in conjunction with the solution of the motion-planning problem. The premise of the proposed approach is that an actor-driven sensor placement sensor placement strategy can improve the actor's performance compared to a typical strategy that places sensors to maximize the information collected. We presented results of simulation experiments with the proposed algorithm. The salient observations were of different types of convergence behaviors of the proposed algorithm, including non-convergence, and of varying levels of sub-optimality of the resultant paths, with different pairs of (N_S, N_P). Future work includes the theoretical characterization of regions in the (N_S, N_P) plane where the proposed algorithm can be shown to converge, and of sub-optimality bounds in these regions. The characterization of the actor's performance improvements with the proposed dynamic actor-sensor interactions in comparison with a information-maximizing sensor placement strategy is also of interest.

Current and future work includes addressing the issue of non-convergence through modification of the least squares estimator, adding stopping criteria based on the sensor repositioning, and identifying relevant subdomain for sensor placement via spatial correlation techniques.

References

1. N. Adurthi, P. Singla, Information driven optimal sensor control for efficient target localization and tracking, in *Proceedings of the 2014 American Control Conference*, Portland, 2014, pp. 610–615
2. R. Alterovitz, T. Siméon, K. Goldberg, The stochastic motion roadmap: a sampling framework for planning with markov motion uncertainty, in *Proceedings of Robotics: Science and Systems* (RSS), Atlanta, MA, USA, 2007
3. M. Athans, P.L. Falb, *Optimal Control* (Dover Publications Inc., Mineola, NY, USA, 2007)
4. D.P. Bertsekas, *Dynamic Programming and Optimal Control* (Athena Scientific, Belmont, 2000)
5. J.T. Betts, Survey of numerical methods for trajectory optimization. J. Guid. Control Dyn. **21**(2), 193–204 (1998)
6. R.A. Brooks, T. Lozano-Pérez, A subdivision algorithm in configuration space for findpath with rotation. IEEE Trans. Syst. Man Cybern. **SMC-15**(2), 224–233 (1985)
7. A.E. Bryson, Y.C. Ho, *Applied Optimal Control* (Taylor & Francis, New York, 1975)
8. S. Chakravorty, R. Saha, Simultaneous planning localization and mapping: a hybrid Bayesian/frequentist approach, in *Proceedings of the American Control Conference*, 2008, pp. 1226–1231. https://doi.org/10.1109/ACC.2008.4586660
9. D. Cochran, A.O. Hero, Information-driven sensor planning: navigating a statistical manifold, in *2013 IEEE Global Conference on Signal and Information Processing, GlobalSIP 2013 – Proceedings*, pp. 1049–1052. https://doi.org/10.1109/GlobalSIP.2013.6737074

10. R.V. Cowlagi, P. Tsiotras, Hierarchical motion planning with dynamical feasibility guarantees for mobile robotic vehicles. IEEE Trans. Robot. **28**(2), 379–395 (2012)

11. M.A. Demetriou, D. Ucinski, State estimation of spatially distributed processes using mobile sensing agents, in *American Control Conference (ACC)*, Jan 2011, San Francisco, CA, USA, pp. 1770–1776

12. M. Demetriou, N. Gatsonis, J. Court, Coupled controls-computational fluids approach for the estimation of the concentration from a moving gaseous source in a 2-d domain with a Lyapunov-guided sensing aerial vehicle. IEEE Trans. Control Syst. Technol. **22**(3), 853–867 (2013). https://doi.org/10.1109/TCST.2013.2267623

13. N. Farmani, L. Sun, D. Pack, Optimal UAV sensor management and path planning for tracking. *The ASME 2014 Dynamic System and Control Conferences*, 2014, pp. 1–8. https://doi.org/10.1115/DSCC2014-6232

14. D. Garg, M. Patterson, W.W. Hager, A.V. Rao, D.A. Benson, G.T. Huntington, A unified framework for the numerical solution of optimal control problems using pseudospectral methods. Automatica **46**, 1843–1851 (2010)

15. S. Karaman, E. Frazzoli, Sampling-based algorithms for optimal motion planning. Int. J. Robot. Res. **30**(7), 846–894 (2011). https://doi.org/10.1177/0278364911406761

16. L.E. Kavraki, P. Švestka, J.C. Latombe, M.H. Overmars, Probabilistic roadmaps for path planning in high-dimensional configuration spaces. IEEE Trans. Robot. Autom. **12**(4), 566–580 (1996)

17. A. Krause, A. Singh, C. Guestrin, Near-optimal sensor placements in gaussian processes: theory, efficient algorithms and empirical studies. J. Mach. Learn. Res. **9**, 235–284 (2008). https://doi.org/10.1145/1102351.1102385

18. C. Kreucher, A.O. Hero, K. Kastella, A comparison of task driven and information driven sensor management for target tracking, in *Proceedings of the 44th IEEE Conference on Decision and Control, and the European Control Conference, CDC-ECC'05*, 2005, pp. 4004–4009. https://doi.org/10.1109/CDC.2005.1582788

19. H. Kurniawati, T. Bandyopadhyay, N.M. Patrikalakis, Global motion planning under uncertain motion, sensing, and environment map. Auton. Robot. **33**(3), 255–272 (2012). https://doi.org/10.1007/s10514-012-9307-y

20. S.M. LaValle, J.J. Kuffner Jr., Randomized kinodynamic planning. Int. J. Robot. Res. **20**(5), 378–400 (2001)

21. R. Lerner, E. Rivlin, I. Shimshoni, Landmark selection for task-oriented navigation. IEEE Trans. Robot. **23**(3), 494–505 (2007). https://doi.org/10.1109/TRO.2007.895070

22. T. Lozano-Pérez, An algorithm for planning collision-free paths among polyhedral obstacles. Commun. ACM **22**(10), 560–570 (1979)

23. R. Madankan, S. Pouget, P. Singla, M. Bursik, J. Dehn, M. Jones, A. Patra, M. Pavolonis, E.B. Pitman, T. Singh, P. Webley, Computation of probabilistic hazard maps and source parameter estimation for volcanic ash transport and dispersion. J. Comput. Phys. **271**, 39–59 (2014)

24. S. Martinez, Distributed interpolation schemes for field estimation by mobile sensor networks. IEEE Trans. Control Syst. Technol. **18**(2), 491–500 (2010). https://doi.org/10.1109/TCST.2009.2017028

25. S. Martinez, F. Bullo, Optimal sensor placement and motion coordination for target tracking. Automatica **42**(4), 661–668 (2006). https://doi.org/10.1016/j.automatica.2005.12.018

26. N. Meuleau, C. Plaunt, D. Smith, T. Smith, A comparison of risk sensitive path planning methods for aircraft emergency landing, in *ICAPS-09: Proceedings of the Workshop on Bridging the Gap Between Task And Motion Planning*, Thessaloniki, Greece, 2009, pp. 71–80

27. B. Mu, L. Paull, M. Graham, J. How, J. Leonard, Two-stage focused inference for resource-constrained collision-free navigation. *Proceedings of Robotics: Science and Systems*, Rome, Italy, 2015. https://doi.org/10.15607/RSS.2015.XI.004

28. N.J. Nilsson, *Artificial Intelligence: A New Synthesis* (Morgan Kauffman Publishers Inc., San Francisco, 1998)

29. S.L. Padula, R.K. Kincaid, Optimization strategies actuator placement sensor and actuator placement. NASA Report, Apr 1999
30. R. Prentice, N. Roy, The belief roadmap: efficient planning in belief space by factoring the covariance. Int. J. Robot. Res. **28**(11–12), 1448–1465 (2009)
31. R. Siegwart, I.R. Nourbakhsh, D. Scaramuzza, Introduction to autonomous mobile robots (MIT Press, Cambridge, 2011)
32. P. Skoglar, J. Nygards, M. Ulvklo, Concurrent path and sensor planning for a uav – towards an information based approach incorporating models of environment and sensor, in *IEEE International Conference on Intelligent Robots and Systems*, 2006, pp. 2436–2442. https://doi.org/10.1109/IROS.2006.281685
33. D. Ucinski, Sensor network scheduling for identification of spatially distributed processes, in *Conference on Control and Fault-Tolerant Systems, SysTol'10 – Final Program and Book of Abstracts*, vol. 20(3), 2010, pp. 493–504. https://doi.org/10.1109/SYSTOL.2010.5675945

Part VII
Energy-Aware: Power Systems

Chapter 20
Energy-Aware Dynamic Data-Driven Distributed Traffic Simulation for Energy and Emissions Reduction

Michael Hunter, Aradhya Biswas, Bhargava Chilukuri, Angshuman Guin, Richard Fujimoto, Randall Guensler, Jorge Laval, Haobing Liu, SaBra Neal, Philip Pecher, and Michael Rodgers

Abstract An approach is described to apply the dynamic data-driven application systems (DDDAS) paradigm to reduce fuel consumption and emissions in surface transportation systems. This approach includes algorithms and distributed simulations to predict space-time trajectories of onroad vehicles. Given historical and real-time measurement data from the road network, computation resources residing in the vehicle generate speed/acceleration profiles used to estimate fuel consumption and emissions. These predictions are used to suggest energy-efficient routes to the driver. Because many components of the envisioned DDDAS system operate on mobile computing devices, a distributed computing architecture and energy-efficient middleware and simulations are proposed to maximize battery life. Energy and emissions modeling and mobile client power measurements are also discussed.

Keywords Vehicle activity monitoring · Energy and emissions modeling · Distributed simulation · Transportation systems

20.1 Introduction

According to the US Energy Information Administration, motor gasoline fuel consumption comprised 29% of all energy carbon dioxide emissions in the U.S. in 2015 [1]. One approach to help reduce this significant source of energy consumption and pollution is to provide drivers with information and travel recommendations

---

M. Hunter · B. Chilukuri · A. Guin · R. Guensler · J. Laval · H. Liu · M. Rodgers
School of Civil & Environmental Engineering, Georgia Institute of Technology, Atlanta, GA, USA

A. Biswas · R. Fujimoto (✉) · S. Neal · P. Pecher
School of Computational Science & Engineering, Georgia Institute of Technology, Atlanta, GA, USA
e-mail: fujimoto@cc.gatech.edu

© The Author(s), under exclusive license to Springer Nature Switzerland AG 2022
E. P. Blasch et al. (eds.), *Handbook of Dynamic Data Driven Applications Systems*,
https://doi.org/10.1007/978-3-030-74568-4_20

in real time to facilitate energy efficient travel decisions. This chapter describes an energy aware DDDAS based system architecture implemented on mobile computing devices that offers the potential to provide up-to-date, adaptive assessments of emissions and fuel consumption based on dynamic data.

Dynamic Data Driven Application Systems (DDDAS) continuously monitor, analyze, and adapt operational systems in order to better assess and/or optimize their behavior or improve the monitoring system [2]. DDDAS has been applied to many areas including natural disaster management, transportation and manufacturing, among others [3–5]. This chapter describes recent results in developing DDDAS technologies and applying them to transportation system management. Prior work in this multi-year study focused on the development of data-driven distributed simulation techniques and application of the DDDAS paradigm to traffic management problems to address congestion issues [6, 7]. The results described here focus on using DDDAS to reduce emission and fuel consumption.

The ubiquity of mobile computing devices such as smart phones and in-vehicle devices make them an attractive platform for realizing DDDAS-based traveler-assistance systems. In such systems, drivers' smartphones act as traffic condition sensors and can serve as computation engines in addition to displaying information to the user. However, the performance and power limitations of mobile processors are a significant concern. While mobile platforms continue to improve in performance and battery life, battery management and performance will remain an issue for some time. Alternatively, fully-vehicle-embedded systems are able to provide ample computational performance and practically unlimited power, but sacrifice the versatility of the full-mobile platform, particularly limiting the system's usefulness in multi-mode travel. Hence, *power-aware mobile systems management* will remain a critical issue, motivating the need for efficient algorithms and careful management of communications without sacrificing accuracy.

Figure 20.1 depicts the overall approach that is envisioned. The objective of the system is to provide the driver with information regarding fuel-efficient, emission-friendly routes. To achieve this goal the driver first supplies the intended destination (and origin if different from the driver's current location) to the client computer, in this case, a smartphone (*Step 1* in Fig. 20.1). The client identifies potential routes for the indicated origin-destination pair and then computes the predicted vehicle space-time trajectory (i.e., second-by-second vehicle position-speed-time) along each potential route (*Step 2*). Next, fuel consumption and emissions are determined for each route (Step 3). Finally, the driver is presented with the route alternatives, along with corresponding travel times, fuel consumption, and emissions values (Step 4), for use in route decision making.

To accomplish these tasks cached on the phone are requisite background data, such as maps and historical traffic information. In addition, as approximately 75% of travel is repetitive, the client maintains subscriptions to a base set of relevant dynamic online data sources for typical travel routes (home-to-work, home-to-school, etc.) (see Fig. 20.1). The smartphone requests supplemental data from one or more online data sources for those links not in the maintained cached data. Historic and dynamic data are stored in a *space-time memory* within a maintained server

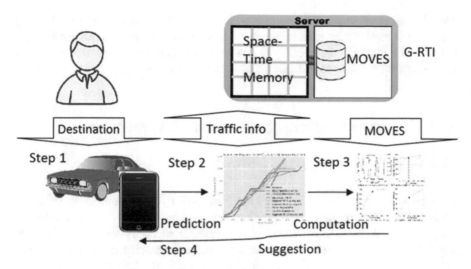

Fig. 20.1 System architecture for computing fuel-efficient, emission-friendly routes

as will be discussed later. In-client simulation or statistical models determine high-resolution vehicle trajectories. This effort currently utilizes two approaches. In most cases, a "Bayesian Inference" (conditional probability) model based on historic and near-real time trajectories is used. In cases where exceptional road conditions exist, such as the presence of a recent accident or unexpected road blockage, sufficient reliable data for the Bayesian model may not be available. In these instances, a microscopic traffic simulation supplements the historical projections. In either case, real-time traffic information is continually updated and passed to clients as needed to improve predictions.

The *MOtor Vehicle Emissions Simulator (MOVES) Matrix modeling approach* [15] is applied to vehicle trajectories to compute second-by-second or link-based fuel consumption and emissions. The methodology takes into account vehicle-specific information such as vehicle classification and model year, and roadway-specific information such as road classification and roadway grade. The specific elements required for these MOVES-Matrix client-level calculations are cached on the mobile device and periodically updated from the server.

Finally, a distributed simulation middleware termed the Green Runtime Infrastructure (G-RTI) provides communications services to interconnect these components. The design of both the middleware and client computations seek to maximize battery life. The concurrent and temporally-evolving data streams requested by the clients motivate the use of a dynamic space-time memory (STM) data structure on the server. The STM contains the historic information about network element performance over time used in the simulation modeling of route alternatives.

This chapter provides an overview of the envisioned approach. The first section presents the two approaches to predict the vehicle trajectory over its route: (1) a cellular automata-based microscopic traffic simulation and (2) a Bayesian inference model. Next is a discussion of energy consumption and emissions modeling. Finally, the power-aware system architecture is presented, along with communication and computation tradeoffs. Specifically described is the G-RTI development supporting the deployment of the proposed DDDAS system on energy-constrained devices.

20.2   Research Components: Models and Architecture

20.2.1   Cellular Automata Modeling

Cellular Automata (CA) models were first proposed by Von Neumann in 1952 [9]. Their popularity in traffic flow simulation increased after Nagel and Schreckenberg proposed simple rules to replicate traffic dynamics on transportation networks in 1992 [10]. Their simple rule-based design enabled efficient simulation of large-scale networks. Since then, various versions of CA-based methods have been developed for traffic flow modeling.

The kinematic wave (KW) model is a popular traffic flow model based on the classical hydrodynamic theory of Lighthill, Witham [11] and Richards [12]. The KW model is a scalar conservation law for the density of vehicles on a road supplemented with a fundamental diagram that gives flow as a function of local traffic density. The KW model is the simplest traffic flow model able to capture congestion dynamics such as the propagation of stop-and-go waves in traffic.

Daganzo [13] showed that a particular CA model gives vehicle trajectories as predicted by the kinematic wave model with a triangular fundamental diagram. We implement this CA model in the CA-Simulation application and extend the CA model to include multiple vehicle classes, their bounded accelerations, and lane changing.

As with all microscopic models, our CA-Simulation application needs traffic data, geometric data, control data, driver behavior data, etc. (see Fig. 20.2) to simulate the traffic dynamics of each vehicle. In the CA-simulation, each lane of the roadway section is discretized spatially; i.e., divided longitudinally into cells of jam-spacing length (that is a cell length is set as the length of a single vehicle plus the gap to the next vehicle, in breakdown (stop) conditions). A vehicle occupies a single cell and its position and speed are updated in discrete time steps. The

Fig. 20.2 CA-simulation
input data collections

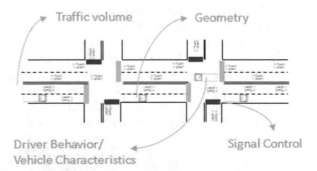

current CA-simulation implementation models three classes of vehicles; passenger cars, high performance cars (i.e. higher acceleration), and trucks. Class-specific vehicle kinematics models are used to predict vehicle accelerations as a function of the speed when unobstructed by the leading vehicle. The lane-changing model implemented in this application is based on velocity incentive, i.e., vehicles change lanes if they perceive an improvement to their speeds due to the lane-changing maneuver. The pseudocode given below describes the CA-simulation steps in more detail.

20.2.1.1   Methodology

In CA models, a vehicle occupies one or multiple cells of the matrix (link) depending on the desired resolution of speed and position updates (needless to say, single vehicle-single cell models require fewer computations than the single vehicle-multiple cell models). In this research, a single vehicle-single cell model is used (for maximum computational efficiency) with a cell size (Δx) of 22 feet and time step (Δt) of 1.2 seconds, i.e. the speed increment ($\Delta x/\Delta t$) of 12.5 miles per hour (mph). Thus, for a roadway with a speed limit of 50 mph, the free flow speed for a vehicle is 4 cells (50 mph/12.5 mph), i.e. the vehicle can move *up to* 4 cells during the next time step. Thus, the current speed of a vehicle is represented in terms of the number of cells it can reach in the next time step.

The CA-Simulation application has three vehicle classes, passenger cars, high performance cars, and trucks and implements their class-specific acceleration models (also called bounded accelerations). The acceleration model is a linearly decreasing function of speed with class-specific values for the intercept and the slope. A vehicle's current velocity is used to determine the acceleration rate from the model to determine its velocity in the next time step, i.e., the number of cells a vehicle can move in the next step. For example, if a vehicle is stopped, it cannot attain its free flow speed in the next time step but will require multiple time steps. In this implementation trucks have the lowest acceleration rates and high performance vehicles the highest.

Lane changing is implemented in the CA-Simulation based on the velocity incentive, i.e., perceived velocity improvement due to the lane changing maneuver. At every time step, each vehicle will first estimate its "desired speed" (i.e. the maximum speed allowed on the roadway or the highest speed the vehicle may achieve without exceeding the maximum speed) in the next time step using its current speed and the class-specific acceleration model. Then, it will check the location of the preceding vehicle to determine if it can achieve its desired speed. If the desired speed cannot be achieved, it will check for the possibility of a lane change maneuver to improve its speed. The vehicle position and speed are updated every time step until the user defined termination criteria is achieved.

Figure 20.3 shows sample vehicle trajectory in space and time from the CA-simulation (without bounded acceleration) which closely represents the traffic

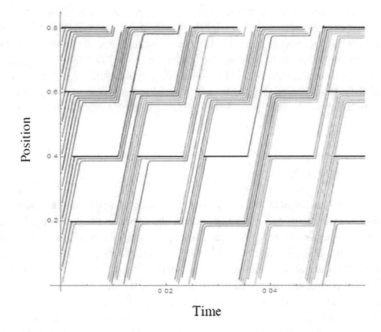

Fig. 20.3 Sample cellular automata results

dynamics on a signalized corridor. The horizontal axis is time, and the vertical axis vehicle position along the test corridor.

The CA modeling approach has several drawbacks in the context of the current application, including requiring a significant quantity of input data to drive the model and that the model is computationally complex. Also, the CA approach requires simulation of all the vehicles on the corridor to obtain the trajectory prediction of the client vehicle, necessary for the client energy consumption and emissions estimates. The Bayesian inference approach (described next) seeks to provide client trajectory predication with fewer data demands, focusing on the client trajectory without direct simulation of the other corridor vehicles. Thus, for the client application the CA-simulation may be limited to non-recurrent congestion scenarios such as accidents where the Bayesian inference approach may be insufficient.

20.2.2   Bayesian Inference Approach

The Bayesian Inference approach seeks to utilize historic and near-real time data to construct a predicted trajectory of the client. In the current implementation, the Bayesian Inference approach implementation is on a segment-by-segment basis, where a segment consists of the section of roadway between two adjacent intersections and the downstream intersection. The overall vehicle trajectory is then the accumulation of the predicted vehicle trajectories over each traversed segment. In this current effort only arterial corridors are considered, although other segment definitions could be considered, such as between freeway ramp junctions. In the least-informed approach, trajectory prediction uses simple averaging or sampling of the segment historic or near-real time data. However, alternatives are explored where a given segment trajectory prediction may be conditioned on other predicted or near-real time behavior such as stopping (e.g., was the vehicle predicted to stop at an upstream intersection?), path similarity (e.g., sample only vehicles with similar upstream or downstream routes), or other trip variables.

Implementation In the implementation of the Bayesian Inference models, a *routing table* defines what road segments a given vehicle will traverse for a given route, in time order. An example of a routing table is R = [4, 3, 2], where the numbers encode roadway segments. The routes are determined based on the driver input origin-destination pair.

In several of the prediction models, a *trail* (also, called *history*, *window*, or *subsequence* in other literature) of realized random variables is used in the prediction of the vehicle trajectory for a segment. For example, if a vehicle is predicted to stop at a segment intersection the likelihood of stopping at the downstream segment intersection will be conditioned on the realization of a stop at the upstream intersection. In some prediction models, the trail is multidimensional and contains multiple random variables (stops and time at crawl speed, for example). The *key type* in each model defines the random variable(s) used for the respective model.

The variable *segment_trail* $(-k)$ expresses a past trail of segment identifiers of length k, up to, but not including the current segment. For example, an instance of *segment_trail* (-2) for Segment 3 may be [1,2,3]. In other words, the vehicle has traversed Segments 1 and 2 and now needs information about its potential behavior on Segment 3, conditioned on it previous path. As another example an instance of *segment_trail* $(+2)$ for Segment 3 may be [3,4,5]. In other words, the vehicle will traverse Segments 4 and 5 in the future, and now some information about its potential behavior on Segment 3 is desired, conditioned on its future path.

Different models may use different trail lengths, referred to here as a *lag*; this is sometimes referred to as *depth* and *order*. For instance, we may condition the likelihood of stopping on a given segment by the predicted stopping on the previous k segments. In the subsequent discussions, *M(k)* will refer to a *Markovian* predictor that has a lag of k. Although most of the investigated random processes are unlikely to be memoryless, in this effort models are referred to as being Markovian by collapsing the current trail into the current state, even if the Markov property is still violated for lower lag values. Hash tables are used for some of the models, which are keyed by the exact match of the trail (of some random variable(s) over a window of size *lag*). Currently the returned value is a mean value obtained from observations in the training set that share the same trail.

The current prediction models make use of a kinematics tuple in the format *<mean running time, mean running speed, mean crawl time, mean crawl speed>* (abbreviated in variable format as $<t_r, v_r, t_c, v_c>$), defined below:

- *Mean crawl time* refers to the average time the vehicle spends on a segment at a speed of less than 5 mph, including time stopped.
- *Mean crawl speed* refers to the average speed of the vehicle on the segment while its speed is less than 5 mph.
- *Mean running time* and *mean running speed* are defined in terms of the velocity complement (over 5 mph) of the preceding definitions, respectively.

It is important to distinguish these categories to generate accurate predictions of emissions. A vehicle trajectory is constructed by accumulating the predicted speeds v_i for time Δt_i, for all i over trip duration T. Where v_i is the speed over Δt_i at time step t_i of the total trip time $\mathbf{T}$. Thus, the sum of Δt_i over all i is $\mathbf{T}$. For example, the predicted segment vehicle trajectory represented by kinematic tuple <22, 35, 12, 3> would be the vehicle traveling at 35 mph for 22 seconds followed by 3 mph for 12 seconds. The next traversed segment's kinematic tuple represents the next portion of the vehicle trip.

Global Segment Estimation This method seeks to predict vehicle trajectories using the global (historic) average travel times and speeds of prior vehicles that traverse a segment during a similar time period (e.g., peak travel period data). During the training phase, the kinematics tuple is updated for each observed segment. There is no further conditioning; the key consists solely of the segment identification number (*id*). During the training phase, the data structure being populated is *segment_to_kinematics_tuple*, which is keyed by segment *id* and has values $<t_r,$ $v_r, t_c, v_c>$. During the testing phase, a vehicle's segment routing table is supplied to the prediction model in its sequential ordering. To produce a trajectory for each segment the segments kinematics tuple is retrieved, i.e., the mean running speed and the mean running time, followed by the mean crawl speed and the mean crawl time. The trip trajectory is then constructed through the accumulation of the individual segment trajectories.

Local(n) Segment Estimation This method is similar to the Global Segment Estimation, although it reduces data needs by using only the data from the *n*-most-recent vehicles to traverse the segment, rather than all historical data. During the training phase, the predicted kinematics tuple is estimated from the preceding *n* vehicles that traversed each particular segment. The *segment_to_kinematics_tuple* is again keyed by segment *id* and also has floating point values $<t_r, v_r, t_c, v_c>$. During the testing phase, the vehicle trip trajectory is then constructed in the same manner as in the Global Segment Estimation, however, using the Local(*n*) Segment Estimation kinematics tuples.

Segment M(−k) Estimation This method seeks to improve the prediction for a client vehicle by sampling only those vehicles that travel the same *k* prior segments. During the training phase, the kinematics tuple $<t_r, v_r, t_c, v_c>$ over the considered segment is estimated for each segment trail of lag k. An example (for $k = 2$) is <[1, 2, 3]> which means that the vehicle has traversed Segment 1 and 2; the relevant segment for the kinematics information extraction and tuple update is Segment 3, as this is the last element (i.e., the segment of interest) in the segment trail. The data structure is segment_trail_to_kinematics_tuple, which is keyed by segment_trail(k) (a vector) and has values <t_r, v_r, t_c, v_c> (i.e., the kinematics tuple). During the testing phase, the segment routing table of each tested vehicle is supplied to the prediction model. The vehicle trip trajectory is then constructed in the same manner as in the Global Segment Estimation, however, using the Segment $M(-k)$ Estimation kinematics tuples.

Segment $M(+k)$ Estimation Ignoring Stops This is identical to the previous model, with the exception that the conditioning for each segment occurs over the future routing table. For example (if $k = 2$), [3, 4, 5] supplied as a key from a test vehicle means that we wish to obtain the kinematics tuple for Segment 3 given that the vehicle will traverse Segments 4 and 5 immediately thereafter.

Segment $M(-k)$ Estimation Including Stops Here stop information, is included in the conditioning, attempting to further improve prediction by not only conditioning on similar paths but also on similar stop histories on those paths. During the training phase, *the kinematics tuple* <t_r, v_r, t_c, v_c> over the considered segment is estimated for each stopped-segment trail of lag k. An example (for k = 2) is <[1, 2, 3], [true, false]>, which means that the vehicle has traversed Segment 1 and 2, and has stopped in Segment 1 (the first element of the stop list is true), but not Segment 2 (the second element is false); the relevant segment for the kinematics information extraction and tuple update is Segment 3, as this is the last element (i.e., the segment of interest) in the segment trail. The data structure is segment_stop_trail_to_kinematics_tuple, which is keyed by <segment_trail(k), stopped_trail(k)> (each of these is a vector) and has values <t_r, v_r, t_c, v_c>. During the testing phase, the segment routing table along with the stop history of each tested vehicle is supplied to the prediction model. The dimensionality of the input is larger as the conditioning occurs over not only the visited segments, but also the stop history of the visited segments. Upon querying, only the point estimates generated from the training set that share the exact segment trail and stop history of the visited segments are considered. During the testing phase, the vehicle trip trajectory is then constructed in the same manner as in the Global Segment Estimation.

Evaluation For the evaluation of these models, we used the Federal Highway Administrations Next Generation Simulation (NGSIM) data. This data contains high-resolution vehicle trajectory data collected for enhancing existing traffic flow models and developing new microscopic models [8]. The current efforts utilize NGSIM data collected on the Peachtree Street in Atlanta, Georgia, between 10th Street and 14th Street. The section is approximately 2100 feet in length, with five intersections and two to three arterial through lanes in each direction. Figure 20.4 depicts the section. The speed limit on this corridor is 35 mph with multiple midblock driveways. The data were collected from 4:00 p.m. to 4:15 p.m. on

Fig. 20.4 Peachtree Street from 10th Street to 14th Street. (Map data: Google, 2018)

November 8, 2006, at a resolution of 10 frames per second. These data provide complete coverage of all vehicle trajectories on this section of roadway, during the specified time, resulting in one of the most robust data sets available. In the current evaluation of the models, only NGSIM vehicle trip trajectories that cover the entirety of all segments traversed are considered. This avoids the complication of incomplete trajectories in the tables. Most of these trajectories have [1, 2, 3, 4, 5]-realized segment routing tables (i.e., the entire corridor is visited). Future efforts will expand to include vehicles that with partial segment data.

The NGSIM data was used to "train" the model (to establish conditional performance distributions), allowing each model to run and predict vehicle trajectories. While robust, the NGSIM is limited in size so this effort does not reserve a subset of the data for comparison to the predictions. Current efforts are limited to a comparison of the quality of the prediction with the training data. However, ongoing efforts are using simulated data sets and probe vehicle data to further explore the robustness of the predicted trajectories.

Data Preprocessing The NGSIM data were first loaded into client memory by using a table data structure. To provide the segment prediction models with the required point estimates, dictionaries are first populated to map segment identifiers to mean velocities and mean travel times. The latter is calculated by counting the number of rows (in the table) along each specific segment id, for each vehicle id (each row corresponds to a tenth-of-a-second). Further, the minimum and maximum y-coordinates for each segment are extracted from the dataset.

Vehicle Trajectory Generation Before control is given to the main training and testing loops, the predicted and actual trajectory containers, as well as the Markov tables are initialized. In the first main loop structure, the first and last row for each considered vehicle in the NGSIM data are first obtained. The direction of travel and all visited intersections along a trajectory are saved for each vehicle. The relevant Markov tables are populated and the actual trajectory is stored in a container. As mentioned previously, the kinematics tuple is the central piece of information used for the models. It contains point estimates for the stop duration, the stop velocity,

Fig. 20.5 Flow graph of trajectory generation procedure for a single segment

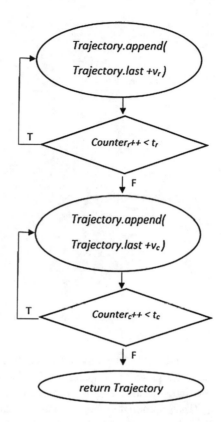

the running duration, and the running velocity. The trajectories are built segment-by-segment. The following subroutine shows how this is accomplished for a given segment. The inputs are `kinematics`, the kinematics tuple, and `trajectory`, a reference to the working trajectory being built. Figure 20.5 shows how the trajectories are generated for a specific segment using the variable names from the kinematics tuple.

First, the trajectory is augmented, for each tenth-of-a-second (0.1 second) timestep, with the displacement values inferred from the run speed point estimate of the kinematics tuple (v_r) over the expected run duration (t_r). Second, the vehicle's trajectory is extended with the crawl movement over the expected crawl duration. The model assumes that vehicles first travel in an unobstructed fashion, and then slow down in response to intersection queues. For each tenth-of-a-second within each interval, the procedure takes the last accumulated displacement that was appended and adds the next value to it. In this case, the value is based upon the historical travel speeds (v_r and v_c) across the segment. Both crawling and running could occur on the same segment. Further, the stopping speed (i.e., speed less than 5 mph) is inferred from historical information across that segment.

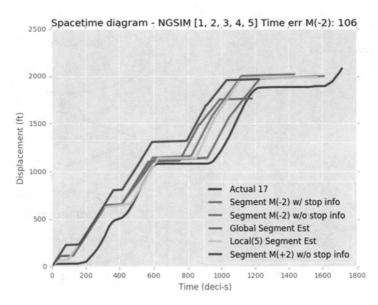

Fig. 20.6 Actual and predicted trajectories in the space-time diagram

Figure 20.6 shows the observed NGSIM trajectory of Vehicle 17 in red, along with the predicted trajectories for Vehicle 17; the line colors for the respective prediction models may be decoded by the included legend.

The accumulated displacement of the vehicle is plotted against the elapsed travel time. The given vehicle traversed all five segments of the data set. The predicted trajectories appear to capture the overall behavior of Vehicle 17 from 40 seconds to 120 seconds. The underpredicted crawl duration, during the first 20 seconds, in Segment 1 results in overestimation of the displacement throughout the trajectory (for all the models). The deceleration curves of the actual trajectory are relatively smooth compared to the predicted trajectories. Future research is aimed at resolving both these issues: the accurate modeling of intersection stop times, as well as the smoothing of the deceleration curves.

20.3   Energy and Emission Modeling with MOVES-Matrix

MOVES-Matrix is a high performance vehicle fuel and emission modeling system based entirely on the U.S. Environmental Protection Agencies' MOtor Vehicle Emissions Simulator (MOVES) model [14]. To develop the MOVES-Matrix, MOVES was run more than one hundred thousand times to obtain multiple arrays of emission rates for all combinations of MOVES input variables, including engine load bins, vehicle types, model age, fuel types, calendar year, temperature, humidity, fuel supplies, and the regional inspection and maintenance strategy. These emission

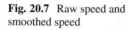

Fig. 20.7 Raw speed and smoothed speed

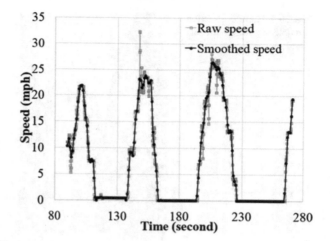

rates are stored in MOVES-Matrix. Use of MOVES Matrix allows for significant decrease in computational time (approximately 200 times faster) required to determine fuel and emissions for a vehicle trip while generating the exact same results as MOVES (the regulatory emission model approved by the U.S. Environmental Protection Agency (USEPA)) [14]. More details on setup and implementation of MOVES-Matrix can be found in [15].

Before energy and emissions calculations are undertaken, the vehicle trajectory data are pre-processed to filter out any unrealistic speed fluctuations. A Savitzky-Golay filter [16] is applied to smooth the observed vehicle traces. For every frame, the current frame, the previous 15 frames, and the following 15 frames (1 frame = 0.1 second) are fitted with least-squares cubic function. From the function, the speed value of the current frame is then calculated. Figure 20.7 shows the example of the raw and smoothed speed data. Here, NGSIM data were again used. The derivative of smoothed speed in each second is then taken to calculate acceleration. Figure 20.8 shows an example of the raw acceleration and the derivative acceleration. The smoothed speed and derivative acceleration are used for emission calculation to avoid over-estimation of vehicle engine power due to data fluctuations.

Figure 20.9a shows an example of second-by-second speed in mph from one vehicle trajectory, and associated NOx emission rates in grams per second. Higher speed and acceleration activities are related to higher power demand, and, thus, a higher emission rate. Figure 20.9b–d represent cumulative sorted NOx emissions, CO emissions, and fuel consumptions by time from trajectories of 550 vehicles (46,833 seconds) recorded in Atlanta NGSIM data. This data implies that 88% of NOx, 90% of CO emissions, and 65% of fuel consumptions are from 40% of operation time, which is related with high engine power. As seen it is of critical importance to estimate vehicle speed and acceleration for fuel consumption and emission prediction. This needs drives the development of client simulation capable of predicting trajectory data.

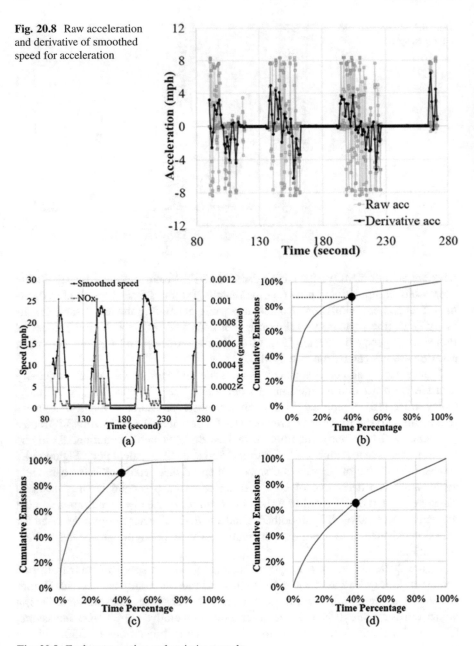

Fig. 20.8 Raw acceleration and derivative of smoothed speed for acceleration

Fig. 20.9 Fuel consumption and emissions results

20.4   Distributed Simulation Middleware

The envisioned distributed simulation system includes multiple simulating entities exchanging data and synchronizing as needed. Middleware is needed to support hand held devices such as smartphones, in-vehicle computers, computing systems operating on mobile platforms such as drones, and centralized servers, as well as sensors, databases, and other resources that all need to interact with one another. Distributed simulation middleware provides the services to interconnect these elements. A well-known example of an approach to defining distributed simulation middleware services is the High Level Architecture (IEEE 1516). Major services of the required distributed simulation middleware include system management, communication, and synchronization.

In contrast to traditional distributed simulations, the DDDAS paradigm used here includes energy-constrained devices such as smartphones and computers executing on drones. Therefore, it introduces new requirements to the development of the simulation middleware services. Energy efficient middleware not only allows for a longer usability of the simulation system elements, but also allows for easier penetration of such systems among existing technologies.

This effort has identified three main avenues for energy optimization in an energy efficient middleware. First, in time management services, an energy efficient synchronization algorithm could significantly reduce energy consumption [17]. The second avenue is an energy efficient data distribution management algorithm [18]. The third component is an applications program interface (API) for the simulation middleware services that supports application-controlled energy optimization. Cooperation between the middleware and application is required so that tradeoffs such as that between energy consumption and latency can be made in a way that is consistent with application requirements. The API supports application controlled tunable energy-efficient algorithms (e.g., data aggregation and energy optimized data subscription).

The *Green Run Time Infrastructure* (G-RTI) is an energy efficient distributed simulation middleware that exploits these three approaches. Apart from being energy efficient, other major considerations in the development of G-RTI were that it should be able to scale to support a large number of clients (perhaps tens of thousands or more) and a wide range of applications written in different programming languages and running on different operating systems and networks.

20.4.1   G-RTI Architecture

To address these considerations, G-RTI was developed using a client-server architecture. The interface between G-RTI and the clients is web-based. A web-based implementation supports a wide array of client types, as any device that is able to make an HTTP request (e.g., Internet of Things devices) can potentially be a G-

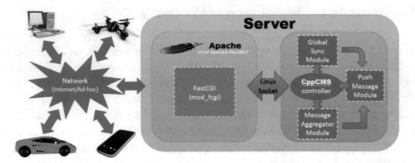

Fig. 20.10 High-level depiction of the Green Run Time Infrastructure (G-RTI) architecture

RTI client. It also eases client side development because it imposes few design restrictions. Support for different types of networks such as the Internet, small private networks, and ad hoc networks is easily provided. The backend allows for easy integration of existing applications with the G-RTI controller.

As shown in Fig. 20.10, the current G-RTI implementation utilizes an *Apache* webserver [19] as well as a CppCMS based controller [20]. Both of these open-source software systems are widely used and are known to scale. CppCMS provides a high performance framework for the development of the bulk of the G-RTI code, shown in the right half of the box labeled "Server" in Fig. 20.10. G-RTI supports "pull-based" data communications through a query service and "push-based" communications through a pub-sub (publish-subscribe) communications mechanism. Data aggregation mechanisms are used to help reduce energy consumption, as discussed later. To understand the breakdown of the energy consumed by a distributed simulation, or in other words to attribute the energy consumed by different components of the distributed simulation, energy profiling techniques such as that described in [21] can be used.

20.4.2   *Energy Consumption Measurements*

An experimental study using the G-RTI client-server architecture was conducted to develop a better understanding of energy consumption issues in distributed simulations. For this study, a cellular automata traffic simulation based on [22] was developed, and configured to model the NGSIM section of Peachtree Street in midtown Atlanta. This simulation was executed on the client, a cellular phone. In addition, a simulation of the same area based on a queueing network model was also developed to provide an additional point of comparison. The queueing network simulation uses an event-driven time advance mechanism in contrast to the cellular automata model that is time-stepped.

The experimental setup consisted of an Android® smartphone (Google Nexus® 5), running Android 5.1 as the client, and a Lenovo ThinkPad® running Ubuntu

14.04, as the G-RTI server. All the communications in the experiments were conducted using 802.11n Wi-Fi over public Wi-Fi access points. The client runs a multithreaded Native Android application with the simulation developed in C and communication using Volley, an HTTP Android library. The Trepn® application developed by Qualcomm was used to measure energy and power consumption of the client machine.

An initial set of data-driven simulation experiments were conducted using the traffic simulations executing on the phone streaming data to and from the server. The first set of experiments show the power utilized for data communications alone. Specifically, the power consumed by the DDDAS application sending and receiving a stream of data was measured. The data stream pertains to vehicles in the traffic network, and includes an identification number and x and y position coordinates of individual vehicles. The parameter that was varied is the frequency that update messages are sent and received. At each update point, the data for all the vehicles are placed into a single message, and sent to/from the embedded traffic simulation executing on the client.

Figure 20.11 shows the average power consumption (energy per unit time) observed in sending and receiving data continuously (effectively no time between update points) and at intervals of 0.01 second and 0.1 second. These data illustrate that power consumption for data communications is substantial, and not surprisingly, greatly affected by the frequency of communication. Power consumption includes a static component that is expended even when there is no communication, and a dynamic component that is proportional to the amount of communications that takes place. The figure illustrates the amount of power consumed including

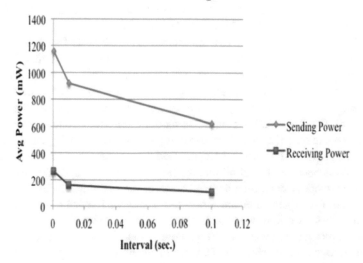

Fig. 20.11 Data streaming power

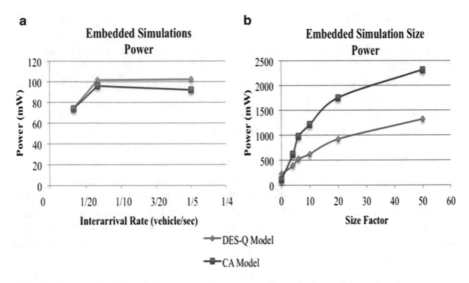

Fig. 20.12 Embedded simulation power (**a**) varying traffic arrival rate. (**b**) varying size

both of these components. The power consumed on the client both to send and receive data are shown in this figure. It is seen that the power needed to send data is approximately five times larger than that required to receive data.

The second set of experiments examined the power consumed by the two traffic simulation applications installed on the Android® phone and run under the conditions that no data streaming is occurring. Experiments were conducted to compare the power drawn by the cellular automata and discrete event queuing network simulation. Figure 20.12a shows the average power drawn by both the discrete event simulation and the cellular automata model under different vehicle arrival rates: 1/30, 1/ 15, and 1/5 (vehicles per second).

The power consumed by the two simulators is comparable for different vehicle arrival rates, although the cellular automata model draws somewhat less power than the queuing model as the arrival rate of vehicles into the system increases. However, one should point out that power consumption quantifies the amount of energy consumed per unit time, not the total amount of energy expended by the computation. While the cellular automata model draws slightly less power, it takes more time to simulate the same scenario compared to the queueing network model, resulting in greater total energy consumption and a greater draw on the phone's battery. This is because the cellular automata must update the state of every cell in the traffic network at each time step, whereas in the queuing model, only vehicles at the front of each queue area are processed during each event time in the system. Figure 20.12b shows that as we increase the network size the cellular automata model consumes more power than the queueing model because the cellular automata model must touch every vehicle in the system, consuming more power to update the network state because larger networks allow more vehicles to reside in the system.

In comparing Figs. 20.11 and 20.12a, these measurements show that the power drawn to stream data is much larger than the power that is needed to run the embedded simulations. One should note, however, that these experiments correspond to a relatively small transportation network. When simulating much larger networks the amount of power consumed by the simulations relative to that for communications may be different.

Finally, one approach to reducing energy consumption was evaluated. If the simulation must send a stream of update messages to the server, one could aggregate several messages into a single message, and send one larger message rather than a sequence of smaller messages. This approach, termed *message aggregation*, is commonly used in distributed systems in order to reduce communication overheads. Message aggregation comes at the cost of increasing latency as some messages must be held at the sender in a buffer while the data is being accumulated, rather than immediately sending the data to the receiver. A set of experiments were conducted to consider the impact of aggregation on energy consumption.

In each experimental run, the number of updates, and the size of the data in each update remains constant and the only variable is the number of updates aggregated to form a message. In these experiments the application executed the cellular automata based traffic simulation; and in addition the application also aggregated and sends messages. The amount of energy consumed per byte of transmitted data was measured. Figure 20.13 shows the results of this experiment. As expected, an initial reduction in the energy consumed is observed as message aggregation increases. This is because fewer messages are sent, thereby reducing the energy consumed to process the message and send overhead information such as message headers. However, an inflection point is reached and the energy consumed per byte of data starts increasing beyond a certain level of aggregation. This is because the operating system will automatically divide large messages into packets, and transmit each packet as a separate unit of data. Thus, from the standpoint of energy

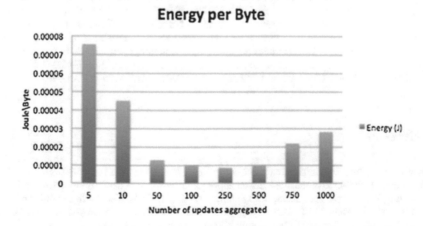

Fig. 20.13 Effect of message aggregation on client energy consumption

consumption, data aggregation is only effective up to the maximum data packet size used by the underlying operating system.

20.5 Concluding Comments and Future Work

Transportation systems can clearly benefit from exploiting the DDDAS paradigm because unexpected events such as crashes and unpredicted demand-induced congestion require real-time response to adapt to changing conditions. While the concern in many situations is increased travel time and delay, the system described here illustrate how DDDAS can also reduce emissions and fuel consumption.

Current research involves investigations concerning several of the topics described in this chapter. Given the discrete position and velocity measurements possible with the cellular automata models, efforts are underway to identify potential improvements to the CA methods and also appropriate post processing techniques to replicate the vehicle trajectories. Investigations are also ongoing concerning issues such as potential biases that may result from excluding vehicles that traverse only a portion of the corridor from the Bayesian approaches. Enhanced smoothing methods are being developed for trajectory analysis and extrapolation methods are being developed for incomplete trip traces (e.g., those vehicles that enter Peachtree Street via one of the side roads). In addition, on-going work is exploring the energy usage of the different simulation methods and various potential implementations of a given method. A particular area of investigation is energy usage with increased scale of the simulation models. Another area of research concerns using deep learning methods to predict one or more relevant factors for the generation of trajectories.

Acknowledgments and Disclaimer The information, data, or work presented herein was funded in part by the Advanced Research Projects Agency - Energy (ARPA-E), U.S. Department of Energy, under Award Number DE-AR0000613. The views and opinions of authors expressed herein do not necessarily state or reflect those of the United States Government or any agency thereof. The contents do not necessarily reflect the official views or policies of the State of Georgia or any agency thereof. This report does not constitute a standard, specification, or regulation. We also thank the Air Force Office of Scientific Research and National Science Foundation for their support of this research (NSF Award 1,462,503 and AFOSR award FA9550-17-1-022).

References

1. US Energy Information Admin., http://www.eia.gov/tools/faqs/faq.cfm?id=307&t=10
2. Darema, F. 2004. "Dynamic data driven applications systems: A new paradigm for application simulations and measurements." *Computational Science-ICCS 2004*, Springer: 662–669.
3. Chen, H., J. Wang and L. Feng. 2012. "Research on the Dynamic Data-driven Application System Architecture for Flight Delay Prediction." *JSW* 7(2): 263–268.

4. Long, Q. 2017. "A framework for data-driven computational experiments of inter-organizational collaborations in supply chain networks." *Information Sciences* **399**: 43–63.
5. Mandel, J., L. Bennethum, M. Chen, J. Coen, C. Douglas, L. Franca, C. Johns, M. Kim, A. Knyazev and R. Kremens. 2005. "Towards a dynamic data driven application system for wildfire simulation." *Computational Science–ICCS 2005*: 197–227.
6. Henclewood, D., W. Suh, A. Guin, R. Guensler, R.M. Fujimoto, and M. Hunter, *A Real-Time Data-Driven Traffic Simulation for Performance Measure Estimation*. IET Intelligent Transportation Systems, 2016. **10**(8): p. 562–571.
7. Suh, W., D. Henclewood, G. Angshuman, R. Guensler, M. Hunter, and R.M. Fujimoto, *Dynamic Data Driven Transportation Systems*. Multimedia Tools and Applications,, 2017. **76**(23): p. 25253–25269.
8. NGSIM Community Home. http://ngsim-community.org
9. Von Neumann, John, and Arthur W. Burks. "Theory of self-reproducing automata." IEEE Transactions on Neural Networks 5.1 (1966): 3–14.
10. Nagel, K., & Schreckenberg, M.: A cellular automaton model for freeway traffic. Journal de physique I, 2(12), 2221–2229 (1992).
11. Lighthill, M. J., Whitham, G. B.: On kinematic waves. II. A theory of traffic flow on long crowded roads. In Proceedings of the Royal Society of London A: Mathematical, Physical and Engineering Sciences (Vol. 229, No. 1178, pp. 317–345). The Royal Society (1955).
12. Richards, P. I.: Shock waves on the highway. Operations research, 4(1), 42–51 (1956).
13. Daganzo, Carlos F. "In traffic flow, cellular automata= kinematic waves." Transportation Research Part B: Methodological 40.5 (2006): 396–403.
14. US EPA, U.S. Environmental Protection Agency: Population and Activity of On-road Vehicles in MOVES2014. EPA Report EPA-420-R-16-003a. 2015. Available at: https://www3.epa.gov/otaq/models/moves/documents/420r16003a.pdf
15. Guensler, R., Liu H., Xu X., Xu Y., Rodgers M.: MOVES-Matrix: Setup, Implementation, and Application. In 95th Annual Meeting of the Transportation Research Board. Washington, DC. (2016).
16. Savitzky, A., Golay, M. J.: Smoothing and differentiation of data by simplified least squares procedures. Analytical chemistry, 36(8), 1627–1639 (1964).
17. Fujimoto, R. M., Biswas, A.: An Empirical Study of Energy Consumption in Distributed Simulations, IEEE/ACM International Symposium on Distributed Simulation and Real-Time Applications (DS/RT) (2015).
18. S. Neal, G. Kanitkar, R. M. Fujimoto, "Power Consumption of Data Distribution Management for On-Line Simulations," *Principles of Advanced Discrete Simulation,* May 2014.
19. The Apache Software Foundation, httpd.apache.org
20. Beilis, A., Tonkikh, M., http://cppcms.com/wikipp/en/page/main
21. Biswas, A., Fujimoto, R.: Profiling Energy Consumption in Distributed Simulations. Proceedings of the 2016 annual ACM Conference on SIGSIM Principles of Advanced Discrete Simulation. ACM (2016).
22. Rickert, M., Nagel K., Schreckenberg M., Latour A.: Two Lane Traffic Simulations using Cellular Automata. Physica A: Statistical Mechanics and its Applications 231(4): 534–550. (1996).

Chapter 21
A Dynamic Data-Driven Optimization Framework for Demand Side Management in Microgrids

Haluk Damgacioglu, Mehrad Bastani, and Nurcin Celik

Abstract The efficient utilization of distributed generation resources (DGs) and demand side management (DSM) in large-scale power systems play a crucial role in satisfying and controlling electricity demand through an economically viable and environmentally friendly way. However, uncertainties in power generation from DGs, variations in load demand, and conflicts in objectives (emission, cost, etc.) pose major challenges to determine the optimal operation planning of microgrids. In this chapter, we propose a dynamic data-driven multi-objective optimization model for a day-ahead operation planning for microgrids, integrating interruption load management (ILM) as a DSM program, while collectively considering the total cost and emissions as objective functions. The proposed model includes three modules that interact with each other: (1) a simulation module that captures the behavior of operating components such as solar panels, wind turbines, etc. and provides the data for the optimization model; (2) an optimization module that determines the optimal operational plan, which includes utilization of diesel generators, purchased electricity from utility and interrupted load, considering cost and emissions objective functions using ϵ-constraint method; and (3) a rule-based real-time decision making module that adapts the operation plan from the optimization model based on dynamic data from the microgrid and sends the revised plan back to the microgrid. The capabilities and performance of the proposed dynamic data-driven optimization framework are demonstrated through a case study of a typical electrical power system. The resultant operation plan is quite promising regarding total cost and CO_2 emission.

Keywords Multi objective optimization · Demand side management · Microgrid · Interruption load management (ILM) · CO_2 emission · Dynamic data-driven multi-objective optimization model (DDD-MOM) · Electricity price model

H. Damgacioglu · M. Bastani · N. Celik (✉)
Department of Industrial Engineering, University of Miami, Coral Gables, FL, USA
e-mail: haluk.damgacioglu@uth.tmc.edu

© The Author(s), under exclusive license to Springer Nature Switzerland AG 2022   497
E. P. Blasch et al. (eds.), *Handbook of Dynamic Data Driven Applications Systems*,
https://doi.org/10.1007/978-3-030-74568-4_21

21.1   Introduction

The concept of microgrids emerged from a rapid increase of distributed energy resources and technological advances in distributed generation (DG) units. A *microgrid* is a localized group of electricity sources and loads that can operate either connected to the main grid or isolated from the main grid. While a microgrid can buy electricity from the main grid in grid-connected mode, in an isolated mode, it has to satisfy its own demand using its energy sources [13, 22, 38]. Moreover, utilization of renewable energy combined with distributed generation in microgrids has become vitally important to reduce greenhouse gas emissions, as global energy demands continues to increase. Microgrids typically employ a variety of DG resources such as solar arrays, wind turbines, and diesel generators. This diversity of energy resources promises adequately reliable, and economically viable power generation for customers. However, increasing the penetration level of the individual DG units in a microgrid also brings about challenges that require complex mechanisms for operation planning since power generation from solar panels and wind turbines heavily depends on weather conditions. Furthermore, the intermittency and stochastic nature of renewable energies has become the major obstacle to large market penetration of renewable energies [35, 39] that can cause energy shortages during energy peak demand periods.

Energy shortage can cause minor to severe failures in power networks, which can lead to significant and irrecoverable costs. One possible way to overcome the energy shortage issue is to use fast-responding generators (diesel generators) or buying energy from the main grid; however, this solution might be expensive and generate a large amount of greenhouse gas. Alternatively, an advanced demand side management (DSM) program can be implemented to adjust the controllable loads to match the available power generation during energy shortage. Demand side management (DSM) programs provide the most practical way to control energy consumption on the customer side of the load [27, 41] and promise a cheaper and more effective way to keep supply and demand balanced.

The final challenge is posed by the non-linearities in both cost and the emissions functions for the diesel generators, which increase the complexity of the problem. The aforementioned challenges make microgrid operational planning an arduous research problem and creates a necessity for complex models that consider not only the utilization of renewable energy and a DSM programs, but also conflicting objectives such as total cost and carbon dioxide emission.

In this paper, we present a novel, dynamic data-driven multi-objective optimization model (DDD-MOM) for determining the detailed real-time operation planning of a microgrid. The proposed model is inspired by the dynamic data-driven application systems (DDDAS) paradigm founded by [8–12] that entails the ability to create a symbiotic feedback loop between the incorporation of the dynamic data in an application system (i.e., bi-objective optimization model in our case) and, in reverse, the ability to steer the measurement process of the real system (i.e., response of the real system in this study). Here, the ultimate goal of the DDDAS paradigm may be summarized as: to make application systems more robust by adding more accurate yet efficient modeling and simulation capabilities through a symbiotic feedback loop. This makes DDDAS a promising and emerging framework which has been applied to a variety of areas such as supply chain systems [6, 7], distributed self-healing electric microgrids [34, 38], electric load dispatching [19, 33], operation planning of a microgrid [32], data fusion analysis [3, 4, 36, 37], smart energy management [17, 18, 20] transportation systems [16, 24], and surveillance and crowd control [5, 23] amongst many others.

Our proposed DDD-MOM approach consists of a simulation model, a bi-objective optimization model, and a rule-based real-time decision making module. In the *simulation model*, the hourly electricity prices are modeled based on historical data using the Bayesian Information Criteria (BIC) method. Solar and wind power generations are simulated using the data from the environmental sensors (i.e., solar radiation, wind speed, ambient temperature), and the load behavior of each demand point is a function of the peak demand and the power factor. After the components of the microgrid under the aforementioned conditions is simulated considering the system uncertainties by the simulation model, the *bi-objective optimization model* is formulated to find the Pareto Frontier solutions in terms of total cost and emission using the ϵ-constraint method. Once the Pareto Frontier is obtained, the best compromise solution is selected among knee solutions which are the preferred trade-off solutions in the Pareto Frontier [31]. Based on the best compromise solution, the operation plan, which includes utilization of diesel generators, purchased electricity from utility, and interrupted load, is determined and sent to the microgrid. In the final stage of the proposed framework, a *rule-based real-time decision-making module* adapts the operation plan obtained from the optimization model with respect to real-time dynamic data collected from the microgrid. The capabilities of the proposed framework are demonstrated via a connected synthetic microgrid that has 50 load points, solar, wind and diesel generators. The proposed framework can be employed to any microgrid that has similarly distributed energy resources by importing the necessary characteristics such as solar capacity, wind turbine capacity, diesel generator characteristics, historical main grid prices, and historical load information.

21.2   Proposed Framework

The proposed DDD-MOM framework aims to determine the (near-) optimal and robust operation planning for microgrids, including demand side management and utilization of diesel generators, in an economically and environmentally friendly way, considering uncertainties of renewable power generation and load demand. The overview of the proposed approach is shown in Fig. 21.1 where the components of the proposed approach are explained in detail in the following subsections.

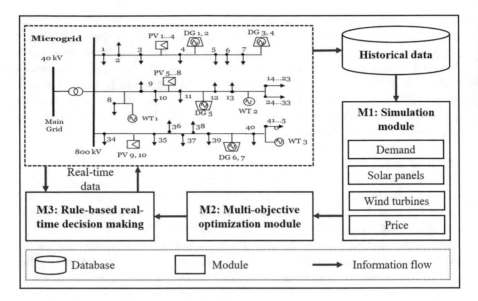

Fig. 21.1 Proposed DDD-MOM approach applied to a considered microgrid

21.2.1   Simulation Module

The simulation module creates a valuable imitation of the operation of different microgrid components while capturing uncertainty associated with these components. In this study, load demand, solar power generation, wind power generation, and hourly electricity prices are simulated as the microgrid operating components. Since the other components, including diesel generators and DSM program, are controllable components, they are utilized only in the optimization model.

Demand The demand data in this study is assumed to follow the microgrid system from [34]. Particularly, the forecasted hourly demand of each building (F_{it}) is a function of peak demand (PD_i) and power factor (PF_{it}) of the building i at a time t. In this study, power factors are determined based on customer type; values are collected from [29] for residential customers and from [34] for commercial and industrial customers. A Gaussian distribution is assumed in modeling the demand uncertainty with 5% standard deviation as used in [40]. The calculation of load demand for each hour and building is shown in (21.1).

$$F_{it} \sim N\left(\mu_{it,\sigma_i}\right) \quad where \quad \mu_i = \sum_{i=1}^{N} PD_i \times PF_{it} \quad and \quad \sigma_i = 0.05\mu_i \quad (21.1)$$

Solar The power generation from solar panels depends on panel characteristics such as solar irradiance and ambient temperature as shown in (21.2)–(21.4). In these equations, the hourly solar generation (S_{out}) is a function of fill factor (FF), which is a constant related to panel characteristics, voltage (V) and current (I). Voltage and current are associated with attributes of solar panel and cell temperature (T_c) calculated by the term $T_a + \frac{(T_n - 20)}{0.8} \cdot SI$ where T_a is ambient temperature, T_n is a nominal cell temperature and SI is the solar irradiance.

$$S_{out} = FF.V.I \tag{21.2}$$

$$V = V_{oc} - k_v\,[T_c - 25] \tag{21.3}$$

$$I = SI \cdot (I_{sc} + k_i\,[T_c - 25]) \tag{21.4}$$

Wind The power generation from wind turbines is calculated by a piecewise function that is dependent on wind speed (v_w) at the site and the parameters of the power performance curve which are rated power (P_w), cut-in speed (v_{ci}), cut-off speed (v_{co}) and rated speed (v_r). Total output power generated from the wind turbine (W_{out}) is computed as follows.

$$W_{out} = \begin{cases} 0 & if \quad v_w < v_d \\ P_w \times \frac{v_w - v_{ci}}{v_r - v_{ci}} & if \quad v_{ci} \le v_w \le v_r \\ P_w & if \quad v_r \le v_w \le v_{co} \\ 0 & if \quad v_w \ge v_{co} \end{cases} \tag{21.5}$$

Price The price of electricity from the main grid is modeled using historical data from [28]. In this study, it is assumed that hourly electricity prices for an entire month follow a similar pattern. In the calculation of prices, the data for the entire month are taken into account for each hour. Here, we analyze several distributions including: Weilbull, Gamma, etc. using the maximum likelihood estimation. After our analysis of the historical data, an inverse Gaussian distribution is determined as the best-fit distribution to explain hourly prices using the Bayesian Information Criteria [21, 30]. The probability density function of the inverse Gaussian distribution is given in (21.6).

$$f(x; \mu, \lambda) = \left[\frac{\lambda}{2\pi x^3}\right]^{\frac{1}{2}} exp\left(\frac{-\lambda\,(x - \mu)^2}{2\mu^2 x}\right) \tag{21.6}$$

In Eq. (21.6), x is the random variable (electricity price in our case), μ is the distribution mean and λ is the shape parameter. As λ increases, the distribution tends toward the Gaussian distribution. In this study, based on the historical data obtained from [28], the parameters of the Inverse Gaussian distribution are estimated using maximum likelihood estimation procedure. Then these parameters are used to generate electricity prices in the simulation model.

21.2.2 Optimization Module

After obtaining the load demand for each building, solar and wind power generation available, and hourly electricity prices from the simulation module, the optimization module minimizes the cost and emission by determining utilization of diesel generators, the amount of electricity that is bought from utility, and the schedule of interruptible load under the interruptible load management (ILM). ILM, as an incentive based DSM program, which attempts to decrease the energy consumption of buildings during the peak demand; however, the energy providers must pay the interruption incentives to consumers to encourage them to participate in this program. In this study, a bi-objective optimization model is formulated to minimize the cost and emission. It should be noted that quadratic cost and emission functions of diesel generators are linearized using an upper piecewise linear approximation method [25]. While the cost function can be represented with one linear curve, the emission function can be written by two linear curves called segments. The notation used in the model is shown in Table 21.1 and the model is represented in (21.7)–(21.19).

Table 21.1 Notation used in bi-objective optimization model

Indices	
i	Buildings $i \in \{1, \cdots, I\}$
t	Hours $t \in \{1, \cdots, 24\}$
j	Diesel generators $j \in \{1, \cdots, J\}$
k	Segments $k \in \{1, 2\}$
Parameters	
F_{it}	Forecasted load of building i at time t
D_t	Demand at time t after solar and wind generation
PG_j^{min}	Minimum amount of electricity that can be produced by generator j
RI_{it}	Interruption rate ($\$/kW$) (dependent on type of customer)
CS_j	Slope of cost function for generation unit j
CI_j	Intercept of cost function for generation unit j
ES_j^k	Slope of emission function for generation unit j at segment k
EI_j	Emission value for PG_j^{min}
GR_j^r	Reference for energy generation where $r \in \{1, \cdots, k+1\}$
U_{lb}	Minimum amount that can be bought from utility
U_{ub}	Maximum amount that can be bought from utility
U_r	Energy rate (price) from utility
Variables	
g_{jt}^k	Energy produced by diesel generator g at time t and segment k
u_{jt}^k	Binary variable for the intercept of generator j at time t and segment k
x_{it}	Amount of interruption of building i at time t
b_t	Amount of electricity bought from utility
v_t	Binary variable for electricity from utility

Objective functions:

$$Min \ z_1 = \sum_{t=1}^{24} \left[\sum_{i=1}^{I} x_{it} RI_{it} + \sum_{j=1}^{J} \left(u_{jt} CI_j + \sum_{k=1}^{2} g_{jt}^k CS_j \right) \right.$$
$$\left. + U_{lb} U_r v_t + (b_t - U_{lb}) U_r \right] \tag{21.7}$$

$$Min \ z_2 = \sum_{t=1}^{24} \sum_{j=1}^{J} \sum_{k=1}^{2} g_{jt}^k ES_j^k + u_{jt} EI_j \tag{21.8}$$

Subject to:

$$D_t = \sum_{i=1}^{I} F_{it} - S_t - W_t \tag{21.9}$$

$$D_t - \sum_{i=1}^{I} x_{it} \le \sum_{j=1}^{J} \left[\sum_{k=1}^{2} g_{jt}^k + u_{jt}^1 PG_j^{min} \right] + b_t, \quad \forall t \tag{21.10}$$

$$g_{jt}^k \le \left(GR_j^{k+1} - GR_j^k \right) u_{jt}^k \quad \forall j, t \quad and \quad k = 1 \tag{21.11}$$

$$u_{jt}^{k+1} \le u_{jt}^k \quad where \quad k = 1 \tag{21.12}$$

$$\left(GR_j^{k+1} - GR_j^k \right) - gs_{jt}^k \le M \left(1 - u_{jt}^{k+1} \right) \quad \forall j, t \quad and \quad k = 1 \tag{21.13}$$

$$x_{it} \le 0.3 \cdot F_{it} \quad \forall i, t \tag{21.14}$$

$$\sum_{t=1}^{24} x_{it} \le 0.02 \sum_{t=1}^{24} F_i t \quad \forall i \tag{21.15}$$

$$b_t \ge U_{lb} \cdot v_t \tag{21.16}$$

$$b_t \le U_{ub} \cdot v_t \tag{21.17}$$

$$u_{jt}^k, y_{it}, v_t \in \{0, 1\} \tag{21.18}$$

$$x_{it}, g_{jt}, g_{jt}^k, b_t \ge 0 \tag{21.19}$$

Equation (21.7) denotes the first objective function that minimizes the total cost including interruption cost $\sum_{t=1}^{24} \sum_{i=1}^{I} x_{it} RI_{it}$, linearized form of diesel generators cost ($\sum_{j=1}^{J}\sum_{t=1}^{24} u_{ij}CI_j + g_{jt}CS_j$), and electricity cost ($\sum_{t=1}^{24} U_{lb}U_r v_t + (b_t - U_{lb})U_r$) that is bought from the utility. Equation (21.8) minimizes the CO_2 emission of diesel generators.

In the constraint set, Eq. (21.9) defines the desired demand at time t, which is the summation over time of forecasted loads minus generated energy from wind and solar at time t. Equation (21.10) prevents the model from exceeding the desired demand at time t. Since the linearized form of the emission function includes two segments, (21.11)–(21.13) ensure that the model does not assign any value to the second segment before fulfilling the first segment. Equations (21.14)–(21.15) ensure that the amount of interruption for each building satisfies hourly and daily by regulations for ILM. Equations (21.16)–(21.17) show the upper and lower limit of the energy that can be bought from utility. Finally, (21.18)–(21.19) are sign constraints. The optimization model (Eqs. (21.7)–(21.19)) is a generic model and it can be applied in any microgrid with the corresponding parameters obtained from the microgrid and ILM program. In this paper, ϵ-constraint method is used to obtain the Pareto Frontier for the proposed mathematical model.

21.2.3 ϵ-Constraint Method for Multi-objective Optimization

In this paper, ϵ-constraint method, first proposed by [26], is used to solve the bi-objective optimization model. In order to implement the ϵ-constraint method in the optimization problem described in Sect. 21.2.2, the optimization problem is first solved for each objective function separately to find the minimum and maximum value for each objective function (pay-off table). Next, the secondary objective function is added to the optimization model as a constraint and the optimization problem is formulated as a single objective optimization problem (based on the primary objective). In this work, the total operation cost is selected as the primary objective and the emission function is determined as the secondary objective. Based on the pay-off table, the range of the secondary objective function is divided into n equal intervals. Then, the new optimization problem that minimizes the total operation cost is solved for n different right hand side and left hand side values of constrained emission function in order to obtain n Pareto Frontier solutions (Fig. 21.2).

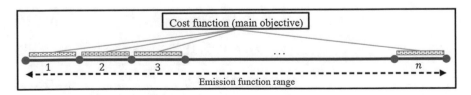

Fig. 21.2 ϵ-constraint method for bi-objective optimization

21.2.4 Real-Time Decision Making Module

Load demand and generation from solar panels and wind turbines cannot be forecasted precisely, so the optimal solution based on simulation results requires modifications in order to adapt the solution to real-time data gathered from the microgrid. However, these modifications should satisfy the constraints without significantly harming the optimal solution. Within this context, we propose a rule-based real-time decision-making module (RTDM) that makes myopic decisions based on the real-time data from microgrid considering both cost and emission as it steps through time. The proposed rule-based RTDM is responsible for decisions regarding utilization of diesel generators, ILM and amount of electricity that will be bought from main grid (Fig. 21.3). It should be noted that the method is terminated if $\Delta D_t = 0$ at any checkpoints.

21.3 Experiments and Results

In order to present the capabilities and performance of the proposed approach, a case study of a synthetic microgrid was carried out. The microgrid analyzed in this work includes 50 buildings composed of 35 residential, 10 commercial, and 5 industrial type of load profiles, solar panels that have a capacity of 10 MW in total, 3 wind turbines, and 7 diesel generators from 4 different types (see Table 21.3 for the types of generators). The characteristics of the solar panel and wind turbines used in this study are shown in Table 21.2. Here, the attributes of the diesel generators are obtained from the study [1]. Then, variable cost and emissions values for each diesel generator type are linearized using a piecewise linear approximation method. The obtained values for diesel generators are shown in Table 21.3.

As mentioned earlier, due to weather changes and variations in customers' load profiles, the operation plans will be different for any day of a year. However, it is commonly believed that, changes within a season have minimal impact. Therefore, in this study, we present results of DDD-MOM for the two best representative days of each season, which are July 15th for summer and January 15th for winter. Here, the simulation model determines the hourly forecasted demand for each

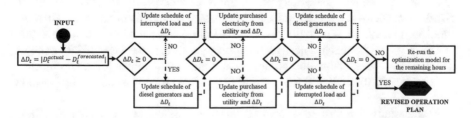

Fig. 21.3 Rule-based real time decision making module for microgrid operational planning

Table 21.2 Attributes of the wind turbines and solar panels [2]

Attribute	Value
Solar panel	
Open circuit voltage	21.98 V
Short circuit current	5.32 A
Voltage temperature coefficient	14.4 mV/°C
Current temperature coefficient	1.22 mA/°C
Nominal cell operating temperature	43°C
Fill factor	0.17
Wind turbine	
Turbine capacity	3000 kW
Cut-in speed	4 (m/s)
Cut-out speed	25 (m/s)
Rated speed	16 (m/s)

Table 21.3 Attributes of the diesel generators

Thermal generators				
Attribute	Type I	Type II	Type III	Type IV
Number of generators	2	2	1	2
Minimum power generation	50	40	30	20
Maximum power generation	300	250	175	120
Fixed cost	16.52	12.02	9.89	7.47
Variable cost coefficient	0.0224	0.0229	0.0235	0.0223
Emission for minimum power generation	0.88	0.76	1.01	0.66
Emission coefficient for segment I	0.0277	0.0214	0.0277	0.0195
Emission coefficient for segment II	0.0599	0.0432	0.0459	0.0364

Table 21.4 Resulted pay-off table for Bi-objective optimization model

Summer	Cost	Emission	Winter	Cost	Emission
Cost	**1320.59$**	6.71 kg	Cost	**1077.07$**	5.39 kg
Emission	2597.00$	**4.78 kg**	Emission	2218.76$	**3.51 kg**

building and hourly solar and wind generation according to the data shown in Tables 21.2, 21.3. It should be noted that weather data is obtained from the Florida Automated Weather Network (FAWN) subsidiary of the University of Florida [14], and winter and summer electricity prices are determined using an Inverse Gaussian distribution where parameters are estimated based on the historical data. Then the simulation results are sent to the bi-objective optimization model. The optimization model is solved for each objective function to construct the pay-off table shown in Table 21.4. In the table, the minimum and maximum values for each objective function ([1077.07–1320.59] for cost and [3.51–4.78] for emission)' were shown in bold.

In this study, the cost function is selected as the primary objective function. Then the emission function is embedded into the model as a constraint as shown in Eq. (21.20).

$$\sum_{t=1}^{24}\sum_{j=1}^{J}\sum_{k=1}^{2} g_{jt}^{k} ES_{j}^{k} + u_{jt} EI_{j} \geq \epsilon_{iter} \qquad (21.20)$$

In Eq. (21.20), ϵ_{iter} represents the right-hand value of ϵ-constraint for each iteration. In this study, in the ϵ-constraint method, the emission function ranges ([4.78, 6.71] for summer and [3.51, 5.39] for winter) are divided into 100 intervals. Here, the ϵ_1 values for summer and winter are 4.78 and 3, 51, respectively. In each iteration, these values are increased by approximately 0.019 for both summer and winter. Then, the optimization problem for minimizing the cost is solved for every ϵ value by using AMPL (A Mathematical Programming Language, [15]) software. Each iteration in ϵ-constraint method takes about 0.7 s on a computer with i7 processor and 16 GB RAM. Based on the results of the optimization problem, the Pareto Frontier is obtained and represented in Fig. 21.4. Then, the best compromise solution is selected by determining the knee-of-the-curve solutions which are the preferred trade-off solutions in the Pareto Frontier [31]. Since our primary objective here is to minimize the cost, the knee solutions, better in terms of total cost, are chosen as the best compromise solutions for winter and summer.

Based on the selected solutions, the optimal operation plans for summer and winter are demonstrated in Fig. 21.5. It should be noticed that in both cases, there is unused generator capacity, showing that the microgrid has enough resources for electricity generation. In fact, even during the peak hours in summer, the utilization of generator type I, which has the highest capacity, does not exceed 60% in total. From Fig. 21.5, it can be understood that in winter, the microgrid does not need electricity from main grid, while in summer, the microgrid buys electricity from the main grid for four hours a day. However, during these hours, the microgrid can produce its own energy. This study also demonstrates that the total amount of interrupted electricity is very small for both seasons; meaning that the microgrid can satisfy the customers in terms of their electricity production. Finally, although the generation from renewable energy sources in summer is almost twice as the generation from renewable energy sources in winter, the higher demand in summer causes more cost and more emissions compared to those of winter.

In the next step, DDD-MOM collects the real-time data from microgrid and performs RTDM to adapt the best compromise solution from optimization module based on these data. In this study, real-time microgrid data is simulated using slightly different parameters from the parameters that are used in the simulation module. The results of RTDM are demonstrated in Fig. 21.6. As can be seen in Fig. 21.6, the changes in the cost function value between the optimization module solution and RTDM solution reach at most a level of 0.9% and 0.6% in summer and winter, respectively. The differences in the emission values obtained from the optimization model and actual case are smaller than 0.4% and 0.6% in winter and summer, respectively. Hence, it can be concluded that the results obtained from the optimization model are robust in terms of cost and emission objectives

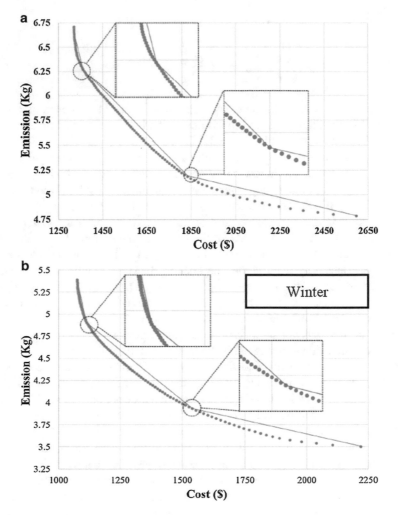

Fig. 21.4 Resulting Pareto Frontier from multi-objective optimization model. (**a**) Summer. (**b**) Winter

against uncertainties of power generation from renewable energy resources and load demand in real-time operation.

21.4 Conclusion

In this study, we propose a dynamic, data driven multi-objective optimization model (DDD-MOM) for the operation planning of a microgrid. The proposed framework consists of three main modules including data simulation, bi-objective optimization

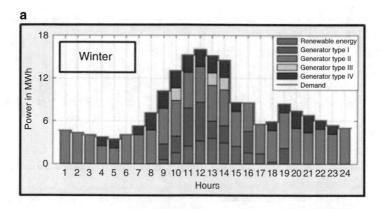

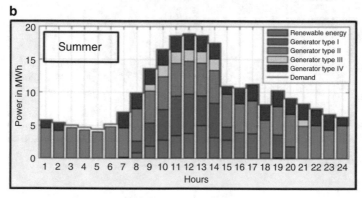

Fig. 21.5 Operation plan of best compromise solutions. (**a**) Winter. (**b**) Summer

model, and a real-time decision-making module. First, the simulation module takes historical data and mimics the behavior of components of the microgrid, considering uncertainties associated with power generation from distributed energy resources and load demand. In the next step, the results of the simulation and linearized form of the quadratic cost and emission functions of diesel generators are imported into the bi-objective optimization model. Then, the biobjective optimization model is solved using an ϵ-constraint method to obtain the best compromise solution. In the last module, the rule-based real-time decision-making module modifies the solution obtained from the optimization module to finalize the operation plan based on dynamic data from the microgrid to satisfy all operational constraints. The performance of the proposed approach is demonstrated through a synthetic microgrid that includes solar panels, wind turbines, and 4 types of diesel generators. The results have shown that DDD-MOM can provide the real time hourly operation plan of a microgrid without harming the feasibility and optimal solution obtained from the optimization model. Our proposed approach is designed in a generic manner that can be implemented in any microgrid with similar types of DGs. In future works, storage devices, such as batteries, and maintenance periods of

a

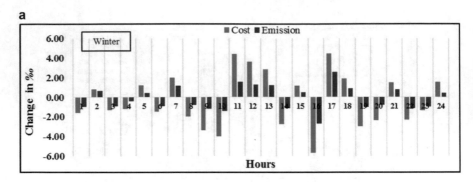

b

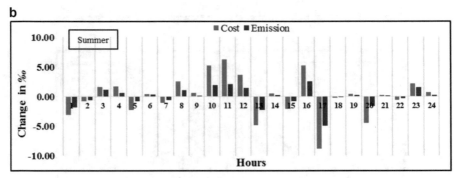

Fig. 21.6 Result of the RTDM module. (**a**) Winter. (**b**) Summer

diesel generators can be considered in order to make the proposed approach more applicable to the wide variety of energy sources in an electrical grid system.

Acknowledgments This project is supported by the AFOSR DDDAS Award No: FA9550-13-1-0105.

References

1. Abido M (2009) Multiobjective particle swarm optimization for environmental/economic dispatch problem. Electric Power Systems Research 79(7):1105–1113
2. Atwa Y, El-Saadany E, Salama M, Seethapathy R (2010) Optimal renewable resources mix for distribution system energy loss minimization. IEEE Transactions on Power Systems 25(1):360–370
3. Aved A (2013) Scene understanding for real time processing of queries over big data streaming video. University of Central Florida
4. Blasch E, Al-Nashif Y, Hariri S (2014) Static versus dynamic data information fusion analysis using dddas for cyber security trust. Procedia Computer Science 29:1299–1313
5. Blasch E, Aved A (2015) Dynamic data-driven application system (dddas) for video surveillance user support. In: Procedia Computer Science, vol 51, pp 2503–2517

6. Blasch E, Xu R, Nikouei S, Chen Y (2018) A study of lightweight dddas architecture for real-time public safety applications through hybrid simulation. In: Winter Simulation Conference (WSC) 2019, pp 762–773
7. Celik N, Lee S, Vasudevan K, Son YJ (2010) Dddas-based multi-fidelity simulation framework for supply chain systems. IIE Transactions 42(5):325–341
8. Darema F (1996) On the parallel characteristics of engineering/scientific and commercial applications: differences, similarities and future outlook. In: Keane J (ed) Parallel Commercial Processing
9. Darema F (2002) Dynamic data driven application systems. Internet Process Coordination p 149
10. Darema F (2004) Dynamic data driven applications systems: A new paradigm for application simulations and measurements. In: International Conference on Computational Science, Springer, pp 662–669
11. Darema F (2011) Computational model and environments. Journal of Algorithms and Computational Technology 5(4):545–600
12. Darema F (2012) New frontiers through computer and information science. International Conference on Computational Science (ICCS)
13. Darville J, Celik N (2020) Simulation optimization for unit commitment using a region-based sampling (rbs) algorithm. In: Institute of Industrial and Systems Engineers, IEEE
14. FAWN (2014) Ftp: Yearly csv data. http://agrofawn-prod01.osg.ufl.edu/fawnpub/data/hourly_summaries
15. Fourer R, Gay DM, Kernighan B (1993) Ampl, vol 117. Boyd & Fraser Danvers, MA
16. Fujimoto R, Guensler R, Hunter M, Kim HK, Lee J, Leonard II J, Palekar M, Schwan K, Seshasayee B (2006) Dynamic data driven application simulation of surface transportation systems. In: International Conference on Computational Science, Springer, pp 425–432
17. Fujimoto RM, Celik N, Damgacioglu H, Hunter M, Jin D, Son YJ, Xu J (2016) Dynamic data driven application systems for smart cities and urban infrastructures. In: Winter Simulation Conference (WSC), 2016, IEEE, pp 1143–1157
18. Fujimoto RM, Celik N, Damgacioglu H, Hunter M, Jin D, Son YJ, Xu J (2016) Dynamic data driven application systems for smart cities and urban infrastructures. In: Winter Simulation Conference (WSC), 2016, IEEE, pp 1143–1157
19. Hunter M, Biswas A, Fujimoto R (2018) Energy efficient middleware for dynamic data driven application systems. In: Proceedings of the 2018 Winter Simulation Conference, pp 628–639
20. Jin D, Nicole D (2015) Parallel simulation and virtual-machine-based emulation of software-defined networks. In: ACM Transactions on Modeling and Computer Simulation (TOMACS), vol 1, pp 1–27
21. Kass RE, Raftery AE (1995) Bayes factors. Journal of the american statistical association 90(430):773–795
22. Katiraei F, Iravani MR (2006) Power management strategies for a microgrid with multiple distributed generation units. IEEE transactions on power systems 21(4):1821–1831
23. Khaleghi AM, Xu D, Wang Z, Li M, Lobos A, Liu J, Son YJ (2013) A dddams-based planning and control framework for surveillance and crowd control via uavs and ugvs. Expert Systems with Applications 40(18):7168–7183
24. Lecerf M, Allaire D, Willcox K (2015) Methodology for dynamic data-driven online flight capability estimation. AIAA Journal 53(10):3073–3087
25. Li HL, Chang CT, Tsai JF (2002) Approximately global optimization for assortment problems using piecewise linearization techniques. European Journal of Operational Research 140(3):584–589
26. Mavrotas G (2009) Effective implementation of the ε-constraint method in multi-objective mathematical programming problems. Applied mathematics and computation 213(2):455–465
27. Mohsenian-Rad AH, Wong VW, Jatskevich J, Schober R, Leon-Garcia A (2010) Autonomous demand-side management based on game-theoretic energy consumption scheduling for the future smart grid. IEEE transactions on Smart Grid 1(3):320–331

28. National Grid (2015) Hourly electric supply charges. https://www.nationalgridus.com/niagaramohawk/business/rates/5_hour_charge.asp
29. Parker DS (2003) Research highlights from a large scale residential monitoring study in a hot climate. Energy and Buildings 35(9):863–876
30. Raftery AE (1986) Choosing models for cross-classifications. American sociological review 51(1):145–146
31. Setämaa-Kärkkäinen A, Miettinen K, Vuori J (2006) Best compromise solution for a new multiobjective scheduling problem. Computers & operations research 33(8):2353–2368
32. Shi X, Damgacioglu H, Celik N (2015) A dynamic data-driven approach for operation planning of microgrids. Procedia Computer Science 51:2543–2552
33. Thanos AE, Shi X, Sáenz JP, Celik N (2015) System of systems modeling and simulation for microgrids using DDDAMS. Modeling and Simulation Support for System of Systems Engineering Applications, John Wiley & Sons, 337
34. Thanos AE, Moore, DeLante E, Shi X, and Celik N (2015) System of systems modeling and simulation for microgrids using DDDAMS. Modeling and Simulation Support for System of Systems Engineering Applications, John Wiley & Sons, 337
35. Wu C, Mohsenian-Rad H, Huang J, Wang AY (2011) Demand side management for wind power integration in microgrid using dynamic potential game theory. In: 2011 IEEE GLOBECOM Workshops (GC Wkshps), IEEE, pp 1199–1204
36. Xu J, Zhang S, Huang E, Chen C, Lee L, Celik N (2014) Efficient multi-fidelity simulation optimization. Winter Simulation Conference, pp 3940–3951
37. Xu J, Zhang S, Huang E, Chen C, Lee L, Celik N (2016) Multi-fidelity optimization with ordinal transformation and optimal sampling. Asia-Pacific Journal of Operational Research 33(3):165–170
38. Yavuz A, Darville J, Celik N, Xu J, Chen C, Langhals B, Engle R (2020) Advancing self healing capabilities in interconnected microgrids via ddas with relational database management. In: Proceedings of the 2020 Winter Simulation Conference
39. Ye C, Ding Y, Wang P, Lin Z (2019) A data-driven bottom-up approach for spatial and temporal electric load forecasting. In: IEEE Trans Power Syst, vol 34, pp 1966–1979
40. Yu DC, Nguyen TC, Haddawy P (1999) Bayesian network model for reliability assessment of power systems. IEEE Transactions on Power Systems 14(2):426–432
41. Zhou K, Chen Y, Xu Z, Lu J, Hu Z (2018) A smart-community demand response load scheduling method based on consumer clustering. In: IEEE Conference Energy Internet Energy System Integration, pp 1–4

Chapter 22
Dynamic Data Driven Partitioning of Smart Grid for Improving Power Efficiency by Combinining K-Means and Fuzzy Methods

Antonia Nasiakou, Miltiadis Alamaniotis, Lefteri H. Tsoukalas, and Manolis Vavalis

Abstract A plethora of energy management opportunities has emerged for electricity consumers and producers by way of the transition from the current grid infrastructure to a smart grid. The aim of this chapter is to present a new dynamic data-driven application systems (DDDAS) methodology for partitioning the smart distribution grid based on dynamically varying data. In particular, the proposed methodology uses the k-means algorithm for performing partitioning and a fuzzy decision making method for increasing power efficiency and reliability. The network is divided into a set of "similar" subnetworks; where the subnetworks are comprised of residential customers (i.e., residencies) who share the same characteristics pertaining to the energy needs but not necessarily the same geographic vicinity or belong to the same grid node. A fuzzy logic method is used to make decisions on which partitions could be offered energy at lower prices available from Renewable Energy Sources (RES). Various scenarios based on the GridLAB-D simulation platform exhibits how the operation of the smart grid is affected from the partition of the distribution grid. The illustrative example utilizes the IEEE-13, IEEE-37 and

A. Nasiakou (✉)
Applied Intelligent Systems Laboratory, School of Nuclear Engineering, Purdue University, West Lafayette, IN, USA

Department of Electrical and Computer Engineering, University of Thessaly, Volos, Greece

M. Alamaniotis
Deparment of Electrical and Computer Engineering, University of Texas at San Antonio, San Antonio, TX, USA
e-mail: malamani@ecn.purdue.edu

L. H. Tsoukalas
Applied Intelligent Systems Laboratory, School of Nuclear Engineering, Purdue University, West Lafayette, IN, USA

M. Vavalis
Department of Electrical and Computer Engineering, University of Thessaly, Volos, Greece

© The Author(s), under exclusive license to Springer Nature Switzerland AG 2022
E. P. Blasch et al. (eds.), *Handbook of Dynamic Data Driven Applications Systems*,
https://doi.org/10.1007/978-3-030-74568-4_22

513

IEEE-123 bus test feeders in the experiments from a distribution grid composing 3004 residencies and both conventional and distributed generators.

Keywords Dynamic data driven · Partitioning · GridLAB-D · Fuzzy logic · Renewable energy sources · Demand response

22.1 Introduction

The primary goal of both transmission and distribution networks is to retain stable, reliable and efficient operations in routine and emergency situations. An anomaly or disruption in the operation of the electricity network could be mitigated through advances in robust decision making mechanisms. Those mechanisms enable the electricity network to react in an efficient way to various types of disturbances. For instance, a huge disturbance in electricity network could be handled by partitioning it, and subsequently targeting at isolating the problem to prevent diffusion in the whole grid. Further, the delivery of electricity has to be non-stop, so that the isolation of the disturbance, aided bypartitioning methods, could be conducted in an efficient way.

In particular, the authors in this study propose a dynamic data driven partitioning of the smart distribution grid focusing on introducing renewable energy sources (RES) in the electricity network and subsequently reducing the wasted energy produced by RES [1]. RES belong to the wide area of the Distributed Energy Sources (DES), with an increasing number of energy companies using emerging RES power systems. The utilities exploiting the features provided by the RES, thus being, more reliable and viable in the energy market. Occasionally, several studies relying on dynamic data driven adaptive simulation techniques have been conducted in order to find the best way to install and integrate RES into the electricity network [1].

The DDDAS concept entails "the ability to dynamically incorporate data into an executing application simulation, and in reverse, the ability of applications to dynamically steer measurement processes", creating "application simulations that can dynamically accept and respond to 'online' field data and measurements and/or control such measurements" paradigm which was presented by Darema in [2]. The creation of a microgrid into the power grid is one of the most widely used and most safest methods to integrate RES into the power grid. For example, in order to reduce the 9 billion dollar cost of satisfying the demand for its installations, the US could adopt RES following a two stage decision making method for reducing its cost as proposed in [3]. A set of microgrids, equipped with RES and distributed communications, could provide energy resources to meet the level of demand satisfaction. The proposed method is based on a DDDAS, allows a simulation model retrieving data from a specific database to dynamically predict the system's reaction under particular conditions. Moreover, in [4], a DDDAS approach is proposed for operation planning of microgrids. It consists of three main components: (a)

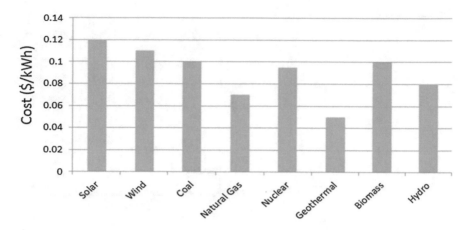

Fig. 22.1 Cost of electricity in dollars per kWh

a database with information about the state of the power network (total demand, market price) and weather conditions, (b) a simulation platform used to simulate the microgrid and (c) a multi-objective optimization problem. Based on the DDDAS concept, the authors in [5], (similar to [4]), propose a novel framework which consists of three main components associated with (a) information about the grid and the weather, (b) an agent based simulation platform and (c) an optimization algorithm. The goal of the study was to develop of a framework for microgrids focusing on the minimization of the computation time of the resource allocation and on the optimization of the operational cost. Additionally, in [6, 7], the authors developed a DDDAS framework for the power network to solve the economic load dispatch problem.

In [8], a DDDAS method is used in health monitoring. To increase data for a set of sensors for the surveillance and crowd control through an efficient way is conducted via a dynamic data driven adaptive multi-scale simulation framework proposed in [9]. In [10], the authors focus on retaining a balance between dynamic data driven solutions and static solutions. In [11], the authors formulate the prediction of wide-area motion imagery data as a DDDAS problem. DDDAS applications are of paramount importance because they provide accurate analysis and predictions, more reliable and efficient outcomes, and more accurate controls [12].

In general, the RES, because of their stochasticity and the high installation cost, offer their produced energy at higher prices than the conventional generators (see Fig. 22.1). Therefore, much of the generated energy may be wasted or stored to batteries due to the fact that the consumers would prefer to buy energy at lower prices than at RES prices. The proposed DDDAS methodology tries to minimize the wasted energy by allowing specific consumers, which belong to the same partition, to buy the potential available energy at lower prices. In other words, the physical constraints of the grid that due to limited delivery capacity may be overcome by using data-driven methods that exploit on the fly the grid state.

Fig. 22.2 Marginal seller
case [14]

Fig. 22.3 Marginal buyer
case [14]

In this study, the market is organized as a double auction market [13]. Both producers and consumer appliances submit their bids for a specific time period into the market framework. More specifically, once the submission period ends, the bids of both appliances and producers are sorted, from highest to lowest price and from lowest to highest price, respectively. The aggregation of the quantities combined with the sorted prices provides the final curve for both producers and appliances. The clearing price and the clearing quantity correspond to the intersection point of the appliances' and producers' curve. The clearing price in which the market offers the clearing quantity is the highest price that a buyer prefers to pay for energy and the lowest price that a seller prefers to sell its produced energy.

In Figs. 22.2 and 22.3, the most widely used scenarios of how the market calculated the clearing quantity and the clearing price are depicted. In this study, we consider that the sellers are the producers and the buyers are the appliances. In particular, Fig. 22.2 depicts the marginal seller case, where the seller offers part of its produced energy. In that case, the clearing price of the market is the bid price of the marginal seller. The clearing quantity is the aggregation of all the buyers' quantities which submit bids with the bid price be higher than the bid price of the marginal seller. In Fig. 22.3, the exact opposite case, known as marginal buyer, is depicted. However, there are cases where the clearing quantity is less than the overall demand, despite the fact that the offered energy that is also the produced energy, is enough to meet the energy requirements of the buyers. In this third case, the buyers, in our case the appliances of all the residencies in the distribution grid that prefer to buy energy at lower than the clearing price, are not included in the market dispatch. So if the overall demand is not satisfied by the market, some appliances won't be in operation for the particular time instance. In other words, these appliances may stay idle and operate in a next clearing of the market framework.

The proposed methodology consists of two phases: the first performs the grid partitioning using input data representing the information pertained to the current state of the power grid. The second phase corresponds to the use of a fuzzy logic decision making method [15–17]. Regarding the partitioning procedure, it is driven by three dynamic factors: (i) the aggregated power demand /total load of the residencies attached to a particular node of the distribution grid, (ii) the average value of a factor for each node of the grid, called schedule skew (each appliance is characterized by this factor), that indicates the estimated time in seconds the householder "starts" their consumption in a given time interval, and (iii) the aggregated number of appliances in operation at each node of the distribution grid each particular time. For comparison purposes, in this study, the proposed methodology is applied every 1 hour and every 4 hours. It is worth mentioning in that point, that the methodology may not be executed, for example, exactly every 1 hour. It may be executed every 55 minutes, or every 70 minutes. Therefore, there is a time window, where the methodology takes place. Actually, this is due to the synchronization of the core module, the most significant module of the GridLAB-D platform.

The fuzzy decision making method uses information regarding the partitions, the number of appliances in operation and the satisfaction of the overall demand. The output of this method is the portioned groups, i.e. the nodes of the distribution grid, which will be the recipient of offered benefits (usually in the form of price incentives); such that the stability of the power grid is also ensured. The two phases of the proposed methodology are:

- The k-means [18] clustering algorithm is utilized to partition the distribution grid using the dynamically driven data from each node. The number of clusters is selected arbitrary; it is set to 3. A distribution grid consists of various nodes; the ones that can handle load and the ones that are used for connectionpurposes. The input data for the proposed partitioning procedure is associated with the nodes in which residencies are attached and in particular the available information, such as the load associated with each of these nodes.
- A fuzzy logic rule based decision making method is utilized. The fuzzy rule is applied when the partitioning procedure ends and when the clearing quantity of the under consideration time interval is not enough to satisfy the overall demand during a particular time interval. In other words, when the demand is satisfied with the quantity provided by the market framework, the fuzzy logic method is not applied. Therefore, the energy produced by RES that is not being

dispatchedwill be offered at a lower price to the appliances of the partition which is selected by the fuzzy logic decision making method. The RES continue to offer their produced energy at lower prices at the selected partition since the demand isnot satisfied from the market.

Going back to the primary goal of this study, after the clearing of the market, appliances that are forced not to operate because their bidding price is lower than the clearing price should not work. Based on that fact, we propose a novel methodology where energy provided by RES that may be wasted, could be sold in a specific partition at a lower price. So, appliances that otherwise should stay idle, with respect to our proposed methodology, they can operate by buying energy at a lower price than the clearing price and closer to their preferred bidding price. More than that, the excessive energy from the RES is not wasted. Therefore, the current study presents our initial efforts to develop a novel methodology for implementing a DDDAS-based smart grid power management method that among many, is also applicable in smart cities [19].

DDDAS is beneficial for a time-limited partitioning of the power grid becauseof its dynamic and evolving nature. The grid is identified as a highly complex system whose modeling is extremely difficult, and as a result data-driven methods are appropriate for its management. In particular, the DDDAS paradigm is efficient for processing the monitored data and subsequently promote respective decisions leading to safe and efficient operation of the power grid. The proposed methodology which makes use of two intelligent tools, the k-means and a fuzzy inference system for intelligent management of the distribution grid based on dynamic driven data during a simulation. Moreover, it implements an elitist approach where the grid is divided into partitions, and at the end only one of them is selected. Both partition and selection procedures are dynamically driven and depend on the current conditions of the grid. The partitioning of the power grid is conducted in such a way that in each partition the nodes have similar energy consumption patterns. Moreover, in each run the selected partition by the fuzzy logic method consists of different nodes.

The rest of this paper is organized as follows. In the next Section, the two tools, i.e., k-means and the fuzzy logic decision making method, are presented in detail. In Sects. 22.3 and 22.4, the simulation configuration and results are presented respectively. Concluding remarks and future plans can be found in Sect. 22.5.

22.2 Methodology

22.2.1 k-means Partitioning Algorithm

Clustering algorithms belong to the class of unsupervised learning methods. In the power grid research field, the load is commonly used for the grid partitioning using the k-means [20] algorithm. The ultimate goal of each partitioning algorithm is to divide the data points of a particular data set into clusters-partitions where the members of the same partition have similar characteristics while the members of different partitions have different characteristics. The k-means algorithm consists of two stages; (a) the determination of a set of k initial clusters that are randomly selected, and (b) the assignment of each data point to the nearest cluster center according to the values of a distance measure. The k-means algorithm aims at minimizing the function in Eq. (22.1).

$$E = \sum_{i=1}^{k} \sum_{p \in X_i} ||p - c_i||^2 \tag{22.1}$$

where p is a data point from the data set and c_i is a cluster centroid.

The k-means algorithm uses the Euclidean distance for the calculation of the distance between each data point of the data set and the cluster center. In this study, the Minkowski distance [21] is utilized. The k-means algorithm runs periodically until the error criterion defined by Eq. (22.1) converges to a predefined threshold. In particular the algorithm converges, when there are no differences between the cluster centers along two sequentially runs of the algorithm. The steps of the k-means algorithm that are conducted in each run are given below:

1. k data points are selected randomly to be the initial cluster centers,
2. repeat the following steps until the error criterion converges to the threshold

   (a) Assign each data point to the closest cluster center by Eq. (22.2)
   (b) Recompute the new cluster centers

$$S_i{}^{(t)} = \left\{ x_p : \left\| x_p - m_i{}^{(t)} \right\|^2 \le \left\| x_p - m_j{}^{(t)} \right\|^2 \right\} \forall j, 1 \le j \le k \tag{22.2}$$

In this study, the calculation of the distance between each data point and the cluster center is based on the Minkowski distance as it is defined in Eq. (22.3).

$$d(x, y) = \left(\sum_{i=0}^{n-1} |x_i - y_i|^p \right)^{1/p} \tag{22.3}$$

There are some special cases for the Minkowski distance. In particular, when p = 1, the distance is known as the Manhattan distance and when p = 2, the distance is the known Euclidean distance.

22.2.2 Fuzzy Logic Decision Making Model

Once the partitioning procedure ends, a fuzzy logic decision making method is utilized to decide which of the partitions may be selected in order the appliances of that partition to benefit from the lower prices of the RES. The produced RES energy is offered at lower prices in the case that their energy is not being dispatched by the market. A fuzzy logic inference system (FIS) consists of four main components, the fuzzifier, the rules, the inference and the defuzzifier. The proposed FIS, utilized in this study, uses as input:

- the load of all the appliances attached to each node that are indicated as cluster centers after the partitioning procedure, named Load. Each node that accommodates residencies can potentially be one of the next cluster centers. The corresponding variable has three fuzzy sets; LOW, MEDIUM and HIGH.
- an index Devices_ON which indicates the aggregated number of appliances in operation of the nodes which are the cluster centers at the particular time that the proposed methodology is applied. The corresponding variable has two fuzzy sets; LOW and HIGH.
- an index, named Satisfaction, with values from 0 to 2, which indicates whether the demand is satisfied or not. A value in the range [0 1] corresponds to the satisfaction of the overall demand while a value in the range [1 2] corresponds to the un-satisfaction of the demand. The former is indicated as SATISFY while the latter is indicated as NO_SATISFY.

The Satisfaction index is the ratio of the clearing quantity of the current bidding period to the total appliances' quantity. On one hand, if it is greater than 1, then the demand is satisfied and the value of the index is the inverse value of this ratio. On the other hand, if it is lower than 1, then the ratio's value is normalized between 1 to 2. If the new value is greater than 2 then the index's value is set equal to 2 and if the normalized value is lower than 1 then the normalized value is accumulated by 1. The FIS implements the following fuzzy rules for associating the input variables Load, Satisfaction and Devices_ON to the output variable Priority:

- IF Load is LOW and Satisfaction is SATISFY and Devices_ON is LOW, THEN Priority is LOW
- IF Load is LOW and Satisfaction is NO_SATISFY and Devices_ON is LOW, THEN Priority is LOW
- IF Load is MEDIUM and Satisfaction is SATISFY and Devices_ON is LOW, THEN Priority is LOW
- IF Load is MEDIUM and Satisfaction is NO_SATISFY and Devices_ON is LOW, THEN Priority is MEDIUM
- IF Load is HIGH and Satisfaction is SATISFY and Devices_ON is LOW, THEN Priority is LOW
- IF Load is HIGH and Satisfaction is NO_SATISFY and Devices_ON is LOW, THEN Priority is HIGH
- IF Load is LOW and Satisfaction is SATISFY and Devices_ON is HIGH, THEN Priority is LOW
- IF Load is LOW and Satisfaction is NO_SATISFY and Devices_ON is HIGH, THEN Priority is MEDIUM
- IF Load is MEDIUM and Satisfaction is SATISFY and Devices_ON is HIGH, THEN Priority is MEDIUM

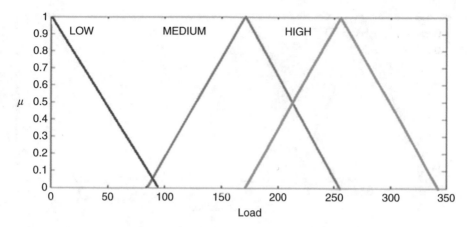

Fig. 22.4 Membership function of the Load input variable

- IF Load is MEDIUM and Satisfaction is NO_SATISFY and Devices_ON is HIGH, THEN Priority is HIGH
- IF Load is HIGH and Satisfaction is SATISFY and Devices_ON is HIGH, THEN Priority is MEDIUM
- IF Load is HIGH and Satisfaction is NO_SATISFY and Devices_ON is HIGH, THEN Priority is HIGH

The output variable Priority indicates which of the partitions is selected over the other partitions to utilize the energy offered from RES at lower prices than their offered price. The membership functions for all the input variables, i.e., Load, Satisfaction, and Devices_ON are based on the triangular form as depicted in Figs. 22.4, 22.5, and 22.6; respectively The Priority variable is also based on the triangular form shown in Fig. 22.7. It is worth mentioning in that point that the Fuzzy Inference System runs independently for each partition (see Fig. 22.8), and the partition with the highest value of the variable Priority is selected.

The proposed DDDAS methodology is executed iteratively until the simulation time ends. More specifically, in each run of the proposed methodology, the aggregated total load, the aggregated number of appliances in operation, the factor schedule skew, the Satisfaction index and the number of clusters are needed for the execution of the proposed methodology (partitioning and fuzzy logic procedures). The data points used by the k-means algorithm is 2-D. One dimension corresponds to the sum of the aggregated total load with the schedule skew factor while the second one corresponds to the number of appliances in operation. In other words, the first dimension is associated with the load at a specific node and the second one with the number of appliances of the same node that need the specific amount of load.

It is worth noting that in the GridLAB-D [22] only the thermostatically controlled appliances submit their bids in the market through the controller object; the aggregated total load which is used in the partitioning procedure, is the total load of

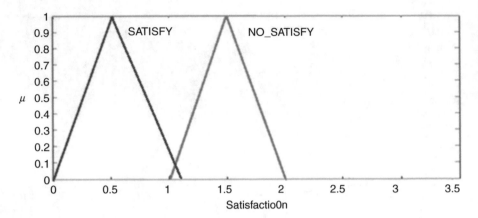

Fig. 22.5 Membership function of the Satisfaction input variable

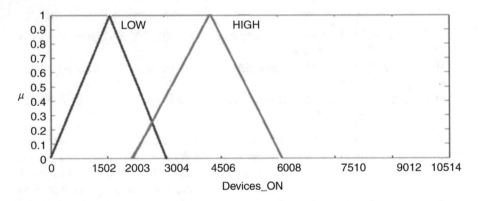

Fig. 22.6 Membership function of the Devices_ON input variable

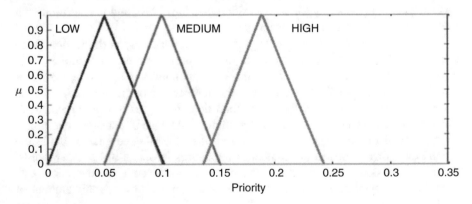

Fig. 22.7 Membership function of the Priority output variable

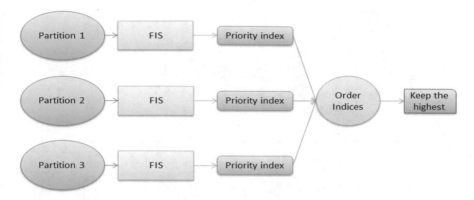

Fig. 22.8 Architecture of the fuzzy logic inference system

Table 22.1 Capacities-prices of the generators

Generators	Price	Max capacity (kW)
Solar panel (116,000 sf)	0.11$/kWh	1917
Wind turbine (GE_25MW, GE_25MW, SYNC_SMALL)	0.10$/kWh	5500
Transmission G1	0.07$/kWh	3300
Transmission G2	0.07$/kWh	3000
Transmission G3	0.07$/kWh	3000

all the appliances in a residency. The fuzzy logic decision making method provides the partition which can benefit from lower prices. The price of produced by the RES energy is defined to be 50% lower than the initial one. We made this assumption because in most of the cases, the clearing price of the market framework is the bid price of one of the producers (0.07$/kWh). In our case, this price is based on conventional natural-gas based generators (See Table 22.1). So, if we reduce the price of RES by 50%, the new price (approx. 0.05$/kWh; 50% lower of the average price of RES) is lower than the clearing price and probably is closer to the preferred by the appliances' price. Therefore, the final price, that the appliances are called to pay for, is the average value of two prices; the price when they belong to the selected partition and they buy energy at the price offered by the RES, and the price when they are satisfied from the market framework.

22.3   Simulations Configuration

For demonstrating the capabilities of the proposed DDDAS methodology, test cases are designed and implemented. The test cases are conducted using the GridLAB-D [22] simulation platform. A DDDAS intelligent simulation engine combines

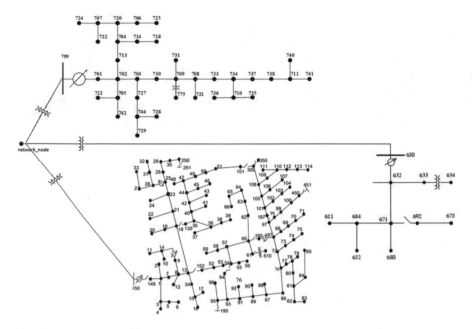

Fig. 22.9 The under consideration distribution power grid

two libraries; the *dlib* library[1] and the *fuzzylite*[2] library. The former provides the implementation of the *k*-means algorithm while the latter provides a C++ based library for the development and the design of fuzzy logic controllers. Three test feeders, the IEEE-13, IEEE-37 and the IEEE-123 [23] are utilized for creating the simulation model test cases presented in this study (see Fig. 22.9).

The simulation model is composed of 3004 residencies, 4 solar panels, 3 wind turbines and 3 conventional natural gas based generators. Each residency can accommodate four individuals and it consists of non-responsive loads, like a refrigerator and responsive loads, like a HVAC (heating, ventilating/ventilation, and air conditioning) system and a water heater. The responsive loads participate in the market using the demand response technique provided by the GridLAB-D. Each RES or conventional generator act as a different energy provider with his own offer price.

The *Transactivec ontroller* or *controller* [24], object of **market** module, implements the demand response technique by submitting on behalf of the appliances the offers in the market. Moreover, the resident is responsible to set his desired setpoints at the thermostatically controlled appliances. The refrigerator, which belongs to the non-responsive loads, is designed through the *ZIPload*, object of **residential**

---

[1] http://dlib.net/ml.html

[2] http://www.fuzzylite.com/

module. For the appliances modelled by utilizing the*ZIPload*object, the *schedule* object of the GridLAB-D is used to provide the energy requirements of the appliance for the overall simulation time. The participation of the refrigerator in the market framework is achieved through the *stub_bidder*, object of **market** module. Its main features are the fixed price and the quantity which actually reflects the energy requirements of the appliance.

Regarding the generators, both transmission and distributed generators are simulated. The dirtibuted generators are associated with RES such as solar panels and three wind turbines. Four solar panels of total area 116,000 sf are simulated. The max output of the threewind turbines is 5500 kW, while the max output of the solar panel area is 1917 kW. For simulation purposes, we use two different types of wind turbines; the GE_25 MW and the GENERIC_SYNC_SMALL, and details about their configuration and their parameters can be found at the GridLAB-D's user guide.[3] Table 22.1 depicts the operating costs for each type of generator including the max power output as well.

The *stub_bidder* object of the **market**module, is designed to submit the offers in the market on behalf of the conventional generators. It is characterized by the fixed price and the fixed quantity during the simulation. Regarding the distributed generators (the associated objects are developed in **generators** module of GridLAB-D), they participate in the market through the *generator_controller*, object of the **market** module. The price in that case is also fixed, but the bidding quantity depends on the weather conditions. For the weather data, the WA-SEATTE.tmy2 file contains weather information for the Seattle, Washington.

22.4 Simulation Results

For assessing the validity and the reliability of the proposed DDDAS methodology, various simulations are conducted whose results are presented in this section. For comparison purposes, we are going to present, compare and analyze the simulation results of the three cases: (CASE I) when the proposed methodology is applied every 1 hour, and (ii) when it is not applied (Case II). Moreover, for proving the dynamic nature of the proposed methodology, we run more simulations by varying the time that the proposed methodology isexecuted. In particular, we are going to analyze and compare the results when the proposed methodology is applied every **one** hour (Case I), every **four** hours (Case III) and when it is not applied (Case II).

For all of the presented test cases, the simulation time is 24 hours, and the simulation day is 08/01/2000. Both producers and appliances can submit their bids in the market framework every 15 minutes. The clearing price and the clearing quantity are available when the bidding period expires. Regarding the proposed methodology, every hour or every 4 hours, information about the state of the

---

[3]http://www.gridlabd.org/documents/doxygen/1.1/files.html

Table 22.2 The average load for the partitions for each run where the fuzzy logic decision making method takes place

Time	Partition #1	Partition #2	Partition #3
2:00 am	26.82	167.25	**61.52**
4:00 am	165.62	26.44	**41.01**
6:00 am	115.67	31.98	**49.94**
8:00 am	203.2	**26.16**	127.57
10:00 am	7.74	16.94	**65.63**
12:00 pm	8.68	**20.70**	5.27
2:00 pm	4.44	**64.80**	15.23
4:00 pm	17.14	**110.57**	28.28
6:00 pm	**94.58**	138.26	25.39
8:00 pm	**27.31**	160.25	69.16
10:00 pm	78.22	161.60	**78.60**
12:00 am	30.46	149.94	**90.28**

distribution grid regarding the load, the *schedule_skew*, the number of appliances in operation and the satisfaction of the demand are available to be utilized.

Table 22.2 presents the average total load of each partition, for each particular time the fuzzy logic procedure is executed. The partitions that are selected from the fuzzy logic decision making method are presented in bold font. The information depicted in the Table 22.2 corresponds to the Case I. It is worth mentioning in that point, that the whole procedure takes place every 1 hour, but the fuzzy logic methodology takes place when the demand of the residential consumers is not fully satisfied. Because of that in the Table 22.2 the results are depicted every 2 hours.

In Figs. 22.10 and 22.11, the HVAC load of two residencies that buy energy at lower prices is depicted. Moreover, for comparison purposes, the HVAC load of the residency when our methodology is not applied (Case II) is also presented. The *x*-axis and the *y*-axis correspond to the simulation time and the HVAC load (in kW) of the residency respectively. It is clear that the HVAC system works more frequently in the case of applying the proposed methodology (Case I). We choose the HVAC system to show the effect of the proposed DDDAS methodology to the operation of the distribution grid because it needs more energy to meet its consumption requirements and operates more frequently as compared with the other thermostatically controlled appliances. The HVAC system and the water heater are the only appliances of which their operation is adjusted by configuring the setpoints. Moreover, it is observed that the operation of the HVAC system is shifted from the on-peak hours to the off-peak hours.

In Fig. 22.12, the clearing quantity for a whole day in both cases I and II is presented. The blue line corresponds to the Case I while the red dots to the Case II. We can observe that the clearing quantity in the Case I is higher, especially during the hours where the proposed methodology is applied. The results associated with the total load of each residency of the Figs. 22.10 and 22.11 of both the Cases I and II are depicted in Table 22.3. It is shown that the proposed methodology gives the opportunity to the residential consumers to buy energy at lower prices. More specifically, the consumer that belongs to the cluster selected by the fuzzy logic

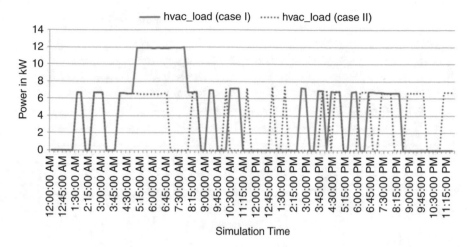

Fig. 22.10 HVAC load for a residency that benefits from the lower prices in some time intervals when the partitioning process is taking place every 1 hour

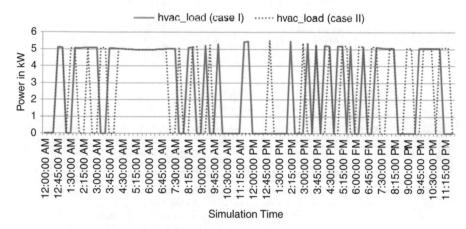

Fig. 22.11 HVAC load for a residency that benefits from the lower prices in some time intervals when the DDDAS proposed methodology is taking place every 1 hour

decision making method can buy one kWh at **0.061$** instead of **0.07$**. This price is the average price for the 24 hours of the simulation.

As mentioned in the introduction, despite the fact that the offered energy, both from the conventional generators and RES, is enough to satisfy the overall demand; the clearing price allows only the appliances that bid in a price equal or higher than the clearing price to buy energy. So, in this study, we run the simulation with the opportunity of the appliances to stay idle because of the high clearing price until they can buy energy at lower prices.

In Fig. 22.13, it is clear that despite the fact that there is wasted or undispatched energy, this amount of energy is comparatively less. The market framework offers

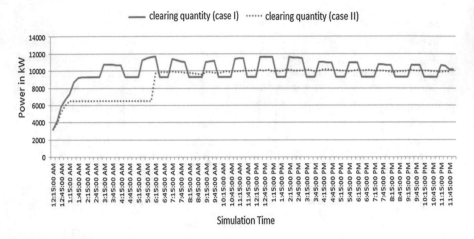

Fig. 22.12 Clearing quantity offered by the market for the Case I and Case II

Table 22.3 Comparison of the cost and the load of a residency in two case studies

		Case I	Case II
Total load (kWh)/ cost ($\kWh)	Residency Fig. 22.10	*7464 / 0.061*	7176 / 0.07
	Residency Fig. 22.11	*5184 / 0.058*	4584 / 0.07

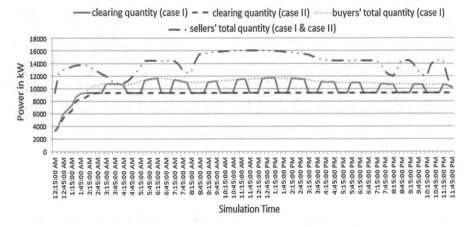

Fig. 22.13 Clearing Quantity, buyers' (or appliances') total quantity and sellers' (or generators')
total quantity regarding the Case I and Case II

less energy than the produced one, because that some amount of energy is offered at
higher prices, especially when this part of energy offered by RES. It is observable,
that the clearing quantity when the proposed methodology is applied is closer to the
supply curve (sellers' total quantity in Fig. 22.13). Therefore, the amount of wasted
energy is lower. So, less amount of energy can be stored in the batteries.

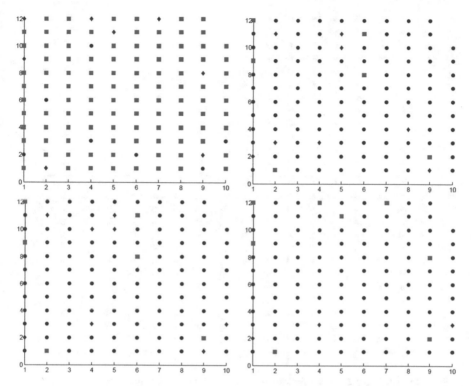

Fig. 22.14 The every 2 hours results starting from 02:00 to 08:00 when the proposed methodology is applied every 2 hour. The red circle points indicate the nodes that are selected to buy energy at lower prices

In Figs. 22.14, 22.15, and 22.16, the results associated with Case I are presented. More specifically, each sub figure corresponds to a specific hour during the simulation while each point in each sub figure corresponds to one node of the distribution grid. The points depicted with red circles are associated with the nodes, that is the appliances, that are selected from the proposed methodology to buy energy at lower prices. The green square and blue rhombus points represent the nodes of the other two partitions. The Fig. 22.14 corresponds to the time interval 02:00 to 08:00 (early morning, off peak demand) with each sub figure from left to right to be associated with a specific hour with 2 hours time interval. Note that as time increase, more nodes are able to buy energy at lower prices.

Regarding Figs. 22.15 and 22.16, the results associated with the time interval 10:00 to 16:00 (daytime) and 18:00 to 24:00 (nighttime), respectively, are shown. It is clear from the figures that the nodes that belong to the selected each time partition are not the same. However, in some cases there are nodes that belong to two consecutive runs of the proposed methodology are of the selected partition. Therefore, the residencies that will be privileged to buy energy at lower prices supplied by the RES in some cases are the same but in most of them, differ. So,

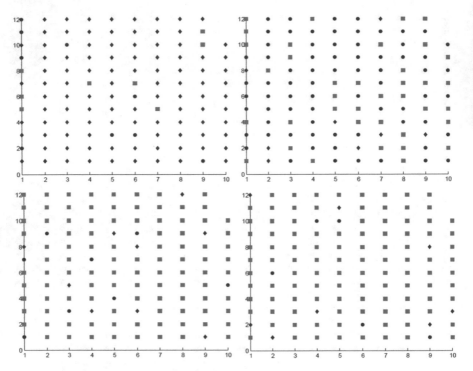

Fig. 22.15 The every 2 hours results starting from 10:00 am when the proposed methodology is applied every 2 hours. The red circle points indicate the nodes that are selected to buy energy at lower prices

we can point out that there are few residencies that are excluded from the benefits provided.

For experimental reasons and for presenting the flexibility of the proposed dynamic data driven methodology, the time of execution of the both the partitioning procedure and the fuzzy logic decision making method has changed from 1 hour (Case I) to 4 hours (Case III). In fact, the average total load of each partition for each run and the partition that is selected (bold font) from the fuzzy logic decision making method are presented. Moreover, it is clear, that in most of the cases, the partition with the biggest average total load is chosen from the fuzzy logic decision making method.

As it is mentioned in the beginning of this Chapter, the information associated with the total load of each residency is dynamically driven during the simulation. Due to the fact that in each simulation, the proposed methodology may not be executed exactly at the same time, we observe that the sum of the average total load of all of the three partitions at 4:00 am in Tables 22.2 and 22.4 differ.

In Fig. 22.17, the clearing quantity of both Case I (every hour) and Case III (every 4 hours) is depicted. It could be noticed that the amount of the demand satisfied when the methodology is applied every 4 hours is higher. This is due to the fact that

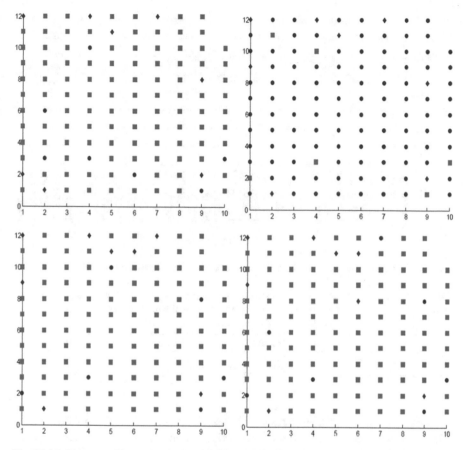

Fig. 22.16 The every 2 hours results starting from 18:00 to 24:00 when the proposed methodology is applied every 2 hours. The red circle points indicate the nodes that are selected to buy energy at lower prices

Table 22.4 The average load for the runs where the proposed methodology is applied every 4 hours

Time	Partition #1	Partition #2	Partition #3
4:00 am	75.21	**485.67**	19.22
2:00 pm	53.46	**23.08**	7.66
6:00 pm	**85.039**	12.65	34.41

the RES offer their energy in lower prices for longer time (4 hours in that case)thus more demand is satisfied.

This is also shown in Table 22.5, where the aggregated clearing quantity of all the cases (Case I, II and III) is depicted. It is also observed that the percentage of the non satisfied power, when the proposed methodology is applied, is at lower levels in Case III. As it is appeared, the amount of demand that is satisfied is higher. Moreover, it is satisfied at a lower than the cleared price, while there is also a reduction in the lost energy that it is produced by the RES.

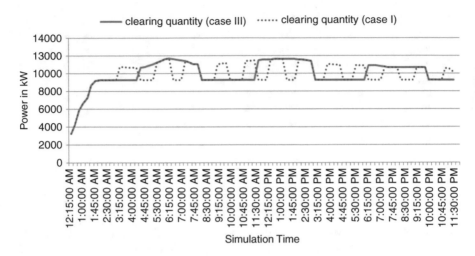

Fig. 22.17 Clearing quantity offered by the market for the Case I and the Case III

Table 22.5 The aggregated clearing quantity in MW and the percentage of the unsatisfied demand demonstrated the 24 hours of the simulation in the case where the methodology is not applied (Case II), is applied every **one** hour (Case I) and every **four** hours (Case III)

	Case I	Case II	Case III
Clearing quantity (MW)	942	855	946
% of non satisfied demand	7.28%	15.84%	6.88%

In Fig. 22.18, the simulation results of Case III are presented. The points depicted with red circles are associated with the nodes that are selected from the proposed methodology to buy energy at lower prices. The green square and blue rhombus points represent the nodes for the other two partitions. It is observed that the second phase of the proposed methodology is applied three times. It is clear that even in the case where the partitioning procedure is taking place every 4 hours, the residencies, that are selected to buy energy at lower prices vary.

22.5 Conclusion

The current work presents our efforts to develop a DDDAS methodology for implementing a smart grid management method. The proposed methodology which makes use of two intelligent tools, namely, the *k*-means clustering method and a fuzzy decision making method to provide intelligent management of the distribution grid. In particular, it implements an elitist approach where the grid is partitioned into clusters and one of them is selected to benefit of buying energy generated by RES at a lower price. Both the partition and selection procedures are dynamically driven and depend on the current grid conditions [25]. The number of clusters used by the

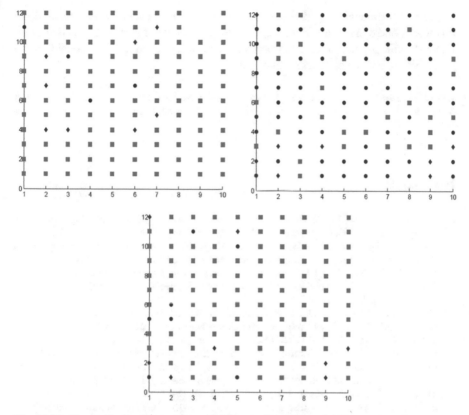

Fig. 22.18 The results for the time interval 4:00 am, 12:00 pm and 6:00 pm when the proposed methodology is applied every 4 hours. The red circle points indicate the nodes that are selected to buy energy at lower prices

k-means algorithm is user-defined, but in our future plans we are planning to use the available information of the grid to decide the number of clusters.

With respect to test results, we observed that the proposed methodology minimizes the wasted energy and satisfies a higher number of residential consumers as compared to cases when no partitioning is performed. The dynamic partitioning process takes place every 1 hour or 4 hours with different nodes at each time be privileged to buy energy offered (RES) at lower prices. Overall it is concluded from the results, that the methodology achieves a reduction in the amount of wasted energy generated by RES.

In the future DDDAS paradigms will play a significant role in the efficient management of the power grid and overall of smart energy systems in smart cities [26]. The advent of smart grid technologies together with the advances in big data processing will demand the utilization of DDDAS paradigm to promote efficient decision making pertained to power grid management. Regarding the grid partitioning method the prospectives of DDDAS contains grid partitioning that is performed at time intervals defined by the grid itself (not every 2 hours as we do in this work), and dynamically defining the size and number of partitions. Furthermore, DDDAS will promote automated partition with the grid taking into consideration power state data as well market state data.

Acknowledgements This work is supported by the US National Science Foundation (NSF) in collaboration with the Air Force Office of Scientific Research (AFOSR) under the grant no 1462393.

References

1. Aghaei, J., Alizadeh, M. Demand response in smart electricity grids equipped with renewable energy sources: A review, Renewable and Sustainable Energy Reviews, **18**, pp. 64–72.
2. Darema, F. Dynamic data driven applications systems: A new paradigm for application simulations and a new paradigm for measurement systems, NSF Workshop, 2000.
3. Moore, D. E., Celik, N. DDDAS-based Communication in Distributed Smartgrid Networks, In Proceedings of the Annual Industrial and Systems Engineering Research Conference 2014, Montreal, Canada, 2014.
4. Shi, X.,Damgacioglu, H.,Celik, N.A. Dynamic Data-driven Approach for Operation Planning of Microgrids, International Conference On Computational Science,**51**,pp. 2543–2552, 2015.
5. Thanos, A.,Bastani, M., Celik, N., Chen, C.H. Dynamic Data Driven Adaptive Simulation Framework for Automated Control in Microgrids,IEEE Transactions on Smart Grid, 2015.
6. Celik, N., Thanos, A. E., Saenz, J. P. DDDAS-based dispatch control in power networks,13th Annual International Conference on Computational Science, pp. 1899–1908,2013.
7. Thanos, A. E., Shi, X., Saenz, J. P., Celik, N. A. DDDAMS framework for real-time load dispatching in power networks,Proceedings of the 2013 Winter Simulation Conference - Simulation: Making Decisions in a Complex World, pp. 1893–1904, 2013.
8. Park, C., Tang, J., Ding, Y. Aggressive data reduction for damage detection in structural health monitoring,Structural Health Monitoring , **9**, pp. 59–74, 2010.
9. Khaleghi, A. M., Xu, D., Wang, Z., Li, M., Lobos, A., Liu, J., Son, Y.A. A DDDAMS-based planning and control framework for surveillance and crowd control via UAVs and UGVs,Expert Systems with Applications,**40**, pp. 7168–7183, 2013.
10. Blasch, E., Al-Nashif, Y., Hariri, S. Static versus dynamic data information fusion analysis using DDDAS for cyber security trust,Procedia Computer Science, **29**, pp. 1299–1313, 2014.
11. Blasch, E.,Seetharaman, G., Darema, F. Dynamic Data Driven Applications Systems (DDDAS) modeling for automatic target recognition,inProc. SPIE 8744, Automatic Target Recognition XXIII, **8744**, 2013.
12. Darema, F. Dynamic Data Driven Applications Systems: New Capabilities for Application Simulations and Measurements, Lecture Notes in Computer Science, **3515**, pp. 610–615, 2005.
13. Fainti, R., Nasiakou, A., Tsoukalas, E., Vavalis, M. Design and early simulations of next generation intelligent energy systems', *International Journal of Monitoring and Surveillance Technologies Research,2*, pp. 58–82,*2014.*
14. GridLAB-D Market Module Documentation.[http://gridlab-d.sourceforge.net/wiki/index.php/ Spec:Market]
15. Tsoukalas, L.H., Uhrig, R.E. Fuzzy and Neural Approaches in Engineering, 1997.
16. Mendel, J. Fuzzy logic systems for engineering: a tutorial, Proceedings of the IEEE, **83**, pp. 345–377, 1995.
17. Alamaniotis, M., Agarwal, V., Jevremovic, V. Anticipatory monitoring and control of complex energy systems using a fuzzy based fusion of support vector regressors, 5th International Conference on Information, Intelligence, Systems and Applications, pp. 33–37, 2014.

18. Nasiakou, A., Alamaniotis, M., Tsoukalas, L.H. Extending the k-meansclustering algorithm to improve the compactness of the clusters. Journal ofPattern Recognition Research, **11**(1),pp. 61–73, 2016.
19. Alamaniotis, M., Bourbakis, N., & Tsoukalas, L.H., "Enhancing Privacy in Smart Cities through Morphing of Anticipated Demand Utilizing Self-Elasticity and Genetic Algorithms," *Sustainable Cities and Society*, Elsevier, vol. 46, April 2019, pp. (101426)1–12.
20. Zhou, K., Yang, S., Shen, C. A review of electric load classification in smart grid environment, Renewable and Sustainable Energy Reviews, **24**, pp. 103–110, 2013.
21. Singh, A., Yadav, A., Rana, A. K-means with Three different Distance Metrics, International Journal of Computer Applications, **67**(10), pp. 13–17,2013
22. Nasiakou, A., Vavalis, M., Bargiotas, D. Simulating active and reactive energy markets, 6th International Conference on Information, Intelligence, Systems and Applications, pp. 1–6,2015.
23. Kersting, W. H. Radial Distribution Feeders, Transactions on Power Systems,**6**, pp. 975–985, 1991.
24. Fuller, J.C., Schneider, K., Chassin, P. D. Analysis of residential demand response and double-auction markets. IEEE Power and Energy Society General Meeting, 2011.
25. Alamaniotis, M., & Gatsis, N., "Evolutionary Load Morphing in Smart Power System Partitions Ensuring Privacy and Minimizing Cost," *Mediterranean Conference on Power Generation, Transmission, Distribution, and Energy Conversion (MEDPOWER 2018)*, Dubrovnik, Croatia, November 12–15, 2018.
26. Bourbakis, N., Tsoukalas, L.H., Alamaniotis, M., Gao, R., & Kerkman, K., "DEMOS: A Distributed Model based on Autonomous, Intelligent Agents with Monitoring and Anticipatory Responses for Energy Management in Smart Cities," *International Journal of Monitoring and Surveillance Technologies Research*, IGI Global Publications, vol. 2(4), October-December 2014, pp. 80–98.

Part VIII
Process-Aware: Image and Video Coding

Chapter 23
Design of a Dynamic Data-Driven System for Multispectral Video Processing

Honglei Li, Yanzhou Liu, Kishan Sudusinghe, Jinsung Yoon, Erik P. Blasch, Mihaela van der Schaar, and Shuvra S. Bhattacharyya

Abstract Driven by recent advances in video capture technology, multispectral video analytics is gaining increased interest due to its potential to exploit increased spectral resolution and diversity across sets of multispectral bands. In this chapter, methods are developed for integrated band subset selection and video processing parameter optimization in multispectral video processing. The methods are designed to systematically trade off processing requirements and accuracy, as well as to maximize accuracy for a given set of processed bands. Using the proposed methods together with the Dynamic Data Driven Applications Systems (DDDAS) paradigm, dynamic constraints and measurements can be incorporated into embedded software adaptation in real-time, bandwidth-constrained applications. While the methods developed in the chapter are demonstrated concretely in the context of background subtraction, the underlying approach is more general and can be adapted to other video analysis solutions.

Keywords Dataflow · Embedded signal processing · Hyperspectral imaging · Video processing

H. Li · Y. Liu · K. Sudusinghe · S. S. Bhattacharyya
Department of Electrical and Computer Engineering, University of Maryland, College Park, MD, USA
e-mail: honglei@umd.edu; yzliu@umd.edu; kishans@umd.edu; ssb@umd.edu

J. Yoon · M. van der Schaar
Department of Electrical Engineering, University of California, Los Angels, CA, USA
e-mail: mihaela@ee.ucla.edu

E. P. Blasch (✉)
Air Force Office of Scientific Research, Arlington, VA, USA
e-mail: erik.blasch.1@us.af.mil

E. P. Blasch et al. (eds.), *Handbook of Dynamic Data Driven Applications Systems*,
https://doi.org/10.1007/978-3-030-74568-4_23

539

23.1 Introduction

Recent advances in multispectral video capture technology along with system design trade-offs introduced by these advances present new challenges and opportunities in the area of dynamic data driven applications systems (DDDAS) for video analytics. The additional spectral bands available in multispectral video streams offer the potential for more accurate knowledge extraction, but also increase costs associated with real-time processing, energy consumption, and storage requirements. In this chapter, we develop data-driven models and methods that address these trade-offs to systematically perform design optimization of multispectral video processing systems. For concreteness, we develop and demonstrate these methods in the context of a specific video processing application—that of background subtraction, which is widely-used in many application areas that require automated detection of moving targets.

More specifically, background subtraction is investigated for multispectral video streams in our recently developed system design framework for dynamic, data-driven video processing using lightweight dataflow (LD) techniques. LD is a model-based methodology and accompanying set of application programming interfaces (APIs) for design and implementation of embedded signal, image, and video processing systems [17, 20]. The design framework developed in this chapter, called LDspectral, provides systematic optimization of relevant trade-offs in real-time implementation of multispectral video processing systems. Capabilities in LDspectral derive a sequence of increasing subsets of the given multispectral bands that correspond to the subsets to process when increasing amounts of computational resources or energy consumption budget are available. The objective is to enable strategic, dynamic selection across the available bands based on constraints imposed by the given operational scenario.

Jointly with the selection of band subsets, methods are presented to optimize background subtraction parameters for multispectral processing. The targeted parameters include the type of fusion strategy (pixel-level or feature-level) to employ across bands; weighting coefficients for pixel-level fusion; and pooling thresholds for feature-level fusion.

In addition to providing methods to adapt video processing configurations in response to dynamically changing operational constraints, the novel approach to parameterization and configuration optimization leads to more accurate background subtraction on a relevant data set as compared to previously developed techniques for multispectral background subtraction.

In the methods developed in this chapter, we model and optimize video processing trade-offs across algorithm and implementation aspects through the DDDAS paradigm. Using the DDDAS paradigm, LDspectral is designed to apply performance data that is collected through execution time instrumentation, and adapt video processing configurations dynamically according to their trade-off models, and according to constraints on real-time performance.

While the methods developed in the chapter are demonstrated concretely in the context of background subtraction, the underlying approach is more general and can be adapted to other video analysis situations.

The remainder of this chapter is organized as follows. Section 23.2 introduces background and related work in multispectral video processing. In Sect. 23.3, we provide an introduction to the LDspectral system and discuss the specific problems in optimized, DDDAS-based video processing that it is designed to address. Sections 23.4, 23.5, and 23.6 present details of the proposed models and methods for addressing the applications in LDspectral. Section 23.7 discusses our experimental setup for demonstrating and assessing these new methods, and reports on the experimental results. Finally, Sect. 23.8 summarizes the contributions, and outlines directions for future work that are motivated by the developments in the chapter.

23.2 Related Work

Multispectral sensor technology is used in a variety of applications for monitoring and surveillance in ground and air environments, such as land cover classification, and thermal mapping. Multispectral images typically cover three to ten spectral bands that range from near infrared to visible light. In recent years, advances in sensor technology have helped to increase the effectiveness and decrease the cost of multispectral imaging systems, and make these systems practical to employ in an increasing variety of applications (e.g., see [8]).

Like hyperspectral imaging, multispectral imaging provides increased spectral discrimination compared to traditional imaging methods. However, multispectral imaging systems employ much fewer spectral bands—in the range of 3 to about 10—while hyperspectral imaging systems can involve hundreds, thousands or even more bands [8]. In addition to being more numerous, the bands employed in hyperspectral imaging systems also have narrower bandwidths. Although the contributions of this chapter are introduced in the context of multispectral imaging systems, they have the potential for adaptation to hyperspectral systems. Investigating such adaptations is a useful direction for future work.

In the extraction of knowledge from the diverse channels provided by multispectral and hyperspectral imaging sensors, image fusion is an important class of algorithms. Liu et al. present a comparative study of different multiresolution algorithms for image fusion [11]. Bhateja et al. develop a non-subsampled contourlet transform approach for multispectral image fusion in medical applications [5]. Wei et al. propose an image fusion method for multispectral and hyperspectral images that is based on a sparse representation, and results in less spectral error and spectral distortion compared to related fusion techniques [22]. Chen et al. develop an approach for fusing low-spatial-resolution hyperspectral images and high-spatial-resolution multispectral images of the same scene using pan-sharpening methods [7].

Benezeth et al. have performed an extensive experimental investigation on the application of multispectral video processing to the detection of moving objects [4]. Benezeth's contributions also include a publicly available dataset with foreground truth for experimenting with multispectral background subtraction techniques. Uzkent, Hoffman, and Vodacek have developed a DDDAS framework for controlling hyperspectral data collection [21]. Sobral et al. proposed an online stochastic tensor decomposition algorithm for robust background subtraction. Sobral's results demonstrate that red-green-blue (RGB) features are not sufficient to handle color saturation, illumination variations and problems due to shadows, while incorporating six visible spectral bands together with one near-infra-red band helps to address these limitations [18]. Reddy et al. present a multispectral video visualization method, and propose in this context a fusion technique to retain color, texture, relative luminance and sharpness [14]. Recently, Aved et al. [1] applied a difference criteria to weight hyperspectral bands.

Babayan et al. reported an object tracking algorithm for multispectral video. The algorithm independently processes the images in different spectral ranges and fuses the tracking results [2]. The authors used performance indicator analysis to select preferred subsets of spectral bands. Scebba et al. presented an algorithm for respiratory rate estimation and apnea detection based on multispectral data fusion. The algorithm first addresses respiratory rate estimation and apnea detection independently, and then fuses the results to determine the final outputs [15]. Xie et al. propose a model-based deep learning approach for merging high resolution multispectral images and low resolution hyperspectral images. The merged results are produced in order to construct high-resolution hyperspectral images [23].

Earlier work on LDspectral was presented in [9]. The early version considered only pixel-level fusion, and focused primarily on identifying two-band subsets for very lightweight processing. In this chapter, we extend the developments of the earlier version by integrating feature-level fusion and arbitrarily-sized band subsets into LDspectral.

The distinguishing aspects of the contributions in this chapter compared to the related work include the (1) focus on integrating DDDAS methods into trade-off optimization between accuracy and real-time performance in multispectral video processing systems, and (2) emphasis on supporting flexible optimization involving the subset of available multispectral bands that is processed, and the associated algorithm and dataflow configurations. The design methodologies and tools developed in this chapter are largely complementary to the methods surveyed above in the area of image fusion, and in our experimental evaluation (Sect. 23.7), we apply the dataset mentioned above that has been introduced by Benezeth et al.

23.3 Lightweight Dataflow (LD) Spectral

As motivated in Sect. 23.1, this chapter develops new capabilities in LDspectral, which is a software tool for optimized design and implementation of multispectral video processing systems. The objective of LDspectral is to enable efficient, dynamic processing across the available bands based on constraints imposed by the given operational scenario, and instrumentation data collected "M" is in Figure 23.1 from the underlying embedded platform.

In the class of DDDAS-driven video processing systems that is targeted by LDspectral, the input data comes from a set $Z = \{B_1, B_2, \ldots, B_M\}$, where M is the total number of available multi-spectral bands. The multispectral image stream with this number of bands is processed by a given dataflow graph $G = (V, E)$, where V is the set of graph vertices (*actors*), which correspond to functional modules, and E is the set of edges. Each edge $e \in E$ corresponds to a first-in-first-out (FIFO) communication channel that buffers data as it passes from the output of one actor to the input of another. The actors and edges in G have associated sets of parameters P_v and P_e, respectively. Parameters of an edge may include a Boolean "activation parameter", in the spirit of Boolean parametric dataflow [3]. Such activation parameters allow edges to be enabled and disabled. In this context, disabling an edge means effectively removing the associated connection (between the edge's source and sink actors) from the graph. Such use of dynamic parameter adjustment can be used to configure dataflow within the system model.

We assume a given constraint C_r (in units of time) on execution time performance for a particular video processing scenario. The run-time system for video processing is equipped with instrumentation for periodically determining the execution time performance of the current video processing configuration. The problem addressed by LDspectral is to select the subset $S \in 2^Z$ of spectral bands to store and process, and an assignment of valid parameter values for all dataflow graph parameters in $(P_v \cup P_e)$ such that video processing accuracy is maximized subject to the real-time constraint specified by C_r. Here, 2^Z denotes the power set of Z.

The LDspectral tool addresses novel video processing design spaces introduced by multispectral image acquisition technology. It enables efficient experimentation and data-driven optimization of video processing configurations for multispectral video analytics. The remainder of this chapter discusses details on design optimization models and methods employed in LDspectral, and demonstrates the tool through a case study involving background subtraction for moving object detection.

23.4 Run-Time System Model

Figure 23.1 shows a block diagram of the run-time system model that is targeted by LDspectral. We refer to this model as the *LDspectral Run-time System Model* (*LRSM*). In the LRSM, Dataflow Configuration Profiles refer to performance profiles of alternative actor configurations. These profiles provide estimates of accuracy and execution time for alternative algorithmic configurations associated with selected functional modules in the given video processing application system. The profiles are determined at design time, through simulation or through instrumented execution on the targeted embedded platform.

Similarly, the Subset Selection Profiles provide estimates of trade-offs between accuracy and execution time for different subsets of spectral bands. Each entry in this collection of profiling data corresponds to a subset $S \in 2^Z$ of the available spectral bands, and provides estimates of the achievable accuracy and the execution time cost when subset S is used as input for the core video processing functionality

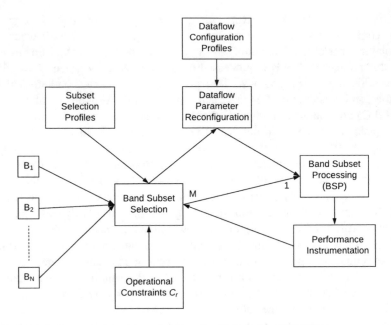

Fig. 23.1 Block diagram of the LDspectral Run-time System Model (LRSM)

(and the remaining bands $(Z - S)$ are discarded or ignored). In the current version of LDspectral, one subset is selected for each cardinality value in the range of $1, 2, \ldots, M$, where M is the total number of available bands in the multispectral sensor subsystem. An entry is then stored within the Subset Selection Profiles for each of these selected subsets. Methods used to select and evaluate these subsets are discussed further in Sect. 23.6.

The Subset Selection Profiles and Dataflow Configuration Profiles are used at run-time to adapt algorithmic and dataflow parameters associated with the core video processing functionality of the targeted embedded system. This core functionality is represented by the block in Fig. 23.1 labeled *Band Subset Processing (BSP)*. Details about the BSP subsystem are discussed in Sect. 23.5. The dynamic, data-driven adaptation of system parameters in the LRSM is performed by the blocks in Fig. 23.1 that are labeled Dataflow Parameter Reconfiguration and Band Subset Selection. *Dataflow Parameter Reconfiguration* is performed using techniques that involve parameterized dataflow [6] and Boolean parametric dataflow [3]. The *Band Subset Selection* block takes as input design time information provided by the Subset Selection Profiles, and run-time information derived from Performance (execution time) Instrumentation. Band Subset Selection produces as output the subset $\sigma(i) \in 2^Z$ of multispectral bands that are to be processed in the next iteration i of LRSM execution. This subset is taken from among the entries in the Subset Selection Profiles as the band subset that provides the highest accuracy while satisfying the current Operational Constraint C_r.

23.5 Band Subset Processing

This section details the BSP subsystem, which was introduced in Sect. 23.1 as one of the blocks in Fig. 23.1. A dataflow representation of the BSP subsystem is illustrated in Fig. 23.2, including pixel-level fusion (PLF) and feature-level fusion (FLF) [10].

The BSP subsystem in LDspectral is designed through integrated used of the lightweight dataflow environment (LIDE) and OpenCV. LIDE is a model-based tool for design and implementation of embedded software and firmware using coarse-grained dataflow representations [17, 20]. OpenCV is a computer vision software framework that includes a large library of software components for video processing (e.g., see [12]). In the integrated use of LIDE and OpenCV employed in BSP, actors in LIDE incorporate calls to relevant OpenCV functions that perform selected image/video processing operations. This approach provides an efficient means for integrating model-based system design techniques with the large library of image/video processing implementations in OpenCV.

As shown in Fig. 23.1, the BSP subsystem consists of several actors. The Input Interface actor provides an interface for accessing and operating on input image frames for a given invocation I of the BSP subsystem. These input frames

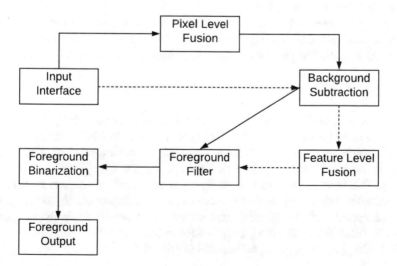

Fig. 23.2 Dataflow representation of the band subset processing (BSP) subsystem shown in Fig. 23.1

correspond to the selected subset of spectral bands that are to be accessed during invocation I.

The *Background Subtraction* actor computes an initial background subtraction result that is further refined in later stages of the BSP subsystem. The core operation applied by this actor is carried out by the OpenCV function called `BackgroundSubtractorMOG2`, which applies a Gaussian Mixture Model (GMM) [19, 25, 26].

The *Foreground Filter* actor is used to remove noise from the output of the Background Subtraction actor. Such noise can result from the moving of background objects, such as trees that are shaken by the wind. This actor applies two morphological operations—erosion and dilation—through their implementations in OpenCV. The erosion function removes objects in the foreground that are smaller than the filter-size (a parameter of the BSP subsystem), while the dilation function corrects distortion at foreground object boundaries that results from the erosion operation.

The *Foreground Binarization* actor takes the output of the foreground filter, and converts it into a binary form, where each pixel is classified as being either a foreground or background pixel. This actor applies a threshold that is determined empirically (off-line) to optimize classification accuracy. In BSP, the OpenCV function called `cvThreshold` is employed for foreground binarization.

The BSP subsystem provides two different fusion methods—PLF and FLF—to fuse the individual images from different bands in the subset of selected bands. PLF is applied to the input image before applying background subtraction, while FLF is applied to the result of preliminary background subtraction from each band. Using the configurable dataflow capabilities in the BSP subsystem (represented by the dashed edges in Fig. 23.2), designers or the LDspectral run-time system can select flexibly between PLF and FLF.

For a band subset with two elements, a "pairwise band combination" parameter α is used to configure PLF in the BSP subsystem. The value of α must be a real number in the range [0, 1]. The parameter α is used to configure the fusion operation by:

$$y = \alpha \times x_1 + (1 - \alpha) \times x_2, \tag{23.1}$$

where x_1 and x_2 are two corresponding pixel values (at the same image coordinates) in the two input bands, and y is the pixel value at same coordinate in the output.

This fusion approach is extended to band subsets having arbitrary size N using an N-dimensional vector $\alpha(N) = (\alpha_1, \alpha_2, \ldots, \alpha_N)$, where $\sum_i \alpha_i = 1$. A vector $\alpha(N)$ of this form is referred to a *PLF weight vector*. When subsets of bands are constructed incrementally, as they are constructed in LDspectral, the vectors $\{\alpha(N)\}$ can be computed efficiently using grid search. More details about the grid search approach employed in this work are provided in Sect. 23.6.

Following [4], we apply a pooling strategy for FLF:

$$Z_t(s) = \begin{cases} 1 & \sum_i Y_{i,t}(s) > \rho \\ 0 & otherwise \end{cases}, \tag{23.2}$$

where $Y_{i,t}$ represents the input image for fusion at frame t and spectral band i; Z_t represents the tth output frame derived by FLF; and ρ, called the *majority* parameter, provides a threshold for the fusion operation. The symbol s in Eq. (23.2) represents a given pixel index. The value of ρ ranges from 1 (a logical OR operation) to the total number bands (a logical AND operation). Each binary pixel value $Z_t(s)$ in the fused result represents a prediction about whether the pixel corresponds to foreground (1) or background (0).

23.6 Band Subset Selection

As described in Sect. 23.4, the Subset Selection Profiles in Fig. 23.1 are derived at design time to provide a set, called *bandseq*, of strategic multispectral input configurations (subsets of the available multispectral bands) that are made available to the LRSM for dynamic, data-driven adaptation. We first discuss the approach used in LDspectral for deriving Subset Selection Profiles based on PLF, and then the approach is extended to incorporate both PLF and FLF.

The derived set of Subset Selection Profiles *bandseq* contains one carefully-selected subset of bands for each cardinality value in the range of $1, 2, \ldots, M_b$, where M_b is the total number of available bands in the multispectral sensor subsystem. Thus, *bandseq* can be viewed as a sequence or array whose ith element is the subset of selected bands that has cardinality i. Along with each subset of bands, an optimized PLF weight vector is derived to heuristically maximize the accuracy of PLF for the associated subset of bands.

Algorithm 1 provides a pseudocode sketch of the algorithm employed in LDspectral to derive the Subset Selection Profiles *bandseq* along with the array of associated PLF weight vectors *alpha*. For each i, *bandseq*[i] is derived to be an i-element set of selected multispectral bands. The algorithm presented here is a greedy algorithm in that for each $j = 2, 3, \ldots, N_b$, *bandseq*[j] is derived by extending *bandseq*[$j-1$] with one band from (*bands*−*bandseq*[$j-1$]), where *bands* represents the complete set of available bands in the multispectral video processing system. Thus, *bandseq*[j][k] = *bandseq*[$j - 1$][k] for $k < j$.

The weight vector for each *bandseq*[j] is derived using the constraint that:

$$alpha[j][k] = g \times alpha[j - 1][k] \text{ for } k < j, \text{ and some coefficient } g \in [0, 1]. \tag{23.3}$$

A grid search is then performed, using a training dataset for evaluation, to optimize the value of g. This evaluation, represented by the call to *evaluateBSP* in Algorithm 1, is performed by invoking the BSP subsystem (Fig. 23.2) on all images in the training dataset to assess the average accuracy using the given band subset and PLF weights. Accuracy evaluation is performed in terms of the harmonic mean performance measure $F_{measure}$. The average $F_{measure}$ computed across the training set is returned from the call to *evaluateBSP*. This metric is discussed in more detail in Sect. 23.7.2.

Since the components of $alpha[j - 1]$ sum to 1 (see Sect. 23.5) and the components of $alpha[j]$ must also sum to 1, the last component of $alpha[j]$ can be derived during the grid search as

$$alpha[j][j] = (1 - g). \tag{23.4}$$

The constraint in Eq. (23.3) is imposed during the search process to reduce the search complexity. Investigating efficient ways to relax this constraint and achieve more thorough search, while keeping the overall time required for optimization in an acceptable range, is a useful direction for future work.

In our experiments, we use a grid spacing (the *gridspacing* parameter in Algorithm 1) of 0.1.

Algorithm 1

> parameter M_b: number of available spectral bands
> parameter *bands*: set of spectral bands
> parameter *grid_spacing*: granularity for grid search
> output *bandseq*[M_b]: sequence of selected bands
> output *alpha*[M_b]: weight vectors for band subsets
> *unprocessed = bands*
> *processed = ∅*
> **for** $i = 1; i \leq N_b; i++$ **do**
> $f_M = -1$
>   **for** $u \in unprocessed$ **do**
> $S = processed \bigcup \{u\}$
>   **for** $0 = 0; g \leq alpha[i - g; g += grid\_spacing)$ **do**
> $f_m = evaluateBSP(S, w)$
>   **if** $f_m > f_M$ **then**
> $bandseq[i] = u$
> $alpha[i] = w$
> $measure[i] = f_M$
> $unprocessed - = \{\overline{u}\}$

> $processed + = \{\overline{u}\}$

Algorithm 1 is adapted for FLF by configuring the dataflow in the BSP subsystem to perform fusion at the feature level, and replacing the grid search to optimize PLF weights with a grid search to optimize the majority threshold ρ (see Eq. (23.2)). This is a relatively straightforward replacement of one kind of grid search with another grid search having a similar form. We omit the details for brevity. This replacement allows us derive an optimized sequence of band subsets using FLF along with an accuracy-optimizing majority value $rho[i]$ for each subset cardinality i.

LDspectral Band Subset Selection (*LBSS*) operates by first applying both Algorithm 1 and the adapted version of Algorithm 1 that employs FLF instead of PLF. We refer to the resulting band subsets (*bandseq* outputs) as β_{plf} and β_{flf}, respectively. Similarly, the resulting average accuracy results (*measure* outputs) are denoted M_{plf} and M_{flf}, respectively.

Then for each band subset cardinality $i \in \{2, 3, \ldots, N_b\}$, LBSS selects either $\beta_{plf}[i]$ (along with the associated weight vector *alpha*[i]) or $\beta_{flf}[i]$ (along with the associated majority value *rho*[i]) depending on whether $M_{plf}[i] \geq M_{flf}[i]$ or $M_{plf}[i] < M_{flf}[i]$, respectively. For $i = 1$, there is no fusion involved so the singleton subset selected by LBSS is simply equal to the common value of $\beta_{plf}[1]$ and $\beta_{flf}[1]$.

23.7 Experimental Results

23.7.1 Experimental Setup

Multispectral video sequences used for training and testing in our experiments were obtained from a multispectral dataset published by Benezeth et al. [4]. The parts of this dataset that we used include foreground truth to enable assessment of background subtraction accuracy.

The video data in this dataset was acquired from a commercial multispectral camera, the FD-1665-MS from FluxData, Inc. The dataset incorporates 7 bands in total, including 6 different channels in the visible spectrum (B_1 through B_6) with wavelengths ranging from 400 nm to 700 nm, and one near-infrared band (B_7) with a wavelength in the range of 700 nm to 1000 nm.

We used 1102 multispectral images from the dataset described above. We divided this set of images into 735 images (approximately 2/3) for training and 367 images for testing.

Our experiments were performed using a desktop computer equipped with a 3.10 GHz Intel i5-2400 CPU, 4 GB RAM, and the Ubuntu 15.10 LTS operating system. Results from these experiments are discussed in Sects. 23.7.2 and 23.7.5.

23.7.2 Accuracy Metric

We use the harmonic mean performance measure $F_{measure}$ as the primary metric to evaluate system accuracy. This metric is used widely in the literature to assess accuracy in object detection contexts (e.g., see [16]). The $F_{measure}$ metric is defined as:

$$F_{measure} = 2 \times \frac{recall \times precision}{recall + precision}, \tag{23.5}$$

where *precision* and *recall* are defined by:

$$precision = \frac{n_c}{n_f}, \text{ and } recall = \frac{n_c}{n_g},$$

where n_c is the number of correctly classified foreground pixels, n_f is the number of pixels classified as foreground, and n_g is the number of foreground pixels in the ground truth.

23.7.3 Example Images

Figure 23.3 shows a composite (all-band) scene; 7 different images corresponding to single-band foreground results on the 7 available multispectral bands; and the foreground result that is derived by LDspectral using background subtraction along with PLF across all 7 bands. This scene is selected here from Benezeth's dataset as an example to illustrate techniques for fusion and background subtraction that are employed in LDspectral. The foreground fusion result derived by LDspectral is shown in the image at the bottom right corner of Fig. 23.3.

Examination of these images shows that performing background subtraction in conjunction with image fusion yields more accurate results compared to the results of performing background subtraction on individual bands in isolation—for example, the hollow portions in the single band results are largely filled in within the fused result.

While it is intuitively clear and concretely illustrated in the example of Fig. 23.3 that fusion can significantly improve accuracy, the overall objective of LDspectral is to enable efficient, dynamic adaptation across video processing configurations that trade-off accuracy and real-time performance subject to operational constraints. The utility of LDspectral for performing such trade-off optimization is demonstrated in the remainder of this section.

23.7.4 Accuracy Evaluation

Figure 23.4 shows foreground accuracy results for all possible one- and two-band subsets for both PLF and FLF. The results shown here are derived using search processes within the LBSS algorithm presented in Sect. 23.6. Each off-diagonal table entry in Fig. 23.4 consists of two values that are stacked vertically—the top value corresponds to PLF and the bottom value to FLF. The entries on the diagonal correspond to singleton (one-band) subsets, while each off-diagonal entry at row i and column j represents the two-band subset $\{B_i, B_j\}$. The values in the table are the average $F_{measure}$ values computed across the training part of our multispectral

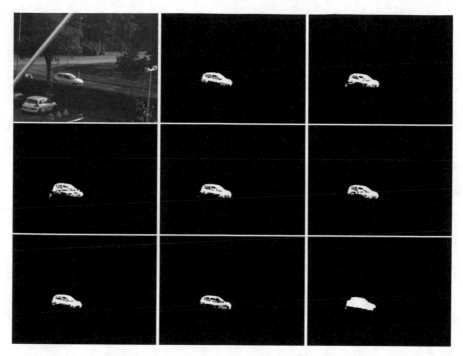

Fig. 23.3 An example from Benezeth's dataset that is used to illustrate the techniques for fusion and background subtraction that are employed in LDspectral: the scene, 7 bands, and foreground fused image

dataset. The boldface values in Fig. 23.4 show the accuracy values for FLF in cases where FLF achieves higher accuracy than PLF.

These results show that FLF achieves higher accuracy compared to PLF in only a small fraction of the evaluated band subsets. Furthermore, as we show in Sect. 23.7.5, FLF requires significantly higher execution time on our experimental platform compared to PLF. Thus, for the remaining experiments reported in this section (Sect. 23.7.4), we "turn off" or disable FLF in LBSS so that only weight-optimized configurations of PLF are considered. However, the option of enabling FLF in LBSS may be useful in general for other target platforms, such as platforms that have more parallelism available to speed up the performance of the FLF-enabled BSP dataflow graph.

From the results in Fig. 23.4, we also see that when the number of bands increases from one to two, a significant improvement in accuracy results. This helps to confirm and quantify the utility of maintaining progressively larger subsets of spectral bands as alternative configurations for dynamic adaptation in LDspectral.

Figure 23.5 shows the results of incremental band subset construction using the LBSS algorithm in LDspectral. The columns correspond to progressively larger subsets of bands that are derived by LBSS, while the rows correspond to individual bands that are incrementally added and evaluated in the search process. For example,

band	1	2	3	4	5	6	7
1	0.934	0.940	0.943	0.945	0.943	0.943	0.933
		0.942	**0.944**	0.940	**0.947**	**0.946**	0.933
2		0.931	0.942	0.936	0.942	0.937	0.930
			0.942	**0.937**	0.942	0.937	0.926
3			0.939	0.939	0.943	0.940	0.939
				0.938	0.941	0.937	0.935
4				0.929	0.940	0.932	0.930
					0.937	0.929	0.926
5					0.942	0.938	0.937
						0.937	0.933
6						0.919	0.925
							0.922
7							0.843

Fig. 23.4 Accuracy results for different one- and two-band subsets using LDspectral with both PLF and FLF. In each off-diagonal table entry, the top value corresponds to PLF, and the bottom value corresponds to FLF

Band(s)	1-4	1-4-6	1-4-6-3	1-4-6-3-5	1-4-6-3-5-2
1	-	-	-	-	-
2	0.948	0.957	**0.957**	**0.958**	-
3	0.946	**0.957**	-	-	-
4	-	-	-	-	-
5	0.949	0.950	0.957	-	-
6	**0.949**	-	-	-	-
7	0.918	0.935	0.938	0.940	**0.961**

Fig. 23.5 Results of incremental band subset construction using the LBSS algorithm in LDspectral

the entry corresponding to Row 3 and Column 1-4-6 shows the best accuracy achieved (across all PLF configurations that are evaluated through grid search) for the band subset $\{B_1, B_3, B_4, B_6\}$.

The boldface values in Fig. 23.5 correspond to the best configurations represented in the corresponding columns. These are the configurations that are "picked up" by the search process in LBSS. For example, band B_6 exhibits the best accuracy when combined with bands B_1, B_4 (the tie here with band B_5 is broken arbitrarily or based on less significant digits that are not shown in the table), and thus, the union $\{B_1, B_4, B_6\}$ of these two subsets is taken as the best 3-element subset. This subset is then represented in the next column of the table (labeled 1-4-6).

The results in Fig. 23.5 are shown based on the band subset $\{B_1, B_4\}$ as a starting point—i.e., as the initial two-band sequence that defines the first column of data in the table. This pair of bands is selected because it corresponds to the best two-band

	Precision	Recall	F_measure
LDspectral	0.969	0.953	0.961
[Benezeth 2014]	0.870	0.925	0.897
Improvement	11.4%	3.0%	7.1%

Fig. 23.6 Accuracy improvement compared with results from [4] using the same multispectral dataset

PLF results in Fig. 23.4, and as motivated above, we have disabled FLF in LBSS for this part of the experimental evaluation.

From the results in Fig. 23.5, we see that, as expected, $F_{measure}$ increases as the cardinality of the set of selected bands increases. The improvement is larger at first (when constructing smaller band subsets), and then becomes smaller when constructing larger subsets. These trends are important as they influence trade-offs between the increased accuracy provided by processing additional bands and the increased computational cost incurred by such processing. The execution time aspects of these trade-offs are investigated in Sect. 23.7.5.

Figure 23.6 shows the improvement in accuracy provided by LDspectral compared to related methods reported in the literature that are evaluated on the same multispectral dataset. These results are for the full set of (7) available multispectral bands. The $F_{measure}$ value is improved by 7.1% through methods in LDspectral. This is a relatively large improvement given that an upper bound on the achievable improvement (represented by $F_{measure} = 1$) is $(1 - 0.897)/0.897 = 11.4\%$. Factors that contribute to this improvement include the integrated use in LDspectral of a GMM model for PLF, and the grid search optimization of the PLF configurations.

23.7.5   Execution Time Evaluation

Figure 23.7 shows the variation in execution time for different numbers of processed bands and different fusion modes. These results are given in terms of milliseconds per video frame that are required to execute the BSP dataflow graph (Fig. 23.2). The columns in the table correspond to different band subset sizes. The first column corresponds to the execution time required for BSP when only one spectral band is involved, and hence no fusion is performed. Thus, the execution times reported in both rows are the same for the first column.

The execution times reported in Fig. 23.7 are obtained by averaging over ten iterations through the training dataset for a band subset of each given cardinality. These results demonstrate that the execution time of FLF exhibits a significantly more rapid increase compared to PLF as the number of bands increases. For

	1	2	3	4	5	6	7
PLF	31.1	34.9	38.8	43.0	47.5	51.6	55.4
FLF	31.1	52.7	81.3	93.7	101.8	121.0	138.5

Fig. 23.7 Variation in execution time for different numbers of processed bands and different fusion modes. The units of execution time in this table are milliseconds/frame

example, from the trends shown in Fig. 23.7, we see that the execution time required to perform FLF on 2 bands exceeds the time required to perform PLF on 6 bands. This kind of result further highlights the need for careful, joint selection of fusion configurations and band subsets in a system that is geared toward optimizing trade-offs between accuracy and real-time performance.

23.8 Conclusions

In this chapter, we have developed new methods for integrated band subset selection and video processing parameter optimization in LDspectral, which is a software tool for model-based system design, prototyping, and optimization of data-driven, multispectral video processing systems. LDspectral is developed for optimization in the context of novel video processing design spaces introduced by multispectral image acquisition techniques. The methods developed in this chapter enable experimentation with and optimization of data-driven video processing for DDDAS. The methods are demonstrated in terms of accuracy and execution time using a case study involving background subtraction, and a relevant multispectral data set for this application.

Useful directions for future work include adapting the developed methods and tools to video analysis contexts other than background subtraction, and to hyper-spectral video processing systems; further improving the search process involved in optimizing weights for image fusion [13, 24]; and experimenting with other kinds of target platforms, such as applications that are based on graphics processing units or field-programmable gate arrays.

Acknowledgments This research was supported in part by the Air Force Office of Scientific Research as part of the DDDAS Program. The views and conclusions contained herein are those of the authors and should not be interpreted as necessarily representing the official policies, either expressed or implied, of AFRL, or the U.S. Government.

References

1. Aved, A.J., Blasch, E.P., Peng, J.: Regularized difference criterion for computing discriminants for dimensionality reduction. IEEE Transactions on Aerospace and Electronic Systems 53(5), 2372–2384 (2017)
2. Babayan, P.V., Smirnov, S.A., Strotov, V.V., Muraviev, V.S., Ershov, M.D.: Object tracking algorithm based on the multispectral template matching. In: Proceedings of the Mediterranean Conference on Embedded Computing (2018)
3. Bebelis, V., Fradet, P., Girault, A., Lavigueur, B.: BPDF: A statically analyzable dataflow model with integer and Boolean parameters. In: Proceedings of the International Workshop on Embedded Software. pp. 1–10 (2013)
4. Benezeth, Y., Sidibé, D., Thomas, J.B.: Background subtraction with multispectral video sequences. In: Proceedings of the Workshop on Non-classical Cameras, Camera Networks and Omnidirectional Vision (2014)
5. Bhateja, V., Srivastava, A., Moin, A., Lay-Ekuakille, A.: NSCT based multispectral medical image fusion model. In: Proceedings of the IEEE International Symposium on Medical Measurements and Applications. pp. 1–5 (2016)
6. Bhattacharya, B., Bhattacharyya, S.S.: Parameterized dataflow modeling for DSP systems. IEEE Transactions on Signal Processing 49(10), 2408–2421 (October 2001)
7. Chen, Z., Pu, H., Wang, B., Jiang, G.M.: Fusion of hyperspectral and multispectral images: A novel framework based on generalization of pan-sharpening methods. IEEE Geoscience and Remote Sensing Letters 11(8), 1418–1422 (2014)
8. Ferrato, L.J., Forsythe, K.W.: Comparing hyperspectral and multispectral imagery for land classification of the lower Don River, Toronto. Journal of Geography and Geology 5(1), 92–107 (2013)
9. Li, H., Sudusinghe, K., Liu, Y., Yoon, J., van der Schaar, M., Blasch, E., Bhattacharyya, S.S.: Dynamic, data-driven processing of multispectral video streams. IEEE Aerospace & Electronic Systems Magazine 32(7), 50–57 (2017)
10. Liu, Z., Blasch, E., John, V.: Statistical comparison of image fusion algorithms: Recommendations. Information Fusion 36, 251–260 (2017)
11. Liu, Z., Blasch, E., Xue, Z., Zhao, J., Laganiere, R., Wu, W.: Objective assessment of multiresolution image fusion algorithms for context enhancement in night vision: A comparative study. IEEE Transactions on Pattern Analysis and Machine Intelligence 34(1), 94–109 (2012)
12. Pulli, K., Baksheev, A., Kornyakov, K., Eruhimov, V.: Real-time computer vision with OpenCV. Communications of the ACM 55(6), 61–69 (2012)
13. Rangnekar, A., Lentilucci, E., Kanan, C., Hoffman, M.J.: Uncertainty Estimation for Semantic Segmentation of Hyperspectral Imagery, International Conference on Dynamic Data Driven Application Systems, 163–170, Springer, 2020.
14. Reddy, B.C.S., Shah, P., Merchant, S.N., Desai, U.B.: Visualization of multispectral video with moving background based on background extraction and fusion. In: Proceedings of the International Conference on Information, Communications and Signal Processing. pp. 1–5 (2011)
15. Scebba, G., Da Poian, G., Karlen, W.: Multispectral video fusion for non-contact monitoring of respiratory rate and apnea. IEEE Transactions on Biomedical Engineering 68(1), 350–359 (2021)
16. Sepulveda, J., Velastin, S.A.: F1 score assesment of Gaussian mixture background subtraction algorithms using the MuHAVi dataset. In: Proceedings of the International Conference on Imaging for Crime Prevention and Detection. pp. 1–6 (2015)
17. Shen, C., Plishker, W., Bhattacharyya, S.S.: Dataflow-based design and implementation of image processing applications. In: Guan, L., He, Y., Kung, S. (eds.) Multimedia Image and Video Processing, pp. 609–629. CRC Press, second edn. (2012), http://www.crcpress.com/product/isbn/9781439830864, chapter 24

18. Sobral, A., Javed, S., Jung, S.K., Bouwmans, T., Zahzah, E.: Online stochastic tensor decomposition for background subtraction in multispectral video sequences. In: Proceedings of the International Conference on Computer Vision Workshop. pp. 946–953 (2015)
19. Stauffer, C., Grimson, W.E.L.: Adaptive background mixture models for real-time tracking. In: Proceedings of the IEEE Conference on Computer Vision and Pattern Recognition (1999)
20. Sudusinghe, K., Won, S., van der Schaar, M., Bhattacharyya, S.S.: A novel framework for design and implementation of adaptive stream mining systems. In: Proceedings of the IEEE International Conference on Multimedia and Expo. pp. 1–6. San Jose, California (July 2013), http://ieeexplore.ieee.org
21. Uzkent, B., Hoffman, M. J., Vodacek, A.: Integrating Hyperspectral Likelihoods in a Multidimensional Assignment Algorithm for Aerial Vehicle Tracking. In: IEEE Journal of Selected Topics in Applied Earth Observations and Remote Sensing 9(9), 4325–4333 (2016), https://doi.org/10.1109/JSTARS.2016.2560220.
22. Wei, Q., Bioucas-Dias, J., Dobigeon, N., Tourneret, J.Y.: Hyperspectral and multispectral image fusion based on a sparse representation. IEEE Transactions on Geoscience and Remote Sensing 53(7), 3658–3668 (2015)
23. Xie, Q., Zhou, M., Zhao, Q., Meng, D., Zuo, W., Xu, Z.: Multispectral and hyperspectral image fusion by MS/HS fusion net. In: Proceedings of the IEEE Conference on Computer Vision and Pattern Recognition. pp. 1585–1594 (2019)
24. Zheng, Y., Blasch, E., Liu, Z.: Multispectral Image Fusion and Colorization, SPIE Press, 2018
25. Zivkovic, Z.: Improved adaptive Gaussian mixture model for background subtraction. In: Proceedings of the International Conference on Pattern Recognition. pp. 28–31 (2004)
26. Zivkovic, Z., van der Heijden, F.: Efficient adaptive density estimation per image pixel for the task of background subtraction. Pattern Recognition Letters 27(7), 773–780 (2006)

Chapter 24
Light Field and Plenoptic Point Cloud Compression

Li Li and Zhu Li

Abstract Light field, or plenoptic images are richer representation of the visual information in 3D. It contains not only the color intensity of a particular view angle at the time of capture, but also much richer photometric and geometric information for re-rendering and viewing from new view angles. This is the key enabling technology for the future immersive visual communication with many applications. There are mainly three types of light field images based on the capturing technology, lenslet camera based, dense camera array based, and non-regularly sampled light field or plenotpic point cloud. In this chapter we will review and discuss the current state of the art in compression for these light field images.

Keywords Light field · Plenoptic images · Point cloud · Compression · Optimization

Light field images, also known as plenoptic images, contain information about not only the intensity of light in a scene but also the direction of the light rays in space. Since light field images contain very rich photometric and geometric information, they will have very widespread applications in the future. For example, immersive content capture for virtual and mixed reality presentation; depth from light fields for auto driving applications. To be more specific, light field images can be enhanced with physical models for an autonomous decision-making process, which is also an important task of the Dynamic Data Driven Applications Systems (DDDAS) [1]. In addition, the rich geometry and photometric information contained in light field images can be updated with real-time measurements, which is a focus of DDDAS such as smart-city-related image and video processing tasks. However, to make light field images easier to be utilized, one of the most important tasks is to compress light field images efficiently so they can be easily distributed over the current communication infrastructure.

L. Li · Z. Li (✉)
University of Missouri-Kansas City, Kansas City, MO, USA
e-mail: lil1@umkc.edu; zhu.li@ieee.org

© The Author(s), under exclusive license to Springer Nature Switzerland AG 2022
E. P. Blasch et al. (eds.), *Handbook of Dynamic Data Driven Applications Systems*,
https://doi.org/10.1007/978-3-030-74568-4_24

557

Typically, there are three kinds of light field images [18]. The first kind is the lenslet-based light field image. The second kind is the camera-array-based light field image. The third kind is the surface light field image. These three kinds of light field images are captured using various equipment and thus contain totally different characteristics. The data collected can be processed with methods to provide real-time imagery. In this chapter, we will give a detailed description of the state-of-the-art compression methods for these three kinds of light field images to be considered when included in a DDDAS system.

24.1 Lenslet-Based Light Field Image Compression

Generally speaking, lenslet-based light field images (LFIs) are acquired with plenoptic cameras, which place an array of micro-lenses in front of a conventional image sensor. The light beams coming from the object with various angles are firstly refracted through the microlens array. Then they are captured by the traditional 2-D image sensor to generate the raw sensor data of LFIs. A simple example of a typical light field capture system is shown in Fig. 24.1.

In a lenslet-based LFI, each micro-lens works as an individual small low-resolution image camera conveying a particular perspective of the object in slightly different angles. The raw sensor data is then converted into a LFI after demosaicing, devignetting, and data structure conversion. As shown in Fig. 24.2, the light field Toolbox v0.4 [2] can convert the raw sensor data generated by the commercial light field camera Lytro Illum in Fig. 24.2a into the light field structure as shown in Fig. 24.2b. In Fig. 24.2b, each rectangle represents a 2-D view obtained from the contributions of all micro-lenses of the camera. From Fig. 24.2b, the LFI is actually with 4-D information including not only the spatial information (similar to 2-D images) but also the angular information (different views).

Since a LFI records the light rays of a scene of interest, it can naturally provide the benefits of rendering new views not only for the changed viewpoint but also for the changed focal point. Recently, especially due to the emergence of the commercial light field cameras, the LFI is becoming a more and more attractive

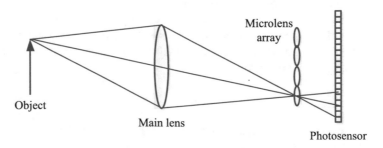

Fig. 24.1 Conceptual schematic of a light field camera

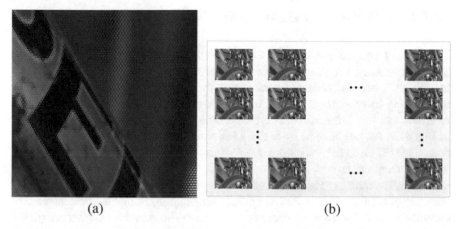

Fig. 24.2 Example of the raw sensor data and its corresponding LFI data. (**a**) Plenoptic camera raw sensor data after demosaicing and devignetting. (**b**) Light-field data structure

solution to 3-D imaging and sensing. However, the widespread use of LFIs is still restricted by their massive size. Since LFIs are with 4-D information, even if the spatial resolution of one view is quite small, the raw data of LFIs with hundreds of views is still very large. For example, the resolution of a raw LFI generated by Lytro Illum [34] containing the captured field of light information is 7728 × 5368 pixels. Besides the huge image size, since the LFI is generated from a micro-lens array, its characteristic is entirely different from the general 2-D image as shown in Fig. 24.2a, which makes it even harder to compress.

There are typically three kinds of methods to compress lenslet-based LFIs making full use of the classic image/video coding standards, such as JPEG [45], H.264/AVC [47], and H.265/HEVC [43]. The first kind of method, called as the self-similarity-based LFI compression [11], tries to compress LFIs using the commonly used image compression standards. The second kind of method, named as the pseudo-sequence-based LFI compression [27], attempts to decompose LFIs into multiple views and tries to utilize the inter prediction in video coding standards to exploit the temporal correlations between various views. The third kind of method is to use the dictionary learning [30] to compress the lenslet-based LFI. In all these methods, there are also some choices for us to abandon some of the views and synthesize them in the decoder since the number of views is really too dense for compression [28]. By removing some views, more bitrate is saved but the choices of the abandoned views remain an open problem. In the following subsections, we give a basic overview and analysis of all those methods.

24.1.1   Self-similarity-Based Light Field Image Compression

Since a LFI can be considered as a sequence of 2-D frames, a simple coding approach by using a regular 2-D video encoder, such as High Efficiency Video Coding (HEVC), can also be used. In this sense, the inherent cross-correlation between neighboring micro-images in a LFI can be seen as a type of spatial redundancy, referred to as "self-similarity". A typical example of the "self-similarity" is shown in Fig. 24.3. As can be seen from Fig. 24.3, the "self-similarity" mode or image-B coder [26] [25] is in fact very similar to the intra block copy mode [49] in the HEVC screen content extension [48].

Just as illustrated in Fig. 24.3, under a self-similarity-based LFI encoder, all the previously coded areas of the current picture are searched to find the best match. The commonly used distortion metrics such as Sum of the Absolute Difference (SAD) and Sum of the Square Difference (SSD) can be used during the searching process. As a result, the chosen block becomes the candidate block and the relative position between the two blocks is defined as a self-similarity vector. Under the standard-based coding framework, the self-similarity vector can be coded in a similar way as the motion vector except for some temporal candidates.

One of the advantages of the self-similarity-based LFI encoder is that it can be easily combined with the standard-based image/video coding framework [9]. A typical example of the self-similarity mode combined with the HEVC intra encoder is shown in Fig. 24.4 [11]. In Fig. 24.4, the self-similarity estimation module is used to derive the self-similarity vector by searching the block one after another in the previously coded areas. And the self-similarity compensation module is used to obtain the most similar block according to the self-similarity vector. Each coding block in the LFI chooses to use the intra mode or the self-similarity mode based on rate-distortion optimization (RDO) to achieve the optimal performance.

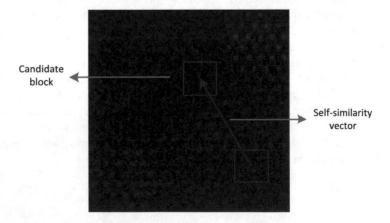

Fig. 24.3 Typical example of the "self-similarity"

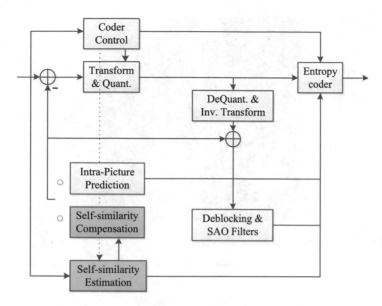

Fig. 24.4 Self-similarity mode combined with the HEVC intra encoder

The above only gives an example of the uni-predicted self-similarity compensation. Motivated by the bi-directional motion estimation and motion compensation in the video coding framework, it is also very natural to use bi-predicted self-similarity compensation [10]. As its name implies, the candidate of a bi-predicted self-similarity compensation can be derived from a linear combination of two blocks within the same searching window. To be more specific, the first candidate is given by the best matching block during the uni-predicted self-similarity estimation and the second candidate is selected by jointly searching the first and the second candidates. A typical example of the bi-predicted self-similarity compensation is shown in Fig. 24.5.

In addition to using one or two blocks to perform self-similarity compensation, the locally linear embedding which employs multiple blocks can also be applied to predict the current block [31]. The essence of the local-linear-embedding-based method is to obtain a linear combination of the K-nearest neighboring (K-NN) blocks to estimate the current block. To find the linear coefficients, the locally linear embedding obtains the coefficients by solving a least-squares problem with a constraint on the sum of the coefficient that has to be 1. Also, to save the bits to transmit the coefficients, template matching is used to obtain the coefficients. As shown in Fig. 24.6, the search window W is used for searching the K-NN template patches that represent the lowest matching error with template C. Then the linear coefficients are optimized to make the linear combinations of the K best template matches approximate the template C. Finally, the current block P is predicted using the same linear coefficients using the square blocks associated with each template patch.

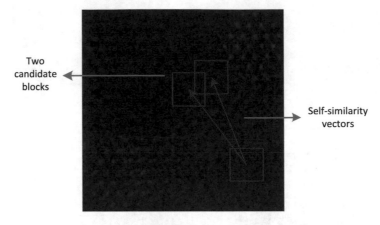

Fig. 24.5 Bi-predicted self-similarity compensation

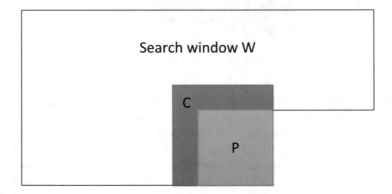

Fig. 24.6 Local-linear-embedding-based self-similarity compensation

24.1.2 Pseudo-Sequence-Based Light Field Image Compression

The "self-similarity" is one kind of correlation that can be exploited to improve the LFI compression efficiency. Since the light field is actually with 4-D information, it can also be decomposed into a pseudo sequence. In this way, the well designed inter prediction coding tools in video coding standards can be fully utilized to improve coding efficiency. As shown in Fig. 24.7, a LFI can be decomposed into multiple sub-images to organize a pseudo sequence [33]. In the early times, the 3-D Discrete Cosine Transform (DCT) [3] and 3-D Discrete Wavelet Transform (DWT) [4] are used to exploit the correlations between various views and improve the coding efficiency. Later, results show that the video-coding-standards-based framework such as H.264/AVC and HEVC are able to better exploit the data redundancy in both spatial and directional domain. In the following, we introduce the 2-D hierarchical

Fig. 24.7 Tiling the raw light field as a pseudo sequence

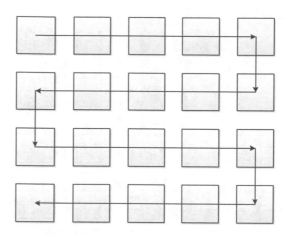

coding structure in detail since it is the state-of-the-art compression method [44] for the LFI especially in low bitrate scenarios [20, 21].

24.1.2.1 The 2-D Hierarchical Coding Structure

Within the DDDAS framework, there are many methods, algorithms, and statistical methods to provide real-time computation [8, 53]. Among all the image and video compression methods, the hierarchical coding structure is able to provide substantial performance improvements in typical video sequences. For a LFI with 4-D information, the decomposed multiple sub-images can be naturally organized into a 2-D coding structure. Since the four corner views may not be beneficial for the overall LFI quality, they are usually deleted from the original coding structure. As a typical example, the LFI generated by Lytro can be decomposed into 165 views and organized into the 2-D coding structure as shown in Fig. 24.8. Then each view is assigned a picture order count (POC) from 0 to 164. In the scheme, the center view is assigned POC 0 and coded as an intra frame since it is with the highest correlation with the other frames. The other views are assigned the POC from the top left to the bottom right and coded as inter frames. Note that the POC here is just a symbol to represent each view instead of the display order in usual videos.

In the 1-D hierarchical coding structure [39], both the coding order and reference frame management are carefully designed to optimize the R-D performance. Under the 2-D hierarchical coding structure, these two key factors should also be considered to improve the LFI coding efficiency. In the 1-D hierarchical coding structure, the depth-first coding order is used to achieve very good R-D performance as well as a very small reference buffer size. For example, as shown in Fig. 24.9, the encoding order of 1-D hierarchical coding structure with group of pictures (GOP) size 16 is 0, 16, 8, 4, 2, 1, 3, 6, 5, 7, 12, 10, 9, 11, 14, 13, and 15. The minimum size of the reference buffer is 5.

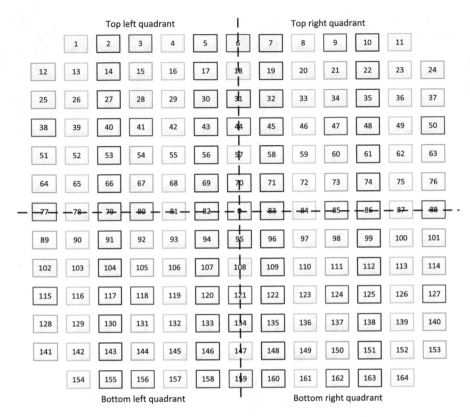

Fig. 24.8 This figure depicts the 13 × 13 views (excluding the 4 corner views) to be compressed. The views are assigned picture order counts ranging from 0 to 164 as shown in the figure. The views are divided into four quadrants

The situation in the 2-D hierarchical coding structure is quite similar. To reduce the reference buffer size as much as possible, all the frames are divided into four quadrants as shown in Fig. 24.8. Then each quadrant is coded in clockwise order from the top left, the top right, the bottom right, to the bottom left. In this way, except for the views in the border of the two quadrants, each quadrant can be considered as an independent one. Therefore, the reference frames belonging to only one quadrant can be popped out of the reference frame buffer as soon as possible to keep a relatively small reference buffer without influencing the coding efficiency.

Inside each quadrant, the depth-first coding order is used for both the horizontal and vertical directions to make full use of the correlations between various views. Take the top left quadrant as an example. The detailed encoding order can be seen from Fig. 24.10. In Fig. 24.10, the number inside each rectangle means the encoding order of each view. In both horizontal and vertical directions, the encoding order of 0, 6, 3, 5, 4, 2, 1 is followed. To be more specific, the 0th row and the 0th column is first encoded. Then according to the hierarchical coding structure in the vertical

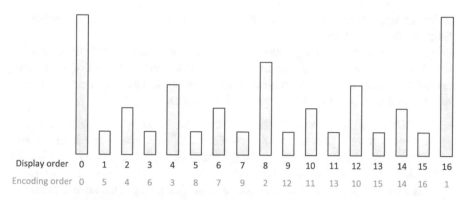

Fig. 24.9 1-D hierarchical coding structure with GOP size 16

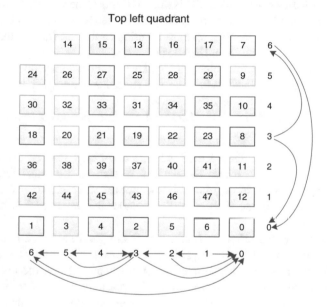

Fig. 24.10 Coding order of the top left quadrant

direction, the 6*th* row is coded and followed by the 3*rd* row. Finally, the 5*th*, 4*th*, 2*nd*, and 1*st* rows are coded sequentially. Inside each row or column, the order of 0, 6, 3, 5, 4, 2, 1 is also used. Note that to guarantee the smallest reference buffer size, the coding orders of the other three quadrants are symmetrical to that of the top left quadrant. To be more specific, the encoding order for each row of the top right and bottom right quadrants is from right to left, and the encoding order for various rows of the bottom right and bottom left quadrants is from bottom to top. Take the row with frames 19, 20, 21, 22, 23, 24 as an example, the encoding order of the row is from right to left as 24, 21, 23, 22, 20, 19. In this way, the frame 24 is only stored in the reference buffer of the frame 23 and thus this scheme can keep the reference frame buffer as small as possible.

In addition to the encoding order, reference frame management is important for the R-D performance. As shown in Fig. 24.8, all the views are divided into four groups according to their frequencies to be referenced. The frequency means the times a reference frame is referenced by other frames.

- The frames with the red block. This kind of frame is the most frequently referenced frame. They are always stored in the reference buffer until the end of encoding the current quadrant. All the frames including the to-be-encoded red block frames in the current quadrant can take the red block frames as references. In the current quadrant, the existence of these frames can guarantee that all the frames have a good prediction.
- The frames with the green block. This kind of frame is the second most frequently referenced frame. They are referenced by the frames belonging to the current row in the same quadrant. For example, in addition to the red frames, the frame 26 can also take the frames 25 and 28 as references.
- The frames with the yellow block. This kind of frame is only referenced by the frame encoded immediately after them in the same quadrant. For example, the frame 27 can take the frame 26 as a reference.
- The frames with the black block. This kind of frame such as the frame 27 belongs to the non-reference frames.

It should be noted that the method uses a row-based coding order, to save the reference buffer size, where the vertical references are much less than the horizontal references for most frames. For example, when encoding the frame 29, the immediate above frame 16 is unavailable under the proposed 2-D hierarchical coding structure.

In the following, the reference buffer size is analyzed for this 2-D hierarchical coding structure. In the top left quadrant, according to a careful analysis, the maximum number of reference frames appears when encoding the non-reference frames such as the frame 27. For the frame 27, not only the eight frequently used red reference frames should be stored in the reference buffer, but also the frames 26 and 28. Therefore, a maximum of 10 reference frames are needed for the top left quadrant. For the top right and bottom right quadrants, the situation is more complicated. As HEVC provides the constraint that the reference frames of the next frame can only be chosen from the reference frames of the current frame and the current frame itself [41], the frames 77 and 80 should always be stored in the reference buffer because they are used as the reference frames for the bottom left quadrant. Therefore, a maximum of 12 reference frames are needed for the top right and bottom right quadrants. The situation of the bottom left quadrant is the same as that of the top left quadrant, for which a maximum of 10 reference frames is needed. Therefore, in summary, the reference buffer size needed for encoding the entire pseudo sequence is 12.

24.1.2.2   Distance-Based Reference Frame Selection and Motion Vector Scaling

According to the analysis in the last subsection, the maximum number of reference frames is 12. If all these reference frames are applied to both list0 and list1, the encoder traverses all the reference frames to obtain the best prediction block, which may increase the encoding complexity dramatically. In addition, the large reference index introduced by a large number of reference frames may increase the overhead bits. Therefore, in this section, a *distance-based reference frame selection* algorithm is introduced to reduce the overhead bits and decrease the encoding complexity. Then since the spatial positions of various views may have influences on the motion vector (MV) scaling process in the merge and advanced motion vector prediction modes, a *spatial-coordinates-based MV scaling* algorithm is introduced to further improve the coding efficiency.

In the 1-D hierarchical coding structure, the frames with the smaller POC differences are put in a relatively earlier position of the reference lists since they are nearer to the current frame and have larger possibilities to be referenced. However, in the proposed 2-D hierarchical coding structure, the POC is just a symbol to represent each view so the POC difference cannot reflect the distance between two frames. For example, as shown in Fig. 24.8, the POC difference between the frames 18 and 6 is 12, which is larger than the POC difference between the frames 18 and 15. However, the distance between the frames 18 and 6 is much smaller than that between the frames 18 and 15. Therefore, the distances among various views need to be calculated before selecting the suitable reference frames. In this work, a coordinate system is established to derive the spatial coordinates of all the views, and then the spatial coordinates are used to calculate the distances between various views. The spatial coordinate of the most top left position of Fig. 24.8 is set as $(0, 0)$, and the right and down directions are set as positive. For example, the spatial coordinates of the frame 0 and the frame 1 is $(6, 6)$ and $(1, 0)$, respectively. Then the correspondence between the POC and the spatial coordinate of each frame (x, y) is derived as follows,

$$x = \begin{cases} 6 & if\ POC = 0 \\ POC\%13 & else\ if\ POC \leq 11 \\ (POC+1)\%13 & else\ if\ POC \leq 82 \\ (POC+2)\%13 & else\ if\ POC \leq 153 \\ (POC+3)\%13 & otherwise \end{cases} \tag{24.1}$$

$$y = \begin{cases} 6 & if\ POC = 0 \\ POC/13 & else\ if\ POC \leq 11 \\ (POC+1)/13 & else\ if\ POC \leq 82 \\ (POC+2)/13 & else\ if\ POC \leq 153 \\ (POC+3)/13 & otherwise \end{cases} \tag{24.2}$$

After the spatial coordinates are determined, the distance between the frames (x_1, y_1) and (x_2, y_2) can be easily calculated through the Euclidean distance,

$$d = \sqrt{(x_1 - x_2)^2 + (y_1 - y_2)^2}. \tag{24.3}$$

Using Eqs. (24.1), (24.2), and (24.3) can construct both the list0 and list1 according to the distances between the current frame and its reference frames. In the 1-D hierarchical coding structure, the forward (smaller POC compared with the current frame) and backward (larger POC compared with the current frame) reference frames are put into list0 and list1, respectively. Similarly, under the 2-D hierarchical coding structure, we first define the forward and backward directions. In this work, the above frames are all treated as the forward frames, and the below frames are all treated as the backward frames. For example, for the frame 17, the frames 1 to 16 are considered as the forward frames, and all the other frames including the frame 0 are considered as the backward frames. According to the above introduction, the totally available reference frames for the frame 17 are frames 16, 15, 6, 3, 38, 41, 44, 77, 80, and 0. If we set the number of reference frames in both lists as 4, according to the distances between the current frame and its reference frames in increasing order, the reference frames in list0 are 16, 6, 15, and 3, and the reference frames in list1 are 44, 41, 0, and 80.

In addition to the reference frame selection, the spatial coordinates may have significant influences on the MV scaling operations in both merge [13] and advanced motion vector prediction modes. The MV scaling operations are performed when the spatial neighboring blocks or temporal co-located blocks are pointing to a different reference frame from the current block. The MV scaling is divided into two kinds: spatial and temporal MV scaling. In a 2-D hierarchical coding structure, we should perform MV scaling based on the distance in x and y directions separately instead of POC.

The detailed processes are presented in Fig. 24.11. For the spatial case, the spatial coordinate of the current frame is (x_0, y_0), the spatial coordinate of the current reference frame is (x_1, y_1), and the spatial coordinate of the reference frame of the neighboring block is (x_2, y_2). The MV of the current block is $(MV_{1,x}, MV_{1,y})$, and the MV of the neighboring block is $(MV_{2,x}, MV_{2,y})$. Assuming that the motions among various frames are uniform, the spatial MV scaling process is derived as follows,

$$MV_{1,x} = \frac{MV_{2,x}}{x_2 - x_0} \times (x_1 - x_0). \tag{24.4}$$

$$MV_{1,y} = \frac{MV_{2,y}}{y_2 - y_0} \times (y_1 - y_0). \tag{24.5}$$

For the temporal case, except for the current frame and its reference frame, there are temporal co-located frame and its corresponding reference frame whose spatial coordinates are (x_3, y_3) and (x_2, y_2), respectively. The MV of the current

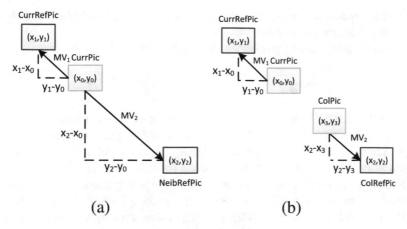

Fig. 24.11 Distance-based MV scaling. (**a**) Spatial case. (**b**) Temporal case

block is $(MV_{1,x}, MV_{1,y})$, and the MV of the co-located block is $(MV_{2,x}, MV_{2,y})$. Assuming that the motions among various frames are uniform, the temporal MV scaling process is derived as follows,

$$MV_{1,x} = \frac{MV_{2,x}}{x_2 - x_3} \times (x_1 - x_0). \tag{24.6}$$

$$MV_{1,y} = \frac{MV_{2,y}}{y_2 - y_3} \times (y_1 - y_0). \tag{24.7}$$

24.1.3 Dictionary-Learning-Based Light Field Image Compression

Dictionary learning [29] aims at finding a sparse representation of the original signal by expressing it as a linear combination of only a few atoms from an over-complete dictionary. The most important part of dictionary learning is to obtain the over-complete dictionary so that the signal can be accurately represented by the smallest possible number of atoms. The over-complete Discrete Cosine Transform (DCT) can be used as the dictionary [36]. However, it is shown that the dictionary from the signal itself [35] for a specific application yields better results.

Given a set of N input signals $\{y_i\}_{i=1,2,\dots,N}$, where each signal y_i contains n data samples, $y_i = [y(1) \ y(2) \ \dots \ y(n)]^T$, corresponds to a macro-pixel (the macro-pixel corresponds to a microlens). The proposed method represents the input matrix $Y = [y_1 \ y_2 \ \dots \ y_N]$, of size $n \times N$, using a reduced number of atoms from the dictionary Φ, of size $n \times d$, where d is the number of atoms in the dictionary. The atoms are selected using the sparse matrix $X = [x_1 \ x_2 \ \dots \ x_N]$, of size $d \times N$, where each sparse vector x_i, of length d, is constrained to have a sparsity s so that x_i combines only s nonzero elements from Φ.

The dictionary learning problem is then formulated as

$$\underset{\Phi,X}{\arg\min} ||Y - \Phi X||_F^2 \quad s.t. \, ||x_i||_0 \le s \;\; \forall \, i, \tag{24.8}$$

where $||\cdot||$ is the Frobenius norm. There are also some works trying to use the L2 norm instead of Frobenius norm [30]. A wide variety of iterative algorithms [6] can be used to solve a non-convex problem. Among them, an Online Sparse Dictionary Learning (OSDL) algorithm [42] is suitable for this case. The OSDL algorithm builds structured dictionaries based on the double-sparsity model, which combines a fixed base dictionary ϕ with an adaptable sparse component A, i.e., $\Phi = \phi A$. The OSDL approach allows for working with larger datasets and it is shown to have a faster convergence rate over traditional dictionary learning methods.

The dictionary problem can then be rewritten using OSDL [54] as follows,

$$\underset{\phi,X}{\arg\min} ||Y - \phi A X||_F^2 \quad s.t. \, ||x_i||_0 \le s \;\; \forall \, i \quad ||a_j||_0 = v \;\; \forall \, j, \tag{24.9}$$

where v is the sparsity for A, and the base dictionary ϕ consists of cropped fully separable wavelets, enabling a multi-scale analysis.

To apply the dictionary-learning-based method to compression, it is better to take the bitrate of the nonzero coefficients into consideration. Specifically, the input signal Y is reconstructed as $\hat{Y} = [\hat{y}_1 \; \hat{y}_2 \; ... \; \hat{y}_N] = \phi A X$, where only the nonzero elements found in X are transmitted to the decoder using their positions in X and their values. Therefore, the following information is transmitted to the decoder:

- The positions of the nonzero coefficients, denoted by P_{nonz}, which are losslessly encoded to guarantee an accurate reconstruction of the input signal.
- The nonzero coefficient values in the coefficient matrix, denoted by X_{nonz}, which are first quantized and then coded using Context Adaptive Binary Arithmetic Coding (CABAC).

Considering the bits of the positions and values of the nonzero coefficients, the dictionary learning problem is finally formulated as

$$\underset{\phi,X}{\arg\min} ||Y - \phi A X||_F^2 + \lambda R_{DL} \quad s.t. \, ||x_i||_0 \le s \;\; \forall \, i \quad ||a_j||_0 = v \;\; \forall \, j. \tag{24.10}$$

The bits R_{DL} are the sum of the bits of the positions and values of the nonzero coefficients,

$$R_{DL} = R_P + R_X, \tag{24.11}$$

where R_P and R_X are the number of bits needed to code the P_{nonz} and X_{nonz}, respectively. The two components are estimated using the following two formulas

Table 24.1 A summary comparison of the lenslet-based light field image compression

	Complexity	Compression efficiency	Quality variance
Self-similarity	Low	Low	Low
Pseudo-sequence	High	High	High
Dictionary learning	Medium	Medium	Low

in the RDO process,

$$R_P = \alpha_1 \cdot N_m, \tag{24.12}$$

$$R_X = \alpha_2 \cdot q + \beta_2, \tag{24.13}$$

where α_1 is the parameter which depends on the sparsity level s and the length of the coefficients vectors d, computed as $\alpha_1 = s log_2 d$. The (α_2, β_2) is the pair of parameters of the least square regression line used to encode the coefficients. N_m is the number of vectors from X_{nonz} transmitted to the decoder.

Three typical compression methods have been introduced above. A summary comparison of these methods is shown in Table 24.1. The self-similarity-based method is with the lowest complexity but also with lower compression efficiency compared with the other methods. The pseudo-sequence-based method is with the highest compression efficiency but also the highest complexity due to the flexible inter partitions in HEVC. The dictionary-based method is also with medium compression efficiency and medium complexity. The users can choose to use different compression methods according to applications.

24.2 Camera-Array-Based Light Field Image Compression

Lenslet-based LFIs sacrifice the spatial resolution to improve the view resolution. Therefore, it is not easy to improve the spatial resolution of each view for lenslet-based LFIs. Camera-array-based LFIs can simultaneously with high spatial resolution and view resolution. For example, the newest dataset from JPEG-Pleno is with 101 views horizontally and 21 views vertically. For each view, it is with 3840×2160 spatial resolution.

Just because camera-array-based LFIs are with very high view resolution and also spatial resolution, the compression requirement of camera-array-based LFIs is even more serious compared with lenslet-based LFIs. For camera-array-based LFIs, they are usually acquired through the dense camera array devices as shown in Fig. 24.12. Various dense camera arrays can have totally different characteristics. Based on the characteristics of the devices, the dense-camera-array-based LFI compression methods can be divided into two groups. One group of methods tries to deal with the case where different cameras are treated as one camera with obvious

Fig. 24.12 Typical dense camera array devices

affine or perspective motions. The other group of methods attempts to handle the situation in which the cameras are mostly with translational motions.

24.2.1 Compression of Dense-Camera-Array-Based Light Field Images with Obvious Perspective Motions

Similar to lenslet-based LFIs, dense-camera-array-based LFIs are also with 4-D information. Therefore, it is very natural to also apply the 2-D hierarchical coding structure to the dense camera array to improve the coding efficiency. For the dense camera array with obvious perspective motions, the number of views is usually not too much. In [12], the 4 × 4 camera array is taken as an example to explain the detailed coding algorithm. The 2-D hierarchical coding structure is first introduced and then the global perspective motion model and local affine motion model are introduced to improve the performance.

24.2.1.1 The 2-D Hierarchical Coding Structure

The frame encoding order and frame types of the 16 views are shown in Fig. 24.13. The frame encoding order is designed following the hierarchical approach suggested by Schwarz et al. [39] in order to code the views efficiently. The method of precedence chosen is weighted on the frame location relative to the light field capture. The top-left frame is the initial frame for the encoder and is the only frame that uses intra prediction. The heaviest weight is given to the other corners and outside frames, whereas the center frames are given the lowest precedence. The reasoning for this is due to the fact that most of the information stored in the center frames is redundant with the exception of obscured objects in the scene and/or occlusions. The parallax phenomenon has been shown to have a direct impact on

Fig. 24.13 2-D hierarchical
coding structure for the dense
camera array LFIs

1_{I_0}	5_{B_2}	6_{B_2}	2_{B_1}
12_{B_2}	13_{B_3}	14_{B_3}	7_{B_2}
11_{B_2}	15_{B_3}	16_{B_3}	8_{B_2}
4_{B_1}	10_{B_2}	9_{B_2}	3_{B_1}

these occlusions and has a greater effect on objects closer to the camera source. In addition, under the 2-D hierarchical coding structure, all the previous coded frames can be used as the reference frames of the current frame to exploit the correlations among various frames as much as possible.

In addition to the benefits of the flexible encoding order, the 2-D hierarchical structure provides the benefit to code each frame with a more reasonable quantization parameter (QP) to further optimize the R-D performance. As shown in Fig. 24.13, four hierarchical layers are used in the 2-D hierarchical coding structure. For different hierarchical layers, since the influence of the frame distortions on the following frames is quite different from each other, the QPs of various frames should also be set according to the influence of the frame distortions. The QPs of layer 1, 2, and 3 are set to the QP of the intra frame plus 2, 4, and 8, respectively.

24.2.1.2   Global Perspective Model

The global affine or perspective motion model was once developed to characterize the global complex motions [46, 50]. To calculate the *global perspective model* between two neighboring frames, two methods are provided below with different trade-offs between the prediction accuracy and the computational complexity. The first one is the direct calculation method using the intrinsic and extrinsic matrices. The second one is key-points-matching-based methods.

The direct calculation method allows the reference frame prediction to be expanded to other frames by using a global space transform. An understanding of relative camera positions in the sequence is required in order to match subsequent frames with the correct camera. This method leverages the encoding order previously stated to predict the next frame in the sequence using a reference frame.

This approach involves leveraging the intrinsic and extrinsic parameters of the camera to reconstruct camera views for frame prediction. The intrinsic matrix provides a transformation from camera coordinates to image coordinates using translation, scaling, and shearing as follows,

$$K = \begin{bmatrix} f_x & s & x_0 \\ 0 & f_y & y_0 \\ 0 & 0 & 1 \end{bmatrix}, \tag{24.14}$$

where the intrinsic matrix K includes x-axis focal length f_x, y-axis focal length f_y, axis skew s, x-axis offset x_0, and y-axis offset y_0. The second matrix used to calibrate the camera is the extrinsic matrix. This matrix describes the transformation from camera coordinates to world coordinates,

$$Q = \begin{bmatrix} r_{1,1} & r_{1,2} & r_{1,3} & t_1 \\ r_{2,1} & r_{2,2} & r_{2,3} & t_2 \\ r_{3,1} & r_{3,2} & r_{3,3} & t_3 \end{bmatrix}, \tag{24.15}$$

where the extrinsic matrix Q includes the rotation and the translational matrices about the x, y, and z axis. The intrinsic matrix K and extrinsic matrix Q can then form a transformation from world coordinate to one perspective,

$$\begin{bmatrix} x_i \\ y_i \\ 1 \end{bmatrix} = s_i K_i Q_i \begin{bmatrix} x_w \\ y_w \\ z_w \\ 1 \end{bmatrix}. \tag{24.16}$$

In (24.16), x_i and y_i are the perspective shifted image coordinates, x_w, y_w, and z_w are the world coordinates, s_i is a scaling factor, K_i is the intrinsic matrix, Q_i is the extrinsic matrix.

Then the perspective transformation, which uses geometric properties to relate planar surfaces to one another, is derived to transform the coordinates from one perspective to the next. This does not use any motion estimation algorithms and can be solved using matrix operations as long as the translation and rotation vectors are known for each camera pose. The perspective transform can be easily derived as follows.

$$\begin{bmatrix} x_i \\ y_i \\ w_i \end{bmatrix} = \begin{bmatrix} c_1 & c_2 & c_3 \\ c_4 & c_5 & c_6 \\ c_7 & c_8 & 1 \end{bmatrix} \begin{bmatrix} x_j \\ y_j \\ 1 \end{bmatrix} \tag{24.17}$$

This is a projection using translation, rotation, and scaling parameters that are contained in a previously calculated camera intrinsic and extrinsic matrix from calibration. As can be seen from (24.17), there are 8 unknown coefficients, they are coded using 32 bits per coefficient.

A comparison of the predicted frame versus the actual frame is achieved by visualizing the residual as shown in Fig. 24.14. The residual produces a PSNR value of 21 dB which can be seen by the abundance of white pixels in the image. The parallax effect is evident in this approach and the objects closer to the camera

Fig. 24.14 Residue of the stitched image using the direct homography projection

Fig. 24.15 SURF extraction and matching

exhibit more adherent noise. For this reason, the global homography transformation is optimal for planar surfaces that are in the far-field range. Although this approach only exhibits marginal PSNR gains, this is a relatively fast operation as only the matrix operation needs to be performed on the frame.

In the feature-matching-based method, the homography matrix estimation is calculated using random sample consensus (RANSAC) and speeded up robust features (SURF) [5] of the two known frames. This is an iterative feature matching process that provides an estimated homography result based on a back projection from one view to another. The SURF method allows features to be extracted from the two reference frames and then the features are matched using key-points which can be observed in Fig. 24.15. Because of the abundance of key-points yielding erroneous matches, RANSAC is used to filter out the outliers. Once the appropriate key-points are mapped, the resulting projection can be achieved by averaging the key-point vectors to approximate the translation, rotation, and scaling.

Fig. 24.16 Residual of the predicted frame using SURF feature matching

As shown in Fig. 24.16, the residual of the RANSAC/SURF method yields a PSNR of 23 dB, which is 2 dB higher compared with the direct calculation method. This gain hints at the possibility that the provided camera parameters are not calculated as precisely needed for the direct calculation method. Although the RANSAC/SURF estimation yields slightly better results, it should be noted that the algorithm estimation time increased by a factor of 150 times. This is a consequence of the iterative method inherent in the RANSAC algorithm.

24.2.1.3 Local Four-Parameter Affine Motion Model

Originally, the local affine model [14] includes the six degrees of freedom (6-DOF) to solve camera motions such as camera track, boom, pan, tilt, zoom, and roll. The six parameters of the affine motion model are reduced to four parameters by Li et al. [19] to get a better balance between the model accuracy and the number of header bits. The *four-parameter affine motion model* is also applied here to code the LFI to try to achieve better coding efficiency. Also, since the camera lens is calibrated and stationary relative to the camera sensor, the four-parameter affine motion model can be better approximated to the camera and object motions for the LFI.

The use of the four-parameter affine motion model allows the complexity of the local affine model to decrease substantially by reducing the calculations by 1/3 compared with the six-parameter affine motion model. As shown in Fig. 24.17, since four parameters are needed for the local transformation, two MVs in the top left corner and top right corner are used to represent the four parameters within a given block of pixels. These MVs are used to interpolate the reference block to the encoded block and are needed to transmit to the decoder to reconstruct the block. Similar to the newest video coding standard Versatile Video Coding (VVC), two MV determination methods, e.g., advanced affine motion vector determination method and affine model merge, are applied to determine the two MVs more efficiently.

Fig. 24.17 Representation of
the local 4-parameter affine
motion model

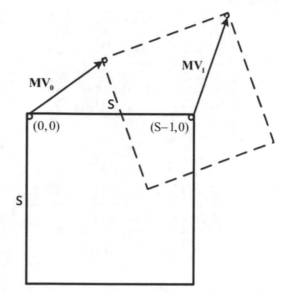

More detailed information about the proposed four-parameter affine motion model
can be found in [19].

24.2.2   Compression of Dense-Camera-Array-Based Light Field Images with Translational Motions

From the data provided by the JPEG standardization group, this kind of camera-
array-based LFI is very dense. As we have mentioned above, the size of the dense
camera array can be as high as 101×21. Since each view of the light field is also
with very high resolution, it is not easy to directly apply the 2-D hierarchical coding
structure due to the quite large memory needed to store all the reference views.
Therefore, a segmented 2-D hierarchical coding structure is designed here to reduce
the reference buffer size while maintaining the coding efficiency.

A segmented 2-D hierarchical coding structure can be seen from Fig. 24.18. All
the views are divided into overlapped segments to reduce the buffer size as shown
in Fig. 24.18. Each small square represents a view and each colored square means
a segment cut from the segment. The array direction means the encoding order of
each segment to save the reference buffer size as much as possible.

Except for the 2-D hierarchical structure, it is also suggested to design a large
background frame [7] [52] for all the views since they are all with very simple
translational motions. The background is composed of the common parts of all the
views. The background frame can be encoded with very high quality and used as
a long term reference frame for all the views. This scheme can absolutely provide
some benefits to coding performance.

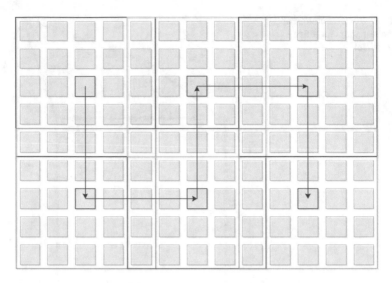

Fig. 24.18 Segmented 2-D hierarchical coding structure

Some compression methods have been introduced above for the multi-camera light field compression. Overall, not many researches have been performed on the compression of the multi-camera LFI yet. Since the multi-camera LFI is really large and redundant, more efforts are appreciated on this topic.

24.3 Surface Light Field Image Compression

The previous two kinds of LFI representations are essentially images from multiple views as they lack explicit geometry information. Surface LFIs are LFI representations with explicit geometry. Sometimes, surface LFIs are also called as plenoptic point clouds. Depending on whether the view synthesis is considered within the scope of compression, the surface LFI compression is divided into two groups: interpolation-based surface LFI compression and plenoptic point cloud compression.

24.3.1 Interpolation-Based Surface Light Field Image Compression

Under the interpolation-based surface LFI compression [51], the multiview images of a scene are first mapped onto a 3D geometric point cloud. The color of each point in the point cloud is a function of viewing direction known as a view map.

The authors represent each view map efficiently using a B-Spline wavelet basis. The representation is capable of modeling diverse surface materials and complex lighting conditions in a highly scalable and adaptive manner. The coefficients of the B-Spline wavelet representation are then compressed using existing point cloud compression methods.

On the decoder side, the scene is rendered efficiently from any viewing direction by reconstructing the view map at each point using interpolation. In contrast to the multiview-image-based LFI compression methods, the method can support photo-realistic rendering of real-world scenes from arbitrary viewpoints.

24.3.2   Plenoptic Point Cloud Compression

There are not many works focusing on the plenoptic point cloud compression. The plenoptic point clouds are first introduced in [37] and [38]. As plenoptic point clouds contain both high spatial and view correlations, both of them need to be fully exploited to improve the plenoptic point cloud compression efficiency. It is proposed in [37] and [38] that the region adaptive hierarchical transform (RAHT) is used to exploit the correlations between different spatial points while the RAHT, DCT, or KLT is used to exploit the correlations between various views. It is reported by the authors that the combination of RAHT and KLT leads to the best performance among various combinations of transforms. Most recently, prior color clustering and specular/diffuse component separation are used to derive a better KLT for each local region [16]. Some performance improvements are observed compared with the combination of RAHT and KLT.

In addition to the transform-based methods, some video-based methods have been proposed to compress plenoptic point clouds. The plenoptic point clouds are first projected onto videos using patch-based methods in the same way as the video-based point cloud compression (V-PCC) [40]. The video projection process can be roughly summarized as patch generation, patch packing, and patch padding. The patched videos [32] are then compressed using video coding standards such as HEVC. As plenoptic point clouds contain the information from multiple views, the multiview-HEVC is also proposed to compress plenoptic point clouds [22]. In addition, some encoder optimization methods such as block-based group dilation and occupancy-map-based RDO [23] can be further used to improve the coding efficiency.

24.4   Conclusion

In this chapter, we have investigated various methods on light field image compression. We mainly focus on three kinds of light field images: the lenslet-based light field image, the camera-array-based light field image, and the surface light field image. For each kind, we have discussed several representative strategies and methods.

Despite the fast development in the light field image compression, the current compression ratio is still far from enough. In the future, we may need to consider some kinds of light field display technologies [15] [17] to better exploit the correlations among various views to improve the coding performance. Also, the correlations among various views and frames for the future light field video compression will be even more complex, we will need some more advanced methods to compress them efficiently, for example, deep learning-based super-resolving techniques [24] for light field images. Current efforts are to explore the algorithms as a DDDAS method to find a satisfactory compression ratio based on the measurements for the light field image or video, the rich geometry and photometric information contained in the light field will enable many new capabilities to the DDDAS related image and video applications.

References

1. Dynamic Data Driven Applications Systems. http://www.1dddas.org/.
2. Light Field Tool box 0.4. http://www.mathworks.com/matlabcentral/fileexchange/49683-light-field-toolbox-v0-4.
3. A. Aggoun. A 3D DCT compression algorithm for omnidirectional integral images. In *2006 IEEE International Conference on Acoustics Speech and Signal Processing Proceedings*, volume 2, pages II–II, May 2006.
4. A. Aggoun. Compression of 3D integral images using 3D wavelet transform. *Journal of Display Technology*, 7(11):586–592, Nov 2011.
5. H. Bay, A. Ess, T. Tuytelaars, and L. V. Gool. Speeded-up robust features (surf). *Computer Vision and Image Understanding*, 110(3):346 – 359, 2008. Similarity Matching in Computer Vision and Multimedia.
6. O. Chabiron, F. Malgouyres, J.-Y. Tourneret, and N. Dobigeon. Toward fast transform learning. *International Journal of Computer Vision*, 114(2-3):195–216, 2015.
7. F. Chen, H. Li, L. Li, D. Liu, and F. Wu. Block-composed background reference for high efficiency video coding. *IEEE Transactions on Circuits and Systems for Video Technology*, PP(99):1–1, 2016.
8. H.-M. Chen, E. Blasch, K. Pham, Z. Wang, and G. Chen. An investigation of image compression on niirs rating degradation through automated image analysis. In *Sensors and Systems for Space Applications IX*, volume 9838, page 983811. International Society for Optics and Photonics, 2016.
9. C. Conti, J. Lino, P. Nunes, L. D. Soares, and P. L. Correia. Spatial prediction based on self-similarity compensation for 3D holoscopic image and video coding. In *2011 18th IEEE International Conference on Image Processing*, pages 961–964, Sept 2011.
10. C. Conti, P. Nunes, and L. D. Soares. HEVC-based light field image coding with bi-predicted self-similarity compensation. In *IEEE International Conf. on Multimedia and Expo - ICME*, pages 1– 4, July 2016.
11. C. Conti, L. D. Soares, and P. Nunes. HEVC-based 3D holoscopic video coding using self-similarity compensated prediction. *Signal Processing: Image Communication*, 42:59–78, March 2016.

12. E. Cornwell, L. Li, Z. Li, and Y. Sun. An efficient compression scheme for the multi-camera light field image. In *2017 IEEE 19th International Workshop on Multimedia Signal Processing (MMSP)*, pages 1–6, Oct 2017.

13. P. Helle, S. Oudin, B. Bross, D. Marpe, M. O. Bici, K. Ugur, J. Jung, G. Clare, and T. Wiegand. Block merging for quadtree-based partitioning in HEVC. *IEEE Transactions on Circuits and Systems for Video Technology*, 22(12):1720–1731, Dec 2012.

14. H. Huang, J. Woods, Y. Zhao, and H. Bai. Control-point representation and differential coding affine-motion compensation. *Circuits and Systems for Video Technology, IEEE Transactions on*, 23(10):1651–1660, Oct. 2013.

15. A. Jones, I. McDowall, H. Yamada, M. Bolas, and P. Debevec. Rendering for an interactive 360 light field display. In *ACM Transactions on Graphics (TOG)*, volume 26, page 40. ACM, 2007.

16. M. Krivokuća and C. Guillemot. Colour compression of plenoptic point clouds Using RAHT-KLT with prior colour clustering and specular/diffuse component separation. In *ICASSP 2020 - 2020 IEEE International Conference on Acoustics, Speech and Signal Processing (ICASSP)*, pages 1978–1982, 2020.

17. D. Lanman, G. Wetzstein, M. Hirsch, W. Heidrich, and R. Raskar. Polarization fields: dynamic light field display using multi-layer lcds. *ACM Transactions on Graphics (TOG)*, 30(6):186, 2011.

18. M. Levoy and P. Hanrahan. Light field rendering. In *Proceedings of the 23rd Annual Conference on Computer Graphics and Interactive Techniques*, SIGGRAPH '96, pages 31–42, New York, NY, USA, 1996. ACM.

19. L. Li, H. Li, D. Liu, Z. Li, H. Yang, L. Sixin, H. Chen, and F. Wu. An efficient four-parameter affine motion model for video coding. *IEEE Transactions on Circuits and Systems for Video Technology*, PP(99):1–1, 2017.

20. L. Li, Z. Li, B. Li, D. Liu, and H. Li. Pseudo sequence based 2-d hierarchical coding structure for light-field image compression. In *Data Compression Conference (DCC), 2017*, pages 131–140. IEEE, 2017.

21. L. Li, Z. Li, B. Li, D. Liu, and H. Li. Pseudo-sequence-based 2-d hierarchical coding structure for light-field image compression. *IEEE Journal of Selected Topics in Signal Processing*, 11(7):1107–1119, Oct 2017.

22. L. Li, Z. Li, S. Liu, and H. Li. Video-based compression for plenoptic point clouds. In *arxiv 1911.01355*, 2019.

23. L. Li, Z. Li, S. Liu, and H. Li. Occupancy-map-based rate distortion optimization and partition for video-based point cloud compression. *IEEE Transactions on Circuits and Systems for Video Technology*, pages 1–1, 2020.

24. Y. Li, D. Liu, H. Li, L. Li, F. Wu, H. Zhang, and H. Yang. Convolutional neural network-based block up-sampling for intra frame coding. *IEEE Transactions on Circuits and Systems for Video Technology*, PP(99):1–1, 2017.

25. Y. Li, R. Olsson, and M. Sjöström. Compression of unfocused plenoptic images using a displacement intra prediction. In *2016 IEEE International Conference on Multimedia Expo Workshops (ICMEW)*, pages 1–4, July 2016.

26. Y. Li, M. Sjöström, R. Olsson, and U. Jennehag. Coding of focused plenoptic contents by displacement intra prediction. *IEEE Transactions on Circuits and Systems for Video Technology*, 26(7):1308–1319, July 2016.

27. D. Liu, L. Wang, L. Li, Z. Xiong, F. Wu, and W. Zeng. Pseudo-sequence-based light field image compression. In *2016 IEEE International Conference on Multimedia Expo Workshops (ICMEW)*, pages 1–4, July 2016.

28. M. Magnor and B. Girod. Data compression for light-field rendering. *IEEE Transactions on Circuits and Systems for Video Technology*, 10(3):338–343, 2000.

29. J. Mairal, F. Bach, J. Ponce, and G. Sapiro. Online dictionary learning for sparse coding. In *Proceedings of the 26th annual international conference on machine learning*, pages 689–696. ACM, 2009.

30. K. Marwah, G. Wetzstein, Y. Bando, and R. Raskar. Compressive light field photography using overcomplete dictionaries and optimized projections. *ACM Transactions on Graphics (TOG)*, 32(4):46, 2013.
31. R. Monteiro, L. Lucas, C. Conti, P. Nunes, N. M. M. Rodrigues, S. Faria, C. Pagliari, E. Silva, and L. D. Soares. Light field HEVC-based image coding using locally linear embedding and self-similarity compensated prediction. In *IEEE International Conf. on Multimedia and Expo - ICME*, pages 1– 4, July 2016.
32. D. Naik, M. Pesonen, and S. Schwarz. [V-PCC] On surface light field support for TMC2. Document ISO/IEC JTC1/SC29/WG11 MPEG2019/M46057, Marrakesh, MA, Jan. 2019.
33. C. Perra and P. Assuncao. High efficiency coding of light field images based on tiling and pseudo-temporal data arrangement. In *2016 IEEE International Conference on Multimedia Expo Workshops (ICMEW)*, pages 1–4, July 2016.
34. M. Rerabek, T. Bruylants, T. Ebrahimi, F. Pereira, and P. Schelkens. ICME 2016 Grand Challenges: Light-Field Image Compression. In *2016 IEEE International Conference on Multimedia Expo Workshops (ICMEW)*, July 2016.
35. Y. Romano, M. Protter, and M. Elad. Single image interpolation via adaptive nonlocal sparsity-based modeling. *IEEE Transactions on Image Processing*, 23(7):3085–3098, 2014.
36. R. Rubinstein, A. M. Bruckstein, and M. Elad. Dictionaries for sparse representation modeling. *Proceedings of the IEEE*, 98(6):1045–1057, 2010.
37. G. Sandri, R. De Queiroz, and P. A. Chou. Compression of plenoptic point clouds using the region-adaptive hierarchical transform. In *2018 25th IEEE International Conference on Image Processing (ICIP)*, pages 1153–1157, Oct 2018.
38. G. Sandri, R. L. de Queiroz, and P. A. Chou. Compression of plenoptic point clouds. *IEEE Transactions on Image Processing*, 28(3):1419–1427, March 2019.
39. H. Schwarz, D. Marpe, and T. Wiegand. Analysis of hierarchical B pictures and MCTF. In *2006 IEEE International Conference on Multimedia and Expo*, pages 1929–1932, July 2006.
40. S. Schwarz, M. Preda, V. Baroncini, M. Budagavi, P. Cesar, P. A. Chou, R. A. Cohen, M. Krivokuća, S. Lasserre, Z. Li, et al. Emerging MPEG standards for point cloud compression. *IEEE Journal on Emerging and Selected Topics in Circuits and Systems*, 9(1):133–148, 2018.
41. R. Sjoberg, Y. Chen, A. Fujibayashi, M. M. Hannuksela, J. Samuelsson, T. K. Tan, Y. K. Wang, and S. Wenger. Overview of HEVC high-level syntax and reference picture management. *IEEE Transactions on Circuits and Systems for Video Technology*, 22(12):1858–1870, Dec 2012.
42. J. Sulam, B. Ophir, M. Zibulevsky, and M. Elad. Trainlets: Dictionary learning in high dimensions. *IEEE Transactions on Signal Processing*, 64(12):3180–3193, 2016.
43. G. J. Sullivan, J. R. Ohm, W. J. Han, and T. Wiegand. Overview of the High Efficiency Video Coding (HEVC) Standard. *IEEE Transactions on Circuits and Systems for Video Technology*, 22(12):1649–1668, Dec 2012.
44. I. Viola, M. Rerabek, T. Bruylants, P. Schelkens, F. Pereira, and T. Ebrahimi. Objective and subjective evaluation of light field image compression algorithms. In *2016 32nd Picture Coding Symposium*, Dec. 2016.
45. G. K. Wallace. The JPEG still picture compression standard. *IEEE Transactions on Consumer Electronics*, 38(1):xviii–xxxiv, Feb 1992.
46. T. Wiegand, E. Steinbach, and B. Girod. Affine multipicture motion-compensated prediction. *Circuits and Systems for Video Technology, IEEE Transactions on*, 15(2):197–209, Feb. 2005.
47. T. Wiegand, G. J. Sullivan, G. Bjontegaard, and A. Luthra. Overview of the H.264/AVC video coding standard. *IEEE Transactions on Circuits and Systems for Video Technology*, 13(7):560–576, July 2003.
48. J. Xu, R. Joshi, and R. A. Cohen. Overview of the emerging HEVC screen content coding extension. *IEEE Transactions on Circuits and Systems for Video Technology*, 26(1):50–62, Jan 2016.
49. X. Xu, S. Liu, T. D. Chuang, Y. W. Huang, S. M. Lei, K. Rapaka, C. Pang, V. Seregin, Y. K. Wang, and M. Karczewicz. Intra block copy in HEVC screen content coding extensions. *IEEE Journal on Emerging and Selected Topics in Circuits and Systems*, PP(99):1–11, 2016.

50. H. Yu, Z. Lin, and F. Teo.   An efficient coding scheme based on image alignment for H.264/AVC. In *Circuits and Systems, 2009. ISCAS 2009. IEEE International Symposium on*, pages 629–632, May 2009.
51. X. Zhang, P. A. Chou, M.-T. Sun, M. Tang, S. Wang, S. Ma, and W. Gao. Surface light field compression using a point cloud codec. *IEEE Journal on Emerging and Selected Topics in Circuits and Systems*, 9(1):163–176, 2018.
52. X. Zhang, T. Huang, Y. Tian, and W. Gao. Background-modeling-based adaptive prediction for surveillance video coding. *IEEE Transactions on Image Processing*, 23(2):769–784, 2014.
53. Y. Zheng, G. Chen, Z. Wang, and E. Blasch. Image quality (iq) guided multispectral image compression. In *Sensing and Analysis Technologies for Biomedical and Cognitive Applications 2016*, volume 9871, page 98710C. International Society for Optics and Photonics, 2016.
54. R. Zhong, I. Schiopu, B. Cornelis, S.-P. Lu, J. Yuan, and A. Munteanu. Dictionary learning-based, directional, and optimized prediction for lenslet image coding. *IEEE Transactions on Circuits and Systems for Video Technology*, 29(4):1116–1129, 2018.

Chapter 25
On Compression of Machine-Derived Context Sets for Fusion of Multi-modal Sensor Data

Nurali Virani, Shashi Phoha, and Asok Ray

Abstract Dynamic data-driven applications systems (DDDAS) operate on a sensing infrastructure for multi-modal measurement, communications, and computation, through which they perceive and control the evolution of physical dynamic processes. Sensors of different modalities are subject to contextually variable performance under varying operational conditions. Unsupervised learning algorithms have been recently developed to extract the operational context set from multi-modal sensor data. A context set represents the set of all natural or man-made factors, which along with the state of the system, completely condition the measurements from sensors observing the system. The desirable property of conditional independence of observations given the state-context pair enables tractable fusion of disparate information sources. In this chapter, we address a crucial problem associated with unsupervised context learning of reducing the cardinality of the context set. Since, the machine-derived context set can have a large number of elements, we propose a graph-theoretic approach and a subset selection approach

The work reported in this chapter has been supported in part by U.S. Air Force Office of Scientific Research (AFOSR) under Grant Nos. FA9550-12-1-0270 and FA9550-15-1-0400. Any opinions, findings, and conclusions in this chapter are those of the authors and do not necessarily reflect the views of the sponsoring agencies.

N. Virani (✉)
GE Global Research, Niskayuna, NY, USA

Department of Mechanical and Nuclear Engineering, The Pennsylvania State University, University Park, PA, USA
e-mail: nurali.virani@ge.com

S. Phoha
Applied Research Laboratory, The Pennsylvania State University, University Park, PA, USA
e-mail: sxp26@arl.psu.edu

A. Ray
Department of Mechanical and Nuclear Engineering, The Pennsylvania State University, University Park, PA, USA
e-mail: axr2@psu.edu

for the controlled reduction of contexts to obtain a context set of lower cardinality. We also derive an upper bound on the error introduced by the compression. These proposed approaches are validated with data collected in field experiments with unattended ground sensors for border-crossing target classification.

Keywords Border security · Conditional independence · Context learning · Graph-theoretic methods · Information fusion · Machine learning · Multimodal measurements · Nondeterministic algebraic structure · Probabilistic finite state automata · Symbolic dynamics · Symbolic time series analysis · Target detection and classification · Unsupervised learning

25.1 Introduction

Dynamic data-driven applications systems (DDDAS) rely on information from a multitude of sensors to assess the state of any observed system [1]. A DDDAS system can not only observe and control states of a physical system, but also adapt the sensing system to obtain better understanding of the system. It is well known that the measurements from the (possibly) multi-modal sources of information are affected not only by the state, but also by the operational conditions around the system [2]. These natural or man-made factors are known as context in literature [3–6]. For example, soil moisture, soil porosity, and ground temperature are contexts for seismic sensors, whereas wind speed and air temperature are those for acoustic sensors. Physics-based analytical models try to capture some of the contextual effects in great detail, but they need accurate estimates of several time-varying environmental parameters. On the other hand, there have been efforts to develop data-driven models for unsupervised discovery of contexts from sensor data. The complexity and accuracy of context-aware DDDAS in state estimation and measurement system adaptation is directly affected by the size of the context set obtained from data-driven or physics-based techniques. This chapter will focus on unsupervised data-driven learning of context with a specific emphasis on techniques to compress the set of contexts and also to understand the effect of this compression. The compression enables to ensure real-time implementation of DDDAS without significantly affecting the performance, such as accuracy of the system.

Recently, in [5] the notion of *context* was mathematically formalized to enable machines to learn from data and then use context in decision-making. However in [3], context was defined as a parameter which along with user-defined state set of the system completely conditions the measurements. Unlike several existing contextual reasoning frameworks, where context is usually associated with a specific modality, proposing context as the enabler of conditional independence unifies the notion of context across all modalities in the system. Bayesian fusion uses the likelihood of a new measurement given all previous measurements from other sensors to correctly obtain the posterior density. A Bayesian process can become intractable for systems which have more than a couple of sensors. Thus, context enables tractable fusion of multi-modal sensors without relying on the possibly incorrect assumption of conditional independence given only the system state (Naïve Bayes assumption). Unsupervised learning of context using clustering as well as density-estimation based approaches have been reported in literature. These approaches either focused on single sensor systems, such as ground penetrating radars in [4] or video sensors in [7], or it is just assumed that the machine-derived context would provide conditional independence in measurements given the state-context pair [5]. However, the nonparametric density-estimation approach for context learning in [3] guarantees that given any user-defined state and machine-defined context pair, the conditional independence property holds true.

The size of context set directly affects the memory required and computation time of the context-aware decision-making approaches for sensor selection [8], tracking [9], multi-modal fusion [6], and pattern recognition [5]. In wireless sensor network applications, such as border surveillance, where power, memory, and execution time are severely constrained, we need to be able to restrict the size of context sets to enable tractable execution of context-aware approaches on resource-constrained platforms. Thus, in this work, we explore different approaches for context set compression. The context learning approach in [3] relies on a convex optimization formulation using the concept of kernel-based density estimation [10, 11]. Thus, adding any explicit sparsity constraint makes the problem nonconvex and hard to solve. Moreover, enforcing strict sparsity constraint on the solution can severely affect the performance of the solution as model order and accuracy are known to be competing objectives [12] and one might have to repeat the nonconvex optimization several times before obtaining a solution with acceptable error. This motivates the need for augmenting the original *convex optimization formulation* with a separate compression step in which the additional maximum error incurred is directly controlled.

This chapter will first review some important aspects of the original optimization problem in Sect. 25.2. The main objective of the chapter is to introduce two distinct techniques to compress the set of contexts and quantify the effect of this compression on the accuracy of the density estimate. The first proposed technique uses the classical graph-theoretic problem of *maximal clique enumeration* [13] for compression of context sets by using a depth-first search strategy [14]. The second technique presents a *subset-selection approach* and establishes a relation of the compression ratio with the upper bound on the additional error incurred by compression on the density estimate. These techniques are explained in Sect. 25.3. The techniques developed in this work are validated using data collected in field experiments from a border surveillance testbed with two geophones to classify whether a human target is walking or running. Finally in Sect. 25.5, the concluding remarks are presented.

25.2   Learning Context from Data

Data-driven modeling of context has been only recently explored in the field of machine learning to enhance the process of information fusion. Unsupervised learning methods using k-means and modularity-based clustering have been reported for obtaining modality-specific context sets [5]. Density estimation has also been used for learning context from data. A parametric approach for context learning to obtain Gaussian mixture models was presented in [4], whereas a nonparametric approach using kernel-based regression was proposed in [3]. In this section, we first present a definition of context, which mathematically formalizes this widely-used notion of context, and then we review some existing methods to derive context sets from data.

Definition 25.2.1 (Context and Context Set [3]) Suppose that the measurements Y_1 and Y_2 take values in $\mathcal{Y}_1$ and $\mathcal{Y}_2$, respectively. Suppose that the state X takes values from a finite set $\mathcal{X}$. Then, a nonempty finite set $\mathcal{C}(X)$ is called the *context set* and each element $c \in \mathcal{C}(X)$ of the set is called a *context*, if the measurements Y_1 and Y_2 are mutually independent conditioned on the state-context pair (x, c) for all $x \in \mathcal{X}$ and for all $c \in \mathcal{C}(X)$.

According to this definition, the following relation holds:

$$p(Y_1, Y_2 \mid X, c) = p_1(Y_1 \mid X, c) p_2(Y_2 \mid X, c) \quad \text{for all } c \in \mathcal{C}(X). \tag{25.1}$$

Here, the left-hand side of (25.1) denotes the conditional density of (Y_1, Y_2) given (X, c), and the right-hand side gives the product of conditional densities of Y_1 and Y_2 given (X, c). The Definition 25.2.1 enables to obtain a single context set from multi-modal sensor data, when the measurement space $\mathcal{Y}_1$ and $\mathcal{Y}_2$ corresponds to heterogeneous sensors. In order to generate a context set $\mathcal{C}(x)$ for each $x \in \mathcal{X}$, so that (25.1) holds, kernel-based density estimation [10] was used in [3].

The problem of obtaining all contexts, which satisfy the relation in (25.1), is nontrivial and the concept to pose it as a nonparametric mixture modeling problem was first proposed in [3]. In view of Definition 25.2.1, the measurement likelihood function is of the form

$$p(Y_1, Y_2 \mid X) = \sum_{c \in \mathcal{C}(X)} \pi_c(X) p(Y_1, Y_2 \mid X, c)$$

$$= \sum_{c \in \mathcal{C}(X)} \pi_c(X) p_1(Y_1 \mid X, c) p_2(Y_2 \mid X, c), \tag{25.2}$$

where $\pi_c(X)$ is the prior probability that, conditioned on the state X, the true context is c. In order to estimate this likelihood model, the conditional density was represented as the following mixture model

$$p(Y_1, Y_2 \mid X) = \sum_{c \in \mathcal{C}(X)} \pi_c(X) \, K_1\big(s_1^{(c)}(X), Y_1\big) K_2\big(s_2^{(c)}(X), Y_2\big), \tag{25.3}$$

where the prior probability $\pi_c(X)$ denotes the weight of the component corresponding to context c in the context set $\mathcal{C}(X)$ and the component is represented by the product of kernel functions $K_i : \mathcal{Y}_i \times \mathcal{Y}_i \to \mathbb{R}$ for $i = 1, 2$. Also, $s_i^{(c)}(X) \in \mathcal{Y}_i$ is a support vector [10] obtained by solving the kernel regression problem using training data consisting of the triples (Y_1, Y_2, X). Thus, the problem of learning a context set was reduced to that of identifying support vectors of a regression problem. The details of this technique are available in [3]. The context set identified by regression has error bounded above by an insensitivity parameter, which is chosen by the user. Although, one can use this error margin parameter to indirectly influence the size of context set, there is no explicit relationship for the set cardinality with the chosen error margin. Thus, the main contribution of the chapter is explained in the next section, which enables controlled compression of context sets.

25.3   Cardinality Reduction of Context Sets

This section will explain the two proposed techniques for cardinality reduction of context sets, as shown in Fig. 25.1, using the maximal clique enumeration algorithm from graph theory and a simple subset selection approach. These techniques assume that the density estimation step for unsupervised context learning has already been solved and the resulting density estimate is used in both of these techniques.

25.3.1   Graph-Theoretic Compression

In graph theory, a clique is a complete subgraph and it is maximal, if it is not contained in a bigger clique. Maximal clique enumeration (MCE) is a classical problem in graph theory, which was addressed in detail in [13, 14] using depth-first search strategy. We use the MCE concept to identify all machine-derived contexts whose effect on sensor measurements is almost identical. The context set is used as the vertex set of a weighted graph and the edge weights denote the pairwise distance

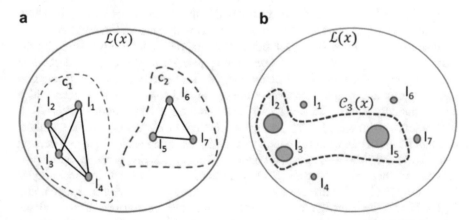

Fig. 25.1 Concept of context set compression. (**a**) Maximal clique enumeration. (**b**) Subset selection

---

Algorithm 1: Context set compression by maximal clique enumeration

---

Input: Observation densities $p(Y \mid X, L)$ and threshold ε.
Output: Context set $\mathscr{C}(X)$.

1 **for** *all* $x \in \mathscr{X}$ **do**
2 $\quad\mid\quad$ Compute weight matrix $\mathbf{W}(x)$;
3 $\quad\mid\quad$ $\mathscr{G}_{x,\varepsilon}$ =ConstructGraph($\mathbf{W}(x), \varepsilon$);
4 $\quad\mid\quad$ $\mathscr{M}$ =MCE($\mathscr{G}_{x,\varepsilon}$);
5 $\quad\mid\quad$ $\mathscr{C}(x)$ =Minterms($\mathscr{M}$).

---

between contextual observation densities. The MCE-based context set compression approach is explained next.

Let $l_1, l_2, \ldots, l_{|\mathscr{L}(x)|}$ denote the distinct machine-derived contexts for the state $x \in \mathscr{X}$ before compression and let c denote an element of the compressed context set $\mathscr{C}(x)$ for the state $x \in \mathscr{X}$. The algorithm defines a weight matrix $\mathbf{W}(x) = [w_{ij}(x)] \in \mathbb{R}^{|\mathscr{L}(x)| \times |\mathscr{L}(x)|}$ by

$$w_{ij}(x) = d\big(p(Y \mid X = x, L = l_i), p(Y \mid X = x, L = l_j)\big)$$

for $x \in \mathscr{X}$ and $i, j = 1, \ldots, |\mathscr{L}(x)|$, where $Y = (Y_1, Y_2, \ldots, Y_N)$ is the concatenated measurement from all sensors. Here, denoted by $d(\cdot, \cdot)$ is a distance function on the space of observation densities, such as symmetric Kullback-Leibler divergence [15] or the Bhattacharyya distance [16]. For a chosen positive real number ε, let $\mathscr{G}_{x,\varepsilon}$ denote the ε-context graph for state $x \in \mathscr{X}$, which is defined by the tuple $(\mathscr{L}(x), \mathscr{E}(x, \varepsilon))$, where the vertex set $\mathscr{L}(x)$ represents the set of all machine-derived contexts corresponding to the state $x \in \mathscr{X}$ and the edge set is given as

$$\mathscr{E}(x, \varepsilon) = \{(l_i, l_j) \in \mathscr{L}(x)^2 \colon w_{ij}(x) \leq \varepsilon, \, i, j = 1, \ldots, |\mathscr{L}(x)|\}$$

for each $x \in \mathscr{X}$. The graph $\mathscr{G}_{x,\varepsilon}$ is constructed in the ConstructGraph function. The edge set $\mathscr{E}(x, \varepsilon)$ represents all pairs of context whose measurement densities are at most distance ε away from each other. This graph $\mathscr{G}_{x,\varepsilon}$ is then processed by the Maximal Clique Enumeration function, which implements the depth-first search strategy given in [14], to obtain the set of all maximal cliques denoted by $\mathscr{M}$. Each maximal clique is a subset of the context set consisting of contexts which are all mutually at most distance ε away from each other. The maximal cliques will form a *set cover* of the set $\mathscr{L}(x)$ (i.e., union of maximal cliques equals the complete set), but they can end up being overlapping, thus, denoting each clique as a context can lead to the loss of the desired conditional independence property. Moreover, it is known that for an n-vertex graph, the maximum number of maximal cliques is given by $3^{n/3}$ [17], thus, the resulting context set might become exponentially larger. Hence, the function Minterms($\mathscr{M}$) uses the method in [18] to evaluate all minterms of $\mathscr{M}$ (i.e., nonempty set differences and intersections formed by the members of $\mathcal{M}$) to obtain a mutually exclusive and exhaustive collection $\mathcal{C}(x)$ of cliques that partition the set $\mathcal{L}(x)$; for example, Minterms($\{\{1, 2, 3, 5\}, \{2, 4\}\}$) gives $\{\{1, 3, 5\}, \{2\}, \{4\}\}$. These steps are given in the Algorithm 1, which lead to the construction of the compressed context set denoted by $\mathcal{C}(X)$.

Each element $c \in \mathcal{C}(X)$ of the context set is a collection of the machine-defined contexts $l \in \mathcal{L}(X)$. The corresponding contextual observation density and prior distribution need to be derived for the compressed context set. We will first assign values to $p(c \mid X, l)$ as follows:

$$p(c \mid X, l) = \begin{cases} 1, & \text{if } l \in c \\ 0, & \text{otherwise.} \end{cases} \tag{25.4}$$

In (25.4), the conditional density is well-defined as $\mathcal{C}(X)$ is a partition of $\mathcal{L}(X)$ and it will assume the value of 1 for only one $c \in \mathcal{C}(X)$. Now, we can compute the prior density using (25.4) as follows:

$$p(c|X) = \sum_{l \in \mathcal{L}(X)} p(c \mid X, l) p(l \mid X) = \sum_{l \in c} p(l \mid X), \tag{25.5}$$

where $p(l|X)$ is the state-dependent prior probability of the machine-defined context which is known. The observation density can be shown to be given accurately by the mixture model

$$p(Y \mid X, c) = \sum_{l_i \in c} \frac{p(l_i \mid X)}{p(c \mid X)} p(Y \mid X, l_i). \tag{25.6}$$

The overall model complexity stays the same as the number of mixture components still remain the same. In order to reduce the model complexity, we define the observation density $p(Y \mid X, c) = p(Y \mid X, l^*)$, where, l^* is an element in c. Theorem 25.3.1 derives an approach to choose l^* and provides the bound for the error induced by this process.

Theorem 25.3.1 (Bound for error introduced in compression by clique enumeration) *If the distance function d used in Algorithm 1 is symmetric Kullback-Leibler divergence (sKL), then for any fixed threshold $\varepsilon > 0$, the error induced by defining $p(Y \mid X, c) = p(Y \mid X, l^*)$ for some $l^* \in c$ is upper-bounded by the value $\varepsilon\left(1 - \frac{p(l^*|X)}{p(c|X)}\right)$, which is strictly less than ε. This error bound is minimized for $l^* = \arg\max_{l \in c} p(l \mid X)$.*

Proof At first, a known result from literature will be shown and then, we will use it to prove the theorem. Let p_0 denote a mixture model with component densities f_i^0 and weights π_i^0 for $i \in \{1, \ldots, n_0\}$, and similarly p_1 denotes another mixture model with n_1 components. The convexity upper bound on KL-divergence [15] is given by

$$KL(p_0 \parallel p_1) \leq \sum_{i=1}^{n_0} \sum_{j=1}^{n_1} \pi_i^0 \pi_j^1 KL(f_i^0 \parallel f_j^1)$$

$$\implies d(p_0, p_1) \leq \sum_{i=1}^{n_0} \sum_{j=1}^{n_1} \pi_i^0 \pi_j^1 d(f_i^0, f_j^1), \tag{25.7}$$

since, $d(p_0, p_1) = sKL(p_0, p_1) = KL(p_0 \parallel p_1) + KL(p_1 \parallel p_0)$. Let us consider p_0 to be the density from (25.6) with $\pi_i^0 = \frac{p(l_i|X)}{p(c|X)}$, $f_i^0 = p(Y \mid X, l_i)$, and $n_0 = |c|$, and assign $p_1 = p(Y|X, l^*)$, i.e., $\pi_j^1 = 1$, if $l_j = l^*$, $\pi_j^1 = 0$, otherwise. Using (25.7) and substituting for the mixture models, we get

$$d(p_0, p_1) \leq \sum_{l_i=1}^{|c|} \pi_i^0 d(p(Y \mid X, l_i), p(Y \mid X, l^*)) =$$

$$\sum_{l_i \in c \setminus \{l^*\}} \pi_i^0 d(p(Y \mid X, l_i), p(Y \mid X, l^*))$$

using that l^* belongs to c and the positive definiteness property of the distance function. Since we know that ε is the distance threshold and clique c consists only of elements l, whose observations densities are at most ε away from each other, we obtain $d(p_0, p_1) \leq \sum_{l_i \in c \setminus \{l^*\}} \pi_i^0 \varepsilon$. Substituting the values for π_i^0 and using (25.5), we will obtain the desired result as follows:

$$d(p_0, p_1) \leq \varepsilon \sum_{l_i \in c \setminus \{l^*\}} \frac{p(l_i \mid X)}{p(c \mid X)} = \varepsilon \left(1 - \frac{p(l^* \mid X)}{p(c \mid X)}\right). \tag{25.8}$$

Since l^* belongs to c, we have $p(l^*|X) \leq p(c|X)$. Thus, we verify that $d(p_0, p_1)$ is indeed less than ε and the error bound is minimized for $l^* = \arg\max_{l \in c} p(l \mid X)$. □

The Theorem shows us that, if we choose acceptable level of error (ε), then we can use it as the graph threshold in the function ConstructGraph of Algorithm 1. The two limitations of this approach are that: (i) the compression level is not known a priori, and (ii) the computations have to be redone if we decide to change the value of ε. In order to alleviate these two issues, we will look at another approach called subset selection.

25.3.2 Compression by Subset Selection

In the subset selection approach, we directly choose the size of the desired compressed context set (say k) and not the acceptable error. The proposed approach is to select a set of k distinct contexts from the machine-derived context set $\mathcal{L}(X)$

and assign those to a compressed context set $\mathscr{C}_k(X)$. Thus, we will end up with $\mathscr{C}_k(X) \subsetneq \mathscr{L}(X)$ for $k < |\mathscr{L}(X)|$. This section explains the approach to select the subset and derive a bound on the error introduced by subset selection.

Let us denote $\bar{\mathscr{C}}_k(X)$ as the relative complement of $\mathscr{C}_k(X)$ with respect to $\mathscr{L}(X)$, given by $\bar{\mathscr{C}}_k(X) = \mathscr{L}(X) \setminus \mathscr{C}_k(X)$. We consider that the set $\mathscr{C}_k(X)$ is constructed by arbitrary selection of any k elements from the set $\mathscr{L}(X)$. Theorem 25.3.2 will derive a bound for the error introduced by subset selection and provides a technique to choose the subset in a systematic way.

Theorem 25.3.2 (Bound for error introduced in compression by subset selection) *Let* $p_{\mathscr{L}}(Y \mid X)$ *be the density estimated using the machine-derived context set* $\mathscr{L}(X)$ *for the state* X, *which is given as*

$$p_{\mathscr{L}}(Y \mid X) = \sum_{i \in \mathscr{L}(X)} \alpha_i K_X(Y, y_i), \tag{25.9}$$

where $K_X(\cdot, \cdot)$ *is a kernel function and* α_i *is the context prior probability associated with the context* $i \in \mathscr{L}(X)$. *If* $\mathscr{C}_k(X)$ *denotes a subset of machine-derived context set* $\mathscr{L}(X)$ *consisting of* k *elements, such that* $\sum_{i \in \mathscr{C}_k(X)} \alpha_i > 0$, *then the density estimate obtained using this subset is given as*

$$p_{\mathscr{C}}(Y \mid X) = \sum_{i \in \mathscr{C}_k(X)} \tilde{\alpha}_i K_X(Y, y_i), \tag{25.10}$$

where $\tilde{\alpha}_i = \frac{\alpha_i}{\sum_{i \in \mathscr{C}_k(X)} \alpha_i}$ *is the associated prior. The upper bound of the supremum norm of error in density estimation due to subset selection is proportional to the sum of context priors from the set* $\bar{\mathscr{C}}_k(X)$, *i.e.,* $\mathscr{L}(X) \setminus \mathscr{C}_k(X)$. *In other words,*

$$\|p_{\mathscr{C}}(Y \mid X) - p_{\mathscr{L}}(Y \mid X)\|_\infty \leq \beta_X \sum_{i \in \bar{\mathscr{C}}_k(X)} \alpha_i \tag{25.11}$$

where $\beta_X \in \mathbb{R}$ *satisfies* $0 \leq K_X(\cdot, \cdot) \leq \beta_X < \infty$.

Proof Using (25.9) and (25.10), after some algebraic manipulations one can show that the difference in estimates for any $y \in \mathscr{Y}$ is given as

$$p_{\mathscr{C}}(y \mid X) - p_{\mathscr{L}}(y \mid X) = \frac{1}{\sum_{l \in \mathscr{C}_k(X)} \alpha_l} \left(\sum_{i \in \mathscr{C}_k(X)} \sum_{j \in \bar{\mathscr{C}}_k(X)} \alpha_i \alpha_j \left(K_X(y, y_i) - K_X(y, y_j) \right) \right).$$

The supremum norm in this setting of continuous functions is given as

$$\|p_{\mathscr{C}}(Y \mid X) - p_{\mathscr{L}}(Y \mid X)\|_\infty = \sup_{y \in \mathscr{Y}} \left| p_{\mathscr{C}}(y \mid X) - p_{\mathscr{L}}(y \mid X) \right|.$$

Using absolute homogeneity and triangle inequality property for the norm, we obtain

$$\|p_{\mathscr{C}}(Y \mid X) - p_{\mathscr{L}}(Y \mid X)\|_\infty \leq \frac{1}{\sum_{l \in \mathscr{C}_k(X)} \alpha_l} \left(\sum_{\substack{i \in \mathscr{C}_k(X) \\ j \in \bar{\mathscr{C}}_k(X)}} \alpha_i \alpha_j \sup_{y \in \mathscr{Y}} \left| K_X(y, y_i) - K_X(y, y_j) \right| \right)$$

$$\leq \frac{1}{\sum_{l \in \mathscr{C}_k(X)} \alpha_l} \left(\sum_{i \in \mathscr{C}_k(X)} \sum_{j \in \bar{\mathscr{C}}_k(X)} \alpha_i \alpha_j \beta_X \right).$$

Since β_X is the maximum value assumed by the nonnegative-valued kernels. Thus, we obtain the desired result,

$$\|p_{\mathscr{C}}(Y \mid X) - p_{\mathscr{L}}(Y \mid X)\|_\infty \leq \beta_X \sum_{j \in \bar{\mathscr{C}}_k(X)} \alpha_j. \qquad \square$$

Remark 25.3.1 (Optimal k-subset) Since the error upper bound is directly proportional to $(1 - \sum_{i \in \mathscr{C}_k(X)} \alpha_i)$, the k-subset with minimum error bound is one for which $\sum_{i \in \mathscr{C}_k(X)} \alpha_i$ is maximum. Thus, if the elements in the context set $\mathscr{L}(X)$ are sorted in descending order of their priors $p(l_i \mid X)$, i.e., α_i, then the best subset $\mathscr{C}_k^*(X)$ corresponds to the first k elements of this sorted sequence. The corresponding error upper bound is $\beta_X(1 - \sum_{j \in \mathscr{C}_k^*(X)} \alpha_j)$.

Remark 25.3.2 (Optimal choice of k) Without loss of generality, we can assume that $\alpha_1 \geq \alpha_2 \geq \cdots \geq \alpha_{|\mathscr{L}(X)|}$ represents the sorted sequence of context priors. If the error upper bound for a k-subset for any $k \in \{1, 2, \ldots, |\mathscr{L}(X)|\}$ is denoted by e_k, then $e_k = \beta_X(1 - \sum_{j=1}^{k} \alpha_j)$ using result in Remark 25.3.1. We can verify that, the sequence $\{e_k\}$ is monotonically decreasing with $e_{|\mathscr{L}(X)|} = 0$. These values represent the accuracy of representation of the density. If in certain application we also have a model complexity function $g(k)$, then we can trade-off accuracy with complexity using a criterion, such as Akaike Information Criterion [12], to find the optimal value of k, which minimizes the chosen criterion.

The error bound derived in Theorem 25.3.2 is usually conservative, but this conservative analysis leads to a simple expression for e_k, which can readily be evaluated for all $k \in \{1, 2, \ldots, |\mathscr{L}(X)|\}$. Unlike the technique in Sect. 25.3.1, the subset selection approach can give a relationship of subset size or compression ratio with maximum error in estimation, which in turn can lead to choosing appropriate compression as shown in Remark 25.3.2. However, the subset selection approach directly ignores the contexts with low priors and does not use information of overlap/distance between individual components, which might not be desirable for certain applications.

This section presented two techniques for compression of context sets along with the main results of the upper bound of error due to approximation. The error bound evaluated in first approach was in terms of statistical distance functions, whereas in second case we derive a more intuitive bound in terms of the supremum norm. In the next section, we will use these techniques for cardinality reduction of context sets derived from multiple seismic sensor data for a target classification problem.

25.4 Experiments and Results

The procedure and results of experimental validation of the context set compression techniques are presented in this section. We conducted field experiments to collect data from unattended ground sensors, such as seismic, acoustic, and passive infrared sensors, for a border-crossing target detection and classification problem. In this study, we use time-series data from two different seismic sensors which were separated by 7 m and the target is passing almost parallel to the line joining the two sensors at various distances between 2 to 8 m. The hypothesis set consists of human target walking ($x = 1$) and human target running ($x = 2$) class and the goal is to classify the activity of the target using data from both the seismic sensors, as shown in Fig. 25.2.

The dataset consists of 110 runs for walking and 118 runs for running. We partition the sample into a training set and testing set consisting of 60% and 40% of the data respectively. All results are generated for 10 different partitions of the sample and average results are available for the different steps. In the first step, low-dimensional features are extracted from time-series data using *symbolic dynamic filtering* (SDF) [19]. In SDF, we partition the measurement space into several regions and assign a symbol to each region. The set of these symbols is known as the alphabet. Bias is removed from the measurement time-series data to make it zero-mean and it is also normalized to have unit variance to remove the effect of target distance on signal amplitude. The resulting time-series data is then represented by a symbol sequence and the statistics of evolution of this sequence is represented by a D-Markov model [20]. In this analysis, we used alphabet size of 6 and depth D of 2, resulting in a D-Markov model of 7 states after state-splitting and state-merging. The left eigenvector of state transition matrix of the D-Markov model corresponding to the eigenvalue of 1 is the stationary state probability vector, which is used as a low-dimensional feature vector for each time-series data. The details on the D-Markov model construction and feature extraction techniques are given in [20].

The second step is of *unsupervised context learning* which uses nonparametric density estimation for obtaining machine-derived context sets from kernel-based mixture models as shown in Sect. 25.2. The density estimation process is used for computing the joint likelihood of obtaining a feature Y_1 from seismic sensor 1 and a feature Y_2 from seismic sensor 2, given that the state is X. The kernels used in the mixture modeling process are Gaussian with diagonal covariance matrix having identical entries, i.e., $K_i(y, y_i) = (2\pi\gamma)^{-d_i/2}\exp(-\frac{(y-y_i)^{\mathrm{T}}(y-y_i)}{2\gamma^2})$, where d_i is the dimensionality of feature Y_i for $i = 1, 2$ and γ is the kernel shape parameter. Using $\gamma = 0.01$, the resulting context sets for state 1 have cardinality (i.e., number of elements in the set) has mean 14.80 and standard deviation 1.47, whereas for state

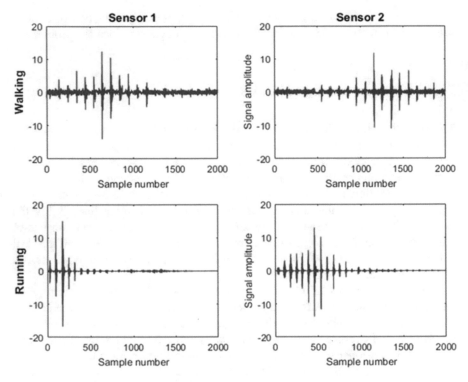

Fig. 25.2 Seismic sensor time series data for walking and running classes

2, the cardinality has mean 20.60 and standard deviation 1.65. The analysis uses maximum likelihood decision rule for classification that gives state estimate as

$$\hat{x} = \arg\max_{x \in \mathcal{X}} p(Y_1, Y_2 \mid x) = \arg\max_{x \in \mathcal{X}} \sum_{c \in \mathcal{C}(x)} p(c|x)p(Y_1, Y_2 \mid x, c). \tag{25.12}$$

For the machine-derived context set with $\gamma = 0.01$, the classification accuracy was 99.78% on average using the decision rule in (25.12).

In the third step, we use the two proposed *context set cardinality reduction* techniques to obtain the compressed context sets. In the maximal clique enumeration (MCE) technique, the contextual observation densities are multivariate Gaussian distributions with mean $\mu_i(x)$ and identical covariance matrix $\Sigma_\gamma(x)$, which is parametrized by the kernel shape parameter γ, thus $p(Y \mid X = x, L = l_i) \sim \mathcal{N}(\mu_i(x), \Sigma_\gamma(x))$. In order to construct the weight matrix, we use the closed form expression of the Bhattacharyya distance for Gaussian densities [16], given as

$$w_{ij}(x) = d\big(p(Y \mid X = x, L = l_i), p(Y \mid X = x, L = l_j)\big)$$

$$= \frac{1}{8}(\mu_i(x) - \mu_j(x))^{\mathrm{T}} \Sigma_\gamma(x)^{-1}(\mu_i(x) - \mu_j(x)) \tag{25.13}$$

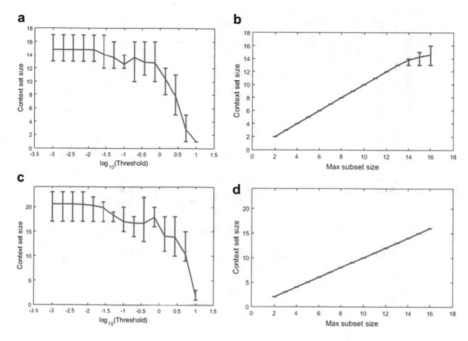

Fig. 25.3 Mean and range of cardinality of the compressed context set. (**a**) MCE for $x = 1$. (**b**) Subset selection for $x = 1$. (**c**) MCE for $x = 2$. (**d**) Subset selection for $x = 2$

for $i, j = 1, 2, \ldots, |\mathscr{L}(x)|$. The threshold parameter ε to be used in the ConstructGraph function of the MCE approach is varied from 10^{-3} to 10^1 in 15 equal steps in the log scale. For the graph obtained from the ConstructGraph function, we perform the maximal clique enumeration process and compute minterms of the obtained set of cliques. Note that as threshold increases, the cardinality of the compressed set shows a nonmonotonic reducing trend in Fig. 25.3a, c as number of cliques need not reduce monotonically with reduction of the edge set of the graph. The Minterms procedure ensures by definition that the number of cliques in the resulting set is upper-bounded by cardinality of the machine defined context set, that is, $|\mathscr{C}(x)| \leq |\mathscr{L}(x)|$ for all $x \in \mathscr{X}$, thus, we will get some compression. The classification performance summary using compressed context sets using MCE is given in Fig. 25.4a. The results show that for $\varepsilon = 10^{0.42} = 2.68$, the mean cardinality of context sets is $|\mathscr{C}(1)| = 7.8$ and $|\mathscr{C}(2)| = 13.9$, where the average classification accuracy is same as the full context set. This result demonstrates that cardinality reduction need not significantly affect the class performance. However, reducing cardinality further by increasing ε leads to significant deterioration in performance in this case. Cross-validation can be used to choose the appropriate value for the threshold ε.

In the subset selection approach, the maximum size of the subset, denoted by k, is varied from 2 to 16. If the original context set is smaller than the chosen set size, we do not perform any other computation, else we choose the best k-subset using

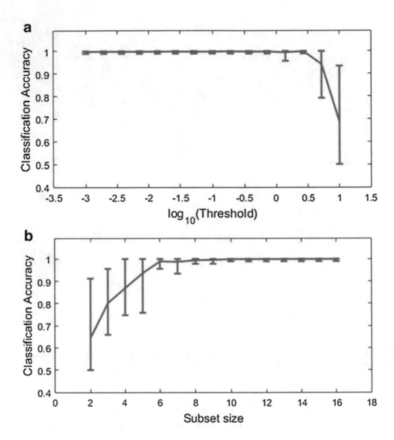

Fig. 25.4 Mean and range of classification accuracy with compressed context sets. (**a**) MCE. (**b**) Subset selection

Remark 25.3.1. Thus, Fig. 25.3b, d shows a monotonic trend of context set size with the chosen parameter k. The classification performance shows an increasing trend with the size of context set. For $k = 8$, the performance is 99.56% and for $k > 8$, the performance is as good as the original set. Thus, compression of context sets can be achieved by subset selection techniques as well. A suitable context set size can be chosen by using cross-validation, if classification accuracy is the selection criterion, else one can use the method outlined in Remark 25.3.2 to choose context set size.

25.5 Conclusion

This chapter presents two different approaches to control the size of context sets in an unsupervised learning setting. Learning approaches with density estimation to obtain machine-defined context set from multi-modal sensor data is reviewed in this chapter and the resulting density estimate is used in both the proposed approaches. One approach relies on the *graph-theoretic concept of maximal clique enumeration* to identify contexts which affect the sensor data in a similar way and it creates approximate equivalence classes of the machine-defined contexts. The upper bound of error introduced by this compression was identified. A *subset selection approach* is also presented in this chapter and the upper bound of error introduced by subset selection is derived. In this approach, the prior probabilities over context played an important role to obtain the best subset. We could derive a conservative relation between the error upper bound and cardinality of the context set. These approaches were then used with seismic sensor data collected in field experiments for walking-type classification of border crossing targets. The results validate that these techniques are indeed useful for compression of context sets and can maintain similar classification performance with a much smaller context set. In future, an agglomerative clustering approach that can provide an estimate of the error introduced by compression will be explored to find a computationally inexpensive approach to allow representation of data from all relevant regions in the measurement space.

References

1. F. Darema, Dynamic data driven applications systems: new capabilities for application simulations and measurements, in *Computational Science–ICCS 2005*, ed. by J.J. Dongarra, P.M.A. Sloot, V.S. Sunderam, G.D. Van Albada (Springer, Berlin/Heidelberg, Atlanda, GA, USA, 2005), pp. 610–615
2. B. Kahler, E. Blasch, L. Goodwon, Operating condition modeling for ATR fusion assessment, in *Defense and Security Symposium* (International Society for Optics and Photonics, Orlando (Kissimmee), FL, USA, 2007), pp. 65710D–65710D
3. N. Virani, J.-W. Lee, S. Phoha, A. Ray, Learning context-aware measurement models, in *American Control Conference (ACC)* (IEEE, Chicago, IL, USA, 2015), pp. 4491–4496
4. C.R. Ratto, P. Torrione, L.M. Collins, Exploiting ground-penetrating radar phenomenology in a context-dependent framework for landmine detection and discrimination. IEEE Trans. Geosci. Remote Sens. **49**(5), 1689–1700 (2011)
5. S. Phoha, N. Virani, P. Chattopadhyay, S. Sarkar, B. Smith, A. Ray, Context-aware dynamic data-driven pattern classification. Procedia Comput. Sci. **29**, 1324–1333 (2014)
6. E. Blasch, J. Nagy, A. Aved, E.K. Jones, W.M. Pottenger, A. Basharat, A. Hoogs, M. Schneider, R. Hammoud, G. Chen et al., Context aided video-to-text information fusion, in *2014 17th International Conference on Information Fusion (FUSION)* (IEEE, Salamanca, Spain, 2014), pp. 1–8
7. L. Snidaro, J. García, J. Llinas, E. Blasch, *Context-Enhanced Information Fusion: Boosting Real-World Performance with Domain Knowledge* (Springer, Cham, 2016)
8. N. Virani, J.-W. Lee, S. Phoha, A. Ray, Dynamic context-aware sensor selection for sequential hypothesis testing, in *2014 IEEE 53rd Annual Conference on Decision and Control (CDC)*, Los Angeles, CA, USA, Dec 2014, pp. 6889–6894
9. E. Blasch, J. G. Herrero, L. Snidaro, J. Llinas, G. Seetharaman, K. Palaniappan, Overview of contextual tracking approaches in information fusion, in *Proceedings of SPIE*, Geospatial InfoFusion III, 87470B (Baltimore, Maryland, USA, May 2013)

10. S. Mukherjee, V. Vapnik, Support vector method for multivariate density estimation, in *Center for Biological and Computational Learning. Department of Brain and Cognitive Sciences, MIT. CBCL*, vol. 170, 1999
11. N. Virani, J.-W. Lee, S. Phoha, A. Ray, Information-space partitioning and symbolization of multi-dimensional time-series data using density estimation, in *American Control Conference (ACC)* (IEEE, Baltimore, MA, USA, 2016), pp. 3328–3333
12. C.M. Bishop, *Pattern Recognition and Machine Learning* (Springer, New York, 2006)
13. C. Bron, J. Kerbosch, Algorithm 457: finding all cliques of an undirected graph. Commun. ACM **16**(9), 575–577 (1973)
14. E. Tomita, A. Tanaka, H. Takahashi, The worst-case time complexity for generating all maximal cliques and computational experiments. Theor. Comput. Sci. **363**(1), 2842 (2006)
15. J.R. Hershey, P. Olsen, Approximating the Kullback Leibler divergence between gaussian mixture models, in *IEEE International Conference on Acoustics, Speech and Signal Processing. ICASSP 2007*, vol. 4 (IEEE, Honolulu, Hawai, USA, 2007), pp. IV–317
16. F.J. Aherne, N.A. Thacker, P.I. Rockett, The Bhattacharyya metric as an absolute similarity measure for frequency coded data. Kybernetika **34**(4), 363–368 (1998)
17. J.W. Moon, L. Moser, On cliques in graphs. Isr. J. Math. **3**(1), 23–28 (1965)
18. D. Avis, K. Fukuda, Reverse search for enumeration. Discret. Appl. Math. **65**(1–3), 21–46 (1996)
19. A. Ray, Symbolic dynamic analysis of complex systems for anomaly detection. Signal Process. **84**, 1115–1130 (2004)
20. K. Mukherjee, A. Ray, State splitting and merging in probabilistic finite state automata for signal representation and analysis. Signal Process. **104**, 105–119 (2014)

Part IX
Cyber-Aware: Security and Computing

Chapter 26
Simulation-Based Optimization as a Service for Dynamic Data-Driven Applications Systems

Yi Li, Shashank Shekhar, Yevgeniy Vorobeychik, Xenofon Koutsoukos, and Aniruddha Gokhale

Abstract Dynamic data-driven systems must be adaptive in the face of highly fluctuating and uncertain environments. An important means to such adaptability is through the use of simulation models which can be leveraged in a dynamic decision support system. To provide high quality decision support, one can use simulations in an optimization loop to derive the best values of system parameters for a given system state particularly when the system has too many parameters and traditional means to optimize the outcomes are intractable. To that end, simulation-based optimization (SBO) methods have emerged to enable optimization in the context of complex, black-box simulations obviating the need for specific and accurate model information, such as gradient computation. An important challenge in using SBO is determining the decision parameters. However, to ensure scalability and real-time decision support, one must be able to rapidly deploy SBO in a way that makes the best use of available computing resources given the time and budget constraints. To address these needs, this chapter presents a cloud-based framework for simulation based optimization as a service (SBOaaS) to enable a flexible and highly parallelizable dynamic decision support for such environments. The chapter

Shashank Shekhar work performed while at Vanderbilt University.

Yevgeniy Vorobeychik work performed while at Vanderbilt University

Y. Li · X. Koutsoukos · A. Gokhale (✉)
Dept of Electrical Engineering and Computer Science, Vanderbilt University, Nashville, TN, USA
e-mail: yi.li@vanderbilt.edu; xenofon.koutsoukos@vanderbilt.edu; a.gokhale@vanderbilt.edu

S. Shekhar
Siemens Corporate Research, Princeton, NJ, USA
e-mail: shashankshekhar@siemens.com

Y. Vorobeychik
Washington University in St. Louis, Dept of Computer Science and Engineering, St. Louis, MO, USA
e-mail: yvorobeychik@wustl.edu

© The Author(s), under exclusive license to Springer Nature Switzerland AG 2022   603
E. P. Blasch et al. (eds.), *Handbook of Dynamic Data Driven Applications Systems*,
https://doi.org/10.1007/978-3-030-74568-4_26

illustrates the framework by using it to design a dynamic traffic light control system through simulation-based optimizations using the SUMO traffic simulation model.

Keywords Simulation-based optimizations · DDDAS · Optimal control · Cloud · Simulation of Urban Mobility (SUMO) traffic simulation · Container manager

26.1   Introduction

Critical cyber-physical infrastructure, such as the national power grid, transportation network [42] and smart cities [10], are large-scale and complex systems that illustrate highly dynamic and uncertain nature of the operations, as well as significant heterogeneity in the end systems, network protocols and technologies, and software systems that support the system operations. In such systems, human intervention becomes infeasible to handle problems stemming from cyber-physical events such as failures or deliberate attacks.

The *dynamic data driven applications systems* (DDDAS) [11] principles are a promising approach to address the need to manage and control the next generation of cyber-physical systems. DDDAS prescribes a data-driven model learning process of real-world systems and subsequently simulating these models within a decision support system to control the system behavior and maintaining its intended trajectory. The use of simulations in decision support is fundamental as a means to enable dynamic data-driven decision support in a wide array of systems. However, the success of any DDDAS approach depends on its ability to learn and simulate models of the target system. In turn, the quality of the learned models will determine how effectively the real-world system can be managed and controlled.

With the advent of data-acquisition technology in the past decade, using simulation-based optimizations provides a low cost alternative to emulation of physical phenomena including stochastic processes and solving optimal control problems in dynamic systems as has been demonstrated in many industrial applications [15, 17, 21, 32]. To provide high quality decision support, simulations in an optimization loop can derive good values of system parameters for a given system state, particularly when the system has too many parameters and traditional means to optimize the outcomes are either intractable or infeasible (for example, if gradient information is not available or is hard to compute). To that end, simulation-based optimization (SBO) methods have emerged to enable optimization in the context of complex, black-box simulations obviating the need for specific and accurate model information, such as gradient computation.

Despite this promise, the traditional simulation-based approaches without dynamic data driven capabilities are not able to synchronize with real-world conditions, which often results in inaccurate prediction and failure of the system control. To that end, DDDAS, as an innovative paradigm for real-time computer simulations, effectively overcomes setbacks in traditional simulation approaches. Two key challenges emerge in this context. First, although SBO has become an important subject in various areas, to solve large scale problems, simulations sometimes are extremely complex and require tremendous computing power. Second, even with DDDAS as an enabling paradigm, SBO methods are not intended for anytime use, and do not account for real-time constraints and associated trade-offs between solution quality and time to decision, which may be critical considerations for the systems that utilize these approaches for control.

To that end, Cloud computing provides an economical solution for individuals and organizations with limited resources to execute compute-intensive tasks, which has become a highly demanded utility due to the advantages of potentially unlimited computing power available on-demand, affordable cost of services without incurring any capital and operation expenditures, elasticity of resources, and its ability to autoscale on demand. Thus, cloud-based simulation services have opened up new avenues to address the challenges stemming from the simulation based optimizations noted above.

To address the known challenges with simulation-based optimizations while exploiting emerging computing paradigms, this chapter presents a cloud-based framework that provides a "simulation-based optimization as a service (SBOaaS)," in which real-time considerations are explicitly accounted for making optimal use of limited but parallel computational resources in order to obtain the best answer in the given time constraints. Specifically, this chapter presents a generic optimization process for deploying simulation-based optimization on a cloud architecture. The framework consists of (a) the implementation of SBOaaS, which describes for a given optimization problem, how to decompose the input problem into a group of parallel simulations and efficiently use the existing computing power; and (b) an anytime parallel simulation-based optimization approach, which admits significant flexibility in both time and computational resource constraints to obtain the best (but possibly suboptimal) solutions given the available resources and time constraints on decisions.

The SBOaaS framework supports solving an optimal control problem in decentralized feedback control, such as an urban traffic light scenario. To validate the ideas and provide a platform to realize SBOaaS, this chapter leverages the authors' prior work on simulation-as-a-service (SIMaaS) [39], which is a cloud-based simulation framework to manage multiple simulation instances on a distributed system. The traffic light simulations use the Simulation of Urban Mobility (SUMO) [3] simulator to implement the traffic light controller logic and evaluate the SBOaaS' optimization algorithm.

The rest of the chapter is organized as follows: Sect. 26.2 provides an overview of our simulation-based optimization as a service concept; Sect. 26.3 describes the algorithms behind realizing SBOaaS particularly in the context of Anytime computations; Sect. 26.4 describes the system architecture we have developed to deploy SBOaaS; Sect. 26.5 validates our claims; Sect. 26.6 compares our work to related efforts; and finally Sect. 26.7 describes concluding remarks alluding to future challenges.

26.2   Problem Statement and Overview of SBOaaS

In this section we use a motivational case study to develop the problem statement we have formulated and solved in this chapter. To that end we first present a traffic light control system as an example of a real-world system where high-quality configuration of the traffic light controller requires an iterative black-box optimization process based on data-driven model simulations. Owing to the high demand for resources and real time performance constraints, such a capability requires cloud computing resources. We designed and implemented SBOaaS, a framework for simulation-based optimization as a service. This section presents key features and a case study illustrating those challenges that SBOaaS should address.

26.2.1   Motivating Case Study: Dynamic Traffic Light Control System

To formulate the problem statement, we use a dynamic traffic light control scenario as our motivating example. In this scenario, each intersection traffic light controller switches its traffic light phases according to the observed vehicle flow. In general, a traffic light phase is related to a collection of lanes dominated by such a phase; if the number of waiting vehicles in the lanes related to the current phase is small and the number of waiting vehicles in the lanes related to the next phase is large, the controller will switch the traffic light phase. Figure 26.1 provides a visual demonstration of the controller logic.

Formally, a feedback controller has a predefined phase sequence $(p_0, ..., p_n)$. For each phase p_i, m_i is the minimum interval, M_i is the maximal interval, q_i is the average queue length of the lanes related to the ith phase, and θ_i is the threshold on the queue length of lanes blocked in the ith phase. If t is the current time point, the control logic is as depicted in Algorithm 1.

Algorithm 1 Feedback controller

1: Current Phase $P := p_0, t' := t, i := 0$.
2: **loop**
3:     $i_{next} := (i + 1) \mod n$
4:     **if** $t - t' > m_i$ **then**
5:         **if** Reach to the maximum interval, $t - t' = M_i$ **then**
6:             Switch phase, $P = p_{i_{next}}, i = i_{next}$
7:         **else if** Find the congestion, $q_i < \theta_i, q_{i_{next}} \geq \theta_{i_{next}}$ **then**
8:             Switch phase, $P = p_{i_{next}}, i = i_{next}$
9:         **end if**
10:    **end if**
11: **end loop**

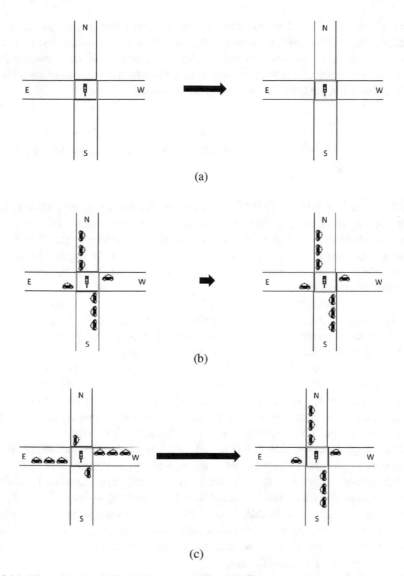

(a)

(b)

(c)

Fig. 26.1 The control logic for feedback controllers. (**a**) Non-feedback controllers have a fixed interval between two phases. (**b, c**) Feedback controllers dynamically change the interval according to the length of their vehicle queues

The controller must solve an optimization problem as follows: for a given vehicle flow of an area in a certain time period and a set of controlled intersections $I\{I_0, ..., I_m\}$, find the optimal thresholds $(\Theta_0, ..., \Theta_m)$, where $\Theta_i = (\theta_0, ...\theta_{n_i})$ are the thresholds of the ith intersection.

The scenario with a single intersection with similar control logic has been discussed in many prior research efforts, e.g., [24]. However, the situation becomes much more complicated when generalizing the controller model to cases with multiple intersections and correspondingly multiple traffic lights. Many factors, such as densities of vehicle flows and topological structures of road networks, may affect the outcomes of such road systems, which leads to the issue of defining the model describing the interactions among the intersections.

26.2.2 DDDAS-Specific Problem Statement and the SBOaaS Approach

Examples, such as the traffic light for multiple intersections, say, in a city downtown, pose significant challenges due to the compute-intensive nature of the solution approach. Moreover, the dynamic nature of traffic patterns (e.g., morning and evening rush hour versus afternoon and night hours) will require periodically recomputing the optimal parameters, which further complicates the problem and its demands on resources.

Two fundamental problems exist in this realm. First, it is likely that the DDDAS feedback loop may have access to only black box models of the dynamic systems, yet will require that the DDDAS infrastructure obtain optimal parameters to be used in the DDDAS feedback loop. Second, the significantly compute intensive nature of the solution approaches makes it infeasible to deploy such model simulations in-house. Rather, there is a need for elastic computing capabilities. Thus, the DDDAS problem we solve in this work can be posed as: (a) How to obtain the optimal parameters, and (b) How to elastically scale the compute resources as the computational needs of the solution approach dynamically changes?

This chapter solves this fundamental problem using the following duo of synergistic approaches: First, we use simulations in an optimization loop to derive the best values of system parameters for a given system state particularly when the system has too many parameters and traditional means to optimize the outcomes are intractable. The approach is called *simulation-based optimization*. To address the need for elastic resources, we exploit Cloud computing as the means to address these needs and provide a framework to realize what we call *Simulation-based Optimization-as-a-Service (SBOaaS)*.

Figure 26.2 visually represents how SBOaaS can be used to deploy the dynamic traffic light control system with online simulation-based optimization. The control system is a closed loop, periodically receiving the real time distribution of vehicle flows—which represents the dynamic and data-driven traits of DDDAS—running multiple simulations in parallel to find the optimal thresholds, and sending the feedback to the traffic light controllers—which represents the closing of the loop in DDDAS.

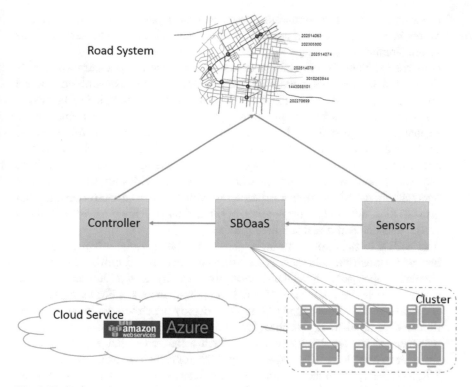

Fig. 26.2 SBOaaS for dynamic traffic light control system

26.2.3 Key Features of SBOaaS

The following represent the key features of SBOaaS.

- **A cloud based solution for parallel execution of multiple simulations.**
  Applying computationally expensive online simulation-based optimization is
  usually time consuming and often fails to address the real-time constraints
  of applications. Moreover, for stochastic simulation models, every simulation
  process can vary and yield different results. To analyze the temporal properties
  of a stochastic system, a large number of simulation tasks needs be executed
  to obtain the probability distribution of simulation results. Thus, the simulation
  service needs to have the ability to execute multiple simulations in parallel. In our
  solution, to overcome this problem, we present a cloud-based approach, which
  is an orchestration middleware helping people to deploy DDDAS applications
  to the platforms of various cloud service providers without considering platform differences. It integrates the simulation manager having the capability to
  spawn and execute simulations in parallel and the result aggregation component
  using several aggregation strategies to recycle the results from the terminated
  simulations. A web-based interface is also implemented, which allows a user

to customize both the simulation model and the input parameters, as well as to monitor the optimization process. Section 26.4 delves into the details of our system architecture.

- **Generic problem decomposition schemes for large scale discrete variable decision problems.** In simulation-based optimization, the results of simulations are often quite different depending on the input parameters supplied to the model. To find the optimal solution, the search space sometimes can be extremely large so that such large-scale problems are intractable to naïve brute force search. In this situation, even parallel computations do not help. In our framework, a collection of generic problem decomposition schemes based on coordinate descent methods is demonstrated, which not only provides an efficient way to parallelize the optimal decision problems with discrete variable domains, but also has the ability to execute anytime optimizations providing a flexible balance between fast response and solution quality.

- **The ability to decouple simulation based problem designs from the problem decomposition schemes.** For traditional model-based online learning and simulation approaches in DDDAS, developers usually need to face and maintain several parts of the system at different levels simultaneously. For example, there is domain-specific knowledge to setup and deploy the simulation environments, different parallelism approaches for various optimization tasks, and system management for regular maintenance. Such a method is not a good practice for a developer team that expects rapid deployment on available resources. SBOaaS leverages Linux container-based infrastructure which aims to create an abstraction layer that helps decouple simulation-based problem designs from the problem decomposition schemes. This approach allows domain experts to encapsulate the simulation environment in a container, while developers design the parallelism process according to the pre-defined interface and system administrators can simply combine both parts to run an optimization without knowing the implementation detail. Moreover, such an approach provides low runtime overhead, negligible setup and tear down costs when deploying the simulations on computing nodes, and fast data exchange among cluster hosts with incremental updates.

26.3   Anytime Optimization Using Parallel Greedy Algorithm

We now describe the approach. SBOaaS estimates the value of an objective, measured using simulation runs, for a given setting of input variables. In order to use this in optimization, one must run this process for many inputs, aiming to choose the best input vector in terms of the objective value. Since such optimization routines can be extremely time consuming in general, they may be of limited utility in dynamic control environments in which real-time decision constraints impose severe limits on the time alloted for simulation-based optimization.

We present several anytime simulation-based optimization algorithms used in our framework which ensure that the optimization process returns the best solution found thus far to the controller even if it is interrupted before it converges. The key feature of these algorithms is that they are directly parallelizable, thereby allowing us to implement them using a cloud-based platform we developed, described below.

Consider a single target optimization problem,

$$\min_{\vec{x}} f(\vec{x}),$$

where $\vec{x} = (x_1, x_2, ..., x_n)$ is a vector of decision variables. In our setting, $f(\vec{x})$ is not known directly, but can be evaluated by simulations for a given $\vec{x}$. If f is stochastic and we wish to minimize the expectation, we can estimate the expectation by running multiple simulations for a given $\vec{x}$ and taking the sample average. Since such a generalization is direct, we assume henceforth that simulations produce a deterministic evaluation of $f(\vec{x})$. We further assume that the domain of variables x_i is discrete. This too is a mild assumption since a continuous, bounded domain can be discretized arbitrarily finely. We developed a framework for anytime simulation-based optimization as a service by making use of a *coordinate greedy* algorithm.

26.3.1 Coordinate Greedy

Coordinate Greedy is a heuristic optimization method which minimizes the function value one variable at a time. The *Sequential coordinate greedy* framework is shown in Algorithm 2.

Algorithm 2 Sequential coordinate greedy($f, \vec{x}^{(0)}$)

1: **input** problem f, initial state $\vec{x}^{(0)} = (x_0^{(0)}, ..., x_n^{(0)}) \in \mathbb{R}^n$
2: **output** $\vec{x}^{(*)} = \arg\min_{\vec{x}} f(\vec{x})$
3: Set $p \leftarrow 0$
4: **repeat**
5:     **for** $i \leftarrow 1, ..., n$ **do**
6:         $x_i^{(p+1)} \leftarrow \arg\min_{x_i} f(x_1^{(p+1)}, ..., x_{i-1}^{(p+1)}, x_i, x_{i+1}^{(p)}, ..., x_n^{(p)})$
7:     **end for**
8: **until** termination test satisfied

In each iteration, it updates one input variable of f by solving the sub-problem:

$$f_i^{(p)} = \min_x f(x_1^{(p+1)}, ..., x_{i-1}^{(p+1)}, x, x_{i+1}^{(p)}, ..., x_n^{(p)})$$

For the discrete variable domain problem, it converges to the local optimum f^* when there is no further improvement found in one iteration ($\exists P \forall i, f^{(P)}(x_0) = f^{(P)}(x_i)$). Similarly, *stochastic coordinate greedy* selects one variable uniformly at random instead of following the vector order in each iteration. Shalev-Shwartz and Tewari [38] provide the best known convergence bounds for stochastic coordinate greedy.

To parallelize this method, in each step consisting of evaluation of a single component x_i, the framework tries to activate multiple simulations for all possible values in the variable domain. This process keeps running until it is suspended by users or reaches a local optimum, in either case returning the best solution found.

26.3.2 K-Coordinate Greedy

With increasing problem dimensionality even the fast coordinate greedy approach becomes expensive. However, limited by the degree of parallelism of basic coordinate greedy, for larger scale problems coordinate greedy does not fully use the provided computing power. K-**Coordinate Greedy** is an algorithm that adds another parallelization level to coordinate greedy to accelerate the rate of convergence of the optimization process, as described in Algorithm 3. It initially

---

Algorithm 3 K coordinate greedy ($f, \vec{x}^{(0)}, k$)

1: **input** problem f, initial state $\vec{x}^{(0)} = (x_0^{(0)}, ..., x_n^{(0)}) \in \mathbb{R}^n$, parallelism degree k
2: **output** $\vec{x}^{(*)} = \arg\min\limits_{\vec{x}} f(\vec{x})$
3: Set $p \leftarrow 0$
4: **repeat**
5:     Choose index set, $I^{(p)} = \{i_0^{(p)}, i_1^{(p)}, ..., i_k^{(p)}\}$
6:     **In parallel** on k
7:     $x_i^{(p+1)} \leftarrow \arg\min\limits_{x_i} f(x_1^{(p)}, ..., x_i, ..., x_n^{(p)}), i \in I^{(p)}$
8: **until** termination test satisfied

---

chooses K, the number of variables to update, according to the available computing resources. In each iteration, it chooses a subset of K variables and optimizes these in parallel using the same update as the coordinate greedy algorithm.

Different parallelism modes do affect the performance and behaviors of K-coordinate greedy. *Synchronous* K-coordinate greedy synchronizes frequently across all K partitions at certain points in time, which ensures that all updates are shared across all processors before further computation occurs, while *asynchronous* one assumes the variable vector x can be accessible to each processor, and available for reading and updating at anytime. Because of eliminating the requirement of consistent information across computing nodes, asynchronous algorithms are supposed to have better performance in practice, while the behaviors of synchronous algorithms are more predictable and easier to analyze. Both synchronous and asyncronous K-coordinate greedy are included and evaluated in our framework.

26.3.3   Adaptive K-Coordinate Greedy

Unlike coordinate greedy, K-coordinate greedy cannot guarantee convergence to the local optimum. The risk of divergence of the algorithm might be increased when there are too many correlated features in the variable vector, which also makes it difficult to define the termination test. In this section, we present adaptive K-coordinate greedy that tries to address these gaps.

Adaptive K-coordinate greedy is a hybrid approach of combining coordinate greedy and K-coordinate greedy, as illustrated by Algorithm 4, which is supposed to speed up the rate of convergence in early stages, and avoid the correlation problems when it gets close to the local optimum. We improve the greedy process by continuously reducing K as the time taken by the algorithm to find the next sub-optimal solution. With decreasing the value of K, the optimization process will be less likely to select correlated features and avoid divergence. When K equals one, the algorithm is exactly the stochastic coordinate greedy algorithm, which has a well-defined termination condition and convergence guarantees.

Algorithm 4 Adaptive K coordinate greedy($f, \vec{x}^{(0)}, k_0$)

1: **input** problem f, initial state $\vec{x}^{(0)} = (x_0^{(0)}, ..., x_n^{(0)}) \in \mathbb{R}^n$, initial parallelism degree k_0

2: **output** $\vec{x}^{(*)} = \arg\min_{\vec{x}} f(\vec{x})$

3: Set $p \leftarrow 0, \Delta t \leftarrow 0$

4: **repeat**

5:     $k \leftarrow k_0 * exp(-\Delta t / T)$

6:     Choose index set, $I^{(p)} = \{i_0^{(p)}, i_1^{(p)}, ..., i_k^{(p)}\}$

7:     **In parallel** on k processors

8:         $x_i^{(p+1)} \leftarrow \arg\min_{x_i} f(x_1^{(p)}, ..., x_i, ..., x_n^{(p)}), i \in I^{(p)}$

9:     **if** find a better solution **then**

10:         $\Delta t \leftarrow 0$

11:     **else**

12:         Increase Δt

13:     **end if**

14: **until** termination test satisfied

26.4   System Architecture

The cloud based SBOaaS architecture is based on our existing framework called SIMaaS (simulation-as-a-service) [39]. We enhanced the SIMaaS architecture to account for various modes that SBOaaS has to operate in. In addition, we added a new scheduling policy based on the SBOaaS requirements. The architecture is composed of both design time and runtime components that we describe in this section.

26.4.1   Runtime Architecture

Figure 26.3 illustrates the key components of SBOaaS. **SIMaaS Manager (SM)** is at the core of the framework and is responsible for coordinating other components, handling user requests and decision-making. SM's pluggable architecture allows it to switch between various virtualization technologies and scheduling policies. The earlier framework was composed of a deadline based scheduler where the number of simulation tasks to execute was a known a priori. However, in the current work, the simulation count is not known a priori and additional constraints were introduced for synchronous and asynchronous modes that required relaxation of system level deadline constraints in favor of resource optimization based on the intermediate results. Thus, we introduced a greedy scheduling policy that leverages the intermediate results to maximize performance of the optimization algorithm and saturates the resources to minimize under utilization.

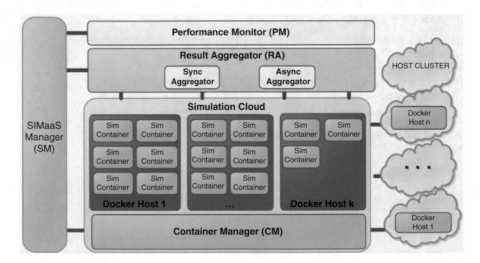

Fig. 26.3 System architecture

The simulation cloud deploys on a host cluster constructed by using the Docker [28] container virtualization technology. A Docker host can run multiple Docker containers, each representing a single computational node in the cloud system. Each simulation-based optimization task runs in a single container. The entire life cycle is managed by the **Container Manager (CM)** shown in Fig. 26.3. CM supports various virtualization technologies such as KVM, however, due to its low startup and tear-down duration, we opted for Docker containers. The role of the CM includes management of hosts, execution, tear-down and deployment of the containers. The CM also maintains a registry for Docker images submitted at design time (explained in Sect. 26.4.2).

Another key component of SBOaaS is the **Result Aggregator (RA)** which is responsible for the collection of results from the simulation containers after they finish their tasks. It also performs result aggregation and informs the SM. The aggregator applies a message queue such that it does not get overloaded with simultaneously finishing simulation tasks. Based on the different aggregation requirements for SBOaaS compared to SIMaaS, we developed sync and async modes for the RA.

- **ASync Aggregator**. The asynchronous aggregator informs the SM as soon as the client aggregator logic aggregates the intermediate results based on the finished simulation task. The SM in turn replaces the old simulation instance and hence keeps the allocated resources 100% utilized.
- **Sync Aggregator**. Sync aggregator waits for all the simulation tasks to finish from the current cycle and invokes the client aggregation logic to obtain the intermediate result such that the next set of tasks can be executed. This helps in initializing the next cycle with the best result. However, this also results in resource under-utilization.

The final piece in the runtime architecture is the **Performance Monitor (PM)** which works with the CM to collect performance metrics from the host cluster and periodically informs the SM for decision making.

26.4.2 Design Time Architecture

The application designer interacts with the SBOaaS interface at design time to provide the configuration, executables and aggregation logic. The designer enters a list of configuration properties using a template that includes the execution command for the simulation task, the expected runtime input parameters, and desired resources among others. The designer also provides the simulation executable in the form of a container image which is uploaded by the system to the image registry and later deployed on the hosts by the CM during runtime. Please note that the first iteration of the simulation tasks incurs an additional deployment cost due to the image download time. This can be avoided by scheduling the simulation jobs *a priori*.

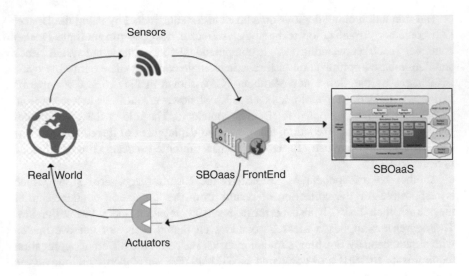

Fig. 26.4 System interaction

Another key role of the designer is to provide the aggregation logic using the SBOaaS aggregator template which is hooked to the Result Aggregator (RA). In this work, the aggregation logic is the optimization algorithm. However, this may vary from one use case to the other.

26.4.3   User Interaction Framework

The SBOaaS interface resides on a light-weight web framework to interact with the system designers, users or APIs and also to provide the result to the invoker. If the deadline is not immediate, a user can provide the runtime parameters using web forms and collect the result from the download link returned by the simulation manager (SM) from the web server.

In a typical system, the manual steps are eliminated with the use of APIs. Figure 26.4 depicts how the SBOaaS interacts with the real world and provides solutions to the optimization problems. Another server labeled as SBOaaS FrontEnd receives runtime parameters for the simulation based optimization in the form of aggregated sensor data. This FrontEnd invokes RESTful APIs from the SBOaaS interface to start a simulation job. Once the job is completed, the results are collected by the SBOaaS FrontEnd and actuation is performed based on the optimization results.

26.5 Evaluation

26.5.1 Online Simulation-Based Optimization for Dynamic Traffic Light Control System

26.5.1.1 Environment

The simulation environment is defined according to the dynamic traffic light control scenario described in Sect. 26.2. To simulate the controlled traffic flow, we employ a simulation suite called SUMO [3] (short for "Simulation of Urban MObility"). SUMO is an open source, highly portable, microscopic road traffic simulation package designed to handle large road networks. SUMO also provides a Traffic Control Interface (TraCI) to let external controllers control the traffic. In our work, we use a Python script to control the simulation through TraCI and implement our control algorithm. The experiment environment is encapsulated into a Docker image in order to be distributed among the computing nodes through SBOaaS.

Our framework was deployed on NSF Chameleon cloud services, which is a cloud platform funded by National Science Foundation (NSF), providing such a large-scale platform to the research community allowing them to explore transformative concepts in deeply programmable cloud services, design, and core technologies. In the experiments, we created a distribution system with 8 computing nodes and 384 cores.

The input data are the map of the Vanderbilt University campus including all exogenously specified parameters (phase sequences and min-max intervals) and the corresponding vehicle flows in a morning scenario based on observations of road sensors. 9 intersections were selected to deploy the feedback controllers. In addition, we only consider two phases for each intersection to have dynamic intervals, which means there are two thresholds for each intersection that need to be optimized. Thus, for 9 intersections, the optimization problem dimension is 18. We consider variable domain {1, ..., 20} and use the vehicle average speed to measure performance.

26.5.1.2 Experiment 1

We first evaluate the performance of anytime optimization methods used in SBOaaS. The experiments ran until either the local optimum is found or the deadline (7000 s) is reached (K-coordinate greedy does not check convergence because there is no well-defined termination test).

26.5.1.3 Results

The experiment results can be seen in Fig. 26.5, which shows simulation outcome (average vehicle speed) as a function of the running time of the optimization

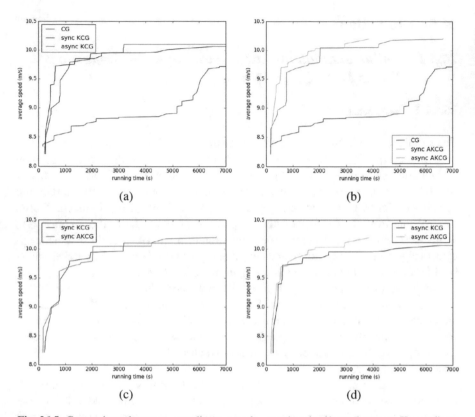

Fig. 26.5 Comparison between coordinate greedy, synchronized/asynchronous K-coordinate greedy, as well as synchronized/asynchronous adaptive K-coordinate greedy decentralized solutions

process. Figures 26.5a and b, respectively, compare the coordinate greedy algorithm (Algorithm 2) with both K-coordinate greedy algorithm and adaptive K-coordinate greedy algorithm (Algorithms 3 and 4). The optimization process is significantly accelerated by the variable-level parallelism. In general, both K-coordinate greedy and adaptive K-coordinate have the same rate of convergence. However, Figs. 26.5c and d indicate that K-coordinate greedy failed to converge within the deadline while adaptive K-coordinate greedy found the local optimum. The asynchronous algorithm has better performance, and a "smoother" curve than the synchronized one, which means better anytime response for returning sub-optimal solutions.

26.5.1.4   Experiment 2

Figure 26.6 illustrates the control processes of DDDAS with traditional simulation-based optimization and any simulation-based optimization. For the current observation, the former one gets and updates the optimum control parameters at the

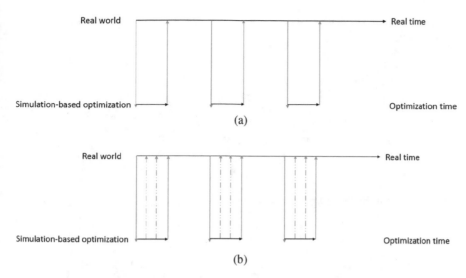

Fig. 26.6 (**a**) DDDAS with traditional simulation-based optimization (**b**) DDDAS with anytime simulation-based optimization

end of optimization process, while the latter one can continuously refresh the control parameters. We now compare both approaches. In this experiment, one simulation was run to simulate the morning scenario in real world. We also start the optimization service simultaneously with the initial road vehicle flow observation, and periodically updated the corresponding sub-optimal control parameters with real time line. We used asynchronous adaptive K-coordinate greedy algorithm and only consider the first optimization period, which is from 7:00 am to 7:30 am (asynchronous adaptive K-coordinate greedy converged within 30 min according to the last experiment). We considered several different periods for updating control parameters.

Period	Overall average speed (m/s)
Baseline	8.703
1 s	9.961
5 min	9.918
10 min	9.566

26.5.1.5   Results

The experiment results can be seen in Fig. 26.7, which shows the average instantaneous vehicle velocity in simulation area as a function of real time and the overall average speed is given by the table. The baseline is the situation that the "real

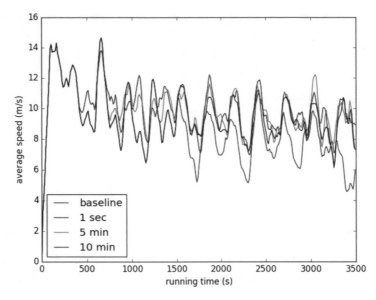

Fig. 26.7 Experiment 2

world" run without control parameters updating, which is the behavior of DDDAS with traditional simulation-based optimization. In Fig. 26.7, the instantaneous outcomes of the tested optimization methods do not show significant differences at the early stage. As the process of optimization gets better and better sub-optimal control parameters, the anytime optimization services gradually improve the outcomes. From the overall performance, the optimization processes with shorter updating intervals gained better outcomes, but got less improvements. Limited by technologies and costs, a real world DDDAS usually will need to choose a suitable updating frequency by considering its marginal benefit.

26.5.2 System Evaluation

We measured the system metrics to validate its robustness and evaluated the overhead. The test bed was setup in accordance with the architecture shown in Fig. 26.3. The SIMaaS Manager and the Result Aggregator were deployed on the same machine. Eight simulation hosts were added to the setup each having 48 cores. Two experiments were performed to assess the performance when the system is running in both synchronous and asynchronous modes. Each experiment was performed for 90 min duration.

26.5.2.1   Result

The results of the experiments are illustrated in Fig. 26.8. We observed that during the 90 min duration, 2520 simulations were performed in synchronous mode and 11,037 in asynchronous mode. The higher number of simulations for asynchronous mode is expected as the goal is to fully utilize the available servers. The figure also displays the utilization metrics of the management server. In both the modes, the CPU and network utilization is less than 1%. The memory utilization is around 3% for asynchronous mode and around 7% for synchronous mode. Even though we see an initial upward trend in memory utilization due to auditing of simulation tasks, it stabilizes towards the end of the experiment because of the cleanup operations running periodically to clear the old simulation containers. We also observe that the spikes in CPU and network usage is low when the simulation tasks are scheduled and when they finish. These results demonstrate that our architecture is robust with low overhead.

Figure 26.9 is the scatter plot for the simulation task execution times for both the modes. Figure 26.9 shows the periodicity in the number of simulation tasks completing in the two modes. There are stragglers in the system which have higher impact on the synchronous mode compared to asynchronous mode as all the tasks of the next cycle have to wait for few stragglers to perform execution. In future, straggler management policies will be implemented which will significantly benefit the synchronous mode.

26.6   Related Work

26.6.1   Coordinate Greedy Algorithm

Coordinate Greedy is one of the class of Coordinate Descent (CD) algorithms. Due to the simplicity of the CD approach and its acceptable performance in many situations, CD methods have a long history for solving various optimization problems. However, the apparent lack of sophistication made CD become an unpopular research field at the end of the last century [43]. Most of the works at that time focused on the convergence properties. Bertsekas and Tsitsiklis [4] first considered the convergence properties for parallel CD methods. Luo and Tseng [25, 26] proved that the convergence of CD methods for twice differentiable convex functions is at least linear.

Since different applications have yielded a wide array of optimization problems for which CD algorithms are competitive, the situation has changed in recent years. One important reason is the rise of machine learning. With increased interest in deploying large-scale machine learning enhanced applications, CD methods have been shown to be competitive to other optimization methods in many tasks, such as training linear support vector machines [18] and non-negative matrix

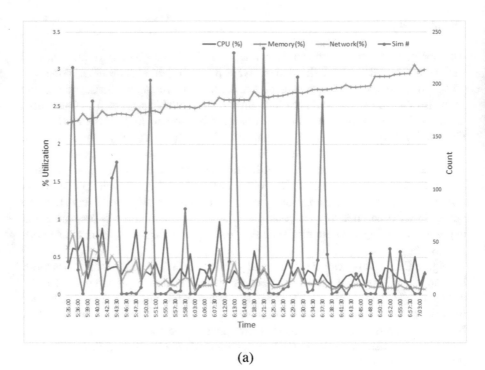

(a)

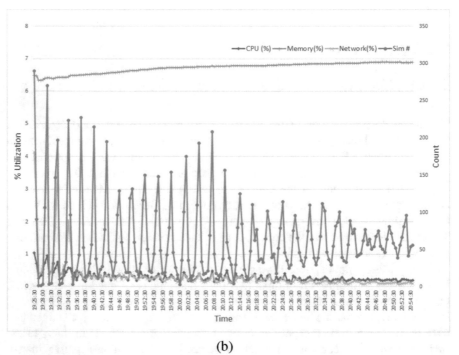

(b)

Fig. 26.8 Comparison of system utilization vs completed simulation count. (**a**) Sync mode. (**b**) Async mode

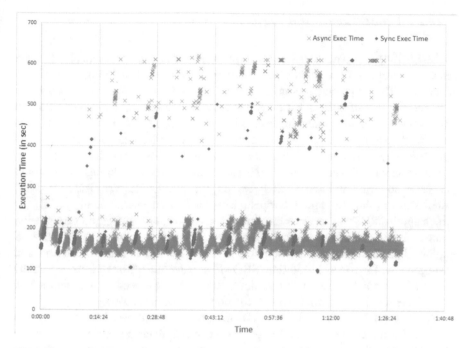

Fig. 26.9 Execution time

factorization [19]. Moreover, the efficiency of CD methods has been recently demonstrated in deep neural network (DNN) training including block coordinate descent (BCD) methods [7, 22, 46] and alternating direction method of multipliers (ADMM) [40, 47].

Compared to mainstream gradient-based approaches such as stochastic gradient descent (SGD) methods [37], the family of CD methods is a kind of gradient-free approaches that can effectively address the vanishing gradient issue [16] for training DNN and be easily implemented in a distributed and parallel architecture [5, 27]. On the other hand, CD algorithms can usually be modified and improved to fit all kinds of problem backgrounds, which can also be easily modified to adapt them well to modern computer architectures. Niu [30] presented a lock free parallel CD algorithm based on traditional stochastic gradient descent. Bradley [6] developed a parallel coordinate descent algorithm for minimizing L_1 regularized losses and proved its convergence bounds. Recently numerous efforts demonstrated that CD methods can be adapted to address problems within many fields, including statistics [14, 20] and many other applications [35, 36].

In distributed systems, parallel CD methods are often implemented using the concept of parameter servers which usually focus on machine learning and neural network [12, 23, 44]. Compared with previous works, SBOaaS combines asynchronous CD algorithms with a container-based simulation framework, which is specifically designed for simulation-based optimization problems.

26.6.2   Cloud-Based Simulation Service

mJADES [34] is a Java-based simulation engine that can automatically acquire resources from various cloud providers and perform simulations on virtual machines. This approach is similar to ours in spawning simulations, however, the objective is different and it does not provide aggregation based optimization logic. The distributed simulation execution (DEXSim) [8] is another simulation framework based on distributed systems principles that can provide two-level parallelism by accounting for CPU threads and availability of multiple systems. On the other hand, SBOaaS relies on the Linux kernel for scheduling of container processes to avail multiple CPU cores on the physical server. Another cloud middleware is the RESTful interoperability simulation environment (RISE) [1] which applies RESTful services for remote management of simulation server using Android-based hand-held devices. The user interaction framework of SBOaaS explained in Sect. 26.4.3 also applies RESTful APIs for user interaction and management of services. In addition, SBOaaS architecture utilizes Linux containers which allows quick startup and tear down alleviating the need to maintain a VM pool, thus providing performance benefits compared to these works.

Resilient DDDAS-As-A Service (rDaaS) [2] is a cloud-based trustworthy and resilient infrastructure for developing secure crisis management systems using DDDAS principles of instrumentation, continuous monitoring and adaptation. The rDaaS architecture's goal is to align the cloud technology required for providing crisis management system in accordance with DDDAS paradigm by combining the design and runtime stages. Similar to rDaaS, SBOaaS leverages the DDDAS paradigm to provide cloud services, however, the objective of SBOaaS is to solve optimization problems using cloud based simulations and the methodology requires managing cloud resources at scale as the number of application instances required by SBOaaS is much larger compared to rDaaS. Nguyen and Khan [29] describe a framework for supporting DDDAS applications in cloud that proactively performs resource optimization and allocates resources when the sampling rate of the DDDAS application changes. This work does not consider the virtualization layer present on the cloud servers and the effects of co-location of multiple different jobs, in contrast, SBOaaS considers the virtualizaton overhead imposed by Docker containers and optimizes the resources for all the scheduled jobs.

26.6.3   Traffic Light Optimal Control Problem

Fundamentally, traffic light control problem is a form of scheduling problems for switching control actions on stochastic hybrid systems. Various models have been well-studied in this area. A decision tree model with Rolling Horizon Dynamic Programming was presented by Porche [33]. The approach based on multi-objective Mixed Integer Linear Programming formulation was proposed by Dujardin [13].

A Markov Decision Process approach was proposed in Yu and Recker [45] and Reinforcement Learning was used in Thorpe [41]. Choi [9] implemented a first-order Sugeno fuzzy model and integrated it into a fuzzy logic controller, while an Infinitesimal Perturbation Analysis approach, using a Stochastic Flow Model to represent the queue content dynamic of road at an intersection was presented by Panayiotou [31].

However, to find the optimal control parameters for a traffic light system via close loop simulations is still a big challenge due to its high computational complexity and the requirement on real time reactions. In this chapter, we illustrate that SBOaaS is a suitable framework to address such issues.

26.7   Conclusions

This chapter presented anytime optimization approaches including several coordinate descent method algorithms for solving simulation-based optimization problems in parallel that is offered as a cloud-based Simulation-based Optimization as a Service (SBOaaS). The benefits of the SBOaaS were demonstrated for a dynamic traffic light control system as a case study. Evaluations of the SBOaaS show enhanced efficiency for anytime optimization algorithms and the online closed loop pattern.

Acknowledgments This work was supported in part by the AFOSR DDDAS program under grants #FA9550-13-1-0227 and #FA9550-18-1-0126 , the System Science of SecUrity and REsilience for Cyber-Physical Systems (SURE) project funded by AFRL contract #FA8750-14-2-0180, and the Office of Naval Research under contract #N00014-15-1-2621. Experimental results presented in this chapter were conducted on the National Science Foundation's Chameleon cloud computing testbed. Any opinions, findings, and conclusions or recommendations expressed in this material are those of the author(s) and do not necessarily reflect the views of AFOSR, AFRL and NSF.

References

1. K. Al-Zoubi and G. Wainer. Distributed Simulation using RESTful Interoperability Simulation Environment (RISE) Middleware. In *Intelligence-Based Systems Engineering*, pages 129–157. Springer, 2011.
2. Y. Badr, S. Hariri, A.-N. Youssif, and E. Blasch. Resilient and trustworthy dynamic data-driven application systems (dddas) services for crisis management environments. *Procedia Computer Science*, 51:2623–2637, 2015.
3. M. Behrisch, L. Bieker, J. Erdmann, and D. Krajzewicz. Sumo–simulation of urban mobility. In *The Third International Conference on Advances in System Simulation (SIMUL 2011)*, *Barcelona, Spain*, 2011.
4. D. P. Bertsekas and J. N. Tsitsiklis. *Parallel and distributed computation: numerical methods*, volume 23. Prentice hall Englewood Cliffs, NJ, 1989.

5. S. Boyd, N. Parikh, and E. Chu. *Distributed optimization and statistical learning via the alternating direction method of multipliers.* Now Publishers Inc, 2011.

6. J. K. Bradley, A. Kyrola, D. Bickson, and C. Guestrin. Parallel coordinate descent for l1-regularized loss minimization. *arXiv preprint arXiv:1105.5379*, 2011.

7. M. Carreira-Perpinan and W. Wang. Distributed optimization of deeply nested systems. In *Artificial Intelligence and Statistics*, pages 10–19. PMLR, 2014.

8. C. Choi, K.-M. Seo, and T. G. Kim. Dexsim: an experimental environment for distributed execution of replicated simulators using a concept of single-simulation multiple scenarios. *Simulation*, page 0037549713520251, 2014.

9. W. Choi, H. Yoon, K. Kim, I. Chung, and S. Lee. A traffic light controlling flc considering the traffic congestion. In *AFSS International Conference on Fuzzy Systems*, pages 69–75. Springer, 2002.

10. H. Chourabi, T. Nam, S. Walker, J. R. Gil-Garcia, S. Mellouli, K. Nahon, T. A. Pardo, and H. J. Scholl. Understanding smart cities: An integrative framework. In *System Science (HICSS), 2012 45th Hawaii International Conference on*, pages 2289–2297. IEEE, 2012.

11. F. Darema. Dynamic Data Driven Applications Systems: A New Paradigm for Application Simulations and Measurements. *Computational Science-ICCS 2004*, pages 662–669, 2004.

12. J. Dean, G. Corrado, R. Monga, K. Chen, M. Devin, M. Mao, A. Senior, P. Tucker, K. Yang, Q. V. Le, et al. Large scale distributed deep networks. In *Advances in neural information processing systems*, pages 1223–1231, 2012.

13. Y. Dujardin, F. Boillot, D. Vanderpooten, and P. Vinant. Multiobjective and multimodal adaptive traffic light control on single junctions. In *2011 14th International IEEE Conference on Intelligent Transportation Systems (ITSC)*, pages 1361–1368. IEEE, 2011.

14. J. Friedman, T. Hastie, H. Höfling, R. Tibshirani, et al. Pathwise coordinate optimization. *The Annals of Applied Statistics*, 1(2):302–332, 2007.

15. M. C. Fu and J.-Q. Hu. Sensitivity analysis for monte carlo simulation of option pricing. *Probability in the Engineering and Informational Sciences*, 9(03):417–446, 1995.

16. I. Goodfellow, Y. Bengio, A. Courville, and Y. Bengio. *Deep learning*, volume 1. MIT press Cambridge, 2016.

17. G. Gurkan, A. Y. Ozge, and T. Robinson. Sample-path optimization in simulation. In *Simulation Conference Proceedings, 1994. Winter*, pages 247–254. IEEE, 1994.

18. C.-J. Hsieh, K.-W. Chang, C.-J. Lin, S. S. Keerthi, and S. Sundararajan. A dual coordinate descent method for large-scale linear svm. In *Proceedings of the 25th international conference on Machine learning*, pages 408–415. ACM, 2008.

19. C.-J. Hsieh and I. S. Dhillon. Fast coordinate descent methods with variable selection for non-negative matrix factorization. In *Proceedings of the 17th ACM SIGKDD international conference on Knowledge discovery and data mining*, pages 1064–1072. ACM, 2011.

20. C.-J. Hsieh, I. S. Dhillon, P. K. Ravikumar, and M. A. Sustik. Sparse inverse covariance matrix estimation using quadratic approximation. In *Advances in Neural Information Processing Systems*, pages 2330–2338, 2011.

21. P. Kim and Y. Ding. Optimal engineering system design guided by data-mining methods. *Technometrics*, 47(3):336–348, 2005.

22. T. T.-K. Lau, J. Zeng, B. Wu, and Y. Yao. A proximal block coordinate descent algorithm for deep neural network training. *arXiv preprint arXiv:1803.09082*, 2018.

23. M. Li, D. G. Andersen, J. W. Park, A. J. Smola, A. Ahmed, V. Josifovski, J. Long, E. J. Shekita, and B.-Y. Su. Scaling distributed machine learning with the parameter server. In *OSDI*, volume 14, pages 583–598, 2014.

24. J. Lima Fleck and C. G. Cassandras. Infinitesimal perturbation analysis for quasi-dynamic traffic light controllers. In *Discrete Event Systems*, volume 12, pages 235–240, 2014.

25. Z.-Q. Luo and P. Tseng. On the convergence of the coordinate descent method for convex differentiable minimization. *Journal of Optimization Theory and Applications*, 72(1):7–35, 1992.

26. Z.-Q. Luo and P. Tseng. Error bounds and convergence analysis of feasible descent methods: a general approach. *Annals of Operations Research*, 46(1):157–178, 1993.

27. D. Mahajan, S. S. Keerthi, and S. Sundararajan. A distributed block coordinate descent method for training l1 regularized linear classifiers. *The Journal of Machine Learning Research*, 18(1):3167–3201, 2017.

28. D. Merkel. Docker: Lightweight Linux Containers for Consistent Development and Deployment. *Linux J.*, 2014(239), Mar. 2014.

29. N. Nguyen and M. M. H. Khan. A closed-loop context aware data acquisition and resource allocation framework for dynamic data driven applications systems (dddas) on the cloud. *Journal of Systems and Software*, 109:88–105, 2015.

30. F. Niu, B. Recht, C. Ré, and S. J. H. Wright. A lock-free approach to parallelizing stochastic gradient descent. arxiv preprint. *arXiv*, 1106, 2011.

31. C. G. Panayiotou, W. C. Howell, and M. Fu. Online traffic light control through gradient estimation using stochastic fluid models. *IFAC Proceedings Volumes*, 38(1):90–95, 2005.

32. E. L. Plambeck, B.-R. Fu, S. M. Robinson, and R. Suri. Throughput optimization in tandem production lines via nonsmooth programming. In *Proceedings of the 1993 Summer Computer Simulation Conference*, pages 70–75, 1993.

33. I. Porche, M. Sampath, R. Sengupta, Y.-L. Chen, and S. Lafortune. A decentralized scheme for real-time optimization of traffic signals. In *Control Applications, 1996., Proceedings of the 1996 IEEE International Conference on*, pages 582–589. IEEE, 1996.

34. M. Rak, A. Cuomo, and U. Villano. Mjades: Concurrent simulation in the cloud. In *Complex, Intelligent and Software Intensive Systems (CISIS), 2012 Sixth International Conference on*, pages 853–860. IEEE, 2012.

35. P. Richtárik and M. Takáč. Distributed coordinate descent method for learning with big data. 2013.

36. P. Richtárik and M. Takáč. Iteration complexity of randomized block-coordinate descent methods for minimizing a composite function. *Mathematical Programming*, 144(1-2):1–38, 2014.

37. H. Robbins and S. Monro. A stochastic approximation method. *The annals of mathematical statistics*, pages 400–407, 1951.

38. S. Shalev-Shwartz and A. Tewari. Stochastic methods for l 1-regularized loss minimization. *The Journal of Machine Learning Research*, 12:1865–1892, 2011.

39. S. Shekhar, H. Abdel-Aziz, M. Walker, F. Caglar, A. Gokhale, and X. Koutsoukos. A simulation as a service cloud middleware. *Annals of Telecommunications*, 71(3):93–108, 2016.

40. G. Taylor, R. Burmeister, Z. Xu, B. Singh, A. Patel, and T. Goldstein. Training neural networks without gradients: A scalable admm approach. In *International conference on machine learning*, pages 2722–2731. PMLR, 2016.

41. T. L. Thorpe. Vehicle traffic light control using sarsa. In *Online]. Available: citeseer. ist. psu. edu/thorpe97vehicle. html*. Citeseer, 1997.

42. N. Tomizawa. On some techniques useful for solution of transportation network problems. *Networks*, 1(2):173–194, 1971.

43. S. J. Wright. Coordinate descent algorithms. *Mathematical Programming*, 151(1):3–34, 2015.

44. E. P. Xing, Q. Ho, W. Dai, J. K. Kim, J. Wei, S. Lee, X. Zheng, P. Xie, A. Kumar, and Y. Yu. Petuum: A new platform for distributed machine learning on big data. *IEEE Transactions on Big Data*, 1(2):49–67, 2015.

45. X.-H. Yu and W. W. Recker. Stochastic adaptive control model for traffic signal systems. *Transportation Research Part C: Emerging Technologies*, 14(4):263–282, 2006.

46. Z. Zhang and M. Brand. Convergent block coordinate descent for training tikhonov regularized deep neural networks. *arXiv preprint arXiv:1711.07354*, 2017.

47. Z. Zhang, Y. Chen, and V. Saligrama. Efficient training of very deep neural networks for supervised hashing. In *Proceedings of the IEEE conference on computer vision and pattern recognition*, pages 1487–1495, 2016.

Chapter 27
Privacy and Security Issues in DDDAS Systems

Li Xiong, Vaidy Sunderam, Liyue Fan, Slawomir Goryczka, and Layla Pournajaf

Abstract With the rapidly increasing prevalence of the DDDAS paradigm, privacy and security issues have come to the forefront. In the measurement, feedback, and control phases of dynamic data driven adaptive systems, protecting data integrity (security) and inferred sensitive information (privacy) from inadvertent release or malicious attack is crucial. The PREDICT (Privacy and secuRity Enhancing Dynamic Information Collection and moniToring) project investigates secure dynamic and adaptive techniques for distributed data collection and fusion, sampling and monitoring, and data modeling that preserve privacy and integrity. These approaches deliver provable guarantees of privacy and security while ensuring high fidelity, and complement encryption-based techniques. Application scenarios include health surveillance data release, traffic analysis, situation awareness and monitoring, and fleet tracking.

Keywords PREDICT (Privacy and secuRity Enhancing Dynamic Information Collection and moniToring) · Encryption · Security · Privacy preserving · Trusted aggregator · Differential privacy · Uncertainty quantification

27.1 Introduction

New technological tools are being developed that facilitate the continuous collection and analysis of information in novel and sophisticated ways. Applications based on participatory sensing [5, 26] are becoming ubiquitous and utilize data in important and valuable ways. At the same time, the Dynamic Data Driven Applications Systems (DDDAS) paradigm [3, 8, 9] established in the last decade offers the promise of augmenting the effectiveness of such data collection and analysis. DDDAS entails a synergistic feedback loop between application simulations and

L. Xiong (✉) · V. Sunderam · L. Fan · S. Goryczka · L. Pournajaf
Emory University, Atlanta, GA, USA
e-mail: lxiong@emory.edu

© The Author(s), under exclusive license to Springer Nature Switzerland AG 2022
E. P. Blasch et al. (eds.), *Handbook of Dynamic Data Driven Applications Systems*,
https://doi.org/10.1007/978-3-030-74568-4_27

629

data collection, in which data are dynamically integrated into an executing simulation to augment or complement the application model, and, conversely the executing simulation steers the data collection processes of the application system. However, in DDDAS systems, the dimensions of privacy and security to protect sensitive data are assuming tremendous importance. Incorporating such attributes into DDDAS platforms will significantly enhance their value and usefulness for transformative applications in a variety of domains.

In distributed data systems, encryption is commonly used to secure data, but it is both restrictive and incomplete. Encryption does not allow constructive data use without divulging content, and does not explicitly protect against disclosure of location or identity of data sources or data subjects. Privacy techniques provide a viable solution: privacy-preserving methods modify data in such a manner that critical attributes are obscured, while presenting meaningful data with a high level of utility to applications. The overall objective of the PREDICT project is to build a holistic framework that applies DDDAS concepts for feedback-driven dynamic information collection/monitoring with provable data privacy and data integrity guarantees. Our approach uses a combination of perturbation, aggregation, and cloaking to enable controlled information gathering and dissemination while preserving data integrity and privacy. As a result, confidentiality is preserved, while simultaneously making available valid high fidelity data to enable use by applications [3, 32, 37, 40].

- *Challenges and Potential Advances.* Data perturbation and aggregation are two main techniques used for privacy-preserving data release, but they introduce error. Therefore one of the main research challenges is to accomplish these transformations with very high fidelity and low error, such that the released data is still highly useful. Moreover, it is necessary to guarantee that released or disseminated data is indeed secure and private, necessitating strong provable mechanisms. Another challenge concerns second order issues; inferred information may be used by adversaries to compromise security and privacy, therefore robust techniques that protect against indirect analysis must be developed. Last but not least, some scenarios including battlefields or hostile environments may be untrustworthy, necessitating communication protocols and aggregation/fusion [24, 25] that are safe in untrusted settings.
- *DDDAS Motivated Solutions.* The PREDICT project extends the base DDDAS mechanism to use feedback loops from both estimates and previous observations to dynamically control the collection, aggregation and perturbation of data (in terms of frequency and values) in real-time to optimally balance error and privacy (control). In addition, it incorporates dynamic data modeling with uncertainty quantification for both single- and multidimensional data. In mobile participatory sensing settings, our work develops cloaking mechanisms with feedback loops and 2-phase task assignment to optimize target coverage while ensuring location privacy of data contributors (task management). In addition, techniques are included to protect against inferred information by adversaries who have access to external or sequence data by using adaptive feedback.

The PREDICT model is a generalized concept that uses DDDAS principles to guarantee privacy and security of both data and data providers. The PREDICT approach allows valuable (processed) data to be made available to authorized entities, without divulging data components, individual values, or provider information. Many applications in health surveillance, traffic analysis, situation awareness and monitoring, flash crowd control and fleet tracking benefit from these methods.

27.2 Background

The DDDAS paradigm is useful in numerous settings; our focus is on scenarios in which data is collected across many distributed, typically autonomous entities, but must be fused and analyzed by users or applications, with either explicit or implicit feedback driving subsequent collection and integration processes. Below we provide several examples:

- *Syndromic Surveillance*. The terrorist attacks in 2001, various disease outbreaks such as the 2009 outbreak of H1N1 Flu [1] and the recent outbreak in Germany of E.coli [2] have prompted much attention in syndromic surveillance systems [6, 41, 43]. Such systems seek to use health data in real time for early detection of large-scale disease outbreaks and bioterrorism attacks. Different statistical algorithms can be applied for detecting outbreaks, once a threshold number of early symptomatic cases or suspicious pattern is identified. Traditional syndromic surveillance systems mainly rely on health data from clinical and emergency room encounters. The recent proliferation of wireless and mobile technologies provides the opportunity for individuals to produce continuous streams of data about themselves (*self surveillance* [32]). A vast amount of data can be captured, such as detailed information about individuals' physical activities, locations (e.g., through text messages), and physiological responses (e.g., through small sensors).

    In the existing syndromic surveillance systems and research conducted to date, issues of privacy and confidentiality of the individuals (*data subjects*) as well as the sheer volume of the data have been known to hamper researchers' efforts. With dynamic feedback loops coupled with privacy protection, data can be anonymized to preserve individual privacy and then injected to real time simulations using diffusion models to simulate and predict the outbreak patterns. The predicted patterns in turn can be used to steer further data collection (e.g., from regions with increased risks) as well as for prevention and intervention purposes.
- *Intelligence Data Collection*. As recent events demonstrate, numerous situations exist where intelligence gathering is performed in crowd settings both non-deliberately by the general public and by principals who are anonymously embedded in the crowds. A canonical example is an uprising in a major city under hostile governmental control – the general public uses smart devices to report on

various field data (*third party surveillance* [32]), but there may also be agents among the crowd, reporting similar data using similar media (e.g., Twitter) to avoid identification. In such situations, central agencies (or the distributed agent network) desire to dynamically steer the data collection through feedback loops (e.g., directing agents to specific data collection locations or requesting finer-grained data). A feedback loop may also take place on open media and it is important to protect the identity and location of the agents (*data contributors*).

27.3   Overview and Goals

Most existing surveillance systems have focused on analytical and modeling methods, with little attention to dynamic feedback loops and privacy requirements. In parallel, typical privacy protection techniques today [12, 13, 20] deal with static and persistent data or the video content [23] but are not sufficient in the surveillance systems where high-volume, complex data are acquired dynamically. New mechanisms are needed urgently to support privacy enhancing dynamic data monitoring with feedback loops while maintaining provable and quantifiable *privacy* guarantees and *data integrity* guarantees.

In this chapter, we present an overview of our ongoing project PREDICT (Privacy and secuRity Enhancing Dynamic Information Collection and moniToring). The overall aim of the project is to develop a framework with algorithms and mechanisms for privacy and security enhanced dynamic data collection, aggregation, and analysis with feedback loops, which will be valuable in situations such as the ones outlined above. We discuss each of our research thrusts with research challenges and potential solutions, and report some preliminary results.

Figure 27.1 depicts an architectural overview of PREDICT. The key innovation of PREDICT is the privacy enhanced feedback loops between data collection, data aggregation, and data modeling. The dynamic approach that leverages real time pre-

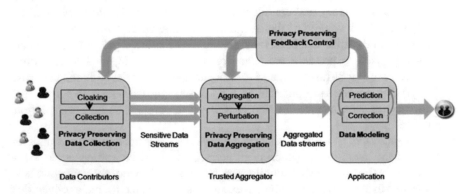

Fig. 27.1 PREDICT overview

dictive data models and feedback loops to steer further data collection and privacy mechanisms is crucial to both enhance privacy and address the big data problem in real time surveillance systems. Implementing these feedback loops presents several unique challenges: (1) how to design the feedback control mechanisms for the privacy preserving data collection and aggregation while minimizing the privacy risk of data subjects and maximizing data integrity; (2) how to model and guarantee data integrity in the presence of perturbations introduced by the privacy mechanisms in addition to measurement uncertainty; and (3) how to guarantee the privacy of data contributors in the feedback loops when there is no trusted aggregator as the data contributors are mutually untrusted. Our project consists of the following major focus areas:

- *Privacy Preserving Data Collection and Aggregation with Feedback Control.* Sensitive data streams are collected, aggregated, and perturbed at selected time points to formally guarantee state-of-the-art differential privacy for data subjects. We are designing a number of feedback loops to control the collection, aggregation, and perturbation process, including collection assignment (*how* to collect), sampling (*when* to aggregate), grouping (*how* to aggregate), and perturbation (*how* to perturb), based on feedback from previously observed aggregates and predictions as well as the privacy and integrity requirements from executing applications.
- *Dynamic Data Modeling and Uncertainty Quantification.* Aggregated and perturbed data streams are injected into predictive data models, which in turn correct the predictive data model. Data integrity is investigated in the presence of data perturbation introduced by the privacy protection mechanisms.
- *Secure Data Aggregation and Feedback Control without Trusted Aggregator.* While the privacy preserving data collection and aggregation can be implemented either by a centralized trusted aggregator or a decentralized group of data contributors, the decentralized case introduces additional privacy concerns of the data contributors (in addition to the data subjects). Decentralized mechanisms are developed to allow data contributors to securely aggregate their data with perturbations and receive feedback from applications without disclosing additional information to other data contributors.

By proactively building privacy into the design of a DDDAS, privacy protections are integrated directly into the DDDAS loop. The effect is to minimize the unnecessary collection and uses of personal data by the system and guarantee the anonymized participation of individuals in the system. The PREDICT project will produce a suite of algorithms and mechanisms that enhance privacy for DDDAS, and have significant impact in enabling and promoting confidence and trust in surveillance systems for critical applications in a variety of application domains.

27.4   Conceptual PREDICT Model

27.4.1   System Model

We consider a dynamic set of *data contributors* who are participating and contributing their own data (self surveillance) or other data (third party surveillance) in a surveillance system. We use *data subjects* to refer to the individuals represented in the collected data, which are the same as data contributors in the self surveillance case. We consider two system models: centralized model and decentralized model, depending on whether or not there is a trusted aggregator. In both models, there is an untrusted application or application run by an untrusted party for analysis and modeling (e.g., disease outbreak detection or intelligence analysis). Privacy preserving data collection and aggregation with feedback control, and dynamic data modeling and uncertainty quantification are applicable to both the centralized and decentralized models, while secure data aggregation and feedback control in the absence of a trusted aggregator is only applicable to the decentralized model.

- *Centralized model with a trusted aggregator.* In the centralized model, the trusted aggregator (e.g., Centers for Disease Control and Prevention (CDC) offices in the syndromic surveillance scenario) collects the data, aggregates them, performs appropriate data perturbation, and outputs perturbed aggregates with privacy guarantee, which can be in turn used for modeling and predictive studies. In the feedback loops, the trusted aggregator receives the control from the running application for further data collection, aggregation, and perturbation.
- *Decentralized model without a trusted aggregator.* In some scenarios, a trusted aggregator is not available. The data contributors need to perform aggregations and perturbations among themselves if needed and submit the aggregated result to the untrusted aggregator or the application directly. In the feedback loops, control is sent to individual contributors as well.

27.4.2   Privacy Model

Privacy of Data Subjects In both centralized and decentralized models, we need to protect the privacy of data subjects represented in the collected data. We assume the end application and end users are untrusted – they may passively observe information to infer sensitive values of the data subjects. Further the analysis results may be shared with other untrusted parties. So our goal is to provide a provable privacy guarantee such that the end application will not learn anything about participating users in the system and whether they participated in the data collection.

Traditional approaches such as removing identifying attributes, generalizing or perturbing individual attribute values, have been shown to be susceptible to various attacks [20]. We use the state-of-the-art *differential privacy* [12, 13, 33] as our privacy model, which gives a strong and provable privacy guarantee. Differential privacy requires that the output of an aggregation or computation should not change significantly even if a single data subject had opted out of the data collection. Therefore, this assures an individual that any privacy breach will not be a result of presence of her record in the collected data. Formally, differential privacy is defined as follows.

Definition 1 (α-Differential privacy [11, 33]) A randomized mechanism $\mathscr{A}$ satisfies unbounded α-differential privacy if for any neighboring databases D_1 and D_2 where D_1 can be obtained from D_2 by either adding or removing one tuple, and any possible output set S, $Pr[\mathscr{A}(D_1) \in S] \leq e^{\alpha} Pr[\mathscr{A}(D_2) \in S]$.

A common mechanism to achieve differential privacy for a single aggregated value is Laplace perturbation (LPA) [12], which adds systematically calibrated Laplace noise to the aggregates. Given an aggregate query Q, the global sensitivity [14] of Q, denoted by Δ_Q, measures the sensitivity of the query result $Q(D)$ if a data subject had opted out. In order to achieve α-differential privacy, the LPA mechanism returns $Q(D) + N$ in place of the original result $Q(D)$, where N is a random noise of Laplace distribution $Lap(\Delta_Q/\alpha)$ with a probability density function $Pr(x) = \frac{\alpha}{2\Delta_Q} e^{-|x|\alpha/\Delta_Q}$ [14].

Any sequence of aggregations from the same set of data subjects that each provides differential privacy in isolation also provides differential privacy in sequence (with accumulated privacy cost), known as *sequential composition* [36]. If a sequence of aggregations is conducted on *disjoint* data subjects, the privacy cost does not accumulate, but depends only on the worst guarantee of all aggregations, known as *parallel composition*.

Privacy of Data Contributors in Decentralized Model In our decentralized system model with no trusted aggregator, the privacy of the data contributors need to be protected from the aggregator and other data contributors. We assume data contributors are either semi-honest – follows the protocol correctly but may passively observe information to infer sensitive information of other data contributors or data subjects, or malicious – can lie about the values being reported, but otherwise follows the protocol correctly. As in general cryptographic solutions, we make an assumption that at least a fraction of data contributors (e.g., a majority) are semi-honest. The remaining data contributors and the aggregator can be arbitrarily malicious.

In the feedback phase, our goal is to ensure that each contributor learns only whether and what data is being requested or collected from her and no additional information about whether and what data is collected from other contributors. In the data aggregation phase, our goal is to ensure the data aggregator or participating data contributors can only learn the aggregates and no additional information about the private data contributed by other data contributors, in addition to ensuring differential privacy of the aggregates for the data subjects. We use the notion of secure multi-party computation (SMC) for this purpose [10, 27, 34]. In a multi-party computation protocol, a set of parties wish to jointly compute a function of their private data inputs. The protocol is *secure* if the parties learn only the result of the function but nothing else.

27.5 PREDICT Framework: Technical Approaches and Results

27.5.1 *Privacy Preserving Data Collection and Data Aggregation with Feedback Control*

The key idea in PREDICT is to use feedback loops from estimates and predictions based on previously observed aggregates and predictive models to dynamically control the collection, aggregation, and perturbation process. We briefly describe feedback control, including data collection (how to collect), the sampling rate (when to aggregate), aggregation grouping (how to aggregate), perturbation level (how much to perturb).

Dynamic data collection assignment The first feedback loop is to control how to collect data. When multiple individual data contributors are available for collecting data (third party surveillance), the aggregator can coordinate the data collection process such that data collection coverage is maximized and data collection cost is minimized. Since we need to protect the identity as well as location privacy for individual data contributors, they can query the central aggregator for data collection tasks anonymously using cloaked locations.

We have designed stochastic optimization algorithms for coordinated data collection assignment [21]. The goal is to optimally assign individual data contributors for data collection tasks (i.e., points of interest) based on feedback and data integrity requirements from applications as well as the cloaked (uncertain) locations of individual data contributors. The optimization goals may include maximizing data collection coverage, maximizing data integrity guarantee, and minimizing data collection cost (e.g., distance traveled by individual data contributors).

We have developed a technique based on cloaked locations to perform task assignment in an efficient manner, while protecting the privacy of participant locations [22]. In our scheme, a tasking server performs a first-approximation task assignment based on cloaked (uncertain) participant locations. This yields the feedback to participants who then perform local refinement, based on the true knowledge of their current locations and feedback data on the server's estimation of target subsets assigned to them. Our preliminary experiments show that this scheme achieves cost-coverage levels that are comparable to the baseline, while ensuring location privacy of participants. We are currently extending our work to situations with dynamic targets.

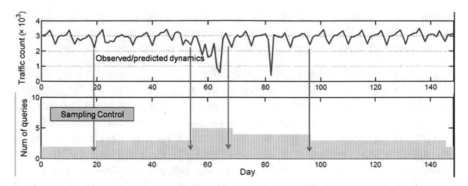

Fig. 27.2 Sampling control using feedback

Once the data are collected via the above mechanism (which protects locations of data contributors), the next central challenge of applying differential privacy for continuous data monitoring is how to minimize privacy cost by avoiding unnecessary aggregations and perturbations. Ideally, we should only compute the aggregates for desired regions at desired time points to preserve privacy cost, and hence preserve data integrity.

Sampling Control using Error Feedback We first study how to dynamically monitor a pre-defined aggregate with sampling control. The key question is when to compute the aggregate (when to sample) such that the data dynamics can be accurately captured while maintaining the accumulated privacy cost below a given privacy bound α. Figure 27.2 illustrates the idea of sampling control using feedback. It shows an original aggregate data stream, *traffic count*, with different dynamics at different time periods. It also shows a desired aggregation strategy with different query rate or sampling rate at different time periods. We observe that the number of queries per time unit (sampling rate) increases at day 55, adapting to the significant fluctuations exhibited by the traffic count, and it drops beyond day 100, when there is little variation among the aggregated values. Ideally, the sampling control mechanism will achieve such dynamic and adaptive behavior. While this is intuitive, it is not a trivial task due to the inherent uncertainty of input data streams. The underlying dynamics of the aggregated data can not be observed directly and need to be carefully modeled. In addition, the raw aggregated data is not accessible to the application or feedback control mechanism due to privacy protections.

PREDICT uses an adaptive sampling controller that adjusts the sampling rate based on the feedback. The feedback is defined as the relative error between the a posteriori estimate and the a priori estimate at a particular time step. Note that the posterior estimate is only available when a noisy observation is sampled from the input stream at time step k_n. Thus no error is defined at non-sampling points. The model error measures how well the internal predictive model describes current data dynamics, supposing the a posteriori estimate $\hat{x}_{k_n}$ is close to the true value. We may infer that data is going through rapid changes if the error E_{k_n} increases with time. In response, the controller in our system will detect the errors and adjust the sampling rate accordingly. Given the model error as feedback, we adopt a PID (Proportional-Integral-Derivative) controller for the sampling control [15, 18].

Aggregation Control using Prediction Feedback The LPA based privacy mechanism is sensitive to the density of the data, e.g. an aggregated statistic from a sparse region will incur a higher relative error compared with a dense region with the same amount of perturbation. On the other hand, if we group multiple cells and compute the aggregate for a partition, the count for each cell has to be estimated assuming certain distribution of the data points in the partition. The dominant approach in histogram literature is making the *uniform distribution assumption*, where the frequencies of records in the bucket are assumed to be the same and equal to the average of the actual frequencies [30]. The uniform distrbution introduces an *approximation error*. Ideally, when the density reaches a certain level, we may wish to have a finer grained statistic for the sub-regions. In other scenarios, we may wish to have a finer grained statistic when there are variances or uneven distributions in the region. In our information collection scenario, once the crowd center is identified for an uprising, it may be desired to collect more fine-grained data around the borders of the crowd to monitor how the crowd moves. Therefore PREDICT uses aggregation control in the multidimensional data space based on predicted data values to jointly minimize privacy cost and the noise introduced by the perturbation and the approximation. Building on our prior work [42], PREDICT uses predictions or estimates from applications and applies partitioning strategies based on k-d trees, binary space partitioning (BSP) and quad-trees to dynamically partition the multidimensional data space based on the predicted state such that data will be aggregated from similar sub-cubes.

Perturbation Control using Error Feedback We also attempt to dynamically determine the level of perturbation for each partition using the feedback of the model error and the uncertainty requirement of the application. If the model error is high, which suggests significant data dynamics, the perturbation control mechanism can adjust the perturbation level so that a more precise aggregate with less noise can be obtained at the next sampling point.

In addition, applications may impose an uncertainty bound or requirement for a perturbed aggregate. In such cases, a perturbation with minimum privacy budget required is invoked in order to satisfy the uncertainty requirement while minimizing the overall privacy cost. In general, when there is no specified integrity requirement, we can consider the overall privacy bound as a resource or budget, and model the perturbation control problem as an online resource allocation problem, which we plan to explore in the future.

27.5.2   Dynamic Data Modeling with Uncertainty Quantification

An essential component that enables the feedback loop is the data modeling that provides real-time model-based prediction and correction based on the sampled or observed aggregates. The key challenge is how to model the data in the presence of perturbation error injected by the LPA privacy mechanism. Thus, the PREDICT project explores robust data assimilation and spatial interpolation techniques for estimating the current state of the system using sampled aggregates with uncertainty quantification in real time.

Data Modeling in Time Domain   In order to model perturbed aggregates in the time domain, we have applied several filtering (or data assimilation) techniques. Data assimilation [4, 31] is a general approach in which observations (or perturbations in our context) of the current (and possibly, past) state of a system are combined with the results from a prediction model (the forecast) to produce an analysis, which is considered 'the best' estimate of the current state of the system. The model is then advanced in time and its result becomes the forecast in the next analysis cycle.

In our design, the prediction, is released at a non-sampling point, while the correction, i.e. posterior estimate based on the noisy observation and prediction, is released at a sampling point. We adopt a constant process model for a single pre-defined aggregate which is given by $x_{k+1} = x_k + \omega$ where k is the discrete time index and ω is a white Gaussian noise $p(\omega) \sim N(0, Q)$ with variance Q. The observed aggregate is perturbed by the Laplace mechanism and can be modeled by $z_k = x_k + \nu$ where ν is a Laplacian noise which follows $p(\nu) \sim Lap(0, \lambda)$ with λ being the magnitude parameter determined by differential privacy mechanism.

Since the measurement noise is non-Gaussian, the posterior density cannot be analytically determined without a Gaussian assumption about the measurement noise. We adopted two solutions to the posterior estimation challenge. One is to approximate the Laplace noise with a Gaussian noise, which can be then solved by the classic Kalman Filter [31]. The other is to simulate the posterior density function via Monte Carlo methods based on the Sampling-Importance-Resampling (SIR) particle filter. Detailed descriptions of these approaches are reported in our recent paper [15].

Preliminary Results   We have completed the design of a framework with Filtering and Adaptive Sampling for monitoring single time-series to address the challenge of sampling control using error feedback, and to model data in the time domain. We performed a set of experiments using the Kalman Filter and Particle Filter in combination with PID based sampling control on synthetic datasets as well as real traffic monitoring and flu datasets. Our approaches consistently outperform the baseline Laplace perturbation algorithm and the state-of-the-art Discrete Fourier Transform (DFT) based algorithm [38], which can be only applied in batch processing settings rather than real-time settings. For more detailed results and a demonstration description, please refer to [15, 18, 19]. We also extended the work to multi-dimensional time-series with spatial partitioning techniques [16, 17].

Data Modeling in Multi-Dimensional Data Space The spatial dependencies or homogeneities of neighborhood characteristics legitimize the use of spatial interpolation methods to predict values for specified spatial locations using a limited number of sample data aggregates at nearby locations. In general, this is also applicable in the multi-dimensional data space. We are currently exploring both deterministic and stochastic methods, and in particular, two commonly adapted interpolators, Inverse Distance Weighting (IDW) and Kriging.

A widely used deterministic interpolation method is Inverse Distance Weighting (IDW). It is a local exact interpolator that interpolates values based only on the surrounding measured values of the interpolating location and functions of the inverse distances between the interpolating location and locations of the surrounding sample. On the other hand, stochastic methods, such as Kriging [39], interpolate values not only based on the surrounding data values, but also based on the overall autocorrelation calculated by applying statistical models to all the known data points. Because of this, not only do stochastic methods have the capability of producing a prediction surface, but they also provide some measure of the certainty or accuracy of the predictions. We are analyzing detailed interpolation algorithms based on Kriging with uncertainty quantifications [7] and incorporating these approaches into the PREDICT framework.

27.5.3 Secure Data Aggregation and Feedback Control Without Trusted Aggregator

In our decentralized system model with no trusted aggregator, the privacy of data contributors need to be protected from the aggregator and other data contributors. Such protection needs to be maintained in the entire feedback loop, i.e. both the feedback control phase and the data aggregation phase.

Secure Feedback Control In the feedback phase, our goal is to ensure that each contributor learns only whether and what data is being requested or collected from her and no additional information about whether and what data is collected at other contributors. Depending on the current data model, applications may need to send feedback to individual data contributors, e.g. to collect more crowd data in certain geographic locations in the intelligence collection for city uprising scenario, without disclosing the control command to other data contributors or entities in the network.

A simple idea we are investigating is based on *public key encryption*. The data contributors send their public keys to the application as they contribute their data. The application can in turn encrypt individual feedback control commands using corresponding public keys such that the contributor who is intended to receive the control commands can decrypt the message and follow the command for future data collection. We are also exploring other potential crypto and secure computation mechanisms and study the effectiveness of their relative performance and functionality.

Secure Data Aggregation In the data aggregation phase, our goal is to ensure the data aggregator or participating data contributors can only learn the aggregates and no additional information about the private data contributed by other data contributors, in addition to ensuring differential privacy of the aggregates for the data subjects. The problem can be formulated as a secure multiparty computation (SMC) or distributed privacy preserving data sharing problem [27, 34], in which a set of parties jointly computes a function of their private data inputs such that the parties learn only the result of the function but nothing else.

In addition to leveraging existing SMC protocols, one particular challenge for secure data aggregation is that when the collected data involves personal data, where the aggregates need to be perturbed (as described earlier) to protect the privacy of data subjects. Suppose a set of n semi-honest data collectors need to compute a perturbed sum to satisfy α-differential privacy. If we have one data contributor generate a Laplace noise and add it to the secure sum result, the sum will be disclosed to this contributor. Thus, the perturbation needs to be distributed as well. Our goal is to minimize the total noise added to the result, and ensure that each data contributor generates a noise such that the summation of the noise is sufficient to achieve α-differential privacy.

Preliminary Results We have designed several SMC protocols for various privacy preserving aggregation and analytical tasks [28, 35]. We also conducted a comprehensive comparative study for the secure sum problem with differential privacy [29]. We studied several secure multiparty computation schemes: Shamir's secret sharing, perturbation-based, and various encryption schemes. Differential privacy of the final result is achieved by distributed Laplace perturbation mechanism (DLPA). Partial random noise is generated by all participants, which draw random variables from Gamma or Gaussian distributions, such that the aggregated noise follows Laplace distribution to satisfy differential privacy. We also introduced a new efficient distributed noise generation scheme with partial noise drawn from Laplace distributions and performed studies on these protocols to compare complexity, security characteristics, and scalability both analytically and experimentally in real distributed environments [29].

27.6   Conclusion

This chapter describes the PREDICT framework for privacy and security enhanced dynamic information collection and monitoring with feedback loops. Our key contributions are: (1) mechanisms for privacy preserving data aggregation with perturbations that can simultaneously achieve condensed data representation and privacy protection; (2) a dynamic privacy preserving approach that leverages real time predictive data models and feedback loops to drive iterative data collection – valuable in big data and real time surveillance systems; (3) a mechanism for monitoring single time-series with differential privacy; and (4) prototype secure aggregation schemes with differential privacy for data collection when there is no trusted aggregator. This chapter described the use of the DDDAS paradigm to enhance privacy and security by utilizing effective dynamic data-driven systems approaches to achieve differential privacy, prepare for timely responses, and monitor system performance. Future work will address secure and private situational awareness in dynamic environments, private information retrieval, and data fusion techniques in DDDAS systems.

Acknowledgments This research is supported by the Air Force Office of Scientific Research (AFOSR) DDDAS program under grants FA9550-12-1-0240 and FA9550-17-1-006.

References

1. 2009 H1N1 Flu. http://www.cdc.gov/h1n1flu/
2. Investigation update: Outbreak of shiga toxin-producing E.coli o104 (stec o104:h4) infections associated with travel to germany. http://www.cdc.gov/ecoli/2011/ecolio104/index.html
3. *Report of the August 2010 Multi-Agency Workshop on InfoSymbiotics/DDDAS, The Power of Dynamic Data Driven Applications Systems*. Workshop sponsored by: Air Force Office of Scientific Research and National Science Foundation
4. M.S. Arulampalam, S. Maskell, N. Gordon, A tutorial on particle filters for online nonlinear/non-Gaussian bayesian tracking. IEEE Trans. Signal Process. **50**, 174–188 (2002)
5. J. Burke, D. Estrin, M. Hansen, A. Parker, N. Ramanathan, S. Reddy, M.B. Srivastava, Participatory sensing, in *Workshop on World-Sensor-Web (WSW'06): Mobile Device Centric Sensor Networks and Applications*, 2006
6. B. Cakici, K. Hebing, M. Grünewald, P. Saretok, A. Hulth, Case: a framework for computer supported outbreak detection. BMC Med. Inform. Decis. Mak. **10**, 14 (2010)
7. J. Chilès, P. Delfiner, *Geostatistics: Modeling Spatial Uncertainty*. Wiley Series in Probability and Statistics (Wiley, New York, 2009)
8. F. Darema, Dynamic data driven applications systems: a new paradigm for application simulations and measurements, in *Computational Science – ICCS 2004*. Lecture Notes in Computer Science, vol. 3038 (Springer, Berlin/Heidelberg, 2004), pp. 662–669
9. F. Darema, InfoSymbioticSystems/DDDAS and Large-Scale Dynamic Data and Large-Scale Big Computing for Smart Systems, in *Proceedings of the 2016 Annual ACM Conference on Principles of Advanced Discrete Simulation, SIGSIM-PADS, Banff, Canada*, 2016
10. W. Du, M.J. Atallah, Secure multi-party computation problems and their applications: a review and open problems, in *NSPW'01: Proceedings of the 2001 Workshop on New Security Paradigms*, New York (ACM, 2001), pp. 13–22
11. C. Dwork, Differential privacy, in *Automata, Languages and Programming, Pt 2* (Springer, Berlin/Heidelberg, 2006), p. 4052
12. C. Dwork, Differential privacy: a survey of results, in *TAMC* ed. by M. Agrawal, D.-Z. Du, Z. Duan, A. Li. Lecture Notes in Computer Science, vol. 4978 (Springer, Berlin, Heidelberg, 2008), pp. 1–19
13. C. Dwork, A firm foundation for private data analysis. Commun. ACM **54**, 86–95 (2011)
14. C. Dwork, F. McSherry, K. Nissim, A. Smith, Calibrating noise to sensitivity in private data analysis, in *3rd Theory of Cryptography Conference, New York, US*, 2006

15. L. Fan, L. Xiong, An adaptive approach to real-time aggregate monitoring with differential privacy. IEEE Trans. Knowl. Data Eng. **26**(9), 2094–2106 (2014)
16. L. Fan, L. Bonomi,L. Xiong, V. Sunderam, Monitoring web browsing behaviors with differential privacy, in *World Wide Web Conference (WWW'14), Seoul, Korea*, 2014
17. L. Fan, L. Xiong, V. Sunderam, Differentially private multi-dimensional time-series release for traffic monitoring, in *27th IFIP WG 11.3 Conference on Data and Applications Security and Privacy (DBSec), Newark, US*, 2013
18. L. Fan, L. Xiong, Real-time aggregate monitoring with differential privacy, in *CIKM*, Maui, US, 2012, pp. 2169–2173
19. L. Fan, L. Xiong, V. Sunderam, Fast: differentially private real-time aggregate monitor with filtering and adaptive sampling (demonstration track), in *ACM SIGMOD, New York, US*, 2013
20. B.C.M. Fung, K. Wang, R. Chen, P.S. Yu, Privacy-preserving data publishing: a survey on recent developments. ACM Comput. Surv. **42**(4), 1–14 (2010)
21. L. Pournajaf, L. Xiong, D.A. Garcia-Ulloa, V. Sunderam, Participant privacy in mobile crowd sensing task management: a survey of methods and challenges. ACM SIGMOD Rec. **44**(4), 23–34 (2015)
22. L. Pournajaf, L. Xiong, V. Sunderam, S. Goryczka, Spatial task assignment for crowd sensing with cloaked locations, in *IEEE 15th International Conference on Mobile Data Management (MDM), Melbourne, Australia*, 2014
23. A. Aved, K. Hua, A general framework for managing and processing live video data with privacy protection. Multimedia Systems **18**(2), 123–143 (2012)
24. Y. Badr, S. Hariri, Y. AlNashif, E. Blasch, Resilient and trustworthy dynamic data-driven application systems (DDDAS) services for crisis management environments, in *Proceedings of the International Conference on Computational Science (ICCS), Reykjavik, Iceland*, 2015
25. E. Blasch, Y.B. Al-Nashif, S. Hariri, Static versus dynamic data information fusion analysis using DDDAS for cyber security trust, in *Proceedings of the International Conference on Computational Science (ICCS), Cairns, Australia*, 2014
26. S.L. Garfinkel, M.D. Smith, Guest editors' introduction: data surveillance. IEEE Secur. Privacy **4**(6), 15–17 (2006)
27. O. Goldreich, *Foundations of Cryptography: Volume 2, Basic Applications* (Cambridge University Press, New York, 2004)
28. S. Goryczka, L. Xiong, B. Fung, m-privacy for collaborative data publishing, in *IEEE Transactions on Data and Knowledge Engineering (TKDE)*, **26**(10), 2520–2533 (2014)
29. S. Goryczka, L. Xiong, V. Sunderam, Secure multiparty aggregation with differential privacy: a comparative study, in *6th International Workshop on Privacy and Anonymity in the Information Society (PAIS), Genoa, Italy*, 2013
30. Y. Ioannidis, The history of histograms (abridged), in *Proceedings of VLDB Conference*, Trento, Italy, 2003
31. R.E. Kalman, A new approach to linear filtering and prediction problems. J. Basic Eng **82**(1), 35–45, 1960
32. J. Kang, K. Shilton, D. Estrin, J. Burke, M. Hansen, Self-surveillance privacy. Iowa Law Rev. **97**, 809–847 (2012)
33. D. Kifer, A. Machanavajjhala, No free lunch in data privacy, in *Proceedings of the 2011 International Conference on Management of Data, SIGMOD'11*, Athens Greece, 2011
34. Y. Lindell, B. Pinkas, Secure multiparty computation for privacy-preserving data mining. Cryptology ePrint Archive, Report 2008/197, 2008. http://eprint.iacr.org/
35. J. Liu, L. Xiong, J. Luo, J.Z. Huang, Privacy preserving distributed dbscan clustering. Trans. Data Privacy **6**, 69–85 (2013)
36. F. McSherry, Privacy integrated queries: an extensible platform for privacy-preserving data analysis, in *SIGMOD*, Providence, US, 2009
37. M. Mun, S. Reddy, K. Shilton, N. Yau, J. Burke, D. Estrin, M. Hansen, E. Howard, R. West, P. Boda, Peir, the personal environmental impact report, as a platform for participatory sensing systems research, in *Proceedings of the 7th International Conference on Mobile Systems, Applications, Services, MobiSys*, Krakow, Poland, 2009

38. V. Rastogi, S. Nath, Differentially private aggregation of distributed time-series with transformation and encryption, in *SIGMOD*, Indianapolis, US, 2010
39. D. Shepard, A two-dimensional interpolation function for irregularly-spaced data, in *Proceedings of the 1968 23rd ACM National Conference, ACM'68*, 1968, pp. 517–524
40. K. Shilton, Four billion little brothers? Privacy, mobile phones, and ubiquitous data collection. Commun. ACM **52**, 48–53 (2009)
41. M.M. Wagner, A.W. Moore, R.M. Aryel (eds.), Elsevier Academic Press. 2011
42. Y. Xiao, L. Xiong, C. Yuan, Differentially private data release through multidimensional partitioning, in *Secure Data Management*, at VLDB, Singapore, 2010, pp. 150–168
43. W. Yih, S. Deshpande, C. Fuller, D. Heisey-Grove, J. Hsu, B. Kruskal, M. Kulldorff, M. Leach, J. Nordin, J. Patton-Levine, E. Puga, E. Sherwood, I. Shui, R. Platt, Evaluating real-time syndromic surveillance signals from ambulatory care data in four states. Public Health Rep. **125**(1), 111–120 (2010)

Chapter 28
Multimedia Content Analysis with Dynamic Data Driven Applications Systems (DDDAS)

Erik P. Blasch, Alex J. Aved, and Shuvra S. Bhattacharyya

Abstract With ubiquitous data acquired from sensors, there is an ever increasing ability to abstract content from the environment. Multimedia content exists in many data forms such as surveillance data from video, reports from documents and twitter, and signals from sensor systems. Current discussions revolve around dynamic data-driven applications systems (DDDAS), big data, cyber-physical systems, and Internet of things (IoT) each of which requires data modeling. Key elements include a computing environment that should match the application, time horizon, and queries for which the data is needed. In this paper, we discuss the DDDAS paradigm of sensor measurements, statistical processing, environmental modeling, and software implementation to deliver content on demand, given the context of the environment. DDDAS provides a framework to control the information flow for rapid decision making, model updating, and being prepared for the unexpected query. Experimental results demonstrate the DDDAS-based Live Video Computing DataBase Modeling approach to allow data discovery, model updates, and query-based flexibility for awareness of unknown situations.

Keywords Data Fusion Information Group (DFIG) model · Human machine interface (HMI) · Qualia-based Exploitation of Sensing Technology (QuEST) · Unexpected query · Situation awareness · Autonomy · Contextual awareness · Data-base management system (DBMS) · Knowledge driven · Unknown-unknown · Content-based image retrieval (CBIR) · Cyber-physical systems (CPS) · Live-video computing (LVC) database management system (LVC-DBMS) · Target tracking

E. P. Blasch (✉)
Air Force Office of Scientific Research, Arlington, VA, USA

A. J. Aved
Air Force Research Lab, Rome, NY, USA

S. S. Bhattacharyya
University of Maryland, College Park, MD, USA

© This is a U.S. government work and not under copyright protection in the U.S.; foreign copyright protection may apply 2022
E. P. Blasch et al. (eds.), *Handbook of Dynamic Data Driven Applications Systems*,
https://doi.org/10.1007/978-3-030-74568-4_28

28.1 Introduction

Dynamic Data Driven Application Systems (DDDAS) require system-level coordination between applications modeling, measurement systems, statistical algorithms, and software methods. Applications modeling include physical, geometrical, or relational models that support control techniques that utilize streaming data to update the theoretical-, data-, and systems-level models as shown in Fig. 28.1. The *application* composes scenarios which include elements of designing systems for challenging situations to handle uncertainty. *Data* includes the models (e.g., theory) and signals (e.g., measurements) which are incorporated into statistical analysis. The *software methods* include techniques to manage the data for real-time performance such as streaming dataflow architectures for information management. Finally, as with most data-to-application designs, there is need for *visualization and user-input* that supports metrics and refinement actions such as model updates. This chapter focuses on dataflow modeling which allows discovery and analysis for model updates.

DDDAS has a rich history in many application for which different information computing solutions have been reported. Given the wealth of capabilities, some of the key developments include: health monitoring, object tracking, object classification, cyber analysis, and systems coordination. The orchestration of these applications supports actionable information for user support from component-level control to system-level information fusion. For the review that follows, we focus on recent developments as to the extent of DDDAS implementations and highlight in Table 28.1.

A historical example of DDDAS success includes **Health Monitoring**. A typical example includes component-level analysis of parts such as the performance of a aircraft wing during disturbances [1]. The DDDAS methods include theoretical performance models matched against sensor measurements such as stress and strain, useful for aircraft performance [2] for which failure modes can be detected [3]. Using the component-level analysis, these results can be used for UAV swarm analysis [4] and network health mentoring [5].

Fig. 28.1 Elements of Dynamic Data-Driven Application Systems (DDDAS) concept

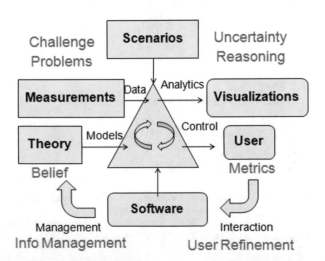

Table 28.1 DDDAS instantiations

	Model	Measurement	Application	References
Health monitoring	Aircraft	Piezo-electric wing	UAV flights	[1–5]
Tracking	Kinematic	Radar	Surveillance	[6–13]
Classification	Shape	Visual	Detection	[14–17]
Architecture	Software	Networked sensors	Dataflow	[18–26]
Cyber-physical	Patterns	Cyber attacks	Security	[27–29]
Environment	Natural	Energy	Power, wind	[30–34]

A common example of DDDAS techniques includes *multiple object tracking*. Object tracking using the DDDAS approach has been applied to hyperspectral data [6], single video [7], and multiple cameras [8]. Using the adaptive streaming of video data [9] provides an interface between visual surveillance [10] and user analysis [11]. Advanced methods include the drift homotopy particle filter [12] for Network Selection and Tracking [13].

In support of analysis of tracking, there are also examples for data analysis for *classification*. Tracking methods include combinations with classification and identification [14]. Examples include DDDAS solutions for fusion techniques for object classification from an array of sensors [15] for object recognition [16]. Using the data available, spectrum information can be used through DDDAS for enhanced object analysis [17].

The various techniques of DDDAS require *software solutions* to enable distributed processing, big data analytics, and model coordination. Software developments include middleware [18], cloud techniques [19], and dataflow architectures [20]. Methods for parallelization support variational inference problems [21] as well as multi-objective design optimization [22]. Our result focused on multimedia database for context analysis which we extend here. Multimedia constructs include content (data), entities (features), and scenes (context). Context enhanced information fusion examples include imagery [23], user queries [24], text and tracking [25] and content-based image retrieval (CBIR). The multiple applications of data fusion require resource management [26] to facilitate the ability of the user-defined queries to be determined from the information management system.

In the support of the network of sensors and software architectures, there is a growing support to *cyber-physical system* analysis and support. Recent examples include cyber trust analytics [27], services for crisis management [28], and security and privacy of networks [29] which can use a variety of data techniques.

As with DDDAS, there is a need to understand how the sensor measurements, dataflow, and application relate to the *environment* of the application. Inherently the environment model provides context-aware capabilities [30]. Key examples include analysis of air flow of wind models affecting control [31, 32]. The analysis of the wind flow can detect plumes [33] as well as power sources of systems [34]. These monitoring applications of DDDAS are important in this research as related to the streaming video processing that can be affected by power and line-of-sight obstructions.

Using these concepts from DDDAS, we seek to use context environment data in analysis of multimedia content of user queries, video streaming processing, and object tracking. We build on our previous work in DDDAS to explore data analysis for tracking and identification techniques [35] and query-based multimedia processing [36].

The DDDAS has been used for combinations of multimedia data sources [37], semantic and video queries [38], analysis of patterns [39], and object tracking [40] for analytical model updates. Advances in sensor analysis for multispectral imaging [41], radar [42] and object tracking [43] have enabled better processing for DDDAS-enabled systems. For example, developments in machine learning had afforded the ability to process big data for visual and infrared data [44], signal features [45], and radar signatures [46]. Exploiting the situational context [47] can be used for data augmentation that combines with the instrumentation from which current DDDAS applications include robotics [48], surveillance security [49], and unsupervised feature queries of edge devices [50] for situation awareness.

The remainder of this Chapter proceeds as follows. Section 28.2 describes multimedia context analysis to support the unexpected query and Sect. 28.3 focuses on data to support modeling of reality. Section 28.4 describes data-oriented and analytical models. Section 28.5 presents the live video computing database management system (LVCDBMS) examples. Section 28.6 draws conclusions.

28.2 Multimedia Analysis

Information fusion has been applied to many applications. One commonly accepted model is the approach (shown in Fig. 28.2) as a common processing framework for the cognitive, information, and physical domains [51]. The levels (L) determine the processing in the system such as L0 data registration, L1 object tracking and identification assessment [52], L2 situation awareness activity analysis, [53], and L3 impact assessment [54]. The complementary control levels are: L4 sensor management, L5 user refinement and L6 mission (SUM) management [55]. Together, these levels of processing could be represented in a DDDAS framework.

Human-machine interaction (HMI) incorporates decision support, human centered design, and user augmentation. In each of these approaches, a user interacts with the system for which DDDAS would enable system analysis, model updates, and queries as shown in Fig. 28.3. Using information fusion as an example, kinematic models support estimation of the incoming physical data for object tracking. Likewise, semantic models process the human-derived queries. The data is fused using a statistical method such as Bayes' rule for a given software architecture for query-based responses.

Utilization of contextual information by a machine includes the database system, the sensor type (e.g., video), the context data, the extracted features (e.g., the object), and the scenes (e.g., the environment). These operating conditions of the sensor, object, and environment need to established together to support information exploitation and contextual analysis [56]. The software architecture includes a

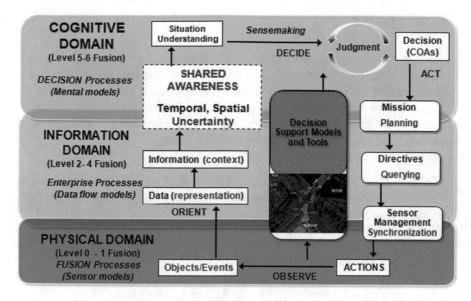

Fig. 28.2 Information fusion physical, information, and cognitive domains

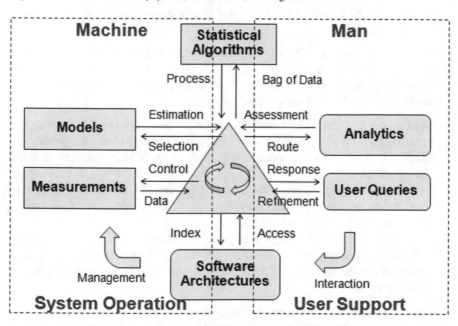

Fig. 28.3 Man-Machine systems operation for DDDAS query-based analysis

database, services, and methods of access. To process multimedia queries, modeling is needed to provide context which is fundamental to the ***Qualia-based Exploitation of Sensing Technology (QuEST)*** concept [57].

28.2.1 QuEST

QuEST is a new approach to situational assessment (processes that are used to achieve situational awareness), situation understanding (comprehension of the meaning of the data as integrated with individual's goals. It is the "*so what*" of the data), or sensemaking ("a motivated, continuous effort to understand connections which can be among people, places, and events in order to anticipate their trajectories and act effectively" [58]) for decision quality.

Three processes are defined in QuEST:

- *QuEST agent processes* implement blended dual process cognitive models (have both artificial conscious and artificial subconscious/intuition processes) for situational assessment.
- *QuEST artificially conscious processes* all are constrained by the fundamental laws of the QUEST Theory of Consciousness (structural coherence, situation based, simulation/cognitively decoupled).
- *QuEST subconscious/intuition processes* do not use working memory and thus considered autonomous (do not require consciousness to act). Current approaches to data-driven artificial intelligence provide a wide range of options for implementing instantiations of capturing experiential knowledge used by these processes.

QuEST is developing a 'Theory of Knowledge' – to provide the foundations to understand what an agent or group of agents can know to support machine learning and human-computer decision making. QuEST seeks principles on which a belief or theory is based. The three tenets are:

- *Structurally Coherent* – the conscious representation has to have enough mutual information with physical reality to facilitate *interaction* with the world in a stable, consistent and useful manner (e.g., learned predictable explanations, links, and outcomes).
- *Situated Conceptualization* – the fundamental units of conscious deliberation are situation entities (e.g., context-based gists, time/space/multi-modality representations, and plausible narratives).
- *Cognitively Decoupled* – the conscious representation is a hypothetical explanation of the present, past or imagined future, it is a simulation which is not a posting of sensor data (e.g., exformation and conceptual combination to generate a new meaning).

Three related ideas from tenets include compression, exformation, and events. *Compression* encodes an infinite number of stimuli into a single quale (e.g., low bandwidth 50 bits/sec) for interaction. *Events* in situations may be communicated to another agent as an event potential akin to an evoked potential (i.e., brain response to a cognitive stimulus). Finally, *exformation* (pattern completion inferring mechanism) affords a conscious representation. The conscious representation is blended with data-driven processing. The deliberation from using these representations complements the conventional data-based representation with the ability to incorporate context. Context can either be stored or inferred by situating the hypothetical representation to generate a cohesive narrative of the sensed data.

Together, the situated coherent experience extends processing, exploitation, and dissemination of information. For processing, it is the formation of structured and coherent understanding of collected data. For exploitation, it is the conceptualization of the situation. Finally, for dissemination, the reported results are appended by experiences where the pre-experienced or by imagined interpretations.

QuEST is exploring the concepts such as DDDAS that shed insights into the current models for sensing-based situation reasoning, exploitation-based decision making, and technology-based information analysis. A key issue is solving the unexpected query.

28.2.2   Unexpected Query

One contemporary issue for query-based multimedia analytics is determining the unexpected query. In many cases, the user has a notion of the scene content and the expected analytics desired (such as tracking vehicles on roads). Future systems must be able to answer, and or provide updates on an unexpected result. As an example of a possible solution, Hendricks et al., [59] develop three systems to meet the challenge. It is a group of systems evaluating an analysis for knowledge reasoning. An example of an unexpected query is asking for something not stored in a semantic or model data base. Using the context of related information, responses to the unexpected query can be provided. The three systems designed [59] include a video system, a semantic library, and a method to link the video analytics to the stored semantic descriptions. However the results come from only previously learned information that combines data and models through semantic queries. Inherent in the approach is a method needed for measuring the similarity of context through adjacency of relations.

While solving the unexpected query is a difficult problem, methods for enhancing the opportunities comes from multi-media data such as that of video supporting text and text supporting video. Another option is transfer learning [60]. In transfer learning, the domain requires learning the probability distribution functions for modeling as well as applying them to the task such as labeling and then matching features to labels.

28.3   Multimedia Contextual Reality

Future human-machine designs require the balance between automation and autonomy. For automation, systems designs require the user to input desired requests such as the rules for object detection, activity analysis, and situation results. For autonomy, the goal is to allow the machine to discover attributes of the scene and report techniques to the user. The challenge comes when the situation is unknown and that the models of reality have also not been completely modeled. Typical video processing techniques assume limited human involvement; however most video technology is employed for use by an analyst (automation) or for mission objectives (autonomy). The definitions of autonomy and automation are:

- **Automation**: The system functions with no/little human operator involvement, however the system performance is limited to the specific actions it has been designed to do. Typically these are well-defined tasks that have predetermined responses, i.e. rule-based responses. (Note: we rather suggest data-driven AI)
- **Autonomy**: Systems which have a set of intelligence-based capabilities that allow it to respond to situations that were not pre-programmed or anticipated in the design (i.e., decision-based responses). Autonomous systems have a degree of self-government, self-directed behavior (with the human's proxy for decisions) [61].

For *automation*, functions for *estimation* are organized as those supporting queries. The system estimates events as states in time, whereas users denote activities which are semantically described intervals of situation-based relationships. Activities are thus composed on multiple events. Event-recognition is dependent on analyst involvement as the enormous amounts of activities are not semantically exhaustibly defined by a machine [62]. The techniques for *autonomy* include *control* functions such as those supporting the data-base management system (DBMS) to include resource management, data storage, and indexing. The use of automation and autonomy provide the processing that affords decisions to data [63]. The real world consists of sensor, environment, and target (SET) operating conditions that need to be assessed for the user [64] to determine the unexpected query.

There are many challenges that come from discovering the **unexpected queries**. The problem is that autonomy also has to understand **reality** in order to update the user on the outputs of the system. The *assumptions* from analysis of multimedia context includes: (1) Problems Statement is precise, (2) Data can be acquired, (3) Data/Evidence can be integrated, (4) Decisions are reproducible, (5) Decisions are actionable, and (6) Error quantified.

Being aware of a **situation** can help guide DDDAS systems, but it might also constrain the results. Thus modeling the situation includes multiple representations of fidelity. For many situations, reality is understood and the proper reaction is known – such as expecting cars to be at road intersections. This requires awareness of the environment or the context of information. The challenge is when the reality is unknown and the proper awareness of the environment is unknown. Figure 28.4 showcases the four cases from the unknown-known perception versus reality.

When *reality* is unknown and the environment is unknown, it requires learning and analysis to deal with the high degree of uncertainty and complexity. When the reality is unknown and the proper mode is understood, such a situation can be overcome with diagnostics such as object classification. DDDAS requires contextual modeling to address the common assumptions to relate perceived data to from the unknown reality to the known reality. Thus, there is a need for data-driven, knowledge-driven, and context-driven approaches to solve the unexpected query.

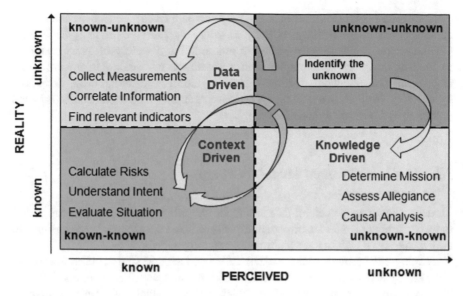

Fig. 28.4 Known versus unknown for perception versus reality

- **Data-driven** implies that the assumption that the error can be quantified and that data can be acquired which moves from the unknown-unknown to the unknown reality, but known modeling.
- **Knowledge-driven** is based on the fact that the problem is specific (such as object tracking) and that decisions are actionable.
- **Context-driven** brings together both data and knowledge. Fusing data helps to move from the unknown reality to the known reality – such as removing false assertions. Likewise, decisions that are reproducible help to verify from the unknown perceptions to the known perceptions as the data is related through the appropriate model.

Here we focus on the assumption that actions and decisions are reproducible from the models.

28.4   Modeling for Multimedia Content

Modeling has many approaches from analytical, experimental, or processing. Many of these approaches focus on the data such as collections of experiments which map results from data to modeling instances. A current question for DDDAS is the types of modeling approaches for which we combine physical modeling (e.g., theoretical) with data modeling (i.e., software).

Multimedia context is established through content (data) which has been termed content-based image retrieval (CBIR) or *query by image content* (*QBIC*) [65]. CBIR systems facilitate retrieval by accommodating a variety of query methods, to include query by example, sketching an image by hand, random browsing, text search (i.e., keyword, speech/voice recognition) and hierarchical navigation by category [66]. Two modeling types that are interrelated include data-oriented modeling and analytical modeling.

28.4.1 Data Oriented Models (Cyber)

Modeling and management of data and model-based representation of computation to be performed on data are important aspects to take into account in the design and understanding of DDDAS for multimedia content analysis.

A *data model* provides common definitions and formats so that different applications and systems can communicate data effectively. Careful consideration of data models is important in multimedia content analysis, which by definition involves heterogeneous forms of data, and also in many cases involves heterogeneous formats for the same basic form of data (e.g., different compression formats for images). Various research efforts have explored the development and application of data modeling techniques for multimedia systems (e.g., see [67–69]).

Data structures to efficiently store and manipulate multimedia data content are also critical in design and integration of multimedia content analysis systems. For example, use of common data structures can facilitate the efficient exchange of content and extracted information. Figure 28.5 illustrates several data structures that are commonly used in multimedia systems. Typical methods for a single measurement system include a stack where data is stored and retrieved in a common location. An array helps to align data in different locations for ease of access. If the data is distributed, a linked-list can help associate information. Current techniques are based on a hash table to rapid storage, access, and retrieval.

Dataflow is a form of model-based design that is useful in the design and implementation of hardware and software for complex multimedia systems [70]. In this context, dataflow can be viewed as a model of computation in which applications are represented as directed graphs that correspond to block diagrams for signal and information processing. Individual dataflow processing blocks, called actors, execute in a data-driven manner, which means that they can be invoked whenever they have sufficient data on their inputs, and sufficient empty space on their outputs to support their associated computations. Where and when (on which processors and at what times) actors in a dataflow graph get executed are determined by a scheduler, which is developed or synthesized as part of the process of implementing a dataflow graph on a particular platform. This separation of concerns between scheduling and behavioral specification is an important aspect of dataflow-based design, and leads to powerful capabilities for design verification and optimization. For more details on dataflow techniques for multimedia systems

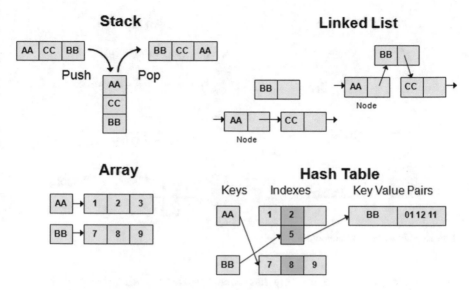

Fig. 28.5 Examples of commonly-used data structures

and other forms of signal and information processing systems, we refer the reader to [71]. Combined with a dataflow method, there is a need for the physical model. Hence, what is stored and accessed has to be related to the application.

28.4.2   Analytical Models (Physical)

Analytical modeling of physical data typically comes from an empirical investigation of the environment and the regressing on the results as shown in Fig. 28.6. Such an empirical model is then supported by a theoretical model. For typical object tracking, this is a kinematic model of the object movement [72]. However, behaviors can be non-typical such as monitoring a car or vehicle against the physical and social norms. Thus, models need to be updated based on emergent behavior and ad-hoc updates such as determine the unexpected query. Here we seek to combine these approaches to performance DDDAS model updating. A related concept is cyber-physical modeling.

28.4.3   Cyber-Physical Models

DDDAS is closely associated with sensor and software systems. Loosely defined, the cyber-physical approach discusses these concepts. The combination of the software (e.g., cyber) and hardware (e.g., physical) could be a form of cyber-physical

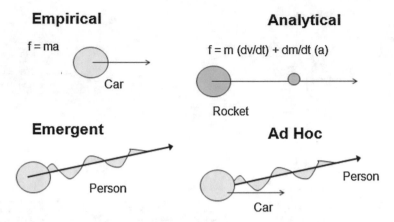

Empirical

$f = ma$

Car

Analytical

$f = m\,(dv/dt) + dm/dt\,(a)$

Rocket

Emergent

Person

Ad Hoc

Person

Car

Fig. 28.6 Physical modeling types

systems analysis. Video tracking has been associated with privacy, distributed processing and connections to instrumentation systems. Data should be in a format so as to curate the data and metadata for analysis for a combination of cyber and physical analysis. Thus, the collaboration of distributed computational elements would be used to control the physical entities.

With image captioning, there is a need for query analysis from sensors. To measure performance, there is a need for credit assignment on how to select models that support improved control. One way to assign credit is on the how the current action relates to the previous result. To exploit the concept, we need to let the CPS explore its environment from which policies can be adapted to model the update. One such example for a temporal query credit assignment is that of low-frame rate systems from which understanding the video methods could alter the processing analysis [73]. Various methods could be done in autonomy by the system or by outputting the processing evaluation to the user for analysis [74].

Using the DDDAS concept with data-oriented models, analytical models, and cyber-physical concepts, we present use case to explore activity analysis for processing of streaming video data.

28.5   Results: Activity Analysis

In order to develop a multimedia content analysis, the goal is to utilize both the known modeling as well as allow the system to discover unknown relationships. These unknown expectations should be developed from a combination of physical modeling, computational data-oriented processing, and contextual reasoning [75]. In order to investigate such an analysis, the live-video computing (LVC) database management system (LVC-DBMS) system is allowed to stream data from which

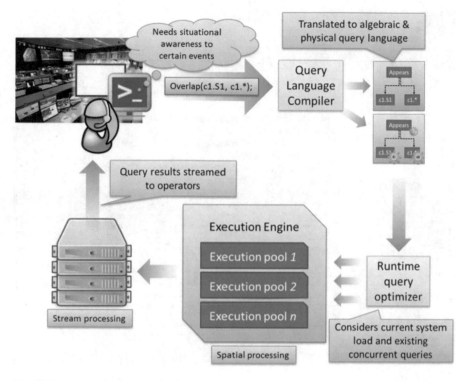

Fig. 28.7 Process flow of LVBDMS

statistical analysis is done by varying the sample rate, detection size, and activity analysis.

28.5.1 Interface

In order to provide queries for the analysis, an interface was designed to allow a user to select the tracking results for object detection by varying the sample rate, detection size, and activity analysis. These queries were generally defined such that the analysis would afford some unexpected queries to be processed for model updates (e.g., person detection outside the parking lot). Figure 28.7 shows the LVDB concept and Fig. 28.8 shows the query interface.

The LVC-DBMS uses a query optimizer and associated execution environment that is designed for the LVC environment [36]. It performs query optimization at runtime, taking a new query and finding any possible overlap with the existing queries in the system and rewriting the new query in order to minimize duplicate subexpressions and optimize the utilization of the query execution engine (Fig. 28.7). Using the LVC environment interface (Fig. 28.8) and implemented in the LVC-DBMS prototype reduce query execution overhead by merging the physical

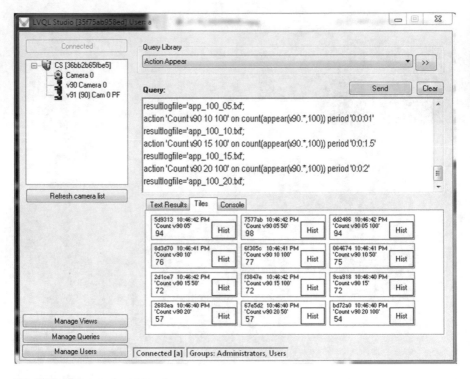

Fig. 28.8 The query-based interface

algebra query trees. The merging of query trees is done through context associations. To facilitate the performance evaluation and the impact of the query optimization, a query cost metric (credit assignment) was derived and used to update modeling performance results.

Using the LVC-DBMS, a relationship was established for the scene content from text analysis (shown in Fig. 28.9). Two videos were selected from the *Defense Advanced Research Projects Agency* (DARPA) Video and Image Retrieval and Analysis Tool (VIRAT) data set of related scene characteristics and the goal was intelligent situation analysis. The first is that of a parking lot and the second is a parking lot located near an intersection. In the first case, the modeling is known as people get in and out their cars. In the second scenario, there is the expectation that people normally enter and exit the car, however, there is a need for the system to discover new information.

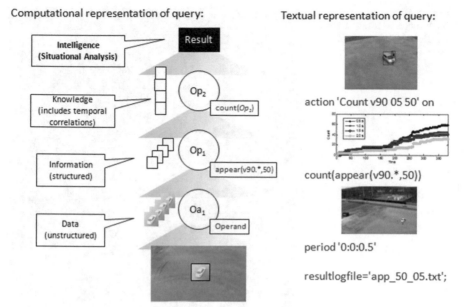

Fig. 28.9 Multimedia (text, video) query relations

28.5.2   Case 1: Intersection

In the first scenario, a video was selected that had both the parking lot as well as background clutter from the road. With the cars traveling at the intersection and people entering their cars in the streaming video (Fig. 28.10), a stable count rate is maintained at the intersection as shown in Fig. 28.11.

28.5.3   Case 2: Parking Lot

In the second scenario, there are many people moving in and out of the cars in unexpected fashion, so the object count is higher for the activity detection. As an example, in the Fig. 28.12, when the parking lot is viewed there is detection from the car and person while variations in the scene clutter are also a result of the scene complexity. Open queries were run on different sampling rates (computation) and object sizes (image processing). As the object size query is increased, then the update rate is not as distinguishing (Fig. 28.13). Thus, for real-time analysis when bandwidth limitations exist, then the analytics could be subsampled without loss of performance analysis.

The second analysis is counts for the activities that were analyzed for the size and frequency intervals from which the sampling was conducted. In Fig. 28.14, it is

Fig. 28.10 Case 1:
Intersection with road traffic,
mostly vehicle maneuvers

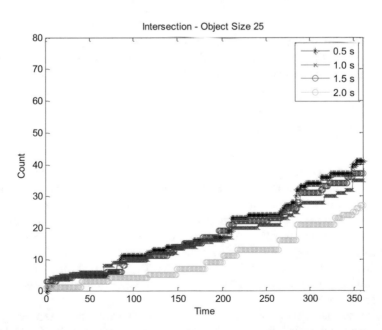

Fig. 28.11 Intersection activity recognition for different sampling rates for a fixed object size

Fig. 28.12 Case 2: Parking lot: clutter and object detection with people entering/exiting scene

shown that the frequency interval of analysis for different object sizes has the ability to distinguish new activities. For the object size, there is a difference in the count which establishes the need for a query-based system to determine the object size (in relation to the resolution of the image) and the selection of the sampling rate.

It is noted that the jump in the object count, from time step 150, indicates when the significant number of activities happens. Thus, the absolute count is not the key feature, but the relative change in the number of objects in the image. The analytics highlight that to get the unexpected query; there is a need for dynamically varying the detector size and sampling rate.

28.6   Conclusions

The paper focused the DDDAS concept for multimedia analysis which includes both video tracking and query-based analytics. Large scale multimedia applications will require dynamic data-driven applications systems (DDDAS) approaches to bring together context, activity, and query analysis. The live-video computing (LVC) database management system was used to explore unexpected queries for

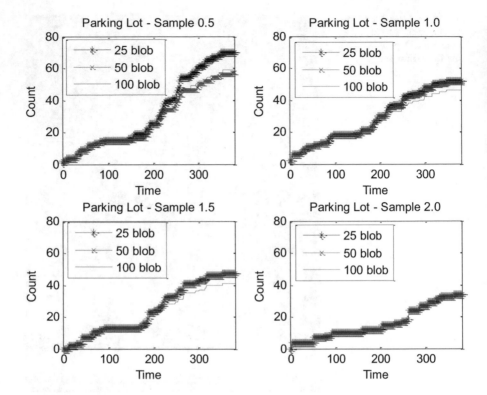

Fig. 28.13 Varying the update rate of the analysis

model updates. The system provides context-aware, query-aware, and activity-aware analysis both on the object size (application) and sampling rate (computation) for data-oriented and analytical modeling updates. Results demonstrate the need for open queries to determine unexpected situations in which defined queries cannot determine all activities within a scene.

Acknowledgements This work is partly supported by the Air Force Office of Scientific Research (AFOSR) under the Dynamic Data Driven Applications Systems program and the Air Force Research Lab. The views and conclusions contained herein are those of the authors and should not be interpreted as necessarily representing the official policies or endorsements, either expressed or implied, of the United States Air Force.

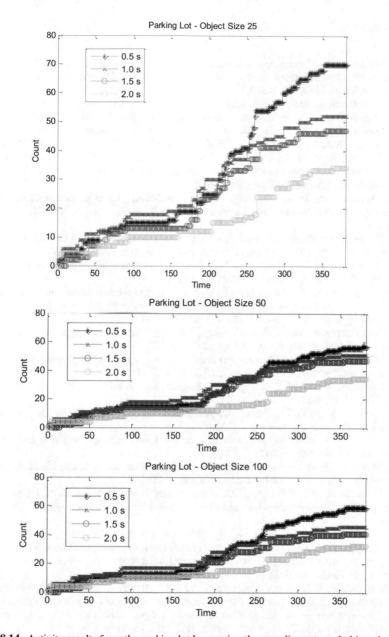

Fig. 28.14 Activity results from the parking lot by varying the sampling rate and object size

References

1. Y. Bazilevs, A.L. Marsdan, et al., Toward a computational steering framework for large-scale composite structures based on continually and dynamically injected sensor data. Procedia Comput. Sci. **9**, 1149–1158 (2012)
2. B. Peherstorfer, K. Willcox, Detecting and adapting to parameter changes for reduced models of dynamic data-driven application systems. Procedia Comput. Sci. **51**, 2553–2562 (2015)
3. S. Imai, A. Galli, C.A. Varela, Dynamic data-driven avionics systems: Inferring failure modes from data stream. Procedia Comput. Sci. **51**, 1665–1674 (2015)
4. R. McCune, R. Purta, M. Dobski, A. Jaworski, G. Madey et al., Investigations of dddas for command and control of uav swarms with agent-based modeling, in *Proceedings Winter Simulation Conference* (2013) pp. 1467–1478
5. T. Henderson, A. Joshi, W. Wang, N. Tirpankar, et al., Bayesian computational sensor networks: small-scale structural health monitoring. Procedia Comput. Sci. **51**, 2603–2612 (2015)
6. B. Uzkent, M.J. Hoffman, A. Vodacek, et al., Feature matching and adaptive prediction models in an object tracking DDDAS. Procedia Comput. Sci. **18**, 1939–1948 (2013)
7. R. Fujimoto, A. Guin, M. Hunter, et al., A dynamic data driven application system for vehicle tracking. Procedia Comput Sci **29**, 1203–1215 (2014)
8. S.S. Bhattacharyya, M. van der Schaar, O. Atan, et al., Data-driven stream mining systems for computer vision, Ch12, in *Advances in Embedded Computer Vision*, ed. by B. Kisacanin, M. Gelautz (Springer International Publishing, Cham, 2014).
9. S. Chakravarthy, A. Aved, S. Shirvani, et al., Adapting stream processing framework for video analysis. Procedia Comput. Sci. **51**, 2648–2657 (2015)
10. E. Blasch, A.J. Aved, Dynamic data-driven application system (DDDAS) for video surveillance user support. Procedia Comput. Sci. **51**, 2503–2517 (2015)
11. A.J. Aved, E. Blasch, Multi-INT query language for DDDAS designs. Procedia Comput. Sci. **51**, 2518–2523 (2015)
12. V. Maroulas, K. Kang, I.D. Shizas, A learning drift homotopy particle filter, in *International Conference on Information Fusion*, (2015)
13. I.D. Schizas, V. Maroulas, Dynamic data driven sensor network selection and tracking. Procedia Comput. Sci. **51**, 2583–2592 (2015)
14. E. Blasch, L. Hong, Data association through fusion of object track and identification sets, International Conference on Information Fusion, (2000)
15. N. Virani, S. Marcks, S. Sarkar, K. Mukerjee, A. Ray, S. Phoha, Dynamic data driven sensor Array fusion for object detection and classification. Procedia Comput. Sci. **18**, 2046–2055 (2013)
16. E. Blasch, G. Seetharaman et al., Dynamic data driven applications systems (DDDAS) modeling for automatic object recognition, in *Proceedings of SPIE*, vol. 8744 (2013)
17. B. Uzkent, M.J. Hoffman, A. Vodacek, Spectral validation of measurements in a vehicle tracking DDDAS. Procedia Comput. Sci. **51**, 2493–2502 (2015)
18. J.B. Weissman, V. Kumar, V. Chandola et al., DDDAS/ITR: A data mining and exploration middleware for grid and distributed computing, in *Int'l. Conf. on Comp. Science* (2007)
19. B. Liu, Y. Chen, et al., Information fusion in a cloud computing era: A systems-level perspective. IEEE Aerosp. Electron. Syst. Mag. **29**(10), 16–24 (2014)
20. X. Li, J. Dennis, G. Gao, W. Lim, H. Wei, C. Yang, R. Pavel, FreshBreeze: A data flow approach for meeting DDDAS challenges. Procedia Comput. Sci. **51**, 2573–2582 (2015)
21. V. Hebbur, V.S. Rao, A. Sandu, Parallel solution of DDDAS variational inference problems. Procedia Comput. Sci. **51**, 2474–2482 (2015)
22. K. Sudusinghe, Y. Jiao, H.B. Salem, M. van der Schaar, S. Bhattacharyya, Multiobjective design optimization in the lightweight dataflow for DDDAS environment (LiD4E). Procedia Comput. Sci. **51**, 2563–2572 (2015)

23. Z. Liu, E. Blasch, Z. Xue, R. Langaniere, W. Wu, Objective assessment of multiresolution image fusion algorithms for context enhancement in night vision: A comparative survey. IEEE Trans. Pattern Anal. Mach. Intell. **34**(1), 94–109 (2012)

24. E. Blasch, S. Plano, Cognitive fusion analysis based on context, in *Proceedings of SPIE*, vol. 5434 (2004)

25. E. Blasch, I. Kadar, K. Hintz, et al., Resource management coordination with level 2/3 fusion issues and challenges. IEEE Aerosp. Electron. Syst. Mag. **23**(3), 32–46 (2008)

26. E. Blasch, E. Bosse, D.A. Lambert, *High-Level Information Fusion Management and Systems Design* (Artech House, Norwood, 2012)

27. E. Blasch, Y. Al-Nashif, S. Hariri, Static versus dynamic data information fusion analysis using DDDAS for cyber trust. Procedia Comput. Sci. **29**, 1299–1313 (2014)

28. Y. Badr, S. Hariri, Y. Al-Nashif, E. Blasch, Resilient and trustworthy dynamic data-driven application systems (DDDAS) Services for Crisis Management Environments. Procedia Comput. Sci. **51**, 2623–2637 (2015)

29. L. Xiong, V. Sunderam, Security and privacy dimensions in next generation DDDAS/Infosymbiotic systems: A position paper. Procedia Comput. Sci. **51**, 2483–2492 (2015)

30. N. Nguyen, M.M.H. Khan, Context aware data acquisition framework for dynamic data driven applications systems (DDDAS), in *IEEE MILCOM* (2013) pp. 334–341

31. P. Tagade, H. Seybold, S. Ravela, Mixture ensembles for data assimilation in dynamic data-driven environmental systems. Procedia Comput. Sci. **29**, 1266–1276 (2014)

32. S. Ravela, Dynamic data-driven deformable reduced models for coherent fluids. Procedia Comput. Sci. **51**, 2464–2473 (2015)

33. L. Peng, M. Silic, R. O'Donnell, K. Mohseni, A DDDAS plume monitoring system with reduced Kalman filter. Procedia Comput. Sci. **51**, 2533–2542 (2015)

34. X. Shi, H. Damgacioglu, N. Celik, A dynamic data driven approach for operation planning of microgrids. Procedia Comput. Sci. **51**, 2543–2552 (2015)

35. E. Blasch, *Derivation of a Belief Filter for Simultaneous High Range Resolution Radar Tracking and Identification,* Ph.D. Thesis, Wright State University, (1999)

36. A.J. Aved, *Scene Understanding for Real Time Processing of Queries over Big Data Streaming Video*, PhD Dissertation, University of Central Florida, (2013)

37. A. Panasyuk, E. Blasch, et al., Extraction of semantic activities from twitter data, in *Proc. on Semantic Technologies for Intelligence, Defense, and Security* (STIDS) *Conf.* (2013)

38. E. Blasch, R. Cruise, A. Aved, et al., Methods of AI for Multimodal Sensing and Action for Complex Situations. *AI Magazine***40**(4): 50–65 (Winter 2019) https://doi.org/10.1609/aimag.v40i4.4813

39. J. Gao, H. Ling, et al., Pattern of life from WAMI objects tracking based on visual context-aware tracking and infusion network models, in *Proceedings of SPIE*, vol. 8745 (2013)

40. J. Dunık, O. Straka, M. Simandl, et al., Random-point-based filters in object tracking. IEEE Trans. Aerosp. Electron. Syst. **51**(2), 1403–1421 (2015)

41. Y. Zheng, E. Blasch, Z. Liu, *Multispectral Image Fusion and Colorization* (SPIE Press, 2018).

42. U. Majumder, E. Blasch, D. Garren, *Deep Learning for Radar and Communications Automatic Target Recognition* (Artech House, Norwood, 2020)

43. J. Duník, O. Kost, O. Straka, E. Blasch, Covariance Estimation and Gaussianity Assessment for State and Measurement Noise. *AIAA Journal of Guidance, Control, and Dynamics***43**, No. 1, Jan (2020) DOI: https://doi.org/10.2514/1.G004348

44. S. Liu, H. Liu, V. John, Z. Liu, et al., Enhanced Situation Awareness through CNN-based Deep MultiModal Image Fusion. *Optical Engineering***59**(5): 053103, (April 2020) DOI: https://doi.org/10.1117/1.OE.59.5.053103

45. T. Mukherjee, P. Kumar, D. Pati, et al., LoSI: Large Scale Location Inference through FM Signal Integration and Estimation. *IEEE Big Data Mining and Analytics***2**(4): 319–348 (Dec 2019) DOI: 10.26599; BDMA.2019.9020013; ISSN 2096-0654.

46. D. Roy, T. Mukherjee, M. Chatterjee, et al., RFAL: Adversarial Learning for RF Transmitter Identification and Classification. *IEEE Transactions on Cognitive Communications and Networking* **6**(2):783–801, (2020) DOI: https://doi.org/10.1109/TCCN.2019.2948919
47. L. Snidaro, J. Garcia, et al., Recent Trends in Context Exploitation for Information Fusion and AI. *AI Magazine* **40**(3):14–27, (Fall 2019)
48. D. Shen, E. Blasch, K. D. Pham, G. Chen, Computer vision and pursuit-evasion game theoretical controls for ground robots. *Adv. in Mechanical Eng.*, **11**(8):1–15 (2019) https://journals.sagepub.com/doi/10.1177/1687814019872911
49. J. Liu, H. Mu, A. Vakil, R. Ewing, et al., Human Occupancy Detection via Passive Cognitive Radio. *Sensors* **20**, 4248 (2020). doi:https://doi.org/10.3390/s20154248
50. S. Y. Nikoueia, Y. Chen, A. Aved, E. Blasch, I-ViSE: Interactive Video Surveillance as an Edge Service using Unsupervised Feature Queries. *IEEE Internet of Things Journal*, Sept, (2020).
51. E. Blasch, G. Seetharaman, K. Reinhardt, Dynamic data driven applications system concept for information fusion. Procedia Comput. Sci. **18**, 1999–2007 (2013)
52. H. Ling, L. Bai et al., Robust infrared vehicle tracking across object pose change using L1 regularization, *International Conference on Information* Fusion, (2010)
53. E. Blasch, Z. Wang, H. Ling, et al., Video-based activity analysis using the L1 tracker on VIRAT data, IEEE Applied Imagery Pattern Recognition Workshop, (2013)
54. G. Chen, D. Shen, C. Kwan, et al., Game theoretic approach to threat prediction and situation awareness. J. Adv. Inf. Fusion **2**(1), 1–14 (2007)
55. E. Blasch, Sensor, user, mission (SUM) resource management and their interaction with level 2/3 fusion, in *International Conference on Information Fusion*, (2006)
56. E. Blasch, A. Steinberg, S. Das, J. Llinas, et al., Revisiting the JDL model for information exploitation, in *International Conference on Information Fusion*, (2013)
57. E.P. Blasch, S.K. Rogers, H. Holloway, J. Tierno, E.K. Jones, R.I. Hammoud, QuEST for information fusion in multimedia reports. Int. J. Monit. Surveill. Technol. Res. **2**(3), 1–30 (2014)
58. G. Klein, B. Moon, R. Hoffman, Making sense of sensemaking 1: Alternative perspectives. IEEE Intell. Syst. **21**(4), 70–73 (2006)
59. L. A. Hendricks, S. Venugopalan, et al., Deep compositional captioning: Describing novel object categories without paired training data, arXiv:1511.05284 [cs.CV], Nov. (2015)
60. S.J. Pan, Q. Yang, Survey on transfer learning. IEEE Trans. Knowl. Data Eng. **22**(10), 1345–1359 (2009)
61. Department of Defense Science Board, The role of autonomy in DoD systems, July, (2012)
62. R.I. Hammoud, C.S. Sahin et al., Automatic Association of Chats and Video Tracks for Activity Learning and Recognition in Aerial Video Surveillance, Sensors **14**, 19843–19860 (2014)
63. E. Blasch, Decisions-to-data using level 5 information fusion, in *Proceedings of SPIE*, vol. 9079 (2014)
64. B. Kahler, E. Blasch, Sensor management fusion using operating conditions, in *Proceedings of IEEE National Aerospace Electronics Conference (NAECON)* (2008)
65. M. Flickner, H. Sawhney,W. Niblack, J. Ashley, Q. Huang, et al., Query by image and video content: The QBIC system. Computer **28**, 23–32 (1995)
66. S.F. Chang, A. Eleftheriadis, R. McClintock, Next-generation content representation, creation, and searching for new-media applications in education. Proc. IEEE **86**, 884–904 (1998)
67. Y. Jianfeng, Z. Yang, L. Zhanhuai, A multimedia document database model based on multilayered description supporting complex multimedia structural and semantic contents, in *Proc. of the Int'l Multimedia Modelling Conf,* (2004) pp. 33–39
68. J.D.N. Dionisio, A.F. Cárdenas, A unified data model for representing multimedia, timeline, and simulation data. IEEE Trans. Knowl. Data Eng. **10**(5), 746–767 (1998)
69. A. Yoshitaka, T. Ichikawa, A survey on content-based retrieval for multimedia databases. IEEE Trans. Knowl. Data Eng. **11**(1), 81–93 (1999)
70. C. Shen, S. Wu, N. Sane, et al., Design and synthesis for multimedia systems using the objected dataflow interchange format. IEEE Trans. Multimedia **14**(3), 630–640 (2012)

71. S.S. Bhattacharyya, E. Deprettere, R. Leupers, J. Takala (eds.), *Handbook of Signal Processing Systems*, 2nd edn, (Springer, 2013). ISBN: 978-1-4614-6858-5 (Print); 978-1-4614-6859-2 (Online)

72. E. Blasch, T. Connare, Improving track maintenance through group tracking, in *Proceedings of the Workshop on Estimation, Tracking, and Fusion; A Tribute to Yaakov Bar Shalom*, May (2001) pp. 360–371

73. H. Ling, Y. Wu et al., Evaluation of visual tracking in extremely low frame rate wide area motion imagery, in *International Conference on Information Fusion* (2011)

74. S.G. Alsing et al., Three-dimensional receiver operating characteristic (ROC) trajectory concepts for the evaluation of object recognition algorithms faced with the unknown object detection problem. Proc. SPIE **3718**, 449–458 (1999)

75. L. Snidaro, J. Garcia, et al. (eds.), *Context-Enhanced Information Fusion: Boosting Real-World Performance with Domain Knowledge*, Springer, (2016)

Part X
Systems-Aware: Design Methods

Chapter 29
Parzen Windows: Simplest Regularization Algorithm

Jing Peng and Peng Zhang

Abstract Nonparametric learning methods such as Parzen Windows have been applied to a variety of density estimation and classification problems. In this chapter we derive a "simplest" regularization algorithm and establish its close relationship with Parzen Windows. We derive the finite sample error bound for the "simplest" regularization algorithm. Because of the close relationship between the "simplest" algorithm and Parzen Windows, this analysis provides interesting insight to Parzen Windows from the view point of learning theory. Our work is a realization of the design principle of dynamic data driven applications system (DDDAS) introduced in Chapter 1. Finally, we provide empirical results on the performance of the "simplest" regularization algorithm (Parzen Windows) and other methods such as nearest neighbor classifiers, and the regularization algorithm on a number of real data sets. These results corroborate well our theoretical analysis.

Keywords Convergence · Parzen windows · Regularized least squares · Ridge regression · Weight decay

29.1 Introduction

Learning from examples, or supervised learning, refers to the task of constructing a predictive model from a set of training examples in the form of input-output pairs. The resulting model is used to predict the output value of a test input. Examples include regression, where output values are continuous, and classification, where output values are discrete. There are other learning paradigms such as clustering and reinforcement learning. This chapter focuses on supervised learning.

J. Peng (✉)
Montclair State University, Montclair, NJ, USA
e-mail: pengj@montclair.edu

P. Zhang
Allston Trading, Chicago, IL, USA

© The Author(s), under exclusive license to Springer Nature Switzerland AG 2022   671
E. P. Blasch et al. (eds.), *Handbook of Dynamic Data Driven Applications Systems*,
https://doi.org/10.1007/978-3-030-74568-4_29

It is argued that a good predictive model is the one that generalizes well over future unseen data [40]. In general, the problem is ill-posed [39, 40]. To mitigate the unknown data problem, one can build predictive models by exploiting ideas developed in regularization theory [39, 40]. That is, a predictive model can be constructed by simultaneously minimizing an empirical error on the sample data and controlling the complexity of the model. The most relevant to this work is the regularization algorithm described in [30], among others [14, 23, 24, 33, 35, 40, 46].

Other widely used techniques such as Parzen Windows and nearest neighbors however do not require optimization [7, 13, 15, 21, 28]. These techniques build a predictive model by estimating class conditional probabilities from the sample data, and then select the class having the maximum class probability. Parzen Windows and nearest neighbors have several attractive properties. For example, they produce continuous and overlapping, rather than fixed, neighborhoods and use a different neighborhood for each individual query so that all points in the neighborhood are close to the query. Furthermore, empirical evaluation shows that these methods are rather robust in a variety of classification problems [2, 11, 12, 16, 20, 21, 29].

Theoretically, it is known that in the asymptotic limit, the probability estimates by these methods converge to the true unknown probabilities [7, 15]. Thus, the classifier based on the estimated probabilities will converge to the optimal Bayes decision rule. Also, a well-known observation is that at least half of the classification information in an infinite data set resides in the nearest neighbor. However, when the training sample size is limited, little systematic work has been carried out on generalization performance. The known generalization performance for these methods are typically obtained empirically. While empirical analysis can be justified statistically, which only provides limited insights into algorithms' performance.

In this chapter, we address the problem implied by the above discussions by first deriving an algorithm that approximates the regularization algorithm (RA) proposed in [30]. The regularization algorithm requires matrix inversion, while our approximation does not. We call the resulting algorithm *Simplest Regularization* algorithm, denoted by SR. This is particularly useful for on-board processing, where resources are limited. Dynamic-data driven applications systems (DDDAS) approaches focus on the combination of modeling, measurements statistical analysis, and software. Successful applications of the DDDAS principle can be found in [1, 3–5]. By addressing the computational requirements such as reducing matrix inversions, using statistical analysis to reduce overfitting, and reporting for increasing classification accuracy; efficient approximate learning is proposed for robust performance, which is a realization of the design principle envisioned in DDDAS. We also establish an error bound for the SR method based on the error bound for the RA given finite samples. Finally we show that SR is closely related to Parzen Windows, thereby providing insight into the performance of the Parzen Windows classifier as well as nearest neighbor methods in finite settings. Thus, the Chapter contributions are:

1. Derive the simplest regularization algorithm and establishing its relation to Parzen Windows; and

2. Establish an error bound for the SR classifier and providing conditions under which the method may not perform well.

The rest of the chapter is organized as follows. Section 29.2 describes research related to this work. Section 29.3 introduces the regularization learning algorithm, and the corresponding error analysis. Section 29.4 derives the simplest regularization algorithm based on the analysis of the learning algorithm described in Sect. 29.4. Section 29.5 introduces our main result: finite sample error bound for the simplest regularization algorithm. Section 29.6 analyses the tradeoff between approximation and sample errors in terms of regularization constant. Section 29.7 discusses computational complexity of the proposed technique. Section 29.8 demonstrates a close relationship between the simplest regularization algorithm and Parzen Windows, thereby providing insights into characteristics of Parzen Windows classifiers. Section 29.9 provides experimental results that validate our theoretical analysis. Finally, Sect. 29.10 summaries our contributions and points out future research directions.

29.2 Related Work

Work in statistical learning theory [9, 40] provides a framework for analyzing error bounds for predictive models given a finite sample data set. The error bound for such a model usually contains two parts: the approximation error (bias), and the sample error (variance). While a general approximation error bound is established [9, 30, 34], these bounds are infinite, unless the smoothness of the regression function f_ρ (see below) matches the smoothness of the chosen kernel.

The regularized least squares methods has been studied for a long time, under different names. In statistics, ridge regression [18] has been very popular for solving badly conditioned linear regression problems. After Tikhonov published his book [39], it was realized that ridge regression uses the regularization term in Tikhonov's sense. In the 1980s, weight decay was proposed to help prune unimportant neural network connections, and was soon recognized that weight decay is equivalent to ridge regression [17].

In [27], the relationship was established between kernel principal component analysis and spectral cut-off regularization. It was shown that the regularization parameter in spectral cut-off analysis represents exactly the number of principal components to retain for kernel principal component analysis.

A generalized regularized least squares algorithm was proposed in [23]. In this algorithm, regularization is restricted to part of the input space. The rationale is that in a well defined part of the input space, regularization is unnecessary. Experimental results showed that the algorithm is effective.

Recently, regularization is applied to penalize solutions away from a predefined subspace [45]. The motivation is that searching for a solution in a predefined subspace may result in loss of discriminant information. Allowing search to take place in the original space increases the flexibility of resulting solutions. A potential drawback is an increase in computation.

More recently, potential function rules are investigated extensively in a very closely related work [37]. It is shown that under appropriate conditions potential function rules are equivalent to the Bayes decision rule. It introduces classifiers based on potential functions and establishes generalization performance on these classifiers. For a given input, the class potential measures on average how close the input is to examples in that class. The measure in many ways is quite similar to the nearest neighbor rule, where each neighborhood is the entire class. When classifiers based on potential functions are estimated from training data, they are closely related to the approximate regularized least squares algorithm proposed in this chapter. Also, experimental results show very competitive performance registered by potential function classifiers.

We note that the concept of margin is also closely related to regularization, that is, the larger the margin, the less complex a classifier, resulting in better generalization [22, 31, 41, 44]. Various large margin learning algorithms have been developed that show very competitive performance [6, 11, 19, 25, 32, 38, 43]. We focus on regularized least squares algorithms in this chapter.

29.3   Regularized Least Squares Method

In the framework of statistical learning theory, regularized least squares methods have been revisited in [30], and discussed in [14] as regularization networks. Most recently, error bounds for these techniques given a finite sample data set were developed in [10]. Here we briefly summarize the theory.

Let X be a compact domain in Euclidean space and $Y = \mathbb{R}$. Also let

$$z = \{(x_1, y_1), \cdots, (x_m, y_m)\} \tag{29.1}$$

be a set of m training examples drawn from $X \times Y$ according to a (unknown) probability measure ρ on $X \times Y$.

The regularization algorithm minimizes the following regularized functional:

$$\frac{1}{m} \sum_{i=1}^{m} (y_i - f(x_i))^2 + \lambda \|f\|_k^2, \tag{29.2}$$

where λ is the regularization parameter, and $\|f\|_k^2$ the norm in the hypothesis space $\mathcal{H}_k$ induced by the kernel function k. A variety of kernel functions can be used. In this work, we focus on the Gaussian kernel

$$k(x, x') = e^{-\frac{\|x - x'\|^2}{\sigma^2}}, \tag{29.3}$$

where σ denotes the kernel width parameter.

It is shown that the minimizer of Eq. (29.2) exists [30]. Furthermore, the minimizer is unique and given by

$$f_{RA}(x) = \sum_{i=1}^{m} c_i k(x, x_i),$$ (29.4)

where the coefficients c_is can be computed by solving the following key system of linear equations

$$(\lambda m I + K)c = y,$$ (29.5)

where $K_{ij} = k(x_i, x_j)$ is the kernel matrix. Matrix $(\lambda m I + K)$ should possess a good condition number. Thus, there should be no numerical problem in computing $(\lambda m I + K)^{-1}$.

Let f_ρ be the true input-output function defined by $f_\rho(x) = \int_Y d\rho(y|x)$, where $\rho(y|x)$ is the conditional probability measure on Y [9, 30]. It is shown that [9, 30]

$$\int (f_{RA} - f_\rho)^2 d\rho_X \leq A(\lambda) + S(\lambda),$$ (29.6)

where ρ_X is the marginal probability measure on X,

$$A(\lambda) = \lambda^{1/2} \| L_k^{-\frac{1}{4}} f_\rho \|^2$$ (29.7)

represents the approximation error in this context, and

$$S(\lambda) = \frac{32 M^2 (\lambda + C_k)^2}{\lambda^2} v^*(m, \delta)$$ (29.8)

represents the sample error. Here L_k is an operator defined as

$$L_k f(x) = \int_X f(x') k(x, x') d\rho_X.$$ (29.9)

Note that the Gaussian kernel (29.3) is generally a smooth function, and the eigenvalues of L_k decay exponentially fast. This requires the target function f_ρ to be smooth as well. Otherwise, $A(\lambda)$, as defined in (29.7), may be infinite.

In (29.8), M is a positive constant, which is chosen to satisfy $|f(x) - y| \leq M$, and $v^*(m, \delta)$ is the unique solution of $\frac{m}{4} v^3 - \ln(\frac{4m}{\delta})v - c_v = 0$, where $c_v > 0$ is a constant. C_k is defined by:

$$C_k = \max\{1, \sup_{x,t \in X} |k(x, t)|\},$$ (29.10)

where $k(x, t)$ is a kernel function, and for the Gaussian kernel, $C_k = 1$.

More recently, an improved error analysis has been proposed based on Shannon sampling [34]. Sharper bounds are obtained using McDiarmid inequalities [26, 42] and by replacing covering number arguments by integral operator estimates. While these improved bounds can applied to both L^2 and reproducing kernel Hilbert spaces, the major shortcoming remains, as we shall see later.

Finding the optimal solution of the RA is equivalent to finding the best tradeoff between $A(\lambda)$ and $S(\lambda)$ for given training data. That is, to minimize $S(\lambda) + A(\lambda)$ over $\lambda > 0$. There is a unique solution – a best λ choice in theory [10]. In real applications, we usually find λ values through cross-validation.

29.4 Approximate Regularized Least Squares

In this section we derive our simplest regularization algorithm. In the discussion, we use the ∞-norm for both matrices and vectors. Also for the sake of simplicity, we use the notation $\| \cdot \|$ to represent the ∞-norm in the following discussion. This norm, however, should not be confused with the norm used in the previous sections.

Lemma 1 *Let $B = K - I$, where K is the kernel matrix $K_{ij} = k(x_i, x_j)$, k is the Gaussian kernel (29.3), and I is the identity matrix of proper size. If*

$$\lambda > \frac{\|B\| - 1}{m}, \tag{29.11}$$

we have

$$(K + \lambda m I)^{-1} = \sum_{i=0}^{\infty} (-1)^i d^{-i-1} B^i,$$

where $d = 1 + \lambda m$.

Proof

$$\|d^{-1}B\| = d^{-1}\|B\| = \frac{\|B\|}{(1 + \lambda m)} < \frac{\|B\|}{(1 + \|B\| - 1)} = 1.$$

Using $B = K - I$, we can write $(K + \lambda m I) = dI + B = d(I + d^{-1}B)$. We have that $(K + \lambda m I)^{-1} = d^{-1}(I + d^{-1}B)^{-1}$. When $\|d^{-1}B\| < 1$, it follows that (the Neumann series) $(I + d^{-1}B)^{-1} = \sum_{i=0}^{\infty}(-1)^i d^{-i} B^i$. Thus, $(\lambda m I + K)^{-1} = \sum_{i=0}^{\infty}(-1)^i d^{-i-1} B^i$. □

Let

$$\hat{c} = d^{-1}y. \tag{29.12}$$

We arrive at the simplest regularization algorithm, or SR:

$$f_{SR}(x) = \sum_i \hat{c}_i k(x_i, x) = \frac{1}{d}(\sum_i y_i k(x_i, x)). \tag{29.13}$$

Note that λ is a decreasing function of m. This follows from that the fact as the number of samples m goes infinity, σ in Eq. (29.3) goes to zero. This implies that K approaches I. Therefore, $\|B\|$ approaches zero.

Notice that SR (Eq. (29.13)) is closely related to potential function classifiers investigated in [37]. For simplicity, we focus on the two class problem, where $y \in \{-1, 1\}$. In particular, if we treat $k(x, x')$ (Eq. 29.3) as a Gaussian point potential function, we can write the sample class potential function as $\phi_y(x) = \frac{1}{m}\sum_{y_i=y} k(x_i, x)$, where $y \in \{-1, +1\}$ [37]. This allows us to rewrite SR (Eq. 29.13) as $f_{SR}(x) = \frac{1}{d}\{\phi_{+1}(x) + \phi_{-1}(x)\}$. Therefore, instead of determining the sample class potential function classifier according to $f_Z(x) = \arg\max_y \phi_y(x)$, the sample class potential function classifier can be computed as $f_Z(x) = sign(f_{SR}(x))$, where $1 = sign(x)$ if $x > 0$, and $-1 = sign(x)$ if $x < 0$. Since potential function classifiers demonstrate very competitive performance on a number of problems [37], this connection shows the strength and applicability of SR.

Let $c = (\lambda m I + K)^{-1} y$. We now ask: How well does our $\hat{c}$ approximate c? From Lemma 1 we have that $(\lambda m I + K)^{-1} = d^{-1}(I - d^{-1}B + d^{-2}B^2 + \cdots)$. Let

$$E = (I - d^{-1}B + d^{-2}B^2 + \cdots). \tag{29.14}$$

Then

$$c = d^{-1}Ey. \tag{29.15}$$

We can now establish a upper bound for the approximation error $\|c - \hat{c}\|$.

Lemma 2 *Let c and $\hat{c}$ as in (29.15) and (29.12), respectively. Then*

$$\|c - \hat{c}\| \leq \frac{\|B\|}{d(d - \|B\|)},$$

where $d = 1 + \lambda m$ and $B = K - I$.

Proof From Eqs. (29.12), (29.14) and (29.15) we have

$$c - \hat{c} = -d^{-2}By + d^{-3}B^2y - d^{-4}B^3y + \cdots.$$

Then, observing that $\|y\| = 1$ (since $y \in \{-1, +1\}$), $\|c - \hat{c}\| \leq \frac{\|B\|}{d^2}(1 + \|d^{-1}B\| + \|d^{-2}B^2\| + \cdots)$. Since $\frac{\|B\|}{d} < 1$, it follows that $1 + \|d^{-1}B\| + \|d^{-2}B^2\| + \cdots \leq \frac{d}{d-\|B\|}$. Therefore, $\|c - \hat{c}\| \leq \frac{\|B\|}{d^2} \frac{d}{d-\|B\|} = \frac{\|B\|}{d(d-\|B\|)}$.   □

29.5   Error Bound for SR

We now establish the error bound for the approximate regularization function f_{SR} in (29.13). We split the error for f_{SR} into two parts. The first part is the error between f_{SR} and RA f_{RA}. The second part is the error between f_{RA} and the true target f_ρ. By combining these two terms we obtain the error bound for SR.

Lemma 3 Let $\lambda > \frac{\|B\|-1}{m}$. Then

$$\int_X (f_{SR} - f_\rho)^2 d\rho_X \leq 2(D(\lambda) + S(\lambda) + A(\lambda)), \tag{29.16}$$

where

$$D(\lambda) = \frac{\|B\|^2}{\lambda^2(\lambda m + 1 - \|.B\|)^2}, \tag{29.17}$$

Here $S(\lambda)$ and $A(\lambda)$ are given by (29.8) and (29.7).

Proof First we prove: $\int_X (f_{SR} - f_{RA})^2 d\rho_X \leq D(\lambda) = \frac{\|B\|^2}{\lambda^2(\lambda m + 1 - \|B\|)^2}$. From (29.4) and (29.13), we have that

$$\int_X (f_{SR} - f_{RA})^2 d\rho_X = \int_X (\sum_{i=1}^m (c_i - \hat{c}_i)k(x_i, .))^2 d\rho_X \tag{29.18}$$

$$\leq \max_x |\sum_{i=1}^m \frac{\|B\|}{d(d-\|B\|)} k(x_i, .)|^2 \tag{29.19}$$

$$\leq \frac{\|B\|^2}{\lambda^2(\lambda m + 1 - \|B\|)^2}. \tag{29.20}$$

Thus $\int_X (f_{SR} - f_\rho)^2 d\rho_X \leq 2(D(\lambda) + A(\lambda) + S(\lambda))$. $\square$

To have a better understanding of $D(\lambda)$, we state the following lemma.

Lemma 4 (Corollary 5 of [34]) Let the training data z (29.1) be randomly drawn according to ρ. If f_ρ is in the range of L_k (29.9), then for any $0 < \delta < 1$, with confidence $1 - \delta$ we have that

$$\|f_{RA} - f_\rho\|_\rho \leq \tilde{C}(\frac{\log(4/\delta)^2}{m})^{1/4} \tag{29.21}$$

by taking

$$\lambda = (\frac{\log(4/\delta)^2}{m})^{1/4}. \tag{29.22}$$

Here $\|\cdot\|_\rho$ is the norm induced by the inner product $\langle f, g\rangle_{\rho_X} = \int_X f(x)g(x)d\rho_X$, and $\tilde{C}$ is a constant independent of the dimension $\tilde{C} = 30\kappa M + 2\kappa^2 M + \|L_k^{-1} f_\rho\|_\rho$. Here $\kappa = \sqrt{\sup_{x \in X} k(x, x)}$.

Note that for the choice of the Gaussian kernel (29.3), $\kappa = 1$. Thus, $\tilde{C}$ reduces to $\tilde{C} = 32M + \|L_k^{-1} f_\rho\|_\rho$.

For the choice of λ (29.22), we see that $\lambda = (\log(4/\delta)^2)^{1/4} m^{-1/4} = C_\delta m^{-1/4}$, where C_δ is a constant for a given δ. This also implies that $\lambda m^{1/4} = (\log(4/\delta)^2)^{1/4} = C_\delta$. Therefore, λm has the following growth rate

$$\lambda m = C_\delta m^{3/4} = \mathcal{O}(m^{3/4}). \tag{29.23}$$

From (29.17) and (29.23), we have that $\lambda^2 (\lambda m + 1 - \|B\|)^2 = C_\delta^4 m (1 - \frac{\|B\|-1}{C_\delta m^{3/4}})^2$. It is clear that $1 - \frac{\|B\|-1}{C_\delta m^{3/4}} \to 1$, as $m \to \infty$. Also, as discussed earlier, $\|B\|$ approaches zero as m goes to infinity. It follows that

$$D(\lambda) = \mathcal{O}(1/m). \tag{29.24}$$

That is, $D(\lambda)$ goes to zero at the rate of $\mathcal{O}(1/m)$. We note that condition $\lambda > \frac{\|B\|-1}{m}$ is guaranteed by condition (29.22).

29.6 Bias, Variance and Regularization Constant

In this section, we further examine the error bound (29.6) and regularization constant λ, where approximation error $A(\lambda)$ (29.7) corresponds to bias, and sample error $S(\lambda)$ (29.8) corresponds to variance.

29.6.1 Regularization Constant

The error bound is a function of regularization constant λ, training data size m, indirectly the kernel function k (affecting $v^*(m, \delta)$), and M. Notice that M is a positive constant that is chosen to satisfy $|f(x) - y| \leq M$, while C_k is determined by the kernel function. For the Gaussian kernel it is 1, as we showed before (29.10). Here we consider that we are given a fixed training data size m and the kernel function k. The error bound becomes a function of λ only. We will minimize the regularization error bound $S(\lambda) + A(\lambda)$ for $\lambda > 0$.

In order to achieve the minimum of $S(\lambda) + A(\lambda)$, it is necessary that $-S'(\lambda) = A'(\lambda)$. Taking derivatives with respect to λ, we obtain that $A(\lambda) = \lambda^{1/2} \|L_k^{-\frac{1}{4}} f_\rho\|^2$, and $A''(\lambda) = -\frac{1}{4} \lambda^{-3/2} \|L_k^{-\frac{1}{4}} f_\rho\|^2$. Similarly, we have $S(\lambda) = \frac{32M^2(\lambda + C_k)^2}{\lambda^2} v^*(m, \delta)$, and $-S''(\lambda) = -64M^2 (\frac{2C_k}{\lambda^3} + \frac{3C_k^2}{\lambda^4}) v^*(m, \delta)$.

Since $\|L_k^{-\frac{1}{4}} f_\rho\|^2 > 0$ and $v^*(m, \delta) > 0$, both $A(\lambda)$ and $S(\lambda)$ are positive functions. $A(\lambda)$ is strictly increasing in $(0, +\infty)$, while $S(\lambda)$ is strictly decreasing in $(0, +\infty)$ and converges to a positive constant $32M^2v^*(m, \delta)$. Furthermore, $A'(\lambda)$ is a positive function strictly decreasing in $(0, +\infty)$, while $-S'(\lambda)$ is a positive function monotonically decreasing in $(0, +\infty)$. The question becomes: is there a unique $\lambda^* > 0$ such that

$$- S'(\lambda^*) = A'(\lambda^*). \tag{29.25}$$

Let the left hand side of (29.25) be: $L(\lambda) = -S'(\lambda)$. Also, let the right hand side be: $R(\lambda) = A'(\lambda)$. Notice that both $L(\lambda)$ and $R(\lambda)$ are monotonically decreasing functions. Now consider $\lambda R(\lambda) = \lambda A'(\lambda) = \frac{1}{2}\lambda^{1/2}\|L_k^{-\frac{1}{4}} f_\rho\|^2$, and $\lambda L(\lambda) = -\lambda S'(\lambda) = 64M^2(\frac{C_k}{\lambda} + \frac{C_k^2}{\lambda^2})v^*(m, \delta)$. Clearly, $\lambda R(\lambda)$ is a monotonically increasing positive function in $(0, +\infty)$, and $\lim_{\lambda \to 0^+} .\lambda R(\lambda) = 0^+$.

On the other hand, $\lambda L(\lambda)$ decreases monotonically in $(0, +\infty)$, and $\lambda L(\lambda)$ approaches $+\infty$ as λ approaches 0. Thus, there must be a unique solution $\lambda^* > 0$ such that $\lambda^* L(\lambda^*) = \lambda^* R(\lambda^*)$. It follows that if $L(\lambda) = R(\lambda)$ has more than one distinct solutions in $(0, +\infty)$, so does $\lambda L(\lambda) = \lambda R(\lambda)$. That contradicts the fact that there is a unique λ such that $\lambda L(\lambda) = \lambda R(\lambda)$. Therefore, $L(\lambda) = R(\lambda)$ must have a unique solution. That is, there is a unique λ^* in $(0, +\infty)$ such that $A'(\lambda^*) = -S'(\lambda^*)$.

Figure 29.1 shows the relationship between $A(\lambda)$ and $S(\lambda)$ in order to achieve the minimum of $A(\lambda) + S(\lambda)$. It can be seen that the minimum is attained at λ^* when the optimal tradeoff between bias and variance is achieved.

Fig. 29.1 Regularization error bound: Minimum is attained when optimal tradeoff between sample error and approximation error is achieved

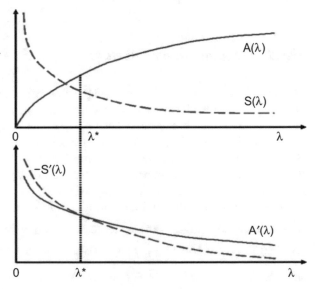

29.6.2   Regularization Constant and Simplest Regularization

A similar argument can be made about the bias and variance tradeoff for SR. Consider $D(\lambda)$ (29.17). The first term of the upper bound for the SR classifier (29.16). Taking derivatives of $D(\lambda)$ with respect to λ, we have that $D(\lambda) = \|B\|^2/(\lambda^2(\lambda m + 1 - \|B\|)^2)$, $-D'(\lambda) = (2\|B\|^2)/(\lambda^3(\lambda m + 1 - \|B\|)^2) + (2\|B\|^2 m)/(\lambda^2(\lambda m + 1 - \|B\|)^3)$, and $-D''(\lambda) = -(6\|B\|^2)/(\lambda^4(\lambda m - 1 + \|B\|)^2) - (8\|B\|^2 m)/(\lambda^3(\lambda m + 1 - \|B\|)^3) - (6\|B\|^2 m^2)/(\lambda^2(\lambda m + 1 - \|B\|)^4)$.

Notice that λ can not be chosen arbitrarily in $(0, +\infty)$ in the upper bound (29.16). Instead, it is only in the range $(\max\{\frac{\|B\|-1}{m}, 0\}, +\infty)$. It can be seen that $D(\lambda)$ is a positive function strictly decreasing in $(\max\{\frac{\|B\|-1}{m}, 0\}, +\infty)$. $-D'(\lambda)$ is positive function decreasing in $(\max\{\frac{\|B\|-1}{m}, 0\}, +\infty)$. We now show that there is a unique $\lambda^{\#} \in (\max\{\frac{\|B\|-1}{m}, 0\}, +\infty)$ such that

$$-2D'(\lambda^{\#}) - 2S'(\lambda^{\#}) = 2A'(\lambda^{\#}). \tag{29.26}$$

The analysis is very similar to the proof for RA. In this case, the left hand side of (29.26) is $L(\lambda) = -2D'(\lambda) - 2S'(\lambda)$, while the right hand side is $R(\lambda) = 2A'(\lambda)$. It follows that $\lambda L(\lambda)$ decreases monotonically in $(\max\{\frac{\|B\|-1}{m}, 0\}, +\infty)$. Therefore

$$\lim_{\lambda \to \max\{\frac{\|B\|-1}{m}, 0\}} \lambda L(\lambda) = +\infty. \tag{29.27}$$

Similarly, $\lambda R(\lambda) = \lambda A'(\lambda) = \frac{1}{2}\lambda^{1/2}\|L_k^{-\frac{1}{4}} f_\rho\|^2$. Thus, $\lambda R(\lambda)$ is a monotonically increasing positive function in $(0, +\infty)$, and

$$\lim_{\lambda \to 0^+} \lambda R(\lambda) = 0^+. \tag{29.28}$$

Combining (29.27) and (29.28), we obtain that there is a unique $\lambda^{\#}$ in $(\max\{\frac{\|B\|-1}{m}, 0\}, +\infty)$ such that $-2D'(\lambda^{\#}) - 2S'(\lambda^{\#}) = 2A'(\lambda^{\#})$.

It is important to note that λ is not a parameter of SR. When $\lambda > \frac{\|B\|-1}{m}$, SR is an approximation to RA and its error bound can be derived from that for RA. However, the error bound for SR does not depend on λ. We thus establish the following:

Theorem 1   *The error bound for SR is:*

$$\int_X (f_{SR} - f_\rho)^2 d\rho_X \leq 2(D(\lambda^{\#}) + A(\lambda^{\#}) + S(\lambda^{\#})), \tag{29.29}$$

where $D(\lambda)$, $A(\lambda)$, and $S(\lambda)$ are defined in (29.17), (29.7), and (29.8), respectively, and $\lambda^{\#}$ is the unique solution to $A'(\lambda) = -S'(\lambda) - D'(\lambda)$.

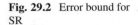

Fig. 29.2 Error bound for SR

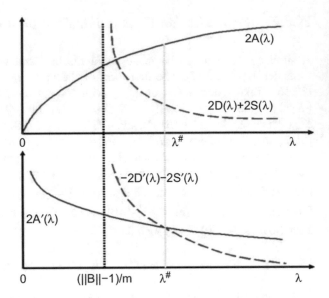

Compared to RA, the minimal point of the error bound for SR is pushed toward right. That is, the crossing between $2A'(\lambda)$ and $-2D'(\lambda) - 2S'(\lambda)$ is shifted to the right, as shown in Fig. 29.2. The error bound for SR is at least twice that for RA. In addition, optimal performance may require λ^* to be less than $\frac{(\|B\|-1)}{m}$, the barrier that the SR algorithm can not cross. As a consequence, the performance of the SR algorithm will be much worse than RA in such situations.

Figure 29.2 shows the error bound curves. It may be argued that the error bound for SR may not be as tight as the bound for RA. However, this is reasonable because SR, as a special case of RA, lacks the capacity to approximate complex functions, while RA has no such restrictions.

29.7 Computational Complexity

During training, f_{RA} (29.4) is computed by inverting matrix $(\lambda m I + K)$ to obtain the coefficients c_is (29.5). Computing $(\lambda m I + K)^{-1}$ requires $\mathcal{O}(m^{2.807})$ operations on a serial machine [36], where m represents the number of training examples. When m is large, inverting $(\lambda m I + K)$ becomes problematic in terms of space and time. On the other hand, no operation is required for SR during training. During testing, $\mathcal{O}(m)$ is required for both the regularization and the simplest regularization algorithms.

29.8   SR and Parzen Windows

Parzen Windows [13, 15, 28] is a technique for density estimation that can be used for classification. Using a kernel function, Parzen Windows approximate a given training data distribution via a linear combination of the kernels centered on the training points. Here, each class density is approximated separately and a test point is assigned to the class having maximal (estimated) class probability.

Given a training sample (Eq. 29.1), Parzen Windows can be defined as

$$f_{Parzen}(x) = \sum y_i k(x_i, x)$$ (29.30)

where $k()$ is a kernel function. For the binary case, the resulting Parzen Windows classifier is very simple

$$\tilde{f}_{Parzen}(x) = sign(\sum y_i k(x_i, x)).$$ (29.31)

Since multiplying $\tilde{f}_{Parzen}$ by any positive constant will not change it, one can see that in the binary classification case, approximate RA (29.13) and Parzen Windows behave the same. Thus Lemma 1 states that under appropriate conditions, the Parzen Windows classifier is an approximation to RA. Although the Parzen Windows classifier performs well asymptotically [13], it may fail to do so in applications with limited samples. Therefore, our analysis of approximate RA provides insight into the characteristics of Parzen Windows in a finite setting.

The Parzen Windows does not require any training and can be viewed as a generalization of k-nearest neighbor techniques. Rather than choosing the k nearest neighbors of a test point and labelling the test point with the majority of its neighbors' votes, one can consider all points in the voting scheme and assign their weight by the kernel function. With Gaussian kernels, the weight decreases exponentially with squared distance, so far away points are practically irrelevant. The width σ of the Gaussian kernel determines the relative weighting of near and far points. Tuning this parameter controls the predictive power of the system.

29.9   Experiments

We now examine the performance of SR and RA on a number of simulated and real examples.

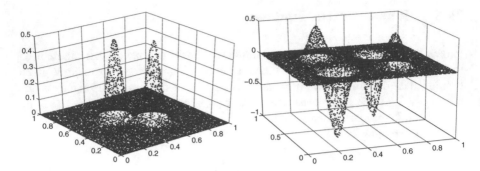

Fig. 29.3 Toy examples: left: two Gaussians f_2. right: four Gaussians f_4

29.9.1 Simulated Data Experiment

We use two simulated examples to illustrate the relationship between RA and SR. The function in the left panel in Fig. 29.3 is defined by

$$f_2(x) = 0.5 \sum_{i=1}^{2} \exp(-(x - \mu_i)^t \Sigma^{-1}(x - \mu_i)), \, x \tag{29.32}$$

where $\mu_1 = (0.4, 0.6)^t$, $\mu_2 = (0.6, 0.4)^t$, and $\Sigma = \begin{pmatrix} 0.005 & 0 \\ 0 & 0.005 \end{pmatrix}$. The function in the right panel in Fig. 29.3 is defined by

$$f_4(x) = 0.5 \sum_{i=1}^{2} \exp(-(x - \mu_i)^t \Sigma^{-1}(x - \mu_i)) - \sum_{i=3}^{4} \exp(-(x - \mu_i)^t \Sigma^{-1}(x - \mu_i)), \tag{29.33}$$

where $\mu_1 = (0.3, 0.7)^t$, $\mu_2 = (0.7, 0.3)^t$, $\mu_3 = (0.3, 0.3)^t$, $\mu_4 = (0.7, 0.3)^t$, and $\Sigma = \begin{pmatrix} 0.005 & 0 \\ 0 & 0.005 \end{pmatrix}$.

In both experiments, we varied the number of training examples from 500 to 2000, with 100 example increment. For each training example, (x, y), x was drawn uniformly randomly from $[0, 1]$, while y was determined according to $f_2(x)$ (29.32) in the first experiment, and $f_4(x)$ (29.33) in the second experiment, respectively. For each training set, 2000 test examples were generated independently from $[0, 1]^2$.

There are two procedural parameters, σ (29.3) and λ (29.5). σ is common to both RA and SR, and was set 0.1 throughout the experiments. For RA, λ was fixed to 0.01 throughout. For SR, since $\lambda > \frac{\|B\|-1}{m}$, $d = 1 + \lambda m > \|B\|$. We thus set d to $\|B\| + 0.1$ in (29.13). Note that in this case, d was not fixed. Rather, d depended on the value of $\|B\|$.

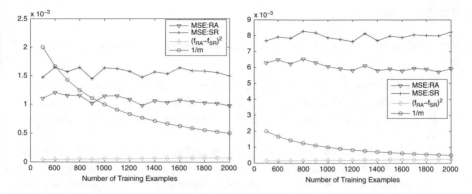

Fig. 29.4 Mean squared errors of RA and SR, mean squared difference between RA and SR, and $\frac{1}{m}$ as a function of the number of training examples averaged over 50 runs on two Gaussians (left), and four Gaussians (right)

Figure 29.4 shows the mean squared errors of both RA and SR, the mean squared difference between RA and SR, and $\frac{1}{m}$ as a function of the number of training examples averaged over 50 runs on the two toy examples. The results show that both RA and SR performed better on the two Gaussian function f_2 (29.32). In both cases, the mean squared difference between f_{SR} and f_{RA}, i.e., $D(\lambda)$ is bounded by $\mathcal{O}(\frac{1}{m})$, which corroborates well with our theoretical analysis, characterized in (29.24).

29.9.2 Real Data Experiment

29.9.2.1 Methods

The following methods are evaluated in the real data experiment.

- SR–Simplest regularization algorithm proposed in this chapter (29.13).
- RA–Regularization algorithm (29.5).
- SVMs–Support Vector Machines with the Gaussian kernel [8].
- 3NN–Three nearest neighbor method. We included this method, because as we discussed before, the Parzen Windows classifier can be viewed a generalization of the nearest neighbor classifier.

For the SR (Parzen Windows) classifier, there is only one parameter to tune: σ of the Gaussian kernel. That is, d in (29.13) does not influence classification performance. For the RA, there are two parameters to tune: σ and λ. For SVMs, there are also two parameters to tune: σ and C (which controls the softness of the margin [8]). These parameters are chosen by ten-fold cross-validation.

29.9.2.2   Data Sets

The following two class problems are used to evaluate the four competing methods.

1. Sonar data (**Sonar**). This data set consists of $n = 60$ frequency measurements made on each of 208 data of $J = 2$ classes ("mines" and "rocks"). The problem is to classify each test point in the 60-dimensional feature space to its correct class.
2. Glass Identification data (**Glass**). The data set has $n = 9$ continuous numerical features describing each of 214 instances in two classes: Window vs non-Window glasses. The objective is to assign the class label to each test instance.
3. Credit Approval data (**Credit**). There are 690 examples and two classes in this data set. Each example is represented by 15 features. The features are a mix of continuous, nominal with small numbers of values, and nominal with larger numbers of values. There are 307 instances in one class, and 383 in the other class.
4. Heart disease diagnosis data (**Heart Cleve**). This data set consists of 303 instances in two classes (There are five original classes. However, we regrouped these five classes into two.) Each of these instances is represented by 13 numerical attributes. The data was collected at Cleveland Clinic Foundation. The goal is to predict the presence of heart disease in the patient.
5. Heart disease diagnosis data (**Heart Hungary**). Similar to **Heart Cleve**, this data set consists of 294 instances represented by 13 numerical attributes. The data was collected at Hungarian Institute of Cardiology, Budapest. The objective is to predict whether a patient has heart disease.
6. Iris data (**Iris**). This data set consists of $n = 4$ measurements made on each of 100 iris plants of $J = 2$ species. The two species are iris versicolor and iris virginica. The problem is to classify each test point to its correct species based on the four measurements.
7. Ionosphere data (**Ionosphere**). The data consists of 34 electromagnetic features that are used to determine "good" or "bad" ($J = 2$) radar returns characterizing evidence of some type of structure in the ionosphere. The data set of 351 instances.
8. Thyroid Gland data (**New thyroid**). Five ($n = 5$) lab tests are used to predict whether a patient's thyroid is normal or hypo and hyper functioning (two classes). All five attributes are continuous. There are total 215 instances, of which 150 are in the normal class, while the remaining ones (65) are in the hypo and hyper class.
9. Letter data (**Letters**). This data set consists of a large number of black-and-white rectangular pixel arrays as one of the 26 upper-case letters in the English alphabet. Each letter is randomly distorted through a quadratic transformation to produce a set of 20,000 unique letter images that are then converted into $q = 16$ primitive numerical features. For this experiment we select letters "U"

and "W", where there are 813 "U" instances and 752 "W" instances. Thus, the data set consists of 1565 letter images.

10. Pima Indians Diabete data (**Pima**). This data set consists of $n = 8$ numerical attributes measured for each of 768 samples of $J = 2$ classes. The problem is to classify each test point in the 8-dimensional space to its correct class.

11. Breast cancer data (**Breast cancer**). The data consists of 9 medical input attributes that are used to make a binary decision on the medical condition: determining whether the cancer is recurring (recurrence vs no-recurrence). The data set has 286 instances, of which 201 are in the no-recurrence class, while the remaining 85 are in the recurrence class.

12. Wisconsin breast cancer data (**Cancer Wisconsin**). The data consists of 9 medical input features that are used to make a binary decision on the medical condition: determining whether the cancer is malignant or benign. The data set consists of 683 instances after removing missing values.

13. Central Nervous System data (**Cns**). This problem is about predicting patient outcome for central nervous system embryonal tumor. It consists of patients who are alive after treatment while the failures are those who succumbed to their disease. The data set contains 60 patient samples, 21 are survivors (class 1) and 39 are failures (class 2). There are $q = 7129$ genes (features) in the dataset.

14. Colon data (**Colon**). This dataset is similar to the yeast data. It contains expression levels of $q = 2000$ genes taken in 62 different samples. For each example it is indicated whether it came from a tumor biopsy or not (two classes).

15. Leukemia data (**Leuk**). The leukemia dataset is a collection of leukemia patient samples. This dataset often serves as benchmark for microarray analysis methods. It contains measurements corresponding to acute lymphoblast leukemia (ALL) and acute myeloid leukemia (AML) samples from bone marrow and peripheral blood. The dataset consisted of 72 samples: 25 samples of AML, and 47 samples of ALL. Each sample is measured over 7,129 genes.

16. Reuturs-21578 data (**Op**). The Reuters-21758 corpus contains Reuters news articles from 1987. It has hierarchical structures. The task is to classify the top-category documents. For this experiment, we use two top categories (Organizations or class 1 and People or class 2). There are 1,175 examples in class 1 and 1,270 examples in class 2. Each example is described by $q = 1000$ numerical features.

17. Reuturs-21578 data (**Opl**). The Reuters-21758 corpus contains Reuters news articles from 1987. Similar to the **Op** data set, the task is to classify the top-category documents. For this experiment, we use two top categories (Organizations or class 1 and Places or class 2). There are 1,175 examples in class 1 and 884 examples in class 2. Each example is described by $q = 1000$ numerical features.

18. Cat and Dog data (**CatDog**). This image data set consists of two hundred images of cat and dog faces. Each image is a black-and-white 64×64 pixel image, and the images have been registered by aligning the eyes.

29.9.2.3 Experimental Results

Each data set was randomly split into 60% training and 40% testing. We repeated this process 30 times to obtain average error rates. All training data had been normalized to have zero mean and unit variance along each variable. The test data were similarly normalized using training mean and variance. Table 29.1 shows the average error rates of the four competing methods over 30 runs on the 18 data sets described above.

Columns RA-3NN and RA-SR in the table show the difference in performance between RA and 3NN, and between RA and SR, respectively, using the paired-sample t-test. 1 indicates the difference is significant at the 95% confidence level, while 0 indicates the difference is insignificant. Out of the 18 data sets, the simplest regularization algorithm registered similar performance to that of the regularization algorithm on 10. They performed differently on the remaining data sets. A closer look at these data sets shows that the average λ values chosen (through cross-validation) by RA were less than 0.019. On the other hand, the average values of $\frac{\|B\|-1}{m}$ were at least 0.608. Recall that, SR (Parzen Windows), as an approximation to RA, only approximates RA when the value of λ is greater than $\frac{\|B\|-1}{m}$ (29.11).

Table 29.1 Error rates of the competing methods: 3NN, SR (Parzen), RA and SVMs on the 18 data sets averaged over 30 runs. Columns RA-3NN and *RA-SR* show performance difference between RA, 3NN, and SR, respectively, using paired t-test: 1 significant and 0 otherwise. Average λ values chosen by RA and average $(\|B\| - 1)/m$ values are also shown

	3NN	SR (Parzen)	RA	SVMs	RA-3NN	RA-SR	λ	$\frac{\|B\|-1}{m}$
Sonar	0.200	0.167	0.165	0.203	1	0	0.008	0.153
Glass	0.074	0.065	0.063	0.065	1	0	0.008	0.324
Credit	0.155	0.158	0.138	0.139	1	1	0.023	0.632
Heart-c	0.178	0.171	0.171	0.168	0	0	0.218	0.634
Heart-h	0.201	0.200	0.191	0.184	1	1	0.069	0.592
Iris	0.059	0.074	0.053	0.073	0	1	0.008	0.683
Ionosphere	0.156	0.132	0.100	0.052	1	1	0.005	0.583
Thyoid	0.065	0.052	0.050	0.046	1	0	0.022	0.186
Letter	0.004	0.005	0.004	0.005	0	0	0.005	0.009
Pima	0.275	0.260	0.231	0.253	1	1	0.007	0.753
Cancer-w	0.035	0.039	0.033	0.034	0	1	0.013	0.568
Cancer	0.315	0.280	0.274	0.296	1	0	0.710	0.433
Cns	0.422	0.390	0.388	0.356	0	0	0.005	0.024
Colon	0.457	0.389	0.381	0.353	1	0	0.005	0.019
Leuk	0.413	0.339	0.339	0.353	1	0	0.005	0.021
Op	0.470	0.464	0.432	0.432	1	1	0.022	0.450
Opl	0.488	0.425	0.420	0.415	1	0	0.031	0.364
CatDog	0.416	0.395	0.188	0.118	1	1	0.005	0.600
AVE	0.244	0.223	0.201	0.197				

Table 29.2 Performance of RA on the data sets where the difference between SR and RA is insignificant, averaged over 30 runs. Second column shows the error rates when λ value was chosen through cross-validation. Forth column shows the error rates when the λ value was set to the average $\frac{\|B\|-1}{m}$ value shown in Table 29.1 (also shown in column five) throughout the runs

	RA	$ave(\lambda)$	RA	$ave(\frac{\|B\|-1}{m})$	Diff
Sonar	0.165	0.008	0.169	0.153	0
Glass	0.063	0.008	0.064	0.324	0
Heart-c	0.171	0.218	0.168	0.634	0
Thyoid	0.050	0.022	0.053	0.186	0
Letter	0.004	0.005	0.004	0.009	0
Cancer	0.274	0.710	0.280	0.433	0
Cns	0.388	0.005	0.390	0.024	0
Colon	0.381	0.005	0.392	0.019	0
Leuk	0.339	0.005	0.348	0.021	0
Opl	0.420	0.031	0.401	0.364	0

When a problem demands a complex decision function, RA can choose a smaller λ value to meet this demand. On the other hand, SR can not. The simplest regularization algorithm (Parzen Windows) lacks the ability to choose complex functions to fit the data.

For the data sets in which the difference in performance between SR and RA is insignificant, it turns out that either RA favored large λ values (**Cancer** data set), or when using larger λ values, its performance does not degrade significantly. Table 29.2 shows a case in point. The fourth column in Table 29.2 shows the performance of RA, averaged over 30 runs, when the λ value was set to the average $\frac{\|B\|-1}{m}$ value shown in Table 29.1 (also shown in column five in Table 29.2) throughout the runs. The results lend support to our theoretical analysis.

The results also show that the 3NN classifier performed slightly worse than SR. 3NN performed similar to RA in 5 out of the 18 data sets, compared to 10 for SR. We note that nearest neighbor classifiers can potentially perform better with varying number of nearest neighbors or with adaptive distance metrics.

The main advantage of the simplest regularization algorithm is computational. As the number of training examples increases, computing the inverse of $(\lambda m I + K)^{-1}$ can be costly, in terms of space and time. In addition, as the number of training examples increases, $D(\lambda)$ diminishes (29.17) and (29.24). As a result, the error bound is at most twice the error bound for RA. In applications where resources are at premium, SR can be advantageous.

29.10 Summary

In this chapter, we have developed a "simplest" regularization algorithm, and shown its relation to Parzen Windows. The development is a realization of the DDDAS design principle, which finds success in many real world applications. We have also established the error bound for the SR algorithm based on the error bound for RA given finite samples. Our analysis shows that SR, thus the Parzen Windows classifier, has an asymptotic error rate that is at most twice that for RA under appropriate conditions. Our analysis also brings insight into the performance of the nearest neighbor classifier. We have provided the conditions under which when SR (Parzen Windows) is a good approximation to RA and the conditions under which it is not. Finally, the experimental results corroborate with our theoretical analysis.

References

1. A.J. Aved, E.P. Blasch, Multi-int query language for DDDAS designs. Proc. Comput. Sci. **51**, 2518–2532 (2015). International Conference On Computational Science, ICCS 2015
2. G.A. Babich, O.I. Camps, Weighted parzen windows for pattern classification. IEEE Trans. Pattern Anal. Mach. Intell. **18**(5), 567–570 (1996)
3. E.P. Blasch, A.J. Aved, Dynamic data-driven application system (DDDAS) for video surveillance user support. Proc. Comput. Sci. **51**, 2503–2517 (2015). International Conference On Computational Science, ICCS 2015
4. E. Blasch, G. Seetharaman, F. Darema, Dynamic data driven applications systems (DDDAS) modeling for automatic target recognition. Autom. Target Recognit. XXIII **8744**, 87440J (2013)
5. E. Blasch, G. Seetharaman, K. Reinhardt, Dynamic data driven applications system concept for information fusion. Proc. Comput. Sci. **18**, 1999–2007 (2013). 2013 International Conference on Computational Science
6. Y. Chen, E. Garcia, M. Gupta, A. Rahimi, L. Cazzanti, Similarity-based classification: concepts and algorithms. J. Mach. Learn. Res. **10**, 747–776 (2009)
7. T.M. Cover, P.E. Hart, Nearest neighbor pattern classification. IEEE Trans. Inf. Theory **13**, 21–27 (1967)
8. N. Cristianini, J. Shawe-Taylor, *An Introduction to Support Vector Machines and Other Kernel-Based Learning Methods* (Cambridge University Press, Cambridge, 2000)
9. F. Cucker, S. Smale, On the mathematical foundations of learning. Bull. Am. Math. Soc. **39**(1), 1–49 (2001)
10. F. Cucker, S. Smale, Best choices for regularization parameters in learning theory: on the bias-variance problem. Found. Comput. Math. **2**(4), 413–428 (2002)
11. C. Domeniconi, J. Peng, D. Gunopulos, Locally adaptive metric nearest neighbor classification. IEEE Trans. Pattern Anal. Mach. Intell. **24**(9), 1281–1285 (2002)
12. C. Domeniconi, D. Gunopulos, J. Peng, Large margin nearest neighbor classifiers. IEEE Trans. Neural Netw. **16**(4), 899–909 (2005)
13. R. Duda, P. Hart, D. Stork, *Patten Classification*, 2nd edn. (John-Wiley & Son, New York, 2000)
14. T. Evgeniou, M. Pontil, T. Poggio, Regularization networks and support vector machines. Adv. Comput. Math. **13**(1), 1–50 (2000)
15. K. Fukunaga, *Introduction to Statistical Pattern Recognition* (Academic, Boston, 1990)

16. T. Hastie, R. Tibshirani, Discriminant adaptive nearest neighbor classification. IEEE Trans. Pattern Anal. Mach. Intell. **18**(6), 607–615 (1996)
17. J. Hertz, A. Krough, R. Palmer, *Introduction to the Theory of Neural Computation* (Addison Wesley, Redwood City, 1991)
18. A. Hoerl, R. Kennard, Ridge regression: biased estimation for nonorthogonal problems. Technometrics **12**(3), 55–67 (1970)
19. M. Kim, Large margin cost-sensitive learning of conditional random fields. Pattern Recogn. **43**(10), 3683–3692 (2010)
20. N. Kwak, C. Choi, Input feature selection by mutual information based on parzen window. IEEE Trans. Pattern Anal. Mach. Intell. **24**(12), 1667–1671 (2004)
21. L. Lan, H. Shi, Z. Wang, S. Vucetic, An active learning algorithm based on parzen window classification. J. Mach. Learn. Res. Work. Conf. Proc. **10**, 1–14 (2010)
22. J. Langford, J. Shawe-Taylor, Pac-Bayes and margins, in *Advances in Neural Information Processing Systems*, vol. 15 (MIT Press, Cambridge, 2002), pp. 439–446
23. W. Li, K. Lee, K. Leung, Generalized regularized least-squares learning with predefined features in a Hilbert space, in *Advances in Neural Information Processing Systems*, ed. by B. Schlkopf, J. Platt, T. Hoffman (MIT Press, Cambridge, 2007)
24. S. Lin, X. Guo, D. Zhou, Distributed learning with regularized least squares. J. Mach. Learn. Res. **18**, 1–31 (2017)
25. A. Maurer, Learning similarity with operator-valued large-margin classifiers. J. Mach. Learn. Res. **9**, 1049–1082 (2008)
26. C. McDiarmid, Concentration, in *Probabilistic Methods for Algorithmic Discrete Mathematics* (Springer, Berlin/Heidelberg, 1998), pp. 195–248
27. S. Mosci, L. Rosasco, A. Verri, Dimensionality reduction and generalization, in *Proceedings of International Conference on Machine Learning*, 2007, pp. 657–664
28. E. Parzen, On the estimation of a probability density function and the mode. Ann. Math. Stats. **33**, 1049–1051 (1962)
29. J. Peng, D. Heisterkamp, H. Dai, Adaptive quasi-conformal Kernel nearest neighbor classification. IEEE Trans. Pattern Anal. Mach. Intell. **26**(5), 565–661 (2005)
30. T. Poggio, S. Smale, The mathematics of learning: dealing with data. Not. AMS **50**(5), 537–544 (2003)
31. G. Ratsch, M. Warmuth, Efficient margin maximizing with boosting. J. Mach. Learn. Res. **6**, 2131–2152 (2005)
32. S. Rosset, J. Zhu, T. Hastie, Boosting as a regularized path to a maximum margin classifier. J. Mach. Learn. Res. **5**, 941–973 (2004)
33. B. Scholkopf, A. Smola, *Learning with Kernels* (MIT Press, Cambridge, 2002)
34. S. Smale, D.X. Zhou, Shannon samping II: connection to learning theory. Appl. Comput. Harmon. Anal. **19**(3), 285–302 (2005)
35. A.J. Smola, B. Schölkopf, K.R. Müller, The connection between regularization operators and support vector kernels. Neural Netw. **11**(4), 637–649 (1998). citeseer.nj.nec.com/smola98connection.html
36. V. Strassen, Gaussian elimination is not optimal. Numer. Math. **13**, 354–356 (1969)
37. F. Teng, Y. Chen, X. Dang, Multiclass classification with potential function rules: margin distribution and generalization. Pattern Recogn. **45**(1), 540–551 (2012)
38. R. Tibshirani, T. Hastie, Margin trees for high-dimensional classification. J. Mach. Learn. Res. **8**, 637–652 (2007)
39. A.N. Tikhonov, V.Y. Arsenin, *Solutions of Ill-Posed Problems* (Wiley, Washington, DC, 1977)
40. V. Vapnik, *Statistical Learning Theory* (Wiley, New York, 1998)
41. V.N. Vapnik, Statistical learning theory, in *Adaptive and Learning Systems for Signal Processing, Communications, and Control* (Wiley, New York, 1998)
42. E.D. Vito, A. Caponnetto, L. Rosasco, Model selection for regularized least-squares algorithm in learning theory. Found. Comput. Math. **5**, 59–85 (2005)

43. J. Wang, X. Shen, Large margin semi-supervised learning. J. Mach. Learn. Res. **8**, 1867–1891 (2007)
44. Y. Guermeur, Vc theory of large margin multi-category classifiers. J. Mach. Learn. Res. **8**, 2551–2594 (2007)
45. Y. Zhang, J. Schneider, Projection penalties: dimension reduction without loss, in *Proceedings 27th International Conference on Machine Learning* (Morgan Kaufmann, San Francisco, 2010)
46. Y. Zhao, J. Fan, L. Shix, Learning rates for regularized least squares ranking algorithm. Anal. Appl. **15**(6), 815–836 (2017)

Chapter 30
Multiscale DDDAS Framework for Damage Prediction in Aerospace Composite Structures

A. Korobenko, M. Pigazzini, X. Deng, and Y. Bazilevs

Abstract In recent years, there has been a significant increase in the use of Unmanned Aerial Vehicles (UAV). UAVs are expected to fly a large number of long (48 or more hours) missions, and operate without failure. Furthermore, in order to increase the durability of these vehicles and to decrease weight, composite materials are currently experiencing a widespread adoption in applications related both to military and civilian aerospace structures. As a result, in order to decrease costs associated with the operation, maintenance, and, in some cases, loss of these vehicles, it is desirable to have a Dynamically Data-Driven Applications Systems framework that can reliably predict the onset and progressions of structural damage in geometrically and materially complex aerospace composite structures operating in the environments typical of UAVs. In this chapter we present a multiscale DDDAS Interactive Structure Composite Element Relation Network (DISCERN) framework. The proposed multiscale DISCERN framework is successfully deployed on a full-scale laminated composite structure to predict the damage onset, evolution, and the structure remaining fatigue life.

Keywords DDDAS Interactive Structure Composite Element Relation Network (DISCERN) · Continuum Damage Mechanics (CDM) · Isogeometric Analysis (IGA) · Structural health model · Classical Laminated Plate Theory (CLPT) · Non-Uniform Rational B-Splines (NURBS) · Airfoil · Piezoelectric transducers · Self-aware UAV

A. Korobenko (✉)
Department of Mechanical and Manufacturing Engineering, University of Calgary, Calgary, AB, Canada
e-mail: artem.korobenko@ucalgary.ca

M. Pigazzini
Department of Structural Engineering, University of California, San Diego, CA, USA

X. Deng
Department of Civil Engineering, University of Hong Kong, Hong Kong, China

Y. Bazilevs
School of Engineering, Brown University, Providence, RI, USA

© The Author(s), under exclusive license to Springer Nature Switzerland AG 2022   693
E. P. Blasch et al. (eds.), *Handbook of Dynamic Data Driven Applications Systems*,
https://doi.org/10.1007/978-3-030-74568-4_30

30.1   Introduction

Sensor and measurement data alone are, in general, insufficient for making predictions about damage initiation and progression. Although measurement data corresponds to an actual physical system of interest, it is typically limited to a small number of spatial points, and involves quantities that are not directly related to structural damage. By the same token, data coming from standalone high-fidelity computational models are also not sufficient for making predictions about damage initiation and progression. Indeed, while three-dimensional and time-dependent data sets may be extracted, including quantities directly related to damage; the underlying computational model makes many assumptions about geometry, materials, constitutive models, boundary and initial conditions, etc., which are often approximations of physical reality. DDDAS [8] is a framework in which sensor and measurement data collected for a given physical system are used to dynamically update a computational model of that system. Using measurement data, the computational model geometry, boundary conditions, external forces, and material parameters may be updated to better represent physical reality. At the same time, the updated computational model can produce higher-fidelity outputs for the quantities of interest for which measurements are not readily available, and provide feedback to a measurement system. As such, DDDAS is a framework in which measurement and simulation co-exist in a symbiotic environment.

Biuilding upon an early version of the DDDAS Interactive Structure Composite Element Relation Network (DISCERN) framework, the multiscale DISCERN framework reflects the multiscale nature of laminated composites by applying the DDDAS concept at all spatial and temporal scales involved in the modeling of composite materials damage. This improve the overall predictive capability for damage initiation and evolution in real-life aerospace structures.

In this chapter we present the first part of the framework, focusing on the computational modeling for the prediction of the damage growth in multi-layered composites. The dynamic coupling between computational model and measurement data will be presented which supports future experiments.

First, we introduce the multiscale DISCERN framework for damage prediction in composite aerospace structures. Then we provide an overview of the computational framework. We focus in particular on the isogeometric discretization of the continuum fields and on the progressive damage model implemented in the framework of the Continuum Damage Mechanics (CDM) for thin-shell elements. The computational framework is then applied to predict the fatigue-damage in full-scale wind turbine blade and predict the damage growth in the Orion Unmanned Aerial Vehicle (UAV), designed by Aurora Flight Science, under a severe landing condition. In the last section we draw conclusions and present future research directions.

30.2   The Multiscale DDDAS Framework

Damage in composite laminates exhibits complex behavior due to heterogeneous failure mechanisms occurring across different spatial scales. A damage model may be either discrete or continuous depending on the scales involved. The model is typically discrete for atomistic voids and lattice defects, and continuous for micro-, meso-, and macroscales. At the microscale, a Representative Volume Element (RVE) is typically introduced to model phenomena such as separation (or debonding) at the fiber-matrix interface or the initiation, growth, and coalescence of microcracks. The RVE must be small enough to distinguish the microscopic hetero-geneities and large enough to represent the overall behavior of the heterogeneous medium. At the mesoscale, various damage modes such as fiber fracture, matrix cracking, and delamination may be incorporated at the lamina or laminate level. At the macroscale, a composite laminate is typically modeled as a collection of plies, where each ply is an orthotropic medium with continuously distributed material properties and damage indexes.

In order to reflect the multiscale nature of laminated composites, we propose a multiscale DDDAS paradigm for damage prediction in aerospace composite structures. In essence, in order to improve the overall predictive capability for damage initiation and propagation in real-life aerospace structures, we propose to apply the DDDAS concept at all spatial and temporal scales involved in the modeling of composite damages:

- At the *microscale level*, RVE computations are often employed to obtain material properties such as directional elastic moduli or failure stresses. X-ray digital micro-tomography may be employed concurrently with the RVE simulations for precise strain measurements intended to calibrate the RVE model parameters.
- At the *mesoscale level* (i.e., the "coupon" level) smaller-scale experiments may be performed concurrently with the simulation of simple geometry specimens (rectangular and, possibly, notched) to extract the parameters for the damage model and to assess the sensitivity of the damage model with respect to these parameters. The optimal set of damage-model parameters can be obtained, for instance, by minimizing a misfit functional between the experimental and computational results. For this purpose, we envision the use of a derivative-free optimizer based on the Surrogate Management Framework (SMF) [7].
- The full richness and power of DDDAS can be exercised at the *macroscale level* (i.e., the structural component level) where the accelerometer and strain-gauge data can be used to adjust the external forces, the boundary conditions and other structural-model input data to better represent physical reality and predict damage onset and growth [9]. The location(s) of the damage-zone formation predicted by the steered computational model may be, in turn, used to make decisions about future sensor placement. This represents a true feedback loop between the actual structure and its computational model. Furthermore, given a combination of measured data and predicted response, a control strategy may be

employed in order to steer the structure out of harm's way (see [3] for an example of the adjoint-based control strategy developed and applied to a two-dimensional model problem).

30.3 Computational Structural Model

The structural components of interest in this work (i.e., the fuselage, the wing and the empennage of the UAV) consist of curved thin composite plates, stiffeners and spars. The structural model adopted for the analysis is based on the thin Kirchoff-Love shell theory. By neglecting the presence of the transverse shear, this rotation-free formulation does not suffer from mesh locking effects in the limit of the elements' thickness tending to zero. In addition, compared to the thick-shell element formulation, it allows to reduce the number of degrees of freedom by a factor of two.

The *Isogeometric Analysis (IGA)* concept is used to discretize the structural mechanics equations. The IGA is a FEM-like simulation methodology that relies on the same basis function technology of computer-aided design, computer graphics, and computer animation. In IGA, both the geometry and the solution fields are represented using the same functional description. The most widely used discretization in IGA makes use of Non-Uniform Rational B-Splines (NURBS), but other alternatives, such as T-splines and subdivision surfaces and solids are possible. In the framework of the IGA, the integration of structural design and numerical analysis is greatly simplified. Indeed, the single representation of the geometry and solution fields allows for a simple integration of different software components needed for different stages of modeling and simulation. In addition, the IGA is an inherently higher-order accurate technique and NURBS shape functions allow to easily enforce higher-order continuity between the elements. This distinguishing feature of IGA is beneficial in many applications of computational mechanics.

The IGA was recently proposed [5, 13] to address the shortcomings of standard finite element technology for thin shells listed above. It was found that the higher-order continuity (C^1 and above) of the IGA basis functions significantly improved per-degree-of-freedom accuracy and robustness of thin shell discretization as compared to the FEM. Furthermore, the increased continuity of the IGA discretization enabled the use of rotation-free shells elements, such as the Kirchhoff-Love shell, leading to further computational cost savings. In the lead author's work on wind turbines, the rotor blade geometry was modeled as a thin shell. The isogeometric rotation-free Kirchhoff-Love shell formulation for structures composed of multiple structural patches, called "the bending-strip method", was developed in [13] and applied to Fluid Structure Interactions (FSI) of wind turbine rotors in [2, 4]. Besides the significant computational savings, the rotation-free shell discretization makes FSI coupling simpler than for shells with rotational degrees of freedom.

The computational performances have been significantly improved by taking advantage of the multi-thread capabilities of modern multi-core processors. We envision the use of Graphics Processing Units (GPU), which provide dense and enormous computing power.

30.3.1 Progressive Damage Model

The material model adopted for the analysis in based on the Kirchhoff-St.Venant linear relationship for stresses and strains. A residual stiffness damage model [15] is introduced at sub-lamina level in order to simulate the intralaminar damages in the framework of the CDM.

The model is based on the assumption that the equivalent effects of the micro- and meso-scale intralaminar damages, such as matrix cracking, fiber kinking and debonding, can be modeled at the macro-scale level in terms of degradation of the pristine elastic properties of the material. Therefore, the material constitutive stiffness matrix is parametrized as a function of three damage indexes, namely d_1, d_2 and d_6, which are respectively associated to the amount of damage in the fiber, in the matrix and in the in-plane shear direction. For each k-th sub-lamina, we define the modified constitutive stiffness matrix as follow:

$$\tilde{\mathbf{C}}_k = \frac{1}{D} \begin{bmatrix} E_1 (1 - d_1) & E_1 v_{21} (1 - d_1) (1 - d_2) & 0 \\ E_1 v_{21} (1 - d_1) (1 - d_2) & E_2 (1 - d_2) & 0 \\ 0 & 0 & G_{12} D (1 - d_6) \end{bmatrix}$$

(30.1)

where $D = 1 - v_{21} v_{12} (1 - d_1) (1 - d_2)$. The Hashin damage criteria [11] are used to detect the onset of the permanent damage. After the initiation of the damage, we make use of a bilinear softening law in order to determine the evolution of the damage indexes based on the current deformation state. As proposed by Bažant [1], a characteristic length is introduced in the bilinear law in order to mitigate the dependency of the results from the discretization adopted for the analysis.

The Classical Laminated Plate Theory (CLPT) is used to compute the extensional, coupling and bending stiffness matrices for the entire laminate, by summing the contribution of all the sub-lamina. This allows to propagate the effects of the intralaminar damage from the sub-lamina level to the macroscale level. The matrices $\mathbf{K}^{\text{exte}}$, $\mathbf{K}^{\text{coup}}$ and $\mathbf{K}^{\text{bend}}$ are then used in the principle of virtual work to compute the deformation energy starting from the measures of the in-plane strain $\varepsilon_{\alpha\beta}$ and from the curvature tensor $\kappa_{\alpha\beta}$. In the framework of the thin shell theory, the presence of the curvature tensor requires the use of, at least, quadratic NURBS shape functions.

30.4 Fatigue Damage Simulation of a Full-Scale CX-100 Wind Turbine Blade Driven by Test Data

This section shows the deployment of the multiscale DISCERN framework using data from a fatigue test of a full-scale wind turbine blade. We describe the blade geometry and material composition, the fatigue test setup and sensors employed, and the computational procedure for fatigue damage identification and prediction that involves dynamic computational model updating based on sensor and measurement data collected during the test.

30.4.1 Blade Structure and Its IGA Model

We use a Sandia CX-100 conventional carbon-spar wind-turbine blade design [6, 14, 22], which is based on the ERS-100 blade [6], but with a substantially reduced spar cap. The blade surface geometry definition is provided in Table 30.1. Up to a 1-m station from the root the blade has a circular cross-section. At a 1.4-m station the blade transitions into the NREL S821 airfoil with a twist angle of 17.5°. At a 4.2-m station the blade blends into the NREL S819 airfoil, which is used almost all the way to the tip where the NREL S820 airfoil is placed. The airfoils are lofted along the blade axis direction to produce a NURBS blade surface.

The blade material composition is as follows. The blade surface is comprised of five primary zones: leading edge, trailing edge, root, spar cap, and shear web. The zones are shown in Fig. 30.1. Each zone is made up of a multilayer composite layup. The different materials used for the layup are summarized in Table 30.2. The root area has several layers of fiberglass plies to strengthen the region where the blade

Table 30.1 Blade cross-section geometry data for the CX-100 blade

Radial distance (m)	Chord length (m)	Twist angle (degrees)	Airfoil type
0.200	0.356	29.6	Cylinder
0.600	0.338	24.8	Cylinder
1.000	0.569	20.8	Cylinder
1.400	0.860	17.5	NREL S821
1.800	1.033	14.7	NREL S821
2.200	0.969	12.4	NREL S821
3.200	0.833	8.3	NREL S821
4.200	0.705	5.8	NREL S819
5.200	0.582	4.0	NREL S819
6.200	0.463	2.7	NREL S819
7.200	0.346	1.4	NREL S819
8.200	0.232	0.4	NREL S819
9.000	0.120	0.0	NREL S820

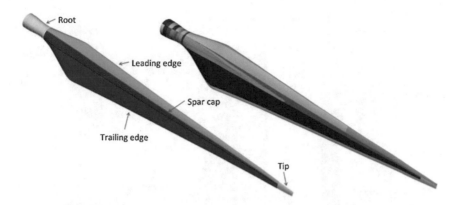

Fig. 30.1 Left: Five primary sections of the CX-100 blade; Right: 32 distinct material zones of the CX-100 blade

Table 30.2 Lamina properties of the materials employed in the CX-100 blade

Material name	E_1 (GPa)	E_2 (GPa)	G_{12} (GPa)	ν_{12}	ρ (kg/m^3)
Gel coat	3.44	3.44	1.38	0.30	1,235
Fill epoxy	2.41	2.41	0.96	0.30	1,154
Fiberglass	7.58	7.58	4.00	0.30	1,678
End-grain balsa	0.12	0.12	0.02	0.30	230
DBM1708 (+/− 45° fiberglass)	9.58	9.58	6.89	0.39	1,814
DBM1208 (+/− 45° fiberglass)	9.58	9.58	6.89	0.39	1,814
C520 (0° fiberglass)	37.30	7.60	6.89	0.31	1,874
0° Carbon, 500 gsm	105.40	6.82	3.32	0.28	1,480
Carbon-fiberglass triaxial fabric	84.10	8.76	4.38	0.21	1,560

is mounted on the hub flange. The leading and trailing edge zones have a similar layup. Both include an outer gel coat and fiberglass layers, with the total thickness of 0.51 mm, as well as additional layers of fiberglass material DBM-1708, 0.89 mm each, and one 6.35 mm layer of balsa wood. Balsa wood is only present in the core section of the blade and not on the edges. The leading edge zone has additional layers of fiberglass material DBM-1208, with a total thickness of 0.56 mm, located between DBM-1708 and balsa core. The layup of the core regions of the trailing and leading edge zones is shown in Fig. 30.2. The spar-cap zone has a nonuniform thickness distribution, ranging from 5.79 to 9.65 mm, due to the decreasing number of carbon fiber laminate layers (from seven to three) along the blade length. The spar-cap layup is also shown in Fig. 30.2, and has the thickest carbon fiber layer. The shear web, which is designed to carry most of the surface loads, has a C-shape structure containing four layers of DBM-1708 fiberglass, 0.74 mm each, and 9.53 mm of balsa wood core. The balsa wood layer is terminated in the tip zone. As a result, the tip region is only comprised of one layer of gel coat and several layers of fiberglass material. This layout leads to 32 zones with constant total thickness

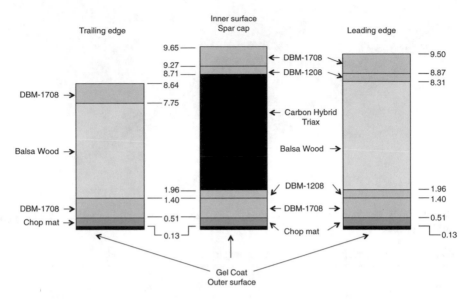

Fig. 30.2 Example of the layup of the trailing edge, leading edge, and spar cap

and unique laminate stacking. All 32 zones are identified on the blade surface and are shown in Fig. 30.1.

30.4.2 Blade Fatigue-Test Setup and Sensor Layout

The CX-100 blade was fatigue loaded until failure using a hydraulic displacement excitation technique at the National Wind Technology Center (NWTC) in Golden, CO as a part of the Los Alamos National Laboratory Wind Turbine Program [10, 16, 18]. During the test the blade was clamped at the root and turned such that the high pressure (HP) side was facing up, and, at a 7-m station, the local chord was parallel to the laboratory floor (see Fig. 30.3). The blade was driven at the natural frequency of the first flap-wise bending mode, which is 1.82 Hz. The cyclic load was applied at a 1.6-m station using UREX hydraulic actuators. The applied-force magnitude during the test was adjusted by changing the stroke of the hydraulic actuators. To amplify the blade response, an additional mass of 164.65 kg was placed at a 6.7-m station. Fig. 30.4 shows the fatigue cycle count versus time (where the number of runs was conducted over a month). The fatigue test lasted from 8/5/2011 to 11/13/2011, until a fatigue-induced crack formed in the blade root region after about 8.0 M loading cycles.

The CX-100 blade was equipped with a number of sensors for both active and passive sensing applications [10, 16–21]. All the sensors were located on the blade exterior with most of them concentrated near the root where fatigue failure was

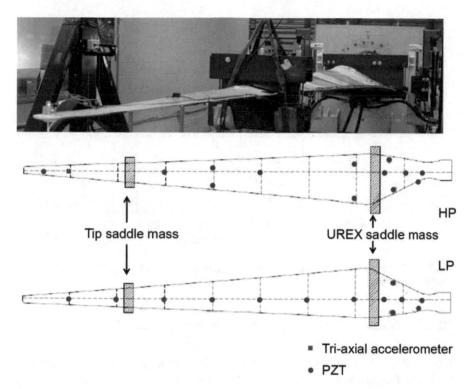

Fig. 30.3 Blade fatigue test setup and sensor layout. Blue square gives the location of the accelerometer providing dynamic acceleration data for displacement amplitude and fatigue-model parameter calibration

expected to occur (and, indeed, occurred). The primary sensors employed were piezoelectric transducers (PZTs), in particular, WASP-1, Metis-1, and LASER. Also, several macro-fiber-composite (MFC) sensors were used as a backup sensors. The layout of PZT sensors on both high- and low-pressure (LP) sides of the blade is shown in Fig. 30.3. Traditional accelerometers that record acceleration during 10-s intervals at a sampling rate of 1.6 kHz were also installed at several locations on the blade surface. Additional devices included strain gages for strain measurements and moment calibration, and temperature sensors. A rich dataset from these sensors was collected and analyzed in [10, 16–18]. In particular, SHM techniques for fatigue crack detection and their comparison were discussed at length in [18]. In the chapter, we present the accelerometer data to steer the fatigue damage computations, as detailed in the following section.

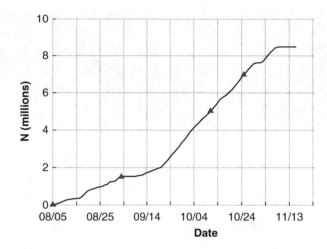

Fig. 30.4 Fatigue cycle count versus date. Triangular symbols indicate calibration points for fatigue damage simulations

30.4.3 Blade Fatigue Simulation Driven by Test Data

The dynamic data collected during the CX-100 blade fatigue test is employed for blade fatigue damage simulation. Although, ideally, the computation would be executed concurrently with the fatigue test, here the measurements from the fatigue test are employed as historic or archival data used to steer the fatigue damage computation. To carry out the simulation, the IGA model of the CX-100 blade is placed in the same orientation as the test specimen and is also clamped at the root. A time-periodic vertical displacement with frequency of 1.82 Hz is applied at a 1.6-m station to mimic the hydraulic-system forcing. The effect of extra mass of 164.65 kg added to the 6.7-m station is achieved by locally increasing the blade material density in this region. The dynamic sensor data are employed to simultaneously calibrate the magnitude of the applied displacement loading, as well as to obtain a good estimate of the input parameters of the fatigue damage model. To this end, we devise two DDDAS loops in DISCERN – the *inner loop* responsible for displacement forcing amplitude calibration, and the *outer loop* responsible for simulation of damage growth and calibration of the associated material constants. The flowchart for each of the two DDDAS loops is shown in Fig. 30.5.

The amplitude of the applied displacement used to actuate the blade is calibrated at four points during the fatigue test, corresponding to cycle number 0 M, 1.5 M, 5 M, and 7 M (see Fig. 30.4). At each one of these points, a dynamic simulation consisting of a few flapping cycles is performed with material parameters corresponding to the blade damage state at that cycle, as predicted by the fatigue damage model. The prescribed displacement amplitude is adjusted until the acceleration time history at location 8.05 m predicted by the simulation matched that measured by the accelerometer placed in this location (see Fig. 30.3). Figure 30.6 shows

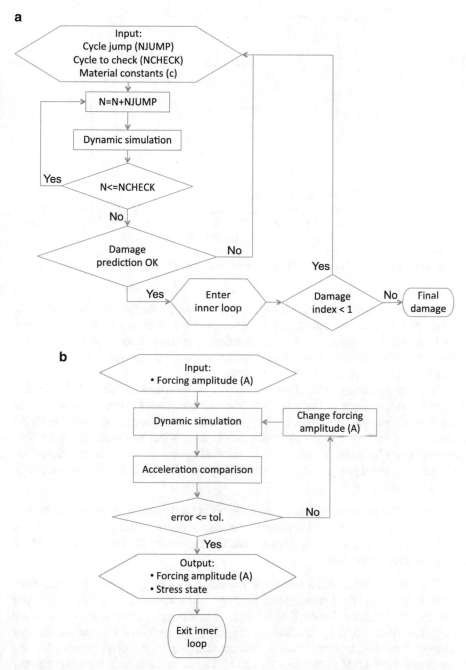

Fig. 30.5 (**a**) Flowchart of the outer DDDAS loop responsible for fatigue damage prediction and model parameter calibration; (**b**) Flowchart of the inner DDDAS loop responsible for applied displacement amplitude calibration

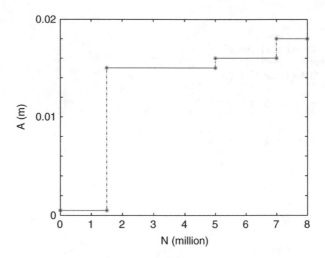

Fig. 30.6 Amplitude (A) of applied displacement forcing as a function of cycle number (N)

the calibrated displacement forcing amplitude as a function of cycle number, while Fig. 30.7 shows the degree to which we are able to match the predicted and measured accelerations. The acceleration data comparison is presented in the time and frequency domains. Note that both the displacement and acceleration amplitudes are increasing with cycle number.

The fatigue damage model parameters are summarized in Table 30.3. We start with the values close to those used for the test specimen in Sect. 30.1, and adjust the model parameters c_1 and c_3 to properly reflect the current damage state of the structure at the same four calibration points during the fatigue test. Figure 30.8 shows the evolution of c_1 and c_3 as a function of cycle number. This evolution gives the predicted blade fatigue life of about 8 M cycle, which is in good agreement with the test data.

Remarks The three points chosen for calibration correspond to the points in the test where the acceleration measurements showed the biggest change. In principle one is free to choose as many calibration points as necessary for good accuracy of the fatigue damage prediction.

Figures 30.9 and 30.10 show the evolution of damage index D_1 (i.e., fiber direction) in the DBM plies. (Note that two different color scales are employed for the two figures.) For the first 1.5 M cycles, damage grows faster in the blade midspan. After 1.5 M cycles damage begins to concentrate and grow in the root section. This is likely due to a significant increase in the displacement forcing amplitude after 1.5 M cycles (see Fig. 30.6). Closer to 8 M cycles a part of the root section is fully damaged, and the damage location is in excellent agreement with that of the crack observed on the blade surface during the fatigue test. (See Fig. 30.11 for a visual comparison of the fatigue-test and simulation results.)

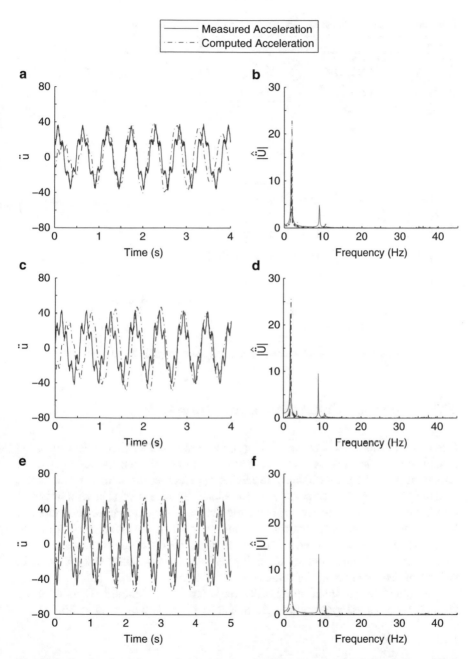

Fig. 30.7 Acceleration data comparison between the fatigue test and simulation at three calibration points. Left: Time domain comparison; Right: Frequency domain comparison

Table 30.3 Damage model parameters of CX-100 blade employed in the computations

Cycle	c_1	c_2	c_3	c_4	c_5	c_6	c_7	c_8	c_9
$\leq 1.5\,\text{M}$	4×10^{-6}	30.0	2.0×10^{-6}	0.8	80.0	0	0	0	0
$1.5\,\text{M} \sim 5.0\,\text{M}$	4×10^{-6}	30.0	2.0×10^{-6}	0.8	80.0	0	0	0	0
$5.0\,\text{M} \sim 7.0\,\text{M}$	1.6×10^{-4}	30.0	4.0×10^{-5}	0.8	80.0	0	0	0	0
$7.0\,\text{M} \sim 8.0\,\text{M}$	4×10^{-4}	30.0	1.0×10^{-4}	0.8	80.0	0	0	0	0

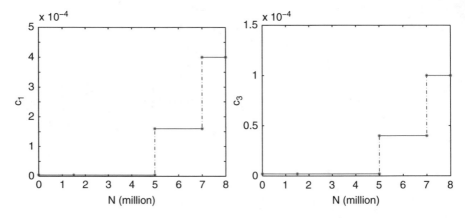

Fig. 30.8 Damage model material parameters c_1 (Left) and c_3 (Right) plotted versus cycle number

30.5 Numerical Simulation of the Orion UAV

One of the intended applications of the proposed multiscale DDDAS framework is in multi-fidelity models for real-time decision support of "self-aware" UAVs. An important part of the multifidelity modeling approach is the library, or database, of damage modes. The database is accumulated by means of a large number of offline computations performed by using medium to high fidelity simulation models. Indeed, these high-fidelity models have little chance of producing results in real time. The database is then used to inform surrogate models which are fast to execute and, as such, are much better suited for real-time online/onboard simulation in support of decision making for self-aware air vehicles.

The simulation presented in this Chapter is based on a simplified model of the Orion UAV, designed by Aurora Flight Sciences, which is shown in Fig. 30.12a.

30.5.1 Parametric UAV Model

As a first step, we construct a parametric IGA model of a close approximation of the full-scale Orion UAV. We make use of a sketch-like vehicle design model

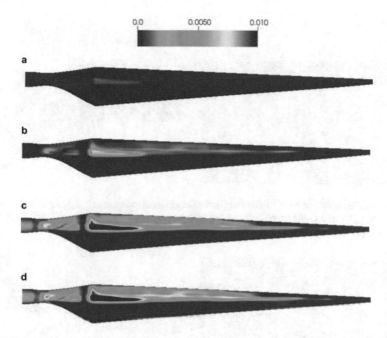

Fig. 30.9 Progression of damage index D_1 up to 1.5 M cycles in a DBM layer: (**a**) Cycle $N = 10,000$; (**b**) Cycle $N = 100,000$; (**c**) Cycle $N = 1,000,000$; (**d**) Cycle $N = 1,500,000$

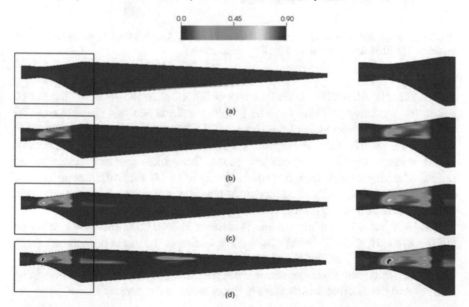

Fig. 30.10 Progression of damage index D_1 from 1.5 M to 8.0 M cycles in a DBM layer: (**a**) Cycle $N = 1,500,000$; (**b**) Cycle $N = 5,000,000$; (**c**) Cycle $N = 7,000,000$; (**d**) Cycle $N = 8,000,000$

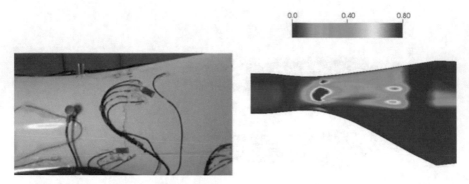

Fig. 30.11 Visual comparison of the fatigue-test and simulation results. Location and shape of the damage zone in a DBM layer near the root are in very good agreement with the location and orientation of the crack observed in the fatigue test

Fig. 30.12 Representation of (**a**) the Orion UAV designed by Aurora Flight Sciences and (**b**) the parametric NURBS based model used for IGA simulations

and of the 3D ASWING[1] model as input. We employ the recently developed parametric modeling platform for IGA [12] to construct analysis-suitable NURBS and T-Spline surface models of the Orion UAV. The resulting parametric model is shown in Fig. 30.12b. One of the principal advantages of having a parametric UAV model is that a handful of parameters govern the vehicle geometry. As a result, instead of having a single design, a whole family of UAVs with different design and configuration can be easily constructed. In addition, the parametric representation of the geometry allows to perform shape optimization analyses.

The UAV has a 16 m wingspan and is made of Hexcel 8552 IM7 PW composite with a symmetrical [0/45/90/45/0] lay-up and nonlinear thickness distribution along the fuselage, wings, horizontal and vertical tails. The main wing is reinforced with two spars, which run along the entire wing pass through the fuselage. The engine nacelles and the external fuel thanks are disregarded in the current model.

---

[1]http://web.mit.edu/drela/Public/web/aswing/

30.5.2   Landing Simulation

In this Chapter, we report the result obtained for a particular loading condition corresponding to a severe hard landing. We focus the attention on the damage developed in the main wing, where the computational mesh has been refined, while the damage model is not active for the shell elements of the fuselage and of the empennage.

The model is further simplified by disregarding the interaction of the landing gear with the ground. Instead, an upward acceleration is imposed on the nodes in the area corresponding to the location of the landing gear, from the bottom of the fuselage to the intersection with the main spar. This area is assumed to behave like a rigid body. This simplification underlies the assumption that the compliance of the fuselage is drastically reduced by the presence of bulkheads designed to transfer the loads from the wing to the landing gear.

In order to simulate the hard landing condition, a downward velocity of 3 m/s is imposed on all the nodes as an initial condition. The upward acceleration increases linearly from 0 to 3 g in the time frame of 0.1 s. A steady value of 3 g is then maintained until the vertical velocity of the UAV decreases to 0 m/s.

The results of the numerical simulation are shown in Figs. 30.13 and 30.14. The maximum deflection of the wing tip is equal to 0.175 m, measured with respect to the wing root.

The model predicts the development of permanent damage in the matrix phase on the wing, from the root up to 70% of the span. A localized permanent damage is also predicted toward the tip of the wing, where a stress concentration is introduced

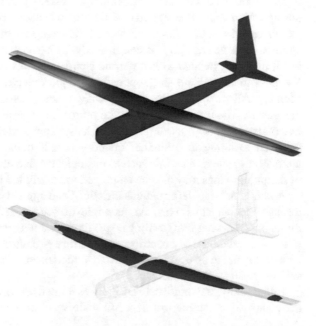

Fig. 30.13 IGA result: comparison of the deformed and the undeformed configuration at the moment of the maximum deflection. Contour plot: vertical displacement

Fig. 30.14 IGA result: identification of the critical area where the matrix phase is completely damaged. Contour plot: area where $d_2 \geq 0.95$ are highlighted in red

by a discontinuity in the thickness of the spar's cap. The critical areas, where the complete failure of the matrix phase is predicted, are highlighted in Fig. 30.14. The results of the numerical analysis provides a powerful predictive tool that can be used in the DDDAS framework, for example, to support the decision for sensor placement.

30.6 Conclusions

The multiscale DDDAS framework for damage prediction in aerospace composite structures is presented in this Chapter. The multiscale DDDAS Interactive Structure Composite Element Relation Network (DISCERN) framework represents a synthesis of the technology developed to predict the development of damage in composite materials at micro-, meso-, and macroscales. With the parametric UAV model in place, we simulate a critical hard landing scenario to provide accurate information about the stresses and damage state. In this paper the damage analysis is limited to the intralaminar damage. The model can be enriched in order to include the interlaminar damage, or delamination, which occurs between distinct layers of the laminate.

The improved accuracy provided by the IGA simulation will enhance the library of damage states and, as a result, will enhance the predictive power of fast surrogate models that rely on these information. The maneuvering simulations, which will be obtained by combining the structural model with a fluid solver, will produce better estimates of the UAV air loads and its response to them.

In the context of UAVs, it is important to not only understand the vehicle response during critical maneuvering scenarios, but also to take protective measures to shelter the air vehicle from excessive structural damage that may occur as a result of an aggressive maneuver. To this end, the adjoint-based control techniques developed in [3] may be extended to incorporate smart materials into the overall framework. We plan to investigate the application of piezoelectric actuators and/or Shape-Memory Alloys (SMA) to control UAV's wing deformation during aggressive maneuvers. The use of SMAs may be preferable over piezoelectric actuators since larger strains (and, thus, larger force density per material surface area) may be achieved resulting in a smaller quantity of additional material required. As an alternative to smart materials such as piezoelectric actuators and SMAs, the concept of morphing wings may also be employed to control the response of the air vehicle.

A family of wing deformations is defined and applied directly to the wing surface through mechanical forces. An example of such a deformation is a continuous morphing of a wing flap (trailing edge) through a wide range of angles. The results of these simulations may contribute to a library of control scenarios, which may also be used to inform fast-executing surrogate models in support of decision making for self-aware air vehicles.

Additionally, the multiscale DISCERN framework was successfully deployed in the context of a fatigue test of a full-scale wind-turbine blade structure and good results are obtained for the prediction of damage zone formation and evolution, eventually leading to blade failure. Such good prediction of the failure location and fatigue-cycle number is only possible with the utilization of the DDDAS concept.

Acknowledgments This work was supported by the AFOSR Grant FA9550-16-1-0131. The authors greatly acknowledge this support.

References

1. Z.P. Bažant, B.H. Oh, Crack band theory for fracture of concrete. Mater. Struct. **16**, 155–177 (1983)
2. Y. Bazilevs, M.-C. Hsu, I. Akkerman, S. Wright, K. Takizawa, B. Henicke, T. Spielman, T.E. Tezduyar, 3D simulation of wind turbine rotors at full scale. Part I: geometry modeling and aerodynamics. Int. J. Numer. Methods Fluids **65**, 207–235 (2011)
3. Y. Bazilevs, M.-C. Hsu, M.T. Bement, Adjoint-based control of fluid-structure interaction for computational steering applications. Proc. Comput. Sci. **18**, 1989–1998 (2013)
4. Y. Bazilevs, M.-C. Hsu, J. Kiendl, R. Wuechner, K.-U. Bletzinger, 3D simulation of wind turbine rotors at full scale. Part II: fluid-structure interaction. Int. J. Numer. Methods Fluids **65**, 236–253 (2011)
5. D.J. Benson, Y. Bazilevs, M.-C. Hsu, T.J.R. Hughes, A large-deformation, rotation-free isogeometric shell. Comput. Methods Appl. Mech. Eng. **200**, 1367–1378 (2011)
6. D. Berry, T. Ashwill, Design of 9-meter carbon-fiberglass prototype blades: CX-100 and TX-100. Report of the Sandia National Laboratories (2007)
7. A.J. Booker, J.E. Dennis Jr., P.D. Frank, D.B. Serafini, V. Torczon, M.W. Trosset, A rigorous framework for optimization of expensive functions by surrogates. Struct. Optim. **17**, 1–13 (1999)
8. F. Darema, Dynamic data driven applications systems: a new paradigm for application simulations and measurements, in *Proceedings of ICCS 2004 – 4th International Conference on Computational Science*, Kraków, Poland, 2004, pp. 662–669
9. X. Deng, A. Korobenko, J. Yan, Y. Bazilevs, Isogeometric analysis of continuum damage in rotation-free composite shells. Comput. Methods Appl. Mech. Eng. **284**, 349–372 (2015)
10. K.M. Farinholt, S.G. Taylor, G. Park, C.M. Ammerman, Full-scale fatigue tests of CX-100 wind turbine blades. Part I: testing, in *SPIE Smart Structures/NDE*, 2012, pp. 83430P–8
11. Z. Hashin, Failure criteria for unidirectional fiber composites. J. Appl. Mech. **47**, 329–334 (1980)
12. M.-C. Hsu, C. Wang, A.J. Herrema, D. Schillinger, A. Ghoshal, Y. Bazilevs, An interactive geometry modeling and parametric design platform for isogeometric analysis. Comput. Math. Appl. **70**, 1481–1500 (2015)
13. J. Kiendl, Y. Bazilevs, M.-C. Hsu, R. Wuechner, K.-U. Bletzinger, The bending strip method for isogeometric analysis of Kirchhoff-Love shell structures comprised of multiple patches. Comput. Methods Appl. Mech. Eng. **199**, 2403–2416 (2010)
14. A. Korobenko, M.-C. Hsu, I. Akkerman, J. Tippmann, Y. Bazilevs, Structural mechanics modeling and FSI simulation of wind turbines. Math. Models Methods Appl. Sci. **23**, 249–272 (2013)
15. A. Matzenmiller, J. Lubliner, R.B. Taylor, A constitutive model for anisotropic damage in fiber-composites. Mech. Mater. **20**, 125–152 (1995)
16. S.G. Taylor, K.M. Farinholt, H. Jeong, J.K. Jang, G. Park, M.D. Todd, C.R. Farrar, C.M. Ammerman, Wind turbine blade fatigue tests: lessons learned and application to shm system development, in *European Workshop on Structural Health Monitoring*, Dresden, Germany, 3–6 July 2012

17. S.G. Taylor, H. Jeong, J.K. Jang, G. Park, K.M. Farinholt, M.D. Todd, C.M. Ammerman, Full-scale fatigue tests of CX-100 wind turbine blades. Part II: analysis, in *SPIE Smart Structures/NDE*, 2012, pp. 83430Q–10

18. S.G. Taylor, G. Park, K.M. Farinholt, M.D. Todd, Fatigue crack detection performance comparison in a composite wind turbine rotor blade. Struct. Health Monit. **12**, 252–262 (2013)

19. J. Tippmann, F. Lanza di Scalea, Experiments on a wind turbine blade testing: an indication for damage using the causal and anti-causal Green's function reconstructed from a diffuse field, in *Proceedings of SPIE (International Society for Optical Engineering) Smart Structures/NDE Annual International Symposium Health Monitoring of Structural and Biological Systems*, ed. by T. Kundu, vol. 9064, 2014, pp. 1–7

20. J. Tippmann, F. Lanza di Scalea, Passive-only damage detection by reciprocity of Green's functions reconstructed from diffuse acoustic fields with application to wind turbine blades. J. Intell. Mater. Syst. Struct. **26**(10), 1251–1258 (2014)

21. J. Tippmann, P. Zhu, F. Lanza di Scalea, Application of damage detection methods using passive reconstruction of impulse response functions, in *Philosophical Transactions of the Royal Society A–Mathematical, Physical and Engineering Sciences*, vol. 373, 2015, pp. 1–16. Special Issue on New Perspectives in Offshore-Wind and Sea-Wave Energy Production

22. J.R. Zayas, W.D. Johnson, 3X-100 blade field test. Wind Energy Technology Department, Sandia National Laboratories, page Report (2008)

Chapter 31
A Dynamic Data-driven Stochastic State-Awareness Framework for the Next Generation of Bio-inspired Fly-by-feel Aerospace Vehicles

Fotis Kopsaftopoulos and Fu-Kuo Chang

Abstract In this work, a novel Data-driven State Awareness (DSA) framework is introduced for the next generation of intelligent "fly-by-feel" aerospace vehicles. The proposed framework is based on two entities: (i) bio-inspired networks of micro-sensors that can provide real-time information on the dynamic aeroelastic response of the structure and (ii) a stochastic "global" identification approach for representing the system dynamics under varying flight states and uncertainty. The evaluation and assessment of the proposed DSA framework is based on a prototype bio-inspired self-sensing intelligent composite wing subjected to a series of wind tunnel experiments under multiple flight states. A total of 148 micro-sensors, including piezoelectric, strain, and temperature sensors, are embedded in the layup of the composite wing in order to provide the sensing capabilities. A novel data-driven stochastic "global" identification approach based on functionally pooled time series models and statistical parameter estimation techniques is employed in order to accurately interpret the sensing data and extract information on the wing aeroelastic behavior and dynamics. The method's cornerstone lies in the new class of Vector-dependent Functionally Pooled (VFP) models which allow for the analytical inclusion of both airspeed and angle of attack (AoA) in the model parameters and, hence, system dynamics. Special emphasis is given to the wind tunnel experimental assessment under various flight states, each defined by

F. Kopsaftopoulos (✉)
Intelligent Structural Systems Laboratory (ISSL), Department of Mechanical, Aerospace, and Nuclear Engineering, Rensselaer Polytechnic Institute, Troy, NY, USA
e-mail: kopsaf@rpi.edu

F.-K. Chang
Structures and Composites Laboratory, Department of Aeronautics and Astronautics, Stanford University, Stanford, CA, USA
e-mail: fkchang@stanford.edu

© The Author(s), under exclusive license to Springer Nature Switzerland AG 2022   713
E. P. Blasch et al. (eds.), *Handbook of Dynamic Data Driven Applications Systems*,
https://doi.org/10.1007/978-3-030-74568-4_31

a distinct pair of airspeed and AoA. The obtained results demonstrate the high achievable accuracy and effectiveness of the proposed state-awareness framework, thus opening new perspectives for enabling the next generation of "fly-by-feel" aerospace vehicles.

Keywords Fly-by-feel · Data-driven State Awareness · Vector-dependent Functionally Pooled (VFP) models · Angle of attack (AoA) · Airfoil · Wing design · Composite laminates · Genetic Algorithms (GA)

31.1 Introduction

The next generation of intelligent aerospace structures and air vehicles will be able to "feel," "think," and "react" in real time based on high-resolution state-sensing, awareness, and self-diagnostic capabilities [1, 3, 16–18, 23, 30, 32]. They will be able to sense and observe phenomena at unprecedented length and time scales allowing for real-time optimal control and decision making, significantly improved performance and extended flight envelope, safer operation, reduced mission and maintenance costs, and complete life-cycle monitoring and management. One of the main challenges of the current state-of-the-art research is the development of technologies that will lead to autonomous "fly-by-feel" air vehicles inspired by the unprecedented sensing and actuation capabilities of biological systems. Such intelligent air vehicles will be able to (i) sense the external environment (temperature, air pressure, humidity, etc.), (ii) sense their flight state (airspeed, flutter, stall, aerodynamic loads, etc.) and internal structural state (stresses, strains, damage), and (iii) effectively interpret the sensing data to achieve real-time state awareness and health monitoring [12–15, 19, 24], and improve the vehicle's performance and control characteristics. Towards this end, novel dynamic data-driven approaches are needed for the accurate interpretation of large volumes of data that are being collected under varying flight states and uncertainty in complex dynamic environments.

The most critical challenge for the postulation of a complete and applicable data-driven state-awareness framework for aerospace vehicles is the effective modeling and interpretation of sensory data obtained under constantly changing dynamic environments, multiple flight states and varying structural health conditions. Evidently, all these different operating conditions affect the vehicle dynamics and aeroelastic response. Oftentimes, the operating conditions are characterized by one or more measurable variables, such as the airspeed, angle of attack (AoA), altitude, temperature, and so on, that may vary over time, and consequently affecting the system dynamics. In such cases the problem of identifying a single "global" model of the system that is capable of representing the dynamics under any admissible operating condition based on available response and/or excitation signals poses a major challenge that needs to be properly addressed [18, 20, 21, 28].

This challenge is typically tackled via either the identification of a number of distinct time series or state space models based on strain or acceleration data, with each model corresponding to a distinct flight state[9, 11, 26, 34–36, 38], or via the use of Linear Parameter Varying (LPV) models [10, 27, 37]. The latter are dynamical models with parameters expressed as functions of the measurable variable(s)—referred to as scheduling variable(s)—designating the operating condition. In this context, model identification is based on the so-called local approach [37], the rationale of which is based on a two-step method that splits the problem into two distinct subproblems: (i) first, a number of local (or else frozen) models—with each corresponding to a single operating condition for which response signals are available—are identified using conventional identification techniques [25, 33], and (ii) second, the identified models are interpolated in order to provide a single global model [37].

This approach is a straightforward extension of classical identification. Yet, when viewed within a stochastic framework in which the response signals are random in nature (stochastic), it leads to suboptimal accuracy. The intuitive explanation may be readily understood from the fact that the signal pairs are not treated as a single entity, but rather in complete isolation from each other in the process of obtaining each local model. This not only neglects potential cross-correlations among the signal pairs, thus resulting into information loss, but additionally leads to an unnecessarily high number of estimated parameters, thus violating the principle of statistical parsimony [25, p. 492]. In addition, this further leads to increased estimation variance and thus reduced accuracy (lack of efficiency in statistical terminology) [25, pp. 560–562]. Finally, additional loss of accuracy and increased error is involved in the subsequent interpolation of the obtained local models when constructing the LPV (global) model. This identification process leads to a final global, but suboptimal, LPV model characterized by reduced accuracy.

In an effort to effectively tackle the aforementioned challenges, in this work we introduce a data-driven stochastic state-awareness framework for aerospace vehicles operating in dynamic environments under varying flight states and uncertainty. This framework incorporates: (i) bio-inspired networks of micro-sensors that can provide real-time information on the dynamic aeroelastic response of the structure [17, 23, 30, 32], and (ii) stochastic "global" identification techniques for representing the system dynamics under varying flight states and uncertainty. The "global" identification is based on the novel class of stochastic Functionally Pooled time series models recently proposed by the authors and co-workers [18–21, 28]. More specifically, in this study, and for the first time in the context of aeroelastic state awareness, the authors introduce the use of Vector-dependent Functionally Pooled (VFP) models [18, 20, 21] that enable explicit functional dependencies between the flight states and the model parameters. The class of VFP models resembles the form of LPV models, with some critical differences: (i) the signals are treated as a single entity and potential cross-correlations are accounted for, (ii) the number of estimated parameters is minimal, (iii) and the estimation is accomplished in a single step (instead of two subsequent steps) for achieving optimal accuracy.

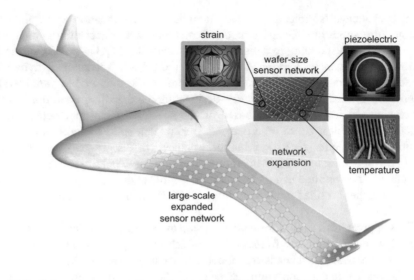

Fig. 31.1 Schematic representation of the intelligent UAV concept with bio-inspired multi-modal stretchable sensor networks embedded inside the composite structural components

This VFP-based identification is based on three important entities [20, 21]:

(i) A *stochastic Functionally Pooled (FP) model structure* that explicitly allows for system modeling under multiple operating conditions via a single ("global") mathematical representation. This representation is characterized by parameters that functionally (explicitly) depend on the flight state and additionally includes proper cross-correlation terms. This leads to more complete model forms, but also paves the way for accurate parameter estimation.

(ii) *Data pooling techniques* in a functional form which simultaneously treat, as a single entity, the data records corresponding to all available flight states. This allows for the simultaneous treatment of all response signals and is important for accounting for cross-correlations and achieving optimal estimation accuracy.

(iii) Properly formulated *statistically optimal techniques* for model estimation.

The aim of the present study is the introduction of the data-driven stochastic state-awareness framework and the experimental evaluation and assessment via a series of wind tunnel experiments under varying conditions. A prototype intelligent composite UAV wing [17] designed and fabricated in the Structures and Composites Laboratory (SACL) at Stanford University is outfitted with four bio-inspired stretchable sensor networks [7, 23, 30, 32] consisting of micro-sensors that are embedded inside the composite layup. The schematic representation of the proposed bio-inspired vehicle concept is presented in Fig. 31.1. Each sensor network contains 8 piezoelectric lead-zirconate titanate (PZT) sensors, 6 strain gauges, and 23 resistive temperature detectors (RTDs). Piezoelectric sensors are used to sense the vibration of the wing and allow the stochastic global identification of the dynamics and aeroelastic behavior under varying flight states, as well as the early detection of incipient dynamic flutter and stall. A series of 285 wind tunnel experiments under various AoA and freesrteam velocities are conducted for data collection under a broad range of flight states. The experimental evaluation of the data-driven identification approach will result in a single "global" time series model capable of accurately representing all the admissible flight states; that is all airspeeds and angles of attack that are considered in the wind tunnel experiments and may form the flight envelope of the vehicle.

The rest of the chapter is organized as follows: The bio-inspired stretchable sensor networks and the wing integration are briefly presented in Sect. 31.2. The wind tunnel experiments are described in Sect. 31.3, while the VFP-based stochastic global identification approach is outlined in Sect. 31.4. The experimental results are provided in Sect. 31.5, while the conclusions are summarized in Sect. 31.6.

31.2   Bio-inspired Sensor Networks and Wing Integration

Recently, micro-fabricated expandable sensor networks have been developed and deployed micro-scale sensors over macroscopic areas [7, 8, 23, 29–32]. In order to survive the large strains that occur in expansion, the sensors are created on polymer substrates with nonstandard and unique micro-fabrication processes. The resulting components have dimensions on the order of tens of micrometers (Fig. 31.2).

These networks are created on standard 100 mm diameter substrates and expanded to span areas orders of magnitude larger than the initial fabrication area deploying numerous micro-meter scale devices over meter scale areas. The resulting web-like network consists of distributed small scale components (nodes, wires, pads, etc.) intended to have a minimal parasitic effect on the host structure. The component size is on the same order as an individual fiber in typical composite materials or scrim in film adhesives and small enough to be placed into a composite without structural modifications. These networks can be used in-situ, from the material fabrication throughout its service life, to monitor the cure process of composite materials, characterize material properties post-cure, and monitor the structural dynamics along with the health of the structure during its life cycle.

In this work four stretchable sensor networks with integrated distributed PZT, strain, and RTD sensors have been designed and fabricated [7, 8, 23, 29, 30, 32] so that they can be embedded inside the layup of the composite wing. Extensible wires connect the network nodes and serve as the signal communication channels. Before stretching, the network dimensions are 52.8 mm by 39.6 mm that after the stretching process expand to 140 mm by 105 mm yielding a 700% total surface area increase [7]. Each of the four sensor networks contains 8 piezoelectric sensors (round PZTs 3.175 mm in diameter), 6 strain gauges, and 24 RTDs. The total number of embedded sensors in the composite wing is 148.

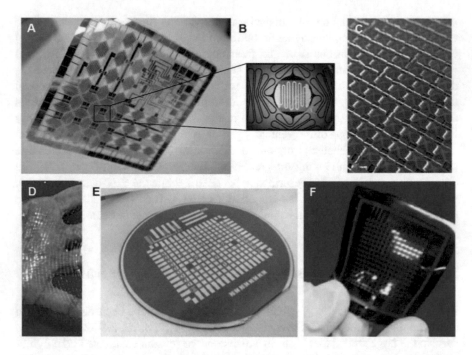

Fig. 31.2 (**a**) A 16-node sensor network on a wafer can be expanded up to $1,057\%$ in each dimension after release. (**b**) Close-up of the sensor node demonstrating the design of the microwires. (**c**) A sensor network with 169 nodes before expansion. (**d**) An expanded 5041-node network is shown in contrast to a hand, which illustrates the flexibility of the membrane. (**e**) Network before release on a 4-inch wafer. (**f**) A fabricated 256-node network on polyimide is easily held by hand without damaging the network. It is characterized by 16 μm wide, 50 μm thick microwires

Table 31.1 Test wing geometry

Semispan b	0.86 m
Chord c	0.235 m
Area S	0.2 m^2
Aspect ratio	7.32
Airfoil	SG6043

31.2.1 The Composite Wing

The prototype wing was designed, constructed and tested at Stanford University. The designed wing is based on the cambered SG6043 high lift-to-drag ratio airfoil with a 0.86 m half-span, 0.235 m chord, and an aspect ratio of 7.32. Table 31.1 presents the wing dimensions. In order to achieve the successful integration and fabrication of the wing prototype, an appropriate network-material integration process had to be developed for embedding the micro-fabricated sensor networks inside the composite materials.

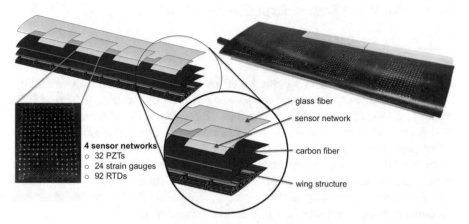

Fig. 31.3 The intelligent composite wing design with a total of 148 (32 piezoelectric, 24 strain gauges, and 92 RTDs) micro-sensors embedded in the composite layup

The micro-scale, aspect ratio, and fragile nature of the stretchable network components, including both the wires and the sensor nodes, requires the use of appropriate integration and network transfer processes. The geometry and material of the network nodes and contact pads may cause the electrical shorting with the carbon fibers if not properly addressed. In order to tackle these integration and manufacturing challenges, a new process had to be developed for the transfer, electrical interfacing and electrical insulation of the network components based on multilayer flexible PCB technologies and epoxy armoring. Via the use of the developed approach the sensor networks were successfully integrated into carbon fiber based composite materials using a multi-step fabrication process. The composite wing structure was manufactured based on carbon and glass laminated composites. The layup consists of carbon fiber (CF) plain weave fabric 1K T300 and glass fiber (GF) plain wave fabric 18 g/m^2 infused with Araldite LY/HY5052 epoxy. The stacking sequence of the layers was [0° GF, 0° CF, 45° CF, 45° CF, 0° CF, 0° GF] (Fig. 31.3).

Four sensor networks were embedded between the two top layers at 0° of the layup (near the wing surface) during the lamination process. The glass fiber was employed due to its transparency, so that the embedded stretchable sensor networks could be evident to the eye. The supporting wing structure consists of wooden (basswood) ribs and spars.

31.3   The Wind Tunnel Experimental Process

31.3.1   The Wind Tunnel

The prototype composite wing was tested in the open-loop wind tunnel facility
at Stanford University. The wind tunnel has a square test section of 0.76×0.76
m (30×30 in) and can achieve continuous flow speeds up to approximately 40
m/s. A custom basis was designed and fabricated to support the wing and permit
adjustments in the AoA. The wing was mounted horizontally inside the test section.
Eight commercial strain gauges were attached on appropriate locations of the basis
to measure the aerodynamic forces. The axis of rotation coincided approximately
with the quarter of the wing chord. Figure 31.4 presents the composite wing with
the corresponding locations of the PZTs and strain sensors.

31.3.2   The Experiments

A series of wind tunnel experiments were conducted for various angles of attack
and free-stream velocities U_∞. For each AoA, from 0 degrees up to 18 degrees with
an incremental step of 1 degree, data were sequentially collected for velocities from
9 m/s up to 22 m/s (incremental step 1 m/s). The above procedure resulted in 285
different experiments covering the complete range of the considered experimental
conditions. The experimental conditions along with the Reynolds numbers are
outlined in Table 31.2.

For each experiment the vibration and strain responses were recorded at different
locations on the wing via the embedded network piezoelectric sensors (initial
sampling frequency $f_s = 1000$ Hz, initial signal bandwidth 0.1–500 Hz) and

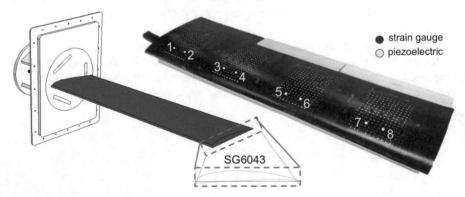

Fig. 31.4 The intelligent composite wing with the embedded sensor networks and the locations
of the piezoelectric and strain sensors

Table 31.2 The conditions considered in the wind tunnel experiments

Re ($\times 10^3$)	124	155	171	187	202	217	233	248	264	280	295	311	326	342
U_∞ (m/s)	9	10	11	12	13	14	15	16	17	18	19	20	21	22
	AoA: 0 – 18 degrees; Total number of experiments: 285													

Table 31.3 Signal pre-processing and details

	Piezoelectric sensors	Strain gauges
Number of sensors:	8	15
Sampling frequency:	$f_s = 1000$ Hz	$f_s = 100$ Hz
Bandwidth:	[0.1–500] Hz	[DC-50] Hz
Signal length:	$N = 90,000$ samples (90 s)	$N = 9000$ samples (90 s)

strain gauges (sampling frequency $f_s = 100$ Hz, signal bandwidth 1–100 Hz), respectively. The sensor signals were driven through a custom designed and built signal conditioning device into the data acquisition system (National Instruments X Series 6366). The total number of the sensor signals that were obtained was limited by the available number of channels of the data acquisition system. Table 31.3 presents the sensors, data acquisition, signal details.

31.4 Stochastic Global Identification Under Multiple Flight States

In this section, the identification of the wing dynamics is presented via the use of stochastic functional models, or more precisely Vector-dependent Functionally Pooled AutoRegressive (VFP-AR) models. These models are capable of representing the system dynamics for the complete range of operating (flight) conditions (airspeeds and angles of attack). The identification of stochastic systems operating under multiple conditions is addressed based on data records obtained under a sample of these conditions. The problem is important in a number of practical applications and is tackled within the recently introduced Functional Pooling framework [20, 21, 28]. This study focuses on the case of flight states characterized by two parameters, namely the airspeed and the AoA of the wing.

31.4.1 Baseline Modeling Under a Single Flight State

The modeling of the wing under a single flight state is an initial step performed in order to facilitate (in the sense of providing approximate model orders) the subsequent step of the global modeling under all the admissible flight states.

A single wind tunnel experiment is performed, based on which an interval estimate of a discrete-time model (or a vector model or an array of models in the case of several response measurement locations) representing the system dynamics is obtained via standard identification procedures [25, 33]. In this study a single response AutoRegressive (AR) model is used.

An AR(n) model is of the form[1] [25]:

$$y[t] + \sum_{i=1}^{n} a_i \cdot y[t - i] = e[t] \qquad e[t] \sim \text{iid} \, \mathcal{N}\left(0, \sigma_e^2\right) \tag{31.1}$$

with t designating the normalized discrete time ($t = 1, 2, 3, \ldots$ with absolute time being $(t - 1)T_s$, where T_s stands for the sampling period), $y[t]$ the measured vibration response signals as generated by the piezoelectric sensors of the wing, n the AR order, and $e[t]$ the stochastic model residual (one-step-ahead prediction error) sequence, that is a white (serially uncorrelated), Gaussian, zero mean with variance σ_e^2 sequence. The symbol $\mathcal{N}(\cdot, \cdot)$ designates Gaussian distribution with the indicated mean and variance, and iid stands for identically independently distributed. Finally, the AR model parameters are designated as a_i.

The model is parameterized in terms of the parameter vector $\bar{\theta} = [a_1 \ \ldots \ a_n \vdots \sigma_e^2]^T$ to be estimated from the measured signals [25]. Model estimation may be achieved based on minimization of the Ordinary Least Squares (OLS) or the Weighted Least Squares (WLS) criteria [25]. The modeling procedure involves the successive fitting of AR(n) models for increasing order n until an adequate model is selected [5]. Model order selection is based on the Bayesian Information Criterion (BIC) and the residual sum of squares normalized by the series sum of squares (RSS/SSS). Final model validation is based on formal verification of the residual (one-step-ahead prediction error) sequence uncorrelatedness (whiteness) hypothesis [25, pp. 512–513].

31.4.2 Global Modeling Under Multiple Flight States

The VFP-AR representation allows for complete and precise modeling of the global wing dynamics under multiple flight states with each state defined by

---

[1]Lower case/capital bold face symbols designate vector/matrix quantities, respectively.

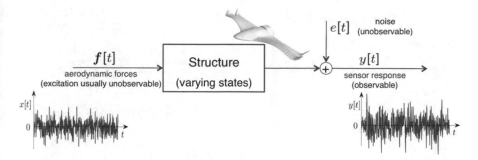

Fig. 31.5 Schematic representation of the system identification problem

a specific airspeed and AoA. Figure 31.5 presents the schematic representation of the identification problem. The VFP model parameters and residual series covariance depend functionally on both airspeed and AoA, while the corresponding interrelations and statistical dependencies between the different flight states are taken into account within the VFP model structure.

The VFP-AR representation belongs to the recently introduced broader class of stochastic functionally pooled models, which make use of functional data pooling techniques for combining and optimally treating (as one entity) the data obtained from various experiments corresponding to different structural states and statistical techniques for model estimation [21, 28].

The global modeling of the composite wing via a VFP-AR model involves consideration of all the admissible airspeeds and angles of attack that define the flight envelope of the wing. A total of $M_1 \times M_2$ experiments is performed (physically or via analytical models and simulations), with M_1 and M_2 designating the number of experiments under the various airspeeds and angles of attack, respectively. Each experiment is characterized by a specific airspeed k^1 and a specific AoA k^2, with the complete series covering the required range of each variable, say $[k^1_{min}, k^1_{max}]$ and $[k^2_{min}, k^2_{max}]$, via the discretizations $\{k^1_1, k^1_2, \ldots, k^1_{M_1}\}$ and $\{k^2_1, k^2_2, \ldots, k^2_{M_2}\}$. For the identification of a global VFP model the vector operating parameter k containing the airspeed and AoA components, is defined as:

$$k = [k^1_i \; k^2_j]^T \iff k_{i,j}, \quad i = 1, \ldots, M_1, \quad j = 1, \ldots, M_2 \tag{31.2}$$

with $k_{i,j}$ designating the flight state of the wing corresponding to the i-th airspeed and the j-th AoA. This procedure yields a pool of response signals (each of length N):

$$x_k[t], y_k[t] \text{ with } t = 1, \ldots, N, \; k^1 \in \{k^1_1, \ldots, k^1_{M_1}\}, \; k^2 \in \{k^2_1, \ldots, k^2_{M_2}\}. \tag{31.3}$$

A schematic representation of the data collection process for the identification of the global model is presented in Fig. 31.6.

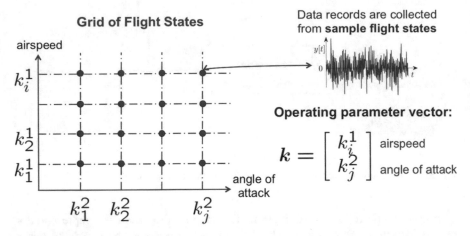

Fig. 31.6 Schematic representation of data collection under different flight states characterized by varying airspeed and AoA

A proper mathematical description of the wing structure may be then obtained in the form of a VFP-AR model. In the case of several response measurement locations an array of such models (or else a vector model) may be obtained, with each scalar model corresponding to each measurement location.

The VFP-AR model is of the following form [21]:

$$y_k[t] + \sum_{i=1}^{n} a_i(k) \cdot y_k[t-i] = e_k[t] \tag{31.4}$$

$$e_k[t] \sim \text{iid}\,\mathcal{N}\left(0, \sigma_e^2(k)\right) \qquad k \in \mathbb{R}^2 \tag{31.5}$$

$$a_i(k) = \sum_{j=1}^{p} a_{i,j} \cdot G_j(k) \tag{31.6}$$

$$E\{e_{k_{i,j}}[t] \cdot e_{k_{m,n}}[t-\tau]\} = \gamma_e[k_{i,j}, k_{m,n}] \cdot \delta[\tau] \tag{31.7}$$

with n designating the AR order, $y_k[t]$ the piezoelectric sensor's response signal, and $e_k[t]$ the model's residual (one-step-ahead prediction error) sequence, that is a white (serially uncorrelated) zero mean sequence with variance $\sigma_e^2(k)$. This may potentially be cross-correlated with its counterparts corresponding to different experiments (different k's). The symbol $E\{\cdot\}$ designates statistical expectation, $\delta[\tau]$ the Kronecker delta (equal to unity for $\tau = 0$ and equal to zero for $\tau \neq 0$), $\mathcal{N}(\cdot, \cdot)$ Gaussian distribution with the indicated mean and variance, and iid stands for identically independently distributed.

As (31.6) indicates, the AR parameters $a_i(k)$ are modeled as explicit functions of the vector k (which contains the airspeed and AoA components) by belonging to p-dimensional functional subspace spanned by the mutually independent basis functions $G_1(k), G_2(k), \ldots, G_p(k)$ (*functional basis*). The functional basis consists of polynomials of two variables (bivariate) obtained as tensor products from their corresponding univariate polynomials (Chebyshev, Legendre, Jacobi, and other families [20, 21]). The constants $a_{i,j}$ designate the AR coefficients of projection.

The VFP-AR model of (31.4)–(31.7) is parameterized in terms of the parameter vector to be estimated from the measured signals:

$$\bar{\theta} = [\, a_{1,1}\; a_{1,2}\; \ldots\; a_{i,j} \;\vdots\; \sigma_e^2(k)\,]^T \quad \forall\, k \tag{31.8}$$

and may be written in linear regression form as:

$$y_k[t] = \left[\varphi_k^T[t] \otimes g^T(k)\right] \cdot \theta + e_k[t] = \phi_k^T[t] \cdot \theta + e_k[t] \tag{31.9}$$

with:

$$\varphi_k[t] := \left[-y_k[t-1] \ldots -y_k[t-n]\right]_{[n\times 1]}^T \tag{31.10}$$

$$g(k) := \left[G_1(k) \ldots G_p(k)\right]_{[p\times 1]}^T \tag{31.11}$$

$$\theta := \left[a_{1,1}\; a_{1,2}\; \ldots\; a_{n,p}\right]_{[np\times 1]}^T \tag{31.12}$$

and ^{T} designating transposition and $\otimes$ Kronecker product [2, Chap. 7].

Pooling together the expressions (31.9) of the VFP-AR model corresponding to all vector operating parameters k $(k_{1,1}, k_{1,2}, \ldots, k_{M_1,M_2})$ considered in the experiments (cross-sectional pooling) yields:

$$\begin{bmatrix} y_{k_{1,1}}[t] \\ \vdots \\ y_{k_{M_1,M_2}}[t] \end{bmatrix} = \begin{bmatrix} \phi_{k_{1,1}}^T[t] \\ \vdots \\ \phi_{k_{M_1,M_2}}^T[t] \end{bmatrix} \cdot \theta + \begin{bmatrix} e_{k_{1,1}}[t] \\ \vdots \\ e_{k_{M_1,M_2}}[t] \end{bmatrix} \implies y[t] = \Phi[t] \cdot \theta + e[t]. \tag{31.13}$$

Then, following substitution of the data for $t = 1, \ldots, N$ the following expression is obtained:

$$y = \Phi \cdot \theta + e \tag{31.14}$$

with

$$
y := \begin{bmatrix} y[1] \\ \vdots \\ y[N] \end{bmatrix}, \quad \Phi := \begin{bmatrix} \Phi[1] \\ \vdots \\ \Phi[N] \end{bmatrix}, \quad e := \begin{bmatrix} e[1] \\ \vdots \\ e[N] \end{bmatrix}. \tag{31.15}
$$

Using the above linear regression framework the simplest approach for estimating the projection coefficient vector θ is based on minimization of the Ordinary Least Squares (OLS) criterion $J^{\mathrm{OLS}} := \frac{1}{N} \sum_{t=1}^{N} e^{T}[t]e[t]$.

A more appropriate criterion is (in view of the Gauss-Markov theorem [6]) the Weighted Least Squares (WLS) criterion:

$$
J^{\mathrm{WLS}} := \frac{1}{N} \sum_{t=1}^{N} e^{T}[t] \Gamma_{e[t]}^{-1} e[t] = \frac{1}{N} e^{T} \Gamma_{e}^{-1} e \tag{31.16}
$$

which leads to the *Weighted Least Squares (WLS)* estimator:

$$
\widehat{\theta}^{\mathrm{WLS}} = \left[\Phi^{T} \Gamma_{e}^{-1} \Phi \right]^{-1} \left[\Phi^{T} \Gamma_{e}^{-1} y \right]. \tag{31.17}
$$

In these expressions $\Gamma_e = E\{ee^T\}$ ($\Gamma_e = \Gamma_{e[t]} \otimes I_N$, with I_N designating the $N \times N$ unity matrix) designates the residual covariance matrix, which is practically unavailable. Nevertheless, it may be consistently estimated by applying (in an initial step) Ordinary Least Squares (details in [21]). Once $\widehat{\theta}^{\mathrm{WLS}}$ has been obtained, the final residual variance and residual covariance matrix estimates are obtained as:

$$
\widehat{\sigma}_{e}^{2}(k, \widehat{\theta}^{\mathrm{WLS}}) = \frac{1}{N} \sum_{t=1}^{N} e_{k}^{2}[t, \widehat{\theta}^{\mathrm{WLS}}], \quad \widehat{\Gamma}_{e[t]} = \frac{1}{N} \sum_{t=1}^{N} e[t, \widehat{\theta}^{\mathrm{WLS}}] e^{T}[t, \widehat{\theta}^{\mathrm{WLS}}]. \tag{31.18}
$$

The estimator $\widehat{\theta}^{\mathrm{WLS}}$ may, under mild conditions, be shown to be asymptotically Gaussian distributed with mean coinciding with the true parameter vector θ^{o} and covariance matrix P_{θ}:

$$
\sqrt{N}(\widehat{\theta}_{N} - \theta^{o}) \sim \mathcal{N}(0, P_{\theta}) \quad (N \longrightarrow \infty) \tag{31.19}
$$

based on which interval estimates of the true parameter vector may be constructed [21].

The problem of VFP-AR model structure selection (structure estimation) for a given basis function family (such as Chebyshev, Legendre, and so on) refers to the model order determination for the AR polynomial and determination of their corresponding functional subspaces. Usually, the AR model order is initially selected via customary model order selection techniques (BIC, RSS, frequency stabilization diagrams) [25], whereas the functional subspace dimensionality is selected via a Genetic Algorithm (GA) procedure [21]. Initially, the maximum functional subspace dimensionality is selected, which defines the search space of the functional subspace estimation subproblem. The determination of the exact subspace dimensionality is achieved via the use of Genetic Algorithms (GA) based on minimization of the BIC with respect to the candidate basis functions. In the current study, the estimation of the functional subspace dimensionality was achieved via the use of the BIC criterion for increasing functional subspace dimensionality.

31.5   Results

31.5.1   Numerical Simulations

In order to extract the aerodynamic properties of the fabricated wing based on which the experimental results will be interpreted and assessed, a series of numerical simulations was conducted using XFOIL, an interactive program developed at MIT for the design and analysis of subsonic isolated airfoils [4].

Figure 31.7a and b present the lift coefficient versus the AoA and lift to drag coefficient ratio C_L/C_D results of the SG6043 airfoil, respectively, for various Reynolds numbers ($U_\infty = 7, 10, 12$ and 15 m/s). It may be readily observed that the wing exhibits stall (loss of lift shown as shaded area in Figure 31.7a) starting from an AoA of approximately 12 degrees for a Reynolds number of $Re = 100,000$. Moreover, observe that the maximum C_L/C_D ratio is obtained for angles between 4 and 8 degrees (shaded areas in Fig. 31.7b).

Figure 31.8 presents indicative signals obtained from piezoelectric sensor 2 (see Fig. 31.4 for the sensor location) under various angles of attack and freestream velocities of $U_\infty = 11$ m/s and $U_\infty = 15$ m/s (see Table 31.2). Observe the random (stochastic) nature of these signals, which is due to the wind tunnel airflow actuation and the aeroelastic response of the wing. In addition, it is evident that for higher angles of attack and as the wing approaches stall, the signal amplitude

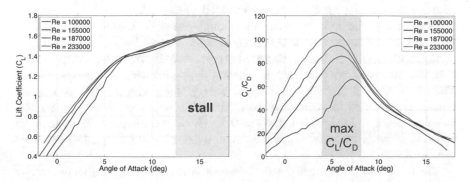

Fig. 31.7 Indicative simulation results: (**a**) lift coefficient C_L (left subplot) and (**b**) lift-to-drag coefficient ratio C_L/C_D (right subplot) versus AoA for the SG6043 airfoil and various Reynolds numbers

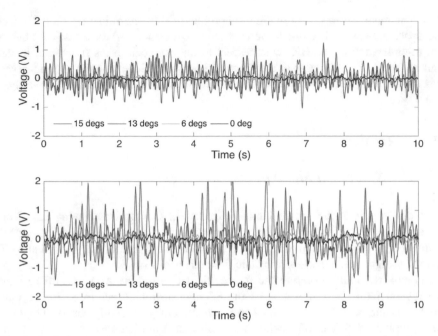

Fig. 31.8 Indicative signals obtained from piezoelectric sensor 2 under various angles of attack: (**a**) freestream velocity $U_\infty = 11$ m/s (top subplot) and (**b**) freestream velocity $U_\infty = 15$ m/s (bottom subplot)

(voltage) increases. In the case of $U_\infty = 11$ m/s that corresponds to the top subplot in Fig. 31.8, the maximum signal amplitude for AoA 13 and 15 degrees seems to be similar as there is no evident increase. For this freestream velocity and based on Fig. 31.7, stall occurs at an AoA of approximately 13 degrees. In the case of $U_\infty = 15$ m/s that corresponds to the bottom subplot in Fig. 31.8, occurs at approximately 15 degrees, and it may be readily observed that there is an obvious increase in the signal amplitude from 13 to 15 degrees AoA.

In order to further investigate the signal amplitude of the sensors with respect to varying AoA we conducted the statistical signal energy analysis of the wing based on the wind tunnel experiments. Figure 31.9 presents indicative signal energy (volt^2· t) results obtained from piezoelectric sensor 1 during the wind tunnel experiments. The mean value of the vibrational signal energy along with the 99% confidence bounds are depicted for increasing AoA. The initial signal of 90 s ($N = 90,000$ samples) was split in signal windows of 0.5 s ($N = 500$ samples). Then, for each signal window the mean value and the standard deviation of the signal energy were estimated.

The AoA is varied between 0 and 15 degrees with a constant freestream velocity of $U_\infty = 11$ m/s. The goal is to correlate the signal energy in the time domain with the airflow characteristics and aeroelastic properties in order to identify and track appropriate signal features that can be used for the wing vibration monitoring, the

Fig. 31.9 Indicative signal energy versus AoA wind-tunnel results for piezoelectric sensor 1 and freestream velocity $U_\infty = 11$ m/s. The mean value of the signal energy is shown as red line. The 99% confidence bounds are shown as green shaded areas

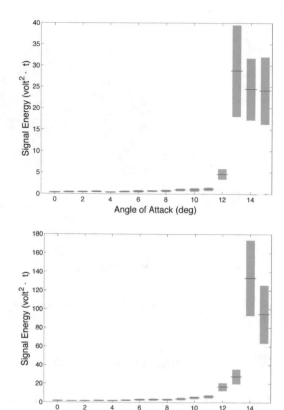

Fig. 31.10 Indicative signal energy versus AoA wind-tunnel results for piezoelectric sensor 1 and freestream velocity $U_\infty = 15$ m/s. The mean value of the signal energy is shown as red line. The 99% confidence bounds are shown as green shaded areas

localization of the flow separation over the wing chord, and the early detection of stall under various flight states.

As the wing angle exceeds the value of 12 degrees the signal energy significantly increases and reaches the maximum value as it approaches stall (AoA of 13 degrees), while slightly decreases after stall has occurred (14 and 15 degrees). The statistical analysis of the wind tunnel signals for the various sensors indicated that for velocities of 11 m/s and 12 m/s the stall angle is 13 degrees, whereas for the higher velocities of 14 m/s and 15 m/s the stall angle appears at 14 degrees.

Figure 31.10 presents similar statistical energy results for freestream velocity $U_\infty = 15$ m/s. These results are in agreement with the trend of signals in Fig. 31.8 as in both cases the signal amplitude/energy is maximized within the stall range of the wing. Also, the results are in agreement with the numerical simulations presented in Fig 31.7.

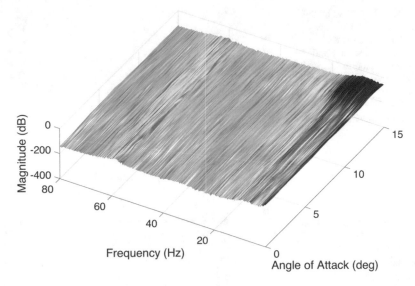

Fig. 31.11 Indicative non-parametric Welch-based PSD estimates (piezoelectric sensor 1) versus AoA for $U_\infty = 13$ m/s ($Re = 202,000$) freestream velocity

31.5.2 Non-parametric Analysis

Non-parametric identification is based on $90,000$ (signal duration of 90 s) sample-long response signals obtained from the embedded piezoelectric sensors (see Table 31.3. A 5096 sample-long Hamming data window (frequency resolution $\Delta f = 0.24$ Hz) with 90% overlap is used for the Welch-based spectral estimation (MATLAB function *pwelch.m*).

Figure 31.11 presents indicative non-parametric power spectral density (PSD) Welch-based estimates of the piezoelectric response signals obtained from sensor 1 for increasing AoA and freestream velocity $U_\infty = 13$ m/s ($Re = 202,000$). Notice that as the AoA increases the PSD amplitude in the lower frequency range of [1–12] Hz significantly increases as well. More specifically, as the angle of the wing approaches the critical stall range of 13–14 degrees, the low frequency vibrations become dominant and thus indicating the proximity to the stall of the wing. It is evident that monitoring the identified lower frequency bandwidths that are sensitive to increasing AoA provides a strong indication of stall. All the embedded piezoelectric sensors of the wing exhibit a similar performance, but for the sake of brevity the results are omitted.

Similarly, Fig. 31.12 presents indicative non-parametric power spectral density (PSD) Welch-based estimates obtained from piezoelectric sensor 1 for increasing airspeed and an constant AoA of 0 degrees. Again, notice that as the airspeed increases, the PSD amplitude in the lower frequency range increases as well. In this case, it is expected that as the airspeed increases for a constant AoA the

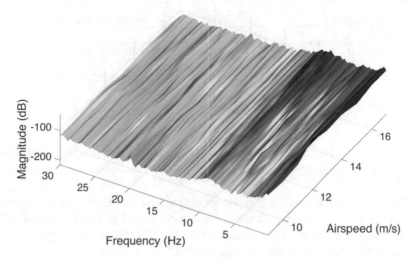

Fig. 31.12 Indicative non-parametric Welch-based PSD estimates (piezoelectric sensor 1) versus airspeed for an AoA of 0 degrees

wing will approach its flutter speed which will be triggered by the coupling of aeroelastic modes. By carefully observing Fig. 31.12 it may be observed that the frequency at approximately 5 Hz increases with increasing airspeed and approaches the frequency at approximately 9 Hz, thus providing an indication of incipient flutter. This observation will be clarified by the global parametric modeling of the next subsections.

31.5.3   Baseline Parametric Modeling

Conventional AR time series models representing the wing dynamics are obtained through standard identification procedures [5, 25] based on the collected piezoelectric response signals (MATLAB function *arx.m*). The response signal bandwidth is selected as 0.1–100 Hz after the initial signals were low-pass filtered (Chebyshev Type II) and sub-sampled to a resulting sampling frequency $f_s = 200$ Hz (initial sampling frequency was at 1000 Hz). Each signal resulted in a length of $N = 4000$ samples and was subsequently sample mean corrected (Table 31.4). For piezoelectric sensor 1, this leads to an AR(72) model for a collected data set corresponding to an airspeed of 11 m/s and an AoA of 3 degrees. This model is used as reference and for providing approximate orders for the identification of the global VFP-AR models of the next section. For the sake of brevity, in the following sections indicative results from sensor 1 only will be presented.

Table 31.4 Piezoelectric signal pre-processing for the parametric identification

Sampling frequency:	$f_s = 200$ Hz (after filtering and subsampling)
Final bandwidth:	[0.1–100] Hz
Digital filtering:	Low-pass Chebyshev Type II (7th order)
Signal length:	$N = 4000$ samples (20 s)

31.5.4   Global Modeling Under Multiple Flight States

The parametric VFP-based identification of the wing dynamics is based on signals collected from the piezoelectric sensors under the various wind tunnel experiments (see Table 31.2).

The global modeling of the composite wing is based on signals obtained from a total of $M_1 \times M_2 = 144$ experiments. Airspeeds up to 17 m/s and angles of attack up to 15 degrees were currently considered for the VFP-based modeling procedure. The airspeed and AoA increments used are $\delta k^1 = 1$ m/s and $\delta k^2 = 1$ degree, respectively, covering the corresponding intervals of [9, 17] m/s and [0, 15] degrees.

Model order selection starts with the orders selected for the conventional AR models representing the wing structure for a constant indicative experimental condition. The final model orders being presently selected are based on the BIC criterion [5] and model validation techniques, such as checking the whiteness (uncorrelatedness) and the normality of the model residuals (MATLAB functions *acf.m* and *normplot.m*, respectively) [5, 25]. The functional subspaces are selected via a similar BIC-based process. The functional subspace consists of 25 Chebyshev Type II bivariate polynomial basis functions[20–22]. The final identified global model is VFP-AR(72)$_{25}$. Thus, the model order of the AR polynomial is 72, while the functional subspace consists of the first $p = 25$ shifted Chebyshev Type II 2-dimensional polynomials.

Indicative VFP-based frequency response function (FRF) results obtained from the VFP-AR(72)$_{25}$ model (for set airspeed of 11 m/s) are, as functions of frequency and AoA, depicted in Fig. 31.13. The frequency resolution is 0.01 Hz, while the AoA resolution is 0.1 degrees. The desired resolutions can be properly defined due to the analytical functional dependence of the flight state with the model parameters. By observing the frequency evolution versus the AoA it may be assessed that the amplitude of the parametric power spectral density increases for lower frequencies with the increase of the AoA. More specifically, the spectral amplitude of the frequency at 9 Hz exhibits a sharp increase for an AoA of 13 degrees in which stall occurs (compare with Fig. 31.7). In addition, by comparing the parametric spectral estimates with the corresponding non-parametric Welch-based analysis of Fig. 31.11 it may be concluded that high accuracy achieved by the global modeling approach which also employs a significantly shorter signal length (see Table 31.3).

Indicative parametric FRF results obtained from the VFP-AR(72)$_{25}$ model (for set AoA of 0 degrees) are, as functions of frequency and airspeed, depicted in Fig. 31.14. It may be observed that the wing mode at 4.5 Hz for 9 m/s gradually

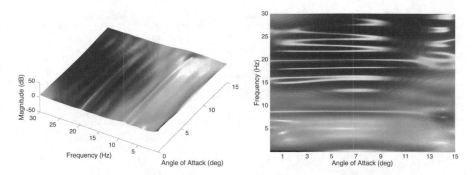

Fig. 31.13 Indicative parametric results obtained via the VFP-AR$(72)_{25}$ model for set airspeed of 11 m/s: frequency response function estimates as function of frequency and AoA. Observe the sharp increase in the spectral amplitude of aeroelastic mode at 8.5 Hz at an AoA of 13 degrees that provides a clear indication of stall

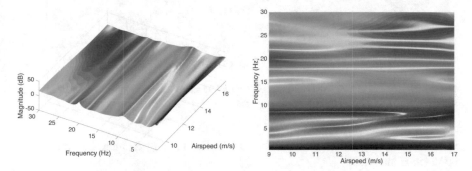

Fig. 31.14 Indicative parametric spectral results obtained from the VFP-AR$(72)_{25}$ model (set AoA of 0 degrees): frequency response function estimates as function of frequency and airspeed. Observe the convergence and final coupling of the aeroelastic modes at 4.5 Hz and 8.5 Hz that provides a clear indication of wing flutter

increases with the increasing airspeed until unified with the mode at 8.5 Hz at approximately 16 m/s. This aeroelastic behavior corresponds to the generation of the dynamic flutter phenomenon. It may be readily observed that the results of Fig. 31.14 are extremely accurate in comparison with the corresponding non-parametric analysis of Fig. 31.12. Via the use of such a global VFP model it is possible to improve the aircraft control in order to suppress, minimize, and even predict dynamic flutter via appropriate real-time monitoring techniques.

Indicative model parameters of the VFP-AR$(72)_{25}$ model are depicted in Fig. 31.15 as functions of the airspeed for a constant AoA of 11 degrees. The corresponding 99% confidence intervals are also depicted in red color. In most of the cases as shown in the subplots, it may be readily observed that the confidence intervals are extremely narrow, which demonstrates the accuracy of the parameter estimation approach. In case of increased uncertainty reflected in the recorded signals, the stochastic identification approach will compensate by increasing

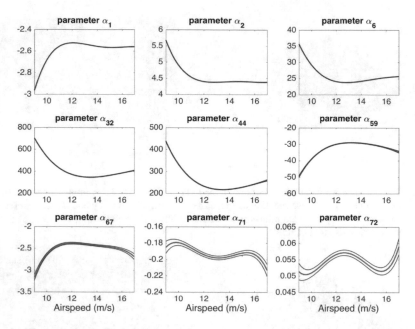

Fig. 31.15 Indicative VFP-AR$(72)_{25}$ model parameters along with their 99% confidence intervals versus airspeed for a set AoA of $k^2 = 11$ degrees

the parameter estimation uncertainty and hence, leading to increased parameter confidence intervals.

However, as previously mentioned, the VFP model parameters are explicit functions of both the airspeed and the AoA based on the selected functional subspace and the estimated coefficients of projections. Towards this end, Fig. 31.16 presents indicative VFP-AR$(72)_{25}$ model parameters as functions of both the airspeed and angel of attack.

31.6 Concluding Remarks

The objective of this work was to introduce a novel data-driven state awareness framework for the next generation of intelligent "fly-by-feel" aerospace vehicles. The proposed framework was based on (i) bio-inspired networks of micro-sensors that can provide real-time information on the dynamic aeroelastic response of the structure and (ii) stochastic "global" models for representing the system dynamics under varying flight states and uncertainty. In the context of aeroelastic state awareness, the use of Vector-dependent Functionally Pooled (VFP) models that allow explicit functional dependencies between the flight states and the model parameters was introduced. The class of VFP models resembles the form of LPV models, with some critical differences: (i) the signals are treated as a single entity

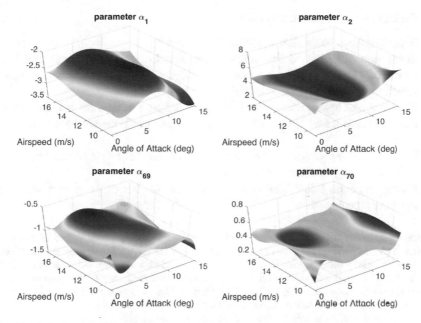

Fig. 31.16   Indicative VFP-AR(72)$_{25}$ model parameters as function of airspeed and AoA

and potential cross-correlations are accounted for, (ii) the number of estimated parameters is minimal, and (iii) the estimation is accomplished in a single step (instead of two subsequent steps) for achieving optimal accuracy.

For the experimental assessment and evaluation of the proposed stochastic framework, a prototype intelligent composite UAV wing was designed and fabricated at Stanford University. The composite wing was outfitted with bio-inspired stretchable networks consisting of 148 micro-sensors that were embedded inside the composite layup. A series of wind tunnel experiments was conducted under various AoA and freesrteam velocities for data collection under varying flight states. A total of 285 wind tunnel experiments covering the complete range of the considered flight states was conducted. The postulated data-driven stochastic identification approach that is based on the novel VFP time series model structure achieved the accurate representation of the wing dynamics for all the admissible flight states and enabled the detection of dynamic stall and flutter phenomena. The obtained results demonstrated the successful integration of the bio-inspired sensor networks with the composite wing, but most importantly the effectiveness and accuracy of the stochastic data-driven "global" identification approach, as a first step towards the next generation of "fly-by-feel" aerospace vehicles with state sensing and awareness capabilities.

Current and future work addresses:

- Real-time implementation of the DSA framework.
- Integration with high-fidelity structural and aeroelastic computational models for increased physical insight, data generation for training purposes, and complete structural awareness in the material.
- Postulation of appropriate control schemes for flutter mitigation, stall avoidance, gust alleviation, and optimized maneuvering and performance based on global model.
- Extension of the global VFP models to the mutlivariate case to simultaneously account for large numbers of sensors.
- Extension of the global VFP models to account for fast evolving non-stationary dynamic signals.

Acknowledgments This research was supported by the U.S. Air Force Office of Scientific Research (AFOSR) Multidisciplinary University Research Initiative (MURI) program under grant FA9550-09-1-0677 with Program Manager Byung-Lip (Les) Lee. The authors would like to thank Dr. Yu-Hung Li for the fabrication of the stretchable sensor networks, Mr. Raphael Nardari for the fabrication of the composite wing, and Mr. Pengchuan Wang, Dr. Jun Wu and Dr. Shaobo Liu for their help during the wind tunnel experiments. Finally, the authors would like to acknowledge the support of Dr. Lester Su and Prof. John Eaton in the wind tunnel facility at Stanford University.

References

1. Ahmed, S., Amer, A., Varela, C.A., Kopsaftopoulos, F.: Data-driven state awareness for fly-by-feel aerial vehicles via adaptive time series and gaussian process regression models. In: International Conference on Dynamic Data Driven Application Systems, pp. 57–65. Springer (2020)
2. Bernstein, D.: Matrix Mathematics. Princeton University Press (2005)
3. Breese, S., Kopsaftopoulos, F., Varela, C.: Towards proving runtime properties of data-driven systems using safety envelopes. In: International Workshop on Structural Health Monitoring 2019 (IWSHM 2019). Stanford, CA, U.S.A. (2019)
4. Drela, M., Youngren, H.: XFOIL. http://web.mit.edu/drela/Public/web/xfoil/. URL http://web.mit.edu/drela/Public/web/xfoil/
5. Fassois, S.D.: Parametric identification of vibrating structures. In: S. Braun, D. Ewins, S. Rao (eds.) Encyclopedia of Vibration, pp. 673–685. Academic Press (2001)
6. Greene, W.H.: Econometric Analysis, 5th edn. Prentice–Hall (2003)
7. Guo, Z.: Robust design and fabrication of highly stretchable sensor networks for the creation of intelligent materials. Ph.D. thesis, Department of Aeronautics and Astronautics, Stanford University (2014)
8. Guo, Z., Kim, K., Lanzara, G., Salowitz, N., Peumans, P., F.-K.Chang: Bio-inspiredsmart skin based on expandable network. In: F.K. Chang (ed.) Proceedings of the 8th International Workshop on Structural Health Monitoring 2011 — Condition Based Maintenance and Intelligent Structures. Stanford, CA, USA (2011)
9. Henshaw, M.C., Badcock, K.J., Vio, G.A., Allen, C.B., Chamberlain, J., Kaynes, I., Dimitriadis, G., Cooper, J.E., Woodgate, M.A., Rampurawala, A.M., Jones, D., Fenwick, C., Gaitonde, A.L., Taylor, N.V., Amor, D.S., Eccles, T.A., Denley, C.J.: Non-linear aeroelastic prediction for aircraft applications. Progress in Aerospace Sciences **43**, 65–137 (2007)

10. Hjartarson, A., Seiler, P.J., Balas, G.J.: LPV aeroservoelastic control using the LPVTools toolbox. In: Proceedings of AIAA Atmospheric Flight Mechanics (AFM) Conference. Boston, MA, U.S.A. (2013)
11. Huang, R., Zhao, Y., Hu, H.: Wind-tunnel tests for active flutter control and closed-loop flutter identification. AIAA Journal 54(7), 2089–2099 (2016)
12. Ihn, J., Chang, F.K.: Detection and monitoring of hidden fatigue crack growth using a built-in piezoelectric sensor/actuator network, part i: Diagnostics. Smart Materials and Structures 13, 609–620 (2004)
13. Ihn, J., Chang, F.K.: Detection and monitoring of hidden fatigue crack growth using a built-in piezoelectric sensor/actuator network, part ii: Validation through riveted joints and repair patches. Smart Materials and Structures 13, 621–630 (2004)
14. Ihn, J., Chang, F.K.: Pitch-catch active sensing methods in structural health monitoring for aircraft structures. Structural Health Monitoring 7(1), 5–19 (2008)
15. Janapati, V., Kopsaftopoulos, F., Li, F., Lee, S., Chang, F.K.: Damage detection sensitivity characterization of acousto-ultrasound-based structural health monitoring techniques. Structural Health Monitoring 15(2), 143–161 (2016)
16. Kopsaftopoulos, F.: Data-driven stochastic identification for fly-by-feel aerospace structures: Critical assessment of non-parametric and parametric approaches. In: AIAA Scitech 2019 Forum, p. 1534 (2019)
17. Kopsaftopoulos, F., Nardari, R., Li, Y.H., Chang, F.K.: Experimental identification of structural dynamics and aeroelastic properties of a self-sensing smart composite wing. In: F.K. Chang, F. Kopsaftopoulos (eds.) Proceedings of the 10th International Workshop on Structural Health Monitoring (IWSHM). Stanford University, USA (2015)
18. Kopsaftopoulos, F., Nardari, R., Li, Y.H., Chang, F.K.: A stochastic global identification framework for aerospace structures operating under varying flight states. Mechanical Systems and Signal Processing 98, 425–447 (2018)
19. Kopsaftopoulos, F., Nardari, R., Li, Y.H., Wang, P., Chang, F.K.: Stochastic global identification of a bio-inspired self-sensing composite uav wing via wind tunnel experiments. In: Proceedings of the SPIE 9805, Health Monitoring of Structural and Biological Systems 2016, 98051V. Las Vegas, NV, USA (2016)
20. Kopsaftopoulos, F.P.: Advanced functional and sequential statistical time series methods for damage diagnosis in mechanical structures. Ph.D. thesis, Department of Mechanical Engineering & Aeronautics, University of Patras, Patras, Greece (2012)
21. Kopsaftopoulos, F.P., Fassois, S.D.: Vector-dependent functionally pooled ARX models for the identification of systems under multiple operating conditions. In: Proceedings of the 16th IFAC Symposium on System Identification, (SYSID). Brussels, Belgium (2012)
22. Kopsaftopoulos, F.P., Fassois, S.D.: A functional model based statistical time series method for vibration based damage detection, localization, and magnitude estimation. Mechanical Systems and Signal Processing 39, 143–161 (2013). http://dx.doi.org/10.1016/j.ymssp.2012.08.023
23. Lanzara, G., Salowitz, N., Guo, Z., Chang, F.K.: A spider-web-like highly expandable sensor network for multifunctional materials. Advanced Materials 22(41), 4643–4648 (2010)
24. Larrosa, C., Lonkar, K., Chang, F.K.: In situ damage classification for composite laminates using gaussian discriminant analysis. Structural Health Monitoring 13(2), 190–204 (2014)
25. Ljung, L.: System Identification: Theory for the User, 2nd edn. Prentice–Hall (1999)
26. Pang, Z.Y., Cesnik, C.E.: Strain state estimation of very flexible unmanned aerial vehicle. In: Proceedings of 57th AIAA/ASCE/AHS/ASC Structures, Structural Dynamics, and Materials Conference. San Diego, CA, U.S.A. (2016)
27. Ryan, J.J., Bosworth, J.T., Burken, J.J., Suh, P.M.: Current and future research in active control of lightweight, flexible structures using the X-56 aircraft. In: Proceedings of AIAA 52nd Aerospace Sciences Meeting. National Harbor, MD, U.S.A. (2014)
28. Sakellariou, J.S., Fassois, S.D.: Functionally pooled models for the global identification of stochastic systems under different pseudo-static operating conditions. Mechanical Systems and Signal Processing 72-73, 785–807 (2016). http://dx.doi.org/10.1016/j.ymssp.2015.10.018

29. Salowitz, N., Guo, Z., Kim, S.J., Li, Y.H., Lanzara, G., Chang, F.K.: Screen-printed piezoce-ramic actuators/sensors microfabricated on organic films and stretchable networks. In: F.K. Chang (ed.) Proceedings of the 9th International Workshop on Structural Health Monitoring 2013. Stanford, CA, USA (2013)

30. Salowitz, N., Guo, Z., Li, Y.H., Kim, K., Lanzara, G., Chang, F.K.: Bio-inspired stretchable network-based intelligent composites. Journal of Composite Materials **47**(1), 97–106 (2013)

31. Salowitz, N., Guo, Z., Roy, S., Nardari, R., Li, Y.H., Kim, S., Kopsaftopoulos, F., Chang, F.K.: A vision on stretchable bio-inspired networks for intelligent structures. In: F.K. Chang (ed.) Proceedings of the 9th International Workshop on Structural Health Monitoring 2013. Stanford, CA, USA (2013)

32. Salowitz, N., Guo, Z., Roy, S., Nardari, R., Li, Y.H., Kim, S.J., Kopsaftopoulos, F., Chang, F.K.: Recent advancements and vision toward stretchable bio-inspired networks for intelligent structures. Structural Health Monitoring **13**(6), 609–620 (2014)

33. Söderström, T., Stoica, P.: System Identification. Prentice–Hall (1989)

34. Sodja, J., Werter, N., Dillinger, J., Breuker, R.D.: Dynamic response of aeroelastically tailored composite wing: Analysis and experiment. In: Proceedings of 57th AIAA/ASCE/AHS/ASC Structures, Structural Dynamics, and Materials Conference. San Diego, CA, U.S.A. (2016)

35. Suh, P.M., Chin, A.W., Mavris, D.N.: Virtual deformation control of the X-56A model with simulated fiber optic sensors. In: Proceedings of AIAA Atmospheric Flight Mechanics (AFM) Conference. Boston, MA, U.S.A. (2013)

36. Suh, P.M., Chin, A.W., Mavris, D.N.: Robust modal filtering and control of the X-56A model with simulated fiber optic sensor failures. In: Proceedings of AIAA Atmospheric Flight Mechanics (AFM) Conference. Atlanta, GA, U.S.A. (2014)

37. Toth, R.: Modeling and Identification of Linear Parameter-Varying Systems, *Lecture Notes in Control and Information Sciences*, vol. 403. Springer, Germany (2010)

38. Zeng, J., Chen, P.C., Kukreja, S.L.: Investigation of the prediction error identification for flutter prediction. In: Proceedings of AIAA Atmospheric Flight Mechanics (AFM) Conference. Minneapolis, MS, U.S.A. (2012)

Chapter 32
The Future of DDDAS

Erik P. Blasch, Frederica Darema (iD), Sai Ravela (iD), and Alex J. Aved

Abstract This second edition of the first volume of the Handbook of Dynamic Data Driven Applications Systems (DDDAS) highlights DDDAS research over the last two decades, with an emphasis on the key areas of theory, modeling, and examples. Recent developments have demonstrated the successful use of the DDDAS paradigm for contemporary engineering systems as well as complex natural systems. DDDAS seeks to leverage high-dimensional models to provide data that augments real time estimation, analysis, and control. Many examples were presented in the book that highlight recent approaches, designs, and use of the DDDAS concept towards advancing science through data understanding, analysis, and discovery. The future would further develop these DDDAS concepts towards a better understanding of scientific principles, engineering systems design, and multi-domains applications. DDDAS advances will leverage and influence such areas as machine learning analytics, multi-domain autonomy, and contextual awareness.

Keywords Big data · Infosymbiotics · Machine learning · Multi-dimensional · Physics-based and human-derived information fusion (PHIF) · Uncertainty quantification · Adaptive sampling · High-performance computing · Multi-domain autonomy

E. P. Blasch (✉)
Air Force Office of Scientific Research, Arlington, VA, USA

F. Darema
InfoSymbiotics Systems Society, Boston, MA, USA

S. Ravela
Massachusetts Institute of Technology, Cambridge, MA, USA

A. J. Aved
Air Force Research Lab, Rome, NY, USA

© This is a U.S. government work and not under copyright protection in the U.S.;
foreign copyright protection may apply 2022
E. P. Blasch et al. (eds.), *Handbook of Dynamic Data Driven Applications Systems*,
https://doi.org/10.1007/978-3-030-74568-4_32

32.1   DDDAS Methods for Systems Science

The updated book from the first edition [1] has demonstrated that many applications have been furthered from the use of the DDDAS paradigm including areas of analytics, autonomy, and awareness. DDDAS methods incorporate dynamic data that predated the trends in big data *analytics*. The future techniques will align with the efforts in artificial intelligence and machine learning that leverage data from high-dimensional modeling.

A second area includes the many applications in *autonomy* to include sensing, robotics, and filtering across many domains: space, air, and ground. The DDDAS methods focused on the machine processing of techniques; however developments will be aligned with user decision support, scenario assessment, and real-world deployment of the methods towards practical applications.

In general, the DDDAS themes include improvements in *awareness*, such as space situational awareness (SSA), structural health awareness, and environment awareness; where newer themes have emerged in context awareness, computational awareness, cyber and materials awareness (as shown in Table 32.1). In many cases, awareness could be replaced by monitoring the surroundings of the application. DDDAS builds on situational monitoring to leverage high-dimensional models for real-time, dynamic, and run-time assessment.

Other demonstrated examples included bio-medical approaches to medical diagnostics, human health, and urban pandemics. The rich exploration of DDDAS for the sciences is only emerging; with impact in data analytics, machine leaning, and artificial intelligence, as these areas would continue to grow. DDDAS fosters the use of high-dimensional, large-scale, and big data models to augment performance. The book follows the advancements since the 2010 workshop which had a focus on the sciences [2], towards engineering results in the last few years. The developments moved from situation awareness to that of situation understanding.

Table 32.1 DDDAS methods applied to awareness

Awareness	Models/measurements	Contributions
Structural health	Solids models Temperature measurements	Self-healing damage recovery Fly-by-feel aircraft
Environment	Weather models Wind measurements	Autonomous UAVs Air-breathing engine safety
Space situational	Atmospheric models Electron density	Resident object tracking Satellite detection
Context	Terrain models Target kinematics	Knowledge-aided radar Multi-sensor planning
Computational	Data flow models Buffer measurements	Computer vision surveillance Container-based optimization
Cyber	Instrumentation modeling IoT, SCADA measurements	Power/micro grid management System level security
Materials	Nano-Meso modeling SEM, EBSD measurements	Grain boundaries detection Nano-fabrication

SCADA supervisory control and data acquisition, *SEM* scanning electron microscope, *EBSD* electron backscatter diffraction

32.2 DDDAS Has Universal Appeal

32.2.1 Paradigm for Theory-Data Symbiosis

Throughout time man has sought to learn from data using to better understand the world around them. From a physics-based analysis, DDDAS formalized this process, initially for computational science, but subsequently for different applications beginning in the first decade before the introduction of big data and recently with data sciences. The DDDAS paradigm seeks to introduce the use of high-dimensional models (theory) as a method for accessing simulated data, when the environmental analysis cannot be fully measured. Pragmatic collection of *data*, whether sparse or voluminous, can be carefully processed to better understand the world and support model refinement. DDDAS seeks to leverage the foundations of mathematics [3] for modeling and control. The **theory-data symbiosis** is the hallmark of the DDDAS approaches. Figure 32.1 highlights the DDDAS conceptual loop when considering awareness (sensor, machine, or mission) to that of the measurement collection, modeling, and methods used for the theory-data symbiosis.

Learning models from data and producing models from theory [4] are both limiting; however the symbiosis occurs at all levels of abstraction. Symbiosis takes many forms: at the highest level, learned models are coupled with derived models, while at the lowest level theory constrains learning from data, from which data provides the mechanism for estimation and control. Key aspects of many of the solutions included **multi-dimensional, multi-resolution, multi-sensor, and multi-perspective** analysis. The diversity of information supports the opportunity to refine models with non-traditional sensing. Examples were provided of emerging concepts that include the use of Internet of Things (IoT) data in addition to electrical output

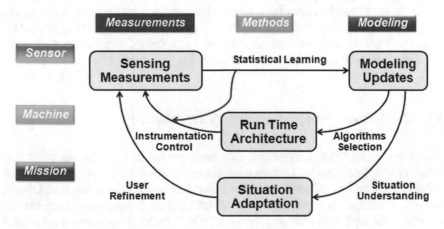

Fig. 32.1 The DDDAS loop

for cyber-physical power and micro-grid analysis, urban monitoring from text and space data, as well as imagery and strain measurements for structural health monitoring. In each case, there was a benefit for management, sensor collection, and healing; respectively. The *future applications* of DDDAS will incorporate public domain information emerging in complexity from the environment (e.g., weather), sensors (e.g., polarization), and objects (e.g., power grids).

32.2.2   Mitigates the Curse of Dimensionality

DDDAS mitigates the challenge of big data collection and analysis from instrumentation systems [5]. From a theoretical point of view, the curse of dimensionality is mitigated through the **intelligent collection of data**. Many theoretical models from physical to social, behavioral, economic, and cultural phenomenon are reduced to a set of salient parameters. In a similar way, the limitations of mathematical tractability can be supported with the assumption that there is a fundamental set of information that is needed to execute run-time applications. In the book, many examples highlighted approaches to support the data analytics with that of data collection and control. Essentially, DDDAS will *push the frontier* of explaining the unknown unknowns; such as how the unknown weather (e.g., hurricanes) effects on the unknowns on sensors (e.g., autonomous aircraft) for control and action.

DDDAS is **valid across many scales** from recent trends in IoT data and instrumentation systems to that of high-dimensional environmental models [6]. The many examples presented in the book demonstrate that DDDAS works across many spectrums, such as time, space, frequency, and modalities such as electro-optical [7] and radar [8]. DDDAS provides solutions for multi-resolution situations from the local to the global spatial, micro to macro frequencies, and small to large time scales. Examples were shown from time series, language processing, and structural analysis. The *explosion of data* is an area were DDDAS-based learning of models, generates new models, uses the models for surrogate information, and provides predictive multi-dimensional control for enhanced performance.

32.2.3   A Prediction and Discovery Instrument

The power of DDDAS is to use the simulated models so as to predict the future behavior of systems. As with the curse of dimensionality, there is the analysis of the unknown unknowns. To be able to utilize a model to predict the **unknown unknowns** through simulation is a unique feature of DDDAS as demonstrated with the use of contextual models [9]. To employ the DDDAS methods, assumptions are made (Fig. 32.2) such as (A1) problem is specific, (A2) data can be acquired, (A3) context data (from the models) can be fused, (A4) decision are actionable such as in future collections, (A5) decisions reproducible (for model updates), and (A6) error can be

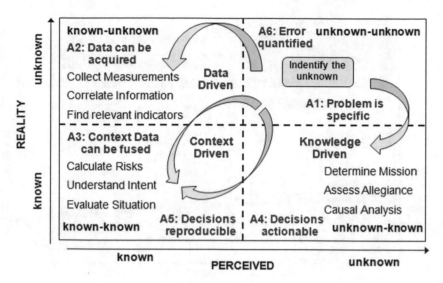

Fig. 32.2 DDDAS for context driven solutions to the unknown unknowns

quantified. The book begins with methods for uncertainty quantification (A6) and ends with domain-specific examples (A1). The domain-specific application supports knowledge-driven approaches, while the error-analysis supports the data-driven approaches. With modeling from various methods of the environment, structures, energy, and network analysis; high-dimensional information is used to support DDDAS approaches for context-based systems support.

32.3 Emerging Opportunities

As highlighted in Chap. 1, DDDAS include: (1) real-world applications, (2) instrumentation methods, (3) modeling and simulation, and (4) systems software. The future of each area and their intersection should forage new efforts using the DDDAS methods.

32.3.1 Applications Systems

DDDAS can be applied to specific problem domains which resolve around the fidelity of the models of those communities. Emerging communities in big data (e.g., IoT), data control (e.g., fog computing), and data science (e.g., multimedia analytics) augment the traditional methods for engineering analysis, as shown in Fig. 32.3. Such information as terrain information can be used for urban tracking

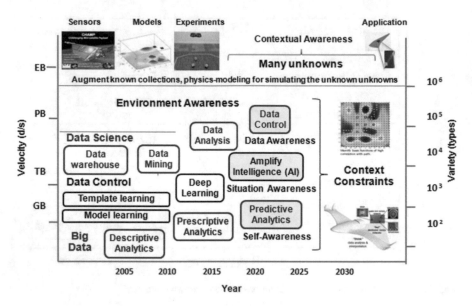

Fig. 32.3 DDDAS developments for data science, data control, and data size

while the intersection of structures, environments, and avionics is shown in Fig. 32.3 as a future application in the fly-by-feel autonomous UAV. Big data metrics includes velocity, volume, veracity, and variety (4 V's) while DDDAS has focused on the *value of data* – whether in collection or from models. DDDAS focuses on value by integrating the correct simulation data into the model and assessment for updates to control the big data collection issues.

It would be difficult to restrict DDDAS to specific application areas; however the book highlights many that could inspire other paradigms such a drug delivery in medicine, aid distribution for emergency dilatators, and social policies for effective management for energy and food resources. Figure 32.3 highlights that the future of DDDAS will leverage data control, artificial intelligence, and predictive analytics forging new applications and products.

32.3.2 Instrumentation

Specific sensors are being designed at every scale, while at the same time there is a growing amount of data being collected from all types of sensors, from the physical to the human. Future instrumentation systems support the processing, exploitation, and dissemination of information for knowledge (shown in Fig. 32.4). The ability of physics-based and human-derived information fusion (PHIF) extends the joint sensing capability over distributed situations. A second construct of instrumentation is that the sensor design and collection includes the processing and

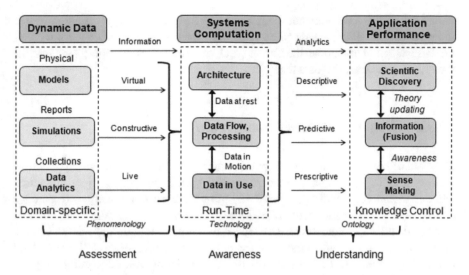

Fig. 32.4 DDDAS Future concepts for situation assessment, awareness, and understanding

exploitation of the data from the sensors. Using a sensor model can help better understand the data that is being collected and assessed. A third concept is the dissemination of the information for indexing and analysis. The instrumentation methods need to consider where the data is being sent for various scales analysis. For example, local data collections could support a single UAV for safe flight, while that information can be sent to air traffic management for a global analysis of the swarm of UAVs operating in various weather conditions. The future of DDDAS will include advanced computation methods for indexing of data, ontological models to categorize the data for human and machine analysis, as well as the control and management of instrumentation data for distributed networks.

32.3.3 Modeling and Simulation Methodology

The growth in data science helps to enhance model building, simulation analysis, and prediction for domain applications. Many times, the models are developed for specific communities in specific forms. Hence, one challenge is in model matching such that multiple types of information can be used (e.g., environment and structures models). Chapter 1 highlighted the data-assimilation loop, but bringing-in multiple (modal) data assimilation loops is still a challenge. For simulation, there is a need for effective and efficient methods to support run-time operations such as dissemination the full-scale results to the on-line system for performance optimization. Deep learning is a method that first learns the global elements and then focuses on learning the specific variations that change (e.g., learning the general aspects of a vehicle and then focusing on the moving parts such as door opening and closing variations or the environmental changes do to luminance effects). Learning over independent paradigms needs to be integrated for useful simulations. As with all DDDAS-inspired methods, the future goal of DDDAS is to bring together the models, simulations, and data analytics.

32.3.4 Systems Software Computation

The field of high-performance computing has many directions, including data flow architectures (e.g., container-based processing), electronic design (e.g., quantum computers and computation), as well as high-end to run-time analysis (e.g., edge computing). The measurement collections of DDDAS can be made more efficient through data flow architectures. The high-dimensional modeling of DDDAS could be developed for quantum computing. Finally, the integration of modeling at a cloud computing center can be integrated with fog computing and edge computing for large scale data collections.

32.4   Example: Hurricane Prediction

As highlighted in the Chap. 1, the modeling from the *data augmentation loop* can support the *information reconfiguration loop*. An example case was presented in hurricane analysis. Figure 32.5 showcases the importance of DDDAS-like processes of the power from the advancements in modeling. The hurricane Katrina incident was based on the capabilities to capture the current data, predict the direction of the hurricane, and determine the "control" of the population and disaster relief. As seen from high-dimensional NASA modeling [10], the updates from 2015 methods demonstrate higher resolution, lower uncertainty, and direction assessment of the hurricane as it moved towards the coastline.

32.5   Conclusions

The DDDAS community is rigorous, unique, and interdisciplinary. The information presented in the book highlights advances in DDDAS with emphasis on the integration of instrumentation, modeling, analytics, and architectures. Hopefully the book presented useful ideas to the reader to inspire their own developments and applications. The organization and methods presented provide a discussion for which the community can utilize DDDAS paradigms for scientific discovery, information analytics, and sense-making for real-time awareness. Follow-up volumes in the book-series, expand on the areas and aspects of DDDAS impact.

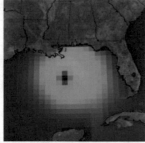

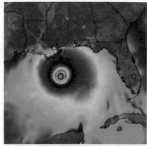

(2005 Model) 10-Meter Wind Speed   (2015 Model) 10-Meter Wind Speed

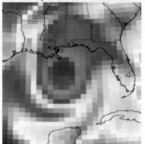

(2005 Model) Water Vapor   (2015 Model) Water Vapor

Fig. 32.5 Contribution of modeling in support of DDDAS [10]. Each image shows the near surface wind speed and water vapor of Hurricane Katrina on Aug. 29, 2005, but at different resolutions. The left image is at a 50-km resolution, the resolution of most global models in 2005. The right image shows a 2015 version of the Goddard Earth Observing System model, Version 5 (GEOS-5), at a 6.25-km global resolution. (*Credits: NASA Goddard Space Flight Center/Bill Putman, accessed at:*https://www.nasa.gov/feature/goddard/since-katrina-nasa-advances-storm-models-science)

Acknowledgements The editors, and contributing authors, would like to thank the support of AFOSR and other funding sources, as acknowledged in individual chapters; also thanks to the broader community who have contributed in DDDAS-based science and technology advances. The views and conclusions contained herein are those of the authors and should not be interpreted as necessarily representing the official policies or endorsements, either expressed or implied, of the United States Air Force or other funding Agencies.

References

1. E. Blasch, S. Ravela, A. Aved (eds.), *Handbook of Dynamic Data Driven Applications Systems*, (Springer, Cham, 2018)
2. F. Darema, *Multi-Agency Workshop on Info/Symbiotics/DDDAS: The power of Dynamic Data Driven Application Systems*, Report Output from AFOSR, August (2010)
3. D.S. Bernstein, *Matrix Mathematics: Theory, Facts, and Formulas with Application to Linear Systems Theory* (Princeton University Press, Princeton, 2005)

4. F. Gini, M. Rangaswamy, *Knowledge Based Radar Detection, Tracking, and Classification* (Wiley-Interscience, Hoboken, 2008)
5. E.P. Blasch, E. Bosse, D.A. Lambert, *High-Level Information Fusion Management and Systems Design* (Artech House, Norwood, 2012)
6. S. Ravela, A. Sandu, *Dynamic Data-Driven Environmental Systems Science*, International Conference, DYDESS 2014, LNCS 8964 (Springer, Cham, 2015)
7. Y. Zheng. E. Blasch, Z. Liu, *Multispectral Image Fusion and Colorization*, (SPIE Press, Bellingham, 2018)
8. U. Majumder, E. Blasch, D. Garren, *Deep Learning for Radar and Communications Automatic Target Recognition*, (Artech House, Norwood, 2020).
9. L. Snidaro, J. Garcia Herrero, J. Llinas, E. Blasch (eds.), *Context-Enhanced Information Fusion: Boosting Real-World Performance with Domain Knowledge* (Springer, Cham, 2016)
10. B. Puttman, *NASA Goddard Space Flight Center,* "Since Katrina: NASA Advances Storm Models Science," Aug. 21, 2015. Accessed 2018 at: https://www.nasa.gov/feature/goddard/since-katrina-nasa-advances-storm-models-science

Index

Printed in the United States
by Baker & Taylor Publisher Services